Child Development

Child Development

SECOND EDITION

Laura E. Berk
Illinois State University

Allyn and Bacon

BOSTON · LONDON · TORONTO · SYDNEY · TOKYO · SINGAPORE

Copyright © 1991, 1989 by Allyn and Bacon
A Division of Simon & Schuster, Inc.
160 Gould Street, Needham Heights, MA 02194

Library of Congress Cataloging-in-Publication Data

Berk, Laura E.
    Child development / Laura E. Berk.
       p.   cm.
    Includes bibliographical references and index.
    ISBN 0-205-12682-0
    1. Child development.   I. Title.
HQ767.9.B464   1991   90-1267
649'.1--dc20   CIP

Series Editor: Diane McOscar
Series Editorial Assistant: Laurie Frankenthaler
Production Coordinator: Marjorie Payne
Editorial-Production Service: York Production Services
Text Designer: Glenna Collett
Cover Administrator: Linda Dickinson
Cover Designer: Susan Slovinsky
Manufacturing Buyer: Megan Cochran

Printed in the United States of America

10 9 8 7 6 5 4 3 2 1   96 95 94 93 92 91 90

With gratitude, admiration, and love
To Esther M. Lentschner
and in memory of my cousin
Walter S. Lentschner

Brief Contents

Detailed Contents

PART II DEVELOPMENTAL FOUNDATIONS

9   Language Development   343

PART IV   PERSONALITY AND SOCIAL DEVELOPMENT

10   Emotional Development   383

PART V   CONTEXTS FOR DEVELOPMENT

Preface

For many years, I have taught courses in child development to students with diverse college majors, future goals, interests, and needs. Some are students in my own academic department, psychology, while many others come from other child-related fields, such as education, home economics, sociology, anthropology, and biology, to name just a few. Each semester, the professional aspirations of my students have proved to be as varied as their fields of study. Many look toward careers in applied work with children — teaching, caregiving, nursing, counseling, social work, school psychology, and program administration. A few plan to teach child development at the college level, and some want to do research. Most hope someday to have children of their own, and a number are already parents who come with a desire to better understand the development of their own youngsters. And almost all my students arrive with a deep curiosity about how they themselves developed from tiny infants into the complex adults they are today.

Finding a textbook that serves the instructional goals of the course as well as the varied needs of students is a challenging task. I wanted a book that was intellectually stimulating; that provided depth as well as breadth of coverage; that did not oversimplify the complexities of child development; that captured the preciousness, beauty, and wonderment of childhood; and that did all this in a clear, approachable, and engaging writing style. It is my goal, in preparing this second edition of *Child Development,* to continue to meet all of these needs.

PHILOSOPHICAL ORIENTATION

My own professional and personal history — as student, teacher, researcher, and parent — shaped the basic approach of this book. I believe that a text must communicate seven essential ingredients for students to emerge from a course in child development with a thorough understanding of the field. Each is emphasized in every chapter of the book, and together they form the philosophical orientation of the text:

1. An appreciation of the diverse array of theoretical perspectives in the field and the strengths and shortcomings of each. This text takes an eclectic approach to describing and explaining child development. In each topical domain, a variety of theoretical perspectives is presented and critiqued. If one or two have emerged as especially prominent in a particular area, I indicate why, in terms of the theory's broad explanatory power. Moreover, I show how each new theory highlights previously overlooked aspects of development, and I argue that only knowledge of multiple theories can do justice to the complexities of childhood and the course of human development. Consideration of contrasting theories also serves as the context for an evenhanded analysis of many controversial issues throughout the text.

2. A sense of the history of child development as a field of study and of the impact of historical trends on current theories. Throughout this book, I emphasize that the modern field of child development is the culmination of a long history — of changes in cultural values, changes in philosophical thinking about children, and scientific progress. A thorough understanding of the current status of the field depends on an appreciation of this history. The first chapter presents an overview of child study, from its philosophical origins in earlier centuries to the current refinement of theories and empirical methods. In each succeeding topical chapter, I describe how theories build on earlier contributions and are related to the cultural belief systems of their times. Thus the text provides students with a broad perspective on the emergence of child study and with a sense of its progress.

3. An understanding of both the sequence of child development and the processes that underlie it. This book provides students with a description of the organized sequence of child development, along with a discussion of processes of change. An understanding of process — how multiple biological and environmental factors produce developmental change — has been the focus of most research during the last few decades. Accordingly, the text discussion reflects this emphasis. But new information about the timetable of development has also emerged in recent years. In virtually all developmental domains, the young child has proved to be a far more competent being than was believed to be the case in decades past. I give thorough attention to recent evidence on the timing and sequence of development, along with its implications for developmental process, throughout the text.

4. An appreciation of basic research strategies used to investigate child development. The continued existence of child development theories depends on scientific verification. To evaluate theories rationally, students need a firm grounding in basic research design and methodology. I devote an entire chapter to a description and critique of research strategies. In each topical chapter, numerous research studies are discussed in sufficient detail for students to use what they have learned to critically evaluate the findings, conclusions, and theoretical implications of research.

5. An understanding of the impact of context and culture on children's development. A wealth of current research reveals more forcefully than ever before that children live in richly influential physical and social settings that combine in complex ways with their genetic heritage to shape the course of development. The text narrative takes the student to many parts of the world as it summarizes a growing body of cross-cultural research on children's development. It also discusses findings on socioeconomically and ethnically diverse groups of children within the United States and other nations. The impact of culture is brought forward in a new series of boxes that highlights the abundant variety of children's experience. Students are encouraged to question the universality of findings obtained on restricted samples and in contexts divorced from children's everyday lives.

6. A sense of the interdependency of all aspects of development — physical, cognitive, emotional, and social. The basic organization of this text is topical — an approach that permits a continuous, coherent discussion of each aspect of child development. At the same time, a wealth of current research reveals that the separate domains of development are interdependent; they mutually influence one another. In every chapter, an integrated approach to child development is emphasized. Students are shown how physical, cognitive, emotional, and social development are interwoven. In many instances, they are referred back to sections in earlier topical chapters that enhance their understanding of relationships among the various components of development.

7. **An appreciation of the interrelatedness of theory, research, and applications.** Throughout this book, I illustrate the vital connections that exist among theory, research, and applications. I show how major research methods have been stimulated by and are intimately related to dominant theories. In addition, I emphasize that theories of child development and the research generated by them provide an essential foundation for sound, effective interventions aimed at improving the welfare and treatment of children. The linkage between theory, research, and applications is reinforced by an organizational format in each chapter that presents theoretical perspectives first, followed by an analysis of the research stimulated by them. Then practical applications are discussed in light of theories and research findings. As in the first edition, a series of boxes highlights the theory, research, and applications theme. In addition, a new priority in the field — harnessing child development research to stimulate social policies that support children's needs — is represented in many sections of the text narrative. It is also accentuated by a new series of social policy boxes and a new chapter entirely devoted to the topic of child development and social policy.

ORGANIZATION AND CONTENT

The text retains the same basic organization that received praise from users in its first edition. The book is divided into 5 parts and 16 chapters, each of which develops the seven themes described above. The salient features of each part and chapter are summarized below:

Part I. Theory and Research in Child Development. This section offers an overview of the history of the field, modern theories, and research strategies. **Chapter 1** introduces students to the importance of theories as organizing frameworks for understanding the child and traces the evolution of views of childhood from medieval to modern times. Separate sections on behaviorism and social learning theory, the ecology of human development, ethology, Piaget's cognitive-developmental theory, information processing, social cognition, the study of emotions, and Vygotsky's dialectical theory provide an overview of the current status of the field. The study of child development is depicted as an interdisciplinary endeavor that draws from psychology as well as a variety of applied fields, including education, home economics, medicine, and social service. **Chapter 2** is devoted to a consideration of strategies for conducting scientifically sound research. Commonly used research methods, as well as general and developmental research designs, are explained and critiqued. The chapter closes with a discussion of special ethical concerns in research with children.

Part II. Developmental Foundations. A trio of chapters introduces students to the foundations of development. **Chapter 3** combines a discussion of genetic mechanisms and prenatal and perinatal environmental influences into a single, integrated analysis of these earliest determinants of development. A concluding section discusses the various ways in which behavioral geneticists and child development specialists conceive of the relationship between heredity and environment, as a prelude to revisiting the nature-nurture controversy in subsequent chapters of the book. **Chapter 4** is devoted to a discussion of the burgeoning literature on infancy. Research on neonatal reflexes, states, and learning capacities is reviewed, followed by a consideration of motor and perceptual development during the first two years of life. The chapter closes with the question of whether infancy is a critical period in which certain experiences must occur to ensure a healthy course of child development. **Chapter 5** addresses physical growth. The orderly, asynchronous nature of physical development is described, followed by a special section on development of the brain. The intimate connection between physical and psychological development is emphasized. The chapter concludes with a discussion of factors affecting physical growth — heredity, nutrition, disease, and affection and stimulation.

Part III. Cognitive and Language Development. Four chapters summarize the diverse theoretical perspectives and wealth of research on cognitive and language development. **Chapter 6** is devoted to a comprehensive description and critique of Piaget's theory. Although Piaget's work has recently been questioned, no other single individual has contributed more to our understanding of child development. Students are offered a thorough grounding in Piagetian theory as a prerequisite for understanding many areas of child study in subsequent chapters, including language development, social cognition, emotional development, and moral reasoning. The chapter concludes with a consideration of an important competing approach to children's thinking that has gained in prominence in the field — Vygotsky's dialectical perspective. **Chapter 7** provides an introduction to information processing, the leading current alternative to Piaget's theory. General as well as developmental models of information processing are reviewed, along with research on each major component of the information processing system. Recent applications of information processing to children's academic learning are discussed, as well as the strengths and weaknesses of the information processing perspective. **Chapter 8** presents the psychometric approach to children's intellectual development. The chapter begins with an overview of the intelligence testing movement and then addresses a wide variety of controversial issues and research findings, including the stability and predictability of IQ, the origins of racial/ethnic and social class differences in IQ, the extent to which intelligence is heritable, and cultural bias in the tests. A concluding section moves beyond IQ to a discussion of creativity. **Chapter 9** offers a comprehensive introduction to language development, including a review of nativist, environmentalist, and interactionist theories. The main body of the chapter is organized around the four basic components of language — phonology, semantics, grammar, and pragmatics. The chapter also addresses such controversial questions as: Is there a critical period for language learning? Does early bilingualism interfere with or enhance development?

Part IV. Personality and Social Development. Coverage of personality and social development is divided into four chapters. **Chapter 10,** on emotional development, provides an overview of current theory and research on general emotional development from infancy through adolescence. It also examines research on the stability and heritability of temperamental traits and the contribution of temperament to cognitive and social development. The chapter concludes with a review of theory and research on infant-mother attachment. The impact of infant temperament on the attachment bond, fathers as attachment figures, and the effects of maternal employment and day care on attachment security are among the special issues discussed. **Chapter 11** offers an overview of the development of social cognition. The discussion is divided into three sections: children's understanding of self, other people, and relationships between people. Among the topics included are the development of self-esteem, achievement-related attributions, perspective-taking, friendship, and social problem solving. **Chapter 12** addresses moral development and self-control. It includes a review and critique of psychoanalytic, behaviorist, and cognitive-developmental approaches to children's morality. Child-rearing practices that foster moral internalization, cross-cultural research on moral reasoning, and the controversial issue of whether sex differences exist in moral understanding are among the special features of this chapter. **Chapter 13** focuses on the development of sex differences and sex roles. Biological and environmental influences on sex-role adoption, the development of sex-role identity, and sex differences in cognitive abilities and personality attributes are reviewed. The chapter also includes an applied section on raising non-sex-stereotyped children.

Part V. Contexts for Development. A final trio of chapters examines five highly influential contexts for children's development — family, peers, media, schooling, and the larger society. **Chapter 14** considers the family from both an ethological and a social systems perspective. The bidirectional nature of parent-child interaction and the significance of linkages between family and community for optimal child development are emphasized. The central portion of this chapter discusses the impact of current changes in the American family, including smaller family sizes, divorce and remarriage, and maternal employment and day care. The chapter concludes with a section on child maltreatment, a serious national problem in the United States. In **Chapter 15,** the social systems perspective is carried over to extrafamilial contexts for development. In the section on peer relations, the development of peer sociability, peer popularity, peer groups, and peers as socialization agents are discussed. The second section of the chapter addresses the impact of television and computers on social and cognitive development. A concluding section on schooling considers such topics as teacher expectations for children's academic performance, mainstreaming, school desegregation, and the current crisis in the quality of American education. **Chapter 16** examines the social policy process — the complex social, political, and economic forces that affect a nation's responsiveness to child and family concerns. The chapter reviews the general condition of children in the United States and around the world, the role of child development research in policymaking, and progress toward improving the well-being of the large numbers of children currently at risk for developmental problems.

NEW COVERAGE IN THE SECOND EDITION

A burgeoning contemporary literature on child development stimulated updating of information throughout the text. Research drawn from over 700 new citations is included. Foremost among the revisions is the addition of a new chapter — Child Development and Social Policy — described in the section above. Other major changes include:

■ Updated coverage of prenatal teratogens, prepared childbirth and home delivery, and developmental consequences of prematurity in Chapter 3.

■ Expanded treatment of neonatal behavioral assessment and inclusion of new evidence on infant learning, motor development, and visual perception in Chapter 4.

■ Coverage of new research on pubertal change and parent-child relationships and expanded treatment of brain plasticity, lateralization, and the development of handedness in Chapter 5.

■ New findings on the validity of Piaget's theory and an indepth consideration of Vygotsky's dialectical perspective and its implications for education in Chapter 6.

■ Increased attention to developmental models of information processing and a new section on applications of the information processing perspective to academic learning in Chapter 7.

■ Discussion of Sternberg's triarchic theory and new research on the impact of children's sociocultural background on intelligence test performance in Chapter 8.

■ Expanded treatment of cross-cultural variations in language acquisition and childhood bilingualism in Chapter 9.

■ Inclusion of a new section on emotional self-regulation, coverage of the recently identified disorganized/disoriented attachment pattern, and analysis of the current controversy over infant day care and attachment in Chapter 10.

■ New ideas on the relationship between children's social experience and social-cognitive development in Chapter 11.

■ Expanded coverage of research on the cross-cultural universality of Kohlberg's stages in Chapter 12.

■ Examination of new evidence on the origins of children's preference for same-sex peer associates, the development of gender constancy, and sex differences in cognitive and personality attributes in Chapter 13.

■ Updated treatment of research on the black extended family, divorce, remarriage, maternal employment, day care, and child maltreatment in Chapter 14.

■ New coverage of adolescent substance abuse and expanded treatment of cross-national research on academic achievement in Chapter 15.

SPECIAL PEDAGOGICAL FEATURES

Writing Style. In writing this book, I made a concerted effort to adopt a prose style that is both engaging and scholarly. I aimed for clear, precise exposition that facilitates student interest and understanding. To encourage critical thinking about the material, I use an interactive approach that poses student-directed questions in many parts of the text discussion. My intent is to offer students a model of good writing and, at the same time, prepare them for reading more advanced, original source material.

Boxes. Boxes reflect three major themes. *Theory, research, and applications* boxes, which are set off by a blue background, illustrate the interrelatedness of these three basic elements of child study. Two types of *contemporary issues* boxes — *cultural differences* and *child development and social policy* — underscore the impact of context on children's development. These are set off by a peach background.

Chapter Introductions and Summaries. An overview of chapter content in each introduction provides students with a helpful preview of what they are about to read. Especially comprehensive summaries, organized according to the major divisions of each chapter and highlighting key terms, remind students of major concepts, principles, and discussion points and reinforce their learning.

Brief Reviews. Brief Reviews, which provide students with interim summaries of what they have read, are introduced at critical points in chapter narratives.

Important Terms and Concepts. Terms and concepts that make up the basic vocabulary of the field appear in boldface type. They are also listed at the end of each chapter to assist students with reviewing chapter content. Each term is page-referenced to its point of introduction in the text narrative. A secondary set of important terms is italicized throughout the text discussion.

Footnotes. Footnotes help students understand the interdependencies among domains of development by reminding them of earlier presented text material and encouraging them to turn back for review.

Tables and Illustrations. Tables distributed throughout the book succinctly summarize and elaborate on text discussion, and colorful, easy-to-interpret graphs and illustrations depict research methods and findings.

Photos. Photographs have been carefully selected to illustrate important points in each chapter. The photos and accompanying captions teach students about development, rather than serving as mere adornments on the page.

Glossary. A glossary of over 500 terms is provided at the end of the book. It includes items appearing in boldface type as well as a large selection of italicized terms. Students can access the text page on which each glossary item is introduced by looking it up in the index.

Reference List. The text contains an extensive list of reference citations, including historically important as well as current sources. The up-to-date nature of the book is reflected in nearly 2,000 references published during the past ten years, including more than 500 since 1988. The citation list is comprehensive enough for students to use as a primary basis for research papers and projects.

A set of carefully prepared supplements accompanies this text. Judy DeLoache of the University of Ilinois at Urbana-Champaign has prepared an excellent book of supplementary readings that incorporates student study aids. Patricia Jarvis, Gary Creasey, and I have written a study guide that includes chapter summaries, learning objectives, study questions emphasizing important points in the text narrative, short-answer essay questions highlighting critical issues, student activities, self-tests, and exercises for mastery of basic terms. I have prepared an instructor's manual that is coordinated with the Study Guide. It contains chapter outlines and summaries, lecture topics, essay test questions, student activities, class demonstrations, suggested readings, and a comprehensive listing of available media materials. A set of transparencies is also available. Amye Warren of the University of Tennessee at Chattanooga has written a test bank of 2,000 multiple choice questions, each of which is page-referenced to chapter content and classified according to type (factual, applied, or conceptual). The test bank comes in both printed and computerized formats.

As part of Allyn and Bacon's Inside Psych series, a VHS videotape presentation entitled "Children's Private Speech" is available as a supplement to the book. The presentation describes the contrasting theories of Piaget and Vygotsky on the significance of children's private speech, summarizes recent research on the topic (including my own), and discusses educational implications of current findings. An instructor's guide that contains discussion questions and multiple choice test questions is enclosed.

ACKNOWLEDGMENTS

The dedicated contributions of a great many individuals helped make this book a reality and contributed to refinements and improvements in the second edition. An impressive cast of reviewers provided many helpful suggestions, constructive criticisms, and much encouragement and enthusiasm for the organization and content of the book. I am grateful to each one of them:

Reviewers of the First Edition

Dana W. Birnbaum
  University of Main at Orono
Kathryn N. Black
  Purdue University
Cathryn L. Booth
  University of Washington
Sam Boyd
  University of Central Arkansas
Celia A. Brownell
  University of Pittsburgh
Toni A. Campbell
  San Jose State University
Beth Casey
  Boston College
John Condry
  Cornell University
James L. Dannemiller
  University of Wisconsin, Madison

Darlene DeSantis
  West Chester University
Elizabeth J. Hrncir
  University of Virginia
Kenneth Hill
  Saint Mary's University, Halifax
Alice S. Honig
  Syracuse University
Mareile Koenig
  George Washington University
  Hospital
Gary W. Ladd
  Purdue University
Frank Laycock
  Oberlin College
Robert S. Marvin
  University of Virginia

Carolyn J. Mebert
University of New Hampshire
Gary B. Melton
University of Nebraska, Lincoln
Mary Evelyn Moore
Indiana University at Bloomington
Larry Nucci
University of Illinois at Chicago
Carol Pandey
Pierce College, Los Angeles
Thomas S. Parish
Kansas State University
B. Kay Pasley
Colorado State University
Ellen F. Potter
University of South Carolina at
Columbia

Kathleen Preston
Humboldt State University
Maria E. Sera
The University of Iowa
Beth Shapiro
Emory University
Gregory J. Smith
Dickinson College
Harold Stevenson
The University of Michigan
Ross A. Thompson
University of Nebraska, Lincoln
Barbara A. Tinsley
University of Illinois at Urbana-
Champaign
Kim F. Townley
University of Kentucky

Reviewers of the Second Edition

James Dannemiller
University of Wisconsin, Madison
Darlene DeSantis
West Chester University
Claire Etaugh
Bradley University
Katherine Green
Millersville University
Daniel Lapsley
University of Notre Dame
Mary D. Leinbach
University of Oregon

Gary B. Melton
University of Nebraska, Lincoln
Daniel Reschly
Iowa State University
Rosemary Rosser
The University of Arizona
Phil Schoggen
Cornell University
Ross A. Thompson
University of Nebraska, Lincoln
Janet Valadez
Pan American University

I am also grateful to my colleagues at Illinois State University who willingly read chapters and offered feedback and consultation in areas of their expertise. They are Raymond Bergner, Gary Creasey, Barbara Goebel, Patricia Jarvis, Steven Landau, Elmer Lemke, Leonard Schmaltz, and Mark Swerdlik. Felissa Cohen, Chairperson of the Department of Medical Surgical Nursing, University of Illinois Medical School, offered helpful consultation on Chapter 3. A special thank you is extended to Benjamin Moore, Clinical Director of the Baby Fold, Normal, Illinois, for his critique of Chapter 16 and for the inspiration of his dedicated work with children.

Many students contributed in important ways to the content and quality of the text. Students enrolled in my child development classes offered suggestions as they studied each portion of the book. Their enthusiasm for a social policy chapter helped stimulate this feature of the new edition. Susan Phelps and Christine Sartoris, my graduate assistants during the year in which I prepared the revision, provided invaluable assistance with literature reviews, proofreading, securing permissions for use of copyrighted material, and preparation of the glossary. I am indebted to Deborah Petrillo for devoting many hours to indexing the text.

I have been especially fortunate to work with an outstanding publishing staff at Allyn and Bacon. Diane McOscar, Senior Editor, amassed an excellent team of reviewers, solicited many useful suggestions from current users of the book, and brought her keen aesthetic sense to bear on a beautiful text design. Her encouragement, support, and wise counsel through all phases of the project have contributed greatly to the quality of the book. Susan Badger, Executive Editor, reviewed and commented on the text revision plan and graciously met with me during the year in which I worked on the new edition. Marjorie Payne, Production Coordinator, and Mary Jo Gregory of York Production Services masterfully handled the complex, time-consuming tasks that transformed my typescript copy into a finished textbook. Laurie Frankenthaler, Senior Editorial Assistant, processed manuscript reviews, co-ordinated the preparation of text supplements, and attended to a wide variety of pressing, last-minute details. Elizabeth Brooks, Developmental Editor, planned the photographic illustrations, and Jennifer Ralph of Picture Research Consultancy secured the photos that so aptly illustrate points in the text discussion. Glenna Collett is responsible for the book's artistic design.

A final word of gratitude goes to my husband and children, whose love, patience, and understanding have enabled me to be wife, mother, teacher, researcher, and text writer since the inception of this project in 1986. My sons, David and Peter, have provided me with many valuable lessons in child development and have enriched my understanding of adolescence in recent years. I thank them for their good-humored interest in this project ("Unreal! She's *still* working on the same textbook!") and their expressions of pride in having a mom who wrote a book. My husband, Ken, willingly made room for this project in our family life and communicated his belief in its importance in a great many unspoken, caring ways.

Laura E. Berk

About the Author

Laura E. Berk is Professor of Psychology and coordinator of the graduate sequence in developmental psychology at Illinois State University, where she has taught child development to undergraduate and graduate students for the past two decades. She received her Bachelor's degree from the University of California, Berkeley, and her Masters and Doctoral degrees from the University of Chicago. She was visiting scholar at Cornell University in 1975–1976, at the University of California, Los Angeles, in 1982–1983, and at Stanford University in 1990–1991. She has published extensively on effects of school environments on children's development and, more recently, on the development of children's private speech. Her research has been funded by the U.S. Office of Education and the National Institute of Child Health and Human Development. It has appeared in such journals as *Child Development, Developmental Psychology, Merrill-Palmer Quarterly, Child and Youth Care Quarterly,* and the *American Journal of Education.* Recently, she wrote the chapter on the extracurriculum for the American Educational Research Association's *Handbook of Research on Curriculum.* She is coeditor of and contributing author to the forthcoming volume, *Private Speech: From Social Interaction to Self-Regulation.*

Child Development

Breakfast in Bed, by Mary Cassatt.
The Virginia Steele Scott Collection, Huntingdon Library and Art Gallery.

1

History, Theory, and Method

Child development is a field of study devoted to the understanding of all facets of human growth and change from conception through adolescence. It is part of a larger discipline known as **developmental psychology** or (as it is referred to in its interdisciplinary sense) **human development**, which encompasses all changes that human beings experience throughout the life span. In fact, no branch of human behavior is broader in scope than the study of development, for every facet of the individual — physical, mental, social, and emotional — changes over time. Great diversity characterizes the interests and concerns of the thousands of investigators who study child development. But all have a single goal in common: the desire to describe and identify those factors that influence the dramatic changes in young people during the first two decades of life.

The field of child development poses many questions about children that you may have wondered about yourself:

How do human beings grow before they are born, and what can be done to ensure a healthy newborn baby?

Can infants "make sense" of their complex perceptual world at birth? What do they already understand about their surroundings, and what must they learn over time?

How do children become such amazingly effective users of their complex language system during the first few years of life? Is it harder or easier for young children to learn a second language than it is for older children and adults?

1

Where do individual differences in intelligence and personality come from? Does heredity play a role in whether children are bright or dull, active or passive, sociable or shy? What aspects of children's home environments make a difference?

Why do most babies begin to show a strong affectional tie to their mothers in the second half of the first year? Do infants who do not become emotionally attached to a caregiver show impaired development in later life?

What kinds of child-rearing practices promote the development of academically motivated, socially competent youngsters? Should parents try to be permissive or strict with their children, or should they aim for something in between?

Look at these questions, and you will see that they are not just of scientific and intellectual interest. Each is of practical importance as well. In fact, scientific curiosity about what makes children the way they are is just one factor that led child development to become the exciting field of study it is today. Knowledge about development has also been stimulated by social pressures to better the lives of children. For example, the growth of public education in the early part of the twentieth century led to a demand for scientific knowledge about what and how to teach children of different ages. The interest of pediatricians in improving children's health required systematic understanding of physical growth and nutrition. The social service profession's desire to alleviate children's anxieties and behavior problems required comprehensive knowledge about personality and social development. And parents have continually sought advice from child development specialists about child-rearing practices and experiences that would promote the optimum growth of their children.

Our current vast storehouse of information about child development grew through the combined efforts of people from many fields of study. Because of the need for solutions to everyday problems concerning children, academic psychologists joined forces in research endeavors with professionals from a variety of applied fields, including education, home economics, medicine, and social service, to name just a few. Today, the field of child development is a melting pot of interdisciplinary contributions stimulated by both intellectual and practical concerns. Its body of knowledge is not only scientifically significant, but also relevant and useful.

THE ROLE OF THEORY

Before scientific study of the child, questions about children were answered by turning to common sense, opinion, and belief. Efforts at systematic study of children began to flourish in the early part of the twentieth century. These activities led to the construction of theories of child development, to which professionals and parents could turn for understanding and practical guidance. Although there have been many scientific and philosophical definitions, for our purposes we can think of a **theory** as an orderly, integrated set of statements that explains and predicts behavior. As we will see later on, child development theories, like the speculations and convictions parents exchange with one another about how best to raise children, are heavily influenced by the cultural values and belief systems of their times. However, theories differ in an important way from mere opinion and belief in that their continued existence depends on scientific verification. Such verification takes place when the assumptions of the theory are tested by means of a fair set of methods and procedures agreed upon by the scientific community.

In the field of child development, there are many theories with dramatically opposing assumptions about the nature of the child and the course of human development. In reading this chapter, you will soon see that basic to some theories is the idea that children are passive reactors to environmental stimuli, whereas other theories view children as active contributors to their own development. Some theories maintain that children and adults respond to the world in much the same way; others assume that children are qualitatively different from adults and must be understood on their own terms. Finally, some theories regard genetic influences as most important in development, others stress the environment, while still a third group strikes a balance between the two.

The study of child development provides no single, ultimate truth. Instead, it offers a smorgasbord of explanations about how the child grows, forcing us to pick and choose, leaving us uncomfortable about our current convictions, and motivating us to seek additional knowledge as the basis for our choices (Scarr, 1985). The field of child development is not deficient because it has no all-encompassing theory. The child's behavior is too complex and multifaceted for any single theory to adequately explain all its aspects. Moreover, the existence of multiple theories leads to advances in knowledge. Theoretical variety stimulates new research aimed at affirming, contradicting, and reconciling different perspectives. Multiple theories also serve as organizing frameworks for observing the child and provide a systematic, rational basis for practical action.

Theories as Guides to Observing the Child

Imagine yourself as a forerunner in the field of child development, confronted with investigating children's growth and behavior for the first time. Faced with the child who is your object of study, what will you observe? Perhaps you can think of many possibilities — relationships with parents, siblings, and peers; school performance; thought processes; language and communicative abilities; eating habits; play preferences; and motor coordination, to name just a few. There is an infinite range of possible aspects to select for study. One solution to your problem might be to observe everything about the child. But should you try this, you would probably find yourself overwhelmed by a multitude of observations and measurements. These discrete, unintegrated facts about the child would seem meaningless and trivial because you would have no organizing framework for guiding and interpreting your observations.

Theories are essential tools for advancing knowledge because they tell us what aspects of child behavior are important to observe, at least for the moment, and why they are important. In addition, theories provide us with an explanation of how facts about children fit together. Thomas (1985) likens them to camera lenses through which we view the child, organizing and highlighting certain observations while filtering out many others. Thus, theories provide orderly, meaningful direction to our research efforts. If we carry our camera analogy a step further, the benefits of multiple theories discussed earlier become even clearer. New theories can serve as eye openers in the quest for knowledge about the child, causing us to attend to new or previously overlooked facts so that we "see" things differently than we did before. Adherence to only a single theory can be obstructive. It may blind us to the existence of new facts that do not fit with currently held beliefs.

Theories as a Rational Basis for Practical Action

For the researcher, theories provide essential frameworks for generating new knowledge. Increasing our understanding of the developing child is a worthwhile goal in itself. In addition, the more we *understand* about development, the better we will know *what to do* in our efforts to improve the welfare and treatment of children. When understanding precedes action, coherent plans replace floundering and groping attempts at solution.

The diffusion of child development knowledge to practitioners and the general public has already had a profound impact on the modern child's experiences. For example, research findings indicating negative consequences from using punishment to discipline children have led to an emphasis on positive motivational techniques in both child-rearing and educational practice. Years of research on the importance of mother-infant attachment has influenced the way mothers and, more recently, fathers and substitute caregivers interact with very young children.

Child development specialists have, over the last two decades, made a special effort to improve our knowledge base in areas directly related to the health and welfare of children. A new emphasis in the field, *child development and social policy*, has recently emerged, consciously concerned with how to translate theory and research into practical situations. These efforts range from finding ways to help individual parents do a better job of raising children to the design and implementation of governmental policies that protect the development of all our youngest citizens. In view of these advances, dissemination and application of child development knowledge may, in the longer perspective, be regarded as one of the most significant achievements of the twentieth century (Horowitz & O'Brien, 1989b; Zigler & Finn-Stevenson, 1988).

THE HISTORY OF CHILD STUDY

The modern science of child development is the culmination of centuries of change in Western cultural values, philosophical thinking about children, and scientific progress. The current structure of the field has deep roots extending far back into the past. In the sections that follow, we consider major historical influences, beginning with those preceding scientific study of the child, that linger on as important forces in current theory and research.

Early Views of Childhood

Medieval Times. In medieval times, little importance was placed on childhood as a separate phase of the life cycle. The idea so commonly accepted today, that the child's nature is unique and to be distinguished from youth and adulthood, was much less common then. Instead, once children emerged from infancy, they were regarded as miniature, already-formed adults, a view called **preformationism.** This attitude is reflected in the art, language, and everyday games and entertainment of the times. If you look carefully at medieval paintings, you will see that children are depicted in dress and expression as immature adults. Moreover, before the sixteenth century, the word "child" did not have the very specific meaning we now give to it. Instead, it was used indiscriminately to refer to sons, lads, and young men. Toys and games were not specially designed to occupy and amuse children but were used by all people. Even age, so important an aspect of modern personal identity and a fact about the self that today's children can recite almost as soon as they can talk, was unimportant in medieval custom and usage. People did not refer to it in everyday conversation, and age was not recorded in family and civil records until the fifteenth and sixteenth centuries (Aries, 1962).

Nevertheless, glimmerings of the idea that children are unique were present during medieval times. For example, some laws recognized that children needed protection from adults who might mistreat or take advantage of them. In addition, medical works had pediatric sections acknowledging the fragility of infants and young children and providing special instructions for their care. But even though in a practical sense there was some awareness of the smallness and vulnerability of children, as yet there were no theories about the individuality of childhood and no conceptions of separate developmental periods (Borstelmann, 1983; Kroll, 1977).

The Sixteenth and Seventeenth Centuries. By the sixteenth century, a revised conception of childhood sprang from religious ideas—in particular, the Protestant conception of original sin. According to this view, the child was a fragile creature of

God who needed to be safeguarded but who also needed to be reformed. Born evil and stubborn, children had to be led away from their devilish ways. Therefore, it was necessary to take them in hand and civilize them toward a destiny of virtue and salvation. Schools, in which boys of the middle classes were separated from the corrupt world of older youths and adults, prolonged the period of childhood beyond infancy. However, girls and lower-class children were excluded, their limited childhood still the same as it was in medieval times (Aries, 1962; Suransky, 1982).

Harsh, authoritarian, and restrictive child-rearing practices were recommended as the most efficient means for transforming the depraved child. Infants were tightly swaddled, and children's clothing was heavily corseted to hold them in adultlike postures. Moral training was an essential feature of schooling, as demonstrated by the text of the *New England Primer*, originally published in Puritan American in 1687. *"A — In Adam's fall we sinned all"* served as the child's first introduction to reading and the alphabet. Pictures of schools showed the rod or birch, and disobedient pupils were routinely beaten by their schoolmasters.

Although these attitudes represented the prevailing child-rearing philosophy of the times, it is important to note that they may not have been typical of day-to-day practices in Puritan families. Recent historical evidence indicates that love and affection for their children made many New England parents reluctant to exercise extremely repressive measures. Instead, they preferred to adopt a more moderate balance between discipline and indulgence, severity and permissiveness (Moran & Vinovskis, 1986).

Early Philosophies of Childhood: Locke and Rousseau. The seventeenth-century Enlightenment brought new philosophies of reason and fostered ideals of human dignity and respect. Revised conceptions of childhood appeared that were more humane and benevolent than those of centuries past.

The writings of John Locke (1632–1704), a leading British philosopher during this Age of Reason, served as the forerunner of an important twentieth-century perspective that we will discuss shortly: *behaviorism.* Locke conceived of the child as **tabula rasa.** Translated from Latin, this means blank slate or white piece of paper. According to this view, children were not basically evil. They were, to begin with, nothing at all, and their characters could be shaped by all kinds of experiences during the course of growing up. Locke (1690/1892) described parents as rational tutors who

This drawing of "The Five Senses," published in an elementary reader in 1744, reflects the new, humane attitudes toward children that developed during the Enlightenment. The illustration depicts children learning through direct experience, with gentle, understanding teachers looking on.

could mold the child in any way they wished, through use of associations, repetitions, imitation, rewards, and punishments. Moreover, Locke was ahead of his time in recommending to parents child-rearing practices whose soundness was eventually validated by twentieth-century research (e.g., Parke, 1977). For example, he suggested that parents not reward children with money or sweets, but rather with praise and approval. He also expressed opposition to physical punishment because it works only when the rod is in sight, does not foster self-control, and establishes unfavorable associations: "The child repeatedly beaten in school cannot look upon books and teachers without experiencing fear and anger." Locke's philosophy heralded a change from punitiveness and brutality toward children to kindness and compassion.

In the eighteenth century, children were dressed more comfortably, babies were not swaddled, and the use of corporal punishment declined. A new, natural theory of childhood was expressed by a French philosopher of the Enlightenment, Jean-Jacques Rousseau (1712–1778). Children, Rousseau thought, were not blank slates and empty containers to be filled by adult instruction. Instead, they were **noble savages,** naturally endowed with a sense of right and wrong and with an innate plan for orderly, healthy growth. In his book *Emile* (1762/1955), Rousseau described the development of a fictitious boy whose upbringing took place according to nature's plan. Unlike Locke, Rousseau thought children's built-in moral sense and unique modes of thinking and feeling would only be obstructed by adult training and restriction. His was a child-centered, permissive philosophy. The adult should be responsive to the child's expressed needs at each of four stages of development: infancy, childhood, late childhood, and adolescence.

Rousseau's philosophy is often thought of as the first truly developmental position (Crain, 1980). It includes two vitally important concepts that are found in modern developmental theories. The first is the concept of **stage** of development. Stages are qualitatively distinct organizations of thought, feelings, and behavior at particular periods of development. The second is the concept of **maturation,** which refers to a genetically predetermined, naturally unfolding plan of growth. If you accept the notion that children mature through a sequence of stages, then they cannot be preformed, miniature adults. Rather, they are unique and different from adults, and their development is determined by their own inner promptings. Rousseau's philosophy foreshadowed several important twentieth-century developmental perspectives, such as Arnold Gesell's maturational theory and Jean Piaget's stage theory of cognitive development, which will be introduced later on in this chapter. Perhaps it is not mere coincidence that Piaget spent most of his research career at the Rousseau Institute at the University of Geneva.

Darwin — Scientific Father of Child Development

In the mid-nineteenth century, Charles Darwin (1809–1882), a British naturalist, joined a scientific expedition to distant parts of the world where he made careful observations of fossils and animal and plant life. Darwin observed the infinite variation among species. He also noticed that within a species, no two members were exactly alike. From these observations, he constructed his famous theory of evolution, reported in *On the Origin of Species by Means of Natural Selection*, published in 1859.

The theory emphasized two related principles of evolution: *natural selection* and *survival of the fittest.* Darwin explained that certain species were selected by nature to survive in particular parts of the world because they possessed characteristics that fit with, or were adapted to, their surroundings. Other species died off because their traits were not well suited to their environments. Reproduction and survival within a species followed a pattern that facilitated the evolution of that species. Individuals that best met the survival requirements of the environment were those that lived long enough to reproduce and transmit their more favorable characteristics to future generations. Darwin observed that the earliest forms of embryos of many species were strikingly alike in physical appearance. He concluded that all species, including human beings, were descended from a few common ancestors and that each had evolved over millions of years according to the process of natural selection.

Darwin's earliest writings focused on the survival value of each species' physical characteristics. Later he came to believe that certain behaviors promoted survival as well (Darwin, 1871/1936), an idea that influenced many child development theories of the twentieth century. For example, it is present in Sigmund Freud's psychosexual theory. Freud believed that development culminates in mature heterosexual behavior and family life, which ensures the birth and survival of the next generation. As we will see shortly, evolutionary ideas also underlie the work of G. Stanley Hall and Arnold Gesell. Their maturational theories of predetermined growth are based on the (no longer accepted) belief that *ontogeny recapitulates phylogeny* — the development of the child (ontogeny) follows the same overall plan as the evolution of the human species (phylogeny).

Today, the work of Hall, Gesell, and Freud is considered to be largely of historical importance in the study of child development. Nevertheless, Darwin's influence remains alive in a wide variety of contemporary theories. For example, Piaget was centrally concerned with how the development of thinking enables children to achieve a successively better adaptive fit with environmental demands. A strong Darwinian flavor is also present in modern ethological theory. As we will see later on, ethological researchers compare human children with the offspring of other animal species to discover how various behaviors promote adaptation to the environment and thereby ensure survival.

Beginnings of Empirical Child Study

The Baby Biographies. The first attempts to study the child directly occurred in the late nineteenth and early twentieth centuries in the form of biographical records of a single child's behavior. These accounts involved day-by-day narrative descriptions of the sequential growth of an infant or young child who was generally well known to the observer. An excerpt from one of them, Millicent Shinn's *The Biography of a Baby*, published in 1900, is given below. Here, Shinn begins the record by reflecting on the birth of her young niece, whose growth she followed during the first year of life:

Charles Darwin's (1809–1882) belief that the physical and behavioral characteristics of each species have survival value influenced many important twentieth century theories of child development.

> Its first act is a cry, not of wrath, . . . nor a shout of joy, . . . , but a snuffling, and then a long, thin, tearless á—á, with the timbre of a Scotch bagpipe, purely automatic, but of discomfort. With this monotonous and dismal cry, with its red, shriveled, parboiled skin . . . , squinting, cross-eyed, pot-bellied, and bow-legged, it is not strange that, if the mother . . . has not come to love her child before birth, there is a brief interval occasionally dangerous to the child before the maternal instinct is fully aroused.
>
> It cannot be denied that this unflattering description is fair enough, and our baby was no handsomer than the rest of her kind. The little boy uncle, who had been elated to hear that his niece resembled him, looked shocked and mortified when he saw her. Yet she did not lack admirers. I have never noticed that women (even those who are not mothers) mind a few little aesthetic defects, . . . with so many counterbalancing charms in the little warm, soft, living thing. (pp. 20–21)

Can you can tell from this passage why the baby biographies have often been upheld as examples of how *not* to do research on children? These first empirical records were eventually criticized for emotional investment in their subjects of study, naive and unobjective recording, absence of theoretical direction, and unwarranted interpretation of behavior (Frank, 1943). However, we must keep in mind that the baby biographers were like explorers first setting foot on alien soil. When a field is new, we cannot expect the theories and methods of study to be completely formulated. Moreover, some astute observations did appear in these records, and the biographical approach did have some advantages. Direct recording and description offered potential for preserving the richness and complexity of children's behavior and its continuity over time. Today, the legacy of the baby biographies lives on in contemporary methods of naturalistic observation and in longitudinal research design, in which the development of individual children is followed over time. The baby biographies also provide us with a sense of progress. We can see where we began and how far we have come in our attempts to study the child scientifically.

The Normative Period and Testing. G. Stanley Hall (1846–1924), one of the most influential psychologists of the early twentieth century, is generally regarded as the founder of the child study movement (Dixon & Lerner, 1988). Profoundly influenced by Darwin, Hall devised a theory in which he argued that the development of the child repeated the evolutionary history of species (Hall, 1904). Today, his theory is all but forgotten. However, one of Hall's lasting contributions was his attempt to enhance the scientific value of research on children.

Hall set out to collect a sound body of objective facts on children's development, an effort that launched the **normative approach** to child study. In a normative investigation, quantitative measurements of children's behavior are taken, and age-related averages are computed to chart the course of growth. Bent on creating instruments that would permit the scientific measurement of children's traits and capacities, Hall constructed elaborate questionnaires asking schoolchildren almost everything they could tell about themselves — interests, fears, imaginary playmates, dreams, friendships, everyday knowledge, and more. But because there was no theoretical framework to give meaning to Hall's questions, the findings of his studies were of little value. However, the normative approach did take hold, and it dominated the field until the middle of the twentieth century. The result was a large body of descriptive facts about children's characteristics at different ages, but little information about process — the how and why of development. Yet the child's development had to be described before it could be understood, and the normative tradition became the basis for more sophisticated research that followed later.

One of Hall's students was Arnold Gesell (1880–1961). Like Hall, Gesell based his theory on evolutionary recapitulation. He believed that maturation was the primary force in children's development and that environment had little effect on the overall sequence and rate of growth (Gesell, 1933). Gesell devoted a major portion of his career to collecting detailed normative information on the behavior of infants and children that charted their genetically determined path of development. His schedules of infant development were particularly complete and comprehensive, and they continue to serve as the basis for many items included in modern-day infant intelligence tests. In addition, Gesell tried to make knowledge about child development meaningful to parents. He wrote for the layperson, providing age-related, typical descriptions of children's motor achievements, social behaviors, and personality characteristics (Gesell & Ilg, 1943/1949, 1946/1949). Gesell hoped to relieve parents' anxieties by providing them with information about what to expect at each age. If, as he believed, the timetable of development is the product of millions of years of evolution, then children are inherently knowledgeable about their needs. His child-rearing advice, in the tradition of Rousseau, was a permissive approach that recommended sensitivity and responsiveness to the child's cues.

Another of Hall's students was Lewis Terman (1877–1956). In 1916, at Stanford University, he published the first widely used intelligence test for children — the *Stanford-Binet Intelligence Scale*. The Stanford-Binet was a revision of the work of Alfred Binet and his colleague Theodore Simon in Paris. In the early 1900s, Binet and Simon were given the task of devising a method to identify retarded children in the Paris school system who required placement in special classes. Thus, the measure of intelligence they developed, which provided the impetus for objective testing in the United States, grew out of practical educational concerns.

Previous attempts to create a useful intelligence test had met with little success. However, Binet's approach was unique in that he began with a sophisticated, well-developed theory. In contrast to earlier conceptions of intelligence, which stressed sensitivity to physical stimuli and speed of reaction (Cattell, 1890; Galton, 1883), Binet defined intelligent thought as good judgment, planning, and critical reflection. Then he selected test items that directly reflected these complex abilities. Because of its sound theory and careful construction, the Binet test was successful in discriminating among children who varied in school achievement, and it became the primary yardstick for measuring children's intelligence for decades to come.

Using the Binet test, Terman initiated the first, and the longest-lasting, longitudinal study, the purpose of which was to chart the development of highly intelligent children. In 1921, about 1,500 youngsters with IQs above 135 were selected and followed from childhood well into mature adulthood. The research performed a great practical service in dispelling the once common belief that gifted children were odd and freakish — physically weak, one-sided in their abilities, and socially maladjusted. Terman's subjects proved to be healthier, emotionally more stable, and socially better adjusted than the rest of the population. In adulthood, they showed extraordinary professional accomplishment (Terman, 1925; Terman & Oden, 1959).

Terman's work provided an educationally useful instrument as well as clear evidence that intelligence tests could help in understanding children's development. The mental testing movement was in motion. The study of intellectual differences among children who vary in sex, ethnicity, birth order, family background, and other characteristics became a major focus of research. Intelligence tests also rose quickly to the forefront of the scientific controversy over nature versus nurture that has continued throughout this century.

Contributions from Practitioners

In the 1930s and 1940s, a growing suspicion of the usefulness of norms for understanding the individual case arose among pediatricians and child guidance professionals who had daily contact with the living, growing child. Diminished faith in the normative approach led these professionals to seek alternative conceptions of health and adjustment that took into account the unique life histories of individual children.

Pediatrics. Pediatricians started with an interest in norms because they needed representative information about the physical development of children as the basis for pinpointing deviations from normality. However, from direct contact with individual children, they quickly became aware that, even in bodily dimensions and physical capacities, practically no child fell at the norm (Frank, 1943). With tremendous strides in treating childhood diseases, some pediatricians turned toward a concern for the overall development of the well child and helping parents rear children with behavior problems. Parents also asked pediatricians for advice, and several exceptional practitioners provided it on a national scale by writing best-selling books, such as Benjamin Spock's influential *Baby and Child Care* (first edition, 1946; recent edition, Spock & Rothenberg, 1985) and, more recently, T. Berry Brazelton's popular volumes for parents of infants and young children (1983, 1989; Brazelton & Cramer, 1990).

The interest of pediatricians in child rearing laid the foundation for important collaborative efforts between child development specialists and pediatricians. Mutual interchange between these two fields has had an important payoff in the recent emergence of a new emphasis called *developmental pediatrics*, which integrates physical and psychological assessment of children, traditional health care, and parental guidance. Special contributions of developmental pediatricians to the field of child development include instruments for assessing the developmental status of newborn infants that permit very early diagnosis of neurological impairments (Brazelton, 1984). Another growing specialty within developmental pediatrics concerns the other end of the child development continuum: adolescent health. For many years, the unique physical and psychological changes that take place during adolescence were all but ignored by the medical field. Today, pediatricians recognize that a number of modern teenage problems, including pregnancy, suicide, and drug abuse, demand a combination of both psychological and medical intervention (Hamburg, 1985).

Child Guidance and the Psychoanalytic Approach. Historically, children identified as problem cases were brought to child guidance professionals, many of whom were psychiatrists and social workers. Behavioral misconduct, school failure, and difficulties in parental and peer relations could not be understood and dealt with in the context of normative tests and measurements. While the normative movement had answered the question, "What are children like?," child guidance clinicians had to address the question, "How and why did children become the way they are?" to diagnose and treat their difficulties. They turned for answers to Freud's **psychoanalytic theory** because of its emphasis on understanding the unique developmental history of each child.

Freud's Theory. Sigmund Freud (1856–1939), a Viennese physician and neurologist, encountered patients in his practice with a variety of nervous symptoms, such as hallucinations, fears, and paralyses, that appeared to have no physical basis. Seeking a cure for these troubled adults, Freud found that symptoms could be alleviated by having patients talk freely about painful events of their childhood past that had been forgotten or repressed. Using this "talking cure," he carefully examined the recollections of his patients. Startling the straightlaced Victorian society in which he lived, Freud concluded that infants and young children were sexual beings and that the way they were permitted to express their impulses lay at the heart of their adult behavior. Based on adult remembrances, Freud constructed his *psychosexual theory* of development, emphasizing that how parents manage their youngster's sexual and aggressive drives in early childhood is crucial for healthy personality development.

In Freud's theory, three portions of the personality — the id, ego, and superego — become integrated with one another during a sequence of five stages of development. The **id,** the largest agency of the mind, is inherited and present at birth. It is the seat of basic biological needs and desires. Because the id seeks to satisfy its impulses head-on, without delay, babies soon experience frustration as tensions mount until the drives can be gratified in the real world. The **ego** emerges in early infancy to ensure that the id's desires are satisfied in accordance with reality. Using its mental powers of attending to the environment and storing up experiences in memory, the ego moderates and redirects the id's urgent demands so they are discharged on appropriate objects at acceptable times and places. At the end of early childhood, the **superego,** or seat of conscience, appears. It contains the values and dictates of society and is often in conflict with the id's desires. The superego develops from social interactions with parents, in whom is vested the task of helping children harness their biological impulses. Once the superego is formed, the ego is faced with the increasingly complex task of mediating among the demands of the id, the external world, and the repressive dictates of conscience (Freud, 1923/1974).

Freud (1938/1973) believed that over the course of childhood, sexual impulses shift their place of expression from the oral to the anal to the genital regions of the body. In each stage of development, parents walk a fine line between permitting too much or too little gratification of their child's basic needs. Either circumstance can result in fixation of psychic energies at a particular stage. Too much satisfaction makes the child unwilling to move on to a more mature level of behavior, while too

Sigmund Freud's (1856–1939) psychosexual theory was the first child development theory to focus on the importance of early experience for later development.

little leads the child to continually seek gratification of the frustrated drive. Here is a brief account of Freud's stages of development:

1. **The oral stage** (birth–1 year): In this stage, the id focuses on obtaining sensual pleasure through the oral zone of the body. The newly emerging ego directs the baby's sucking activities toward breast or bottle to satisfy urgent pangs of hunger and for pleasurable oral stimulation. If oral needs are not gratified appropriately during infancy, the individual is likely to discharge them through such obsessive habits as thumb sucking, fingernail biting, and pencil chewing in childhood and overeating and smoking later in life.

2. **The anal stage** (1–3 years): Pleasure is now derived from the anal and urethral areas of the body, and young toddlers and preschoolers enjoy retaining and expelling urine and feces at will. At this stage, the ego must learn to postpone pleasurable release to an appropriate time and place, and toilet training becomes a major issue between parent and child. If parents insist that children be trained before they are physiologically ready or make too few demands, conflicts about anal control may become evident later on in the form of obsessive punctuality, orderliness, and cleanliness or the alternative extreme of messiness and disorder.

3. **The phallic stage** (3–6 years): The focus of id impulses transfers to the genitals, and the child now derives pleasure from genital stimulation. During this stage, Freud's famous _Oedipal conflict_ takes place. The young boy feels a sexual desire for his mother but eventually represses this urge out of fear that his father will punish him for his unacceptable impulses. To retain his parents' love and approval, the boy _identifies_ with, or adopts, his father's characteristics and social values. Becoming like the father also serves as a means of vicariously enjoying the adult's power and pleasures. Freud believed that a similar _Electra conflict_ takes place for girls that leads them to identify with their mothers. With the resolution of the Oedipal conflict, the superego is formed, and the relations between id, ego, and superego established at this time determine the individual's basic personality orientation.

4. **The latency stage** (6 years–puberty): During this stage, sexual instincts lie repressed and dormant. The child works on solidifying the superego by playing and identifying with same-sex children and assimilating social values from adults beyond the family.

5. **The genital stage** (post-puberty): Pubertal maturation causes the sexual drive of the earlier phallic stage to be reactivated, but now it can be gratified through love relationships outside the family. If development has proceeded appropriately during the earlier stages, it culminates at this time in marriage, mature genital sexuality, and the birth and rearing of children.

Freud's theory highlighted the importance of family relationships for children's development and provided a framework for understanding children's emotional problems. In addition, it was the first theory to emphasize the importance of early experience for later development. Nevertheless, Freud's perspective was eventually criticized. First, the theory overemphasized the influence of erogenous zones and sexual feelings in development. It failed to recognize that developmental tasks of a social and intellectual nature also prepare children for adulthood and that important ones are dealt with beyond the early childhood years. Second, because it was based on the problems of sexually repressed, middle-class adults, some aspects of Freud's theory did not apply to child development in cultures differing from nineteenth century Victorian society. Finally, another reason Freud's ideas were called into question was that he never really studied children directly.

Erik Erikson's Expansion of Freud's Theory. Several of Freud's contemporaries and followers took what was useful from his theory and stretched and rearranged it in

*Erik Erikson (1902–)
expanded Freud's stages of
development and was one of
the first theorists to address
development throughout the
life span.*

ways that improved upon Freud's vision. The most important of these neo-Freudians for the field of child development is Erik Erikson (1902–). Erikson's interest in children began with his work as teacher of the sons and daughters of Freud's psychoanalytic circle in Vienna. Although he originally intended to become an artist, Erikson was captivated by Freud's ideas. Eventually, he graduated from the Vienna Psychoanalytic Institute, having developed a deep concern for the development, treatment, and education of children. The European upheaval of World War II brought Erikson to the United States, where he made major advances in psychoanalytic theory by building upon Freud's work. In 1950, Erikson's most important contributions were published in *Childhood and Society*, which is still among the books most widely read by child development specialists today.

Although Erikson accepted Freud's basic psychosexual framework, he provided an expanded picture of the tasks of development at each stage. He emphasized the *psychosocial* outcomes of development — how each Freudian stage contributes to the development of a unique personality and at the same time helps the individual become an active, contributing member of society. A series of basic psychological conflicts, each of which is resolved along a continuum from positive to negative outcomes, characterizes the course of development. As shown in Table 1.1, Erikson's first five stages parallel Freud's stages. However, Erikson did not regard important developmental tasks as occurring only in early childhood. Instead, he believed that significant psychosocial problems are addressed at all stages of life and was one of the first to recognize the life-span nature of development. Finally, unlike Freud, Erikson emphasized that normal development at each stage must be understood in relation to the child's unique life situation and cultural context. Here is a brief description of each of Erikson's stages:

1. **Basic trust versus mistrust** (birth – 1 year): From warm, responsive maternal care and pleasurable sensations while feeding, infants gain a sense of trust, or confidence, that people who care for them are predictable, good, and gratifying. Mistrust of others is promoted when infants have to wait too long for comfort and are handled harshly and insensitively.

2. **Autonomy versus shame and doubt** (1 – 3 years): During this stage of achieving muscular control and exercising new exploratory skills of walking, climbing, and manipulating, the child develops mental powers of choosing and deciding. Autonomy is fostered when parents offer guided opportunities for free choice and do not overly restrict, force, or shame the child.

3. **Initiative versus guilt** (3 – 6 years): Through make-believe play, children learn about the roles and institutions of society and gain insight into what kind of person they can become. Initiative, involving a sense of ambition and social responsibility, develops when parents support their child's emerging sense of purpose and direction. The danger at this stage is that parental demands for self-control will lead to overcontrol or too much guilt.

4. **Industry versus inferiority** (6 years – puberty): This is the school age, during which children develop an industrious capacity for productive work, cooperative participation with others, and pride in doing things well. Inferiority, the sense that one will never be good at anything, develops when children's experiences at school, in the peer group, and with parents do not foster feelings of competence and mastery.

5. **Identity versus identity diffusion** (adolescence): This is a culminating stage, marking the transition between childhood and adulthood. In it, the tasks of the earlier stages become integrated into a lasting sense of identity. Past and present experiences, along with expectations for the future, are brought together into a coherent sense of who one is and one's place in society. The negative outcome, identity diffusion, is marked by confusion about one's sexual, occupational, and self-definition.

Table 1.1. The Relationship between Freud's and Erikson's Stages

PERIOD OF DEVELOPMENT	FREUD'S PSYCHOSEXUAL STAGES	ERIKSON'S PSYCHOSOCIAL STAGES
Birth–1 year	Oral stage	Basic trust versus mistrust
1–3 years	Anal stage	Autonomy versus shame and doubt
3–6 years	Phallic stage	Initiative versus guilt
6 years–puberty	Latency stage	Industry versus inferiority
Adolescence	Genital stage	Identity versus identity diffusion
Young adulthood		Intimacy versus isolation
Middle adulthood		Generativity versus stagnation
Old age		Ego integrity versus despair

6. **Intimacy versus isolation** (young adulthood): Once a sense of personal identity is achieved, young people turn toward the task of establishing meaningful, intimate ties to other people. Although important relationships with members of the opposite sex are established at this time, close friendships with members of the same sex also occur. Both enhance the individual's sense of identity and provide gratifying feelings of connectedness to others. Young adults who experience negative outcomes at this stage are unable to establish close relationships. They cannot risk the possibility of rejection or disagreement and remain isolated from others.

7. **Generativity versus stagnation** (middle adulthood): Generativity means giving of oneself to the next generation, a task accomplished through child rearing, caring for other people, and productive work. The person who fails to contribute in one or more of these ways to the continuation of society feels a sense of stagnation, boredom, and absence of meaningful accomplishment.

8. **Ego integrity versus despair** (old age): In this final stage, individuals look back on the kind of person they have been and what they have accomplished over their lifetime. Integrity results from the feeling that life was worth living as it happened,

According to Erikson, these school-age children have already developed a sense of initiative and have some insight into what kinds of people they can become. They now display an industrious capacity for work and cooperative participation.

and with it, death is not threatening. Old people who are dissatisfied with their life course feel a sense of despair. Since time is too short to correct life's shortcomings, they fear death.

All psychoanalytic theorists accept the *clinical method* as the most effective way to gather information about a child's development and emotional health. Sometimes referred to as the case study approach, the clinical method combines interview material obtained from the child, family members, and others who know the child well; results on psychological tests; and observations of the child in a clinic setting and sometimes in everyday contexts as well. The information gathered is synthesized into a description of the unique personality functioning of the individual child so that professionals can better understand the child's problems and come up with effective ways to solve them. Because data obtained through the clinical method are often selective and subjective in nature, it is risky to rely on them for conclusions about children in general. Nevertheless, clinical records serve as rich sources of ideas about child development that can be tested systematically by using other procedures.

Currently, psychoanalytic theory is no longer in the mainstream of child development research. There are various speculations as to why this is the case. Psychoanalytic theory may have become isolated from the rest of the field because it was so strongly committed to the clinical approach that it failed to acknowledge the importance of other methods (Sears, 1975). In addition, many psychoanalytic concepts, such as the unconscious, infantile sexuality, and the Oedipal conflict, seem so vague that they are either difficult or impossible to test empirically (Nagel, 1959; Schultz, 1975).

Despite its shortcomings, psychoanalytic theory provided a tremendous stimulus to research on many aspects of child development, including mother-infant attachment, aggression, sibling and peer relationships, child-rearing practices, moral development, sex-role development, and adolescent identity. Also, the clinical method was applied to areas other than personality. For example, we will see later on that it was adopted and modified by Piaget, who used a flexible, open-ended means of questioning children to investigate their developing cognitions.

THE RISE OF MODERN THEORY AND METHOD

Behaviorism

In the late 1930s and 1940s, child study was profoundly influenced by a perspective that differed radically from psychoanalysis: **behaviorism,** a tradition consistent with Locke's tabula rasa. Behaviorist theory originated in several preceding decades of research by academic psychologists, beginning with the work of John B. Watson (1878–1958). Watson wanted to create an objective science of psychology. He believed that directly observable events — stimuli and responses — should be the focus of study, not fuzzy internal constructs of the mind.

Impressed with the work of Ivan Pavlov in the Soviet Union, who taught dogs to salivate at the sound of a buzzer by pairing it with the presentation of food, Watson performed an historic experiment in which he applied Pavlov's principles of *classical conditioning* to children's behavior. Albert, a 9-month-old baby, was taught to fear a neutral stimulus — a furry white rat — after Watson presented it several times in the company of a loud, obnoxious sound. Little Albert, who initially reached out eagerly to touch the soft white object, soon cried vehemently and turned his head away at the mere sight of it (Watson & Raynor, 1920). On the basis of findings like these, Watson concluded that environment was the supreme force in child development. Children, he thought, could be molded in any direction adults desired if they carefully controlled stimulus-response associations.

With Watson's behaviorism, an American experimental child psychology was born. Learning became its key element, and biological factors (such as those empha-

John B. Watson (1878–1958) was the founder of behaviorism, a theory that led to the emergency of experimental child psychology.

sized by Gesell and Freud) were important only in providing a basic foundation for learned responses. Following Watson, American behaviorism underwent several lines of development. The first was Clark Hull's *drive reduction* theory. According to this view, the organism continually acts to satisfy physiological needs and reduce states of tension. As *primary drives* of hunger, thirst, and sex are met, a wide variety of stimuli associated with them become *secondary*, or learned *drives*. For example, a Hullian theorist believes that infants will seek the closeness and attention of adults who have given them food or that children will agree to wash dishes to get their allowance because money has been paired with the purchase of ice cream, candy bars, and soft drinks, which are pleasurable reducers of primary drives indeed!

Another variant of behaviorism was B.F. Skinner's *operant conditioning* theory. Skinner rejected Hull's idea that primary drive reduction was the only way to get an organism to learn. According to Skinner's theory, a child's behavior can be increased by following it with a wide variety of *reinforcers* besides food and drink, such as praise, a friendly smile, or a new toy; and it can be decreased with such *punishments* as withdrawal of privileges, parental disapproval, or being sent to be alone in one's room. As the result of Skinner's work, operant conditioning became a broadly applied behaviorist learning paradigm in child psychology.

Social Learning Theory

Psychologists quickly became interested in whether behaviorism might offer a more direct and effective explanation of the development of children's social behavior than the less precise constructs of psychoanalytic theory. This concern sparked a vigorous effort by researchers to take those psychoanalytic predictions that seemed testable, translate them into learning theory terms, and subject them to rigorous experimental verification. For example, Freudian theory predicted that intense frustration of the child's basic desires would lead to anxiety and maladaptive behaviors, such as aggression. Behaviorists adopted this frustration-aggression hypothesis and studied it thoroughly. Children's aggressive responses were related to the degree of frustration experienced and to rewards and punishments for aggressive behavior (Dollard et al., 1939). With such investigations, the field of child development entered the scientifically controlled environment of the laboratory, and a new **social learning theory** of childhood emerged. Social learning theorists accepted the principles of conditioning and reinforcement identified by the behaviorists who came before them. They also built upon these principles, offering expanded views of how children and adults acquire new responses. After World War II, social learning theory became one of the dominant forces in child development research.

B. F. Skinner (1904–1990) rejected primary drive reduction as the basis for all learning. He developed an alternative learning paradigm, operant conditioning, that has been broadly applied in the field of child development.

Although several varieties of social learning theory emerged, the most influential one was devised by Albert Bandura and his colleagues. Bandura (1967, 1977) is responsible for an extensive line of laboratory investigations demonstrating that observational learning, often referred to as *modeling*, is the basis for a wide variety of children's behaviors, such as aggression, helping, sharing, and sex-typed responses. Bandura recognized that from an early age, children acquire many skills in the absence of direct rewards and punishments, simply by watching and listening to others around them. Why do children imitate some models more readily than others? Research by Bandura and his followers has shown that children are drawn to models who are warm and powerful and who possess desirable objects and characteristics. By acting like these models, children hope to obtain their valued resources for themselves sometime in the future.

Bandura's work continues to influence much research on children's social development. However, like changes in the field of child development as a whole, his theory has become more cognitive, acknowledging that children's abilities to listen, remember, and abstract general rules from complex sets of observed behavior affect their imitation and learning (Bandura, 1986). In fact, Bandura's (1989) most recent theoretical update places such strong emphasis on how children think about themselves and other people that he has come to identify more strongly with the social-cognitive approach (which we take up shortly) than with traditional social learning theory. However, he continues to regard modeling as the foundation for virtually all aspects of social development.

Behaviorism and social learning theory have had a major impact on applied work with children. *Behavior modification* refers to a set of practical procedures that combines reinforcement, modeling, and the manipulation of situational cues to eliminate children's undesirable behaviors and increase their adoption of socially acceptable responses. These principles have largely been used with children who have behavior problems, but they are also effective in dealing with relatively common problems of childhood. For example, in a recent study, preschoolers' anxious reactions during dental treatment were reduced by reinforcing them with small toys for answering questions about a story they were read while the dentist worked. Because the children could not listen to the story and kick and cry at the same time, their disruptive behaviors quickly subsided (Stark et al., 1989).

Although the techniques of behaviorism have proved to be invaluable applied tools, we must keep in mind that making something happen by conditioning children does not mean that these principles provide a complete account of development in natural contexts (Horowitz, 1987). We will see in the following sections that many theorists believe behaviorism offers too narrow a conception of important environmental influences. Behaviorism has also been criticized for underestimating the extent to which children actively contribute to their own development.

The Ecological Perspective

While a great many psychologists embraced the laboratory in the middle part of this century, others had serious reservations about it as an appropriate context for studying child development. Urie Bronfenbrenner, a contemporary leader of theory and research in the **ecology of human development**, suggested that an overemphasis on laboratory research had caused developmental psychology to become "the science of strange behavior of children in strange situations with strange adults for the briefest possible periods of time" (1979, p. 19). A new breed of psychologists advocated the study of children in their natural environments. Laboratory research, while scientifically *rigorous*, was not necessarily *relevant*, that is, generalizable to the everyday contexts in which children were living their lives and growing up.

In the late 1940s, Roger Barker began research that led to the emergence of a field of study called *ecological psychology*. Its basic premise was that natural environments were a major source of influence on human behavior. Research demonstrating the explanatory power of the environment involved recording behavior as it happened. Naturalistic observation, first introduced by the baby biographers decades before, was refined into a major tool for gathering information about children's development.

Many of the first ecological studies of children focused on the impact of school settings. An early investigation was Barker and Gump's (1964) *Big School, Small School*. The findings showed that pupils attending small as opposed to large high schools received an enhanced extracurricular experience. A greater percentage felt an obligation to become involved in activities, actually participated, and held positions of leadership and responsibility. Consequently, in small schools there were proportionately fewer outsiders—that is, pupils on the fringe who did not participate at all.

Other ecological studies have compared such environments as open versus traditional classrooms, day care versus home rearing experiences, and different housing arrangements, such as living in high-rise versus low-rise buildings. Results on this last topic provide a vivid illustration of the usefulness of ecological research for the design of safe, healthy rearing environments for children. For example, apartment noise increases as one moves from higher to lower stories in high-rise city buildings.

Children living for four or more years on lower floors have poorer auditory discrimination skills and read less well than those living on the upper floors (Cohen, Glass, & Singer, 1973). However, living on the higher floors contributes to social isolation, health-related complaints, family tension, and an increase in child abuse (Parke & Collmer, 1975). Upper floor residence hampers family members' easy access to environmental escape valves in the form of playgrounds and the out-of-doors.

Bronfenbrenner (1979, 1989) has expanded Barker's conception of important environmental influences. In Bronfenbrenner's theory of the ecology of human development, the environment is envisioned as a series of nested structures that extend beyond the home, school, and neighborhood settings in which children spend their everyday lives (see Figure 1.1). Each layer is regarded as having a powerful impact on children's development.

The innermost level is called the **microsystem,** which refers to the activities, roles, and relationships in the child's immediate surroundings. Traditionally, child development specialists emphasized adults' effects on children when studying two-person, or *dyadic*, relationships at the microsystem level. Bronfenbrenner points out that not only do adult agents affect children's behavior, but children also influence the behavior of adults. In other words, all dyadic relationships are bidirectional and reciprocal. Today, much more research in child development recognizes the impact of children's characteristics on the reactions they receive from others. Also, dyadic

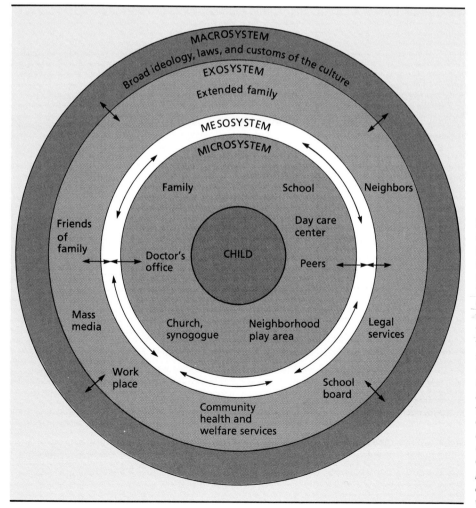

Figure 1.1. Bronfenbrenner's ecological model of the environment as a series of nested structures. The microsystem refers to relations between the child and the immediate environment, the mesosystem to connections among the child's immediate settings, the exosystem to social settings that affect but do not contain the child, and the macrosystem to the overarching ideology of the culture. *(Adapted from* The Child: Development in a Social Context, *edited by* C. B. Kopp and J. B. Krakow. © 1982, Addison-Wesley Publishing Co., Reading, Massachusetts. P. 648. Reprinted with permission.)

interaction is indirectly influenced by the presence of *third parties* within the microsystem. If other individuals in the setting are supportive, the quality of dyadic exchange is enhanced. For example, when fathers give mothers encouragement in their caregiving role, mothers are more effective in feeding their babies. In contrast, marital tension and conflict is associated with inept infant feeding (Pedersen, 1976). Child development within the microsystem must be understood in terms of these complex, interacting relationships.

At the second level of Bronfenbrenner's model is the **mesosystem.** It refers to relationships among microsystems, such as home, school, neighborhood, and child care center. Bronfenbrenner believes that child development is facilitated by interconnections among these settings. For example, a child's ability to learn to read may depend not just on learning activities that take place in the first grade, but also on the extent to which those activities carry over to and are encouraged in the home environment. A mother's interaction with her child may be affected by the child's relationships with caregivers in a day care center and vice versa. Mother-child and caregiver-child relationships are each likely to support child development when there are links, in the form of mutual visits and exchange of information, between the home and the center.

The **exosystem** refers to social settings that do not actually contain children but that nevertheless affect their experiences in immediate settings. Exosystems can be formal, such as the parent's workplace and organizational memberships or health and welfare services in the community. They can also be informal, such as parents' social networks—friends and extended family members who provide advice and support

---

◆ **THEORY, RESEARCH, AND APPLICATIONS** ◆

T*he Neighborhood Walk: Sources of Support in Middle Childhood*   Box 1.1

Theory. In an unusual study, Brenda Bryant (1985) examined children's everyday environments as important sources of support for their social and emotional development in middle childhood. Consistent with Bronfenbrenner's ecological perspective, Bryant reasoned that children are affected not just by the environments others establish for them, but also by the ones they select and create for themselves. She predicted that as children get older, they form their own *mesosystems*—complex networks of supportive settings extending beyond the immediate family. In addition, she expected that such networks would be positively related to children's socioemotional functioning—the way they think and feel about themselves and their ability to get along with others.

Research. To assess children's environmental supports, a unique interviewing procedure called the "neighborhood walk" was used. Seven- and 10-year-old children each toured their neighborhood with an investigator and reported on important aspects of their personal and social worlds—friends, relatives, neighbors, pets, clubs, organizations, and places to go off alone. Once the walk was complete, a wide variety of assessments of children's socioemotional capacities were made.

The findings showed that children's networks of social support expand with age. Ten-year-olds had established more complex mesosystem relationships than had 7-year-olds. For example, older children felt that adults of their parents' and grandparents' generations were more salient in their lives, and they more often viewed pets as special friends. An important part of development during middle childhood seems to involve building bridges from immediate family to extended family and community ties.

Consistent with Bronfenbrenner's concept of the mesosystem, Bryant found that children's networks of support predicted their socioemotional functioning better than did any single source of support. However, the relationship of these networks to development was complex, depending on such factors as the child's age and family size. For example, several aspects of support—intimate talks with pets and with adults of the grandparents' generation, visits to mother's workplace, and involvement in organizations such as scouting or 4-H—were related to more positive socioemotional functioning among 10-year-olds, but not among 7-year-olds. Bryant speculated that either older children use environmental supports more effectively or by age 10 the influence of these supports has had more time to take ef-for child rearing. Bronfenbrenner emphasizes the importance of goals and activities within the exosystem that support actions on behalf of the developing child. For example, flexible work schedules, paid maternity and paternity leave, and sick leave for parents whose children are ill are ways that work environments can help parents in their parenting roles and, indirectly, enhance child development. Research also demonstrates the potentially negative impact of a breakdown in exosystem activities. Families who are socially isolated, that is, who have few personal or community-based relationships on which to rely, and families who are affected by unemployment show an increased incidence of child abuse (Emery, 1989).

The outermost level of Bronfenbrenner's model is the **macrosystem.** It is not a specific environmental context. Instead, it refers to the overarching ideology, values, laws, regulations, and customs of a particular culture. The priority given by the macrosystem to children's developmental needs is especially crucial in determining children's experiences within lower levels of the environmental structure. For example, child abuse is likely to be prevalent in cultures that positively sanction violence and physical force (Belsky, 1980). In addition, in countries that place a priority on developing high quality standards for child care and allocate public funds to ensure that those standards are met, children are likely to experience positive, stimulating interactions with peers and adults in day care centers.

According to Bronfenbrenner (1989), we must keep in mind that the environment is not a static entity that impinges on the child in a uniform way. Instead, it is a dynamic, ever-changing force in development. Important events, such as the birth of a sibling, entering school, or moving to a new neighborhood, modify the existing

In middle childhood, children establish their own social networks that extend beyond the immediate family. The support they receive from these sources enhances their social and emotional development.

fect. For children from large families, close relationships with adults outside the home were positively related to children's empathy, or ability to understand and respond to the feelings of others. In contrast, opportunities for independence from adults were more important for children from small families. Children who had more places to go off by themselves or with friends—a treehouse, a fort, or a neighbor's garage—were more tolerant of individual differences among people. These findings suggest that in small families where adult involvement with children is fairly intense, an occasional opportunity to break away from it leads to enhanced socioemotional development. In contrast, parental attention is less readily available in large families. Consequently, supplementary rela-

tionships with adults in the community are more important.

Applications. Bryant's findings indicate that children's own social networks and community ties, not just those of their parents, have important implications for children's socioemotional development. Relationships with pets and with adults outside the immediate family sphere appear to be particularly supportive, perhaps because both offer unconditional acceptance of children's feelings and special opportunities to explore and acknowledge those feelings. Bryant's investigation suggests that it is vitally important to foster children's informal ties to kin and community during middle childhood.

relationship between the child and the environment, thereby creating new conditions that affect the course of development. Moreover, the timing of environmental change influences its impact. Arrival of a new sibling has very different implications for the home-bound toddler than for the self-reliant adolescent, who has established a world of gratifying relationships and activities beyond the family. This example, along with research reviewed in Box 1.1, suggests an additional point we must keep in mind to fully appreciate the complex interplay between person and environment. Children select, modify, and create some of their own external conditions. How they do so depends on their age, their distinctive physical, personality, and intellectual characteristics, and the environmental opportunities available to them. Consequently, in ecological theory, development is neither driven by inner forces nor automatically controlled by environmental circumstances. Instead, children are products as well as producers of their environments, both of which form a network of interdependent effects on development. We will see many more examples of these important principles in later chapters of this book.

Finally, Bronfenbrenner (1979) calls for more research on the complex interrelationships among different parts of the environment. He recommends *ecological experiments*, or experiments of nature, as ideal ways to understand the impact of the environment on the developing child. In an ecological experiment, the investigator intervenes in the natural environment, changes it, and looks to see what effect the intervention has on the individual. Ecological experiments can be conducted at any level of Bronfenbrenner's model. At the level of the exosystem, an example is providing socially isolated parents of abused children with support in the form of parenting groups where they can discuss child-rearing problems and experience gratifying social relationships. Ecological experiments at the overarching level of the macrosystem, where established values and social policies are restructured in directions that are more favorable to children's development, are considered by Bronfenbrenner to be especially important.

Ethology

Another theoretical perspective that emphasizes the relevance of environmental contexts to behavior is **ethology.** It began to be applied to research on children in the 1960s and continues to be influential today. Ethology is concerned with understanding the adaptive, or survival, value of behavior and its evolutionary history (Hinde, 1989). The origins of ethology can be traced to the work of Darwin; its modern foundations were laid by two European zoologists, Konrad Lorenz and Niko Tinbergen. Watching the behaviors of diverse animal species in their natural habitats, Lorenz and Tinbergen observed a number of built-in behavior patterns that promote survival. The most well-known of them is *imprinting*, the early following behavior of certain baby birds that ensures the young will stay close to the mother and be fed and protected from predators. Imprinting occurs during an early, restricted time period of development. If the mother is not present during this time, but an object resembling her in important features is, such as a squatting, quacking adult or a moving milk bottle, young ducklings may imprint on it instead (Lorenz, 1952). Observations of imprinting led to a major theoretical concept that has since been widely applied in child development: the *critical period*. It refers to a limited time span during which the organism is biologically prepared to acquire certain behaviors but requires the support of an appropriately stimulating environment. Many investigators have conducted studies to find out whether complex cognitive and social behaviors of human beings must be learned during a restricted time period, and we will discuss their findings in subsequent chapters of this book.

Inspired by observations of imprinting, John Bowlby (1969) applied ethological theory to the understanding of the human mother-infant relationship. Bowlby argued that attachment behaviors of infants to their mothers, in the form of smiling, babbling, grasping, and crying, were built-in social signals that encouraged the mother to approach the infant. They could best be understood from an evolutionary perspective, as behaviors that had evolved because they favored survival of the young. By promoting proximity to the mother, attachment behaviors ensure that the infant will be adequately cared for and protected from danger. Notice how this ethological view of attachment, with its focus on innate infant signals, differs sharply from the behaviorist drive reduction explanation we mentioned earlier — that the baby's desire for physical closeness to the mother is a secondary drive based on feeding.

Observations by ethologists of a wide variety of animal behaviors have recently stimulated ethological investigations of dominance hierarchies, aggression, play, cooperation, and nonverbal communication among human children. Results of these studies provide us with a stark reminder that our evolutionary ancestry is retained in many of our everyday social behaviors. For example, Strayer and Strayer (1976) recorded naturally occurring conflicts among preschoolers and found evidence of a stable dominance hierarchy. The low frequency of counterattacks in children's conflicts suggests that the adaptive value of the dominance hierarchy is to reduce aggression within the group, just as it does in other primates. Other investigations have identified specific nonverbal cues in human children that signal dominance and submission. For example, Zivin (1977) observed a facial expression, involving raised eyebrows and chin combined with a direct stare toward another child's eyes. When used in competitive encounters between children, the child who displays it almost always wins. The facial expression is similar to dominance-related threat stares in nonhuman primates.

The research methodology of ethology begins with naturalistic observation. To understand the evolutionary and adaptive significance of behavior, it must first be observed in its natural context. Then ethologists may conduct laboratory investigations in which the specific environmental eliciting conditions for behaviors are studied. Harry Harlow's research, in which the behavior of monkeys reared under a variety of conditions — in isolation, with various types of surrogate mothers, and with peers — is an example of the latter type of investigation (Suomi & Harlow, 1978). Another powerful laboratory procedure that has been employed to study attachment in human infants is Mary Ainsworth's *Strange Situation*. Infants' responses to a series of brief separations from and reunions with their mothers are observed. On the basis of the pattern of the babies' reactions, the security of the attachment bond is assessed (Ainsworth et al., 1978).

The ethological perspective is an excellent example of how child development has borrowed from other disciplines. Research efforts emphasize the genetic and biological bases of behavior, but learning, because it lends flexibility and greater environmental adaptiveness to behavior, is also considered important. Since ethologists believe that behavior can best be understood in terms of its adaptive value, they are interested in a full understanding of environmental contexts, including physical, social, and cultural aspects. Thus, the interests of ethologists are broad; they aim to understand the entire organism-environment system (Hinde, 1989; Miller, 1989).

Ethological research is also of practical significance. Social changes over the last two decades, such as the rise in single parent families and in substitute child care as mothers enter the labor force in increasing numbers, have led to dramatic changes in the early environments of children. Ethological theory can help us understand which aspects of the environment are essential to maintain and what kinds of changes are likely to strain the adaptive resources of the infant and young child.

Piaget's Cognitive-Developmental Theory

If there is any single individual who has had more influence on the modern field of child development than any other, it is the Swiss psychologist Jean Piaget (1896 – 1980). Although American psychologists had been aware of Piaget's work since 1930, they did not grant it much attention until the 1960s. A major reason was that his theory and methods of studying children were very much at odds with the behaviorist tradition that dominated American psychology during the middle of the twentieth century.

Recall from our earlier description of behaviorism and social learning theory that the child was considered to be a passive organism whose responses were shaped by environmental stimuli. Behaviorists such as Watson and Skinner did not speculate about internal mental processes. Thinking could be reduced to simple connections between stimuli and responses, and the course of development was quantitative, consisting of a gradual increase in the number and strength of these connections with age. In contrast, Piaget did not think that knowledge was bestowed upon a passive child. He believed that children construct it actively as they manipulate and explore their world.

Piaget's view of development was greatly influenced by his early training in biology. Central to his **cognitive-developmental theory** is the biological concept of *adaptation* (Piaget, 1971). Just as the structures of the body are adapted to fit with the environment, so the structures of the mind develop over the course of infancy and childhood to achieve a better adaptive fit with external reality. In early childhood, children's understanding of their world is very different from that of adults. For example, preschoolers say that a quantity of liquid changes when it is poured into a differently shaped container and that dreams are real objects visible to other people. These ideas are revised as a result of the child's constant efforts to achieve an *equilibrium*, or balance, between internal structures and the demands of the external world (Beilin, 1989; Kuhn, 1988).

Piaget believed that the child traverses a series of four broad stages of development, each characterized by a qualitatively different organization of cognitive structures. During the *sensorimotor stage* of infancy, the structures are action patterns aimed at recognizing and exploring objects and events with the senses. Sensorimotor behaviors gradually become internalized and representational during the *preoperational stage* of the preschool years. Preschoolers' new symbolic capacities are most evident in the rapid progress they make in language acquisition. In the *concrete operational stage*, internalized mental structures become the more organized and accurate thinking of the elementary school child, who can think about concrete problems in a logical fashion. For example, during this stage, children understand that a quantity of liquid is unchanged after it is poured from a tall, narrow container into a short, wide one. Finally, in the *formal operational stage* of adolescence, the structures become the abstract, logically organized system of adult intelligence. When faced with a complex problem, the adolescent speculates about all possible solutions before trying them out systemically in the real world, much like a scientist experimenting in the laboratory. Piaget (1966) thought that adults could do little to deliberately teach, train, or accelerate the child's movement through these stages. Instead, children had to act directly on experience and initiate their own cognitive transformations. However, the availability of a rich, stimulating environment was still considered important as a general context for developmental change.

Piaget used research methods that were designed to uncover the child's unique construction of reality. He made careful observations of his own three children in infancy and showed an intuitive genius for arranging situations that revealed the infant's understanding of actions and objects in the surrounding world. With older children, he used the method of the *clinical interview* (Piaget, 1926/1930). Unlike a test, in which the form of the question is the same for all children and the examiner's interest is in whether the child's answer is right or wrong, the clinical interview is flexible and open-ended. Verbal probes are used in which questions are varied and rephrased in an effort to ensure that children's responses truly represent their way of thinking. Here is an excerpt from a clinical interview in which Piaget tried to find out about a young child's understanding of dreams (the child's name and age in years and months are given at the beginning):

METR (5:9): "Where does the dream come from? — *I think you sleep so well that you dream.* — Does it come from us or from outside? — *From outside.* — What do we dream with? — *I don't know.* — With the hands? . . . With nothing? — *Yes, with nothing.* — When you are in bed and you dream, where is the dream? — *In my bed, under the blanket. I don't really know. If it was in my stomach, the bones would be in the way and I shouldn't see it.* — Is the dream there when you sleep? — *Yes, it is in the bed beside me . . .* — You see the dream when you are in the room, but if I were in the room, too, should I see it? — *No, grownups don't ever dream.* — Can two people ever have the same dream? — *No, never.* — When the dream is in the room, is it near you? — *Yes, there!* (pointing to 30 cms. in front of his eyes)." (Piaget, 1926/1930, pp. 97–98)

Piaget's clinical interviewing approach has been criticized because it is not applied in the same way to all children. However, the method reflects the central core of Piaget's theory in that it is a systematic effort to understand and explore the child's point of view and to avoid an adult-centered interpretation of responses.

Piaget's cognitive-developmental perspective has stimulated more research on children's development than any other single theory. Nevertheless, recent research has raised questions about the accuracy of his stages of development. Some investigators have concluded that the quality of children's thinking at each stage forms a far less unified whole than Piaget assumed and that the maturity of children's cognitions may depend on their familiarity with the task and the kind of knowledge sampled. Furthermore, many studies have shown that children's performance on Piagetian tasks can be improved with training, raising questions about his conclusion that little can be done in the way of direct teaching to foster the child's developmental progress (Gelman & Baillargeon, 1983).

Despite these challenges, Piaget convinced many developmental psychologists that children are active learners and that their minds are inhabited by rich structures of knowledge. Piaget's emphasis on an active and adaptive organism has been especially influential in the recent expansion of research on infant development, including perceptual, motor, cognitive, and social competencies.

Practically speaking, Piaget's theory encouraged the development of educational philosophies and programs that emphasize children's discovery learning and direct experimentation with the environment. His work also stimulated the design of new intelligence tests that assess children's progress in terms of Piagetian stage-related milestones. In Chapter 6, we will consider Piaget's theory in greater detail.

CURRENT AND FUTURE DIRECTIONS

New ways of thinking about and studying the child are constantly emerging — questioning, building upon, and enhancing the discoveries of earlier theories. Today, a burst of fresh approaches and research emphases — information processing, social cognition, a renewal of enthusiasm for studying children's emotions, and cross-cultural investigations — are broadening our understanding of children's development.

Information Processing

Child development specialists had become disenchanted with behaviorism as a complete account of children's learning and disappointed in their attempts to fully validate Piaget's stage theory. They turned to the field of cognitive psychology as a whole for new ways to understand the development of children's thinking. Today, a leading approach for studying children's cognition is **information processing.** Influenced by research in adult cognition, psycholinguistics, and computer science, information processing is not so much a unified theory as a general approach in which the human being is viewed as a system through which information flows (Klahr, 1989). Between presentation to the senses at *input* and behavioral responses at *output*, information is actively coded, transformed, and organized.

Information processing is often thought of as a field of scripts, frames, and flow-charts. Sequential diagrams are used to map the precise series of steps individuals use to solve problems and complete tasks, much like the representations devised by programmers to get computers to perform a series of "mental" operations. The flowchart approach ensures that information processing models of child and adult cognitive functioning will be highly explicit, not vague and imprecise. However, the use of these computerlike analogies does not mean that psychologists believe the thinking of human beings is identical to that of a computer. Instead, since human beings design and program computers, information processing theorists believe that important insights can be gained from computers about the strategies people use to represent experience and solve problems (Klahr, 1989).

Several lines of research were especially influential in the current embrace of information processing by child development specialists. The popularity of the computer metaphor for human problem solving may be traced to important advances in the field of computer science following World War II. Of no less consequence were the ground-breaking discoveries of linguist Noam Chomsky (1957) that children comprehend and produce novel utterances they have never heard before. Chomsky argued that children are *rule-oriented* in their acquisition of language. His idea that children use internal rules that must be inferred from the language they hear (input) and the language they produce (output) is consistent with an information processing framework. By the 1960s, Chomsky's work had sparked a tremendous upsurge in developmental studies of children's language. Psychologists' excitement concerning new evidence for rule-governed aspects of language spread to the search for corresponding rules and strategies in children's thinking.

Today, the information processing approach to child development encompasses a wide variety of research activities, including studies of children's attention, memory, planning strategies, comprehension of written and spoken prose, and problem solving. Unlike Piaget's theory, there is no assumption of stages of development. Rather, since the processes studied apply to all ages but may be present to a lesser extent in children, the developmental viewpoint is largely one of quantitative increase rather than qualitative change.

The methods used are mostly experimental and laboratory-based. For example, researchers use reaction times to examine the temporal course of information flow, eye movement data to find out how infants and young children process visual information, and patterns of errors and verbal reports to determine the strategies children use to remember and solve problems.

The information processing approach has begun to provide important practical implications for children's education. Successful learning is more likely if the tasks required of children are within their perceptual, memory, and problem-solving capabilities. Already, there is a trend in information processing to study educationally important domains of learning, such as reading, mathematics, and scientific problem solving, in which children's performances are described and factors that give them difficulty are identified (Hall, 1989; Resnick, 1989; Siegler, 1983b).

Social Cognition

So far, information processing has not had much impact on the understanding of social and personality development. However, another area has evolved over the past two decades that has led to substantial advances in our understanding of these two topics. It is called the development of **social cognition.** In earlier theories, such as psychoanalytic and social learning, the child was not described as a *thinking* social being. Now social and cognitive development have been brought together.

Research in social cognition examines how children of different ages think about themselves and their social world and how this reasoning is related to their social behaviors. Like information processing, there is no single unified theory, but rather an approach emphasizing children's active efforts to make sense of their social experiences. A major influence has been Piaget's theory. For example, his stages of cognitive development sparked new theories of children's conceptions of self, friendship, and morality (Damon, 1977; Kohlberg, 1969, 1976; Montemayor & Eisen, 1977). In each of these theories, the development of *perspective-taking*—children's capacity to understand what another person is thinking and feeling—is central and believed to underlie a wide variety of positive social behaviors, such as cooperativeness, kindness, helpfulness, friendliness, and generosity (Selman, 1980).

The interest of child development specialists in social cognition has also been stimulated by work in the mainstream of academic social psychology, especially *attribution theory*. Attributions are everyday explanations people give for the causes of their own and others' behavior. For example, in achievement situations, children can attribute their successes and failures to ability (how smart they are), effort (how hard they try), or luck. Such attributions originate in part from children's social experiences with teachers and parents, and they predict how hard children are willing to try again at a given activity and whether they expect to succeed in the future (Dweck, 1983).

Since the research topics are diverse, a variety of methods have been employed to study children's social cognition. The Piagetian clinical interview is often used to probe for children's social understanding—for example, what children of different ages mean by a "best friend." Children have also been presented with a variety of tasks in the laboratory, such as perspective-taking problems in which they must describe another person's point of view. Sometimes children are observed in the natural environment interacting with one another, and their social behaviors and statements are used to infer their social knowledge.

Research in social cognition also has important practical implications. Children's attributions of success and failure are of concern to educators, and children profit from interventions designed to help them change attributions that lead to self-defeating behaviors in learning situations (Dweck, 1975, 1986). Programs that train children in perspective-taking and others that provide experiences in social problem solving, such as how to gain entry into peer play groups and sustain positive interactions with agemates, have been developed to help children who have interpersonal problems (Asher & Renshaw, 1981; Chandler, 1973; Shantz, 1983).

The Study of Emotions

Although a cognitive emphasis dominated child development during the middle part of this century and continues to be vigorously influential today, a rebirth of interest in children's emotions has occurred over the last decade, and it shows every indication of gathering additional momentum in the future. Once the impact of the psychoanalytic perspective began to recede in the 1950s and 1960s, emotions were no longer credited with playing a central role in children's development. Instead, they were treated as mere by-products of cognitive processing. For example, smiling and laughter were regarded as indications of children's delight at being able to process a new stimulus, and fear was thought to be produced by events so different from those to which the young child was accustomed that cognitive processing was disrupted, producing anxiety and withdrawal (Kagan, Kearsley, & Zelazo, 1978; McCall & McGhee, 1977). Although these cognitive explanations of emotional reactions proved

The field of child development is currently experiencing a rebirth of interest in children's emotions.

to be partially correct, they failed to account for many emotional phenomena. For example, cognitive theorists could not explain why infants' fear of strangers varies depending on whether they sit close to their mothers or some distance away and why some familiar events and people continue to elicit positive responses from children rather than disinterest and boredom. The deficiencies of the cognitive perspective, coupled with the discovery during the 1970s of innovative laboratory methods that permitted researchers to study emotional reactions more accurately than was previously possible, touched off a new theoretical perspective called the **organizational approach to emotional development** (Campos et al., 1983).

The organizational approach has much in common with ethology in emphasizing the adaptive role of emotions in promoting survival of the organism. In addition, it regards emotions as centrally important in all facets of human behavior. Emotions play a major role in determining what we perceive and remember and how we interpret events in the surrounding world. Moreover, emotions powerfully influence social interaction. For example, infants' and children's smiles elicit positive emotional reactions from their caregivers, and the exchange of smiles draws adults and children closer to one another and encourages them to continue their pleasurable interaction. Emotional reactions also affect physiological processes and physical health, as is illustrated by cases of children who fail to grow normally because they lack the experience of warm, caring parenting (Drotar, 1985).

Over the past two decades, organizational theorists have generated a large body of research on the development of a variety of emotional reactions, such as happiness, interest, surprise, anger, fear, and sadness. Child development specialists have also been interested in studying *temperament*, or individual differences in style of emotional responding. Assessments of children's temperamental styles, such as sociability, activity level, and irritability, are usually derived from parental reports of children's typical emotional reactions or from ratings made by other adults familiar with the child. In some instances, direct observation in the home or laboratory as well as physiological measures of emotional arousal have also been used. Researchers are investigating the long-term stability of temperamental characteristics, the origins of temperament in both heredity and child-rearing practices, and the extent to which early temperament is predictive of adult personality.

Cross-Cultural Research and Vygotsky's Dialectical Theory

Another recent trend in child development research is a dramatic increase in cross-cultural studies. Investigations that make comparisons across cultures and between ethnic and social-class groups within cultures provide insight into whether developmental sequences are universal and characteristic of all children or limited to particular environmental circumstances. Cross-cultural research also aids child development specialists in untangling the respective contributions of biological and environmental factors to the timing and order of appearance of children's behaviors.

Recently, cross-cultural investigations have moved away from examining broad cultural influences on development — for example, whether children in one culture are more advanced in motor development or do better on intellectual tasks than children in another culture. This approach can lead researchers to conclude incorrectly that one culture is superior in enhancing development, while another promotes developmental deficiencies. In addition, it does not help us understand the specific experiences that contribute to cultural differences in children's behavior.

Today, more research is examining the relationship of *culturally specific practices* to children's development. The contributions of the Soviet psychologist Lev Semanovich Vygotsky (1896–1934) have played a major role in this trend. Although Vygotsky developed his theory in the early part of this century, many of his writings were not translated from Russian until quite recently. Once American and European investigators became familiar with his work, it sparked a new wave of research on how children's participation in activities with mature members of their society promotes the development of unique, culturally adaptive competencies.

Vygotsky's (1934/1987, 1930–1935/1978) perspective on development is called **dialectical theory.** The term dialectic, meaning discussion and reasoning through social interaction, is used because cooperative dialogues between children and their socializing agents are regarded as essential for developmental progress. Vygotsky believed that as knowledgeable members of society help children master culturally meaningful activities, the communication occurring between them is gradually incorporated into children's thinking. Once children internalize the essential features of these dialogues, they can use the diverse skills embedded in them to accomplish tasks on their own.

Perhaps you can tell from this brief description that Vygotsky's theory has been especially influential in the study of children's cognition. However, as we will see in greater detail in Chapter 6, Vygotsky's approach to cognitive development is quite different from Piaget's. Recall that Piaget did not regard direct teaching by adults as important for stimulating cognitive change. Instead, he emphasized children's active, independent efforts to make sense of their world. Vygotsky agreed with Piaget that children are active, constructive beings. But unlike Piaget, he regarded cognitive development as a *socially mediated* process — as heavily dependent on the communicative support that adults and more mature peers provide as children try new tasks.

A major contribution of recent cross-cultural research has been the demonstration that cultures select different contexts for children's learning. In line with Vygotsky's theory, social interaction surrounding particular tasks and goals leads to the acquisition of knowledge and skills essential for success in a particular culture. For example, among the Zinacanteco Indians of southern Mexico, girls become expert weavers of complex garments at an early age through the informal guidance of adult experts (Childs & Greenfield, 1982). In Brazil, child candy sellers with little or no schooling develop sophisticated mathematical abilities as the result of buying candy from

Consistent with Vygotsky's theory, cross-cultural research highlights the importance of cooperative dialogues between children and more mature members of society for many aspects of development. Here Kenyan children learn to play a complicated game with the help of a more skilled peer.

wholesalers, pricing it in collaboration with adults and experienced peers, and bargaining with customers on city streets (Saxe, 1988). Moreover, as Box 1.2 illustrates, dramatic transformations in the tasks and relationships that support children's learning can occur in response to broad cultural change.

Findings like these reveal that there are strengths in every culture not present in others because children adapt to the demands of their culture through the mastery of particular activities. The field of child development has again borrowed from another discipline — anthropology — to achieve this understanding. A cross-cultural perspective reminds us that the majority of child development specialists reside in the United States, and their usual subjects of study comprise only a small minority of humankind. We cannot assume that the developmental sequences observed in our own children are "natural" or that the experiences fostering them are "ideal" without looking around the world (Heron & Kroeger, 1981; Laboratory of Comparative Human Cognition, 1983).

SUMMARY OF MAJOR THEORETICAL PERSPECTIVES

The history of child study is a chronicle of contrasting themes of childhood and child development. The major theories and approaches we have discussed, along with their dominant methods and representative applications, are summarized in Table 1.2.

◆ CONTEMPORARY ISSUES: CULTURAL DIFFERENCES ◆

*C*ultural *Change and Child-Rearing Among the* !Kung   Box 1.2

How does change in one part of a culture affect other parts? Recently, Patricia Draper and Elizabeth Cashdan (1988) capitalized on rapid transformations in the subsistence economy of the !Kung[1] people of Botswana, Africa, to find out how child rearing is affected by broad economic and social conditions.

Over the last 30 years, many !Kung have changed from a nomadic hunting and gathering economy to a settled agricultural life supported by gardening and livestock raising. Currently, both foraging and sedentary groups exist in the same geographic area, creating ideal conditions for observing the impact of economic practices on children's everyday lives.

!Kung hunters and gatherers lead a life believed to be similar to conditions under which our species evolved. A temporary camp, consisting of a central yard surrounded by grass huts, comprises the main living area where families spend most of their time. Daily hunting and gathering missions take small numbers of adults several miles from the home base, but most obtain enough food to contribute to group subsistence by working only three out of every seven days. When adults are not foraging, there are tasks to be done in the campground, such as food preparation and tool making. However, a mobile way of life prevents the accumulation of

many possessions that require extensive care and maintenance, and !Kung adults have many free hours to relax around the campfire. Children do not participate in the major work activities of the culture until adolescence because they lack sufficient endurance to keep up on lengthy foraging missions. Moreover, the vast, uniform desert area where the !Kung live contains little of interest to draw children away from the central campground. Consequently, the traditional !Kung way of life produces ample spare time for children and adults alike, and they spend it in intimate social contact with one another. Adults, particularly women and mothers, lavish attention on young children. Infants are breast fed for the first three years of their lives, and intense parent-child bonds develop. In addition, since children are seldom assigned chores that, in many other cultures, train boys and girls in different skills, there is little sex-role differentiation among !Kung youngsters. Instead, boys and girls grow up in strikingly similar social and physical settings.

Life in !Kung agricultural villages contrasts sharply with that of the hunting and gathering communities. A semicircle of permanent houses spread farther apart than the nomadic huts faces outward toward livestock enclosures. The surrounding yard is complex and differentiated, mirroring the many activities that accompany

Three *metatheoretical issues*, or larger questions about the nature of the child and developmental change, which we mentioned at the beginning of this chapter, emerge from comparisons of the theories. Because these metatheoretical issues help us summarize basic similarities and differences among the major theories, let's consider them in greater detail.

1. *Are children active organisms who play a major role in determining the course of their own development, or are they passive recipients of environmental inputs?* This issue contrasts the **organismic model** of child development, reflected in maturational, psychoanalytic, and cognitive-developmental theories, with the **mechanistic model,** represented by behaviorist and social learning theories.

Organismic theorists assume the existence of organizing structures internal to the child that underlie and exert control over development. The organismic model holds that children are active and purposeful contributors to their own development. The environment facilitates growth, but it does not play a major causal role.

In contrast, the mechanistic view focuses on relationships between environmental inputs and behavioral outputs. The model is called mechanistic because children's behavior is likened to the workings of a machine. Change is initiated by the environment, which actively impinges on the child who is a passive reactor. Development is treated as a predictable, manageable consequence of learning, based on fundamental principles of conditioning and modeling.

sedentary life, including farming, harvesting, food storage, and animal grazing. This rich, stimulating physical world offers children many enticing opportunities for play and exploration. At the same time, demanding agricultural tasks occupy adults for most of the daylight hours. Together, these factors cause children to spend more time with peers and less time interacting with parents than their hunting and gathering counterparts. Moreover, village children are expected to help with the farming and livestock workload, and a sex-differentiated pattern of childhood economic participation has recently emerged. Boys (like their fathers) do chores, such as herding livestock, that take them substantial distances from home. In the process, they are granted considerable independence from adult supervision. Girls more often perform food preparation and gardening tasks at or near the central household, where they are closely monitored and instructed by older women. The types of tasks assigned contribute to marked sex differences in children's skills and behavior that do not exist in the hunting and gathering context. For example, the wider spatial range of village-reared boys promotes autonomy, familiarity with life outside the home compound, and proficiency in the languages of nearby peoples. These opportunities are less available to the typical !Kung girl, who receives extensive practice in domestic skills and in compliance with adult directives.

The child-rearing consequences of the changing !Kung economy provide a forceful illustration of how cultures shape children's learning by selecting the daily company they keep and the activities that engage their time. The long-term implications of the new !Kung lifestyle for children's cognitive, social, and personality development remain to be investigated. However, the findings to date indicate that, at the very least, sex-role flexibility is lessened by sedentary agricultural life.

At this point, you may be wondering how nomadic !Kung children are initiated into adult work roles, since unlike village-reared youngsters, they are not directly taught in childhood. Fortunately, many societies create substitutes for adult-child participation in essential activities when it is not possible. In foraging groups, the groundwork is laid informally as children listen to their elders recount previous hunts and swap exciting stories and tales (Super, 1980).

[1] The !Kung speak a language characterized by clicking sounds. The exclamation point represents a click in the pronunciation of their name.

Table 1.2. Summary of Major Theories, Methods, and Practical Applications

MAJOR THEORY OR APPROACH	VIEW OF CHILD DEVELOPMENT	DOMINANT METHODS	REPRESENTATIVE APPLICATIONS
Maturational theory (Hall, Gesell)	Genetically predetermined, naturally unfolding plan of growth	Normative study using questionnaires, observations	Child-rearing advice
Psychoanalytic theory (Freud, Erikson)	Qualitative change through a series of psychosexual and psychosocial stages	Clinical method	Child-rearing advice; treatment of children with emotional problems
Behaviorism and social learning theory (Watson, Skinner, Bandura)	Quantitative increase in learned responses as the result of reinforcement and modeling	Laboratory study	Behavior modification to eliminate undesirable responses and increase socially acceptable behavior
Ecological theory (Barker, Bronfenbrenner)	Natural environments as sources of influence on children's development. The child's relationship to the environment as bidirectional and constantly changing over time	Naturalistic observation	Design of environments that enhance development
Ethology (Bowlby, Ainsworth, Harlow)	Evolutionary origins and adaptive value of behavior. Existence of built-in behavior patterns that promote survival	Naturalistic observation, follow-up laboratory study	Alleviation of features of child-rearing environments that strain children's adaptive resources
Piaget's cognitive-developmental theory	Mental structures change through qualitatively distinct stages. Children actively construct their world	Infant observation, clinical interview	Educational programs emphasizing discovery learning; stage-based assessments of intelligence
Information processing	Quantitative increase in knowledge and active use of processing strategies	Laboratory study	Educational interventions that improve children's processing strategies
Social cognition	Changes in social understanding through qualitatively distinct stages. Children actively think about their social world	Clinical interview, laboratory tasks, and naturalistic observation	Training in perspective-taking and social problem solving for children with interpersonal problems
Organizational approach to emotional development	Adaptive value of emotions. Emotions as central in all aspects of development	Naturalistic observation, laboratory study	Using knowledge about children's emotions to optimize cognitive and social development as well as physical health
Vygotsky's dialectical theory	Cooperative dialogues between children and more knowledgeable members of their culture as essential for developmental progress	Cross-cultural comparisons of children's social experiences and development	Interventions promoting adult-child and peer-child interaction that enhance acquisition of knowledge and skills

2. *Is child development a matter of quantitative or qualitative change?* The quantitative position suggests that development is a linear, cumulative process that proceeds in gradual, continuous increments. Differences between the immature and mature organism are viewed as merely a matter of amount or complexity of behavior, and children are assumed to be similar to adults. Behaviorism, social learning theory, and the information processing approach share this view. In contrast, stage theories of development — psychoanalytic, cognitive-developmental, and social cognition —

view children as having unique, qualitatively distinct ways of thinking, feeling, and responding to the world that must be understood on their own terms. Development is a discontinuous rather than continuous process in which fundamentally new and different modes of behavior emerge following periodic revisions and reorganizations in underlying structures.

3. *Are genetic or environmental factors the most important determinants of child development and behavior?* This is the age-old nature-nurture controversy. Almost all theories have at least given lip service to both sides, but nevertheless, a few have taken extreme positions. For example, in maturational theory, inherited potential for growth is of paramount importance, while the child's experiences are supreme in behaviorism and social learning theory.

Some theories, especially the more recent ones, steer a middle course on these controversial issues. The thinking of many theorists has moderated, and they recognize the importance of both sides. For example, on the nature-nurture issue, psychoanalytic theory, cognitive-developmental theory, and social cognition all recognize biological foundations by describing development in terms of a universal, maturationally determined sequence of stages. However, the child's experiences during each stage are regarded as important for developmental progress. The importance of both maturation and experience can also be seen in the ethological concept of critical period, in which nature determines timing and nurture influences how well the needs of the individual are met during a particular phase of development. Finally, a position intermediate between the mechanistic and organismic extremes characterizes information processing, the ecological perspective, and Vygotsky's dialectical theory. In information processing, an input-output machinelike model coexists with active processing strategies going on within the organism. In ecological and dialectical theories, environmental conditions combine with children's active efforts to master their world.

CHILD DEVELOPMENT AS A RAPIDLY CHANGING FIELD

Six "Great Handbooks," summarizing theory and research in the field of child development, have been published during the last 60 years. The most recent, which appeared in 1983, reveals that child development in the latter part of the twentieth century is still questioning and refining its theories and methods and confronting more directly than ever before the complexity of the child's development (Kessen, 1983). The latest *Handbook of Child Psychology* contains four volumes and over 4,000 pages. There are new chapters on such topics as play, logical thinking, information processing, social cognition, emotional development, and schooling. Three chapters are devoted to language development (as opposed to one in the 1970 Handbook), and an entire volume is given over to the burgeoning research literature on infant development. The 1983 Handbook reflects the use of diverse methods and varied settings to study the child. The scientific respectability of research on children no longer rests as exclusively on laboratory investigations as it did a few decades ago.

The field of child development continues to be influenced by pressing unresolved problems faced by today's children. High infant mortality rates, poor health care for pregnant women and children, teenage pregnancy, widespread child abuse, rising rates of divorce, developmental risks of poverty, and increased demand for child care as women enter the labor force are pervasive national concerns. The need to incorporate lessons from scientific theory and research into our efforts to solve these problems is now recognized, since solutions must be based on good theories of what the child is like and how development occurs. For this reason, child development specialists are no longer exclusively confined to academic settings. As we will see in Chapter 16, they have entered the arena of government policy, and their theoretical principles and methods of study have benefited, in turn, from the stimulus of direct experience with the realities of children's lives (Horowitz & O'Brien, 1989; Zigler & Finn-Stevenson, 1988).

This reciprocity between theory, research, and the applied needs of children is a major driving force behind the ever-changing, continuously evolving field of child development. It also offers child development specialists unique opportunities to contribute in significant ways to the improvement of human life.

CHAPTER SUMMARY

The Role of Theory

■ **Child development** is the study of human growth and change from conception through adolescence. Its knowledge base is unique in having been stimulated by both scientific curiosity and social pressures to better the lives of children. Theories lend structure and organization to this knowledge base, provide frameworks from which to generate new knowledge, and offer a rational basis for practical action.

The History of Child Study

■ Modern theories of child development are the product of centuries of change in cultural values, philosophical thinking, and scientific progress. In medieval times, children were regarded as miniature adults, a view called **preformationism**. By the sixteenth and seventeenth centuries, childhood began to be regarded as a distinct phase of the life cycle, but the Protestant conception of original sin led to a harsh, authoritarian philosophy of child rearing.

■ The Enlightenment brought new philosophies favoring more humane child treatment. Locke's **tabula rasa** furnished the philosophical basis for modern behaviorism, while Rousseau's **noble savage** foreshadowed the developmental concepts of **stage** and **maturation**. In the nineteenth century, Darwin's theory of evolution provided the scientific foundation for many twentieth century theories.

■ Efforts to study the child directly began in the late nineteenth and early twentieth centuries with the baby biographies. Although methodologically naive, they served as forerunners of naturalistic observation and longitudinal research. From the early normative period emerged Gesell's maturational theory, a large body of descriptive facts about child development, and the intelligence testing movement.

■ Some professionals sought alternatives to the normative approach that would take into account the unique life histories of individual children. Child guidance professionals turned to **psychoanalytic theory** for help in understanding children with emotional difficulties. Pediatricians devoted greater attention to the well child and provided parents with child-rearing advice. Eventually, they collaborated with child development specialists in the prevention and treatment of children's health problems.

The Rise of Modern Theory and Method

■ In the 1930s and 1940s, academic psychology began to influence child study. From **behaviorism** and **social learning theory** came controlled laboratory investigations and practical procedures for modifying children's behavior.

■ The **ecology of human development**, in which layers of the natural environment are seen as major influences on children's well-being, emerged in part as a reaction to contrived laboratory investigations. In addition, child development researchers turned to **ethology** for an understanding of the adaptive or survival value of children's behavior and its origins in human evolutionary history. Enthusiasm for Piaget's **cognitive-developmental theory** in the 1960s stimulated a cognitive revolution in child development.

Current and Future Directions

■ Child development specialists continue to refine existing theories and seek new directions. The strong cognitive flavor of current research is apparent in the approaches of **information processing** and **social cognition**. Interest in the central role played by emotions in all aspects of children's behavior has been revitalized by the **organizational approach to emotional development**. Vygotsky's **dialectical theory** has enhanced our understanding of cultural influences, especially in the area of cognitive development.

Summary of Major Theoretical Perspectives

■ Three controversial questions about the nature of the child and the course of development emerge from comparisons of major theories: (1) Is the child an **organismic** or **mechanistic** being? (2) Is development a quantitative, continuous process or a stage-wise, discontinuous process? (3) Is development primarily determined by genetic or environmental factors? While some theories take extreme positions on these issues, others incorporate elements from both sides.

Child Development as a Rapidly Changing Field

■ Reciprocity between theory, research, and the applied needs of children stimulates the field of child development to move rapidly forward. In the last twenty-five years, pressing problems faced by today's children have attracted the attention of academic researchers, and their findings have, in turn, affected programs and policies.

IMPORTANT TERMS AND CONCEPTS

child development   (p. 1)
developmental psychology   (p. 1)
human development   (p. 1)
theory   (p. 2)
preformationism   (p. 4)
tabula rasa   (p. 5)
noble savage   (p. 6)
stage   (p. 6)
maturation   (p. 6)
normative approach   (p. 8)
psychoanalytic theory   (p. 10)
id   (p. 10)

ego   (p. 10)
superego   (p. 10)
Freud's stages of psychosexual
   development   (p. 11)
Erikson's stages of psychosocial
   development   (p. 12–13)
behaviorism   (p. 14)
social learning theory   (p. 15)
ecology of human
   development   (p. 16)
microsystem   (p. 17)
mesosystem   (p. 18)

exosystem   (p. 18)
macrosystem   (p. 19)
ethology   (p. 20)
cognitive-developmental
   theory   (p. 22)
information processing   (p. 23)
social cognition   (p. 24)
organizational approach to emotional
   development   (p. 26)
dialectical theory   (p. 27)
organismic model   (p. 29)
mechanistic model   (p. 29)

Eleanor Holding a Shell, by Frank W. Benson.
Private Collection. Photo Courtesy R. H. Love Galleries, Chicago.

2

Research Strategies

In Chapter 1, we discussed the relationship of theory to child development research. We saw how theories structure the research process by identifying important questions to ask and preferred methods for collecting data. We also considered how theories guide the interpretation of findings and their application to real-life circumstances and practices with children. In fact, research usually begins with a prediction about behavior drawn directly from a theory, or what we call an **hypothesis.** Think back to the diverse array of child development theories we reviewed in Chapter 1. A myriad of hypotheses can be drawn from any one of them that, once tested, would reflect back on the accuracy of the theory.

Sometimes research pits an hypothesis taken from one theory against an hypothesis taken from another. For example, a maturationist would predict that parental encouragement will have little effect on the age at which children take their first steps or say their first words, while a behaviorist would speculate that these skills can be accelerated through systematic reinforcement. At other times, research tests predictions drawn from a single theory. For example, an ecologist would hypothesize that providing isolated, divorced mothers with social supports will increase their sensitivity and patience with children. An ethologist might speculate that a tape recording of a baby's cry will stimulate strong physiological arousal in mothers who hear it.

Occasionally, little or no theory exists in an area of child development. In these instances, rather than making a specific prediction, the investigator may start with a *research question*, such as: "Are children reaching puberty earlier and growing taller than they did a generation ago?" "Do first-grade girls learn to read more easily and quickly than first-grade boys?"

But theories, hypotheses, and research questions are only the beginning of the many activities that culminate in sound information about child development. Conducting research according to scientifically accepted procedures involves many important steps and choices. Investigators must work out the particulars of which subjects, and how many, will be asked to participate. Then they must decide what the subjects will be asked to do and when, where, and how many times each will need to be seen. Finally, they must examine relationships and draw conclusions from their data.

This chapter is devoted to a close look at the steps of the research process. We begin by considering why an appreciation of research strategies is important—not just for researchers who are immersed in the research enterprise, but also for students who want to understand child development and practitioners who work directly with children. Next, we consider two vitally important research concepts—validity and reliability—that help scientists evaluate the accuracy of their procedures and, ultimately, the trustworthiness of the conclusions they draw from a research study.

Our discussion then turns to the strengths and weaknesses of a variety of research strategies commonly used to study children. Deciding on an appropriate research strategy involves two main tasks. The first concerns selecting one or more *research methods*, the specific activities in which subjects will participate, such as taking tests, answering questionnaires, responding to interviews, or being observed, and where those activities will take place—in the laboratory or in the natural environment. The second task involves choosing a *research design*, or overall plan for the study that permits the best possible test of the researcher's question.

You have probably already heard of some common research designs. Correlational and experimental designs are broadly applied strategies in psychological research of all kinds, and we will discuss them in this chapter. But research in child development is often complicated by the fact that age differences in behavior are of central interest. Longitudinal and cross-sectional designs are two *developmental* research strategies that permit investigators to examine age-related changes. As we discuss these designs later on in this chapter, you will see that drawing conclusions about age differences presents investigators with special problems, and innovative modifications of developmental designs have been devised to overcome some of these difficulties.

Finally, we consider ethical issues involved in research on children. Research on any subjects, whether animal or human, must meet certain ethical standards that protect participants from stressful and harmful treatment. Because of children's immaturity and vulnerability, extra precautions must be taken to ensure that their rights are not violated in the course of a research study.

WHY KNOW ABOUT RESEARCH STRATEGIES?

Investigators in the field of child development need to understand scientific procedures for studying human behavior to ensure as accurate a representation of children's development as possible. But students of child development and practitioners who work with children in applied settings might ask why they, too, should know about research strategies. Why not leave these matters to research specialists and concentrate on what is already known about the child and how this knowledge can be applied?

There are several reasons. First, students and practitioners must be wise and critical consumers of knowledge, not naive sponges who indiscriminately soak up facts about children. As we saw in Chapter 1, the field of child development is full of many contrasting theories, findings, and conclusions. Therefore, a basic appreciation of research strategies becomes important as a rational means through which dependable information can be separated from misleading and erroneous results. Without an understanding of the research process, you must rely on authorities to tell you about the worth of child development information, not on your own well-reasoned judgment.

Second, ideally, researchers and practitioners should be partners in the quest for knowledge about the child. The researcher needs to find out about behavior in the everyday environments in which teachers, caregivers, social workers, and others deal with children. Moreover, research questions and plans often benefit from the astute insights and suggestions of practitioners. When this partnership happens, research findings are generally more relevant and useful in our search for new ways to enhance children's development. But for researchers and practitioners to work fruitfully together, they must try to understand each other's goals and activities. Part of this mutual understanding involves a shared appreciation of accepted research strategies.

Finally, practitioners are sometimes in a position to carry out small-scale research studies to answer practical questions about the children with whom they work. At other times they may have to provide systematic information on how well their goals for children are being realized to justify continued support for their programs and activities. Under these circumstances, a basic understanding of research strategies is essential practical knowledge.

RELIABILITY AND VALIDITY: KEYS TO SCIENTIFICALLY SOUND RESEARCH

Two essential concepts — reliability and validity — must be kept in mind during each step of the research process to ensure that a study provides a trustworthy answer to an hypothesis or research question. **Reliability** refers to the consistency, or repeatability, of measures of subjects' behavior. **Validity** concerns how accurately the measures reflect what the investigator intended to measure in the first place. Let's discuss each of these important criteria for scientifically sound research, first as they apply to the methods researchers use to collect information on their subjects and second as they apply to the overall findings and conclusions of a research study.

Reliability and Validity of Research Methods

Suppose you go into a classroom and record the number of times a child behaves in a helpful and cooperative fashion toward others, but your research partner, in simultaneously observing the same child, comes up with a very different set of measurements. Or you ask a group of children some questions about their interests, but a week later when you question them again, their answers are very different. To be *reliable*, observations of children cannot be unique to a single observer. People must agree on what they see. Also, a test, questionnaire, or interview, when given again within a short period of time (before subjects can reasonably be expected to change or develop in their responses) must yield similar results on both occasions. If a method turns out to be unreliable, it tells us that we did not manage the conditions of observation or testing carefully enough. In observational studies, the behaviors of interest may have been so poorly defined, and observers so casually trained, that they could not record children's behavior consistently from moment to moment (Anastasi, 1988). With tests and interviews, perhaps instructions to subjects were vague, questions were not phrased clearly, or the content of the instrument did not engage the interest of research participants. Any one of these factors could have caused our methods to be so unreliable that they would be useless for answering our research questions.

Investigators estimate the reliability of the information they collect in different ways. In observational research, they need to know whether two or more people applying the same method of observation will come up with identical codes and scores. To find out, pairs of observers can be asked to record the same behavior sequences independently. Then the researcher can examine their judgments of subjects' activities and behaviors to see whether they agree. With tests and questionnaires, reliability can be demonstrated by finding out how similar children's responses are when the test is retaken, or children's scores can be compared on different forms of the same test. If necessary, reliability can also be estimated from a single testing by comparing children's scores on different halves of the test.

Research methods are *valid* if they yield measurements of those subject characteristics they were intended to measure in the first place. Perhaps you have already noticed from our discussion that reliability is absolutely essential for valid research techniques. Methods that are implemented carelessly, unevenly, and inconsistently cannot possibly represent what an investigator originally intended to study. But reliability is not sufficient by itself to ensure that a research strategy will accurately reflect an investigator's goals. Investigators must go further to ensure that their methods are valid indicators of their research intentions, and they generally do so in a number of different ways. They may carefully examine the content of tests and observation instruments to see that they provide thorough coverage of the behaviors of interest. For example, a test intended to measure fifth-grade children's knowledge of arithmetic would not be valid if it contained only addition problems and no subtraction, multiplication, or division problems (Miller, 1987). Another approach to validity is to see how effective a method is in predicting behavior in other situations that we would reasonably expect it to predict. If scores on an arithmetic test are valid, we might expect them to be related to how well children do on their arithmetic assignments in school or even to how quickly and accurately they can make change in a game of Monopoly.

Reliability and Validity of Research Findings

Aside from their relevance to research methods, the concepts of reliability and validity can be applied more broadly, to the overall findings and conclusions of research studies (Achenbach, 1978). An investigator's findings are reliable if **replication** is possible — that is, if the investigation, when carried out again with a new group of subjects, yields the same findings. Replication studies give investigators important information about the consistency of research findings, and they take place far too seldom in child development research.

Two special kinds of validity are important for the accuracy of research findings and conclusions. The first is called **internal validity.** It applies to factors within the context of the study itself (Miller, 1987). To assess internal validity, investigators must look carefully at every aspect of their research procedures and ask, "Have my results really come about for the reasons I hypothesized, or can they be attributed to some other factor in my research design?" To ensure internal validity, each of the methods chosen by the researcher must be reliable and valid in ways we discussed above. But beyond the choice of trustworthy methods, if during any phase of the research process the investigator permits factors unrelated to the hypothesis to influence subjects' behavior, then internal validity is in doubt, and the study cannot be considered a fair test of the investigator's theory. There are many factors against which researchers must be on guard to make sure their work is internally valid. To illustrate the most important ones, let's take a look at a hypothetical investigation.

Suppose a researcher predicts that attending an open classroom, where children are offered plenty of free choice in learning activities, causes elementary school pupils to be more creative than their counterparts in traditional classrooms, where teachers structure and assign most of the learning experiences. But what if parents who choose to send their youngsters to open schools happen to encourage autonomy and freedom of expression more often than parents of children in traditional schools? In this case, *children's background characteristics* are a threat to the internal validity, or accuracy, of the study's findings because we cannot tell whether parental encouragement or school experiences (or both) are responsible for differences in children's creativity scores.

In addition, imagine that our researcher arrives at the classrooms to give the creativity test on a day when many pupils are home with the flu, and several children who take the test in the traditional school are not feeling well and do poorly. If this happens, an _inadequate sample size_ can account for the results. The number of children tested is so small to begin with that when a few subjects respond atypically, the findings are severely distorted.

Finally, suppose that our investigator believes so zealously in the superiority of open classrooms that he inadvertently gives children in the open school more time to complete the creativity test than those in the traditional school. This time, _researcher bias_—subtle efforts on the part of the investigator to obtain the results he desires—taints the outcome. This last example shows how researchers can contaminate their own findings if they do not take special precautions. In most studies, it is wise to have people who have no knowledge of the investigator's hypotheses, or who at least have little personal investment in them, collect the data. Throughout this chapter, we will encounter additional examples of "extraneous" influences that can jeopardize the internal validity of a research study. When investigators cannot take steps to reduce the impact of these factors, they need to qualify the conclusions they draw by indicating that more than one possible explanation may account for their findings.

A second type of validity that applies to the overall accuracy of research findings is **external validity.** It refers to whether results can be generalized to other groups of children and situations in which the same findings are expected to prevail. Investigators may limit this kind of validity by using _biased samples_—for example, children of only one sex or subjects of a single social class or ethnic background—so that results are applicable only to restricted groups of children. External validity is also compromised when researchers assume that their findings have meaning in everyday contexts, but they conduct the investigation in contrived, artificial situations that induce children to behave in ways that do not represent their usual behaviors (Achenbach, 1978; Bracht & Glass, 1968). However, we should keep in mind that some kinds of behavior, such as infant perceptual abilities, can be investigated only in the laboratory. For example, if we want to know whether infants can perceive colors, we need precision instruments that permit control of brightness and wavelength to measure responses with scientific accuracy. In addition, there is no reason to suspect that infants' color perception in the laboratory is very different from their responses in everyday contexts (Seitz, 1988). Nevertheless, in the case of many cognitive and social behaviors, children's responses may differ substantially in strange and familiar places. In these instances, researchers can determine the external validity of their findings by conducting **cross-validation studies** in which they try to replicate their results in new situations or with different samples of children. Refer to Box 2.1 for an interesting example of cross-validation research.

In the following sections of this chapter, we review a diverse array of methods and designs from which child development specialists choose as they plan a research study. As you read about the strengths and weaknesses of each of these research alternatives, note how matters of internal and external validity are continually at the heart of investigators' efforts to choose wisely among them.

COMMON RESEARCH METHODS FOR STUDYING CHILDREN

In this section, we consider the researcher's choice of a basic approach to gathering information about children. Commonly used methods in the field of child development include systematic observation, self-report techniques (such as questionnaires and interviews), and clinical or case studies of the behavior and development of a single child.

Systematic observation involves observing and recording behavior as it happens. Observations of the behavior of children, and of the adults who are important in their development, can be made in different ways. One approach is to go into the field or natural environment and observe the behavior of interest, a method called **naturalistic observation.** Recall from Chapter 1 that this method is especially useful for testing hypotheses generated by the theoretical perspectives of ecology and ethology, but social-cognitive theorists, investigators interested in emotional development, and individuals of a variety of other theoretical persuasions use it as well.

A study by Barrett and Yarrow (1977) provides a good example of the application of naturalistic observation to the study of children's social development. Observing 5-

---

◆   THEORY, RESEARCH, AND APPLICATIONS   ◆

"Don't Forget to Take the Cupcakes Out of the Oven": A Study of Children's Prospective Memory

Box 2.1

Theory. How well can laboratory studies inform us about children's memory performance in the everyday world? To find out, Stephen Ceci and Urie Bronfenbrenner (1985) conducted a cross-validation study in which they observed children in the laboratory as well as in the familiar context of their own homes.

Most research on memory is concerned with *retrospective* memory, or recalling information learned in the past. However, in daily life, an important part of remembering is *prospective*. Children must learn to attend to future events, such as catching the morning bus on time, turning off the sprinklers in the front yard, or taking one's spelling book to reading class on Fridays. To remember to do something in the future, children often use external retrieval cues, such as setting the kitchen buzzer for the time when they must leave or placing the spelling book in a conspicuous place on Friday mornings. Ceci and Bronfenbrenner decided to examine another approach for remembering future events, which they called *strategic time-monitoring*. If there is something you need to do very soon, strategic time-monitoring is an efficient memory strategy that permits less frequent clock-checking during the waiting period so you can turn your attention to other activities.

Strategic time-monitoring consists of three phases: (1) an early calibration phase, in which individuals engage in frequent clock-checking to synchronize their "psychological clocks" with the passage of real clock time; (2) an intermediate phase, in which there is reduced clock-checking along with freedom to pursue other activities; and (3) a scalloping phase, in which clock-checking increases sharply as the time limit approaches. If children are using strategic time-monitoring, it should be reflected in a U-shaped distribution of clock-checking over time. This is in contrast to another memory strategy, called *anxious time-monitoring*, in which restless uncertainty about remembering results in

a constantly rising rate of clock-checking during the waiting period and more clock-checking overall (see the figure below).

Strange environments induce anxiety in children, and anxiety interferes with efficient memory processing. Therefore, Ceci and Bronfenbrenner hypothesized that

Strategic and anxious time-monitoring strategies in the Ceci and Bronfenbrenner (1985) study.

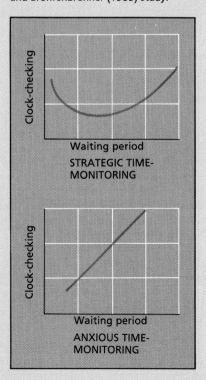

STRATEGIC TIME-MONITORING

ANXIOUS TIME-MONITORING

to 8-year-old children at a summer camp, the researchers recorded the number of times each child provided another person with physical or emotional support in the form of comforting, sharing, helping, or expressing sympathy. In addition, they noted the occurrence of cues from other people nearby, such as a tearful playmate, that indicated a need for comfort or assistance. The great strength of naturalistic observation in studies like this one is that investigators can see directly the everyday behaviors they hope to explain (Miller, 1987).

However, Barrett and Yarrow's research also highlights an important weakness of naturalistic observation: Not all children have the same opportunity to display a particular behavior in everyday life. In their investigation, some children happened to be exposed to more cues for positive social behaviors than others, and for this reason they showed higher rates of helpful and comforting actions. Barrett and Yarrow

when children have to remember a future event, they will be more likely to show anxious time-monitoring in the laboratory and strategic time-monitoring in the comfortable and familiar setting of their own home. Memory strategies should also change with age. Older children, because they are more advanced in cognitive development, should show more strategic time-monitoring than younger children. In addition, Ceci and Bronfenbrenner expected differences in memory performance between boys and girls, depending on the sex-typed nature of the task they were asked to perform. If the task is "sex-appropriate"—baking cupcakes for girls, charging a motorcycle battery for boys—children should be more likely to respond with anxious clock-watching because of an especially strong desire to do well.

Research. Nearly 100 children, half 10-year-olds and half 14-year-olds, half boys and half girls, were each offered $5 either to bake cupcakes or to charge a motorcycle battery. Half the children did the baking or charging in their own homes and the other half in the laboratory. Children asked to bake cupcakes were told to put them in the oven at a certain time and remove them exactly 30 minutes later. Those charging the battery were asked to remove the cables after the battery had charged for 30 minutes. To make sure that an attractive activity was available while children waited, an exciting video game was placed in an adjoining room. An observer pretending to read a magazine recorded children's clock-checking behavior during the waiting period.

Ceci and Bronfenbrenner took special precautions to protect the internal validity of their study. They ruled out family socioeconomic status and living in a single-parent household as alternative explanations for their findings by making sure these characteristics were equally distributed across children's age and sex groups. They also checked their data carefully to ensure that in-terest and success in playing video games was not the factor responsible for clock-checking behavior. Furthermore, reliability was determined by seeing whether different observers watching the same child could record clock-checking in the same way. Also, none of the observers knew the purpose of the study until after it had been completed.

As predicted, strategic time-monitoring was more pronounced in the home, while anxious time-monitoring was more prevalent in the laboratory. Apparently, many children took special precautions in the lab to ensure that they would live up to adult expectations. Interestingly, all age, sex, and task differences in clock-watching occurred *only* in the laboratory. For example, 14-year-olds spent less time clock-watching and made greater use of strategic time-monitoring than 10-year-olds while in the lab, but no age differences in behavior appeared in the home environment. The expected sex differences occurred only for older boys and, again, just in the lab, where these boys were more anxious and less efficient clock-checkers when asked to disconnect a battery than when requested to bake cupcakes. These findings indicate that laboratory settings may bring out differences among children and tasks that do not necessarily exist in the natural environment.

Applications. Ceci and Bronfenbrenner's results indicate that children as young as 10 years of age are able to use a complex, sophisticated strategy to remember future events and that they are more likely to do so in the familiar environment of their own home than in an unfamiliar laboratory setting. Their study shows that we cannot assume children's performances in contrived, unfamiliar contexts are a valid indication of the cognitive competencies that prevail in their everyday activities.

adjusted for this problem in the way they scored each child's responses. However, researchers commonly deal with this difficulty by making **structured observations** in a laboratory. In this approach, the investigator sets up a cue for the behavior of interest, and since every subject is exposed to it in the same way, each has an equal opportunity to manifest the response. In one recent study, researchers made structured observations of children's helping behaviors by having an adult "accidentally" spill a box of stars in a laboratory and recording how each participating child reacted (Stanhope, Bell, & Parker-Cohen, 1987).

Structured observations permit investigators to exert more control over the research situation. In addition, the method is particularly useful for evoking behaviors that researchers rarely have an opportunity to see in everyday life. For example, Cummings, Iannotti, and Zahn-Waxler (1985) wanted to know how preschoolers react emotionally to arguing and bickering among family members. Having little or no chance to watch families argue in real-life settings, they set up a laboratory to resemble a homelike atmosphere, brought in pairs of preschoolers to play with one another, and had two adults speak angrily in the background. Of course, the great disadvantage of structured observations, as you already know from the study described in Box 2.1, is that children do not always behave in the laboratory as they do in everyday life.

The procedures used to collect systematic observations may vary considerably from one study to another, depending on the nature of the research problem posed. Some investigators may choose to use a **specimen record,** a description of the subject's entire stream of behavior in which everything that is said and done for a specified time period is recorded (Wright, 1967). Recently, a researcher wanted to find out how sensitive, responsive, and verbally stimulating caregivers were when they interacted with preschool children in day care centers (Berk, 1985). In this case, everything each caregiver said and did and even the amount of time she spent away from the children taking coffee breaks and talking on the phone was important.

By making structured observations in a laboratory, researchers can ensure that all subjects have the same opportunity to display the behavior of interest in a research study. However, subjects may not respond in the laboratory as they do in everyday life.

In other studies, information on only one or a few kinds of behavior is needed, and it is not necessary to preserve the entire behavior stream. In these instances, researchers may choose more efficient observation procedures. One approach is to do an **event sampling,** in which the observer records all instances of a particular behavior of interest during a specified time period and leaves the rest out of the record. For example, in an observational study of children's antisocial behavior, every episode of physical aggression during a one-hour observation period on each child could be noted. Another approach is **time sampling.** In this procedure, the investigator records whether or not certain behaviors occur during a sample of short time intervals. First, a checklist of the behaviors of interest is prepared. Then the observer divides the entire observation period into a series of brief time segments. For example, a half-hour observation period might be divided into 120 15-second intervals. The observer collects data by alternately watching the child for an interval and then checking off behaviors during the next interval, repeating this process until the entire observation period is complete. Whether an investigator chooses event sampling or time sampling as the basis for collecting observations depends on the goals of the research as well as how convenient the procedure is to use in a particular setting (Miller, 1987).

A major problem in collecting systematic observations is the influence of the observer on the behavior to be observed. The presence of a watchful unfamiliar individual may cause the children and adults who are targets of the observation to change their behavior in unnatural ways. For children below the age of 7 or 8, observer influence is generally limited to the first session or two that the strange adult is present in the setting. Young children cannot stop "being themselves" for very long, and they quickly get used to an observer's presence. Older children and adults are more likely to be affected, but their manner of responding is usually biased in a positive, socially desirable direction. Therefore, the investigator can take their responses as indications of the best behavior the subjects typically display under the circumstances. However, not all older subjects will conceal socially undesirable behavior while being observed. In a number of studies, parents who had developed severely maladaptive patterns of family interaction continued to engage in harsh methods of disciplining their children, including physical punishment, even when they were well aware that an observer was watching and recording their behavior (Reid, Taplin, & Lorber, 1981).

There are several ways in which researchers can minimize the behavioral distortion introduced by placing an observer in the same environment as research subjects. Adaptation periods are helpful. In these, observers make frequent visits to the research setting so subjects have a chance to get used to their presence. Another approach is to have individuals who are typically a part of the child's natural environment do the observing. In several studies, parents have been trained to record children's behavior. This method has the advantage of reducing observer influence while permitting information to be gathered on behaviors that occur so infrequently that researchers would have to remain in the natural setting for a very long time to obtain enough data themselves. In one such study, mothers kept diary records of each episode in which their infants showed evidence of recall memory (Ashmead & Perlmutter, 1980). The information obtained provided important new insights into the emergence of memory capacities during the first year of life.

Several decades ago, most naturalistic observations were recorded by jotting down notes on a pad of paper. This was a cumbersome technique, and information was missed in instances in which investigators tried to capture a complete account of each subject's behavior. Today, sophisticated equipment and recording devices are available to increase the efficiency and accuracy of observational research. Tape recorders with mouthpieces that muffle the sound of an observer's voice enable investigators to dictate on-the-spot descriptions of subjects' activities. Cordless microphones attached to children's collars permit researchers to pick up verbal data that are not easily heard by even the most astute observer, such as soft-spoken conversations with peers and adults (Tizard et al., 1980). Videotaping is often used to obtain a complete record of subjects' behavior in the laboratory. Sometimes it can be used effectively in natural settings as well, if the equipment is placed in an inconspicuous location so that subjects are not distracted by or made to feel self-conscious by its presence.

Systematic observation provides invaluable information on how children and adults actually behave, but the records that result generally tell us little about the thinking and reasoning that lie behind their behavior. For this kind of information, researchers must turn to another type of method — self-report techniques.

Self-Reports: Interviews and Questionnaires

Self-reports are instruments that ask subjects to answer questions of various kinds so that information can be obtained on their perceptions, thoughts, abilities, feelings, attitudes, beliefs, and past behaviors. Self-reports include relatively unstructured clinical interviews, the method used by Piaget to assess the quality of children's thinking, as well as highly structured interviews, questionnaires, and tests.

Turn back to page 23 in Chapter 1 to study the sample **clinical interview** in which Piaget questioned a young child about his understanding of dreams. Notice how the child is encouraged to follow his own train of thought; the investigator prompts only enough to get a full picture of the child's thinking on the topic. Piaget's use of the clinical interview to study children's cognition is the method's most well-known application, but it has been applied to the study of other areas of child development as well. For example, Sears, Maccoby, and Levin (1957) conducted one of the most comprehensive studies on child-rearing practices and young children's behavior that has been completed to date. Mothers were questioned about a wide range of topics, including their handling of weaning, feeding problems, aggression, dependency, exploration, and more. Although a basic set of questions was given to each mother, an open-ended format was used in which participants were free to respond at any length and in any way they wished. In addition, follow-up probes were used in which what was asked and how the question was worded varied from mother to mother, depending on her initial response.

Taken together, Piaget's and Sears, Maccoby, and Levin's research highlight two major strengths of the clinical interviewing procedure. The first is that it permits subjects to display their thoughts in terms that come as close as possible to the way they think about events in everyday life. The second is the breadth and scope of information yielded by the clinical interview in a relatively brief period of time. For example, in a session that lasted about two hours, Sears, Maccoby, and Levin obtained a wide range of child-rearing information from each mother, much more than could be captured in the same amount of time by making observations of parent-child interaction.

A major weakness of the clinical interview has to do with the accuracy with which subjects report their own thoughts, feelings, and behaviors. Some interviewers tend to probe too little, so that a full understanding of the subject's point of view is not revealed. At the opposite extreme, some interviewers press, prompt, and suggest too much. Under these conditions, many young children, desiring to please the adult, may make up answers that really do not represent their way of thinking. Furthermore, the clinical interview depends on children's verbal ability and expressiveness. There is a danger that the capacities of subjects who have difficulty putting their thoughts into words will not be adequately reflected by the method. However, a skillful interviewer knows how to minimize these problems by wording questions carefully and by being sensitive to cues that indicate a child may not have clearly understood a question or may need extra time to feel comfortable in the situation.

Using the clinical interview, this investigator asks a mother to describe her child's development. The method permits large amounts of information to be gathered in a short period of time.

Interviews in which adults are asked about their child-rearing practices and the behaviors of their youngsters are known to be subject to distortion, particularly under certain conditions. When parents are asked to recall events that happened during an earlier period in the child's life, they often give responses that depict their child in glowing terms. In cases in which it has been possible to compare recall of early events with information obtained at the same time the events actually occurred, mothers have been found to report faster development, fewer childhood problems, and child-rearing practices more in line with contemporary expert advice than with the records of their actual behaviors (Robbins, 1963; Yarrow, Campbell, & Burton, 1970). In addition, most parents find it difficult to recall specific instances of early events, although they can report general tendencies more readily — the child as "fussy" versus "easy to manage" or their disciplinary approach as "permissive" versus "strict." But strictness to one parent may register as permissiveness to another. Parents may have very different subjective definitions of these general terms, causing their retrospective accounts to be inconsistent and virtually useless as predictors of children's later behaviors (Maccoby & Martin, 1983). It is now recommended that parent interviews focus on obtaining concurrent rather than retrospective information and that parents be asked for specific practices and behaviors, not just global judgments and interpretations (Kochanska, Kuczinski, & Radke-Yarrow, 1989).

We mentioned in Chapter 1 that the clinical interview has been subject to criticism because of its nonstandardized administration procedures. When questions are phrased differently for each subject, variations in responses may be due to the manner of interviewing rather than real differences in the way subjects think about a certain topic. **Structured interviews** and **questionnaires,** in which each participant is asked an identical set of questions, can eliminate this difficulty. In addition, their administration and scoring procedures are much more efficient. For example, when using a questionnaire, a researcher can obtain written responses from an entire class of children or group of parents simultaneously. Furthermore, when these instruments make use of multiple-choice, yes-no, or true-false formats, as is done in many tests, the responses can be tabulated quickly by machine. However, while these approaches gain in impartiality and efficiency, they do not yield the same depth of information about the subject's perspective as does a clinical interview. Moreover, they are not immune to inaccurate reporting, although investigators can minimize this effect by telling subjects that their answers will be recorded anonymously and phrasing questions in nonevaluative ways. In addition, when asking for opinions and beliefs, researchers can remind subjects that there are no right or wrong answers.

The Clinical Method

In Chapter 1, we discussed the **clinical method** (sometimes called the case study approach) as an outgrowth of psychoanalytic theory, which stressed the importance of understanding the unique individual child. Recall that the clinical approach synthesizes a wide range of data about one subject, including interview material, test scores, and observations. The aim is to obtain as complete a picture as possible of that child's psychological functioning and the experiences that led up to it.

Clinical studies are generally carried out on children who have serious emotional problems, but they do exist on normal, well-adjusted youngsters as well (e.g., Coles, 1977). The method yields case narratives that are rich in descriptive detail and that frequently offer important insights into the processes of development. We will discuss the findings of a number of well-known clinical studies in subsequent chapters of this book. One example is the case of Genie, a child who was isolated in the back room of a house from the time she was 20 months old until she was an adolescent of 13 (Curtiss, 1977). Her story sheds important light on whether there is a critical period for early language learning.

The clinical method, like all others, has drawbacks. Collection and recording of information are often unsystematic and subjective, and investigators cannot assume that conclusions generalize to anyone other than the particular child studied. Therefore, the insights drawn from clinical investigations need to be tested further using other research strategies.

BRIEF REVIEW

Table 2.1 provides a summary of the strengths and weaknesses of each of the research methods discussed above. You may wish to review them at this time, as a prerequisite for moving on to a consideration of research designs — general investigative plans that permit researchers to use the data obtained from various methods to test hypotheses and answer research questions.

GENERAL RESEARCH DESIGNS

In deciding on a research design, investigators choose a way of setting up a study that enables them to identify relationships among events and behaviors and the causes of those relationships with the greatest certainty possible. Two main types of designs are used in all research on human behavior: correlational and experimental.

Correlational Design

In a **correlational design,** the investigator gathers information on already existing groups of individuals, generally in natural life circumstances, and no effort is made to manipulate or intervene in the subjects' experiences in any way. Once the data are obtained, relationships among various pieces of information can be examined, but the correlational design does not permit exact determination of the causes of those relationships.

Suppose we want to answer such questions as: Do structure and organization in the home make a difference in children's school performance? Does attending a day care center promote children's friendliness with peers? Do mothers' styles of interacting with and disciplining children have any bearing on children's intelligence? In these and many other instances, although we can observe and measure the events of interest, it is very difficult, if not impossible, to deliberately arrange, manipulate, and control them. Consequently, if we find in a correlational study that maternal interac-

Table 2.1. Strengths and Weaknesses of Common Research Methods

METHOD	DESCRIPTION	STRENGTHS	WEAKNESSES
Naturalistic observation	Observations of behavior taken in natural contexts	Observations are applicable to children's everyday lives and experiences	Conditions under which children are observed cannot be controlled and may not be the same for all children
Structured observation	Behavior of interest recorded in a laboratory situation designed to evoke it	Offers a standardized observation situation for all children	Observations may not be typical of the way children behave in everyday life
Clinical interview	Flexible, open-ended interviewing procedure in which the investigator obtains a complete account of the subject's train of thought	Provides a full picture of each subject's perceptions, thoughts, and feelings about an experience or event. Great breadth and depth of information can be obtained in a limited time period	Subjects may report information in a selective, distorted fashion. Nonstandardized administration procedures make comparisons of subjects' responses difficult
Structured interview and questionnaire	Self-report instruments in which each subject is asked the same questions in the same way	Standardized method of asking questions permits comparisons of subjects' responses and efficient administration and scoring	Does not yield the same depth of information as a clinical interview. Responses are still subject to inaccurate reporting
Clinical method (case study)	Synthesis of interview, test, and observational data to yield a full picture of an individual child's development and psychological functioning	Provides rich, descriptive insights into processes of development	Collection of information is often unsystematic and subjective. Conclusions cannot be applied to individuals other than the subject child

tion style does relate to children's intelligence, we would not know for sure whether maternal behavior was actually responsible for the intellectual differences among the children. In fact, the reverse direction of causality is certainly possible. The behaviors of highly intelligent children may be so attractive and inviting that they cause mothers to interact more favorably. Alternatively, a third variable that we did not even think about studying, such as amount of noise and distraction in the home, may be causing both the quality of maternal interaction and children's intelligence to change simultaneously in a particular direction.

In correlational investigations, and in other types of research designs, researchers often examine relationships among variables by using a **correlation coefficient.** (Other statistical approaches to examining relationships are also available.) We will encounter the correlation coefficient many times in discussing the findings of research throughout this book, so let's look at what it is and how it is interpreted. A correlation coefficient provides a numerical estimate of how two measures, or variables, are associated with one another. It can range in value from $+1.00$ to -1.00. The magnitude of the number gives an indication of the strength of the relationship. A zero correlation indicates no systematic association, but the closer the value is to $+1.00$ or -1.00, the stronger the relationship that exists. The sign of the number ($+$ or $-$) refers to the direction of the association. If it is positive ($+$), this means that as one measure of performance *increases*, the other also *increases*. If the sign is negative ($-$), this indicates that as one measure *increases*, the other *decreases*.

Does a rich, supportive home environment bear any relationship to a child's performance in school? A correlational design can be used to answer this question, but it does not enable researchers to determine the precise cause of their findings.

Let's take several examples to illustrate how a correlation coefficient works. In one study, a researcher found that a measure of maternal attentiveness at 11 months of age was positively correlated with infant mental test scores during the second year of life, at +.60. This is a moderately high correlation, which indicates that the more attentive the mothers were to their babies in infancy, the better their youngsters did on an intelligence test as toddlers several months later (Clarke-Stewart, 1973). In another similar study, a researcher reported that uninvolved behavior on the part of mothers—the extent to which they ignored their 10-month-old infants' bids for attention—was negatively correlated with children's willingness to comply with parental demands one year later, at −.46 for boys and −.36 for girls (Martin, 1981). These moderate correlations reveal that the more the mothers ignored their babies, the less cooperative their children were during the second year of life. Although in both of these investigations the researchers suspected that maternal behavior played a causal role in affecting children's mental test performance and compliance, in neither could they really be sure about what caused the variables of interest to be associated with one another.

Let's take just one more example to illustrate the usefulness of correlational research. This time, the researchers asked parents of preschoolers to indicate how much time their children spent watching television and the kinds of programs they viewed. The findings revealed a correlation of +.33 between time spent watching action-oriented TV shows with high violent content and children's display of aggression during play periods at nursery school (Singer & Singer, 1981). Once again, we cannot conclude from the evidence that watching violent TV caused these children to behave aggressively. It can just as easily be argued that children who are inherently aggressive prefer to watch violent TV. But television viewing is a factor that investigators *can* manipulate and control to some degree. The identification of a relationship between violent TV and aggressive behavior in a correlational study suggests that it would be worthwhile to try to track down its cause with a more sensitive research strategy. We will see in the following section that a number of investigators have pursued the causal basis of the television-aggression connection using more powerful experimental procedures.

In contrast to correlational studies, **experimental designs** permit precise determination of cause and effect relationships. In an experiment, the events and behaviors of interest are divided into two types: independent and dependent variables. The **independent variable** is the one anticipated by the investigator, on the basis of an hypothesis or research question, to cause changes in another variable. The **dependent variable** is the one that the investigator expects to be influenced by the independent variable. In an experimental design, inferences about cause and effect relationships are possible because the researcher directly controls or manipulates changes in the independent variable. This is done by assigning subjects to two or more treatment conditions and then comparing the performance of the different treatment groups on measures of the dependent variable. For example, if an investigator wants to know whether watching violent television programs (independent variable) causes aggressive behavior (dependent variable), an experiment could be designed in which some children are deliberately exposed to violent films and others to alternative treatments. Then the groups could be compared on the basis of a measure of their aggressiveness.

The Laboratory Experiment. A classic **laboratory experiment** aimed at answering this very question was carried out by Bandura and his associates in the early 1960s (Bandura, Ross, & Ross, 1963). Nearly 100 preschoolers were brought individually into the investigators' research laboratory. Each was assigned to one of three treatment conditions—an adult model portraying aggression on film, an aggressive cartoon character, or a real-life aggressive adult model—or to a control group that experienced no treatment. In the three treatments, children watched adult or cartoon models repeatedly punch a Bobo doll on the nose, hit it with a mallet, toss it into the air, and kick it harshly. Afterward, children from all conditions were brought individually into a playroom and given an opportunity to use a variety of toys. Some were

In a classic experiment by Bandura, some preschoolers watched an aggressive model punch, kick, and hit a Bobo doll, while others received no treatment. Then each child was given an opportunity to play with toys. Those who observed an aggressive model displayed far more aggressive behavior in the playroom than did children in the no treatment condition.

designed to stimulate aggressive behavior, while others were chosen for their nonaggressive play possibilities. Bandura found that children in all three experimental treatments engaged in far more aggressive play with the toys than control children, and many of their behaviors were exact replicas of the model's aggressive responses. Furthermore, film-mediated models were just as effective as live adult models in promoting a variety of aggressive behaviors.

In experimental studies, investigators must take special precautions to control for unknown characteristics of subjects that could reduce the validity of their findings. In Bandura's study, if a greater number of children who had learned before the experiment to behave in hostile and antagonistic ways happened to end up in one of the treatment groups, we could not tell whether the independent variable or the children's background characteristics were responsible for the obtained differences in aggressive behavior. **Random assignment** of subjects to different conditions offers protection against this problem. By using an evenhanded procedure, such as drawing numbers out of a hat or flipping a coin, the experimenter increases the chances that children's characteristics will be equally distributed across treatment groups. Bandura took even more stringent precautions to make sure that his results would not be contaminated by children's background characteristics. Before the study, nursery school teachers were asked to rate each child on aggressive attributes. Then a **matching** procedure was used in which equal numbers of children having high and low aggressive tendencies were randomly assigned to each of the four conditions. Matching ensures equal distribution of certain subject characteristics across experimental groups. They are matched, or deliberately made equivalent, on subject qualities that have an especially strong chance of distorting the results.

The Field Experiment. Like Bandura's study, most experiments are conducted in laboratories because laboratory conditions enable researchers to achieve the maximum possible control over the treatments to which subjects are exposed. Consequently, the strength of laboratory experiments resides in their high internal validity, but this is often obtained at some sacrifice to external validity. The ideal solution to this problem is to do ecological experiments, or experiments in the field, as a complement to laboratory investigations. In **field experiments,** investigators capitalize on rare opportunities to assign subjects to different treatments in natural settings. In the case of Bandura's laboratory experiment, we are able to conclude that filmed aggression *can* cause children to behave more aggressively, but *does* it do so when children are exposed to violent television fare in everyday life?

A field experiment conducted by Friedrich and Stein (1973) helps answer this question. They began their research by hypothesizing that if television programs can cause children to imitate antisocial and aggressive responses, then the opposite may also be true. Perhaps programs with the right kind of content can teach socially desirable behaviors, such as cooperation, sharing, sympathy, and self-control. Consequently, Friedrich and Stein designed a study to investigate both the positive and negative outcomes of children's television programming. Over 90 children enrolled in a summer nursery school session were randomly assigned to watch one of three types of TV shows each day for a period of four weeks: aggressive cartoons ("Batman" and "Superman"), a prosocial program ("Mister Rogers' Neighborhood"), and neutral films that had neither aggressive nor prosocial content (e.g., farm and animal scenes). The investigators had groups of children come to a small room near their nursery school classroom to watch the films for a half-hour period each day. Before, during, and after the children experienced the treatments, their aggressive and prosocial free play behaviors in the nursery school were observed and recorded. To study the effects of the different viewing conditions, children's behavior before watching the programs was compared to their behavior during and after television viewing.

Friedrich and Stein found that television treatments had a dramatic influence on children's behavior. Preschoolers who watched aggressive films showed a decline in tolerance of delay (being able to wait for materials or adult attention) and rule obedience in the classroom. Interpersonal aggression, such as hitting, teasing, name-calling, tattling, and yelling at others, also increased for children assigned to this treatment, but only for those who were above average in aggressive behavior to begin with. In contrast, children exposed to prosocial programming displayed higher levels of task persistence, rule obedience, and tolerance of delay. Positive interpersonal behaviors (cooperating with, helping, comforting, and verbalizing feelings to others) also increased, but only for children in the sample who came from low-income families.

Friedrich and Stein's field experiment extends Bandura's earlier work by showing that imitation of film-mediated aggression does occur in everyday life. However, it suggests that this effect may be limited to children who are initially high in aggression. The study also reveals that television has as much potential for helping children learn positive social behaviors as it has for teaching aggression and violence.

The Natural Experiment. We have already indicated that in the case of many hypotheses and research questions, investigators cannot randomly assign subjects and manipulate conditions in the real world, as Friedrich and Stein were able to do. However, sometimes researchers can select naturally occurring treatments, such as different school environments, day care centers, and preschool programs, in which children's backgrounds and prior experiences are as similar as possible. Studies of existing variations in children's experiences are sometimes referred to as **natural experiments** because investigators try to find situations that at least approximate the controlled conditions of a true experiment. In this way, they rule out as best as they can alternative explanations for their treatment effects. Despite such efforts, natural experiments are unable to achieve the precision and rigor of true experimental research (Achenbach, 1978; Campbell & Stanley, 1966). An example of this kind of study is described in Box 2.2.

DESIGNS FOR STUDYING DEVELOPMENT

Scientists interested in child development are unique in requiring information about the way their subjects change over time. To answer questions about development, they must extend the experimental and correlational approaches discussed above to include measurements of subjects at different ages. Longitudinal and cross-sectional designs are special *developmental* research strategies. In each, age comparisons form the basis of the research plan.

The Longitudinal Design

In a **longitudinal design,** one sample of children is observed repeatedly at different ages, and changes are noted as they mature. The time period spanned may be relatively short — a few months to several years — or it may be very long — a decade or even a lifetime. In the 1920s and 1930s, several longitudinal studies were initiated in which samples of infants were followed through childhood, adolescence, and well into the adult years. Important examples are the Fels Institute Study, begun in 1929 in Yellow Springs, Ohio, and two investigations carried out at the University of California at Berkeley, the Berkeley Growth Study and the Guidance Study, both initiated in 1928 (Kagan, 1964). The investigators of each major study hoped that collection of a massive data base on a group of individuals over a long period of time would provide important insights into the course and continuity of development. Therefore, they obtained repeated measurements on a wide range of characteristics, behaviors, and experiences, including physical growth, intelligence, personality, child-rearing practices, and more. We will use findings from these classic studies to illustrate the unique kinds of information about development that can be obtained only from a longitudinal design.

Advantages of the Longitudinal Design. The first major strength of the longitudinal approach is that it permits researchers to examine developmental changes in various attributes for each individual in the sample. By tracking the performance of each subject over time, investigators can identify common patterns of development as well as individual differences in the paths children follow to maturity (Wohlwill, 1973).

Data gathered from the Fels and Berkeley studies on changes in children's mental test performance illustrate the value of this kind of information. During the early part of this century, it was commonly assumed that intelligence was a largely inherited capacity that remained fairly stable over an individual's lifetime. The Berkeley and Fels studies offered the first major challenge to this assumption. Many children followed during childhood and adolescence showed marked changes in their intelligence test scores. Of the 222 youngsters tested repeatedly as part of the Berkeley Guidance Study, 85 percent showed changes of 10 or more IQ points and a third showed changes of more than 20 IQ points between 6 and 18 years of age (Honzik, Macfarlane, & Allen, 1948). In the Fels Study, the changes were even more dramatic. Among 80 children studied, the average shift between 2½ and 17 years of age was 28.5 points (McCall, Appelbaum, & Hogarty, 1973; Sontag, Baker, & Nelson, 1958).

◆ **THEORY, RESEARCH, AND APPLICATIONS** ◆

*S*ex-Typed *Social Behaviors in Traditional and Open Schools*: A Natural *Experiment*   Box 2.2

Theory. A large body of research on children's peer relations indicates that by the preschool years, children prefer playmates of the same sex. But what happens when school environments are designed to deliberately minimize sex-typed play and peer associations? Barbara Bianchi and Roger Bakeman (1978) conducted a natural experiment to answer this question. They hypothesized that if social learning theory is correct that modeling contributes to children's play choices, then school environments that hold less extreme views of acceptable sex-role conduct should be able to modify children's sex-typed behavior.

Research. Over 50 4- to 6-year-old children, half enrolled in a traditional kindergarten and half in an open classroom school, were observed. The philosophies and learning activities of the two schools were markedly different. The traditional environment stressed children's acquisition of conventional values and standards of conduct, including established sex-role behavior. In contrast, the goal of the open school was to respond to children on the basis of their unique characteristics, and sex-typed expectations about children's interests, abilities, and personalities were consciously avoided. In the

open school, both male and female teachers translated this philosophy into classroom practice by modeling a wide range of activities and roles for children.

Observations of children in both schools were made during free play by using a time-sampling technique. Over a six-day period, observers repeatedly worked through a list of the children in each classroom, recording how often each child played with other children as well as the number of times their playmates were all of the same sex.

In line with expectations, the findings showed that traditional school pupils largely played in a sex-segregated fashion, while open school boys and girls could frequently be seen playing together, as shown in the adjacent figure. In fact, on the average, open school pupils spent more than half their time in mixed-sex play activities, and boys and girls were equally affected.

Bianchi and Bakeman's results suggest that school environments can modify children's sex-typed social behaviors. However, since the study was limited to comparisons of intact, already existing groups of children, the authors were careful to point out that factors other than schooling may be responsible for the findings. Parents of open school children had made a conscious deci-

Furthermore, those children who changed radically in test performance usually showed patterns of change that were orderly and predictable, not random, haphazard fluctuations. As is illustrated in Figure 2.1, some children had steadily increasing scores, while others had steadily decreasing performances over childhood and adolescence.

The existence of these stable patterns of change raises provocative questions about the factors responsible for them. A second strength of the longitudinal design is that investigators can compare age changes in different aspects of behavior to see whether the timing of change in one is similar to the timing of change in another (Wohlwill, 1973). When correspondences are identified, they often lead to valuable insights into why certain changes occur. For example, the Berkeley investigators carefully examined the information they had collected on children's emotional and physical health and compared it to changes in children's IQ scores. The results revealed that emotional factors and illness closely paralleled major shifts in intellectual performance. For example, Case 567, whose increase in IQ is shown in Figure 2.1, experienced improved health and emotional well-being at the same time that she showed an upward shift in the test scores. The researchers wrote:

> The early preschool history of this girl (the period of her lowest scores) was characterized by the critical illnesses of her mother and brother and the emotional and financial strain that these entailed. Further, the girl . . . was very shy and reserved. At 6½ years she had pneumonia. From ten on, she had many supports in her life—

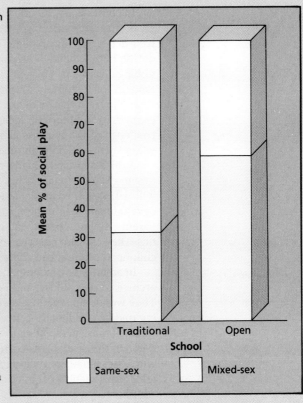

Same-sex and mixed-sex social play in a traditional and open school in the Bianchi and Bakeman (1978) study. Pupils attending an open school played far more often than traditional school pupils with children of the opposite sex. *(Adapted from Bianchi & Bakeman, 1978.)*

sion to enroll their youngsters in an alternative school environment, so it is possible that parental and school attitudes concerning sex typing were highly similar in this investigation. Consequently, the natural experiment does not permit us to rule out the likelihood that observed school differences were merely a reflection of modeling and reinforcement patterns implemented by parents at home.

Applications. Despite ambiguity regarding the causes of school differences in social behavior, Bianchi and Bakeman's study does indicate that young children's same-sex peer associations can be modified by the environments to which children are exposed. The results suggest that teachers think carefully about the social experiences they encourage in their classrooms. Providing children with a broader range of social opportunities, like those observed by Bianchi and Bakeman in the open school, may have an important impact on the acquisition of less sex-stereotyped attitudes and behavior.

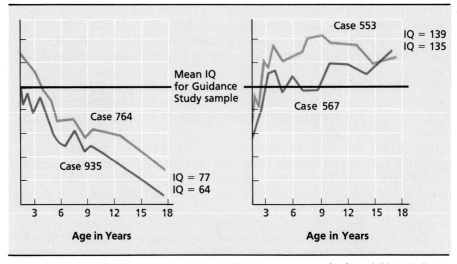

Figure 2.1. Individual patterns of change in intelligence test scores for four children in the Berkeley Guidance Study sample. Cases 935 and 764 showed age-related declines in performance, while Cases 567 and 553 showed gradual gains. The overall magnitude of change for each of these subjects was between 70 and 79 IQ points. *(From M. P. Honzik, J. W. Macfarlane, & L. Allen, 1948, "The Stability of Mental Test Performance Between Two and Eighteen Years," Journal of Experimental Education, 17, 319. Adapted by permission.)*

music, athletic success, summer camps, the honor roll at school. Eighteen years marks her first year in college and away from home and her first really completely satisfying social life. (Honzik, Macfarlane, & Allen, 1948, p. 314)

In contrast, the IQ of Case 935 dropped steadily over time. Although she experienced an early satisfying home life, serious emotional and economic stress characterized her family in middle childhood, and she experienced repeated school failure during her elementary school years. The Berkeley investigators reported that emotional adjustment, physical health, and changes in intelligence test scores varied in tandem for a substantial number of children in their sample. Although we cannot conclude from this evidence that variations in emotional and physical health cause changes in children's IQ scores, the existence of these associations presents a serious challenge to the traditional assumption that IQ is largely a reflection of hereditary endowment and only minimally influenced by environmental factors.

A third and final advantage of the longitudinal design is that it permits investigators to examine relationships between early and later events and behaviors (Wohlwill, 1973). For example, to increase our understanding of factors that contribute to development, researchers can look at the extent to which early experiences with parents, siblings, peers, and teachers are related to children's emerging characteristics. They can also observe whether children with particular personality attributes in childhood retain those characteristics in adult life.

In an intensive examination of interview data from the Berkeley Guidance Study archives, Caspi, Elder, and Bem (1987, 1988) sought answers to this very question. They wondered whether youngsters who showed extreme styles of responding during middle childhood—either ill-tempered and explosive or shy and withdrawn—retained these personality dispositions when assessed as adults many years later. To find out, the researchers correlated ratings of subjects' behavior in middle childhood with assessments of their personality at age 30. In addition, they explored the long-term consequences of childhood dispositions for work, marital, and parenting roles in adulthood.

Results revealed that the two contrasting personality styles were moderately stable from childhood into adulthood. In addition, childhood dispositions had implications for many areas of adult functioning, but these outcomes were not the same for males and females. For men, the consequences of early explosiveness were most apparent in the occupational sphere, in the form of conflicts with supervisors, frequent job changes, and unemployment. Since few women in this sample of the 1930s and 1940s worked after marriage, their family lives were most affected. Ill-tempered girls grew up to be hotheaded and irritable wives and parents who were especially prone to divorce. (Explosive men also showed an elevated incidence of marital breakup.) Gender differences in life course consequences of shyness were even more pronounced. When compared to their more gregarious counterparts, men who had been withdrawn in childhood were considerably delayed in marrying, becoming fathers, and establishing stable careers. In contrast, women who were reserved as children showed no special adjustment problems. Interestingly, recent sex-role changes in our society do not seem to have altered this pattern of findings. Research on contemporary samples reveals that the negative social consequences of shyness continue to be greater for males than for females (Jones & Briggs, 1984).

Despite these striking longitudinal outcomes, we must keep in mind that continuity in personality over the life course characterized only some, not all, of the Guidance Study participants. Caspi and his collaborators believe that explosiveness and shyness are sustained through a kind of "snowballing" effect, whereby children and adults evoke responses from others that serve to perpetuate their current dispositions. Clearly, many youngsters were eventually successful in breaking this cycle or received help from others in doing so.

Problems in Conducting Longitudinal Research. Despite their many strengths, longitudinal investigations confront investigators with a wide variety of problems. There are practical difficulties, such as obtaining adequate financial support and waiting the many years it takes for meaningful results to accrue in a long-term study. Beyond these drawbacks, many threats to internal and external validity plague longitudinal investigations that can create serious difficulties for the meaningfulness of the findings.

Biased sampling is a prevalent problem in longitudinal research. People who willingly participate in a study that requires them to be continually observed and tested over many years are likely to have unique characteristics, and we cannot easily generalize from them to the rest of the population. In the Fels and Berkeley Growth studies, the families who volunteered to participate were better educated and socioeconomically more advantaged than average, and they probably had a unique appreciation of the scientific value of the research. Furthermore, longitudinal samples generally become more biased as the investigation proceeds, due to **subject attrition.** Some people may move or drop out of the study for other reasons, and the ones who remain are likely to be different from the ones who do not continue. To minimize this problem, participants are sometimes chosen on the basis of their long-term availability as residents in a particular community. But in view of the mobility of many American families, this criterion for subject selection reduces the generalizability of longitudinal findings still further.

The very experience of being repeatedly interviewed, observed, and tested can also threaten the validity of a longitudinal study. If the measures concern attitudes, feelings, or moral judgments, **subject reactivity** may pose problems. Participants may gradually be alerted to their own thoughts and feelings, think about them, and revise them in a way that has little to do with age-related change (Nunnally, 1982). In addition, with repeated testing, subjects may become "test-wise," and their performance may improve as the result of better test-taking skills and increased familiarity with the test. Investigators can check for such **practice effects** by introducing new children into the testing program and comparing their scores with those of longitudinal subjects of the same age who have experienced repeated testing. If longitudinal subjects obtain higher scores, then practice effects may be operating. In addition, researchers can carefully examine the developmental trends of children in their sample to determine whether they are consistent with the influence of practice effects. When children who are studied longitudinally show a wide variety of developmental profiles, including the steady increases and declines over many years that we described for the Fels and Berkeley children's IQ scores, then we know the findings cannot simply be due to repeated assessments.

The most widely discussed threat to the validity of longitudinal investigations is **cultural-historical change,** or what are commonly called **cohort effects.** Longitudinal studies examine the growth and development of cohorts, or children born in the same historical era who are influenced by a particular set of cultural conditions. Findings based on one cohort may not be universal and generalizable to children growing up at other points in time. For example, children's intelligence test performance may be affected by differences in the quality of public schooling from one decade to another or by generational changes in parental values regarding the importance of stimulating children's intellectual abilities. A longitudinal study of social development would probably result in different findings if children were observed during the Vietnam War of the 1960s and 1970s, around the time of World War II, or during the Great Depression of the 1930s (see Box 2.3).

◆ CONTEMPORARY ISSUES: CULTURAL DIFFERENCES ◆

*C*hildren of the Great Depression   Box 2.3

Economic disaster, wars, and periods of social ferment can produce major reorientations in people's lives. Glen Elder (1974) took advantage of variations in the extent to which families experienced economic hardship during the Great Depression of the 1930s to study its consequences for children's development.

To examine the impact of the Great Depression, Elder capitalized on the extensive research archives of the Oakland Growth Study, a longitudinal investigation begun in the early 1930s and originally intended to chart the growth of 167 youngsters from late childhood into adolescence. The research was eventually extended over several decades to cover long-term development well into the adult years. Elder subdivided the sample into individuals whose adolescent years were marked by severe economic deprivation during the Depression and those whose youth was relatively free of economic strain. Then he compared the two groups on a wide range of information, including ratings of family relations, social behaviors, and personal attributes.

The findings showed that unusual responsibilities were placed on adolescents from deprived families as their parents' roles and responsibilities changed. Mothers entered the labor force, fathers sought work outside the immediate community, and the emotional stress of economic hardship led to a rising rate of parental divorce and illness. In response, young people experienced an accelerated entry into the adult world as they were challenged to take on many of the burdens of family maintenance. The nature of these new responsibilities depended on the child's sex, with girls assuming more domestic duties and boys seeking part-time jobs outside the home. These changes in adolescents' lives had major consequences for their future aspirations. Girls' early immersion in domestic responsibilities led their interests to be centered around home and family and decreased their aspirations to enter careers. The experience of economic insecurity exposed many boys to the realities of self-support, convinced them that economic resources could not be taken for granted, and fostered an early commitment to occupational roles and career choices.

Relationships also changed in economically deprived homes. Unemployment led fathers to lose status in the family, and mothers became increasingly prominent in family affairs. This reversal of traditional sex roles was distressing for many couples, and it tended to provoke dissention and conflict. Fathers became explosive, punitive, and arbitrary in their behaviors toward children (Elder, Liker, & Cross, 1984). In response, boys turned toward peers and adults outside the family as substitute sources of emotional support during a time when parents' ability to provide it was impaired. Economic hardship seemed to increase fathers' rejecting behavior toward daughters in particular, perhaps because girls'

Cultural-historical change (cohort effects) is a major threat to the generalizability of longitudinal research findings. These children growing up in Belfast, Northern Ireland, have experienced civil warfare as part of their daily lives. Their childhoods are substantially different from those of Irish youngsters who grew up during peacetime.

greater involvement in household affairs made them readily available targets of family tension. Also, fathers may have been particularly resentful toward daughters as family power and status were given over to females during the period of economic misfortune (Elder, Van Nguyen, & Caspi, 1985).

The impact of the Depression continued to be apparent in family and work roles as these youngsters entered adulthood. Girls who grew up in economically deprived households remained strongly committed to domestic life as adults, and many married at a relatively early age. As a result, their educational goals were restricted, and fewer entered college. Twenty-five years after the Depression, commitment to family life continued to be stronger for them than for women with nondeprived upbringings. Men reared in deprived homes had an especially intense desire for occupational security, and they changed jobs less frequently during adulthood than those from nondeprived backgrounds. Those from middle-class families showed higher adult occupational attainment than their nondeprived counterparts, perhaps because of their early vocational focus and a strong sense of responsibility and commitment acquired early in life. Finally, the chance to bear and rear children was particularly important to men from deprived backgrounds. For those who had experienced the failure of economic security, children may have been viewed as the most re-

warding and enduring benefit of their adult lives.

Elder's findings reveal that the Great Depression substantially altered the life course of many youngsters who experienced it. But the fact that the Oakland study participants were adolescents and, therefore, beyond the early years of intense family dependency, may explain why most weathered this period of economic strain so successfully. Recently, Elder and his colleagues conducted a similar investigation of the Berkeley Guidance Study sample, who were born later and were therefore much younger when the Great Depression struck. For young boys (who, as we will see in later chapters, are especially vulnerable to adjustment difficulties in the face of family stress), the long-term consequences of economic hardship were particularly severe. Lack of energy, poor psychological health, and dispirited attitudes toward school and work characterized these children as they moved through adolescence and adulthood (Elder, Caspi, & Van Nguyen, 1986; Elder & Caspi, 1988). Clearly, cultural-historical change is not associated with identical outcomes for all children. With respect to the Great Depression, the consequences varied considerably, depending on the youngster's sex and the period of development in which social change occurred (Stewart & Healy, 1989).

Finally, changes occurring within the field of child development may create problems for longitudinal studies that last many years. Theories and dominant methods for studying children are constantly changing, and those that originally inspired a longitudinal study may become dated and obsolete (Nunnally, 1982). For this reason, as well as others mentioned above, many recent longitudinal studies have been short-term, spanning only a few months or years in a child's life. Consequently, investigators are spared some of the formidable obstacles that threaten longitudinal findings that cover an extended period from childhood to maturity.

The Cross-Sectional Design

The sheer length of time it takes for many behaviors to change, even in limited longitudinal studies, has led researchers to turn toward another strategy for studying development. In the **cross-sectional design,** groups of children of different ages are studied at the same point in time. For example, we could choose a group of 5-year-olds, a group of 10-year-olds, and a group of 15-year-olds and compare their responses. In cross-sectional studies, researchers do not have to worry about many of the difficulties that plague the longitudinal design. When participants have to be measured only once, it is much easier to obtain representative samples, and investigators do not need to be concerned about subjects dropping out of the study, practice effects, or transformations in the field of child development that might make the research obsolete by the time it is complete.

However, when researchers choose the more convenient cross-sectional shortcut, they are short-changed in the kind of information they can obtain about development. Evidence about change at the level at which it actually occurs — the individual — is not available. Instead, the study of development is limited to comparisons of the average performance of different age groups of children.

Furthermore, to conclude from a cross-sectional study that a true age-related change has occurred, researchers must make a special, sometimes unwarranted assumption: that the behavior of the younger subjects reflects how the older subjects behaved at an earlier age. In cross-sectional investigations that cover a large age range, this assumption is especially risky because the separate age groups contain individuals born in widely separated years. Differences found between 10-year-old cohorts who were born in 1981 and 20-year-old cohorts who were born in 1971 may not really represent age-related changes. Instead, they may be due to unique experiences associated with the different time periods in which the age groups were growing up. Thus, the validity of cross-sectional studies can also be threatened by cultural-historical change, and cross-sectional research is likely to suffer from fewest problems if the age range sampled is fairly narrow.

Despite these limitations, the cross-sectional design is an efficient strategy for identifying developmental trends, and results from such studies frequently lead to fruitful speculations about the reasons for age-related changes. A cross-sectional study by Loney (1974) serves as a good example. Loney wanted to find out whether hyperactive boys, whose behavior is characterized by impulsiveness, inattentiveness, and overactivity, differ from normal agemates in the development of intelligence and self-esteem during middle childhood. To find out, she obtained intelligence test scores and teacher ratings of self-esteem on hyperactive and normal boys enrolled in second- and fifth-grade classrooms. The results, displayed in Figure 2.2, show that the scores of both types of boys were similar in second grade. However, in fifth grade, hyperactive boys' self-esteem and IQ scores were considerably below those of their normal counterparts. Loney suggested that hyperactive boys' poor self-control probably leads to negative reactions from teachers and repeated failure in school. Between second and fifth grade, these experiences may lower the children's self-esteem and motivation, which, in turn, may depress their intelligence test performance. Loney's study does not offer definite proof for this intriguing explanation. Nevertheless, it

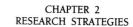

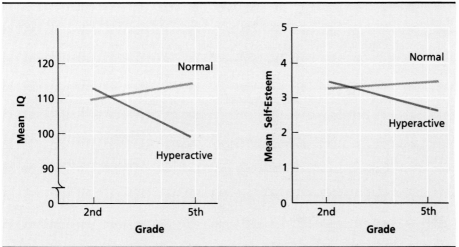

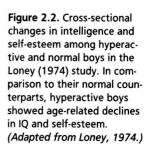

Figure 2.2. Cross-sectional changes in intelligence and self-esteem among hyperactive and normal boys in the Loney (1974) study. In comparison to their normal counterparts, hyperactive boys showed age-related declines in IQ and self-esteem. *(Adapted from Loney, 1974.)*

highlights some thought-provoking developmental trends that deserve to be followed up in subsequent research.

Improving Developmental Designs

To overcome some of the limitations of longitudinal and cross-sectional designs, several new approaches for studying development have been devised. One of them, called the **longitudinal-sequential design,** is depicted in Figure 2.3. It is called a sequential design because it is composed of a sequence of samples, each of which is followed longitudinally for a number of years (Schaie & Hertzog, 1982). In the example shown here, three samples of children born in different years have been selected. Each group is followed longitudinally during 1990, 1991, and 1992. Because the design includes several different samples that are followed over time, it actually combines longitudinal and cross-sectional strategies (Achenbach, 1978).

The new design has several advantages. First, it enables investigators to find out whether cultural-historical effects are operating by making a *time-lag comparison.* This entails comparing the samples born in different years with one another when they have reached the same age. Using the example shown in Figure 2.3, we can compare the behaviors of the three samples of children when they are each 7 years of age. Because the ages of the three groups of children are identical, any differences that we find among them can be attributed to cultural-historical influences associated with their different birth years. Second, it is possible to do both longitudinal and cross-sectional comparisons among the samples of children. Therefore, the design permits us to find out whether age-related changes can be replicated by using the two different developmental approaches. Third, the design is efficient, in that it enables us to obtain information over a fairly long period of development in less time than it takes the development to occur. In our example, it takes only two years, from 1990 to 1992, to carry out the study. However, as long as there are no cultural-historical influences to contaminate our age-related findings, we have obtained information about development over a 4-year period, from 5 to 9 years of age (Achenbach, 1978).

Finally, perhaps you noticed that all of the examples of longitudinal and cross-sectional research we have discussed provide only correlational, and not causal, inferences about development. Yet, ideally, causal information is desirable, both for verifying theories and for coming up with ways to improve children's development. If we find that some aspect of children's experiences and behavior are related in a developmental design, in some instances we can explore the causal relationship between them by experimentally manipulating the early experience in a subsequent

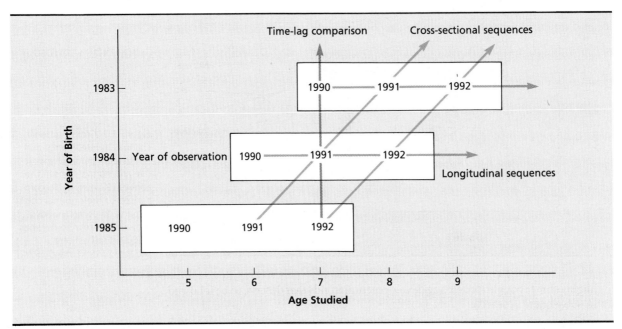

Figure 2.3. The longitudinal-sequential design. Three samples of children born in 1983, 1984, and 1985, respectively, are observed longitudinally in the years 1990 to 1992. The design permits both longitudinal and cross-sectional comparisons. In addition, a time-lag comparison allows the investigator to as- sess cultural-historical effects. *(Adapted with permission of The Free Press, a Division of Macmillan, Inc., from* Research in Developmental Psychology: Concepts, Strategies, Methods, *by Thomas M. Achenbach. Copyright © 1978 by The Free Press.)*

study. If, as a result, child development is enhanced, this would provide strong evidence for a causal relationship between the early experience and later behavior. Today, research that combines an experimental strategy with either a longitudinal or a cross-sectional approach appears with increasing frequency in the research literature. Such designs are a vital force in helping child development specialists move beyond mere identification of correlated variables toward a causal account of factors responsible for developmental change.

BRIEF REVIEW

In the sections above, we discussed a wide variety of research designs commonly used in the field of child development, each of which presents investigators with advantages and disadvantages. To help you review and compare the various designs, Table 2.2 provides a brief descriptive summary of each, along with its major strengths and weaknesses.

ETHICS IN RESEARCH WITH CHILDREN

In any study, investigators must address fundamental questions about whether or not the research presents ethical risks to the subjects involved. Research into human behavior creates ethical issues because, unfortunately, the quest for scientific knowledge can sometimes be turned to manipulative and exploitative purposes as well. When children are research participants, the ethical considerations are especially complex. Children are more vulnerable than adults to physical and psychological harm, and immaturity makes it difficult or impossible for children to evaluate for themselves what participation in research may mean. For these reasons, special ethical guidelines for research involving children have been developed by the federal government, by funding agencies, and by research-oriented associations such as the American Psychological Association (1968) and the Society for Research in Child

Table 2.2. Strengths and Weaknesses of Common Research Designs

DESIGN	DESCRIPTION	STRENGTHS	WEAKNESSES
GENERAL DESIGNS			
Correlational design	Information obtained on existing groups of individuals, without researcher intervention	Permits study of relationships between variables in natural life circumstances	Does not permit determination of cause and effect relationships among variables
Laboratory experiment	Under controlled laboratory conditions, investigator manipulates an independent variable and looks at what effect this has on a dependent variable. Requires random assignment of subjects to treatment conditions	Permits determination of cause and effect relationships between variables	Findings may not generalize to the real world
Field experiment	Experimental design involving random assignment of subjects to treatments in natural settings	Permits generalization of experimental findings to the real world	Control over treatment is generally weaker than in a laboratory experiment
Natural experiment	Comparison of existing real-world treatments to which subjects cannot be randomly assigned	Permits study of many naturally occurring variables not subject to experimenter manipulation	Observed differences may be due to variables other than the treatment
DEVELOPMENTAL DESIGNS			
Longitudinal design	A group of subjects is observed repeatedly at different ages	Permits study of individual developmental trends and relationships between early and later events and behaviors	Age-related changes are subject to distortion if biased sampling, subject attrition, subject reactivity, practice effects, or cultural-historical change occurs
Cross-sectional design	Groups of subjects of different ages are observed at a single point in time	More convenient and efficient than the longitudinal design	Does not permit study of individual developmental trends. Age differences are subject to distortion due to cultural-historical change
Longitudinal-sequential design	Several groups of children born in different years are followed longitudinally over the same time span	Provides both longitudinal and cross-sectional data. Time-lag comparison reveals existence of cultural-historical change	Is subject to the same problems as longitudinal and cross-sectional strategies, but the design itself helps identify difficulties

Development (1990). A summary of children's basic research rights drawn from these guidelines is presented in Table 2.3.

Most studies in which children are observed, questioned, or tested present little potential for harm. However, investigators occasionally find it difficult to study important topics without asking anxiety-provoking questions, deceiving children, or exposing them to some stress. For example, the following research situations pose serious ethical dilemmas. On the basis of the guidelines given in Table 2.3, what precautions do you think should be taken in each instance? Is any one of them so threatening to children's well-being that it should not be carried out at all?

To study young children's separation distress, an investigator decides to ask mothers of 1- and 2-year-olds to leave their youngsters alone for a brief period of time in a

Table 2.3. Children's Research Rights

Protection from Harm. Children have the right to be protected from physical or psychological harm in research. If in doubt about the harmful effects of research, investigators should seek the opinion of others. When harm seems possible, investigators should find other means for obtaining the desired information or abandon the research.

Informed Consent. Informed consent of parents as well as others who act on the child's behalf (such as school officials) should be obtained for any research involving children, preferably in writing. All research participants, including children, have the right to have explained to them all aspects of the research that may affect their willingness to participate in language appropriate to their level of understanding. Adults and children should be free to discontinue participation in research at any time.

Privacy. Children have the right to concealment of their identity on all information collected in the course of research. They also have this right with respect to written reports and in any informal discussions about the research.

Knowledge of Results. Children have the right to be informed of the results of research in terms that are appropriate to their understanding.

Beneficial Treatments. If experimental treatments believed to be beneficial are under investigation, children in control groups have the right to alternative beneficial treatments if they are available.

Sources: American Psychological Association, Division on Developmental Psychology, 1968; Society for Research in Child Development, Committee for Ethical Conduct in Child Development Research, 1990.

strange playroom. The researcher knows that under these circumstances, some children become very upset.

In a study of moral development, an investigator wants to assess children's ability to resist temptation by videotaping their responses without their knowledge. Seven-year-olds are promised an attractive prize for solving some very difficult puzzles. They are also told to refrain from looking at a peer's correct solutions, which are deliberately placed at the back of the room. If the researcher has to tell children ahead of time that cheating is being studied or that their behavior is being closely monitored, he will destroy the phenomenon under investigation.

An investigator interested in peer relations plans to have third graders name the children they like best and those they like least in their classroom. The teacher complains that asking pupils to evaluate one another in this way sensitizes them to their own social preferences and encourages them to share these opinions with others. Thus, the method may cause disliked children to be further ostracized by their peers.[1]

Did you find it difficult to decide on the best course of action in the examples given above? Virtually every committee that has worked on developing ethical principles for research has concluded that the conflicts raised by such studies cannot be resolved with simple right or wrong answers. Consequently, the ultimate responsibility for the ethical integrity of research resides with the investigator. However, researchers are advised or, in the case of federally funded research, required to seek advice from others, and **institutional review boards** exist in colleges, universities, and other

[1] Sometimes additional research can help resolve perplexing ethical dilemmas. In a recent study, Bell-Dolan, Foster, and Sikora (1989) found that asking elementary school children to nominate disliked peers did not lead them to interact less frequently or more negatively with these youngsters. Nevertheless, the authors recommend that special precautions be taken by investigators when requesting such information. For example, children can be asked to keep their peer nominations confidential, and assessments can be made just before periods in which classmates have limited opportunities to interact with one another.

research-oriented organizations for this purpose. These review boards evaluate research studies on the basis of a **risks-versus-benefits ratio.** This involves weighing the costs of the research to the individual participant in terms of time, stress, and inconvenience against its value for advancing knowledge and increasing our capacity to better children's conditions of life (Cooke, 1982). The general ethical question that must be asked about every research study is whether there are any negative implications for the safety and welfare of participants that the worth of the research findings really does not justify. If so, priority should always be given to the research participant.

The ethical principle of **informed consent** requires special interpretation when research participants are children. The competence of youngsters of different ages to make choices about their own participation must be taken into account. Parental consent is meant to protect the safety of children whose ability to make these decisions is not yet fully mature. Besides parental consent, agreement of other individuals who act on children's behalf, such as institutional officials when research is conducted in schools, day care centers, or hospitals, should be obtained. This is especially important when research includes children with special characteristics, such as maltreated youngsters, whose parents may not always represent their best interests (Thompson, 1990). Furthermore, researchers should seek the agreement of children as soon as they begin to develop some ability to understand verbal explanations. Children's ability to make such judgments varies tremendously. Infants and preverbal toddlers certainly cannot make reasoned judgments, and parental consent should usually be the deciding factor. By the time children enter the preschool years, they have some capacity to understand investigators' explanations if these are conveyed concretely, in terms that refer to the immediate situation and the child's recent experiences. Therefore, in addition to obtaining parental consent, investigators should provide preschool children with simple explanations, such as "We want to find out more about how children play, how they solve problems, what they think about these questions" (Ferguson, 1978, p. 118).

For children 7 years and older, their own informed consent should be obtained in addition to parental consent (National Commission for the Protection of Human Subjects, 1977). Around the age of 7, changes in children's thinking permit them to better understand simple scientific principles, the perspectives of others, and the consequences of their behavior for those around them. Researchers should respect and enhance these new capacities by providing school-age children with a full explanation of research activities in everyday language that children can understand (Cooke, 1982; Ferguson, 1978; Thompson, 1990).

Finally, young children rely on a basic faith in the trustworthiness of adults for feeling secure in unfamiliar situations. Therefore, it is possible for some types of research to be particularly disturbing to them. Virtually all ethical guidelines advise that special precautions be taken in the use of deception and concealment, as occurs in studies in which researchers give children false feedback about their performance, observe them surreptitiously from behind one-way mirrors, or do not tell children the truth regarding what the research is all about. When these kinds of procedures are used with adults, **debriefing,** in which a full account and justification of the activities is provided by the experimenter, occurs after the research session is over. Debriefing should also take place with children, but it does not always work as well. Despite explanations, children may come away from the research situation thinking that some adults do not tell the truth and having their basic faith in adults undermined. Ethical standards permit deception in research with children if investigators satisfy institutional review boards that such practices are necessary. Nevertheless, since deception may have serious emotional consequences for some youngsters, many child development specialists take the position that its use is always unethical and that investigators should use their ingenuity to come up with alternative research procedures when children are involved (Cooke, 1982; Ferguson, 1978).

Introduction

■ Research generally begins with an **hypothesis,** or prediction about behavior drawn from a theory. In areas in which there is little or no existing theory, it starts with a research question. On the basis of the hypothesis or question, the investigator selects research methods (specific activities in which each subject will participate) and a research design (overall plan for the study).

Why Know about Research Strategies?

■ Investigators must understand scientific procedures for conducting research to ensure as accurate a representation of child development as possible. To be wise and critical consumers of knowledge, students and practitioners also need to be familiar with research procedures. In addition, sometimes practioners are in a position to conduct small-scale studies to answer questions about the children with whom they work.

Reliability and Validity: Keys to Scientifically Sound Research

■ Reliability and validity are concepts that help investigators determine whether a research strategy produces accurate and meaningful information. A research method is **reliable** if it produces consistent, repeatable results. A method is **valid** if, after examining its content and relationships with other measures of behavior, the investigator finds that it reflects what it was intended to measure.

■ Two special kinds of validity refer to the accuracy of the researcher's overall findings and conclusions. The **internal validity** of a study is jeopardized if factors unrelated to the researcher's hypothesis serve as alternative explanations for the results. **External validity** refers to the generalizability of research findings. It is compromised when investigators use biased samples or conduct research in contrived, artificial situations.

Common Research Methods Used to Study Children

■ Commonly used research methods in child development include systematic observation, self-reports, and the clinical or case study method. **Naturalistic observations** are made in children's everyday environments, while **structured observations** take place in laboratories where investigators deliberately set up cues to elicit the behaviors of interest. Depending on the researcher's purpose, observations can preserve the entire behavior stream of the subject, as in the **specimen record**, or they can be limited to one or a few behaviors, as in **event sampling** and **time sampling**.

■ Self-report methods can be flexible and open-ended, like the **clinical interview,** which yields a full picture of each subject's thoughts and feelings. Alternatively, **structured interviews** and **questionnaires** can be given, which permit easy comparison of subjects' responses and efficient administration and scoring.

■ Investigators use the **clinical method** when they desire an in-depth understanding of a single child. In this approach, a wide range of interview, test, and observational information is synthesized into a description of the subject's development and unique psychological functioning.

General Research Designs

■ Two basic kinds of research designs are correlational and experimental. The **correlational design** examines relationships between variables as they happen to occur, without the researcher's intervention. Correlational studies do not permit identification of the precise causal links between variables, but their use is justified when investigators find it difficult or impossible to control the variables of interest.

■ In contrast, **experimental designs** permit determination of cause and effect relationships. In a typical experiment, researchers manipulate an **independent variable** by exposing groups of subjects to two or more treatment conditions. Then they determine what effect this has on changes in a **dependent variable. Random assignment** and **matching** are techniques used in experiments to ensure that characteristics of subjects do not contaminate the findings.

■ To achieve high degrees of control, most experiments are conducted in laboratories. The strength of the **laboratory experiment** is the achievement of high internal validity, but this is often obtained at some expense to external validity.

■ Researchers have tried to improve the external validity of experimental findings by conducting **field experiments,** in which they manipulate treatment conditions in the real world. When this is impossible, they resort to **natural experiments,** in which already existing, naturally occurring treatments are compared with one another.

Designs for Studying Development

■ Longitudinal and cross-sectional designs are uniquely suited for studying human development. The **longitudinal design,** in which a sample of children is observed repeatedly at different ages, permits the study of individual developmental trends, relationships among changes in different aspects of behavior, and relationships among early and later events and behaviors.

■ Investigators face a variety of problems in conducting longitudinal research. These include **biased sampling, sub-**

ject reactivity, **practice effects, cultural-historical change (cohort effects),** and outdated theories and methods in long-term studies.

■ The **cross-sectional design,** in which groups of children of different ages are observed at a single point in time, provides an expedient approach to studying development. However, the information available is restricted to comparisons of the average performance of different age groups. In addition, cross-sectional studies that span a wide age range are threatened by the effects of cultural-historical change.

■ To deal with some of the limitations of longitudinal and cross-sectional designs, new approaches for studying development, such as the **longitudinal-sequential design,** have been devised. In addition, experimental procedures can be combined with longitudinal or cross-sectional designs to examine causal influences on development.

Ethics in Research with Children

■ Research involving children raises special ethical concerns. Because of their immaturity, children are especially vulnerable to harm and cannot always make informed choices about research participation. Ethical guidelines for research and **institutional review boards** help ensure that children's research rights are protected.

■ As soon as children are old enough to understand the researcher's verbal explanations, investigators should seek their **informed consent** for research participation, in addition to the consent of their parents. The use of deception in research with children is especially risky, since it may leave emotional scars and undermine children's basic faith in the trustworthiness of adults.

IMPORTANT TERMS AND CONCEPTS

hypothesis   (p. 35)
reliability   (p. 37)
validity   (p. 37)
replication   (p. 38)
internal validity   (p. 38)
external validity   (p. 39)
cross-validation study   (p. 39)
naturalistic observation   (p. 40)
structured observation   (p. 42)
specimen record   (p. 42)
event sampling   (p. 43)
time sampling   (p. 43)
clinical interview   (p. 44)
structured interview   (p. 45)

questionnaire   (p. 45)
clinical method   (p. 46)
correlational design   (p. 46)
correlation coefficient   (p. 47)
experimental designs   (p. 49)
independent variable   (p. 49)
dependent variable   (p. 49)
laboratory experiment   (p. 49)
random assignment   (p. 50)
matching   (p. 50)
field experiment   (p. 50)
natural experiment   (p. 51)
longitudinal design   (p. 51)
biased sampling   (p. 55)

subject attrition   (p. 55)
subject reactivity   (p. 55)
practice effects   (p. 55)
cultural-historical change (cohort effects)   (p. 56)
cross-sectional design   (p. 58)
longitudinal-sequential design   (p. 59)
institutional review board   (p. 62)
risks-versus-benefits ratio   (p. 63)
informed consent   (p. 63)
debriefing   (p. 63)

Frederick Carl Frieseke: *Peace.*
In the collection of The Corcoran Gallery of Art, Museum Purchase, 1921.

3

Biological Foundations, Prenatal Development, and Birth

In this chapter, we consider the beginnings of development. In a brief nine-month period, a tiny, one-celled fertilized ovum miraculously unfolds into a newborn baby equipped with complex physical and behavioral characteristics specially suited for life outside the womb. Because nature has prepared the human infant for survival, all healthy newborns have many characteristics in common. At the same time, a glance around a hospital nursery reveals that each baby's uniqueness is evident soon after birth. Excited relatives looking for family resemblances find that one infant shows combined features of both parents, another resembles only one parent, while a third bears characteristics unlike those of either parent. These visibly apparent differences, referred to as **phenotypes,** depend in part on genetic, or **genotype,** differences among children.

In this chapter, we consider basic genetic principles of transmission that underlie important individual differences in appearance and behavior. Then we trace development during the most rapid phase of growth, the prenatal period, in which complex transactions between heredity and environment begin to shape the course of future development. The prenatal environment is far more constant than the world the infant will encounter after birth. Nevertheless, it can have major consequences for the child's physical and behavioral characteristics. Our discussion considers environmental supports that are necessary for normal intrauterine growth as well as damaging environmental influences that have irrevocable consequences for the unborn child's future. Then we turn to the drama of birth and a consideration of developmental risks for infants born prematurely, before prenatal growth is complete.

Finally, we take a look ahead. This earliest period of development introduces us to the operation of two basic determinants of development: heredity and environment. We discuss how child development specialists think about and study the relationship between heredity and environment as they continue to influence the child's emerging characteristics from infancy through adolescence.

GENETIC FOUNDATIONS

Genetics is the science of heredity, of how traits are passed from one generation to the next. The study of genetic mechanisms of transmission began over a century ago, with the famous crossings between varieties of garden peas made by the Austrian monk Gregor Mendel. Conducting experiments in which he recorded the number of times each generation of white- and pink-flowered plants had offspring with white or pink flowers, Mendel inferred the presence of genes, factors controlling the physical traits he studied. While peas and humans may seem completely unrelated, the transmission of heredity conforms to the same basic principles among diverse forms of life. Since Mendel's ground-breaking observations, more knowledge has accumulated about the precise makeup of genetic material.

The Genetic Code

Each of us is made up of trillions of independent units called cells. Inside every cell is a control center or nucleus, which contains, among other things, **chromosomes,** the bearers of our genetic fate. When cells are chemically stained and viewed through a powerful microscope, the chromosomes, or "colored bodies," are visible as rod-like structures in the nucleus. Chromosomes store and transmit genetic information, control how the cells are made, and play an important role in determining our development and characteristics. The number of chromosomes varies from species to

Figure 3.1. Human chromosomes. (Left) A *karyotype*, or photograph of human chromosomes from a white blood cell. (Right) The chromosomes have been assembled in pairs and ordered according to decreasing size. Note the 23rd pair, XY. The cell donor is a male. The chromosomes in this photo have just replicated themselves in preparation for mitosis, or cell duplication. *(From E. Frankel, 1979,* DNA: The Ladder of Life, *New York: McGraw-Hill. P. 16. Reprinted by permission.)*

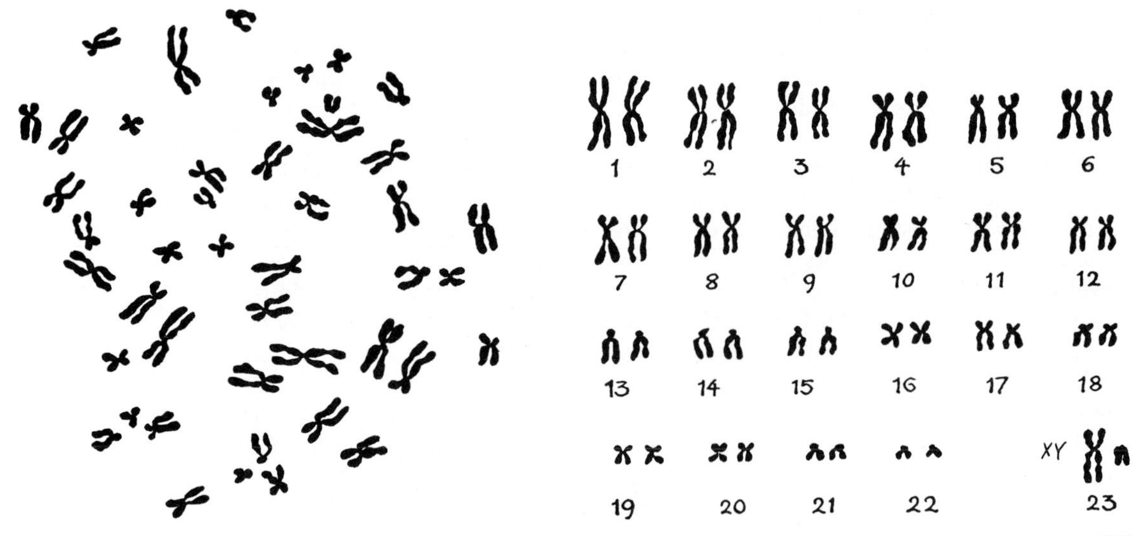

species — 48 for the chimpanzee, 64 for the horse, 40 for the mouse, and 46 for the human being. Chromosomes come in duplicates, or what are called **homologous** pairs (an exception is the XY pair in males, which we will discuss later). Each pair member corresponds to the other in size, shape, and genetic functions, with one inherited from the mother and one from the father. Therefore, in humans, we speak of 23 *pairs* of chromosomes residing in each human cell (see Figure 3.1).

Chromosomes contain long, double-stranded molecules of a chemical substance called **deoxyribonucleic acid,** or **DNA.** In the early 1950s, Watson and Crick's (1953) discovery of the chemical architecture of the DNA molecule unlocked the genetic code. As shown in Figure 3.2, DNA has a "double-helix" structure that resembles a twisted ladder. Notice that each rung consists of a specific pair of chemical bases joined together between the two sides of the ladder. Although the bases occur in fixed association across the ladder rungs, they can occur in any order along its sides, and it is the sequence of bases that provides specific genetic instruc-

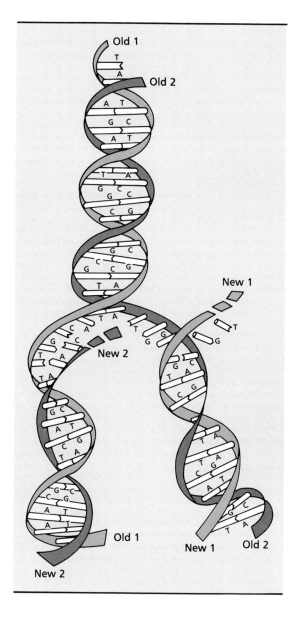

Figure 3.2. DNA's double-helix structure. The pairings of bases across the rungs of the ladder are very specific: adenine (A) always appears with thymine (T) and cytosine (C) with guanine (G). Here, the DNA ladder is shown duplicating itself by splitting down the middle of its ladder rungs. Then each free base picks up a new complementary partner from the cytoplasm of the cell. The result is two identical strands of DNA. *(From E. Frankel, 1979,* DNA: The Ladder of Life, *New York: McGraw-Hill. P. 54. Reprinted by permission.)*

tions. A **gene** is a segment of DNA along the length of the molecule. Genes can be of different lengths—perhaps 100 to several thousand ladder rungs long—and each differs from the next because of its special sequence of base pairs. Thus, each new individual begins life with a set of hereditary instructions built into the structure of its DNA that determines what kind of organism it is and many of its unique characteristics.

A unique feature of DNA, one that distinguishes it from all other molecules, is that it can duplicate itself. This special ability makes it possible for the one-celled fertilized ovum to develop into a complex human being composed of trillions of cells. The precise mechanism of cell duplication is called **mitosis.** In mitosis, the DNA ladder splits down the middle (as shown in Figure 3.2). Then each base is free to pick up a new complementary mate from the cytoplasm of the cell. Notice how this results in two identical DNA ladders, each containing one new side and one old side of the previous chain. At the chromosome level, mitosis involves each chromosome replicating itself. As a result, each new cell contains an exact copy of the original chromosomes and the identical genetic material.

The Sex Cells

The new individual is created by the union of two special cells, a sperm and an ovum, which are referred to as **gametes.** Gametes are unique in that they contain only 23 chromosomes, half as many as a regular body cell. They are formed through a special process of cell division called **meiosis.**

Meiosis takes place according to the sequence of steps displayed in Figure 3.3. First, homologous chromosomes pair up within the original cell, and each member of the pair replicates itself. Then the paired and duplicated chromosomes align themselves at the middle of the cell. While they are there, a special event called **crossing over** takes place, in which adjacent pair members break at one or more points along their length and exchange corresponding segments, so that genes from one chromosome are replaced by genes from another. Then the two chromosomes in a pair separate into different cells. However, chance governs which chromosomes from a homologous pair will gather with others and eventually end up in the same gamete. Finally, in the last phase of meiosis, each pair member separates from its partner and becomes part of a sex cell containing 23 chromosomes.

In the male, the meiotic process results in the formation of four gametes, or sperm cells, from the original cell. In the female, the end product is slightly different in that it results in only one unfertilized ovum; the leftover cellular material soon degenerates. When the sperm and ovum unite at fertilization to form the beginning of the new individual, the cell that results, called a **zygote,** will again have 46 chromosomes.

The process of meiosis guarantees that a constant quantity of genetic material will be transmitted from one generation to the next. In addition, it also increases genetic variability among offspring. Crossing over and independent assortment of the members of chromosome pairs ensure that no two gametes will ever be genetically identical (except for identical twins, which result when a zygote duplicates itself). Although half the new individual's genes are drawn from the mother and half from the father, each offspring receives a different selection of genes from each parent. Thus, meiosis explains why siblings differ from one another in appearance and characteristics, although they also share features in common, since their genotypes come from a common pool of parental genes.

The genetic variability produced by meiosis is important in an evolutionary sense. Certain combinations of genes enable individuals to adapt better to the environment. When these individuals reproduce, their favorable genetic makeup has the opportunity to undergo further modifications, and some new genetic combinations may prove even better suited to the environment than the original ones. In addition, environments also undergo change, so the greater the genetic variability present among

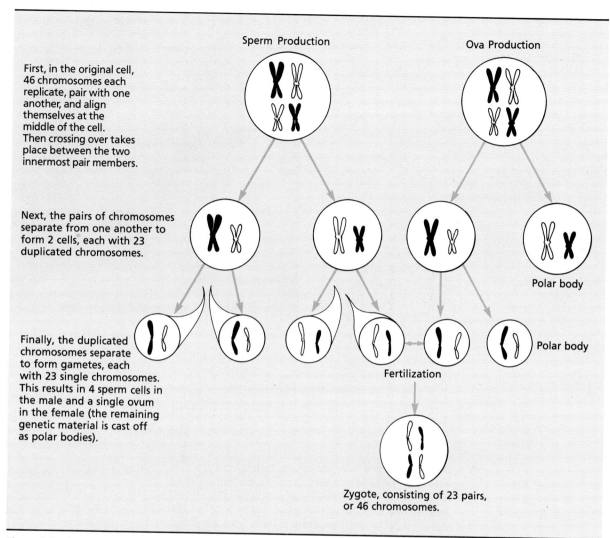

Sperm Production

Ova Production

First, in the original cell, 46 chromosomes each replicate, pair with one another, and align themselves at the middle of the cell. Then crossing over takes place between the two innermost pair members.

Next, the pairs of chromosomes separate from one another to form 2 cells, each with 23 duplicated chromosomes.

Polar body

Finally, the duplicated chromosomes separate to form gametes, each with 23 single chromosomes. This results in 4 sperm cells in the male and a single ovum in the female (the remaining genetic material is cast off as polar bodies).

Fertilization

Polar body

Zygote, consisting of 23 pairs, or 46 chromosomes.

Figure 3.3. The cell division process of meiosis, leading to gamete formation. Original cells are depicted with two rather than the full complement of 23 chromosome pairs.

members of a species, the greater the chances that some will be able to cope with new environmental conditions. Thus, the genetic variability that results from the meiotic production of sex cells is essential for evolutionary progress and the survival of a species.

In the male, the cells from which the sperm arise are produced continuously, from puberty onward. In the female, gamete production is more restricted. The ovum-producing cells are formed and enter the early stages of meiosis before birth, and the female is born with all her potential gametes present in her ovaries. Still, there is no shortage of female reproductive cells. About 1 to 2 million are present at birth, 40,000 remain at puberty, and approximately 350 to 450 will mature during a woman's childbearing years (Sadler, 1990).

Patterns of Genetic Inheritance

Using special microscopic techniques, the pairs of chromosomes can be distinguished from one another. The 22 pairs that are homologous are called **autosomes,** and they are numbered by geneticists from longest to shortest (refer back to Figure 3.1). The

Heredity manifests itself in many visible human characteristics; sometimes the resemblance between parent and offspring is striking.

23rd pair is made up of the **sex chromosomes.** In females, this pair is called XX; in males, it is called XY. The single X is a relatively long chromosome, while the Y is short and carries very little genetic material. In gamete formation in males, the X and Y chromosomes separate into different sperm cells; in females, all gametes carry an X chromosome. Therefore, the sex of the individual is determined by whether an X-bearing or Y-bearing sperm fertilizes the ovum. In fact, scientists recently isolated a single gene on the Y chromosome that triggers male sexual development. When this gene is absent, the fetus that develops is female (Page et al., 1987).

Two forms of each gene occur at the same locus, or place, on the autosomes: one inherited from the mother and one from the father. Each is called an *allele.* If the alleles from both parents are alike, the new individual is said to be **homozygous** and will display the inherited trait. If the alleles are different, the individual is **heterozygous.** Under heterozygous circumstances, the way that the two alleles interact determines the phenotypic trait that the individual will display, and there are a number of different possibilities.

Dominant-Recessive Relationships. Under many heterozygous conditions, only one of the alleles becomes phenotypically apparent. It is termed **dominant,** while the second allele whose influence does not appear in the phenotype is called **recessive.** Hair color is an example of this dominant-recessive pattern of inheritance. The allele for dark hair is known to be dominant (we can represent it with a capital H), while the one for blond hair is recessive (symbolized by a small h). Individuals who inherit a homozygous pair of dominant alleles (HH) or a heterozygous pair (Hh) will display the same dark-haired phenotype, even though their genotypes are different. Blond hair can result only when the individual inherits the combination of two recessive alleles (hh).

A list of some of the human characteristics that operate according to the dominant-recessive mode of inheritance is given in Table 3.1. As you can see by examining the table, many serious disease conditions are the product of two recessive genes. One of the most frequently occurring of such disorders is *phenylketonuria*, or *PKU.* PKU is an especially good example of genetic transmission, since it shows that inheritance of unfavorable genes does not necessarily mean that the resulting condition is permanent and unmodifiable. For PKU, we know the specific biochemical consequences of recessive gene inheritance. Consequently, we can use this information to intervene with the environment and prevent the most serious aspects of the disease.

PKU occurs about once in every 8,000 births (March of Dimes, 1983). Inheritance of two autosomal recessive alleles (pp) affects the way the body metabolizes proteins contained in many foods, such as cow's milk and meat. Infants born with PKU lack an enzyme that converts a potentially harmful amino acid contained in proteins (phenylalanine) into a harmless by-product. In the absence of this enzyme, a toxic excess of phenylalanine quickly accumulates and damages the central nervous system. By 3 to 5 months of age, infants with untreated PKU start to lose interest in their surroundings, and by 1 year of age, they are permanently mentally retarded.

Most states require that every newborn be tested for PKU. If the disease is diagnosed, treatment involves placing the baby on a diet low in phenylalanine and monitoring the concentration of this substance in the bloodstream to make sure it never reaches toxic levels. Children who receive this dietary treatment show near-normal levels of intelligence, and the most harmful effects of the disorder are averted. Frequently, the special diet is discontinued by 5 or 6 years of age, when many physicians believe the central nervous system is sufficiently mature to resist the effects of phenylalanine. However, others disagree and recommend lifetime dietary maintenance because of declines in intelligence test scores of some children who were removed from the diet at school age (Michals et al., 1988; Pietz et al., 1988).

There is another reason for long-term dietary intervention. If a woman who had PKU as a child but stopped the diet becomes pregnant, her baby is likely to be born retarded. Toxic levels of phenylalanine in the mother's bloodstream enter the baby's circulatory system before birth and interfere with development of the central nervous system. In this case, the unborn child may not have inherited the disorder but will nevertheless bear its effects because of a damaging intrauterine environment provided by the PKU mother. Retardation can be prevented if the mother goes back on a low-phenylalanine diet before and during pregnancy (Lowitzer, 1987).

Table 3.1. Examples of Dominant and Recessive Characteristics and Diseases

DOMINANT	RECESSIVE
Dark hair	Blond hair
Curly hair	Straight hair
Facial dimples	No dimples
Normal hearing	Some forms of congenital deafness
Normal vision	Nearsightedness
Farsightedness	Normal vision
Normal vision	Congenital eye cataracts
Normal color vision	Red-green color blindness
Normally pigmented skin	Albinism
Type A blood	Type O blood
Type B blood	Type O blood
Rh positive blood	Rh negative blood
Normal respiratory and gastrointestinal functioning	Cystic fibrosis
Normal blood-clotting factors	Hemophilia
Normal protein metabolism	Phenylketonuria (PKU)
Normal red blood cells	Sickle cell anemia
Normal central nervous system development	Tay-Sachs disease
Huntington's chorea	Normal central nervous system functioning in adulthood

Sources: McKusick, 1988; Stanbury, Wyngaarden, & Fredrickson, 1983.

Note: Many normal characteristics that were previously thought to be governed by the single-gene dominant-recessive mode of inheritance, such as eye color, are now regarded by geneticists as polygenically determined (due to multiple genes). For the characteristics listed here, there still seems to be fairly common agreement that the simple dominant-recessive relationship holds.

In dominant-recessive autosomal inheritance, if we know the genetic makeup of the parents, we can predict the proportion of offspring in a family who are likely to manifest the recessive trait or be heterozygous carriers of it. Figure 3.4 shows one hypothetical example for PKU. Note that for a child to inherit the condition, a recessive allele (p) must be carried and transmitted by each parent. One good reason for cultural and legal prohibitions against marriages between close blood relatives is that related parents have an increased risk of inheriting the same damaging recessive allele from a common ancestor and passing it along to their offspring. Recessive disorders like PKU are more common among children born to parents who are first or second cousins (Reed, 1975).

Co-Dominance. In the case of a few characteristics attributable to single gene inheritance, the dominant-recessive pattern of expression does not hold completely. There are some heterozygous allele combinations in which it is possible for both alleles to be expressed in the individual's phenotype. This is called **co-dominance.** ABO blood typing provides an illustration. Three possible alleles—A, B, and O—can be inherited in any paired combination. Therefore, three heterozygous conditions are possible: AO, BO, and AB. When paired with O, the A and B alleles will determine the phenotype, and the usual dominant-recessive mode of expression applies. But when both A and B alleles are inherited, the result is the combined phenotypic expression known as type AB blood, in which both A and B antigens are present.

Sickle cell anemia, a recessive blood disorder that afflicts one out of every 500 African-Americans, is another instance in which co-dominance applies. However, in the case of the sickle cell trait, special circumstances in the environment are responsible for triggering the expression of both alleles in heterozygous individuals. Thus, the sickle cell genetic disorder is an illustration of the subtle interaction of hereditary and environmental factors that can contribute to phenotypic results.

Sickle cell anemia occurs when a person inherits a pair of recessive alleles that cause the usually round red blood cells to assume a sickle shape, a response that is especially acute under low-oxygen environmental conditions. The sickled cells clog the blood vessels, interfere with the flow of blood, and interrupt the delivery of oxygen to body tissues. Organs whose demand for oxygen is particularly great—the brain, kidney, liver, heart, spleen, and muscles—are most affected. Individuals afflicted with the disorder suffer severe attacks involving intense pain, swelling, and

Figure 3.4. Dominant-recessive mode of inheritance as illustrated by PKU. When both parents are heterozygous carriers of the recessive allele, we can predict that 25 percent of their offspring will be normal, 50 percent will be carriers, and 25 percent will be afflicted with PKU. *(From March of Dimes, 1983.* PKU *[Genetic Series: Public Health Education Information Sheet], White Plains, NY. March of Dimes Birth Defects Foundation. Reprinted by permission.)*

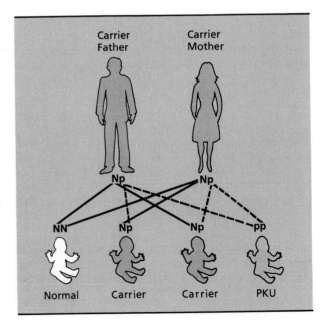

tissue damage. They generally die in the first two decades of life; few live past age 40. Heterozygous individuals are protected from the disease under a broad range of environmental conditions. However, when they are exposed to oxygen deprivation —for example, at high altitudes or after intense physical exertion—the single recessive allele asserts itself, and mild sickling accompanied by painful swelling and fatigue occurs (Sullivan, 1987). Thus, under specific environmental circumstances, the otherwise dominant allele does not completely overcome the effects of the sickle cell gene, and the combined, or co-dominant, effects of both alleles are apparent in a less severe and temporary form of the illness.

Natural Selection, Mutation, and Unfavorable Genes. Inheritance of unfavorable genes decreases the chances that afflicted individuals will reproduce and pass them on to their offspring. Why, then, do some harmful alleles continue to survive? In some instances, natural selection provides the answer. In the case of the sickle cell trait, African heterozygous carriers are more resistant to malaria than individuals with two genes for normal red blood cells. In malaria-ridden regions of the world, these carriers survived and reproduced more frequently than others, leading the gene to be transmitted to their offspring and maintained in the population.

Perhaps you are also asking yourself, "How do genes with unfavorable consequences come to be present in the gene pool in the first place?" The answer is **mutation,** a sudden but permanent change in genetic material. A mutation may involve many genes, as is the case in the chromosomal abnormalities we will discuss later in this chapter, or it may affect only one or two alleles. Some mutations occur spontaneously, while others are provoked by hazardous environmental agents, such as agricultural and industrial chemicals that enter the food supply or are present in the air we breathe. For many years, ionizing radiation has been known to cause mutations. Several studies show a relationship between increased exposure of mothers to radiation before conception and chromosomal defects in their children, with large doses more likely to cause damage than the same amount of radiation received in low doses over time. Other investigations have found chromosomal abnormalities to be higher among the offspring of fathers subjected to high levels of radiation in their occupations (Schrag & Dixon, 1985).

Not all mutations are due to environmental toxins. As we mentioned above, there are also random, spontaneous mutations. Virtually all of those that have been studied are harmful. However, others are necessary and desirable from an evolutionary perspective. They contribute to genetic variability in a population, thereby helping it adapt to unexpected environmental challenges and survive. Scientists seldom go looking for the mutagenic origins of favorable characteristics, such as an exceptional talent or an especially sturdy immune system. Instead, they are far more concerned with identifying and eliminating unfavorable mutations that threaten the healthy development of the organism.

X-Linked Inheritance. Recessive disorders like PKU and sickle cell anemia are due to the inheritance of homozygous pairs of alleles on the autosomes, and males and females have an equal chance of being affected. When a recessive characteristic is carried on the X chromosome, a special pattern of genetic transmission called **X-linked inheritance** applies. Males (XY) are more likely to be affected than females (XX) because the male sex chromosomes are not homologous. In females, any X-linked recessive allele has a reasonable chance of being suppressed by a dominant allele on the other X. Males have only one X chromosome, and there are no complementary alleles on the Y to dominate or soften the effects of those on the X. This leads the genes carried by the X chromosome to be expressed in the male phenotype when they are present in only a single copy, regardless of whether they have dominant or recessive consequences for females. Red-green color blindness is one example of a frequently occurring X-linked recessive trait. Its phenotypic appearance in Caucasians is twice as great for males (eight out of 100) as it is for females (four out of 100), due to the X-linked pattern of genetic transmission (Cohen, 1984).

Hemophilia, a disorder in which the blood fails to clot normally, was one of the earliest known instances of an X-linked recessive disease, appearing relatively frequently in the royal families of Europe. In the general population, it occurs about once in every 4000 to 7000 male births (the disease seldom occurs in females). Hemophilia may become evident shortly after birth if the male infant is circumcised, or it may be recognized later in the first year in a baby who seems to bruise easily or who bleeds excessively after an accidental fall. The major problem is internal bleeding into the joints and muscles that, if not stopped, can lead to deformity, loss of function, and even death. However, with improved medical treatment, bleeding is often preventable, and the life span of afflicted males has increased so that many live long enough to reproduce (Cohen, 1984). Provided that he marries a woman without the recessive gene, none of the sons of a hemophiliac male will manifest the disease, since they inherit his Y chromosome. However, all daughters will be carriers, since they receive his X chromosome. Consequently, the sons of these daughters will have a 50 percent chance of inheriting the disease.

A wide variety of X-linked recessive disorders with increased prevalence in males have been identified—blood clotting deficiencies, metabolic diseases, one form of diabetes, and one type of muscular dystrophy, to name just a few (McKusick, 1988). In addition, many sex differences in development reveal the male to be at a general disadvantage. The rates of spontaneous abortion, stillbirths, and infant and childhood mortality are greater for males, and males show a higher incidence of learning disabilities, behavior disorders, and mental retardation than do females. It is possible that these sex differences may have their origins in the genetic code. The female, with two X chromosomes, benefits from a greater variety of genetic material, while the male's single rather than double dose of X-linked genes contributes to his disadvantage. However, nature seems to make an adjustment for the greater male vulnerability. About 106 boys are born for every 100 girls, and judging from miscarriage and abortion statistics, a still greater number of boys appear to be conceived (Rugh & Shettles, 1971).

Pleiotropism and Modifier Genes. So far, we have considered only one-to-one relationships between genes and phenotypic attributes. However, it is possible for a single gene to affect more than one characteristic. This is known as **pleiotropism,** and the recessive gene responsible for PKU provides an example. Untreated PKU children differ from normal children not only in intelligence, but also in hair color. Hair pigment is formed from the protein tyrosine, and the blond coloring of PKU victims is due to their inability to metabolize phenylalanine into tyrosine.

It is also possible for some genes to modify the phenotypic expression of other genes by either enhancing or diluting their effects. Because of the influence of **modifier genes** on the two recessive alleles for PKU, children differ from one another in the degree to which abnormally high levels of phenylalanine accumulate in their tissues. They also differ in the extent to which they respond to dietary treatment. Other genetic diseases, such as hemophilia and cystic fibrosis (see Table 3.1) also vary in severity, and modifier genes are thought to be responsible.

Polygenic Inheritance. Over 1,000 characteristics are thought to be inherited according to the rules of dominant-recessive genetic transmission (McKusick, 1988). In most of these instances, either people display a particular phenotypic trait or they do not. Such relatively cut-and-dried individual differences are much easier to trace to their genetic origins than characteristics that vary continuously among people. Many physical and behavioral traits of interest to developmental psychologists, such as height, weight, intelligence, and personality, are of the latter type. People are not just tall or short, bright or dull, outgoing or shy. Instead, they show various gradations between these extremes. For continuous characteristics like these, **polygenic inheritance** is more likely (Plomin, 1989). More than one gene, and perhaps a great many, affect the characteristic in question, and the rules of genetic transmission are complex and as yet unspecified. Therefore, scientists have had to study the influence of polygenic inheritance on important human characteristics indirectly. In the final section of this chapter, we will discuss ways that have been used to *infer* the influence of heredity on behavior when knowledge of specific genetic influences is unavailable.

CHROMOSOMAL ABNORMALITIES

In addition to the inheritance of recessive genes, chromosomal abnormalities are a principal cause of serious developmental problems. Most chromosomal defects are the result of imperfect meiosis during gamete formation, in which a chromosome pair does not separate properly or part of a chromosome breaks off. Since these errors involve far more DNA than problems associated with a single gene, they usually produce disorders that display many physical and mental symptoms, with depressed intellectual functioning being one common outcome. Child development specialists are particularly interested in chromosomal abnormalities because they provide insights into biological factors that affect the development of normal children. However, as will be apparent when we discuss some of the more frequent chromosomal problems in the sections below, the phenotypic results of inheriting a particular disorder are not completely clear-cut. Aside from the affected chromosomes, thousands of other genes act on the individual's development, and each affected person is exposed to unique environmental influences from conception on. These factors can minimize or intensify the chromosomal condition.

Physical abnormalities and impaired intellectual functioning characterize Down syndrome children. These youngsters require extra attention to get them to become actively engaged in their surroundings.

Down Syndrome

The most common chromosomal abnormality, occurring in one out of every 800 live births, is *Down syndrome* (Baird & Sadovnick, 1987). It is due to one of several different types of chromosomal mistakes. In over 90 percent of the cases, Down syndrome results from a failure of the 21st pair of chromosomes to separate during meiosis, so the new individual inherits three of these chromosomes rather than the normal two. In other less frequent forms, an extra broken piece of a 21st chromosome is present. In these instances, the phenotype can vary from one that is practically normal to one that bears the typical characteristics of Down syndrome, depending on how much additional genetic material is involved (Rosenberg & Pettegrew, 1983).

Children with Down syndrome have a variety of seemingly unrelated defects. These include distinct physical features—a short stocky build, a flattened face, a protruding tongue, almond-shaped eyes, and an unusual crease running across the palm of the hand. In addition, infants with Down syndrome are often born with such congenital[1] problems as heart abnormalities, malformations of the intestinal tract, and eye cataracts, and their facial deformities often lead to breathing and feeding difficulties in infancy. Because of medical advances, early mortality of Down syndrome children due to heart defects and respiratory infections has been reduced, but it is still common. About 14 percent die by age 1 and 21 percent by age 10, the rest usually living until middle adulthood (Baird & Sadovnick, 1987).

[1] The term *congenital* refers to any malformations that have their origins during the early weeks of prenatal life when the organs of the body are being formed. The concept includes defects that are due to hereditary influences, prenatal environmental influences, or both factors.

The behavioral consequences of Down syndrome include mental retardation, poorly articulated speech, limited vocabulary, and slow motor development. These deficits become increasingly apparent with age, since Down syndrome children show a progressive slowing down in development from infancy onward when compared to normal children (Kopp, 1983). Most fall within an IQ range of 20 to 50, and only about 5 percent ever learn to read. Interestingly, these youngsters seem to find ways early on to compensate for their severe verbal deficits. When compared to normal children of the same level of mental development, Down syndrome preschoolers display strengths in certain aspects of nonverbal communication, such as gesturing to get an adult's attention and turn-taking in simple social games (Mundy et al., 1988).

Typically, children with Down syndrome have been described as friendly, easy-going, and placid in disposition. However, recent research suggests that as a group, they are more variable in personality than this stereotype suggests. Parent ratings indicate that they show the same range of basic temperaments as normal youngsters (Bridges & Cicchetti, 1982; Gunn & Berry, 1985; Huntington & Simeonsson, 1987). Some are passive and easy to please, while others are overactive, prone to angry outbursts, and difficult to manage. Other evidence suggests that Down syndrome babies are less emotionally expressive than their normal counterparts. They smile less readily, show poor eye-to-eye contact, and explore objects less persistently. Consequently, parents may have to play a more assertive role in getting these infants to become actively engaged in their surroundings (Cardoso-Martins & Mervis, 1985; Loveland, 1987; MacTurk et al., 1985). However, when parents make this effort, their children show better developmental progress. In one study, mothers who actively stimulated, played with, and were sensitively responsive to their Down syndrome 2-year-olds had children who scored higher in social responsiveness and play maturity (Crawley & Spiker, 1983). Down syndrome infants enrolled in early and long-term intervention programs also show more optimal development, although social, emotional, and motor skills improve more readily than intellectual performance (Gibson & Harris, 1988). These findings indicate that even though Down syndrome is genetic in origin, environmental factors play an important role in these children's progress.

Down syndrome rises dramatically with maternal age, from one in every 1,900 births for mothers 20 to 24 years of age to one in every 30 births for mothers over age 45 (Baird & Sadovnick, 1988). The unfertilized ovum released by the older mother has remained in the early stages of meiosis for over three or four decades, ever since her own prenatal period of development. Geneticists believe that the condition is caused by a weakening or deterioration of cell structures necessary for the proper separation of chromosomes in meiosis. Paternal age has also been implicated as a cause of Down syndrome, with fathers over 40 showing a strongly increased risk of having offspring with the disorder (Hook, 1980; Stene, Stene, & Stengel-Rutkowski, 1981).

Abnormalities of the Sex Chromosomes

Although there are other disorders of the autosomal chromosomes besides Down syndrome, they generally disrupt development so severely that they account for about 50 percent of spontaneous abortions. Affected individuals rarely survive beyond early childhood. In contrast, deviations of the sex chromosomes generally result in fewer problems. According to geneticists, the shortness of the Y chromosome leads little genetic material to be involved, and additional X chromosomes may be inactivated early in development (Cohen, 1984). In fact, disorders related to sex chromosomes often go unrecognized until the adolescent years when, in some of the deviations, pubertal development is delayed. The most common problems involve the presence of an extra chromosome (either X or Y) or the absence of one X chromosome in females.

Turner Syndrome. That both X chromosomes are needed for normal physical development in females is shown by *Turner syndrome,* in which all or part of the second X chromosome is missing (the disorder is symbolized as XO). The estimated incidence of Turner syndrome is one in every 2,500 to 8,000 live births. Phenotypically, these individuals are females, but the ovaries usually do not develop during the prenatal period. Therefore, sex hormone levels are low, secondary sexual characteristics and menstruation generally do not appear at puberty, and afflicted girls remain childlike in physical appearance. Other features include short stature (usually below 57 inches) and a webbed neck. Heart abnormalities are present in 25 percent of the cases. If Turner syndrome is diagnosed early enough, hormones can be administered in childhood to stimulate physical growth and at puberty to induce breast development and vaginal maturation (Cohen, 1984).

Unlike other chromosomal abnormalities, general intelligence is not impaired by this disorder. In fact, the majority of Turner syndrome girls seem to show above-average educational attainment. In one study, 80 percent of those surveyed were reported to have finished college (Hall et al., 1982); in another, they performed better than their chromosomally normal sisters in school (Nielsen, Nyborg, & Dahl, 1977). However, despite their overall normal intelligence, girls with Turner syndrome have specific cognitive deficits in spatial perception and orientation. Such children have trouble with handwriting, distinguishing right from left, copying geometric designs, and constructing "mental maps" that help them find their way from one place to another in the real world. By the time they reach high school, it is not surprising that they begin to avoid courses like geometry and those that demand drawing skills (Pennington et al., 1982).

Youngsters with Turner syndrome have been described as socially immature and unassertive in personality (McCauley, Ito, & Kay, 1986). Although these difficulties could stem from reactions of others to their physical appearance, a recent study showed that in comparison to short-stature controls, Turner syndrome girls had difficulty interpreting emotional cues from facial expressions (McCauley et al., 1987). The ability to process facial affect is another area of cognitive weakness that may underlie these children's social problems.

Girls with Turner syndrome usually have a typical feminine gender identity. In childhood, they show the same feminine interests and play preferences as genetically normal girls. In one medical clinic specializing in treatment of Turner syndrome, more than half of the adult patients were married (Hall et al., 1982). However, the vast majority are sterile and cannot bear children.

Triple X and Klinefelter's Syndromes. In contrast to Turner syndrome, in which the afflicted child is missing an X, in *triple X syndrome (XXX)* and *Klinefelter's syndrome (XXY),* the opposite is the case: an extra X is present. These chromosomal abnormalities occur far more frequently than Turner syndrome, about once in every 500 to 1,250 births (Cohen, 1984).

Intellectual deficits related to Turner syndrome involve spatial and not verbal abilities, but the reverse is the case in triple X and Klinefelter's syndromes. When compared to normal siblings and agemates, these youngsters score consistently low in verbal intelligence, and they show delays in speech and language development. School performance in spelling and arithmetic, which depend heavily on verbal memory skills, is particularly affected (Pennington et al., 1982; Netley, 1986). Taken together, the mental test scores of children with Turner, triple X, and Klinefelter's syndromes indicate that adding to or subtracting from the usual number of X chromosomes leads to very specific intellectual problems. However, at present, geneticists do not know exactly why this is the case.

Other than diminished verbal abilities, triple X syndrome does not produce a consistent pattern of physical or behavioral anomalies. Afflicted girls are no different in appearance from normal children, except for a greater tendency toward tallness. In adolescence, they show typical development of sexual organs and characteristics, and they can bear children. As a result, this disorder frequently remains unnoticed by parents and pediatricians (Cohen, 1984).

Boys with Klinefelter's syndrome are also unusually tall, but unlike their triple X counterparts, they have a variety of physical problems. The disorder is usually diagnosed at puberty, when incomplete development of the secondary sex characteristics is evident. However, hormone therapy can remedy this problem. In addition, XXY boys are likely to be overweight, to have a body fat distribution resembling that of females, and to show poor muscle development. In personality, they often display a tendency toward shyness, timidity, and low self-esteem — difficulties that probably result from the reactions of others to their physical characteristics (Bancroft, Axworthy, & Ratcliffe, 1982). Despite these problems, XXY boys show typical masculine interests and activities in childhood and develop a normal male gender identity. As adults, most of them marry, although the additional X chromosome usually renders them sterile (Cohen, 1984).

XYY Syndrome. In the 1960s, it was widely believed that *XYY syndrome* was linked to aggression and antisocial behavior, but by the end of the decade, scientists recognized that these individuals were being unfairly stigmatized. Early studies concluding that XYY males were dangerous were based on small and highly select groups of individuals housed in prisons and mental institutions. Carefully conducted follow-up research showed that although the incidence of XYY males in penal institutions was greater than their frequency in the general population, they were not among the most violent and physically aggressive inmates. In fact, their crimes were generally less serious than those of XY prisoners (Hook, 1973). Moreover, in studies of noninstitutionalized XYYs, deviant and aggressive behavior is not a common finding (Jarvik, Klodin, & Matsuyama, 1973; Schaivi et al., 1984).

Contrary to popular opinion, the typical characteristics of XYY males are not violence and criminality, but above-average height, large teeth, and in some cases severe acne. Development of sexual characteristics and fertility are normal. The combined results of nine longitudinal studies in which 59 XYY boys were followed through childhood indicated that their intelligence test performance was not depressed and that the incidence of behavior problems among them was no different from that of XY controls (Stewart, 1982; see also Netley, 1986).

Fragile X Syndrome. Fragile sites on chromosomes are special spots where abnormal gaps and breaks occur. Recently, the identification of a fragile site in a special place on the X chromosome has been linked to a unique constellation of physical, intellectual, and behavioral deficits known as *fragile X syndrome*. About one in every 1,500 male births and one in every 2,000 female births are affected (Borghgraef et al., 1987). Currently, the disorder ranks second only to Down syndrome as a major chromosomal cause of mental retardation. Besides moderate to severe intellectual deficits, afflicted children generally have a distinct set of mild facial deformities, including large ears, an elongated jaw, and a prominent forehead. Many also exhibit a rapid, staccato speech rhythm along with hyperactive behavior. Moreover, about 12 percent are afflicted with a serious emotional disorder of early childhood called infantile autism, involving bizarre, self-stimulating behavior and delayed or absent language and communication (Ho, Glahn, & Ho, 1988).

At first, fragile X syndrome was thought to operate according to X-linked principles of inheritance, since the disorder appears more often in males than females. However, recent studies show that it does not conform perfectly to the classic X-linked pattern. Twenty percent of males who inherit the fragile site display no symptoms at all, while 30 percent of females with only one damaged X are affected (Ho, Glahn, & Ho, 1988). As fragile X syndrome reveals, scientists still have much to learn about even the most basic principles of genetic transmission.

GENETIC COUNSELING AND
PRENATAL DIAGNOSIS

81

CHAPTER 3
BIOLOGICAL
FOUNDATIONS, PRENATAL
DEVELOPMENT, AND BIRTH

In the past, many couples with genetic disorders in their families chose not to bear a child at all rather than take the risk of giving birth to an abnormal baby. Today, the availability of genetic counseling and prenatal diagnosis helps people make informed decisions about the risks involved in conceiving or carrying a particular pregnancy to term.

Individuals most likely to seek **genetic counseling** are those who have a history of genetic disorders in their family, have already given birth to an abnormal child, or have experienced reproductive problems such as repeated miscarriages and still-births. The genetic counselor interviews the couple and prepares a *pedigree*, a pictorial representation of the family history in which affected relatives are identified and their relationships to others are made clear. The pedigree is examined for *consanguinity*, the extent to which the couple is genetically related through descent from a common ancestor within the last few generations. Consanguinity increases the chances of homozygous pairing of recessive alleles and, therefore, of having offspring with genetic disorders. The pedigree is also used to determine modes of inheritance and to calculate the odds that parents may bear an abnormal child, using the same basic principles of genetic transmission we discussed earlier.

When all the relevant information is assembled, the genetic counselor helps people consider appropriate options — "taking a chance" and conceiving a child, adoption, artificial insemination, or new reproductive options such as test tube fertilization or surrogate motherhood. Box 3.1 describes these new medical technologies, as well as the host of serious legal and ethical dilemmas that have recently arisen in their application.

If individuals at risk decide to conceive a child, a variety of **prenatal diagnostic methods** are available that permit early detection of fetal problems. Currently, such recessive disorders as cystic fibrosis, muscular dystrophy, Tay-Sachs disease, and Huntington's chorea, along with all the chromosomal abnormalities discussed above, can be identified through biochemical analysis of fetal cellular material (Martin, 1987; Seligman, 1989). In addition to a family history of genetic problems, another reason for prenatal testing is maternal age, since the overall rate of chromosomal abnormalities rises dramatically after age 35, from one in every 100 to as many as one in every three pregnancies at age 48 (Hook, 1988).

The most widely applied prenatal diagnostic technique is *amniocentesis*. A hollow needle is inserted through the abdominal wall to obtain a sample of amniotic fluid. Then fetal cells are extracted and cultured for chromosomal analysis. In the past, a major limitation of amniocentesis was that the test could not be performed until considerable amniotic fluid was available, at 15 to 16 weeks gestation. Since 3 more weeks were required to culture the cells, the decision to terminate a pregnancy had to be delayed until 18 weeks or later, at which time abortion is medically, legally, and emotionally more difficult. Recent advances now make earlier amniocentesis possible, at 11 to 14 weeks, although the waiting period for test results is still the same (Benacerraf et al., 1988). Consequently, a new prenatal diagnostic approach called *chorionic villi biopsy* may soon replace amniocentesis, since it can be performed by 6 to 8 weeks gestation, and results are available immediately. However, chorionic villi biopsy does entail a slightly greater risk of procedure failure and spontaneous abortion than does amniocentesis (Rhoads et al., 1989).

In both amniocentesis and chorionic villi biopsy, *ultrasound* is used to guide the extraction of fetal material. High-frequency sound waves are beamed at the uterus, and their reflection is translated into a picture that reveals the size, shape, and placement of the fetus. Ultrasound is also used to support another technique called *fetoscopy*. Between 18 and 22 weeks gestation, a small tube with a light source at one end can be inserted into the uterus to inspect the fetus for malformations of the limbs and face. In addition, fetoscopy allows a sample of fetal blood from the placenta or umbilical cord to be obtained, permitting diagnosis of such disorders as hemophilia and sickle cell anemia. Besides its combination with other prenatal diagnostic techniques, ultrasound is frequently used by itself to estimate gestational age, monitor fetal growth, and detect gross structural abnormalities.

Technological advances in prenatal diagnosis have led to remarkable developments in fetal medicine. Today, some medical problems can be treated before birth. For example, drug therapy has been introduced to treat some genetically transmitted metabolic defects, and surgery in utero has been performed to correct such problems as urinary tract obstructions and neural defects (Kolata, 1989). Medical interventions like these promise new hope for fetuses that otherwise would have little or no chance of survival.

If prenatal diagnosis reveals the fetus to have an abnormal condition that cannot be corrected, parents are faced with the difficult choice of whether to have an abortion. The decision to terminate a desired pregnancy is anguishing for all who have to make it. Parents must deal with the emotional shock of the news and make a decision within a very short period of time. If they choose to have an abortion, they face the grief that comes with having lost a wanted child, worries about future pregnancies, and ambivalence and guilt about the abortion itself. Fortunately, 95 percent of fetuses examined through prenatal diagnosis are perfectly normal (Benacerraf et al., 1988). Because modern medicine makes such tests possible, many individuals whose age or family history would have caused them to avoid pregnancy entirely can now have healthy children.

◆ CONTEMPORARY ISSUES: SOCIAL POLICY ◆

The Pros and Cons of New Reproductive Technologies   Box 3.1

Currently, one sixth of all married couples are involuntarily sterile, and others are hesitant to risk pregnancy because of a family history of genetic disease. The high incidence of reproductive problems among individuals seeking to have children has resulted in a variety of alternative methods of conception and gestation. For several decades, *donor insemination* (artificial insemination of a woman with sperm from an anonymous man) has been used routinely to overcome male reproductive difficulties. In the United States alone, approximately 20,000 children are conceived this way each year (Sokoloff, 1987). Although donor insemination has achieved widespread acceptance by the medical community and the public, two new and far more controversial practices — in vitro fertilization and surrogate motherhood — have become increasingly common during the last 10 years.

Since the first "test tube" baby was born in England in 1978, more than 5,000 infants have been created through *in vitro fertilization* (Ryan, 1989). In this method, hormones are administered to a woman, which stimulate the ripening of several ova. These are extracted through a delicate surgical process and placed in a dish of nutrients, to which sperm are added. Once an ovum is fertilized and begins to divide into several cells, it is injected into the mother's uterus, where, hopefully,

it will implant and develop. Used most often to treat infertility in women whose fallopian tubes are permanently damaged, in vitro fertilization is successful for 20 percent of those who try it. These results are sufficiently encouraging that the technique has been expanded. By mixing and matching gametes of donors and recipients, pregnancies can be brought about when either or both partners have a reproductive problem. Also, fertilized ova can be frozen and stored in embryo banks early in marriage for use at some future time, thereby guaranteeing healthy infants for older mothers who have an increased risk of bearing children with genetic defects.

Both donor insemination and in vitro fertilization appear to be physically as safe for the child as unassisted procreation. Nevertheless, serious questions have arisen about their implementation. Many states have no legal guidelines for these procedures. As a result, donor screening is extremely lax, and biochemical analyses for genetic or sexually transmitted diseases are not always conducted. In addition, some doctors report using the same donor for many pregnancies. In these instances, a substantial number of genetically related children may grow up in the same community, creating opportunities for genetic inbreeding and repetition of a genetic defect (Andrews, 1987; Sokoloff, 1987). Moreover, because

In the first portion of this chapter, we took an intensive look at the basic biological subtrate of human development. First, we located genes, segments of DNA that determine our species and unique characteristics, within the 23 pairs of chromosomes residing in each human cell. Then we traced the hereditary transmission of traits attributable to single genes, including dominant-recessive, co-dominant, and X-linked inheritance. Through such examples as PKU, sickle cell anemia, and hemophilia, we illustrated the serious developmental problems that can occur when just one unfavorable allele is passed from parent to child. Next, we discussed a variety of chromosomal abnormalities that can result when the process of gamete formation (meiosis) goes awry. An understanding of these basic principles of genetic transmission helps us appreciate the complexities involved in the determination of polygenic characteristics, such as height, weight, intelligence, and personality. However, even for traits governed by the simplest modes of inheritance, developmental outcomes are not perfectly predictable, since moderator genes, medical interventions, and rearing environments play important roles.

PRENATAL DEVELOPMENT

The sperm and ovum that will unite to form the new individual are uniquely suited for the task of reproduction. The ovum is a tiny sphere measuring $1/175$ of an inch in diameter that is barely visible to the naked eye as a dot the size of the period at the end of this sentence. Nevertheless, in its microscopic world, it is a giant. The sperm are

donors usually want to remain completely anonymous, records of their characteristics are kept by only a minority of physicians. Yet the resulting children may someday want information about their biological roots or actually need it for medical reasons.

The most controversial form of medically assisted conception is *surrogate motherhood*. In this procedure, sperm from a man whose wife is infertile are used to artificially inseminate a woman, who is paid a substantial fee for her childbearing services. In return, the surrogate signs an agreement to relinquish her parental rights and turn the baby over to the man (who is the natural father). The child is subsequently adopted by his wife. Although most of these arrangements proceed uneventfully, those that end up in court highlight serious risks for all concerned. In one instance, both parties rejected the handicapped infant that resulted from the pregnancy. In several others, the surrogate mother changed her mind and wanted to keep the baby. Thus, the child came into the world in midst of family conflict that threatened to last for years to come. To date, most court decisions have found that surrogacy contracts conflict with adoption statutes, which prohibit payment of money to obtain a baby. Since the arrangement favors the wealthy as contractors for infants and the less

economically advantaged as surrogates, it may also violate basic constitutional guarantees that guard against exploitation of one sector of society by another. In addition, most surrogates already have children of their own, who may be deeply affected by the experience. Knowledge that their mother would sell a half-sibling for profit is likely to cause these youngsters to question the security of their own family circumstances (McGinty & Zafran, 1988; Ryan, 1989).

Although new reproductive technologies permit many barren couples to rear healthy newborn babies, legislation is desperately needed to regulate these methods. In the case of surrogate motherhood, the legal and ethical problems are so complex that many European governments have banned the practice entirely (McGinty & Zafran, 1988), and a few U.S. states have taken steps to do so as well. Furthermore, at present, practically nothing is known about the psychological consequences of being a product of these procedures. Research on how such children grow up, including what they know and how they feel about their origins, is crucial for weighing the pros and cons of these techniques.

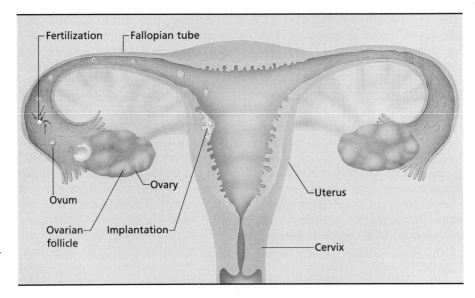

Figure 3.5. Journey of the ovum toward the uterus after its release from the ovarian follicle.

much tinier, measuring but ⅟₅₀₀ of an inch. In the middle of a woman's menstrual cycle, the ovum matures. Surrounded by thousands of nurse cells that will nourish it along its path, the ovum ruptures from the ovary and is drawn into one of the two *fallopian tubes* — long, thin structures that convey the ovum from the ovaries to the uterus (see Figure 3.5). The ruptured ovarian follicle or cavity, now known as the *corpus luteum*, begins to secrete hormones that prepare the lining of the uterus for implantation of a fertilized ovum. If pregnancy does not occur, the corpus luteum shrinks, and the lining of the uterus is discarded in two weeks with menstruation (Rugh & Shettles, 1971).

The sperm are produced in profuse numbers, at a rate of 300 million a day. In the final process of maturation, they develop a tail that permits them to swim long distances, upstream through the female reproductive tract and into the fallopian tube, where fertilization takes place. The journey is arduous. Of the 360 million sperm released in a single ejaculation, only 100 or so reach the vicinity of the ovum, if one happens to be there. The sperm have an average life of 48 hours and can lie in wait for the ovum for up to two days until one appears, while the ovum survives for up to 24 hours. Therefore, the maximum fertile period during each monthly cycle is about 72 hours long (Nilsson, 1986).

With fertilization and the formation of the zygote, the story of prenatal development begins to unfold. Although prenatal growth is a continuous, 9-month process, the dramatic changes that transform the one-celled zygote into a complex, differen-

Fertilization occurs when sperm and ovum unite in the fallopian tube.

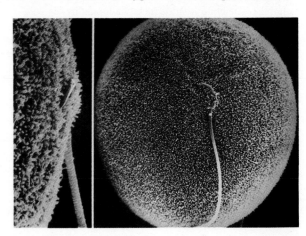

tiated organism comprised of trillions of cells are best understood in terms of three periods of development: the period of the zygote (sometimes called the germinal period), the period of the embryo, and the period of the fetus. These three periods of prenatal development are useful in two ways: (1) for organizing individual growth and (2) for understanding the impact of environmental agents on the developing person.

The Period of the Zygote

The period of the zygote lasts approximately two weeks, from fertilization until the first tiny mass of cells attaches itself to the wall of the uterus and becomes deeply embedded in the uterine lining. Thirty-six hours after fertilization, the zygote has undergone its first cell duplication by the process of mitosis. Occasionally, the first two cells produced separate completely and give rise to two individuals, called **identical** or **monozygotic twins** because they develop from a single zygote and have identical genetic blueprints. **Fraternal** or **dizygotic twins** are the result of the ripening and release of two ova from the mother's ovaries. If both are fertilized, two offspring develop who are genetically no more alike than ordinary siblings.

While the first cell division of the zygote takes many hours, each successive one occurs with increasing rapidity. By the end of the fourth day, 60 to 70 cells exist, and as shown in Figure 3.6, they have begun to differentiate into separate structures. The mass of cells, now known as a *blastocyst*, forms a hollow sphere around a fluid-filled cavity. An inner cell mass projecting into the cavity becomes the *embryonic disk*, which will develop into the new individual. The rest of the cells will provide protective covering. Seven to nine days after conception, the blastocyst bores into the uterine lining. Engulfed by the mother's nourishing blood, the cell mass begins to grow at a much more astounding rate. At first, the protective outer layers multiply more rapidly than the embryonic disk. An inner membrane, the *amnion*, is formed that encases the baby in amniotic fluid, helping to keep the temperature of the prenatal environment constant and cushioning the organism against any jolt the

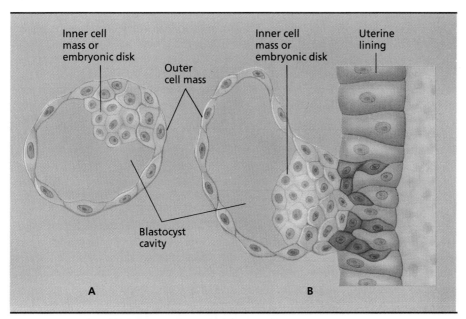

Figure 3.6. The human blastocyst. (A) The blastocyst at about 4½ days. The blue cells represent the inner cell mass or embryonic disk, the brown cells the outer cell mass that will soon become the amnion and chorion. (B) At the end of the first week, the blastocyst begins to bore into the uterine lining. (*From T.W. Sadler, 1990.* Langman's Medical Embryology *(6th ed.)*, *Baltimore: Williams & Wilkins. P. 32. Adapted by permission.*)

mother might suffer. Additional protection is provided by an outer membrane, called the *chorion*, which, along with its fingerlike villi, has appeared by the end of the second week (Moore, 1989; Sadler, 1990). A *yolk sac* emerges and begins to produce blood cells for the embryo until its liver, spleen, and bone marrow are mature enough to take over this process independently. By the second month, the yolk sac is no longer needed and disappears.

As soon as implantation takes place, the **placenta** starts to form as chorionic villi burrow into the uterine wall. The villi rupture uterine capillaries, and maternal blood is freed to circulate in spaces around the villi. Each villus contains blood vessels that send nutrients and oxygen to the embryo and take away waste products to be excreted by the mother. A semipermeable placental membrane forms through which these substances are exchanged but which, at the same time, keeps the maternal and fetal blood from mixing directly with one another. The placenta is connected to the developing organism by the **umbilical cord** (in the period of the zygote, it first appears as a primitive body stalk). The umbilical cord contains one vein that delivers blood loaded with nutrients and two arteries that remove waste products. During the course of pregnancy, the umbilical cord grows to a length of 1 to 3 feet. The force and volume of blood flowing through the cord keep it taut, much like a garden hose, so it seldom tangles or forms knots while the baby, like a space-walking astronaut, floats freely in its fluid-filled chamber (Rugh & Shettles, 1971).

By the end of the period of the zygote, the primitive organism has already found food and shelter by submerging itself in the uterine lining. Though it does not yet resemble a human being, it has begun to grow and differentiate in earnest. These momentous beginnings take place before all but the most sensitive mother even knows that she is pregnant.

The Period of the Embryo

From implantation to 8 weeks gestation, the developing organism is called an **embryo.** During this brief 6 weeks, the most rapid and dramatic changes in prenatal development take place as the groundwork for all body structures and internal systems is laid down.

By the middle of the first month, the embryonic disk folds over to form three layers of cells — the *ectoderm*, from which will emerge the nervous system, outer skin, hair, and sweat glands; the *mesoderm*, which will form the deeper layers of skin, the muscles, the skeleton, the circulatory system, and a variety of internal organs; and the *endoderm*, which will differentiate into the digestive system, lungs, urinary tract, and internal glands. Thus, the three layers give rise to all the tissues and organs of the body. At first, the emphasis is on development of the nervous system, although other organs begin to form as well. The ectoderm folds over to form a neural tube or primitive spinal cord, the top of which swells to form a brain, and nerve fibers begin to emerge along with the rudiments of the embryo's eyes. While the nervous system is developing, a primitive heart begins to pump blood around the embryo's circulatory system, and muscles, vertebrae, ribs, and digestive organs start to appear. At the end of the first month, the curled embryo consists of millions of intricately organized groups of cells with specific functions, although it is only a fourth of an inch long. Most of this length is taken up by the head and upper region of the body, since the brain and heart develop sooner than the other organs. A rudimentary tail (an extension of the spinal column) and primitive gill arches (like those found in fish and tadpoles) are present as vestiges of our primordial past, but they soon disappear.

In the second month, growth and differentiation continue rapidly. The eyes, ears, nasal organs, and jaw form, so the face is clearly human and no longer resembles the embryos of a variety of other developing species. Protruding buds gradually become arms, legs, fingers, and toes. Internal organs are more distinct: the intestines grow, the heart develops separate chambers, the kidneys and genital and eliminative passages appear, and the liver takes over the manufacture of blood cells so that the yolk sac is

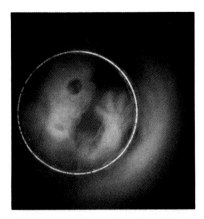

This embryo, which is approximately six weeks old, has developed the protruding buds that will become arms, legs, fingers, and toes.

no longer needed. The head continues to enlarge, and a distinct neck is formed. Skeletal growth and changing body proportions lead the embryo's posture to be more upright. By the end of the second month, the major muscle groups have developed, and some movement is possible, but it is still too light to be felt by the mother. Although only an inch long and one seventh of an ounce in weight, the developing organism is now human in form. Growth in size must occur and details must be perfected, but everything is present that will be found in the newborn infant, and the threshold has been crossed between embryo and fetus (Nilsson, 1986).

The Period of the Fetus

Lasting until the end of pregnancy, this longest prenatal phase is the "growth and finishing period." Now called a **fetus,** the new organism begins to enlarge in size. As shown in Figure 3.7, the rate of body growth during the fetal period is extraordinary, especially from the ninth to the twentieth week (Moore, 1989).

In the third month, the newly differentiated organs, muscles, and nervous system start to become organized and interconnected. The brain signals, and in response, the

Figure 3.7. Rate of body growth during the fetal period. The drawings are about one fifth of actual size. The average duration of pregnancy is 38 weeks from fertilization. Premature infants of 24 weeks or more have some chance of survival. *(From K. L. Moore, 1989. Before We Are Born (3rd ed.), Philadelphia Saunders. P. 68. Reprinted by permission.)*

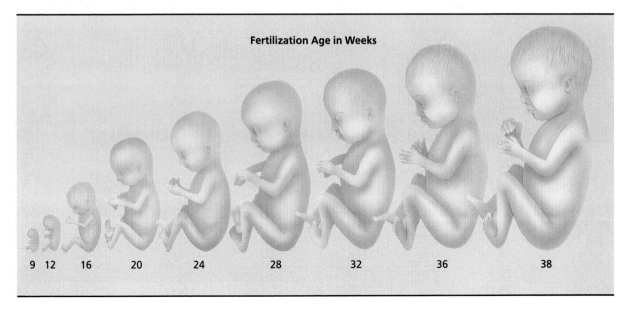

Fertilization Age in Weeks

9 12   16   20   24   28   32   36   38

fetus kicks, bends its arms, forms a fist, curls its toes, and grimaces by squinting, frowning, and opening its mouth. The primitive lungs begin to expand and contract in an early rehearsal of breathing movements. The external genitalia become increasingly refined, and the baby's sex is evident by the twelfth week. Finishing touches appear — fingernails, toenails, hair follicles, tooth buds, and eyelids that open and close. The fetal heartbeat is now stronger and can be heard through a stethoscope.

Prenatal development is often divided into three trimesters. At the end of the third month, the first trimester is complete.

The Second Trimester. By the middle of the second trimester, between 17 and 20 weeks of age, the fetus has lengthened sufficiently that its movement — at first a tiny flutter and later a firm kick or turn of the entire body — can be felt by the mother. The body of the fetus is now covered with a white cheeselike substance called *vernix,* which protects the skin from chapping and hardening due to the long months spent bathing in the amniotic fluid. A white, downy hair covering called *lanugo* appears over the entire body and helps the vernix stick to the skin. At the end of the second trimester, almost all the fetal organs are so well developed that one might wonder why the 1½ pound infant, if born prematurely, cannot yet survive. The reason is that the lungs, although structurally formed, are still quite immature, and the central nervous system has not yet developed to the point at which it can control breathing movements and body temperature (Moore, 1989).

The Third Trimester. The final trimester of development differs from the previous six months in that the fetus now has a chance for survival if born prematurely — a probability that improves with each successive day the baby remains in the uterus. If born between the seventh and eighth months, breathing would still be a problem, and oxygen assistance would be necessary. This is not because the respiratory center of the brain is poorly developed, but because the alveoli (tiny air sacs) in the lungs are not yet ready to inflate and exchange oxygen for carbon dioxide.

The brain makes tremendous strides during this final phase of fetal development. The cortex, the seat of human intelligence, enlarges, and its convolutions, wrinkles, and crevices form. At the same time, the fetus begins to react to external stimuli — the sudden whir of the electric mixer, the vibrating washing machine, the sound of the mother's voice. In one clever study of fetal responsiveness, researchers had mothers-to-be read Dr. Seuss's lively poem *The Cat in the Hat* to their unborn children twice a day for the last 6 weeks of pregnancy. After the babies were born, they showed a clear preference for listening to the familiar poem over a different rhyming story. Clearly, third trimester fetuses experience their mothers' speech sounds and even learn to prefer them while still in the womb (DeCasper & Spence, 1986).

During the last trimester, the fetus gains 5 pounds and grows 7 inches. As the end of the prenatal phase approaches, the rapidly enlarging baby finds its difficult to move

At about 20 weeks, this fetus looks distinctly human and can move about within the uterus.

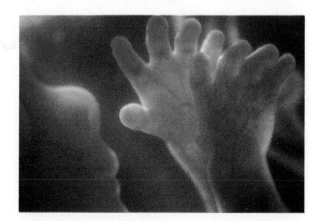

about in the confines of the uterus and becomes less active. In the eighth month, a layer of fat begins to be deposited under the skin to assist with temperature regulation after birth. In the ninth month, the baby acquires antibodies from the mother's blood, granting it temporary protection from illnesses that could be dangerous to the new-born (its own immune system does not function effectively until several months after birth). In the final weeks, most infants assume an upside-down position, partly due to the shape of the uterus and because the baby's head is heavier than its feet. Growth slows as the placenta starts to degenerate, and birth is imminent (Moore, 1989).

PRENATAL ENVIRONMENTAL INFLUENCES

Teratogens

In the first half of this century, it was commonly believed that the unborn child, safely cradled in the mother's uterus and surrounded by her protective body, was com-pletely shielded from the adversities of the environment. All deviations from normal development were attributed to the genes. However, the increasing medical use of X-rays in the 1920s and 1930s led to a growing realization that the structures and functions of the fetus could be profoundly damaged by environmental agents. In the 1940s, it was established that maternal rubella (German measles) during the first 3 months of pregnancy was associated with a variety of physical defects in the newborn infant. The 1960s brought the shocking demonstration that a tranquilizer called thalidomide, made available with the best intentions for benefit of the mother, could have disastrous consequences for the unborn child.

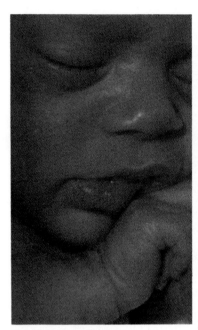

This fetus looks like a sleep-ing newborn. During the final weeks of gestation, a layer of fat is laid down in preparation for life outside the warm, protective womb.

The term **teratogen** refers to environmental agents that cause damage during the prenatal period. The modern science of teratology has revealed that the consequences of toxic environmental agents for the unborn child are complex and varied. Effects depend on amount and length of exposure, combination with other teratogenic and environmental agents, and the genetic constitution of the mother and fetus, which affects their ability to withstand the harmful influence. Furthermore, whereas physi-cal deformities are easy to notice, important psychological consequences may be harder to identify. Some may not be evident until later in development; others may occur as the indirect consequence of physical damage. For example, an anatomical defect resulting from the mother's ingestion of drugs during the prenatal period can affect such experiences as parent-child interaction, peer relations, and exploration of the environment during childhood. These, in turn, may have implications for cogni-tive, social, and emotional functioning (Vorhees & Mollnow, 1987; Kopp & Kaler, 1989).

In addition, the effects of teratogens depend on the age of the embryo or fetus at the time of exposure. We can best understand this if we conceive of the prenatal phase as a sequence of carefully timed **critical periods,** or moments when body structures are developing most rapidly and are therefore acutely sensitive to both facilitating and disruptive environmental influences. Figure 3.8 provides a schematic summary of prenatal critical periods. It shows that they vary from one organ or tissue to another, depending on the timing and duration of development. Some structures, such as the brain and the eye, have long critical periods that extend throughout the embryonic and fetal stages of growth, while others, such as the limbs and palate, are of more restricted duration. Figure 3.8 also indicates that some general statements can be made about the effect of teratogens during prenatal growth. During the period of the zygote, before implantation, the organism is rarely influenced by teratogens. When it is, the primitive mass of cells is so completely affected that the result is usually death and spontaneous abortion. The embryonic period is the time of maximum susceptibi-lity to environmental influences. During this phase, the foundations for all essential body systems are rapidly emerging, and teratogens generally produce gross structural abnormalities. The fetal period involves growth toward size and body proportions of

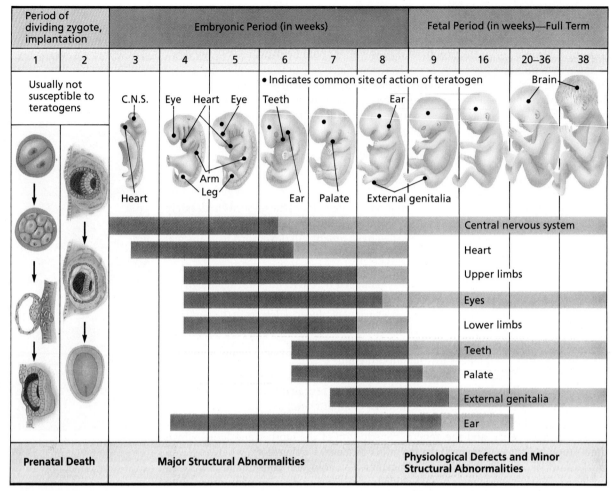

Figure 3.8. Critical periods in prenatal development. Each organ or structure has a critical period during which its development may be disturbed. Black indicates highly sensitive periods; pink indicates periods that are less sensitive to teratogens *(From K. L. Moore, 1989,* Before We Are Born *(3rd ed.), Philadelphia: Saunders. P. 111. Reprinted by permission.)*

the newborn infant, along with some completion of body systems. When teratogenic agents interfere, the result is often minor structural alterations. However, some organs, such as the central nervous system and genitals, can still be strongly affected. Now let's consider what is known about a variety of teratogenic agents.

Prescription and Nonprescription Medications. Almost any agent dissolved in the mother's bloodstream can pass to the developing organism, although the placenta offers some protection by slowing the transfer of substances so that the maternal system has a chance to break them down and reduce their concentration. A tragic lesson was learned from the drug thalidomide, a sedative widely available in Canada and Europe during the early 1960s. Thalidomide showed that the human embryo can be extraordinarily sensitive to a substance that has little or no harmful impact on human adults or most test animals employed in teratogenic research. When ingested by mothers between the 21st and 36th days after conception, thalidomide produced gross deformities of the embryo's arms, legs, and ears. In addition, an unexpectedly high proportion of these youngsters had subnormal IQs (Vorhees & Mollnow, 1987).

Despite the bitter lesson of thalidomide, pregnant women continue to take a wide variety of drugs. In one study, 65 percent reported taking self-prescribed medications;

when physician-prescribed drugs were also considered, the total number taken during pregnancy ranged from 3 to 29, with an average of 10.3 (Hill, 1973). Among commonly used medications, regular prenatal exposure to aspirin has been linked to low birth weight, increased infant mortality, and depressed childhood intelligence (Streissguth et al., 1984b; Vorhees & Mollnow, 1987). Heavy consumption of caffeine has been associated with prematurity, spontaneous abortion, early induction of labor, and newborn withdrawal symptoms, including irritability and vomiting (Aaronson & MacNee, 1989; McGowan, Altman, & Kanto, 1988). However, all of these findings require additional research to be confirmed. Because mothers often take multiple drugs, it is difficult to evaluate their independent effects, and dosage levels that endanger the fetus are as yet unknown. In the absence of conclusive evidence on the prenatal consequences of over-the-counter medications, the safest course of action for pregnant women is to avoid them.

Illicit Drugs. A wide variety of illegal mood-altering drugs severely damage the offspring of pregnant laboratory animals, but until recently, human research on most of them has been scant and inconsistent. The clearest evidence exists for heroin and methadone (a less addictive substance used to wean individuals away from heroin). Infants of heroin-addicted mothers are at risk for a wide variety of problems, including prematurity, low birth weight, physical malformations, respiratory distress, and increased mortality at birth. Substitute use of methadone reduces the incidence of many of these complications (Cushner, 1981). However, infants exposed prenatally to either heroin or methadone become, like their mothers, physiologically addicted. They exhibit withdrawal symptoms at birth, including tremors, vomiting, fever, irritability, and disturbed sleep, along with an abnormal, high-pitched cry (East & Steele, 1987; Vorhees & Mollnow, 1987). Behavioral disturbances persist through the first year of life, with heroin- and methadone-exposed babies exhibiting less attentiveness to the environment and poorer performance on assessments of infant motor skills. Beyond the period of infancy, findings on prenatal narcotics exposure are mixed. Some investigations report persisting attentional deficits into the childhood years, while others show no lasting consequences (Hutchings & Fifer, 1986; Vorhees & Mollnow, 1987). Why long-term effects exist for some youngsters but not for others is not yet completely understood. Certainly, the jitteriness of these babies makes them very difficult to care for, so perhaps the kind of parenting they receive is a crucial factor in whether they recover.

New studies on infants born to women who smoke marijuana or take cocaine suggest that these infants display all the problems of heroin-exposed babies, including withdrawal symptoms and a shrill cry in the days following birth (Chasnoff et al., 1989; Fried et al., 1987; Lester & Dreher, 1989; Little et al., 1989; Zuckerman et al., 1989). In addition, growing evidence reveals that cocaine is associated with a specific set of structural anomalies, including genital and urinary tract deformities, heart defects, and brain seizures (Chasnoff et al., 1989). Infants born to mothers who smoke crack (a cheap derivative of cocaine that delivers high doses through the vascular bed of the lungs) seem to be worst off in terms of low birth weight and damage to the central nervous system (Kaye et al., 1989).

Hormones. During normal prenatal development, the organism secretes hormones that affect development of the reproductive system. The presence of androgens (male sex hormones) influences the development of the male structures, while its absence leads to the emergence of female reproductive organs. Irregularities and imbalances in the quantities of hormones available prenatally can lead to structural abnormalities of the genital organs as well as other defects. In a few studies, exposure of the embryo to oral contraceptives, which sometimes occurs in the early weeks when the mother is not aware she is pregnant, has been linked to cardiovascular problems and limb deformities (e.g., Kricker et al., 1986). However, additional evidence is needed to verify these associations (Grimes & Mishell, 1988).

Between 1945 and 1970, a synthetic estrogen, diethylstilbestrol (DES), was widely used to prevent miscarriages in women who had a history of spontaneous abortion. As the female offspring of these mothers reached adolescence, the relationship between prenatal DES exposure and a rare form of cancer of the vagina became apparent. It was later discovered that DES causes abnormal development of the vaginal cells and structural abnormalities of the uterus in virtually all female babies exposed to it (Nevin, 1988). Although there are millions of daughters whose mothers were treated with DES, only a limited number — 16 out of every 1,000 — eventually develop cancer (Robboy et al., 1984). However, the long-term impact of the hormone is also manifested in other ways. When DES daughters bear children themselves, their pregnancies are more likely to result in prematurity, low birth weight, and spontaneous abortion (Linn et al., 1988). In addition, DES-exposed sons are not left unaffected. Research shows that they are subject to a variety of genital abnormalities, as well as an increased risk of testicular cancer (Herbst, 1981; Stenchever et al. 1981; Stillman, 1982).

Smoking. An estimated 30 percent of women continue to smoke during pregnancy (Brooke et al., 1989), despite abundant evidence that nicotine intake leads to serious consequences for the fetus and newborn child. Babies of smoking mothers experience higher rates of prematurity, low birth weight, spontaneous abortion, and death during the period surrounding birth. The more cigarettes smoked, the greater the risk of these adverse outcomes. However, a mother who stops smoking during pregnancy, even as late as the third trimester, can reduce her baby's chances of being born underweight (Aaronson & Macnee, 1989; Sexton & Hebel, 1984).

Newborn babies of smoking mothers appear less responsive to the surrounding environment when compared to infants of nonsmokers. For example, they turn to the sound of an auditory stimulus (such as the jingle of a bell) more slowly, and they habituate, or stop responding to it, more rapidly than other infants (Picone et al., 1982a). Infants of smoking mothers also seem more irritable in that they cry more during physical examinations (Woodson et al., 1980). As we mentioned earlier, behavioral deficits like these can negatively influence the adjustment of newborn babies to their physical and social surroundings and may be the beginning of a spiraling incidence of problems extending into the childhood years. Several extended follow-up studies have linked prenatal nicotine exposure to slightly reduced school achievement, shorter attention span, and increased motor activity in early and middle childhood (Butler & Goldstein, 1973; Naeye & Peters, 1984; Streissguth et al., 1984a).

Why do unfavorable outcomes appear in babies of mothers who smoke? Are they simply due to the fact that smokers eat less well, so that inadequate maternal nutrition is at the root of these babies' problems? This is apparently not the case, since infants of smokers continue to weigh less than infants of nonsmokers in research in which maternal weight gain is controlled (Haworth et al., 1980). Instead, at least two other mediating mechanisms seem to be operating. First, smoking is linked to severe structural abnormalities in the placenta. This reduces maternal blood flow and, consequently, transfer of nutrients to the fetus. Second, smoking raises the concentration of carbon monoxide in both maternal and fetal bloodstreams. Carbon monoxide exposure promotes central nervous system damage and low birth weight in the fetuses of laboratory animals, and similar effects may operate in humans as well (Aaronson & MacNee, 1989; Nash & Persaud, 1988).

Finally, one recent study showed that infants of smoking fathers also experience the familiar reduction in birth weight that occurs with nicotine exposure (Schwartz-Bickenbach et al., 1987). Passive smoking, it seems, can also adversely affect the unborn child.

Alcohol. A specific cluster of abnormalities appearing frequently in the offspring of alcohol-abusing mothers was described and named *fetal alcohol syndrome (FAS)* by Jones and his collaborators in 1973. Since then, thousands of research studies have confirmed that heavy prenatal alcohol consumption produces a severe and complex set of handicaps for children. Among the distinguishing features of this disorder are prenatal and postnatal growth retardation and a particular pattern of facial abnormalities, including widely spaced eyes, short eyelid openings, a small upturned nose, a thin upper lip, and minor ear deformities. The fetal brain is highly sensitive to damage from alcohol. Microcephaly (a small, underdeveloped brain) occurs in 80 percent of children with FAS. Most are mentally retarded, with IQ scores averaging about 65 or 70. Behavior problems appear in infancy and persist into childhood; the most common are irritability and hyperactivity. Sometimes affected children show a variety of other physical problems, including defects of the eyes, ears, nose, throat, heart, genitals, urinary tract, and immune system (Aaronson & MacNee, 1989; Hoyseth & Jones, 1989; Streissguth, Sampson, & Barr, 1989).

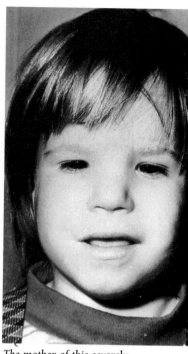

All reported cases of FAS are infants whose mothers drank heavily throughout pregnancy. But sometimes babies do not display all the abnormalities associated with FAS—only some of them. In these instances, the infant is said to suffer from *fetal alcohol effects (FAE)*. Generally, these youngsters have been subjected to smaller or less frequent quantities of alcohol, with the precise consequences depending on the timing and length of exposure (Hoyseth & Jones, 1989).

Alcohol quickly diffuses through the placental barrier. Once in the baby's system, it impedes cell duplication and differentiation, thereby causing central nervous system impairment and physical anomalies. Fetal tissues are further damaged through oxygen deprivation, since to metabolize alcohol, the mother's liver draws large quantities of oxygen away from the placenta. Finally, alcohol promotes contraction of the umbilical arteries and vein, an effect that contributes further to fetal oxygen and nutrient deprivation. In fact, the high incidence of spontaneous abortion among alcoholic women may be due to severe umbilical cord contraction, which results in fetal death (Hoyseth & Jones, 1989).

How much alcohol consumption is safe during pregnancy? Is it all right to have just one drink, either on a daily basis or every once in a while? So far, a dividing line between safe and dangerous drinking levels has not been established (Aaronson & MacNee, 1989; Hoyseth & Jones, 1989). However, a recent study indicated that the more alcohol consumed during pregnancy, the lower a child's IQ score at 4 years of age, even after many other potentially influential variables had been controlled (Streissguth et al., 1989). Findings like these indicate that the safest course of action for pregnant women is to abstain from alcohol entirely.

The mother of this severely retarded boy drank heavily during pregnancy. His widely spaced eyes, thin upper lip, and short eyelid openings are typical of fetal alcohol syndrome. [Streissguth, A. P., Clarren, S. K., & Jones, K. L. (1985, July). Natural History of the Fetal Alcohol Syndrome: A Ten-Year Follow-up of Eleven Patients. Lancet, 2, 85–92.]

Ionizing Radiation. In addition to its mutagenic consequences, discussed earlier in this chapter, high doses of ionizing radiation are associated with severe damage to the developing embryo and fetus, including spontaneous abortion, growth retardation, microcephaly, and structural malformations, particularly of the skeleton, central nervous system, and eyes (Michel, 1989). Even when an exposed child appears normal at birth, the possibility of problems appearing later in development cannot be ruled out. For example, research suggests that even low-level radiation, as a result of industrial leakage or medical X-rays, can increase the risk of childhood cancers (Forman et al., 1987; UNSCEAR, 1986). Since dosage levels that damage the developing baby are still unknown, at present no amount of radiation during pregnancy can be considered safe.

Environmental Pollution. The number of potentially dangerous chemicals in the environments of industrialized nations is astounding. In the United States, roughly 100,000 are in common use, and 1,000 new ones are introduced each year

(Dye-White, 1986). The human teratogenic effects of only a small number are known, although many more have been found to cause serious birth defects in animals.

Among heavy metals, mercury and lead are established teratogens that cause serious central nervous system damage. In the 1950s, an industrial plant discharged mercury-containing waste into a bay providing food and water for the town of Minamata, Japan. Many children born at the time were mentally retarded and showed serious neurological symptoms, including abnormal speech, difficulty in chewing and swallowing, and uncoordinated movements. Autopsies of those who died revealed extensive brain damage (Vorhees & Mollnow, 1987). High maternal lead absorption resulting from traffic emissions, lead-based paint, or industrial employment has been linked to stillbirths, prematurity, low birth weight, neurological damage, and congenital malformations (Dye-White, 1986). Even a low level of prenatal lead exposure seems to result in slightly impaired mental development over the course of infancy (Bellinger et al., 1984; Ernhart et al., 1985).

Polychlorinated-biphenyls (PCBs) are an additional group of environmental pollutants for which there is evidence of teratogenic effects. Used for many years as an insulating substance in electrical equipment, PCBs were banned in 1977 after research showed that, like mercury, they found their way into waterways, moved up the food chain, and were eventually ingested by human beings. In one investigation, newborn babies of women who frequently consumed PCB-contaminated fish were compared with newborns whose mothers ate little or no seafood. PCB-exposed newborns had a wide array of problems, including low birth weight, reduced head circumference, and decreased responsiveness to external stimulation (Jacobson et al., 1984). When assessed again at 7 months of age, these infants showed deficient memory performance, an early cognitive ability that is moderately related to intelligence during the preschool years (Jacobson et al., 1985).

In view of the sensitivity of the human fetus to environmental toxins, pregnant women should do everything possible to avoid them. An expectant mother who refinishes baby furniture in her garage or permits her garden to be sprayed with pesticides comes into contact with chemical levels thousands of times greater than judged occupationally safe by the federal government (Samuels & Samuels, 1986).

Maternal Disease. Most diseases that cause prenatal defects are viruses, probably because the majority of other disease-producing microorganisms are so toxic that they usually lead to spontaneous abortion rather than malformations. Viral infections occur in about 5 percent of all pregnancies. While most exert no effect, a few can cause serious damage to the child before birth.

A worldwide epidemic of rubella (three-day or German measles) led to the birth of over 20,000 American babies with *congenital rubella syndrome* in the mid-1960s. Twenty percent of these babies died shortly after birth (Cochi et al., 1989). Consistent with the critical period principle, the consequences of rubella depend on the timing of prenatal infection. The severest damage occurs when the disease strikes during the fourth to eighth week of embryonic development (see Figure 3.8). Common symptoms include heart defects; eye cataracts; deafness; genital, urinary, and gastrointestinal anomalies; and mental retardation. Infection during subsequent weeks is associated with less extreme consequences, including low birth weight, hearing loss, encephalitis (inflammation of the brain), and bone abnormalities (Samson, 1988). Since development of the rubella vaccine in 1966, the number of prenatal cases in the United States has dropped dramatically. Still, 10 to 20 percent of American women of childbearing age lack the rubella antibody, so the possibility still exists for new outbreaks of congenital rubella syndrome (Cochi et al., 1989).

The harmful impact of other common viruses is summarized in Table 3.2. The developing organism is particularly sensitive to the family of herpes viruses, for which there is no vaccine or treatment. Cytomegalovirus, a form of herpes affecting the salivary glands that may remain latent for years, only to be reactivated during

Table 3.2. Effects of Some Infectious Diseases during Pregnancy

DISEASE	INCREASED SPONTANEOUS ABORTION	PHYSICAL MALFORMATIONS	MENTAL RETARDATION	PREMATURITY OR PRENATAL GROWTH RETARDATION
VIRAL				
Cytomegalovirus	+	+	+	+
Rubella	+	+	+	+
Chicken pox	0	+	+	+
Herpes simplex 2	+	+	+	+
Mumps	+	?	0	0
Rubeola (red measles)	+	0	0	+
BACTERIAL				
Syphillis	+	+	+	?
Tuberculosis	+	?	+	+
PARASITIC				
Malaria	+	0	0	+
Toxoplasmosis	+	+	+	+

+ = established finding, 0 = no present evidence, ? = possible effect that is not clearly established. (Adapted from *Clinical Genetics in Nursing Practice* (p. 16) by F. L. Cohen, 1984, Philadelphia: Lippincott. Reprinted by permission. *Additional sources*: Samson, 1988; Sever, 1983; Vorhees, 1986.)

pregnancy, is the most frequent cause of fetal infection, invading 0.3 to 0.5 percent of all fetuses and 1 to 2 percent of infants during the birth process. Herpes simplex 2, a common sexually transmitted disease in the United States, can also infect the fetus either prenatally or during birth. The herpes viruses are associated with a wide variety of congenital malformations. Since they attack the central nervous system, the long-term consequences for child development, including mental retardation and learning problems during the school years, are only beginning to be appreciated (Samson, 1988).

Also listed in Table 3.2 are several bacterial and parasitic diseases. Among the most common is toxoplasmosis, acquired from eating raw or undercooked meat or from contact with infected cats. Toxoplasmosis has been linked to eye and central nervous system damage during the first trimester (Marcus, 1983). In view of what we now know about the disease, advice to women that they not eat red meat and avoid direct contact with cats during pregnancy should not be dismissed as an old wives' tale.

A relatively new illness that is spreading rapidly among certain sectors of the American population is Acquired Immune Deficiency Syndrome (AIDS). Recent research reveals that, like other viruses, AIDS can cross the placental barrier. You can read more about the prenatal transmission of AIDS in Box 3.2.

Other Maternal Factors

Emotional Stress. A large number of studies demonstrate that women who report severe and prolonged stress just before or during pregnancy experience more medical complications and give birth to infants with a greater number of abnormalities than women who are relatively free of anxiety. Emotional stress is associated with spontaneous abortion, labor difficulties, prematurity, low birth weight, newborn respiratory problems, and physical deformities such as cleft palate and infantile pyloric stenosis, a defect involving tightening of the infant's stomach outlet that must be treated surgically (Norbeck & Tilden, 1983; Omer & Everly, 1988; Revill & Dodge, 1978).

Medical research has led to increased understanding of the specific mechanisms by which stress can affect the developing baby. Anxiety activates the autonomic nervous system, stimulating the release of adrenal hormones into the mother's bloodstream. The hormones cause large amounts of blood to be diverted to parts of the mother's body involved in the defensive response — the brain, the heart, and the voluntary muscles in the arms, legs, and trunk. Blood flow to other organs, including the uterus, is diminished. Transfer of stimulant hormones across the placenta and inadequate oxygen supply resulting from reduced maternal blood flow cause fetal heart rate and activity level to rise dramatically. At the same time, muscles in the body, including those in the uterus, increase in tension. Contractions occur, which may be responsible for the higher incidence of preterm births among chronically anxious mothers (Omer & Everly, 1988).

Stress has also been associated with low weight gain in pregnant women (Picone et al., 1982b). Anxious mothers do not eat less. Rather, the physiological consequences of their intense anxiety reduce the utilization of food by their bodies, and this may, in turn, contribute to the low birth weights of their infants. Some researchers believe that prolonged exposure to stress hormones during the prenatal period is responsible for the increased irritability, restlessness, and digestive disturbances observed in these babies. However, the quality of maternal interaction with the infant during the period after birth may be just as important in causing these difficulties (Sameroff & Chandler, 1975). Intense stress experienced in utero may also have lifelong consequences for the ability of the developing person to cope with anxiety. A long-term follow-up of infants born to mothers who experienced the trauma of their

---

◆ CONTEMPORARY ISSUES: SOCIAL POLICY ◆

AIDS *and Prenatal Development*

Box 3.2

AIDS is a relatively new viral disease that is rapidly increasing among certain sectors of the population. The AIDS virus ravages the immune system. Afflicted individuals eventually die of a variety of intractable illnesses that invade and destroy the body. Groups at high risk for contracting AIDS are male homosexuals and bisexuals, intravenous drug abusers, and heterosexual partners of these individuals. Transfer of body fluids from one person to another, either directly or through use of contaminated needles, must take place for the disease to spread.

According to the U.S. Centers for Disease Control, more than 2,000 childhood cases of AIDS were diagnosed in the United States between 1981 and 1990. The large majority (78 percent) are infants infected prenatally, usually because of their mother's use of intravenous drugs. Since AIDS has an extended incubation period of up to 5 years in adults, expectant women carrying the virus are usually not aware at the time of their pregnancies that they can transmit the illness to their offspring.

In contrast to adults, AIDS seems to have a relatively short incubation period in infants. The average age at which symptoms appear in babies for whom prenatal transmission is suspected is 6 months. Weight loss, chronic fever and diarrhea, and a number of infectious illnesses appear. Affected infants rarely survive more than 5 to 8 months after symptom onset (Minkoff et al., 1987; Task Force on Pediatric AIDS, 1989).

Recent research suggests that like other intrauterine viral infections, AIDS may cause serious malformations in the developing embryo and fetus. A pattern of congenital abnormalities has been linked to prenatal infection, including microcephaly and a set of facial deformities involving a prominent boxlike forehead, widely spaced and obliquely positioned eyes, thickened lips, and other distortions. Infants who manifest more of these abnormalities show an earlier onset of AIDS symptoms during the first year of life, suggesting to researchers that the defects are caused by early intrauterine transfer of the AIDS virus (Marion et al., 1986). Additional problems are recurrent illnesses, neurological impairment, and delayed physical and mental development (Novick, in press).

Most prenatal AIDS babies are born to urban, poverty-stricken parents. Lack of money to pay for medical treatment, social ostracism because of prejudices and misunderstandings about the disease, and anxiety about the child's uncertain future undermine the functioning of these already stressed families. At present, specialized medical and psychological support services for stricken youngsters and their parents are badly needed. In addition, with no cure likely in the near future, widespread education of high-risk adults is the only way to prevent further spread of the virus to children (Task Force on Pediatric AIDS, 1989).

husbands' death during pregnancy revealed a higher incidence of psychiatric disorders by the time the offspring reached adulthood in comparison to a control group whose mothers experienced the same loss during the first year after birth (Huttunen & Niskanen, 1978).

It is important to note that high stress experienced during pregnancy does not always lead to negative outcomes. The problems mentioned above are greatly reduced when mothers have ready access to supportive social relationships. One study showed that among women experiencing severe life stress during pregnancy, those who reported having other people on whom they could count for help had a complication rate of only 33 percent, compared to 91 percent for those who had few or no social supports (Nuckolls, Cassel, & Kaplan, 1972). These results suggest that finding ways to strengthen supportive social ties during pregnancy can have a strong preventive impact on prenatal complications.

Nutrition. At one time it was commonly believed that under conditions of inadequate nutrition, the growing fetus, like a parasite, would take whatever it needed from its mother's body, and only the mother would suffer. The parasite theory was eventually proved wrong. Offspring of mothers with poor diets have higher prematurity and mortality rates, an increased incidence of congenital malformations, lower birth weights, and reduced head circumferences (Burke et al., 1943; Jeans, Smith & Stearns, 1955; Kaplan, 1972; Philipps & Johnson, 1977).

The critical period principle operates with nutrition, as it does with other environmental agents. In a study of pregnancy outcomes of women who experienced severe famine in Holland during World War II, nutritional deprivation during the first trimester was associated with congenital malformations and spontaneous abortion. In contrast, during the third trimester, it was related to low birth weight and reduced head circumference (Stein et al., 1975). These findings indicate that during the embryonic period, the organism is so small that it does not require much nutritional energy; however, very severe malnutrition during this time can cause structural damage and death. Inadequate maternal diet has its greatest impact on prenatal growth late in pregnancy. Cells are increasing rapidly in number and size, and a maternal diet high in all the basic nutrients is necessary for optimal development.

Prenatal malnutrition has especially severe consequences for the development of the central nervous system. Nutritionally deprived infants are apathetic, unresponsive to environmental stimulation, and irritable when aroused. They also have an abnormal, high-pitched cry that may be particularly distressing to their caregivers. Intellectual deficits and learning problems become increasingly apparent as these children get older (Zeskind & Lester, 1981). Autopsies of those who die reveal a dramatic reduction in number of brain cells, and the weight deficits of their brains are sometimes as high as 36 percent. The greater the nutritional deficiency, the greater the loss in brain weight, especially if the malnutrition occurs during the last three months of gestation or the first three months of postnatal life (Naeye, Blanc, & Paul, 1973; Parekh et al., 1970; Winick, Rosso, & Waterlow, 1970).

Prevention or recovery from prenatal malnutrition is possible only if adequate feeding is resumed early in development, while cell production is still taking place in the brain. The human brain grows by cell division during gestation and into the second year of postnatal life. Studies show that providing inadequately nourished women with dietary supplements during pregnancy is successful in reducing prenatal and infant mortality rates (Toverud, Stearns, & Macy, 1950). The consequences of maternal dietary enrichment for intellectual and behavioral development are less clear because malnutrition is highest among low socioeconomic sectors of the world's population. Therefore, it is difficult to separate nutritional influences from the host of other high-risk environmental factors to which children of poverty are exposed (Lozoff, 1989). However, several studies suggest that prenatal dietary enrichment leads to improved motor development in infancy (Herrera et al., 1980; Joos et al.,

1983), higher intelligence test scores at age 3 (Harrell, Woodyard, & Gates, 1955), and greater social involvement, affect expression, and interest in the environment during middle childhood (Barrett, Radke-Yarrow, & Klein, 1982).

After birth, intervention with prenatally malnourished infants may require more than just dietary enrichment. The lethargic and irritable dispositions of these babies may lead parents to withdraw from them and be less supportive and sensitive in caregiving. A self-perpetuating system is formed in which disturbed social experiences compound the behavioral and intellectual deficits of fetal malnutrition (Lozoff, 1989). The most successful intervention programs break this apathetic infant–nonsupportive caregiver feedback system. Some do so by providing parents with guidance in how to interact in optimal ways with the baby (Grantham-McGregor, Schofield, & Powell, 1987), while others focus on cognitive stimulation of infants to promote active engagement with their social and physical surroundings (Zeskind & Ramey, 1978, 1981).

Maternal Age. The number of women over 30 giving birth has quadrupled over the last decade and a half (U.S. Bureau of the Census, 1989a). Today, many women choose to delay motherhood until their careers are well underway. Others decide to have second families after divorce and remarriage. What risks do mothers take when they bear children at a more mature age? The most significant one was discussed earlier in this chapter: an increased likelihood of giving birth to an infant with chromosomal abnormalities. Because of this problem, women over 35 also experience a higher rate of spontaneous abortion.

For many years, aging of the mother's reproductive organs was also thought to make her more susceptible to a variety of pregnancy and birth complications. However, this assumption has recently been questioned. New studies indicate that when major medical problems are accounted for, even women in their forties do not show a greater incidence of these difficulties than do women in their twenties (Spellacy, Miller, & Winegar, 1986; Stein, 1983). Therefore, as long as the woman is in good health, having a child at an older age poses few risks to the mother and her developing infant.

In the case of very young teenage mothers, it has been conjectured that immaturity of the reproductive organs may promote pregnancy and delivery complications. However, like the findings on older mothers, research indicates that teenage mothers are not at risk because of physiological immaturity. Rather, many of them do not seek or have access to prenatal medical care and come from low-income backgrounds where nutrition and general health status are more likely to be inadequate. Studies that have taken socioeconomic status and prenatal care into account report few if any differences in pregnancy outcomes between teenagers and women 20 to 30 years of age (Mednick, Baker, & Sutton-Smith, 1979; Roosa, 1984; Rothenberg & Varga, 1981). Offspring of teenage mothers are at serious risk for developmental problems because adolescent pregnancy is associated with poverty and lack of psychological readiness for raising a child. We will consider teenage parenthood in greater detail in Chapter 5.

Parity. Parity refers to the number of children to whom a mother has given birth. Many women are surprised to find that length of labor is less than half as long with subsequent deliveries as it is with the first. Additional use seems to "break in" the uterus, but can repeated pregnancy also lead to "overuse" and damaging consequences for the developing child? Bearing a great many children has commonly been thought to magnify the number of pregnancy complications and birth defects in later offspring. However, a study of the relationship of prior pregnancies to a wide range of problems in over 50,000 births showed no such effect (Heinonen, Slone, & Shapiro, 1977). In instances in which parity seems to be related to complications, they are not caused by overuse of the reproductive organs, but rather by the cumulative effect of poor health or long-term exposure to damaging environmental agents. For example, when alcoholic mothers have had several children, the youngest offspring are most affected, largely because years of alcohol abuse leads to progressive deterioration of the mother's internal organs (Abel, 1988).

Prenatal development is divided into three phases—the period of the zygote, the period of the embryo, and the period of the fetus—that help us understand the impact of environmental agents on the developing organism. Teratogens—drugs, hormones, environmental pollutants, and maternal diseases that interfere with prenatal growth —operate according to the critical period principle. The greatest damage usually occurs during embryonic development, when the foundations of all organ systems are rapidly emerging. Malnutrition and maternal stress can also undermine prenatal growth. As with other environmental factors, the precise consequences depend on the timing and extent of the influence and the constitutional makeup of the mother and baby. Finally, as long as they are in good health, teenagers, women in their forties, and women who have already given birth to several children are not at greater risk for pregnancy and birth complications.

CHILDBIRTH

The nine-month period of gestation culminates in *labor*, a complex series of events that physically separate the mother and baby. The hard work of labor consists of muscular contractions that open the lower part of the uterus so the baby can be pushed down the birth canal and out into the external world. Labor naturally divides into the following three stages (see Figure 3.9):

1. *Dilation and effacement of the cervix.* This is the longest stage of labor, lasting, on the average, 12 to 14 hours with a first baby and 4 to 6 hours with subsequent births. Contractions cause the cervix, or bottom of the uterus, to thin and widen so the baby can enter the birth canal. The contractions gradually become more intense and closely spaced, but they take place quite automatically, and there is nothing the mother can do to speed up the process.

2. *Expulsion of the fetus.* This is a much shorter stage than the first, lasting about 50 minutes in a first delivery and 20 minutes in later births. The baby is moved into and down the birth canal and is finally born. During this stage, if the mother is not medicated, she feels a reflexive urge to squeeze and push with her abdominal muscles. It is the mother's pushing combined with further contractions of the uterus that forces the baby down and out.

3. *Expulsion of the placenta.* In this final stage, which lasts about 5 to 10 minutes, the placenta detaches from the uterine wall, and a few contractions and pushes by the mother cause it to be expelled from the birth canal (Samuels & Samuels, 1986).

These events that thrust the baby from the warm, dark, protective womb into a cold, brightly lit external world may strike you as a traumatic and perilous ordeal. The fetus is, after all, squeezed through the birth canal for many hours, during which time its head is subjected to considerable pressure. Furthermore, constriction of the placenta and umbilical cord during the contractions causes all infants to experience periodic oxygen deprivation.

In response to the trauma of labor, the infant produces extraordinarily high levels of stress hormones. We have already discussed how, during the prenatal period, the physiological effects of maternal stress can threaten the organism's development. In contrast, production of stress hormones by the fetus during labor has positive, highly adaptive consequences. Stress hormones help the baby withstand oxygen deprivation

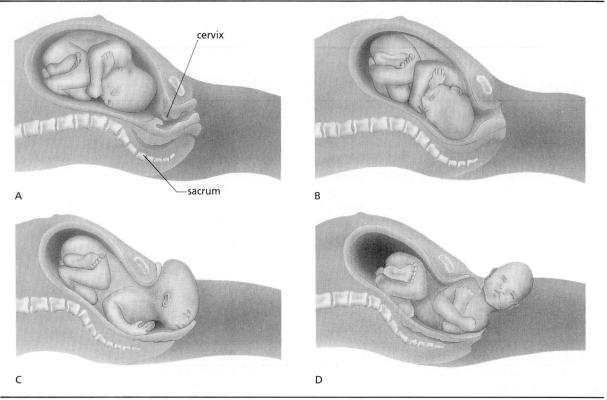

Figure 3.9. Progress through the birth canal during the first two stages of labor. Stage 1. *(A)* Before contractions commence, the baby still floats freely in the uterus. *(B)* Uterine contractions cause the cervix to thin and widen in anticipation of the baby's entry into the birth canal. Stage 2. *(C)* Uterine contractions combine with the mother's reflexive pushing to force the baby down the birth canal, and the head appears for the first time. *(D)* Near the end of Stage 2, the shoulders emerge and are followed quickly by the rest of the baby's body. After the baby is born, Stage 3, the final stage of labor, is completed when the placenta is expelled.

by ensuring that a rich supply of blood is delivered to the brain and heart. In addition, they help the infant breathe effectively when first separated from the mother by dilating the bronchial tubes and facilitating the absorption of liquid from the lungs. Because high levels of stress hormones also arouse the infant into alertness at birth, researchers believe they may facilitate the neonate's readiness to interact with the environment and promote attachment between mother and child (Emory & Toomey, 1988; Lagercrantz & Slotkin, 1986).

Infants who have difficulty meeting the survival demands of the external world must be given special assistance immediately. To quickly assess the infant's physical condition at birth, physicians use the **Apgar Scale** (Apgar, 1953), which provides a rating from 0 to 2 on each of five characteristics at 1 and 5 minutes after birth (see Table 3.3). An Apgar score of 7 or better indicates that the infant is in good physical condition. If the score is between 4 and 6, the infant requires special help in establishing breathing and other vital signs. If the score is 3 or below, the baby is in serious danger, and emergency medical attention is needed.

Prepared Childbirth and Home Delivery

In many preindustrial societies, prospective mothers are well acquainted with the events of childbirth, and they are supported by the presence of friends and family members. For example, the Navaho Indians of the southwestern United States treat

Table 3.3. The Apgar Scale

101

CHAPTER 3
BIOLOGICAL
FOUNDATIONS, PRENATAL
DEVELOPMENT, AND BIRTH

SIGN	SCORE		
	0	1	2
Heart rate	No heartbeat	Under 100 beats per minute	100 to 140 beats per minute
Respiratory effort	No breathing for 60 seconds	Irregular, shallow breathing	Strong breathing and crying
Reflex irritability	No response	Weak reflexive response	Strong reflexive response (sneezing, coughing, and grimacing)
Muscle Tone	Completely flaccid	Weak flexion of arms and legs	Strong flexion of arms and legs
Color[1]	Blue body and extremities	Body pink with blue extremities	Body and extremities completely pink

Source: Apgar, 1953.

[1] Color is the least reliable of the Apgar signs. Vernix, the white cheesy substance that covers the skin, often interferes with the physician's rating, and the skin tone of nonwhite babies makes it difficult to apply the "pink" criterion. However, physicians can rate newborns of all races for a pinkish glow that results from infusion of oxygen through the body tissues, since skin color is generally lighter at birth than the baby's inherited pigmentation.

birth as a major social event. Many members of the community attend to lend moral support to the mother. Among the Pukapukans of the Pacific Islands, childbirth is of interest to everyone, including children. A favorite pretend game of young girls involves stuffing coconuts inside their dresses, imitating the progress of labor, and permitting the nut to be born at the proper moment (Mead & Newton, 1967).

In the history of our own culture, childbirth typically occurred at home and was a shared family experience. However, nineteenth-century industrialization and urbanization brought new health problems that led to a rise in maternal and infant mortality. As a result, childbirth moved from home to hospital, where the health of mothers and babies could be protected. Once the responsibility for childbirth was placed in the hands of physicians, women's access to knowledge about it was reduced, and other family members no longer participated (Lindell, 1988).

In the 1950s and 1960s, a *prepared*, or *natural*, *childbirth* movement arose in Europe and quickly spread to the United States. Its fundamental purpose was to make birth as comfortable and rewarding an experience for mothers as possible in the context of hospital delivery. Most prepared childbirth techniques incorporate aspects of the methods of the English obstetrician Grantly Dick-Read (1959) or the French physician Ferdinand Lamaze (1958). All of them provide educational classes about what to expect during childbirth, teach relaxation and breathing exercises to counteract pain and increase the amount of oxygen available to the baby, and offer support to mothers through the presence of their husbands or a sympathetic and responsive companion during labor and delivery.

Although research on prepared childbirth has only begun to accumulate, the evidence to date suggests a variety of benefits, including more favorable maternal attitudes toward labor and delivery, a decrease in stress during the birth process, and more sensitive interaction with the newborn baby (Lindell, 1988). Prepared childbirth also seems to prevent the declines in marital satisfaction that typically occur for first-time parents once the baby goes home and they must adjust to new caregiving responsibilities (Cowan & Cowan, 1988; Markman & Kadushin, 1986).

Despite the widespread availability of hospital birthing centers that are family-centered in approach and homelike in appearance, approximately 1 percent of American women choose to have their babies at home. These mothers desire to recapture

In this natural childbirth class, expectant parents prepare for the experience of labor and delivery. Fathers learn how to serve as involved, sympathetic companions as mothers give birth.

the time when birth was an important part of domestic life (McClain, 1987). Most also want to avoid certain medical interventions, such as the uncomfortable fetal heart rate monitors (used to detect fetal distress) that are routinely strapped across the abdomen during a hospital labor. Although some home births are attended by physicians, many more are overseen by certified nurse-midwives who are specially trained in childbirth management.

Is it just as safe to give birth at home as in a hospital? For healthy women who are assisted by a medical professional, it appears so, since mortality rates are very low. However, when attendants are untrained or minimally trained, the neonatal death rate is considerably higher (Schramm, Barnes, & Bakewell, 1987). Moreover, for mothers who are at risk for any kind of complication, the appropriate place of birth is clearly the hospital, where life-saving treatment is available should it be needed.

Labor and Delivery Medication

When natural childbirth techniques are successful in reducing stress and pain experienced by the mother, they also lessen or eliminate the need for obstetric medication. Anesthetics and analgesias administered during labor rapidly cross the placenta, and when given in fairly large doses, they produce a depressed state in newborn infants that may last for several days. Attentiveness to sights and sounds in the environment as well as motor movements decrease in affected babies, and such infants also suck poorly during feedings and are more irritable (Brackbill, McManus, & Woodward, 1985; Stechler & Halton, 1982). The baby's depressed condition affects the early mother-infant reciprocal relationship. One study found that obstetrically medicated mothers engaged in less smiling and touching of their babies and that this effect persisted throughout the first month of postpartum life (Hollenbeck, Gewirtz, & Sebris, 1984). Although some research suggests poorer mental and physical development in infants of heavily medicated mothers throughout the first year, the longer-lasting effects of obstetric medication are controversial and still unproved (Broman, 1983).

Some form of medication is used in a great many births in the United States, but in most instances, it is mild and administered quite late in delivery. Since obstetric drugs can be helpful in easing long labors and difficult births, it is not practical to try to eliminate them entirely. Nevertheless, the impact of obstetric medication on early infant behavior and maternal caregiving is well documented, supporting the current trend in the medical profession toward restrained and limited use.

Perinatal[2] Complications

The great majority of births take place quite normally and result in healthy newborn infants. However, sometimes the mother's labor is long and drawn out, or serious complications occur that result in medical emergencies. Abnormal separation of the placenta before the baby is born and breech births (in which the baby's buttocks or feet emerge first and both the umbilical cord and infant's head have an increased chance of being compressed) are situations in which damage due to **anoxia,** or lack of oxygen, may occur. In addition, premature labor is one of the most significant complications of pregnancy. When infants are born too soon, they are at greater risk for a variety of physical and behavioral problems of development.

Anoxia. Although all infants experience some oxygen deprivation during labor and delivery, a small percentage are subjected to high levels of anoxia when they fail to breathe spontaneously within a minute or two after birth. Prolonged suspension of breathing is called *apnea*, which can occur if there is delay between the time the baby is no longer receiving oxygen through the umbilical cord and when the infant starts to breathe on its own. Newborns can survive periods of apnea longer than adults, but there is risk of brain damage if breathing is suspended for more than 3 minutes (Stechler & Halton, 1982).

Severe anoxia may occur during labor if the umbilical cord is squeezed or excessive pressure is applied to the baby's head, as may happen in a breech birth or when forceps are used in a difficult delivery to assist the baby out of the birth canal. Rh blood incompatibility is another cause of perinatal anoxia. If the mother's blood is Rh negative (lacking Rh antigens) and she carries an Rh positive baby, it is possible for the infant's antigens to cross the placenta and enter the mother's bloodstream. When this happens, the mother produces antibodies against the infant's blood cells. The antibodies may travel back into the baby's system and lead to *erythroblastosis*, a condition in which the red blood cells are destroyed and the oxygen supply to the fetus is reduced. The exchange of blood leading to erythroblastosis is more likely to occur during labor and delivery, although it can happen earlier. Since it takes time for the mother's system to produce Rh antibodies, first-born children are rarely affected, but the danger increases with successive offspring. Fortunately, erythroblastosis can be prevented by giving the mother an injection of a substance called RhoGam after the birth of each Rh positive baby to prevent the buildup of antibodies in the mother's system. However, sometimes errors are made in maternal blood typing, and the mother's production of antibodies is not controlled. In these cases, if the baby is in danger, it is possible to perform blood transfusions immediately after birth or, if necessary, even before the baby is born (Simkin, Whalley & Keppler, 1984).

Results of a major longitudinal study of over 100 anoxic newborns revealed sensorimotor impairments during the first few days of life that were greatest for infants experiencing the most severe oxygen deprivation (Graham et al., 1957). Studied again during the preschool years, the anoxic infants continued to show intellectual and behavioral deficits (Graham et al., 1962). However, by age 7, differences between anoxic children and controls had largely disappeared (Corah et al., 1965). Evidence from this study, as well as many others, indicates that although

---

[2] The perinatal period begins with the onset of labor and ends with the expulsion of the baby from the birth canal and the cutting of the umbilical cord.

deficits persist through the first few years of life, by school age most infants who suffered from anoxia have caught up with their agemates (Stechler & Halton, 1982).

In instances in which perinatal anoxia is associated with severe problems, the oxygen deprivation was probably especially acute. Moreover, it may have occurred because of earlier damage to or immaturity of the respiratory system, thereby serving as only one among a number of contributing factors to serious developmental problems. For example, infants born more than 6 weeks premature are commonly afflicted with *respiratory distress syndrome*, otherwise known as *hyaline membrane disease*. The tiny lungs of these babies are so underdeveloped that the air sacs collapse, causing serious breathing difficulties and, in some cases, death by suffocation. Today, use of mechanical ventilators keeps many such infants alive. Nevertheless, some experience permanent impairment due to oxygen deprivation or lung damage from the treatment itself (Vohr & Garcia-Coll, 1988). Respiratory distress syndrome is only one of a number of risks for youngsters born weeks before their due date. We turn to a more detailed consideration of these infants in the following section.

Preterm and Low-Birth-Weight Infants. The term premature has traditionally been used to refer to babies born 3 weeks or more before the end of a full 38-week gestational period or to infants weighing less than 2,500 grams (5½ pounds). Several decades of research reveals that premature babies show high mortality rates and are at risk for developmental problems. Birth weight is the best available predictor of survival and long-term developmental outcomes. A substantial number of infants below 1,500 grams (3.3 pounds) experience developmental difficulties that are not overcome later, an effect that becomes stronger as birth weight decreases (Hoy, Bill, & Sykes, 1988; Kopp & Kaler, 1989; Vohr & Garcia-Coll, 1988).

Nevertheless, many premature babies — even some who weigh only a couple of pounds — fare reasonably well (Vohr & Garcia-Coll, 1988). Child development specialists and pediatricians now believe that the category of "prematurity" is too global to help us fully understand the factors affecting outcomes for these infants. Currently, low-birth-weight babies are divided into two groups. The first consists of **preterm** or short-gestation infants who are born several weeks or more before their due date. Although small in size, their weight may still be appropriate for their gestational age. The second group includes infants who are **small for dates.** These babies are born below their expected weight when their gestational age is taken into account. Some of them are full term, while others are preterm infants who are especially underweight.

Though all low-birth-weight babies are developmentally at risk, a review of the few studies in which infants have been separated into subgroups suggests that small-for-dates babies are somewhat more disadvantaged than are preterm infants. During the first year of life, they show higher rates of mortality, susceptibility to illness, and neurological problems. By school age, low intelligence test scores, school achievement difficulties, hyperactivity, and poor motor coordination are more common among small-for-dates youngsters (Teberg, Walther, & Pena, 1988). Small-for-dates babies are believed to have experienced inadequate prenatal nutrition, because of either their mother's diets, faulty functioning of the placenta, or congenital anomalies of their own. Nutritional deprivation is a serious problem that we discussed earlier, and it may help to explain the continuing developmental problems of these children.

The largest body of research exists for infants labeled preterm, regardless of the relationship between their gestational age and weight. Twins are usually born about 3 weeks early, and because of restricted space inside the uterus, they gain less weight than singletons after the twentieth week of pregnancy. Otherwise, preterm births are more prevalent among women from low socioeconomic backgrounds. They are probably caused by many factors, including poor maternal health, drug abuse and smoking during pregnancy, lack of prenatal care, or a uterus that is insufficient for carrying a baby to term. The number of preterm infants experiencing serious developmental consequences is markedly reduced today because of advanced medical technology that permits feeding, temperature control, and constant monitoring of the physiological status of even the tiniest babies. Nevertheless, preterm infants are still highly vulnerable to later intellectual deficits and school difficulties. However, developmental outcomes vary with family rearing conditions. Problems are much more prevalent among infants who grow up in impoverished and nonsupportive home environments (Kopp & Kaler, 1989; Teberg, Walther, & Pena, 1988).

In an effort to understand the origins of later developmental problems, researchers have amassed an extensive literature on the early characteristics and experiences of preterm infants. Results of these studies indicate that low gestational age is associated with infant behavior that is more variable and less competent than that of full-term newborns. For example, preterm babies are less alert and responsive and more difficult to feed, and they show poorer motor coordinations, less well organized sleep patterns, and hyper-responsiveness to sounds (Tronick, Scanlon, & Scanlon, in press). In addition, at birth they look quite different from babies of full gestational age. Scrawny, thin-skinned, and still covered with hairy lanugo on their shoulders and backs, preterms are regarded by most people as far less attractive and appealing than their round-faced, chubby, full-term counterparts (Maier et al., 1984; Stern & Hildebrandt, 1986).

The appearance and behavioral disorganization of preterm infants create strains for parents that may adversely affect their relationship with the baby (Pederson et al., 1987). An added factor is that parents are initially separated from and have infrequent early contacts with preterm infants, a circumstance that may interfere with maternal attachment. In one study, observations were made of parents interacting with their preterm babies after hospital discharge. During feedings, parents less often held the babies close and touched and talked to them than they did full-term infants (Goldberg, Brachfeld, & DiVitto, 1980). Behavioral differences between most preterm and full-term babies diminish over the course of the first year of life, but preterms who are sickly at birth continue to be more irritable and less responsive to their environment for many months. When their poorly adapted behaviors are combined with parents who have difficulty coping because they are young, impoverished, uneducated, or lacking in social supports, unfavorable developmental outcomes are likely to occur. Research shows that sick preterms tend to be responded to by parents with more intrusive and controlling behaviors by the middle of the first year of life. Parents probably use more interfering touches, verbal commands, and criticisms in an effort to obtain a higher level of response from an infant who is, to begin with, passive, slowly developing, and not a very rewarding social partner (Beckwith & Cohen, 1980). Some parents may accelerate these intrusive efforts in the face of continuing ungratifying and irritable infant behavior, and this may explain why preterm infants as a group are susceptible to child abuse (Kennell, Voos, & Klaus, 1979; Parke & Collmer, 1975).

By the early school years, most preterm babies exposed to sensitive, caring parenting catch up in development and show intelligence test scores that are within normal range (Cohen & Parmelee, 1983). If positive caregiver-infant interaction can overcome the negative consequences of early birth, then intervention programs directed at supporting this relationship should help these infants make a successful recovery.

A variety of interventions have been tried with preterm babies. Some treat the infant side of the relationship by providing increased stimulation to ameliorate the baby's initially passive, poorly organized behavior. In a number of these efforts, infants have been rocked in suspended hammocks or placed on waterbeds to simulate the gentle motion they would have experienced in their mother's womb. In general, these stimulus enrichment programs have led to increased weight gain, more predictable sleep patterns, and improved visual alertness and motor maturation during the early postnatal period (Cornell & Gottfried, 1976; Schaefer, Hatcher, & Bargelow, 1980). Touch seems to be an especially important form of intervention for preterm infants. In animal research, tactile stimulation has been found to release certain brain chemicals that support physical growth, and these effects are believed to hold for humans as well (Schanberg & Field, 1987). In one recent study, long-term benefits accrued for preterm infants who were gently massaged several times each day in the hospital. They not only gained weight faster, but were advantaged over infants who did not receive the tactile stimulation in mental and motor ability at 8 and 12 months of age (Field et al., 1986). Nevertheless, to be effective, stimulation must be carefully adjusted to each preterm baby's capacity to tolerate and make use of it. Some very small or sick infants are too fragile to handle much visual, auditory, or tactile input. In fact, the noise, bright light, and invasive medical procedures of the intensive care nursery are already too overwhelming and stressful for them. At present, not much is known about how to regulate the amount and kind of stimulation so it fits with the individual needs of preterm infants (Korner, 1987).

Other intervention programs have focused on the maternal side of the relationship by providing training to mothers who are at risk for poor parenting skills. In one such program, Field and her collaborators (1980) taught low-income teenage mothers to provide age-appropriate stimulation to their preterm infants and educated these mothers about developmental milestones. Those who received the training, in comparison to controls who did not, had more desirable child-rearing attitudes, rated their infants' temperaments as less difficult, and were more verbally responsive and emotionally involved with their babies. At 4 months of age, their infants had greater weight and length measurements, and at 8 months, they had higher mental test scores. However, programs for parents, like those for infants, must be carefully tailored to the needs of the individual participants. Recent evidence indicates that mothers who benefit most are those with few alternative sources of support. When friends and family members provide help and encouragement and mothers feel secure about interacting with their preterm baby, intervention is not especially helpful. In fact, it can be counterproductive if it causes the mother to question her own effectiveness as a caregiver (Affleck et al., 1989, in press).

UNDERSTANDING REPRODUCTIVE RISK

Throughout this chapter, we have discussed how biological risks can interfere with the development of the child at conception and during the prenatal and perinatal periods. We have emphasized that developmental outcomes can vary from severely damaging to near normal, depending on the type and timing of influence. Pasamanick and Knobloch (1966) refer to this variation in severity of biological insults as the **continuum of reproductive casualty.** In general, the earlier the insult, the greater the damage to the developing organism. However, we have also shown that even when the nature of the early biological trauma is known, definite predictions about the ultimate course of development are not always possible. As Sameroff and Chandler point out (1975), reproductive risk is also affected by an equally important **continuum of caretaking casualty.** Caretaking can vary from severe abuse and neglect to stimulating, sensitive, and supportive parenting. In many instances, it can perpetuate or break the relationship between early trauma and later disorders.

The results of a major longitudinal study conducted in Hawaii illustrate how the continua of reproductive and caretaking casualty work together. In 1955, 670 infants born on the island of Kauai were rated as having experienced mild, moderate, or severe perinatal complications and then matched, on the basis of socioeconomic status and race, with infants who had uncomplicated births. In childhood, their family environments were rated on extent of emotional support and educational stimulation. By age 10, early developmental differences between children who differed in perinatal problems had become less pronounced. Any persisting effects were found largely among a very small group of children who had experienced the most severe complications. At age 18, this group had 10 times the incidence of mental retardation, five times the number of mental health problems, and twice the number of physical handicaps as the remainder of the children studied. Among mild to moderately stressed children, quality of the caretaking environment was the best predictor of later developmental deficits. Homes rated low in family stability and in educational stimulation produced lasting behavior and learning problems. Among homes rated high, the consequences of perinatal complications were less and less evident as the child matured (Werner & Smith, 1979, 1982).

In summarizing the joint effects of the continua of reproductive and caretaking casualty, Sameroff and Chandler (1975) state:

> When the child's vulnerability is heightened through massive reproductive trauma, only an extremely supportive environment can help to restore the normal integrative growth process. . . . On the other extreme, a highly disordered caretaking setting might convert the most sturdy and integrated of children into a caretaking casualty (pp. 235–236).

For the great majority of children who have experienced reproductive risk, familial and socioeconomic characteristics of the caretaking environment provide the most potent predictors of long-term developmental outcomes.

HEREDITY, ENVIRONMENT, AND BEHAVIOR: A LOOK AHEAD

Most infants emerge from the prenatal period of development unscathed. Born healthy and vigorous, as developing members of the human species they soon show considerable variation in attributes and abilities. Some are outgoing and sociable, others are incessantly curious explorers of their physical environment, while still others are quiet, shy, and reserved. By school age, one child shows a penchant for arithmetic, another loves to read, while a third excels at music or athletics. *Behavioral geneticists* are scientists interested in discovering the origins of this great diversity in human behavior and characteristics. We have already seen that they are only beginning to understand the genetic and environmental events preceding birth that ensure a healthy, intact organism or place limits on the individual's potential. How, then, do they unravel the hereditary and environmental roots of the many complex characteristics that emerge after birth and that are the focus of the remaining chapters in this book?

All behavioral geneticists acknowledge that *both* heredity and environment are indispensable for the development of any behavior. There is no real controversy on this point because the organism can develop only through the joint action of genetic information and environmental contexts that allow this information to be expressed (Scarr, 1988). No child can learn to talk without being exposed to verbal communication or learn to read without access to and instruction in how to decipher the printed word. However, for polygenic traits like intelligence and personality, scientists are a very long way from being able to identify the genes responsible for individual differences and the biochemical mechanisms through which they exert their effect. Therefore, they must study the relationship of genetic factors to these behaviors indirectly, and an unresolved nature-nurture controversy exists because scientists do not agree on how heredity and environment influence these complex characteristics.

Some believe that it is both useful and possible to answer the question of *how much* each factor contributes to differences among children. To find out whether one factor is more important than the other, behavioral geneticists use special research methods to separate individual differences into their hereditary and environmental components. In doing so, they try to determine which factor plays the major role. A second group of scientists regards the question of which factor is more important as neither useful nor answerable. These individuals believe that heredity and environment do not make separate contributions to human behavior. Instead, they are interdependent, and the nature and extent of influence of one factor depend upon the contribution of the other. Since these scientists see development as a complex transaction between nature and nurture, they think the real question we need to explore is *how* heredity and environment work together (Anastasi, 1958; Lerner, 1986). Let's consider each of these two positions in turn.

The Question of "How Much"?

Behavioral geneticists use **heritability estimates** to measure the extent to which variation among individuals in complex behaviors can be attributed to genetic factors. Investigators have obtained heritabilities for intelligence and a variety of personality characteristics. We will review their findings in greater detail in later chapters devoted to these topics, while providing only a brief overview of the issues involved in estimating heritability here. Heritability estimates are obtained from **kinship studies,** investigations in which individuals within a family who have different degrees of genetic relationship to one another are compared. The most common type of kinship study compares identical twins, who, because they develop from a single zygote, share all their genes in common, with fraternal twins, who are genetically no more alike than ordinary siblings. The assumption made in these comparisons is that if individuals who are of greater genetic similarity also resemble each other more closely in behavior, then the behavior must be at least partly genetically determined.

Because they share the same genetic makeup, identical twins are a fascinating and common subject in studies of the heritability of behavior.

Findings from kinship studies on the heritability of intelligence provide one of the most controversial sets of data in the field of child development. While some experts claim a high degree of genetic determination, others believe there is no convincing evidence that genetic factors have anything to do with individual differences in intelligence. Currently, most behavioral geneticists support a moderate role for heredity. When many twin studies are compiled, correlations between the intelligence test scores of identicals are consistently higher than those for fraternals. In one summary of over 30 such investigations, the mean correlation for intelligence was .86 for identical twins and .60 for fraternal twins (Bouchard & McGue, 1981). Using special statistical procedures, behavioral geneticists compare the two correlations to arrive at a heritability estimate, ranging from 0 to 1.00, which refers to the proportion of differences among individuals in behavior that can be explained by their genetic differences (Plomin, 1986). Depending on the particular twin studies used to calculate heritability, the values for intelligence range from .30 to .70. Scarr and Kidd (1983) suggest that a likely value is probably about .50. Other kinship comparisons—for example, between identical twins and ordinary siblings or siblings and half-siblings—also support a moderate heritability of about this magnitude. In addition, the measured intelligence of adopted children consistently shows a stronger correlation with the scores of their biological parents than those of their adoptive parents, offering further evidence that heredity plays an important role (Scarr & Weinberg, 1983; Skodak & Skeels, 1949).

Research indicates that heredity also influences personality. In fact, for personality traits that have been studied extensively, such as sociability, emotionality, and activity level, heritability is at about the same moderate level as that reported for intelligence (Plomin, 1989).

Although heritabilities derived from kinship studies provide evidence that genetic factors make important contributions to individual differences, they are limited statistics, and questions have been raised about their validity. A heritability index is heavily influenced by the range of environments to which kinship pairs have been exposed. For example, pairs of identical twins raised together under highly similar conditions have more strongly correlated intelligence test scores than those reared apart in very different environments. When the former are used to compute heritability estimates, the higher correlation causes the contribution of heredity to be overestimated. To remedy this difficulty, researchers try to compute heritabilities on pairs of twins who have been reared apart in foster or adoptive homes. But few separated twin pairs are available for study, and when they are, social service agencies often place them in advantaged home environments that are similar in many ways. These problems suggest a major concern about the heritability measure. The variety of home environments most twin pairs experience is far more restricted than that found in the general population. This limitation makes it difficult to generalize heritability estimates to the population as a whole (Bronfenbrenner, 1972; Scarr & Kidd, 1983).

Another criticism of heritability estimates is that subtle environmental pressures may contribute to the substantially greater correlations between pairs of identical than fraternal twins. Knowing that identical twins are genetically the same, perhaps parents simply expect them to behave more similarly and therefore treat them more alike than fraternals. Although this idea seems plausible, there is actually little support for it. In one study, Lytton (1977) carefully observed the interactions of mothers with their 2-year-old twin sons. He found that although parents of identical twins do behave more similarly toward their children than parents of fraternals, they do so only in response to the identical twins' more similar behaviors. Parent-initiated behaviors not contingent on the child's actions do not differ between identical and fraternal twin pairs. In addition, twins whose zygosity has been misclassified (identicals who were thought to be fraternals and fraternals who were thought to be identicals) show behavioral similarities more in line with their actual twin status than their perceived status (Scarr, 1968; Scarr & Carter-Saltzman, 1979). These findings also indicate that parents do not alter the way they treat twins on the basis of knowledge of their genetic similarity.

Heritability estimates are controversial measures because they can easily be misapplied. For example, high heritabilities obtained from kinship studies have been used to suggest that racial differences in intelligence, such as the generally poorer test performance of blacks in comparison to whites in the United States, have a genetic basis (Jensen, 1969, 1973). As we will see in greater detail in Chapter 8, heritability estimates offer no direct evidence about genetically determined intellectual differences between the races, and the hypothesis that heredity is responsible for the black-white intelligence gap has been disproved. Research shows that when black and white children are raised in similar environments, they do not differ in performance on intelligence tests (Scarr & Weinberg, 1976, 1983).

Perhaps the most serious criticism leveled at heritability estimates has to do with their usefulness. While they are interesting statistics that tell us heredity is undoubtedly involved in the determination of complex behaviors like intelligence and personality, they give us no information on how these behaviors develop or how children might respond when exposed to novel environments designed to help them develop as far as possible. Behavioral geneticists respond to these criticisms by arguing that their efforts can be regarded as a first step. As more evidence accumulates to show that genetic factors underlie important individual differences in behavior, then scientists can begin to ask about the specific genes involved, the biochemical pathways through which the genes exert their influence, and how these pathways are modified by environmental factors.

The Question of "How?"

According to a second perspective, heredity and environment do not influence behavior independently of one another. Instead, behavior is the result of a dynamic interplay between these two fundamental sources of development. How do heredity and environment work together to influence development? Several important concepts shed light on this complex question.

The first is the concept of **range of reaction** (Gottesman, 1963). According to this idea, there is no simple, one-to-one correspondence between our genes and the characteristics we develop. Instead, each person's genotype establishes its own upper and lower boundaries for development because it responds uniquely to a given range of environmental conditions. Range of reaction applies to any phenotypic characteristic. In Figure 3.10, it is illustrated for intelligence. The figure depicts reaction ranges for three hypothetical children. As environments vary from extremely impoverished to highly stimulating and enriched, child A's score changes dramatically, child B's only moderately, and child C's hardly at all. Reaction range assumes a complex interdependency between heredity and environment. First, it shows that when environments vary, a single genotype will produce different phenotypes. At the same time, identical environments do not have the same effect on all genotypes. A poor environment will result in a lower phenotypic intelligence for child C than child A, while an advantaged environment will elevate child A's performance far above what is possible for child C. Second, different genotypes can lead to identical phenotypes when combined with appropriate environmental conditions. For example, children who show the same intelligence test score arrive there through distinct genetic and environmental routes. A score of 100 may be the result of a disadvantaged environment for a child with a favorable genotype, but a superior home and special schooling may produce the same score for a child with a less favorable genotype. Thus, different children vary in their range of possible responses to different environments, and

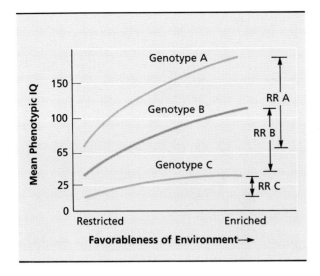

Figure 3.10. Intellectual ranges of reaction (RR) for three hypothetical children in environments that vary from unstimulating to highly enriched. *(From I. I. Gottesman, 1963, "Genetic Aspects of Intelligent Behavior." In N. R. Ellis [Ed.],* Handbook of Mental Deficiency, *New York: McGraw-Hill. P. 255. Adapted by permission.)*

unique genotype-environment combinations are responsible for both similarities and differences in human behavior.

The concept of **canalization** provides another view of how heredity and environment combine. A behavior that is strongly canalized follows a genetically predetermined growth path, and only strong environmental forces can deflect it from one or a few possible outcomes. Waddington's (1957) "developmental landscape," shown in Figure 3.11, is a pictorial representation of this concept. A ball, representing the developing phenotype, rolls down a tilted surface toward its final end state at the bottom edge. The surface is grooved by a number of possible paths or channels of development. Early on, the ball can easily be diverted by an environmental push into one groove instead of another. Once the ball has rolled into a channel, however, it becomes increasingly difficult for the environment to redirect its course. Strongly canalized behaviors have channels that are relatively deep, and their course of development is not easily modified by the environment. Infant sensorimotor development is said to be strongly canalized, since all normal human infants suck on objects, smile, roll over, and eventually crawl and walk. Only extreme environmental conditions can modify these behaviors or cause them not to appear. Intelligence and personality are less strongly canalized characteristics that are more modifiable (Scarr-Salapatek, 1975). However, the developmental landscape also shows that over time, even weakly canalized attributes like these become entrenched in a groove, and they become less subject to environmental modification after the early years of life. The concept of canalization reveals that the often-heard statement, "Heredity sets the limits within which environment determines the eventual outcome" is only partly true. The environment also sets limits by deflecting the phenotype into a particular channel, and early environmental forces affect the extent to which later experiences can modify the course of development. Can you think of examples from our discussion of prenatal development that illustrate this idea?

There is still another way in which heredity and environment are interdependent. Scarr and McCartney (1983) point out that a major problem in trying to separate genetic and environmental factors is that they are often correlated with one another. In other words, our genetic predispositions have some influence on the environments to which we are exposed (Plomin, DeFries, & Loehlin, 1977; Plomin, 1986). The way this happens changes with development.

At younger ages, two types of genetic-environmental correlation are common. The first is called *passive correlation* because the child has no control over it. Early on,

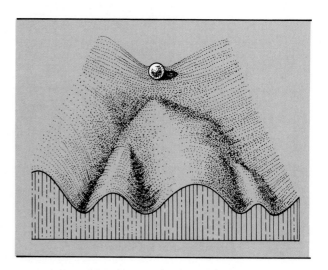

Figure 3.11. Waddington's developmental landscape, a pictorial illustration of the concept of canalization. *(Extract taken from* The Strategy of the Genes, *by C. H. Waddington, reproduced by kind permission of Unwin Hyman Ltd. © 1957, Allen & Unwin, London.)*

parents provide rearing environments that are compatible with their own genotypes. Since they share genes in common with their offspring, the environments are also likely to be congruent with their children's genetic predispositions. For example, parents who enjoy reading offer their children a home environment rich in books, magazines, and encouragement to read, and their children are likely to become good readers for both genetic and environmental reasons. The second type of genetic-environmental correlation is *evocative*. Children evoke responses from others that are influenced by the children's genotypes, and these responses strengthen their original predispositions. For example, an active, gregarious infant is likely to receive more social stimulation from those around her than a quiet, passive baby; a conscientious, attentive preschooler will probably receive more positive interactions from parents than an inattentive, distractible child.

At older ages, *active* genotype-environmental correlation becomes common. As children extend their experiences beyond the immediate family and are granted the freedom to make more of their own choices, they play an increasingly active role in seeking out environments that are compatible with their genetic inclinations. The well-coordinated, muscular child spends more time at after-school sports, the musically inclined youngster enrolls in the school orchestra and practices his violin, and the intellectually curious child is a well-known patron at the local library and reads avidly during her spare time. Scarr and McCartney refer to this tendency to actively choose environments that complement our heredity as **niche-picking.** Infants and young children cannot do much niche-picking, since adults select the environments to which they are exposed. In contrast, older children and adolescents can create their own environments to a much greater extent. Scarr and McCartney's niche-picking idea explains why pairs of identical twins reared apart during childhood and later reunited often find, to their great surprise, that they have similar hobbies, food preferences, friendship choices, and vocations. It also helps us understand some curious longitudinal findings from kinship studies that reveal declining similarities between fraternal twins and adopted siblings from infancy to adolescence (Bouchard, 1981; Scarr & Weinberg, 1983). According to Scarr and McCartney, the relative influence of heredity and environment is not constant but changes over the course of development. With age, genetic inclinations become increasingly important in determining the environments we experience and choose for ourselves.

A major reason that child development specialists are interested in the nature-nurture issue is that they want to find ways to improve environments in order to help children realize their genetic potential. The concepts of range of reaction, canalization, and niche-picking remind us that the development of individual differences is best understood as a series of complex transactions between nature and nurture. When a characteristic is strongly determined by heredity, this does not mean that it cannot be modified. However, children are not infinitely malleable. The effectiveness of any attempt to enhance development depends on the characteristics we want to change, the genetic makeup of the individual child, and the type, timing, and strength of the environmental intervention.

CHAPTER SUMMARY

Genetic Foundations

■ Development begins at conception, with the joining of sperm and ovum into the one-celled **zygote.** Within the cell nucleus are 23 pairs of **chromosomes,** and beaded along their length are the **genes,** segments of **DNA** that make us distinctly human and are responsible for many of our unique characteristics.

■ Through the process of cell duplication known as **mitosis,** the zygote develops into a complex human being composed of trillions of cells. The **gametes**—sperm and ovum—that merge to form the zygote are produced by a special process of cell division known as **meiosis.** By ensuring that each offspring receives a unique complement of genes from each parent, meiosis promotes genetic variability important for survival of the species.

■ **Dominant-recessive** and **co-dominant** relationships are basic patterns of genetic transmission that apply to traits governed by a single gene. Because most harmful genes are recessive, they have a reduced likelihood of becoming phenotypically apparent. However, when recessive disorders are **X-linked** (carried on the X chromosome), males are more likely to be affected because there are no complementary genes on the Y chromosome to overcome the effects of those on the X. Unfavorable genes arise from **mutations,** which can occur spontaneously or be provoked by hazardous environmental agents.

■ Most relationships between genes and phenotypic attributes are not one-to-one. Even when characteristics are attributable to a single gene, other **modifier genes** can affect the outcome. Moreover, complex attributes such as intelligence and personality are **polygenic,** or influenced by many genes. In these cases, the specific rules of genetic transmission may never be known.

Chromosomal Abnormalities

■ Chromosomal abnormalities can cause serious developmental problems, but the outcomes for any single disorder are not clear-cut and depend on a host of additional genetic and environmental factors. Down syndrome is an **autosomal** disorder that results in physical defects and severe intellectual impairment. However, sensitive, responsive parenting and early intervention make an important difference in how well children with Down syndrome develop.

■ Disorders of the **sex chromosomes** are milder than autosomal abnormalities. Studies of the intellectual abilities of children with Turner, triple X, and Klinefelter's syndromes are beginning to provide important insights into the biological bases of intellectual abilities. Contrary to popular belief, males with XYY syndrome are not prone to violence, criminality, and below-average intellectual functioning. Fragile X syndrome, a disorder involving abnormal gaps and breaks in a special place on the X chromosome, has recently been identified as a major cause of mental retardation.

Genetic Counseling and Prenatal Diagnosis

■ **Genetic counseling** helps couples at risk for bearing offspring with genetic abnormalities decide whether to conceive a child or consider other options, such as adoption, artificial insemination, in vitro fertilization, or surrogate motherhood. New **prenatal diagnostic methods** now make it possible to examine the condition of the developing organism early in pregnancy.

Prenatal Development

■ Prenatal development is usually divided into three phases. The period of the zygote lasts approximately 2 weeks, from fertilization until the first tiny mass of cells becomes fully embedded in the uterine lining. The period of the **embryo** extends from 2 to 8 weeks gestation. During this time, the foundations for all body systems are laid down. The period of the **fetus,** lasting until the end of pregnancy, involves a dramatic increase in body size and completion of physical structures.

Prenatal Environmental Influences

■ **Teratogens** are environmental agents that cause damage during the prenatal period. Although teratogens can be harmful throughout pregnancy, the developing organism is especially sensitive during the embryonic period, since all essential body structures are rapidly emerging at this time. Drugs, hormones, alcohol, smoking, radiation, environmental pollution, and infectious diseases are teratogens that pose a significant danger to the child before birth.

■ Other maternal factors can also complicate prenatal development. Severe emotional stress has been linked to pregnancy and birth complications, and prenatal malnutrition interferes with body growth and the development of the central nervous system. Although maternal age and **parity** were once thought to be major causes of pregnancy complications, recent research indicates that (except for the increased risk of chromosomal abnormalities in older women) this is not the case. Instead, poor health, inadequate prenatal care, and environmental risk factors associated with poverty are related to an increased incidence of prenatal and perinatal problems at all maternal ages.

Childbirth

■ Childbirth takes place in three stages, beginning with muscular contractions that open the lower part of the uterus so the baby can be pushed down the birth canal and ending with delivery of the placenta. During labor, infants produce high levels of stress hormones, which help them withstand oxygen deprivation and arouse them into alertness at delivery. The **Apgar Scale** is used to quickly assess the infant's physical condition at birth.

■ Prepared, or natural, childbirth techniques reduce stress and pain for the mother during labor and delivery. They may also lessen or eliminate the need for obstetric medication, which can produce a depressed state in the newborn infant.

■ Birth complications, such as anoxia, premature delivery, and low birth weight, present serious risks for the adjustment and behavior of the newborn infant. In terms of childhood development, **small-for-dates** babies generally fare less well than **preterm** infants whose weight is appropriate for their gestational age.

Understanding Reproductive Risk

■ For youngsters who experience reproductive risks, the **continuum of reproductive casualty** and the **continuum of caretaking casualty** combine to affect long-term development outcomes. As long as biological insults are not too severe and children are raised in supportive home environments, the adverse consequences of pregnancy and birth complications gradually diminish and often disappear by middle childhood.

Heredity, Environment, and Behavior: A Look Ahead

■ Child development specialists have only begun to understand the genetic and environmental events preceding birth that ensure a healthy organism or place limits on the child's developing potential. Unraveling the genetic and environmental roots of complex characteristics emerging after birth, such as intelligence and personality, is even more challenging, since the contribution of heredity must be studied indirectly.

■ Some scientists believe that it is useful and possible to determine "how much" genetic factors contribute to individual differences by computing **heritability estimates** from **kinship** studies. Although heritability estimates show that genetic factors play an important role in the development of intelligence and personality, they are limited statistics that can easily be misapplied.

■ Other scientists think that separating individual differences into hereditary and environmental components is neither useful or valid. They believe that the important question is "how" heredity and environment depend on one another and work together. The concepts of **range of reaction, canalization,** and **niche-picking** remind us that development is best understood as a complex series of transactions between nature and nurture.

IMPORTANT TERMS AND CONCEPTS

phenotypes   (p. 67)
genotypes   (p. 67)
chromosomes   (p. 68)
homologous   (p. 69)
deoxyribonucleic acid (DNA)   (p. 69)
genes   (p. 70)
mitosis   (p. 70)

gametes   (p. 70)
meiosis   (p. 70)
crossing over   (p. 70)
zygote   (p. 70)
autosomes   (p. 71)
sex chromosomes   (p. 72)
homozygous   (p. 72)

heterozygous   (p. 72)
dominant   (p. 72)
recessive   (p. 72)
co-dominance   (p. 74)
mutation   (p. 75)
X-linked inheritance   (p. 75)
pleiotropism   (p. 76)

Mother & Child, by Diego Rivera.
Oakland Museum of Art.

4
Infancy

The Organized Newborn
Motor Development in Infancy
Perceptual Development in Infancy
Early Deprivation and Enrichment: Is Infancy a Critical Period of Development?

Infancy refers to the period of development that begins at birth and ends at about 18 months to 2 years of age with early language use. Though it comprises only 2 percent of the life span, it is one of the most remarkable and busiest times of development. The newborn baby enters the world with a surprisingly sophisticated set of perceptual and motor abilities, a repertoire of behaviors for interacting with people, and a capacity to learn that is put to use immediately after birth. By the end of infancy, the small child is a sociable, self-assertive, purposeful being who walks on her own, has developed refined manual skills, and is prepared to acquire the most unique of human abilities — language.

Since the 1960s, investigators have been intensely interested in how such vast changes can take place in a period so brief in duration. An explosion of research now offers answers to such questions as: What capacities are present in the infant from the very beginning? Which must wait to mature with the passage of time? And which ones must be learned through constant interaction with the physical and social world?

Our view of the infant has changed drastically over the course of this century. At one time, the newborn baby was considered a passive, incompetent organism whose world was, in the words of turn-of-the-century psychologist William James, a "blooming, buzzing confusion." Recently developed methods and equipment enabling researchers to test the young baby's capacities have permitted a very different picture to emerge. It is now well-accepted that infants are, from the outset, skilled, competent beings who display the roots of many complex human abilities.

In this chapter, we explore the infant's remarkable capabilities — early reflexive behavior, learning mechanisms, motor skills, and perceptual functioning. Through-

117

out our discussion we will see how research on infant development adds to our practical understanding of environmental factors necessary to support the dramatic changes of these first two years of life.

THE ORGANIZED NEWBORN

Although excited new parents may be inclined to disagree, the newborn infant is a homely-looking creature. At birth, the average baby is 7½ pounds in weight and 20 inches long. Consistent with sex differences that prevail later on, male infants are slightly heavier and larger than females. Infants' body proportions, which are very different from those of older children and adults, contribute to their strange and unflattering appearance. Head and eyes are disproportionately large in comparison to the pot-bellied trunk and bow-legged lower portion of the body. In addition, the pressure of passing through the narrow birth canal usually causes the baby's head to be molded and misshapen, and the newborn's skin is generally red, wrinkled, and "parboiled" in appearance. At first glance, this odd-looking little newcomer appears vulnerable and helpless, and naive parents may assume that their infant can do nothing but eat and sleep. However, these casual impressions are wrong. The neonate's[1] active capabilities are evident in a set of innate reflexes that enable the baby to adapt to the environment; an organized sleeping-waking cycle; clearly communicable cries that summon the caregiver, and the capacity to learn, which babies exercise as soon as they emerge from the womb.

Early Reflexes

Reflexes are the newborn infant's most obvious organized patterns of behavior. Dozens of neonatal reflexes have been identified, including reactions of the head, mouth, hands, feet, and entire body. The major ones are described in Table 4.1. As you examine this table, you will see that the ability to react to stimulation with motor responses is a built-in property of the infant's nervous system (Touwen, 1984).

Some reflexes are thought to have survival value. For example, if we had to teach infants the complex reactions involved in sucking, the human species would be unlikely to survive for a single generation! Other reflexes probably had survival value at some time during our evolutionary history but no longer seem to serve an adaptive purpose (Kessen, 1967). For example, the Moro or "embracing" reflex is believed to represent the infant's primitive tendency to clasp and cling to its mother. If the baby happened to lose support, the Moro reflex would immediately cause the infant to embrace and, in cooperation with the grasp reflex, regain its hold on the mother's body (Prechtl, 1958). In fact, the grasp reflex is so strong during the first week of life that infants are able to use it to support their entire weight (Kessen, Haith, & Salapatek, 1970). Another purpose of neonatal reflexes is to protect the infant from unwanted stimulation. The optical blink reflex helps shield the baby from intense bright light, while the withdrawal reflex is a response to unpleasant tactile stimulation. Organized reflexive behavior also plays a role in the control of infant distress. As any new mother is aware who remembers to bring a pacifier on an outing with her young infant, sucking will inhibit the mass, uncoordinated motor activity of a fussy neonate almost immediately.

Most neonatal reflexes disappear during the first 6 months of life. Experts in infant development believe that this is due to a gradual increase in voluntary control as the cortex of the brain gains influence over behavior and suppresses subcortical reflexive responses (Touwen, 1984). However, opinions differ about the role that reflexes play

[1] The term *neonate* is used to refer to infants from birth through the first month of life.

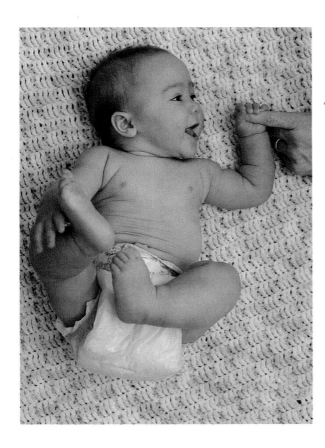

This baby displays two re-flexes at the same time — the palmar grasp and the tonic neck reflex. Both pave the way for voluntary reaching.

in the development of voluntary action. Do infant reflexes simply wane before voluntary behavior appears? Or can the beginnings of human complexity be found in these early reactions, and do the reflexes play a facilitating role in organizing voluntary motor abilities (Sheppard & Mysak, 1984)?

The fact that babies adapt their reflex actions to changing environmental conditions immediately after birth suggests that many reflexes form the basis for, and are gradually incorporated into, more complex, purposeful behaviors. An experiment by Sameroff (1968) on sucking behavior illustrates how newborn infants modify reflexive responses adaptively. Infant sucking can be analyzed into two basic, alternating components: suctioning and expression. In the usual sucking response, delivery of milk occurs after suctioning (not after expression), but in a special experimental condition, Sameroff arranged a nipple in such a way that delivery of milk actually followed expression (and not suctioning). When newborns were given milk each time they expressed, in just a few minutes the amount of suctioning began to decrease, and expression increased. Babies also adapted the level of their expression pressure, depending on how much was required to get the milk.

Infants suck in an organized fashion involving bursts of sucks separated by pauses, a pattern that is unique to the human species. In a study of neonatal feeding, Kaye and Wells (1980) concluded that this burst-pause pattern is an evolved behavior that helps parents and babies establish satisfying interaction with one another as soon as possible. The investigators observed that most mothers jiggle their babies during the pause, expressing the belief that this "wakes the baby up" and leads to a resumption of sucking. In response, neonates soon learn to anticipate and wait for their mother's jiggle before continuing to suck. As a result, mothers and babies build an early pattern of interaction that fits the turn-taking characteristics of the human dialogue. Neonates, even with their limited reflexive capacities, participate as active, cooperative partners.

Table 4.1. Major Neonatal Reflexes

REFLEX	FORM OF STIMULATION	RESPONSE	DEVELOPMENTAL COURSE	SIGNIFICANCE
Optical or acoustic blink	Bright light shined suddenly at eyes or hand clap 12 in. (30 cm) from head	Quick closure of eyelids	Permanent	Protection from strong stimulation. Absent in some infants with impaired visual or auditory systems
Tonic neck reflex	Turn baby's head to one side while infant lies awake on back	Infant assumes a fencing posture. Arm is extended on side toward which head is turned. Opposite arm is flexed with the hand resting near or in the head-chest region	Characteristic of first 12 weeks, but is not consistently present. Fades by 16th week	If constantly present, may indicate neurological abnormalities
Biceps reflex	Tap on tendon of the biceps muscle in the elbow area	Short contraction of the biceps muscle	Brisker in first 2 days of life than later	Absent or difficult to obtain in anoxic, anesthetized, or narcotics-exposed newborns and in cases of congenital muscular disease
Knee jerk	Tap on tendon just below the knee	Quick extension of the knee	More pronounced during first 2 days of life than later	Absent or difficult to obtain in anoxic, anesthetized, or narcotics-exposed newborns and in cases of congenital muscular disease
Palmar grasp reflex	Place finger into infant's hand and press against palmar surface	Spontaneous grasp of examiner's finger	Less intense during first 2 days of life than later. Disappears at 3 to 4 months of age	Preparatory movement for voluntary grasping. Absent or difficult to obtain in anoxic, anesthetized, or narcotics-exposed newborns and in cases of congenital muscular disease

Sources: Prechtl & Beintema, 1965; Knobloch & Pasamanick, 1974.

Additional research reveals similar complexity and variability for other reflexive behaviors. For example, different sequences of finger flexion appear in the palmar grasp reflex, depending on how the palm of the baby's hand is stimulated (Touwen, 1978). Also, some reflexes that appear rather purposeless may be related to later voluntary behavior in subtle ways. The tonic neck reflex is believed to pave the way for visually guided reaching because it channels the infant's attention toward the hand and, by gradual stages, to active approach and manipulation of objects (Knobloch & Pasamanick, 1974).

Some reflexes drop out in early infancy, and the motor functions involved are renewed later in development. An example is the walking reflex (see Table 4.1), which usually recedes by the end of the second month of life. However, in an experiment conducted by Zelazo, Zelazo, and Kolb (1972), babies given daily stimulation of the walking reflex from the second through the eighth week of life not only

Table 4.1. Major Neonatal Reflexes *(Continued)*

REFLEX	FORM OF STIMULATION	RESPONSE	DEVELOPMENTAL COURSE	SIGNIFICANCE
Babinski reflex	Stroke sole of foot from toes toward heel	Extension of big toe and spreading of smaller toes	Disappears between 8 months and 1 year	Absent in infants with defects of the lower spinal cord
Withdrawal reflex	Prick sole of foot with a pin	Withdrawal, with flexion of foot, knee, and hip	Constantly present during first 10 days. Weaker thereafter	Protection from unpleasant tactile stimulation. Absent in infants with defects of the lower spinal cord. Weakened by breech birth and sciatic nerve damage
Rooting reflex	Tickle skin at one corner of the mouth	Head turns toward source of stimulation. Infant tries to suck the stimulating finger	Less vigorous during first 2 days. Easily elicited in infants 1 to 2 weeks old. Is transformed into a voluntary head-turning response by 3 weeks	Assists baby in finding the nipple. Absent or difficult to obtain in anoxic, anesthetized, or narcotics-exposed newborns
Sucking reflex	Place index finger 1 in. (3 cm) into mouth	Rhythic sucking of the finger	Less intense and regular during the first 3 to 4 days	Permits feeding. Absent or difficult to obtain in anoxic, anesthetized, or narcotics-exposed newborns
Moro reflex	With body supported horizontally by examiner, permit infant's head to drop slightly or produce a sudden loud sound against the surface supporting the infant	Infant arches back, extends legs, and throws arms outward, then brings them in toward the midline of the body, as if to grab on for support	Disappears by middle of the first year	If absent or weak, indicates serious central nervous system dysfunction
Walking reflex	Hold infant under arms, permit bare feet to touch a flat surface	Infant lifts one foot after another in walking response	Usually disappears by 8 weeks. Retained longer in babies who are lighter in weight or who are given opportunities to exercise the reflex	May be absent in infants born by breech presentation or in anoxic, anesthetized, or narcotics-exposed newborns

retained the reflex, but showed a strong increase in stepping movement (see Figure 4.1). In contrast, walking motions gradually became sluggish and poorly executed among control groups receiving either daily passive exercise (movement of their arms and legs in a pumping motion while they lay on their backs) or no exercise at all. Also, babies who received reflexive practice walked on their own over 1 month earlier than infants in the two control conditions.

Exactly how does neonatal stimulation contribute to earlier emergence of independent walking? There are different answers to this question. Zelazo (1983) concluded that exercising the walking reflex facilitates the emergence of voluntary cortical control over the behavior at the end of the first year. However, research by Thelen suggests a much more direct explanation. She showed that babies who gained the most weight during the first month of life took the fewest reflexive steps at 4 weeks of age. In addition, neonatal stepping movements increased when babies' legs

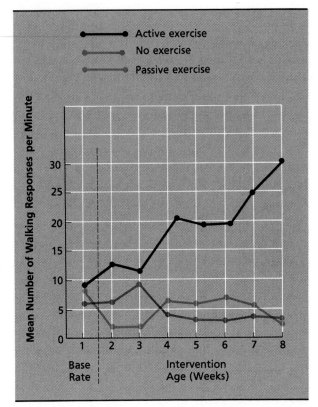

Figure 4.1. Mean number of walking responses for the experimental and control groups during the first 8 weeks of life in the Zelazo, Zelazo, and Kolb (1972) study. *(From P. R. Zelazo, N. A. Zelazo, & S. Kolb, 1972, "'Walking' in the Newborn," Science, 176, 314–315. Copyright 1972 by the AAAS Reprinted by permission.)*

were submerged under water (Thelen, Fisher, & Ridley-Johnson 1984). Thelen proposed that the walking reflex drops out because early infant weight gain is not matched by a comparable gain in muscle strength that permits babies to lift their increasingly heavy legs. Reflexive walking movements simply lie dormant until improved muscle strength allows them to be displayed again at the end of the first year. But the baby given an opportunity to exercise the walking reflex builds leg strength early, in much the same way that exercise leads an athlete to gain in muscle power. Such babies are strong enough to retain the reflexive stepping movements over the first year, and their greater leg strength also permits them to stand and walk at an earlier age (Thelen, 1983). Regardless of which position is correct, the findings of both Zelazo and Thelen reveal that although reflexive stepping subsides in many infants for a period of time, the mechanism responsible for it is eventually used by the brain at a later age.

Aside from their adaptive value, neonatal reflexes provide a window through which the pediatrician can assess the intactness of the infant's neurological system. In babies who are brain damaged, reflexes may be weak or absent, or in some cases they may be exaggerated and overly stereotyped (Touwen, 1984). Brain damage may also be indicated when a number of reflexes persist past the point in development when they normally disappear.

Newborn States

Newborn babies spend their days in various gradations of sleep and wakefulness. Observing a sample of healthy newborns, Wolff (1966) described seven different neonatal states along a continuum from lesser to greater arousal, as follows:

1. *Regular sleep.* The infant is at full rest and shows little or no diffuse motor activity. The eyelids are closed, no spontaneous eye movements occur, and the facial muscles are in repose. The rate and depth of respiration are even and regular.

2. *Periodic sleep.* This state is intermediate between regular and irregular sleep. The infant shows slightly more motor activity than in regular sleep. Respiratory movements are periodic; bursts of rapid, shallow breathing alternate with bursts of deep, slow respiration.

3. *Irregular sleep.* Motor activity is greater than in periodic sleep and varies from gentle limb movements to occasional stirring. Facial grimaces and mouthing occur, and occasional rapid eye movements can be observed through the eyelids. The rate and depth of respiration are irregular, and breathing occurs at a somewhat faster pace than it does in regular sleep.

4. *Drowsiness.* In this state, the infant is either falling asleep or waking up. The baby is less active than in periodic or irregular sleep, but more active than in regular sleep. Eyes open and close intermittently. When open, they have a glazed appearance and are poorly focused. If the infant is waking up, spurts of gross motor activity occur. Respiration is usually even but somewhat quicker than during regular sleep.

5. *Alert inactivity.* The infant is relatively inactive, with eyes open, attentive, and focused. Respiration is constant in frequency and depth.

6. *Waking activity.* The infant shows frequent bursts of diffuse motor activity. The face may be relaxed, or tense and wrinkled as if the infant is about to cry, and respiration is very irregular.

7. *Crying.* Crying is accompanied by diffuse, vigorous motor activity.

Using these state classifications or very similar ones, researchers have recorded the amount of time young infants spend at different levels of arousal. In the first month after birth, infants sleep most of the time — on the average, about 16 to 17 hours per day — with frequent, alternating periods of sleep and wakefulness evenly distributed across the day and night (Berg & Berg, 1987).

Much to the relief of their fatigued parents, babies in industrialized societies show more consolidated patterns of sleeping and waking by 5 to 6 weeks of age. By this time, fewer periods of longer duration occur, and they have also become diurnally organized, with wakeful states occurring during the day and sleep states at night (Berg & Berg, 1987). By 4 months of age, the average American baby's nightly sleep period resembles that of the parents, in that it is 8 hours long.

Western investigators take these early changes in the organization and predictability of the sleep-wakefulness cycle as an important indicator of brain maturation. However, cross-cultural research suggests that this is true only when parents push young infants to the limits of their neurological capacities. In our culture, night waking is inconvenient, and parents try to get their babies to sleep through the night by offering an evening feeding before putting them down in a separate, quiet room. In contrast, infants in rural Kenya are in constant physical contact with their mothers. During the day they are carried about, and at night they lie in the mother's bed, sleeping and waking to nurse at will. For these babies, the average sleep period remains constant, at about 3 hours, from 1 to 8 months of age. Only at the end of the first year do they move in the direction of an adultlike sleep-waking schedule (Super & Harkness, 1982).

Although the timing and duration of states become more patterned and regular for all babies, striking individual differences in these daily rhythms do exist. Variations among infants in time spent asleep and awake are likely to affect Western parents' attitudes and caregiving in significant ways. Infants who sleep for long periods at an early age increase the amount of rest their parents receive and the energy they have available for sensitive, responsive care. Babies who cry a great deal require that parents try harder to soothe them. If these efforts are not successful, parents' feelings of competence and attitudes toward their infants may be adversely affected. Babies who spend a great deal of time in an attentive, focused state are likely to receive more social stimulation from their parents. Furthermore, since the alert, focused state provides infants with greater opportunities to explore the environment, babies who favor it may be advantaged in cognitive development.

Besides their concern with overall changes in infant sleep-waking patterns, child development specialists are interested in the organization of behavior *within* particular states because such knowledge contributes to our understanding of both normal and pathological development. In the sections below, we turn to a more detailed consideration of the two most extreme infant states: sleeping and crying.

Sleep. Sleep is made up of at least two distinct states that correspond to Wolff's (1966) classification, presented above, of regular and irregular sleep. Most investigators refer to these two basic sleep states as **REM sleep** and **NREM sleep** because a distinguishing feature of irregular sleep is the occurrence of rapid eye movements (REM), whereas in regular sleep they are absent. The two states also differ in physiological organization, as revealed by electroencephalograpic (EEG) brain wave recordings, polygraph records of heart rate and respiration, and direct observation of motor activity.

We are used to thinking of sleep as a time of rest and reversal of fatigue. However, the characteristics of REM sleep indicate that this commonly accepted explanation of why we sleep is far from complete, especially where the young infant is concerned. During REM sleep, the brain and portions of the body are intensely active. Electrical brain wave activity, as measured by the EEG, is remarkably similar to that of the waking state, and heart rate, blood pressure, and respiration are uneven and slightly accelerated. In addition to the darting of the eyes beneath the lids, slight but continuous body movements occur. Sleeping neonates grimace, whimper, smile, and engage in twitches of the face and extremities, behaviors suggesting that this state signifies something other than restful repose! In contrast, NREM sleep is almost devoid of muscular activity. Except for an occasional twitch, the infant is passive and motionless, and heart rate, respiratory rhythms, and EEG activity are slow and regular (Dittrichova et al., 1982).

Like older children and adults, neonates demonstrate an alternating REM-NREM sleep cycle, but its organization changes substantially with age. As shown in Figure 4.2, infants spend far more time in REM sleep than do adults. REM comprises 20 percent of the average adult's sleep, but it consumes 50 percent of the newborn baby's sleep time. In fact, because neonates spend so much of their day asleep, the REM state accounts for about a third of their entire existence! Between the newborn period and young adulthood, REM sleep diminishes 80 percent, from a total of 8 hours to 1 hour and 40 minutes. In comparison, NREM sleep changes very little. Between infancy and adulthood, it declines only 25 percent, from 8 to 6 hours. These statistics indicate that the great sleep requirement of infancy is largely a need for REM sleep (Roffwarg, Muzio, & Dement, 1966).

Another difference between the sleep of infants and adults concerns the sequence of REM and NREM cycles. Adults do not enter REM sleep until 70 to 100 minutes after sleep onset, but newborn infants routinely begin sleep with REM activity. The transition to NREM sleep onset occurs around the middle of the first year (Berg & Berg, 1987), suggesting that by this time, infants have moved from the primitive sleep pattern of the young baby to a more mature sleep organization.

According to **autostimulation theory,** REM sleep offers intense stimulation to the central nervous system, turned on from within the organism. In children and adults, the REM state is associated with dreaming. Babies probably do not dream, at least not in the same way we do. However, young infants are believed to have a special need for the stimulation of REM sleep because they spend relatively little time in an alert, conscious state. REM sleep seems to be a way in which the immature organism compensates for unavailable activity. Sleep researchers believe that such stimulation is vitally important for the growth of the central nervous system and that, without it, the structures of the brain may be impaired (Roffwarg, Muzio, & Dement,

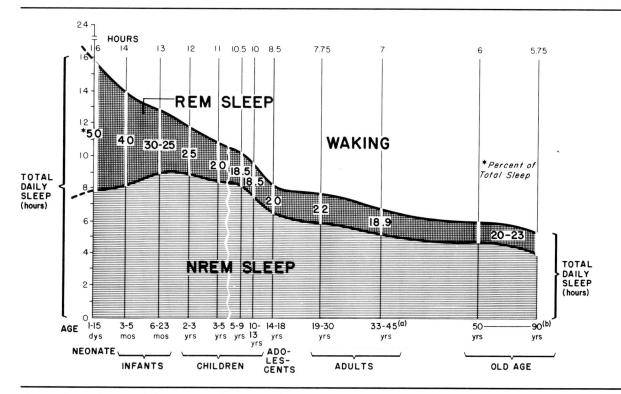

Figure 4.2. Developmental changes in total amount and percentage of REM sleep, NREM sleep, and the waking state from birth to old age. *(From H. P. Roffwarg, J. N. Muzio, & W. C. Dement, "Ontogenetic Development of the Human Sleep-* *Dream Cycle," Science, 152, 608. Copyright 1966 by the AAAS. Revised from original publication by the authors in 1969 on the basis of additional data.)*

1966). The autostimulation function of REM sleep fits with research indicating that when newborn babies are encouraged to spend more time awake, their REM sleep is reduced in quantity, while their NREM sleep remains unchanged (Anders & Roffwarg, 1973; Boismier, 1977). In preterm infants, whose capacity to take advantage of external stimulation is especially limited, the percentage of sleep devoted to the REM state is greater than in full-term newborns, and it increases with extent of prematurity (Parmelee et al., 1967).

Because the normal sleep behavior of the neonate is organized and patterned, sleep studies are useful in the newborn period for identifying central nervous system dysfunction. Disturbances in REM-NREM cycling are common among infants who are brain damaged or premature or who have experienced prenatal or perinatal complications (Dreyfus-Brisac, 1970; Prechtl, Theorell, & Blair, 1973; Theorell, Prechtl, & Vos, 1974).

Crying. Crying is the first way that infants communicate with their surrounding world. At delivery, a lusty cry signals the doctor that the baby has begun to breathe. Soon after, it informs caregivers of the infant's need for food, comfort, and stimulation. Careful analyses reveal that the cry of the newborn infant is a complex expressive behavior. Wolff (1969) identified four different patterns of crying in neonates:

1. *the basic cry*, which is usually associated with hunger but has a fundamental rhythmic pattern into which all infant cries eventually resolve;
2. *the anger cry*;
3. *the pain cry*; and
4. *the attention cry*, which develops later than the other types, at about the third week after birth.

Today, investigators recognize that the acoustics of these cries vary along a continuum that reflects that baby's level of distress. There is not a perfect correspondence between the dynamics of the cry and the baby's need state. However, the intensity of the cry helps guide the caregiver toward one of the above hypotheses about the cry's cause (Gustafson & Harris, 1990).

Events that cause newborn infants to cry are largely physical and physiological. Hunger is, of course, a common cause, but young infants may also cry in response to temperature change, to being undressed, or when startled by loud, sudden sounds. An infant's state is an important factor in influencing whether a baby will cry in response to visual or auditory stimuli. Infants who, when alert and inactive, regard their mother's face, a colorful object, or the sound of a toy horn with interest and pleasure may react to the same events with a sudden burst of tears during a state of mild discomfort and diffuse activity (Tennes et al., 1972; Wolff, 1969). Perhaps this reaction is the result of momentary overstimulation, since it lessens with age as infants become better able to tolerate more sensory input and turn away when there is too much (Sroufe, 1979).

Newborn crying can also be induced by the sound of another crying baby. Infants less than a day old cry when exposed to a recording of another infant's cry, a response that may indicate the existence of an inborn distress reaction to the experience of distress in others. Interestingly, a tape recording of the infant's own cry has the opposite effect. It causes a crying baby to stop crying, and it does not induce crying in a calm infant. Newborns seem able to make the fine distinction between their own cry and that of another baby, although how they do so is not yet understood (Martin & Clark, 1982).

Adult Responsiveness to Infant Cries. A crying baby stimulates strong feelings in just about anyone within earshot. In several studies, heart rate and skin conductance measures have been taken while adults listened to sound recordings of infant cries. The crying response induced intense physiological arousal in both mothers and fathers (Boukydis & Burgess, 1982; Frodi et al., 1978), as well as in adults of both sexes who have no children (Freudenberg, Driscoll, & Stern, 1978; Murray, 1985). The powerful effect of the infant's cry is probably biologically programmed in all human beings to make sure that babies receive the necessary care and protection to survive.

Parents quickly become aware of differences in infant cries. Although they are not always correct in interpreting the meaning of the cry, experience improves their accuracy (Green, Jones, & Gustafson, 1987). Parents are somewhat better at distinguishing the cries of their own baby than those of a strange infant (Wiesenfeld, Malatesta, & DeLoache, 1981). In addition, first-time parents respond to their infants' cries with somewhat more arousal than do parents who already have one or more children. Mothers and fathers of a first baby probably have a greater investment in learning to interpret infant cries than do seasoned parents of several children (Boukydis & Burgess, 1982).

Observing maternal responses to crying infants less than 6 months of age, Wolff (1969) found that mothers do not react to the hunger, anger, and attention cries in the same way. For example, in response to the basic hunger cry, mothers may or may not come immediately, and when they do, some try feeding, while others change the infant's diaper first. The anger cry leads mothers to stop and check on the baby, but they do not seem alarmed or unduly concerned, and some react with tolerant amusement at this early expression of indignation in the tiny new being.

Only the pain cry produces an immediate and dramatic response. Mothers rush to the baby, anxious and worried (Wolff, 1969). An intense reaction to the pain cry even occurs in adults who are not parents of the crying infant. Among the Zhun/twasi hunting and gathering people of Africa, an observed instance of the pain cry caused everyone in the village to orient in the direction of the sound, and a dozen concerned adults jumped up and approached the crying child. In contrast, hunger cries of Zhun/twasi infants produce no reaction in anyone but the mother or substitute caregiver (Konner, 1972). In a study in which parents were played recordings of both anger and pain cries, they rated the pain cry as more unpleasant and as causing more tension. It also produced greater physiological arousal, as measured by skin conductance and heart rate responses (Wiesenfeld, Malaesta, & DeLoache, 1981). By eliciting strong emotion and a fixed reaction in all adults, the pain cry is an adaptive mechanism that ensures an infant in danger will quickly get help.

Soothing a Crying Infant. Fortunately, there are ways to soothe a crying baby. Observing techniques that mothers used to calm their infants at the beginning and end of the first year, Bell and Ainsworth (1972) found that picking up the baby and providing close physical contact constitute the most frequent maternal intervention, and also the most successful. As shown in Figure 4.3, it soothed crying infants in over 80 percent of the instances in which it was observed. More specifically, lifting the baby to the shoulder, a method that involves at least three dimensions of stimulation —physical contact, motion, and the upright posture—is the technique that works the best. It not only encourages infants to stop crying, but also causes them to become quietly alert and visually attentive to the environment (Reisman, 1987). Not surprisingly, Figure 4.3 also indicates that feeding is another highly successful soothing technique. In fact, any other method is bound to be just a temporary stop-gap if the baby is hungry. Additional soothing methods that mothers use are offering their infants pacifiers or toys and talking to them. Although these are less successful than picking the baby up, they still work fairly well. Rhythmic sounds (the ticking of a clock, music, or singing), rocking, and swaddling (wrapping babies so their limbs are restricted) are also effective (Lester, 1985).

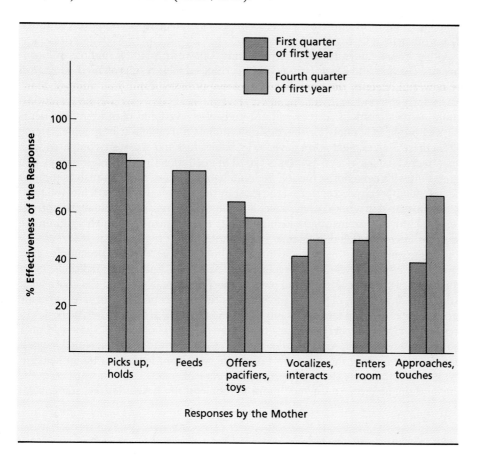

Figure 4.3. Effectiveness of various maternal responses to crying in the first and fourth quarters of the first year in the Bell and Ainsworth (1972) study. *(From S. M. Bell & M. D. S. Ainsworth, 1972, "Infant Crying and Maternal Responsiveness."* Child Development, 43, *1182. © The Society for Research in Child Development, Inc.)*

The type of discomfort and the infant's age are two factors that influence the effectiveness of different soothing techniques. In a recent study, Campos (1989) compared the ability of pacifiers and swaddling to reduce the pain cries of young babies. Pacifiers soothed more rapidly, but crying often reappeared when the pacifier was removed. In contrast, swaddling was less immediately successful, but its effect lasted longer. When babies were unwrapped after quieting down, they remained placid and content. However, as Figure 4.3 suggests, with increasing age, infants gradually become more receptive to soothing techniques that do not involve such extensive tactile stimulation, such as the sight of the mother or the reassuring sound of her voice.

How quickly and how often should a mother respond to her infant's cries? Will reacting promptly and consistently strengthen crying behavior and produce a demanding, miniature tyrant? Or will it give infants a sense of confidence that their needs will be met and, over time, reduce their tendency to fuss and complain? Available answers to this question are controversial and conflicting. In a widely publicized study, Bell and Ainsworth (1972) concluded that responding consistently to a young baby's cries will not lead to dependency and spoiling. They found that mothers who delayed or failed to respond had babies who engaged in more frequent and persistent crying in the latter part of the first year. In addition, by 1 year of age, these infants were less mature in their communicative behaviors. They had developed fewer noncrying modes of expressing their needs and desires, such as facial expressions, gestures, and vocalizations. Bell and Ainsworth used *ethological theory* to interpret their findings. According to this perspective, crying is viewed as the earliest possible proximity-promoting, signaling behavior in infants. Maternal responsiveness is adaptive in that it ensures the infant's basic needs will be met and provides protection from danger. At the same time, it brings baby and mother into close proximity where the mother can be sensitively responsive to a wide range of infant behaviors and, in the process, can encourage her infant to communicate through means other than crying.

Other investigators disagree with Bell and Ainsworth's (1972) findings and conclusions. Gewirtz and Boyd (1977a, 1977b) criticized their results on methodological grounds and, instead, adhered to a *behaviorist* position. From this point of view, consistently responding to a crying infant rewards the crying response and results in a whiny, demanding child. A cross-cultural study of several child-rearing environments in Israel provides support for this position. Infants of Bedouin tribespeople, among whom there is an explicit norm never to let babies fuss and cry, were compared with home-reared babies as well as infants raised in institutional and kibbutz[2] settings. In agreement with behaviorist theory, Bedouin babies (whose mothers rush to them at the first whimper) fussed and cried the most throughout the first year of life, followed by infants reared in homes, where there is greater opportunity to respond promptly to a crying baby than in institutional and kibbutz environments in which children are cared for in groups (Landau, 1982).

These contrasting theories and findings indicate that there is no simple, easy formula for how parents should respond to their infants' cries. The conditions under which babies cry are complex, and parents must make reasoned choices about what to do based on a variety of factors, including culturally accepted practices, the specific circumstances evoking the cry, its intensity, and the general context in which the cry occurs — for example, in the privacy of the parent's own home, while having dinner at a restaurant, or while visiting friends or relatives. Certainly no one would suggest that a mother prolong the discomfort of a hungry baby or ignore her infant's urgent cry of pain. However, the communicative intent of infant cries changes over the course of the first year to include more psychologically based desires, such as de-

---

[2] A kibbutz is an Israeli agricultural settlement in which children are reared together in children's houses, freeing both parents for full participation in the economic life of the community.

mands for attention and expressions of impatience and frustration. As infants get older and cry less often for purely physical reasons, both ethological and behaviorist theory would probably agree that one way parents can lessen their babies' need to cry is to encourage them to choose other more mature ways of communicating their desires.

The fact that newborn babies produce typical cries has led investigators to search for abnormal patterns of infant crying. Spectrographic analyses indicate that the pitch of the baby's cry is a fundamental indicator of central nervous system distress. The cries of brain-damaged infants and those who have experienced prenatal and perinatal complications are especially shrill and piercing (Lester, 1987; Zeskind & Lester, 1978, 1981). The nature of the high-risk infant's cry has implications for the caregiver-infant relationship. The higher the pitch of an infant's cry, the more urgent and distressing parents perceive it to be (Zeskind & Marshall, 1988). In some cases, the cry may be so unpleasant that it does not induce the care necessary to facilitate recovery of a sick baby. In infant child abuse cases, a high-pitched, grating cry is sometimes mentioned as a causal factor (Boukydis, 1985; Frodi, 1985).

Neonatal Behavioral Assessment

A variety of instruments are available for assessing the overall behavioral status of the infant during the newborn period. The most widely used is Brazelton's (1984) **Neonatal Behavioral Assessment Scale (NBAS).** It provides a general overview of the newborn infant's behavioral repertoire, including responsiveness to social and physical stimuli, state changes, autonomic reactivity, reflexes, and other motor capacities. Some examples of NBAS items are shown in Table 4.2.

Neonatal assessment is useful for a variety of reasons. When scores are combined with information from a physical examination, they enable all but a very few cases of severe neurological impairment to be diagnosed in the first few weeks of life (Amiel-Tison, 1985). The NBAS and other similar instruments have also helped investigators describe the effects of prenatal and perinatal risk factors on infant behavior (Brazelton, Nugent, & Lester, 1987; Eldredge & Salamy, 1988). In fact, a special adaptation of the NBAS has been developed for use with preterm infants (Als et al., 1980).

Neonatal assessment can also help determine how infant behavior contributes to later development. Research indicates that babies scoring high on the NBAS are slightly advantaged in terms of visual responsiveness and mental test performance during the first year of life (Moss et al., 1988; Vaughn et al., 1980). Since neonatal behavior is thought to affect the way parents respond to their infants, and parental responsiveness, in turn, contributes to later behavior, additional research using the NBAS may help clarify the course of early development. In fact, as indicated by Box 4.1, the NBAS has been used to study relationships between neonatal behavior and early caregiving practices in different cultures. These findings have led to a better understanding of the adaptive value of infant care routines in different parts of the world.

Nevertheless, investigators caution against trying to predict future development from a single NBAS score, since many babies change considerably in how well they respond over the first few weeks of life (Asch et al., 1986; Francis, Self, & Horowitz, 1987). Because some neonates require time and caregiver assistance to recover from the trauma of birth, a profile of scores over the first week or two seems to be a better way to assess each baby's resilience and adaptability. In fact, research indicates that such NBAS "recovery curves" predict intellectual functioning with modest success well into the preschool years (Brazelton, Nugent, & Lester, 1987).

Although the NBAS has largely been employed for research, it has also been used practically. In some hospitals, portions of the scale are given in the presence of parents to teach them about newborn capabilities and to sensitize them to their baby's individual characteristics. These programs have been found to enhance early parent-

Table 4.2. Sample Items from Brazelton's Neonatal Behavioral Assessment Scale (NBAS)

SAMPLE ITEM	DESCRIPTION
Reflexes	See Table 4.1 for examples.
Motor capacities	
Pull to sit	The examiner gently pulls the baby to a sitting position. Ability of the infant to support the head is assessed.
Defensive movements	A small cloth is held lightly over the infant's eyes. The baby's effort to work free of the cloth is assessed.
Responsiveness to stimuli	
Light	A flashlight is shined briefly but repeatedly in the infant's eyes. The baby's capacity to decrease responsiveness to a disturbing stimulus is assessed.
Animate auditory	The examiner speaks softly into one of the baby's ears, with face out of the baby's line of vision. The baby's ability to alert and turn to the sound is assessed.
Animate visual	A brightly colored ball is moved horizontally and then vertically before the baby's eyes. The infant's ability to track the ball is assessed.
Alertness	The examiner rates the overall alertness of the baby during the examination.
State changes	
Irritability	The number of times during the exam that the infant fusses and the kind of stimuli that lead to irritability are assessed.
Cuddliness	The infant's willingness to relax and mold to the examiner's body when held in an alert state is assessed.
Consolability	The number of maneuvers the examiner must use to bring the baby from an upset to a quiet state is assessed, from simply moving into the infant's line of vision to dressing, holding, rocking, and offering a pacifier at the same time.
Autonomic reactivity	
Tremulousness	Tremors of the infant's body are rated. If very severe, tremulousness is an indication of central nervous system irritation.
Lability of skin color	Changes in skin color during the entire examination are noted. A normal newborn demonstrates mild color changes after being undressed, disturbed, or upset, but the original color returns quickly. Difficult to score in nonwhite babies.

Source: Brazelton, 1984.

infant interaction in many types of participants—mothers and fathers, adolescents and adults, lower- and middle-class parents, and full-term and preterm newborns (Brazelton, Nugent, & Lester, 1987; Worobey, 1985). Although lasting effects on development have not been demonstrated, NBAS-based interventions are clearly useful in helping the parent-infant relationship get off to a good start.

Learning in Infancy

Learning refers to changes in behavior over time as the result of experience. In studying infant learning, investigators have sought answers to the following questions: To what extent are newborn babies capable of profiting from experience? Are some kinds of experiences more effective in modifying infant behavior than others? Most research aimed at answering these questions has involved two basic learning paradigms: classical and operant conditioning. However, the ability of infants to profit from experience is not limited to conditioning. As we will see shortly, very young infants also learn through their remarkable capacity to imitate and remember events in the surrounding world.

Neonatal Behavior and Infant Rearing in Cultural Context

Box 4.1

Do newborn babies differ in behavioral capacities from one culture to another, and if so, do these variations have some adaptive value? How do culturally specific caregiving practices protect the survival and development of neonates in harsh physical environments? A wealth of cross-cultural research with the NBAS is providing answers to these questions.

Observations of newborns in a variety of Oriental and Indian cultures indicate that they are less irritable and more easily soothed than Caucasian-American infants (Chisholm, 1989; Freedman & Freedman, 1969; Murett-Wagstaff & Moore, 1989; Woodson & da Costa, 1989). For example, neonatal assessments of Zinacanteco Indian babies of Southern Mexico reveal them to be quieter and less demanding than Caucasian infants. Since these characteristics are well suited to the culture's emphasis on restrained, subdued behavior, they are promoted by caregivers immediately after birth. Through swaddling, close physical contact, and nursing the infant at the earliest signs of restlessness, the Indian mothers encourage their babies' placid dispositions (Brazelton, Robey, & Collier, 1969).

The research described above indicates that cultural practices can sustain behavioral continuity from early infancy onward. Sometimes, however, infant-rearing customs have the opposite effect: they change neonatal behavior patterns that do not have cultural meaning or that threaten the baby's survival and development. In one study, Zambian babies who were undernourished and dehydrated at birth scored low in responsiveness to stimulation on the first day of life. But by the tenth day, these babies obtained high scores on alertness, social interest, and soothability. Their rapid recovery was attributed to the willingness of Zambian mothers to provide their infants with vigorous stimulation, including active handling and a rich variety of visual, auditory, and tactile experiences as the result of being carried about on the mother's hip for most of the day. These maternal practices also fit with Zambian cultural expectations for early physical and social development (Brazelton, Koslowski, & Tronick, 1976). Among the Efe hunters and gatherers of Zaire, NBAS assessments show newborn babies to be unusually fussy and difficult to console

Similar to women in the Zambian culture, Senegalese mothers carry their babies about all day, providing close physical contact and a rich variety of stimulation.

(Winn, Tronick, & Morelli, 1989). A caregiving system in which infants are passed back and forth from one adult to another, as often as 3 to 8 times an hour, may be especially suited to calming these babies. Moreover, the responsibility for infant soothing is shared by members of the group, thereby reducing the burden of care placed on the baby's mother (Brazelton, 1989).

Cross-cultural research with the NBAS reveals that early rearing practices either encourage or discourage distinct neonatal behavior patterns, depending on their adaptiveness. As long as threats to early development are not extreme, cultures generate strategies of infant caregiving that protect the survival and growth of their youngest members.

Classical Conditioning. Classical conditioning involves learning a new association between a neutral stimulus and a stimulus that reliably elicits a reflexive response. In other words, control of the response is transferred to a new stimulus that did not evoke it in the first place. You may already be familiar with the famous experiment of the Russian psychologist Ivan Pavlov, who first identified the components of the classical conditioning paradigm. At the beginning of Pavlov's experiment, the taste of food powder automatically caused a dog to salivate, but a neutral stimulus, the sound of a bell, did not. After several repeated pairings of the bell with the food powder, Pavlov's dog learned to salivate at the sound of the bell alone.

The key steps in classical conditioning are as follows:

1. Before learning takes place, an **unconditional stimulus (UCS)** must reliably elicit a reflexive, or **unconditioned response (UCR),** while a neutral, or **conditioned stimulus (CS)** does not.

$$UCS \longrightarrow UCR$$
Food powder   Salivation

CS   (does not elicit salivation)
Bell

2. To produce learning, the CS and UCS are presented in close temporal sequence. Optimally, the CS is presented just before the UCS.

CS
Bell
$$UCS \longrightarrow UCR$$
Food powder   Salivation

3. To find out whether learning occurred, the CS presented by itself must produce the reflexive response, which, if it occurs, is now called a **conditioned response (CR).**

$$CS \longrightarrow CR$$
Bell   Salivation

Of course, if the CS is presented by itself enough times without further presentations of the UCS, the CR will eventually cease to occur. This is referred to as **extinction**. The occurrence of responses to the CS during the extinction phase of a classical conditioning experiment is the main indicator that learning has taken place.

Many attempts to classically condition newborn infants have been unsuccessful, and only recently has it become clear why this is the case. To be easily learned, a new association must be of biological significance to the neonate. Not surprisingly, most CRs occur in the feeding context; their adaptive value is to increase the efficiency of food-getting behavior. In one study that obtained classical conditioning at 2 hours after birth, tactile stimulation was chosen as the CS because it is a natural means of mother-infant communication that may help young babies predict when nursing is about to occur. Experimental group infants were offered a sugar water solution as the UCS, with resultant sucking as the UCR. Just before delivery of the sugar water, the babies' foreheads were stroked (CS). When the CS was presented alone during extinction, the experimental group showed a much higher incidence of sucking (CR) than did control group babies (Blass, Ganchrow, & Steiner, 1984). In fact, infants are so sensitive to stimulus cues in the feeding situation that even the passage of time between meals can serve as an effective CS. Most newborns are fed about every 3 to 4 hours. As the end of this interval approaches (CS), mouthing, sucking, and salivation (CR) increase in frequency and intensity (Rovee-Collier, 1987; Rovee-Collier & Lipsitt, 1982).

In contrast to feeding-associated responses, defensive reactions are very difficult to condition in young babies. Until the latter part of the first year, infants do not have the motor abilities to escape or avoid unpleasant events. Because they depend on their parents for this kind of protection, they do not yet have a biological need to form these associations. But between 8 and 12 months of age, the conditioning of fear and avoidance is easily accomplished, as the famous example of little Albert, conditioned by John Watson to withdraw and cry at the sight of a furry white rat, clearly indicates.[3]

[3] Return to Chapter 1, page 14, to review this classic investigation. To test your knowledge of the classical conditioning paradigm, identify the UCS, UCR, CS, and CR in Watson's study.

Another reason that many classical conditioning studies have not met with uniform success is that in the laboratory, investigators usually hold the baby's state constant, assuming that alert wakefulness is always best for conditioning. Recent research indicates that this is not true for all types of associations. For example, when the baby is highly aroused and crying, the sight of the mother or the sound of her footsteps (CS) predicts relief from discomfort. Under these state conditions, babies quickly learn to inhibit crying and to mouth and suck (CR) in anticipation of feeding. However, when the baby is quietly alert, the mother's approach does not have this meaning, and the same response rarely appears (Gekoski, Rovee-Collier, & Carulli-Rabinowitz, 1983).

In summary, efforts to classically condition young infants show that some CS-UCS combinations produce learning, while others do not. Because processes intrinsic to the infant play an important role in determining which associations are learned, it is a mistake to conclude from classical conditioning research that babies are merely passive reactors to environmental contingencies. At the very least, the adaptive significance of what is to be learned and the state and developmental maturity of the infant are major influences on the range of associations that infants will make.

Operant Conditioning. In **operant conditioning,** a spontaneously emitted behavior is followed by an outcome that changes the probability that the behavior will occur again. Outcomes that increase the occurrence of a behavior are called **reinforcers,** whereas those that decrease its occurrence are called **punishments.** In contrast to classical conditioning, in which the subject's behavior is controlled by a stimulus that precedes it, in operant conditioning, behavior is affected by the stimulus that follows it.

Operant conditioning of young infants has been demonstrated in a wide variety of studies. However, because the newborn lacks voluntary control over many behaviors, successful operant conditioning is limited to sucking and head-turning responses, with many types of stimuli serving as reinforcers. For example, very young infants vary their sucking patterns according to the sweetness of the fluid they receive. When water is delivered after a sugar solution, newborns display their apparent aversion to the water by dramatically reducing their rate of sucking (Lipsitt & Werner, 1981). Neonates also quickly learn to turn their heads to the side when this response is followed by a sugar water reinforcer (Siqueland & Lipsitt, 1966).

Stimulus variety and change are just as reinforcing as food for young infants. Researchers have created special laboratory environments in which the baby's rate of sucking on a nonnutritive nipple produces visual or auditory feedback. Newborns readily suck faster to control the appearance and brightness of a visual display, and they also increase their sucking when music, speech sounds, and human voices serve as reinforcers. In fact, even preterm infants can be conditioned in this way (Rovee-Collier, 1987). Because stimuli from such a wide variety of sensory modalities can modify infant behavior, the operant conditioning paradigm has become a powerful research tool for clarifying the baby's perceptual and memory capacities.

As infants get older, successful operant conditioning expands to include a wider range of behaviors and environmental events. In several studies, special mobiles have been hung over the cribs of 2-month-olds. By making small head movements on a pressure-sensitive pillow (Watson & Ramey, 1972) or kicking a foot connected to the mobile by means of a long silk cord (Rovee-Collier, 1984), babies can, through their own activity, make the mobile shake or turn. Infants who receive contingent visual stimulation from the mobile show a dramatic increase in response rate in comparison to controls who experience either noncontingent stimulation or a mobile that does not move at all.

Studies like these show that infants quickly develop active modes of controlling the environment and that they will repeat behaviors that lead to interesting outcomes. Since the operant conditioning label is generally taken to reflect the traditional behaviorist position of an infant passively responding to environmental contingencies, Sameroff and Cavanaugh (1979) prefer the term *action-consequence learning* to describe the *active* efforts of infants to explore and control their surrounding world. In fact, when infants' environments are so disorganized and unpredictable that stimulation is rarely contingent on their own behavior, serious developmental problems, ranging from retarded learning to apathy and depression, may result (Cicchetti & Aber, 1986; Seligman, 1975). In addition, as Box 4.2 reveals, disruptions in the infant's inherent capacity to engage in these active learning efforts may be related to a major cause of infant mortality: sudden infant death syndrome.

Habituation and Memory. Habituation refers to the gradual waning of response when subjects are exposed to repetitive stimulation. Provided that the repetitive stimulus is mild or only moderately intense, both physiological and behavioral responses of infants gradually decrease in strength, even though the initial presentation of the stimulus may have produced strong reactions, such as a marked startle, intense looking, and a change in heart rate. Once behavior has waned, presentation of a new stimulus causes the baby's response to **dishabituate,** or return to its original level. This habituation-dishabituation sequence indicates that the infant has stored some

---

◆ CONTEMPORARY ISSUES: SOCIAL POLICY ◆

T*he Mysterious Tragedy of Sudden Infant Death Syndrome* 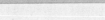 Box 4.2

In *sudden infant death syndrome (SIDS),* a baby stops breathing, usually during the night, and dies silently without apparent cause. SIDS is responsible for nearly 13 percent of America's infant mortality rate and results in more deaths among infants between 10 days and 1 year of age than any other factor (Colón & Colón, 1989). The tragedy is especially difficult for parents to bear because of the absence of definite answers as to why SIDS occurs. However, more information has recently come to light about the characteristics of SIDS victims, and promising hypotheses about the causes of SIDS are being followed up with new research.

Several studies indicate that babies who succumb to SIDS show biological vulnerabilities from the very beginning. Birth records and early pediatric examinations of victims reveal a higher incidence of prematurity and low birth weight, lower Apgar scores, respiratory abnormalities, flaccid muscle tone, and poor visual performance in terms of ability to focus on objects (Buck et al., 1989; Lipsitt, Sturner, & Burke, 1979; Shannon et al., 1987). Abnormal fluctuations in heart rate and respiratory activity as well as disturbances of sleeping and waking states throughout the night are also thought to be involved (Gordon et al., 1984; Harper et al., 1981). At the time of death, many SIDS babies are reported to have a mild respiratory infection, a circumstance that seems to heighten the chances of respiratory failure in the already vulnerable baby (Morris, 1989).

Lewis Lipsitt (1982) believes that the biological fragility of SIDS infants makes it difficult for them to benefit from experience in ways that prepare them to respond defensively when their survival is threatened—for example, when respiration is suddenly interrupted.

According to Lipsitt, SIDS babies may suffer from a basic learning disability in the first few months of life. In the period between 2 and 4 months of age, when the incidence of SIDS reaches its peak, unconditioned reflexes diminish and are supplanted by voluntary learned responses. Lipsitt believes that respiratory inadequacy, general lethargy, and visual inattentiveness at birth may lead SIDS infants to engage the environment less well and to experience fewer opportunities for learning than normal babies. When a respiratory threat occurs, appropriate voluntary behaviors may not have been learned in time to supplant the defensive reflex that wanes between 2 and 4 months of age, leading to oxygen deprivation and death. Lipsitt's hypothesis about the origins of SIDS suggests that besides monitoring physiological signs, intervention programs may need to provide infants with special help in the acquisition of life-saving defensive responses.

In addition, cross-national differences in SIDS rates are providing new insights into caregiving customs that may increase or reduce the risk in susceptible babies. Although investigators do not yet know why, widespread adoption of the practice of placing infants in a prone sleeping position (on their stomachs) in Holland during the 1970s coincided with a rise in SIDS (de Jonge et al., 1989). In Hong Kong, where the normal caregiving routine is to lay babies on their backs, the incidence of SIDS is especially low. Hong Kong's overcrowded living conditions may also confer an advantage, by providing extra stimulation to poorly developing infants and the watchful eye of several extended family members residing in the same household (Lee et al., 1989).

information about the original stimulus in memory and recognizes that the new one is different from the old.

Let's take an example to explore this important paradigm for studying infant memory more closely. In one investigation, Fagan and Singer (1979) used the habituation-dishabituation sequence to find out whether 5- to 6-month-old infants could discriminate between two similar photographs, one of a baby's face and another of a bald-headed man. As shown in Figure 4.4, during phase 1 of the study (habituation phase), infants were presented with a baby picture and allowed to look at it for a short period of time. The researchers measured visual fixation to be sure the infants had studied the photo. In phase 2 (dishabituation phase), the infants were shown the same baby picture, but now it was presented simultaneously with a picture of a bald-headed man. During this part of the procedure, the investigators kept careful track of which photo the infants looked at most. Because subjects paid more attention, or dishabituated, to the bald-headed man than to the baby, the researchers concluded that infants both remembered the baby face and identified the picture of the man as something new and different.

A large number of habituation studies demonstrate that infants several months of age remember visual stimuli to which they have been exposed. Can this ability be found even earlier, during the first few weeks of life? As long as neonates are given a long time to study the initial stimulus and the stimulus patterns used are very distinct, the ability to remember aspects of the environment can be detected from birth onward. In fact, memory for a visual stimulus has even been found in 6-day-old infants born 5 weeks preterm (Werner & Siqueland, 1978). However, memory processing of preterm babies is slower than that of full-term infants. Preterm babies require an especially lengthy exposure to stimuli to demonstrate the habituation-dishabituation response (Rose, 1980).

As infants get older, they make successively finer distinctions among stimuli in a habituation-dishabituation paradigm, and from 5 months onward, they require as little as 5 to 10 seconds of study time for immediate recognition. When given more time to examine the first stimulus, the older infant's recognition that two stimuli are different persists over delays of several minutes between presentation of the visual patterns, even in the face of potential interference from other stimuli to which the infant is exposed during the delay (Fagan, 1971, 1977).

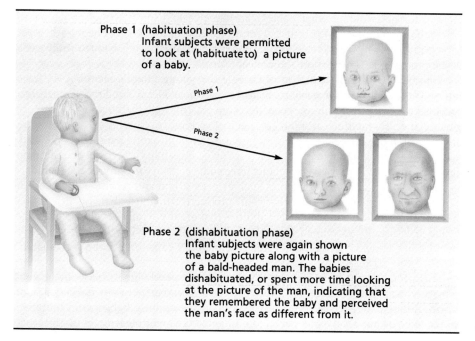

Phase 1 (habituation phase)
Infant subjects were permitted
to look at (habituate to) a picture
of a baby.

Phase 1

Phase 2

Phase 2 (dishabituation phase)
Infant subjects were again shown
the baby picture along with a picture
of a bald-headed man. The babies
dishabituated, or spent more time looking
at the picture of the man, indicating that
they remembered the baby and perceived
the man's face as different from it.

Figure 4.4. Example of the habituation-dishabituation paradigm, as applied in the Fagan and Singer (1979) study. *(Adapted from Fagan & Singer, 1979.)*

Habituation can also be used to test how long an infant's memory for a single stimulus lasts. Infants can be exposed to a stimulus pattern until they habituate. Then they can be shown the same pattern at a later time. If habituation takes place more rapidly on the second occasion, this indicates that babies must recognize that they have seen the pattern before. Using this method, studies show that by 3 months of age, infants remember a visual stimulus for as long as 24 hours (Martin, 1975). By the end of the first year, recognition increases to several days and, in the case of very familiar stimuli such as the human face, even weeks (Fagan, 1973).

However, other research indicates that the habituation paradigm may underestimate infants' capacity to remember, perhaps because the still photos and designs commonly employed in habituation studies are harder to remember than animated stimuli. Recall the operant conditioning research described earlier in which babies learned to activate a mobile through footkicking. In a series of investigations, Rovee-Collier and her associates showed that 2- and 3-month-olds can remember how to make the mobile move for as long as a week after initial exposure. Moreover, when given a visual reminder of how the mobile works after forgetting (the examiner briefly rotates it for the baby), young infants vigorously reactivate their footkicking as long as 2 weeks after they were first trained (Linde, Morrongiello, & Rovee-Collier, 1985; Rovee-Collier, Patterson, & Haye, 1985).

Nevertheless, a wealth of research indicates that habituation measures are the best available infant predictors of later cognitive development. The extent to which infants habituate and dishabituate to novel stimuli is moderately correlated with IQ scores during the preschool years. In addition, infants expected to show depressed intelligence in later life, such as Down syndrome babies, habituate and dishabituate to new stimuli more slowly than do normal infants. On the basis of this evidence, several investigators have concluded that response to novelty may tap a fundamental intellectual process that underlies a variety of tasks on traditional intelligence tests (Bornstein & Sigman, 1986; Fagan, 1984; Rose, Feldman, & Wallace, 1988; Rose et al., 1989).

Although most habituation studies have been concerned with the visual modality, neonates also habituate to auditory and olfactory stimuli. Besides enhancing our understanding of infant memory, habituation research provides much information about the perceptual world of infants. As we will see later in this chapter, by varying the nature of the stimuli presented, investigators rely on habituation as a major method for determining what babies can perceive and for charting the course of perceptual development. We will also return to habituation in later chapters devoted to cognitive development, since the method has been used extensively to study early development of categorization and concept formation.

You may have noticed that in discussing the young infant's memory, we have referred to it as *recognition memory*. By this we mean an infant's ability to recognize a previously observed stimulus when it reappears (through habituating to it more quickly the second time around) or that two stimuli presented successively are different from one another (as in the habituation-dishabituation paradigm). We have not discussed *productive memory*, which involves the ability to recall something no longer present. By 1 year of age, infants have some capacity for productive memory, as they spontaneously imitate games such as peek-a-boo and recall the locations of familiar objects (Nelson, 1984). However, productive memory depends heavily on mental representation and language, abilities that are more fully developed after age 2, and it is usually examined through verbal recall. We will take up productive memory in Chapter 7 when we consider the memory capacities of the verbal child.

Imitation. If you have had an opportunity to spend some time with infants, perhaps you noticed the extent to which they readily **imitate** or copy the behavior of others. Adults capitalize on this tendency when they amuse babies with imitative games, such as pat-a-cake and peekaboo. Infants take great pleasure in these activities and respond with smiles, gleeful vocalizations, and excited motor activity.

For many years, theorists of infant development believed that imitation was beyond the cognitive competence of young infants; it was not expected to appear before the end of the first year (Bayley, 1969; Piaget, 1945/1951). Then a growing literature began to report that newborn babies have the capacity to engage in rudimentary imitation of a visual model. These findings suggest that neonates are far more sophisticated in their ability to process stimulation than was previously thought.

Meltzoff and Moore (1977) conducted one of the first studies of neonatal imitation. Infants between 12 and 21 days of age were presented with four different gestures to imitate. Three were facial gestures (tongue protrusion, mouth opening, and lip protrusion), and one was a manual gesture (sequential finger movements). By showing that infants frequently exhibited the same gesture as the adult, Meltzoff and Moore claimed that neonates were capable of imitating all these behaviors. In another investigation, Field and her collaborators (1982) reported that infants less than 2 days old imitated an adult's happy, sad, and surprised facial expressions. The researchers concluded that newborn babies come into the world with a sophisticated ability to translate many behaviors they see into equivalent motor responses. Convincing photographic records offer further support for this conclusion (see Figure 4.5).

Claims that newborns can imitate the gestures of other human beings seem so extraordinary that it is not surprising they have been disputed. Several studies failed to replicate Meltzoff and Moore's and Field's findings (Hayes & Watson, 1981; McKenzie & Over, 1983). In other investigations that did find evidence of imitation, the imitative capacity of young babies was much more limited than in the first studies described above. Among a variety of modeled behaviors, tongue protrusion was the only one that elicited imitation, and infant responses were partial and incomplete

Figure 4.5. Photographs from two studies of neonatal imitation. Photographs from the Meltzoff and Moore (1977) study show 2- to 3-week-old infants imitating tongue protrusion *(A)*, mouth opening *(B)*, and lip protrusion *(C)* by an adult experimenter. In photographs from the Field et al. (1981) study, 2-day-old infants imitate happy *(D)* and sad *(E)* adult facial expressions. *(From T. M. Field et al., 1982, "Discrimination and Imitation of Facial Expressions by Neonates," Science, 218, 180 [Copyright 1977 by the AAAS]; A. N. Meltzoff & M. K. Moore, 1977, "Imitation of Facial and Manual Gestures by Human Neonates," Science, 198, 75 [Copyright 1977 by the AAAS].)*

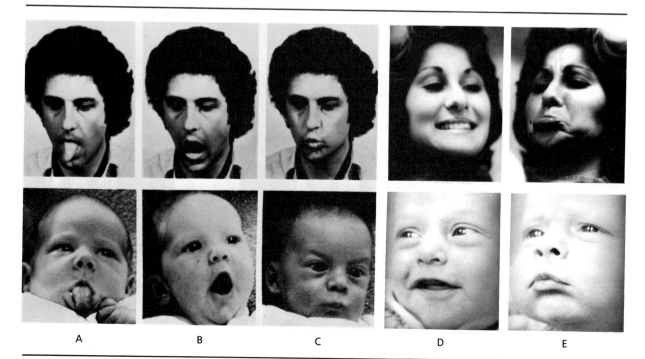

A   B   C   D   E

versions of the modeled action, not well-formed copies (Abravanel & Sigafoos, 1984; Kaitz et al., 1988).

However, a recent study by Reissland (1988) helps make sense of these conflicting findings. Reissland points out that all previous research on neonatal imitation has been carried out in North America and Europe, where use of obstetric medication may interfere with this remarkable capacity. In addition, investigators reporting positive findings looked at very young babies (no more than 2 weeks old), while those failing to replicate worked with slightly older infants. In Reissland's research, babies born in rural Nepal who were tested minutes after a drug-free delivery showed clear imitation of two adult facial expressions: lips widened and lips pursed. Reissland believes that neonatal imitation may be a temporary adaptive capacity that recedes after the first few weeks of life, only to return in more coordinated and purposeful form later on.

Reissland's results also indicate that neonatal imitation is not limited to a single stereotyped movement, such as tongue protrusion. Instead, newborn babies flexibly copy a variety of adult-modeled behaviors. In fact, new evidence by Meltzoff and Moore (1989) suggests that the neonate's imitative repertoire extends beyond facial gestures to include head movements as well! Still, it is important to keep in mind that this early capacity is quite rudimentary, and imitative abilities undergo considerable change over the first two years of life. Imitation in newborns is restricted to common actions within the baby's behavioral repertoire. Later on, as infants make strides in the development of skilled motor actions, they can imitate increasingly complex and unfamiliar behaviors, and in the latter part of the first year, their imitation becomes less approximate and far more exact (Kaye & Marcus, 1981). Finally, deferred imitation — the ability to replicate the behavior of a model hours or days after it was first observed — is a complex cognitive achievement that is not well developed until the second year of life. We will discuss its emergence in Chapter 6.

However basic and elemental, the capacity to imitate provides newborn babies with another powerful mechanism for learning. Imitation is a way to get young infants to express desirable behaviors, and once they are demonstrated, adults can encourage them further. Imitation also plays an important role in infant social development. Adults take great pleasure in a baby who imitates their facial gestures and actions, and as infants and adults trade imitative responses back and forth, both enjoy the interaction. Such imitative interchanges are common in infancy and serve as an important ingredient in the development of caregiver-infant attachment.

BRIEF REVIEW

In the sections above, we have seen that the newborn baby is a remarkably well-organized being with an amazing set of capacities for adapting to the environment. Reflexes help ensure the baby's survival, facilitate the development of voluntary action, and provide a ready indicator of the intactness of the neurological system. Short, cyclical periods of sleeping and waking gradually consolidate over the first year of life, and REM sleep diminishes as infants spend more time in the waking state. A set of recognizable cries permits newborn babies to communicate their needs effectively to adults. And, as research on conditioning, habituation, and imitation reveals, neonates are marvelously equipped to learn from their experiences immediately after birth.

MOTOR DEVELOPMENT IN INFANCY

Virtually all parents eagerly anticipate their infant's achievement of new motor skills. Baby books are filled with proud notations, and parents are quick to inform friends and relatives as soon as the infant holds up her head, reaches for objects, sits by herself, and walks alone. Parental enthusiasm for these motor accomplishments is not at all misplaced, for they are, indeed, milestones of development. With each additional skill, babies gain control over their bodies and the environment in a new way. Infants who sit alone are granted an entirely different perspective on the world from those who spend much of their day on their backs or stomachs. Coordinated reaching opens up a whole new avenue for investigating objects, and when babies can move about, their opportunities for exploration are multiplied. As new ways of controlling the environment are achieved, motor development provides infants with a growing sense of competence and mastery. It also contributes importantly to their perceptual and cognitive understanding of the world.

Babies' emerging motor competencies also have a powerful effect on their social relationships. For example, the appearance of crawling leads parents to restrict the infant's activities in ways that were previously unnecessary when the baby, placed on a blanket, would stay there! New motor skills, such as pointing and showing toys, permit infants to communicate more effectively with others. In response, parents place less emphasis on physical caregiving and engage in more game playing and verbal requests, and these new ways of interacting provide further encouragement for infants' rapidly expanding motor abilities. Modifications in motor skills and in the infant's social environment are bidirectional and mutually supportive. Changes in one area promote and sustain those that occur in the other (Green, Gustafson, & West, 1980).

The Organization and Sequence of Motor Development

Most tests that measure infant development rely heavily on motor skills because they are the most obvious accomplishments of infancy. Table 4.3 provides the average age at which a variety of motor skills are achieved, as well as the age range during which the majority of infants accomplish each skill, based on a major infant test, the *Bayley Scales of Infant Development* (Bayley, 1969). Whereas most infants adhere fairly closely to the sequence given in the table, the age ranges indicate that there are substantial individual differences in the rate at which motor development proceeds. Besides individual differences, there is another reason to consider age averages for motor skills with caution. Like height and weight (which we will discuss in Chapter 5), motor development is subject to a **secular trend,** in that infants achieve

Table 4.3. Milestones of Infant Motor Development

MOTOR SKILL	AVERAGE AGE ACHIEVED	AGE RANGE WITHIN WHICH ACHIEVED BY MOST INFANTS
Holds head erect and steady when held upright	7 weeks	3 weeks–4 months
When prone, elevates self by arms	2 months	3 weeks–5 months
Rolls from side to back	2 months	3 weeks–5 months
Rolls from back to side	4½ months	2–7 months
Grasps cube	3 months, 3 weeks	2–7 months
Sits alone, good coordination	7 months	5–9 months
Crawls	7 months	5–11 months
Pulls to stand	8 months	5–12 months
Uses neat pincer grasp	9 months	7–10 months
Plays pat-a-cake	9 months, 3 weeks	7–15 months
Stands alone	11 months	9–16 months
Walks alone	11 months, 3 weeks	9–17 months

Source: Bayley (1969).

these milestones earlier today than they did a half century ago (Appleton, Clifton, & Goldberg, 1975). A variety of factors could be responsible for this gradual acceleration in infant motor progress, including better nutrition, better health care, and changing ways of rearing infants.

Look carefully at Table 4.3 once more, and you will see that there is organization and direction to the infant's motor achievements. Two well-known, general developmental trends are reflected in the order of the entries. First, motor control of the head comes before control of the arms and trunk, and control of the arms and trunk is achieved before control of the legs. This head-to-foot sequence is called the **cephalo-caudal trend** of development. Second, motor functioning proceeds from the center of the body outward, in that head and arm control is achieved before coordination of the hands and fingers. This is the **proximo-distal trend** of development. It is interesting that physical growth during the prenatal period, as well as during infancy and childhood, follows these same trends. Because motor control shows the same directional course as early physical development, the cephalo-caudal and proximo-distal patterns are believed to be genetically preprogrammed maturational phenomena (Shirley, 1933).

Once research in the early half of this century had documented the basic sequence of motor milestones, interest in motor development waned for several decades. Then in the 1980s, a resurgence of work appeared, this time from a much broader perspective. Modern child development specialists no longer regard motor development as the emergence of isolated, functionally discrete skills. Today, motor control is viewed as the acquisition of progressively more complex *systems of action*. New investigations show how previously mastered motor components are gradually modified and integrated into more intricate and effective modes of exploring and controlling the environment (Hofsten, 1989; Pick, 1989; Thelen, 1989). For example, in gross motor development, control of the head and upper chest contribute to sitting with support; kicking, rocking on all fours, and reaching are reorganized into crawling (Goldfield, 1989); and crawling, standing, and stepping are united into walking alone. The way simple motor acts are eventually absorbed into complex behaviors is even more evident in the development of fine motor skills. As we will see when we discuss the special significance of visually guided reaching, the component acts of grasping, looking, and arm movements at first emerge independently and then are coordinated into successful reaching (Manchester, 1988). Once this is accomplished, reaching is available as a separate element to be combined into even more complex activities, such as stacking blocks, putting objects in containers, and eating with a spoon (Connolly & Dagleish, 1989).

Dennis and Dennis (1940) found that confinement to the cradle board did not impede the development of walking in Indian babies and concluded that the emergence of motor skills was largely under maturational control. Later studies revealed that both maturation and experience influence the course of motor development.

Maturation versus Experience and the Development of Motor Skills

We have described the organized, sequential quality of motor development and noted its profound impact on other areas of functioning, but the question still remains: What processes explain the emergence of motor skills?

The research of early investigators of the 1930s and 1940s led them to conclude that motor skills were under the control of biological maturation and that experience had little to do with the timing or form into which motor behaviors were cast. For example, Gesell (1929) conducted a famous study of a pair of identical twins in which one was given early practice at stair climbing and fine motor manipulation of cubes and the other was not. Without intensive practice, the untrained twin quickly caught up with the trained twin after exposure to the stairs and cubes at a more mature age. Dennis and Dennis (1940) studied age of walking among the Hopi Indians, some of whom bound their infants to cradle boards, while others, influenced by Western ways, had given up this practice. Despite severe restriction of movement among the cradle board infants throughout the first year of life, both groups of infants walked unaided at precisely the same age — around 15 months. However, these studies were deliberately designed to decide between two extreme theories of development, and little attention was paid to subtle experiences that could have influenced the motor skills in question. For example, in Gesell's study, unknown aspects of the untrained twin's everyday experiences, such as opportunities to climb on furniture, could have facilitated stair climbing. In Dennis's investigation of infant walking, constant exposure to the upright posture on the cradle board could have compensated for early movement deprivation among the Hopi babies.

It is now recognized that both maturation and experience influence the course of motor development. In fact, later in his career, after observing infants reared in Iranian institutions who spent their days lying on their backs in cribs, Dennis (1960) recognized the vital importance of postural experience and a generally stimulating environment for the emergence of motor skills. These Iranian babies were severely retarded in gross motor achievements such as sitting, creeping, and walking. When they finally did move about (which for the great majority was not until after 2 years of age), the constant experience of lying on their backs led most of them to scoot in a sitting position, rather than crawl on their hands and knees the way family-reared babies do. Thus, the early experiences of these infants changed not just the rate, but also the form of motor development. Moreover, the preference for scooting may have further retarded the institutionalized infants' motor progress. Babies who scoot encounter furniture and objects with their feet, not their hands, and they are far less likely to pull themselves to a standing position in preparation for walking.

Cross-cultural research also shows how experience affects motor development. The emergence of certain gross motor skills is advanced among African and West Indian infants who experience highly stimulating handling as an important feature of their culture's child-rearing practices. For example, West Indian babies attain head control, sit alone, and walk considerably earlier than their Caucasian counterparts. As shown in Figure 4.6, passive stretching of the legs, arms, and neck, vigorous massaging of the body after the daily bath, propping with cushions to encourage an upright posture, and exercising of stepping responses by their mothers are responsible for this precocity (Hopkins & Westra, 1988).

Fine Motor Development: The Special Case of Visually Guided Reaching

The ability to extend the hand and touch or grasp an object is a major advance in exploration and manipulation of the environment, and its perfection is believed to play an important role in infant cognitive development (Piaget, 1936/1952). Therefore, investigators have gone beyond merely identifying when visually guided reaching emerges to carefully charting its developmental course.

The development of reaching and grasping provides an excellent example of how motor development proceeds from gross, diffuse activity to skilled mastery of fine motor movements. Even newborns exhibit primitive reaching behavior. Placed upright in an infant seat, neonates direct their arms in the general vicinity of an object dangled before them, but their movements are not well coordinated, and they rarely contact the object successfully. In fact, the newborn's primitive reaching movements have been called *prereaching*, since they resemble swipes or swings. Unlike older infants, neonates cannot carefully guide their hands with their eyes, and if they miss the object, they are unable to correct their error (Hofsten, 1982). Like the neonatal reflexes we discussed earlier, prereaching eventually drops out. It decreases abruptly around 7 weeks of age, and at about 3 months, visually guided reaching first appears (Hofsten, 1984).

The reaching behavior of infants who are a few months of age is far more successful than that of neonates, since now infants use their eyes to guide their arms and hands. As a result, the imprecise movements and misses that occur between 3 and 5 months can be compensated for and corrected (Bushnell, 1985). Nevertheless, visually guided reaching is limited at first. The 3-month-old will only contact objects

Figure 4.6. West Indian mothers use a formal handling routine with their babies (shown above). Exercises practiced in the first few months include stretching each arm in suspension (A); holding the infant upside down by the ankles (B); grasping the baby's head on both sides, lifting upwards, and stretching the neck (C); and propping the infant with cushions that are gradually removed as the baby begins to sit independently (D). Later in the first year, the baby is "walked" up the mother's body (E) and encouraged to take steps on the floor while supported (F). *(Adapted from B. Hopkins & T. Westra, 1988, "Maternal Handling and Motor Development: An Intracultural Study," Genetic, Social and General Psychology Monographs, 14, pp. 385, 388, 389. Reprinted with permission of the Helen Dwight Reid Educational Foundation. Published by Heldref Publications, 4000 Albemarle St., N.W., Washington, DC 20016. Copyright © 1988.)*

offered on the same side of the body as the reaching hand. Reaching for objects at the midline and on the opposite side of the body develops gradually. By 4½ months, infants can successfully obtain objects in all three positions (Provine & Westerman, 1979).

Over the course of the first year, infants also improve the nature of their grasp so that they can better adapt to objects of different sizes and characteristics. When the palmar grasp reflex weakens, it is replaced by primitive swiping and then by the **ulnar grasp,** a clumsy motion in which the fingers close against the palm. Soon,

Infant motor milestones follow a cephalo-caudal trend of development. This 4-month-old baby achieves control over the head and upper body before the trunk and legs.

infants begin to adjust the forearm and hand to match the size and orientation of the object they are about to grasp (Hofsten & Rönnqvist, 1988), and by 4 to 5 months, both hands are increasingly coordinated in the exploration of objects. Babies of this age can hold an object in one hand while the other scans it with the tips of the fingers, and they frequently transfer the object from hand to hand (Rochat, 1989). By the end of the first year, infants use the thumb and index finger opposably in a well-coordinated **pincer grasp** (Halverson, 1931). Once the pincer grasp appears, babies start to engage in far more refined and elaborate manipulation of objects, such as picking up raisins and blades of grass, turning knobs, manipulating latches, and opening small boxes.

By 8 to 11 months of age, reaching and grasping are so well practiced that they are executed smoothly and effortlessly, and infants no longer need to monitor the movements of their arms and hands with their eyes to be successful. This decreased need for visual guidance is of major developmental significance, because the infant's attention is released from executing the motor skill itself and can be used for integrating events that occur before and after obtaining the object. The perfection of reaching at the end of the first year is thought to pave the way for new cognitive advances, such as those described by Piaget, who indicated that infants first began to search for hidden objects at this time (Bushnell, 1985).

As with the gross motor accomplishments discussed earlier, experience plays an important role in the development of visually guided reaching. In a classic experiment, White and Held (1966) modified the early experiences of two groups of institutionalized infants. In the massively enriched group, between 1 to 4 months of age, babies were exposed to an elaborate, multicolored mobile hung above their cribs, and patterned sheets and crib bumpers were substituted for the usual white ones. In the moderately enriched group, infants were initially provided with a far simpler form of stimulation. Between 1 and 2 months of age, two red and white patterned disks were hung on each side of the crib rails. Later on, between 2 and 4 months, the quantity of enrichment was augmented by exposing the babies to the same mobile and crib bumpers provided to the massively enriched group at an earlier age. Although both groups mastered reaching for objects 6 to 8 weeks earlier than a control group exposed to the usual institutional conditions, the investigators did not find that more stimulation was necessarily better! Instead, the moderately enriched group was the most advanced in development. In fact, during the first month of exposure to the mobile, massively enriched babies were the least attentive to their surroundings. Overwhelmed by so much stimulation, they looked away and cried a great deal.

White and Held's findings do not imply that parents must make a deliberate effort to teach their babies to reach, since almost all home environments offer sufficiently varied stimulation to ensure that visually guided reaching will emerge quite adequately on its own. However, the study does suggest that some forms of stimulation —in particular, those that provide too much all at once — can undermine the optimal emergence of important infant skills.

PERCEPTUAL DEVELOPMENT IN INFANCY

In this section, we explore the baby's sensitivity to touch, postural orientation, taste, smell, sound, and visual stimulation. Research on infant perception has largely addressed two questions: (1) What can infants perceive at birth, and (2) how do these capacities change over the first few months of life? Child development specialists have sought answers to these questions for a number of reasons. One is the relevance of infant perception to the age-old nature-nurture controversy. Is an adultlike perceptual world given to the infant, or must it be acquired through experience? As we will see shortly, infants exhibit a remarkable constellation of perceptual capacities from the very beginning. However, since improvements occur as the result of both maturation and experience, an appropriate resolution to the nature-nurture debate seems, once again, to lie somewhere between the two extremes. A second reason for interest in infant perceptual abilities is that they shed light on other areas of development. For example, because visual and auditory capacities enable us to interact with other human beings, they are a basic part of social development. Through the auditory sense, language is learned. Furthermore, perceptual development provides the foundation for cognitive development, since knowledge about the world is first gathered through the senses.

Studying infant perception is especially challenging because babies cannot verbally describe their experiences. Instead, the infant's perceptual world must be inferred from the repertoire of behaviors babies do have. Fortunately, the young infant's behavioral competence permits investigators to make use of a variety of responses that change in accord with stimulation — looking, sucking, head turning, facial expressions, and startle responses, to name just a few. Advances in research technology have also permitted physiological indicators, such as changes in respiration and heart rate, to be used. Researchers have also capitalized on the baby's ability to learn. The habituation-dishabituation paradigm serves as a means for finding out whether infants can discriminate among certain stimuli. Operant conditioning procedures, in which infants are trained to respond to one stimulus rather than another, are also sometimes used.

Touch

As we will see in Chapter 10, the sense of touch is especially important for early emotional development. Therefore, it is not surprising that tactile sensitivity appears quite early in prenatal life and is well developed at birth. Responsiveness to touch in the area of the mouth is present by 7½ weeks gestation. Sensitivity in the oral and genital areas and on the palms of the hands and soles of the feet matures first, followed by other regions of the body. Reactions to temperature change also appear prenatally, and both the fetus and the neonate are more sensitive to stimuli that are colder than body temperature than to those that are warmer (Humphrey, 1978). In addition, the newborn infant responds to pain, as reports of high-pitched infant crying during circumcision, generally performed without anesthesia in the first few days of life, indicate (Porter, Porges, & Marshall, 1988). Research with the habituation-dishabituation paradigm reveals that newborns can discriminate different touch stimuli, such as a brush stroke across the mouth and one across the ear (Kisilevsky & Muir, 1984). However, little information exists on the refinement of tactile sensitivity over the course of infancy.

Vestibular Sensitivity

Vestibular sensitivity refers to awareness of body orientation and motion. As motor skills develop during the first year of life, infants rely increasingly on it for maintenance of an upright posture. The vestibular system is controlled by displacement of fluid in the semicircular canals of the inner ear as the body sways. Even young infants are sensitive to these cues, as the soothing effect of rocking and being held in a vertical position indicates. Later in the first year, the vestibular apparatus becomes integrated with vision in controlling postural stability. In a series of ingenious studies, infants were placed in a room with walls that could be moved, while the floor (and therefore the baby) remained stationary. Under these conditions, most individuals perceive themselves to be leaning in a direction opposite to the movement of the walls and initiate postural compensations. Between 5 and 9 months of age (the period during which infants learn to sit and crawl), body adjustments to the moving walls increasingly resembled those of older children and adults. Newly walking 1-year-olds staggered and fell, with movement of the side walls producing a greater effect than movement of the front wall alone. This finding suggests that the edges of the visual field induce greater postural responsiveness than the center, which the baby seems to reserve for other important aspects of visual perception (Bertenthal & Bai, 1989; Lee & Aronson, 1974).

Taste

The taste buds are structurally mature long before birth (Bradley, 1972), and neonates use them to discriminate the four basic tastes of sweet, sour, bitter, and salty. When permitted to suck for a sugar solution instead of water, newborn infants show an immediate rise in heart rate. In addition, they begin to suck more continuously with fewer pauses, and their overall rate of sucking slows down. Researchers believe these changes indicate that infants prefer sweetness and modify their sucking in such a way as to savor the taste of their favorite food (Crook & Lipsitt, 1976). Sucking bursts to salt solutions are shorter than those to sugar, suggesting that newborns react negatively to salty tastes (Crook, 1978). Research has not shown that infants vary their sucking in response to other taste qualities, but changes in facial expressions indicate that neonates differentiate sweet, sour, and bitter solutions. Sweet stimulation promotes facial relaxation, sour stimulation pursing of the lips, and bitter stimulation a distinct archlike mouth opening. Since these same facial responses have been observed in anencephalic infants (born with only a brain stem and no cortex), they operate at a very primitive, reflexive level. Facial expressions are a basic form of human communication, and all infants seem to come into the world with a built-in ability to convey their taste preferences to others (Steiner, 1979).

Smell

Like taste receptors, the olfactory apparatus is well developed at birth, and newborn babies can differentiate among odors. Given a sufficiently strong stimulus, even preterm infants as young as 28 weeks gestation respond to an unpleasant odor by increasing their activity level and respiration rate (Sarnat, 1978). The strength of an odor stimulus needed to produce a response declines over the first few days of life, suggesting that the sense of smell becomes increasingly sensitive during this time (Lipsitt, Engen, & Kaye, 1963).

Newborn infants show expected facial reactions to pleasant and unpleasant food odors. For example, the smell of bananas or chocolate provokes a relaxed facial response, whereas the odor of rotten eggs leads to arching of the lips, turning down of the corners of the mouth, spitting, and salivation (Steiner, 1979). The fact that distinct facial reactions resembling those of adults appear so early in life indicates that at least some odor preferences are innate. Neonates also exhibit a surprising ability to respond to the location of an odor and, if it is unpleasant, to defend themselves accordingly. When a whiff of ammonia is presented to one side of the baby's nostrils, infants less than 6 days old quickly turn their heads in the opposite direction (Reiser, Yonas, & Wikner, 1976).

In lower mammals, the sense of smell plays an important role in eating, avoidance of predators, and mother-infant attachment. Though smell is less well developed in human beings, vestiges of its survival value may still be present in young babies. In a study in which newborns were simultaneously exposed to the odor of their own mother's breast pad and that of a strange mother, by 6 days of age, they turned more often in the direction of the odor of their own mother (MacFarlane, 1975). This olfactory recognition occurs only in breast-fed babies; bottle-fed newborns cannot detect a difference between their mother's underarm odor and that of an unfamiliar woman (Cernoch & Porter, 1985). Nevertheless, bottle-fed female neonates do show a nonspecific preference for the breast odors of lactating women (Makin & Porter, 1989).[4] Taken together, these findings suggest that newborn babies' attraction to the smell of the lactating breast may serve two adaptive functions: (1) helping infants recognize their own mother and (2) assisting infants in locating an appropriate food source.

Hearing

Because anatomical development of the ear is nearly complete at birth (Accredolo & Hake, 1982), newborn babies can hear a wide variety of sounds. However, they are more responsive to some than to others. For example, neonates react more consistently to complex sounds composed of a variety of frequencies (e.g., noises and voices) than to pure tones (Bench et al., 1976). Their sensitivity to pitch and loudness, particularly at low frequencies, is not as keen as that of an adult (Morrongiello & Clifton, 1984), but it improves markedly over the first few days of life and continues to do so throughout the first year (Olsho, 1984; Sinnott, Pisoni, & Aslin, 1983). Besides sensitivity to single sounds, babies' recognition of sound patterns improves substantially. Newborns can discriminate between a series of tones arranged in ascending and descending order, but 12-month-olds can detect quite subtle changes in complex melodic patterns, an achievement that is probably influenced by gains in recognition memory during the latter half of the first year (Morrongiello, 1986).

Responsiveness to sound provides support for the infant's visual exploration of the environment. Babies as young as 3 days of age turn their eyes and head in the general direction of a sound. However, precise localization of sound sources is not present at birth and only gradually improves over the first 18 months of life (Field et al., 1980; Morrongiello & Rocca, 1988). In addition, neonates have difficulty localizing auditory stimuli under complex conditions in which more than one sound is present. The ability to selectively attend to one sound while suppressing interfering auditory stimulation does not emerge until about 5 months of age (Clifton et al., 1981).

Neonates are particularly responsive to auditory stimuli within the frequency range of the human voice, and they show a special sensitivity to the sounds of human speech. Habituation studies reveal that newborn infants can make fine-grained distinctions among a wide variety of speech sounds — "ba" and "ga," "ma" and "na," and the short vowel sounds "a" and "i," to name just a few. In fact, there are only a very few speech discriminations that infants cannot detect, and their ability to perceive sounds not found in their language environment is more perfect than an adult's

---

[4] Females are superior to males in the ability to discriminate odors throughout the life span (Doty et al., 1984). Makin and Porter (1989) believe that future studies using more refined methodologies may find that male infants also prefer the smell of the lactating breast.

(Aslin, Pisoni, & Jusczyk, 1983). Babies seem to come into the world biologically prepared to respond to the sounds of any human language, although by the end of the first year, exposure to a single language starts to limit the sounds to which babies are sensitive (Werker & Tees, 1984).

Newborns prefer to listen to high-pitched, expressive voices with rising intonation patterns (Sullivan & Horowitz, 1983; Turnure, 1971). In addition, they suck more often on a nipple to hear their own mother's voice than that of a strange female (DeCasper & Fifer, 1980), a preference that may have developed from hearing the muffled sounds of the mother's voice prenatally (Spence & DeCasper, 1987). Infants' special responsiveness to maternal speech undoubtedly encourages mothers to talk to babies who are not yet verbal themselves. As mothers and infants are increasingly drawn into reciprocal interaction, both early language acquisition and the emotional bond between mother and baby are simultaneously facilitated.

Vision

It is not surprising that more research has been done on the development of vision than on any other perceptual system. More than any other sense, humans depend on vision for active exploration of the environment. Long before coordinated reaching and crawling are possible, infants scan the environment, track moving objects, and bring sources of sound into sight. How mature are the visual capacities of newborn infants? Is their visual reality fashioned like that of adults—a world of distinct, recognizable objects in which such features as brightness, colors, patterns, and depth can be distinguished? Or do these visual competencies have to mature or be learned over the course of time?

The visual apparatus is less well developed at birth than that of any other sense. The *retina* is the portion of the eye that captures light and transforms it into nerve signals that are transmitted to the brain. The *fovea,* the area at the center of the retina where images are focused most sharply, contains visual receptors that are not as mature nor as densely packed in the neonate as they are in adults. In addition, the muscles controlling the shape of the *lens,* that part of the eye that enables us to adjust our focus to varying distances of objects, are weak at birth. Although newborns cannot focus the eye as well as adults, their ability to do so over a wide range of distances is still considerable. However, young infants rarely make full use of the focusing ability they have. This is because their **visual acuity**, or fineness of discrimination, is severely restricted. Applying the same parameters doctors use to describe our own visual acuity, researchers estimate that newborn babies perceive objects at a distance of 20 feet about as clearly as adults do at 440 to 800 feet (Appleton, Clifton, & Goldberg, 1975). Furthermore, unlike adults, young infants see *equally unclearly* across a wide range of distances. As a result, there are no visual cues available to help them notice that a near or far image can be sharpened by refocusing the lens (Banks, 1980).

The infant's visual system matures rapidly over the first few months of life. The ability to focus on objects at varying distances approximates that of adults by 3 months of age (Banks, 1980). Visual acuity develops over a somewhat longer period. It can be estimated by determining the narrowest distance between a series of stripes that the infant can detect visually. At 10 inches from the eye, newborns distinguish a striped stimulus from an unpatterned surface only if the stripes are at least ⅛ of an inch in width. By 6 months of age, they can discriminate stripes that are ¹⁄₆₄ of an inch wide, indicating that their acuity is comparable to that of an adult with 20/100 vision (Fantz, Ordy, & Udelf, 1962). During the second half of the first year, visual acuity improves even more. It is supported by continuous structural maturation of the fovea, which reaches adultlike status at about 11 months of age (Abramov et al., 1982). The optic nerve and visual cortex also undergo development during the first year, contributing to the infant's gradually improved visual capacities (Banks & Salapatek, 1983).

Scanning and Tracking. The scanning behavior of newborn infants indicates that they are, from the outset, active, organized visual explorers of the environment. The eye movements we use to explore the visual field are called **saccades.** A saccade is a rapid, accurate motion that goes smoothly from a starting point to a visual target, bringing it from the periphery to the center of the field of vision so it can be inspected more carefully. Although somewhat slower and less accurate than those of adults, saccadic eye movements exist in newborns. Apparently, this basic mechanism for responding to visual information does not have to be learned, and it quickly improves during the first few months of life (Aslin, 1987).

Once newborn infants bring a target to the center of the visual field, they begin to explore it, but the nature of their visual exploration changes markedly in the first 2 months. When scanning a simple outline shape, 1-month-olds show very restricted visual exploration in that they tend to look only at a single feature, such as one corner of a triangle. However, by 2 months of age they scan more broadly, covering the entire perimeter (see Figure 4.7). Complex stimuli that have internal features, such as the eyes and mouth of the human face, are treated similarly. One-month-olds show eye fixations limited to the external boundaries of the visual target, and they are captured by a single feature, such as the hairline or chin. At about 2 months of age, infants shift from restricted scanning of the external border to a thorough examination of its internal features (Bushnell, Gerry, & Burt, 1983; Salapatek, 1975). However, if internal features are made very salient — for example, by embedding a bull's eye or checkerboard within a square or circle — even 1-month-olds will notice and inspect them (Ganon & Swartz, 1980). Apparently, visual scanning by the neonate is governed by high contrast and salience. Only at 2 months does the infant respond to the entire configuration of a stimulus, including less salient, fine-grained features and details.

When tracking a moving target, we use **smooth pursuit eye movements,** which are much slower and more sustained than saccades, enabling us to hold fixation on the

Figure 4.7. Visual scanning of simple and complex targets by young infants. When scanning a simple triangle, newborns focus only on a single feature, whereas 2-month-olds scan the whole shape. When targets are complex and have internal features, such as the human face, 1-month-olds limit their scanning to single features on the perimeter of the stimulus, whereas 2-month-olds examine the internal features. *(From P. Salapatek, 1975, ''Pattern Perception in Early Infancy.'' In L. B. Cohen & P. Salapatek [Eds.], Infant Perception: From Sensation to Cognition. New York: Academic Press, Pp. 195, 201. Reprinted by permission.)*

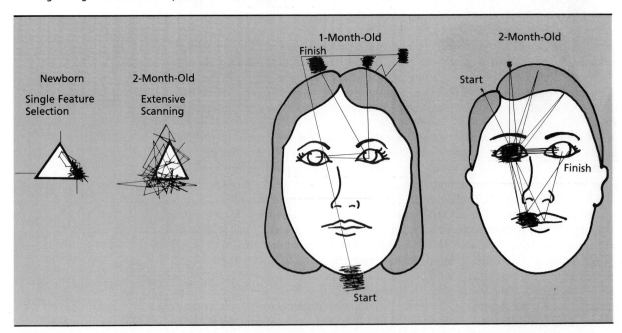

moving stimulus. The eye movements of neonates while following a moving stimulus are jerky and uncontrolled (Kremenitzer et al., 1979). As long as objects move very slowly, smooth pursuit appears at about 1 month of age, and it continues to improve during the first 6 months of life (Hainline, 1985).

Brightness and Color. Young infants are attracted to bright objects, such as lights, and on the basis of the length of time they spend looking at lights of different brightness, they prefer those of medium intensity to ones that are very bright or dim (Hershenson, 1964). The extent to which infants can discriminate among lights of different brightness can be determined by testing for whether they distinguish a bar of light from its background. By 2 months of age, infants discriminate lights of different brightness almost as well as adults do (Peeples & Teller, 1975).

Color perception is difficult to investigate in infants. Colors differ from one another in brightness, and since the relationship between brightness and color is thought to be different for infants than adults, it is impossible to be sure that pairs of color presentations are equalized for brightness in research involving infants. Investigators have tried to surmount this problem in a number of ways. One is to present pairs of colors repeatedly so that sometimes the first is brighter than the second and sometimes the second is brighter than the first. Under these conditions, if infants consistently look longer at one color, then their response cannot be based on brightness. Research using this technique indicates that color perception is not well developed at birth (Adams, Maurer, & Davis, 1986). Although newborns prefer to look at colored rather than gray stimuli, preference for particular colors does not appear until 2 to 3 months of age (Adams, 1987). Around this time, infants show a markedly improved ability to discriminate different hues (Teller & Bornstein, 1987).

Depth Perception. Depth perception—the process by which we gauge the distance of objects from one another and from ourselves—is important for understanding the spatial layout of the environment and for guiding motor activity. We live in a three-dimensional world, but the surface of the retina onto which visual images are projected is two-dimensional. Therefore, we depend on a variety of visual cues for converting this two-dimensional representation into a three-dimensional image of reality. Research on the development of depth perception has largely been aimed at answering two questions: Do very young infants perceive depth? How does sensitivity to various perceptual cues for depth develop during the first year of life?

Early studies of depth perception used a famous apparatus called the **visual cliff** (see Figure 4.8). Developed by Gibson and Walk (1960), it consisted of a table covered by glass, at the center of which was a platform. On one side of the platform (the shallow side), a checkerboard pattern was placed just under the surface of the glass, whereas on the other (the deep side), the checkerboard was positioned several feet beneath the glass. Infants were placed on the platform, and their mothers were asked to coax them to crawl over both the deep and shallow sides by calling to them and holding out a toy. Using this technique, Walk and Gibson (1961) found that although infants between 6 and 14 months could easily be enticed to cross the shallow side, all but a very few reacted with fear and avoidance to the deep side. At least by the time they are able to crawl, the majority of infants discriminate deep from shallow surfaces and behave in such a way as to avoid potentially dangerous dropoffs.

The Gibson and Walk research demonstrates that infants distinguish surfaces of different depths as soon as they can move about independently, but it does not tell us whether they do so earlier. To clarify when depth perception first appears and how it develops, investigators have turned toward the study of babies' responsiveness to particular depth cues, using methods that do not require independent locomotion. Three basic cues for depth are available to human beings: kinetic, binocular, and pictorial. Let's discuss each of them in turn.

Figure 4.8. The visual cliff. By refusing to cross the deep side and showing a preference for the shallow surface, this infant demonstrates the ability to perceive depth. (*William Vandivert*/Scientific American)

Kinetic Cues. **Kinetic depth cues** result from changes in retinal images created by movements of the infant's head or body or by moving objects in the environment. For example, when an object approaches us, its retinal image expands, and when it recedes, the image gradually shrinks. The cue for depth in this instance is the changing size of the object. The way infants respond to stimuli loomed at their faces indicates sensitivity to kinetic depth cues. As early as 3 weeks of age, babies blink defensively to visual information specifying an impending collision (Nanez, 1987). Complex habituation-dishabituation procedures in which infants are shown a rotating object and then required to recognize its three-dimensional shape in a new context are also used to study kinetic depth perception. Sensitivity to this kind of kinetic cue is present by 3 to 4 months of age (Arterberry & Yonas, 1988; Yonas, Arterberry, & Granrud, 1987). Kinetic responsiveness appears to be the earliest form of depth perception to develop.

Binocular Cues. **Binocular depth cues** arise from the fact that our eyes are separated, and each receives a slightly different view of the visual field. The mature visual system blends these two views into a single image but also registers the difference between them to provide strong cues for three-dimensionality, an ability that is called *stereopsis.* The infant's responsiveness to stereoscopic cues can be tested with a method similar to a 3-D movie. Two overlapping images are projected before the infant, and goggles worn by the baby allow one image to reach one eye and the other to reach the other eye. If infants are capable of stereopsis, they see an organized stereoscopic form that they track with their eyes instead of a randomly distributed series of dots or elements. Using this method, research shows that responsiveness to stereoscopic cues is absent in 10-week-old infants but undergoes gradual improvement between 3 and 6 months of age (Fox et al., 1979). Another indication that infants of this age use binocular information is that they adjust their reach in accord with the distance of an object when responding to a stereoscopic display (Field, 1977).

Pictorial Cues. Human beings also depend on **pictorial depth cues,** the kind used by artists to create the effect of three-dimensionality in a painting. Examples are linear perspective, texture gradients (nearby textured surfaces appear more fine-grained than distant surfaces), the interposition of objects (an object partially hidden by another object is perceived to be farther away), and shading (variations in lighting across the surface of an object give the impression of three-dimensionality). Since all these cues can be distinguished with only a single eye, they are often called *monocular depth cues*.

Yonas and his colleagues investigated sensitivity to a variety of pictorial depth cues by seeing whether babies are guided by them in reaching for objects. In two recent studies, they showed that 7-month-olds, but not 5-month-olds, could use *texture gradients* and *linear perspective* as cues for depth. Infants were presented with the display shown in Figure 4.9. The two ducks, one suspended lower than the other, were equal in size and distance from the infant, but texture gradients and linear perspective in the background combined to create the illusion of two objects resting at different distances on a horizontal surface. When viewing this display with one eye covered (monocular viewing condition), the older infants were more likely to reach for the nearer-appearing toy. With both eyes uncovered (binocular condition), there was no difference in 7-month-olds' reaching preference. These outcomes imply that in the monocular condition, 7-month-olds perceived the two objects' relative distances on the basis of textural and linear cues. The absence of a difference in preferential reaching between the two conditions for 5-month-olds suggests that they did not respond to these pictorial depth cues (Arterberry, Yonas, & Bensen, 1989; Yonas et al., 1986).

Sensitivity to *interposition* also emerges by the middle of the first year. When 7-month-olds are presented with the three stimuli depicted in Figure 4.10, they reach

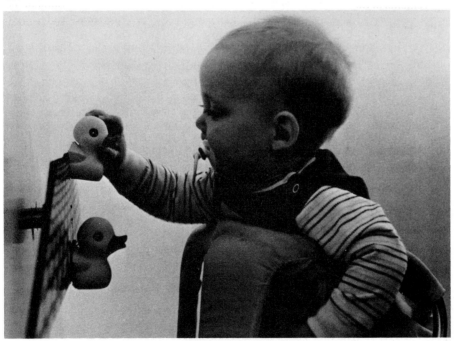

A

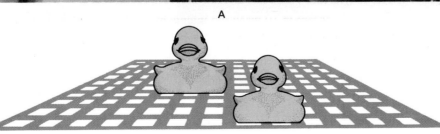

B

Figure 4.9. Test of infant's ability to perceive relative distance from pictorial cues in the Yonas et al. (1986) study. *A* provides a side view of an apparatus in which two toy ducks—equal in size and in distance from the infant—are placed in front of a background combining texture gradient and linear perspective cues to depth. Preferential reaching is recorded under both a binocular viewing condition (as above) and a monocular viewing condition. *B* shows the experimental display as viewed by an infant who can perceive distance based on these cues. *(Adapted from Yonas et al., 1986. Photo courtesy of Albert Yonas, University of Minnesota.)*

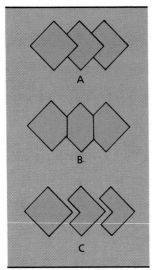

Figure 4.10. Interposition displays presented to 5- and 7-month-old infants in the Granrud and Yonas (1984) study. Seven-month-olds showed a reaching preference for the apparently "nearer" area of stimulus *A*. *(From C. E. Granrud & A. Yonas, 1984, "Infants' Perception of Pictorially Specified Interposition,"* Journal of Experimental Child Psychology, *37, 501. Adapted by permission.)*

consistently for the perceptually "nearer" part of stimulus *A*, but they show no reaching preferences toward *B* or *C*. Five-month-olds are not responsive to interposition; they do not reach preferentially for any part of the three stimuli (Granrud & Yonas, 1984).

Finally, babies are also sensitive to *shading* at 7 months of age; they will reach for a photograph of a convex surface rather than a concave surface (see Figure 4.11). Because of its shading, the convex area resembles a protruding sphere, and 7-month-olds, like adults, perceive it as closer to them than a concave surface (Granrud, Yonas, & Opland, 1985).

A consistent finding in all of Yonas's studies is that 7-month-olds respond to pictorial depth cues, whereas 5-month olds do not. The use of pictorial cues seems to emerge around the middle of the first year, much later than infants' sensitivity to kinetic and binocular depth information (Yonas, Arterberry, & Granrud, 1987).

You may have noticed from our discussion so far that research on infant depth perception has largely focused on the ages at which various capacities appear. Little information is available on factors that influence the infant's appreciation of depth. One intriguing hypothesis is that self-produced movement, especially locomotion, facilitates babies' perception of a three-dimensional world. Although crawling emerges at about the same time as sensitivity to pictorial depth cues, recent evidence indicates that neither crawling onset nor crawling experience affects infants' responsiveness to pictorial information in the laboratory (Arterberry, Yonas, & Bensen, 1989). Nevertheless, locomotion may enable babies to use their newfound sensitivity to depth more effectively in situations, such as the visual cliff, that resemble edges and dropoffs encountered in the everyday world (Campos & Bertenthal, 1989). In fact, the role that crawling plays in depth perception is at the heart of a recent debate on whether maturation or experience is responsible for infants' avoidance of the deep side of the visual cliff. Turn to Box 4.3 to explore this issue.

Pattern Perception. Early research by Fantz (1961, 1963) indicated that even newborn babies prefer to look at some visual patterns rather than others. Fantz measured infants' preferences for the six stimuli shown in Figure 4.12 and found that babies from birth to 6 months of age fixated longer on patterned targets than on plain targets. This finding of an early preference for patterned stimuli gave rise to a massive research literature on the features of patterns to which infants are sensitive at various ages. In addition, the preference exhibited by Fantz's subjects for the pattern of the human face led subsequent investigators to pursue the question of whether neonates are innately equipped to recognize and respond to the human facial configuration.

Sensitivity to Pattern Features. Research that followed Fantz's early work showed that as infants get older, they prefer increasingly complex visual patterns. For example, when babies of 3, 8, and 14 weeks of age were exposed to black-and-white checkerboard patterns, younger infants looked longest at the one composed of only a few large squares, whereas older infants preferred checkerboards having many

Figure 4.11. Convex and concave surfaces depicted by shading in the Granrud, Yonas, and Opland (1985) study. *(From C. E. Granrud, A. Yonas, & E. A. Opland, 1985, "Infants' Sensitivity to the Depth Cue of Shading,"* Perception and Psychophysics, *37, 416. Reprinted by permission.)*

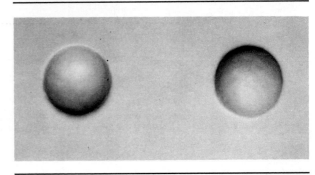

Maturation, Experience, and Avoidance of the Dropoff on the Visual Cliff

Box 4.3

Theory. In Gibson and Walk's research on the visual cliff, most infants refused to cross the deep side, but a few did cross. To explain the unusual behavior of these babies, some child development specialists have taken a maturational position. They claim that avoidance of the deep side eventually matures with age, independent of early experience. Others emphasize the role of experience and maintain that practice in independent movement facilitates the avoidance response. Several attempts to sort out the relative importance of maturation and experience in visual cliff behavior have been made.

Research. Nancy Rader and her colleagues (Rader, Bausano, & Richards, 1980; Richards & Rader, 1981) concluded that a special visual program controlled by maturation governs infants' avoidance of the visual cliff. Results from two experiments showed that babies who began crawling earlier were more likely to cross the deep side than those who crawled later, regardless of amount of prior crawling experience. Rader conjectured that infants who begin crawling early, before depth perception is fully mature, rely on tactile rather than visual cues to guide their crawling movements. However, among late crawlers, the capacity to use visual information emerges just before or at about the same time as crawling. For these babies, visual cues supersede tactile cues for guiding performance on the visual cliff, and they avoid the dropoff. Rader also reasoned that if experience in independent movement is important for the development of the depth response, then the opportunity to use a walker, as well as practice in crawling, should be related to visual cliff avoidance.

To investigate these issues, infants between 4½ and 8½ months of age were given daily practice sessions in using a walker over several weeks to several months. Then they were tested on the visual cliff both crawling and in a walker. Neither prior experience in crawling nor practice with the walker predicted avoidance of the deep side. In addition, although many of the infants avoided the dropoff when permitted to crawl, when tested in a walker, almost none of them did! Rader concluded that visual cues that ordinarily guide babies' crawling movements are disrupted when they move about in an artificial locomotion device.

Contrary evidence comes from Bennett Bertenthal and his associates (Bertenthal & Campos, 1987; Bertenthal, Campos, & Barrett, 1984), who argue that maturational factors alone cannot explain avoidance of heights. In one study, groups of precrawling infants were given many hours of artificial locomotor practice in walkers, while another group did not receive this experience. When held over the deep side of the cliff, the "walker" babies showed heart rate accelerations (which the investigators took as an indication of avoidance); their "nonwalker" counterparts did not. In another investigation, visual cliff performance was tested as a function of both age when infants began crawling and duration of crawling experience. Results indicated that at each crawling-onset age, infants with more crawling experience were much more likely to refuse to cross the deep side. The researchers concluded that infants who do not avoid the dropoff are "tenderfoot" crawlers who have had insufficient practice at independent locomotion.

Applications. The relative importance of maturation and experience in visual cliff performance remains unresolved. Until additional research unravels this complex issue, what advice should be given to parents whose youngsters are just beginning to crawl? The old adage, "Better safe than sorry" applies. Parents of precocious crawlers often describe their babies as fearless daredevils who are willing to crawl while looking elsewhere than at the surface ahead of them. Whether their failure to avoid dropoffs is a consequence of an immature visual program or too little experience, parents would do well to take special safety precautions when infants are near common household dropoffs, such as staircases, or when they are placed in walkers.

---

smaller squares (Brennan, Ames, & Moore, 1966). Infant preferences for many other pattern stimuli have also been assessed — curved versus straight lines, connected versus disconnected elements, and whether or not the pattern is organized about a central focus (as in a bull's eye), to name just a few.

For many years, investigators found it extremely difficult to sort out exactly which of these pattern features are most important to infants of different ages. Then, research by Banks and his collaborators showed that a general principle called *contrast sensitivity* accounts for young babies' pattern preferences (Banks & Ginsburg, 1985; Banks & Salapatek, 1981). Contrast refers to the overall quantity of light-dark transitions in a stimulus configuration. If babies can detect a difference in contrast between two patterns, they will prefer the one with more contrast. This explains why

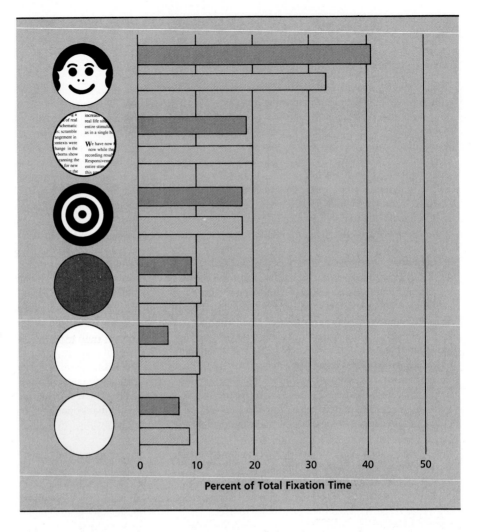

Figure 4.12. Fantz's (1961) findings on infant pattern perception. Preference for patterned stimuli was demonstrated by recording the extent to which infants looked at a face, newsprint, a bull's eye, and plain red, white, and yellow circles. The purple bars show the results for infants from 2 to 3 months of age, the blue bars for infants between 3 and 6 months of age. Even newborns showed pattern preferences similar to these. *(From R. Fantz, 1961, "The Origin of Form Perception,"* Scientific American, 204, *72.*

very young infants prefer to look at large, bold checkerboards. During the early weeks of life, patterns with many small elements cannot easily be resolved by the baby's immature visual system. Consequently, neonates see little or no contrast in them at all. By 2 months of age, contrast sensitivity has improved considerably. Patterns with fine details and subtle, muted edges begin to consume more looking time (Dodwell, Humphrey, & Muir, 1987; Pipp & Haith, 1984). Moreover, patterns that move (such as a flashing field of lights) are especially attractive to young babies (Kaufmann, Stucki, & Kaufmann-Hayoz, 1985). Motion heightens the degree of contrast available in the infant's visual field.

In the early weeks of life, infants respond to the separate parts of a pattern. Only around 2 to 3 months do they begin to integrate pattern elements into a unified whole. For example, after habituating to the cross (A) shown in Figure 4.13, 2-month-olds dishabituate to a change in the stimulus configuration (B), not to a change in its elements (C), indicating that they perceive the overall form (Vurpillot, Ruel, & Castrec, 1977). However, in young infants, sensitivity to pattern structure is limited to simple configurations with a high degree of symmetry. Over the first half year, progressively more complex and less regular pattern arrangements are discriminated (Dodwell, Humphrey, & Muir, 1987). By this time, infants are so adept at detecting pattern organization that they even generate subjective boundaries that are not physically present. Look at the pattern shown in Figure 4.14. Seven-month-old babies perceive a square in the center of this figure, just as you do (Bertenthal, Campos, &

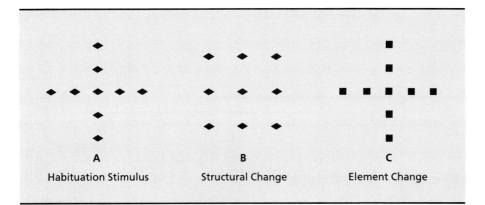

A	B	C
Habituation Stimulus	Structural Change	Element Change

Figure 4.13. Stimuli used to test infants' recognition of a pattern configuration. After habituating to pattern *A*, 2-month-olds dishabituate to a change in the stimulus configuration *(B)*, not to a change in its elements *(C)*. This indicates that they are sensitive to overall pattern form. *(Adapted from Vurpillot, Ruel, & Castrec, 1977.)*

Haith, 1980). Older infants carry this responsiveness to subjective contour even further. Nine-month-olds can detect the organized, meaningful pattern conveyed by a series of moving lights that simulate a human being walking, in that they look much longer at this display than they do at upside down or disorganized versions (Bertenthal et al., 1985). Although 3- to 5-month-olds can discriminate among these configurations, they do not show a special preference for one with both an upright orientation and a humanlike movement pattern (Berthenthal et al., 1987; Bertenthal, Proffit, & Cutting, 1984).

Most investigators believe that maturation of the visual system is largely responsible for the infant's growing preference for complex, integrated patterns. As we saw earlier, both visual acuity and scanning behavior improve during the first few months, and these changes support the infant's exploration of complex stimuli (Pipp & Haith, 1984). Also, direct examination of the visual cortex in animals, along with indirect research on humans, reveals that neural receptors are prewired to respond to very specific pattern stimuli, such as vertical, horizontal, and curved lines. Improvements in the sensitivity and organization of these receptors probably play a major part in the infant's changing pattern preferences (Accredolo & Hake, 1982).

Perception of the Human Face. If it existed, an innate capacity on the part of neonates to recognize and respond to the configuration of the human face would undoubtedly promote survival and be adaptive in an evolutionary sense. Although Fantz (1961) claimed that newborns prefer the regular configuration of the human face to patterns of equal complexity, such as scrambled facial features, his finding has not been replicated. Neither the orientation nor the arrangement of facial features in a stimulus pattern seems to influence the attention of infants under 2 months of age, largely because, as we discussed earlier, 1-month-olds do not scan the internal features of a stimulus.[5] At 2 to 3 months, when scanning is more mature and infants become sensitive to pattern structure, they do prefer a schematic face over scrambled arrangements (Maurer, 1985). By this time, they recognize the **invariant features,** or stable characteristics of the stimulus, that distinguish faceness from nonfaceness in pictures and photos (Dannemiller & Stephens, 1988; Kleiner & Banks, 1987). How-

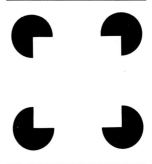

Figure 4.14. Subjective contours in a visual pattern. Do you perceive a square in the middle of this figure? By 7 months of age, infants do, too. *(Adapted from Bertenthal, Campos, & Haith, 1980.)*

[5] Perhaps you are wondering, at this point, how newborn babies can exhibit the remarkable imitative capacities described earlier in this chapter if they do not scan the internal features of a face. Recall that the facial gestures in the neonatal imitation research were live demonstrations. Their dynamic quality probably caused the babies to notice them. In the research described above, all the facial stimuli are static poses.

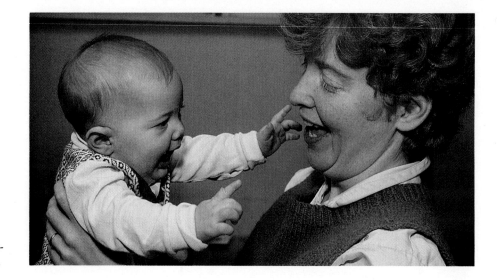

*The human face is a fasci-
nating object of sensory exploration for young babies.*

ever, the infant's emerging recognition of faces does not seem to be a built-in perceptual capacity. Instead, it follows the same developmental course as other aspects of
visual perception.

By 3 months of age, infants can make subtle discriminations among the internal
features of faces. For example, they distinguish between photos of strangers, even
when the faces are judged by adults to be moderately similar to one another (Barrera
& Maurer, 1981a). Around this time, babies also recognize their mother's face in a
photo, as they look longer at it than the face of a stranger (Barrera & Maurer, 1981b).

By 5 months, infants notice the invariant features that make a human face unique.
In other words, they recognize a particular configuration of eyes, nose, and mouth as
stable, even when it appears in a new context. This is evident in 5-month-olds' ability
to recognize a new photo of a person they had previously seen in a different pose
(Fagan, 1976) and to generalize from a real face to a color photograph of the same
person (Dirks & Gibson, 1977). Also, around 7 months, infants recognize the same
facial expression (happiness) in a photograph when it is demonstrated by different
people (Caron, Caron, & Myers, 1982).

The development of face perception contributes to the infant's ability to recognize
and respond to the expressive behaviors of others. For example, one of the earliest
infant behaviors elicited by the human face is the smile, a response that is important
in the affectional bond infants and caregivers build during the first year of life. By the
middle of the second month, infants start to smile in response to a wide range of
high-contrast patterns, including the visual configuration of the human face (Bower,
1982). At 2 months, internal features of the face become important in eliciting
smiling—at first the eyes (a high-contrast feature), followed by the mouth and other
elements (Kagan, 1971). At 3 months, when infants can recognize different facial
configurations, smiling becomes selective in that it occurs more often in response to
familiar than to unfamiliar people. The baby's social smile is rewarding to caregivers;
it draws them closer to the infant and encourages them to continue the pleasurable
interaction. As a result, babies respond by smiling all the more. Thus, the visual
abilities underlying infants' perception of the human face contribute to their recognition of familiar people and to the formation of their earliest social relationships.

Object Perception. Research on pattern perception deals only with two-dimensional stimuli, but as adults, we perceive a world made up of stable, three-dimensional
objects. To what extent is the visual world of infants organized into coherent, independently existing objects in the same way as our own?

Shape and Size Constancy. As we move around the environment and look at objects, the retinal images associated with them undergo constant changes in size and shape. To recognize objects as stable and unchanging, we translate these varying retinal images into a single representation. Perception of an object's shape as stable, despite changes in the shape projected on the retina, is called **shape constancy.** The ability to perceive an object's size as constant, despite changes in retinal image size as we move closer to it or farther away, is called **size constancy.**

Slater and Morison (1985) looked for evidence of shape constancy in newborns. Babies 6 hours to 6 days old were first habituated to one of two stimuli: a square or a trapezoid presented in a sequence of different slants to the eye. Next, the square and trapezoid were paired together, but both were at slants other than those presented in the initial habituation phase. Dishabituation proved to be greatest to the novel shape, indicating that newborns could extract the constant, real shape of the stimulus during the habituation phase and then respond to the novel shape. These findings suggest that shape constancy is an innate perceptual ability. It is interesting that shape constancy is present long before the emergence of controlled reaching and grasping, which permit babies to actively rotate objects and view them from many different angles.

In contrast to shape constancy, size constancy does not emerge until 4 to 6 months of age. In a study in which infants were first habituated to a large mannequin and then were tested to see whether they perceived it as equivalent to a mannequin of the same size but a different distance away, McKenzie, Tootell, and Day (1980) obtained evidence for size constancy in 6- to 8-month-olds. As illustrated in Figure 4.15, the infants regarded a mannequin whose real size was identical to the original stimulus as perceptually equivalent, even when its retinal image size was not the same. In a second, similarly designed study, 4-month-olds showed size constancy when each of the stimuli was displayed in motion, approaching and receding before the baby's eyes (Day & McKenzie, 1981). Size constancy seems to require some appreciation of depth and the third dimension. Recall that infants first become sensitive to kinetic depth cues, so perhaps it is not surprising that younger babies can detect size constancy only

Figure 4.15. Testing infants for size constancy in the McKenzie, Tootell, and Day (1980) study. The procedure illustrated is a simplified version of the one used by the investigators. (1) Infants were first habituated to a large mannequin head 60 cm from their eyes. (2) Then they were tested to see whether they would dishabituate to the same size mannequin 30 cm away (a); or a smaller mannequin 30 cm away (b). Infants dishabituated to 2b, indicating that they regard objects of the same actual size presented at different distances from their eyes (1 and 2a) as perceptually equivalent.

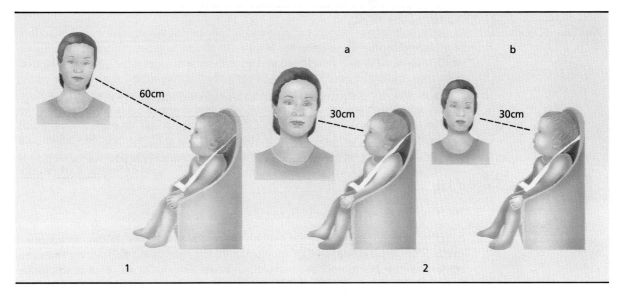

under moving stimulus conditions. Between 4 and 8 months, infants respond to binocular and pictorial depth cues, which may contribute to size constancy with stationary objects at this time (Aslin, 1987).

Perception of Objects as Distinct, Bounded Wholes. The achievement of perceptual constancies does not give us a complete picture of the extent to which infants perceive a world of structured, independent objects like our own. Adults can distinguish a single object from surrounding objects and surfaces by looking for a regular shape and uniform texture and color. Observations by Piaget (1936/1952) of his 6-month-old son Laurent first suggested that young infants do not use these same cues. Piaget dangled a small, attractive object in front of Laurent, who eagerly grabbed it. But as soon as it was placed on top of a bigger object, such as a book or pillow, Laurent no longer reached for it. Instead, he reached for the larger, supporting object. Laurent's behavior indicates that he did not perceive the boundary between the two objects created by their different sizes, shapes, and textures. As long as one object was adjacent to the other, he treated them as a single unit.

Recent carefully controlled studies support Piaget's informal observations, and they also indicate that it is the *movement* of objects relative to one another and to their background that gradually enables infants to construct a visual world of independent objects. In a series of studies, 5-month-olds were shown two box-shaped objects, a smaller one in front of a larger one. In some presentations, the objects touched each other; in others, they were spatially separated. Also, sometimes the objects were stationary, and at other times they moved either independently or together. When the objects touched each other and were either stationary or moving in the same direction, infants reached for them as a whole. But when they were separated or moved in opposite directions, infants behaved as if the objects were distinct, and they reached for only one of them (Hofsten & Spelke, 1985; Spelke, Hofsten, & Kestenbaum, 1989). These findings suggest that the relative motions of surfaces permit infants to organize their visual environment into separately existing objects. When an object moves across a background, its various features remain in the same relationship to one another and move together. Such movement helps the infant differentiate the object from other units in the visual field. The research described above, as well as other studies (Kellman & Spelke, 1983; Kellman, Spelke, & Short, 1986), indicates that during the first 5 months of life, motion seems to exert a stronger effect on the infant's perception of an object as a bounded whole than do stationary cues such as pattern, texture, and color. By the middle of the first year, stationary cues start to become more important for identifying objects as separate units (Bower, 1982).

BRIEF REVIEW

Recent research has led to an exciting and significant expansion of our understanding of infant perceptual development. Sensitivity to touch, postural orientation, taste, smell, and sound is well developed in the newborn baby. Over the course of the first year, the vestibular system becomes integrated with vision, and sensitivity to pitch, loudness, and location of sound improves. Of all the senses, vision is the least mature at birth and undergoes the most dramatic postnatal changes. To help you master the diverse visual achievements of infants, Figure 4.16 provides an overview of visual development during the first 7 months. Look carefully at the figure, and you will see that age 2 months is clearly a turning point in infant visual competence, a finding that investigators attribute to rapid maturation of the visual system during the early weeks of life.

Intermodal Coordination: Bringing the Senses Together

So far we have discussed the infant's sensory systems one by one, but most events we perceive are **intermodal** in that they make information available to more than one sensory system at a time. For example, we know that the shape of an object is the same whether we see it or touch it, that lip movements are correlated with the sound of a voice, and that dropping a rigid object on a hard surface will cause a sharp,

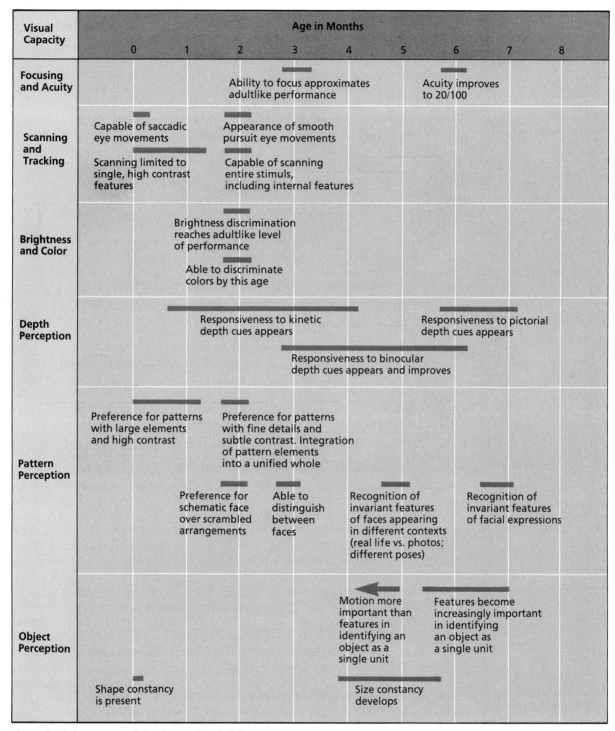

Figure 4.16. Emergence of visual capacities in infancy.

banging sound. As adults, we take information offered to more than one sensory modality at a time and perceive it as an integrated unit. Also, on the basis of information picked up in one modality, we have certain expectations about what we will perceive in another. For example, we expect an object with a smooth, curved surface that we *feel* to *look* round, and we expect to *hear* a voice in synchrony with lip movements that we *see*.

The emergence of intermodal coordination has been a long-debated topic in developmental psychology. Some investigators believe that human beings begin life with sensory modalities that are entirely independent and that over time, they gradually learn intermodal coordination as the result of experiencing the repeated association of one sensory impression with another. Others believe that the detection of intermodal commonalities is a fundamental characteristic of the human perceptual system and that it is available from the start, without benefit of learned correlations. To decide between these two points of view, researchers have examined the extent to which young infants can appreciate the intermodal nature of perceived events.

Recent research sides with the position that infants are innately wired to put intersensory information together (Spelke, 1987). The ability of newborn babies to turn in the general direction of a sound and to engage in primitive reaching for objects suggests that a natural tendency to combine information across modalities is present from birth. In addition, neonates can translate tactile information into visual information. Meltzoff and Borton (1979) gave 1-month-old infants a pacifier to suck on with either a smooth surface or a surface with nubs on it. After exploring it in their mouths, the infants were presented with two pacifiers for visual inspection. They preferred to look at the shape they had sucked, indicating that they could recognize intermodal matches without months of experience in simultaneous tactile-visual exploration.

As early as 4 months of age, infants spontaneously coordinate auditory and visual information appropriately. In one study, babies were shown two films side by side, one depicting two blocks banging and the other showing two sponges being squashed together. At the same time, the sound track for only one of the films — either a sharp, banging noise or a soft, squashing sound — could be heard. Infants looked at the film appropriate to the sound track, indicating that they were able to detect a common rhythmic and temporal structure in both the seen movement and the sound of the objects (Bahrick, 1983). As yet, such immediate integration of auditory and visual information has not been demonstrated in younger babies. However, new research on the emergence of this capacity suggests that infants will not link any visual and auditory input together. Instead, they are primed from the start to pick up *appropriate* connections. Recently, Bahrick (1988) gave 3-month-olds a chance to learn intermodal matches that they did not exhibit spontaneously. Babies were shown either a single large marble or a group of smaller marbles colliding against a surface. In some conditions, an accompanying sound track was synchronous with the movements of the objects and also fit with the way marbles usually sound; in other conditions, these natural visual-auditory relationships were broken. Results showed that infants learned the intermodal association only when the sound track was congruent with both the motion and the composition of the marbles.

Looking, touching, and listening appear to be coordinated in infants from the earliest ages. Then, as babies become increasingly familiar with the action possibilities of objects, they extend that initial coordination. By the middle of the first year, intermodal perception is sophisticated. For example, 5- to 6-month-olds know that male faces go with male voices and female faces with female voices (Francis & McCroy, 1983) and that a noise growing softer matches an object moving away, not one approaching (Walker-Andrews & Lennon, 1985). Moreover, infants pick up intermodal relationships rapidly, often after only one brief exposure to a new situation (Spelke, 1987).

Understanding Perceptual Development

Now that we have reviewed the emergence of infant perceptual competencies, the question arises: How can we put this diverse array of amazing achievements together? Does any general principle account for perceptual development? Eleanor and James Gibson's **differentiation theory** provides the most widely accepted answer to this question in the field today. Earlier we mentioned the concept of *invariant features* in our discussion of infant face perception. According to the Gibsons, infants actively search for and detect invariant features of the environment (those that remain stable) in a constantly changing perceptual world. For example, in pattern perception, we observed that infants first search for salient, high-contrast features along the periphery of a stimulus and then explore its more subtle, internal features. Eventually, they notice *invariant relations* among these features. Consequently, they detect overall patterns, including those that distinguish faces from nonfaces and that discriminate unique facial expressions. Perception of size constancy and the features that identify objects as separate, bounded units are additional examples of the baby's tendency to search for permanence and stability in a changing flux of stimulation. Intermodal coordination also seems to conform to this principle. Infants look for invariant relations, such as the same rhythm and tempo in an object's motion and sound, that unite information across different modalities. Therefore, one way of conceptualizing the general progression of perceptual development is to think of it as a built-in tendency to search for order and stability in a complex, changing world, an ability that becomes increasingly fine-tuned with development (Gibson, 1970; Gibson, 1979).

At this point, it is important to note that differentiation theory is not the only perspective on the emergence of infant psychological competencies. Other researchers believe that babies do not just make sense of stimuli by sorting out their distinctive features. Instead, they attribute *meaning* to what they perceive, constructing categories of objects and events in the surrounding environment. We have already seen the glimmerings of this cognitive point of view in evidence reviewed above. For example, older infants *interpret* a pattern of blinking lights as a moving human being and a familiar face as a source of pleasure, affection, and security. We will save our discussion of infant cognitive development for later chapters of this book, acknowledging for now that the cognitive perspective also has merit in understanding the achievements of infancy. In fact, many investigators combine these two positions, regarding infant psychological development as proceeding from a perceptual to a cognitive emphasis over the first year of life (Salapatek & Cohen, 1987).

EARLY DEPRIVATION AND ENRICHMENT: IS INFANCY A CRITICAL PERIOD OF DEVELOPMENT?

Throughout this chapter, we have discussed how certain experiences affect the development of infant perceptual and motor capacities. In view of the findings already reported, it is not surprising that many other investigations have found that attentive, warm, stimulating caregiving that is responsive to infants' self-initiated efforts promotes active exploration of the environment and early achievement of developmental milestones, (e.g., Belsky, Goode, & Most, 1980; Bradley et al., 1989). In fact, the relationship between early experience and infant competence is bidirectional. Sensitive, responsive caregiving leads to active, exploratory, mature babies, who, in turn, are more likely to evoke stimulating behaviors from parents. As a result, such infants profit from experience even more.

The powerful effect of early experience is even more apparent when we consider how infants develop in settings that lack the rich, varied stimulation of normal homes. We have already seen that infants reared in deprived institutions are severely retarded in motor development. They also engage in less exploration of objects, show stereotyped, immature play behaviors, and are overly fearful of new situations that present attractive opportunities to play and explore (Collard, 1971). After only a few months, the mental development of these babies is far behind that of their home-reared peers (Dennis & Najarian, 1957).

Although these findings indicate that early experience has a profound impact on infant development, they do not tell us for sure whether infancy is a **critical period** of development. That is, if babies do not experience rich and varied stimulation of their senses in the first year or two of life, will there be *permanent* deficits in development

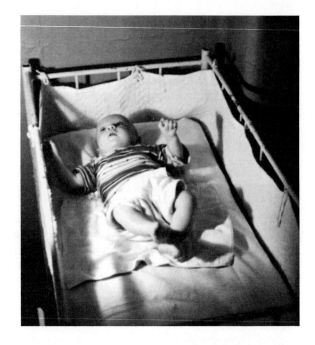

A deprived institutional environment can significantly delay an infant's development. However, if conditions improve, infants usually overcome the effects of early deprivation.

from which they cannot recover later on? This question has been of special interest since the 1940s, when researchers suggested that the consequences of rearing babies under deprived institutional conditions were both dire and irrevocable (Goldfarb, 1945; Spitz, 1945).

For ethical reasons, we cannot conduct experiments in which we deliberately deprive human infants of normal rearing experiences and wait to observe the long-term consequences. However, a number of natural experiments in which children were the unfortunate victims of deprived conditions in early infancy but were later exposed to stimulating, sensitive care provide the best available test of whether human infancy is a critical period of development. A unique feature of these studies is that they allow us to examine the long-lasting effects of early deprivation without the contaminating influence of later deprivation. If the critical period hypothesis is correct, then the effects of deprivation during infancy should persist, even when children are moved into enriched settings.

In a classic study of this kind, Skodak and Skeels (1945, 1949) investigated the consequences of transferring 13 orphanage infants whose development was extremely delayed to an institution for the retarded at an average age of 19 months. The retarded adult residents eagerly welcomed the youngsters into their wards, played with them, talked to them, and even competed to see whose baby was developing the fastest! The average IQ of the children when they were transferred was 64, but after a stay of 1 to 2 years, they showed dramatic gains, attaining a mean performance of 96. Eleven of the children were eventually adopted, and a follow-up after 2½ years in their adoptive homes revealed an average IQ of 101. As adults, half completed high school, 4 attended college, and 1 eventually earned a Ph.D. at a major university. All were self-supporting in skilled jobs, 11 married, and 9 became parents. Skodak and Skeels contrasted the development of these transferred infants with a group of 12 children who remained at the original orphanage. Their initial IQ was higher (mean of 87) than those who had been placed with the retarded adults, but their subsequent performance was markedly inferior. By 2½ years of age, they had lost an average of 26 points. In adulthood, only half completed the third grade. Five continued to reside in institutions, 5 of the 6 who worked held unskilled jobs, and 1 had died. Only 2 eventually married (Skeels, 1966).

The Skodak and Skeels research demonstrates that the effects of early deprivation can be overcome if children are provided with a more stimulating environment at an early age. Although their study has been criticized on methodological grounds (e.g., Longstreth, 1981), other investigations support the conclusion that deprived infants show striking gains when the quality of their rearing environment improves (Dennis, 1973; Kagan et al., 1979). In the most remarkable of these, Dennis studied a Lebanese institution called the Creche, where infants lay in their cribs through most of the first year and received practically no individual attention from caregivers. Extreme retardation in motor and language development was the result. Many babies did not sit up until 1 year of age or walk until well into the preschool years, and their average IQ between 1 and 6 years was 53. In 1956, adoption was legalized in Lebanon, and children of a variety of ages left the Creche and entered normal homes. By comparing children adopted early (before 2 years of age) with those adopted later, Dennis obtained a more precise answer to the question of whether a stimulating environment during infancy is critical for later development. The findings showed that children adopted before age 2 overcame their initial retardation, gaining an average of almost 50 IQ points and achieving a score of about 100 within 2 years time. In contrast, those adopted later, although they gained steadily in IQ over the period of childhood, never fully recovered from their earlier retardation. After 6 to 8 years with their adoptive families, their IQ scores were in the high 70s. Dennis concluded that environmental improvement by age 2 is necessary for complete recovery of deprived infants.

Taken together, the findings described above suggest that the critical period concept is too strict a notion to apply to psychological development during the first 2 years of life. Babies seem to be remarkably resilient beings who can withstand serious deprivation without being ruined or permanently stunted. However, the evidence is consistent with a modified notion that considers infancy to be a **sensitive phase** of development. A sensitive phase is a time that is optimal for certain capacities to emerge, but its boundaries are less well defined than those of a critical period. It is possible for development to occur later, but it is harder to induce it at that time. The research we have considered fits the conclusion that a sensitive phase of infant development may end somewhere around 2 years of age.

Unfortunately, most infants raised in underprivileged settings are likely to continue to be affected by the same disadvantaged conditions during their childhood years. Interventions that try to break this pattern by teaching caregivers about infant development and training them to engage in attentive, stimulating behaviors with infants have been shown to be markedly effective and to have lasting benefits (Andrews et al., 1982; Hunt et al., 1976). One of the most important outcomes of these programs is that passive, apathetic babies become active, alert beings with the capacity to evoke positive interactions from caregivers and initiate stimulating play for themselves.

Research on early deprivation and enrichment also indicates that there are individual differences in how easily children recover from impoverished rearing conditions. Reports exist on several children who made dramatic recoveries, even though systematic treatment did not begin until 5 or 6 years of age (Davis, 1947; Koluchova, 1972), whereas a few children barely changed at all, despite much earlier improvement in their environmental conditions. These cases suggest that in addition to the timing and quality of intervention, the long-term consequences of early deprivation depend on infant constitutional factors. To help us understand what kinds of interventions work best with particular children, the joint effects of these variables need to be understood (Gardner, Karmel, & Dowd, 1985).

Finally, there is currently a popular trend toward "educating" babies in infancy even when no early biological or environmental handicaps are evident. The rationale for such efforts is that even if infants are healthy, reared in sensitive, responsive environments, and not obviously in need of intervention, more stimulation can only make things better. In recent years, expensive early learning centers have sprung up around the United States where infants under 1 year of age are trained with letter and number flash cards and slightly older toddlers grapple with a full curriculum of reading, math, art, music, gym, and more. There is no evidence to date that such programs offer methods for raising infants that are superior to the natural inclinations of sensitive, caring parents or that they are actually successful in producing smarter, better, "super babies." In fact, programs designed to "hot house" or "jump start" infants may actually pose serious risks to their development. As we saw earlier in White and Held's (1966) study of visually guided reaching, more stimulation is not necessarily better, and it can be harmful. Trying to stuff infants with knowledge for which they are not ready may cause them to withdraw, ultimately threatening their spontaneous interest and pleasure in learning. The first 2 years of life are a time when infants learn to use their bodies, make sense of their perceptual world, and relate to people—learning that proceeds quite well without a deliberate adult lesson plan. Programs promising precocity that continue over many months are in danger of subtracting from the time babies have available for these vitally important developmental tasks (Siegel, 1987). In addition, when they promise but do not produce young geniuses, such programs are likely to lead to disappointed parents who view their children as failures at a very tender age (White, 1985). Thus, they rob infants of a psychologically healthy start on the long road to maturity, and they deprive parents of relaxed, pleasurable participation in their infant's early growth.

CHAPTER SUMMARY

The Organized Newborn

■ Infants are well-organized, competent beings who begin life with remarkable skills for relating to their physical and social worlds. The neonate's most obvious organized patterns of behavior are innate reflexes. A number of reflexes have survival value, while others provide the foundation for more complex motor behaviors that emerge later on.

■ The neonate has an organized sleep-waking cycle that becomes increasingly patterned and predictable over the first year of life. Infant sleep is also well organized. It can be divided into two distinct states: **REM** and **NREM sleep.** Babies spend far more time in the active, REM phase than do adults. According to **autostimulation theory,** the central nervous system depends on internal stimulation from REM sleep for normal growth and development.

■ Infants begin life with a set of distinct, clearly communicable cries. A crying baby stimulates strong physiological arousal in all human adults, with the pain cry producing an especially intense reaction. Events that cause a young infant to cry are largely physical and physiological, while older infants use the cry to express more psychologically based desires. Lifting the baby to the shoulder is the most effective way to soothe a crying infant. However, ethological and behaviorist theories disagree on how promptly caregivers should respond to infant cries. A high-pitched neonatal cry is a fundamental indicator of central nervous system distress.

■ The most widely used instrument for assessing the overall behavioral status of the newborn infant is Brazelton's **Neonatal Behavioral Assessment Scale (NBAS).** NBAS scores are modestly related to later intellectual functioning. The scale has also been used to teach parents about their baby's capacities and unique characteristics.

■ Newborn infants demonstrate a remarkable capacity to learn. Neonates can be **classically conditioned** when **CS-UCS** pairings are of biological significance to the organism. **Operant conditioning** has been demonstrated in a wide variety of investigations. **Habituation** studies reveal the neonate's impressive ability to recognize and remember prior experiences and to distinguish one stimulus from another. Newborn babies also have a rudimentary capacity to **imitate** adult gestures.

Motor Development in Infancy

■ Infants' rapidly emerging motor competencies support their perceptual and cognitive understanding of the world. Motor development is subject to a **secular trend,** as babies achieve motor milestones earlier today than they did a half century ago. The general maturational sequence of motor development follows the **cephalo-caudal** and **proximo-distal** trends. Today, motor control is understood as the progressive integration of separate behaviors into increasingly complex systems of action.

■ Experience has a profound effect on motor development, as shown by research on infants raised in deprived institutions. Visually guided reaching is gradually perfected during the first year and plays a major role in infants' exploration and manipulation of the environment.

Perceptual Development in Infancy

■ Infants exhibit a remarkable constellation of perceptual capacities from the very beginning. Touch, vestibular sensitivity, taste, and smell are well developed at birth, and the vestibular system becomes integrated with vision during the first year of life. In addition, neonates can hear a wide variety of sounds, and sensitivity to pitch, loudness, and sound location improves over the first year. Newborns are particularly responsive to auditory stimuli within the frequency range of the human voice. They can distinguish among almost all speech sounds in human languages.

■ The visual apparatus is not fully developed at birth, but **visual acuity** and the ability to focus on objects mature rapidly during the first few months. From birth onward, infants use **saccades** to explore the visual field. **Smooth pursuit eye movements** for tracking moving stimuli appear at 1 month and improve over the first half year. By 2 months, infants discriminate between lights of different brightness as well as adults do, and color perception has improved.

■ Research on depth perception indicates that around the time infants are able to crawl, they avoid the deep dropoff on the **visual cliff.** Visual cliff research has not clarified when infants respond to particular depth cues, but recent investigations show that responsiveness to **kinetic cues** appears first, at the end of the first month, followed by sensitivity to **binocular cues** between 3 and 6 months of age. Perception of **pictorial cues** emerges last, around 6 or 7 months of age.

■ Infants' developing preference for more complex patterns has been attributed to rapid maturation of the visual system over the first few months of life. Perception of the human face follows the same course of development as other aspects of visual perception, with single, high-contrast features on the periphery of a stimulus capturing the attention of the 1-month-old. Scanning of internal features appears by 2 months, when infants recognize the **invariant features** that distinguish faceness from nonfaceness. At 3 months, infants can discriminate between different faces, and at 5 months, they notice the invariant features that make a particular face unique.

■ Infants gradually build a visual world made up of stable, three-dimensional objects during the first 6 months of life. **Shape constancy** is present at birth, while **size constancy** does not appear until 4 to 6 months of age. The contrasting movements of objects help infants learn to perceive them as separate entities.

■ Young infants have a remarkable built-in capacity for **intermodal coordination.** Research suggests that a natural tendency to combine and integrate information across perceptual modalities exists from birth onward.

■ **Differentiation theory** is the most widely accepted account of perceptual development. Over time, infants detect increasingly fine-grained, invariant features of stimulation in a constantly changing perceptual world.

Early Deprivation and Enrichment: Is Infancy a Critical Period of Development?

■ Attentive, warm, stimulating caregiving is vitally important for development in the first 2 years of life. Rather than being a **critical period** of development, infancy is a **sensitive phase** in which a variety of milestones emerge easily and optimally. Children can compensate for early deprivation after 2 years of age, but recovery may not be complete.

IMPORTANT TERMS AND CONCEPTS

REM sleep   (p. 124)
NREM sleep   (p. 124)
autostimulation theory   (p. 124)
Neonatal Behavioral Assessment Scale
   (NBAS)   (p. 129)
classical conditioning   (p. 131)
unconditioned stimulus
   (UCS)   (p. 132)
unconditioned response
   (UCR)   (p. 132)
conditioned stimulus (CS)   (p. 132)
conditioned response (CR)   (p. 132)
extinction   (p. 132)
operant conditioning   (p. 133)

reinforcer   (p. 133)
punishment   (p. 133)
habituation   (p. 134)
dishabituation   (p. 134)
imitation   (p. 136)
secular trend in motor
   development   (p. 139)
cephalo-caudal trend   (p. 140)
proximo-distal trend   (p. 140)
ulnar grasp   (p. 142)
pincer grasp   (p. 143)
visual acuity   (p. 147)
saccades   (p. 148)

smooth pursuit eye
   movements   (p. 148)
visual cliff   (p. 149)
kinetic depth cues   (p. 150)
binocular depth cues   (p. 150)
pictorial depth cues   (p. 150)
invariant features   (p. 155)
shape constancy   (p. 157)
size constancy   (p. 157)
intermodal coordination   (p. 158)
differentiation theory   (p. 160)
critical period   (p. 161)
sensitive phase   (p. 163)

John Singer Sargeant: *Young Boy on the Beach* (Sketch for the Oyster Gatherers of Cancale). Oil on canvas, 38.
1980 © Daniel J. Terra Collection, Terra Museum of American Art, Chicago.

5
Physical Growth

The Course of Physical Growth
Development of the Brain
Factors Affecting Physical Growth

As time passes during the first two decades of life, the child's body changes continuously and dramatically, until it reaches the mature adult state. Think, for a moment, about the vast physical differences between a newborn infant and a full-grown young adult. From birth to maturity, the average individual's height multiplies more than threefold, and weight increases as much as fifteen- to twentyfold. The top-heavy, chubby infant, whose head represents a quarter of the body's total length, is gradually transformed into the better proportioned youngster and eventually into the longer, broader, more muscular adult, whose head now consumes only a seventh of the body's total length. As we examine the changes that take place from infancy through adolescence, you will quickly see that the story of physical growth is not just a matter of becoming taller and larger. Physical development involves a highly complex series of changes in body size, proportion, and composition. In this chapter, we describe the general course of human growth, along with biological and environmental factors that regulate and control it. Then we turn to the development of the brain, the seat of our intelligence and adaptive functioning. We consider how its complex structure is generated during the early years of life and how its growth depends on precise interaction between the environment and developing nerve cells.

Although a basic overall plan for growth is shared by all members of the human species, there are marked individual differences in the rate at which physical growth proceeds. These differences exist to some degree at all ages, but they are most evident at *puberty*, a period of rapid physical change leading to an adult-sized body and sexual maturity at adolescence. Try to arrange a time to observe a group of 12-year-old girls or 14-year-old boys. You will see that obvious differences in progress toward maturity

167

exist among them. These variations have important consequences for social and emotional adjustment. In this chapter, we take up the interplay and connectedness between physical and psychological development. We also address sex differences in physical growth and the extent to which they mediate the development of body strength and athletic ability.

Finally, in several sections of this chapter, we consider disorders of physical growth—failure to thrive in infants, deprivation dwarfism in children, childhood obesity, and anorexia nervosa during the adolescent years. These special problems reveal that physical growth is a prime indicator of the child's mental health, and they illustrate the intimate connection between the physical and psychological domains of development.

THE COURSE OF PHYSICAL GROWTH

Compared to other animals, primates (including human beings) experience an extended period of postnatal growth. For example, in mice and rats, the interval between birth and puberty is a matter of weeks, comprising only 1 to 2 percent of the life span. In chimpanzees, who are closest to humans in the evolutionary hierarchy of primates, the time between birth and puberty is extended to about 7 years, consuming about one sixth of the life span. This expansion of the period of physical immaturity is even more exaggerated in human beings, who devote about one fifth of their total years to growth and development (Napier, 1970). Evolutionary reasons for the long period of human growth are not hard to find. Prolonged immaturity increases the dependency of the young on parents and other agents of socialization. In so doing, it provides added time for children to acquire the knowledge, skills, and behavior patterns necessary for life in a complex physical and social world. In the words of anthropologist Weston LaBarre (1954), "Biologically, it takes more time to become human. Obviously, too, it is the human brain and human learning which gain particular advantages by this biological slow-down" (p. 153).

Growth Curves and Changes in Overall Body Size

To parents, the most obvious signs of physical growth are changes in the dimensions of the child's body as a whole. During infancy, these changes are rapid. In the first 3 months of life, infants gain an average of 2 pounds per month. By 5 months of age, their birth weight has doubled, by the end of the first year it has tripled, and at 2 years of age it has quadrupled. Height undergoes similar dramatic gains during infancy. At the end of the first year, the infant's length is 50 percent greater than it was at birth, and by 2 years of age, it is 75 percent greater. In comparison, body growth during the preschool and middle childhood years is slow and steady. Increments average about 2 inches in height and 5 pounds in weight per year until the ninth or tenth birthday. Adolescence follows and is marked by a sharp acceleration in rate of growth. Large increases in height and weight are accompanied by sexual maturity. Then a deceleration in growth occurs as human beings reach their adult stature.

Investigators of physical growth describe these age-related changes in height and weight using two types of growth curves. The first, shown in Figure 5.1, is a **distance curve.** It records the height and weight of a single child, or the average height and weight of a group of children, at each age. It is called a distance curve because it indicates typical yearly progress toward maturity, or the average distance traveled at each age along the general path of growth. Besides serving as a useful set of growth standards, a number of interesting facts about children's growth can be obtained from these curves, especially since boys and girls are plotted separately. During infancy and childhood, the two sexes are very similar, with the typical girl just slightly shorter and lighter than the typical boy. Shortly after 11 years of age, the girl becomes taller

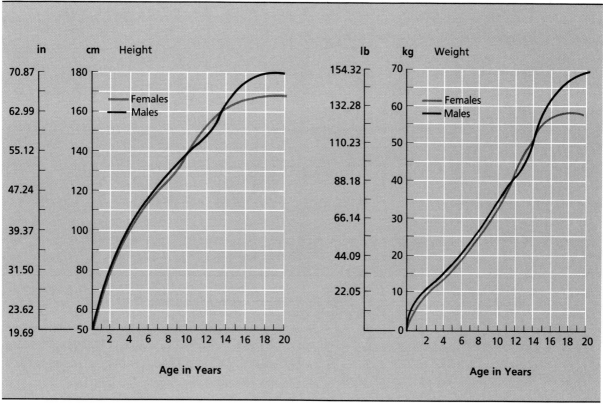

Figure 5.1. Height and weight distance curves for boys and girls, drawn from longitudinal measurements on approximately 175 individuals. *(From R. M. Malina, 1975,* Growth and Devel- opment: The First Twenty Years in Man. *P. 19. Minneapolis: Burgess. Adapted by permission.)*

and heavier for a time because, on the average, her adolescent growth spurt takes place 2 years earlier than the boy's. However, this advantage is short-lived. At age 14, she is surpassed in height by the typical boy, whose adolescent growth spurt has now started, while hers is almost finished. Growth in stature is complete for most girls by 16 years of age and for boys by age 17½ (Tanner, 1978b).

A second kind of growth curve is the **velocity curve,** depicted in Figure 5.2. It plots the absolute amount of growth at each yearly interval. Velocity curves are much better than distance curves at identifying the exact timing of growth spurts. There- fore, Figure 5.2 makes plain some growth facts we have already mentioned. Two large spurts in general body growth occur during human postnatal growth—one during the first year of life and the other at adolescence. Notice how the figure clearly reveals that the adolescent spurt takes place, on the average, 2 years earlier for girls than it does for boys.

The growth curves for height and weight shown in Figures 5.1 and 5.2 are often referred to as *general growth curves,* since most of the external body dimensions, as well as a number of internal organs such as the liver, spleen, and kidney, grow in a similar manner—rapid growth during infancy, slow and steady growth during mid- dle childhood, rapid growth once more during adolescence, and slowing and cessa- tion of growth during late adolescence. However, there are exceptions to this pattern. Among them are the brain and skull, the reproductive organs, and lymphoid tissues located throughout the body. As depicted in Figure 5.3, the brain and skull undergo rapid early growth, so rapid that the brain attains 70 percent of its adult size by age 3 and 95 percent by age 7. The genital curve shows a slight early rise, followed by a latent period during childhood and then a rapid growth spurt at adolescence. The

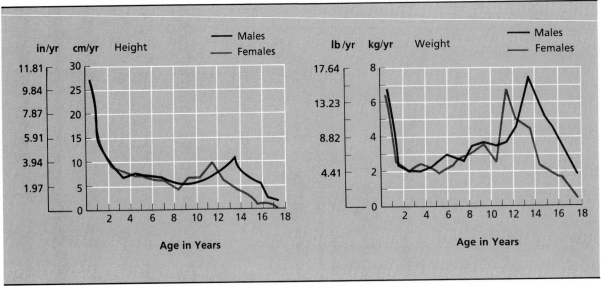

Figure 5.2. Height and weight velocity curves for boys and girls, drawn from longitudinal measurements on approximately 175 individuals. *(From R. M. Malina, 1975,* Growth and Devel- opment: The First Twenty Years in Man. *P. 20. Minneapolis: Burgess. Adapted by permission.)*

lymphoid curve is unique in that it rises rapidly in infancy and early childhood to a peak just before adolescence, at which time the amount of lymphoid tissue decreases into adulthood. This path of development is adaptive, in that the lymph system plays a central role in the body's defense against infection and is also believed to increase nutritional absorption (Shields, 1972). Figure 5.3 depicts the orderly but *asynchronous* nature of human growth. Various systems of the body have their own carefully timed, unique patterns of maturation (Malina, 1975).

Changes in Body Proportions

As the child's overall size increases, different parts of the body grow at different rates, and body proportions change accordingly. For example, during the prenatal period and throughout infancy, the upper part of the body is better developed than the lower limbs, but this imbalance is gradually corrected as the legs lengthen at a faster rate than the trunk throughout childhood. Perhaps you recognize this pattern of growth as the familiar *cephalo-caudal trend* we discussed in Chapter 4. You can see it depicted visually in Figure 5.4. Note that the ratio of leg length to total height is less than 1:4 in the early prenatal period, increases to 1:3 at birth, and then rises to 1:2 by adulthood. Physical growth during infancy and childhood also conforms to the *proximo-distal trend*, since it begins near the center axis of the body and moves outward, with the upper arms growing before the lower arms, which grow before the hands.

However, some exceptions to these basic trends appear just before puberty. During this time, growth actually proceeds in the reverse direction. The hands and feet enlarge just before the dramatic pubertal increase in height and weight. Also, at the beginning of the adolescent growth spurt, leg length peaks first. This is followed by additional growth in the length of the torso and trunk and, finally, by expansion of the shoulders and chest. This pattern of development explains why young adolescents stop growing out of their shoes and trousers before they stop growing out of their jackets and why parents, after doing a double-take at their rapidly transforming youngsters, often describe them as ''all legs.'' It also helps us understand why early adolescence is often regarded as an awkward phase. When the adolescent's trunk length starts to increase, the body's center of gravity shifts, causing new problems of

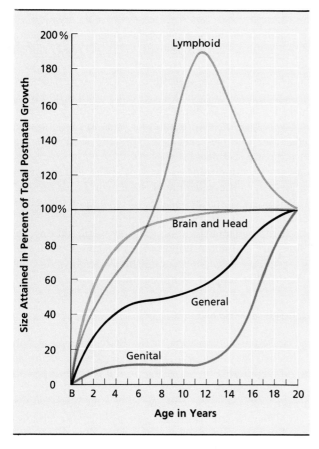

Figure 5.3. Growth curves of four different organ systems and tissues of the body. All are distance curves plotted in terms of percentage of change from birth to 20 years. *(From J. M. Tanner, 1962, Growth at Adolescence [2nd ed.]. Oxford: Blackwell. P. 11. Reprinted by permission.)*

balance and a period of temporary awkwardness in gross motor skills. However, this seldom lasts longer than 6 months (Tanner, 1978b).

The body proportions of boys and girls are similar during infancy and childhood. However, at adolescence, differences start to appear that are typical of young adults. The most obvious are the broadening of the shoulders relative to the hips that is characteristic of males and the broadening of the hips relative to the shoulders and

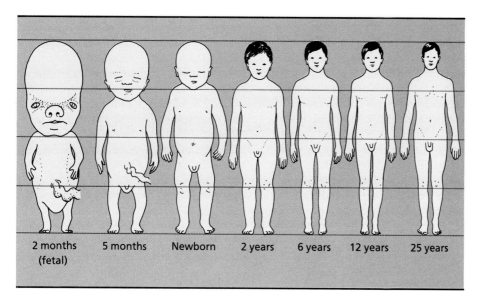

Figure 5.4. Changes in body proportions from the early prenatal period to adulthood. The figure illustrates the cephalo-caudal trend of growth. *(From Robbins et al., 1982, p. 118.)*

waist that is typical of females (Malina, 1975). These differences are the result of the influence of sex hormones on skeletal development during adolescence. Cartilage cells in the hip joints are specialized to respond to the rise in female sex hormones (estrogens), whereas those in the shoulder region are specialized to respond to an increase in male hormones (androgens, especially testosterone). Of course, males also grow substantially larger than females, and their legs are longer in proportion to the rest of the body. These sex differences are partly due to boys' delayed pubertal growth spurt. In comparison to girls, boys benefit from 2 additional years of preadolescent growth. Also, as we mentioned earlier, during the last part of preadolescence, the legs grow faster than the trunk of the body (Tanner, 1978b).

Sex differences in body size and proportions evolved over the history of our species because of their adaptive value. The widening of the female's hips provides room for the uterus and fetus to grow and a large enough pelvic opening so that a baby can be born. Broad shoulders, a muscular body, and long legs that contribute to running speed lead the male body to be adapted for tasks of heavy work, fighting, and hunting. Although these abilities are of limited importance in technologically advanced cultures where many strenuous tasks are accomplished with the aid of machines, the physical characteristics that support them continue to exist.

Changes in Body Composition

Major changes in the fat and muscular composition of the body take place with development. Body fat (most of which lies just beneath the skin) begins to accumulate in the last few weeks of prenatal life, gradually increasing until it reaches a peak at about 9 months of age. Thereafter, it declines until about 6 to 8 years of age, when it begins to rise again. Thus, newborn infants quickly fill out into round, plump babies over the course of the first year. Then, beginning in the second year of life, children start to become more angular and slender, a trend that continues into the school years. Girls have slightly more total fat at birth than do boys, a difference that becomes greater over the course of childhood and is especially marked after 8 years of age. Although both sexes show increases in fat on the trunk of the body until adulthood, girls accumulate fat at a substantially greater rate than boys. In addition, girls continue to add limb fat during adolescence, whereas the limb fat of boys decreases at this time (Tanner & Whitehouse, 1975).

Muscle tissue grows according to a very different early pattern than fat, accumulating very slowly and gradually at a decelerating rate throughout infancy and childhood. Then it increases dramatically at adolescence (Tanner, 1978a). Although both sexes gain in muscle at puberty, the increase is much greater for males than females. Adolescent boys develop larger hearts, larger skeletal muscles, and a greater vital capacity of the lungs than do girls. In addition, the number of red blood cells, and therefore the amount of hemoglobin available to carry oxygen from the lungs to the muscles, increases in boys at adolescence but remains unchanged in girls (Tanner, 1962). The combined result of all these changes is that boys' gains in muscle strength at adolescence are substantial and far outstrip those of girls, whose increases trail off earlier and remain at a much lower level. Boys' muscle strength shows its largest rise in the latter part of pubertal growth (Stolz & Stolz, 1971), a pattern of gain that plays a major role in their steady increase in athletic performance throughout the teenage years. When adolescent boys and girls were compared on a series of basic athletic skills, such as distance throw, broad jump, and 50-yard dash, girls' performance increased up to age 14 and then leveled off, whereas boys' performance continued to improve through their 17th year (Espenschade, 1971). However, girls receive far less encouragement and social approval for athletic accomplishment throughout childhood than do boys, a factor that dampens the development of physical skills in many girls and exaggerates the differences that do exist between the sexes (Thomas & French, 1985).

Since the growth spurt for boys occurs later than it does for girls, females generally tower over their male peers during early adolescence.

Skeletal Growth

Because children of the same age differ in their rates of growth, a variety of methods for estimating progress toward physical maturity have been devised. These estimates are useful to researchers studying the causes and consequences of individual differences in physical growth. They also provide rough estimates of children's chronological age in areas of the world where birth dates are not customarily recorded. One type of maturity estimate involves an assessment of the state of development of the primary and secondary sexual characteristics. This is an excellent indicator of maturity status, but it is useful only during the adolescent years. The best method for assessing growth maturation in children is **skeletal age,** because the development of the skeleton spans the entire period of physical growth and is related to the percentage of growth completed at any age (Tanner et al., 1983).

The forerunners of bones appear as cartilage early in prenatal life and start to be replaced by bone in the sixth week of gestation, a process that continues until individuals are in their 20s. Each bone begins as a primary center of **ossification** (place where cartilage hardens into bone) from which it enlarges and takes on a basic shape. Shortly before birth, secondary centers of ossification start to appear called **epiphyses** (see Figure 5.5). In the long bones, the epiphyses emerge at the two extreme ends of the bone. Immediately beneath each epiphysis is a growth plate, where cartilage cells proliferate and are gradually converted into bone. Thus, long bones extend their length by growing inward from each end. As growth nears completion, the growth plate gets thinner and eventually disappears. When this occurs, no more growth of the bone is possible. New epiphyses appear in various parts of the skeleton until puberty. The developing child has approximately 400 epiphyses at birth and twice that number by the beginning of adolescence (Delecki, 1985).

Skeletal age can be estimated by X-raying the bones of the body and seeing how many epiphyses there are and the extent to which they are not yet fused (see Figure 5.6). The x-rays are compared to norms established for bone maturity based on large numbers of children. Such estimates show that girls exceed boys in skeletal maturity throughout development. During the prenatal period, girls are already about 3 weeks ahead in skeletal growth. At birth, the difference amounts to about 4 to 6 weeks, and

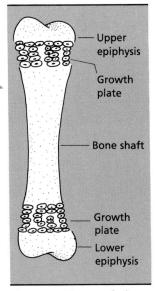

Figure 5.5 Diagram of a long bone showing growth plates beneath upper and lower epiphyses. *(Reprinted by permission of the publisher from* Fetus into Man *by J. M. Tanner, Cambridge, Mass.: Harvard University Press, Copyright © 1978 by J. M. Tanner. All rights reserved.)*

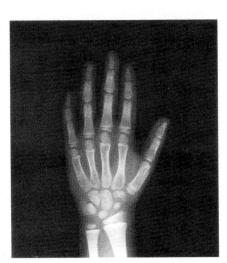

6½ Years

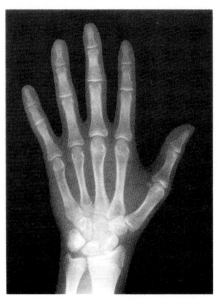

14½ Years

Figure 5.6. X-rays of the hand of a girl at two chronological ages, showing different degrees of skeletal maturity. Note the difference in ossification of the wrist bones and fusion of the epiphyses on the long bones of the forearm. *(From J. M. Tanner, R. H. Whitehouse, N. Cameron, W. A. Marshall, M. J. R. Healey, & H. Goldstein, 1983,* Assessment of Skeletal Maturity and Prediction of Adult Height *[TW2 method, 2nd ed.]. Academic Press, Inc. [London, Ltd.]. P. 86. Reprinted by permission.)*

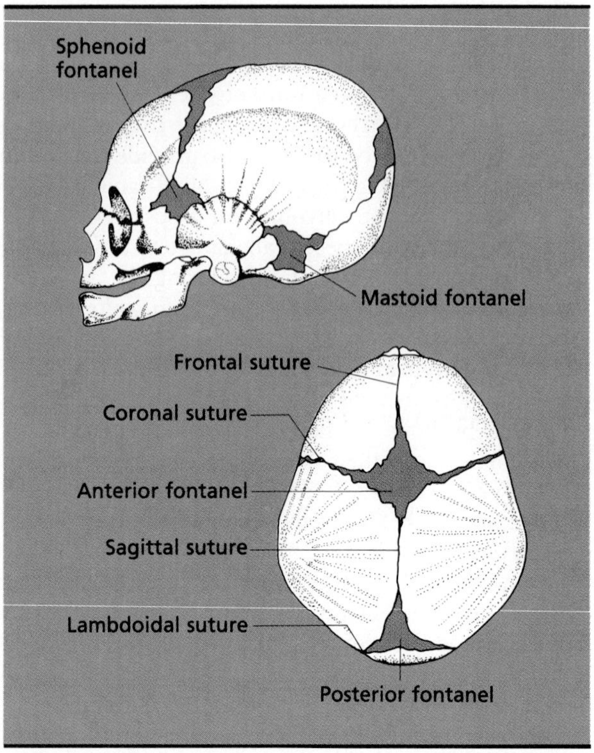

Figure 5.7. The skull at birth, showing the fontanels and sutures. *(From J. Delecki, "Principles of Growth and Development." in P. M. Hill [Ed.],* Human Growth and Development Throughout Life. *Copyright © 1985 by John Wiley & Sons, Inc. Reprinted by permission of John Wiley & Sons, Inc.)*

by puberty, it has increased to 2 years. Girls are advanced in the development of other organ systems as well. Their greater physiological maturity beginning in prenatal life may be partly responsible for their superior resilience in the face of environmental stressors and for the lower infant and early childhood mortality rates that exist for girls in comparison to boys (Tanner, 1978b).

Pediatricians are concerned with another aspect of skeletal development when they routinely measure the head circumference of babies from birth until 2 years of age. The pattern of skull growth is very different from that of the rest of the skeleton. Its growth is rapid during the first 2 years of life. By 6 years of age, its size is nearly complete, although slight increases continue to occur through adolescence. At birth, the bones of the cranial vault are separated by six gaps, or "soft spots," filled with fibrous tissue called **fontanels** (see Figure 5.7). The gaps allow the bones to slide over one another to some degree as the relatively large head of the baby passes through the narrow birth canal. The largest gap, the anterior fontanel, can easily be felt at the top of a baby's skull; it is slightly more than an inch across. It gradually shrinks and is filled in during the second year of life. The other fontanels are smaller and close more quickly. As the cranial bones come in contact with one another, they form sutures, or seams, which permit continued skull expansion as the brain enlarges in size. The sutures disappear completely after puberty, when skull growth ceases entirely (Delecki, 1985).

Besides increasing in length, the bones of the skeleton also grow in width, a process that takes place without the intervention of cartilage. Much like a tree expanding in girth, new layers are deposited as the result of cell duplication taking place just under the surface of the bone. The bones of the skull and the face grow in this manner. Small increases in the width of the long bones continue throughout the life span (Tanner, 1978b).

Puberty: The Physical Transition to Adulthood

Puberty is the time of development in which individuals become sexually mature and capable of producing offspring. It is also the period of greatest sex differentiation since intrauterine life. As we have already seen, dramatic changes in size, proportion, and muscular and fat composition of the body take place during this phase of development. Although the sequence of physical changes occurring at adolescence is fairly uniform among children, timing and speed of maturation differ substantially from individual to individual (see Figure 5.8). As we will see shortly, both the physical events of puberty and the rate at which they proceed have important implications for adolescent social and emotional adjustment.

Pubertal Development in Girls. Although **menarche,** or first menstrual period, is generally regarded as the major sign that puberty has arrived in girls, it actually occurs fairly late in the sequence of pubertal events. The first indicators of female puberty are the budding of the breasts and the beginning of the growth spurt—the swift increase in height and weight and expansion of the pelvis that we discussed earlier in this chapter. The average age at which these early signs appear in European and North American girls is around age 11, but the range extends from 8 to 13. The first appearance of pubic hair generally occurs slightly later than the budding of the breasts, usually between the eleventh and twelfth birthdays (Tanner, 1978b).

Menarche typically happens around the thirteenth birthday, although, again, the age range is large, extending from as early as 10½ to as late as 15½ years of age. By the time the girl has experienced her first menstrual period, her rapid gain in body size is

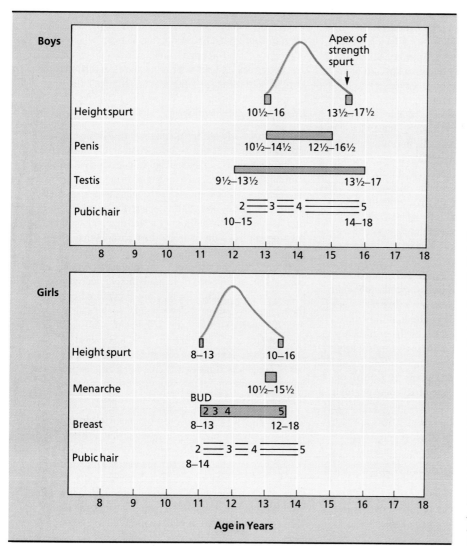

Figure 5.8. Range of ages for onset and completion of pubertal changes in boys and girls. To show the extent of individual variability, the beginning and completion of most changes are marked with a range of chronological ages. Pubic hair and breast development are rated on scales of 2 (initial signs) to 5 (completed growth). Note especially the relationship of the height spurt to other pubertal changes. It occurs earlier in the sequence of events for girls than it does for boys. *(From J. M. Tanner, 1962. Growth at Adolescence [2nd ed.], Oxford: Blackwell, Pp. 30, 36. Adapted by permission. Age ranges from Faust, 1977, and Tanner, 1978b.)*

starting to taper off, and the growth spurt is nearly over. The average girl adds almost 8 inches of total height during puberty, with only about 2 of these occurring after menarche. In the year following the appearance of menstruation, pubic hair and breast development are completed, and underarm hair appears. Although a 3-year time line for female pubertal growth is the norm, some girls pass far more rapidly through these milestones, taking as little as a year and a half. Others require an extended period, sometimes as long as 5 years (Marshall & Tanner, 1969).

Age of menarche is closely synchronized with the attainment of an appropriate level of skeletal maturity. In other words, menarche does not initiate the girl's physical growing up, but follows it (refer again to Figure 5.8). This sequence of events has clear adaptive value. It makes sense from a biological standpoint to delay menarche until sufficient physical and pelvic size is attained to permit the successful

---

CONTEMPORARY ISSUES: SOCIAL POLICY

Teenage Pregnancy: A Growing National Concern

Box 5.1

Each year, more than a million American teenagers become pregnant, four out of five of them unmarried and some 30,000 of them under the age of 15. The United States leads nearly all other developed nations in the incidence of teenage pregnancy, making it a pervasive national problem (Jones et al., 1985). Not all adolescents who conceive give birth to a baby. Approximately 40 percent of pregnant teenagers choose to have an abortion, and 13 percent of adolescent pregnancies end in miscarriage. Nevertheless, the number of out-of-wedlock births to mothers under 20 years of age increased from under 100,000 in 1960 to over 375,000 in the 1980s. The trend is due to a gradual rise over this period in teenage sexual activity, along with a sharp drop in the number of pregnant teens who marry before childbirth. Moreover, increased social acceptance of a young single mother raising a baby has probably contributed to the fact that relatively few of these infants are given up for adoption (Baldwin, 1983; Brooks-Gunn & Furstenberg, 1989; Furstenberg, Brooks-Gunn, & Chase-Landsdale, 1989).

When a baby is born to a teenage girl, it imposes lasting hardships on two generations—both adolescent parent and child. Teenage mothers are many times as likely as older women with young children to be poor, and a high proportion of adolescent births occur among members of low-income ethnic minority groups. Early pregnancy further reduces these youngsters' life chances, since it is educationally disruptive. Only 50 percent of girls who give birth before the age of 18 complete high school, compared to 96 percent of those who postpone childbearing. Both teenage mothers and fathers are likely to be on welfare, and if they are employed, their educational background limits them to unsatisfying, low-paid jobs (Elster & Panzarine, 1983; Furstenberg, Brooks-Gunn, & Chase-Landsdale, 1989; Osofsky & Osofsky, 1983).

Why does teenage pregnancy occur? In part, it is due to pervasive sexual activity among adolescents,

combined with inadequate sexual knowledge and lack of easy access to contraception. Estimates indicate that over 40 percent of 16-year-old girls have had sexual intercourse (Brooks-Gunn & Furstenberg, 1989). Yet even when school courses in sex education exist, adolescents often misunderstand reproductive facts or believe that pregnancy "can't happen to me." However, when earlier and better sex education programs are coupled with efforts to help teenagers obtain contraceptives, the pregnancy rate drops sharply (Furstenberg, Brooks-Gunn, & Chase-Landsdale, 1989).

The roots of teenage pregnancy are not just lack of sex education or access to birth control. Often the lives of these youngsters are troubled in many ways. Succumbing to peer pressure for premarital sex occurs more often among adolescents who feel alienated from their immediate family. Pregnant teenagers report less affection, less communication, and fewer demands and expectations placed on them by their parents than their nonpregnant counterparts (Olson & Worobey, 1984). In addition, academic achievement, interest in school, and educational aspirations of sexually active youngsters tend to be low. Such teenagers are also more likely than their peers to engage in deviant acts, such as alcohol and drug use, petty stealing, and defiance of adult authority (Brooks-Gunn & Furstenberg, 1989; Rowe et al., 1989). So premature sexuality seems to be one among a number of behaviors through which adolescents express feelings of frustration, failure, and opposition to conventional society.

Adolescent pregnancy also repeats itself from generation to generation. One study found that a third of girls and a seventh of boys who were teenage parents had been born to teenage mothers themselves (Furstenberg, Brooks-Gunn, & Morgan, 1987). Generally, these youngsters are from poor families, and having little sense of a promising future, the girls in particular imagine that a baby will fill the void in their lives (Wallis, 1985).

bearing of children. Higher rates of stillbirths and obstetric complications occur among women who are short in stature and who have small pelvic dimensions (Ellison, 1982).

Menarche is generally taken as the sign that a girl has reached sexual maturity. It does mark a mature state of uterine development, but in many girls, there is a period of 12 to 18 months following the beginning of menstruation in which mature ova are not yet produced. However, this temporary period of sterility cannot be counted on (Tanner, 1978b). Pregnancies resulting from early sexual activity among adolescents are on the rise, and many babies are being born to mothers who are younger than 15 years of age. As indicated in Box 5.1, teenage pregnancy is a major problem in the United States; the development of both young adolescent girls and their newborn infants is seriously at risk.

Most teenagers are not fully mature in their own right. As a result, they are often overwhelmed by the responsibilities of parenthood.

The process of becoming a parent constitutes a major life transition that brings with it stress and disequilibrium for any individual, but it is especially difficult for adolescents. They must accept the responsibilities of parenting before they have established a clear sense of direction for their own lives, a circumstance that can create serious disruptions for both teenage parent and child. Research addressing the adequacy of adolescent girls as mothers has reported them to be less verbal, less nurturing, more impatient, and more prone to punish their children than controls (Lawrence, 1983). Also, the younger the teenage mother, the more limited her capacity to cope with the simultaneous stresses of adolescence and motherhood, and the less effective her parenting behaviors. In one study, mothers in the mid-adolescent years were seen engaging in aggressive actions such as pulling and pinching their infants—behaviors that are the early precursors of the high levels of child abuse experienced by the offspring of teenage parents (Lawrence et al., 1981). In another study, the younger the adolescent mother, the less she engaged in the typical maternal behaviors of touching, speaking to her infant in a gentle high-pitched voice, and holding her baby close (McAnarney, Lawrence, & Aten, 1979).

In view of these findings, it is not surprising that children of adolescents score low on intellectual measures, achieve poorly in school, and engage in disruptive social behavior (Kinard & Klerman, 1983; Lawrence, 1983). Still, how well an adolescent fares as a parent varies considerably. Adolescent parenting and infant development are more favorable when teenage mothers return to school immediately after giving birth and continue to reside in their parents' homes, where child care responsibilities can be shared with mature, experienced caregivers (Sahler, 1983). If the teenager is successful in avoiding additional early births, finishing high school, finding a stable marriage partner, and achieving at least moderate economic security, long-term disruptions in her own and her child's development are less severe (Furstenberg, Brooks-Gunn, & Morgan, 1987).

Few adolescents under the age of 18 are ready for parenthood. In view of the magnitude of the teenage pregnancy problem in the United States, there is an overwhelming need for public programs to assist young people in avoiding unwanted pregnancies and for interventions that offer health and medical services, educational and vocational counseling, child care, and training in parenting skills to adolescent mothers and fathers.

Pubertal Development in Boys. The first sign of puberty in boys is the enlargement of the testes, accompanied by modifications in the texture and color of the scrotum. These changes begin to appear, on the average, in the middle of the eleventh year, although growth of the testes does not show a steep rise until much later, around 14 years of age. Pubic hair first appears in boys around age 12½, about the same time that the penis begins to enlarge in size. The penis is fully developed around age 14½, but there are wide individual differences; in some boys this occurs as early as 12½, whereas in others it happens as late as 16½ (Tanner 1978a, 1978b).

Refer once more to Figure 5.8, and you will see that the spurt in height occurs much later in the sequence of pubertal events for boys than it does for girls. It begins about a year after the initial enlargement of the testes, but it does not reach its maximum peak until a year later, at about 14 years of age. Around this time, the growth of pubertal hair is complete, and underarm hair appears soon after. Male facial and body hair emerges slightly after the peak growth spurt, but it progresses very slowly and does not reach completion until several years after puberty is over. Another landmark of male physical maturity is the deepening of the voice, an event that results from the enlargement of the larynx and lengthening of the vocal cords. Voice change also occurs late in the sequence of pubertal events, just after the peak spurt in general body growth (Tanner, 1978b).

At the same time as the penis is growing, the prostate gland and the seminal vesicles enlarge, and about a year later, around the age of 15, **spermarche,** the first spontaneous ejaculation of seminal fluid, occurs. The first fluid produced generally contains few viable sperm, and so, like adolescent females, males have an initial period of reduced fertility (Tanner, 1978b). Spermarche may be as psychologically significant a pubertal event for boys as menarche is for girls (Gaddis & Brooks-Gunn, 1985), an issue that we address in the next section.

The Psychological Impact of Pubertal Events. How do adolescent boys and girls adapt to the massive physical changes that occur during puberty? Most research aimed at answering this question has focused on girls and deals with reactions to the first menstrual period.

Originally, reactions to menarche were studied retrospectively in samples of women being treated for emotional difficulties. Because these subjects tended to remember their experiences as traumatic and upsetting, puberty came to be viewed as a period of crisis and negative emotion (Brooks-Gunn, 1984). However, recent investigations, in which adolescents have been asked to report their feelings and experiences directly, indicate that girls' reactions to their first menstrual period are not singularly unfavorable. The most common response is "surprise," undoubtedly provoked by the sudden nature of the event. In addition, the majority of girls report a mixture of positive and negative emotions — "excited and pleased" as well as "scared and upset" (Petersen, 1983; Ruble & Brooks-Gunn, 1982; Whisnant & Zegans, 1975). Whether their feelings lean more in the positive or the negative direction depends on a number of factors, including prior knowledge and support from family members, both of which are influenced by social and cultural attitudes toward physical maturation and sexuality (Greif & Ulman, 1982).

For girls who have no advance information about menstruation, its onset can be quite traumatic. Both girls who are early and those who are unprepared report more negative experiences. Of course, it is difficult to separate the effects of these two variables, since being early is positively correlated with not being prepared. Nevertheless, the absence of prior knowledge seems to have long-term negative consequences. Adults and adolescent girls who remember being unprepared report more severe physical symptoms, more unfavorable attitudes about menstruation, and more embarrassment and self-consciousness (Koff, Rierdan, & Sheingold, 1982; Ruble & Brooks-Gunn, 1982). Fortunately, the percentage of girls with no advance preparation is much smaller today than was the case several decades ago. In the 1950s, up to

50 percent of all girls were given no prior information (Shainess, 1961), whereas by the 1970s, only 5 to 10 percent were uninformed. This shift is probably due to greater openness on the part of modern parents to discussing sexual matters with their youngsters. Currently, almost all girls acquire some information from their mothers (Brooks-Gunn & Ruble, 1980). Also, the widespread addition of health education classes to the school curriculum makes it likely that today's girls have at least heard about menstruation, even when their mothers have been reluctant to discuss it (Brooks-Gunn & Ruble, 1983).

The family environment also makes a difference in how girls respond to menarche. In a study in which adolescent girls were asked about family communication, those who reported that their fathers were not told about their first menstruation, or who did not know whether their fathers were told, described more negative attitudes and more severe menstrual symptoms than did those who stated that their fathers knew. Whether or not fathers are told may say something about family attitudes toward physical and sexual matters, which may be one of the most important factors in encouraging more positive emotional reactions to menarche among adolescent girls (Brooks-Gunn & Ruble, 1980).

Menarche is unique among pubertal events in that it happens suddenly without warning, a fact that could contribute to girls' mixed feelings about it. Other pubertal changes are more gradual, providing the adolescent girl with time to get used to them. Consequently, girls' reactions to these events may be more consistently favorable. The scant evidence available on girls' attitudes toward their more feminine-shaped bodies supports this idea. Brooks-Gunn and Warren (1988) found that among 9- to 11-year-olds, breast development was associated with a positive body image (e.g., responding "yes" to such questions as "I am proud of my body"), feelings of peer acceptance, and superior psychological adjustment.

Very little information exists on boys' attitudes and feelings about puberty. One older study reported that almost all boys reacted to their first ejaculation in negative terms (Shipman, 1971). However, like the findings of early research on menarche, these results are probably related to boys' lack of preparation, since only 15 percent of

In many primitive cultures like the Warusha tribe of Africa, puberty is recognized through ceremonies that involve face painting and circumcision rituals.

the sample understood the concept of ejaculation before its occurrence. In a more recent investigation, Gaddis and Brooks-Gunn (1985) found that, like girls' reactions to menstruation, boys' responses to spermarche were not intensely negative, and most reported mixed feelings. All had some advance knowledge about ejaculation. But in contrast to girls, most of whom talk with their mothers and learn about menarche at school, very few of the boys in this study received information from others, and most obtained it from reading material.

Both boys and girls behave quite secretively about spermarche and menarche when it comes to telling their peers. Girls tell far fewer friends than they predicted they would tell before their first menstruation occurred, and only a fourth tell anyone besides their mothers. However, girls' reluctance to talk about menarche is temporary and lasts only about 6 months. By then, almost all have talked to their peers and know that some of their friends are also menstruating (Brooks-Gunn et al., 1986; Danza, 1983; Ruble & Brooks-Gunn, 1982). Far fewer boys ever tell anyone about spermarche. In the Gaddis and Brooks-Gunn (1985) study described above, the small minority of boys who eventually did confide in someone were those who had been given prior information by an adult male, and they told only that one person. Therefore, spermarche, in contrast to menarche, is rarely discussed with others either before or after the experience, yet research shows that information transmitted by parents and friends leads to better acceptance and adjustment to the physical changes of puberty (Brooks-Gunn et al., 1986). In this regard, girls receive far more social support than boys, a finding which suggests that boys might benefit from special opportunities to ask questions and discuss feelings about pubertal changes with a sympathetic male teacher at school.

At this point, it is important to note that all the evidence described above has been gathered on white middle-class youngsters. To date, no studies have looked at whether reactions to puberty differ across social-class and ethnic groups. Yet the experience of puberty takes place in the larger cultural context in which pubescent boys and girls live. In many nonindustrialized societies, puberty is recognized as a crucial time in the adolescent's physical, psychological, and social development. It is openly acknowledged through ceremonial rituals that mark entry into the adult world. In contrast, in our society, little formal recognition is granted to the advent of puberty. There are no special customs to mark it, and no obvious changes in social status follow it.[1] Although school health programs provide information about some physical changes, the topic of puberty is generally approached from the standpoint of hygiene rather than as a recognized maturational milestone (Greif & Ulman, 1982). Yet research indicates that menarche is an emotionally charged event that relates to a girl's emerging identity as a woman, her newly acquired ability to reproduce, and her changing relationships with others. Although boys remain underresearched, it is likely that puberty has a similarly profound significance for them. As Whisnant and Zegans (1975) point out, because puberty brings with it many new psychological adjustments, there is a need for us to develop "a more socially and culturally appropriate substitute to serve the emotional function that more primitive societies have met with familial and social rituals" (p. 814).

The Importance of Early versus Late Maturation. Think back to your late elementary school and junior high school days. Were you early, late, or about on time in physical maturation with respect to your peers? Research indicates that matura-tional timing makes an important difference in social and emotional adjustment, since having physical characteristics that help gain social acceptance from others can be very comforting to adolescent boys and girls.

---

[1] An exception is the Jewish *bar* or *bat mitzvah* ceremony, which takes place for a boy at age 13 and for a girl at age 12. This religious rite of passage celebrates the young adolescent's entry into the adult Jewish community.

The well-known Berkeley longitudinal studies, to which you were introduced in Chapter 2, first explored the relationship of early versus late maturation to adolescent adjustment. Findings revealed that early-maturing boys were advantaged in many aspects of social and emotional functioning. They were seen as relaxed, independent, self-confident, and physically attractive by both adults and peers. Socially poised and popular with their agemates, early-maturing boys held a high proportion of positions of leadership in school, and they also tended to be athletic stars. In comparison, late-maturing boys were not well liked, and peers and adults viewed them as anxious and attention-seeking in behavior (Clausen, 1975; Jones, 1965; Jones & Bayley, 1950). These differences were long-lasting, as they were still present when the subjects reached adulthood (Clausen, 1975).

In contrast, the Berkeley studies showed that early-maturing girls were not socially advantaged. They scored below average in popularity, appeared withdrawn and lacking in self-confidence, and held few positions of leadership. Instead, their late-maturing counterparts were especially well off. Late-maturing girls were regarded as physically attractive, buoyant, sociable, and poised by peers and adults, and they held more positions of prestige and leadership at school (Jones & Mussen, 1958). However, the consequences of being an early versus late maturer were not as long lasting for girls as they were for boys. Negative outcomes associated with being an early maturer weakened between sixth and eighth grade as other girls caught up in physical status and the peer group as a whole developed heterosexual interests (Faust, 1960). By the time female subjects reached adulthood, differences associated with rate of maturation were nonexistent (Peskin, 1973).

The research on maturational timing described above was largely completed in the 1950s and 1960s, but current evidence indicates that the same differences continue to be true of adolescents today. Recent studies also help us understand why the consequences of maturational timing are so consistent and pervasive. Two factors seem especially important. First, early and late maturers bring to social situations body types that match ideal standards of physical beauty to different degrees. Second, at adolescence, it is especially important to "fit in" physically with one's peers. Let's discuss each of these factors in turn.

Flip through the pages of your favorite popular magazine, and take a look at the figures of men and women portrayed in the ads. You will see convincing evidence for our society's view of a physically attractive female as exceptionally thin and long-legged and an attractive male as tall, broad-shouldered, and muscular. The female image portrayed throughout the media is a prepubertal shape that favors late-developing girls. Because of delayed closing of the epiphyses at the growth points of the long bones, the late-maturing girl has a longer time to grow. As a result, she is longer-legged than her early-maturing agemate (Faust, 1983). In addition, early-maturing children of both sexes are generally heavier and stockier than late-maturing children (Malina, 1975), a circumstance that conflicts with the lithesome female ideal but is consistent with the value of male physical robustness.

Recent evidence suggests that a preference for physical attractiveness, at least in terms of facial features, begins in infancy (Langlois et al., 1987; Langlois, Roggman, & Riesser-Danner, 1990). By the preschool years, children have acquired cultural ideals of physical beauty through exposure to media and the preferences of others around them (Styczynski & Langlois, 1977). By fifth grade, children apply these standards of physical appearance consistently (Cavior & Lombardi, 1973). As early and late maturers bring different physical characteristics to social situations, others react to them in terms of accepted standards of physical beauty. This feedback strongly affects how comfortable and satisfied adolescents are with their physical selves and, ultimately, their social and emotional well-being (Lerner, 1985).

A consistent finding of many studies is that early-developing girls have less positive body images than their on-time and late-maturing agemates. Among boys, the opposite is the case: early maturation is linked to a positive body image, while late maturation is associated with dissatisfaction with the physical self (Blyth et al., 1981; Blyth, Simmons, & Zakin, 1985; Brooks-Gunn, 1984; Brooks-Gunn & Ruble, 1983; Simmons & Blyth, 1987; Tobin-Richards, Boxer, & Petersen, 1983). Both male and female adolescents who have physical characteristics regarded by themselves and others as less attractive are less well liked by peers and have a lower sense of self-esteem (Langlois & Stephan, 1981; Lerner & Brackney, 1978). Thus, the adoption of society's "beauty is best" stereotype seems to be an important mediating factor in the adjustment of early- and late-maturing boys and girls.

A second way of explaining differences in adjustment between early and late maturers is in terms of their physical status in relation to the rest of the peer group. From this perspective, since early-maturing boys are about as physically mature as the average girl of the same age, and late-maturing girls are about as mature as the average boy, these groups of adolescents should experience few problems. However, because girls who mature early are much earlier than the rest of their peers and boys who mature late are much later, it is these two groups that are most likely to experience difficulties as the result of being different from their agemates. This analysis is certainly consistent with the evidence described above, and additional support comes from results indicating that adolescents are most comfortable interacting with peers who match their own level of biological maturity. For example, individuals in the same stage of physical development are regarded as preferred companions and as closer friends by adolescent girls (Brooks-Gunn et al., 1986; Magnusson, Stattin, & Allen, 1986). But because few agemates of the same biological status are available to early-maturing girls, many seek older companions, who may influence them in ways that promote school behavior problems as well as lower academic performance — difficulties that are more prevalent among early-maturing girls. However, these problems generally disappear as agemates catch up in physical development and as early-maturing girls merge with the majority in terms of their physical status (Magnusson, Stattin, & Allen, 1985; Simmons & Blyth, 1987; Simmons, Blyth, & McKinney, 1983).

The fact that adolescents easily incorporate and apply socially transmitted ideals of physical attractiveness and are especially sensitive to peer pressures suggests that maturational timing effects can be modified by social contexts. Indeed, several studies reveal this to be the case. For example, Blyth, Simmons, and their colleagues found that early-maturing sixth-grade girls had more positive body images when they attended kindergarten through sixth-grade (K–6) schools rather than kindergarten through eighth-grade (K–8) schools. Despite the scarcity of other children who were just as physically mature, early-maturing girls in K–6 schools were relieved of pressures from older adolescents to adopt behaviors for which they were not yet ready, particularly in dating and sexual activity. However, the same school context was not as advantageous for on-time maturing girls. They fared better in self-esteem if they attended K–8 environments, where they were not faced with making the transition to a new school (between sixth and seventh grade) at the same time as they experienced the physical changes of puberty (Blyth, Simmons, & Zakin, 1985; Simmons et al., 1979). Additional research indicates that simultaneous physical and social changes in an early adolescent's life are stressful for both boys and girls. They have a negative impact not only on self-esteem, but also on grade-point average and extracurricular participation (Simmons et al., 1987).

The standards and expectations of special social contexts can also modify maturational timing effects. For example, in a study of girls enrolled in dance company schools, on-time maturers had poorer body images, rated themselves as heavy (although they were thin by usual standards), and were less emotionally healthy than their counterparts in nondance environments. Because the dance world places an especially strong value on a thin, petite feminine form, it favors girls who are late maturers. In such schools, delayed passage through the physical changes of puberty is normative rather than unique (Brooks-Gunn & Warren, 1985). Taken together, the results of the studies described above demonstrate that the effects of maturational timing can only be fully understood as a complex interplay between the biological changes of puberty, the social contexts to which adolescents are exposed, and the psychological aspects of development.

An additional example of the way in which biological, social, and psychological factors interact during adolescence is provided by a serious emotional and growth disturbance of adolescence called anorexia nervosa. It most commonly affects girls who have special difficulties accepting the physical changes of puberty and the new behavioral expectations that go along with a more grown-up appearance. To find out more about anorexia nervosa, refer to Box 5.2.

Pubertal Change and Parent-Child Relationships. The onset of puberty affects not only peer relationships, but also family functioning. Many studies indicate that pubertal maturation leads to increased emotional distance between youngsters and their parents. Boys as well as girls and mothers as well as fathers report less closeness in the parent-child relationship, greater adolescent autonomy, and a slight increase in conflict over mundane issues of daily living with advancing physical maturity (Papini & Sebby, 1987; Steinberg, 1987, 1988a). Observations of parents and their youngsters interacting in the laboratory also indicate that petty arguments and standoffs become more frequent as adolescents move toward the apex of pubertal growth (Hill, 1988).

Why should an adolescent's more adultlike appearance trigger emotional distance between parent and child? Researchers believe the association may have evolved because of its adaptive value. Among nonhuman primates, the young typically leave the family group around the time of puberty, an event that discourages inbreeding and promotes genetic diversity (Caine, 1986). Departure of adolescents from the family is also common in many non-Western cultures (Cohen, 1964). But because children in industrialized societies remain economically dependent on parents long after they reach physical and sexual maturity, a modern substitute for leaving the family seems to have emerged. As Steinberg (1987) suggests, "Psychological distance — in the form of increased conflict, increased autonomy, and decreased (family) cohesion — may be an atavism related to a pattern of behavior that at one time protected the genetic integrity of the species" (p. 128).

Although more family quarreling does occur during adolescence, it is usually mild and rarely results in severing of the parent-child bond. In actuality, parents and children display both conflict and affection toward one another throughout the adolescent years. This also makes sense from an evolutionary perspective. Although separation from parents is adaptive, both generations benefit from warm, protective family relationships that last for many years to come (Steinberg, 1989).

The Endocrinology of Growth

The vast physical changes that take place at puberty, as well as the growth that occurs earlier in development, are controlled by the endocrine glands of the body. These glands manufacture chemical agents known as *hormones*, substances secreted by specialized cells in one organ or part of the body that pass to and have an influence on cells in another. Because there are receptors in our cells that respond to some hormones and not to others, the action of each hormone is unique. The most important ones for human growth are released from the anterior portion of the *pituitary gland*, which is located at the base of the brain near the *hypothalamus*, a central nervous system structure that initiates and regulates pituitary secretions. Once pituitary hormones enter the bloodstream they act directly on body tissues to produce growth, or they stimulate the release of other hormones from endocrine glands located elsewhere in the body.

Figure 5.9 diagrams the way in which the hypothalamus, pituitary gland, and other endocrine glands work together to affect physical growth. You may want to refer to this chart as we briefly discuss each of the five major endocrine influences.

Growth hormone (GH) is the only pituitary secretion produced continuously throughout life. It affects cell duplication of almost all body tissues, except the central nervous system and possibly the adrenal glands and gonads. While GH does not seem to be crucial for fetal growth, it is necessary for normal growth from birth to adulthood. Children who lack it reach a mature height of only 4 feet, 4 inches (130 cm), although they are normal in physical proportions and healthy in all other respects. When treated with injections of GH, such children show catch-up growth and then begin to grow at a normal rate. However, the extent to which they attain their genetically expected height depends on initiating treatment early, before the skeletal growth centers are very mature (D'Ercole & Underwood, 1986). At puberty, GH must be present for the sex hormones to exert their full impact on body growth. In its absence, the height spurt is only about two thirds of normal, and the broadening of the hips in girls and expansion of the shoulders in boys are also reduced (Tanner, 1978b).

Thyroid stimulating hormone (TSH) stimulates the thyroid gland to release *thyroxin*, which is necessary for proper development of the nerve cells of the brain. Infants born without it must be treated with synthetic thyroxin at once, because an early deficiency results in mental retardation. At older ages, children with too little thyroxin experience slow skeletal maturity. However, the central nervous system is no longer affected, since the most rapid period of brain growth is complete. With prompt treatment, such children catch up in body growth and eventually reach normal adult size (Tanner, 1978b).

◆ CONTEMPORARY ISSUES: SOCIAL POLICY ◆

Anorexia Nervosa: Self-Inflicted Adolescent Starvation

Box 5.2

Anorexia nervosa is a tragic disorder in which adolescents starve themselves because of an aversion to food or weight gain. Its incidence is on the rise; some estimates indicate that it afflicts as many as a million Americans (Brumberg, 1988). The large majority of victims are white middle-class females, most of whom are between the ages of 12 and 25. The symptoms include such severe restriction of food intake that body weight loss is as great as 25 percent or more, along with *amenorrhea*, or cessation of menstrual periods. Victims take on a painfully thin appearance, and the serious malnutrition that accompanies the disorder leads to a cluster of additional physical effects, including brittle, discolored nails, pale skin, fine dark hairs appearing all over the body, and extreme sensitivity to cold. Anorectics show a constant preoccupation with food coupled with a persistent determination not to eat. Most lose weight by following a stringent, self-imposed diet, but some also achieve it through *bulimia*, an accompanying disorder involving eating binges followed by intestinal purges in which the individual vomits or ingests large doses of laxatives. Anorectics deny their hunger and extreme physical fatigue by combining dieting with strenuous physical exercise. Most have such a distorted perception of their physical condition that they continue to regard themselves as fat, even after they have become grotesquely emaciated (Gilbert & DeBlassie, 1984).

Anorexia nervosa is the result of a complex combination of cultural, familial, and psychological conditions. The American societal preoccupation with thinness seems to be one factor that contributes to the anorectic's compulsion to lose weight. In fact, the rapid accumulation of body fat during puberty appears to trigger eating problems in susceptible girls (Brooks-Gunn, 1988). Early maturers, especially those who feel quite negative about their bodies, are at greatest risk (Attie & Brooks-Gunn, 1989). But while almost all adolescent girls go on diets at one time or another, anorectics persist in their efforts to lose weight long after they have attained the cultural ideal of slimness. Many appear to be perfectionists who have very high standards for their own behavior and performance. Conscientious, well-behaved, and excelling academically, most of these girls presented few problems at home or school before the appearance of their anorectic behavior.

However, researchers who have studied the interaction of parents with their anorectic daughters have identified family problems surrounding issues of adolescent autonomy that may precipitate the compulsive dieting. The parents often appear controlling and

Adrenocorticotropic hormone (ACTH) stimulates the adrenal cortex (the outer part of the adrenal glands located on top of each kidney) to produce *corticoids*, which regulate the body's protein and carbohydrate metabolism, and also *androgens*. During childhood, androgen secretion is low, but at puberty, it rises to a level higher than that occurring in adults. In girls, androgens are largely responsible for the adolescent growth spurt and for the emergence and maintenance of underarm and pubic hair. In boys, adrenal androgens play a lesser role, since skeletal growth and secondary sex characteristics are mainly influenced by the androgen hormone *testosterone*, which is secreted from the testes.

Follicle stimulating hormone (FSH) and **luteinizing hormone (LH)** are two pituitary hormones whose concentrations in the bloodstream rise at the beginning of puberty. This causes the ovaries and testes to release additional hormones that affect the growth and sexual changes of adolescence. In females, FSH initiates the production of *estrogens*, which cause the pelvis to broaden and promote maturation of the breasts, uterus, and vagina (Malina, 1975). FSH and LH also work together to control the menstrual cycle. FSH initiates ripening of the ovum, and LH causes the ovary to release it and produce the hormone *progesterone*. Progesterone, in combination with estrogen, results in thickening of the uterine lining. If a fertilized ovum does not implant, estrogen and progesterone levels decline, the uterus sheds its lining, and the menstrual cycle starts again. In males, FSH causes the testes to produce sperm, and LH stimulates testicular production of androgens, which bring about male sexual characteristics, muscle growth, and large increase in body size.

Exactly what provokes the rise in pituitary hormones leading to the onset of puberty is not yet fully understood. As we mentioned earlier in this chapter, skeletal

overprotective and do not seem to recognize their daughter as an individual in her own right. Having compliantly accepted the values of her parents and fulfilled all their hopes and expectations for a model daughter, the anorectic girl has developed little in the way of an independent sense of self. As a result, she meets adolescent physical and social changes with anxiety and lack of self-confidence, and she responds by avoiding them through self-starvation and changing her body's appearance to a much younger, prepubescent image (Bruch, 1978; Leon et al., 1985; Minuchin, Rosman, & Baker, 1978). The strange eating habits and excessive jogging and calisthenics of anorectics lead to social isolation and estrangement from family and friends, a circumstance that compounds feelings of loneliness, insecurity, and inadequacy. Yet attempts on the part of others to intervene in the anorectic's rigid, compulsive regime are met with angry and desperate resistance (Gilbert & DeBlassie, 1984).

When anorexia nervosa is prolonged and severe, it becomes a life-threatening illness. Mortality rates are estimated to be about 5 percent of those afflicted with the disorder (Romeo, 1986). Because the roots of anorexia nervosa are in individual and family problems, family therapy, in which efforts are made to change family members' interaction patterns and expectations of one another, is the most successful treatment, with 85 percent of cases showing full recovery (Bemis, 1978). Behavior modification programs, in which hospitalized anorectics are rewarded for gaining weight with praise, social contact, and opportunities for exercise, are less successful as the sole treatment approach, because they do not deal with underlying family dynamics. However, behavior modification has proved to be a useful adjunct to family therapy (Gilbert & DeBlassie, 1984). Since anorexia nervosa involves extreme body image distortion in the form of overestimation of body size, another supplementary treatment involves repeatedly confronting the anorectic girl with her self-image in mirrors, in photographs, and on videotape in order to induce a more realistic physical self-appraisal. Also, some therapists try to provide their patients with insights into social factors that have led them to value their bodies only in terms of how well they meet culturally accepted standards of beauty (Bemis, 1978). Early identification of victims of anorexia nervosa is crucial, permitting treatment to begin before the development of irreversible medical complications and the needless loss of a young life.

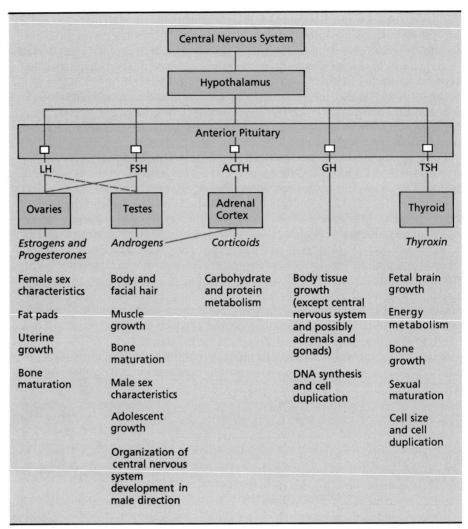

Figure 5.9. Endocrine influences on postnatal growth. *(Adapted with permission of Macmillan Publishing Company from* Children: Development and Relationships *[3rd ed.] by M. S. Smart and R. C. Smart. P. 500. Copyright © 1977, 1972, 1967, Macmillan Publishing Company.)*

age is the best predictor of menarche, and some investigators believe that a large increase in body size and fat composition triggers the pituitary secretions that initiate menstruation in females (Frisch, 1983). In support of this idea, high levels of exercise as well as low nutritional intake, both of which reduce the percentage of body fat, affect female menstrual periods. For example, girls who begin serious athletic training at young ages experience a greatly delayed menarche, sometimes as late as 18 or 20 years of age, a finding that helps explain the high proportion of late-maturing girls in the dance company schools we discussed earlier (Frisch, Wyshak, & Vincent, 1980; Frisch et al., 1981). However, skeletal maturity and body composition show no relationship to other pubertal milestones, such as enlargement of breast tissue or testes (Tanner, 1978b). The underlying causes of these aspects of adolescent maturity are still obscure.

Secular Trends in Physical Growth

Secular trends in human growth are changes that occur from one generation to another. Over the last century, children in modern industrialized countries have been getting larger. Increases in height and weight have been documented in nearly all European nations, in Japan, and among black and white children in the United States.

However, gains have been greater for economically privileged than underprivileged groups in these countries (Roche, 1979).

The secular difference in body size appears early in life and becomes greater over the course of childhood and early adolescence. Then, from midadolescence until mature body size is attained, it diminishes. The fact that the secular gain is greatest at puberty and then contracts indicates that size differences among children of different generations are largely differences in rate of maturation. Today, children reach their adult height and weight earlier than they did in generations past. This acceleration of physical growth is most evident in the secular reduction that has occurred in age of menarche. From 1880 to 1960, menarche advanced about 3 months per decade (Tanner, 1978b). Of course, human beings cannot keep growing larger and maturing earlier indefinitely, since we cannot exceed the genetic limitations of our species. In fact, the secular trend appears to have slowed or ceased entirely in some developed countries, such as England, Japan, Norway, and the United States (Roche, 1979). Also, the generational increase described above is not worldwide. In underdeveloped countries stricken by poverty, famine, or disease, a secular decrease in adult stature has occurred (Tobias, 1975).

Why are many modern children growing larger and reaching maturity earlier than their ancestors? Biologists believe that improved nutrition plays a major role. In addition, the reduction or complete elimination of many growth-stunting diseases has permitted more children to attain their full potential for growth. The end of child labor in industrialized countries early in the twentieth century is also thought to have contributed to secular gains. Research conducted in Japan suggests that children who live under poor nutritional circumstances and are exposed to hard labor experience premature closure of the epiphyses of the long bones and, for this reason, end up shorter in stature (Kato & Ishiko, 1966). Finally, the average number of individuals per household has decreased from 1850 to the present. Children from small families are somewhat larger and mature earlier than those from large families, particularly among low-income groups. It may be that important environmental influences, such as improved nutrition and better health care, are mediated through family size (Malina, 1979). We will take up the impact of these factors on physical growth in greater detail in the last part of this chapter.

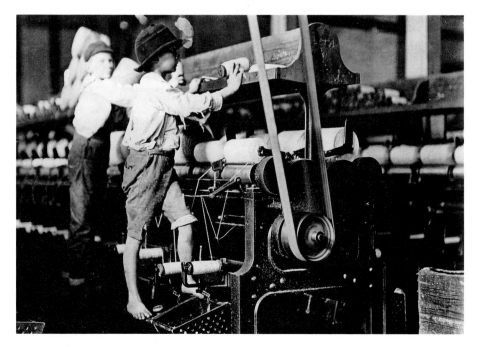

The small stature of children who lived during the nineteenth century was partly due to the hard labor that many endured in factories.

In the sections above, we have seen that human beings experience a prolonged period of physical growth in which changes in body size proceed rapidly during infancy, gradually during the childhood years, and rapidly again at adolescence. Nevertheless, some organs and parts of the body deviate from this general growth plan, and physical development is best described as an organized but asynchronous process. As the child enlarges, changes in body proportions and fat and muscle composition occur that support sex differences favoring boys in physical capacities. However, girls are advanced over boys in physical maturity at all ages, a gap that widens to as much as 2 years at puberty.

Pubertal changes have important psychological and social implications. Overall, girls' reactions to menarche and boys' to spermarche are mixed, and late-maturing girls and early-maturing boys are advantaged in socioemotional adjustment. Pubertal development is also accompanied by increased psychological distance between parents and their physically mature children.

Body growth is controlled by a complex set of hormonal secretions released by the pituitary gland and regulated by the hypothalamus. Finally, secular trends in physical growth have occurred over the past century, with children in industrialized nations growing larger and reaching maturity earlier than they did in generations past.

DEVELOPMENT OF THE BRAIN

The human brain is the most complicated and intricate organ in the human body, and it also ranks as the most effective and elaborate living structure on earth today. The brain is composed of 10 to 20 billion **neurons,** or nerve cells, many of them having thousands of direct connections with other neurons. Although the pattern of connections is not precisely the same for each of us, the basic structure and organization of the brain are fairly constant from one person to another. Like other body structures, the brain follows an orderly, sequential plan of development.

The brain is divided into three major parts: the *forebrain* (the major structure of which is the **cerebral cortex,** containing the "higher brain centers"); the *midbrain* (top of the brain stem, housing part of the visual and auditory systems as well as structures that relay signals between other parts of the brain); and the *hindbrain* (containing, among other structures, the cerebellum, which helps maintain balance and motor coordination). It is the massive cortical areas of the forebrain that make the human central nervous system unique among all species of mammals. The human cortex is much larger and far more structurally complex than that of even the most advanced apes. This is especially true of its *association regions*—areas regarded as "thought centers" and whose capabilities surpass those of the brains of any other living being (Suomi, 1982).

The human brain achieves its peak velocity of growth earlier than other organs. At birth, it is nearer to its adult size than any other body structure, except perhaps the eye (Tanner, 1978b). However, when the growth curves of various parts of the brain are examined separately, the cerebral cortex once again distinguishes itself. It is the last to stop growing and differentiating. The cortical areas undergo greater structural change after birth than any other part of the central nervous system, and because of this, they are believed to be much more susceptible to environmental influences than any other brain structure (Suomi, 1982). But to appreciate how experience can affect the developing brain, it is necessary to understand the basic progression of brain maturation. Some of the principles by which the brain develops are best understood at the level neurons and their interconnections, while others are best appreciated at the larger level of areas of the cerebral cortex.

Neuronal Development

As shown in Figure 5.10, a neuron consists of a cell body, at the center of which is a nucleus. The cell body sends out fibers filled with cytoplasm. One, called an *axon*, is a

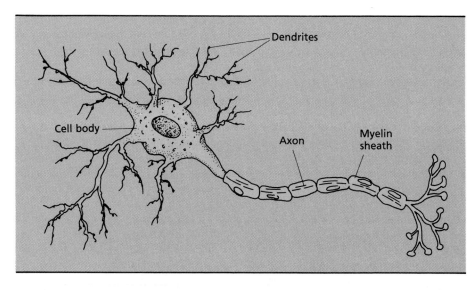

Figure 5.10. Principal structures of the neuron.

long fiber that conducts messages away from the cell body. Others are branch-like fibers called *dendrites*, which carry impulses to the cell body from other neurons. Neurons are not tightly packed together like the cells of most other body tissues. There are tiny gaps, or **synapses,** between them where axons and dendritic fibers come close to one another but do not touch. Information transmitted by a neuron travels electrically from the cell body along the axon to the synapse, where it is transformed into a chemical message that crosses the synapse, after which it is carried along a dendrite to the body of another cell.

Neurons are not the only cellular residents of the brain. About half the brain's volume consists of **glial cells,** which do not carry messages (Tanner, 1978a). Instead, their most important function is **myelinization,** a process whereby the axons in the developing brain become surrounded by an insulating fatty sheath that promotes efficient conduction of nerve impulses. As we will see shortly, the proliferation of neurons takes place during a short and finite period of early brain maturation, but glial cells continue to multiply throughout life (Spreen et al., 1984).

The basic story of brain development concerns how the cells of the nervous system develop and form their intricate communication system. Each neuron passes through three developmental steps: cell proliferation, cell migration, and cell differentiation (Nowakowski, 1987). The *proliferation*, or production, of neurons takes place inside the primitive neural tube of the embryo by the process of cell duplication known as mitosis, which we discussed in Chapter 3. Once formed, neural cells *migrate* to their permanent locations, where they aggregate to form the major parts of the brain (Moore, 1989). When the neurons arrive, they orient their primitive axons in the general direction toward which they will eventually extend. At 8 to 10 weeks gestation, the cortex has started to form in this way. By 6 months gestational age, the proliferation of cortical neurons is complete; no more will be produced in the individual's lifetime. The precise location and orientation of each neuron and the direction of its axonal and dendritic growth are thought to be genetically determined (Spreen et al., 1984). In fact, if the delicate process of neuronal migration is disrupted because of hereditary abnormalities or a defective prenatal environment, a variety of abnormalities can result, ranging from severe mental retardation to specific learning problems. A number of the teratogens we discussed in Chapter 3, such as alcohol and mercury, are believed to exert their damaging effects partly by interfering with neuronal migration (Nowakowski, 1987).

After orienting in the proper direction, cortical neurons begin to grow and *differentiate*, establishing their separate functions by extending their axons and expanding their dendrites, forming an intricate system of synaptic connections with neighboring cells. Because growing neurons require additional space for their axons and dendrites, many surrounding neurons atrophy and die when synaptic junctures are formed. Thus, the peak period of development in any brain area is also marked by the greatest rate of cell death. At first glance, this may strike you as rather surprising, since neurons, unlike other cells, do not replenish themselves over the life span of the individual. Fortunately, the embryonic neural tube produces far more cells than the brain will ever need. In the process of making synaptic contacts, excess neurons degenerate (Suomi, 1982).

In contrast to cell location and orientation, the formation of specific synapses in the brain is probably not under genetic control, because the number of neurons and possible combinations among them are so vast as to be well beyond the quantity of information that can be carried by the human genes (Spreen et al., 1984). Instead, initiation of connections between neurons seems to be largely a matter of random contacts between neuronal cells in the same vicinity that make appropriate chemical offerings to one another (Wolff, 1981). Whether a particular neuron will survive or die off early in development depends, first of all, on whether it is successful at establishing synaptic connections. Once it is successful, another factor becomes crucially important: stimulation. Neurons that are stimulated continue to flourish by growing new dendritic branches and forming myelin sheaths around their axons, increasing the probability that they will form new synapses and continue to receive stimulation in the future. Neurons that are seldom stimulated soon degenerate. Thus, because the location and orientation of neurons is genetically determined, but the maintenance of synaptic connections is a matter of adequate stimulation, growth of the brain is influenced by both hereditary and environmental factors (Greenough, Black, & Wallace, 1987). Also, the phases of neuronal development described above suggest that appropriate environmental input to the brain is crucially important during periods in which the establishment of neuronal connections and myelinization are at a peak.

Glial cells proliferate at different times than neurons. They are relatively immature in the early stages of central nervous system development, but they multiply and mature at a dramatic pace from the fourth month of fetal life into the second year of postnatal life, after which their rate of duplication slows down. Whereas substantial increases in connectivity between neurons can take place with little increase in brain weight, the formation of myelin causes the brain to gain rapidly in overall size and weight. Therefore, glial cell production is largely responsible for the growth curve of the brain depicted in Figure 5.11 (Spreen et al., 1984).

As we will see when we discuss the development of the cerebral cortex, various regions of the brain establish synaptic connections and myelinate at different times. For some areas, the peak period of myelinization is before birth; for others, it is afterward. Researchers have attempted to correlate these myelinization cycles with the emergence of specific capacities, such as memory and language. In most cases, functional activity of an area of the brain seems to follow myelinization. However, it may occur without it, since some unmyelinated neurons have been found to conduct impulses (Spreen et al., 1984).

Development of the Cerebral Cortex

Of all structures of the human brain, the cerebral cortex contains the greatest number of neurons and synapses. At maturity, it surrounds the rest of the brain, somewhat like a half-shelled walnut. The cerebral cortex is divided into two hemispheres, each of which contains several different lobes (see Figure 5.12). These are further divided into different regions. Some are *primary areas*—motor regions that give direct orders to the muscles of the body, premotor regions that provide information to motor regions, and *sensory regions* that receive direct input from the sense organs. *Secondary areas* are made up of *association* or "thought" regions, which are integrative systems having extensive connections to other parts of the brain and through which primary impulses can be combined with other impulses.

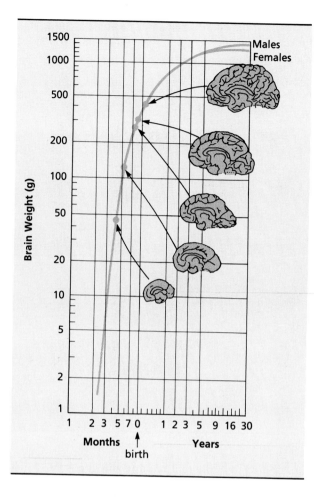

Figure 5.11. Distance curve for the weight of the human brain from the prenatal period into adult life. Note the dramatic early rise between the fetal period and the second postnatal year. *(From R. J. Lemire, J. D. Loeser, R. W. Leech, & E. C. Alvord, 1975, Normal and Abnormal Development of the Human Nervous System. New York: Harper & Row. P. 236. Adapted by permission.)*

Changes in chemical makeup and distribution of myelin suggest that at birth, the cortex is not fully developed and that various portions mature at different rates. If we look at the general order in which regions of the cortex develop, we see that it corresponds to the order in which various capacities emerge in the growing infant and young child. Among the primary areas, the most advanced is the motor region of the precentral gyrus (see Figure 5.12), whose cells initiate gross body movements. Within it, nerve cells that control movements of the head, arms, and upper trunk mature ahead of those that control the legs. (Do you recognize a familiar developmental trend?) Sensory regions are next to mature, and premotor regions follow as the infant gains voluntary control over motor behavior. The last portions of the cortex to develop and myelinate are the association regions. From about 2 months of age onward, the association regions function more effectively, and they continue their growth for years, some of them well into the second and third decades of life (Gibson, 1977; Suomi, 1982; Spreen et al., 1984). Being the last to emerge and having the most extended period of development, the association regions are also the areas of the cortex with the greatest long-term sensitivity to environmental influences (Goldman & Rakic, 1979).

The *corpus callosum*, a large bundle of neural fibers that connects the two hemispheres, matures relatively slowly in comparison to other parts of the brain. Myelinization of the corpus callosum does not begin until the end of the first year of life. By 4 to 5 years of age, its development is fairly advanced (Spreen et al., 1984; Witelson & Kigar, 1988). About this time, children become more proficient at tasks that require transfer of information between the cerebral hemispheres, such as comparing two

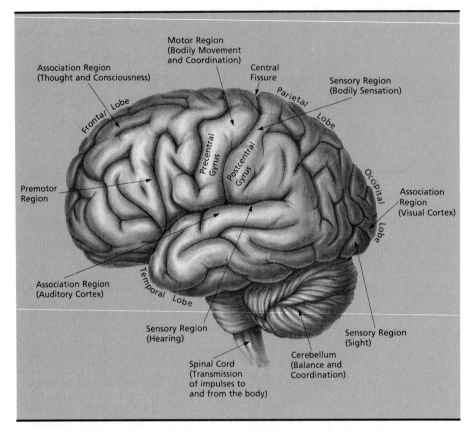

Figure 5.12. A lateral view of the left side of the human brain, showing the major structures. The locations of different functional areas of the cerebral cortex are identified.

tactile stimuli when each is presented to a different hand (Galin et al., 1979). The corpus callosum continues to mature at a slower rate through middle childhood. Investigators believe that more information on how it develops is likely to enhance our understanding of complex human abilities that require efficient communication among many parts of the brain, such as abstract thinking and creativity.

Lateralization of the Cortex

Few topics concerning the brain have stimulated as much interest as **lateralization,** or specialization of functions between the human cerebral hemispheres. Although they look very similar, the two hemispheres of the adult brain are not mirror images of one another. Some tasks are done predominantly by one side, and some by the other. For example, each hemisphere receives sensory input from and controls only one side of the body (the one opposite to it). In addition, for most of us, the left hemisphere governs processing of verbal information, whereas the right hemisphere plays the major role in processing of spatial information, nonspeech sounds, and emotions. This pattern may be reversed in a few left-handed people, but more commonly, the brains of left-handers are less clearly lateralized than those of right-handers.

To determine how flexible various parts of the cortex are in assuming cognitive functions early in life, child development specialists have explored the question of whether a lateralized hemispheric organization exists from the very beginning or whether it emerges gradually during childhood. New studies of infant cortical responsiveness to various kinds of stimulation and of the development of handedness are helping to answer these questions. In addition, since sex differences in cognitive abilities are evident in the verbal and spatial domains, the question arises as to whether the development of cerebral lateralization can help to explain them.

How Early Does Brain Lateralization Occur? Initially, insights into brain lateralization were obtained from studies of individuals afflicted with acquired *aphasia*, a condition in which there is difficulty in either comprehending or producing speech. On the basis of cases of left-hemispheric damaged young children who recovered from aphasia, Lenneberg (1967) suggested that from birth to 2 years of age, the cerebral hemispheres have equal potential for processing language and other lateralized functions. Thereafter, as each hemisphere becomes increasingly specialized, the ability of the brain to compensate after injury is gradually reduced.

Lenneberg's pioneering research contributed to a general principle of brain development that is now widely accepted. In infancy, before a great many neurons have formed synaptic connections and taken on unique functions, there is high brain **plasticity.** That is, if some areas are injured, others compensate by taking over the abilities that would have been allocated to the damaged regions. Dramatic evidence for early brain plasticity comes from research on infants who had part or all of a hemisphere removed to control violent seizures. In these cases, the remaining hemisphere, whether right or left, showed a remarkable ability to assume both language and spatial functions as the child matured (Goodman & Whitaker, 1985).

Nevertheless, additional evidence reveals that the young brain, although very flexible, is not quite as plastic as Lenneberg believed. First, although the surgically treated youngsters described above showed normal development of many basic skills, by the late childhood and adolescent years, severe deficits in complex verbal or spatial abilities were evident, depending on which hemisphere had been removed (Dennis & Whitaker, 1976; Kohn & Dennis, 1974). Second, new studies of brain-damaged patients indicated that the risk of permanent aphasia due to left hemispheric injury is very similar in adults and in children as young as 1 year of age (Satz & Bullard-Bates, 1981). These findings suggest that lateralized functioning is present considerably earlier than Lenneberg's boundary of age 2.

In fact, electroencephalograph (EEG) brain wave recordings taken as normal infants react to a variety of stimuli suggest that the cerebral hemispheres are programmed from the start for specialized functions. For example, newborn babies, as well as infants born several weeks preterm, show a greater amplitude of response to speech sounds in the left hemisphere than in the right (Molfese, 1977; Molfese & Molfese, 1979, 1980). Similarly, right-brain EEG activity is augmented when neonates are exposed to nonspeech sounds, flashes of light, or stimuli (such as a sour-tasting fluid) that cause them to display negative emotions (Crowell et al., 1973; Fox & Davidson, 1986; Molfese, 1977). These findings suggest that left hemispheric superiority for processing linguistic information and right hemispheric superiority for processing nonverbal information and expressing certain emotions are present at birth (Hahn, 1987).

Developmental Changes in Lateralization: Studies of Handedness. Even though the cerebral hemispheres appear to be specialized from the very beginning, considerable evidence indicates that brain lateralization increases with age. A growing literature on the development of handedness is providing fascinating new insights into changes in lateralized functioning during infancy and early childhood.

A strong hand preference is a reflection of the greater capacity of one side of the brain—often referred to as the individual's *dominant* hemisphere—to carry out skilled motor action. Other functions localized on the dominant side may be superior as well. In support of this idea, language, the most highly developed capacity of the human species, is housed with manual dexterity in the left hemisphere for approximately 90 percent of the adult population. For the remaining 10 percent who are left-handed, control of language is often shared between the hemispheres, rather than governed by only one (Curtiss, 1985; Hiscock & Kinsborne, 1987). In line with this reduced laterality for linguistic skills, a great many left-handers are also ambidextrous—that is, although they prefer the left hand, they rely on and use their right hand adeptly as well (Corvitz & Zener, 1962; McManus et al., 1988). Taken together, these findings suggest that verbal dominance and manual dominance are highly correlated. Therefore, by tracking the emergence and refinement of handedness in the early years of life, we can gain insight into how cortical specialization of linguistic functions proceeds.

Consistent with evidence on specialization of the neonate's brain reviewed earlier, research suggests that handedness is genetically determined and probably preset at birth. Similarity of handedness is greater among biological relatives than adopted relatives (Carter-Saltzman, 1980), and most newborns turn toward the right side when tested for the tonic neck reflex. By 5 to 6 months of age, more infants reach for objects with their right hand than with their left hand (McCormick & Maurer, 1988). However, hand preference is not very stable until about 2 years of age, and some intriguing research by Ramsay suggests why. Handedness seems to undergo dips and recoveries during the first 2 years that coincide with advances in infant linguistic skills. Shortly after 6 months, when babbling becomes more complex, infants lose their early reaching bias, only to exhibit it once more around 9 months (Ramsay, 1985). Another dip in handedness occurs about the time babies say their first words and, again, late in the second year, when they begin to combine words (Ramsay & McClune, 1984). Ramsay believes that developmental increments in language skill place extra demands on the left hemisphere. This results in a temporary loss in motor dominance that returns when the baby's early linguistic competencies are well established. These results are certainly consistent with the observations of many mothers, who report that when their infants forge ahead in spoken language, they seem to temporarily postpone the mastery of new motor skills or vice versa.

By the beginning of the preschool years, handedness is clearly defined in most children. A preference for using the dominant hand for many activities, such as drawing, throwing a ball, and using a spoon or a toothbrush, increases into middle childhood, suggesting that hemispheric specialization strengthens during this time (McManus et al., 1988). The development of a lateralized brain is adaptive, because it permits a larger complement of talents to be represented in the cerebral hemispheres than would be possible if both sides served exactly the same functions. But what about children whose hand use suggests an atypical organization of brain functions?

Perhaps you have heard that left-handed individuals are overrepresented among the severely retarded and mentally ill. While this is true, it is highly unlikely that deviant cerebral organization is responsible for the psychological deficits of these individuals. Instead, they probably experienced very early brain damage, which simultaneously contributed to a shift in handedness and caused their disabilities. In the general population, neither direction nor degree of handedness is related to cognitive or behavioral deficits (Hiscock & Kinsbourne, 1987; McManus et al., 1988; Satz & Fletcher, 1987; Van Strien, Bouma, & Bakker, 1987). In fact, left-handed people may have certain cognitive advantages. Benbow (1986) reported that a disproportionate number of adolescents with highly superior verbal and/or mathematical abilities are either left- or mixed-handed. She believes that a genetic predisposition for bihemispheric representation of cognitive functions is responsible for this trend. Still, it is important to keep in mind that many left-handed children and adults may be bilateral and ambidextrous for environmental and not just genetic reasons, since they must learn to live in a right-hand-biased world.

Sex Differences in Brain Lateralization. Are there sex differences in brain lateralization, and if so, how do they develop? One reason child development specialists have been interested in answering this question is to help explain why females tend to excel in verbal rather than spatial tasks, whereas the opposite is true for males. Also, the study of sex differences in lateralization may someday be helpful in understanding disorders of the higher cortical functions. For example, childhood language disabilities, such as stuttering, reading problems, and aphasia, are three times more prevalent among boys than girls (Hier & Kaplan, 1980). Unfortunately, as we will see in Chapter 13, the literature on sex differences in lateralization is inconclusive. All that can be stated definitely at this time is that *both* males and females tend to be left hemispherically specialized for language functions and right hemispherically specialized for nonverbal functions. There are few hard biological explanations for why sex differences in cognitive abilities exist.

Brain Growth Spurts and Critical Periods of Development

In Chapter 3, we pointed out that an important critical period in central nervous system development occurs during the third trimester of pregnancy, a time when axonal and dendritic growth and multiplication of glial cells are taking place at an astounding pace. We showed how damaging prenatal environmental influences — in particular, malnutrition — can lead to a permanent loss in brain weight and reduction in number of brain cells. Critical periods are well established for prenatal growth when the major organ systems of the body are forming. But because neurological structures continue to mature after birth, the concept is also thought to apply to development of the human brain during postnatal life.

The importance of stimulation during periods in which cortical structures are growing most rapidly has been amply demonstrated in experimental studies of baby animals exposed to extreme forms of sensory deprivation. For example, there seems to be a critical period during which suitable visual experiences must occur if the visual cortex is to develop and function normally. Light deprivation for as brief a period as 3 to 4 days can cause severe degenerative changes in the visual cortex of a 4-week-old kitten. If the kitten's eye is sutured closed for as long as 2 months, the cortical damage is permanent (Hubel & Wiesel, 1970). Animal research also suggests that severe stimulus deprivation has an effect on the general growth of the brain. Comparisons of pet-reared animals with animals reared in isolation reveal the brain of the pet to be heavier and thicker, especially in certain cortical lobes (Bennett et al., 1964; Greenough, Black, & Wallace, 1987).

Because we cannot ethically expose human children to such experiments, investigators interested in identifying postnatal critical periods for human brain growth have had to rely on less direct evidence. Epstein (1974a, 1974b, 1980) identified a set of brain growth spurts occurring intermittently from infancy into adolescence, based on velocity curves for brain weight and skull circumference as well as changes in the electrical activity of the cortex. He indicated that the spurts were correlated with peaks in children's mental test performance and with transitions between Piagetian stages. Although the existence of such brain-mind growth spurts has been challenged (Marsh, 1985), Thatcher, Walker, and Giudice (1987) reported renewed evidence for them. Moreover, research on changes in brain physiology that coincide with mastery of Piagetian sensorimotor problems by infant rhesus monkeys suggests that a dramatic rise in synaptic connections throughout the cortex may underlie the earliest brain growth spurts (Goldman-Rakic, 1987). More limited production of synapses, thinning out of excess connections, and myelinization may account for the later ones (Fischer, 1987).

At present, exactly how the brain might be environmentally facilitated or disrupted during such growth spurts is not known. If we had such information, it would have major implications for child-rearing and educational practices. We would know what kinds of environmental enrichment are most effective at different times of development and how to protect the brain of the growing child from potentially damaging environmental influences.

BRIEF REVIEW

The human brain, like the rest of the body, follows an organized, sequential growth plan. Neuronal development takes place in a three-step sequence — cell proliferation, migration, and differentiation — that culminates in the formation of synaptic connections and myelinization of neural fibers. Various regions of the cortex follow a hierarchical pattern of development consistent with the emergence of behavioral capacities in the infant and young child. From birth onward, the two cortical hemispheres are lateralized, or specialized for different functions. Nevertheless, brain plasticity, the ability of intact areas to take over the functions of injured regions, is greatest during early infancy. Research on the development of handedness indicates that lateralization increases over the course of childhood. However, contrary to a widely held belief, a left-hand preference is not associated with cognitive and behavioral deficits in the general population. Finally, new evidence supports the existence of intermittent growth spurts in the human brain from infancy into adolescence. Each may be a critical period during which appropriate stimulation is required for optimal development of human intelligence.

FACTORS AFFECTING PHYSICAL GROWTH

Physical growth, like other human characteristics, is the result of the continuous and complex interplay between heredity and environment. In the following sections of this chapter, we consider genetic and environmental influences on physical growth. A variety of facets of the environment are known to impinge on physical development — the human-made environment (nutrition), the natural environment (disease), and the social environment (stimulation and affection versus deprivation and emotional neglect).

Heredity

Heredity plays a role in the determination of body size and rate of physical maturation. Studies show that identical twins generally resemble each other in height and weight far more closely than do fraternals. However, the extent of resemblance varies with the period of development in which the twins are measured. At birth, differences in the lengths and weights of identical twins are actually greater than those of fraternals. This is because sharing of the same placenta frequently results in one identical twin occupying a more favorable position in the uterus and obtaining greater quantities of nourishment. However, unless the intrauterine disadvantage was extreme, by a few months after birth, the smaller twin has recovered and returned to his genetically determined growth path (Wilson, 1976). The increasing resemblance of identical twins' body size over the first few months of life illustrates a genetic concept that we first discussed in Chapter 3: *canalization*, or the tendency to swing back to a particular channel or trajectory of growth after having been deflected off course. As long as environmental influences are not too severe, this tendency persists throughout childhood and is often called **catch-up growth** (Tanner, 1978a).

When environmental conditions are adequate, individual differences in the linear dimensions of the body — the height and length of the long bones — are largely determined by heredity (Susanne, 1975). But contrary to the popular belief that the physical dimensions of girls are closer to their mothers' and those of boys to their fathers', parents actually make equal genetic contributions to the body dimensions of their children. For example, when elementary school children are grouped according to their parents' height combinations, the offspring of two tall parents are clearly the tallest, while those of two short parents are the shortest. Other parent combinations usually produce children of intermediate stature (Malina, Harper, & Holman, 1970).

Familial studies of age at menarche illustrate the impact of heredity on rate of maturation. Identical twins generally reach menarche within a month or two of each other, whereas fraternal twins differ, on the average, by about 12 months. Again, parents exert equal genetic influence on tempo of growth; an early-maturing girl is as likely to have a mother who matured early as she is to have a father who matured early. Also, genetic influences on rate of maturation are present throughout childhood and adolescence; the same family relationships that apply to menarche hold for skeletal maturity at all ages (Tanner, 1978a).

Nutrition

Nutritional status covers a broad spectrum, ranging from extreme undernutrition to ideal nutrition to overnutrition. Both undernutrition and overnutrition are forms of *malnutrition* — an abnormal condition of the body that results from either a deficiency or an excess of essential nutrients (Tanner, 1978a). A list of essential human nutrients is provided in Table 5.1. It shows the many substances we must regularly ingest for normal growth and body maintenance. Proteins, fats, and carbohydrates are the three basic components of the diet. Each serves different functions with respect to physical development. Proteins are essential for growth, maintenance, and repair of body tissues; carbohydrates supply the primary fuel to meet the energy requirements of the body; and fats contribute to energy reserves and insulate the body against heat loss. The human body also needs minerals, such as calcium for bone tissue, iron for hemoglobin, iodine for thyroid functioning, and vitamins, such as A for sight and D for bone growth. As it stands, the list of essential nutrients is impressive, yet it is probably not exhaustive. Some substances are not included because they are not yet established as essential for humans (Johnston, 1980; Tanner, 1978a).

Undernutrition. In developing countries where food resources are limited and population is on the rise, the most common nutritional problem is *protein-calorie undernutrition*. Recent statistics indicate that 40 to 60 percent of the world's child population is at least mildly afflicted with it (Lozoff, 1989). It therefore ranks as one of the most serious problems confronting the human species today. Among the 4 to 7 percent of children who are severely affected, protein-calorie undernutrition results in two dietary diseases — marasmus and kwashiorkor.

Table 5.1. Essential Human Nutrients

Carbohydrate

Fat

Protein

Water

Minerals

Calcium	Iron	Cobalt
Phosphorus	Zinc	Chrominum
Potassium	Selenium	Fluorine
Sulfur	Manganese	Silicon
Sodium	Copper	Vanadium
Chlorine	Iodine	Nickel
Magnesium	Molybdenum	Tin

Vitamins

A	Riboflavin
D	Niacin
E	Pyroxidine
K	Pantothenic acid
Ascorbic acid	Folacin
Thiamin	B_{12}

Biotin

Source: F. E. Johnston, 1980. ''The Causes of Malnutrition.'' In L. S. Greene & F. E. Johnston (Eds.), *Social and Biological Predictors of Nutritional Status, Physical Growth, and Neurological Development*, New York: Academic Press. Reprinted by permission.

Marasmus is a condition of general starvation that usually makes its appearance in the first year of life. It is due to a diet that is low in all essential nutrients, including both protein and calories. The disease usually occurs when, because of extreme maternal malnutrition, breast milk is insufficient for the growing baby and supplementary feeding is inadequate (Suskind, 1977). A condition of extreme emaciation ensues — severe weight loss, muscular atrophy, and a decrease in subcutaneous fat.

In contrast to marasmus, **kwashiorkor** is not the result of general starvation. It is due to an unbalanced diet, one that is very low in protein. Kwashiorkor commonly occurs between the ages of 1 and 3 after weaning, in areas of the world where protein resources are scarce and young children are provided with diets that are minimally adequate in terms of calories but consist almost entirely of starch. The stricken child shows a wasted condition of the body, accompanied by swelling of the face and limbs, a skin rash, and an enlarged, fatty liver leading to a swollen abdomen.

When such severe forms of malnutrition occur for prolonged periods during the early years of life, growth is permanently stunted. Affected children show retarded physical development, and they grow to be smaller in all body dimensions than their better nourished counterparts (Galler, Ramsey, & Solimano, 1985a; Stoch et al., 1982). Information about the direct effects of postnatal malnutrition on the anatomy of the developing brain is more limited in humans than in animals. However, several studies indicate that children who are severely malnourished during the first few years of life show smaller head circumferences, deviant electrical brain wave recordings, and a drastic reduction in motor nerve conduction velocity — findings that suggest interference with myelinization (Barnet et al., 1978; Engsner & Woldemariam, 1974; Malina, 1980). A 20-year study of the development of a group of grossly marasmic children revealed that nutritional intervention resulted in some catch-up growth in height, but the children failed to catch up in head circumference, suggesting permanent effects of severe malnutrition on the overall weight of the brain (Stoch et al., 1982).

The swollen abdomens of these children are a classic symptom of kwashiorkor, a nutritional condition that results from a diet very low in protein.

Longitudinal studies of severely undernourished children reveal wide-ranging cognitive and socioemotional problems during middle childhood and adolescence, including depressed intelligence, poor fine motor performance, and unfavorable classroom behavior in terms of attentiveness and social skills (Galler et al., 1984; Galler, Ramsey, & Solimano, 1985b; Stoch et al, 1982). These difficulties persist even when dietary supplementation and medical intervention have taken place during the preschool period. When early undernutrition is only mild to moderate, long-term intellectual deficits are less severe, but impaired ability to pay attention and reduced social responsiveness are still evident during the school years (Barrett, Radke-Yarrow, & Klein, 1982).

Since undernutrition of infants and children almost invariably occurs in combination with conditions of social deprivation and poverty, it is usually difficult to know whether behavioral deficits are the result of malnutrition alone, associated social circumstances, or both. Some studies have tried to isolate the influence of protein-calorie malnutrition on behavioral development by comparing malnourished children with sibling controls who were raised in the same family environment but who did not have a history of dietary insufficiency. In such studies, although both groups of children show depressed intellectual functioning, the deficit is greater for children who were malnourished in early childhood. This suggests that malnutrition contributes to low cognitive functioning beyond the influence of social and familial factors (Evans et al., 1980; Richardson & Birch, 1973).

Still, as we indicated in Chapter 3, the long-term consequences of malnutrition are probably the result of complex, bidirectional influences. The passivity and irritability of chronically undernourished children limit their ability to evoke sensitive, stimulating caregiving, thereby contributing to the development of abnormal patterns of social interaction and depressed intelligence. To successfully break this cycle, interventions must improve the environmental situation of the family as well as the child's nutritional status. In addition, prevention programs that provide food supplements and medical care to at-risk mothers and children before the effects of malnutrition run their course are vitally important (Birns & Noyes, 1984). Another effective method of preventing infant protein-calorie malnutrition is breast feeding. To find out more about its nutritional role in infancy, refer to Box 5.3. Interestingly, breast feeding may also help prevent childhood obesity, a growing problem in industrialized nations that we take up in the next section.

Overnutrition. Overweight and **obesity**[2] are prevalent nutritional disorders in more affluent countries, posing significant health risks in terms of heart disease, hypertension, and diabetes and leading to serious psychological and social consequences. Recent statistics indicate that approximately 45 percent of American adults suffer from overnutrition. In spite of the many and varied approaches to weight reduction available, adult efforts to sustain weight loss generally fail (Stephenson et al., 1987).

A number of studies indicate that obese children have a high probability of becoming obese adults, with 80 percent or more retaining their overweight status in later years (Abraham, Collins, & Nordsieck, 1971; Knittle, 1972; Rim & Rim, 1976). In fact, detection of obesity in a substantial number of cases can be achieved by 2 years of age. One survey revealed that 36 percent of individuals who exceeded the 90th percentile of weight as infants became overweight adults, compared to only 14 percent for average and lightweight infants (Charney et al., 1976). Another study showed that among nearly 500 cases of childhood obesity, at least half became overweight by age 2 (Mossberg, 1948). These findings suggest that the first few years of life are very important for establishing lifelong patterns of overnutrition.

---

[2] Obesity is generally defined as a greater than 20 percent increment over average body weight, standardized for age, sex, and stature (Epstein & Wing, 1987).

Not every child is equally at risk for overweight. Fat children tend to have fat parents, a relationship that reflects both hereditary and environmental components. Heredity clearly plays some role, since the weights of adopted children correlate more strongly with those of their biological parents than their adoptive parents (Stunkard et al., 1986). But there is also reason to believe that environment contributes in an important way to a person's weight. For example, socioeconomic status and obesity are consistently related in industrialized nations, with a higher incidence of overweight occurring among low-income individuals (Stunkard et al., 1972).

Researchers have examined early growth patterns for clues about the origins of obesity. The evidence indicates that rapidity of weight gain during the first year of life

---

◆ CONTEMPORARY ISSUES: CULTURAL DIFFERENCES ◆

The Nutritional Importance of Breast Feeding

Box 5.3

The decision by a mother to breast-feed or bottle-feed her baby is influenced by many social, economic, and maternal factors. As long as infants are well nourished, there are no established differences in psychological development between breast-fed and bottle-fed babies. However, breast feeding does have nutritional consequences, and these vary according to the part of the world in which the mother-infant pair lives.

In developing countries, bottle-fed babies are smaller and less viable than breast-fed babies in the first 6 months of life. This is because bottle feeding in many poverty-stricken areas involves low-grade nutrients (such as rice or sugar water, crushed bananas, or highly diluted cow's or goat's milk) that are insufficient for satisfying the requirements of a growing infant. Human breast milk is ideally suited to the nutritional needs of the human baby, and its composition is highly resistant to inadequate maternal nutrition. When mothers are malnourished, breast milk is reduced in volume more than it is in nutritional makeup. In addition, antibodies transmitted from mother to infant via breast milk assist in the baby's immune response, and breast-fed infants experience fewer respiratory and gastrointestinal infections than bottle-fed infants during the first year of life. In fact, bottle feeding in developing countries often increases the danger of infection and disease, since sanitation is poor and sterilization lacking (Stini et al., 1980).

In contrast, in industrialized countries, it is the bottle-fed baby who grows faster, adding extra muscle and fat tissue during the first 9 months of life. Some investigators have speculated that cow's milk formula, artificially blended so that it is as high in fat as breast milk, but higher in protein and sugar, may result in overfeeding of infants. In addition, whereas breast milk serves as a nutritionally complete diet until the baby is 6 months old, bottle feeding necessitates the early introduction of solid foods (by about 3 months of age), which contributes further to early rapid weight gain. The stimulation

of early growth in excess of what breast feeding would ordinarily produce is thought to be one factor, among others, that leads to a tendency toward obesity in childhood and later life (Kramer et al., 1985; Stini et al., 1980).

In breast feeding, the frequency and size of the meal are largely baby-controlled, whereas in bottle feeding, they are more mother-controlled. Breast-fed infants are more likely to be fed on demand and bottle-fed babies on schedule. Also, in breast-fed infants, the quantity of milk intake is correlated with the interval between meals in that larger meals are associated with longer intervals and smaller meals with shorter intervals. Bottle-fed babies tend to receive the same amount of milk regardless of the feeding interval. Wright and Crow (1982) suggest that the infant who establishes early self-control over the frequency of meals and the course of the feed is more likely to become an adult whose food intake is determined by internal physiological signals of hunger rather than external cues, such as the quantity offered, the taste of the food, and the context in which feeding occurs, as is the case with overweight individuals.

The hypothesized connection between bottle feeding and later obesity requires further study, but there is no dispute over the fact that human breast milk is the product of long-term natural selection for uniquely human needs. When compared to the milk of other mammalian species, it is proportionally higher in fat and sugar and lower in protein. The greater fat content suits the needs of a rapidly myelinating central nervous system early in life, while the lower protein content fits with a prolonged period of physical growth in comparison to other mammals. Human beings have an extended timetable of childhood dependency during which a tremendous amount of learning takes place. To facilitate this learning, central nervous system development is emphasized early, while muscle growth is postponed for later. The composition of human milk reflects these adaptive priorities (Stini, et al., 1980).

Obese children often have psychological and social problems; they also have a high probability of becoming obese adults.

predicts overweight during the school years (Eid, 1970; Heald & Hollander, 1965; Taitz, 1971). Animal research shows that excessive fat storage early in development leads to an overabundance of fat cells, which act to support and maintain the overweight condition. It is possible, although not yet proven, that this same biological factor may operate in the development of human obesity, with maladaptive early eating patterns setting it in motion.

Obese individuals are more responsive to external stimuli associated with eating — taste, sight, smell, and time of day — and less responsive to internal hunger cues than are normal-weight individuals (Schachter & Rodin, 1974). This heightened responsiveness to food-related cues is already present in overweight elementary school children and may develop even earlier (Ballard et al., 1980; Constanzo & Woody, 1979). Overweight individuals also eat faster and chew their food less thoroughly than their average-weight and thin counterparts, a behavioral pattern that appears in overweight children as early as 18 months of age (Drabman et al., 1979).

Although the precise origins of the eating patterns of overweight children and adults are not known, a number of investigators believe they are learned early in life. Some mothers interpret almost all the expressed needs of their infants as a desire for food. As a result, they anxiously overfeed their babies and fail to help them learn to distinguish hunger from other physical and emotional discomforts (Weil, 1975). Bruch (1970) reported that parents of obese children frequently employ food as a reward as well as to relieve anxiety. When food is used to reinforce the performance of desirable behaviors (e.g., "Pick up your toys, and then you can have a cookie"), the child's desire for the presented food, as well as for other foods similar to it, is enhanced (Birch, Zimmerman, & Hind, 1980; Birch, 1981). In families in which rewarding children with food happens often, eating acquires important emotional significance beyond the reduction of hunger, a situation that may contribute to the overweight child's heightened responsiveness to food cues.

Overweight children do not just eat more; they are less physically active than their normal-weight peers. Some investigators believe that activity level is at least as important as food intake in the development of obesity. One intriguing hypothesis is that the increase in obesity in the United States over the past 20 years is in part a function of television viewing. Analyzing longitudinal data on a large sample of American children, Dietz and Gortmaker (1985) found that next to prior obesity, television viewing was the strongest predictor of subsequent obesity, a relationship that held even when a variety of controls were introduced. Television watching is certainly a highly sedentary activity, and children tend to eat when they watch. In addition, while viewing, they are repeatedly exposed to food ads, the overwhelming majority of which are for high-calorie snacks containing large amounts of sugar and fat and few beneficial nutrients (Mauro & Feins, 1977).

Unfortunately, physical attractiveness is related to likability, and the psychological and social consequences of childhood obesity are especially severe. Both children and adults hold highly negative stereotypes of overweight children and rate them as less likable than children with a wide variety of physical disabilities (Richardson et al., 1961). This trend is evident as early as kindergarten (Lerner & Schroeder, 1971), and it becomes stronger with age (Brenner & Hinsdale, 1978; Lerner & Korn, 1972). Children even report that they would stand farther away when interacting with a chubby child than they would with an average-build partner (Lerner, Karabenick, & Meisels, 1975; Lerner, Venning, & Knapp, 1975). By middle childhood, obese children display more behavior problems, have poorer self-concepts, and report feeling more depressed than their nonobese counterparts, factors that undoubtedly contribute to the continuation of their maladaptive eating behavior (Banis et al., 1988; Strauss et al., 1985).

Among treatments for obese children, behavior modification programs seem to work the best. Therapists analyze the stimuli and rewards that surround excess eating to arrive at a more suitable eating pattern. For example, tempting high-calorie foods may be eliminated from the household, smaller portions served at meals, television viewing curtailed, and planned opportunities for exercise integrated into daily activities. Programs that involve the entire family rather than just the overweight child are the most successful, since parental eating and exercise patterns serve as influential models for children. Also, parental cooperation and support are especially important in the long-term maintenance of children's weight loss (Epstein & Wing, 1987). Because overnutrition is very difficult to change once it is firmly established, investigators have emphasized the need for early identification as well as efforts at prevention, through such means as nutrition education in the schools and widespread pro-nutrition media campaigns (Peterson et al., 1984).

Disease

In adequately nourished children, ordinary childhood illnesses have no effect on physical growth. However, in undernourished children, disease interacts with malnutrition in a vicious, bidirectional spiral in which one contributes to the detrimental effects of the other, and the consequences for physical growth are compounded.

In developing countries where a large portion of the population lives in a state of poverty, infectious diseases such as measles and chicken pox, which typically do not occur until after age 3, appear much earlier, often afflicting children under 2 and taking the form of severe illnesses (Eveleth & Tanner, 1976). This is because poor diets depress the body's immune system, making children far more susceptible to disease (Salomon, Mata, & Gordon, 1968). The vulnerability of undernourished children to infection is clearly shown by the fact that immunizations containing live disease agents (such as smallpox, polio, and the diphtheria-pertussis-tetanus combination) often lead to substantial weight loss, especially among malnourished infants. These immunizations have little or no growth impact on well-nourished babies (Kielman, 1977).

Disease, in turn, is a major cause of malnutrition and, through it, affects physical growth. Illness reduces children's appetite and limits nutrient absorption. These consequences are especially severe for children afflicted with chronic gastrointestinal infections. Diarrhea is widespread in developing countries and generally increases around the time of weaning, between 6 and 18 months of age, when pathogenic organisms are introduced through supplementary foods. Studies by Martorell (1980) reveal that 7-year-olds growing up in poverty-stricken Guatemalan villages who had been relatively free of gastrointestinal illness since birth were nearly 1½ inches taller and 3½ pounds heavier than their frequently ill peers. This is a large difference, since all the children were quite small to begin with—5 inches shorter and 11 pounds lighter, on the average, than well-nourished children in the United States.

Affection and Stimulation

That parental affection and stimulation are vital for normal physical growth has been known since the thirteenth century, when Frederick II, King of Two Sicilies, tried to determine which of the world's languages was the true natural language of the human species. He took a group of newborn infants away from their mothers and isolated them on an island with wet nurses, who were instructed not to speak to the babies. The king's experiment was a failure. All the infants died, "for they could not live without the petting and the joyful faces and loving words of their foster mothers" (Gardner, 1972, p. 76). Today, failure to thrive and deprivation dwarfism are recognized growth disorders believed to result from lack of attention and affection.

Failure to thrive is a term applied to infants who show growth retardation, with no additional organic signs or obvious nutritional deprivation to account for it. Present in the majority of cases by 18 months of age, its most striking physical feature is a substantial reduction in weight. The loss of both fat and muscle tissue leads the baby to take on an emaciated appearance. The behavior of infants with failure to thrive provides a strong clue to its diagnosis. Along with passivity and apathy toward the physical environment, they show an unusual apprehensive watchfulness of adults, exhibit little smiling and vocalization, and do not react with cuddliness to being picked up (Leonard, Rhymes, & Solnit, 1966; Oates, 1984).

Deprivation dwarfism appears at later ages than failure to thrive. It is generally diagnosed between 2 and 15 years of age. Short stature is its most striking feature, but children's weight is usually in proportion to their height, and they do not present a picture of malnutrition. Children with deprivation dwarfism often show abnormally low levels of growth hormone, and their skeletal ages are immature. It is now believed that the disorder occurs because emotional deprivation affects hypothalamic-pituitary communication, decreasing growth hormone secretions and thereby inhibiting growth. When affected children are removed from their emotionally inadequate environments, their growth hormone levels quickly return to normal, and they grow rapidly. However, if treatment is delayed until late in development, the dwarfism can be permanent (Oates, Peacock, & Forrest, 1985).

The families of children with both failure to thrive and deprivation dwarfism are characterized by non-nurturant communication. However, the conditions surrounding failure to thrive have been studied more intensively. Mothers of these infants take little pleasure in interacting with them and seem cold, impatient, and hostile. Examining videotapes of mothers and their failure-to-thrive infants engaged in feeding and play activities, Haynes and her colleagues (1983) observed the mothers to be either overly intrusive or disengaged. They appeared insensitive to their baby's initiatives—arbitrarily removing toys, offering food efficiently but mechanically, and reprimanding and ridiculing the baby. The infants protected themselves from these negative behaviors by turning their heads away and avoiding the mother's gaze. In another study, the breakdown in mother-infant interaction leading to failure to thrive was already evident in the first few days after birth. Mothers whose infants later developed the disorder spent less time looking at their babies and terminated interaction with them more quickly than did mothers of controls, and feeding problems were evident soon after delivery (Vietz et al., 1980). When treated early, through intensive family intervention or placement in a caring foster home, failure-to-thrive infants show quick catch-up growth. But if the problem is not corrected in infancy, some children remain small and show lasting intellectual and behavioral difficulties (Altemeier et al., 1984; Drotar & Sturm, 1988).

Maternal nurturing problems associated with growth disorders are often grounded in poverty and family disorganization. Job instability, chronic unemployment, and crowded living conditions place parents under severe stress. With their own emotional resources depleted, parents have little energy available to meet the psychological needs of their children. However, failure to thrive and deprivation dwarfism do not occur exclusively among the poor. The syndromes also appear in economically advantaged families in which marital discord or other pressures cause parents to behave in non-nurturant and destructive ways toward their children (Gagan, 1984).

The study of growth disorders permits us to see important influences on physical development that are not readily apparent when we observe the healthy, normally growing child. In the case of failure to thrive and deprivation dwarfism, we become consciously aware of the intimate connection between sensitive, loving care and how children grow.

CHAPTER SUMMARY

The Course of Physical Growth

■ Compared to other species, human beings experience a prolonged period of physical growth, providing ample time for children to learn to live in a complex physical and social world. **Distance** and **velocity curves** display the orderly overall pattern of human growth. Increases in height and weight are rapid during infancy, slow and steady during middle childhood, and rapid again during adolescence. Some tissues and organs, such as the brain and lymph system, do not follow this general growth trend. Human growth is asynchronous, with various parts of the body having their own unique timetables of maturation.

■ Although all individuals adhere closely to the same sequence of growth, individual differences exist in rate of maturation. Determination of **skeletal age** by examining the extent of **ossification** of bone growth centers is the best available method for assessing a child's progress toward physical maturity.

■ Sex differences in growth are relatively small during the infant and childhood years. Girls are ahead in skeletal age, whereas boys are slightly larger in overall body size. At adolescence, obvious sex differences emerge. Girls reach puberty, on the average, 2 years earlier than boys. Girls develop physical characteristics, including a broad pelvic frame and extra fatty tissue, that are uniquely suited for carrying and bearing offspring. Boys' later pubertal growth spurt is partly responsible for the fact that they grow taller and have legs that are proportionately longer than girls'. Males also gain far more muscle tissue than females. As a result, adolescent boys outperform girls in a wide range of athletic skills.

■ The adolescent growth spurt occurs earlier in the sequence of pubertal events for girls than boys, with growth in height mostly complete by the time the girl experiences **menarche.** How girls react to first menstruation depends on a number of factors, including prior knowledge and family support. The little information available on boys' reactions to **spermarche** suggests that it may be of comparable emotional importance.

■ The timing of pubertal maturation influences adolescent social and emotional adjustment. Early-maturing boys and late-maturing girls, who bring to social situations body types that closely match cultural standards of physical attractiveness, are advantaged. In contrast, early-maturing girls and late-maturing boys, who fit in least well with their agemates in physical status, experience social and emotional difficulties. Social contexts, such as the grade makeup of school environments, can modify maturational timing effects.

■ Physical growth is controlled by hormones released from the endocrine glands of the body. The hypothalamus initiates and regulates five important hormonal secretions from the pituitary gland. These either act directly on tissues to produce growth or stimulate the release of other hormones from glands located elsewhere in the body. Without early medical intervention, failure of the child's endocrine system to produce normal levels of hormones leads to serious growth problems.

■ **Secular trends** in physical growth have occurred in modern industrialized nations; children have been growing larger and reaching maturity more quickly over the last century. Attributed to better nutrition, improved health care, and the end of child labor in the early part of this century, these secular gains are now leveling off. Secular increases in growth do not occur in all countries. In some developing nations stricken by poverty, famine, and disease, secular decreases have been found.

Development of the Brain

■ The human brain achieves its peak period of growth earlier than other organs. However, like the rest of the body, its growth is asynchronous, with the **cerebral cortex,** seat of human intelligence, being the last part of the brain to stop growing. Consequently, the cortex is more susceptible to postnatal environmental influences than is any other brain structure.

■ The production of **neurons** ceases by 6 months gestational age, and their migration and orientation during the early weeks of prenatal life are under genetic control. Once neurons begin to differentiate by forming **synapses,** or connections with one another, environmental stimulation determines which neurons will survive and which will die off. To develop optimally, the brain requires appropriate environmental input during periods in which the establishment of neuronal connections is at a peak. **Glial cells,** which are responsible for **myelinization** of the nervous system, continue to multiply long after the production of neurons is complete. They are largely responsible for postnatal gains of the brain in size and weight.

■ Maturation of the cortex closely parallels the acquisition of various capacities in the infant and young child. Sensory and motor regions are the first to mature. Association or ''thought'' regions are last to develop, with some continuing their growth well into the second and third decades of life.

■ **Lateralization** refers to specialization of functions between the two cerebral hemispheres. For most individuals, processing of verbal information is concentrated in the left hemisphere, and processing of spatial information, nonspeech sounds, and emotion in the right hemisphere. In infancy, before many neurons have taken on specialized roles, there is high brain **plasticity.** If some portions of the cortex are injured, others take over their basic functions. However, some brain specialization already exists in newborn infants, and research on handedness indicates that lateralization increases over the childhood years.

■ Research suggests that growth spurts in the human cortex occur intermittently from infancy into adolescence. These may be critical periods during which the brain requires appropriate stimulation for optimal development of human intelligence.

Factors Affecting Physical Growth

■ The course of physical growth is the result of a continuous and complex interplay between heredity and environment. Heredity contributes to children's height, weight, and rate of maturation.

■ A variety of environmental factors affect physical growth. The importance of nutrition is tragically evident in the dietary diseases of **marasums** and **kwashiorkor,** which affect large numbers of children in developing countries. In industrialized nations, overweight and **obesity** are serious nutritional problems caused by maladaptive eating patterns and physical underactivity during childhood.

■ Disease interacts with undernutrition to affect physical growth. **Failure to thrive** and **deprivation dwarfism** are two growth disorders that illustrate the importance of adequate parental stimulation and affection for normal physical development.

IMPORTANT TERMS AND CONCEPTS

distance curve   (p. 168)
velocity curve   (p. 169)
skeletal age   (p. 173)
ossification   (p. 173)
epiphyses   (p. 173)
fontanels   (p. 174)
menarche   (p. 175)
spermarche   (p. 178)
growth hormone (GH)   (p. 184)
thyroid stimulating hormone
 (TSH)   (p. 184)

adrenocorticotropic hormone
 (ACTH)   (p. 185)
follicle stimulating hormone
 (FSH)   (p. 185)
luteinizing hormone (LH)   (p. 185)
secular trends in physical
 growth   (p. 186)
neurons   (p. 188)
cerebral cortex   (p. 188)
synapses   (p. 189)
glial cells   (p. 189)

myelinization   (p. 189)
lateralization   (p. 192)
plasticity   (p. 193)
catch-up growth   (p. 196)
marasmus   (p. 198)
kwashiorkor   (p. 198)
obesity   (p. 199)
failure to thrive   (p. 203)
deprivation dwarfism   (p. 203)

N.C. Wyeth (1882–1945): *The Giant*. Oil on canvas, painted in 1923.
Collection of the Westtown School, Pa. Photo Courtesy of the Brandywine River Museum.

6

Cognitive Development: A Piagetian Perspective

Cognition refers to the inner processes and products of the human mind that lead to "knowing." It includes all human mental activity: remembering, relating, classifying, symbolizing, imagining, problem-solving, creating, and even fantasizing and dreaming. Indeed, we could easily enlarge upon this list; there is no clear place at which to limit a definition of human cognition because mental processes make their way into virtually everything human beings do (Flavell, 1985). Among the great contributions of the eminent Swiss psychologist Jean Piaget (1896–1980) was a theory of development in which human cognition is viewed as a broad, complex phenomenon made up of diverse components that emerge in a richly interwoven fashion. Piaget's perspective stands as one of the two dominant positions on cognitive development in the field, the other being information processing, which we take up in Chapter 7.

The first portion of this chapter is devoted to highlighting Piaget's theoretical and empirical work. Piaget conceived of human cognition as a network of mental structures created by an active organism striving to make sense of its surrounding world. This perspective was revolutionary when it first reached the shores of the United States in the middle of the twentieth century. It represented a radical departure from the then dominant behaviorist position, which steered clear of any internal constructs of mind and conceived of the child as a passive entity shaped and molded from without. By the 1960s, Piaget's ideas were embraced by the American child development community with enthusiasm. The power of his theoretical concepts, the large array of problem-solving tasks he devised to chart the landmarks of cognitive development, and the relevance of his ideas for the education of children made his work especially attractive.

Over the last three decades, many research studies have been aimed at replicating and extending Piaget's research. Currently, there is considerable debate over the adequacy and correctness of his ideas. As we review Piaget's theory, we will pause at various points along the way to represent new evidence that verifies his original conclusions as well as findings that indicate a need for revisions of his ideas. It is possible that Piaget's theory may someday be set aside in favor of an improved alternative. However, even Piaget's staunchest critics agree that without his contributions, we would not have progressed as quickly and as far as we have in our understanding of children's thinking.

The final section of this chapter is devoted to an alternative perspective that the field of child development has only recently begun to explore — the dialectical theory of Lev Semanovich Vygotsky (1896 – 1934), to which you were introduced in Chapter 1. Vygotsky carried out his research in the Soviet Union during the 1920s and 1930s, at about the same time Piaget conducted his formative studies of children's thinking. Early on, the two theorists were aware of each other's work, and they disagreed sharply about the basis of cognitive development.

Vygotsky believed that the child's immature mental structures change from constant exposure to the more mature thinking of adults and peers, with whom the child engages in cooperative dialogues surrounding everyday activities. He regarded social communication (and therefore language) as the primary means through which children become conscious of their own thinking, plan and guide their own behavior, and learn to reason abstractly — mental capacities that distinguish humans from all other animal species. Although Piaget also believed that language facilitates thought, he did not grant it primary status in cognitive development. Instead, Piaget concluded that more mature cognition comes about through the child's active manipulation of the physical world. As children act on objects, they spontaneously generate more effective structures that take newly discovered properties of the environment into account. These discoveries are eventually coded into words and symbols, but it is the child's exploratory activity, not language and social communication, that provides the foundation for them.

On the basis of this brief description, do you find it difficult to decide between Piaget's and Vygotsky's theories? Before we can evaluate these two divergent perspectives, we must become thoroughly acquainted with Piaget's and then Vygotsky's work.

PIAGET'S THEORY OF COGNITIVE DEVELOPMENT

Piaget received his early training in biology and philosophy. As a young boy he spent his afternoons at the Museum of Natural History in Neuchatel, where he became intensely interested in the many species of sea snails that populate the lakes of Switzerland. An intellectually precocious youngster, Piaget studied how the shell structure of each species is uniquely adapted to the animal's habitat. Soon his godfather introduced him to a subdiscipline of philosophy called *epistemology*, which is concerned with the analysis of knowledge and the understanding of various forms of knowing. At age 21, Piaget completed his Ph.D. in zoology. Shortly thereafter, he applied his early grounding in science and philosophy to the construction of a biological account of the origins of knowledge. As a result, his theory of cognitive development came to have a distinctly biological flavor.

Piaget regarded cognitive development as a special case of biological growth in general. Just as the body has physical structures that enable it to adapt to the environment, so the mind builds mental structures that permit it to achieve a progressively better adaptive fit with experience. In the development of these structures, the mind of the child is intensely active. It selects, interprets, and reorganizes experience in terms of its currently existing structures, and it also modifies these structures so that they take into account more subtle and detailed aspects of the surrounding world.

Through careful observations of children, as well as clinical interviews with them, Jean Piaget (1896–1980) developed his comprehensive theory of cognitve development.

Thus, for Piaget, cognitive development is the story of how each of us discovers the nature of reality. Each child's mental reality is very much his or her own unique construction. But since all of us possess the same biological apparatus for acting on and interpreting experience, the course of development is the same for all human beings.

Piaget believed that children move through a sequence of stages — *qualitatively* distinct reorganizations of thought — during infancy and childhood. Therefore, his ideas are different from the mental testing approach that has long dominated the investigation of children's intelligence in the United States. Intelligence tests have largely been concerned with *quantitative* changes — how much of a particular mental skill, such as memory or comprehension of information, children possess at different ages and whether performance at early ages can predict performance at later ages. Piaget was not concerned with these issues (although his theory has served as the basis for several intelligence tests, as we will see in Chapter 8). Instead, he focused on describing the cognitive structures that underlie intelligent behavior and identifying the discrete stages through which these structures are transformed (Brainerd, 1978). He also specified a common set of processes, or functions, that are responsible for all cognitive changes. Thus, the structures describe *what* changes and the functions explain *how* change takes place in Piaget's system.

Key Concepts: Cognitive Contents, Structures, and Functions

Since Piagetian structures and functions are mental phenomena and not directly observable, they must be inferred from cognitive **contents,** the specific intellectual acts in which infants and children engage at any stage of development. As babies experiment with objects, or as children solve problems and demonstrate reasoning skills, they provide raw behavioral data that can be interpreted for structural and functional characteristics.

Structures are organized properties of intelligence that change with age. They are inferred from behavioral content, but they also underlie and determine it. For example, in a child who judges, after water is poured from a tall, thin glass into a short, wide container, that the container has less liquid in it because it is shorter, we witness behavioral content. From it we infer that the child's cognitive structures are organized in such a way that the surface appearance of things dominates. Successive states of objects (a certain amount of water first in one place and then in another) remain unrelated to one another in any logical fashion. This knowledge of the child's structures then allows us to predict what the child might do in other situations.

Schemes. Specific cognitive structures are called **schemes.** Piaget maintained that all schemes are spontaneously exercised; children have a natural tendency to use them repeatedly. This is evident, for example, in the infant's repetitious application of the sensorimotor scheme of grasping to a wide variety of objects and the 2-year-old's tireless exercise of new representational schemes in demanding that a story be read again and again. Piaget believed that repetition of schemes ensures that cognitive change will take place. As schemes are applied, they come into contact with new information, and children modify them to incorporate new experiences. To explain how schemes develop, Piaget identified two important intellectual **functions:** adaption and organization. The fundamental properties of these functions remain the same throughout life, despite the wide variety of schemes that they create.

Adaptation. Adaptation involves building schemes through direct interaction with the environment. It consists of two simultaneous but complementary processes: **assimilation** and **accommodation.** These concepts provide an excellent illustration of the distinctly biological flavor of Piaget's theory, since they are taken directly from principles of biological growth (Piaget, 1936/1952b). In the biological incorporation of food, we *assimilate* edible materials and make them like ourselves. At the same time, we also *accommodate* to them, for we must open our mouths to receive the food, chew some foods more thoroughly than others, and adapt our digestive processes to the physical and chemical properties of each food. Otherwise, digestion cannot take place.

This 5-month-old baby assimilates a rattle into her already well-established sucking scheme.

A similar process takes place on the level of intellectual adaptation. When we assimilate, we interpret the external world in terms of our schemes or currently available ways of thinking about things. For example, the infant who puts a variety of objects in her mouth is assimilating them all into a primitive, sensorimotor sucking scheme. And the preschooler who sees her first camel at the zoo and calls it a "horse" has sifted through her collection of schemes until she arrives at one that will incorporate the object. In accommodation, the schemes are revised to take into account newly apprehended properties of the environment. For example, when the infant begins to suck differently on the edge of a blanket than on a nipple, she has started to modify the sucking scheme. And the preschooler who calls a camel a "lumpy horse" has noticed that certain properties of the camel are not just like horses and has revised the horse scheme accordingly.

So far, we have referred to assimilation and accommodation as separate activities, but Piaget actually regarded them as working together. That is, in every interchange with the environment, the mind interprets information using its existing cognitive structures, and it also refines its structures to achieve a better adaptive fit with experience. Nevertheless, the balance between assimilation and accommodation does vary from one time to another. Since assimilation accounts for the exercise of current schemes and accommodation for their modification, during periods in which the child is largely preoccupied with using recently formed schemes, assimilation predominates over accommodation. During periods of rapid change and development, accommodation prevails over assimilation.

Piaget used the term **equilibration,** which refers to continuous movement between states of cognitive *equilibrium* and *disequilibrium*, to describe the way in which assimilation and accommodation work together in varying balances to produce cognitive change. The term equilibrium implies a steady, comfortable state. It refers to a condition in which we use already formed schemes to interpret reality; in other words, we are largely assimilating rather than accommodating. But in the process of exercising schemes, we notice new information that does not fit with our current structures. This produces a state of disequilibrium, or cognitive discomfort, in which we shift away from assimilation toward accommodation to resolve the discrepancy between the environment and our present schemes. Once we have successfully modified our schemes, we can use the newly formed structures to assimilate reality. As we do so, we reach a new, more stable level of cognitive equilibrium as the breadth of experiences to which our schemes apply expands. The process of equilibrating takes place continuously during development, repeating itself at ever higher levels of cognitive maturity (Piaget, 1985).

Organization. Adaptation involves direct contact between schemes and the environment. However, Piaget was careful to point out that cognitive structures can change in the absence of environmental stimulation. **Organization,** an additional cognitive function, goes on internally quite apart from our interaction with the physical world. Once structures reach a true state of equilibrium, they form an orderly, integrated whole, show a high degree of interdependence, and are part of a strong total system. Piaget believed that this is achieved through organization, the constant internal rearrangement of schemes so they fit tightly with one another (Piaget, 1936/1952b; Flavell, 1963).

The Piagetian Notion of Stage

Each Piagetian stage groups together similar qualitative changes in many schemes that take place during the same period of development (Tanner & Inhelder, 1956). The stages are assumed to be *invariant*; that is, they emerge in a fixed order for all children, and there can be no skipping of stages. Piaget's invariant stage sequence reveals that his theory has a strong maturational component. The order of stages is regarded as genetically determined, although the age at which each stage appears varies considerably from child to child. Piaget cautioned against relying on age as an indicator of stage of development because many factors—both hereditary and environmental—affect the speed with which children move through the stages (Piaget, 1926/1928). In fact, he viewed both maturation and experience as making joint and inseparable contributions to development, since children cannot mature through his stages without opportunities to exercise their schemes in a rich and varied external world.

Piaget acknowledged that not all individuals achieve the final stages of development. For example, retarded children follow the identical sequence of Piagetian stages as do nonretarded children, differing only in the slow rate at which they progress and in the lower stage ceiling they attain (Weisz & Zigler, 1979). Moreover, as we will see later on, attainment of the highest stage of formal operations depends on extensive experience in specific content areas. Therefore, a particular individual may not reach formal operations in all situations (Flavell, 1963).

A final important feature of Piaget's stages is that they are *hierarchically related*. That is, the structures of the early stages are not lost forever once children advance to a new stage. Instead, they are absorbed and integrated into the later stages. For example, crawling infants have developed a basic sensorimotor map of their immediate surroundings, and they use it to move quickly and efficiently from one place to another, making detours and avoiding obstacles. Years later, these sensorimotor action patterns are incorporated into representational schemes, as school-age children imagine spatial relationships and draw organized maps of their surroundings (Flavell, 1963; Piaget, Inhelder, & Szeminska, 1948/1960).

Piaget's Methods of Study

Piaget developed unique methods for investigating the quality of children's thought. In the early part of his career, he made careful observations of his three infant children and also presented them with little problems, such as an attractive object that could be grasped, mouthed, kicked, or searched for when hidden from view. From their reactions, Piaget derived the sequence of cognitive changes that take place during the first two years of life. In studying childhood and adolescent thought, Piaget took advantage of children's ability to verbally report their thinking. For a period of time, he worked in the Paris laboratory of Alfred Binet (creator of the first successful intelligence test), and he quickly discovered the importance of the **clinical interview**[1] for understanding children's thought. Piaget was fascinated by children's wrong answers to intelligence test questions and the reasons for them; their mistakes seemed to follow predictable patterns related to age. He began to interview his subjects in a flexible, open-ended conversational style in which he followed a child's line of thought by permitting an initial explanation to determine the next question he would ask (Piaget, 1952a). As Piaget's work became more widely known, he was criticized by American investigators for using this method because it violated the widely held research principle that procedures be applied in an identical, standardized fashion to every subject. Yet it was this very approach that permitted Piaget to investigate the underlying processes of children's thought.

PIAGET'S STAGES OF DEVELOPMENT

Piaget referred to his stages as sensorimotor, preoperational, concrete operational, and formal operational. To orient you to the complex cognitive changes that occur during these four periods of development, a brief overview is provided below. Then we will embark on a detailed consideration of each stage.

[1] An excerpt from a clinical interview conducted by Piaget is given on page 23 of Chapter 1. You may wish to read it again to refresh your memory of this method for investigating children's thinking.

The **sensorimotor stage** spans the age of infancy, from birth to about 2 years. During this period, infants "think" by acting on the world with their eyes, ears, hands, and other sensorimotor equipment; they cannot carry out many activities "inside their heads." These sensorimotor action patterns become increasingly complex and flexible during the first two years of life. During the **preoperational stage,** which extends from approximately 2 to 7 years of age, children represent their earlier sensorimotor structures internally. As a result, they acquire "thought." However, their thinking is unsophisticated and lacks the rigorous, logical properties of the two remaining stages. The **concrete operational stage** begins around age 7 and ends at about age 11. During this period, children's reasoning takes on logical characteristics, and a far more systematic and rational cognitive framework is applied to the world of concrete objects. When thought processes have this orderly, logical character, Piaget called them **operations.** But operational thinking at this stage falls short of adult intelligence in that it is not yet abstract. The **formal operational stage,** which begins around age 11 and is fully achieved by age 15, brings with it the capacity for abstraction. This permits adolescents to reason beyond a world of concrete reality to a world of possibilities and to operate logically on symbols and information that do not necessarily refer to objects and events in the real world (Flavell, 1963; Brainerd, 1978).

The Sensorimotor Stage (Birth – 2 Years)

Compared to older children and adults, infants are much simpler cognitive beings. Nevertheless, the difference between the newborn baby and the 2-year-old child is so vast that Piaget's sensorimotor period ranks among his most complex statements on the development of intelligence. Unlike the neonate, whose adaptations are limited and reflexive, the child of late infancy and the early preschool years can solve practical, everyday problems and can represent reality in terms of symbols in speech, gesture, and play (Flavell, 1985). Given these enormous changes, it is no surprise that Piaget's sensorimotor period is comprised of six substages.

The fact that Piaget's infant observations were based on the very limited sample of his own three children caused many investigators to question the validity of his sensorimotor stage. Although subsequent research has confirmed Piaget's general sequence of sensorimotor development (Corman & Escalona, 1969; Užgiris, 1973; Užgiris & Hunt, 1975), questions have been raised about his interpretation of several infant intellectual phenomena. It is now generally agreed that Piaget underestimated the young baby's intellectual competence (Gibson & Spelke, 1983). In the sections below, we first describe sensorimotor development as Piaget saw it, noting recent research that supports his observations. Then we consider current differences of opinion that surround his description of this first stage.

Major Achievements of the Sensorimotor Stage. The sensorimotor period results in several landmark intellectual achievements. One of the most important is **object permanence,** the understanding that objects have a permanent existence independent of the infant's interaction with them. Think, for a moment, about your own understanding of objects. You know that when an object is out of sight, it has not miraculously evaporated. You also know that an object's behavior is independent of your contact with it. While an object is out of sight, you are aware that it can change locations. If you look for it again, it may be where you last saw it, or it may have moved or been moved by someone else. This multifaceted understanding of objects, which is basic to a coherent mental life, develops gradually over the first two years.

During the sensorimotor period, infants also develop **intentional,** or **goal-directed behavior.** At the beginning of this stage, the baby's actions are not planful and goal-directed. Instead, they have a random, hit-or-miss quality to them — for example, *accidentally* bringing thumb to mouth and latching on or *happening* to kick the mobile, which yields an interesting visual and auditory effect. But by about 8 months of age, infants have had enough practice with a variety of schemes that they can combine them intentionally in the solution of simple sensorimotor problems.

Two important cognitive capacities, *play* and *imitation*, make their first appearance during the sensorimotor period. Together they serve as important mechanisms for solidifying old schemes and acquiring new ones. Piaget defined play as the exercise of already acquired schemes just for the pleasure and fun of doing so.[2] Therefore, he regarded play as placing its heaviest accent on assimilation. In contrast, imitation, the copying of behaviors that are not yet in the child's repertoire, is accommodation in its purest form. When infants and young children imitate, they put all their effort into modifying behavior to fit with what they perceive in the environment. Piaget believed that what infants and children play at and what they imitate provide excellent indicators of their advancing intellectual achievements.

The Circular Reaction: Basic Sensorimotor Learning Mechanism. Before infants can play, imitate, or engage in intentional behavior, they must have some means for building schemes. Piaget referred to the earliest sensorimotor learning mechanism as the **circular reaction.** It consists of stumbling accidentally onto a new experience that results from the infant's own activity. The reaction is "circular" because the infant tries to repeat this chance event again and again. Through a series of such repetitions, a new response becomes strengthened into a firmly established scheme. The circular reaction, like play and imitation, adapts over the sensorimotor period to reflect major advances in infant intellectual capacities. Circular reactions change from *primary*, or centered around the infant's own body, to *secondary*, directed outward to manipulation of objects, to *tertiary*, concerned with exploration of novel effects in the surrounding world. This sequence indicates that infant intellectual activity gradually becomes less self-centered, less rigid, and more outer-directed and exploratory over the first two years of life.

Sensorimotor Egocentrism. Central to Piaget's theory of cognitive development is the concept of egocentrism — young children's inability to distinguish their own cognitive perspectives from the perspectives of others. **Sensorimotor egocentrism** involves an absence of the understanding that objects exist independently of one's own actions and that the self is an object in a world of objects. It gradually declines as infants become aware that objects are permanent, external entities and that their own actions are separate from the objects themselves. Piaget's concept of infant egocentrism will become clearer to you as we describe his six sensorimotor substages.

The Six Sensorimotor Substages. The major cognitive transformations of the first two years of life are as follows:

Substage 1: Reflexive Schemes (Birth–1 Month). Because the newborn infant's behavior consists of little more than neonatal reflexes, Piaget treated this stage briefly. Nevertheless, he regarded the baby's reflexive adaptations as the building blocks of sensorimotor intelligence. While some reflexes like the Moro and Babinski (which we discussed in Chapter 4) never become cognitively relevant, others such as sucking, grasping, and eye movements begin to change as they are applied to objects and events. During this first substage, infants are completely egocentric. Although equipped with innate responses, they have no understanding of a world of objects existing separately from the self (Piaget, 1936/1952b).

---

[2] There are many definitions of play in the child development literature. Some definitions emphasize the intrinsically motivated nature of children's activity, others the child's active engagement with the environment, and still others a pleasurable emotional state that accompanies play behavior (Rubin, Fein, & Vandenberg, 1983). All of these characteristics fit very well with Piaget's definition of play. However, as we will see later on in this chapter, some theorists believe that play goes well beyond the practice of previously learned skills and actually increases children's repertoire of responses to the environment. They suggest that Piaget underestimated the power of play in children's development.

Substage 2: Primary Circular Reactions: The First Learned Adaptations (1–4 Months). By repeating chance behaviors that lead to satisfying results, infants develop some simple motor habits, such as sucking their thumbs, sticking out their tongues, and opening and closing their hands. In addition, infants of this substage start to vary their behavior more clearly in response to environmental demands, as, for example, when they open their mouths differently to a nipple than to a spoon. The improved coordination of actions with experience is also evident in the 2-month-old's limited ability to anticipate events — for example, when the baby displays anticipatory sucking movements in preparation for feeding. Still, the sensorimotor schemes of Substage 2 are very limited in that they are primarily centered around the baby's own body and motivated by basic physiological needs. As yet, infants do not seem very concerned with the results to which their actions lead in the external world. Therefore, the infant of a few months of age is still a very egocentric being.

By the end of this substage, visually guided reaching appears, and it plays a major role in turning infants' attention outward toward objects. Also, around this time, Piaget believed that infants show the first glimmerings of the capacity to imitate others, but it is limited to copying someone else's imitation of their own actions. However, as we discussed in Chapter 4, recent evidence indicates that even newborn infants have a rudimentary capacity to imitate adults' facial gestures. Therefore, imitation is one of the areas in which Piaget underestimated the young baby's competence. Finally, Substage 2 infants exercise simple motor habits playfully; they can be seen smiling gleefully as they repeat a newly developed action.

Substage 3: Secondary Circular Reactions: Making Interesting Sights Last (4–8 Months). Now infants perform actions that are more definitely oriented toward objects and events outside their own bodies. Using the secondary circular reaction, they try to maintain through repetition interesting effects produced by their own actions. Piaget recorded numerous examples of secondary circular reactions, most involving manual activity such as pulling, striking, swinging, and rubbing. The one described below shows the gradual emergence of the sensorimotor scheme of "hitting" in Piaget's 4-month-old son Laurent:

> At 4 months, 7 days, [Laurent] looks at a letter opener tangled in the strings of a doll hung in front of him. He tries to grasp (a scheme he already knows) the doll or the letter opener but each time, his attempts only result in his knocking the objects (so they swing out of his reach). He then looks at them with interest and starts over again. . . . The next day Laurent tries to grasp a doll hanging in front of him; but he only manages to make it swing. . . . Then he shakes his whole body, waving his arms (another scheme he already knows). But in so doing he hits the doll by accident; then he starts over on purpose, a number of times. . . . At 4 months 15 days, with another doll hung in front of him, Laurent tries to grasp it, then shakes himself to make it swing, knocks it accidentally, and then tries simply to hit it. . . . At 4 months 18 days, Laurent hits my hands without trying to grasp them, but he started by simply waving his arms around, and only afterwards went on to hit my hands. The next day, finally, Laurent immediately hits a doll hung in front of him. The scheme is now completely differentiated. (Piaget, 1936/1952b, pp. 167–168)[3]

Although they are a great cognitive advance over the previous stage, secondary circular reactions are limited in that they involve undifferentiated connections between actions and objects. Infants do not yet explore the objects that give rise to their pleasurable experiences. Instead, they simply repeat a newly acquired action with respect to an object over and over again. Therefore, Substage 3 infants are still egocentric and have little understanding of objects existing independently of their own actions.

[3] Quotations from Piaget (1936/1952b) are reprinted by permission of International Universities Press, Inc.

Notice how similar the example of Laurent's secondary circular reaction is to the evidence on operant conditioning of early infant behaviors, presented in Chapter 4. From this perspective, Laurent's hitting scheme is a conditioned response, and the visual effect it produces serves as a reinforcer. Operant conditioning research shows that the frequency of newborn babies' responses like sucking and head turning increases rapidly when they lead to interesting results, such as sounds and patterned visual displays. Therefore, some version of Substage 3 behavior appears earlier than Piaget indicated. As with imitation, Piaget seems to have underestimated the young infant's capacity to engage in secondary circular reactions.

According to Piaget, infants of Substage 3 show slightly more advanced imitative abilities in that they will spontaneously copy the behavior of a model. However, they can imitate only behaviors that are already within their own repertoire, not those that are novel and as yet unpracticed. Piaget also believed that Substage 3 babies could imitate only behaviors they could see or hear themselves produce. These include vocalizations and manual gestures but not facial expressions, since babies cannot see their own faces. However, once again, the latter conclusion is at variance with research on neonatal imitation described in Chapter 4.

Substage 4: Coordination of Secondary Circular Reactions and Their Application to New Situations (8–12 Months). In Substage 4, previously acquired schemes are combined into new action sequences that are intentional and goal-directed. The clearest example is provided by Piaget's object-hiding tasks, in which he shows the infant an attractive object and then hides it behind his hand, under a cloth cover, or beneath a cup. Infants of this stage can set aside the obstacle and retrieve the object. In doing so, they coordinate two schemes, one serving as the means (pushing aside the obstacle) and the other serving as the goal (grasping the object). Piaget regarded such means-end behavior as the first truly intelligent behavior and the foundation for all later problem solving.

The fact that infants of Substage 4 can retrieve a hidden object indicates that they have achieved some appreciation of the continued existence of objects that have been spirited out of sight. However, Piaget believed that infants' understanding of object permanence is limited at this stage. He claimed that if a hidden object is moved to a new location, infants will search for it only in the first place in which it was concealed. Therefore, he concluded, infants do not really have a clear image of the object as continuing to exist beneath the cover.

Substage 4 also brings advances in imitative abilities; now babies imitate behaviors that are slightly different from those they customarily perform. Infants do this by searching through their current repertoire of schemes and making deliberate modifications to approximate the new behavior. Thus, imitation, like means-end behavior, becomes intentional during this period (Piaget, 1945/1951).

Finally, play expands to include practicing the means in babies' new means-end action sequences. Piaget described an example in which one of his children began by pushing an obstacle aside to obtain a toy but ended up by ignoring the toy and, instead, pushing aside the obstacle (Piaget's hand or a piece of cardboard) again and again for fun (Piaget, 1945/1951).

Substage 5: Tertiary Circular Reactions: The Discovery of New Means Through Active Experimentation (12–18 Months). Presented with an object, babies who are capable of tertiary circular reactions still stumble onto new and intriguing consequences by accident. However, in attempting to recapture them, they *repeat with variation*, trying this, then that, and then another action pattern in a deliberately exploratory approach. In doing so, infants try to provoke new results and are not satisfied with familiar ones. This vigorous experimental orientation makes infants far more effective sensorimotor problem solvers, since they can discover *new means to ends*. For example, they can figure out how to fit objects into container openings and how to tilt a long stick to draw it through the bars of their playpen.

As infants master the nuances of object permanence, they delight in hiding-and-finding games such as peekaboo.

According to Piaget, infants' new capacity to explore permits a more advanced notion of object permanence. Now they can search in successive locations for a hidden toy. In addition, they can imitate behaviors that are much more unfamiliar than those of the previous stage. Infants of Substage 5 can also be seen exercising their more advanced sensorimotor schemes in play when, for example, they bang blocks together in different ways. Moreover, once babies vary their actions with respect to objects, they clearly distinguish themselves and their own actions from the world around them. As a result, sensorimotor egocentrism disappears.

Substage 6: Invention of New Means Through Mental Combinations (18 months – 2 Years). Substage 5 is the last truly *sensorimotor* stage; Substage 6 brings with it the ability to make the first internal representations of reality. Now infants can solve problems through symbolic means instead of trial-and-error behavior. One indication of this new capacity is that infants arrive at solutions to sensorimotor problems suddenly. Piaget infers from this that they go through a covert process that involves experimenting with actions internally. Faced with her doll carriage stuck against the wall, Piaget's daughter Lucienne, had she been in Substage 5, would have pushed, pulled, and bumped it until she finally reoriented it in a new direction. Notice how she handles the problem differently in Substage 6:

> At (1 year, 6 months, and 23 days) for the first time Lucienne plays with a doll carriage. . . . She rolls it over the carpet by pushing it. When she comes against a wall, she pulls, walking backward. But as this position is not convenient for her, she pauses and without hesitation, goes to the other side to push the carriage again. She therefore found the procedure in one attempt, apparently through analogy to other situations but without training, apprenticeship, or chance. (Piaget, 1936/1952b, p. 338)

With the capacity to represent reality internally, infants arrive at the understanding that objects can move or be moved when out of sight. Now they can solve object-hiding tasks involving invisible displacements. If a toy is hidden in a box, the box is placed under a cover, and, while out of the baby's sight, the toy is dumped out of the box, the Substage 6 infant will search in each possible hiding place and eventually find the toy. Younger babies are baffled by this situation.

Representation also brings with it a major advance in imitative ability: the capacity for **deferred imitation,** or the ability to imitate the behavior of models that are not immediately present. A famous and amusing example is Piaget's daughter Jacqueline's delayed imitation of the temper tantrum of another baby:

> At (1 year, 4 months, and 3 days) Jacqueline had a visit from a little boy of (1 year, 6 months) . . . who, in the course of the afternoon, got into a terrible temper. He screamed as he tried to get out of a playpen and pushed it backwards, stamping his feet. Jacqueline stood watching him in amazement. . . . The next day, she herself screamed in her playpen and tried to move it, stamping her foot lightly several times in succession. (Piaget, 1936/1952b, p. 63)

Piaget concluded that Jacqueline's imitation of the little boy's tantrum must have involved a stored representation, since it followed more than half a day after the original encounter. In a recent series of experiments, Meltzoff (1988a, 1988b) showed that 9-month-old infants can reproduce an experimenter's simple action with an unfamiliar toy even when their first opportunity to perform it is delayed for 24 hours. Fourteen-month-olds can retain and duplicate as many as five actions after a one-week delay. These findings reveal that deferred imitation, like other imitative capacities, emerges considerably earlier than Piaget believed.

Finally, the ability to represent reality leads to a major change in the nature of play. At the end of the sensorimotor period, children engage in **make-believe play,** in which they reenact familiar activities such as pretending to eat, go to sleep, or drive a car. As the sensorimotor period draws to a close, mental symbols quickly become major instruments of human thinking.

BRIEF REVIEW

Piaget's sensorimotor substages detail the enormous cognitive changes that take place between birth and 2 years of age. As the result of opportunities to act directly on the environment, the reflexive and egocentric schemes of the neonate are transformed into the more versatile intellectual structures of the young preschool child. Table 6.1 provides an overview of the major intellectual accomplishments of this early period of development.

New Research on Sensorimotor Intelligence. During the past 20 years, many researchers have reinvestigated the accomplishments of Piaget's sensorimotor stage. Although the overall sequence of development has survived quite well, a number of recent studies, such as those mentioned earlier on neonatal imitation and operant conditioning, show that infants attain some sensorimotor milestones earlier than Piaget indicated. Piaget's underestimation of infant cognitive capacities is partly due to the fact that he did not have the sophisticated experimental techniques that are available to modern researchers (Flavell, 1985). Currently, most studies of sensorimotor intelligence deal with the development of object permanence. New findings indicate that when researchers rely on assessments of perception and memory instead of infants' willingness to engage in active search, object permanence shows up earlier than Piaget believed.

One such indirect approach to studying object permanence used the habituation-dishabituation paradigm discussed in Chapter 4. In an intriguing set of experiments, Baillargeon and her colleagues (Baillargeon, 1987; Baillargeon, Spelke, and Wasserman, 1985) found evidence for object permanence in 4½- and even some 3½-month-old infants, months earlier than Piaget concluded it developed! First, infants were habituated to a screen that moved back and forth like a drawbridge through a 180-degree arc. Then a yellow box was placed behind the screen, and two test events were presented. The first was a *possible event,* in which the screen slowly moved up from a flat position until it rested against the box, where it stopped and then returned

Table 6.1. Summary of Intellectual Development During the Sensorimotor Stage

SENSORIMOTOR SUBSTAGE	TYPICAL ADAPTIVE BEHAVIORS	OBJECT PERMANENCE	IMITATION	PLAY
1. Reflexive schemes (birth–1 month)	Neonatal reflexes	None	None, according to Piaget, but recent evidence disputes this (see Chapter 4)	None
2. Primary circular reactions (1–4 months)	Simple motor habits centered around the infant's own body	None	Rudimentary ability to imitate. Believed by Piaget to be limited to copying of another person's imitation of the infant's own behavior	Beginnings of playful exercise of schemes for their own sake
3. Secondary circular reactions (4–8 months)	Actions oriented toward recapturing interesting effects in the external world	Ability to retrieve a partially hidden object	Spontaneous imitation of the behavior of a model, but only if the behavior is currently within the infant's repertoire	Same as previous substage
4. Coordination of secondary circular reactions (8–12 months)	Combination of two object-directed actions, one serving as the means and the other as the end in a goal-directed action sequence	Ability to retrieve a hidden object from the first location in which it is hidden	Imitation of behaviors slightly different from those the infant usually performs	Playful exercise of "means" in means-end behavior sequences
5. Tertiary circular reactions (12–18 months)	Exploration of the properties of objects by acting on them in varied ways	Ability to search in successive locations for a hidden toy	Imitation of unfamiliar behaviors of a model	More varied and less repetitive sensorimotor play
6. Mental combinations (18 months–2 years)	Internal representation of sensorimotor objects and events	Ability to solve object-hiding tasks involving invisible displacements	Deferred imitation. However, new evidence suggests that it may appear as early as Substage 4	First appearance of make-believe play

to its original position. The second was an *impossible event* in which the screen began as before but then miraculously continued its movement as if the box were no longer there. It completed a full 180-degree arc before reversing direction, returning to its initial position, and revealing the box standing intact (see Figure 6.1). The findings showed that infants looked longer, as though surprised, at the impossible event. Apparently, early Substage 3 and some late Substage 2 babies understand that an object continues to exist when it is hidden from view.

If Baillargeon, Spelke, and Wasserman are correct that infants as young as 3½ months have some understanding of object permanence, then what explains the absence of active search in young babies (who are quite capable of visually guided reaching) when they are confronted with toys hidden under blankets or concealed in the palm of an adult's hand? One explanation is that, just as Piaget suggested, they cannot yet coordinate separate actions into means-end sequences. As a result, what they *know* about object permanence is not yet *evident* in their motor activities. Support for this interpretation comes from observations that infants do not spontaneously search for hidden objects until they can engage in combined action sequences — pushing and pulling objects and putting them in and taking them out of containers (Užgiris, 1973).

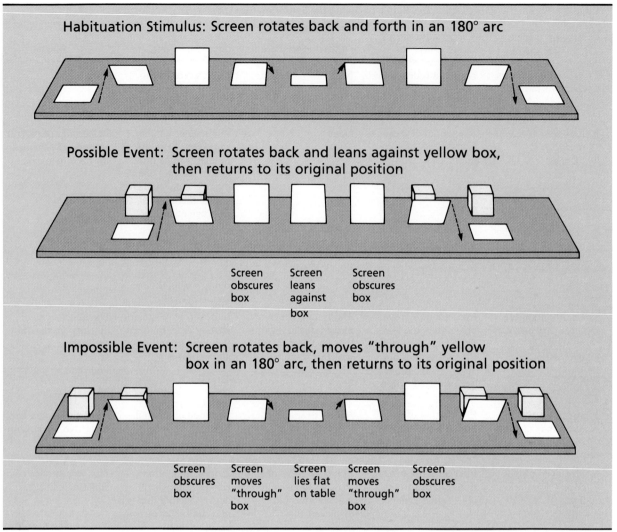

Figure 6.1. Schematic diagram of the habituation stimulus and the possible and impossible events used in the Baillargeon, Spelke, and Wasserman (1985) study. The habituation-dishabi-tuation paradigm predicts that infants should look longer at the possible event, which depicts a novel, shorter screen movement compared to the original habituation stimulus. But subjects looked longer at the impossible event, as if with sur-prise, indicating their understanding of object permanence. *(From R. Baillargeon, E. S. Spelke, & S. Wasserman, 1985, "Ob-ject Permanence in Five-Month-Old Infants," Cognition, 20, 196. Adapted by permission.)*

Once babies actively search for a hidden object, they make errors if it is hidden in more than one place. Remember that in Piaget's Substage 4, infants tend to look for an object in the first place (A) in which it is hidden. If it is moved to a new location (B), many babies search again at A and are perplexed when this does not yield the object. If infants understand that an object still exists when it is out of sight and are capable of retrieving hidden objects, why does this AB search error occur?

A common explanation is that infants have trouble remembering an object's new location after it has been hidden in more than one place (Bjork & Cummings, 1984; Harris, in press). However, considerable evidence indicates that AB errors cannot simply be attributed to poor memory (Wellman, Cross, & Bartsch, 1987). For exam-ple, using the habituation-dishabituation paradigm, Baillargeon and Graber (1988) showed that 8-month-olds can recall behind which of two screens an object was last hidden over delays lasting much longer than those associated with search errors in the standard AB task. These investigators believe that infants make AB errors because they have difficulty translating what they know about an object moving from one place to another into a successful search strategy. Other research indicates that the emergence of correct responses to the AB problem by infant rhesus monkeys coincides with widespread maturational changes in the cerebral cortex (Goldman-Rakic, 1987). Perhaps the ability of human infants to integrate memory for complex events with effective search behavior also depends on brain maturation. But whatever the underlying mechanism, it is clear that older infants (like the 3- and 4-month-olds discussed earlier) know much more about object permanence than is revealed by their actions.

Even though Piaget's assumptions about the development of object permanence require revision, other aspects of the sensorimotor stage have held up quite well. For example, despite some discrepancies in timing of development, research on infant play and imitation fits quite well with Piaget's overall sequence and is consistent with the main tenets of his theory (Belsky & Most, 1981; Kaye & Marcus, 1981; McCall, Eichorn, & Hogarty, 1977).

The Preoperational Stage (2–7 Years)

Symbolic Activity. As children move from the sensorimotor to the preoperational stage, the most obvious change is an extraordinary increase in symbolic activity. Around age 2, tremendous strides in language development take place. But children's new symbolic capacity makes use of a variety of representational media in addition to language, including deferred imitation, make-believe play, and mental images of actions and events. By detaching thought from action, mental symbols permit thought to be more efficient than it was during the sensorimotor stage. Now the child can transcend the confines of immediate time and space and represent several events simultaneously, rather than having to deal with them in a successive, step-by-step, action-oriented fashion (Piaget & Inhelder, 1967/1969).

Language. Piaget acknowledged that language is the most versatile of human symbolic mechanisms, but earlier in this chapter we indicated that he de-emphasized its role in cognitive development. According to Piaget, since thought in the form of sensorimotor intelligence begins long before language, thought is not just a by-product of language. Instead, sensorimotor activity provides the cognitive foundation that makes the very use of language possible, just as it makes possible deferred imitation and make-believe play. In agreement with Piaget's view of the primacy of sensorimotor activity, research shows that children's first words are initially not truly symbolic, in that they are tied to actions and objects in the immediate present. For example, the 1-year-old baby says "ball" only when he kicks or pushes his red rubber ball. When a child uses words in place of things or actions that are not there at the moment, then the true symbolic function has emerged. Also, research on language acquisition reveals that the first words babies use have a strong sensorimotor basis; that is, the objects and events for which they stand are things infants act upon (such as ball or cup), actions that they perform or see others perform (bye-bye, all gone), or things that act themselves and therefore have salient perceptual properties (car, doggie). Thus, the words children learn first reflect their sensorimotor mode of structuring the world (Nelson, 1973).

Additional evidence for the view that language is a matter of learning how to represent what the child knows on a sensorimotor plane comes from habituation studies demonstrating that before infants acquire language, they already have a prelinguistic knowledge of concepts. After being exposed to a series of common objects belonging to one category (e.g., hot dog, piece of bread, slice of salami), infants tend to look longer at noninstances than at new instances (e.g., chair instead of apple). This indicates that they have formed some complex categorical relations. For example, by 12 months of age, babies know that food items, furniture, and stuffed animals belong to separate categories (Ross, 1980; Sherman, 1985; Younger, 1985). This awareness cannot be based on language, since 12-month-olds have not yet learned such words as hotdog, chair, and teddy bear! Instead, it must be based on their wide-ranging sensorimotor experience with objects.

During the second year, babies start to sort objects into categories. At first, around 12 months, they merely touch objects that belong together, without grouping them. A little later, they engage in single-category grouping. For example, when given four balls and four boxes, a 16-month-old will put all the balls together but not the boxes. And finally, around 18 months of age, infants can sort objects correctly into two classes. In a recent study, Gopnik and Meltzoff (1987b) showed that this advanced object-sorting capacity emerges at about the same time that toddlers show a "naming explosion," or sharp rise in vocabulary growth. This finding offers additional support for Piaget's contention that early language builds on advances in nonverbal cognitive skills, rather than the other way around.

Make-Believe Play. Make-believe play provides a further example of the emergence of representational skills during the preoperational stage. Like language, it grows prodigiously over the preschool years. In fact, it is largely confined to this age period. Young infants are not capable of it, and children older than 6 or 7 years of age have largely given it up in favor of other forms of play such as organized games, sports, and hobbies (Fein, 1979). How does make-believe play reflect the development of symbolic activity, and what is its role in the cognitive life of the preschool child?

Piaget believed that pretending, much like language, emerges spontaneously out of sensorimotor activity. Its function, he thought, is largely to strengthen and consolidate newly acquired symbolic skills. Drawing upon Piaget's ideas, a number of investigators have traced the refinement of make-believe play over the preoperational stage. Their findings indicate that it changes in three important ways, each of which reflects children's growing symbolic mastery.

First, over time, play becomes increasingly detached from the real-life conditions associated with it. For example, in early pretending, the toddler uses only realistic objects—for example, a toy telephone to talk into or a wash cloth to wash with. As children get older, use of less realistic toys, such as a block for a telephone receiver, becomes more frequent. This change indicates that children's representations are becoming increasingly flexible in that a play symbol no longer has to resemble the object for which it stands (Bretherton et al., 1984; Corrigan, 1987).

Second, the way in which the "child as self" participates in play changes during the early preoperational period. When make-believe first appears, it is directed toward the self—that is, children pretend to feed or wash only themselves. A short time later, other objects become recipients, as when the child pretends to feed or wash a doll. Around age 2, objects can be used as active agents, and the child becomes a detached participant who makes a doll feed itself or a parent doll feed a baby doll. This sequence reveals that make-believe play gradually becomes less egocentric, as children recognize that agents and recipients of pretend actions can be independent of themselves (Corrigan, 1987; Ungerer et al., 1981).

Finally, early pretending is limited to the use of single schemes. For example, the toddler may pretend to pour cereal into a bowl but cannot yet combine both pouring and eating. Over time, play includes increasingly complex, scheme combinations (Corrigan, 1987; McCune-Nicholich & Fenson, 1984). This is especially evident in the emergence of **sociodramatic play,** the make-believe with others that first appears around 2½ years. By age 5, children collectively create and manage intricate roles and complex plots, indicating that they have developed a sophisticated understanding of object substitutions, role relationships, and story lines.

Although make-believe play provides important insights into children's symbolic development, Piaget's view of it as pure assimilation, or mere practice of symbolic schemes, is now regarded as too limited a perspective. Recent research indicates that play not only reflects, but also contributes to children's cognitive and social development (Rubin, Fein, & Vandenberg, 1983). Sociodramatic play has been studied most extensively. In comparison to social nonpretend activities (such as drawing or putting puzzles together), during social pretend play, preschoolers' interactions last longer, show more involvement, draw larger groups of children into the activity, and are more cooperative (Connolly, Doyle, & Reznick, 1988). In view of this evidence, it is not surprising that children who spend more time in sociodramatic play develop an enhanced ability to understand the feelings of others, are seen as more socially competent by teachers, and are more cognitively advanced (Burns & Brainerd, 1979; Connolly & Doyle, 1984; Saltz, Dixon, & Johnson, 1977). Finally, as Box 6.1 indicates, play seems to help children grasp the conceptual distinction between appearance and reality. As preschoolers step into and out of make-believe, they become increasingly aware of the difference between what is pretend and what is real.

◆　　　THEORY, RESEARCH, AND APPLICATIONS　　　◆

Children's Understanding of the Appearance-Reality Distinction

Box 6.1

Theory. If an object looks and smells like an orange, is it *really and truly* an orange? As adults, we know that appearances can be deceptive, but children must figure out the difference between what is genuine and what is illusory in everyday life. Flavell, Green, and Flavell (1987) hypothesized that mastering the pretend-real distinction in make-believe play helps preschoolers grasp the boundary between appearance and reality in the world of physical objects. This achievement, in turn, may have important implications for the development of logical reasoning. For example, it may help children realize in Piagetian conservation problems that simply rearranging the way an object looks does not mean that its quantity or substance has been transformed.

To what extent can young children discriminate real from fake objects, and how does this understanding change with age? A new research literature has just begun to answer these questions.

Research. Young children have considerable difficulty separating real from look-alike objects, an ability that improves into the elementary school years. In several studies, Flavell presented children with real and apparent objects and asked them questions about what the items were, "really and truly." At age 3, children could discriminate real from unreal features in the tactile domain. For example, they understood that even though an ice cube did not feel cold to their gloved finger, it "really and truly" was cold (Flavell et al., 1989). However, at this age, children's understanding of appearance versus reality remains fragile and incomplete. Three-year-olds are easily tricked by visual and auditory appearances. When asked whether a white piece of paper placed behind a blue filter is "really and truly blue" or whether a can that sounds like a baby crying when turned over is "really and truly a baby," they frequently respond "yes!" Even when efforts are made to train them to make such distinctions, their performance does not improve. By age

6, children do well on these tasks, but they still have much to learn about the dividing line between appearance and reality. Not until late childhood can youngsters handle more complex problems—for example, recognizing that a curved pipe cleaner that looks straight when viewed at a distance is really still curved. Children's ability to put their ideas about appearance versus reality into words also improves around this time (Flavell, Green, & Flavell, 1987).

What underlies development of the appearance-reality distinction? Research suggests that opportunities for make-believe play may be important. The capacity to distinguish pretend play from real experiences is quite sophisticated by the middle of the preschool years (Di-Lalla & Watson, 1988; Wellman & Estes, 1986). In fact, it proceeds considerably in advance of correct solutions to the appearance-reality problems described above (Flavell, Green, & Flavell, 1987). As Flavell points out, over the preschool years, children integrate a wide array of objects into their fantasy play themes. The contrast between playful and everyday use of objects provided by these experiences probably helps children refine their categorization of real and unreal elements in the surrounding world.

Applications. Young children's difficulty in separating appearance from reality helps us understand some curious behaviors of preschoolers that often puzzle their parents. Three- and 4-year-olds may suddenly insist that pictures of zoo animals be removed from the walls of their room at night. Or they may become frightened of their own appearance after dressing up as a witch or goblin on Halloween. The likelihood that make-believe play helps children master the appearance-reality distinction (and other cognitive, social, and emotional skills as well) serves as ample justification for its central role in early childhood programs and the daily life of the preschool child.

Pictorial Representation. Children's drawings are another important vehicle of symbolic expression. Even the scrawls of the 1½- or 2-year-old, which seem at first glance to be little more than indecipherable tangles of lines, are often "experiments in representation" (Winner, 1986, pp. 25–26). At first, children's artful representation is gestural and motoric rather than pictorial. For example, one toddler took her crayon and hopped it around the page, explaining as she made a series of dots, "Rabbit goes hop-hop." By age 3, children's scribbles start to become pictures. Initially, this happens after they make a gestural motion with the crayon, notice that they have drawn a recognizable shape, and then decide to label it. In one case, a 2-year-old made some random marks on a page and then, realizing the resemblance between his scribbles and noodles, named the creation "chicken pie and noodles" (Winner, 1986).

A major milestone in children's artistic development occurs when they begin to use lines to represent the boundaries of objects. This enables them to draw their first picture of a person by age 3 or 4. The tadpole image shown on the left in Figure 6.2 is a universal one in which the limitations of the preschooler's fine motor skills reduce the figure down to the simplest form that still portrays a human image (Gardner, 1980; Winner, 1986). Unlike many adults, young children do not demand that a drawing be realistic. As they get older, their fine motor control improves, and they learn to desire greater realism. Consequently, they begin to create more complex, differentiated drawings, like the one shown on the right in Figure 6.2 made by a 6-year-old child. Still, children of this age are not very particular about mirroring reality in their pictures. There are perceptual distortions, which help to make their work fanciful and

Figure 6.2. Examples of young children's drawings. The universal tadpole-like shape that children use to draw their first picture of a person is shown on the left. The tadpole soon becomes an anchor for greater detail, as arms, fingers, toes, and facial features sprout from the basic shape. By the end of the preschool years, children produce more complex, differentiated pictures, like the one on the right drawn by a 6-year-old child. (*Tadpole drawings from* Artful Scribbles: The Significance of Children's Drawings, *p. 64, by Howard Gardner. Copyright © 1980 by Howard Gardner. Reprinted by permission of Basic Books, Inc., Publishers. Six-year-old's picture from E. Winner [August 1986], "Where Pelicans Kiss Seals," Psychology Today, 20. 35. Reprinted by permission.*)

inventive. Accomplished artists, who also try to represent reality freely, must often work hard to do deliberately what they did without effort as 5- and 6-year-olds (Winner, 1986).

Aside from the development of representation, Piaget largely described preschool children in terms of what they *cannot*, rather than *can*, understand. The very name of the stage — *pre*operational — indicates that Piaget compared preschoolers to older, more capable concrete operational youngsters. As a result, he discovered little of a positive nature about the young child's thinking. Later on, when we discuss new research on preschool thought, we will see that Piaget underestimated the cognitive competencies of early childhood. But first, let's describe the deficiencies of preoperational thought from Piaget's point of view.

Limitations of Preoperational Thought. For Piaget, mental operations — internal representations of actions that obey logical rules — are where cognitive development is going. In the preoperational stage, children are not capable of operations. Instead, their representational thinking is rigid, inflexible, and strongly influenced by momentary appearances. As a result, preoperational reasoning is prelogical and intuitive rather than rational, and when judged by adult standards, it often seems distorted and incorrect.

The most pervasive characteristic of this stage, and the one responsible for all other cognitive deficiencies, is **preoperational egocentrism.** Remember that sensorimotor egocentrism gradually disappears over the first two years of life. Now, with the emergence of new symbolic capacities, egocentrism reappears in a different form. Preoperational children are egocentric with respect to their symbolic viewpoints; that is, they are unaware of points of view other than their own, and they think that everyone experiences the world in the same way they do (Piaget, 1950).

Piaget believed that egocentrism is responsible for young children's belief that inanimate objects have lifelike qualities — in other words, that objects have thoughts, wishes, feelings, and intentions, just like the self. He called this **animistic thinking** (Piaget, 1926/1930). The 3-year-old who charmingly explains that the sun is angry at the clouds and has chased them away is demonstrating this kind of reasoning.

But Piaget's most compelling demonstration of preoperational egocentrism involves a task called the *three mountains problem* (Piaget and Inhelder, 1948/1956). A child stands on one side of a table and views a display of three mountains of different heights. Then a small doll is placed at various locations around the display, and the child must choose from photographs what the display looks like from the doll's perspective. Below the age of 6 or 7, most children select the photo that shows the display from their own perspective.

Piaget believed that egocentrism is largely responsible for the rigidity and illogical nature of young children's thinking. Thought that proceeds so strongly from a single point of view prevents children from accommodating, or adjusting their schemes in accordance with feedback from the physical and social world. Egocentric thinking is also not reflective thought, which critically examines itself. Young children, believing that their own symbolic perspective is universal, cannot think reflectively and are not even motivated to do so. But to fully appreciate these deficiencies of preoperational thought, you must understand the tasks Piaget used to assess children's operational abilities.

The most important set of tasks is the conservation problems. **Conservation** refers to the idea that certain physical attributes of an object remain the same, even though its outward appearance changes. A typical example is the conservation of liquid problem mentioned earlier in this chapter. The child is presented with two identical tall glasses of water and asked to agree that they contain equal amounts of liquid. Then the appearance of the water in one glass (but not its amount) is transformed by pouring it into a short, wide container. The child is asked once more whether the amount of liquid is still the same or whether it has changed. Preoperational children think that the quantity of liquid is no longer the same when it is poured into a differently shaped container. When asked to explain the reasoning behind their answer, they respond in ways like this: "There is less now because the water is way down here" (that is, its level is so low in the short, wide container) or "There is more water now because it is all spread out." There are many types of Piagetian conservation tasks. You will find others illustrated in Figure 6.3.

The inability of children at the preoperational stage to conserve highlights several related aspects of their thinking. First, their understanding of reality is **perception-bound.** They are easily distracted by the concrete, perceptual appearance of objects (it *looks* like there is less water in the short, wide container, and so there *must be* less water). Second, their thinking is "centered," or characterized by **centration.** Preoperational children focus their attention on one detail of a situation to the neglect of other important features. In the case of the conservation of liquid problem, the nonconserver centers on the height of the water level in the two containers, failing to take account of the fact that all changes in height of the liquid are compensated for by changes in width (or vice versa). Third, preoperational children focus on successive states in a situation rather than on dynamic transformations between them. In the conservation of liquid problem, they treat the initial and final states of the water as completely unrelated events. An even more dramatic illustration of this tendency to focus on **states versus transformations** is provided by another problem that Piaget presents to children. A bar is allowed to fall freely from a vertical, upright position to a horizontal one. The child is asked either to draw its movement or to select from a group of illustrations one that depicts what happened. Young children fail to draw or select a picture that represents the intermediate positions of the bar. As shown in Figure 6.4, they focus only on its beginning and ending states, ignoring the transformations in between (Flavell, 1963).

Being perception-bound, being centered, and being focused on states rather than transformations are characteristics that portray the preoperational child as a limited, one-dimensional processor of information. But the most important illogical feature of preoperational thought is its *irreversibility.* **Reversibility,** the opposite of this concept, characterizes every logical operation. It refers to the ability to mentally go through a series of steps in a problem and then reverse direction, returning to the starting point. In the case of the conservation of liquid problem, the preoperational child fails to see how the existence of the same amount of liquid is ensured by imagining it being poured back into its original container.

Reversible thinking is flexible and well organized. Because preoperational children are not capable of it, their reasoning about events often consists of collections of disconnected facts and contradictions. Instead of inductive (proceeding from particular to general) or deductive (proceeding from general to particular), Piaget referred to young children's causal explanations as **transductive reasoning** (proceeding from particular to particular). That is, in providing explanations, they simply link together two events that occur close in time and space. Sometimes this leads to a correct conclusion, as when Piaget's daughter said at 2½ years of age, "Daddy's getting hot water, so he's going to shave" (Piaget, 1945/1951, pp. 230–231). At other times, it leads to some fantastic connections, as illustrated in the following interview that Piaget conducted with a young child on the topic of why the clouds move:

> You have already seen the clouds moving along? What makes them move?— *When we move along, they move along too.* — Can *you* make them move?— *Everybody can, when they walk.* — When I walk and you are still, do they move?— *Yes.* — And at night, when everyone is asleep, do they move?— *Yes.* — But you tell me that they move when somebody walks. — *They always move. The cats, when they walk, and then the dogs, they make the clouds move along."* (Piaget, 1927/1929, p. 62)

Because preoperational children are not yet capable of logical operations, they have difficulty with **hierarchical classification.** According to Piaget, they cannot

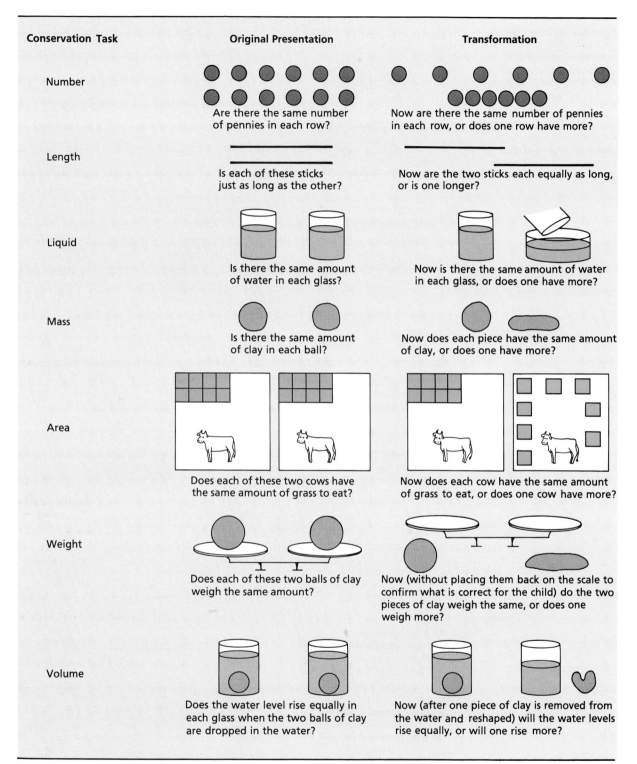

Figure 6.3. Some Piagetian conservation tasks. They are achieved successively over the concrete operational period. Number, length, liquid, and mass are acquired some be- tween 6 and 7 years of age; area and weight between 8 and 10 years; and volume between 10 and 12 years.

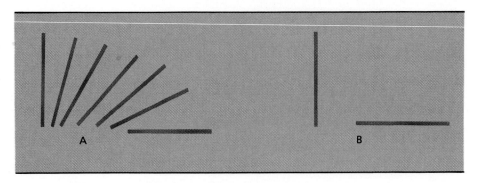

Figure 6.4. Piagetian task illustrating the preoperational child's focus on states rather than transformations. A bar is allowed to fall from a vertical to a horizontal position on a table top. The concrete operational child is capable of representing its successive transformations (A), but the preoperational child represents only the initial and final states (B).

organize objects into hierarchies of classes and subclasses on the basis of similarities and differences between the groups. Piaget illustrates this with his famous class inclusion problem. Children are shown a set of common objects, such as 16 flowers, most of which are yellow and a few of which are blue (see Figure 6.5). Asked whether there are *more yellow flowers* or *more flowers*, preoperational children respond quite confidently, "More yellow flowers!" Their approach to the problem shows a tendency to center on the overriding perceptual attribute of color and an inability to think reversibly by moving from the whole class (flowers) to the parts (yellow and blue) and back again.

Just as they have difficulty with hierarchical classification, very young preoperational children also have trouble with *seriation,* the systematic arrangement of a set of objects according to some quantitative characteristic, such as length. The 2- and 3-year-old cannot arrange ten sticks in order from shortest to longest. Later, preoperational children can arrange a set of concrete objects in a series, but Piaget concluded that they cannot seriate mentally, a logical operation called **transitivity.** For example, Piaget regarded preschoolers as incapable of making the mental inference that stick A is longer than stick C from information that A is longer than B and B is longer than C (see Figure 6.6) (Piaget, Inhelder, & Szeminska, 1948/1960).

Finally, because preoperational children are tricked by perceptual features of objects and events, Piaget believed that they have not yet attained **identity constancy.** In other words, they do not realize that some qualitative characteristics of individuals, such as their sex or species (e.g., dog or cat), are permanent, despite changes in the way they appear. In the best known identity constancy study, DeVries (1969) placed masks resembling a dog or rabbit's head on a black cat named Maynard.

Figure 6.5. Example of a Piagetian class inclusion problem. Children are shown 16 flowers, 4 of which are blue and 12 of which are yellow. Asked whether there are more yellow flowers or more flowers, the preoperational child responds, "More yellow flowers," failing to take account of the fact that both yellow and blue flowers are embedded in the superordinate category of "flowers." In contrast, the concrete operational child understands hierarchical classification.

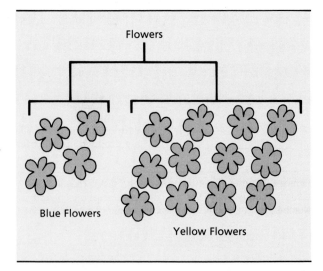

Flowers

Blue Flowers

Yellow Flowers

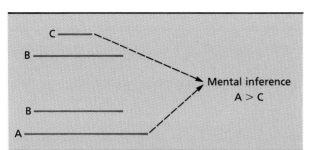

Figure 6.6. Example of a problem that requires children to make transitive inferences. After being shown a pair of sticks in which A > B, followed by a second pair in which B > C, the preoperational child cannot make the mental inference that A >C. In contrast, the concrete operational child is able to do so.

Children between the ages of 3 and 6 were questioned about what they thought the animal was. Then Maynard was unmasked, and the children were questioned again. The youngest subjects showed no identity constancy; the animal changed species whenever the mask was fitted or removed. At an intermediate age, children believed that Maynard's name changed when he wore a mask, but not his species. By 5 and 6 years of age, they understood that Maynard's identity always remained the same, despite alterations in his appearance.

To help you master Piaget's preoperational stage, Table 6.2 lists each of the cognitive limitations discussed above, along with its definition and the tasks that can be used to assess it. At this point, perhaps you are wondering how to pull all these diverse characteristics together into a succinct, unified description of what the preoperational child is like? Flavell (1963), a well-known Piagetian scholar, indicates that Piaget viewed all these traits as expressions of a single, underlying cognitive orientation. Taken together, the attributes point to a view of preoperational thought as

> bear(ing) the impress of its sensory-motor origins. . . . It is extremely concrete . . . slow and static, concerned more with immobile, eye-catching configurations than with more subtle, less obvious components . . . it is unconcerned with proof or logical justification and, in general, unaware of the effect of its communications on others. In short, in more respects than not, it resembles sensory-motor action which has simply been transposed to a new arena of operation. (Flavell, 1963, p. 162)

New Research on Preoperational Thought. The results of many investigations carried out over the last two decades indicate that under optimal conditions, preschoolers are more competent, logical thinkers than Piaget recognized. Piaget's failure to acknowledge the positive thought capabilities of young children can be attributed in large measure to the tasks he used to investigate their cognitions. In many instances, they contained unfamiliar elements or too many pieces of information for a young child to assimilate. As a result, preschoolers' responses did not fully reflect their abilities. Also, Piaget and his followers missed many naturally occurring instances of preschoolers' effective reasoning. Let's look at some examples that illustrate these points.

Egocentrism and Animism. Are young children really so egocentric that they believe an observer standing in a different location in a room sees the same thing that they see? Children's responses to Piaget's three mountains task suggest that the answer is "yes," but more recent studies say "no." The age at which children demonstrate nonegocentric perspective taking seems to be heavily influenced by such task variables as the nature of the visual display and the type of response required of the child. For example, Borke (1975) presented 3- and 4-year-olds with scenes containing

Table 6.2. Limitations of Preoperational Thought

LIMITATION	DEFINITION	RELEVANT PIAGETIAN TASKS
Preoperational egocentrism	The inability to distinguish one's own symbolic viewpoint from the viewpoints of others	Three mountains problem
Animistic thinking	The belief that inanimate objects have lifelike qualities	Interviews with children about living and nonliving things
Perception-bound thought	The quality of being tricked by the concrete, perceptual appearance of objects	Conservation tasks
Centration	The tendency to focus on one detail in a situation to the neglect of other important features	Conservation tasks
States versus transformations	The tendency to attend to successive states in a situation rather than dynamic transformations between them	Falling bar problem
Irreversibility	The inability to mentally go through a series of steps in a problem and then return to the starting point	Conservation tasks
Transductive reasoning	Reasoning from particular to particular instead of from general to particular (deductive reasoning) or particular to general (inductive reasoning)	Interviews with children about everyday events
Absence of hierarchical classification	The inability to organize objects into hierarchies of classes and subclasses based on similarities and differences between groups	Class inclusion problems
Lack of transitivity	The inability to mentally arrange elements in order of increasing or decreasing size	Mental seriation problems
Absence of identity constancy	The inability to recognize that some qualitative characteristics of individuals, such as their sex or species, are permanent, despite superficial changes in appearance	Tasks in which the appearance of an animal or person is changed

familiar toy objects. Children's ability to recognize how a scene looks from a doll's vantage point was assessed by having them rotate an exact replica on a turntable until the doll's view was in front of them. Under these conditions, preschool children could assess the doll's perspective quite well.

Nonegocentric responses also appear in young children's everyday interactions with people. When showing a picture to an adult, children as young as 2 will turn it so that it is oriented to the adult's perspective (Lemperers, Flavell, & Flavell, 1977). Preschoolers also adjust their speech to fit the needs of their listeners. For example, 4-year-olds use shorter, simpler utterances when talking to 2-year-olds than when talking to adults (Gelman & Shatz, 1978). Moreover, in describing objects, children do not use dimensional words, such as "big" and "little," in a rigid, egocentric fashion that makes reference only to their own size and activities. Instead, they adjust their descriptions, taking account of context. For example, by 3 years of age, children judge a 2-inch shoe as small when seen by itself (because it is much smaller than most shoes) but as big when asked about its appropriateness for a very tiny 5-inch doll (Ebeling & Gelman, 1988; Gelman & Ebeling, 1989). These flexible communicative capacities are clearly at odds with Piaget's description of young children as staunchly egocentric.

Piaget concluded that egocentrism was responsible for the young child's tendency to attribute lifelike characteristics to inanimate objects. But recent research indicates that preschoolers correctly categorize even very unfamiliar stimuli as animate or inanimate. In one study, Massey and Gelman (1988) showed 3- and 4-year-olds photos of strange animals, wheeled vehicles, and rigid objects that most adults cannot identify by name. The children indicated whether or not each item could go up and down a hill by itself and then explained their answers. The large majority made accurate predictions for all types of stimuli and based their judgments on features signifying the object's capacity for independent movement—for example, "It can't move. It doesn't have feet" or "It can go by itself because it's an animal" (p. 314). Adults, like these young children, also base their judgments of aliveness on self-movement and animate-appearing features (Richards & Siegler, 1986). Therefore, Massey and Gelman's findings indicate that a mature concept of animacy is present at a surprisingly early age.

This 4-year-old boy adapts to the needs of his 2-year-old sister, indicating that he is not as egocentric as Piaget believed.

Illogical Characteristics of Thought. A host of studies have reexamined the question of whether the collection of illogical characteristics that Piaget ascribed to preschool children really reflects their cognitive capacities. These investigations show that when traditional Piagetian tasks are simplified and children are asked about objects and events with which they are very familiar, preschoolers display some unexpected cognitive competencies.

For example, Anderson and Cuneo (1978; Cuneo, 1980) restudied the issue of whether preoperational children's thinking is centered. Preschoolers were asked to rate how happy a very hungry child would be to get different cookies to eat. The stimuli consisted of rectangular cookies whose height and width varied systematically. Children as young as 3 simultaneously took into account both height and width in judging the desirability of the cookies. They showed no evidence of centering on one relevant dimension to the neglect of the other.

Das Gupta and Bryant (1989) asked children to reason about everyday event sequences and found that by the middle of the preschool years, children competently take account of intermediate steps in a simple reasoning problem. Three- and 4-year-olds were shown "picture stories" depicting familiar occurrences. In some, an object went from its basic state to a changed condition (e.g., a cup became a wet cup), while in others, it went from a changed condition to its basic state (e.g., a wet cup became a [dry] cup). The children were asked to pick an item from three choices (water, drying up cloth, or feather) that caused the object to change. Three-year-olds had considerable difficulty. In the example given above, most simply picked water for both transformations. But 4-year-olds did quite well. They integrated beginning and ending states with appropriate intermediate agents and reasoned effectively in either direction, from basic states to changed conditions and back again. This suggests that at least by age 4, preschoolers deal effectively with transformations in familiar contexts and can represent simple event sequences reversibly.

Other research indicates that the phrasing of an examiner's questions can have a profound effect on how well children perform on Piagetian tasks. Even older children and adults give different responses to Piagetian tasks, depending on the way they are interviewed. For example, instead of the standard conservation of weight problem shown in Figure 6.3, try giving one of your friends this version: "When do you weigh the most, when you are walking or running?" Under these conditions, many adults do not conserve weight! The fact that people who otherwise reason logically can be led astray by deceptive wording suggests that similar factors may affect the performance of young children (Winer, Hemphill, & Craig, 1988). In fact, new evidence indicates that the wording of questions in many identity constancy studies may be ambiguous, causing children's responses not to represent their thinking (Bem, 1989). Because this finding has especially important implications for our understanding of children's concepts of gender, we will return to it in some detail in Chapter 13.

In a study addressing the impact of interviewing procedures on hierarchical classification, Hodges and French (1988) gave preschoolers class inclusion problems involving green and purple grapes. In some presentations, children were questioned in the usual way ("Who would have more to eat, someone who ate the green grapes or someone who ate *the grapes*?"). In others, the superordinate category was referred to as a whole group or collectivity of items ("Who would have more to eat, someone who ate the green grapes or someone who ate *the bunch*?"). Children performed far better in the collectivity condition. Does this mean that referring to objects as collections enables young children to transcend misleading perceptual cues and display more sophisticated reasoning? Markman (1979a, 1989) thinks so, but Hodges and French are not sure. In contrast to class inclusion, conservation of number does not improve when items, such as toy soldiers, are referred to as a group (e.g., "What's more, my *army*, your *army*, or are they both the same?"). Perhaps young children interpret collection labels in class inclusion problems to mean "more," thereby changing the essential nature of the question posed and the task set for the child.

Even though preschoolers have difficulty with Piagetian class inclusion tasks, their spontaneously generated categories are organized into taxonomies of nested relations at a surprisingly early age. A growing literature on the development of categorization reveals that, at first, children work on establishing *basic level categories*—those at an intermediate level of generality (such as "chairs") that share many features in common but, at the same time, are perceptually distinct from related categories (such as "tables," "dressers," and "beds"). Preschoolers' performance on object-sorting tasks indicates that by age 3 or 4, they can link basic categories together at a more general, *superordinate level* ("furniture") as well as break them down into specific, *subordinate level* categories ("rocking chairs" and "desk chairs") (Markman & Hutchinson, 1984; Mervis & Crisafi, 1982; Murphy & Smith, 1982; Rosch et al., 1976). Young children's category systems are not yet very complex and differentiated, and operational reasoning facilitates their development (Ricco, 1989). Nevertheless, the capacity to classify hierchically is present in early childhood.

Finally, new work on children's understanding of a particular type of category—called *natural kinds*—challenges Piaget's assumption that preschoolers' thinking is always perception-bound. Natural kinds are richly structured categories found in nature (such as various types of plants and animals) whose members share both observable and unobservable characteristics. For example, besides fur, four legs, and whiskers, cats resemble one another in diet, life expectancy, sensory capacities, and internal organs. Recently, Gelman and Markman (1987) discovered that even young preschoolers are sensitive to the nonperceptual features of natural kind categories. The investigators taught 3- and 4-year-olds a new fact about an object. Contrary to Piagetian predictions, children more often generalized the information to a new object that *shared the same label* but *looked different* from the target than to an object that *looked similar* to the target but was *given a different label*. For example, when shown the cat with skunk markings depicted in Figure 6.7A and told, "This cat can see in the dark," most preschoolers indicated that the white cat (B) could also see in the dark but that the skunk (C) could not. As Markman (1989) notes, "By age 3 and 4, children expect natural kinds to have a richly correlated structure that goes beyond superficial appearances" (p. 106).

Gelman and Baillargeon (1983) interpret the results of studies like these as indicating that children show the rudiments of logical operations long before the onset of Piaget's concrete operational stage. They acknowledge that preschoolers' ability to reason logically is not as well developed as that of the elementary school child, since preschoolers do fail standard Piagetian tasks of conservation, class inclusion, and seriation. But when the number of elements is scaled down (e.g., when a conservation of number task contains only three items instead of six or seven), preschoolers perform quite successfully (Gelman, 1972). These findings suggest that like other Piagetian tasks, traditional conservation problems mask the preschool child's logical competencies. One study showed that many 5-year-olds who pass a standard conservation of number task will spontaneously count or match the items in each row before giving a conserving response (Fuson, Secada, & Hall, 1983). Three- and 4-year-olds may be able to count and match rows of three items, but having to do so with seven is beyond their capacity. Under such circumstances, they may fall back on less mature,

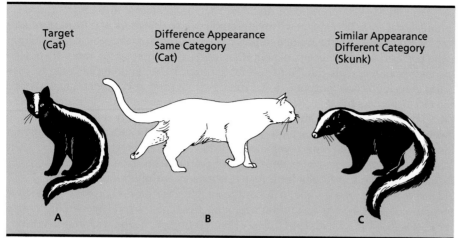

Figure 6.7. Sample set of items in the Gelman and Markman (1987) study of natural kind categories. When generalizing information from one object to another, 3- and 4-year-olds relied on a shared category label, not on perceptual similarity. They assumed that cat B (like cat A) could see in the dark, but skunk C could not. These findings are at odds with Piaget's conclusion that young children's thinking is perception-bound. *(Adapted from S. A. Gelman & E. M. Markman, 1987, "Young Children's Inductions from Natural Kinds: The Role of Categories and Appearances,"* Child Development, 58, *1535. © The Society for Research in Child Development, Inc. Reprinted by permission.)*

perceptual strategies for handling the task. Thus, their ability to approach the problem logically is not evident because of the complexity of the conservation task set before them.

However, a cautious approach to this explanation of young children's failure on standard Piagetian problems is appropriate, since not everyone agrees with it. Halford and Boyle (1985) argue that scaling down conservation of number tasks for young children so they contain a countable number of elements means they are no longer true conservation problems! A child who is capable of logical operations should be able to *mentally reverse* a transformation without counting or matching. Halford and Boyle agree with Piaget that 3- and 4-year-olds do not really understand conservation. Other evidence suggests that even though preschoolers can count small sets, their conceptual understanding of number is still too limited to surmount misleading perceptual cues in typical conservation of number problems (Becker, 1989; Schonfeld, 1990; Sophian, 1988).

But if we combine Halford and Boyle's argument with the research described above on preschoolers' positive cognitive achievements, we obtain a clearer understanding of how children do emerge from the preoperational stage with a flexible capacity for manipulating reality internally and logically. The development of logical operations is a gradual matter that takes place as children rely on increasingly sophisticated mental as opposed to perceptual approaches to solving problems. In the case of conservation of number, the youngest preschoolers seem to rely on their perception of which row is longer in almost all cases — for both large and small arrays of items. But soon they start to solve conservation of number problems that contain very few items using empirical strategies — by counting or pairing objects in the two rows. Later on, they extend these strategies to problems with larger numbers of items. As a result, they develop a mental understanding that number remains the same after a transformation as long as nothing is added or taken away, and they no longer need to rely on outside verification (Siegler & Robinson, 1982). This model of conservation acquisition shows that young children pass through several phases of understanding. In doing so, it acknowledges preschoolers' positive cognitive accomplishments, but it is still consistent with Piaget's conclusion that a true, mental understanding of the principle of conservation is not present until the early school years.

Training Logical Operational Abilities. That attainment of logical operations is a gradual process helps explain why many studies show that more mature performance on Piagetian tasks can be trained in preschool children. It makes sense that children who possess part of a capacity benefit from training, as opposed to those who possess no understanding at all (Inhelder, Sinclair, & Bovet, 1974). Training has been successful in inducing a variety of operational abilities, such as conservation, transitivity, and hierarchical classification (Beilin, 1978; Bryant & Trabasso, 1971; Kingma, 1987; McCabe & Siegel, 1987; Murray, 1978). In addition, a variety of training methods seem to work, including social interaction of nonconservers with more capable peers, adult instruction that points out contradictions in children's logic, and efforts to help children remember the component parts of the problem. However, training is not equally effective for all children. Age is a major controlling factor (Beilin, 1980). Three-year-olds, for example, can be trained, but they do not improve as much as 4-year-olds, and the effects of training young preschoolers rarely generalize to new tasks (Siegler, 1981; Field, 1981). These findings suggest, in line with Piaget's theory, that children with the simplest available cognitive structures try to accommodate to new information, but they cannot do so as effectively as older children with more developed operational schemes.

Taken together, recent research on preoperational thought indicates that preschool children have the beginnings of a variety of organized structures that help them understand and predict their world. Although they still have a great deal of developing to do, new research shows that the young child's mind is considerably more coherent and organized than Piaget indicated it was.

The Concrete Operational Stage (7–11 Years)

Operational Thinking. Piaget viewed concrete operations as a major turning point in cognitive development. When children attain this stage, their thought bears a much closer resemblance to that of adults than to the younger sensorimotor and preoperational child (Piaget & Inhelder, 1967/1969). According to Piaget, concrete operational reasoning is flexible, organized, and logical. This advance is evident in the school-age child's performance on a wide variety of problems involving operational thinking—conservation, transitivity, and hierarchical classification—and, in addition, problems requiring the child to reason about spatial relationships among objects. We will see as we discuss these achievements that children do not grasp them all at once. Rather, they are mastered in a gradual, sequential fashion over the middle childhood years.

The Horizontal Décalage. For Piaget, conservation is the single most important concrete operational achievement because it provides clear evidence of the presence of mental operations (Brainerd, 1978). The conservation tasks depicted in Figure 6.3 are achieved one by one during the concrete operational stage. Piaget used the term **horizontal décalage**[4] to refer to the sequential mastery of concepts across different content areas within a single stage (Brainerd, 1978). In the case of conservation, he predicted that concrete operational children will always conserve number (which can be empirically verified) before they conserve length, mass, and liquid, and this pattern of development has been documented in several investigations (Brainerd & Brainerd, 1972; Gruen & Vore, 1972). Another horizontal décalage is the achievement of conservation of liquid and mass before weight and conservation of weight before volume (Brainerd, 1978). Užgiris (1964) tested this sequence in children from first through sixth grades and found that 93 percent conformed to this order.

Additional horizontal décalages have been discovered at the concrete operational

---

[4] Décalage is a name Piaget used to refer to a progression of development that is uniform, or invariant, for all children. Vertical décalage refers to development through the four major Piagetian stages. In contrast, horizontal décalage is development within a stage that results from the child's efforts to apply newly attained structures to a variety of problems.

stage. Piaget assumed that there was parallel development in transitivity, number conservation, and class inclusion, which he grouped together as *logico-arithmetic operations* (Brainerd, 1978). Although he believed they were all achieved at about the same time during middle childhood, several studies reveal that transitivity tests are passed first (during the late preschool years), then conservation of number (during the early elementary school period), and finally class inclusion (late elementary school years) (Achenbach & Weisz, 1975; Brainerd, 1974; Winer & Kronberg, 1974). Piaget thought that mastery of these operations was closely tied to the elementary school child's increased facility with quantitative and numerical tasks. As we will see in Chapter 7 when we discuss children's mathematical reasoning in greater detail, preschoolers do have some impressive numerical skills, including the ability to count small arrays and add and subtract with small sets of items. However, most of what people come to know about mathematics is acquired after early childhood. Elementary school children do have a more quantitative, measurement-oriented approach to many tasks and problems than do preschoolers (Fuson, 1988).

Spatial Operations. In addition to logico-arithmetic operations, the concrete operational child also masters a variety of *spatial operations*. These are geometrical in nature, since they deal with the *distance* of objects from each other, as well as with *projective concepts*, which tell us about the spatial relationships of objects to one another.

The conservation paradigm provides a good example of the new understanding of distance that Piaget believed is attained at the concrete operational stage. Between two small toy trees standing apart on a table an examiner places a block or thick piece of cardboard. The child is asked whether the trees are still the same distance apart. Preoperational youngsters generally respond that the distance is reduced — in other words, they believe that a filled up space does not have the same value as an empty space. However, recent evidence indicates that preschoolers do show the rudiments of distance conservation when the problem is couched in more concrete terms (Miller & Baillargeon, 1990). As with other operational abilities, it is important to think of spatial reasoning as developing gradually rather than suddenly during middle childhood.

According to Piaget (1946/1969; 1946/1970), operational thinking permits children to integrate distance with other physical dimensions, such as time and speed. However, the understanding of such relationships takes place in steps and seems to form yet another horizontal décalage. Piaget found repeatedly that elementary school children first recognize the *positive* relationship between distance and speed (e.g., in a given amount of time, a bunny travels *farther* down a road than a skunk if the bunny runs *faster*) and between distance and duration (e.g., at a given speed, a bunny travels *farther* down a road than a skunk if the bunny runs for a *longer* period of time). Only later do they understand the *inverse* relationship between duration and speed (e.g., for a given distance, a bunny travels for a *shorter* period of time than a skunk if the bunny runs *faster*). Acredolo, Adams, and Schmid (1984) studied elementary school pupils' grasp of these principles. The children were told several versions of a story in which a bunny and a skunk raided a garden of cabbages. When frightened by a barking dog, the animals ran down a road and out of the garden. In telling the story, the examiner gave the child bits of information about two of the dimensions (e.g., the bunny ran just as fast as the skunk, but the bunny ran farther) and asked the child to determine the third piece of information (in this case, whether the bunny and skunk ran for an equally long period of time or whether one ran longer). As shown in Figure 6.8, from first grade on, children performed at a high level when asked to coordinate distance and speed and almost as well when asked to coordinate distance and duration. But just as Piaget predicted, the inverse relationship between speed and duration was not achieved until later, around the middle of the elementary school years.

Piaget investigated children's projective understanding of space by having them produce representations of large-scale environments — spaces too big to be seen all at

Figure 6.8. Elementary school children's understanding of the relationships between distance, time, and speed in the Acredolo, Adams, and Schmid (1984) study. In agreement with Piaget's work, the speed-distance and duration-distance relationships were understood before the speed-duration relationship. *(From C. Acredolo, A. Adams, & J. Schmid, 1984, "On the Understanding of the Relationships between Speed, Duration, and Distance," Child Development, 55, 2156. © The Society for Research in Child Development, Inc. Reprinted by permission.)*

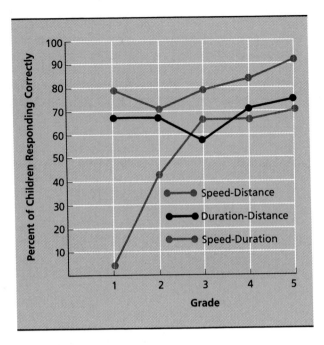

once, so the overall layout has to be mentally inferred. Recent investigators refer to these mental constructions as **cognitive maps.** In one study, Piaget had children build a replica of the vicinity in which they lived using toy objects to represent buildings, parks, bridges, and rivers. He also asked them to draw maps showing how they get from home to school or to other familiar landmarks. Successful performance on such tasks requires advanced perspective-taking skill. Children must coordinate and integrate successive perceptions of an environment, since all parts of it cannot be viewed at the same time. Piaget found that children below age 7 could not arrange landmarks in terms of an organized spatial whole. Instead, they remained unintegrated with one another and with routes of movement through the setting (Piaget & Inhelder, 1948/1956).

Many follow-up studies lend support to Piaget's assumption that children's cognitive maps undergo important changes from the preschool into the elementary school years. Taken together, the research suggests a specific developmental sequence. Preschoolers' representations focus on separate landmarks and are fragmented and disorganized. During the early elementary school years, *landmark knowledge* becomes subordinate to *route knowledge.* Children start to arrange landmarks along an organized route of travel, but the relationship of routes to one another is not well coordinated. Finally, *configurational knowledge* emerges and improves. Children form an overall representation of a large-scale space in which landmarks and routes are spatially coordinated (Newcombe, 1982; Siegel, 1981). However, once again, we must be careful not to underestimate the preschooler's capacity for spatial representation. Younger children's restricted opportunity to travel in unfamiliar environments may limit the complexity of their cognitive maps (Cornell, Heth, & Broda, 1989). In addition, some preschoolers may have considerable spatial understanding but simply not be able to draw or construct what they know as effectively as older youngsters. In support of this idea, recent evidence indicates that children as young as 3 can use a simple map to navigate their way through a space they have never seen before (DeLoache, 1987; Uttal & Wellman, 1989). Nevertheless, "map literacy" does improve substantially during middle childhood (Liben & Downs, 1986).

Limitations of Concrete Operational Thought. Although cognition is much more adultlike than it was earlier, the stage of concrete operations suffers from one important limitation. Elementary school children can think in an organized, logical fashion only when dealing with concrete, tangible information they can directly perceive. Their mental operations work poorly when applied to information that is abstract and hypothetical. Children's solutions to transitivity problems provide a good illustration. During concrete operations, they can easily make the mental inference that if stick A is longer than stick B and stick B is longer than stick C, then stick A is longer than stick C. However, if they are asked to deal with an entirely hypothetical version of the task, such as "Susan is taller than Sally and Sally is taller than Mary. Who is the tallest?", they have great difficulty. It is not until around age 11 or 12 that this type of problem is easily solved. We will see more examples of the "concreteness" of concrete operational thinking shortly when we compare it to formal operational thought.

Extensions and Applications of Concrete Operations: Children's Understanding of Humor. New logical capacities of the concrete operational stage help explain changes in children's appreciation of humor. Humor depends on cognitive surprise, incongruity, and discrepancy from the expected. A Piagetian model of humor comprehension would suggest that joke material moderately divergent from the child's current cognitive structures is likely to be regarded as most interesting and funniest (Brodzinsky & Rightmyer, 1980).

Logical operational abilities permit elementary school children to understand jokes that are beyond the comprehension of the preschool child. In fact, if you observe a group of preschoolers for what they find amusing, you will see that their humor reflects their recent mastery of the symbolic function. Endless play with words and calling of objects by names the child knows to be incorrect are sources of great delight to children below the age of 6. School-age youngsters no longer find such wordplay funny. Instead, exchanges of riddles and puns requiring an understanding of the double meanings of words are common social pastimes among elementary school children:

"Hey, did you take a bath?" "No! Why, is one missing?"

"Order! Order in the court! "Ham and cheese on rye, your honor."

Preoperational children may laugh at these jokes because they are nonsensical, but they cannot explain what is funny about them. In contrast, older children can reverse their thinking, moving back and forth between different meanings of the same key word. This permits them to understand that a joke or riddle can have two possible interpretations, a usual one and an unusual one, the latter of which is funny because it is incongruous (Shultz & Horibe, 1974; Sutton-Smith, 1975). In fact, children can be given a riddle with two possible answers, as follows:

"Why did the old man tiptoe past the medicine cabinet?"

Serious answer: "Because he dropped a glass and did not want to cut his foot."

Joking answer: "Because he didn't want to wake up the sleeping pills."

Under these conditions, preschoolers choose the serious and joking answers with equal frequency. They show no awareness of the double meaning on which the riddle depends. By age 7, children start to choose the joking answer more often, and they improve in their ability to do so over middle childhood (McGhee, 1974).

In comparison to elementary school children, adolescents can understand more sophisticated and abstract humor (Couturier, Mansfield, & Gallagher, 1981). In addition, they tend to favor anecdotes and spontaneous wit over the memorized jokes preferred by younger children. Aside from these differences, once logical operations are attained, the nature of humor appreciation remains essentially the same from middle childhood into adult life (McGhee, 1979).

Concrete operational capacities have also been used to explain elementary school children's more mature understanding of a very serious topic — the concept of death. Refer to Box 6.2 to find out how it changes from early to middle childhood and how effectively Piagetian theory accounts for its development.

The Formal Operational Stage (11–15 Years)

The concrete operational approach to solving problems is rational and logical, but it does not deal with possibilities — that is, potential relationships that are not easily detected in the real world or that may not exist at all. Beginning somewhere around 11 years of age and becoming fully developed at about age 15, the capacity for abstract thinking appears. At the formal operational stage, adolescents become capable of reasoning in a manner like that of the scientist searching for solutions in the laboratory. Concrete operational children can only "operate on reality," but formal operational adolescents "operate on operations." It is in this sense that their thinking is

◆ THEORY, RESEARCH, AND APPLICATIONS ◆

The Development of Children's Understanding of Death   Box 6.2

Theory. As adults, we understand death in terms of three basic components: (1) *permanence:* once a living thing dies, it cannot be brought back to life; (2) *universality:* all living things eventually die; and (3) *nonfunctionality:* all living functions, including thought, movement, and vital signs, cease at death. Many investigators have expressed the belief that concrete operational children's ability to classify, understand transformations, and take the perspective of others leads to a mature appreciation of death. If this is true, then acquisition of the three components of the death concept should appear in the early elementary school years and be associated with successful performance on concrete operational tasks.

Research. A variety of studies confirm that a mature understanding of death is achieved around age 7, at about the same time children make the transition from preoperational to concrete operational thought (Speece & Brent, 1984). Before this time, young children master the three components of the death concept in a particular order. Permanence, the notion that death cannot be reversed, is the first and easiest understood idea. Appreciation of universality comes slightly later. Initially, children think that certain people do not die, especially those with whom they have close emotional ties or who are like themselves — other children. In addition, children usually understand that others will die before they realize that they themselves will die. When they finally grasp their own mortality, they believe that it will be in the very remote future (which is, of course, true for most children). They do not seem to appreciate that their own death could occur at any time. Finally, nonfunctionality is the most abstract and difficult component of the death concept for children to grasp. Many preschoolers view dead things as retaining functional capacities. When they first comprehend nonfunctionality, they do so in terms of its most visible aspects (e.g., heart beating and breathing). Only later do they appreciate that cognitive functioning (e.g., thinking and dreaming)

also ceases (Speece & Brent, 1984; Stambrook & Parker, 1987).

Although a mature understanding of death does appear in the elementary school years, the Piagetian transition to concrete operations does not fully explain it. A close examination of the research literature reveals that the linkage between performance on Piagetian tasks and children's understanding of death is inconsistent from study to study. Also, although 7 is the usual age at which the death concept is adultlike, many investigations report wide individual differences. Children's experiences with death seem to exert just as powerful an influence on their understanding as their stage of cognitive development. For example, terminally ill children under age 6 often have a well-developed conception of death (Bluebond-Langer, 1977). Also, most children find it far more difficult to grasp plant death than human or animal death. Although they have witnessed the revival of wilted plants after watering, they have not seen any comparable kind of event in the death of people or animals (Speece & Brent, 1984). Cultural experiences and mass media exposure may also affect children's understanding, but these influences remain to be studied.

Applications. Children's changing ideas about death are important when the death of a relative or pet places an adult in the position of explaining what has happened. Explanations likely to facilitate children's understanding are ones that are simple, direct, and provide factual information. Since children sometimes have magical answers to questions about death, adults who provide explanations can have children recount what has been told so that opportunities are available to correct distortions and misperceptions (Koocher, 1981). Some investigators believe that providing children with opportunities to talk about death may lead them to worry less about it. If so, then open and honest discussions with children contribute to both their cognitive appreciation of the concept and their emotional well-being.

truly abstract, since they can derive new, more general logical rules through internal reflection. Concrete props and things are no longer required as contents of thought (Brainerd, 1978; Flavell, 1985; Inhelder & Piaget, 1955/1958). The major cognitive achievements of the formal operational stage are spelled out in more detail below, along with some examples.

Abstract, Scientific Thinking. According to Piaget, there are two major characteristics of formal operational thought. The first is **hypothetic-deductive reasoning.** When faced with a problem, adolescents come up with a *general theory* of all possible factors that might affect the outcome and *deduce* from it specific *hypotheses* that might obtain in the situation. Then they systematically test these hypotheses to see which ones do in fact occur in the real world. Thus, adolescent problem solving begins with possibility and proceeds to reality. In contrast, concrete operational children begin with reality, but when the most obvious predictions are not verified, they cannot think of alternatives and fail to solve the problem.

Adolescent performance on Piaget's famous *pendulum problem* illustrates this new hypothetico-deductive approach. Provided with strings of different lengths, objects of different weights to attach to the strings, and a bar from which to hang the strings, subjects are asked to figure out what makes a pendulum swing more rapidly in one case than another. Formal operational subjects come up with four hypotheses: the length of the string, the weight of the object hung on it, how high the object is raised before it is released, and how forceful a push the object is given. Then, by varying one factor at a time while holding all others constant, they try out each of the possibilities systematically, eventually discovering that only string length makes a difference. In contrast, concrete operational children's experimentation is unsystematic; they cannot separate out the effects of relevant variables. For example, they may test for the effect of string length without holding weight constant. In addition, they fail to notice the potential influence of variables that are not immediately suggested by the concrete materials of the task — the height and forcefulness with which the pendulum is released.

The second important characteristic of formal operational thought is that it is **propositional** in nature. Adolescents can focus on verbal assertions and evaluate their logical validity without making reference to real-world circumstances. In contrast, concrete operational children can evaluate the logic of statements only by considering them against concrete, perceptible evidence. A study by Osherson and Markman (1975) illustrates this difference. A pile of poker chips was placed on a table,

During the stage of formal operations, adolescents solve problems by generating all of the possible hypotheses that could occur in a situation. Then they systematically test their predictions to see which ones apply in the real world.

and an experimenter indicated that some statements would be made about them. The subject was to respond to each statement as true, false, or uncertain. In one condition, a chip was concealed in the hand of the experimenter, who then said, "Either the chip in my hand is green or it is not green" or "The chip in my hand is green and it is not green." In another condition, the experimenter held up either a red or a green chip and made the same statements. Elementary school children focused on the concrete properties of the poker chips in the examiner's hand rather than on the purely logical characteristics of the statements. As a result, they replied that they were uncertain to both statements when the chip was hidden from view. When it was visible, they judged both statements to be true if the chip was green and false if it was red. In contrast, adolescents evaluated the logic of the statements as propositions. They could appreciate the fact that the "either-or" statement is always true and the "and" statement is always false, regardless of empirical evidence.

Because the essence of formal operational reasoning is that it is no longer tied to real objects and events, Piaget indicated that language plays a more central role in thinking at this stage than it did earlier. The adolescent's abstract mental abilities rest on the capacity to use language-based systems of representation that are entirely divorced from concrete experience, such as those that exist in higher mathematics. They also depend on the capacity to formulate language-based conjectures dealing with abstract concepts, such as "What is truth?", "What is justice?", and "How are freedom and democracy related?" (Brainerd, 1978).

Adolescent Idealism and Egocentrism. Given these new abstract powers of logical reasoning, it is not surprising that adolescents spend a good deal of time thinking about and constructing grand systems that have to do with religion, ethics, and other philosophical questions. The ability to reason about the way things could be instead of confining themselves to the way they are leads many teenagers to be idealists and social reformers. However, because of their limited life experience, their theories are often naive and unsophisticated. Piaget believed that the insistence of adolescents that reality submit itself completely to their idealistic constructions marks the appearance of a new form of egocentrism. In **formal operational egocentrism,** the young person rigidly insists that it is only through the implementation of their grand idealistic systems that the world can become a better place to live. Gradually, as the result of efforts to implement their hypotheses, adolescents adjust them to take account of the fact that many realities of human behavior do not conform to abstract ideals and systems of logic (Inhelder & Piaget, 1955/1958).

Elkind (1976, 1981) describes two other aspects of egocentrism that result from the adolescent's new abstract reasoning powers — in particular, the ability to imagine what others may be thinking. The first is called the **imaginary audience.** It refers to the belief that other people are as concerned with and critical of the adolescent's behavior as adolescents are themselves. As Elkind puts it:

> When adolescents begin thinking about other people's thinking, they often assume that other people are thinking about them. They become, as a matter of fact, convinced that others are as concerned with them and their appearance as they are with themselves. Hence the "self-consciousness" so characteristic of young adolescents has to be attributed, in part at least, to the appearance of formal operations. While the physical and physiological transformations undergone by the adolescent play a part in this self consciousness, its cognitive determination must also be recognized. (Elkind, 1976, p. 101)

A second facet of adolescent egocentrism is the **personal fable,** the belief that one's own ideas and feelings are so unique that no one else could experience anything like them. This sense of specialness is reflected in the self-searching ruminations that frequently appear in adolescent diaries. It also underlies the following impatient refrain heard often by parents of teenage youngsters: "Forget it! You couldn't possibly understand!"

In line with Piaget's theory, research indicates that adolescents' preoccupation with the imaginary audience increases during the transition from concrete to formal operations and then declines as formal operational abilities become better established (Gray & Hudson, 1984). Nevertheless, some experts reject the assumption that the imaginary audience and personal fable result from egocentrism—an inability to accurately differentiate the abstract perspectives of self and others. They prefer to view these developments as an outgrowth of advances in perspective taking that cause young people to be increasingly concerned with what others think of them (Lapsley, 1985; Lapsley et al., 1986).

In the sections above, we have seen that the last two Piagetian stages—concrete operational and formal operational—are similar in that the child's thinking is logical, rational, and systematic. The major difference is the child's application of these reasoning skills. In concrete operations, thought is bound by concrete reality. In formal operations, it extends to the abstract and hypothetical. The cognitive achievements and limitations of both stages are summarized in Table 6.3.

BRIEF REVIEW

New Research on Formal Operational Thought. Investigators conducting follow-up research on formal operations have asked some of the same questions that were posed about the preceding stages: Is there evidence that formal operational abilities appear earlier in development than expected, and can they be trained in children who, according to Piaget's stage theory, should not yet be capable of formal operational reasoning?

Research indicates that even preschoolers can answer simple propositional questions in which the content of statements is unrelated to the real world. For example, 4- and 5-year-olds recognize the truth value of the following premises about an imaginary animal:

Premise 1: Every banga is purple.
Premise 2: Purple animals always sneeze at people.
Question: Do bangas sneeze at people?
Conclusion: Yes, bangas sneeze at people. (Hawkins et al., 1984)

At the same time, the capacity of young children to engage in propositional reasoning is limited. When statements contradict reality (for example, contain information

Table 6.3. Achievements and Limitations of Concrete and Formal Operational Thought

ACHIEVEMENTS	LIMITATIONS
CONCRETE OPERATIONAL STAGE	
Appearance of organized, logical reasoning, as indicated by: (1) Transitivity, conservation, and hierarchical classification (2) Spatial operations—conservation of distance; relations between distance, time, and speed; and well-organized cognitive maps	Sequential rather than complete mastery of logical reasoning in different content areas, according to the horizontal décalage Logical reasoning limited to concrete, tangible information; cannot think abstractly
FORMAL OPERATIONAL STAGE	
Appearance of abstract, scientific thinking, as indicated by: (1) Hypothetico-deductive reasoning (2) Propositional thought	Emergence of formal operational egocentrism, including the imaginary audience and personal fable. Declines as formal operations become better established

about birds with wheels), preschoolers cannot handle them (Hawkins et al., 1984). And in instances in which 4- to 8-year-olds respond correctly to propositional tasks, their success seems to be due to an "atmosphere effect." Statements phrased in the affirmative are always answered with "yes" and those phrased in the negative are always answered with "no," even though use of this strategy sometimes violates the most basic rules of propositional logic (Markovits, Schleifer, & Fortier, 1989). For example, when given the following premises (one of which is negative), elementary school children usually draw an erroneous negative conclusion:

Premise 1: If there is a knife, then there is a fork.
Premise 2: There is not a knife.
Question: Is there a fork?
Erroneous Conclusion: No, there is not a fork. (Kodroff & Roberge, 1975)

Around age 11, children show an improved ability to analyze the logical structure of a series of propositions (Byrnes & Overton, 1986; Markovits, Schleifer, & Fortier, 1989). However, even adolescents and adults have difficulty with problems like the one given above! Taken together, research indicates that propositional reasoning abilities are present in rudimentary form during early and middle childhood. At the same time, many adolescents and adults are not fully formal operational; they do not differ very much from younger children in some of their spontaneous reasoning abilities.

Can formal operational abilities be trained in concrete operational youngsters? There is evidence that training does lead to improved performance on such tasks as the pendulum problem and conservation of volume[5] (Brainerd & Allen, 1971; Siegler, Liebert, & Liebert, 1973). However, the effects of training last longer and generalize more easily to unfamiliar situations when subjects are adolescents and college students rather than elementary school children (Greenbowe et al., 1981; Kuhn, Ho, & Adams, 1979). Formal operational training research leads to conclusions like those we discussed earlier with respect to training preschoolers in concrete operational skills. Elementary school children show the glimmerings of more complex, abstract reasoning abilities, but they are not as cognitively competent as adolescents and adults (Flavell, 1985).

If the beginnings of formal thinking are present at an early age, then why is it that many college students, and adults in general, do not show spontaneous mastery of formal operational tasks (Keating, 1979; Kuhn, 1979; Neimark, 1975)? The answer cannot be that they lack the capacity to reason abstractly. As we have just seen, adolescents and college students manifest formal operational abilities very quickly and at a high level after training. Instead, it seems that people are most likely to display formal operational thinking in contexts in which they have had extensive experience. This interpretation is supported by DeLisi and Staudt's (1980) finding that college students show formal operational reasoning in accordance with their college majors. Formal operations have also not been found in preliterate cultures. However, lack of experience in solving hypothetical problems, rather than absence of cognitive competency, probably explains these findings as well (Gellatly, 1987; Scribner, 1977).

Nevertheless, the fact that unschooled, village-dwelling people rarely display formal operational reasoning raises an important question about the universality of Piaget's stage sequence. Is the highest stage really a natural outgrowth of children's independent efforts to make sense of their physical world? Or is it a culturally transmitted way of reasoning that is specific to literate societies and that most individuals are taught in school? This issue, along with several others discussed

---

[5] Piaget identified conservation of volume as a formal operational task (see Figure 6.3), since it involves an understanding of the proportional relationship between length, width, and depth. Concrete operational children have difficulty separating out the relevant variables in this problem.

below, has prompted many investigators to doubt the overall validity of Piaget's theory.

LARGER QUESTIONS ABOUT THE VALIDITY OF PIAGET'S THEORY

Clarity, Correctness, and Completeness

We have seen that Piaget's theory has been the subject of intense critical scrutiny in recent years. Taken together, the wealth of accumulated research reveals that it has a number of important shortcomings. Flavell (1982a, 1982b) summarizes these as problems of clarity, correctness, and completeness.

Some of Piaget's ideas about cognitive development are not clearly spelled out. Concepts like adaptation, organization, and equilibration seem fuzzy and imprecise. Exactly what they refer to in the child's cognitive activities is not readily apparent. As an example of this problem, at the beginning of this chapter, we indicated that Piaget considered children's cognitive structures to be characterized by *organization*. That is, he assumed that the structures of each stage form a coherent, integrated whole. But we do not always know the way in which Piaget understood the diverse achievements of each stage — take, for example, conservation, transitivity, hierarchical classification, and the variety of spatial concepts identified with concrete operations — to be bound together by a single, underlying form of thought.

Throughout this chapter, we indicated that several of Piaget's ideas are now regarded as either incorrect or only partially correct. For example, infants achieve a number of sensorimotor milestones at earlier ages than Piaget anticipated. Preschoolers are not egocentric when tasks are simplified and made relevant to their everyday experiences. And both preoperational and concrete operational children can be trained to exhibit more mature thinking, indicating that Piaget's assumption that they must act on the environment to revise their cognitive structures is too narrow a notion of how learning takes place. Cognitive development is not always self-generating, and left to their own devices, children may not necessarily notice important conflicting elements in a situation and come up with an improved interpretation of experience. Current evidence indicates that, in contrast to what Piaget believed, "there is no single, overarching process or principle sufficient to describe how all cognitive-developmental advances are made" (Flavell, 1985, p. 290).

Piaget's theory of development is also regarded as incomplete. Whereas logical structures are an important part of human mental life, investigators have begun to question whether they are the general, underlying basis of all human thought that Piaget believed them to be. Child development specialists now think that the Piagetian model cannot account for the complexity and variety of human cognitive phenomena (Flavell, 1985; Legendre-Bergeron & Laveault, 1983). Other equally important accomplishments in such areas as attention, memory, communication, and creativity have been identified, and we will discuss them in subsequent chapters.

Of all the questions raised about the validity of Piaget's theory, the most hotly debated is whether cognitive development really does advance through a series of broad, qualitatively distinct stages. We take up this issue in the section below.

Are There Stages of Cognitive Development?

The type of developmental pattern emphasized by Piaget is one in which the child masters a set of interrelated cognitive abilities during a specified time period that, taken together, form a major stage. Recently, this idea has come under heavy attack. Stages, in the strict Piagetian sense of the word, are *discontinuous* developmental entities. If they exist, children must display new competencies that they did not have before. But throughout this chapter we have seen that most cognitive changes proceed slowly and gradually; very few abilities are absent during one period and then suddenly present at another. Also, there seem to be few periods of developmental quiescence and equilibrium. Instead, within each of Piaget's stages, children appear to be constantly modifying structures and acquiring new skills.

These difficulties have led some investigators to completely discard the notion of stage as an adequate account of how cognitive development takes place. For example, Gelman and Baillargeon (1983) favor a view that rejects the existence of both stages and broadly applicable cognitive structures. Instead, children are seen as gradually working out their understanding of each type of task separately, and their thought processes are regarded as basically the same at all ages; they are just present to a greater or lesser extent. These assumptions — that children's performance is context-specific and that cognitive development is continuous — form the basis for the major competing approach to Piaget's theory: information processing, which we take up in Chapter 7.

Although some theorists have dismissed the idea of stage, it is important to keep in mind that the existence of cognitive stages is still an unsettled issue. A number of experts think that the stage notion is still valid, even though Piaget's strict definition of it requires modification. For example, Flavell (1982a) argues for a more dynamic, less tightly knit concept of stage, one in which certain competencies take a long time rather than a short time to achieve. From this point of view, a stage simply refers to an extended period of related developmental changes. Flavell retains the stage idea because he finds it difficult to believe the child's cognition is so completely variable across tasks and situations as to have no coherence. As he indicates, "Perhaps what the field needs is another genius like Piaget to show us how, and to what extent, all those cognitive-developmental strands within the growing child are really knotted together" (Flavell, 1985, p. 297).

EDUCATIONAL IMPLICATIONS OF PIAGET'S THEORY

Piaget has had a major impact on the design of educational programs for children, especially at the preschool and early elementary school levels. A number of educational principles derived from his theory have served as the foundation for a wide variety of Piagetian-based curricula developed over the past several decades. These principles include:

1. *A focus on the process of children's thinking, not just its products.* In addition to the correctness of children's answers, teachers must understand the processes children use to get to the answer. Appropriate learning experiences build on children's current level of cognitive functioning, and only when teachers appreciate children's methods of arriving at particular conclusions are they in a position to provide such experiences.

2. *Recognition of the crucial role of children's self-initiated, active involvement in learning activities.* In a Piagetian classroom, the presentation of ready-made knowledge is de-emphasized, and children are encouraged to discover for themselves through spontaneous interaction with the environment. Therefore, instead of teaching didactically, teachers provide a rich variety of activities that permit children to act directly on the physical world.

3. *A de-emphasis on practices aimed at making children adultlike in their thinking.* Piaget referred to the question "How can we speed up development?" as "the American question." Among the many countries he visited, psychologists and educators in the United States seemed most interested in what techniques could be used to accelerate children's progress through the stages. Piagetian-based educational programs accept his firm belief that premature teaching may be worse than no teaching at all

In a Piagetian classroom, children are encouraged to explore their physical world. Activities are designed for individuals and small groups rather than for the total class.

because it leads to superficial acceptance of adult formulas rather than true cognitive understanding (Johnson & Hooper, 1982).

4. *Acceptance of individual differences in developmental progress.* Piaget's theory assumes that all children go through the same sequence of development, but they do so at different rates. Therefore, teachers must make a special effort to arrange classroom activities for individuals and small groups of children, rather than for the total class group (Ginsburg & Opper, 1979). In addition, since individual differences are expected, assessment of children's educational progress should be made in terms of each child's own previous course of development, rather than against normative standards provided by the performance of same-age peers (Gray, 1978).

Criticisms have been made of Piagetian educational applications. Since much of Piaget's work has involved the investigation of mathematical and scientific concepts, some claim that his educational recommendations are useful only for the teaching of these subjects and that they are less relevant to other areas, such as language arts (Roberts, 1984). Also, Piaget's insistence on the primacy of children's physical interaction with the environment is no longer fully accepted (Hooper & DeFrain, 1980). Other theoretical approaches, such as the Vygotskian position that we are about to discuss, show that young children can and do use language-based routes to knowledge. But despite these shortcomings, Piaget left a powerful educational legacy. He provided teachers with new ways of observing, understanding, and enhancing children's development and strong theoretical justification for less traditional, more child-oriented approaches to classroom teaching and learning.

AN ALTERNATIVE PERSPECTIVE: VYGOTSKY'S DIALECTICAL THEORY

Throughout our discussion of Piaget's work, we have noted important controversies and new findings that call for revisions in his theory. Recall that Piaget de-emphasized language as an important source of cognitive development. This idea resulted in yet another challenge quite early in Piaget's career, this time from the creative young Soviet psychologist Vygotsky. Vygotsky's research was unknown in the United States until its gradual translation into English beginning in the 1960s. In recent years, it has quickly gained in stature within the field of child development.

Piaget Versus Vygotsky: Children's Private Speech

Watch preschoolers as they go about their daily activities, and you will see that they frequently talk out loud to themselves while they play and explore the environment. In the 1920s, Piaget and Vygotsky both noticed this intriguing phenomenon and came to strikingly different conclusions about its role in cognitive development.

Carefully observing the speech of children enrolled in the kindergarten at the Rousseau Institute in Geneva, Piaget (1923/1926) recorded instances in which they mimicked the verbalizations of other nearby people, carried on *monologues* while involved in a solitary activity, or engaged in *collective monologues* in which two or more children in a group spoke, but their statements were not meaningful and reciprocal responses to one another. Piaget called these utterances **egocentric speech,** a term expressing his belief that they reflected the preoperational child's cognitive immaturity. Young children, Piaget interpreted, engage in such speech because they have difficulty taking into account of the perspectives of others. For this reason, their talk is often "talk for self" in which they run off thoughts in whatever form they happen to occur, regardless of whether it is understandable to a listener. Piaget believed that increasing cognitive maturity coupled with certain social experiences—namely, disagreements with same-age peers—eventually brings an end to egocentric speech. Through arguments with agemates, children are repeatedly confronted with evidence that others hold viewpoints different from their own. As children become less self-centered and more logical between the ages of 4 and 7, egocentric speech is gradually replaced by socialized speech, in which children adapt what they say to a listener and engage in real social exchange of ideas.

Vygotsky (1934/1987) voiced a powerful objection to Piaget's conclusion that young children's language is largely egocentric and nonsocial and that self-directed speech plays no useful role in the cognitive life of the child. He pointed out that the

During the preschool years, children frequently talk to themselves as they play and explore the environment. Piaget and Vygotsky disagreed about the significance of this egocentric, or private, speech.

monologues noticed by Piaget occur most often in certain situations, a fact that provides an important clue to their significance. When children engage in tasks in which they encounter obstacles and difficulties, the incidence of such speech nearly doubles. Under these circumstances, what children seem to do is to try to solve problems by talking to themselves:

> "Where's the pencil? I need a blue pencil. Never mind, I'll draw with the red one and wet it with water; it will become dark and look like blue." (Vygotsky, 1934/1987, p. 70)

Such speech, Vygotsky believed, was indeed quite communicative. He regarded it as *communication with the self* for the purpose of self-guidance and self-direction. Because language helps children reflect on their own behavior and plan alternative courses of action, Vygotsky viewed it as the foundation for all higher cognitive processes, including self-awareness, concept formation, and problem solving. As children get older, their self-directed utterances gradually become internalized as silent, inner speech—the continuous verbal dialogues we carry on with ourselves while thinking and acting in everyday situations.

Over the past two decades, researchers have conducted many studies to determine which of these interpretations—Piaget's or Vygotsky's—is correct. Almost all the findings have sided with Vygotsky. As a result, most investigators now refer to the phenomenon as **private speech** instead of egocentric speech. It is now well documented that the majority of children's private utterances serve a self-guiding function and that children use more private speech when tasks are difficult, after they make errors, or when they are confused about how to proceed (Berk & Garvin, 1984; Deutsch & Stein, 1972; Kohlberg, Yaeger, & Hjertholm, 1968). In addition, just as Vygotsky predicted, with increasing age, private speech goes underground, changing from clearly audible verbalizations into soft whispers and silent lip movements (Berk, 1986; Berk, Garvin, 1984; Frauenglass & Diaz, 1985; Kohlberg, Yaeger, & Hjertholm, 1968). Look at Figure 6.9, and you will see just this pattern of development in a recent longitudinal study of elementary school children who were observed as they worked at their desks on math problems from first to third grades. Finally, children who use private speech freely when faced with a challenging activity are more attentive and involved in the task and gain in performance relative to their less talkative peers (Behrend, Rosengren, & Perlmutter, 1989; Bivens & Berk, 1990). These findings support Vygotsky's conjecture that private speech helps children master their own behavior and facilitates thought.

If private speech is a central force in cognitive development, where does it come from? Vygotsky's answer to this question highlights the social roots of human cognition, his main point of departure from Piaget.

The Social Origins of Cognitive Development

Vygotsky believed that all higher mental functions have social origins and appear, at first, on an interpersonal plane, between individuals, before they exist on an intrapsychic plane, within the individual (Vygotsky, 1930–1935/1978; Wertsch, 1986). He stressed the role of social communication in cognitive development by conceiving of children's learning as taking place within the **zone of proximal development.** Tasks within a child's zone of proximal development are ones that are too difficult to be done alone but that can be accomplished through cooperative dialogues[6] with adults or more skilled peers. Then children take the language of these verbal instructions,

---

[6] Recall from Chapter 1 that Vygotsky's theory is called *dialectical* because it regards new ways of thinking as emerging out of dialogues, or discussion and reasoning with others.

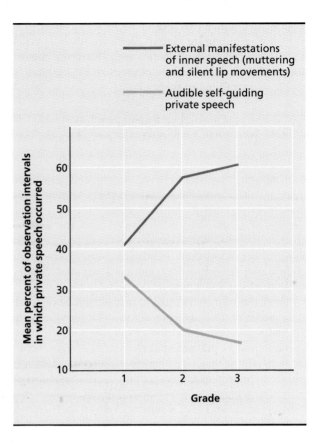

Figure 6.9. Development of elementary school children's private speech in the Bivens and Berk (1990) longitudinal study. During first, second, and third grades, children were observed as they worked at their desks on math assignments. The mirror-image relationship between these two developmental trends suggests that audible self-guiding private speech was gradually replaced by the more internalized speech forms of muttering and silent lip movements. *(Adapted from Bivens & Berk, 1990.)*

make it part of their private speech, and use this speech to organize their own independent efforts in the same way. According to Vygotsky, it is through this process that cognitive skills required for success in each culture are socially transmitted from generation to generation.

To be effective, the adult or peer's communication must have certain features. It must offer a support system, or verbal *scaffold*, that helps the child master new skills (Wood, Bruner, & Ross, 1976). This requires careful coordination of the assistance offered with the current abilities of the child. A mother, for example, helps her youngster learn to tie shoes, work a puzzle, or play a new game by providing help at just the right moment and in the right amount. As the child becomes increasingly proficient, the mother gradually steps back, permitting the child to take over her regulating role and apply it to his own activity.

Is there evidence to support Vygotsky's ideas on the social origins of cognitive development? The literature is growing rapidly, and its findings are capturing the attention of the child development community. In a recent study, Behrend, Rosengren, and Perlmutter (1989) found that maternal support was linked to children's private speech and independent problem solving in ways consistent with Vygotsky's theory. Mothers who used patient, sensitive communication in teaching their preschoolers how to solve a challenging puzzle had youngsters who engaged in more private speech while learning the task. Such children were also more successful when asked to do a puzzle by themselves a week later. Additional research indicates that although preschool children benefit cognitively from working on a task with a same-age peer, their planning and problem-solving skills undergo greater improvement when their partner is either an "expert" peer (especially well versed in the task) or an adult (Azmitia, 1988; Gauvain & Rogoff, 1989; Radziszewska & Rogoff, 1988). Moreover, conflict and disagreement between preschoolers (the dimension of peer interaction emphasized by Piaget) does not seem to be as important in fostering development as the extent to which peers resolve their differences of opinion, share responsibility, and engage in cooperative dialogues. These abilities are less well developed in early childhood but improve markedly during the elementary school years (Nastasi, Clements, & Battista, 1990; Perlmutter et al., 1989; Tudge & Rogoff, 1989).

Finally, recent evidence on the origins of children's make-believe play challenges Piaget's assumption that it simply emerges spontaneously out of sensorimotor schemes. Vygotsky's (1930–1935/1978) theory suggests that once children are capable of representation, they learn how to pretend from their interactions with others. Consistent with this idea, new research indicates that when children begin to use objects as symbols for real activities, their mothers have already started to teach them how to do so (Smolucha, in press). Moreover, during the second year, both the complexity of symbolic play and the length of play episodes increase when mothers are available to play with their youngsters (Slade, 1987). These findings suggest that maternal involvement in young children's play creates a zone of proximal development in which children's make-believe skills expand with support and encouragement.

Vygotsky and Education

Educators have become intensely interested in the implications of Vygotsky's ideas for teaching children in school. Clearly, Piagetian and Vygotskian classrooms have certain features in common, such as opportunities for active participation, an emphasis on process rather than products of thinking, and acceptance of individual differences in cognitive development. But a Vygotskian environment goes beyond arranging activities to promote children's self-initiated discovery. Instead, it maximizes *assisted discovery* (Tharp & Gallimore, 1988). Teachers guide children's learning with explanations, demonstrations, and verbal prompts, carefully tailoring their efforts to each child's zone of proximal development. Gradually, children are encouraged to assist themselves, at first through self-guiding private speech. Then teachers step back as speech-to-self recedes and children move toward independent mastery. The process of assisted discovery is also enhanced through planned opportunities for peer collaboration. Teachers arrange cooperative learning experiences, grouping together classmates whose abilities are moderately discrepant from one another so that peers can teach and help one another (Forman & McPhail, 1989).

At this point, it is important to note that Vygotsky's theory, like Piaget's, has not gone unchallenged. As Rogoff (1990) points out, finely tuned, scaffolded instruction may not be the only means through which children's thought develops, or even the most important one in some cultures. For example, the young child who is inducted into sailing a canoe in Micronesia may learn more from direct observation and practice than from joint participation with and verbal guidance by adults. It is possible that the kind of assistance offered to children varies considerably from one culture to another, depending on the tasks that must be mastered for success in each society. So we are reminded once again that children learn in a great many ways, and as yet, no single theory provides a complete account of cognitive development.

To help you review, Table 6.4 summarizes Piaget's and Vygotsky's contrasting views on the role of egocentric or private speech in children's cognition. We have stressed the differences between them — Piaget's focus on the individual and Vygotsky's concern with the social and cultural context of development — but perhaps a new theory will someday synthesize their respective contributions. In fact, we have already seen in our discussion of educational implications that some essential aspects of Piaget's and Vygotsky's theories are compatible and related — especially a view of the child as an active, sense-making being who is continuously engaged in creative

Table 6.4. Differences Between Piaget's and Vygotsky's Theories of Egocentric or Private Speech

	PIAGET	VYGOTSKY
Developmental significance	Represents an inability to take the perspective of another and engage in reciprocal communication	Represents externalized thought; its function is to communicate with the self for the purpose of self-guidance and self-direction
Course of development	Declines with age	Increases at younger ages and then gradually loses its audible quality to become internal verbal thought
Relationship to social speech	Negative; least socially and cognitively mature children use more egocentric speech	Positive; private speech develops out of social interaction with others
Relationship to environmental contexts	—	Increases with task difficulty. Private speech serves a helpful self-guiding function in situations where more cognitive effort is needed to reach a solution

Source: L. E. Berk & R. A. Garvin, 1984, "Development of Private Speech Among Low-Income Appalachian Children," Developmental Psychology, 20, 272. Copyright 1984 by the American Psychological Association. Reprinted by permission of the author.

commerce with the environment. When put together, the work of these two great theorists promises an expanded view of the human mind as inseparable from the physical and social worlds that it acts upon and transforms.

CHAPTER SUMMARY

Piaget's Theory of Cognitive Development

■ Influenced by his early background in biology, Piaget viewed cognitive development as an adaptive process. As children act directly on the environment, their mental structures evolve through a series of stages in which they achieve a better and better adaptive fit with external reality.

■ In Piaget's theory, **structures,** or **schemes,** undergo qualitative transformations as children move from one stage to another. The functions of **organization** and **adaptation,** with its two complementary processes of **assimilation** and **accommodation,** explain how change in structures takes place.

Piaget's Stages of Development

■ According to Piaget, children pass through four stages of development: (1) the **sensorimotor stage,** (2) the **preoperational stage,** (3) the **concrete operational stage,** and (4) the **formal operational stage.** The stages form an invariant maturational sequence and are hierarchically related.

■ During the six sensorimotor substages, the neonate's reflexive action patterns gradually become more flexible and

refined. The sensorimotor stage brings with it the attainment of **object permanence;** the appearance of **intentional,** or **goal-directed behavior;** and the beginnings of imitation and play.

■ Infants use the **circular reaction** to build and consolidate their earliest schemes. **Sensorimotor egocentrism** diminishes and disappears as the circular reaction becomes less self-centered and more outer-directed and as infants master the permanence of objects.

■ Piaget's general sequence of sensorimotor development has been supported. However, new studies reveal that infants attain some sensorimotor milestones, such as imitation, secondary circular reactions, and object permanence, earlier than Piaget expected.

■ Aside from rapid expansion of the symbolic function, Piaget described preoperational children in terms of cognitive deficits rather than strengths. The most pervasive deficit of this stage is **preoperational egocentrism,** which is responsible for the rigidity and illogical nature of preschoolers' thought.

■ Preoperational thinking is **animistic, perception-bound, centered, irreversible,** and focused on **states rather** than **transformations** of objects. In addition, preoperational children **reason transductively** as opposed to inductively or deductively. Because of these cognitive inadequacies, they fail to pass a wide variety of Piagetian tasks, including **conservation, hierarchical classification,** and **transitivity.**

■ However, when preschool children are given problems that are scaled down in complexity or that contain familiar items, their performance appears more mature. In addition, preoperational children can be trained on Piagetian tasks. These findings suggest that young children have preparatory structures for logical reasoning that were not recognized by Piaget.

■ At the concrete operational stage, children think with logical, reversible **operations** and can pass conservation, transitivity, hierarchical classification, and spatial reasoning tasks. Piaget realized that some concrete operational concepts are mastered earlier than others. He used the term **horizontal décalage** to refer to the gradual, orderly mastery of cognitive milestones within a stage. Concrete operational thought is limited in that children can reason logically only about concrete, tangible information.

■ At the formal operational stage, the capacity for abstract, scientific reasoning appears. Formal operations are characterized by **hypothetico-deductive reasoning** and **propositional thinking.** These new capacities lead to **formal operational egocentrism,** including the **imaginary audience** and **personal fable,** in young adolescents.

■ New studies of formal thought indicate that the glimmerings of abstract reasoning are present before adolescence. In addition, formal thinking is generally limited to those contexts in which individuals have had extensive experience solving hypothetical problems.

Larger Questions About the Validity of Piaget's Theory

■ Piaget's theory has been the focus of intense critical scrutiny in recent years. Currently, the most hotly debated question is whether cognitive development really takes place in stages. Some investigators reject the notion of stage, while others argue for a less tightly knit stage concept than was originally proposed by Piaget.

Educational Implications of Piaget's Theory

■ Piaget's theory has had a lasting impact on the design of educational programs for young children. A Piagetian-based classroom promotes active engagement with the environment and discovery learning.

An Alternative Perspective: Vygotsky's Dialectical Theory

■ While Piaget de-emphasized the role of language in cognitive development, Vygotsky regarded it as the basis for all higher mental functions. According to Vygotsky, children's **private speech,** or self-directed language, helps children plan and guide their own behavior. With age, private speech goes underground to become internal, verbal thought.

■ Private speech emerges out of social communication with others. Adults and more capable peers provide children with verbal guidance in the **zone of proximal development.** Then children integrate the language of these instructions into their private speech and apply it to their own activity. A Vygotskian classroom emphasizes assisted discovery rather than self-discovery. Verbal support from teachers and peer collaboration in learning are important.

IMPORTANT TERMS AND CONCEPTS

contents   (p. 209)
structures   (p. 209)
schemes   (p. 210)
functions   (p. 210)
adaptation   (p. 210)
assimilation   (p. 210)
accommodation   (p. 210)
equilibration   (p. 211)
organization   (p. 211)
clinical interview   (p. 212)
sensorimotor stage   (p. 213)
preoperational stage   (p. 213)
concrete operational stage   (p. 213)
operations   (p. 213)
formal operational stage   (p. 213)
object permanence   (p. 213)

intentional, or goal-directed
   behavior   (p. 213)
circular reaction   (p. 214)
sensorimotor egocentrism   (p. 214)
deferred imitation   (p. 218)
make-believe play   (p. 218)
sociodramatic play   (p. 222)
preoperational egocentrism   (p. 225)
animistic thinking   (p. 225)
conservation   (p. 225)
perception-bound   (p. 226)
centration   (p. 226)
states versus transforma-
   tions   (p. 226)
reversibility   (p. 226)
transductive reasoning   (p. 226)

hierarchical classification   (p. 226)
transitivity   (p. 228)
identity constancy   (p. 228)
horizontal décalage   (p. 234)
cognitive maps   (p. 236)
hypothetico-deductive
   reasoning   (p. 239)
propositional thinking   (p. 239)
formal operational ego-
   centrism   (p. 240)
imaginary audience   (p. 240)
personal fable   (p. 240)
egocentric speech   (p. 246)
private speech   (p. 247)
zone of proximal develop-
   ment   (p. 247)

Girl Drawing by Mary L. Harcourt.
Christopher Wood Gallery, Bridgeman Art Library (London).

7

Cognitive Development: An Information Processing Perspective

The information processing view of cognition arrived on the scene of child development in part as a reaction to the inadequacies of Piaget's theory. Unlike the Piagetian view, information processing does not provide a single, unified theory of children's thinking. Instead, it is an approach adhered to by investigators studying a variety of aspects of cognition, from perceptual, attentional, and memory processes to complex problem solving. Their combined goal is to find out how children and adults operate internally on different kinds of information, coding, transforming, and organizing it as it makes its way through the cognitive system.

This chapter provides an overview of the information processing perspective. First we review its history and major models of the human mental apparatus. Next we turn to the development of three basic operations that enter into all of human thinking: perception, attention, and memory. We also consider how children's growing knowledge of the world and awareness of their own mental activities affect these basic operations. Then we discuss recent applications of the information processing approach to children's learning in school, including reading, mathematics, and scientific problem solving. Our discussion concludes with an evaluation of the strengths and weaknesses of information processing as a framework for understanding cognitive development.

THE INFORMATION PROCESSING APPROACH

Most information processing theorists have in common a view of the human mind as a complex, symbol-manipulating system through which information flows, operating much like a digital computer. Information from the environment is *encoded*, or taken in by the system and retained in symbolic, representational form. Then a variety of internal processes actively operate on the information, *recoding* it, or revising its symbolic structure if its form proves to be initially inadequate, and *decoding* it, or deciphering and interpreting its meaning by comparing and combining it with other previously stored information. Thus, while inside the system, information is manipulated and transformed in a variety of ways that permit the storage and generation of new representations. When these cognitive operations are completed, output in the form of a behavioral response, a final solution to a task or problem, is generated.

Consider this brief description of the information processing view of mental functioning, and perhaps you already see that the computer analogue as a device for understanding cognition has a number of attractive features. It shares with the other major competing approach to cognitive development, Piaget's theory, a view of the human organism as an active processor of information. Beyond this, the computer model offers theoretical exactitude in a way that many vague, holistic Piagetian concepts do not. Information processing researchers use the computer metaphor to articulate the precise series of cognitive operations that children and adults execute when faced with a task or problem. In fact, some try to map the "odyssey of information flow" (Flavel, 1985, p. 76) in such detail that the same mental operations can actually be programmed into and run on a computer. Then such computer simulations can be used to make predictions about how children and adults respond when exposed to particular task conditions (e.g., Klahr & Wallace, 1976). Other information processing theorists do not rely on computer simulations to test their ideas. But all hold in common a strong commitment to explicit models of cognitive functioning that can be subjected to direct, empirical verification (Klahr, 1989; Kuhn, 1988).

Besides growing disillusionment with Piaget's theory, several other influences led information processing to rise to the forefront of research on children's cognition. In the sections that follow, we consider the history of this burgeoning new emphasis in child development.

Behaviorist Foundations

The forerunner of the current preoccupation of information processing with explicitness and precision was *behaviorism* — a popular theoretical approach to the understanding of children's thinking in the middle part of this century. But "thinking," if we take the word, as it is usually taken, to refer to *internal* processes and products of mind, was not thinking at all to traditional behaviorists. They believed that only observable responses of the organism were proper objects of scientific study. Development was merely the progressive shaping of independent acts by environmental stimuli that served as reinforcers. Since all behavior was regarded as under the control of the environment, a **black box model** of the organism prevailed in which research focused on the stimuli that entered and the responses that emerged. Trying to explain behavior through the inner workings of the black box — by postulating internal, unobservable constructs of mind — was regarded as unnecessary and fruitless. But when, in the 1960s, behaviorists began to study children's responses more carefully than they had before, learning as the accumulation of discrete acts by an essentially passive organism could not account for what they saw.

A major turning point in the willingness of behaviorally oriented child psychologists to speculate about what might be going on inside the black box came from some classic research on children's concept formation, involving **reversal and nonreversal learning,** by the Kendlers (Kendler & Kendler, 1962, 1975). Figure 7.1 shows the kind of task the Kendlers gave to children. The stimuli presented, in this case cups, differed on two conceptual dimensions — size and color. Children were first rewarded for responding to one dimension, size; that is, they were reinforced for choosing large instead of small cups. The other dimension, color, was irrelevant. After learning this first discrimination, they were forced to shift to a new response in one of

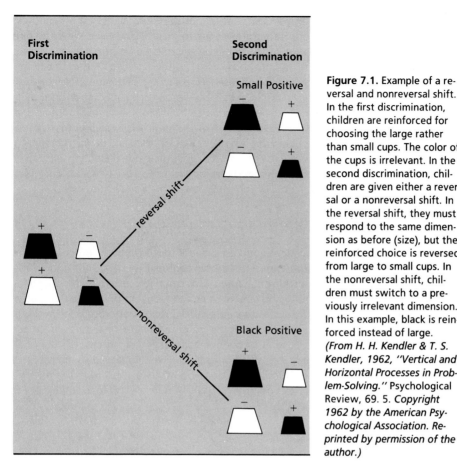

First Discrimination

Second Discrimination

Small Positive

reversal shift

nonreversal shift

Black Positive

Figure 7.1. Example of a reversal and nonreversal shift. In the first discrimination, children are reinforced for choosing the large rather than small cups. The color of the cups is irrelevant. In the second discrimination, children are given either a reversal or a nonreversal shift. In the reversal shift, they must respond to the same dimension as before (size), but the reinforced choice is reversed, from large to small cups. In the nonreversal shift, children must switch to a previously irrelevant dimension. In this example, black is reinforced instead of large. *(From H. H. Kendler & T. S. Kendler, 1962, "Vertical and Horizontal Processes in Problem-Solving." Psychological Review, 69. 5. Copyright 1962 by the American Psychological Association. Reprinted by permission of the author.)*

two ways. In a *reversal shift*, they responded to the same dimension on which they were trained (size), but their choice had to be reversed; they had to learn to pick the small cup instead of the large one. In a *nonreversal shift*, the previously irrelevant dimension, color, became relevant; in our example, black was reinforced instead of white.

A traditional behaviorist who assumes that concept learning consists of direct connections of external stimuli to overt responses would predict that the nonreversal shift would be learned more quickly than the reversal shift. In the nonreversal shift, only two of the originally established discrete connections must be relearned, whereas in the reversal shift all four must be changed. This prediction held for children under age 6, who learned the nonreversal shift faster. But for subjects over age 6, the reversal shift was consistently easier. The inability of traditional behaviorism to account for how more mature children, as well as adults, behaved on these problems led the Kendlers to develop a new, modified behaviorist position called **mediational theory.** What the older subject seemed to learn in the first phase of the task was a covert, mediational response — an internal strategy such as "It's the size of the cup that matters, not the color." Once constructed, this representation of the common features of the stimuli controlled the choice of responses. The nonreversal shift took longer for the mediating subject to establish because not just the overt responses, but also the internal representation used to organize behavior ("Now it's the color of the cup that's important, not its size") had to be changed.

As we will see later in this chapter, a great deal of recent information processing research on children's cognitive strategies, internal techniques used to encode and interpret stimulus information, agrees with the Kendlers' finding that young children are far less effective cognitive mediators of environmental inputs than are older children and adults. But the important point about the Kendler research for now is that it revealed that constructs making reference to mental processes were the *only* route to an adequate explanation of the behavior of children. Without assuming the existence of internal mechanisms of thought, the difference between younger and older subjects' performances simply could not be understood (Kuhn, 1988).

Compared to information processing, the behaviorist verbal mediation approach, in which a word like "big" or "black" intervenes between a stimulus input and an overt response, is a substantial oversimplification of the way in which human beings use symbolic activity to guide behavior. But the more elaborate and detailed models of information processing, which try to specify what goes on inside the black box, can be viewed as sophisticated modern descendants of the behaviorist mediational idea (Brown et al., 1983).

Influences from Cognitive Psychology and Linguistics

The commitment of child development researchers to information processing was strengthened by trends in adult experimental psychology. By the 1940s and 1950s, many psychologists had become disenchanted with behaviorism as a viable approach for understanding adult learning and saw the need to focus on underlying cognitive events (Miller, 1989). In addition, in the mid-1950s, the ground-breaking work of linguist Noam Chomsky made psychologists patently aware of young children's remarkable ability to comprehend and produce novel language utterances they had never heard before. In between input and output, children appeared to operate in a rule-oriented fashion on linguistic information. Chomsky's work was yet another influence in legitimizing complex cognitive activity as a necessary focus of inquiry in child development (Siegler, 1983b).

The Computer Metaphor

The fields of computer science and cybernetics were major forces in the emergence of information processing as well. The computer-inspired representation of the human mind retained the features of precision and explicitness that had made behaviorism so attractive, but it also provided a more adequate and complete conception of human mental functioning. Both human beings and computers could be thought of as complex, symbol-manipulating systems able to deal with difficult tasks and problems. Since computers were made by human beings, they were invaluable tools in the quest to specify and understand the components of human symbol manipulation (Newell & Simon, 1972; Siegler, 1983b). Thus, the computer metaphor was used to help analyze thinking into a series of separate processes that operated individually on stimulus information and then combined to generate a final performance. As a result, frames and flowcharts began to be employed to represent the human mental apparatus.

MAJOR MODELS OF THE INFORMATION PROCESSING SYSTEM

Atkinson and Shiffrin's Store Model

The most influential of the computerlike conceptualizations of mental functioning is Atkinson and Shiffrin's **store model** of the information processing system (Atkinson & Shiffrin, 1968; Shiffrin & Atkinson, 1969). Depicted in Figure 7.2, it is called a store model because information is viewed as being held, or stored, in three parts of the system for processing. The three parts — the sensory register, the short-term memory store, and the long-term memory store — correspond to the *hardware* of the system. Atkinson and Shiffrin regard them as inborn and constant across all individuals. All three stores are limited in the speed with which they can process information. In addition, the sensory register and the short-term store are limited in capacity. They can hold onto only a finite quantity of input, and it can be retained only for a brief period of time before it fades away entirely.

Besides these structural units, the model includes **control processes,** or **strategies,** which are like the *software* of the system. These techniques help people increase the efficiency and capacity of the storage bins. For example, given a list of numbers to learn, a standard **memory span** task that is often used to determine the limits of short-term memory, you can repeat the first ones to yourself while awaiting delivery of the remaining ones, operating on your limited processing space in a fashion that enables more information to be retained than if you used no strategies at all. According to Atkinson and Shiffrin, control processes are not innate; they are learned, and individuals differ in how well they use them.

Look at Figure 7.2 again, and notice how information moves through the system sequentially. First, it enters the **sensory register.** Here, auditory and visual events are represented literally and held very briefly, generally for not more than a few seconds, while being initially processed and transferred to the short-term store. Control processes can be used to influence the workings of the sensory store. For example, people can deploy their attention selectively, screening out information from sensory modalities that are unimportant at the moment, and within a single modality, they can heighten their attention to particular stimuli.

Information flows next to the **short-term memory store,** the central processing unit of the system. Here information is operated on and combined with additional material from long-term memory, the accumulated knowledge base of the system. The short-term store is the conscious part of memory. People are not really aware of the activities of the sensory register or the long-term store, but they are actively conscious of events taking place in short-term memory as information is brought into

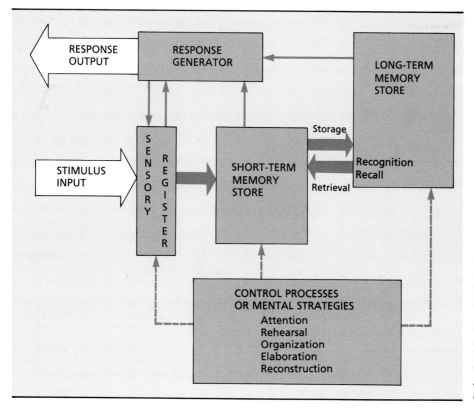

Figure 7.2. Atkinson and Shiffrin's store model of the information processing system. Solid lines indicate paths of information transfer. Dashed lines indicate connections that permit comparison of information residing in different parts of the system; they also indicate paths along which control signals may be sent to activate information transfer. *(From R. M. Shiffin & R. C. Atkinson, 1969, "Storage and Retrieval Processes in Long-Term Memory." Psychological Review, 76. 180. Copyright 1969 by the American Psychological Association. Adapted by permission of the authors.)*

and out of focal attention, stored and retrieved, and compared and combined in various ways (Siegler, 1983b).

As we mentioned earlier, the short-term store is limited in capacity. The sensory register, although also limited, can take in a wide panorama of information, but when the input reaches the short-term store, a bottleneck occurs. The capacity constraint of the short-term store is not a matter of physical units of material. Instead, it is a matter of *meaningful* pieces, or *chunks* of information. For example, you would probably find the task of holding the following line of single-digit numbers in short-term memory very difficult: 101212323434545. But try chunking or combining them into three-digit numbers, as follows: 101 212 323 434 545. Notice how the task becomes much easier, since only five instead of fifteen pieces need to be retained. But even with chunking, once the limited number of slots in the short-term store is occupied, either new information cannot enter the system, or, if it does, it will push out existing information. Information in short-term memory also decays quickly. It will be lost within 15 to 30 seconds (Siegler, 1983b) without the application of control processes, such as *rehearsal* (repeating the information to be remembered). The longer the material is maintained, the greater the probability that it will be transferred to long-term memory.

Atkinson and Shiffrin indicate that besides rehearsal, other important control processes have an even greater effect on retention of information. For example, look at the string of three-digit numbers above once more. Do you see a pattern that makes them easier to remember? If so, you employed the control strategy of *organization;* you recoded the material into a new, more tightly organized form that enabled you to retain it more easily. Perhaps you also noticed that one or more of the units was the same as a familiar house number or the first three digits of your phone number. If you thought of one or more of the chunks in ways like this, you were using a control strategy called *elaboration.* You linked the material to already existing information in long-term memory, thereby greatly increasing the probability that it would be incorporated into this largest processing receptacle.

Atkinson and Shiffrin believe that once information enters the **long-term memory store,** the memory traces are permanent. Also, unlike the sensory and short-term stores, the capacity of long-term memory is assumed to be limitless. Inability to remember information stored in long-term memory is considered to be a problem in retrieval, or getting information back from the system. To aid retrieval, control processes dominate the activities of the long-term store, organizing and elaborating on each bit of material, interconnecting it with many other pieces of information, and filing it according to a master plan that is contingent on contents, very much like a "library shelving system which is based upon the contents of the books" (Atkinson & Shiffrin, 1968, p. 181). Then, if the information is needed at some time in the future, it can be retrieved by following the same strategic plan that was used to store it in the first place.

Research Testing the Validity of the Store Approach

A considerable amount of research is consistent with Atkinson and Shiffrin's store model (Siegler, 1983b). For example, the distinction between short- and long-term memory is supported by the well-known **serial position effect** that occurs in memory tasks involving lists of items. If an item occurs in the middle of a sequence, it is less likely to be remembered than if it occurs at the beginning or the end. The advantage of being at the beginning of the list is called the *primacy effect,* whereas the advantage of being at the end is termed the *recency effect.* However, research shows that over time, items at the end of a list decay from memory, while those at the beginning continue to be retained. The reason, investigators believe, is that those learned last are held only temporarily in short-term memory, while those learned first have had sufficient time to transfer to the long-term store.

In a study of infants, Cornell and Bergstrom (1983) found this very same effect as early as 7 months of age. Babies were presented with a list of three photos of women's faces. Then each of the infants was assigned to a condition in which the photo occupying either the first, middle, or last position in the list was paired with a completely new photo. Memory for the original photo was inferred if infants dishabituated, or spent more time attending to the new picture. As shown in Figure 7.3, when the infants were tested immediately after list presentation, the traditional primacy and recency effects occurred. After delays of 1 and 5 minutes, recognition of the photo in serial position 3 disappeared. Cornell and Bergstrom's study is consistent with Atkinson and Shiffrin's assumption that separate short- and long-term memory stores are fundamental properties of the human information processing system.

Despite such evidence, other findings have led some investigators to question the store model of information processing. The capacity limits of the sensory and short-term stores have been found to be highly variable. For example, depending on the study, estimates of the retention period for visual sensory information range from 250 milliseconds to 25 seconds. Similarly, the short-term store, once thought to be limited to 7 slots, actually ranges from 2 to 20 chunks (Siegler, 1983b). Thus, the existence of separate information stores is called into question by the fact that their capacity parameters are slippery and elusive. As a result, some information processing theorists have turned toward a levels of processing view.

The Levels of Processing Model

The **levels of processing model** abandons the idea of a series of containers with fixed limits on how much information can be grasped at once. Instead, it assumes that retention of information is a function of the depth to which an incoming stimulus is analyzed by the system. For example, a written word might be encoded at a very superficial level, according to its perceptual features (e.g., whether it is printed in capital or lowercase letters). At a slightly deeper level, it could be encoded according

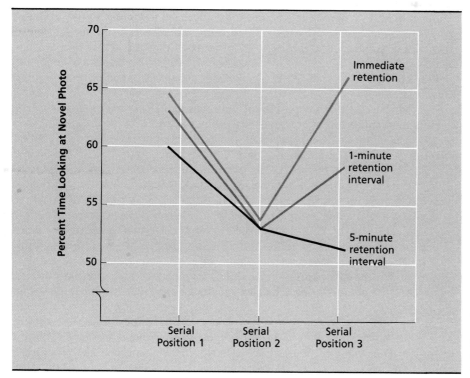

Figure 7.3. Serial position findings in the Cornell and Bergstrom (1983) study of 7-month-old infants. In the immediate retention condition, both primacy and recency effects occurred, but in the delayed retention conditions, recency effects faded and disappeared. *(Adapted from Cornell & Bergstrom, 1983.)*

Once cognitive operations become automatic, they demand little or no attentional resources, and children can engage in several activities at once. For example, this child talks on the phone while writing down a message.

to its phonemic characteristics, or how it sounds. Encoding at this intermediate level is akin to the memory strategy of rehearsal, in which the word is repeated over and over again to oneself. At the deepest level of analysis, the word could be encoded according to its meaning, or *semantic* features. Here the strategies of organization and elaboration lead the incoming stimulus to be subjected to more extensive cognitive processing (Craik & Lockhart, 1972). In the levels of processing model, control processes or strategies are emphasized. Information that is processed superficially quickly decays and is soon forgotten, whereas information processed meaningfully and linked with other knowledge is retained for a longer period of time (Craik & Tulving, 1975).

According to the levels of processing view, our limited capacity to handle a large number of stimulus inputs simultaneously is not due to a fixed-size memory container. Instead, the limit is imposed by the extent to which we can distribute our attention across several activities at once. Consequently, in this model, the limited-slot idea of short-term memory is replaced by the concept of **working memory,** which refers to a general attentional resource pool from which our information processing activities draw (Baddeley, 1986). Attention is demanded by an activity depending on how automatic and well learned the cognitive operations required by the task happen to be. Unskilled subjects must allocate more of their attentional resources, and as a result, attention is drawn away from other operations in which they otherwise could engage at the same time. In contrast, automatic cognitive operations demand little or no attentional capacity, and their execution is not affected by the presence of other tasks occurring simultaneously (Klatzky, 1984). For example, consider the difference between a novice and an expert bicycle rider. The novice is entirely engrossed in controlling the pedals, maintaining balance, and steering, with no attentional resources left over to devote to any other activities. In contrast, the practiced bicyclist negotiates easily around the neighborhood, delivers papers, chews gum, and carries on a conversation with a nearby rider, all at the same time.

Research Comparing the Store and Levels of Processing Approaches

When applied to development, the store and levels of processing models emphasize somewhat different features. The store approach suggests that both the hardware of the system, the basic capacity of the information containers, and the software, or deployment of control processes, change with age. That is, what develops may be both a bigger computer and a wider range of effective programs, or strategies. In contrast, the levels of processing model suggests that all developmental changes have to do with *software*, or functioning of the system. In other words, many operations become less capacity-consuming as the result of years of practice with strategies, which eventually leads to more skillful deployment of the available space (Siegler, 1983b).

The evidence we will review throughout this chapter indicates that, without a doubt, functional capacity, or use of control processes, does improve with age. Children gradually acquire a variety of strategies for allocating space within the limited-capacity systems that they have. They also learn how to supplement their limited systems with external aids to processing, employing calendars, notebooks, libraries, and even computers to enhance their ability to retain information.

It has been difficult to find out whether structural constraints also change, but recent evidence indicates that the basic hardware does not change much. In two studies, developmental increases in memory span (the commonly used measure of the capacity limits of the short-term store) were completely explained by the speed with which children and adults could process information. Adults' memory spans are twice as large as those of first graders, but adults are also able to rehearse words and digits more quickly. Case, Kurland, and Goldberg (1982) gave college students numbers in a foreign language that they could repeat no faster than 6-year-olds can repeat English numbers. Under these conditions, the memory span differences between children and adults completely disappeared. Similarly, Hulme and his colleagues (1984) found that young children who were able to repeat words in a list just as fast as older children and adults remembered an equal number of items. These findings suggest that developmental changes in capacity are the result of changes in deployment of strategies. The structural size of the information processing system seems to be fairly constant from early childhood into adult life.

Children gradually learn to supplement their limited-capacity information processing systems with external memory aids. This child uses a calendar to keep track of how many days remain before an important event.

Developmental Models of Information Processing

The store and levels of processing models are *general* approaches to human information processing. Predictions about development can be derived from them, but neither makes precise statements about how children's thinking changes with age. Although few uniquely developmental information processing models exist, two of them—Case's M-space and Fischer's skill theory—have attracted widespread attention in the field. Interestingly, each is an effort to improve on Piaget's theory by reinterpreting it within an information processing framework.

Case's M-Space. Robbie Case (1985) accepts the levels of processing assumption that the basic size of the information processing system does not change with age. Instead, he sees development as a matter of increases in *available capacity* due to improvements in strategy deployment. Piagetian schemes, in Case's theory, constitute the child's mental strategies. With age, a computerlike construct called mental space, or **M-space,** expands. It refers to the maximum number of schemes the child can apply simultaneously at any given time. Increases in M-space are due to two factors: maturation of the child's central nervous system and greater routinization of schemes. As schemes are repeatedly practiced, they become more automatic and require less attentional capacity, freeing up extra M-space for the child to work on combining and consolidating old schemes and generating new ones. Thus, Case accepts Piaget's stage-wise progression of development but views it as a series of increasingly powerful strategies, each of which is a modified but more effective version of previous ones.

Case's theory also explains horizontal décalage—that many Piagetian achievements (such as conservation) appear in particular situations at different times, rather than being mastered all at once.[1] Case assumes that different forms of the same logical insight vary in the processing demands they make of the child. Therefore, each successive Piagetian task requires more M-space for mastery.

Think back for a moment to the various Piagetian tasks that we discussed in Chapter 6. In line with Case's theory, a notable feature of them is that at each new stage of development, a greater number of items must be held in memory and combined with one another to reach a correct solution. In fact, support for Case's theory comes from evidence that shows a positive correlation between children's ability to pass more advanced Piagetian tasks and the size of their memory spans (Case, 1977, 1978). This finding is consistent with the idea that combining Piagetian schemes in more complex problem solving is accompanied by expansion of a central processing resource pool (M-space) with development.

According to Case's theory, as schemes are repeatedly practiced, they become more automatic, and children can combine them into more complex activities. This preschooler integrates several schemes when putting on his shoes and socks.

Fischer's Skill Theory. Kurt Fischer's **skill theory** also accounts for Piaget's broad stage changes. In addition, it interprets the phenomenon of horizontal décalage in a somewhat different way than Case—by emphasizing children's specific experiences. According to Fischer, a *skill* is a Piagetian scheme applied to a particular task or set of tasks. How broadly applicable a skill is depends on both organism and environment—that is, central nervous system maturation plus the range of environments to which the child has been exposed (Fischer, 1980; Fischer & Pipp, 1984). This will become apparent as we look at the concepts that Fischer uses to describe skill development.

Each child has an *optimal level of skill performance,* or upper limit of processing capacity that cannot be exceeded without further central nervous system development. Fischer identifies three optimal skill levels: sensorimotor actions, representations, and abstractions (note their correspondence with Piaget's stages). However, children (and adults as well) seldom function optimally because using the most

---

[1] Return to Chapter 6, page 234, if you need to review Piaget's concept of horizontal décalage.

advanced skills possible depends on extensive support from the environment. Consequently, within each developmental level, an extended period of *skill acquisition* takes place in which children acquire new competencies in specific contexts, integrate them with others, and gradually transform them into more efficient, generalized, higher-order skills.

For example, a 5-year-old who cannot yet conserve liquid may have some isolated representational skills such as: (1) after water is poured from a tall into a short glass, the height of the liquid is reduced; and (2) after water is poured from a thin into a wide glass, the width of the liquid increases. But until the child has had sufficient experience in transferring liquids from one container to another, she cannot *combine* these two separate skills into the following more effective one: (3) when water is poured from a tall into a short glass, all changes in height are compensated for by changes in width, and liquid is conserved. Once a more advanced skill is mastered in a particular context, it can be *substituted*, or transferred to other similar contexts. In our example, conservation can then be applied to mass or weight. Eventually, the child *intercoordinates* several context-specific skills into a new, more broadly generalizable principle. When this happens, cognition moves to a higher level of functioning (in this case, from representation to abstraction). According to Fischer, skill combination, substitution, and intercoordination are *transformational rules* that describe skill revision at any level of development. Notice how these rules offer a more precise account of cognitive change than Piaget's concepts of assimilation and accommodation.

Skill theory also helps refine our understanding of how working memory develops. Fischer believes that expansion of memory capacity is not just a matter of practice and routinization of separate schemes or skills, as Case's theory suggests. In addition, each transition to a new skill level brings with it a dramatic increase in working memory. As children become capable of representation and finally abstraction, their skills are reorganized into new, more efficient forms that make far fewer demands on cognitive processing. In line with this idea, research shows that simply training children to retain relevant background facts does not always increase their problem-solving performance (Brainerd & Reyna, 1988). Sometimes, more effective ways of representing and manipulating information in working memory seem to be necessary.

BRIEF REVIEW

In the sections above, we discussed two general models of information processing: Atkinson and Shiffrin's store model and the levels of processing perspective. The distinguishing feature of levels of processing, in comparison to the store approach, is an emphasis on allocation of attention as responsible for processing limitations, rather than fixed-size mental containers. Two developmental models of information processing—Case's M-space and Fischer's skill theory—reinterpret Piaget's theory in information processing terms. Each explains broad stage changes as well as the phenomenon of horizontal décalage, or context-specific mastery of Piagetian milestones. Case and Fischer also provide accounts of age-related increases in working memory. While Case emphasizes practice and automaticity of schemes or strategies, Fischer focuses on increments in skill level that result in more efficient and effective thought. Finally, in comparison to Piaget, Fischer offers a more precise description of how cognitive change takes place.

Despite the different emphases of the models described above, all information processing theorists agree that memory is critically important for virtually all kinds of cognitive activity. Since all thinking involves memory, the bulk of developmental research from the information processing perspective has stressed how the ability to remember changes with age. Because many investigators continue to find the demarcations useful, we will retain Atkinson and Shiffrin's fundamental distinctions between the sensory register and short-term and long-term memory stores throughout our discussion, even though some theorists have completely abandoned them. In the following sections, we consider how sensory functioning, deployment of attention, short-term memory, and long-term memory change with age.

SENSORY PROCESSING

Differentiation Theory

The major perspective on the processing of sensory information is Eleanor and James Gibson's **differentiation theory,** to which you were introduced in Chapter 4. In that chapter, we showed that as the result of central nervous system maturation and repeated exposure to stimulation during the first few months of life, infants become increasingly skilled at detecting *invariant features*, stable aspects of an object or pattern that distinguish it from its background and from other stimuli. Detection of these invariants is an adaptive process; it reduces ambiguity and uncertainty for the organism by creating order and continuity out of an initially chaotic and fluctuating sensory world (Gibson, 1970; Gibson, 1979).

As the term *differentiation* suggests, the environmental features noticed by children become increasingly fine-grained and subtle with age. For the young infant, the initial sensory processing task is one of locating objects and establishing a stable organization of space. Once infants can locate objects in space, they sort them out according to their invariant features. For example, in Chapter 4 we showed how infants first notice the features that distinguish human faces from nonfaces and then go on to make more subtle discriminations between the features of particular faces.

During childhood, the process of differentiation, of detecting the detailed, fine structure of stimuli, continues (Gibson & Spelke, 1983). In fact, Eleanor Gibson (1970) has applied differentiation theory to the way in which young children go about distinguishing written symbols from one another when they first learn to read. Preschoolers start by detecting the invariant features of letters as a set of items. By age 3 or 4, they can distinguish numbers and letters from scribbling and pictures, even though they cannot yet identify very many individual graphic forms.

Gibson and her colleagues studied how children tackle the perceptual task of discriminating individual letters by showing them pairs of letters, asking them to

According to Gibson, the early phase of learning to read involves increasingly fine-grained detection of the invariant features of graphic forms.

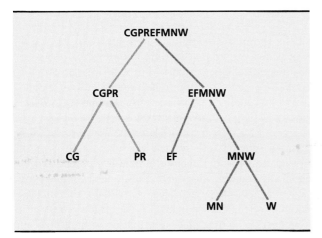

Figure 7.4. A "confusion matrix" indicating how children discriminate among a group of letters according to their distinctive features. *(From E. J. Gibson, 1970, "The Development of Perception as an Adaptive Process."* American Scientist, 58, *106. Reprinted by permission.)*

indicate whether the letters were the same or different, and noting how long it took the children to make each judgment. Using this information, the investigators constructed treelike "confusion matrices" that indicated which letters are most often mistaken for one another. One of these matrices, shown in Figure 7.4, illustrates how children progressively discriminate letters by their invariant features. First, they distinguish the set of curved from straight-line letters. Then, within the curved set, round letters are split from the P and R. Finally, within the straight-line set, square letters are distinguished from diagonals (Gibson, Schapiro, & Yonas, 1968).

Gibson's finding that distinguishing among letters with diagonal lines is difficult for preschool and early elementary school children fits quite well with other research. In a classic study, Rudel and Teuber (1963) gave 3- to 8-year-olds forms to discriminate, as shown in Figure 7.5. All the children easily distinguished the first and third pairs, involving vertical versus horizontal and right-side-up versus upside-down comparisons. However, practically no children younger than 6½ could tell the difference between the two diagonals in the second pair. In addition, the right-left discrimination in the fourth pair was quite difficult.

Does this last comparison remind you of the problems that young children have in differentiating certain letters, such as b and d, that are left-right mirror images of one another? Until 7 or 8 years of age, children reverse such letters frequently in their handwriting. Recently, Casey (1986) showed that young children who confuse left-right mirror images and cannot be trained to make this discrimination fail to attend to the invariant features of such stimulus pairs. In other words, they do not visually search the stimuli systematically enough to notice the subtle difference between them. One reason that young children do not attend to mirror-image and diagonal perceptual distinctions may be that up until the time they learn to read, they do not find it especially useful to notice them. In contrast, children encounter many natural experiences in which objects assume a vertical orientation against a flat surface or have to be placed right side up to be used effectively. Casey presents convincing evidence that the tendency to tune into mirror-image differences, as well as adhere to a left-right order of information flow, depends at least in part on experience with reading materials. Thus, the very activity of learning to read increases the variety of perceptual cues to which children are sensitive.

Of course, becoming a proficient reader entails much more than discriminating graphic symbols. As we will see later when we consider applications of information processing to academic learning, perceptual pick-up from the printed page must be integrated with a variety of other complex cognitive activities, including memory, comprehension, and inference making. So far, we have addressed only one small part of the reading development process.

Figure 7.5. Pairs of forms 3- to 8-year-old children were asked to discriminate in the Rudel and Teuber (1963) study. *(From R. G. Rudel & H. L. Teuber, 1963, "Discrimination of Direction of Line in Children."* Journal of Comparative and Physiological Psychology, 56. *893. Copyright 1963 by the American Psychological Association. Reprinted by permission of the APA.)*

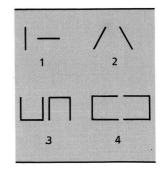

Enrichment Theory

Although differentiation theory is the most widely accepted approach to sensory processing, it is not the only available viewpoint. In differentiation theory, stable aspects of stimuli in the environment — their invariant features — impose order on the child's perceptual world. Development is a matter of becoming better at noticing the structure that already exists in external stimuli. In contrast, **enrichment theory** of perception places the locus of perceptual organization inside the individual. From this point of view, perception involves using internal cognitive schemes to interpret incoming stimulus information. As schemes are refined and elaborated over the course of development, perceptual intake from the environment is enriched accordingly. For example, a young child's interaction with the family cat leads him to build, at first, a scheme for a furry, four-legged, meowing object. Gradually, this image is elaborated to include the slinkiness of the cat's movement, the peacefulness of its sleep, and the contentment of its purr. Each time more information is integrated into the cat scheme, the child's subsequent apprehension of the object is enhanced.

As you probably noticed from this brief description, in viewing perception as largely a matter of mental interpretation of stimulus events, enrichment theory is strongly Piagetian in its orientation. However, some information processing theorists adhere to it as well (e.g., Neisser, 1967). The enrichment position helps remind us of the fine line that exists between perception and cognition. When we consider both differentiation and enrichment positions together, we are provided with a more complete picture. Both the nature of the stimulus material and the individual's mental approach to the world are influential during each phase of information processing. This is a point to which we will return a number of times in the course of this chapter.

ATTENTIONAL PROCESSING

Because attention determines the sources of information that will be considered in any task or problem, it is of fundamental importance in human thinking. When attentional processing is operating at its best, we pick up aspects of the stimulus environment that have optimal utility for the task at hand. As a result, task performance is more efficient and economical (Gibson & Rader, 1979). Attention improves in at least three different ways over the course of childhood. It becomes more controlled, adaptable, and planful.

Control

As children get older, they consciously and deliberately focus their attention on just those aspects of a situation that are relevant to their task goals, ignoring other sources of information. Investigators usually study this increasing control or channeling of attention by introducing irrelevant stimuli into a task. Then children's performance is monitored to see how well they attend to the task's central elements. A large number of studies of this type show that young children are more distractible than older children and adults. Young children have considerable difficulty inhibiting responses to irrelevant information (Lane & Pearson, 1982).

In some cases, researchers use irrelevant input that resembles the background events that are continuously present in children's everyday environments. In one study, Higgins and Turnure (1984) gave preschoolers and second and sixth graders visual discrimination tasks. On each trial, two stimuli were presented, and children had to choose the one of the correct shape and color by pressing a button as quickly as possible. Subjects did the task under one of three conditions: in a quiet room (no extraneous input) or with background music played either softly or loudly. The music impaired the performance of younger children, who made more errors and frequently glanced away from the task. In contrast, the louder the music, the more it facilitated the performance of the older children! The sixth graders actively overcame the background noise by concentrating harder on the task. However, we must keep in mind that extraneous input may not facilitate older children's information processing on all types of tasks, even when it is associated with greater attentional effort. In the case of complex activities, such as comprehension of written text, a great deal of background noise may produce decrements in performance.

In other studies, the irrelevant information is not background stimulation. Instead, it is an intrinsic part of the task itself. Investigations of **incidental learning** are of this type. In an early study of this kind, Maccoby and Hagen (1965) presented third, fifth, and seventh graders with a set of distinctively colored cards with pictures of common objects on them. The cards were shown one by one and then placed face down in a row in front of the child. The central task involved remembering the location in the row of each color. The incidental task, given unexpectedly after a series of trials on the central task, was to match each object with the colored background on which it appeared. Maccoby and Hagen found that central performance improved steadily with age. Incidental learning improved slightly until fifth grade and then decreased sharply by seventh grade (see Figure 7.6).

A variety of other studies also report that incidental learning rises until age 11 and shows a steep decline thereafter (e.g., Hagen & Hale, 1973; Hagen & Stanovich, 1977). The increasing part of this developmental trend probably results from general improvement in processing capacity with age. With the same amount of attention allocated to the incidental stimuli, older children simply remember more of them. But after age 11, children are much better at keeping their attention from being drawn to irrelevant aspects of task stimuli. In contrast, the attentional approach of preschool and early elementary school youngsters is more playful, exploratory, and easily captured by momentarily attractive features of situations (Lane & Pearson, 1982; Vliestra, 1982).

Adaptability

In Maccoby and Hagen's research described above, the central and incidental aspects of the task are completely unrelated to one another. To perform well, it makes perfect sense to ignore the incidental information. But sometimes, a central stimulus is embedded in a context that is meaningfully associated with it. Under these conditions, attending to the incidental material can augment retention of central information. For example, suppose you were told to remember the word sword, presented in one of the following triplets of words: (1) knife, sword, dagger; and (2) cake, sword,

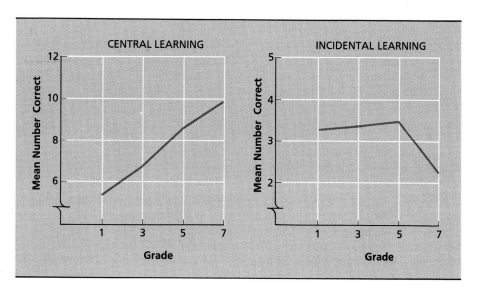

Figure 7.6. Age changes in central and incidental learning in the Maccoby and Hagen (1965) study. *(From E. E. Maccoby & J. W. Hagen, 1965, "Effects of Distraction upon Central Versus Incidental Recall: Developmental Trends,"* Journal of Experimental Child Psychology, 2, 285. *Adapted by permission.)*

pie. In the first case, noticing the relation between the three items helps you distinguish sword from the others. In the second instance, it is best to ignore the incidental words. In a series of studies using stimuli like these, Ackerman (1986) found that in comparison to second graders, fifth graders and college students were better at attending to context when it is helpful and ignoring it when it is not. This indicates that attention gradually becomes more adaptable, flexibly adjusting to momentary requirements of tasks and problems.

In addition to modulating attention in response to task demands, older children shift in response to increments in their own learning. In one investigation, elementary school and college students were given lists of pictures to learn. On each trial but the first, they were allowed to select half the items for further study. First graders' choices did not follow any systematic pattern. But by third grade, children showed a strong tendency to choose the items that they had missed on previous recall attempts (Masur, McIntyre, & Flavell, 1973). When tasks involve more intricate material, such as prose passages, the ability to allocate attention on the basis of previous performance continues to improve into the college years (Brown, Smiley, and Lawton, 1978). This finding indicates that the age at which adaptive attentional strategies emerge is partly a function of task complexity.

Planfulness

Over time, deployment of attention becomes more planful. Investigations of children's visual scanning demonstrate this trend. Vurpillot (1968) studied how children scan pairs of stimuli, such as the houses depicted in Figure 7.7, to decide whether they are the same or different. Preschoolers' eye movement paths indicated that they did

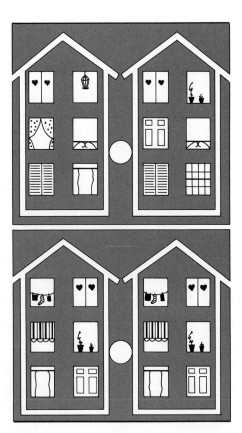

Figure 7.7. Pairs of houses used as stimuli in the Vurpillot (1968) study. After scanning each pair, children indicated whether the houses were the same or different. *(From E. Vurpillot, 1968, "The Development of Scanning Strategies and Their Relation to Visual Differentiation,"* Journal of Experimental Child Psychology, 6, *634. Reprinted by permission.)*

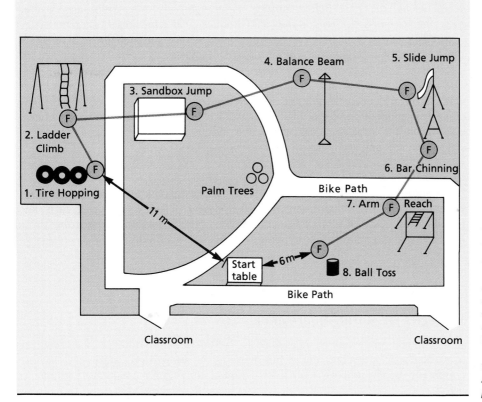

Figure 7.8. Layout of the playground in the Wellman, Somerville, and Haake (1979) study. The figure shows the games the children played at the eight locations. Each location was marked by a flag Ⓕ that displayed a picture of the activity performed there. Red yarn stretched between the flags defined the path from location 1 to 8. Thus, children could easily retrace their steps during the search phase of the study. *(From H. M. Wellman, S. C. Somerville, & R. J. Haake, 1979, "Development of Search Procedures in Real-Life Spatial Environments,"* Developmental Psychology, 15, 532. *Copyright 1979 by the American Psychological Association. Reprinted by permission of the author.)*

not examine all stimulus features and that those they did examine were not studied systematically. As a result, they frequently judged pairs of houses that were different to be the same. In contrast, 6- to 9-year-olds used an exhaustive search strategy in which they compared the details of the houses window to window.

Vurpillot's findings place the beginnings of well-organized, planful search on laboratory tasks in the early to mid-elementary school years. However, strategic search routines are evident during the preschool period when investigators study children in natural environments. For example, Wellman, Somerville, & Haake (1979) looked at how 3- to 5-year-olds search for a lost object in a familiar playground. Each child was taken through the setting by an experimenter, who stopped at eight locations along the way to play a game (see Figure 7.8). In the third location the adult took the child's picture, but by the seventh, the camera was missing. The child completed the path to the eighth location and was then asked to search for the camera. Children of all ages tended to search first in the third area where the picture was taken. When the camera could not be found there, most 3-year-olds gave up. Those who continued to look usually searched outside the "critical area" (the path between location 3 where the picture was taken and location 7 where the camera was first discovered missing). In contrast, older preschoolers were more likely to confine their search to the critical area and to search the possible locations sequentially and comprehensively. These findings, as well as others (Annooshian, Hartman, & Scharf, 1982; Haake, Somerville, & Wellman, 1980), indicate that a tendency to search systematically and exhaustively in familiar environments develops over the preschool years.

Planful allocation of attention is not just a matter of thoroughly examining a stimulus field. Successful performance on complex tasks with several parts requires that children make decisions about what to do first and what to do next in a methodical, orderly fashion. Recently, Gauvain and Rogoff (1989) gave 5- and 9-year-olds lists of 25 items to retrieve in a model grocery store, arranged in an inconvenient order for travel through the space. Before starting on a shopping trip, older children more often took time to scan the store, and they also produced shorter routes through the aisles. With age, children seem better able to plan before acting, and such foresight results in more efficient allocation of attention to parts of a task.

BRIEF REVIEW

The research reviewed above indicates that attentional processing becomes more deliberate and focused, flexible and adaptive, and planful and organized with age. The older child maintains an attentional strategy if it continues to work, changes it when it is inappropriate, and depending on task demands, is capable of enacting a diversity of attentional sets and strategies.

Despite these trends, a surprisingly large minority of children, most of them boys, experience serious difficulties in the development of attention during early and middle childhood. See Box 7.1 for a discussion of the behavioral and learning problems of these attention-deficit hyperactivity disordered children.

SHORT-TERM MEMORY

Strategies for Storing Information

As attentional processing changes with age, so do memory strategies, the voluntary acts we use to store and retain information. As we will see, strategies that are commonly used by adults to keep information in short-term memory and facilitate its

---

◆ CONTEMPORARY ISSUES: SOCIAL POLICY ◆

Attention-Deficit Hyperactivity Disorder

Box 7.1

Just about everyone has, at one time or another, encountered a child whose poorly controlled behavior and extreme distractibility immediately conjure up the term *hyperactive*. Such children often act impulsively without thinking, have difficulty focusing on a single task for more than a few minutes, and find it especially hard to wait patiently for a desired event. In addition, some of them approach what they do with excessive motor activity. Recently, the American Psychiatric Association (1987) introduced the term *attention-deficit hyperactivity disorder (ADHD)* to describe these youngsters. Between 3 and 5 percent of school-age children are affected, most of them boys. Their behavior quickly leads to social friction, academic failure, and low self-esteem. Parents and teachers easily become impatient when a hyperactive child repeatedly fails to listen to directions, talks out of turn, and cannot concentrate long enough to finish a task. Peers also notice the disruptive, off-task behavior and respond to it with annoyance and rejection (Pelham & Murphy, in press).

Attentional difficulties are the fundamental problem area for these children. Research indicates that they do poorly on laboratory tasks requiring controlled, sus-

tained attention and that they also fail to adjust their attentional strategies to task demands (Douglas, 1980; Landau, Milich, & Lorch, in press). Although some outgrow these difficulties, most ADHD children continue to have problems concentrating and finding friends into adolescence and adulthood (Pelham & Murphy, in press). Moreover, because of persisting impulsive behavior and frustration with classroom life, two thirds of these youngsters become serious discipline problems in high school, where they experience high rates of suspensions and expulsions (Weiss & Hechtman, 1986).

ADHD does not seem to have one single cause. Instead, it has been linked to genetic as well as a variety of environmental factors. Some evidence suggests that high degrees of restlessness and school difficulties are more similar for identical than fraternal twins (O'Connor et al., 1980). However, these findings are inconclusive, since genetically identical children may also have been exposed to similar atypical home environments. A somewhat higher proportion of hyperactive children come from homes characterized by marital instability and parental distress (Whalen, 1983). Other evidence indicates that high levels of childhood exposure to lead, an envi-

transfer to the long-term, permanent store are not effectively employed during the early childhood years. But around the time children enter elementary school, they start to become more proficient at generating strategies for remembering (Kail, 1990).

Rehearsal. Children below the age of 5 or 6 are less likely than older youngsters and adults to **rehearse,** or repeat information to themselves that they are trying to memorize. In an early study demonstrating that young children rarely rehearse, Keeney, Canizzo, and Flavell (1967) presented 6- and 10-year-olds with pictures of objects to remember. To determine whether the children rehearsed, a space helmet was used to cover their eyes, but it permitted the experimenter to observe any lip movements they made. Very few 6-year-olds moved their lips, but almost all the 10-year-olds did. Those children who used rehearsal recalled far more of the objects.

Why do young children seldom rehearse? Is the problem simply a **production deficiency,** a failure to generate an already available strategy that would work quite well if only the young child would rely on it? Or is it a **control deficiency,** an inability to skillfully implement a particular strategy even when it is used? Many investigations have been directed at answering these questions. Taken together, research indicates that both strategy production and control difficulties are responsible for younger children's poorer performance on memory tasks.

Studies in which investigators have trained young children to use rehearsal underline the importance of an early production deficiency. When nonrehearsing children are taught to rehearse, their recall improves substantially. However, when later given an opportunity to use rehearsal without prompting, most trained children abandon the strategy (Hagen, Hargrove, & Ross, 1973; Keeney, Canizzo, & Flavell, 1967). Thus, young children can be instructed to rehearse, but they fail to generate the strategy in new situations or maintain it over time.

ronmental pollutant, is related to attentional problems that continue into young adulthood (Needleman et al., 1990). Food additives have also been implicated, but a causal relationship has not yet been established (Whalen, 1983). A common belief is that excessive dietary intake of sugar contributes to hyperactivity, but recent carefully controlled research indicates that it does not play a major role (Milich & Pelham, 1986; Rosén et al., 1988).

Early identification and treatment of ADHD children is crucial in view of the large number of youngsters who are affected and the profound consequences of the disorder for many aspects of development. Currently, the major treatment approach is stimulant medication. For approximately 70 percent of ADHD children, it leads to a reduction in overactivity as well as improvements in compliance, attention, academic performance, and peer relationships (Pelham & Murphy, in press). However, dosage must be carefully regulated; if it is too high, learning will be impaired, despite the fact that overactivity is reduced (Sprague & Sleator, 1977). Some investigators believe that ADHD youngsters are chronically underaroused; that is, normal levels of stimulation are not sufficient to engage their interest and attention. There-

fore, if a task is overly familiar or repetitive, they seek stimulation elsewhere, attending to irrelevant features and engaging in high rates of motor activity. Stimulant drug therapy is thought to be helpful because it has an alerting effect on the central nervous system. As a result, it decreases the child's need to engage in task-irrelevant, self-stimulating behavior.

Nevertheless, drug treatment by itself does not eliminate all these children's difficulties. Therefore, behavior modification programs that model and reinforce appropriate academic and social behavior have also been used. In fact, recent evidence suggests that combining medication with such behavioral treatments is most effective (Pelham & Murphy, in press). In contrast, cognitive interventions that teach ADHD youngsters to use verbal self-instructions to plan and order their task-related activity have not worked well (Whalen, Henker, & Hinshaw, 1985). Perhaps investigators have not yet discovered the best training procedures to help these children gain cognitive mastery over their own behavior.

When children start to use rehearsal spontaneously, control deficiencies are evident. Their first rehearsal efforts differ in quality and effectiveness from those of older individuals. Eight-year-olds commonly rehearse items in isolation. For example, after being given the word cat in a list of to-be-remembered items, they say, "Cat, cat, cat." In contrast, older children combine previously presented words with the newest item, saying "Desk, man, yard, cat, cat." When children use this approach, it substantially increases the serial position primacy effect. In other words, the combined rehearsal strategy results in transfer of much more information to long-term memory (Kunzinger, 1985; Ornstein, Naus, & Liberty, 1975). Second-grade piecemeal rehearsers can be taught to use the more effective approach (Ornstein, Naus & Stone, 1977). However, they require more time to execute the strategy and the extra support of having continuous visual access to all items in a list for training to be effective (Ornstein et al., 1985).

The preschool child's minimal use of rehearsal and the young elementary school child's less effective deployment of it indicate that the development of rehearsal skill is a gradual process. Efficiency is reached only after much time and practice. In one study, Baker-Ward, Ornstein, and Holden (1984) gave preschoolers familiar toys and instructed them to remember as many as possible. Under these conditions, children as young as 3 showed some evidence of intentional memory behavior. They named, visually inspected, and manipulated the toys more and played with them less than a control group that was not instructed to remember them. Although labeling the objects did not increase performance until 6 years of age, the beginnings of rehearsal could be seen in the children's behavior years earlier. These findings indicate that a memory strategy has to be well established before it can serve as an effective memory aid. Until the strategy becomes less effortful and more automatic, young children have difficulty applying it successfully in a memory problem.

Organization. Rehearsal is not the most effective memory strategy available to a resourceful information processor. **Organization** goes beyond mere repetition by relating items to one another, causing recall to improve dramatically.

Like rehearsal, the beginnings of organization can be seen in very young children. When circumstances permit, preschoolers readily use *spatial organization* to aid their recall. In a study of 2- to 5-years-olds, De Loache and Todd (1988) placed either an M&M or a wooden peg in each of 12 identical containers and handed them one by one to the child. The task was to remember where the candy was hidden. By 4 years of age, children spontaneously grouped the candy containers in one place on the table and the peg containers in another, a strategy that almost always led to perfect recall. However, deliberate use of *semantic organization*—grouping objects or words into meaningful categories to aid recall—is a later-developing memory skill that improves steadily from kindergarten into adolescence (Bjorklund & Muir, 1988).

When experimenters train children to use semantic organization by instructing them to sort items into groups of things "that go together or are alike," subjects as young as 4 show enhanced category clustering as well as improved recall (Sodian, Schneider, & Perlmutter, 1986). However, even after training, they rarely do as well as older youngsters who spontaneously organize. The mental effort required to semantically group items is so great for young children that little is left over for the operations of storing and retrieving specific items (Bjorklund & Harnishfeger, 1987). Consequently, it is not surprising that they stop organizing as soon as adults no longer direct them to do so (Liberty & Ornstein, 1973; Williams & Goulet, 1975). These results indicate an early production deficiency for organization that is similar to the one described earlier for rehearsal.

Also like rehearsal, the quality of children's organizational strategies changes with age. Young children are less parsimonious organizers than older children and adults. They divide their lists into a greater number of categories, leave many isolates, and change their grouping schemes from one trial to the next (Frankel and Rollins, 1985; Liberty & Ornstein, 1973; Moely, 1977). The shifting, piecemeal quality of children's first organizational efforts may be partly due to the fact that they are not consciously aware of organizing at all! In comparison to their older counterparts, young children often cannot name their sorting categories or say why they grouped items as they did (Bjorklund & Zeman, 1983; Liberty & Ornstein, 1973).

Why are children initially not aware of how and why they categorize? When investigators study exactly what children do when putting information together, they repeatedly find that younger subjects restrict their grouping to items that are *high in associative strength*—that easily cue one another because they commonly occur together in everyday experience. For example, look at the following set of items:

hat	carrot	head	rabbit
feet	monkey	banana	shoes

When memorizing them, young children spontaneously organize the words into associative pairs, such as "hat-head," "feet-shoes," and "monkey-banana." In contrast, older children and adults group the items using semantic categories of body parts, clothing, animals, and food. The less mature method of organizing by associative relations is probably not very deliberate and effortful. Instead, it may take place quite automatically, without much awareness on the part of the child (Bjorklund & Jacobs, 1985; Frankel & Rollins, 1985).

In a representative study, Bjorklund and de Marchena (1984) found a shift at fourth grade from memory organization based on associative criteria to memory organization based on categorical relations (see Figure 7.9). They believe that the younger child's organizational memory is really not strategic, since it rests on automatic activation of associative relations. However, grouping by associativity may facilitate the development of categorical organization. Once children engage in an automatic grouping process, they may notice it, think about its significance, and start to consciously apply more cognitively mature forms of relating items together (Bjorklund & Jacobs, 1985).

Finally, since young children are primarily associative organizers, whether or not they do organize depends on favorable task circumstances. As long as they are given highly familiar and strongly associated words to memorize, children below age 9 or 10 cluster the words together in recall. When presented with items that have less obvious characteristics in common, they show little if any organization (Best & Ornstein, 1986; Bjorklund & Hock, 1982). As children get older and understand more about semantic relations, they apply this knowledge more broadly (Bjorklund, 1987). As a result, they start to use organizational strategies under less favorable task conditions.

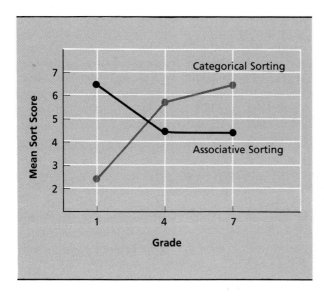

Figure 7.9. Age changes in associative and categorical sorting in the Bjorklund and de Marchena (1984) study. Children were given a set of words on cards, told that they would need to remember them, and then asked to sort them into groups. *(From D. F. Bjorklund & M. R. de Marchena, 1984, "Developmental Shifts in the Basis of Organization Memory: The Role of Associative Versus Categorical Relatedness in Children's Free Recall," Child Development, 55, 956. © The Society for Research in Child Development, Inc. Adapted by permission.)*

Elaboration. Elaboration involves creating a relationship, or shared meaning, between two or more pieces of information that do not bear any natural categorical relationship to one another. It is commonly studied in *paired-associate tasks*, in which the subject is asked to learn pairs of stimulus-response items (e.g., fish-pipe) so that when the stimulus is presented (fish), the response (pipe) is easily recalled. If, in trying to learn this pair, you generated a mental image of a fish smoking a pipe or you recited a sentence to yourself expressing this relationship (e.g., "The fish puffed the pipe."), you were engaging in elaboration. A substantial body of research reveals that elaboration is one of the most effective methods of cementing information in memory (Schneider & Pressley, 1989).

Compared to other strategies, elaboration is a late-developing skill that typically appears after age 11 and gradually increases into young adulthood (Pressley, 1982; Rohwer, & Litrownik, 1983). When individuals finally do use it, elaboration is so effective in producing high memory performance that it tends to replace other memory strategies (Pressley & Levin, 1977).

The very reasons that explain why elaboration is so successful also provide insight into why it is so late to arrive on the scene as a spontaneous strategy. When individuals use mental imagery to elaborate, they must process deeply, going well beyond the information given in a memory problem. Recall that the levels of processing model suggests that the more deeply we process material by weaving meaningful connections with other previously stored information, the more likely it is that new material will be remembered. But deep elaborative processing does not emerge until early adolescence because it makes substantial information processing demands on the individual. For example, when you use mental imagery to elaborate, you must translate the items to be remembered into pictures and then generate an imaginal interaction between them. Children's working memories must expand before they can carry out all these activities effectively at once (Pressley et al., 1987). Increased knowledge about how different items can be combined in an elaborative representation undoubtedly contributes to successful use of the strategy as well (Pressley, 1982).

Investigators used to think that younger children depended on concrete mental imagery as an elaborative device, while older children and adults relied on purely verbal elaboration, of the type that occurs when two unrelated words are connected together in a sentence. Research shows that this once well-accepted assumption is not correct. Even preschoolers can be taught the relatively simple technique of inserting a verb or preposition between two words as a way to improve their memory of the items. In contrast, instruction in mental imagery rarely works below age 5 or 6 but increases in effectiveness until age 11, around the time when the strategy is generated spontaneously. In addition, children below age 7 or 8 profit from instruction in elaborative mental imagery only if the to-be-learned items are concrete objects or pictures of objects. By the late elementary school years, the strategy is used successfully with purely verbal materials (Pressley, 1982).

Even during high school and college, individual differences exist in the extent to which people rely on elaboration in memory tasks. Although virtually all adolescents and young adults use rehearsal and organization, there are still some who never think of using elaboration (Schneider & Pressley, 1989). Why elaboration is a less universally applied strategy than other memory techniques remains a topic for future research.

Environmental Contexts and Memory Strategies

In the many laboratory studies cited above, memory is the one and only goal of the child's activity. But in most everyday tasks, individuals are not just engaged in the business of committing information to memory for its own sake. Rather, they participate in a variety of daily activities that produce excellent memory as a natural by-product of the activity itself (Paris & Lindauer, 1982).

By learning about money within the familiar context of play with a cash register, this child remembers the value of each bill more easily than if he were simply told to learn a list.

Very much like young children, people in non-Western cultures who have no formal schooling do not spontaneously generate or benefit easily from instruction in memory strategies. Such individuals consistently do poorly on tasks in which material is presented as isolated units, devoid of obvious structuring components and removed from external cues of the kind found in everyday life that assist in recall of information (Cole & Scribner, 1977; Paris & Lindauer, 1982). In an intriguing study, Istomina (1975) showed that some of the performance difficulties of young children on laboratory memory tasks reside in learning how to remember information for its own sake when its usefulness is unclear. Soviet 3- to 7-year-olds were required to recall a list of five words under two different conditions. In one, they played a game of grocery store and had to remember the items so they could buy them. In the other, they were simply told to learn the list. Children remembered nearly twice as many items in the grocery store game (in which the information had a clear purpose) as they did in the list-learning condition.

A repeated finding of cross-cultural research is that well-educated subjects remember more than less educated subjects when tasks require memory strategies. This suggests that experiences associated with formal schooling promote the memorizing techniques described above. Deliberate memorization is common in school, and academic tasks provide children with a great deal of motivation for using strategies (Cole & Scribner, 1977; Paris & Lindauer, 1982). In fact, Western children may receive so much practice in learning isolated bits of information that they do not refine other techniques for remembering that rely on spatial location and arrangement of objects, cues that are readily available in daily life. Australian aboriginal and Guatemalan Mayan children are considerably better at these approaches (Kearins, 1981; Rogoff, 1986). Looked at in this way, the development of memory strategies is not just a matter of the emergence of a more competent and facile information processing system. It is also a product of environmental demands and cultural circumstances. Turn to Box 7.2 for additional evidence on how culture and experience influence strategic processing.

BRIEF REVIEW

In the sections above, we have seen that young children's use of memory strategies is characterized by both production and control deficiencies. Preschoolers seldom use techniques to intentionally improve their memory, nor do they show lasting benefits from training. By the time they enter school, children start to acquire greater competence in rehearsal and organization. Elaboration develops later, emerging after age 11 and increasing into young adulthood. Besides improvement in functioning of the information processing system, environment and culture affect the use of memory strategies.

LONG-TERM MEMORY

Retrieval of Information

So far, we have discussed storage mechanisms that put things into memory. Once information enters the long-term store, it must be retrieved, or recovered, to be used again. Information processing theorists study three different types of retrieval: recognition, recall, and reconstruction.

Recognition. Recognition involves noticing that a stimulus is identical or similar to something previously experienced. It is the simplest form of retrieval, since the material to be remembered is fully present during testing to serve as its own retrieval cue. Recognition memory is evident early in infancy, as shown by the habituation research that we discussed in Chapter 4. In fact, by the second year of life, children's recognition of briefly displayed stimuli lasts much longer than most people would expect. Using the habituation-dishabitation paradigm, Daehler & Bukatko (1977) showed toddlers long sequences of pictures. Each was presented only once during the memorization phase of the study. During testing, it was paired with a novel picture. Even when as many as 50 pictures intervened between the two presentations, 19-month-olds consistently dishabituated, or looked longer at the novel picture, indicating that they recognized the familiar picture as one they had seen before.

By the end of the preschool years, recognition memory is very accurate (Perlmutter, 1984). Brown and Campione (1972) found that one week after viewing a series of 80 pictures, 4-year-olds discriminated old from new pictures with 90 percent accuracy. Because recognition appears so early in development and young children can recognize large numbers of stimuli successfully, it is regarded as a rather automatic

---

◆ CONTEMPORARY ISSUES: CULTURAL DIFFERENCES ◆

*S*trategic *Processing in German and American Children*   Box 7.2

Besides formal schooling, home environments have important implications for children's memory development. In a recent cross-cultural study, Martha Carr and her collaborators (1989) tested German and American 8-year-olds on their use of an organizational memory strategy. Children were given a set of magnetized pictures to place on a board for study. Then the pictures were removed, and the children were asked to recall them. The German youngsters outperformed the Americans in strategic processing. While memorizing, they more often rearranged the pictures into semantic categories (such as food and clothing), and they had higher recall scores. In addition, German children were more aware of the usefulness of organization as a memory aid than their American counterparts. When asked which of the following would be easier to learn—a list of related words that could be easily clustered or a list of unrelated words—the German children more often chose the former.

Why do German and American children differ so strikingly in strategy use? Cultural differences in home environments are the likely cause. Carr asked parents of children in her study about encouragement of strategic processing in the home. German parents more often reported checking their children's homework for accuracy, explicitly telling them to use strategies, and initiating games that required strategic thinking. Moreover, the frequency with which parents engaged in these practices was related to their children's use of an organizational strategy when learning new information. Parental encouragement also predicted children's conscious knowledge of a wide variety of effective memorization techniques. Carr's findings highlight the importance of culture, mediated through informal teaching in the home, for the development of strategic processing.

process that is less dependent on systematic search of the memory store than other types of retrieval (Perlmutter & Lange, 1978).

Even though young children's recognition memory approximates that of adults on many tasks, it does show some improvement with age. The ability of older children and adults to apply strategies during storage, such as systematic search of stimuli and verbal rehearsal, increases the number of stimuli later recognized, particularly when they are complex and not very familiar (Hoffman & Dick, 1976; Mandler & Robinson, 1978; Nelson & Kosslyn, 1976). In addition, growth in general knowledge undoubtedly supports improvement in recognition memory. With age, there are simply fewer stimuli around with which children have had no prior experience (Perlmutter, 1984).

Recall. In contrast to recognition, **recall** is a form of *productive memory* in that it involves the ability to spontaneously remember something that is not present. In recognition, the original stimulus is available, but in recall, there may be only a few cues as to what it is, or none at all besides the general context in which it was originally learned. Therefore, recall always demands generation of a mental representation of the absent stimulus. How much must be generated differs from one recall task to another, depending on the degree of contextual support, or availability of external retrieval cues, at time of testing (Perlmutter, 1984).

The beginnings of recall appear before 1 year of age as long as memories are strongly cued. Ashmead and Perlmutter (1980) had parents keep diary accounts of their babies' memories. For infants as young as 7 months of age, many examples of recall for people, places, and objects appeared in the records. The following diary entry of a 7-month-old's memory of his father is an example:

> My husband called from work and I let him talk to Rob. (Rob) looked puzzled for a while and then he turned and looked at the door. Rob thought of the only time he hears his dad's voice when he knows Dad isn't home is when his dad just got home. He heard his dad's voice and based on past experiences, he reasoned that his dad must be home, so he looked at the door (p. 4).

In another diary study, 21- to 27-month-old children were able to remember experiences that happened several months previously, in some cases from a time before they had learned to talk. For example, one child recalled a friend whom he had not seen in several months when passing the friend's house (Nelson & Ross, 1980). Moreover, research on *deferred imitation*, which we considered in Chapter 6, also indicates that recall emerges early, before 1 year of age.[2]

By the time children are 3 or 4, one of the most obvious features of their memory performance is their much poorer recall than recognition. Of course, recognition is much easier than recall for adults as well, but in comparison to adults, children's recall is quite deficient. There is far greater improvement in recall than recognition with age (Perlmutter & Lange, 1978; Perlmutter, 1984). In fact, the ability to recall information accurately over extended periods of time continues to increase through adolescence (Brainerd, Kingma, & Howe, 1985).

Earlier in this chapter, we mentioned a major reason that younger children's recall is poorer than that of older children and adults. Younger and older children differ in the extent to which they meaningfully organize information to aid remembrance. When items are strategically organized at encoding so that they are deeply processed and connected with other material in long-term memory, individuals can rely on a wide variety of internal retrieval cues to stimulate recall. During the elementary school years, semantic organization of the knowledge base increases. Children develop more consistent and stable criteria for defining categories and connect them into hierarchically structured networks of information (Ford & Keating, 1981; Nelson, 1984). In some studies, the degree to which children rely on semantic organiza-

---

[2] Return to Chapter 6, page 218, to review this evidence.

tion for recall has been examined by looking at the extent to which their production of recalled items is clustered into categories. Clustering is related to better recall, and greater spontaneous clustering of information occurs with age (Perlmutter, 1984).

Reconstruction. Read the following passage about George, a convict who has escaped from prison. Then close the book and try to recall it by telling the story to a friend or writing it down:

> George was alone. He knew they would soon be here. They were not far behind him when he left the village, hungry and cold. He dared not stop for food or shelter for fear of falling into the hands of his pursuers. There were many of them; they were strong and he was weak. George could hear the noise as the uniformed band beat its way through the trees not far behind him. The sense of their presence was everywhere. His spine tingled with fear. Eagerly he awaited the darkness. In darkness he would find safety. (Brown et al., 1977, p. 1456)

When you have retold the story, compare your rendition with the original version above. Is it a perfectly faithful reproduction?

In studies of adult memory carried out earlier in this century, Bartlett (1932) showed that when people are given complex, meaningful material to remember instead of isolated bits and pieces of information, an extraordinarily high proportion of inaccuracies, distortions, and additions occur that are not just the result of memory failure. Instead, they are the outcome of a radical transformation of the material. Bartlett advocated a *constructivist* view of human memory. It assumes that much of the meaningful information that we encounter in our daily lives, such as prose passages and spoken language, is not copied verbatim into the system at storage and then faithfully reproduced at retrieval. Instead, new information is selected, interpreted, and embellished on the basis of its correspondence with the individual's existing knowledge base. As a result, exact reproductions of meaningful stimulus events are rare. In fact, once the material is transformed, people may not be able to distinguish what they have internally constructed from what was initially presented (Flavell, 1985; Paris & Lindauer, 1977). Recall from Chapter 6 that Piaget's theory was also a constructivist position. He believed that knowledge could not be imposed ready-made on the child from without. Instead, it is built by the mind through the mental functions of adaptation and organization. Does the constructivist view of human memory remind you of these Piagetian concepts? It is, in fact, very congruent with Piaget's basic ideas (Piaget & Inhelder, 1973).

Constructive processing can take place during any phase of information processing. It can occur during storage. In fact, the memory strategies of organization and elaboration are clearly within the province of constructive memory, since both emphasize generated relationships among stimuli. However, we already know that young children rarely use these encoding strategies efficiently. Constructive processing can also involve **reconstruction** of information while it is in the system and generation of new relationships at retrieval. Do children reconstruct stored information in these ways? The answer clearly is yes.

Children's reconstructive processing has been studied by asking them to recall prose material. Like adults, when children retell a story, they condense, integrate, and add information. For example, by 6 or 7 years of age, children recall the important features of a story and forget the unimportant ones, amalgamate information into more tightly knit units, and reorder the sequence of events to make it more logically consistent (Barclay & Reid, 1974; Bischofshausen, 1985; Christie & Schumacher, 1975; Mandler & Johnson, 1977). Moreover, they frequently report information that fits with the meaning of a passage but that was not really presented. For example, when Brown and her colleagues (1977) told elementary school pupils the story of George, the escaped convict, the following statements were generated as part of their recollections:

All the prison guards were chasing him.
He climbed over the prison walls.
He was running so the police would be so far away that their dogs would not catch his trail. (p. 1459)

In revising and embellishing their recall in meaningful ways, children provide themselves with a multitude of helpful retrieval cues that can be used to remember the information. Thus, from the early elementary school years on, the nature of children's recollection of prose material is similar to that of adults in its emphasis on reconstruction of information.

Between the ages of 4 and 12, reconstruction goes even further as the ability to make inferences about actions and actors within a story improves (Paris & Lindauer, 1977). Preschoolers can draw inferences when story statements concern the physical causes of events. For example, given the sentence "As Jennifer was walking to the store, she *turned a somersault* and lost her dollar," 4-year-olds infer how Jennifer lost her money. But it is not until the early to mid-elementary school years that children can make inferences from information about psychological causes, as in the following sentence: "As Jennifer was walking to the store, she *became very excited* and lost her dollar." Young children's prior understanding of and experience with physical causation is much greater than it is with psychological causation, a difference that affects their ability to comprehend and infer relationships (Thompson & Myers, 1985).

In a recent study, Miller and Pressley (1987) showed that storybook illustrations can help children generate inferences that later serve as useful retrieval cues. Six- and 7-year-olds were read sentences like this one: "The workman dug a hole in the ground." As each sentence was presented, some children viewed a "partial picture" that suggested, but did not depict, the instrument used; the children had to infer it (see Figure 7.10A). Later, when the experimenter cued sentence recall by naming each inferred instrument (in this case, "shovel"), the "partial picture" group remembered just as much as another group that had been directly provided with retrieval cues in "complete pictures" (see Figure 7.10B). Both of these groups recalled nearly twice as much as children who saw no pictures at all. These findings suggest that carefully designed illustrations can enhance children's prose memory by encouraging inferential processing (Pressley & Miller, 1987).

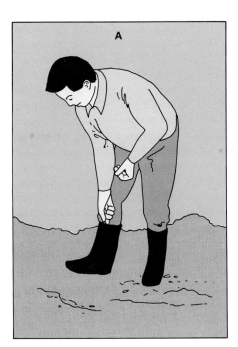 

Figure 7.10. Pictures used to illustrate the sentence "The workman dug a hole in the ground" in the Miller and Pressley (1987) study. (A) Partial picture. (B) Complete picture. (*From G. E. Miller & M. Pressley, 1987, "Partial Picture Effects on Children's Memory for Sentences Containing Implicit Information,"* Journal of Experimental Child Psychology, *42, 303. Copyright © 1987 by Academic Press, Inc. Reprinted by permission.*)

In the sections above, we have seen that memory retrieval evolves from simple recognition of previously experienced stimuli to recall in the presence of salient external retrieval cues over the course of infancy. During childhood and adolescence, recall undergoes marked improvement as stored information becomes better integrated with other knowledge in long-term memory and children rely on a wide variety of internal retrieval cues. Children, like adults, often recall complex, meaningful information in reconstructed forms. Reconstructive processing, including the ability to make inferences, improves during the elementary school years, enabling children to better understand and remember prose material.

The Knowledge Base

Knowledge as an Explanation for Age Differences in Memory Performance. In several earlier sections, we suggested that the child's rapidly developing storehouse of information may be crucial for the deployment of increasingly successful memory strategies. The extent to which expansion of knowledge serves as an adequate explanation for age differences in memory performance is a topic of great interest to information processing investigators. Many now believe that cognitive development is largely a matter of acquisition of **domain-specific knowledge**— knowledge of specific content areas that subsequently renders new, related information more familiar and meaningful and therefore easier to store and retrieve (Bjorklund, 1987; Mandler, 1983; Siegler, 1983b). Becoming more knowledgeable in a particular area also improves strategy use. Chi (1982) demonstrated the importance of knowledge for strategic processing in a study showing that how well a 5-year-old used an alphabetical strategy for retrieving children's names depended on her familiarity with the to-be-remembered material. When asked to retrieve the names of pupils in her own classroom—domain-specific knowledge that she knew very well —the child learned and applied the alphabetical strategy quickly. When required to use it to retrieve names of people she did not know, she had great difficulty doing so.

If children's growing knowledge of task-related stimuli serves as a viable explanation for age-related increments in memory performance, then in content domains in which some children are more knowledgeable than most adults, these child experts should also show superior recall. In an intriguing study, this prediction was, in fact, borne out. Chi (1978) solicited six third- through eighth-grade children from a local chess tournament and compared their recall for legitimate chessboard arrangements with the memory of adult subjects who could play chess to some degree but who were not especially knowledgeable. As shown in Figure 7.11A, children's reproductions on the first trial were far more accurate than those of adults. Even when their initial response was not perfect, the young chess players required fewer repeated recall trials to get the chess configurations completely right (see Figure 7.11B). Chi's striking results cannot be attributed to the selection of an unusual sample of especially bright children with superior memories. On a standard memory span task in which the subjects were asked to recall a list of numerical digits, the adults did better.

In Chi's investigation of chess-playing children, memory differences were largely attributed to differences in *quantity* of knowledge in a specific domain. But the differences may also have been due to the *structure* of knowledge, or the way in which experts versus novices form and interconnect concepts in a particular content area. In another study by Chi and Koeske (1983), the domain-specific knowledge of a 4½-year-old dinosaur enthusiast was studied. Remarkably, his dinosaur knowledge conformed to a hierarchically organized pattern, much like that found among adults. This, as well as other findings, suggests that the basic organization of long-term memory is similar throughout development (Mervis & Crisafi, 1982; Tversky, 1989). Age-related changes seem to be ones of greater differentiation and hierarchical organization as knowledge increases in quantity and becomes more familiar, rather than fundamental revisions in format (Mandler, 1983).

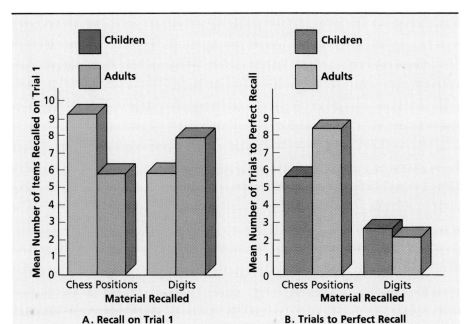

Figure 7.11. Performance of skilled child chess players and adults on two tasks—memory for chessboard arrangements and standard digit span—in the Chi (1978) study. (A) Child chess experts recalled more items on the first trial of the chess task, whereas adults recalled more on the digit span task. (B) Child chess experts required fewer trials to perfect recall on the chess task, whereas adults required fewer on the digit span task. *(Adapted from M. T. H. Chi, 1978.)*

Although knowledge clearly plays a central role in memory development, whether or not it is the only factor involved is still a matter of controversy. Some research indicates that children do not just differ in their available storehouse of information; they also vary in the degree to which they use it to understand and learn new material. Bransford and his colleagues (1981) discovered differences between academically successful and less successful fifth graders in the extent to which they access current knowledge to clarify the significance of new information. In one task, the children were given a written passage describing two different kinds of robots. One (the extendable robot) was used to wash outside windows on two-story houses. The other (the nonextendable robot) was suitable for high-rise apartment buildings. The opening paragraph of the passage provided a brief description of the functions of each robot. Then several additional paragraphs described the robots' properties. For example, the extendable robot was made of heavy steel and had spiked feet that stuck in the ground. The nonextendable robot was light, had suction-cup feet, and was equipped with a parachute in case it should fall. The children had to memorize each robot's characteristics. The academically successful pupils used the information about the robots' functions to understand the meaning of each robot's features, and their recall was exceptionally good. In contrast, even though the same functional knowledge was available to the less successful students, they failed to make use of it in interpreting the significance of the robot characteristics. As a result, they remembered much less.[3]

Bransford believes that failure to approach memory tasks by asking oneself how previously stored information can clarify the meaning of new material may, in the long run, seriously interfere with the development of an adequate knowledge base. Clearly, it restricts the child's opportunity to learn new information. Looked at in this way, inadequate knowledge is not just a cause of memory problems, but an important consequence as well. As Brown and her collaborators (1983) point out, children "vary not only in what they know but also in what they do with what they know. Knowledge

---

[3] Did you use your previously acquired knowledge to process the information in this section more deeply? Notice that what the more successful students did in this study was to engage in *reconstructive processing*. They drew *inferences* about relationships between robot functions and characteristics and then relied on them as retrieval cues when recalling robot properties.

is necessary but not sufficient for performance, for it is the efficiency with which a learner uses whatever is available that defines intelligence" (p. 100).

Young Children's Scripts: Basic Building Blocks of Structured Knowledge. Think back to Chi and Koeske's (1983) investigation of the 4-year-old dinosaur expert that we mentioned earlier. The study provided evidence that young children's semantic knowledge is not fragmented and disorganized. Instead, children seem to form the rudiments of a structured long-term knowledge base at an early age. How do children begin to build a coherent network of knowledge as early as the preschool years, and in what ways does it change with age?

Our vast, intricately organized general knowledge system, which, for purposes of clarity, we now refer to as **semantic memory,** must somehow grow out of the young child's **episodic memory,** or memory for a great many personally experienced events (Tulving, 1972; Posner & Warren, 1972). How semantic memory emerges from a foundation of specific real-world experiences is considered by some researchers to be the quintessential question of memory development (Nelson & Brown, 1978).

Nelson (1986) and her colleagues have explored the nature of young children's episodic memory representations. Like adults, children as young as 3 remember familiar daily experiences in terms of **scripts.** Scripts are organized representations of event sequences that provide a general description of what occurs and when it occurs in a given situation (Schank & Abelson, 1977). An experience coded in script form provides the child with a basic organizing device for interpreting everyday experiences, such as going to nursery school or eating lunch. Scripts that are held in long-term memory can be used to predict what will happen in the future on similar occasions. An example of a script structure, based on the most common actions mentioned by preschoolers about lunchtime at a day care center, is given in Figure 7.12.

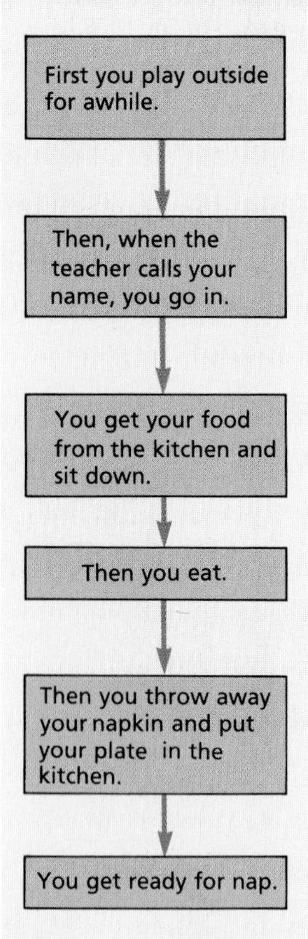

For young preschool children, scripts begin as a very general structure of main acts. For example, when asked to tell what happens when you go to a restaurant, a 3-year-old might say, "You go in, get the food, eat, and then pay." Even though children's first scripts contain few acts, they are almost always recalled in a temporally and causally correct sequence. This is true even for children who are too young to verbally describe scripted events but who act them out with toys (Bauer & Mandler, 1989). With increasing age, children's scripts become more elaborate and complex, as in the following restaurant rendition: "You go in. You can sit in the booths or at a table. Then you tell the waitress what you want. You eat. If you want dessert, you can have some. Then you pay and go home" (Fivush, 1984; McCarthy & Nelson, 1981; Nelson & Gruendel, 1981).

Nelson believes that scripts serve as a basic means through which children organize and interpret their world. For example, young children rely on scripts when listening to and telling stories. They recall more events from stories that are based on familiar event sequences than on unfamiliar ones (Hudson & Nelson, 1983). They also use script structures for the stories they act out in play. Listen carefully to preschoolers' make-believe. You will hear scripts reflected in their dialogues when they pretend to put the baby to bed, go on a trip, or play school (Nelson & Gruendel, 1981).

Nelson regards scripts as the developmental link in the progression from early episodic memory to a mature, semantically organized, long-term memory store (Nelson & Brown, 1978; Nelson & Gruendel, 1981). Objects that share the same function in a script structure provide the basis for the child's early semantic relationships. Lucariello and Nelson (1985) discovered that a list of script-related items (e.g., peanut butter, bologna, cheese [foods often eaten at lunchtime]) was recalled in clustered form and remembered more easily by 3- and 4-year-old children than a typical categorical list (toast, cheese, ice cream [foods]). It appears that relationships among items are first understood in terms of familiar events in which children take part

Figure 7.12. "Lunchtime at the day care center" script. This script is typical of ones generated by children of 5 or 6 years of age. Younger children give scripts that are less detailed and that contain fewer main acts.

First you play outside for awhile.

Then, when the teacher calls your name, you go in.

You get your food from the kitchen and sit down.

Then you eat.

Then you throw away your napkin and put your plate in the kitchen.

You get ready for nap.

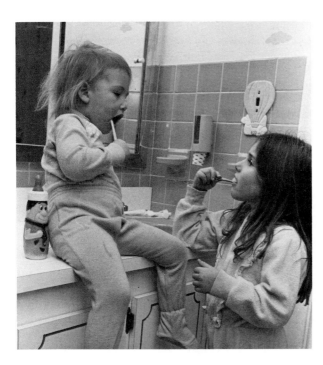

Through repeated experience of daily events, such as brushing teeth before bedtime, young children build mental scripts that help them organize, interpret, and predict their world.

within an organized script framework. Once children develop an array of script sequences, objects that share the same function but occur in different scripts (eating toast for breakfast, peanut butter for lunch) may be joined together under a single, more typical semantic category (food).

A final word about scripts and the development of long-term memory deserves mention. To the extent that any one occasion is like others, it is fused into the same script representation. Consequently, any specific instance of a scripted experience becomes difficult to recall. For example, unless it was out of the ordinary, you probably cannot remember exactly what you had for dinner two days ago. The same is true for young children (Fivush, 1984; Hudson, 1988). The early merging of specific memories with the more general knowledge system is one among several explanations for an intriguing phenomenon called **infantile amnesia**—the fact that practically none of us can retrieve any specific autobiographical events that happened to us before 3 years of age. Nelson and Ross (1980) believe that only after children have formed well-established script sequences can unique experiences stand out from them. This general base of scripted knowledge probably takes the first few years of life to build up.

Age differences in memory processing are at least partly due to changes in the breadth of children's underlying knowledge base. However, the extent to which children spontaneously use their current knowledge to remember information is also important. How our vast, semantically organized storehouse of information evolves from memories of everyday experience is one of the most puzzling questions about memory development. Children's tendency to remember daily events in scripted format is one possible basis for this change.

BRIEF REVIEW

METACOGNITION

In previous sections of this chapter, we made many references to the fact that cognitive processing abilities become more conscious, reflective, and deliberate with age. These trends suggest that another form of knowledge we have not yet considered may have an important bearing on how effectively children can remember and solve problems. **Metacognition** refers to awareness and understanding of our own cognitive processes. Cognitive psychologists believe that to work most effectively, the information processing system must be aware of itself. For example, it needs to be able to arrive at such realizations as: "I had better write that phone number down or I'll forget it." "This paragraph is complicated; I had better read it again to understand the author's point." "I had better try to group these items together in some way if I am going to remember them" (Paris & Lindauer, 1982).

Metacognition can be as wide ranging as the functioning of the information processing system itself. Below we discuss three aspects of metacognitive knowledge: knowledge of self as a cognitive processor, knowledge of strategies, and knowledge of task variables. Once children develop these understandings, they must put them into action while solving a task. They do this through self-regulation — constantly monitoring progress toward a goal, checking outcomes, and redirecting efforts that prove unsuccessful. In the last part of this section, we take up the development of this on-line, continuous monitoring of cognitive activity.

Metacognitive Knowledge

Knowledge of Self as a Cognitive Processor. At what age are children first aware of the existence of their own mental worlds, and how does their understanding change with age? Recent evidence indicates that awareness of mental events appears remarkably early. Such words as "think," "remember," and "pretend" are among the first verbs that young children add to their vocabulary. After age 2½, they use them appropriately to refer to internal states, as when they say, "It's not real, I was just pretending" or "I thought the socks were in the drawer, 'cept they weren't" (Wellman, 1985, p. 176).

Although preschoolers have some understanding of mentality, it is initially rudimentary and incomplete (Miller & Aloise, 1989). Piaget (1930) first suggested that young children have difficulty telling the difference between mental events and external behaviors. Research indicates that they separate these two realms quite well in everyday language, as the examples given above reveal. But when questioned in the laboratory about subtle distinctions between mental terms, young children often confuse mental states with external reality. For example, 4-year-olds define "know" and "remember" as being correct and "guess" and "forget" as being incorrect, regardless of a person's prior knowledge (Miscione et al., 1978; Wellman & Johnson, 1979). Around age 5, children develop a differentiated appreciation of these mental processes. This includes the understanding that saying you "know" something means that you are far more certain of your memory than saying you "think" or "guess" (Moore, Bryant, & Furrow, 1989).

Once children appreciate the existence of an internal cognitive system, when do they recognize that it is a limited-capacity processing device? Even 3- and 4-year-olds understand that noise, lack of interest, and thinking about other things can hinder attentiveness to a task (Miller & Zalenski, 1982). By age 5, most children also realize that their memory is limited — that briefly presented information may be lost, that having to retain information for a long period of time makes memory uncertain, and that at times they do forget (Kreutzer, Leonard, & Flavell, 1975; Wellman, 1978). Nevertheless, elementary school children have a much better understanding of the impact of psychological factors on performance. For example, they recognize that optimal conditions for doing well on a task involve concentrating on it, wanting to do it, and not being tempted by anything else (Miller & Bigi, 1979). They are also aware that mental inferences are an important source of knowledge. In contrast, young children think that all events must be directly observed to be known (Sodian & Wimmer, 1987).

Pillow (1988) and Wellman (1988) sum up children's changing appreciation of their own mental functioning as movement from a passive to an active understanding of the mind in relation to the external world. Preschoolers tend to view the mind as a passive receptacle of information. Consequently, they believe that a person's physical experience with the environment determines mental experience. In contrast, older children regard the mind as an active, constructive agent. They recognize that it selects and transforms information, thereby influencing what and how external events are perceived. Look again at the findings reported above and see whether you can discern this general progression of development.

Knowledge of Strategies and Task Variables. Middle childhood is also the time when children become more conscious of strategies for processing information. By first grade, children recognize systematic visual search as the most effective way to determine which item in an array of similar ones differs from the others (Miller & Bigi, 1979). However, it is not until third grade that knowledge of strategies becomes sophisticated. By this age, children realize that in studying material for later recall, it is helpful to devote most effort to items that you know least well. Moreover, when given a hypothetical memory task, older youngsters can think of many more strategic things to do. Witness the following response of an 8-year-old to the question of what she would do to remember a phone number:

> Say the number is 663-8854. Then what I'd do is — say that my number is 663, so I won't have to remember that, really. And then I would think now I've got to remember 88. Now I'm 8 years old, so I can remember, say, my age two times. Then I say how old my brother is, and how old he was last year. And that's how I'd usually remember that phone number. [Is that how you would most often remember a phone number?] Well, usually I write it down. (Kreutzer, Leonard, & Flavell, 1975, p. 11)

Similarly, older elementary school children have a more differentiated understanding of task variables that affect performance. Kindergartners are aware of some factors that make a memory task easy or hard — for example, the number of items to be learned, their familiarity, the amount of study time available, and whether one is asked to recognize or recall them (Kreutzer, Leonard, & Flavell, 1975; Speer & Flavell, 1979; Wellman, 1977). But during the mid-elementary school years, this understanding is carried much further. By this time, children recognize that a list of semantically related items is easier to remember than a list of unrelated items and that having to recall prose material word for word is more difficult than being asked for a paraphrase (Kreutzer, Leonard, & Flavel, 1975; Tenney, 1975).

Development of a "Naive Theory of Mind." Once children are consciously aware of mental states, strategies, and task variables, they combine this metacognitive knowledge into an integrated understanding of cognition, or what Wellman (1985) calls a "naive theory of mind." Even preschool children are sometimes aware of the simultaneous influence of two variables — for example, that both the amount you must learn and the effort you expend operate jointly to determine mental performance (Wellman, Collins, & Glieberman, 1981). However, older children are far more likely to take account of such interactions. A comprehensive understanding of how many factors — such as age and motivational level of the learner, effective use of strategies, and nature and difficulty of the task — work together is not achieved until well into the elementary school years (Wellman, 1985).

Self-Regulation

Despite growth of metacognitive knowledge over the childhood years, most studies report that it is only weakly related to task performance (e..g., Byrd & Gholson, 1985; Flavell, 1986; Moynahan, 1973). This disappointing finding is due to the fact that a great many factors can intercede between children's knowledge of what to do and the way in which they actually behave when confronted with a problem. Children might know about a strategy but not be good at using it, simply choose to use a different one, think the task is easy enough to do without the strategy, or just not bother to implement it (Flavell & Wellman, 1977; Siegler, 1983b). Still another reason that metacognitive knowledge is only remotely connected to task performance is that younger children are relatively poor at **self-regulation.** They have difficulty using what they know about cognition to continuously monitor their progress toward a goal, and they often continue with an approach when it is obviously ineffective (Brown et al., 1983; Paris & Lindauer, 1982).

Self-regulatory behavior can be assessed by looking at children's sensitivity to how well they understand a spoken or written message. This skill is called **comprehension monitoring.** Markman (1979b) had third, fifth, and sixth graders listen to short essays containing inconsistent information, as in the following passage:

> To make (Baked Alaska) they put ice cream in a very hot oven. The ice cream in Baked Alaska melts when it gets that hot. Then they take the ice cream out of the oven and serve it right away. When they make Baked Alaska the ice cream stays firm and it does not melt. (p. 646)

Children of all grades were poor at noticing such inconsistencies, and similar findings have been reported in other studies of both spoken and written prose (Flavell et al., 1981; Harris et al., 1981). Sixth graders reduce their reading speed and look back through the material to a greater extent than third graders when a text is not clear (Capelli & Markman, 1980; Zabrucky & Ratner, 1986). Younger children sometimes show puzzled facial expressions, although they have trouble verbalizing what is wrong (Flavell et al., 1981). One impediment to young children's self-regulation may be that they have difficulty interpreting their own feelings of uneasiness when they encounter ambiguities that interfere with successful task performance (Brown et al., 1983; Flavell, 1981). Poor readers of all ages are especially deficient in self-regulation. They seldom look forward and backwards to check their understanding as they read (Baker & Brown, 1984).

Current evidence indicates that self-regulation is a late-developing skill. In fact, Piaget (1978) believed that it did not appear in sophisticated form until adolescence. In line with this conclusion, there is evidence that by the adolescent years, metacognitive knowledge and task performance become better related (Waters, 1982; McGivern et al., 1986).

Still, it is possible to facilitate the development of self-regulation. Parents and teachers can help children by promoting conscious awareness of task demands, personal planning, and self-correction. As adults ask children questions and help them monitor their own behavior in circumstances in which they are likely to encounter difficulties, children can internalize these procedures and make them part of their own self-regulatory skills.

Think about these practical suggestions for fostering self-regulation. Do they resemble Vygotsky's theory about the self-guiding role of private speech, which we discussed in Chapter 6? The ideas are much the same, since Vygotsky emphasized that the self-regulatory function of children's speech-to-self has its origins in social dialogues with others. In fact, Vygotsky's theory has been a source of inspiration for research on the effects of *metacognitive training* on children's task performance (Reeve & Brown, 1985). Many studies show that providing children with instructions to check and monitor their progress toward a goal has a substantial effect on how well they do. In addition, training that not only demonstrates an effective strategy, but also informs children of the reasons that the strategy is useful, enhances children's use of it in new situations (Moely et al., 1986). When adults tell children *why* and not just *what* to do, they provide a rationale for future action. Then children learn not just how to get a particular task done, but also what to do when faced with new problems. When adults use such approaches to teach children, as Brown and her colleagues (1983) suggest, they help children "learn how to learn."

Metacognition gradually moves from a passive to an active view of mental functioning as children grasp the impact of a wider array of person, strategy, and task variables. Eventually, children integrate these factors into a coherent view of mental functioning, or a "naive theory of mind." Nevertheless, children's metacognitive understanding shows a disappointingly weak relationship with task performance. One reason is that the ability to apply metacognition in a self-regulatory fashion is not well developed until adolescence. However, younger children can be trained to improve their self-regulatory skills.

APPLICATIONS OF INFORMATION PROCESSING TO ACADEMIC LEARNING

Over the past decade, fundamental discoveries about the development of information processing have been applied to children's mastery of complex academic skills. A rapidly growing literature focuses on learning in different subject matter areas, such as reading, mathematics, and scientific problem solving. Because paths to competence may vary across domains of knowledge, each has been studied separately. Nevertheless, the research has features in common. First, investigators identify the cognitive components that are necessary for skilled performance, try to trace their development, and distinguish good from poor learners by pinpointing the cognitive operations in which they are deficient. Then, using this information, they design instructional procedures to improve children's learning (Glaser, 1988). We turn to a sampling of these efforts in the sections that follow.

Reading

While reading, we execute a large number of skills at once that tax all facets of our information processing systems. Table 7.1 lists the diverse perceptual and cognitive acts that, when put together, result in comprehension, the goal of reading activity. In fact, reading is such a demanding process that skilled performance — extracting meaning while moving fluidly down the printed page — requires highly automated application of all or most separate skills. If one or more skills are insufficiently developed, they will compete for attentional resources in our limited working memories, and performance on the composite task will decline (Frederiksen & Warren, 1987; Perfetti, 1988).

Table 7.1. Cognitive Components of Skilled Reading

LOWER-LEVEL SKILLS
Perceptual encoding of single letters and multiletter combinations
Decoding single letters and multiletter combinations into speech sounds
Sight recognition of high-frequency words, to reduce reliance on time-consuming decoding
Holding chunks of verbatim text in working memory for higher-level processing

HIGHER-LEVEL SKILLS
Locating word referents in long-term memory
Combining word referents into meaningful clauses and sentences
Using prose context to refine word, clause, and sentence meaning
Integrating sentence meanings into higher-order semantic relations
Using previous knowledge to draw inferences about text meaning
Comprehension monitoring to check processing accuracy

Sources: Frederiksen & Warren, 1987; Perfetti, 1988.

Parents who read to their preschoolers provide vital preparation for the complex task of independent reading.

Investigators do not know just how children manage to combine the many components summarized in Table 7.1 into an integrated, functioning whole. If we knew more, we would have clearer answers to questions of how to facilitate reading development. For several decades, a "great debate" has waged among psychologists and educators about how to teach beginning reading. Some advocate a *whole-word method*, sometimes called the "look-say" approach because pupils are taught to read by naming whole printed words and comprehension is emphasized. Others adhere to a *basic skills method*, often referred to as the phonics approach because it stresses rules for decoding graphic symbols into sounds. Yet extensive research comparing these two methods does not show clearcut superiority for either one (Williams, 1979).

At present, our best guess is that children need balanced practice in both lower- and higher-level skills to become expert readers. Learning the basics — relationships between graphic symbols and sounds — enables children to decode new words that they have never seen before. As decoding becomes more automatic, it releases children's attention to the higher-level activities involved in grasping the text's meaning (Frederiksen & Warren, 1987). However, if practice in basic skills is overemphasized, children may lose sight of the fact that the ultimate goal of reading is understanding. Many teachers report cases of pupils who can decode fluently (as indicated by the way they read aloud) but who register little or no meaning. In line with these observations, research indicates that by fourth grade, decoding ability is a poor predictor of text comprehension (Walczyk, 1990). This suggests that effective reading may demand only a certain threshold of facility with lower-level skills. By mid-elementary school, all but the very poorest readers have crossed that threshold. For most older pupils, instruction that emphasizes strategic detection of prose meaning — how to skim, draw inferences, summarize, and engage in comprehension monitoring — appears to be most effective (Paris, Saarnio, & Cross, 1986).

Reading builds on a broad foundation of spoken language and general knowledge about the world. Parents who converse with their children, take them on outings, and frequently read to them have youngsters who arrive at school with a rich appreciation of story structure and content that eases the difficulty of early text processing. Cultural background also affects children's understanding of the written word (Hall, 1989). In recent years, authors of beginning readers have made a concerted effort to provide materials that draw from the experiences of culturally different youngsters. Because this enhances children's access to text meaning, it increases their motivation to learn to read.

Mathematics

Mathematical reasoning, like reading, builds on a foundation of informally acquired knowledge. Using the habituation-dishabituation paradigm, Starkey, Spelke, and Gelman (in press) showed that 6-month-old babies can discriminate the numerosity of small sets. They even recognize the same quantity when it is presented in different sensory modalities (e.g., vision and sound).

In the early preschool period, children start to attach verbal labels (such as lots, little, big, small) to discriminations of amounts and sizes. Between the ages of 2 and 3, many children begin to count. However, at first, counting is little more than a memorized routine. Often numbers are recited in an undifferentiated string, like this: "Onetwothreefourfivesix!" Or children repeat a few number words while vaguely pointing in the direction of objects that they have seen others count (Fuson, 1988).

Very soon, however, counting strategies become more precise. By age 3, most children have established an accurate one-to-one correspondence between a short sequence of number words and the items they represent (Fuson, 1988; Gelman & Gallistel, 1986). Some time between 3 and 4 years of age, they grasp the vital principle of *cardinality*. They understand that the last word in a counting sequence indicates the quantity of items in the set. They also know that if two groups of objects match up (e.g., every jar has its own spoon or every doll its own cup), then each set contains the same number of items (Becker, 1989; Fuson, 1988; Sophian, 1988).[4]

Mastery of cardinality quickly permits children's counting strategies to become more efficient. By the late preschool years, children no longer need to start a counting sequence with the number "one." Instead, knowing that there are six items in one pile and some additional ones in another, they begin with the number "six" and *count up* to determine the total quantity. Eventually, they generalize this strategy and *count down* to find out how many items remain after some are taken away. Once these procedures are mastered, children start to manipulate numbers without requiring that countable objects be physically present (Fuson, 1988). At this point, counting on fingers becomes an intermediate step on the way to automatic performance of basic arithmetic operations. By age 8 or 9, children naturally apply their additive understanding to multiplication, first approaching it as a kind of repeated addition (Nesher, 1988).

Cross-cultural evidence suggests that the arithmetic knowledge described above emerges universally around the world (Resnick, 1989; Saxe, Guberman, & Gearhart, 1987). However, children may acquire it at different rates, depending on the extent to which informal counting experiences are prevalent in their everyday lives (Fuson, 1988). In homes and preschools where adults provide many occasions and requests for quantification, children probably construct these basic understandings sooner. Then they are solidly available as supports for the wide variety of mathematical skills that are taught in school.

---

[4] As Piaget's conservation of number task indicates, at first, preschoolers' understanding of cardinality is fragile. It is easily overcome by the appearance of a set of objects. However, the evidence reviewed above clearly indicates that young children understand much more about numbers than Piaget gave them credit for.

Counting on fingers is an early, spontaneous strategy children use to master basic arithmetic operations.

Variants and extensions of this natural appreciation of number form the core of the elementary and junior high school mathematics curriculum. Yet once in school, some pupils experience difficulties with more complicated skills, such as carrying in addition, borrowing in subtraction, and operating with decimals and fractions. Often these youngsters apply a systematic routine that is close to what they have been taught but that yields a wrong answer. Their mistakes indicate that they have tried to memorize a method, but they do not understand the basis for it (Resnick, 1987). For example, look at the following subtraction errors:

$$
\begin{array}{r}
4\ 2\ 7 \\
-1\ 3\ 8 \\
\hline
3\ 1\ 1
\end{array}
\qquad
\begin{array}{r}
\overset{6}{\not{7}}\ 0\ 0_1\ 2 \\
-5\ 4\ 4\ 5 \\
\hline
1\ 4\ 4\ 7
\end{array}
$$

In the first problem, the child consistently subtracts a smaller from a larger digit, regardless of which is on top. In the second, columns with zeros are repeatedly skipped in a borrowing operation, and whenever there is a zero on top, the bottom digit is written as the answer. Several investigators believe that drill-oriented math instruction that discourages children from using their naturally acquired counting methods to grasp the principles behind new skills is at the heart of these difficulties (Fuson, 1988; Resnick, 1989).

In fact, arguments about how to teach arithmetic closely resemble the positions that we discussed earlier in the area of reading. Extensive speeded practice in basic number combinations to promote automaticity of retrieval is pitted against "number sense" or understanding. Further research is likely to show that some blend of these two aspects of instruction is most beneficial. In the meantime, cross-cultural evidence indicates that American math education may have gone too far in emphasizing computational drill over numerical reasoning. As we will see in Chapter 15, Japanese and Chinese children are ahead of American pupils in mathematical development at all levels of schooling. In Asian classrooms, considerably more time is spent exploring underlying principles and much less on drill and repetition (Stigler & Baranes, in press).

Scientific Problem Solving

Robert Siegler's **rule-assessment approach** is one of the most extensive efforts to trace the development of children's scientific problem solving from an information processing perspective. Recall from Chapter 6 that many Piagetian tasks are drawn from the domain of physical science. Siegler has restudied them, offering a precise analysis of children's strategy use that is designed to compete with Piaget's stage-wise description. According to Siegler, development involves the acquisition of increasingly sophisticated rules, or cognitive procedures for arriving at solutions, that permit children to succeed on a wider array of task items (Siegler, 1981, 1983a, 1983b).

In the best known of Siegler's investigations, children ranging in age from 3 to 17 were shown a balance scale with four pegs on each side of a fulcrum, much like one of Piaget's formal operational tasks (Siegler, 1976, 1978). Weights were placed on a single peg on each side of the scale. On some trials, the total weight on each side was equal, while on others it was unequal. In addition, sometimes the distances of the weights from the fulcrum were the same, and sometimes they differed. Each time, the child was asked to indicate whether the scale would balance or not. Results showed that 3-year-olds answered randomly; they used no systematic procedures at all. But from the late preschool period on, four different developmentally ordered rules were used, each of which predicted a particular pattern of response across balance scale problems (see Figure 7.13):

Rule I: Four- to 6-year-olds took into account only the number of weights on each side of the fulcrum, ignoring distance. If the number of weights was equal, they predicted that the scale would balance. If it was not equal, they predicted that it would not balance.

Rule II: By the mid-elementary school years, many children had modified Rule 1 slightly. They continued to focus only on weight, except when the weights on both sides were equal. Under this circumstance, they predicted that the scale would balance if the two distances were equal. If they were not, children predicted that the scale would not balance.

Rule III: Adolescents considered both weight and distance. If one dimension was equal and the other was not, they based their decision on the unequal dimension. However, if both dimensions were unequal, they had no rule for integrating the information and merely guessed.

Rule IV: Very few subjects used this rule. It involves the principle of torque: only when the product of weight $\times$ distance on both sides of the scale is equal will the scale balance.

Further research by Siegler showed that feedback to children about whether they were correct or not led many of them to use more advanced rules. However, some children profited from this information more than others. For example 8-year-olds who used Rule I generally advanced to Rule II or Rule III, but many 5-year olds did not change at all. Siegler observed that younger Rule I users failed to notice the distance of weights from the fulcrum. When trained to encode distance, they quickly improved their rule-governed solutions (Siegler, 1976). Inadequate encoding also explained the absence of rule use in many preschoolers, who did not notice weight. When trained to detect it, they used Rule I quite effectively. Similarly, 13- and 17-year-olds grasped

Problem Type	RULE			
	I	II	III	IV
1. Equal weight-equal distance 	100%	100%	100%	100%
2. Unequal weight-equal distance 	100%	100%	100%	100%
3. Unequal distance-equal weight 	0% should say "Balance"	100%	100%	100%
4. Conflict-weight (more weight on one side, more distance on the other, configuration arranged so side with more weight goes down) 	100%	100%	33% (chance responding)	100%
5. Conflict-distance (similar to conflict-weight, but side with greater distance goes down) 	0% should say "Right side down"	0% should say "Right side down"	33% (chance responding)	100%
6. Conflict-balance (like the above two problems, except the scale remains balanced) 	0% should say "Right side down"	0% should say "Right side down"	33% (chance responding)	100%

Figure 7.13. Percentage of correct responses expected on Siegler's (1978) balance scale problems for children using different rules. For each problem type, children are asked to indicate whether they think the scale will balance or whether the right or left side will go down. *(From "The Origins of Scientific Reasoning" by R. S. Siegler. In R. S. Siegler [Ed.], Children's Thinking: What Develops? [pp. 104–149]. Hillsdale NJ: Erlbaum. Copyright 1978 by Lawrence Erlbaum Associates. Adapted by permission.)*

Rule IV when given aids that were designed to facilitate discovery of the torque principle (Siegler, 1978). Siegler's approach shows that children profit most from instruction that responds to specific inadequacies in their current knowledge. When children lack detailed knowledge, they rely on what Siegler calls *fallback rules*— approaches that focus on only a single obvious dimension of a situation, such as the Rule I preoccupation with weight described above.[5]

---

[5] Notice how similar Siegler's notion of fallback rules is to Piaget's preoperational characteristic of centration, described in Chapter 6. However, unlike Piaget, Siegler does not regard this tendency to focus on a single aspect of a problem as an inherent property of young children's mental organization. Instead, he views it as a temporary strategy that both children and adults use when they have limited knowledge about a task.

Siegler believes that extending his rule-assessment approach to other domains could lead to a general model of how children of different ages solve problems. Can all of children's problem solving be captured in this way? A number of investigators think not. Some critics suggest that it may apply only to highly structured tasks (Strauss & Levin, 1981). Siegler himself acknowledges that numerous tasks with varying characteristics will need to be studied to build a comprehensive theory of problem-solving development. Nevertheless, his research is a promising start, and it has already generated precise and useful suggestions for education.

EVALUATION OF THE INFORMATION PROCESSING APPROACH TO COGNITIVE DEVELOPMENT

The major strength of information processing is its explicitness and precision in breaking down cognitive performance into a set of distinct, sequentially operating processes. The information processing approach has been successful in generating detailed descriptions of how younger versus older and more skilled versus less skilled individuals perceive, attend, memorize, and solve problems. As information processing continues to generate a multifaceted picture of cognitive development, its investigators have also pressed for a more precise description of how cognitive change takes place than is offered by Piaget's theory (Kuhn, 1988; Siegler, 1988; Sternberg, 1988). Moreover, information processing has underscored the conclusion that many aspects of cognitive development are domain-specific. Few general statements can be made about how children think without specifying the nature of their task environments. Finally, the most recent contribution of information processing has been to the understanding of academic learning and to the design of instructional programs that enhance children's school performance.

Nevertheless, the information processing perspective has a number of limitations that prevent it from serving as a completely adequate account of cognitive development. The first, ironically, stems from its central strength: by breaking cognition down into its components, information processing has had difficulty integrating all the elements into a broad, comprehensive theory. For this reason, there are still many child development specialists who resist abandoning Piaget's view in favor of it. In fact, efforts to build general theories of development within an information processing framework, such as Case's M-space and Fischer's skill theory, have succeeded only by retaining essential features of Piaget's system.

In addition, the computer metaphor, although bringing exactitude and precision to research on the workings of the human mind, has its own inherent limitations. Models of cognitive processing that are based on the computer analogy, while complex in their own right, do not mirror the richness of many real-life learning situations. For example, they tell us little about some facets of cognition that are not linear, logical, and unidirectional in nature, such as daydreaming and creative imagination (Greeno, 1989). In addition, computers cannot feel, and they do not have self-generated goals and intentions. While they can interact with other machines through phone lines and modems, computers do not make friends, develop affectional ties, take another person's perspective, or adopt moral and social values. Perhaps because of the narrowness of the computer metaphor, information processing has not yet told us much about the links between cognition and other areas of development, such as emotion, motivation, and social functioning. Currently, child development specialists are intensely interested in whether information processing can enhance our understanding of how children think about their social world. We will see a few examples of this new emphasis in later chapters of this book. However, it is still the case that extensions of Piaget's work prevail when it comes to research on children's social cognition and moral thought.

Despite its deficiencies, the information processing approach holds considerable promise for the future. New breakthroughs in specifying mechanisms of cognitive change, understanding the processing capacities of infants and toddlers (who at this time remain understudied), and expanding our knowledge of how children master academic skills are likely to take place in the decade to come.

CHAPTER SUMMARY

The Information Processing Approach

■ Information processing rose to the forefront of the field as the result of dissatisfaction with both Piagetian and behaviorist perspectives. The approach views the mind as a complex, symbol-manipulating system, much like a digital computer. The computer metaphor helps investigators analyze thought into separate components that can be studied individually to yield a detailed understanding of what children and adults do when faced with a task or problem.

Major Models of the Information Processing System

■ General models of human information processing include the store and levels of processing approaches. Atkinson and Shiffrin's **store model** assumes that information travels through a sequence of finite-capacity units, where **control processes,** or **strategies,** operate on it so that it can be retained and used efficiently. The **serial position effect** supports Atkinson and Shiffrin's distinction between **short-** and **long-term memory.** However, variable findings on the capacities of the stores have led some investigators to turn toward a levels of processing approach.

■ The **levels of processing model** assumes that memory is a function of the depth to which an incoming stimulus is analyzed. Instead of a fixed-capacity store, levels of processing theorists attribute the limited capacity of **working memory** entirely to attentional resources. With age, cognitive operations become more automatic and efficient because of practice and improved use of strategies. As a result, attention is freed for other concurrent activities.

■ Case's **M-space** and Fischer's **skill theory** are among the few uniquely developmental models of information processing. Both reinterpret Piaget's stages and the phenomenon of horizontal décalage within an information processing framework. Case views age-related increases in working memory as due to automaticity of Piagetian schemes. Fischer believes that working memory expands as increments in optimal skill level (which correspond to Piaget's stages) lead to more efficient cognitive activity.

Sensory Processing

■ The major perspective on sensory processing is **differentiation theory,** which views development as the detection of increasingly fine-grained distinctions among stimuli. Dif-

ferentiation theory helps explain the way in which children discriminate written symbols as they learn to read. **Enrichment theory,** a competing approach to sensory processing, emphasizes the application of cognitive schemes to the interpretation of stimulus events.

Attentional Processing

■ With age, children's allocation of attention becomes more controlled and sustained as well as planful and systematic. Also, older children are better able to adapt attentional resources to task demands and increments in their own learning.

Short-Term Memory

■ Strategies for storing discrete pieces of information are rarely seen in preschool children. Although young children can be trained to use strategies, without continued adult prompting, they quickly abandon them. During middle childhood, children use **rehearsal** and **organization** spontaneously and with greater effectiveness. **Elaboration** is a late-developing memory strategy that typically does not appear until adolescence. Home and school learning experiences affect the use of deliberate memorization.

Long-Term Memory

■ **Recognition** is the simplest form of memory retrieval, and by the early preschool years, it is very accurate. In comparison, young children's **recall** is poorly developed. Recall gradually improves as children encode information in a more organized fashion. Even young children **reconstruct** complex meaningful material when remembering it. During elementary school, children become better at drawing inferences from prose material.

■ Some investigators believe that cognitive development is largely a matter of the acquisition of **domain-specific knowledge** that renders new information more familiar and easier to store and retrieve. However, children differ not only in how much they know, but also in how effectively they use their knowledge to clarify the meaning of new information.

■ Like adults, young children remember repeated experiences in terms of **scripts,** general descriptions of what occurs and when it will occur in a given situation. Scripts may be the intermediate link in the transition from **episodic** to **semantic memory.**

Metacognition

■ Children's **metacognition**—conscious knowledge of self, strategies, and task variables—changes from a passive to an active view of mental functioning as children enter middle childhood. However, metacognitive knowledge bears only a weak relationship to performance, probably because young children are relatively poor at **self-regulation**—using what they know to monitor their task-related behavior.

Applications of Information Processing to Academic Learning

■ Skilled reading requires simultaneous performance of many lower- and higher-level cognitive skills. Beginning readers profit from instruction in both sets of components. By mid-elementary school, most youngsters have mastered the basics, and teaching that emphasizes comprehension seems to be most effective.

■ Children construct a variety of basic mathematical concepts and counting strategies during the preschool years. Fail-ure to make use of their informally acquired knowledge and an overemphasis on drill at the expense of understanding may limit children's mathematical development in school.

■ Examining children's patterns of performance on scientific tasks, Siegler concludes that development involves the acquisition of more broadly applicable **rules** for solving problems. Siegler finds that poor encoding is a major obstacle to better problem-solving performance.

Evaluation of the Information Processing Approach to Cognitive Development

■ A major strength of the information processing approach is its explicitness and precision in conceptualizing mental functioning. As yet, information processing has not led to a broad, integrative theory of cognitive growth. Nor has it shed much light on how cognitive processing is related to other facets of psychological development.

IMPORTANT TERMS AND CONCEPTS

black box model   (p. 254)
reversal and nonreversal
   learning   (p. 254)
mediational theory   (p. 255)
store model   (p. 256)
control processes or
   strategies   (p. 257)
memory span   (p. 257)
sensory register   (p. 257)
short-term memory store   (p. 257)
long-term memory store   (p. 258)
serial position effect   (p. 258)

levels of processing model   (p. 259)
working memory   (p. 260)
M-space   (p. 262)
skill theory   (p. 262)
differentiation theory   (p. 264)
enrichment theory   (p. 266)
incidental learning   (p. 267)
rehearsal   (p. 271)
production deficiency   (p. 271)
control deficiency   (p. 271)
organization   (p. 272)
elaboration   (p. 274)

recognition   (p. 276)
recall   (p. 277)
reconstruction   (p. 278)
domain-specific knowledge   (p. 280)
semantic memory   (p. 282)
episodic memory   (p. 282)
scripts   (p. 282)
infantile amnesia   (p. 283)
metacognition   (p. 284)
self-regulation   (p. 286)
comprehension monitoring   (p. 286)
rule-assessment approach   (p. 291)

The Verandah, by Edgard Wiethase.
Whitford and Hughes, London/Bridgeman Art Library.

8

Intelligence:
A Psychometric Perspective

The psychometric or measurement approach to children's development serves as the basis for the wide variety of intelligence tests currently available for the assessment of children. As we will see shortly, in recent years, the content of some mental tests has been influenced by the Piagetian and information processing perspectives, which we discussed in Chapters 6 and 7. However, when compared to these other two views, the psychometric perspective is far more "product-oriented" than "process-oriented" in its approach to intellectual development. In other words, it focuses on outcomes and results—*how many* and *what kinds* of questions children can answer correctly at different ages. It places less emphasis on *how* children arrive at solutions to problems at various points in development. Psychometricians pose such questions as: What factors or dimensions make up intelligence, and how do they change with age? How can intellectual development be measured quantitatively so that scores are useful for predicting school achievement, career attainment, and other aspects of intellectual success? To what extent do children of the same age differ in intelligence, and what factors explain these differences?

We begin our consideration of the psychometric perspective by reviewing historical and current definitions of intelligence. After discussing how IQ scores are computed and distributed in the population and describing some commonly used intelligence tests, we turn to research on the stability of the IQ score and how effectively it predicts scholastic performance and later life success and satisfaction. Racial/ethnic and social class differences are at the heart of the IQ nature-nurture debate waged over the course of this century. Our discussion continues with a consideration of genetic and environmental determinants of IQ, as well as the controversial issue of whether intelligence tests are biased against ethnic minority children. Finally, we move "beyond IQ" to consider the development of creativity. Although creativity is among the most highly valued of human attributes, it is one mental ability that is not represented on current intelligence tests for children.

DEFINITIONS OF INTELLIGENCE

Take a moment to jot down a list of behaviors that you regard as typical of people who are highly intelligent. Did you come up with just one or two attributes or a great many? Sternberg and his co-workers (Sternberg et al., 1981; Sternberg, 1982) asked nearly 500 laypeople to complete a similar exercise. He found that most people have very definite notions of what intelligence is and that their ideas are surprisingly similar to the views of experts. Psychometricians and laypeople alike typically regard "intelligence" as a complex construct made up of practical problem solving, verbal ability, and social competence. These findings indicate that most people do not consider a single dimension as adequate for describing intelligence. Instead, their definitions incorporate a variety of attributes.

The problem of defining children's intelligence is especially complicated because behaviors judged to reflect intelligent behavior change with age. In a study similar to the one described above, Siegler and Richards (1980) asked students in an introductory psychology course to list five traits they thought characterized intelligent 6-month-olds, 2-year-olds, 10-year-olds, and adults. As shown in Table 8.1, common descriptors of intelligent behavior differed from one developmental period to another, in much the same fashion as Piaget suggested intelligence changes over the course of childhood. For example, with age, problem solving and reasoning became more important as intelligent characteristics, and sensorimotor responsiveness became less so. Furthermore, beyond infancy, respondents stressed verbal and symbolic knowledge as the major basis of intelligence, an emphasis that fits with both the Piagetian and information processing views. The investigators also asked students to estimate correlations among the traits mentioned at each age. Students thought there would be some close connections between different mental abilities, but they predicted considerable distinctiveness as well. In the sections that follow, you will see that the

Table 8.1. Five Traits Most Frequently Mentioned by College Students as Characterizing Intelligence at Different Ages

6-MONTH-OLDS	2-YEAR-OLDS	10-YEAR-OLDS	ADULTS
1. Recognition of people and objects	1. Verbal ability	1. Verbal ability	1. Reasoning
2. Motor coordination	2. Learning ability	2,3,4. Learning ability; problem solving; reasoning (all three tied)	2. Verbal ability
3. Alertness	3. Awareness of people and environment		3. Problem solving
4. Awareness of environment	4. Motor coordination		4. Learning ability
5. Verbalization	5. Curiosity	5. Creativity	5. Creativity

Source: R. S. Siegler & D. D. Richards, 1980. *College Students' Prototypes of Children's Intelligence.* Paper presented at the annual meeting of the American Psychological Association, New York. Adapted by permission of the author.

evolution of scientific theories reveals this same tension between a view of intelligence as a single, overarching characteristic versus a collection of only loosely related cognitive skills.

Early Conceptions of Intelligence

Foundations of the Intelligence Testing Movement. From the end of the nineteenth century to the middle of the twentieth century, the mental testing movement evolved from crude beginnings to an advanced state of development. The rise of mental testing was stimulated by the intellectual, social, and educational climate of this time period. During the latter part of the nineteenth century, Darwin's theory of evolution helped draw the attention of behavioral scientists to individual differences (which at that time were presumed to be largely hereditary) in people's ability to adapt to the demands of a newly industrialized society. The initiation of universal public education in Europe and the United States by the early 1900s opened the schoolhouse doors to children of all social classes, not just society's privileged. As a result, new methods were needed to identify pupils who could not profit from regular classroom instruction. Moreover, the emergence of mental testing coincided with a major war that brought with it the enormous practical problem of selecting and training millions of men for military combat. By the beginning of World War I, test construction had progressed far enough that psychologists were able to apply the new methodology to this mass selection effort (Carroll, 1982).

Sir Francis Galton and James McKeen Cattell. The British psychologist and statistician Sir Francis Galton (1883) and the American psychologist James McKeen Cattell (1890) can be credited with inventing the first mental tests. But like others before the turn of the century, they adhered to a crude conception of intelligence, believing that it could be revealed by simple tests of sensory acuity and speed of reaction. Intelligence test items, such as reaction time to sound and time for naming colors, were chosen to reflect the ability of the nervous system to respond sensitively and quickly. However, these measures proved to have little practical utility. They were poor

By the early 1900s, universal public education had become prevalent in Europe and the United States. Intelligence tests responded to a new need for ways to identify children who could not profit from regular classroom instruction.

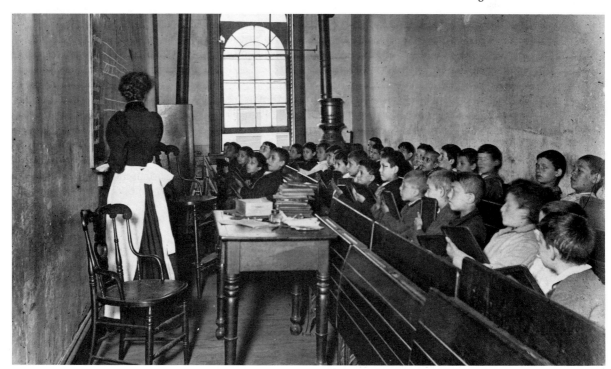

indicators of everyday mental functioning, and they bore no relationship to academic achievement (Wissler, 1901).

Alfred Binet. In the early 1900s, the French psychologist Alfred Binet and his colleague Theodore Simon discovered the first effective way to measure intelligence. Binet's approach was motivated by the challenging task of recommending to the French Minister of Public Instruction a method for identifying Parisian schoolchildren who could not benefit from regular classroom experiences and needed special instruction. Binet concluded that instead of measures of sensory acuity and reaction time, test items resembling the mental activities of everyday life were needed. Believing that intelligence involved sophisticated mental powers of memory, good judgment, and abstraction, he devised a test of "general mental ability" that included a diverse array of complex verbal and nonverbal reasoning tasks. Binet's test was also the first *developmental* approach to test construction. The criterion for including an item on the test was that it had to show a consistent increase in performance with age.

The Binet test proved to be so successful in predicting school achievement that it became the basis for new intelligence tests developed in other countries. In 1916, it was adapted for use with American schoolchildren by Louis Terman at Stanford University. Since then, its American version has been known as the Stanford-Binet Intelligence Scale. The Stanford-Binet has undergone several revisions over the course of this century, but the content of the current test still reflects Binet's original scale.

Alfred Binet (1857–1911) devised the first effective measure of intelligence. His test of "general mental ability" was the first to successfully predict children's school performance.

From Individual to Group Testing. Binet's instrument was designed to be administered individually, but psychologists soon realized that many of its items could be adapted for more efficient group testing. One of the first group tests developed was the Army Alpha Examination, given during World War I to more than a million U.S. army recruits to aid in their selection and rejection. Early trials revealed a surprisingly high rate of illiteracy in the recruit population. As a result, the new group testing approach was attended to by educators, who felt that it might help teachers assess the learning capacities of their pupils. A flood of group intelligence tests soon appeared that imitated the format of the army examination, bringing the concept of intelligence into widespread usage (Carroll, 1982).

Currently, a wide variety of group intelligence tests are available for use in schools. These mass testing instruments permit the simultaneous examination of large numbers of children and require little training of teacher-examiners (Anastasi, 1988). However, most intelligence tests that enter into important educational decisions, such as placement of children in special education programs, are individually administered and demand considerable training and experience to give well. In contrast to group tests, individual tests permit an in-depth diagnosis by a skilled examiner who not only considers the child's answers, but also makes clinical observations of the child's functioning during the test, such as attentiveness to and interest in the tasks. The examiner also looks for evidence of certain internal states, such as anxiety or wariness of the tester, that might lead the results to underestimate the child's ability. This information is combined with additional data on the child's cultural and educational background when the test scores are interpreted (Kaufman, 1979).

Because group tests do not permit the gathering of such clinical evidence, they involve a greater risk of error than do individual tests. Consequently, their practical usefulness is limited to instructional planning for large groups and *screening*, or the identification of children who require more extensive evaluation with individually administered tests. In recent years, heightened sensitivity to the limitations of group tests has led their designers to no longer refer to them as tests of "intelligence" or "mental ability." Instead, they are given less assuming names, such as "academic aptitude," "scholastic aptitude," "school ability," or "cognitive abilities" (Lennon, 1985).

Toward Clearer Definitions: The Early Factor Analysts. The efforts of Binet and others during the early period of the mental testing movement were oriented toward a holistic appraisal of intelligence. A single score was used to measure overall ability (Guilford, 1985). However, as shown in Figure 8.1, a wide variety of tasks appear on typical intelligence tests. Consequently, psychologists seeking clearer definitions of intelligence had to face the important issue of whether it really was an all-inclusive entity that could be represented by a single score or a collection of many different abilities.

To resolve the dilemma, researchers began to carefully study the performances of individuals on intelligence tests. The statistical technique of **factor analysis** was used early on as a tool for identifying various types of intelligence. Factor analysis is a complicated correlational procedure whereby scores on many separate test items are combined together into just a few factors, which substitute for the separate scores. Then the investigator gives each of the factors a name, based on the common characteristics of items that are closely correlated with the factor. For example, if vocabulary, verbal comprehension, and verbal analogies items all correlate highly with the same factor, it might be labeled "verbal ability." Using this technique, many efforts were made to identify the underlying mental abilities that account for successful performance on intelligence tests.

Charles Spearman's "General Factor." An early influential factor analyst was British psychologist Charles Spearman (1927). Spearman found that all the test items he examined correlated to a greater or lesser extent with one another. He therefore proposed that they had in common an underlying **general factor,** or what he termed "**g.**" In addition, since the test items were not perfectly correlated, Spearman suggested that each also measured a **specific factor,** called "**s,**" which was unique to the task. Spearman's identification of "g" and "s" led his theory of mental abilities to be called the *two-factor theory of intelligence.*

Spearman was especially interested in the psychological nature of "g," or whatever it is that produces positive correlations among all mental test scores. With further study, he concluded that "g" represented some kind of abstract reasoning power. Intelligence test problems requiring individuals to extract relationships and apply general principles seemed to be the strongest correlates of "g," and they also offered the best prediction of intellectual performance outside the test situation.

Later in his research, Spearman discovered something that contradicted his earlier two-factor view. He found that some subsets of test items correlated more highly with one another than they did with other items. This finding led him to add to his theory a set of **group factors** (such as verbal, visual, and numerical abilities) that were of moderate degrees of generality, in addition to "g" and "s." Out of these results emerged a new view of intelligence as a set of hierarchically structured abilities. Still, from Spearman's point of view, "g" was central and supreme. Today, the existence of a general factor underlying a wide variety of separate mental abilities is accepted by a great many (but not all) psychometric experts.

Louis Thurstone's "Primary Mental Abilities." Louis Thurstone, an American contemporary of Spearman, did not originally view intelligence as unitary. Instead, he saw it as a multidimensional construct. Thurstone gave 50 intelligence tests to a large number of college students, analyses of which yielded seven clear factors. He concluded that intelligence was composed of seven distinct **primary mental abilities:** verbal meaning, perceptual speed, reasoning, number, rote memory, word fluency, and a spatial or visualization factor. With further research, Thurstone found that his primary mental abilities correlated moderately with one another, and he eventually acknowledged the existence of "g."

Spearman's and Thurstone's respective findings are generally taken to represent two different schools of thought about intelligence, the first stressing one general ability tapped by all tests, the other emphasizing that there are numerous indepen-

Item Type	TYPICAL VERBAL ITEMS
Vocabulary	Tell me what "carpet" means.
General Information	How many ounces make a pound? What day of the week comes right after Thursday?
Verbal Comprehension	Why are policemen needed?
Verbal Analogies	A rock is hard; a pillow is _____ .
Logical Reasoning	Five girls are sitting side by side on a bench. Jane is in the middle and Betty sits next to her on the right. Alice is beside Betty, and Dale is beside Ellen, who sits next to Jane. Who are sitting on the ends?
Number Series	Which number comes next in the series? **4 8 6 12 10** ____

TYPICAL NONVERBAL ITEMS

Picture Oddities	Which picture does not belong with the others?

Spatial Visualization	Which of the boxes on the right can be made from the pattern shown on the left?

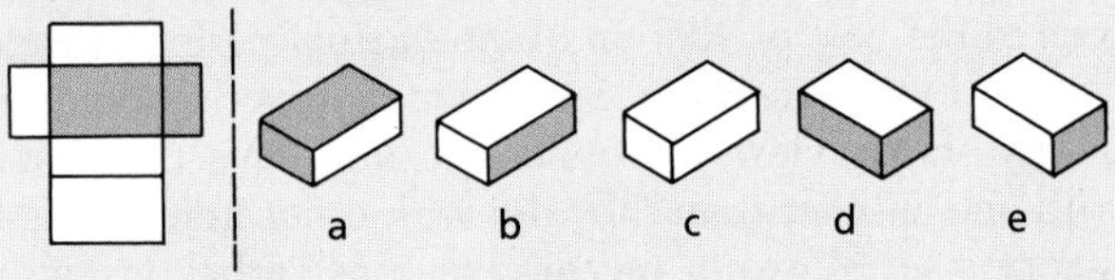

Figure 8.1. Sample intelligence test items appropriate for children of different ages. The items are similar, but not identical, to ones that appear on common individually and group-administered tests. In contrast to verbal items, nonverbal items do not require reading or direct use of language. Performance items are also nonverbal, but they require the individual to draw or construct something rather than merely give a correct answer. As a result, they appear only on individually administered intelligence tests. *(Logical reasoning, picture oddities, spatial visualization, and figure matrices examples are adapted with permission of The Free Press, a Division of Macmillan, Inc. from* Bias in Mental Testing *by Arthur R. Jensen. Pp. 150, 154, 157, 160. Copyright © 1980 by Arthur R. Jensen.)*

dent abilities. In actuality, each view is supported by research and accounts for part of the story. Still, Thurstone's work underlined the notion that intelligence tests were mixtures of very diverse mental tasks. A single, composite score, he believed, could conceal important information about a child's intellectual strengths and weaknesses (Carroll, 1982).

The Modern Factor Analysts

J. P. Guilford's "Structure-of-Intellect" Model. Modern mental ability theorists follow in the tradition of the early factor analysts. One of the most prominent is J. P. Guilford (1967, 1985), who proposes a complex, three-dimensional **structure-of-intellect model** (see Figure 8.2). In the model, mental activity is classified along three dimensions: (1) its mental operation, (2) its contents, and (3) the product resulting from the mental operation. For example, a common memory span task in which a

Figure Matrices   Which pattern fills the blank space?

TYPICAL PERFORMANCE ITEMS

Picture Series   Put the pictures in the right order so
that what is happening makes sense.

Puzzles   Put these pieces together so they make a wagon.

child is asked to remember a list of numbers would be classified as memory (operation), symbolic (content), and units (product). A test that asks a child to decide which of a set of words belong to the same class (e.g., jacket, socks, tie, pencil) involves evaluation (operation), semantic (content), and classes (product). The structure-of-intellect model generates a total of 150 separate ability factors.

Unusual features of Guilford's model include a "behavioral" content category, which is responsive to the idea that a separate "social intelligence" exists, involving sensitivity to the mental states of others. In addition, Guilford added tests of creative thinking to his factor analytic studies, recognizing that items of this type were conspicuously absent from standard intelligence tests. According to Guilford (1950), one mental operation that is centrally involved in creative thinking is *divergent production*, which involves fluent generation of a wide variety of alternatives to meet a particular need (e.g., Think of as many meanings for the word "bolt" as you can). It can be contrasted with the noncreative type of thinking involved in *convergent*

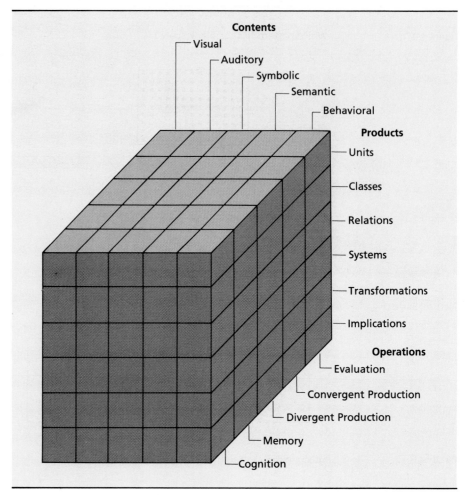

Figure 8.2. Guilford's structure-of-intellect model. *(From J. P. Guilford, 1985, "The Structure-of-Intellect Model." In B. B. Wolman [Ed.],* Handbook of Intelligence. *Copyright © 1985 by John Wiley & Sons, Inc. Reprinted by permission of John Wiley & Sons, Inc.)*

production, in which we are asked to converge on or arrive at a single best answer (e.g., "Bolt" most nearly means: [a] to paint, [b] to sing, [c] to run, [d] to hang). Guilford also conjectured that creative thinking is flexible thinking. It requires a ready ability to switch categories of thought, an aspect represented by the product category *tranformations.* As we will see later when we discuss the development of creativity, test materials commonly used to assess it are based on Guilford's ideas.

Although Guilford's model of mental abilities is the most comprehensive available, many psychologists have questioned his extensive proliferation of mental factors beyond the seven originally identified by Thurstone. Studies providing support for the structure-of-intellect model have been criticized on methodological grounds (Horn & Knapp, 1974). Investigators have also raised such issues as: "Do the factors really correspond to the nature of human mental life?" "To what extent is each of Guilford's mental abilities important in school, everyday life, and other activities?" (Carroll, 1982). As yet, these questions have not been fully answered by research.

Raymond B. Cattell's "Fluid Versus Crystallized Intelligence." A different, more parsimonious approach to defining mental abilities is reflected in the work of Raymond B. Cattell (1963, 1971), who distinguishes between two broad intellectual factors. **Crystallized intelligence** depends heavily on culturally loaded, fact-oriented learning. Tasks that are highly correlated with this factor include vocabulary, general information, and arithmetic problems. In contrast, **fluid intelligence** demands little in the way of specific informational content. It involves the ability to see complex relationships and solve problems, as is the case in the number series, spatial visualization, and figure matrix examples displayed in Figure 8.1.

When samples of children are similar in cultural and educational background, crystallized and fluid intelligence are highly correlated, so much so that they cannot be distinguished by using factor analysis. In such instances, the strong relationship is probably due to the fact that children who are high in fluid intelligence tend to acquire specific information more efficiently and extensively. However, when children have had very different cultural and educational experiences, the two types of ability are easier to separate; children with the same fluid capacity may perform quite differently on tests that emphasize crystallized items. As these findings suggest, R. B. Cattell's theory has important implications for the issue of cultural bias in intelligence testing. Efforts to devise culture-fair tests that do not discriminate against ethnic minority children usually emphasize fluid over crystallized type items.

Recent Developments in Defining Intelligence

Although the factor analytic approach has been the major methodological route to defining mental abilities, a number of investigators believe that its value will remain limited unless it is combined with other theoretical approaches to the study of human cognition. Psychometric researchers have been criticized for devoting too much attention to identifying factors and too little to specifying the cognitive processes that contribute to them. As Carroll (1982) points out, factors by themselves are of little usefulness unless psychologists can explain why the tasks associated with each factor are linked together. Once the underlying basis of IQ scores is understood, we will know much more about why a particular child does well or poorly and what fundamental capacities must be worked on to improve performance.

Combining Psychometric and Information Processing Approaches. To overcome the limitations of factor analysis, investigators have started to combine the psychometric with the information processing perspective. Researchers involved in this effort believe that individual differences in information processing components — sensory apprehension, attention, memory strategies, symbolic comparison and transformation, metacognition, and others — are at the heart of varying performances on intelligence test items (Carroll, 1981; Sternberg, 1985a, 1985b). Consequently, they conduct *componential analyses* of children's IQ scores in which performance on test items is correlated with laboratory measures designed to reveal the speed and effectiveness of information processing skills (e.g., Carroll & Maxwell, 1979; Jensen, 1985b, 1988; Keating & Bobbitt, 1978; Sternberg, 1977).

Evidence from such studies indicates that information processing efficiency is substantially correlated with the "g" factor on intelligence tests (Jensen, 1985a), a finding that has direct implications for the expansion of mental testing procedures. For example, it has been suggested that traditional intelligence tests could be supplemented by items that reflect important information processing components. These tasks may be particularly effective in isolating specific cognitive processes in which improvement is needed to augment general intellectual performance (Sternberg, 1981). In fact, psychometricians have already begun to apply information processing to mental testing. Later in this chapter, we will see that the authors of one of the newest intelligence tests for children, the Kaufman Assessment Battery, relied heavily on information processing theory for the design of their mental tasks (Kaufman & Kaufman, 1983a).

Nevertheless, the componential analyses described above have a major shortcoming: Intelligence test performance is attributed entirely to causes within the child. Yet throughout Chapter 7, we described evidence indicating that cultural and situational factors profoundly affect children's cognitive skills. Recently, Robert Sternberg expanded the componential approach into a comprehensive theory that views intelligence as a product of both internal and external forces. Because Sternberg's theory has attracted widespread attention and is likely to serve as the basis for the construction of more effective intelligence tests in the near future, we describe it in the following section.

Sternberg's Triarchic Theory. As shown in Figure 8.3, Sternberg's (1985a, 1988a) **triarchic theory of intelligence** is made up of three interacting subtheories. The first, the *componential subtheory*, spells out the information processing skills that underlie intelligent behavior. You are already familiar with its main elements— metacognition, strategy application, and knowledge acquisition—from reading Chapter 7.

According to Sternberg, children's application of these components is not just a matter of internal capacity. It is also a function of the circumstances under which intelligence is assessed. The *experiential subtheory* states that highly intelligent individuals, in comparison to less intelligent ones, deploy their cognitive operations more skillfully in novel situations. When confronted with a relatively new task, the bright person learns rapidly, quickly making strategies automatic so attention is freed for more complex and subtle aspects of the situation.

Think, for a moment, about the implications of this idea for measuring children's intelligence. To validly compare children in brightness—in ability to deal with novelty and learn efficiently—all children must be presented with *equally unfamiliar* test items. Otherwise, some children will *appear* more intelligent than others because of their past experiences, not because they are really more cognitively skilled. These children start with an unfair advantage in the form of prior practice and movement toward automaticity on the tasks.

This point brings us to the third facet of Sternberg's model, his *contextual subtheory*. It proposes that intelligent people skillfully *adapt* their processing components to

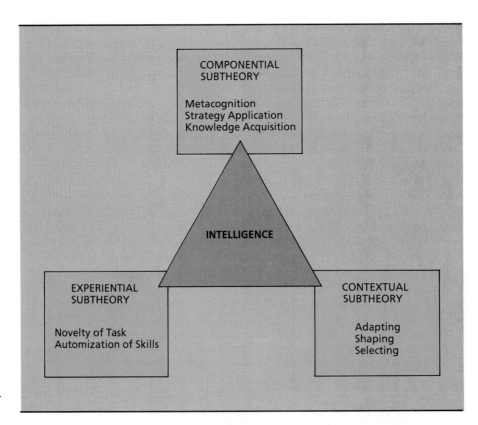

Figure 8.3. A pictorial representation of Sternberg's triarchic theory of intelligence.

fit with their personal desires and the demands of their everyday worlds. When they cannot adapt to a situation, they try to *shape*, or change it to meet their needs. If they cannot shape it, they *select* new contexts that are consistent with their goals. The contextual dimension of Sternberg's theory emphasizes that intelligent behavior is never culture-free. Because of their backgrounds, some children come to value behaviors required for success on intelligence tests, and they readily adapt to the tasks and testing conditions. Others with different life histories easily misinterpret the testing context or reject it entirely because it does not suit their needs. This is despite the fact that such children may display highly sophisticated, adaptive skills in daily life — for example, telling elaborate stories, engaging in complicated artistic activities, or interacting skillfully and sensitively with other people (Sternberg, 1988a).

Sternberg's triarchic theory underscores the complexity of intelligent behavior and the heterogeneity of children's intellectual skills. As you have probably already surmised, his ideas (like R. B. Cattell's distinction between crystallized and fluid intelligence) are particularly relevant to the controversy surrounding cultural bias in IQ testing, to which we return later in this chapter.

In the preceding sections, we have seen that factor analytic research led to the identification of Spearman's "g," a general factor underlying all intelligence test performances, as well as a wide variety of distinct mental abilities. Recently, investigators have combined the psychometric with the information processing perspective in an effort to discover the precise cognitive processes responsible for mental test scores. Sternberg has expanded this componential approach into a comprehensive, triarchic theory of intelligence. It asserts that information processing skills, prior experience with the tasks, and contextual factors (the child's cultural background and consequent interpretation of the testing situation) interact to determine IQ scores.

Now that we have considered the complex issues involved in defining intelligence, let's turn to how the IQ score is computed and what particular score values actually mean.

THE COMPUTATION AND DISTRIBUTION OF IQ SCORES

Once an intelligence test has been given, the examiner computes a raw score on the basis of the child's answers. Then the raw score is converted to an **intelligence quotient (IQ)** that permits the child's performance to be readily compared to the scores of other individuals.

The Traditional IQ Score

In the original Stanford-Binet scale, IQs were obtained by converting the raw score on the test to a **mental age (MA).** The mental age equivalent of a particular raw score is determined by finding the chronological age at which children, on the average, obtain that score. For example, if the mean raw score of 8-year-olds is 40, then a raw score of 40 is equivalent to a mental age of 8. A child's IQ could then be computed by entering the mental age into the following formula:

$$IQ = (MA/CA) \times 100$$

Using this method, children with IQs of 100 are considered average in mental ability, since they do just as well as would be expected for their chronological age (CA). Children with IQs higher than 100 are above average, since they obtain raw scores comparable to those of older children. Children with IQs lower than 100 are below average for a similar reason.

Although the mental age approach provides a convenient way of comparing the test scores of different children, it has come under criticism and is rarely used today. Mental growth is known to be far more rapid at younger ages than at older ages. In other words, the difference in intellectual functioning between a 2- and a 3-year-old is much greater than it is between a 10- and an 11-year-old, but an IQ based on mental age does not take this into account. In addition, the mental age equivalent encourages people who are not familiar with the basis of the score to draw the erroneous conclusion that an 8-year-old child with a mental age of 12 is like a 12-year-old in all respects. Yet the assumption that such a child could keep pace with children four years her senior in academic and social situations is unreasonable (Sattler, 1988). It is best not to make this inference and, instead, to merely regard the 8-year-old as a very intellectually superior child in comparison to her own age group.

The Modern IQ Score

The modern method of arriving at an IQ avoids the problems inherent in the mental age approach by making a direct comparison of a child's raw score to the scores of a representative sample of children of the same chronological age. This approach is often referred to as a **deviation IQ,** because it is based on the extent to which a child's performance deviates from the mean of same-age children. When an intelligence test is standardized, it is given to a large number of individuals, and the performances of children at each age level form a frequency distribution that closely approximates the *normal curve* shown in Figure 8.4. Two important features of the normal curve are its *mean*, or the average of the test scores, and its *standard deviation*, which gives a measure of the average variability, or "spread-outness," of the scores from the mean.

Knowing the mean and standard deviation of the raw scores, we can determine the exact percentage of the population that falls above or below a certain score. Figure 8.4 shows the percentage of individuals within each area of the normal curve when the distribution is marked off in standard deviation units. Most intelligence tests recalibrate their raw scores so that the mean is set at 100 and the standard deviation at 15. Then when we talk about an IQ of a particular magnitude, we know precisely what it means. For example, a child who obtains an IQ of 100 performs better than 50 percent of the population of same-age children. A child with an IQ of 85 does better than only 15.9 percent of her agemates, while a child with an IQ of 130 outperforms 97.7 percent of them. Look at Figure 8.4 again and notice how most of the scores cluster near the mean. The great majority of the population (95.5 percent) falls between IQs of 70 and 130, with only a few people achieving very high or very low scores.

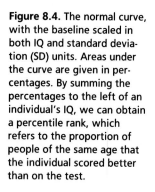

Figure 8.4. The normal curve, with the baseline scaled in both IQ and standard deviation (SD) units. Areas under the curve are given in percentages. By summing the percentages to the left of an individual's IQ, we can obtain a percentile rank, which refers to the proportion of people of the same age that the individual scored better than on the test.

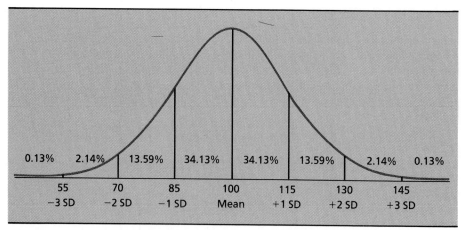

REPRESENTATIVE INTELLIGENCE TESTS
FOR CHILDREN

309

CHAPTER 8
INTELLIGENCE: A
PSYCHOMETRIC
PERSPECTIVE

Given the diversity of scientific models of intelligence, it is not surprising that a multitude of tests have been developed to represent them. Among the variety of instruments available, the Stanford-Binet and Wechsler Scales are most often used to diagnose children with learning problems, identify highly intelligent children, and make decisions about special educational placement.

The Stanford-Binet Intelligence Scale

For over half a century, the *Stanford-Binet* has been the most popular individual intelligence test for children. Translated and adopted throughout the world, it has often served as the yardstick against which the worth of other intelligence tests has been measured. Like earlier editions, the 1986 revision is suitable for testing individuals from 2 through 18 years of age.

In contrast to older versions, the new Stanford-Binet measures both overall intellectual performance and multiple factors. It is based on a hierarchical model of intelligence that incorporates the theories of Spearman, R. B. Cattell, and Horn, whose extensions of Cattell's work identified short-term memory as an additional factor that is independent of crystallized and fluid intelligence (Horn, 1985; Stankov, Horn, & Roy, 1980). As shown in Figure 8.5, the three-level model consists of 15 subtests that permit a detailed analysis of each child's mental abilities (Thorndike, Hagen, & Sattler, 1986). Also, the new test materials are designed to be sensitive to minority and handicapped youngsters and to reduce sex bias. Pictures of children from different racial/ethnic groups, a child in a wheelchair, and "unisex" figures that can be interpreted as either male or female are included (see Figure 8.6).

Nevertheless, the new Stanford-Binet has been criticized on several grounds. Some subtests are not strongly correlated with the factors they are supposed to represent, raising questions about the meaningfulness of the separate mental ability scores and concerns about whether the test actually reflects the model of mental ability adopted by the test designers. In addition, the test takes an especially long time to administer — up to 2 hours for some children (Sattler, 1988).

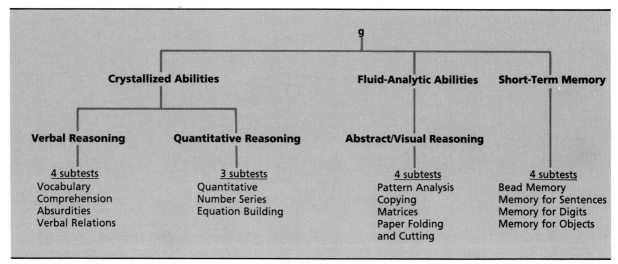

Figure 8.5. Mental abilities appraised by the 1986 revision of the Stanford-Binet Intelligence Scale. *(Adapted from Thorndike, Hagen, & Sattler, 1986.)*

The Wechsler Intelligence Scales

The *Wechsler Intelligence Scale for Children-Revised* (WISC-R) and the *Wechsler Preschool and Primary Scale of Intelligence-Revised* (WPPSI-R) are the only individual tests of mental ability that have successfully competed with the Stanford-Binet in popularity. The Wechsler tests offered differentiated scoring long before it was incorporated into the Stanford-Binet. Consequently, over the past two decades, they have become the preferred mental assessment tools of clinical and school psychologists. The WISC-R is appropriate for children 6 through 16 years of age, the WPPSI-R for children 3 through 8 (Wechsler, 1974, 1989).

Figure 8.7 shows the factor structure of the Wechsler tests. Both consist of verbal and performance subtests that combine to yield Verbal, Performance, and Full Scale IQs. Although the Verbal IQ is a better predictor of academic performance (Wikoff, 1979), the Performance IQ provided one of the first means through which non-English-speaking children and children with speech and language disorders could demonstrate their intellectual strengths.

The Wechsler tests were the first to be standardized on samples representing the total population of the United States, including racial/ethnic minorities (Zimmerman & Woo-Sam, 1978). Their broadly representative standardization procedures have served as models for many later intelligence tests, including the new version of the Stanford-Binet.

Other Intelligence Tests

The Kaufman Assessment Battery for Children. *The Kaufman Assessment Battery for Children (K-ABC)* is the first major assessment instrument to be theoretically grounded in cognitive psychology. Published in 1983, the K-ABC measures the intelligence of children from 2½ through 12 years of age on the basis of two general classes of information processing skills: simultaneous and sequential processing. It provides a unique array of subtests as well as a separate score to represent each (see Figure 8.8).

Sequential processing refers to the capacity to solve problems in a step-wise fashion. Tasks that sample this ability emphasize solutions that depend on temporal or serial relationships among stimulus elements. In contrast, *simultaneous processing* involves the ability to meaningfully integrate a variety of stimuli at the same time. The two processing components combine to yield an overall intelligence or information processing measure, called the Mental Processing Composite.

In the construction of both mental processing scales, a concerted effort was made to reduce cultural bias through the provision of items whose content is familiar to all

Figure 8.6. "Unisex" child in the new Stanford-Binet, designed to reduce sex bias in the test. *(From R. L. Thorndike, E. P. Hagen, & J. M. Sattler, 1986,* The Stanford-Binet Intelligence Scale *[4th ed.], Chicago: Riverside Publishing. Reprinted by permission.)*

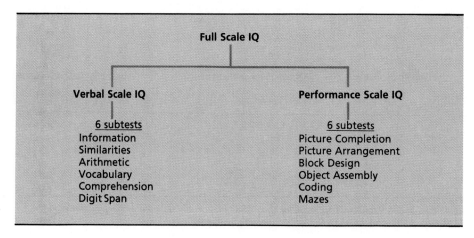

Figure 8.7. Mental abilities appraised by the Wechsler intelligence tests.

children. As a result, the K-ABC mental processing scales are largely nonverbal in nature and heavily laden with items that reflect R. B. Cattell's concept of fluid intelligence. Crystallized items are assessed by a separate intellectual dimension—the Achievement Scale. It includes subtests that are traditionally associated with verbal intelligence as well as measures of school-related skills.

Like the Wechsler tests, the K-ABC's standardization sample is highly representative. Moreover, national norms are supplemented by separate norms for blacks and whites and, within these two racial groups, norms for different income levels. These permit each child to be compared to a representative sample of children who have experienced comparable opportunities for learning (Kaufman & Kaufman, 1983a).

Extra efforts to respond to the needs of minority children are also apparent in the K-ABC's unusually flexible administration procedures. Deviating from virtually all other tests, the K-ABC permits the examiner to "teach the task" to any child who fails one of the first three items on any subtest. The tester may use alternative wording, gestures, and physical prompts and may even communicate in a language other than English (Kaufman & Kaufman, 1983a, 1983b). These special features make the K-ABC stand apart as one of the fairest measures of intelligence currently available for children from ethnic minority and low-income backgrounds.

Like the new Stanford-Binet, the K-ABC is not without critics. Some point out that there is little support in the information processing literature for the simultaneous/sequential processing dichotomy on which the test is based (Goetz & Hall, 1984). The battery has also been criticized for overemphasizing short-term memory and rote learning (Sternberg, 1984). Nevertheless, the test represents a new wave of enthusiasm among psychometricians for measuring intelligence on the basis of contemporary cognitive theory, and it is likely to inspire the construction of new instruments that draw on information processing models.

Piagetian-Based Tests. During the 1960s and early 1970s, psychometricians became interested in whether the tasks that Piaget devised to reflect children's stage-wise progress could be used to assess individual differences in intelligence. Several Piagetian instruments for preschool and school-age children have since been developed (e.g., Goldschmid & Bentler, 1968; Humphreys, Rich, & Davey, 1985). However, assessments of preoperational and concrete operational thinking have not caught hold strongly, largely because they have not worked better than traditional intelligence tests for practical purposes. Piagetian performance correlates well with

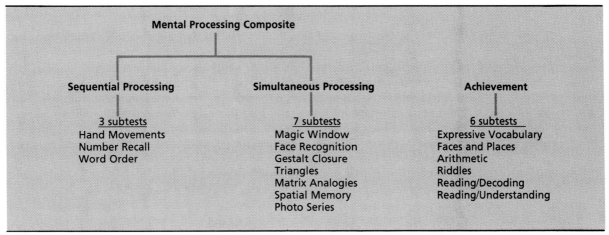

Figure 8.8. Mental abilities appraised by the Kaufman Assessment Battery for Children (K-ABC). *(From A. S. Kaufman & N. L. Kaufman, 1983,* Kaufman Assessment Battery for Children: Interpretive Manual. *Circle Pines, MN: American Guidance Service. Adapted by permission.)*

IQ and school achievement. But most psychometric instruments sample a much wider range of mental abilities than do Piagetian-based tests, which are limited to general reasoning ability (Elkind, 1971).

Piagetian theory has had a greater impact in the area of infant assessment. Two tests that chart progress through the sensorimotor stage have been developed (Escalona & Corman, 1969; Užgiris & Hunt, 1975). The most recent is Užgiris and Hunt's *Infant Psychological Development Scale*. It contains eight subscales, each of which assesses the development of an important sensorimotor capacity, such as object permanence and vocal and gestural imitation. A study by Wachs (1975) revealed that among the Užgiris-Hunt subscales, assessments of object permanence predicted Stanford-Binet IQ during the early preschool years. As will become apparent in the section below, Piagetian-based infant scales are somewhat more successful than traditional infant intelligence tests in predicting later mental ability. Perhaps this is because they focus more directly on infant problem solving and conceptual understanding than do most early assessment devices (Lewis & Sullivan, 1985).

Infant Intelligence Tests. Psychometrically based instruments for infants consist largely of perceptual and motor performances, such as lifting the head, following a moving object with the eyes, and building a tower of cubes. Since babies are often less then cooperative subjects, infant scores are more unreliable than those obtained for older children. Some tests depend heavily on information supplied by parents to compensate for the unpredictability of these very young test-takers. Also, because of skepticism about whether infant scales reflect the same construct of intelligence measured by tests for children and adults, most scores on infant tests are conservatively labeled **developmental quotients (DQ)** rather than IQs. However, the DQ is computed in the same way as an IQ, with a score of 100 indicating average performance.

The roots of tests for babies can be traced to the work of Arnold Gesell, one of the founders of the normative tradition in child development. Virtually all infant tests have either borrowed or adapted items from *The Gesell Developmental Schedules*, first introduced in 1925 and designed to measure the developmental progress of babies from 3 to 24 months of age (Honzik, 1983; Lewis & Sullivan, 1985). Besides the Gesell test, an instrument developed in the 1930s by Nancy Bayley, *The Bayley Scales of Infant Development*, became widely used. Both currently exist in revised forms (Bayley, 1969; Knobloch, Stevens, & Malone, 1980).

The Bayley infant test was the first to be designed for the purpose of predicting future intellectual competence. However, despite its careful construction, it remains a poor predictor of intelligence during the childhood years, at least for samples of normal babies (Bayley, 1970; Lewis & McGurk, 1972; McCall, Hogarty, & Hurlburt, 1972). The consistency of this finding has led investigators to conclude that the perceptual and motor behaviors tapped in infancy are qualitatively different from the verbal, conceptual, and problem-solving skills assessed at later ages.

Some investigators have speculated that infant tests miss early information processing behaviors that might be expected to predict later cognitive functioning, such as response to novelty, as assessed by the habituation-dishabituation paradigm. Recall from Chapter 4 that habituation and dishabituation measures are, at present, the best infant correlates of IQ through the preschool years. Therefore, finding ways to include them in new infant tests holds considerable promise for improving the predictability of these early assessment devices.

Infant tests do show somewhat better long-term prediction for very low scoring babies (Honzik, 1983). Consequently, many investigators believe that the major usefulness of infant testing is for screening purposes — identifying babies for further diagnosis and possible intervention whose initial low scores may mean that they have a high probability of experiencing delayed or abnormal development in the future (Lewis & Sullivan, 1985).

Current widely used intelligence tests for children are based on hierarchical models of intelligence in which both general ability and numerous separate abilities are measured. In addition, each major test has incorporated features into its design that respond to the special needs of ethnic minority children. In general, infant mental test scores are unrelated to later IQs. However, infant tests are useful for identifying babies whose extremely low scores suggest that they may be experiencing serious developmental difficulties.

WHAT AND HOW WELL DO INTELLIGENCE TESTS PREDICT?

We have already seen that in the great majority of cases, infant tests are poor predictors of later cognitive functioning, but what about the more frequently administered childhood tests? Psychologists and educators who use test scores to help make decisions regarding the educational placement of children assume that the scores are good indicators of future intellectual and scholastic performance. Let's see how well the IQ fares as a predictive measure based on research evidence.

The Stability of IQ Scores

Stability refers to how effectively IQ serves as a predictor of itself from one developmental period to another. Do children who obtain a particular IQ at age 3 or 4 perform about the same during the elementary school years and again when tested in high school? To investigate the stability of IQ, psychologists must follow children longitudinally, retesting them at regular intervals. Such studies are expensive and time-consuming to conduct. Therefore, investigators have relied on already existing data from major longitudinal investigations, especially the Berkeley and Fels studies, to which you were introduced in Chapter 2.

Correlational Stability. One way of examining the stability of IQ is to correlate scores obtained from repeated testings on the same group of children. This information tells us whether children who score low or high in comparison to their agemates at one point in time continue to do so at later ages. Drawing from such evidence, two generalizations about the stability of mental test performance can be made:

1. *The older the child at the time of first testing, the better the prediction of later IQ status.* For example, the Berkeley longitudinal data showed that the correlation between IQs taken at 2 and 5 years of age is only .32. It rises to .70 between the ages of 5 and 8 and to .85 between the ages of 9 and 12 (Honzik, Macfarlane, & Allen, 1948). Preschool IQs do not predict school-age scores as well as later measures, but after age 6, there is good stability, with many of the correlations remaining in the .70s and .80s. Relationships between two testings obtained during the adolescent years are as high as the .80s and .90s (Bayley, 1949; Honzik, Macfarlane, & Allen, 1948; Sontag, Baker, & Nelson, 1958).

2. *The closer in time two testings are, the stronger the relationship between the scores.* For example, a 4-year IQ correlates with a 5-year score at .72, but the prediction drops by age 6 to .62. By age 18, it has declined to .42 (Honzik, Macfarlane, & Allen, 1948).

Taken together, these findings indicate that before the age of 5 or 6, IQ should be regarded as largely an indicator of present ability, not as a dependable, enduring measure. Why do preschool scores predict less well than later assessments? One frequently cited reason is similar to the one we discussed earlier with regard to infant tests. Differences in the nature of test items may play an important role. Concrete intellectual knowledge tends to be tested at younger ages and abstract, problem-solving ability later on. It is possible that skill at the former is not necessarily predictive of skill at the latter (Siegler & Richards, 1982). Another explanation is that during early periods of rapid growth, one child may spurt ahead of another and reach a plateau, while a second child, moving along slowly and steadily from behind, may gain on and gradually overtake the first. Because children frequently change places with one another in a distribution during periods of rapid change, all measures of developmental status, including height and weight, are less stable and predictable at these times, and IQ seems to be no exception.

The Stability of Absolute Scores. So far, the stability evidence we have discussed centers on the strength of correlations, which tell us the extent to which children maintain their relative IQ standing among agemates over time. It is also possible to view stability in absolute terms. We can compare each child to himself or herself by examining a profile of IQ scores on a series of repeated testings. Recall the examples of individual IQ growth trends from the Fels and Berkeley studies that we discussed in Chapter 2. The evidence revealed that the majority of children experienced substantial IQ fluctuations. To refresh your memory, the Berkeley findings indicated that 85 percent of the children studied showed changes of ten or more points, and a third of the sample showed changes of 20 or more points, between 6 and 18 years of age (Honzik, Macfarlane, & Allen, 1948). Individual IQ variations of children in the Fels sample were even more dramatic (Sontag, Baker, & Nelson, 1958).[1]

The Berkeley and Fels IQ profiles tended to be orderly. Steadily increasing or decreasing performances rather than random, unpredictable fluctuations occurred. Also, large shifts were often associated with children's personality characteristics and parental child-rearing practices. For example, IQ gainers were more independent and scholastically competitive, and their parents' special interest in their intellectual accomplishments was reflected in greater pressure to succeed in school along with moderate, rational disciplinary techniques. Children who showed IQ declines had parents who made little effort to stimulate them and who showed extremes in discipline—either very severe or very lax punishment techniques (McCall, Appelbaum, & Hogarty, 1973; Sontag, Baker, & Nelson, 1958).

Longitudinal studies generally report IQ gains for their samples as a whole (although a handful of subjects always show decreases). However, when children from low-income and poverty-stricken ethnic minority homes are selected for special study, a large number of them show progressive IQ declines. This decrement has been attributed to the cumulative impact of an underprivileged background on IQ, an explanation referred to as the **cumulative deficit hypothesis.** The cumulative deficit hypothesis suggests that, because of the compounding effects of depressed rearing conditions, early intellectual deficiencies lead to more deficiencies, gradually becoming more difficult to counteract as children get older. This idea has served as the basic rationale for many early intervention programs, which are intensive efforts to offset such declines.

Although cross-sectional studies are consistent with the cumulative deficit hypothesis, they have methodological difficulties. Older and younger age groups could have been exposed to different life experiences and therefore may not have been comparable (Jensen, 1974). Well-designed longitudinal research is scarce, but one British investigation reported supportive evidence. Inner-city disadvantaged youngsters declined steadily on a wide variety of intellectual measures between 7 and 15 years of age, whereas more advantaged controls showed no such trend (Cox, 1983).

Nevertheless, longitudinal findings like these do not tell us for sure that depressed environments are the cause of the IQ decline. A competing hypothesis is that genetic

---

[1] Return to Chapter 2, pages 52–54, to review this evidence in greater detail and to Figure 2.1 on page 54 to examine some sample IQ profiles of individual children.

differences in children's intellectual growth curves exist and are responsible for the progressive drop among the disadvantaged. However, in a study of American black children, Jensen (1977) reported evidence contradicting a genetic explanation. He compared the IQ scores of younger and older children in the same families, reasoning that if a true cumulative deficit exists, older siblings should obtain lower test scores than their younger brothers and sisters. Jensen found just such an effect for black children growing up under severely depressed circumstances in the rural South. Among a sample of less disadvantaged, California-reared black youngsters, the sibling effect did not occur.

A surprising number of youngsters show substantial changes in the absolute value of their IQ scores during childhood and adolescence. Upward shifts are typical for advantaged children, while downward shifts occur often among low-income and ethnic minority youngsters. Nevertheless, IQs obtained after school entry are good indicators of a child's intellectual status in comparison to agemates. Once IQ becomes reasonably stable in a correlational sense, it predicts a variety of outcome measures, as we will see in the following sections.

BRIEF REVIEW

IQ as a Predictor of Scholastic Success

Thousands of studies reveal that intelligence tests have accomplished the goal of predicting academic achievement. IQ shows a moderate to strong relationship with achievement test scores during elementary and high school. The correlations generally range from about .40 to .70, with typical figures hovering around .50 (Jensen, 1980; Siegler & Richards, 1982). Children with higher IQs also get better grades and stay in school longer. As early as age 7, IQ is moderately correlated with adult educational attainment (McCall, 1977).

Why does IQ predict scholastic success so well? Psychologists differ in how they answer this question. Some believe that tests of intelligence and achievement both sample from the same pool of culturally specific information. From this point of view, an intelligence test is at least partly an achievement test, and relevant past experiences determine whether children do well or poorly on both types of measures (Zigler & Seitz, 1982). Support for this position comes from research indicating that crystallized intelligence (which reflects acquired knowledge) does a much better job of predicting achievement than does its fluid counterpart (Kaufman, Kamphaus, & Kaufman, 1985).

Other psychologists believe that the IQ–achievement relationship does not come about because both measures reflect the same body of culturally relevant information. Instead, they believe that IQ predicts achievement because both depend on cognitive processes that underlie Spearman's "g" — the ability to form mental relationships and to reason abstractly. The fact that IQ correlates best with achievement in the more academic and abstract school subjects, such as English, mathematics, and science, has been taken to support this position (Jensen, 1980).

As you can probably imagine, psychologists who believe that experiential factors account for most of the IQ variation among individuals prefer the first of these explanations, whereas those who believe that heredity plays a crucial role prefer the second. But whether one or the other (or both) of these interpretations is correct, it is important to note that the correlation between IQ and achievement is far from perfect. In fact, intelligence accounts for no more than half of the individual differences among children in academic performance.[2] The other half is determined by a different set of

IQ scores are consistently correlated with school achievement. However, investigators disagree on the underlying basis for this relationship.

---

[2] When two variables, such as IQ and achievement, are correlated, investigators determine the proportion of variation in one that can be explained by the other by squaring the correlation. The highest correlations obtained between IQ and achievement are around .70. This figure, when squared, equals .49. The result indicates that only about half of the variation, or differences among individuals, in achievement can be accounted for by IQ.

influences, such as some combination of motivational and personality characteristics that leads some children to try hard and to want to do well in school. These factors are at least as important as IQ in explaining individual differences in scholastic success (Zigler & Seitz, 1982).

IQ as a Predictor of Vocational Success

Psychologists and educators might be less preoccupied with IQ scores if they only predicted only school performance and were unrelated to long-term measures of life success. However, research indicates that childhood IQ predicts adult occupational status just about as well as it correlates with school achievement. By second grade, pupils with the highest IQs are the ones who are most likely to enter prestigious occupations such as physician, scientist, lawyer, or engineer (McCall, 1977). Long-term follow-ups of Terman's famous sample of children with IQs above 135 provide additional support for this association. By middle age, more than 86 percent of the men had entered high-status professions. Also, most had incomes that exceeded the earnings of individuals in the general population who had attained a comparable level of occupational status (Terman & Oden, 1959).[3] Moreover, IQ is not just effective in predicting occupational prestige and income. It also correlates well with job training success and on-the-job performance across the entire range of occupations, from very low to very high status endeavors (Hunter & Hunter, 1984).

But like the IQ–school achievement connection, the relationship between mental test scores and occupational attainment is not perfect; other variables figure importantly into the picture. For example, among Terman's gifted sample, not all individuals were equally professionally successful. Those who fared best seemed to have "a special drive to succeed, a need to achieve, that had been with them from grammar school onward" (Goleman, 1980, p. 31). Moreover, it is possible that factors related to family background are largely responsible for the complex of correlations among IQ, education, occupation, and income, rather than intelligence being at the heart of them. However, home background cannot be the whole story because differences among family members in vocational achievement are also related to their IQ scores (Waller, 1971). Once again, however, the picture is not simple, since IQ cannot account for all such within-family variation in occupational success.

IQ as a Predictor of Psychological Adjustment

Is IQ so influential that it predicts indicators of life success beyond the schoolroom and workplace, such as social and emotional adjustment? A number of studies show that during the elementary school years, pupils with higher IQs are better accepted by their classmates (Hartup, 1983). However, the origins of this association, like the predictive relationships described above, are obscure. Differences among children in social skills are just as likely to originate from factors having to do with socioeconomic status, child-rearing practices, health, physical appearance, and personality (all of which are correlated with IQ) as they are from mental ability.

Another way of exploring the intelligence–psychological adjustment relationship is to look at the IQs of children who are clearly poorly adjusted, such as highly aggressive youngsters who engage in norm-violating acts. IQ and delinquency are negatively correlated, with most delinquents falling in the lower half of the IQ

[3] Born in the early part of this century during an era quite different from our own, nearly half of the women in Terman's study became housewives. However, of those who had professional careers, there were examples of outstanding vocational accomplishments. Among them were scientists (one of whom contributed to the development of the polio vaccine), several novelists and journalists, and a number of highly successful businesswomen (Terman & Oden, 1959).

distribution. Yet several interpretations of this association exist in which IQ itself does not play a causal role. Some investigators believe that delinquency is promoted by negative school experiences in combination with an underprivileged family background. They suggest that children from nonsupportive families who fail repeatedly in the classroom are likely to react to the pain of these events by turning to antisocial behavior (Hirschi & Hindelang, 1977). This explanation is supported by the finding that as soon as delinquent youngsters leave school, their antisocial behaviors decline (Phillips & Kelly, 1979). However, for some children, the relationship between IQ and aggressive, acting-out behavior is present by 3 or 4 years of age (Richman, Stevenson, & Graham, 1982). For these youngsters, the relationship cannot be mediated by school failure, since it is present before school entry. In such cases, personality or familial background variables may simultaneously predispose children to both intellectual deficits and antisocial conduct (Rutter & Garmezy, 1983).

Thus, there are several plausible explanations for the IQ-adjustment connection in which IQ itself does not play a direct causal role. Moreover, it is important to note that a good number of adjustment disorders, such as excessive anxiety, fearfulness, withdrawal, and depression, are unrelated to children's IQ scores (Graham, 1979).

IQ is an effective predictor of a wide variety of measures of personal success and life satisfaction. However, the causal factors involved in these relationships are not clearly established. Home background and personality appear to be just as important as IQ in predicting educational, occupational, and personal success.

BRIEF REVIEW

RACIAL/ETHNIC AND SOCIOECONOMIC DIFFERENCES IN IQ

The academic and vocational outcomes of which IQ is predictive are unevenly distributed among racial, ethnic, and socioeconomic groups (Cleary et al., 1975). In searching for the roots of these disparities, social scientists have compared the intelligence test performance of major sectors of the U.S. population. The results of these investigations are responsible for kindling the IQ nature-nurture debate. If children of various racial/ethnic and socioeconomic classifications differ in IQ, then either there must be genetic differences between rich and poor and black and white children, or children from impoverished sectors of the population must have fewer opportunities to acquire the skills necessary for successful test performance.

What are the origins of racial/ethnic and socioeconomic differences in general intelligence and specific mental abilities? Research aimed at answering this question has been the subject of heated controversy.

The IQ nature-nurture controversy reached epic proportions during the 1970s, following publication of a 1969 *Harvard Educational Review* article by psychologist Arthur Jensen entitled, "How much can we boost IQ and scholastic achievement?" Jensen's answer to this question was *not much* because, he argued, racial and socio-economic differences in IQ are largely traceable to genetic origins.

Jensen's work was followed by an outpouring of responses and research studies, some in favor of and some opposed to his position. In addition, there were ethical challenges from scientists who were deeply concerned that his conclusions would be used inappropriately to fuel existing social prejudices. This concern was intensified by the fact that Jensen's findings were highly tenuous and debatable. The controversy has since died down. Most scientists have come to the reasoned conclusion that individual differences in IQ scores are genetically as well as environmentally determined. Moreover, as we explained in Chapter 3, the two sets of influences are often impossible to disentangle. Before we consider the evidence on this issue, let's look at the nature and extent of racial, ethnic, and socioeconomic differences in IQ, since they are at the heart of the controversy.

Differences in General Intelligence

American black children score, on the average, about 15 points below American white children on measures of general intelligence (Brody, 1985; Cleary et al., 1975; Loehlin, Lindzey, & Spuhler, 1975; Jensen, 1980). Socioeconomic differences in IQ also exist, but they are smaller in magnitude than black-white differences. In one large-scale study, low-income children scored about 9 points below their middle-income counterparts (Jensen & Figueroa, 1975). Since a disproportionate number of black families have low incomes, it is reasonable to ask whether socioeconomic differences in IQ fully account for the racial discrepancy. They explain some of it, but not all of it. When members of both racial groups are matched on the basis of socioeconomic status, the black-white IQ gap is reduced by only a third (Jencks, 1972).

The group differences described above are averages. It is important to keep in mind that substantial IQ variation exists within each race and social class. For example, as shown in Figure 8.9, the IQ distributions of blacks and whites overlap a great deal; 15 to 20 percent of blacks score above the white mean, and the same percentage of whites score below the black mean. Regardless of how high one chooses to draw a line on the intellectual dimension, there will always be blacks who score

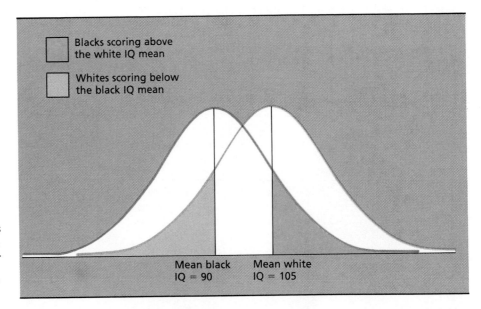

Blacks scoring above
the white IQ mean

Whites scoring below
the black IQ mean

Mean black
IQ = 90

Mean white
IQ = 105

Figure 8.9. Comparison of the distributions of IQ scores for black and white children. The means represent approximate values obtained in studies of children reared by their biological parents.

above it, but there will be proportionately fewer of them than whites (Cleary et al., 1975). In fact, race and socioeconomic status account for only about one fourth of the total variation in IQ (Jensen, 1980). Still, these group differences are sufficiently large and of serious enough consequence that they cannot be ignored.

Differences in Specific Mental Abilities

Although many studies have compared racial and social-class groups in terms of general intelligence, more detailed comparisons of particular mental abilities are less frequent. In one well-known theory about racial and social-class variations in different mental abilities, called the **Level I–Level II theory,** Jensen (1969, 1973, 1980) argued that subgroup disparities are greater for some intellectual abilities than others.

The Level I–Level II theory distinguishes between two kinds of intelligence. Mental test items that reflect Level I emphasize rote memory, or the ability to register, store, and engage in short-term recognition and verbatim recall of information. The digit span items on many intelligence tests are a good example of Level I ability. In contrast, Level II involves complex cognitive processing and problem solving. Items that are highly correlated with Spearman's "g" reflect Level II abilities, such as vocabulary and verbal comprehension, spatial visualization, and figure matrices. Jensen and his collaborators have presented evidence to suggest that black-white IQ differences and, to a lesser extent, socioeconomic differences are largely accounted for by Level II abilities and that population subgroups differ very little in Level I capacity (Jensen, 1985b, 1988; Jensen & Figueroa, 1975; Reynolds & Jensen, 1983).

In addition, Jensen suggested that among Level II abilities, black children do worst on the least culturally loaded, fluid ability, problem-solving type items and best on the most culturally loaded, crystallized items, such as vocabulary and general information. Therefore, Jensen argued, black-white IQ differences cannot be accounted for by any cultural biases inherent in the tests (Jensen, 1980). The conclusion drawn, that blacks obtain lower IQ scores than whites because they are least well endowed with higher-order, conceptual forms of intelligence, is one aspect of Jensen's research that intensified public outcries about the racist connotations of his work.

Jensen's Level I–Level II theory remains controversial. Reviewing a large number of studies, Vernon (1981, 1987) concluded that most were consistent with the theory. However, it has not been substantiated by the work of others. Stankov, Horn, and Roy (1980) found that children's short-term memory performance (Level I) as well as fluid and crystallized scores (Level II) all declined in a similar fashion from high to middle to low socioeconomic classifications. These findings leave open the possibility that a wide variety of factors, among them cultural bias in the tests, affect different mental ability scores in the same way. In another investigation of a large representative sample of black and white adolescents, Scarr and Barker (1981) reported results in opposition to Jensen's. The largest differences between black and white children occurred on the most culturally loaded items (vocabulary) and the smallest differences on tests of memory and conceptual understanding, although black children did worse than white children on all measures.

In one of the most comprehensive investigations of racial/ethnic differences in specific mental abilities, Lesser and his colleagues (Lesser, Fifer, & Clark, 1965; Stodolsky & Lesser, 1967) tested a large sample of lower- and middle-class 6- and 7-year-olds from four ethnic minority groups: Chinese, Jewish, black, and Puerto Rican. Each child was given measures of four mental abilities. As shown in Figure 8.10, both social class and ethnicity made a difference in children's overall performance. Within each ethnic classification, middle-class children consistently outperformed lower-class children. In addition, Chinese and Jewish children did better than blacks and Puerto Ricans. However, the most striking finding was that each ethnic group showed a distinct mental ability profile that remained unaltered across social class.

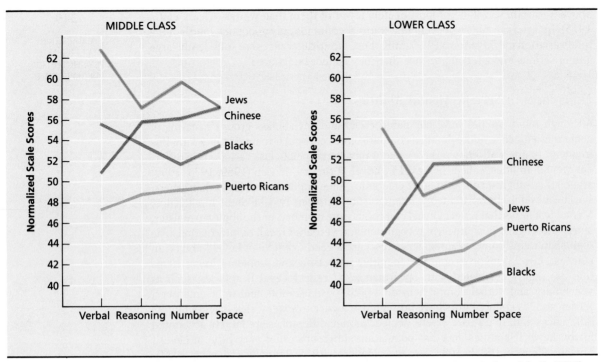

Figure 8.10. Patterns of mental abilities obtained by Lesser and his co-workers among middle-class and lower-class children from four ethnic groups. *(Adapted from S. Stodolsky & G. Lesser, "Learning Patterns in the Disadvantaged."* Harvard Ed- ucational Review, *1967, 37, 546–593. Copyright © 1967 by the President and Fellows of Harvard College. All rights reserved.)*

Lesser's results, like Jensen's, have been challenged. Vernon, Jackson, and Messick (1988) reported that ethnic ability patterns vary considerably from study to study, depending on the ages of children tested, the specific IQ measures given, and the procedures used to compare the scores. Nevertheless, the evidence as a whole suggests that Jensen's theory is an oversimplification of the complex mental ability profiles associated with racial/ethnic identities (Borkowski & Maxwell, 1985; Stankov, 1987). These patterns are subtle, intricate, and unlikely to be accounted for in simple ways.

Now that we have an overall picture of the IQ variations that figure importantly into the nature-nurture debate, let's examine the evidence on genetic and environmental determinants of the IQ score.

EXPLAINING INDIVIDUAL DIFFERENCES IN IQ

Genetic Influences

Heritability of Intelligence. Because intelligence is a polygenic trait (influenced by a complex array of genes), knowledge of the specific hereditary pathways that affect it is a long way off. Many scientists believe that they will never be precisely understood. Therefore, research on the role of genetics in the development of intelligence is limited to indirect methods of study. In Chapter 3, we introduced the most popular of these methods, the **heritability estimate.** Recall that heritability estimates are obtained from *kinship studies*. First, the IQs of pairs of individuals of different degrees of genetic relationship are correlated. Then, using a complicated statistical procedure, the correlations are compared to arrive at an index of heritability, ranging from 0 to 1, that reflects the proportion of IQ variation attributable to genetic factors. Let's begin our consideration of hereditary influences on IQ by examining the correlational evidence on which these estimates are based.

Averaging the results of the most carefully conducted studies, Bouchard and McGue (1981) summarized worldwide findings on IQ correlations between kinship pairs. The correlations, shown in Table 8.2, are consistent with a polygenic model of inheritance because they show that the higher the proportion of genes two relatives have in common, the stronger the relationship between their IQs. In fact, two of the correlations reveal that heredity is, without question, a partial determinant of general intelligence. The correlation for identical twins reared apart (.72) is considerably higher than for fraternal twins reared together in the same household (.60).

Recently, investigators have begun to study how these kinship correlations change with age. The findings of a number of investigations agree that the impact of heredity strengthens with development (DeFries, Plomin, & LaBuda, 1987; Loehlin, Horn, & Willerman, 1989; Wilson, 1983). For example, Wilson (1983) followed a sample of identical and fraternal twins from infancy into the adolescent years. As shown in Figure 8.11, the correlations for identicals gradually increased, and those for fraternals decreased. Do these trends remind you of the *niche-picking* concept that we discussed in Chapter 3? Common rearing experiences support the similarity of fraternal twins during childhood. But as they move toward adolescence and are gradually released from the influence of their immediate family environment, each fraternal twin pursues a course of development, or finds a niche, that fits with his or her unique genotype. As a result, their IQ scores start to diverge. In contrast, the genetic likeness of identical twins leads them to seek out very similar niches in adolescence. Consequently, their resemblance in IQ is even greater than it was during the childhood years.

Although kinship comparisons verify the importance of genetic factors, careful inspection of all of the correlations given in Table 8.2 indicates that the role of heredity in determining IQ is only moderate. For example, the average correlation between identical twins reared apart is considerably less than the perfect value that would be expected if IQ was determined solely by the genes (although its high

Table 8.2. Bouchard and McGue's (1981) Worldwide Summary of IQ Correlations Between Kinship Pairs

KINSHIP PAIR	AVERAGE WEIGHTED CORRELATION	TOTAL NUMBER OF KINSHIP PAIRS INCLUDED	NUMBER OF STUDIES
Identical twins reared together	.86	4,672	34
Identical twins reared apart	.72	65	3
Fraternal twins reared together	.60	5,546	41
Siblings reared together	.47	26,473	69
Siblings reared apart	.24	203	2
Biological parent–offspring living together	.42	8,433	32
Biological parent–offspring living apart	.22[a]	814	4
Nonbiological siblings (adopted–natural pairings)	.29	345	5
Nonbiological siblings (adopted–adopted pairings)	.34	369	6
Adoptive parent–offspring	.19	1,397	6

[a] This correlation is lower than the values obtained in two subsequent American cross-fostering studies (Horn, 1983; Scarr & Weinberg, 1983), which reported correlations of .31 and .43, respectively.
Source: T. J. Bouchard & M. McGue, 1981. "Familial Studies of Intelligence: A Review," *Science, 212*, 1056. Copyright 1981 by the AAAS.

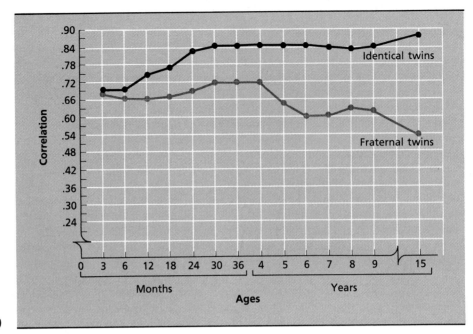

Figure 8.11. Age changes in IQ correlations for identical and fraternal twins in the Louisville Twin study. *(From R. Wilson, 1983, "The Louisville Twin Study: Developmental Synchronies in Behavior," Child Development, 5ᵈ 311. © The Society for Research in Child Development, Inc. Reprinted by permission.)*

magnitude cannot be explained on the basis of a strict environmental hypothesis either). In addition, the correlation between identical twins who are reared apart is substantially less than when they are reared together, a difference that points to the importance of family environment. Other comparisons that stress the role of environment include: the stronger correlation for fraternal twins than for ordinary siblings reared together (attributed to twins' more similar rearing conditions); the stronger correlation for siblings reared together than apart; and the stronger correlation for biological parents and offspring living together than apart. Finally, adoptive parents and their adopted offspring, as well as unrelated siblings, show low positive IQ correlations, again providing support for the impact of common rearing conditions.

Heritability estimates are generally computed using correlations of identical and fraternal twins. The values arrived at in recent investigations, which employ improved statistical methodology over previous research, range from .30 to .70. Scarr and Kidd (1983) suggest that the true value is probably somewhere around .50, which means that half of the variation in IQ can be attributed to differences among people in genetic makeup. This is a much more modest estimate than reported in earlier studies, such as the value of .80 arrived at by Jensen as part of his controversial 1969 article. In addition, as we indicated in Chapter 3, it is still possible that the moderate heritabilities described above are inaccurate, since twins reared together experience very similar overall environments. Even when they are reared apart, they are often placed in foster and adoptive homes that are advantaged and alike in many ways. When the range of environments to which twin pairs are exposed is restricted, heritabilities underestimate environmental influences and overestimate genetic influences. This problem also raises questions about the generalizability of heritability estimates. Because of their placement in similar and superior homes, the rearing conditions of separated twins are unlikely to be representative of the broad range of environments experienced by children growing up in an average community.

Despite inherent limitations of the heritability estimate, Jensen (1969, 1973) relied heavily on it to support the argument that racial and socioeconomic differences in general intelligence have a strong genetic basis. This line of reasoning is widely regarded as inappropriate. Heritability estimates computed *within* a population (largely on white twin samples) provide no direct evidence about what is responsible for *between-group* racial/ethnic and socioeconomic differences in IQ. In a well-known example, Lewontin (1976) showed that using within-group heritabilities to explain between-group differences is like comparing different seeds in different soil. Suppose we take a handful of "white" corn seeds and pot them all with the same special nutrient designed to encourage plant growth. Then we take a handful of "black" seeds and grow them under quite different conditions, with half as much nutrient. We chart plant growth and find that although the plants in each group vary in height, the "white" seeds, on the average, grow taller than the "black" ones. Within each group, we can attribute individual differences in plant height to genetic factors (since growth environments were much the same). But it would be wrong to account for the between-group difference in this way. Instead, it must be largely environmental, since the nutrient given to the "black" seeds was much less plentiful.

Furthermore, high heritabilities have been *assumed* by Jensen to imply that the malleability of the IQ score is very limited. In actuality, the correlational findings on which heritability estimates are based offer no precise information on the extent to which heredity restricts future opportunities for environment to affect IQ. In contrast, **cross-fostering studies,** in which children are reared in environments very different from their family of origin, provide more information. Correlations of children with their biological as well as adoptive family members can be studied for insight into the relative importance of heredity and environment. In addition, changes in the absolute value of IQ as the result of being reared in an advantaged family can be examined.

Cross-Fostering Research. Several classic adoption studies were carried out in the 1930s and 1940s. Then the adoption design lay dormant for nearly three decades until the nature-nurture debate of the 1970s sparked renewed interest in it. The best known of the early studies was conducted by Skodak and Skeels (1949). They gave repeated IQ testings during childhood and adolescence to 100 children placed in adoptive homes before 6 months of age. Although the biological parents were largely from low socioeconomic backgrounds, the adoptive parents were well above average in income and education. Because of advantaged rearing conditions, the absolute value of the adopted children's IQ scores remained above the population mean throughout middle childhood and into the adolescent years. This finding indicates that IQ is, in fact, highly malleable! Nevertheless, the children's IQs still showed considerable correlation with the scores of their biological mothers, providing support for the role of heredity.

Selective placement in adoption procedures is a problem that plagues most cross-fostering studies, and it appeared to be operating in the Skodak and Skeels investigation. When selective placement occurs, both biological and adoptive parents are similar in IQ and other characteristics. As a result, hereditary and environmental influences cannot be disentangled completely. However, Skodak and Skeels's findings have been replicated in a recent adoption study in which selective placement was judged to be minimal. The Texas Adoption Project (Horn, Loehlin, & Willerman, 1979; Horn, 1983; Willerman, 1979) resulted from the discovery of a large private adoption agency that had administered IQ tests routinely to unwed mothers residing in its residential facility. The children of two extreme groups of biological mothers — those with IQs below 95 and those with IQs above 120 — were chosen for special study. As shown in Figure 8.12, when tested during middle childhood, children of low-IQ mothers scored above average in IQ, but they did not do nearly as well as children of brighter natural mothers who were placed in comparable adoptive families. In addition, adopted children's IQs correlated more strongly with the scores of their biological than their adoptive mothers (who had reared them from birth). Thus, cross-fostering research shows that *both* family environment *and* heredity contribute significantly to IQ.

The fact that adopted offspring have repeatedly been found to score above average in IQ suggests that the social-class difference in intelligence has a substantial environmental component. However, concluding that it is entirely due to differences in family environments is probably too extreme. Although children of low-IQ biological

Figure 8.12. IQs of adopted children as a function of biological mothers' IQ in the Texas Adoption Project. A four-point difference between the two groups in the IQs of the adoptive mothers occurred, suggesting a mild selective placement effect. However, it was not great enough to account for the substantial difference in children's IQs as a function of biological mothers' scores. *(Adapted from Willerman, 1979.)*

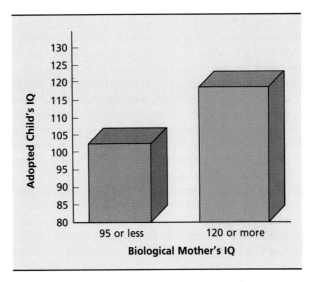

mothers adopted into upper-middle-class families attain above-average IQs, they generally score somewhat lower than their adoptive parents' natural children, with whom they share equally privileged rearing conditions. In addition, cross-fostering studies repeatedly reveal stronger correlations between the IQ scores of biological than adoptive relatives (Horn, 1983; Plomin & DeFries, 1983; Scarr & Weinberg, 1983). On the basis of such evidence, a number of investigators have concluded that the social-class–IQ connection is partly genetic in origin (Bouchard & Segal, 1985; Scarr & Weinberg, 1978).

The adoption findings reviewed above are based on white samples and tell us nothing about the origins of the black-white IQ gap. Yet some additional studies of black children raised in white middle-class homes reveal that the poorer test performance of black youngsters is socioculturally determined and cannot be explained by racially linked, inferior genes. See Box 8.1 for a description of this important research.

BRIEF REVIEW

In the preceding sections, we have seen that heritability estimates support a moderate role for genetic factors in the determination of intelligence. However, heritabilities cannot be generalized to explain social-class and racial differences in IQ, and they do not tell us whether further environmental interventions can raise test scores. In contrast, cross-fostering research reveals that the absolute value of the IQ is highly malleable. It also shows that heredity is clearly important; IQ correlations are consistently stronger for biological than adoptive relatives.

Environmental Influences

Although genetic factors play an undeniable part in the IQ variation in the general population, at present there are no ethically acceptable routes to controlling such influences. It is much more fruitful for people interested in bettering the lives of children to concentrate on things that they can do something about — the environmental factors that explain the sizable remaining variation in IQ once heredity is accounted for. Although predictive of children's IQ, global indices of the environment (such as parental occupation, income, and education) do not tell us much about the specific aspects of experience — details of the child's home environment and schooling — that contribute to intellectual development. Over the last two decades, researchers have made substantial progress in clarifying these environmental effects.

Sociocultural Background and Bias in the Tests. Both professionals and lay-people have raised the question of whether taking the intellectual behaviors of the majority as the standard against which the performance of all children is assessed yields a biased picture of minority children's abilities. The issue of test bias has produced a voluminous and controversial literature. Psychologists are not of one mind, either about how to define test bias or whether it exists.

Some believe that test bias should be viewed strictly in terms of objective assessments of an intelligence test's validity (Ebel, 1975; Jensen, 1980; Oakland & Parmelee, 1985). From this perspective, if a test has the same factor structure and predicts scholastic performance equivalently among minority and majority children, it is not biased. When these criteria are used, intelligence tests have stood up very well (Kaplan, 1985; Oakland & Parmelee, 1985; Reschly, 1978; Reynolds & Nigl, 1981). However, some exceptions do exist (Mercer, 1979a; Oakland, 1978), and the validity of every test needs to be established for children of different backgrounds. Otherwise, a test can have very different meanings for different kinds of children (Kaplan, 1985).

◆ CONTEMPORARY ISSUES: CULTURAL DIFFERENCES ◆

Transracial Adoption: When Black Children Grow Up in White Homes
Box 8.1

Two transracial adoption studies, both focusing on the development of black children growing up in white middle-class homes, provide a critical test of the origins of the black-white IQ gap. If Jensen's claim that black children are limited in intellectual potential is correct, then the IQs of black adoptees should fall considerably below those of other children who are reared in advantaged white families. However, if black children have the hereditary prerequisites to benefit from advantaged rearing conditions, then they should show a substantial rise in test performance when they are raised by white parents "in the culture of the tests and schools."

Scarr and Weinberg (1976, 1983) were the first to study transracially adopted black children. They administered IQ tests during childhood and adolescence to over 100 such youngsters, two thirds of whom were placed during the first year of life and one third after 12 months of age. The white adoptive parents had high-average to superior IQs, were well above average in occupational status and income, and exceeded the educational attainment of the children's biological parents by 4 to 5 years.

Findings paralleled the dramatic results of cross-fostering investigations involving white adoptees. The black children attained an average IQ of 106, considerably above the general population mean, and their school achievement was similarly elevated. The scores of those who had been adopted within the first 12 months of life were even higher. Averaging 110, they achieved 20 points above the mean IQ of children growing up in low-income black communities. The investigators concluded that genetic factors cannot account for black children's typically depressed intelligence test scores.

A second transracial study explored the precise cultural experiences that were responsible for Scarr and Weinberg's findings. Elsie Moore (1986) compared the test-taking behavior and parent-child communication of two groups of black adoptees: one growing up in white and the other in black middle-class families. Tested between 7 and 10 years of age, the traditionally adopted children did well on IQ tests, achieving a mean of 104. But the performance of their transracially adopted counterparts was substantially higher, averaging 117. In line with their superior scores, the transracial group approached the testing situation with attitudes and strategies that were especially conducive to success. For example, they were more task-involved and persistent, and they gave more elaborate responses to the examiner. When they could not answer a question, they spontaneously explained that they had not yet had a chance to learn the information; they seldom attributed failure to personal inadequacies. The transracially adopted children's greater test-taking confidence could, in turn, be attributed to their mothers' special encouragement of problem-solving behavior. When asked to teach their child a difficult IQ task, the white mothers displayed considerably more encouragement and enthusiasm for their youngster's efforts.

These results indicate that ethnicity of the black child's rearing environment, not hereditary endowment, accounts for the black-white IQ gap. However, the investigators were careful to point out that their findings are not an endorsement for widespread adoption of black children into white homes. Instead, they call for more research on specific ways in which culturally different families support a diverse array of intellectual skills.

Once a test behaves in the same way for different subgroups with regard to these issues, people who endorse a strict definition of test bias regard the instruments as equally fair for all children. They claim that intelligence tests were intended to represent important aspects of success in the common culture. As long as they do so, any additional bias (if it exists) is not in the tests so much as it is in the attitudes, values, and child-rearing practices of particular subgroups that do not prepare their children to succeed in the prevailing culture. These psychologists believe that minority interests are not well served by blaming tests for disadvantaged children's poorer scores (Ebel, 1975; Oakland & Parmelee, 1985).

Other psychologists adhere to a much broader definition of test bias. In addition to issues of uniform factor structure and prediction of academic performance, they regard a test as biased if it samples culturally specific knowledge and skills that not all subgroups have had equal opportunity to learn (Mercer, 1975; Sternberg, 1988a; Zigler & Seitz, 1982). These psychologists believe that familiarity of item content, language differences, and motivational variables lead IQ tests to underestimate the abilities of poor and ethnic minority children. To evaluate this position, let's examine each of these important factors in turn.

Familiarity of Item Content. Many researchers argue that IQ scores are affected by knowledge of specific information acquired as part of white, middle-class upbringing. Unfortunately, efforts to change test items so they are fairer to minority children — either by basing them on more familiar content or by eliminating their dependence on culturally based, crystallized knowledge — have not raised the scores of these youngsters very much (Kaplan, 1985). For example, *Raven's Progressive Matrices* is one of the most extensively used culture-fair tests of fluid intelligence. To see a typical item, look back at the figure matrix task shown in Figure 8.1. Despite the Raven's lack of dependence on verbal information and its simple instructions, minority children continue to perform more poorly on it, and on other tests like it, than their white middle-class counterparts do (Jensen, 1980).

Nevertheless, it is possible that high scores on fluid tests like Raven's Matrices depend on subtle learning opportunities. In one study, Dirks (1982) discovered that children's performance on the Block Design subtest of the WISC-R (also a measure of fluid intelligence) was related to the extent to which they had played an expensive commercial game that (like the subtest) required them to arrange cubes to duplicate a geometric pattern as quickly as possible. When children inexperienced at playing the game were given a brief exposure to it, their Block Design scores rose dramatically. Opportunities to interact with games and objects may be especially important for the development of some nonverbal intellectual skills, and many minority children may be especially deficient in such experiences. In fact, it has been suggested that because black children are raised in more "people-oriented" than "object-oriented" homes, they experience fewer opportunities to manipulate objects and discover their properties and relationships (Sternberg, 1988a).

In a recent Israeli study, Cahan and Cohen (1989) found that years of school attendance was a much better predictor of elementary school children's raw scores on crystallized and (to a lesser extent) fluid ability measures than their chronological age. This finding lends added support to the conclusion that specific experiences affect performance on a diverse array of mental ability tasks.

Language Differences. IQ scores are biased indicators of true ability when non-English-speaking and bilingual children are not tested in their native or dominant language. When tests are given in English, these children frequently obtain higher scores on nonverbal and performance scales than on verbal scales. However, under these circumstances, it would be incorrect to conclude that this profile indicates a deficiency in verbal intelligence (Jensen, 1980; Oakland & Parmelee, 1985).

Many black children from low-income backgrounds speak a dialect that is different from standard English. Like bilingual children, they are often assumed to be at a disadvantage on tests administered in standard English. However, when tests are translated into black dialect, black children's scores do not change (Quay, 1972, 1974). This finding does not necessarily generalize to all dialect-speaking youngsters. One study reported that children who spoke a Hawaiian-English dialect did better on a verbal comprehension test when it was administered in their dialect instead of in standard English (Speidel & Tharp, 1985).

Another prevalent claim is that intelligence tests, and the classroom learning experiences that resemble them, are not relevant to the early language customs of many minority children. For example, some investigators believe that black subculture gives rise to unique language skills that are ignored in the usual educational and mental assessment process. Well-known psychometric experts dismiss black children's unique verbal experiences as a source of test bias (e.g., Ebel, 1975; Jensen, 1980; Sattler, 1988). However, anthropologists who have spent many hours observing black youngsters at home and in school disagree. For example, Michaels (1980) studied sharing time in an integrated urban first-grade classroom. When talking to the class, white middle-class pupils used a tightly organized, *topic-centered style* that focused on a single topic or series of related topics. In contrast, low-income black pupils used a *topic-chaining style* that flowed easily from one topic to another and that usually dealt with aspects of personal relationships. The white teacher had trouble understanding and responding to black children's narratives, which appeared to her to be poorly focused, rambling responses.

How do such different verbal approaches to the same classroom learning experience develop? In a study described in Box 8.2, anthropologist Shirley Brice-Heath provides some provocative answers to this question. Brice-Heath and others (Hale, 1982; Havighurst, 1976; Yando, Seitz, & Zigler, 1979) advocate a *difference* rather than *deficit* approach to understanding and helping the minority child. They stress the need for school instruction that recognizes minority children's cognitive strengths and that builds bridges between their natural learning styles and classroom learning and testing situations. Such efforts may be especially critical at school entry, before declining achievement patterns of minority pupils become well established and difficult to change (Alexander & Entwisle, 1988).

Motivational Variables. IQ scores are known to be influenced by motivational factors. When faced with an unfamiliar adult, children from poor backgrounds often reply "I don't know" to the simplest of questions, including "What's your name?" The response does not stem from lack of cognitive competence. Instead, it reflects wariness of the examiner and the test situation. Consequently, the fearful child behaves in ways that are aimed at minimizing interaction and terminating the unpleasant situation as soon as possible. Besides suspicion and discomfort in the presence of strangers, many ethnic minority children do not define testing conditions in achievement terms. They are more motivated to look for signs of attention and approval and less motivated to be correct for the sake of correctness alone. They often settle for lower levels of task success than their abilities allow (Zigler & Seitz, 1982).

Several studies show that IQ gains result when testing conditions are modified so that disadvantaged children have an opportunity to become familiar with the examiner, are provided with generous amounts of praise and encouragement, and are given easier test items immediately after incorrect responses to minimize the emotional consequences of failure (Ali & Costello, 1971; Zigler, Abelson, & Seitz, 1973; Zigler & Butterfield, 1968). In the most impressive of these investigations, preschool children from poor backgrounds scored ten points higher after either being given a ten-minute play period with the examiner before testing or being individually tested a second time by the same examiner who tested them on the first occasion. In contrast, gains of advantaged children under these optimal testing conditions amounted to only about three IQ points (Zigler, Abelson, & Seitz, 1973).

Although these procedures minimize motivational problems related to the testing situation, many disadvantaged children suffer from more deep-seated self-defeating attitudes. More extensive intervention is necessary to treat these difficulties. In one study, Zigler and his colleagues (1982) reported that preschool children who attended a year-long Head Start program showed IQ gains, but comparable children who did not attend experienced IQ declines accompanied by a rise in wariness of strange adults. These findings are consistent with the idea that poor motives underlie disadvantaged children's lower test scores and lesser readiness to profit from instruction at school entry. As such children experience repeated academic failure, a self-defeating motivational style marked by withdrawal, disengagement, and reduced effort be-

---

◆ THEORY, RESEARCH, AND APPLICATIONS ◆

Questioning at Home and School: Early Language Environments of Black and White Children

Box 8.2

Theory. Anthropologist Shirley Brice-Heath (1982, 1989) studied the language customs of Trackton, a small black community in a southeastern American city, and compared them to white teachers' communications with their own children at home and their pupils at school. She predicted that such information would help explain why many ethnic minority youngsters approach school learning situations differently from other children. Brice-Heath also hypothesized that sharing her language observations with white teachers of the Trackton children could spur the development of more effective teaching strategies that incorporate the unique language experiences of black youngsters.

Research. Children of Trackton attended integrated public schools, where they were taught by white teachers. Trackton parents were disturbed by their children's extreme dislike of school and discomfort communicating in the classroom. The teachers commented that many of the children seemed unable to answer even simple questions. Some teachers attributed the difficulty to differences between the black dialect used in Trackton and standard English used at school. Others believed that the communication breakdown was more basic, although they could not pin down exactly what the problem was.

In comparing uses of language in Trackton with language customs in the white community, Brice-Heath concentrated on question asking, since questions are a particularly important classroom communication tool. Watching the white teachers interact with their own young children, Brice-Heath discovered that the white teachers constantly communicated in questions. Over 50 percent of their utterances were interrogatives, most of which were used to train children in knowledge about the world, as in "What color is it?", "Where's the puppy?", and "What's this story about?" Moreover, teachers' classroom discourse also consisted largely of questions, and the types of questions used by teachers at home were the same as the ones used in school.

Compared to white youngsters, black pupils from Trackton were asked questions at home far less frequently. As a rule, Trackton adults postponed question asking until their children were seen as competent conversationalists and realistic sources of information. When black children got older, the questions that were asked were of a very different sort than those white teachers posed to their children. Instead of knowledge-training questions, black parents asked analogy questions (e.g., "What's that like?") or story-starter questions (e.g., "Didja hear Miss Sally this morning?") that called for elaborate responses about whole events for which there was no single "right answer."

Once Brice-Heath got teachers to incorporate these kinds of questions into classroom activities, Trackton children changed from passive, reticent pupils to lively, eager participants. Using photos of the community, teachers started by asking such questions as "Tell me what you did when you were there?" and "What's that like?" Then they taped children's responses and added specific, school-type questions to the tapes. These were placed in learning centers where children could listen to themselves give responses appropriate in their own community alongside ones expected in school. Gradually, the children were helped to prepare new questions and answers for the tapes. As a result of these experiences, they soon caught on to classroom verbal customs and began to realize that school-type questions need not threaten their ways of talking at home.

Applications. Brice-Heath's study illustrates a unique approach to helping ethnic minority children become more successful in school. When teachers understand the cultural experiences that give rise to the distinct verbal customs of black children, they can incorporate these customs into classroom activities. Then effective bridges can be built between black children's natural learning styles and the styles of learning that are necessary for school success.

comes firmly entrenched in their personality dispositions and increasingly difficult to modify.

Overcoming Test Bias. Evidence that IQ scores of disadvantaged children do not reflect their true abilities has become part of a national controversy over whether biased testing procedures lead to overlabeling of minority children as retarded and their disproportionate assignment to special public school classes that provide an inferior education. Studies by sociologist Jane Mercer (1972, 1975) conducted in Riverside, California, during the 1970s revealed that for a total of 812 individuals defined as mentally retarded by community agencies, schools were the principal labelers, contributing 429, or more than half of the diagnoses. Poor children as well as blacks and Hispanics were overrepresented, especially among public school nominees. Recent research indicates that overrepresentation of minority students in special classes for the retarded and their underrepresentation in programs for the academically gifted remain pervasive national concerns (Landesman & Ramey, 1989; Reis, 1989).

As a remedy for these problems, Mercer believes that adaptive behavior inventories, designed to assess children's ability to cope with the everyday demands of the environment, should supplement intelligence testing.[4] In Mercer's research, 90 percent of black and 60 percent of Hispanic children with IQs below 70 appeared to function well in their everyday worlds, demonstrating considerable "street smarts" or practical intelligence. Because of the dangers of unfairly penalizing ethnic minority children, Mercer suggests that only those who fall in the lowest 2 percent on both intelligence and adaptive behavior be labeled retarded. Although current definitions of mental retardation accept this criterion, it has not yet had much impact on educational practice. This is partly because few effective, culturally sensitive measures of adaptive behavior exist (Landesman & Ramey, 1989).

Mercer has also been a strong advocate of assessment approaches that deliberately take cultural differences into account. To that end, she developed the *System of Multicultural Pluralistic Assessment (SOMPA)*, which is based on the assumption that a culturally fair testing system must compare minority children to others with similar life experiences (Mercer, 1979b; Mercer & Lewis, 1978). The SOMPA adds extra points to the child's IQ score to compensate for an underprivileged sociocultural background. Its purpose is, once again, to help prevent minority children from being overidentified as mentally retarded.

Critics of this approach maintain that low-IQ children need extra help in school, and Mercer's system could prevent them from getting it. Because the socioculturally adjusted scores on the SOMPA are poor predictors of school success, critics also claim that the approach is less valid than sticking to traditional IQs (Goodman, 1979; Oakland, 1979; Reschly, 1981; Sattler, 1988). Others take more of a "wait-and-see" attitude toward the SOMPA. They believe that time will tell if minority children not placed in special classes who otherwise would have been are benefiting educationally (Kaplan, 1985).

A less radical approach to reducing test bias is exemplified by the K-ABC. Recall that designers of this test took special steps to increase its fairness, including eliminating items with biased content and permitting flexible administration procedures. These efforts cut the typical IQ discrepancy between black and white children in half and nearly equalized the scores of Hispanic and white youngsters (Kaufman, Kamphaus, & Kaufman, 1985). These findings are encouraging; the K-ABC has managed to reduce racial/ethnic differences in IQ while accumulating a substantial record of reliability and validity (Kaplan, 1985).

Should the problems of test bias and the potential for misusing IQ scores be resolved by banning the tests altogether? A few experts think so (Kamii, 1990). However, most regard this alternative as unacceptable, since it totally relinquishes

[4] Notice how this recommendation places special emphasis on the contextual dimension of Sternberg's triarchic theory, discussed earlier in this chapter.

important decisions about children to subjective impressions, a policy that could increase the discriminatory placement of minority children. As Reschly (1981) points out, IQ tests reduce the degree of overrepresentation in special classes that would exist from teacher referral alone, and when wisely used and interpreted, they yield information not available through other means. Rather than banning the tests entirely, it is better to continue to refine current mental testing practices and build safeguards into decision-making processes involving IQ scores.

BRIEF REVIEW

Psychologists differ in the criteria they use to define test bias. Those who adopt a strict, objective definition find little evidence of bias against low-income and ethnic minority children. In contrast, proponents of culture-fair assessment argue that unfamiliar item content, different language customs, and motivational factors lead IQ tests to underestimate disadvantaged children's true abilities. Test bias and misuse of IQ scores have been held responsible for the overidentification of minority children as mentally retarded in the public schools. Assessments of adaptive behavior and testing procedures that take cultural differences into account have been recommended as remedies for this problem.

Home Environment and IQ. Racial/ethnic and social class differences are not the only important IQ variations with environmental explanations. As we indicated earlier in this chapter, individual children of the *same* ethnic and socioeconomic background also differ in IQ. We now consider some important home environmental factors that contribute to these differences.

Variations in home environments that affect children's IQ scores are of two general types. The first type, **between-family environmental influences,** includes factors that are related to the overall "intellectual climate" of the home. They are called between-family influences because they permeate the general atmosphere of the home and therefore affect all children living in it to the same extent. The availability of stimulating toys and books and modeling by parents of intellectual activities are good examples. The second type, **within-family environmental influences,** has only recently captured the attention of child development specialists. These are factors that make siblings *different* from one another. Examples include differential treatment by parents, birth order and spacing, as well as serendipitous events such as moving to a new neighborhood that affect one sibling more than another. Let's see what research says about each of these classes of environmental influences.

Between-Family Influences. An enormous body of research carried out over the last 40 years has consistently shown that children's concurrent and later IQs can be predicted from assessments of their home environments taken as early as the first two years of life. Longitudinal investigations, such as the Berkeley and Fels studies, were among the first to discover these relationships. Stimulation provided by the physical setting, parental encouragement of intellectual achievement, and the emotional climate created by parent-child interactions loomed as especially important in these first studies (Honzik, 1967; Moore, 1968).

Because of the promising nature of these early findings, Bradley and Caldwell developed the *Home Observation for Measurement of the Environment (HOME),* an instrument for assessing between-family environmental factors that are relevant to children's intellectual performance. HOME gathers information through direct observation as well as parental interview. Separate infancy, preschool, and middle childhood versions exist (Bradley & Caldwell, 1979; Bradley et al., 1988; Elardo, Bradley, & Caldwell, 1975). The subscales measured by each are shown in Table 8.3.

Research with HOME provides overwhelming confirmation of the findings of earlier research—that the quantity of stimulation provided in the early years is linked to cognitive development. All early childhood subscales are correlated with children's intellectual performance, although the most important ones change with age. In infancy, organization of the environment and variety in daily stimulation are

Table 8.3. Home Observation for Measurement of the Environment (HOME) Subscales

INFANCY VERSION (BIRTH–3 YEARS)	PRESCHOOL VERSION (3–6 YEARS)	MIDDLE CHILDHOOD VERSION (6–10 YEARS)
1. Emotional and verbal responsivity of the mother	1. Stimulation through toys, games, and reading material	1. Emotional and verbal responsivity of the parent
2. Avoidance of restriction and punishment	2. Language stimulation	2. Encouragement of social maturity
3. Organization of the physical and temporal environment	3. Physical environment: Safe, clean, and conducive to development	3. Emotional climate of the parent-child relationship
4. Provision of appropriate play materials	4. Pride, affection, and warmth	4. Growth-fostering materials and experiences
5. Maternal involvement with the child	5. Stimulation of academic behavior	5. Provision for active stimulation
6. Variety in daily stimulation	6. Modeling and encouragement of social maturity	6. Family participation in developmentally stimulating experiences
	7. Variety in daily stimulation	7. Paternal involvement in parenting
	8. Avoidance of physical punishment	8. Physical environment: Safe, clean, and conducive to development

Sources: Bradley & Caldwell, 1979; Bradley et al., 1988; Elardo, Bradley, & Caldwell, 1975.

most strongly related to mental development. During the preschool years, warmth, stimulation of language and academic behavior, and provision of appropriate play materials become more powerful predictors (Bradley & Caldwell, 1976; Elardo, Bradley, & Caldwell, 1975, 1977). Also, high HOME scores during infancy are associated with IQ gains between 1 and 3 years of age, while low HOME scores consistently predict declines as large as 15 to 20 points (Bradley et al., 1989).[5]

Studies examining home environments within different social-class and ethnic groups report findings similar to those described above (Bee et al., 1982; Bradley & Caldwell, 1981, 1982; Bradley et al., 1989; McGowan & Johnson, 1984). No matter how economically and ethnically homogeneous the sample, certain aspects of maternal behavior—provision of appropriate play materials, encouragement of achievement and independence, warmth and affection, and verbal stimulation and responsiveness—repeatedly predict infant and early childhood mental test scores. Moreover, HOME scores have proved to be far more effective predictors of intellectual development than global environmental indices such as socioeconomic status.

However, caution should be exercised with regard to these correlational findings, since they tell us nothing definite about causation. In all the investigations reviewed so far, children were reared by their biological parents, with whom they share not only a common environment but also a common heredity. Perhaps parents who have genes for high IQ simply provide better experiences as well as give birth to genetically superior children (Longstreth et al., 1981). Although this idea may account for a portion of the HOME–IQ linkage, it is clearly not the whole story. Prediction of IQ

---

[5] Because the middle childhood version of HOME is new, there is little research with it. Preliminary evidence indicates that provision for active stimulation (e.g., encouraging hobbies, trips to the library, and organizational memberships) and family participation in stimulating experiences (e.g., visiting friends or relatives, attending musical or theater performances) are the strongest predictors of school achievement at 10 and 11 years of age (Bradley, Caldwell, & Rock, 1988).

from early HOME measures is as powerful among adopted children as it is among children reared by their biological parents (Plomin & DeFries, 1983). Also, HOME assessments have been shown to contribute to children's test performance *beyond* the effect of maternal IQ (Plomin & DeFries, 1983; Wilson, 1983; Yeates et al., 1983). These findings indicate that HOME–IQ correlations *are* environmentally mediated.

Still, it is important to keep in mind that the relationship between home environment and intelligence is undoubtedly very complex. We have already seen that different HOME variables exert their strongest influence at different periods of development. Also, as our discussion of genetic-environmental correlation in Chapter 3 indicated, children *evoke* different environmental inputs from their families, and the way they do so changes over the childhood years. Bradley and Caldwell acknowledge that as children get older, the relationship between home environment and IQ probably becomes increasingly bidirectional, with neither serving as the primary cause.

Within-Family Influences. Rowe and Plomin (1981) argue that within-family influences on intelligence — those that make siblings different from one another — are at least as important as between-family influences. The most obvious examples of within-family influences are family configurational variables such as birth order and spacing of children. In an effort to sort out their effects, Zajonc and Markus proposed a complex theory called the **confluence model** (Zajonc, 1976; Zajonc & Markus, 1975; Zajonc, Markus, & Markus, 1979). It regards children's mental growth as a function of the unique environmental quality that each experiences within the family, which is affected by the contributions of other family members. With each new child born into the family, environmental quality is diluted, since infants are cognitively immature beings who consume the attentions of the most mature family members but contribute little to its overall level. However, as children get older and mature intellectually, environmental quality rises. Based on these assumptions, the confluence model leads to a number of specific predictions about the effects of family configurational factors on intelligence. Children's scores should be higher in smaller families with wider spacing among siblings. In addition, IQ should decline with birth order, except when wide spacing cancels the negative effects of being born into a large family.

Do the complex predictions of confluence theory hold up under research scrutiny? An extensive study that analyzed data from military files on almost all males born in Holland at the end of World War II revealed supportive findings (Zajonc, 1976; Zajonc & Marcus, 1975). As shown in Figure 8.13, both family size and birth order had the expected depressing effects on IQ (Belmont & Marolla, 1973). However, exceptions to confluence theory also appeared. The performance of only children, who are from the smallest family size, was lower than expected. Also, the last child in each family size showed a greater drop in intelligence than occurred for other birth order positions. Zajonc and Markus explain these deviations from the overall pattern by suggesting that neither only nor last-born children have the opportunity to serve as intellectual resources to younger siblings. Experiences in teaching younger brothers and sisters, they believe, offer a special intellectual advantage to the older sibling who serves as the teacher.

The confluence model has been the subject of heated controversy. While some studies have confirmed its predictions (Berbaum & Moreland, 1985), others have not (Brackbill & Nichols, 1982; Galbraith, 1982). Some researchers suggest that rather than trying to test the model in its entirety, a more fruitful approach would be to study each configurational variable separately with the aim of discovering the precise processes responsible for its effects (Rodgers, 1984; McCall, 1985). In one effort of this kind, McCall (1984) reported that the IQs of children who experienced the birth of a younger sibling dropped ten points during the following two years, at which point they were lower than the scores of singletons and last-born children in families of the same size. The decline was temporary; the older siblings gradually compensated for it, and these differences were no longer apparent by 17 years of age. In two other studies,

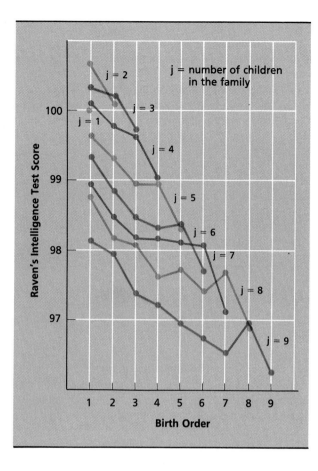

Figure 8.13. Intelligence test scores plotted as a function of family size and birth order from Belmont and Marolla's (1973) Dutch sample of 19-year-old males. *(From L. Belmont & F. A. Marolla, 1973, "Birth Order, Family Size, and Intelligence," Science, 182, 1097. Copyright 1973 by the AAAS.)*

the birth of a baby was associated with less positive and playful communication as well as more negative interaction on the part of mothers with their older children (Dunn & Kendrick, 1980; Stewart et al., 1987). Taken together, these investigations are consistent with an important tenet of confluence theory — that the arrival of a new child reduces the intellectual atmosphere of the home and temporarily slows the mental development of older children. But more than that, the findings help to illuminate just how this effect is set in motion.

Another important assumption of confluence theory has to do with the value of being in a position to teach younger siblings. Many studies indicate that children and adolescents do benefit intellectually from tutoring other children in school (Bargh & Schul, 1980; Devin-Sheehan, Feldman, & Allen, 1976), but to date, only one investigation has explored this issue in connection with sibling relationships. Smith (1984) found that among a large sample of sixth- through twelfth-grade students, the relationship between responsibility for younger siblings and school grades was far more complex than is predicted by confluence theory. Among white students, a moderate amount of sibling responsibility was related to higher grades, but either very little or a great deal of responsibility predicted lower grades. In contrast, among blacks, sibling responsibility was consistently related to lower grades. These findings indicate that sibling teaching opportunities may have quite different meanings for different ethnic groups. They also suggest that burdening any child with too much sibling responsibility may drain time and energy away from schoolwork and other pursuits that are important for intellectual growth.

On the whole, the confluence model has received only mixed support. Perhaps you noticed in examining Figure 8.13 that family size and birth order effects amount to no more than a few IQ points. Does this mean that within-family influences are really not that important? The evidence is not all in on this issue. As McCall (1983) points out, some potentially powerful within-family factors are isolated, one-time events. A particularly inspiring English teacher, a summer vacation spent with an attentive and caring grandparent, and a period of especially intense rivalry with a sibling are examples of such experiences. The most important within-family environmental influences may be of this kind, but understanding their impact requires far more intensive longitudinal study of children in the same family than has been accomplished to date.

BRIEF REVIEW

A stimulating physical environment along with parental warmth, verbal stimulation, and encouragement for achievement are between-family influences that are consistently related to mental test performance during the early childhood years. Within-family factors considered by the confluence model , such as birth order and spacing, also show relationships with IQ, but they are not very powerful. Other within-family influences are probably more important than these configurational variables, but they remain to be studied.

EARLY INTERVENTION AND INTELLECTUAL DEVELOPMENT

A wide variety of early intervention programs for children of poverty were launched in the 1960s, during a decade of great optimism about the malleability of young children's intelligence. The programs were based on the assumption that the learning problems of low-income children were best treated early, before formal schooling began, as well as on the hope that early enrichment would offset the declines in IQ and school achievement common among children from disadvantaged backgrounds.

Intervention programs continue to exist in large numbers today. The most widespread is Project Head Start, initiated by the federal government in 1965. A typical Head Start program provides children with a year of preschool education before school entry, along with nutritional and medical services. In addition, parent involvement is a central part of the Head Start philosophy. Parents serve on policy councils as

Childen who attend Head Start programs show long-term gains in school adjustment.

decision makers in program planning. They also work directly with children in classrooms, attend special programs on parenting and child development, and receive services directed at their own social, emotional, and vocational needs. Although Head Start has had a shaky history with its funding several times in jeopardy, it now stands solidly on its feet. Its 1,300 centers located around the country serve approximately 450,000 children annually (Haskins, 1989).

Fifteen years of research establishing the long-term benefits of early intervention has played a major role in the survival of Head Start. However, the first widely publicized evaluation of the program yielded adverse findings and seriously threatened its existence. Conducted by the Westinghouse Learning Corporation in cooperation with Ohio University (and now known as the Westinghouse Report), the initial study indicated that a year of Head Start had only marginal effects on children's intelligence and school achievement (Cicerelli, Evans, & Schiller, 1969). The study was immediately criticized because it was seriously flawed. Carried out retrospectively, a year or more after children in the sample had already completed Head Start, the evaluation suffered from inadequate matching of Head Start and control children and poor sampling of the variety of Head Start interventions available at the time (Smith & Bissell, 1970). Still, many people were convinced by the Westinghouse Report, and its findings became an important part of Jensen's (1969) argument that the low IQs of poor children were largely genetically determined and could not be raised very much.

Fortunately, new evaluations were completed during the 1970s and 1980s in which powerful longitudinal designs replaced the questionable retrospective approach of the Westinghouse Report. The most important of these was coordinated by the Consortium for Longitudinal Studies, a group of 12 investigators who pooled long-term follow-up data from a variety of preschool interventions. This massive evaluation effort showed that attending programs providing from one to three years of cognitive enrichment increased IQ and school achievement among low-income children through the early elementary school years (although the scores declined thereafter). More important, it revealed that real-life indicators of school adjustment emerged in the primary grades and lasted through adolescence. As shown in Figure 8.14, intervention significantly reduced the number of children who were assigned to special education classes and retained in grade and increased the number graduating from high school. Also, there were motivational and attitudinal benefits. Program children were more likely than controls to give achievement-related reasons for being proud of themselves, and their mothers had higher vocational aspirations for them (Lazar & Darlington, 1982; Royce, Darlington, & Murray, 1983). A separate report on the long-term outcomes of one of the programs revealed benefits that lasted into young adulthood. This intervention was associated with a reduction in delinquency and teenage pregnancy and an increase in the likelihood of employment (Berrueta-Clement et al., 1984). These findings had a tremendous impact on the nation's funding and preservation of early intervention, since scientific evidence clearly supported its value.

Other longitudinal findings are consistent with the Consortium results. Immediate cognitive gains are dramatic, especially for Head Start, which admits the neediest and most cognitively disadvantaged preschoolers (Lee, Brooks-Gunn, & Schnur, 1988). Yet almost all children experience an eventual **washout effect.** In other words, improvements in IQ and achievement do not last for more than a few years beyond termination of the intervention (McKey et al., 1985). This is not surprising, since preschool educational experiences become increasingly less relevant to test and classroom learning content as children mature. For intervention to be most effective, it must be continuous. Dovetailed programs, each appropriate for a particular period of development and extending from infancy into the adolescent years, would undoubtedly produce more permanent cognitive gains (Zigler & Berman, 1983). In fact, some intervention programs *are* starting earlier and lasting longer. Head Start has spawned a successful downward extension, the Parent-Child Centers for infants and

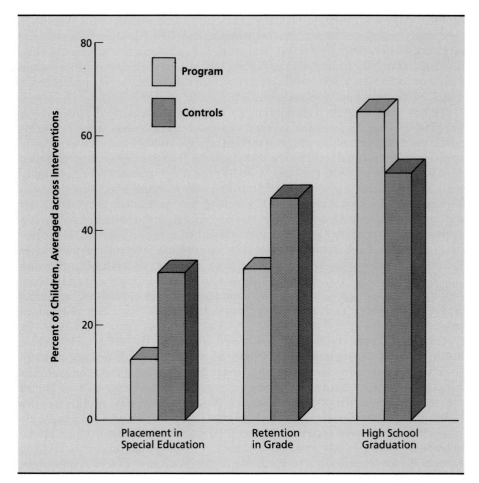

Figure 8.14. Comparisons of children who attended preschool early intervention programs with controls on real-life indicators of school adjustment. *(Adapted from Royce, Darlington, & Murray, 1983.)*

their families (Andrews et al., 1982), and an upward extension, Project Follow Through, which provides classroom enrichment and other support services during the early elementary school years (Becker & Gersten, 1982).

The fact that short-term preschool programs result in impressive changes in children's ability to meet basic school requirements, without permanently changing the IQ score itself, has been one of the most important revelations of intervention research (Becker & Gersten, 1982; Lazar & Darlington, 1982; Seitz, Rosenbaum, & Apfel, 1985; Sprigle & Schaefer, 1985). Are these lasting outcomes mediated by IQ gains during the period following the program, even though the scores themselves do not last? Or are they largely the result of changes in the attitudes and behaviors of program parents, who are more satisfied with their children's schoolwork and develop higher expectations for their performance?

As yet, the precise mechanisms through which these long-term outcomes are achieved are not known, but researchers are working to find out. Many experts believe that the addition of a few extra IQ points does not bring lasting advantages to children of poverty, and programs that have as their singular goal the raising of test scores are regarded as far too narrowly focused (Seitz, Rosenbaum, & Apfel, 1985; Zigler & Berman, 1983; Zigler, 1985). Comparisons of the effectiveness of different interventions reveal that the most successful ones generally work closely with parents (Bronfenbrenner, 1975; Gray and Wandersman, 1980). Involving and supporting parents builds bridges between center and home, thereby making it more likely that program effects will be sustained.

Recently, social scientists have experimented with interventions that direct their primary efforts toward working with parents, and evaluations reveal striking long-term gains comparable to those of programs that emphasize cognitive stimulation of children. One such program provided impoverished mothers with social, psychological, and medical services as well as day care when it was needed during the first 2½ years of their children's lives. The benefits were still evident ten years later. In comparison to controls, program mothers were more likely to be employed and to be better educated, and their enhanced sense of self-esteem and control over their own lives seemed to transfer to their offspring. Though their children showed no lasting cognitive gains, they did show improved school adjustment. Teachers described them as likable, socially well-adapted pupils, and their school attendance was good. Moreover, boys in particular had a lessened need for special educational services. In contrast, control children were often truant and had serious learning and behavior problems. The investigators concluded that the link between early intervention and positive outcomes for children could probably be found in a nurturant, supportive parent-child relationship, which carried benefits for children into later years (Seitz, Rosenbaum, & Apfel, 1985).

Perhaps future research will show that the most effective interventions are those that provide *both* long-term family support *and* cognitive enrichment, leading to improved adjustment as well as higher IQs. Early intervention is an evolving concept, and social scientists continue to experiment with it and to build on its demonstrated achievements (Zigler, 1985). Unfortunately, because of the complex forces associated with poverty that act to limit human intellectual potential, it is unlikely that intervention experiments will ever produce gains for disadvantaged youngsters that equal the life chances of children who are born into economically privileged homes.

BEYOND IQ: THE DEVELOPMENT OF CREATIVITY

As we indicated at the beginning of this chapter, the concept of intelligence, to experts and laypeople alike, means much more than just traditional academic potential that predicts success in school. One type of ability that is not sampled by major intelligence tests is creativity. Some evidence indicates that low-income children demonstrate special capabilities in this area that, besides academic intelligence, deserve to be fostered educationally (Kogan, 1983; Yando, Seitz, & Zigler, 1979).

In adults, creativity is generally regarded as the demonstration of unusual accomplishment at some intrinsically meaningful activity, such as writing, music, painting, science, or mathematics (Wallach, 1985). Of course, children are not yet mature and experienced enough to make such outstanding contributions. Therefore, in childhood, creativity has taken on a more restricted definition that has its origins in Guilford's distinction between convergent and divergent production. **Convergent thinking,** with its emphasis on arriving at a single correct answer to a problem, is the kind of cognition called for by tasks on traditional intelligence tests, whereas **divergent thinking** refers to the generation of multiple possibilities. Tests that measure divergent thinking ask children to describe as many problems as possible that are suggested by particular happenings, to name as many uses for common objects (e.g., a newspaper) as they can, or to think of as many instances of a particular class of objects (e.g., "all the round things") as possible (Wallach & Kogan, 1965). Responses can be scored for their ideational fluency, or the number of different ideas generated, as well as for their originality or unusualness. For example, saying that a newspaper can be used "as handgrips for a bicycle" would be a more unusual response than indicating that it can be used "to clean things."

The above-mentioned tasks are verbal tests of creativity, but figural or drawing measures also exist (Torrance, 1966). For example, Figure 8.15 displays the responses of a highly creative 8-year-old to a figural measure requiring her to come up with as many drawings based on a circular motif as she could.

The ability of children to display creativity on divergent thinking tasks has little to do with whether they are capable of earning high scores on conventional intelligence tests. Among the general population of children, IQ and divergent thinking show only a low positive correlation. At high levels of intelligence, the relationship is virtually nil. Thus, children who are both highly intelligent and highly creative are the exception rather than the rule (Kogan, 1983; Torrance, 1976). The absence of a close association between intelligence and creativity has even been documented in adulthood for a variety of professions, including art, writing, architecture, science, and mathematics (Barron, 1963, 1983; Helson & Crutchfield, 1970; MacKinnon, 1968; MacKinnon & Hall, 1973). These findings underline the importance of sampling a wider range of mental abilities than those encompassed by traditional IQ tests when identifying children who have special intellectual talents (Reis, 1989).

Comparisons of identical and fraternal twins reveal that genetic influences on divergent thinking are extremely weak (Pezzullo, Thorsen, & Madaus, 1972). Thus, there may be an especially wide margin in which creative thinking can be enhanced by experience. Research on family environments reveals that parents of creative children value nonconformity, emphasize intellectual curiosity and freedom of exploration, and are highly accepting of their children's individual characteristics (Getzels

Figure 8.15. Responses of a highly creative child to one of Torrance's (1966) figural measures of creativity. This 8-year-old was asked to make as many objects or pictures as she could from the circles on the page. The titles she gave her drawings, from left to right, are as follows: ''dracula,'' ''one-eyed monster,'' ''pumpkin,'' ''hula-hoop,'' ''poster,'' ''wheel chair,'' ''earth,'' ''moon,'' ''planet,'' ''movie camera,'' ''sad face,'' ''picture,'' ''stop light,'' ''beach ball,'' ''the letter O,'' ''car,'' ''glasses.'' *(Copyright © 1980 by Scholastic Testing Service, Inc. Reprinted by permission of Scholastic Testing Service, Inc. From* The Torrance Tests of Creative Thinking *by E. P. Torrance.)*

& Jackson, 1962). In view of this background of early support, it is not surprising that studies of personality characteristics of creative children and adults reveal them to be broad in their interests, attracted by complexity, and unconcerned about complying with conventional social norms (Barron & Harrington, 1981; Wallach, 1985).

Complementing the home background findings, cross-sectional evidence on the development of creativity suggests that the fact- and memory-oriented emphasis of many school classrooms may inhibit divergent thinking. Moran and his colleagues (1983) found that kindergartners gave a higher proportion of original responses to creativity tasks than did individuals from second grade through the adult years. They suggested that the answer-centered approach of traditional school curricula may make children and adolescents more cautious about expressing unusual ideas than are preschoolers, who spend less time in formal settings. Consistent with this interpretation, open classrooms, which provide greater freedom and choice in learning activities, have a facilitating effect on divergent thinking when compared to traditional classrooms, at least for the young elementary school child (Thomas & Berk, 1981).

A major concern of researchers has been how to foster venturesome and original thinking in childhood. A variety of successful techniques for stimulating divergent thinking have been identified, including modeling of a fluent, freely flowing style of responding and direct instruction in question-asking techniques (Belcher, 1975; Cliatt, Shaw, & Sherwood, 1980; Franklin & Richards, 1977). Question-asking training provides children with experiences in *problem finding* (as opposed to problem solving). This cognitive ability is judged to be so important to creative productivity in all fields of endeavor that Arlin (1975) views it as the zenith of human cognitive capacity and as a qualitatively distinct kind of cognition that lies beyond Piaget's formal operational stage. A strong link between play and divergent thinking has also been established. Because of its imaginative, experimental quality, make-believe play is especially facilitating. Whether young children engage in it spontaneously or it is induced by an experimenter, make-believe play is consistently related to enhanced performance on divergent thinking tasks (Dansky, 1980; Pepler & Ross, 1981).

Despite the availability of successful methods for augmenting divergent thinking, not all experts think these efforts are worthwhile. Wallach (1985) believes that to justify interventions aimed at improving divergent test scores, they must clearly be shown to predict real-life creative accomplishments. Yet evidence is inconsistent on this issue, and at best, divergent thinking seems to be an imperfect predictor of real-world creativity (Kogan, 1983).

Partly because of this finding, many investigators have turned their attention away from a general index of creativity toward the assessment of specialized talents. There is clear evidence that outstanding performances in domain-specific areas, such as mathematics, science, music, art, and athletics, have their roots in specialized skills that are evident in childhood (Wallach, 1985). Recently, researchers have begun to study the unique information processing attributes of children who have superior abilities, seeking answers to such questions as: Are talented youths especially adept at knowledge acquisition, strategy application, metacognitive awareness, or all three? To what extent do processing strengths differ across talent domains and individual children (Sternberg, 1988b; Sternberg & Davidson, 1986)?

At the same time, it is well recognized that the presence of unusual cognitive skill is not sufficient for the development of talent; it must be nurtured in a favorable social environment (Albert & Runco, 1986). Retrospective accounts by highly accomplished adult pianists, research mathematicians, and Olympic swimmers of their childhood years point to the importance of long-term, systematic instruction in their field of achievement from an early age, apprenticeship under eminent and inspiring teachers, and deeply committed parents who assist with their instruction (Bloom, 1982; Bloom & Sosniak, 1981). Sheer natural ability plays an undeniable role in the accomplishments of these outstanding people. But intense, field-specific education over a period of a decade or longer and an especially supportive family are also crucial to their development. These findings suggest that the most effective way to foster creativity it to provide children with systematic training aimed at thorough mastery of a particular domain, helping the talented student to reach the limits of a particular field as quickly as possible and then move beyond.

At present, there are no longitudinal studies of creative children—either those who excel at divergent thinking or those who display exceptional domain-specific talents—that trace the long-term trajectory of their accomplishments and the factors that support their special abilities. Child development specialists agree that longitudinal information is essential, both for improving ways of identifying creative children and for designing educational programs aimed at helping them realize their unique potential (Kogan, 1983; Reis, 1989; Sternberg & Davidson, 1986; Wallach, 1985). How best to maximize the creative resources of the coming generation—the future poet and scientist as well as the everyday citizen—is a challenging task for future research.

CHAPTER SUMMARY

Definitions of Intelligence

■ In the early 1900s, Alfred Binet developed the first successful intelligence test for children. An individually administered test, it was adapted for use in the United States in 1916. Soon it inspired the construction of a multitude of more efficient group-administered instruments.

■ **Factor analysis** surfaced as the central means for arriving at definitions of intelligence. The research of Spearman and Thurstone produced two schools of thought. The first regarded test items as having in common one **general factor** ("**g**"). The second viewed intelligence as a set of distinct **primary mental abilities.**

■ Modern factor analysts follow in the tradition of these early theorists. Guilford's **structure-of-intellect** model defines a total of 150 separate abilities. R. B. Cattell's distinction between **fluid** and **crystallized intelligence** has influenced many attempts to create culture-fair tests.

■ To search for the precise mental processes underlying mental ability factors, investigators have combined the psychometric with the information processing perspective. Sternberg's **triarchic theory of intelligence** extends these efforts. Intelligence is viewed as a complex interaction of cognitive processes, specific experiences, and contextual influences.

The Computation and Distribution of IQ Scores

■ Modern test designers have abandoned the **mental age (MA)** approach to computing test scores in favor of the **deviation IQ.** It offers a direct comparison of a child's raw score to the performance of a normally distributed standardization sample of same-age children.

Representative Intelligence Tests for Children

■ Current widely used intelligence tests for children are the Stanford Binet Intelligence Scale, the Wechsler Scales, and the Kaufman Assessment Battery for Children. Each provides an overall IQ, as well as a profile of subtest scores. Infant tests are useful for identifying babies who are likely to experience delayed or abnormal development. Otherwise, they are poor indicators of later IQ.

What and How Well Do Intelligence Tests Predict?

■ IQs obtained after school entry have substantial correlational stability. At the same time, many children show considerable change in the absolute value of their scores. Longitudinal gains are typical for middle-class children. In contrast, many low-income and ethnic minority youngsters experience progressive declines due to a **cumulative deficit,** or the compounding effects of depressed rearing conditions.

■ IQ is an effective predictor of scholastic success, educational attainment, occupational status, job performance, income, and social and emotional adjustment. However, the underlying causes of these correlational findings are not well established. Besides IQ, home background and personality contribute substantially to academic and personal success.

Racial/Ethnic and Socioeconomic Differences in IQ

■ Low-income and black children score lower on IQ tests than do white middle-class children, a finding that was responsible for kindling the IQ nature-nurture debate. Jensen's **Level I – Level II theory** attributes the poorer scores of these youngsters to genetic deficiencies in complex cognitive processing. However, the theory has been challenged by subsequent research.

Explaining Individual Differences in IQ

■ **Heritability estimates** arrived at through twin comparisons support a moderate role for genetic factors in determining IQ. However, **cross-fostering studies** offer a wider range of information. Advantaged rearing conditions raise the absolute value of adopted children's IQs substantially. At the same time, their performance correlates more strongly with the scores of their biological than adoptive relatives.

■ Research on black children reared in white middle-class homes demonstrates that the black-white IQ gap is socioculturally determined. It cannot be explained by racially linked, inferior genes.

■ Psychologists disagree on how to define test bias and whether it exists. Some believe that if tests have equivalent factor structures and predict scholastic performance to the same degree for different subgroups of children, they are not biased. Others think that tests are biased if some groups of children have less opportunity to learn the knowledge and skills required for successful performance.

■ Research indicates that lack of familiarity with item content, different language customs, and motivational factors lead test scores to underrepresent minority children's true abilities. Cultural bias in the tests is believed by Mercer, as well as others, to result in overlabeling of minority children as mentally retarded and their disproportionate assignment to special education classes.

■ Children of the same racial/ethnic and social class backgrounds also differ in IQ. Besides heredity, **between-family** and **within-family environmental influences** account for this variation. Research with HOME indicates that many aspects of the family environment predict IQ scores. The **confluence model** addresses the impact of several within-family variables, such as birth order and spacing. So far, it has received only limited support.

Early Intervention and Intellectual Development

■ Longitudinal studies of low-income children who have experienced early intervention repeatedly indicate that immediate IQ gains **wash out** with time. However, lasting benefits occur in school adjustment and ability to meet basic educational requirements.

Beyond IQ: The Development of Creativity

■ IQ and creativity are only weakly related in the general child population. Children who score high in **divergent thinking** come from homes that value nonconformity and intellectual curiosity. Research suggests that the fact-oriented emphasis of traditional classrooms may dampen divergent thinking.

■ Divergent thinking is an imperfect predictor of real-life creativity. Therefore, some investigators question the value of efforts to augment it. They regard specialized talent as a better index of creative potential.

IMPORTANT TERMS AND CONCEPTS

factor analysis   (p. 301)
general factor ("g")   (p. 301)
specific factor ("s")   (p. 301)
group factors   (p. 301)
primary mental abilities   (p. 301)
structure-of-intellect model   (p. 302)
crystallized intelligence   (p. 304)
fluid intelligence   (p. 304)
triarchic theory of
    intelligence   (p. 306)

intelligence quotient (IQ)   (p. 307)
mental age (MA)   (p. 307)
deviation IQ   (p. 308)
developmental quotient (DQ)
    (p. 312)
cumulative deficit
    hypothesis   (p. 314)
Level I–Level II theory   (p. 319)
heritability estimate   (p. 320)
cross-fostering study   (p. 323)

between-family environmental influences   (p. 330)
within-family environmental
    influences   (p. 330)
confluence model   (p. 332)
washout effect   (p. 335)
convergent thinking   (p. 337)
divergent thinking   (p. 337)

341

Francis Coates Jones: *Mother and Child (Reading)*. Oil on canvas 7. 1981.
© Daniel J. Terra Collection, Terra Museum of American Art, Chicago.

9

Language Development

"Bah-bah!" waves 1-year-old Mark, snugly strapped into his infant seat as his mother backs the car out of the driveway at grandmother's house. As she pulls onto the freeway and heads for home, Mark calls demandingly, "Bel! Bel!" He tugs at his seat belt, looking alternately at it and his mother seated beside him.

"The seat belt, Mark?" his mother responds. "Let's keep it on." "Look!" she says. "Here's something," handing him a cracker.

"Caa-caa. Caa-caa," says Mark, who begins to eat contentedly.

"Can you shut the front door?" Susan's father shouts from upstairs to his 3-year-old daughter.

"There. Dad, I shutted it," calls Susan up the stairs after closing the door.

Four-year-old Connie reaches for a piece of toast as she looks over the choices of jam and jelly jars at the breakfast table. "Mamma, there's no more honey, is there?" she says.

"That's right, we ran out," her mother acknowledges. "We need to buy some more."

"You go get it because I don't want to," Connie states emphatically.

"All right," Connie's mother agrees. "I can get some later while you're at nursery school."

Language — the most complex and fascinating of human abilities — develops with extraordinary rapidity over the early childhood years. At age 1, Mark can use single words to name familiar objects and communicate his desires. Three-year-old Susan already has a subtle understanding of the conventions of human communication. Even though her father's message is phrased as a question, she knows that he really intends it to be a directive and willingly complies by closing the door. In her report of the accomplished act, she uses grammatical rules to combine words into meaningful sentences. In fact, Susan's incorrect construction, "shutted," attests to her active, rule-oriented approach to linguistic production. She generalizes the "verb + ed" past tense construction to an irregular verb, a common error among children her age. With a larger vocabulary, 4-year-old Connie produces longer utterances and shows that she is in command of sophisticated grammatical forms, including the tag question and use of conjunctions. Connie also follows generally accepted conversational rules as she takes turns in a short discussion with her mother. Research aimed at discovering how young children achieve so much in such a short time has mushroomed over the last two decades. The cumulative literature on language development is vast — larger than the literature on any other aspect of child development research (Flavell, 1985).

A common practice of psycholinguists is to divide human language skill into four components: phonology, semantics, grammar, and pragmatics. **Phonology** concerns how we understand and produce the speech sounds of language. If you have ever visited a foreign country where you had little or no facility with the language, you probably wondered how anyone could segment the rapid, unbroken flow of speech sounds emitted by native speakers into organized strings of words. Yet in English, you easily comprehend and produce complicated sound patterns. How you acquired this facility is the story of phonological development.

Semantics refers to word meaning, or the way in which underlying concepts are expressed in words and word combinations. Over the preschool years, children acquire a vast number of new words. As we will see shortly, intensive study of young children's vocabulary growth lends insight into how they go about the Herculean task of mapping thousands of words onto previously unlabeled concepts.

Once mastery of vocabulary is on its way, children begin to combine words and modify them in meaningful ways. Knowledge of **grammar** includes two main facets: *syntax*, the rules by which words are arranged into comprehensible sentences, and *morphology*, the application of grammatical markers that denote number, tense, case, person, gender, and active versus passive voice, as well as other meanings in various languages (the -s and -ed endings serve as examples in English).

Finally, **pragmatics** refers to the communicative side of language. It deals with how to engage in linguistic discourse with others — how to take turns, maintain topic relevance, and communicate clearly, as well as how to use gestures, tone of voice, and the context in which a verbal message occurs to accurately gauge its meaning. Pragmatics also includes *sociolinguistic knowledge*, since society dictates how language should be spoken. To be successful communicators, children must acquire certain socially accepted interaction rituals, such as verbal greetings and leave-takings. They must also learn to adjust their speech to mark important social relationships between speaker and listener, such as differentials in age and status.

In this chapter, we begin with a brief history of the field of language development, including the fiery theoretical debate of the 1950s between behaviorist B. F. Skinner and linguist Noam Chomsky that inspired the burst of research since that time. Next we take up several current issues in the study of child language, and we discuss infant preparatory skills that set the stage for the child's first words during the second year of life. The central portion of our discussion is organized around the four main areas of language skill. For each area, we describe *what* changes and then treat the more controversial question of *how* young children acquire so much in so little time. As we proceed, you will see that the four areas of language development are really mutually interdependent; acquisition of each one facilitates mastery of the others.

To be successful communicators, children must learn socially accepted interaction rituals, such as verbal greeting and leave-takings.

During the first half of this century, research on language acquisition was primarily descriptive—aimed at establishing norms of development. The first studies identified basic milestones that characterized children growing up around the globe: all babbled by the middle of the first year, said their first words between 8 and 18 months, combined words at the end of the second year, and were in command of a great many grammatical constructions by 4 to 5 years of age. The regularity of these achievements regardless of the language children spoke suggested a maturational process. Given a reasonably stimulating linguistic context in which to grow, it appeared that children could not help but acquire language. Yet at the same time, language seemed to be learned, since without exposure to a spoken language, children who, for example, were congenitally deaf or seriously neglected, did not acquire verbal language (McNeill, 1970). This seeming contradiction set the stage for a nature-nurture debate as virulent as any that has been waged in the field of child development. By the end of the 1950s, two major figures had taken opposite sides in the controversy.

Nature versus Nurture and the Skinner-Chomsky Debate

The Behaviorist Perspective. In his book *Verbal Behavior*, published in 1957, B. F. Skinner took the radical behaviorist stance that language, just like any other behavior, is learned as adults apply the principles of *operant conditioning* to the utterances of their infants and young children. Beginning with spontaneous babbling, parents reinforce the child's utterances until these become more like adult speech. While operant conditioning has been used to account for children's language production, other behaviorists have relied on *classical conditioning* to explain children's ability to respond appropriately to language they hear (Staats, 1971). For example, when a mother says "milk" while feeding her baby, the infant associates the word with the food stimulus. Soon the word elicits a response similar to that evoked by the milk itself. The mechanism of *imitation* has also been added to behaviorist accounts, to explain how children rapidly acquire complex language behaviors, such as whole phrases and sentences (Whitehurst & Vasta, 1975). Moreover, imitation can combine with reinforcement to promote language learning, as when the parent coaxes, "Say I want a cookie" and delivers praise and a treat after the child responds correctly.

Although adherents to a behaviorist view of language acquisition still exist (Moerk, 1983; Whitehurst & Valdez-Menchaca, 1988), they are few in number. Think, for a moment, about the process of language development proposed by Skinner and other behaviorists. Parents must engage in deliberate and intensive language tutoring—shaping, modeling, and reinforcing so that, by kindergarten age, children readily produce complex sentences and have a usable vocabulary of over 14,000 words. We now know that this is a physically impossible task, even for the most conscientious of parents. For this reason, as well as others, the behaviorist view of language as impressed on a passive child who reacts to the reinforcements of intrusive adult tutors is no longer widely accepted.

Nevertheless, the ideas of Skinner and other behaviorists have contributed to our understanding of language development. Throughout this chapter, we will see many examples of how adult responsiveness and example support children's language learning, although they do not fully explain it. Moreover, behaviorist principles continue to be of considerable applied value to speech and language therapists in their efforts to help children with language delays and disabilities overcome their problems (Whitehurst et al., 1989).

The Nativist Perspective. Linguist Noam Chomsky's (1957) book *Syntactic Structures*, published during the same year as Skinner's volume, along with

Linguist Noam Chomsky believes that an innate language acquisition device (LAD) enables children to combine words into grammatically consistent utterances and understand the speech of other people at an early age.

Chomsky's (1959) critical review of Skinner's theory, first convinced the scientific community that even small children assume much of the responsibility for their own language learning. In addition to the problems noted above, Chomsky mentioned other difficulties with Skinner's analysis, including the fact that many things children say, like Susan's use of the word "shutted" in the conversational vignette at the beginning of this chapter, could not have been directly taught. Such utterances are self-generated, novel productions governed by a working knowledge of grammatical rules.

Chomsky's alternative was a staunchly nativist theory that regarded children's amazing linguistic accomplishments as a biologically based, uniquely human attribute. Focusing on children's grammatical achievements, Chomsky reasoned that the structure of language is too complex to be directly taught to or independently discovered by the cognitively immature preschool child. Instead, children are born with a **language acquisition device (LAD)**, an innately given grammatical representation that underlies all languages. It enables children, immediately upon acquiring a sufficient vocabulary, to combine words into novel but grammatically consistent utterances and to understand the meaning of the language they hear. It is the existence of the LAD, according to Chomsky, that permits children to develop language so early and so swiftly.

Chomsky proposed a theory of *transformational grammar* to explain how a single LAD can account for children's acquisition of grammatically diverse language systems around the world. The theory is extremely complex—in fact, Chomsky and others are still trying to clarify it—so we will give only its basic flavor here. Chomsky (1957) distinguished between the *surface structure* of a sentence, which refers to what people actually say, and its *deep structure*, or basic underlying meaning. Upon hearing spoken sentences, we translate grammatically diverse surface structures into their common underlying meanings using *transformational rules* that are contained in the LAD. For example, the following two sentences are grammatically different in their surface structures: "Jim gave Mary a present," and "The present was given by Jim to Mary." Because we can apply a transformational rule that takes us from the two different surface sentences to the same underlying deep structure, we know immediately that the sentences mean the same thing. The above example applies to language comprehension, but language production simply works in the opposite way. We start with the deep structure and apply transformational rules to produce grammatically correct surface sentences. According to Chomsky, language development is a matter of gaining facility with these rules during early childhood. Children are not taught to use them. Instead, the ability to do so matures spontaneously with mere exposure to a language environment.

Are children biologically primed to acquire language? Evidence we mentioned earlier on similarities among children in attainment of basic language milestones lends plausibility to this idea. In addition, Chomsky's belief in a species-specific LAD is consistent with the results of efforts to train nonhuman primates in American Sign Language (a gestural system used by the deaf that is as elaborate as any spoken language) or simplified artificial languages. Chimpanzees (who are closest to humans in the evolutionary hierarchy) have some capacity for linguistic representation, but it is limited. Extensive training and reinforcement are usually required to get them to acquire a basic vocabulary, and to date, there is no convincing evidence that they can master complex grammatical and conversational rules (Berko Gleason, 1989; Terrace et al., 1980). Finally, cross-cultural research discussed in Box 9.1, which suggests that children have a remarkable ability to invent new linguistic systems, is among the most powerful evidence that human beings are prepared for language learning in a specialized way.

Chomsky's theory, especially, has had a lasting influence on our understanding of language acquisition. It is now widely accepted that children are active, rule-oriented beings who acquire much of their language at their own initiative. Nevertheless, Chomsky's ideas, like Skinner's, have been questioned (Maratsos, 1983; Whitehurst,

Critics point out that it is not clear exactly what transformational rules are acquired by children. Currently, at least four competing transformational grammars exist, each devised by different linguists (Fodor, 1977), and Chomsky himself has changed important details of his original theory (Chomsky, 1982). As a result, Chomsky's approach has provided little that is definite about how language development proceeds (Moerk, 1989).

Also, investigators have questioned the "psychological existence" of deep grammatical structures. There is good evidence that the first word combinations of very young children are not based on a consistent application of formal grammatical categories, such as the subject of a sentence and the object of the main verb. Instead,

---

◆ CONTEMPORARY ISSUES: CULTURAL DIFFERENCES ◆

Children Invent Language: The Case of Hawaiian Creole English　　　　Box 9.1

Can instances be found in which children develop complex language systems in the presence of minimal linguistic input? If so, this evidence would serve as strong support for Chomsky's idea that all members of our species are born with a biological program for language acquisition.

In a recent series of studies, Susan Goldin-Meadow and her colleagues reported that congenitally deaf preschoolers who had not been taught conventional sign language spontaneously produced a gestural communication system strikingly similar to hearing children's verbal language (Goldin-Meadow, 1979; Goldin-Meadow & Mylander, 1983; Goldin-Meadow & Morford, 1985). However, Goldin-Meadow's conclusions have been criticized by investigators who believe that the children's competencies may have resulted from subtle gestural exchanges with their parents (Bohannon & Warren-Leubecker, 1989; Whitehurst, 1982).

The study of creole offers an alternative test of the nativist hypothesis. *Creoles* are languages that arise rapidly from *pidgins*, which are minimally developed "emergency" tongues that result when several language communities migrate to the same locale and no dominant language exists to support communication among them. In 1876, the Hawaiian sugar industry imported large numbers of foreign workers from China, Japan, Korea, the Phillippines, Puerto Rico, and Portugal. The multilingual population quickly outnumbered former residents—English speakers and native Hawaiians alike. Out of this melting pot, Hawaiian Pidgin English emerged, a communication system with a small vocabulary and a narrow range of grammatical options that did little more than permit new residents to "get by" in everyday life. In fact, Pidgin English was so restricted in its possibilities and applied so unsystematically that it may have offered growing children insufficient language input from which to learn. Yet within 20 to 30 years after initial foreign settlement, a new complex language (Hawaiian Creole English), which borrowed vocabulary

from its pigdin and foreign language predecessors but bore little structural resemblance to them, became widespread. How could this remarkable linguistic achievement have occurred?

Derek Bickerton (1981, 1984) concludes that the next generation of children must have invented the language, relying on innate mechanisms ensuring the development of an adequate communication system. Support for Bickerton's conclusion is of two kinds. First, the structure of creole languages is similar around the world, suggesting that a common genetic program underlies them. Second, creole grammar bears a striking resemblance to the linguistic structures children first use when acquiring any language and to their incorrect hypotheses about complex grammatical forms. For example, expressions like "He no bite you" and "Where he put the toy?" are perfectly correct in Hawaiian Creole English. Bickerton (1981) believes that:

> The child does not, initially, "learn language." As he develops, the genetic program for language which is his hominid inheritance unrolls exactly as does the genetic program that determines his increase in size (and) muscular control. . . . "Learning" consists of adapting this program, revising it, adjusting it to fit the realities of the cultural language he happens to encounter. Without such a program, the simplest of cultural languages would be quite unlearnable. . . . (pp. 296–297).

According to Bickerton, the child's biological language is always there, under the surface, ready to reemerge when cultural language is shattered—an event experienced by all first-generation creole children. However, as yet, no one has been able to observe the language acquisition of these youngsters directly. Without such evidence, we cannot be entirely sure that adult input to children plays little role in the creation of creole (Bohannon, MacWhinney, & Snow, 1990).

as we will see in greater detail later on, at first children use words belonging to the same grammatical class in unpredictable ways that do not fit with an innate knowledge of grammar (Braine, 1976; Maratsos & Chalkley, 1980).

Finally, children's language acquisition is no longer regarded as accomplished quite as quickly as nativist theory assumes. Although extraordinary strides are made during the preschool years, children's progress in mastering many sentence constructions is steady and gradual, showing little evidence of sudden, innately determined insights (Brown, 1973). In fact, complete mastery of some common grammatical forms (such as the passive voice) is not achieved until well into middle childhood (Horgan, 1978), and some grammatical subtleties continue to be learned into the adult years (Menyuk, 1977).

The Interactionist Perspective

New theories of language development emphasize linkages and interactions between inner predispositions and environmental inputs, replacing the dichotomy that grew out of the Skinner-Chomsky debate. Although several interactionist models exist, all stress the social context of language learning. An active child, well endowed for acquiring language, observes and engages in social exchanges with others. From this experience the child builds a linguistic system that relates the form and content of language to its social meaning. As you can probably see from this brief description, interactionists locate language acquisition squarely within a social framework. Both native endowment and a rich communicative environment assist the child in discovering the functions and regularities of language (Bohannon & Warren-Leubecker, 1989).

Although all interactionists regard the child as an active, communicative being from birth, there is little agreement about the precise nature of children's innate abilities. Some theorists believe that children make sense of their complex language environments by applying powerful analytic capacities of a general cognitive kind (Bates & MacWhinney, 1987; Nelson, 1989). Others continue to agree with Chomsky's basic position that the human brain is uniquely primed for linguistic analysis (Slobin, 1985). As we chart the course of language growth, we will describe some of these new views, but it is important to note that none are completely verified yet. We still know much more about the course of language acquisition than exactly how development takes place (Rice, 1989).

IMPORTANT ISSUES IN LANGUAGE DEVELOPMENT

In this section, we consider three basic issues about language growth. The first two — whether there is a critical period for language acquisition and whether language development proceeds according to a universal sequence — are offshoots of the nature-nurture debate. If children are equipped with something like an LAD that prepares them to learn language easily and rapidly, then we would expect early childhood to be the time of greatest receptivity to language learning. We would also expect development to proceed in a uniform fashion for all children. The third issue that we address is how to assess children's language progress: by means of language production, that is, what they are able to *say*, or through their comprehension, what they are able to *understand* but might not yet produce in their own speech.

Is There a Critical Period for Language Development?

Lenneberg (1967) first proposed that language acquisition must occur during a critical period that parallels the age span during which lateralization (or localization) of language functions takes place in the left hemisphere of the brain. Lenneberg believed that lateralization was complete around puberty; exposure to a linguistic environment, he thought, had to occur before this time, or language development would not be possible. You may recall from Chapter 5 that localization of language in the left hemisphere begins far earlier than Lenneberg speculated. It is present at birth and increases over the childhood years. This evidence does not refute the existence of a critical period, although if the period is tied to lateralization, it may end earlier than Lenneberg believed. To verify the critical period notion, we need to show that when language development is delayed beyond a certain time, it is far more difficult for children to acquire, or it cannot be acquired at all. Two kinds of evidence shed light on this issue. The first are studies of children not exposed to language in early childhood but later given the opportunity to learn it. The second are investigations aimed at finding out whether a second language can be acquired more easily during childhood than later on.

A few investigators have tracked the recovery of severely abused children who experienced minimal human contact during childhood. The most recent and thoroughly studied is *Genie*, a child isolated at 20 months of age[1] in the back room of her parent's house and harnessed to a potty chair. Genie was not discovered until 13½ years of age. Her early environment was linguistically (as well as emotionally) impoverished. No one was permitted to talk to her, and she was severely beaten when she made any noise. When found, she did not vocalize at all; even her crying was silent. Over several years of training with warm, dedicated caregivers, Genie's language developed, but not nearly at the same rate or to the same extent as normal children. Although she eventually developed a large vocabulary and good comprehension of everyday conversation, her grammatical abilities were limited. For example, she never acquired some syntactic forms, such as pronouns. Genie's speech also showed poor pitch control, and she could not use intonation to express some meanings. Although she was eager to join in conversations, she was slow to respond. Asked something, Genie might not answer right away, but would return 5 or 10 minutes later to deliver the requested information (Curtiss, 1977).

Genie's case is consistent with the operation of a "weak" critical period, or the sensitive phase notion we introduced in Chapter 4. Genie *was* able to acquire a first language, but she did not do so as easily, naturally, and competently as preschool children do. Neurolinguistic assessments revealed that Genie used her right hemisphere to process linguistic information. Curtiss (1977) believes that by the time she was found, the developmental period had passed during which specialized language areas in the left hemisphere could accomplish the task of language learning. Nonlanguage areas were forced to take over functioning, but they were limited in their ability to do so. Consistent with this idea, Genie's accomplishments resembled the attainments of other right hemispheric language cases and, to some degree, nonhuman primates, who, when given language training, also have difficulty with grammar. Thus, Genie's development fits with the conjecture that language learning is optimal when it occurs during the period of brain lateralization, although her case does not tell how early and limited that period might be. However, in another study of a child named Isabelle, the daughter of an isolated deaf mute, language remediation initiated at age 6 resulted in complete recovery within two years (Davis, 1947). Isabelle's case suggests that early childhood linguistic deficits are reversible in nonabused children, although more extended deprivation may not be (Snow, 1987).

What about acquiring a second language? Is this task harder during adolescence and adulthood, after a critical or sensitive phase for language development has passed? In one of the most comprehensive studies of second language learning, Snow

---

[1] Pediatric records of Genie's early infancy suggest that she was an alert, responsive baby. Her early motor development was normal, and her mother reported that she said her first words just before her confinement, after which all language disappeared. Therefore, mental retardation is regarded as an unlikely alternative explanation for the course of her later development.

and Hoefnagel-Höhle (1978) spent one year tracking the acquisition of Dutch by native English speakers ranging in age from 3 years to adulthood. All were picking up the language at school or work, with little or no formal instruction. Except for pronunciation (for which attainment at year's end was similar at all ages), virtually all acquisition differences favored the older subjects, with 12- to 15-year-olds learning the fastest and preschoolers the slowest. It seems that increasing age actually predicts faster acquisition of a second language, at least up to a point well beyond the time frame during which the brain is believed to be especially receptive to language learning. These results are contrary to the expectations of a critical period hypothesis. Snow and Hoefnagel-Höhle believe that motivational and social factors, rather than biological readiness, influence second language learning. People of a wide range of ages will acquire a foreign language quickly if it is needed to get along in daily life. Older children, who have developed better learning strategies, will progress more quickly than younger ones.

Taken together, the evidence reviewed above indicates that there may be an extended sensitive phase for first language acquisition. Once a first language has been learned, second language learning does not proceed in a way that is consistent with the critical period hypothesis.

Universals versus Individual Differences in Language Development

As a result of Chomsky's influence, most work on language acquisition before 1970 involved a search for *universals*, or similarities in the way children master their first language. A variety of commonalities were identified that we will discuss in greater detail later on. They were assumed to reflect the maturational unfolding of a genetically determined linguistic competence, and variations among children were not regarded as particularly interesting or important (Goldfield & Snow, 1989; Wells, 1986).

As Chomsky's theory began to be questioned, research on language universals waned. Investigators realized that universal milestones could as easily be attributed to experiences common to all children as to an innate LAD. The genetic versus environmental causes of universals were difficult, if not impossible, to sort out (Hardy-Brown, 1983). Yet researchers wanted to move beyond mere description of language development toward an understanding of factors responsible for its acquisition.

Individual differences in *rate* of language development had long been recognized (McCarthy, 1954). Starting in the 1970s, studies reported differences not just in rate, but also in *route* or form of development. Researchers quickly recognized that studying differences as well as similarities was crucially important if the origins of language were to be fully understood.

Nelson (1973) was among the first to identify important individual differences in route of language development, and her findings have been documented and extended in recent research. Following a sample of 1- to 2½-year-olds as they acquired their first 50 words, Nelson noticed that the children differed in the words and phrases they produced. The majority fit a **referential style** of language learning. Their early vocabularies consisted of many nouns (familiar object names, such as "ball" and "car") and fewer verbs, proper names, and adjectives. A smaller number of children used an **expressive style.** Compared to referential children, they used a large number of pronouns and social formulas, such as "stop it," "I want it," and "what d'you want," and relatively fewer nouns, verbs, and adjectives. Children uttered these social phrases without pause in the form of compressed wholes, much like single words. Nelson suggested that the two types of children had different early notions about the uses of language. Referential children thought language largely served the purpose of talking about things, while expressive children seemed to think it was for talking about the self and other people, as well as for expressing feelings, needs, and social forms. Thus, children's first notions of what language was all about were reflected in the unique makeup of their early vocabularies.[2]

Children's early styles soon became linked to other aspects of language development. Expressive children used more pronouns in their early sentences, whereas referential children showed clearer articulation, and their vocabulary and grammar grew more quickly (Bates, Bretherton, & Snyder, 1988; Nelson, 1973). The referential advantage in vocabulary size is not surprising. Languages provide the child who talks mostly about things with many object labels, but far fewer social phrases are available for the expressively oriented child. Vocabulary differences diminished as children broadened their first primitive notions about the functions of language (Nelson, 1973, 1975), but some referential versus expressive variations persisted well into the preschool years. For example, Horgan (1980, 1981) reported that referential children elaborated noun phrases with descriptive information (e.g., "*The great big mean dog* ran home"). Expressive children elaborated verb phrases (e.g., He *might have been going* home"). Thus, early stylistic variations evolved into new individual differences as children matured.

Recent research on the origins of these individual differences suggests that a rapidly developing, referential-style child has an especially active interest in exploring objects, a home life that provides a rich variety of play materials, and parents who eagerly respond with words for things to the child's first attempts to talk. In contrast, an expressive-style child seems to have a more socially oriented personality and experiences a linguistic environment in which speech is frequently used to mediate social relationships (Furrow & Nelson, 1984; Goldfield, 1987; Lieven, 1978). Moreover, early stylistic variations are linked to culture. For example, while many mothers in Western society stress object labels to children, Vietnamese toddlers learn an honorific pronoun system first (Nelson, 1981). These findings are consistent with an interactionist approach to language development, involving interdependency between children's inherent attributes and their physical and social worlds.

The Comprehension versus Production Distinction

A final important issue is the distinction between **comprehension** (the language children understand) and **production** (the language they use). Most research on early language development is based on what children say rather than what they comprehend. Yet inferences about development based only on production may give a distorted picture, since young children understand many words long before they produce them (Goldin-Meadow, Seligman, & Gelman, 1976).

The distinction we made in Chapter 7 between recognition and recall will help you understand why language comprehension proceeds ahead of production. Comprehension merely requires recognition of a word, along with a memory search for the concept it designates. In contrast, production demands active retrieval of words, plus an evaluation of whether they appropriately express one's intended meaning (Clark, 1983; Kuczaj, 1986). Because production is cognitively more difficult, failure to produce a word is not good evidence that children do not comprehend it. In fact, children with more reserved, cautious personalities may show especially large comprehension-production discrepancies during the early phases of language growth. In comparison to their more outgoing agemates, these youngsters begin to talk later and often show sudden spurts in language production (Nelson, 1973). Thus, relying only on production to make judgments about language functioning leads to underestimates of linguistic knowledge that are greater for some children than for others. In assessing

---

[2] Nelson notes that there are some children who employ both styles from the very beginning, suggesting that the referential-expressive distinction is a continuum rather than two completely separate language learning strategies. Also, nouns were the most frequent words in the vocabularies of all of the children, although some children used more nouns than others.

language competence, it is important to look at not just one, but both of these processes.

Now that we have covered these basic, prefacing issues, let's chart the course of language development itself.

PRELINGUISTIC PREPARATION

From the very beginning, babies are prepared to acquire language. In the following sections, we discuss important inborn capabilities and infant developmental milestones that pave the way for the dawn of linguistic communication.

Receptivity to Speech Sounds

Infants, as we indicated in Chapter 4, are pretuned to respond to human speech sounds. Recall that the newborn baby is especially sensitive to the pitch range of the human voice, that human speech is more rewarding to infants than other sounds, and that neonates have an astonishing ability to detect differences between language sounds that exceeds the performance of adults. Because this latter skill may help children crack the phonological code of their language, let's consider it in greater detail.

As adults, we analyze the speech stream into sound categories, or **phonemes.** That is, when we listen to spoken utterances, we attend to certain features that permit us to divide it into small but distinct units, such as the difference between the initial consonants in "pa" and "ba." Phonemes are not the same across all languages. For example, "ra" and "la" are distinct sounds to English speakers, but Japanese individuals cannot distinguish them (Miyawaki et al., 1975). Conversely, English speakers do not make some distinctions that are important in other languages (Sachs, 1985).

When adults are asked to discriminate artificially generated sounds that belong to the same phonemic category in their native language but are actually slightly different acoustically, they have considerable difficulty in doing so. This tendency to perceive as identical a range of sounds that belong to the same phonemic class is called **categorical speech perception.** Research shows that categorical speech perception is characteristic not only of adults, but also of 1-month-old infants. Furthermore, as we indicated earlier, young infants around the world can discriminate phoneme categories that adults cannot because the particular contrast is not used in the language they speak (Aslin, Pisoni, & Jusczyk, 1983).

Do these findings indicate that infants are born with a speech decoder, an innate device that permits them to analyze the sound stream of any language to which they are exposed? A decade or two ago, psycholinguists thought this was the case, but new research has led this view to be questioned. Recent evidence reveals that babies have a built-in tendency to look for well-defined boundaries in *both* speech and nonspeech sounds. However, the nature of the speech stream is such that it is more easily separable into perceptual categories than are other sound stimuli (Aslin, Pisoni & Jusczyk, 1983).

By 8 to 10 months of age, babies no longer discriminate sounds that are not used in their own language community (Werker & Tees, 1984; Werker, 1989). Jusczyk (1985) believes this shift is not just the result of infants' increased exposure to a particular language environment. That it occurs around the time when infants start to talk suggests that it may be related to their increased desire to communicate. As babies attend selectively to speech sounds that lead to changes of meaning in their own language, they cease to notice speech sounds that are not used. However, the capacity to detect nonnative phonemes is not lost. With training, adults show renewed sensitivity to distinctions they made quite easily as tiny infants (Werker, 1989).

Besides being able to detect a wide range of speech sounds, babies as young as 4 days of age have a remarkable ability to distinguish the overall sound pattern of their native language from that of other languages (Mehler et al., 1988). This finding indicates that neonates are not just innately wired to categorize separate sounds; they quickly group together the sound patterns of the language spoken around them. This natural ability to separate one language from another is of enormous assistance to young language learners growing up in multilingual environments, a topic to which we return at the end of this chapter.

Babbling

Around 2 months of age, babies begin to make vowel-like noises, called *cooing* because of their pleasant, "oo" quality. Gradually, consonants are added, and around 6 months, **babbling** appears, in which infants repeat consonant-vowel combinations in extended strings, like "bababa" and "nanana." The onset and early course of babbling seem to be controlled maturationally, since babies from all linguistic environments start babbling at around the same age and produce a similar repertoire of early sounds. Even deaf babies and infants of deaf parents who cannot respond to their babies' sounds make some typical babbling sounds (Lenneberg, Rebelsky & Nichols, 1965; Stoel-Gammon & Otomo, 1986). However, the continuation of babbling is dependent on the ability to hear human speech. Babbling containing the sounds of mature spoken languages appears in hearing babies around 7 months of age; in hearing-impaired infants, it rarely occurs before the second year of life. In fact, observations of one totally deaf child revealed a complete absence of speechlike babbles (Oller & Eilers, 1988).

Nevertheless, among hearing infants a maturational component continues to be evident in the *form* of babbling throughout the first year. Adults cannot change the babbled sounds that infants make through reinforcement and modeling, although they can, to some extent, influence the overall *amount* of babbling (Dodd, 1972; Todd & Palmer, 1968). Moreover, the phonetic development of babbling follows a universal pattern. Infants initially produce a limited number of vowel and consonant sounds that expands to include a much broader range by 12 months of age. The addition of a wide variety of stress and intonation patterns makes the 1-year-old's babbling stream seem much like conversational speech without intelligible words. Maturation of the vocal structures and of the brain areas responsible for articulation is thought to be responsible for these changes (de Villiers & de Villiers, 1978; Sachs, 1985).

At one time, it was believed that the child's first words emerged directly out of babbling — that infants babbled all possible sounds, and adults simply reinforced the ones that were most similar to their own language (Winitz, 1969). Think about what we have said about the development of babbling so far, and you will see that this explanation cannot possibly be correct. Not only is adult feedback ineffective in changing babbling sounds, but babbling *expands* with development; it does not contract to become more like the language the child will learn. Also, only its intonation patterns, not its sounds, resemble those of the child's language community (Boysson-Bardies, deSagart, & Durand, 1984; Thevenin et al., 1985).

That infants do not stop babbling when they first begin to talk suggests that babbling plays some role in early speech production, although investigators are not entirely certain what it is. In one study, Elbers and Ton (1985) recorded the speech of a young toddler and discovered a continuous interplay between the child's babbling and early word productions. New words influenced the sound characteristics of babbling, and babbling, in turn, seemed to pave the way for the production of additional new words. Babbling may enable speech sounds to develop in a preparatory way that then facilitates their integration into the child's first words.

The Emergence of Communicative Competence

Research suggests biological preparedness for some aspects of conversational behavior. For example, newborn infants can initiate interactions by making eye contact and terminate them by averting their gaze. By 4 months of age (when their tracking is sufficiently mature), infants follow their mother's line of regard. Thus, the attention of mother and infant becomes jointly directed at an early age, and mothers often verbally comment on what their infants are observing (Bruner, 1974). In fact, joint attentional engagement in which an adult labels what the child is looking at seems to facilitate early language development. Mothers who spend more time in this way have infants who start to talk earlier and show faster vocabulary development (Tomasello, 1988).

By about 3 months of age, the beginnings of conversational turn-taking can be observed. **Pseudodialogues,** which mimic the form but do not yet serve the function of verbal exchange, appear between caregivers and infants. The baby vocalizes, the adult vocalizes in return, waits for a response, and vocalizes again (Bateson, 1975). In Western cultures, these vocal exchanges are common, but the mother is largely responsible for sustaining the interaction. She does this by responding to the temporal flow of her baby's behavior—replying, fitting into, and supporting the infant's signals. In this way, the baby's responses become integrated into a dialogue-like sequence before infants have any real awareness that conversational expectations exist (Schaffer, 1979).

Bruner (1977) believes that early social games help infants grasp the conversational routine and pair its turn-taking form with its information exchange function. Between 6 and 12 months, conventional infant games, such as peekaboo and pat-a-cake, increase in frequency and variety. The games contain complementary roles that are almost always reversible. At first, the parent elaborates the game, and the amused infant is a passive spectator. Gradually, the baby learns to anticipate game events, and around age 1, infant and parent alternate the roles of agent and experiencer (Ratner & Bruner, 1978). Simple, predictable game structures are an ideal setting for infants to connect parents' spoken utterances to the ongoing action of the games. In fact, between 13 and 16 months of age, children begin to linguistically mark their own participation (Camaioni & Laicardi, 1985).

At the end of the first year, babies start to intentionally use nonverbal signals to direct and control the behavior of other people. Bates and her colleagues found that infants use two preverbal forms of basic speech acts. The first is the **protodeclara-**

According to Bruner, early social games like pat-a-cake help infants grasp the turn-taking form of conversation along with its information exchange function.

tive, involving assertions about objects, in which the baby touches an object, holds it up, or points to it while looking at others to make sure they notice. The second is the **protoimperative,** in which the infant gets another person to do something by pointing, reaching, and often calling and making sounds at the same time. These preverbal speech acts coincide with Piaget's sensorimotor Substage 5, in which the child learns that it is possible to bring about changes through various means, one of these being to use another person to achieve a goal rather than to carry it out directly oneself (Bates, 1979; Bates, Camaioni, & Volterra, 1975). However, preverbal intentional communication is also encouraged by the caregiver's responses to infant signals. These help babies realize that their cries, smiles, vocalizations, and gestures produce predictable results. In time, babies send out these signals deliberately because they have learned, as the result of maternal responsiveness, to anticipate their effects on others (Bruner, 1977).

Early in the second year, turn-taking and children's preverbal intentional communication are brought together, especially in situations in which children's messages do not communicate clearly. Babies of this age start to negotiate their failed messages. Sometimes these exchanges last for a number of turns before infants achieve their goal, as in the following example of a 14-month-old's efforts to get his mother to give him a sponge from the kitchen counter (Golinkoff, 1983, pp. 58–59):

Jordan: (Vocalizes repeatedly until his mother turns around.)

Mother: (Turns around to look at him.)

Jordan: (Points to one of the objects on the counter.)

Mother: Do you want this? (Holds up milk container.)

Jordan: (Shakes his head "no.") (Vocalizes, continues to point.)

Mother: Do you want this? (Holds up jelly jar.)

Jordan: (Shakes head "no.") (Continues to point.) (Two more offer-rejection pairs.)

Mother: This? (Picks up sponge.)

Jordan: (Leans back in highchair, puts arms down, tension leaves body.)

Mother: (Hands Jordan sponge.)

Soon words are uttered along with the same reaching and pointing gestures that made up the infant's preverbal communicative acts. Then the gestures diminish, eventually becoming a redundant adjunct to vocal language (Goldin-Meadow & Morford, 1985).

Throughout this section, we have stressed that progress toward verbal communication is encouraged by caregivers who involve infants in dialogue-like exchanges. However, caution should be exercised with regard to how essential these interactive experiences are. Recent cross-cultural evidence reveals that there are societies, such as the people of Western Samoa and the Kaluli of Papua New Guinea, who rarely treat their infants as communicative partners and never play social games with them. Yet these children become speakers of their native language within the normal time frame of development (Schieffelin & Ochs, 1987). Perhaps deliberate parental molding of the infant's expressive behavior is not essential, but when it occurs, it facilitates communicative development. Additional cross-cultural comparisons are needed to determine how crucial maternal-infant reciprocal interaction really is for the development of communicative competence (Shatz, 1983).

The Beginnings of Conceptual Understanding

In Chapter 6, as well as in the discussion above, we indicated that certain cognitive acquisitions provide a foundation for early language development. A flexible ability to coordinate sensorimotor means with ends is related to infants' realization that language is a tool for influencing others. The development of the symbolic function in Piaget's sensorimotor Substage 6 underlies the toddler's ability to use words in place of objects and events that are not immediately present. Children must also acquire a foundation of prelinguistic concepts onto which they can map their first words. As we will soon see, children's early vocabulary reflects the cognitive knowledge they have amassed about objects and situations during infancy. Thus, language builds on prior cognitive advances, but as we showed in Chapter 6, the relationship between language and thought quickly becomes reciprocal. Learning new words and verbal expressions also facilitates cognitive development by making meanings salient and explicit, freeing thought from its ties to the here-and-now, and increasing the efficiency and flexibility of human thinking.

BRIEF REVIEW

During infancy, biological predispositions, cognitive-developmental achievements, and a responsive social environment prepare the child for verbal language. Human neonates have a built-in capacity to detect a wide variety of speech sounds and to distinguish the overall sound pattern of the language they hear from that of others. By the end of the first year, babies become increasingly sensitive to the speech categories of their native tongue. Infants also coo, then babble, and finally develop preverbal communicative gestures. Adults in Western cultures shape these prelinguistic initiatives into conversationlike exchanges. Additional cognitive advances combine with these preparatory skills to produce a beginning speaker by the second year of life.

Now that we have charted the course of prelinguistic development, let's turn to a consideration of the various facets of language acquisition — phonological, semantic, grammatical, and pragmatic — during the much lengthier, linguistic period of childhood.

PHONOLOGICAL DEVELOPMENT

Think about the sounds you might hear if you listened in on a 1- or 2-year-old child trying out her first handful of words. You probably conjured up an assortment of rather interesting pronunciations, such as "nana" for banana, "oap" for soap, and "weddy" for ready, as well as some puzzling productions that the child uses like words but that have no resemblance to adult forms. For "translations" of these latter items, you have to ask the child's parent. Acquiring accurate pronunciation skills is a complicated process that depends on children's increasing control over the articulatory apparatus, improved ability to attend to complex phonological sequences, and growing capacity to monitor and revise their faulty productions so they match adult speech. Between 1 and 4 years of age, children make considerable progress at this task (Ingram, 1986).

Experts in phonology view children mastering the pronunciation of their language as young problem solvers. In trying to figure out how to talk like people around them, they adopt a variety of temporary strategies for producing sounds that bring adult words within their current range of physical and cognitive capabilities (Ingram, 1986; Menn, 1989; Menyuk, Menn, & Silber, 1986). Let's look at the characteristics of this progression.

The Early Phase: First Words, Sound Play, and Jargon Stretches

During the transition from babbling to speech, children engage in trial-and-error efforts to pronounce their first words, some of which are produced fairly accurately, while others are only loosely approximated. Children's first productions are limited by the small number of sounds they can voluntarily control. At first, they apply a single phonetic form to a variety of words, a feature of their speech that often makes them difficult to understand. In one case described by Ingram (1986), a child substituted "bat" for as many as 12 different words, including "bad," "bark," "bent," and "bite."

During this period, first words often become the subject of **sound play** episodes as children practice and expand their newfound phonological capacities (Garvey, 1977). Your author's older son, upon acquiring the word "book" at 14 months, was fond of creating vocal variations on it, which sounded something like this: "book-a-book-a-dook-a-dook-a-book-a-nook-a-book-aaaa." Also, children of this phase frequently produce **jargon stretches**—babbled sequences with real words embedded in them that are uttered with eye contact and communicative intent (Menyuk, Menn, & Silber, 1986). Young language learners seem to recognize that adults' words occur in extended sound streams, and they emulate this form with the limited vocabulary and phonological resources that they have.

Early semantic and phonological development are interdependent. The first words children choose to say are partly influenced by what they can successfully pronounce. For example, Menn's (1976) subject Jacob understood many words beginning with "b," "k," and "d" at the time he began to speak, but he attempted to say only those beginning with "d." Some children are quite conservative in this respect and try to say only words within their current phonological repertoire, while others are more daring and will try to say just about anything. Most, however, fall in between these two extremes and are simply more likely to produce words with familiar sounds (Schwartz & Leonard, 1982).

The Appearance of Phonological Strategies

By the middle of the second year, children apply systematic strategies to simplify words so they fit with their phonological capabilities (Preisser, Hodson, & Paden, 1988). These strategies mark an intermediate phase of development in which children's pronunciation of many words is partly right and partly wrong, but their errors are fairly consistent. Although children vary greatly in the rules they adopt, a few typical ones are shown in Table 9.1. Phonological strategies often lead children to pronounce different words identically—for example, both "wing" and "ring" as

Table 9.1. Common Phonological Strategies Used by Young Children to Simplify the Task of Pronouncing Adult Words

STRATEGY	EXAMPLES
Repeating the initial consonant-vowel in a multisyllable word	"TV" becomes "didi," "cookie" becomes "gege"
Deleting of unstressed syllables in a multisyllable word	"banana" becomes "nana," "granola" becomes "nola," "giraffe" becomes "raffe"
Replacing fricatives (hissing sounds) with stop consonant sounds	"sea" becomes "tea," "say" becomes "tay," "sing" becomes "ting"
Replacing consonant sounds produced in the rear and palate area of the vocal tract with ones produced in the frontal area	"shoe" becomes "zue," "shop" becomes "zop," "goose" becomes "doose"
Replacing liquid sounds ("l" or "r") with glides ("j" or "w")	"lap" becomes "jap," "ready" becomes "weddy"
Reducing consonant-vowel-consonant words to a consonant-vowel form by deleting the final consonant	"bib" becomes "bi," "bike" becomes "bai," "more" becomes "muh"
Replacing an ending consonant syllable with a vowel	"apple" becomes "appo," "bottom" becomes "bada"
Reducing a consonant cluster to a single consonant	"clown" becomes "cown," "play" becomes "pay," "train" becomes "tain"

Source: Ingram, 1986.

"wing." Such errors do not result from an inability to perceive sound differences between the words. Children can point to a correct picture when presented with each of the adult pronunciations, even though they cannot yet say both words correctly (Barton, 1980). Here again, comprehension is clearly ahead of production.

Children's pronunciation undergoes marked improvement over the preschool years. Maturation of the vocal apparatus and the child's own active problem-solving efforts are largely responsible for this change, since children's phonological errors are quite resistant to adult correction. However, parents and others provide effective models from which children do learn. When speaking to young children, adults and older children in many cultures tend to limit their communications to simple sentences with exaggerated intonation and very clear pronunciation, a form of speech called **motherese** (Fernald et al., 1989; Newport, Gleitman, & Gleitman, 1977; Papousek & Papousek, in press). Parents do not seem to use motherese in a deliberate attempt to teach language; most of us rely on these same speech qualities when communicating with foreigners. Motherese probably arises unconsciously out of parental efforts to keep children's attention and make sure they understand, and it seems to work effectively in these ways. From birth on, children prefer to listen to motherese over adult-directed speech (Fernald & Kuhl, 1987; Rileigh, 1973). Moreover, parents fine-tune motherese to fit with children's needs, increasing its complexity as language develops and simplifying it when children signal lack of understanding (Bohannon & Warren-Leubecker, 1988). Motherese may not be essential for language acquisition, but it is probably facilitating. In the case of phonological development, its high articulatory precision undoubtedly eases the young child's task of analyzing a complex speech stream.

Later Phonological Development

Although phonological development is largely complete by the time the child goes to school, a few acquisitions involving accent patterns are not mastered until later childhood and adolescence. Pronunciations that signal differences in meaning between such words as "greenhouse" and "green house" develop gradually from first to sixth grade (Atkinson-King, 1973). Changes in syllabic stress after words take on endings, such as -ity ("humid," "humidity") and -al ("method," "methodical"), are not mastered until adolescence. These late developments may have something to do with the semantic complexity of the words to which they apply. Even among young children, pronunciation is best for easily understood words (Camarata & Leonard, 1986). As indicated in Chapter 7, the human information processing capacity is limited. Working on both the form and meaning of a new word at the same time may overload the system, leading form to be sacrificed temporarily until the word's meaning is better understood.

BRIEF REVIEW

Phonological development begins with young children's trial-and-error efforts to pronounce their first words, followed by an intermediate period in which systematic strategies are used to simplify difficult words. Although the sound features of motherese facilitate early phonological development, the child is an active problem solver in mastering the phonology of language. Phonological development is mostly complete by school entry, except for a few complex accent patterns.

SEMANTIC DEVELOPMENT

The Early Phase

Maternal reports indicate that on the average, children utter their first word between 11 and 12 months, with a range of about 8 to 18 months (Whitehurst, 1982). By age 6, children have a vocabulary of around 14,000 words (Templin, 1957). To accomplish this monumental task, between 18 months and 6 years, children add about nine words to their vocabulary each day (Clark, 1983).

Learning words is largely a matter of identifying which concept within one's current cognitive repertoire each label picks out in a particular language community. In view of the sensorimotor foundations that precede language learning, it is not surprising that children's first words generally refer to manipulable or moving objects (e.g., "car," "ball," "cat") and to events that have salient properties of change ("bye-bye," "up," "more"). As Nelson (1973) points out, in their first 50 vocabulary words, children rarely include names for things like table or vase that just *sit there*. A growing body of evidence indicates that these early word acquisitions are linked to specific cognitive attainments. For example, the development of disappearance words ("all gone") coincides with mastery of advanced object permanence problems. Success and failure terms ("there!" and "uh-oh!") appear around the time toddlers can solve sensorimotor problems through insight rather than trial and error (in Piaget's Substage 6) (Gopnik & Meltzoff, 1986, 1987a). As Gopnik and Meltzoff (1986) state, "Children seem to be motivated to acquire words that are relevant to the particular cognitive problems they are working on at the moment" (p. 1052).

Research demonstrates the remarkable ease with which children connect a new word with an underlying concept after only a brief encounter, a process called **fast mapping**. It helps explain how young children build up a large vocabulary with extraordinary speed (Carey, 1978). Dollaghan (1985) presented preschoolers with a novel nonsense word, "koob," and its referent, an oddly shaped plastic ring, in a game in which the object was labeled only once. Children as young as 2 picked up the connection between the novel word and its referent. Preschoolers can even fast map new words they hear on television, as one recent experiment revealed (Rice & Woodsmall, 1988).[3]

Representations for words heard only once or twice do not fade quickly. When children are tested several days after hearing a new label, they are as likely to use it and recognize its referent as are children who heard the label very recently (Dickinson, 1984). Thus, fast mapping provides powerful cognitive support for vocabulary growth. However, once children fast map a word, their acquisition is not yet complete. During a second, extended phase of word learning, children refine their initial representation of the word's meaning on the basis of subsequent encounters with the word.

Careful examination of the kinds of words children acquire and how they use them provides psycholinguists with important information about the course of semantic development. Clark (1983) divides children's early words into three categories: words for objects, words for actions, and words for states (modifiers of objects and actions).

Object Words. Although (as we indicated earlier) children differ in the first words they choose to learn, virtually all early language learners have far more object than action words in their beginning vocabularies (Gentner, 1982; Goldin-Meadow, Seligman, & Gelman, 1976; Greenfield & Smith, 1976; Nelson, 1973). If actions are an especially important means through which infants find out about their world, why this early predominance of object words? Investigators have explained the finding in two different ways.

The first explanation is that concepts referred to by nouns are particularly accessible to young children because they are perceptually bounded, highly cohesive, and

---

[3] Despite these intriguing findings, it would be wrong to conclude that television exposure is sufficient for learning language or that it can substitute for the richness of adult-child communication. Toddlers who are permitted to watch a great deal of TV progress more slowly in vocabulary development than those who watch only a little (Nelson, 1973). Moreover, hearing children raised by deaf parents and exposed to spoken language only through television do not acquire normal speech (Bonvillian, Nelson, & Charrow, 1976).

easily identifiable. By the time children start to talk, all they need to do is match objects with their appropriate linguistic referents (Gentner, 1982).[4] In contrast, verbs are conceptually more complex in that they require an understanding of the connections between objects and actions (Huttenlocher & Lui, 1979).

A second explanation involves the characteristics of adult speech to young children. Although motherese does not contain a greater number of object than action words (Nelson, 1973; Schnur & Shatz, 1984), the way in which nouns are used by adults may lead children to learn them more easily (Bridges, 1985). For example, in one study of mothers' speech to 14-month-olds, the most heavily stressed words were nouns (names of toys). Also, nouns, more often than verbs, occur as single-word utterances or at the ends of sentences (at least in English). There is evidence that children find it easiest to pay attention to the ending parts of adult speech (Kuczaj, 1979; Slobin, 1973).

Nevertheless, cross-cultural evidence indicates that characteristics of the linguistic environment cannot completely account for children's early emphasis on object words. Higher proportions of nouns are found in the vocabularies of children learning a wide variety of languages. In some, word order is such that verbs rather than nouns usually occur in final sentence positions, but verbs are still not acquired with greater frequency. Moreover, in cultures in which adults show little interest in teaching children the names of objects, children still have many more object than action words in their initial vocabularies (Gentner, 1982). Thus, the disproportionate number of nouns in children's early speech largely reflects the dependence of language on cognitive development, a theme, as we will see below, that continues to assert itself as vocabulary growth proceeds.

Action Words. At first, children use a variety of words — verbs ("open"), nouns ("door"), and prepositions ("out") — to refer to actions. As their vocabulary and utterance length expand, children use many more words to refer to actions that, for adults, are verbs (Clark, 1983). By age 3, preschoolers clearly distinguish between words for objects and actions. When presented with a nonsense word embedded in the following sentence, "Do you know what it means *to sib*?", children consistently point to a picture of an action. When asked, "Do you know what *a sib* is?", they point to an object (Brown, 1957).

Researchers have studied how very young children use action words to talk about cause and effect. Between 1 and 2 years, they focus only on the results of actions, saying "broken" for a toy that is broken or "stuck" for a finger stuck in a small hole (Clark, 1983). As early as age 2, they use expressions containing actions plus an indication of the effect they lead to, such as "eat allgone" or "push out." Appropriate usage of such causal terms as "if," "because," and "so" follows shortly thereafter, appearing as soon as children can produce longer utterances, around 3 to 4 years of age (e.g., "If you drink paint, you'll get sick") (French & Nelson, 1985; McCabe et al., 1983; McCabe & Peterson, 1988). The ability to express causal relations when talking about familiar events is one finding, like many others described in Chapter 6, that has led recent investigators to conclude that preschool children's thought is far more orderly and logical than was once believed to be the case.

State Words. Consistent with the sensorimotor underpinnings of early language, children's first state words refer to transient conditions of objects that are the outcome of some action, such as "dirty," "wet," and "hot." Between 2 and 2½ years, children's range of modifiers expands to include labels for salient perceptual attributes, such as

---

[4] You may wish to turn back to Chapter 4 to review how, during the first year of life, infants acquire the concept of the object as a perceptually independent, bounded whole. It is interesting that young children take a word uttered by an adult while pointing at an object as a name for that object as a whole, and not, as would certainly be logically possible, as a name for just some part of it (Markman, 1989).

Children's acquisition of new words takes place in an order that conforms to their mastery of underlying concepts. With respect to state words designating an object's location, "in" is acquired first, followed by "on" and then "under."

their size and color ("big," "red"), as well as possession ("my toy," "Mommy purse"). Modifiers that refer to the functions of objects (e.g., "dump truck," "pickup truck") appear soon after (Nelson, 1976).

In instances in which modifiers are related to one another in meaning, the least conceptually complex and most broadly applicable terms are acquired first. For example, a stable order exists in the acquisition of dimensional adjectives: big-small first; followed by tall-short, high-low, and long-short; and finally wide-narrow and deep-shallow. The same applies to temporal terms, which serve as modifiers of actions. Between 3 and 5 years of age, children first master "now" versus "then" and "before" versus "after," followed by "today" versus "yesterday" and "tomorrow" (Clark, 1983; Stevenson & Pollitt, 1987).

Children's state words designating the location and orientation of objects provide additional examples of how conceptual knowledge influences vocabulary acquisition. In one study, children were asked to imitate an experimenter's actions in placing an object in, on, under, and next to a container or support. Children below age 2 could mimic placing objects in and on, but not under, and their ability to follow verbal instructions containing these prepositions (e.g., "Put the x *in [on, under]* the y") showed an order of acquisition that paralleled their nonlinguistic imitations. "In" was mastered first, followed by "on" and then "under," with all three achieved around 2½ years of age (Clark, 1973). Children's understanding of words describing the orientation of objects — top, bottom, front, and back — reveals a similar pattern of development. "Top" and "bottom" are understood first, around 2½ or 3 years, followed by front and back, between 4 and 5 (Clark, 1980).

State words perform a vital communicative service for children. By permitting distinctions among objects and actions, children can use them to name new concepts that cannot be designated with just a single label. Thus, state terms contribute significantly to the flexible, productive nature of human language.

Mismatches, Underextensions, and Overextensions. During early vocabulary development, children make three types of errors. In fast mapping a new word into their initial vocabularies, they may **mismatch** the new label with an underlying concept, applying it to an inappropriate set of events. For example, your author's younger son, at age 2, was offered a "new" Pooh bear to replace a tattered "old" one that had become a highly treasured toy. He rejected the new bear vehemently and a day later produced the words "new" and "old" for the first time. After refusing a cookie he was offered, he pointed to a box of a different kind and said, "Want *old* cookie, not *new* cookie!" Using "old" to mean "something I want" and "new" to mean "something I don't want," he began with the wrong hypothesis about adult conventions for the words.

Two additional types of errors are **underextension,** which involves applying a term to a smaller collection of events than is acceptable in conventional usage (e.g., using the word "doll" only to denote a particular doll), and **overextension,** applying it to a wider collection of events than is appropriate (e.g., using the word "car" to refer to trucks, trains, and bikes). Underextension is hard to detect, since children use the word in question appropriately, but simply extend it to a very limited range of instances. It is possible that underextension, in the form of picking up a new word in a very specific context, constitutes the first stage of acquisition for a great many words (Clark, 1983).

Overextensions are the most frequently observed word errors between 1 and 2½ years of age (Clark, 1978). Psycholinguists have studied them carefully for information about how children gradually develop adult word meanings. Overextensions reveal a surprisingly early sensitivity to categorical relations in toddlers and young preschoolers. Children do not overextend words randomly. Instead, they apply them to a class of similar referents — for example, taking the word "dog" to refer to a variety of furry, four-legged animals or the word "open" to mean opening a door, peeling fruit, and undoing shoe laces (Behrend, 1988; Clark, 1983). As children enlarge their vocabularies, they make finer distinctions, and overextended words become more constricted in their application (Rescorla, 1980).

Nevertheless, the study of overextensions underestimates what children really know about word meanings, as children overextend many more words in production than they do in comprehension. That is, a 2-year-old may refer to trucks, trains, and bikes as "cars" but point to these objects correctly when given their names in a comprehension task (Clark, 1978; Nelson et al., 1978; Rescorla, 1980). These findings suggest that preschoolers may sometimes overextend deliberately because they have no suitable word or because they cannot remember the right word. From this perspective, overextension is a strategy young children use to stretch their limited language resources to the utmost (Clark, 1978).

Extending Language Meanings: Word Coinages and Metaphors. Children rely on another device to fill in for words they have not yet acquired or cannot retrieve. As early as age 2, they coin new words based on ones they already know. Children's word coinages follow the principles of word formation in their language. The earliest strategies operate on whole words, as in the technique of compounding — "break-machine" for a machine that breaks things and "plant-man" for a gardner. Children also convert verbs into nouns and nouns into verbs, as in one child's use of "needle it" to mend something. Later, children discover more specialized word coinage techniques, such as adding the ending -er to identify a doer of a particular action — for example, a "crayoner" for a child using crayons instead of paints. Children relinquish coined words as soon as they acquire conventional labels for their intended meanings (Clark & Hecht, 1982), but their inventiveness in constructing them attests to their remarkable, rule-governed approach to language learning at an early age.

Preschoolers also show a special affinity for metaphors — a form of expression that permits them to expand the meanings they can understand and express linguistically. Metaphors based on sensory comparisons — "clouds are pillows" and "leaves are dancers" — are easiest for preschoolers to comprehend (Gentner & Stuart, 1983). Once their vocabulary and knowledge of the world expand, they appreciate metaphors based on nonsensory comparisons as well, such as, "Friends are like magnets" (Keil, 1986). In fact, some surprisingly sophisticated metaphoric expressions can be heard in preschoolers' everyday language. One 3-year-old described a new blanket as "full of gas" and an old, shabby one as "out of gas" (Gentner & Stuart, 1983). Another used the expression "fire engine in my tummy" to describe a recent stomachache. Metaphors permit meanings to be communicated in especially vivid, economical, and memorable ways. Also, they are sometimes the only means we have to convey what we want to say (Winner, 1988).

Later Vocabulary Development

Vocabulary continues to increase during middle childhood and adolescence, more than doubling in size from school entry to adulthood; a mature linguistic repertoire consists of more than 30,000 words. During the school years, children use many words more precisely and conventionally, and their semantic knowledge becomes better organized and hierarchically arranged. Recall from Chapter 7 that this occurs earlier in some domains of knowledge than others, especially those that are very familiar to the child.

In adding new words to their vocabulary, 11- and 12-year-olds profit far more than do 6- and 7-year-olds from being given explicit definitions (Dickinson, 1984). Similarly, the ability to use language to explain word meanings improves with age. During the early school years, children's word definitions are highly concrete, consisting primarily of descriptions of a referent's function or appearance (e.g., knife: "when you're cutting carrots"; bicycle: "its got wheels, a chain, and handlebars"). Later on, children give more abstract responses involving synonyms, explanations, and descriptions of categorical relationships (e.g., knife: "something you could cut with. A saw is like a knife. It could also be a weapon"). This advance reflects the older child's ability to deal with word meanings on an entirely verbal plane (Litowitz, 1977). It also indicates that children's definitions move from ones based largely on personal experience to ones based on more general, socially shared information (Wehren, DeLisi, & Arnold, 1981).

Finally, during the school years, children display an improved ability to understand the multiple meanings of words. For example, they recognize that many words, such as "sharp" or "cold," have psychological as well as physical meanings. Consequently, 8- to 10-year-olds comprehend more subtle metaphors, such as "sharp as a tack," "spilling the beans," and "left high and dry" (Winner, 1988). Older children's advanced appreciation of figures of speech and their ability to deal with word meanings on an entirely linguistic plane reflect growth in *metalinguistic awareness*, or conscious ability to reflect on language as a system. We will comment more fully on this aspect of development in a later section of this chapter.

New Ideas about How Semantic Development Takes Place

Adults correct inaccuracies in children's word usage, and research indicates that adult feedback facilitates semantic development. In one study, three types of adult feedback for toddlers' incorrect labeling were compared: (1) correction (e.g., "That's not a car. It's a truck"); (2) correction plus an explanation that points out features of the referent ("That's a truck. See, it has a place to put things in"); and (3) acceptance of an incorrect label ("Yes, that's a car"). Correction with explanation was most effective in helping 1- to 1½-year-old children move toward adultlike word meanings, followed by simple correction, which was more effective than acceptance (Chapman, Leonard, & Mervis, 1986).

Still, there is no way that adults, in naming instances of categories and providing children with feedback, can indicate exactly what each word picks out. For example, if an adult points to a dog and calls it a "doggie," it is not automatically clear whether the word refers to four-legged animals, the dog's shaggy ears, the shape of its wagging tail, or its barking sound. A major role in vocabulary development must be played by the child's own active cognitive processing. Children have to look for consistencies in adult usage, try words out on the basis of initial hypotheses about their meanings, and then make adjustments based on additional examples and feedback from others (Clark, 1983). Finding out exactly how children go about deriving word meanings has been a challenging task for psycholinguists. Major theoretical accounts have been adopted and discarded over the years.

Recently, Clark (1983, 1987) proposed a new explanation of early semantic development called **lexical contrast theory.** It assumes that two fundamental principles govern the acquisition of word meaning. The first is *conventionality*, children's natural desire to acquire words and word meanings that are accepted by their linguistic community. Children attend to conventionality from a very early age; they ask for names of unfamiliar objects, and they drop coined words as well as refine overextensions and underextensions as soon as new labels and meanings are added to their semantic repertoire. The second principle is *contrast*, which explains how new word meanings are acquired. Children assume that the meaning of each word they hear is unique, so when they hear a new label, they immediately try to figure out what it refers to by contrasting it with words they already know. At the same time, each new word provides a comparative basis for revising the understanding of old ones.

Preliminary evidence offers support for Clark's theory. Consistent with the principle of contrast, young children resist accepting two words for the same object (Markman & Wachtel, 1988). In fact, Taylor and Gelman (1988, 1989) recently showed that when 2-year-olds are given a new word for an object for which they already have a label (e.g., "fep" for a dog), they apply the principle of contrast and take the new word to mean a subset of the original category (a particular kind of dog). According to these investigators, young children's tendency to contrast novel with familiar labels helps them build their first concept hierarchies.

At the same time, Gathercole (1987) has challenged lexical contrast theory. Children's everyday application of many words, she suggests, is too variable for the principle of contrast to fully explain it. Gathercole believes that children rely on a wide variety of processing strategies — not just one — to narrow the distance between their first understanding of a word and its conventional usage. Whether Clark's theory is too limited an account of how young children refine word meanings remains to be determined by future research.

BRIEF REVIEW   Semantic development proceeds with extraordinary rapidity as preschoolers fast map thousands of words into their vocabularies. The course of vocabulary growth reflects children's cognitive development. At first, object words predominate; action and state words increase later on. Errors of mismatch, underextension, and overextension occur often but gradually disappear as preschoolers enlarge and refine their vocabularies. An increasingly flexible, abstract understanding of word meanings emerges during middle childhood and adolescence. Adult feedback assists with the monumental task of semantic development, but a major role is played by the child's active cognitive processing. Lexical contrast theory is a new, controversial account of how semantic development takes place.

GRAMMATICAL DEVELOPMENT

Grammar requires that more than a single word be evident in children's speech. Therefore, grammatical progress is charted by using an index called **mean length of**

utterance (MLU). Utterance length is measured in terms of number of **morphemes,** the smallest meaningful unit of adult speech. MLU is strongly related to the number of words in an utterance, but not perfectly so. For example, a young child's utterance, "see boat," is two morphemes long, whereas "see boats" contains three morphemes because of the additional element "-s." MLU is determined by averaging the lengths of a large sample of a child's utterances. During the first few years, the acquisition of grammatical features correlates with children's MLU. Therefore, grammatical development is often divided into phases based on this index.

A major controversy in the area of grammatical development concerns how early children develop an appreciation of adult grammatical categories, such as "subject-verb-object." Evidence for a very early grasp of formal grammatical distinctions would provide Chomsky's nativist theory with continued support. However, if grammar is not present in early word combinations, then factors other than the LAD, such as powerful cognitive processing abilities, could account for the acquisition of grammar. We consider evidence relevant to this issue as we chart the course of grammatical development.

The One-Word Phase: Is an Appreciation of Grammar Already Present?

Between 1 and 2 years of age, most utterances are single words. Yet by combining them with gestures and intonation, children can express meanings that seem sentencelike in nature. One interpretation of single-word utterances is that children already have a full sentence in mind, but they do not display this inherent grammatical knowledge because they cannot yet remember and produce longer word strings. Investigators who accept this explanation call these one-word utterances **holophrases** (meaning one-word sentences). Others reject this idea (e.g., Bloom, 1973; Dore, 1985), preferring to postpone judgments about children's grammatical knowledge until the MLU has expanded and grammar can be studied directly.

First Word Combinations: The Two-Word Utterance Phase

Sometime between 1½ and 2½ years, children combine two words, such as "Mommy shoe," "go car," and "more cookie." Children's two-word utterances have been called **telegraphic speech.** Like a telegram, they omit smaller and less important words, such as articles ("a," "the"), auxiliary verbs ("can," "am," "will"), and prepositions ("on," "at," "in"). Also, as yet there are no grammatical morphemes added to the words, such as "-s" and "-ed" endings (Brown, 1973). Even though 2-year-olds omit these tiny elements from their own utterances, they do detect them in adult speech. Because these markers often occur at the beginning of noun and verb phrases, they may help young language learners divide sentences into basic grammatical units, thereby paving the way for later grammatical achievements (Gerken, Landau, & Remez, 1990).

Despite the restricted form of the two-word utterance, young children the world over use it to express a very similar and impressive variety of meanings, the most common of which are summarized in Table 9.2. In expressing these meanings, do children use a consistent word order that suggests an inherent grasp of grammatical categories? Investigators used to think so, but current evidence argues against it. There is no uniform word order during the two-word phase (Maratsos, 1983; Maratsos & Chalkley, 1980). For example, children are just as likely to say "cookie give" as "give cookie" (which conforms to English grammar).

Children's two-word speech contains some word-bound formulas, such as "want + X" or "more + X." These are productive in nature, as children insert a variety of words in the X position. When a number of these formulas appear at once, they give the appearance that the child has captured a grammatical rule, but such formulas are actually very limited in their initial application. For example, Jonathan, a

Table 9.2. Common Semantic Relationships Expressed by Children During the Two-Word Utterance Phase

MEANING	EXAMPLE
Agent and action	"Tommy hit"
Action and object	"Give cookie"
Agent and object	"Mommy truck" (meaning Mommy push the truck)
Action and location	"Put table" (meaning put X on the table)
Entity and location	"Daddy outside"
Possessor and possession	"My truck"
Entity and attribution	"Big ball"
Demonstrative and entity	"That doggie"
Notice and noticed object	"Hi mommy," "Hi truck"
Recurrence	"More milk"
Nonexistence and nonexistent or disappeared object	"No shirt," "No more milk"

Source: Brown, 1973.

child studied by Braine (1976), produced several actor-action combinations at about the same time, such as "Mommy sit," "Daddy sleep," and "Daddy work." However, they did not represent a general understanding of subject-verb grammatical relations, since Jonathan used them only when an agent was moving from one place to another, such as his father going to bed or leaving for work. He had really constructed a very specific rule for expressing a particular semantic relationship, which was something like this: "mover of self + movement." Furthermore, many of the creative combinations that children produce during the two-word period do not conform to adult grammatical restrictions. For example, based on a "more + X" rule, Andrew, another child studied by Braine (1976), said "more hot" and "more read," but these combinations are not acceptable in English grammar.

The evidence cited above indicates that learning how to express a small set of semantic relations is the prevalent task of the two-word phase. It is now widely agreed that the unification of words into grammatical classes is a later achievement. However, the piece-by-piece learning of word-based rules that goes on during this phase may provide the foundation for the emergence of formal grammatical structures. Pieces that are similar to one another may eventually be drawn together, a general tendency that characterizes much of cognitive development (Maratsos, 1983).

From Two-Word Utterances to Complex Speech

Between 2 and 3 years of age, as the MLU moves from 2 toward 3, simple sentences appear. In English, one of their characteristics is a relatively fixed word order: subject-verb-object. Historically, the subject-verb-object sequence was thought to be close to Chomsky's deep structure and to represent a natural order of thoughts. However, as cross-linguistic research accumulated, it became clear that this order is not basic. It is not characteristic of children learning a wide variety of languages — Finnish, Samoan, Hungarian, Turkish, German, Italian, and Serbo-Croatian, to name just a few — in which different orderings of subject, verb, and object are typical. Children in these linguistic communities adopt the word orders reflected in the adult speech to which they are exposed. Moreover, they find their native tongue no more difficult to learn than children born into English-speaking homes (Maratsos, 1983).

The Acquisition of Grammatical Morphemes. During this period, children acquire grammatical morphemes. Expressions with small additions over the two-word phase, such as "he *is* eating" and "John's dog," become frequent. However, these acquisitions are not the result of sudden, rule-guided insights. They are mastered very gradually, and children do not use them consistently for months or even years after they first appear (Maratsos, 1983).

A striking finding is that morphemes are acquired in a highly regular order by English-speaking children between 1½ and 3½ years of age, a pattern first observed by Brown (1973) in an intensive longitudinal study of the early language development of three children and later replicated on larger cross-sectional samples (de Villiers & de Villiers, 1973b; Kuczaj, 1977a). The sequence of acquisition is displayed in Table 9.3.

Why does this regular order of development occur? One conjecture is that the morphemes children hear most often are those acquired earliest. However, adult usage is unrelated to children's order of acquisition; therefore, it cannot be an important factor (Pinker, 1981). A second explanation has to do with the *structural complexity* of each of the grammatical forms. For example, adding the endings "-ing" or "-s" is structurally less complex than using the various forms of the verb "to be." In these, the child has to figure out the different forms that express tense and also has to make the verb agree with the noun person and number (e.g., "I *am* coming" versus "They *are* coming"). Besides structural complexity, *semantic complexity*, or the number and difficulty of the meanings encoded in the acquisition, can also affect morphological development. For example, noun pluralization by adding "-s" involves just one semantic distinction, the difference between one and more than one. In contrast, distinguishing among the various forms of the verb "to be" involves many more,

Table 9.3. Order of Acquisition of English Grammatical Morphemes

MORPHEME	EXAMPLE
1. Verb present progressive ending (-ing)	"He singing."
2. Preposition "on"	"On horsie."
3. Preposition "in"	"In wagon."
4. Noun plural "-s"	"Cats."
5. Verb irregular past tense	"He ran." "It broke."
6. Noun possessive	"Daddy's hat."
7. Verb uncontractible "be" form used with adjective, preposition, or noun phrase	"Are kitties sleepy?"
8. Articles "a" and "the"	"A cookie." "The bunny."
9. Verb regular past tense ending (-ed)	"He kicked it."
10. Verb present tense, third person singular regular ending (-s)	"He likes it."
11. Verb present tense, third person singular irregular ending (-s)	"She has (from have) a cookie." "He does (from do) eat cookies."
12. Auxiliary verb uncontractible "be" forms	"Are you eating?"
13. Verb contractible "be" forms used with adjective, preposition, or noun phrase	"He's inside." "They're sleepy."
14. Auxiliary verb contractible "be" forms	"He's coming." "Doggie's eating."

Source: Brown, 1973.

including an understanding of number, person, and time of occurrence. Analyzing the structural and semantic complexity of the morphemes shown in Table 9.3, Brown (1973) concluded that both factors predict their order of acquisition fairly well.

Structural and semantic complexity are hard to tease apart, since generally speaking, the more complex the grammatical construction, the more complicated the meaning it expresses. However, cross-linguistic research provides support for the independent contribution of each factor. Because of differences in the structural complexity of the expression, the time of emergence of constructions having similar meanings varies for children learning different languages. For example, Johnston and Slobin (1979) found that acquisition of the morphology used to express location (in English, this would be prepositions such as "in" and "on") occurred earlier for children learning English, Italian, and Turkish than Serbo-Croatian, in which locational expression is structurally more complex. At the same time, semantic complexity is partly responsible for morphological development, since across languages, there is considerable similarity in the order of acquisition of morphemes with the same meaning (Slobin, 1982).

Slobin (1982) uses the analogy of a "waiting room" to show how semantic and structural complexity work together to affect grammatical development. If we think of each linguistic form shown in Table 9.3 as having its own waiting room, children first gain entry to the room with a cognitive appreciation of the expression's underlying meaning as the key. Once in the room, they must figure out how the meaning in question is encoded in the grammatical structure of their language. This task takes varying amounts of time and effort, depending on the complexity of the linguistic features involved, but finally the child leaves the particular waiting room with the completed structure in hand. As Slobin explains, "The important point of the waiting-room metaphor is its two doors: the cognitive entry door and the linguistic exit. . . . we cannot hope to understand language acquisition without understanding the path between these two doors" (p. 169).

Overregularization. Look again at Table 9.3, and you will see that grammatical morphemes with irregular forms are acquired before those with regular forms. For example, children use such past tense irregular verbs as "broke" and "ran" before they acquire the regular "-ed" form. But once children get a regular morphological rule, they **overregularize,** or extend it inappropriately to irregular instances. For example, such expressions as "breaked," "runned," "goed," "feets," and "mouses" are frequent occurrences in the speech of 3-year-olds. Since children do not hear mature English speakers say "breaked" or "feets," the mistakes show that they develop productive grammatical rules at an early age.

Additional evidence for the productive use of morphological rules comes from a famous study by Berko (1958) in which children were shown pictures of unusual objects and actions that were given nonsense syllable names, such as "wug" for a birdlike creature and "rick" for a swinging motion (see Figure 9.1). The nonsense labels were embedded in sentences that Berko asked children to complete. Preschoolers could supply correct morphemes to many novel nouns and verbs (e.g., they completed the sentences shown in Figure 9.1 with the expressions "wugs" and "ricked"). These findings support the conclusion that children construct *mental rules* for the application of grammatical morphemes. They do not learn them in a rote fashion by imitating adult usage.

An interesting question concerns why children use a number of correct irregular forms before they begin to overregularize. Whitehurst (1982) points out that irregular forms in all languages are applied to important, frequently used words. Children may initially learn these instances by rote memory, but as soon as they grasp a morphological rule, they apply it broadly, and irregular words are overregularized for a time. Application of morphological rules does not drive out irregular forms completely. Kuczaj (1977b) showed that there is alternation between overregularized and irregu-

Figure 9.1. Two examples from Berko's (1958) "wug test." *From J. Berko, 1958, "The Child's Learning of English Morphology," Word, 14, pp. 154–155. Reprinted by permission.*

lar versions of words in children's speech for many months and sometimes years until the child has managed the difficult task of sorting out the exceptions from the regular instances.

The Emergence of Formal Grammatical Understandings. Around the time that the MLU reaches 3 and children are about 2½ years old, they first show an appreciation of the formal grammatical categories of their language. Valian (1986) analyzed a large number of utterances of 2-year-old children to see whether words that are members of particular grammatical categories obey the regularities characteristic of adult English usage. If so, Valian suggested, then children's knowledge of these categories could be inferred. For example, we would know that young children have formed the grammatical category of "adjective" (even though they do not consciously label it as such) if they consistently place words adults classify as adjectives before nouns and after articles ("a *big* dog"), understand that adjectives can be sequenced ("a *big bad* dog") or repeated ("a *big big* dog"), and realize that adjectives can appear as predicates ("The dog is *big*"). Valian found that by the middle of the third year, the distributional properties of children's speech were highly consistent, suggesting that they had implicit knowledge of the formal grammatical categories of adjective, article, noun, noun phrase, preposition, and prepositional phrase.

Psycholinguists have different ideas about exactly how children achieve this amazing structural organization of language at such an early age. Some think that the *semantic* properties of grammatical classes play a prominent role in early category formation. For example, children might begin by grouping together words with "object qualities" as nouns and words with "action qualities" as verbs and then merge these basic semantic classes with observations they make about how particular words are used in sentence contexts (Bates & MacWhinney, 1982; Pinker, 1984). Others believe that grammatical categories are largely shaped by observations children make about the *structural* properties of linguistic usage. That is, children notice which words appear in the same positions in sentences, take the same inflectional endings, and are similarly combined with other words and gradually group them together (Braine, 1987; Maratsos & Chalkley, 1980). Perhaps some complex combination of semantic and structural properties leads children to this accomplishment (Maratsos,

1983). Psycholinguists still have much to learn about exactly how children construct their first grammatical classifications.

The Development of Complex Grammatical Forms. The appearance of forms of the auxiliary verb "to be" opens the door to a variety of new expressions around 3 to 3½ years of age. In English, auxiliary verbs play central roles in a great many sentence structures that are variations on the basic subject-verb-object form. Two important examples are negatives and questions.

Negatives. Mastery of negation reflects a complex interaction of grammatical, semantic, and parental input factors that combine to produce some interesting developmental patterns (Tager-Flusberg, 1989). Three semantic types of negation exist, and they appear in children's speech in the following order: (1) *nonexistence*, in which the child remarks on the absence of something, such as "no cookie" or "all gone crackers"; (2) *rejection*, in which the child expresses opposition to something, such as "no take bath"; and (3) *denial*, in which the child denies the truthfulness of something, such as "That not my kitty" (Bloom, 1970; Clancy, 1985). Young children tend to use the rule "no + utterance" to express nonexistence and rejection, but they use an internal form of negation to express denial. de Villiers and de Villiers (1979) suggest that these different forms are derived from parental speech. When parents express nonexistence or rejection, they often use constructions in which "no" appears at the beginning of the sentence, such as "No more cookies" or "No, you can't have another cracker." Around 3- to 3½ years, children add auxiliary verbs to their utterances and become sensitive to the way they are combined with negatives by adult speakers. Consequently, appropriate grammatical constructions for all types of negation appear, such as "There aren't any more cookies" (nonexistence), "I don't want a bath" (rejection), and "That isn't my kitty" (denial).

Questions. Like negatives, questions also emerge over the early to middle preschool years. English-speaking children can use rising intonation to convert an utterance into a *yes-no question* (e.g., "Mommy baking cookies?"). As a result, they produce them at an earlier age than children learning languages in which the construction of yes-no questions is more complex (Bowerman, 1973). Other kinds of questions, the so-called *wh- questions* that begin with "what," "where," "which," "who," "when," "why," and "how," require that children invert the subject and auxiliary verb and place the wh- word at the beginning of the sentence. One of the best-known phenomena in English grammatical development is the initial noninversion of these sentences by children between 2 and 3 years of age. They can be heard using such expressions as "What you doing?" and "Where Daddy going?" A little later, they include the auxiliary without inverting (e.g., "What you are doing?"). Finally, they can incorporate all the rules for producing a correctly formed wh- question.

The acquisition of wh- questions follows an order that conforms to both semantic and structural complexity. "What," "where," "which," and "who" questions, which ask about concrete objects, places, and people, appear first in children's speech. "When," "how," and "why" refer to more difficult concepts (time, manner, and causality), and they appear later on. The latter questions are also structurally more complex, since answers to them generally require whole sentences rather than just a single word (Tyack & Ingram, 1977).

Other Complex Constructions. Between 3 and 6 years of age, and as the MLU advances from 3 to 4 and beyond, children acquire increasingly complex syntactic forms. First, conjunctions appear connecting whole sentences (e.g., "Mom picked me up, *and* we went to the park") and verb phrases ("I got up *and* ate breakfast") (Bloom et al., 1980). Later, children produce embedded sentences (e.g., I think *he will come*"), tag questions ("He isn't coming, *is he*?"), indirect object–direct object constructions

("The boy showed *his friend the present*"), and passive sentence forms ("The dog *was patted* by the girl") (Whitehurst, 1982). In addition, by school entry, children acquire some of the subtleties involved in the use of pronouns. For example, they understand that "he" and "Bill" can co-refer in "After he ate, Bill went to the movies" but not in "He said Bill should eat dinner now" (Solan, 1983). Thus, as the preschool years draw to a close, children have mastered an impressive variety of grammatical constructions. Still, grammatical development is by no means complete. There is still a long period of development beyond early childhood.

Later Grammatical Development

The passive voice is an example of a grammatical construction that is not completely mastered until well into middle childhood. Studying passive sentences that 2- to 13-year-olds used to describe pictures, Horgan (1978) found that children of all ages produced more *truncated passives* (e.g., "It got broken," "They got lost") than *full passives* ("The glass was broken by Mary"). However, the production of full passives increased steadily from the preschool through the early adolescent years. Before children begin to produce very many passives, they show evidence of understanding them, but they comprehend some types more easily than others. Preschool and early school-age children understand passives based on action verbs, such as "hit" or "kiss," better than those based on experiential verbs, such as "like" or "know." The latter are not well understood until the mid–elementary school years (Pinker, Lebeaux, & Frost, 1987; Sudhalter & Braine, 1985). Moreover, when preschoolers are taught to use the passive form, they master sentences with animate subjects ("The *baby* is touched by the frog") more successfully than those with inanimate subjects ("The *drum* is touched by the frog"). Apparently, children's first concept of the subject of a sentence is limited to dynamic, moving entities. Until they broaden this idea, complex grammatical transformations are easier with sentences of this kind (Lempert, 1989). Taken together, research indicates that mastery of the passive form in its full range of possibilities is a long development that is not complete before the end of middle childhood.

Another grammatical achievement that appears during the school years is the understanding of infinitive phrases, such as the difference between "John is eager to please" (in which "John" is the agent of "please") and "John is easy to please" (in which "John" is the object of "please"). Carol Chomsky (1969) tested children's understanding of this construction by presenting them with a blindfolded doll and asking them to respond to the question "Is the doll *easy or hard to see*?" The results indicated that 5-year-old children always equate the grammatical subject ("doll" in this instance) with the agent role. That is, they respond "hard to see," as if they understand the question to mean something like "Is the doll able to see?" Between 5 and 10, children gradually separate subject from agent in these kinds of sentences (Karmiloff-Smith, 1979).

The above examples reflect the broad scope of grammatical development. Like semantic development, later grammatical acquisitions are facilitated by the older child's cognitive maturity and metalinguistic awareness. School-age children can deal with less explicitly stated relationships and are more attentive to subtle linguistic cues. These achievements play major roles in helping them understand the most intricate grammatical constructions (Wallach, 1984).

New Ideas about How Grammatical Development Takes Place

As Chomsky's theory failed to find consistent support, a number of investigators began to view grammar as a product of general cognitive development or children's tendency to search the environment for consistencies and patterns of all sorts (Bates

& MacWhinney, 1987; Bever, 1982; Maratsos, 1983). Other theorists, while also focusing on cognitive processing mechanisms, have not rejected the possibility that they are specially tuned for language learning. For example, Slobin (1985) proposes that children do not start out with an innate knowledge of grammatical rules (as Chomsky believed), but they do have a special **language-making capacity (LMC)** —a set of cognitive procedures for analyzing linguistic input that supports the discovery of grammatical regularities. On the basis of cross-linguistic studies, Slobin has begun to specify the processing procedures that all children may be using to master the grammar of their language. However, whether the LMC actually exists, whether it is innately specified at birth, and whether it is specially tuned to analyze linguistic features of the environment remain controversial issues (Bowerman, 1985).

In addition to children's inherent capacities, investigators have been interested in what aspects of linguistic input may make the task of grammatical mastery easier. In a well-known study, Brown and Hanlon (1970) reported that parents give preschoolers feedback not on the basis of grammaticality, but in response to the "truth value" of their utterances. For example, the statement "Her curling my hair" was met with an approving response because the child's mother was, in fact, curling her hair, whereas "There's the animal farmhouse" led a parent to respond that the building was really a lighthouse and not a farmhouse. These findings suggest that preschool children receive little direct guidance in formulating their grammar and must figure out its intricacies largely on their own.

Nevertheless, many subtle aspects of adult speech facilitate grammatical development. We have already indicated that motherese provides children with input in the form of short, clearly pronounced syntactic structures. In addition, it is slower in tempo than speech to adults and contains distinct pauses between major phrases, to which children are sensitive at an early age (Hirsh-Pasek et al., 1987). Adults also adjust their utterance length so that it is just ahead of the child's MLU, thereby fine-tuning it to children's changing developmental needs (Gleitman, Newport, & Gleitman, 1984).

Furthermore, adults use two techniques, often in combination, that offer children indirect feedback about grammaticality: **expansions** and **recasts.** For example, a parent hearing a child say "go car" may answer, "Yes, we're going to the car now," expanding on the child's statement as well as recasting its primitive structure into a more mature form. Recent evidence indicates that parents and nonparents alike are far more likely to respond in this way after children make grammatical errors. When utterances are well formed, adults either repeat what the child has just said or continue the topic of conversation (Bohannon & Stanowicz, 1988; Penner, 1987). Although these contingencies are far less obvious than direct approval or disapproval, they can be regarded as a kind of feedback to children about grammaticality. In line with this idea, Bohannon and Stanowicz (1988) found that children often imitate adult recasts of their errors, but they rarely imitate adult repetitions of their correct speech. Moreover, research suggests that mothers who frequently expand and recast have preschoolers who make especially rapid progress in language development (Cross, 1978; Nelson et al., 1984).

BRIEF REVIEW

Children are active, rule-oriented learners whose utterances start to conform to the grammar of their language during the early preschool years. By school entry, children have mastered a wide variety of complex grammatical constructions. A number of interacting factors contribute to the course of grammatical development. These include processing strategies for analyzing linguistic input, the difficulty of the meanings expressed by the structures to be learned, the complexity of the structures themselves, and adult feedback about grammaticality. Psycholinguists still have much to discover about each of these ingredients and how they work together. The acquisition of grammar continues to be one of the most awesome achievements of childhood.

During development, children must learn to use language in ways that permit them to send and receive messages successfully in social contexts. To do so, they must supplement linguistic channels of communication with nonlinguistic ones, send messages that are clear and precise, and conform to social conventions that govern how speakers and listeners should relate to one another. In the following sections, we address this pragmatic side of language development.

Becoming an Effective Conversationalist

At age 2, children's ability to participate in a sustained conversation is still limited; they rarely continue a conversation beyond two turns. One reason is that although 2-year-olds *respond* in a relevant fashion to prior utterances, they rarely use conventional techniques that help sustain interaction. One of these is the **turnabout,** in which the conversationalist not only comments on what has just been said, but also adds some other kind of request to get the partner to respond again. Children's production of turnabouts increases over the preschool years (Goelman, 1986; Kaye & Charney, 1980). Its restricted use by very young preschoolers may be due to their limited MLU, since they cannot yet use very many words in each turn. During early childhood, children also become more adept at maintaining a single topic of discussion (Byrne & Hayden, 1980; McDonald & Pien, 1982), and they develop more effective strategies for joining in the conversations of others (Dunn & Shatz, 1989). Between the ages of 5 and 9, more advanced conversational strategies appear, such as **shading,** in which a change of topic is initiated gradually by modifying its focus, rather than through an abrupt topical change (Wanska & Bedrosian, 1985).

Although the child's participatory role increases, adults continue to assume much responsibility for maintaining conversational structure and cohesiveness when interacting with preschoolers (Wanska & Bedrosian, 1985). In doing so, adults demonstrate effective conversational techniques. In fact, opportunities for conversational give-and-take with adults seem to be an especially facilitating context for all aspects of early language development. Conversational extension and topic maintenance between adults and children are positively related to general measures of preschool language growth (Byrne & Hayden, 1980). Moreover, as Box 9.2 suggests, the slower rate of language development among twins than among singletons may be explained by twins' reduced opportunity to engage in conversational participation with their parents.

If children are to carry on effective discourse, they must also become sensitive to the **illocutionary intent** of utterances — that is, what a speaker *means to say*, regardless of whether the linguistic form of the utterance is perfectly consistent with it. For example, the question "Would you like to make cookies?" can be a request for information, an offer to provide an activity, or a directive to do something, depending on the context in which it is said. By age 3, children comprehend a variety of utterances as requests for action even when they are not directly expressed that way, such as "I need a pencil" or "Why don't you tickle me?" (Garvey, 1974). In addition, preschoolers can make requests of others using a variety of linguistic forms (Dore, 1974; Read & Cherry, 1978). Perhaps children come to appreciate the multiple interpretations of verbal messages so early because they are exposed to a wide variety of adult form-intention pairings. Shatz (1979) reported that mothers of 1- and 2-year-olds use many linguistic forms to express a single intention, and they express a variety of intentions with the same form.

During the school years, children grasp illocutionary intentions that are expressed in subtle ways. Around 8 to 10 years of age, they begin to understand irony — for example, that the comment "Gee, this is great soup!" said with mocking intonation really means the opposite of the speaker's statement (Winner, 1988). Comprehending form-intention pairings like this one requires children to make inferences about context and utterance that are beyond the cognitive capacity of preschoolers.

Learning to Communicate Clearly

Effective communication involves the ability to phrase messages we send as clearly as possible, as well as the ability to recognize when messages we receive are unclear so we can ask for more information. These aspects of language development are called **referential communication skills.**

The ability to phrase messages clearly begins to develop during the preschool years, although it is not well developed until middle childhood. Not until age 3 do children revise their own utterances in response to requests for more information (Gallagher, 1981). However, when preschoolers do clarify their messages, they rely heavily on gestures (such as pointing). They are unlikely to give full verbal accounts of

---

◆ **THEORY, RESEARCH AND APPLICATIONS** ◆

Language Learning Environments of Twins and Singletons

Box 9.2

Theory. Twins learn language at a slower rate than singletons during the first few years of life (Slavic, 1980). The difference could be due to twins' less advantaged prenatal conditions. Twins must share space and nutrition in utero, and they are generally born several weeks preterm—factors that may lead to a slower course of early development. Alternatively, twins' language learning environments could be responsible for their slower linguistic growth. Twins' conversational experiences with their mothers are almost always *triadic* rather than *dyadic.* That is, they almost always take place in the presence of a same-age sibling. Michael Tomasello, Sara Mannle, and Ann Kruger (1986) hypothesized that the presence of the second child reduces the effectiveness of the mother's conversational style, thereby delaying twins' early language mastery.

Research. Six pairs of toddler-age twins were matched with singleton children on socioeconomic status and age. Along with their mothers, they were videotaped at home, with each singleton dyad and twin triad interacting with toys and the mothers doing what they normally do when playing and conversing with their children. The videotapes were coded for the amount and quality of mother-child conversations and for the size of children's vocabularies as a general indicator of language development.

The findings indicated that twins were substantially behind singletons in early vocabulary growth. As shown in the accompanying figure, singletons produced nearly four times the total number of words and five times as many different words as twins during the videotaping session. As expected, the triadic interactive situation had

Early language development is often slower for twins than singletons because mothers of twins must divide their attention between two young children.

a substantial effect on the quantity and quality of mother-child conversations. Although mothers of twins spent just as much time interacting with their youngsters as did mothers of singletons, each twin got less than half the quantity of direct input accorded to singletons. Also, the utterances used by mothers of twins were shorter in length and contained a higher proportion of directives and a lower proportion of comments and questions designed to extend the interaction. Moreover, the quantity of maternal utterances and use of conversation-extending devices were positively related (and di-

exactly what they mean (Pechmann & Deutsch, 1982; Van Hekken, Vergeer, & Harris, 1980).

Factors responsible for the production of clear verbal messages are both cognitive and linguistic in nature. Cognitively, skilled speakers must be able to determine the attributes of a referent that discriminate it from other possible alternatives. Linguistically, they must be in command of the vocabulary and grammar that permit them to designate those attributes. Even when preschoolers have these prerequisites, they do not necessarily make full use of them. For example, Deutsch and Pechmann (1982) showed several eight-object arrays to 3- to 10-year-old children as well as adults. In each array, several of the objects were similar in size, shape, and color. Subjects were asked to indicate which object they liked best as a birthday present for an imaginary friend. Most of the 3-year-olds gave ambiguous descriptions, a tendency that declined steadily with age.

An interesting finding is that when children's messages *are* inadequate and there is a breakdown in communication, preschoolers tend to blame their listeners rather

rectives were negatively related) to children's vocabulary development.

Applications. The presence of a twin may dramatically alter parent-child conversations in ways that impede early language learning. Consequently, parents of twins should make a concerted effort to interact separately with each of their children. Arranging special times for one-to-one conversation may also be important for later-born siblings. In a study similar to the one described above, the presence of a closely spaced older sibling led mothers to offer the younger child less responsive verbal stimulation. Some evidence suggests that laterborns are slower than firstborns in early language development (Jones & Adamson, 1987).

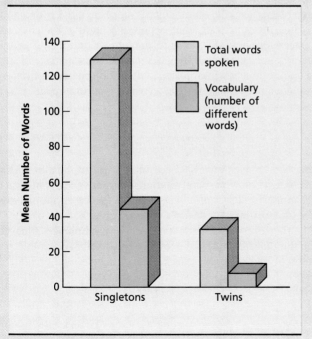

Vocabulary differences between 21-month-old twins and singletons in the Tomasello, Mannle, and Kruger (1986) study. The means indicate the total number of words spoken as well as the number of *different* words spoken (an estimate of vocabulary size) in a 15-minute recording session. *(Adapted from Tomasello, Mannle, and Kruger, 1986.)*

*Referential communication —
the ability to phrase messages clearly and to recognize
when messages received are
unclear — is not well developed until middle childhood.*

than themselves. Young children may have reason to do so, since many parents patiently try to figure out their children's utterances and rarely tell them exactly why their messages are not understood. Laboratory experiments reveal that providing children with explicit feedback (e.g., "There are four balls, and I don't know whether you mean a large or a small one or a red or a green one") increases the clarity of their messages and reduces their listener-blaming tendencies (Robinson, 1981).

Children's capacity to evaluate the communicative adequacy of messages they receive also improves from the preschool years into middle childhood. Around age 3, children start to ask for clarification from others when a message is ambiguous (Revelle, Karabenick, & Wellman, 1981). Still, young children only gradually become aware of the inadequacies of different kinds of uninformative messages. Recognition that a message provides an ambiguous description of a concrete object emerges earlier than recognition that a message is inconsistent with something a speaker said earlier in a conversation. Detection of this last kind of difficulty is more cognitively demanding. Instead of just comparing the content of what is said to stimuli in the environment, the listener must retrieve previous discourse from memory and then match it against the spoken message (Sonnenschein, 1986a). Noticing inconsistencies in spoken language requires the comprehension monitoring skills we discussed in Chapter 7. It is a late-developing achievement that improves gradually during middle childhood and adolescence.

The Development of Sociolinguistic Understanding

Besides expressing meanings, verbal messages have sociolinguistic implications. That is, they carry information having to do with social relationships between people, such as status differentials and familiarity. Psycholinguists refer to speech variations that adapt to changes in social expectations as **speech registers.** As adults, we move through a variety of roles in the course of a single day — parent, employee, supervisor, friend, and casual acquaintance, to name just a few. To be socially acceptable, we have to master several different registers. Over the course of development, children must learn to adjust their speech to fit with social demands, since whether or not they do so may determine whether a listener is willing to receive their message at all.

Children are sensitive to the age, sex, and social status of their communicative partners at an early age. In one study, 4- to 7-year-olds were asked to act out different roles with hand puppets. Even the youngest children understood stereotypic linguistic features of different social positions. They used more imperatives when playing socially dominant and male roles, such as teacher, doctor, and father, and more politeness routines and indirect requests when playing less dominant and feminine roles, such as pupil, patient, and mother (Anderson, 1984). Older children have acquired an even more subtle appreciation of register adjustments that mark social status. Between 5 and 8 years of age, they increase the amount of deference they express in requests they make of preoccupied adults, who can be expected to be disturbed by the interruption (Ervin-Tripp, O'Connor, & Rosenberg, 1984). Speech adjustments based on familiarity also appear during the preschool and early elementary school years. Children give fuller explanations to an unfamiliar listener than to someone with whom they share common experiences, such as a friend or family member (Menig-Peterson, 1975; Sonnenschein, 1986b).

Children learn a great deal about speech registers through direct observation, but parents also deliberately teach some social forms. From age 2 on, children get intensive instruction in politeness routines. When they fail to say "please," "thank you," or "hi" and "goodbye," parents generally demand an appropriate response. This is true not only in our culture, but in others as well (Schieffelin & Ochs, 1983). A child can get by in the world without perfectly correct grammar, pronunciation, and an extensive vocabulary, but failing to use socially acceptable speech can lead to ostracism and rejection. Anything that has such drastic consequences cannot be unimportant, and parents' insistent tutoring in social niceties suggests that they are well aware of this fact (Greif & Berko Gleason, 1980).

BRIEF REVIEW

During early and middle childhood, children acquire pragmatic skills that enable them to participate as competent conversationalists in sustained discourse with others. Over this same period, the ability to detect the illocutionary intent of others and referential communication also improve. Finally, children's sociolinguistic understanding, or sensitivity to social expectations conveyed through language, appears early and undergoes further refinement during the school years.

THE EMERGENCE OF METALINGUISTIC AWARENESS

Earlier in this chapter we indicated that **metalinguistic awareness** — the ability to think about language itself — is involved in a variety of later language achievements. Psycholinguists have been interested in when metalinguistic awareness emerges and the role it plays in a number of language-related accomplishments, especially learning to read.

Laboratory studies show that a diverse array of metalinguistic skills appears during the preschool years. For example, some 3-year-olds and many 4-year-olds are aware that word labels are arbitrary and not an actual part of the objects they denote. When asked whether an object could be called by a different name in a new language, they respond "yes." In addition, 4-year-olds demonstrate some phonological awareness; they are able to pick out words that rhyme from those that do not. They can also make some conscious syntactic judgments — for example, that a puppet who says "nose your touch" or "dog the pat" is saying his sentences "the wrong way around." Furthermore, these beginning metalinguistic accomplishments are strongly correlated with vocabulary and grammatical development during the preschool years (Smith & Tager-Flusberg, 1982).

Still, many metalinguistic abilities do not emerge until middle childhood. For example, around 8 years of age, children can segment spoken words into phonemes (Tunmer & Nesdale, 1982). In addition, they can judge the grammatical correctness of a sentence even if its meaning is false or senseless, whereas preschoolers cannot (Bialystok, 1986). Some investigators believe that refinement of metalinguistic skills may be a function of improved metacognitive control over the information processing system during middle childhood (see Chapter 7). However, much more research is needed to determine the precise links between metacognitive and metalinguistic development (Tunmer & Bowey, 1984).

Many studies report that kindergartners' scores on a variety of metalinguistic measures are good predictors of reading achievement in first grade (Ehri, 1979). That metalinguistic abilities are intimately involved in successful reading makes perfect sense. To map printed text onto oral language effectively, children must have some conscious knowledge of the structural features of spoken language. However, as yet, researchers do not know which metalinguistic abilities are essential. Once more is known, special training in metalinguistic skills could prove to be an especially effective means for facilitating reading progress (Tunmer & Bowey, 1984).

BILINGUALISM: LEARNING TWO LANGUAGES AT A TIME

For most of this chapter, our discussion has focused on children's acquisition of their first language. However, a common occurrence throughout the world is that children must learn two languages, and sometimes more than two, during their childhood years. Current estimates indicate that 2.5 million American school-age children speak a language other than English at home, a figure that is expected to double by the year 2000 (Hakuta & Garcia, 1989).

Until recently, a commonly held belief among Americans was that learning more than one language in childhood undermined proficiency in either language, led to intellectual deficits, and promoted a sense of personal rootlessness because the bilingual child was believed to identify only weakly with mainstream American culture. The long American tradition of negative attitudes toward childhood bilingualism has been fueled by racial and ethnic prejudices, since bilingualism in the United States is strongly associated with low-income and minority status. In addition, during the early part of this century, the view was bolstered by the findings of seriously flawed research (Diaz, 1983). Today, more carefully conducted investigations show that there are no negative consequences from an early bilingual experience. To the contrary, bilingualism actually has intellectually enriching consequences.

Children may become bilingual in two ways: through *simultaneous acquisition* of both languages or through *sequential acquisition* in which second language learning follows mastery of the first. Case studies reveal no serious linguistic retardation in either language as the result of simultaneous acquisition in early childhood. For a short period of time during the second year of life, children who are exposed to two languages appear to develop more slowly. This is because they shift between the two vocabularies, often apply the grammar of one language to the vocabulary of the other, and sometimes mix the two phonological systems. Between the ages of 2 and 3, children become aware that they are dealing with two separate languages. From then on, each develops as an independent system. By age 4, bilingual youngsters show normal native ability in the language of their community and good to native ability in the second language, depending on the extent to which they have been exposed to it. When two languages are learned sequentially (one before and one after age 3), it generally takes about a year to achieve a level of fluency that is roughly comparable to that of native-speaking agemates (Reich, 1986).

A landmark study conducted by Peal and Lambert (1962) showed for the first time that bilingualism has a positive influence on cognitive development. Comparing 10-year-old Canadian children who were equally fluent in both English and French to monolingual controls, the investigators found that the bilinguals performed better on a variety of verbal and nonverbal intellectual measures. Although Peal and Lambert's research suffered from methodological problems, better-designed studies have replicated and extended their findings. Children who are fluent in a second language outperform their monolingual counterparts on tests of analytic reasoning, concept formation, cognitive flexibility, and metalinguistic awareness (Ben-Zeev, 1977; Bialystok, 1986; Diaz, 1985; Galambos & Goldin-Meadow, 1990; Ianco-Worrall, 1972).

The cognitive advantages of bilingualism provide strong justification for the expansion of bilingual education programs to serve children with limited English proficiency in American public schools. Box 9.3 describes the current status of bilingual education in the United States. As you will see, it is still the case that few bilingual

---

◆ CONTEMPORARY ISSUES: SOCIAL POLICY ◆

Bilingual Education in the United States

Box 9.3

Over the last two decades, a wide variety of bilingual education programs designed to serve the growing number of children with limited English proficiency have sprung up around the United States, and state and federal funding to support them has increased. Nevertheless, the question of how bilingual education should be implemented continues to be the subject of heated controversy.

On one side of the debate are individuals who believe that classroom instruction in English should be emphasized for language minority youngsters. According to this view, time spent communicating in the child's native tongue only subtracts from English language achievement, which is crucial for success in the academic and vocational worlds. Consistent with this perspective, most bilingual education programs are conducted largely or entirely in English. The child's native tongue is used only initially and temporarily; it is phased out as quickly as possible.

On the other side are educators committed to truly *bilingual* education—developing the ethnic minority child's native language while fostering mastery of English. Supporters of this view believe that providing instruction in the native language and gradually introducing English as children become ready for it communicates to minority youngsters that their language and culture are respected. In addition, by avoiding abrupt submersion in an English-speaking environment, bilingual education can prevent the cognitive and educational risks of *semilingualism*, or inadequate proficiency in both languages. Semilingualism is one factor believed to contribute to the high rates of school failure and dropout among low-income Hispanic youngsters, who constitute nearly 50 percent of the public school language minority population (August & Garcia, 1988; Ruiz, 1988).

In recent years, public opinion has sided heavily with the first of these two viewpoints. Many states have passed laws declaring English to be their official language, creating conditions in which schools have no obligation to teach minority pupils in languages other than English (August & Garcia, 1988). Yet a growing body of evidence underscores the value of instruction in the child's native tongue. In classrooms where both lan-

When bilingual education programs provide instruction in both the child's native language and in English, children are more involved in learning and show superior language development.

guages are integrated into the curriculum, minority children are more involved in learning, participate more actively in class discussions, and show superior language development. In contrast, when teachers speak only in a language their pupils can barely understand, children exhibit frustration, boredom, and withdrawal (Cazden, 1984; Tikenoff, 1983; Wong-Fillmore et al., 1985).

A number of psycholinguists have pointed out a curious paradox in American educational practice. Although minority children are encouraged to become English monolinguals, academic instruction in foreign languages (many of which are natively spoken by minority youngsters) continues to be highly valued for middle-class, native English-speaking pupils (Hakuta & Garcia, 1989; Ruiz, 1988). Recently, a few schools have experimented with an unusual form of bilingual education designed to benefit both groups of youngsters. In these programs, limited-English-proficient and fluent-English-speaking children are assigned in equal numbers to the same classroom, and instruction is directed at helping all achieve competence in English and a second language. Evaluations of these efforts, in addition to research on existing programs, need to be communicated to policymakers, educators, and the American public with the goal of promoting educational experiences that enhance linguistic opportunities for all children.

children receive much in the way of maintenance of their native language in school. Bilingualism is part of the ethnic minority child's right to be fully educated. Beyond this, it provides one of the best examples of how language, once learned, becomes an important tool of the intellect and fosters cognitive growth. As Hakuta (1986) and Ruiz (1988) suggest, the goals of schooling could justifiably be broadened to include the development of *all* students as functional bilinguals, with the aim of promoting the linguistic, cognitive, and cultural enrichment of the entire populace.

CHAPTER SUMMARY

A Short History

■ Increased interest in language development was sparked by the Chomsky-Skinner debate of the 1950s. Both behaviorist and nativist theories have since been criticized, and an interactionist perspective now dominates the field. Children are viewed as active, hypothesis-testing beings who, supported by a rich linguistic environment, acquire the complexities of language largely at their own initiative.

Important Issues in Language Development

■ Evidence on whether first language acquisition must take place during childhood for development to proceed normally is consistent with a weak version of the critical period, or a sensitive phase. However, second language learning does not conform to the critical period hypothesis.

■ Although some milestones of language development are universal, striking individual differences in rate and route exist. Some children display a **referential style** of language learning, in which nouns are emphasized and early language development is rapid. Others have an **expressive style,** in which pronouns and social phrases are common and development proceeds more slowly.

■ Language **comprehension** is generally ahead of **production.** An accurate appraisal of children's development requires that both processes be assessed.

Prelinguistic Preparation

■ Infants are specially prepared for language learning. Neonates are capable of **categorical speech perception** and can discriminate almost all **phonemes** used in human languages. By the end of the first year, infants focus more intently on the speech sounds of their native tongue.

■ Infants begin to coo at 2 months and **babble** around 6 months. The range of sounds produced gradually expands during the first year. In Western cultures, adults prepare infants for conversational turn-taking by engaging in **pseudodialogues** and playing social games with them.

■ By the end of the first year, babies express preverbal intentions through **protodeclaratives** and **protoimperatives.** Also, they have made considerable progress in acquiring prelinguistic concepts, onto which they map their first words.

Phonological Development

■ Phonological development involves understanding and producing the sound patterns of our native language. During the transition from babbling to speech, children expand their phonological capabilities by engaging in **sound play** and **jargon stretches.** Slightly later, they use systematic phonological strategies to simplify adult pronunciations.

■ Pronunciation undergoes marked improvement during the preschool years. Maturation of the vocal apparatus and children's active problem-solving efforts are largely responsible for this change. However, the features of **motherese** ease the child's task. Although phonological development is largely complete by school entry, a few stress and accent patterns are mastered during middle childhood and adolescence.

Semantic Development

■ Semantic development involves identifying which underlying concept each verbal label picks out in our language community. To build an extensive vocabulary rapidly, children engage in **fast mapping,** a process that permits a new word to be connected with an underlying concept after only a brief encounter.

■ In children's early vocabularies, object labels are most common, while action and state words are less frequent. The order of word acquisitions reflects children's cognitive development.

■ When first learning new words, children make errors involving **mismatches, underextensions,** and **overextensions.** Word coinages and metaphors permit children to expand the range of meanings they can express linguistically.

■ During the school years, children's ability to grasp word meanings from verbal definitions improves. Also, older youngsters understand that many words have multiple meanings; as a result, their appreciation of metaphor expands.

■ **Lexical contrast theory** is a new, controversial theory of early semantic development. Principles of conventionality and contrast are used to account for children's acquisition and refinement of word meanings.

Grammatical Development

■ Early grammatical development can be divided into phases based on children's **mean length of utterance**

(MLU). During the one-word phase, children appear to use single words to express sentencelike meanings, or **holophrases.** However, an understanding of grammar is not yet apparent.

■ Children's two-word utterances are referred to as **telegraphic speech,** since they omit smaller and less important words. During this phase, children combine words to express many meanings, but their utterances do not follow adultlike grammatical rules.

■ As the MLU moves from 2 to 3, simple sentences reflecting word order conventions of the child's language community appear. Grammatical morphemes are added in a consistent order that reflects their structural and semantic complexity. Soon children **overregularize,** or extend morphological rules inappropriately to irregular instances.

■ Around the time the MLU reaches 3, children achieve an implicit appreciation of formal grammatical categories of their language. In addition, complex grammatical constructions, such as negations and questions, appear. The passive voice and infinitive phrases are examples of grammatical forms that continue to develop during middle childhood.

■ Current theorists believe that powerful cognitive processing mechanisms help young children discover the regularities of grammar. However, debate continues about whether or not they are specially tuned to analyze linguistic information. The simple syntactic structure of motherese, along with adult **expansions** and **recasts** of children's utterances, facilitates grammatical development.

Pragmatic Development

■ Pragmatic development involves the communicative side of language. During the preschool years, children become more effective conversationalists, and **referential communication skills** improve. Sociolinguistic understanding is reflected in preschoolers' ability to adjust their speech in accord with the age, sex, and social status of their communicative partners.

The Emergence of Metalinguistic Awareness

■ **Metalinguistic awareness,** the ability to consciously reflect on language as a system, is related to language development as well as language-related accomplishments, such as learning to read. Preschoolers acquire some metalinguistic skills, but many do not emerge until middle childhood.

Bilingualism: Learning Two Languages at a Time

■ Although the United States has a sizable bilingual population, Americans have traditionally held negative attitudes toward multiple language learning in childhood. Recent research shows that bilingual children are cognitively advantaged when compared to their monolingual counterparts.

IMPORTANT TERMS AND CONCEPTS

phonology (p. 344)
semantics (p. 344)
grammar (p. 344)
pragmatics (p. 344)
language acquisition device
    (LAD) (p. 346)
referential style (p. 350)
expressive style (p. 350)
comprehension (p. 351)
production (p. 351)
phonemes (p. 352)
categorical speech
    perception (p. 352)
babbling (p. 353)

pseudodialogues (p. 354)
protodeclarative (p. 354)
protoimperative (p. 355)
sound play (p. 357)
jargon stretches (p. 357)
motherese (p. 358)
fast mapping (p. 359)
mismatch (p. 362)
underextension (p. 362)
overextension (p. 362)
lexical contrast theory (p. 364)
mean length of utterance
    (MLU) (p. 364)
morphemes (p. 365)

holophrases (p. 365)
telegraphic speech (p. 365)
overregularization (p. 368)
language-making capacity
    (LMC) (p. 372)
expansions (p. 372)
recasts (p. 372)
turnabout (p. 373)
shading (p. 373)
illocutionary intent (p. 373)
referential communication
    skills (p. 374)
speech registers (p. 376)
metalinguistic awareness (p. 377)

My Brother Malcolm by Conger Metcalfe.
Cedar Rapids Museum of Art.

10
Emotional Development

In this chapter we turn to a consideration of the child's emotions, a topic that it has captured the attention of investigators from virtually every major theoretical persuasion in the field of child development. Although the affective side of development lay in the shadow of cognition for several decades, today new excitement surrounds the topic. Rapidly accumulating evidence reveals that emotions play a central role in all aspects of human behavior.

Our discussion brings together three lines of evidence. First, we chart the general course of emotional development. In doing so, we describe new methods of study, major theories, and research on children's ability to express as well as recognize and interpret emotional signals. Second, our attention turns to individual differences in children's temperament and personality. We examine both biological and environmental origins of these differences as well as their consequences for later development. Finally, we discuss attachment to the caregiver, the child's first affectional tie that emerges over the course of infancy. This formative social relationship is forged from a complex interplay between the baby's emotional signals and the caregiver's responsiveness to infant cues. The feelings of security that emanate from this bond provide a vital source of support for many aspects of psychological growth. As we consider these diverse topics, you will see that a unifying theme that weaves its way through all current research is that emotions serve as powerful organizing forces in all of human development.

Between the 1940s and 1970s, researchers rarely stopped to consider the possibility that emotions might play a central role in the social and intellectual life of the child. The third *Handbook of Child Psychology*, which summarized the status of the field in 1970, did not even include a chapter on emotional development. This was in stark contrast to the three previous editions, each of which had included a chapter (Campos et al., 1983). The most recent *Handbook of Child Psychology*, published in 1983, compensated for the 1970 omission by devoting over 100 pages to the topic. This rebirth of interest was sparked, in part, by the discovery of new methods that permitted investigators to assess emotional reactions more accurately and at an earlier age than was previously thought possible.

Methods of Measuring Emotional Reactions

A variety of procedures for classifying the patterning of facial expressions as indicators of underlying emotions have recently been developed (Ekman & Oster, 1979; Matias, Cohn, & Ross, 1989). One of them is illustrated in Figure 10.1 to give you an example of the most common methods used to study young children's emotional reactions today. The refinement of these techniques was inspired by cross-cultural evidence indicating that the facial behaviors people associate with basic emotions are universal. For example, Ekman and Friesen (1972) reported that subjects from the United States, Japan, a variety of South American countries, and even preliterate societies discriminate happiness, sadness, disgust, and anger from still photographs in the same way. The consistency of these findings suggested that a number of facial patterns were under biological control, had important adaptive value, and could even be discerned in early infancy.

Recently, the vocal channel has also been used to study children's emotions. Although the techniques are not as well developed as those for facial patterns, different emotions can be identified consistently in vocal expressions (e.g., Scherer, 1982). This is even true early in life. As we indicated in Chapter 4, newborn infants already express some vocal affects through a set of differentiated cries that are clearly recognizable to their caregivers.

Expressions of emotion involving postural movements have received less attention, although they offer promise as measures of children's affects. In one study, Lewis and Michalson (1982) reported that mothers of 1-year-olds often used bodily responses to infer and label their children's emotions. For example, throwing objects, kicking, and stomping were taken as evidence of anger; moving away and refusing to look as fear; and skipping and strutting as happiness.

Finally, physiological measures indexing autonomic nervous system reactivity, such as galvanic skin response, heart rate, blood pressure, and respiration rate, have been used to measure emotional arousal for decades. However, by themselves, physiological measures are limited indices of emotion, since there has been little success in linking them to discrete emotional states. Nevertheless, physiological indices do serve as good measures of the intensity of an emotional response and therefore are useful adjuncts to other methods (Lewis & Michalson, 1983).

Theories of Emotional Development

In the sections to follow, we review three important theoretical approaches to general emotional development — behaviorism and social learning theory, cognitive-developmental discrepancy theory, and the new organizational approach, to which you were introduced in Chapter 1. While organizational theories have gained in popularity because of their broad explanatory power, each of these perspectives has made lasting contributions to our understanding of children's emotions.

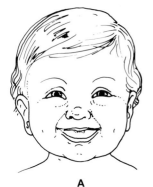

A

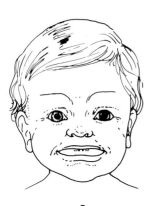

B

Figure 10.1. Examples of emotions assessed by the MAX (Maximally Discriminative Facial Movement) System (Izard, 1979). In this widely used method for classifying infants' emotional expressions, babies' facial muscle movements are carefully rated to determine their correspondence with basic feeling states. For example, cheeks raised and corners of the mouth pulled back and up signal happiness (A). Eyebrows raised, eyes widened, and mouth opened with corners pulled straight back denote fear (B).

Behaviorism and Social Learning Theory. The early behaviorist, John Watson (1913), accorded emotional reactions a prominent role in child development and behavior. Watson proposed three innate emotions that he claimed to have observed in neonates: fear, elicited by loud noises or loss of support; rage, elicited by restriction of bodily movements; and love, evoked by tactile stimulation. As we indicated in Chapter 1, one of Watson's major contributions was his finding that emotional responses to new stimuli could be learned through *classical conditioning*. Recall that the pairing of a furry white rat with a loud, fear-eliciting sound produced a fear reaction (intense crying) to the rat as well as to other white furry objects in a 9-month-old baby. Watson concluded that all emotional reactions came to be associated with novel stimuli in just this way. In the 1960s, a second behaviorist paradigm, *operant conditioning*, became the focus of attention. Several researchers showed that infant smiling, vocalizing, and crying could be manipulated through the careful application of reinforcers and punishments (Etzel & Gewirtz, 1967; Rheingold, Gewirtz, & Ross, 1959).

Bandura's (1986, 1989) social learning theory, a revision and expansion of traditional behaviorism, includes *modeling* of others' emotional reactions as another important means through which children come to associate feelings with particular environmental conditions. Moreover, Bandura deviates sharply from the behaviorist accounts described above by adding a cognitive component to his theory. According to Bandura, as children's representational capacities improve, they can engage in *emotional self-arousal* by thinking about their own affectively charged past experiences or ones they saw happen to other people.

Although some emotional reactions are acquired according to the principles of conditioning and modeling, behaviorist and social learning theory approaches to emotional development are limited. They cannot explain why some emotional responses appear spontaneously, without any prior association with unpleasant experiences. For example, around 8 months of age, normal, family-reared babies often show fear of strangers. The fear occurs despite the fact that infants previously reacted positively to strangers and the strangers continue to smile at and initiate playful interaction with the baby. Throughout this chapter, we will see that children often respond emotionally in ways that cannot be accounted for by basic learning mechanisms. These emergent emotional reactions are better explained by other theories.

Cognitive-Developmental Discrepancy Theory. Instead of viewing emotions as central forces in development, cognitive-developmental theorists explain them in cognitive terms. The first to take this position was Donald Hebb (1946, 1949), who outlined a **discrepancy theory** of emotional development, which explained how distress reactions come to be elicited by novel stimuli. According to discrepancy theory, when the child encounters a new stimulus, it is compared to a mental representation, or scheme, of a familiar object. The degree of similarity between the novel stimulus and the child's internal scheme determines the emotional response. Little discrepancy produces very little distress, but as the magnitude of the discrepancy increases, the child's distress reaction intensifies. When the discrepancy is very great, the stimulus can no longer be assimilated. At this point, the child's distress reaction falls off until there is no reaction at all. As shown in Figure 10.2, Hebb's theory predicts an inverted U-shaped relationship between cognitive discrepancy and emotional distress.

Hebb's theory was later modified by several investigators, who argued that it could account for a wide variety of emotional phenomena (Kagan, Kearsley, & Zelazo, 1978; McCall & McGhee, 1977). For example, the positive emotions of interest and smiling were believed to be produced by a moderate degree of discrepancy between a current scheme and a new event. Fear of strangers was thought to occur just after the child formed a coherent scheme for the mother, but the discrepancy between the maternal scheme and unfamiliar people was still fairly large.

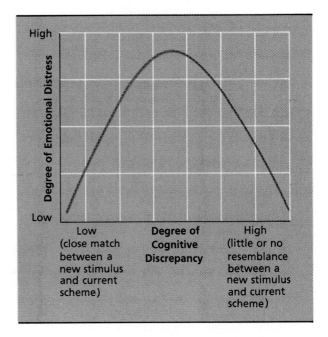

Figure 10.2. Hebb's proposed relationship between cognitive discrepancy and emotional distress.

Cognitive discrepancy is especially effective in explaining children's interest in and exploration of the physical environment. McCall, Kennedy, and Appelbaum (1977) reviewed the results of many studies in which infants were exposed to a wide variety of visual stimulus arrays that varied systematically in their divergence from a standard. In each case, infants looked longest at stimuli that were moderately discrepant from the standard with which they had been familiarized. For example, 10-week-old babies who were first shown a picture of an arrow in one orientation (e.g., ↕) looked longest at new arrows that were moderately discrepant (↗) as opposed to widely discrepant (↔) in orientation from the initial stimulus. Applied to everyday life, discrepancy theory explains why young children play happily with new toys while ignoring familiar ones. It also helps us understand why many parents and teachers find it useful to rotate toys in and out of children's play space to promote absorbed interest in objects.

Nevertheless, discrepancy theory does poorly when it comes to explaining children's emotional reactions to other people. In the case of fear of strangers, a major difficulty is that babies have well-established memories of their mothers long before fear of strangers emerges late in the first year. Yet discrepancy theory implies that as soon as the maternal scheme is present, distress reactions to discrepant stimuli should appear. Furthermore, in one intriguing investigation of emotional reactions to *different* strangers — a normal-sized adult, an adult midget, and a 5-year-old child — infant behavior did not conform to discrepancy theory predictions. The babies responded with fear to the full-sized adult, friendliness to the unfamiliar child, and uncertainty to the midget. If the infants had used a maternal scheme as the reference point for making cognitive comparisons, the strange child and small adult, not the normal-sized adult, should have elicited the greatest negative affect (Brooks & Lewis, 1976).

A final difficulty with discrepancy theory is that it cannot explain why very familiar experiences do not consistently elicit boredom, withdrawal, or a lack of emotional response. For example, the approach of the mother (who is a very familiar person indeed) repeatedly elicits smiling and pleasure from infants, and preschoolers are known for their tireless requests to have the same story read to them over and over again. There is no question that infants and children display positive affect to some events with which they are thoroughly familiar.

✓ **The New Organizational Approach.** New theories, gathered together under the **organizational approach to emotional development,** have emerged as a result of the rediscovery of the importance of emotions. The most prominent of these theories, developed by Joseph Campos and his collaborators (Barrett & Campos, 1987; Campos et al., 1983), stresses that emotions are central, adaptive forces in virtually all aspects of human functioning. To illustrate, let's look at how emotions *organize* experience in each of these areas.

Emotions as Determinants of Cognitive Processing. A large body of evidence indicates that emotions have a profound impact on learning and cognitive processing. Campos and his colleagues (1983) point out that emotional reactions can lead to learning that is crucial for survival. For example, the newly walking infant does not need to receive a shock from an electric outlet or fall down a steep staircase to learn to avoid these dangerous situations. Instead, the caregiver's highly charged command is sufficient to get the baby to acquire self-protective behaviors.

Think about your feelings on several occasions during which you did either well or poorly on a test or oral report. Did your experiences conform to the well-known inverted U-shaped relationship between intensity of emotional arousal and cognitive functioning? The effect of anxiety on children's school performance follows this pattern: Large and small amounts of anxiety lead to poorer outcomes than a moderate amount of anxiety, which can be facilitating (Sarason, 1980). Research also indicates that emotions can have powerful effects on the storage and retrieval of information from memory. For example, we remember many things better when we are in the same emotional state in which we originally learned them — word lists, childhood experiences, and recent personal events, to name just a few (Bower, 1981).

Unlike discrepancy theory, Campos's organizational perspective does not view the relationship between emotion and cognition as unidirectional. Instead, emotion and cognition are regarded as intimately interdependent. Lewis, Sullivan, and Michalson (1984) liken this continuous, dynamic interplay to a musical fugue[1] in which these two major themes of experience are inseparably interwoven into a single stream of behavior. In one study, the investigators reported evidence for reciprocal emotion-cognition relationships as early as the first 6 months of life. Babies were presented with an apparatus in which pulling a lever resulted in a pleasant audiovisual event (a color slide of a happy baby and a recording of a children's song). Tracking facial reactions and vocalizations as the infants learned the task, the researchers found interest high upon first exposure to the situation. Wariness increased as initial arm pulls produced the first recurrences of the rewarding stimulus. A rise in interest, surprise, and happiness followed as a higher rate of arm-pulling revealed that babies had figured out the connection between action and outcome. Finally, indications of sadness emerged at the end of the task (see Figure 10.3).

These findings suggest that emotional reactions serve both as consequences for prior learning and as the foundation for each new learning phase. For example, infants' negative emotion of sadness at the end of the task may have been set off by the peak of enjoyment that followed their discovery of what made the audiovisual stimulus recur. Adults often find that a negative emotion can be precipitated by a preceding positive one, and such "post-task blues" (provided they are not too intense) may help individuals reorient toward new goals. For the infants described above, sadness may have served this very function, acting as "the first note in the next sequence of the cognitive-emotional fugue" (Lewis, Sullivan, & Michalson, 1984, p. 283).

Emotions as Determinants of Social Behavior. Besides their role in cognitive processing, emotions help organize behavior in social contexts. Children's emotional

---

[1] A fugue is a musical composition in which several statements of a theme are interwoven in such a way that they seem to appear, disappear, and reappear as they weave in and out and respond to one another.

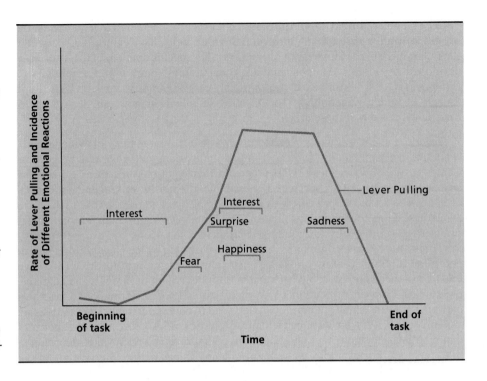

Figure 10.3. Relationship between emotions and learning in the Lewis, Sullivan, and Michalson (1984) study. The figure shows the peaks in various discrete emotional reactions that occurred as infants learned to pull a lever to produce a pleasant audio-visual event. *(From M. Lewis, M. W. Sullivan, & L. Michalson, 1984. "The Cognitive-Emotional Fugue." In C. E. Izard, J. Kagan, & R. B. Zajonc [Eds.], Emotions, Cognition, and Behavior. New York: Cambridge University Press. Pp. 280–281. © Copyright 1984 by Cambridge University Press. Reprinted with the permission of Cambridge University Press.)*

signals, such as smiling, crying, and attentive interest, affect the behavior of care-givers in powerful ways, and the emotional reactions of others also regulate children's emotional responses. Careful analyses of mother-infant face-to-face interaction indicate that a complex communication system in which each partner responds in specific and appropriate ways to the emotional cues of the other is present by 3 months of age (Cohn & Tronick, 1988; Haviland & Lelwica, 1987; Tronick & Cohn, 1989). Moreover, when miscoordination of affective signals occurs — as occasionally happens in all human dialogues — both partners try to repair the interaction. In one series of studies, Tronick and his collaborators instructed mothers to assume either a still-faced, unreactive pose or a depressed emotional state. Three-month-olds used facial expressions, vocalizations, and gestures to get their mothers to behave responsively again. When these efforts failed, the infants looked away from their mothers and engaged in intense crying and protest behavior (Cohn & Tronick, 1983; Tronick, 1989).

Toward the end of the first year, infants deliberately seek emotional information from caregivers and use it to appraise events, such as the approach of a stranger, about which they are uncertain (Campos & Stenberg, 1981). This phenomenon, called *social referencing,* is a clear illustration of the way infants rely on the feelings of others as crucial evaluative resources, and we consider it in detail later in this chapter. Finally, another way emotions regulate social behavior is through *empathy,* the perception and vicarious experience of emotions expressed by others. Because empathy is of crucial significance in fostering prosocial and altruistic behavior, we also consider its development in a subsequent section.

Emotions as Contributors to Physical Health. A growing body of evidence indicates that emotions affect physical health. When experienced for extended periods of time, negative feelings, such as depression, anxiety, and anger, affect the body's immunological system by lowering resistance to infection. Negative emotions also affect physical health when they are associated with prolonged changes in autonomic nervous system functioning. In support of the connection between emotional well-being and physical health, a longitudinal study of 100 Harvard graduates revealed

Emotions are powerful regulators of social behavior. This mutual exchange of smiles draws mother and baby closer and helps sustain their interaction.

that of those considered to be poorly adjusted during college, nearly half became seriously ill or died by their early 50s. Among those in the best mental health, only two became ill or died (Valliant, 1977).

Recent research indicates that certain emotional states that form the basis of enduring personality traits may contribute to the development of life-threatening illnesses. The most widely publicized of these dispositions, the Type A personality, had been linked to heart disease. As indicated in Box 10.1, researchers are currently exploring the childhood origins of Type A behavior in an effort to prevent its later-life consequences as early as possible.

Other Features of the Organizational Approach. Besides the central role of emotions in many aspects of psychological functioning, you will see several additional features of Campos's organizational approach reflected in research throughout this chapter. First, emotions are viewed as important in the development of self-awareness. For example, the sense of interest and excitement associated with acting on novel objects provides infants with their first opportunities to gain a notion of the self as agent, capable of affecting events in their surrounding world.[2] Once a rudimentary sense of self has developed by the second year of life, a new array of emotions that make reference to our self-image — shame, embarrassment, guilt, envy, and pride — begin to appear (Barrett & Campos, 1987; Lewis et al, 1989). Thus emotions facilitate the emergence of self-awareness, and when the glimmerings of a self-concept exist, the door is opened for the experience of new, increasingly complex emotional states.

Second, a core aspect of emotional development involves a growing ability to engage in *self-regulation* of emotional experience (Campos et al., 1983; Thompson, 1990). Young infants have only a limited ability to modulate emotional arousal; their caregivers provide much assistance in helping them sustain interest in the environment or calm down from intense crying. As cognitive and motor development proceed, babies assume more responsibility for maintaining an adaptive level of emotional experience. For example, toddlers can approach or withdraw from an emotion-arousing stimulus in response to their own feelings. Later, representation and language provide an additional means for controlling affective states. In the face of a potentially overwhelming emotional experience, preschoolers can talk about

---

[2] You may wish to return to Chapter 6 to review Piaget's description of how infants' sensorimotor exploratory activity eventually leads to a decline in egocentrism and a growing appreciation of the self as an object in a world of objects.

their feelings or ask for help, while older youngsters can use a variety of sophisticated psychological strategies for reducing stress and anxiety. Perhaps you can already see why the development of emotional self-regulation is so important. When we are underaroused or when emotions escalate to an unmanageable intensity, effective behavioral organization is undermined.

Finally, emotional reactions gradually become socialized. Cultures specify *emotional display rules*—the circumstances under which it is socially acceptable to communicate our feelings. Investigators have begun to study how children learn these rules so that, by late childhood, few emotions are expressed as openly and freely as they were during the early years of life.

BRIEF REVIEW

In the sections above, we reviewed three general approaches to emotional development. Behaviorism and social learning theory rely on conditioning and modeling to explain the acquisition of emotional reactions, while discrepancy theory regards emotions as mere by-products of cognitive processing. In comparison to these two

---

◆   THEORY, RESEARCH, AND APPLICATIONS   ◆

Type A Behavior in Children   Box 10.1

Theory. In the late 1950s, Friedman and Rosenman (1959) first presented evidence that linked the *Type A personality* to increased risk of heart disease in adulthood. When confronted with competition-eliciting circumstances, Type A adults exhibit excessive time consciousness, impatience, restlessness, anger, and competitiveness. The physiological correlates of these responses include elevated blood cholesterol levels and heightened systolic blood pressure during challenging tasks (Dembroski et al., 1979; Glass et al., 1980), factors that increase the chances of arteriosclerosis (hardening of the arteries). In fact, the incidence of heart disease is about twice as high in Type A than Type B individuals. Recently, researchers have begun to explore whether the Type A behavior pattern and its cardiovascular correlates are already evident in childhood.

Research. Investigators generally distinguish Type A from Type B children by asking teachers to rate pupils in their classrooms on a variety of behaviors associated with the Type A personality (e.g., "This child is competitive," "When this child has to wait for others, he/she becomes impatient"). Then children are subjected to a set of tasks designed to elicit Type A responding. In one investigation, Matthews and Angulo (1980) found that Type A second through sixth graders aggressed against a Bobo doll sooner, won a car race against a female adult by a greater margin of victory, and emitted more impatient behaviors (sighed, squirmed, and clicked their tongues) during a frustrating drawing task than their Type B counterparts. In another study of younger children, Type A and Type B 2- to 5-year-olds were paired with one another in competitive games. The Type A children were more often the winners. Furthermore, when observed in their classrooms, they showed more

frequent interruptions of their peers, more signs of facial annoyance, and greater gross motor activity than Type B youngsters (Vega-Lahr et al., 1988).

So far, at least two investigations have reported that Type A children show elevated physiological responsiveness in competitive situations. Lundberg (1983) discovered that Type A preschoolers display a greater rise in systolic blood pressure than their Type B counterparts when confronted with the challenge of running as fast as possible up and down a day care center corridor. Studying 11- and 12-year olds, Lawler and her colleagues (1981) reported a rise not only in systolic blood pressure, but also in heart rate and galvanic skin response for Type A children under challenging task conditions.

Nevertheless, not all Type A children become Type A adults. Recent evidence indicates that Type A behavior does not become stable until the adolescent years (Bergman & Magnusson, 1986; Steinberg, 1988c). Perhaps environmental forces combine with children's dispositions to sustain Type A traits in some youngsters but not in others. In line with this idea, recent evidence indicates that fathers of Type A sons often exhibit Type A behavior themselves (Weidner et al., 1988). When parents model impatience and competitiveness and set unrealistically high goals, Type A traits may be encouraged in children prone to be hard-driving and irritable in the first place.

Applications. Research on Type A children is still in its early stages, and investigators have much to discover about the constitutional and environmental foundations of the Type A personality. When more is known about factors that contribute to the emergence of stable Type A behaviors, intervention programs can be designed to prevent this important cause of heart disease in the fourth and fifth decades of life.

views, the new organizational approach provides a more comprehensive account of emotional development. According to Campos's organizational theory, emotions are major adaptive forces in all aspects of human functioning, are inseparably intertwined with cognition, and become increasingly self-regulated and socialized as the child matures.

Now we turn to a closer look at changes in children's emotional capacities from infancy through adolescence. Our discussion is organized around the two complementary ingredients of emotional communication: (1) changes in children's expression of a variety of emotional states and (2) changes in children's recognition of and responsiveness to the emotional signals of other people.

Development of the Expression of Discrete Emotions

How early are discrete emotional states present in the young baby? Organizational theorists differ in their answers to this question. Some believe that infants are endowed with a set of differentiated emotions at birth. Others think that the neonate's emotional capacities are more limited and that qualitatively distinct emotions gradually emerge from initial global arousal states. Let's begin our discussion of children's emotional development by examining current evidence on this issue.

To What Extent Are Newborns Capable of Discrete Emotional Expressions? In Chapter 4, we indicated that newborn infants respond with distinct facial reactions to the taste and smell of substances regarded as pleasant or unpleasant by adults (Steiner, 1979). These findings offer support for the existence of discrete emotional expressions in the neonate. Even theorists who believe that the neonate's expressive capacity is limited acknowledge that a few emotions, such as interest, distress, and disgust, are already observable in the newborn baby (e.g., Izard & Malatesta, 1987; Sroufe, 1979).

Campos and his colleagues (1983) take the position that all of the **basic emotions**, including happiness, interest, surprise, fear, anger, sadness, and disgust, are probably present in the early weeks of life. Interviews with mothers about their infants' emotional expressions support this view. In two such investigations, the majority of mothers with babies under 3 months of age reported that their infants showed surprise, anger, and fear in addition to the reactions of interest, happiness, distress, and disgust that have been observed in laboratory studies (Johnson et al., 1982; Klinnert et al., 1984). The mothers based their judgments on infant facial, vocal, and gestural cues. For example, when asked how they knew their babies were surprised, they described components of the classic "surprise expression," such as wide open eyes and mouth along with a startle response. These reports indicate that a remarkably diverse core of emotions may be present in early infancy (Emde, 1983).

The Development of Some Basic Emotions. Among the basic emotions, happiness, anger, sadness, and fear have received the most research attention. Infants display these feelings with increasing frequency and consistency over the first 7 months of life.

Happiness. The literature on children's emotions is replete with studies of smiling and laughter. As one of the infant's first emotional and social behaviors, the smile "serves many masters," playing an important role in the child's total development (Kagan, 1971). Smiling provides a mechanism for release of tension and expression of delight in cognitive mastery. The smile also elicits pleasure in adults, binding them to the infant and young child and thereby serving social and survival goals. These functions of smiling are complementary and interrelated. We will see how this is the case as we trace the development of smiling and its more intense and joyful counterpart, laughter, below.

Infants' first smiles and laughs occur in response to tactile and auditory stimulation.

The first smiles, which appear soon after birth, are called **endogenous smiles** because they occur in the absence of external stimulation, most commonly during REM sleep (Emde, Gaensbauer, & Harmon, 1976). Already, the relationship between smiling and tension release is present. Electrical recordings of brain activity indicate that endogenous smiles are associated with spontaneous neural discharge in the brain stem and limbic system[3] (Sroufe & Waters, 1976).

Exogenous smiles, which are provoked by external stimulation, appear during the first and second weeks of life. Initially, they are most easily elicited by low-level tactile and auditory stimulation while infants are asleep or drowsy. By the third week, babies start to smile in response to mild stimulation in the waking state, with light touches or blowing on the skin, gentle jogging, and a soft, high-pitched voice being the most effective stimuli (Emde & Koenig, 1969). By the fourth week, the mother's voice is especially effective, even causing the baby to interrupt a feeding in order to smile. Around the fifth week, infants also smile at visual stimuli, but the stimulus must be active and dynamic — a nodding head or a moving object that jumps suddenly across the baby's field of vision. In the second month, the human face becomes a potent stimulus of smiling as long as it remains in motion, leading the smiling response at this time to be called the **social smile** (Wolff, 1963). Presentation of stationary faces or other static visual stimuli does not consistently produce smiling until about the eighth or tenth week. By this time, the initial soft, turning up of the corners of the mouth that occurred during the neonatal period has become a broad, active grin that is often accompanied by pleasurable cooing (Sroufe & Waters, 1976).

Perhaps you can already see that changes in infant smiling parallel the development of perceptual capacities — in particular, sensitivity to moving stimuli and complex visual patterns, including the human face — that we discussed in Chapter 4. Investigators agree that by 3 months of age, one important elicitor of smiling is active processing of stimulus information, which goes on during physiological excitation–relaxation cycles during the waking state. The smile occurs at the point at which the infant assimilates the stimulus, after which arousal begins to decrease.

Laughter is a more intense expression of positive affect than smiling, requiring a steeper buildup and more rapid release of tension. It generally does not appear until 12 to 16 weeks of age, although it has occasionally been observed as early as 5 to 9 weeks (Wolff, 1963). As with smiling, infants' first laughs are in response to physical

[3] The limbic system is a portion of the forebrain involved in the regulation of emotional behavior and learning.

and auditory stimulation, but the stimulus must be dynamic and intrusive, as when the mother says playfully, "I'm gonna get you" and kisses the baby's tummy. Over the next few months, babies begin to laugh at increasingly subtle stimuli—a soundless game of peek-a-boo or the caregiver's approach with a covered face. By 1 year of age, infants laugh at situations providing obvious elements of discrepancy, such as the mother walking like a penguin or sucking on the baby's bottle. As with early smiling, events that produce laughter go hand in hand with the baby's cognitive achievements. However, laughter reflects faster assimilation of stimuli than smiling. Generally, the infant has already formed an initial representation of the novel stimulus. Then, when it occurs again, the prior mental representation hastens the infant's processing, and a laugh follows (Sroufe & Wunsch, 1972).

In addition to their role in cognitive mastery, expressions of happiness take on a vital social function, eliciting the approach and positive engagement of others. By age 3 months, the smile has become a major component in the infant's greeting behavior and is performed differentially to familiar figures (Vine, 1973). During the second year, babies deliberately use the smile as a social signal. They break their play with an interesting toy to turn around and communicate their delight to an attentive adult (Jones & Raag, 1989). The baby's smile motivates the caregiver to be affectionate as well as stimulating, since it signals well-being and encourages the caregiver to initiate cognitively interesting events. Thus, the social and cognitive consequences of the baby's expressions of happiness support one another. In addition, changes in the stimuli that babies smile at offer a window through which we can observe cognitive growth.

Anger and Sadness. During the first two months, infants express anger in response to physical restraint, such as having their arms forcefully held, and to painful stimuli. In a longitudinal study of 2- to 18-month olds' facial expressions following routine inoculations, the all-out emergency reaction of pain declined and was replaced by an increase in anger, with the largest rise occurring between 7 and 19 months (see Figure 10.4) (Izard, Hembree, & Huebner, 1987). By the end of the first year, anger is

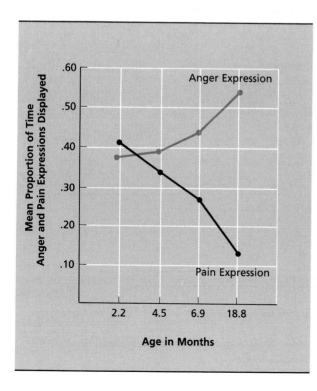

Figure 10.4. Proportion of time following a routine inoculation that infants of different ages showed pain and anger facial expressions in the Izard, Hembree, and Huebner (1987) study. *(From C. E. Izard, E. A. Hembree, & R. R. Huebner, 1987, "Infants' Emotion Expressions to Acute Pain,"* Developmental Psychology, 23, *105–113. © Copyright 1987 by the American Psychological Association. Reprinted by permission of the author.)*

sometimes observed in response to brief separations from the mother (Hyson & Izard, 1983; Shiller, Izard, & Hembree, 1986) as well as other blocked goals, such as the removal of a teething biscuit from the baby's mouth. The intensity of the anger response is affected by situational conditions. Anger rises with the repetition of a frustrating event and when a familiar person whom the infant expects to be warm and comforting is the agent of frustration (Stenberg, Campos, & Emde, 1983).

The sharp rise in anger after 7 months of age may be due to infants' improved cognitive capacity to identify the agent of a painful stimulus or a blocked goal. In addition, maturation of inhibitory mechanisms in the brain may permit infants to cut short a reflexive pain response and substitute an angry emotional reaction. The rise in anger at the end of the first year is also adaptive. New motor capacities permit older babies to use the energy mobilized by anger either to defend themselves or to overcome obstacles (Izard, Hembree, & Huebner, 1987). At the same time, the expression of anger is a potent social signal that motivates adults to comfort a suffering infant and, in the case of separation, may discourage them from leaving again soon.

Expressions of sadness also occur in response to painful stimuli and brief separations, but they are far less frequent than anger (Izard, Hembree, & Huebner, 1987; Shiller, Izard, & Hembree, 1986). However, infants who are separated from their mothers for extended periods of time and who do not experience the care of a sensitive parental substitute show a dramatic increase in sadness that corresponds to a severe depressive reaction (Gaensbauer, 1980; Spitz, 1945). We will discuss the significance of this response later when we take up the topic of infant-mother attachment.

Fear. Fear reactions are infrequent during early infancy, probably for adaptive reasons. Young babies do not yet have the motor capacities to respond to fear-arousing events. Instead, they rely on caregivers to protect them from danger (Izard & Malatesta, 1987). Like anger, fear rises dramatically between 7 and 9 months. Its most frequent expression at this time is to strange adults, a reaction called **stranger distress** (Gaensbauer, Emde, & Campos, 1976). Fear of strangers is best understood in relation to a diverse array of cognitive, social, and exploratory capacities that are emerging in the second half of the first year. But before we see how it fits in, let's discuss the characteristics of this new wariness of unfamiliar people.

Stranger distress typically occurs when an unfamiliar adult approaches and picks up the infant (Emde, Gaensbauer, & Harmon, 1976). However, it is strongly influenced by situational factors. Babies may display friendliness toward strangers if there is a period of infant-controlled acquaintance before the stranger comes near. For example, if the infant is allowed to move around the environment while the stranger sits still, babies often display positive and curious behavior toward unknown adults, including smiling, visual exploration, and spontaneous approach, although they rarely make physical contact (Harmon, Morgan, & Klein, 1977; Horner, 1980). The adult's style of interaction also makes a difference. If the stranger presents an attractive toy, begins to play a familiar game, or approaches the infant slowly as opposed to quickly and abruptly, the baby's fear can be reduced. Close proximity of the mother also serves to allay a fearful reaction (Rheingold & Eckerman, 1973; Ross & Goldman, 1977; Trause, 1977).

The fact that stranger distress is influenced by situational context helps us understand the significance of increased fearfulness around 8 months of age. Like other affective responses, fear has an adaptive function that is especially relevant at the end of the first year. It holds in check the baby's compelling urge to venture away from the caregiver that comes with the onset of crawling and walking (Ainsworth, 1973). The rise in fear permits the familiar caregiver to serve as a **secure base** from which exploration of the environment can be made and as a haven of safety when distress occurs. As part of this adaptive system, encounters with unfamiliar individuals activate two conflicting tendencies in the baby: approach (signified by interest and friendly affiliation) versus avoidance (signified by wariness and fear). The infant's resulting behavior is a matter of a careful balance between the two (Clarke-Stewart, 1978). But what tips this balance in one direction or the other has to do with new cognitive capacities, since the older infant has a more advanced ability to appraise unfamiliar experiences.

As we mentioned earlier, infants do not show the same degree of wariness to all unfamiliar people. They rarely respond with fear to small children, although why this is the case is not completely clear. Lewis and Brooks's (1978) explanation is that once the infant develops a rudimentary sense of self as separate from the surrounding world, the self is used as a basis of comparison in encounters with unfamiliar people. Consequently, the cognitive determination that small children are more like the self than adults leads infants to be less afraid. The unique stimulus value of small children may also play a role, especially their animated and friendly behavior.

Eventually, children's fear of strangers wanes as cognitive development permits them to differentiate more effectively between threatening and nonthreatening encounters. In addition, a broader array of strategies for coping with fear, including improved motor capacities and the ability to represent the whereabouts and return of the mother, lead to more effective control over fearful reactions around 2 years of age (Sroufe, 1977). Thus, infant reactions to strangers can only be understood in terms of a complex set of factors, including the context of the encounter with the stranger, the adaptiveness of the fear response, and the baby's emerging cognitive competencies.

The Emergence of Complex Emotions. Only at the end of infancy do complex emotions such as shame, embarrassment, guilt, envy, and pride emerge. An important feature of these emotions is that they involve either injury to or enhancement of the sense of self. For example, shame and embarrassment signify injury to the self-concept, and guilt represents a failure to live up to the self's moral standards. Envy is a negative appraisal of the self's ability to secure desired goods and experiences, while pride reflects delight in the self's achievements. Complex emotions actually have much in common with basic emotions, including the capacity to influence cognition and social behavior and the fact that they are adaptive. For example, guilt plays an important role in self-responsibility and morality, and shame, envy, pride, and embarrassment motivate people to pursue socially acceptable behaviors and goals.[4]

But complex emotions are also different from basic emotions in that they require both self-awareness and specific socialization experiences to develop (Campos et al., 1983; Harter, Wright, & Bresnick, 1987; Lewis et al., 1989). For example, children must first have experiences in which the parent is ashamed or proud of them to feel shame or pride themselves. In addition, children must discover what situations appropriately elicit complex emotions in their culture. In the United States, children are taught to feel pride over individual achievement. They display happiness and excitement after winning a game or getting good grades. Among the Zuni Indians, children learn that the goals of the individual must be subordinated to those of the group. Shame and embarrassment — signified by lowering the eyes and hanging the head — occur in response to purely personal success (Benedict, 1934).

Children show evidence of shame and embarrassment by 18 months and guilt and pride by age 3 (Lewis et al., 1989; Sroufe, 1979). Envy has also been observed in preschool children (Freud & Dann, 1951). However, even though signs of these emotions are present early, the circumstances under which children experience them change markedly over the elementary school years. For example, when provided with vignettes designed to evoke pride (e.g., a child accomplishing a gymnastic feat) and shame (e.g., a child taking money from a jar that belongs to her parents) and asked

---

[4] It is important to note that any of these emotions can be maladaptive if they are too intense or last for too long a period of time (Campos et al., 1983).

how they would feel, early elementary school children report the appropriate emotion only if an adult is there to observe the act. In contrast, older children report experiencing the emotion in the absence of observation by others, and they can provide much better definitions of shame and pride than their younger counterparts (Harter, Wright, & Bresnick, 1987). In another study, 6- to 11-year-olds were asked to tell about experiences that made them feel guilty. The youngest subjects reported guilt for any act that could be described as wrongdoing, even if it was accidental. Older children reported guilt for clearly intentional wrongdoing, such as ignoring responsibilities, cheating, or lying (Graham, Doubleday, & Guarino, 1984). Taken together, these investigations show that complex emotions are *outcome-related for younger children.* Experiencing them is dependent on others' reactions and obvious consequences of one's behavior. Eventually, complex emotions are experienced in the absence of adult surveillance and are linked to a conscious awareness of the self as a causal agent.

The Development of Emotional Self-Regulation. In addition to expanding their repertoire of discrete emotions, children gradually acquire a variety of techniques for managing their emotional experiences. **Emotional self-regulation** refers to the strategies we use to adjust our emotional state to a suitable level of intensity so we can remain productively engaged with our surroundings (Dodge, 1989; Thompson, 1990). If you drank a cup of coffee to alert yourself this morning, reminded yourself before an anxiety-provoking event that "it would be over soon," or decided not to see a horror film at the local theater because of its fear-arousing consequences, you were engaging in emotional self-regulation.

The diverse strategies we use to maintain an optimal level of emotional arousal begin to emerge in infancy. Development depends on maturation of the central nervous system and cognitive, linguistic, and motor abilities. However, at each step along the way, sensitive parenting supports children's acquisition of effective emotional management skills.

In the early months of life, self-regulation of emotional arousal is rudimentary. Although neonates can turn away from unpleasant stimulation or engage in mouthing and sucking when emotional intensity gets too high, they are easily overwhelmed by internal and external stimuli. Consequently, young infants depend on the soothing interventions of caregivers — lifting the distressed infant to the shoulder, rocking, and talking softly — to modulate their emotional reactions. Rapid growth of association or "thought" regions of the cortex gradually increases the baby's ability to tolerate stimulation. By 2 to 3 months, caregivers start to build on this capacity by initiating face-to-face play and attention to objects. In these rich interactional sequences, parents arouse pleasure in the baby while adjusting the pace of their own activity so the infant does not become overwhelmed and distressed. As a result, the baby's emotional tolerance for stimulation expands, and the foundation is laid for the development of higher-order self-regulatory skills (Kopp, 1989; Thompson, 1990).

During the preschool period, growth in representation and language provides the child with powerful new tools for emotional self-regulation. A vocabulary of emotional terms grows rapidly after 18 months of age. By the third year, children make frequent reference to internal states and engage in active efforts to understand and control them (Bretherton et al., 1986; Dunn, Bretherton, & Munn, 1987). For example, preschoolers know that emotional arousal can be blunted by restricting sensory input (covering your eyes or ears), talking to yourself ("Mommy said she'll be back soon"), or changing your goals (deciding that you don't want to play anyway after being excluded from a game). Caregivers' conversations with and instructions to children enhance these self-regulatory efforts. When adults prepare children for potentially arousing experiences (a trip to the dentist's office or the first day of nursery school) by describing what to expect and suggesting ways to handle anxiety, they offer coping techniques that children can later apply to themselves (Thompson, 1990).[5]

From middle-childhood into adolescence, emotional self-regulation increases in variety and sophistication. Band and Weisz (1988) asked 6- to 12-year-olds to describe their responses to common stressful situations, such as peer teasing, getting a bad grade on a test, or being the target of adult anger. Efforts to modify the situation —studying harder to get a better grade, telling a playmate not to be so mean—were common at all ages. However, older youngsters seemed more aware that some life circumstances cannot be changed. Consequently, they mentioned a greater number of subtle psychological techniques aimed at helping themselves accept current conditions—for example, lowering expectations to minimize the threat of failure or redefining the situation (telling themselves "it's all for the best" or "it's not so bad after all"). The capacity to generate a diverse array of self-regulatory strategies and flexibly adjust them to situational demands permits adolescents to handle unanticipated daily stresses more successfully than younger children (Altshuler & Ruble, 1989).

Unfortunately, not all children acquire effective emotional self-regulatory skills. The emotional climate of the home makes an important difference. In a recent study, Gottman and Katz (1989) observed unhappily married couples behaving coldly, unresponsively, and angrily toward their 4- and 5-year-olds, a response style that predicted hostility, noncompliance, and high levels of stress hormones in their children. Interestingly, these youngsters tended to avoid intense play when interacting with familiar agemates, perhaps as a way of protecting themselves from being flooded with feelings that they had not yet learned to control.

✓Acquiring Emotional Display Rules. Besides regulating internal emotional states, children must learn when and where it is appropriate for certain emotions to be expressed in their culture. Acquisition of conventionally accepted **emotional display rules** is crucial for successful social interaction. For example, a person who openly expresses dislike for an unattractive birthday present or who laughs in response to the injury of another runs the risk of serious negative social consequences, ranging from disapproval to outright scorn and rejection.

As early as the first few months of life, American middle-class infants are exposed to socialization experiences aimed at suppressing the display of negative affect. Malatesta and her colleagues filmed mothers playing with their 2- to 7-month-old babies. Mothers sometimes imitated their infants' emotional reactions, but they were selective in how they did so. Imitations were restricted to the positive emotions of interest, happiness, and surprise; mothers rarely duplicated anger and sadness (Malatesta & Haviland, 1982; Malatesta et al., 1986).

At slightly older ages, parents provide children with direct instruction in emotional display rules. Miller and Sperry (1987) studied the everyday interactions of three mother-toddler pairs in an urban working-class neighborhood. Consistent with the social values of this community, the mothers encouraged their young children to express anger and aggression in self-defense (e.g., when a playmate grabbed a toy or hit the child) but not to do so under other conditions. In addition, children learned about how to behave emotionally by watching parents modulate their own affective displays and hearing them talk about their own and others' reactions to daily experiences.

Although caregiver shaping of acceptable emotional behavior begins early, children only gradually become adept at modifying their own emotional displays. Not

[5] The central role of language in emotional self-regulation should remind you of Vygotsky's ideas on the self-guiding function of children's private speech. Return to Chapter 6, pages 245–250, if you need to review Vygotsky's theory.

until 3 years of age can children pose an expression they do not feel. Moreover, these emotional "masks" are largely limited to the positive feelings of happiness and surprise. Children of all ages (and adults as well) find it much more difficult to act sad, angry, or disgusted than to seem pleased (Lewis, Sullivan, & Vasen, 1987). In fact, over the elementary school years, children become especially skilled at suppressing negative affect. In contrast, they often leak their true feelings when asked to hide a positive emotional state (Shennum & Bugental, 1982). Socialization pressures are undoubtedly responsible for these trends. To foster social interaction, many cultures encourage children to communicate positive feelings and to inhibit unpleasant emotional displays.

Besides greater conformity to emotional display rules, a conscious awareness and understanding of them emerges in middle childhood. Saarni (1979) presented 6-, 8-, and 10-year-olds with hypothetical scenarios involving a child in a stressful situation with an onlooker present. For example, in one, the child boasted about his skating ability and afterward fell down. The subjects were asked to choose from a set of pictures the facial expression that best ended the scene and to explain why the choice was appropriate. Ten-year-olds exceeded 6- and 8-year-olds in the number of display rules they used. In addition, older children justified display rules by referring to social norms (e.g., "It's impolite to show you feel that way"). In contrast, younger children justified them as a way to avoid scolding and ridicule (e.g., "He'd be pretty stupid to show he's hurt after he's been bragging how good he is"). These findings suggest that children initially obey display rules to avoid punishment and gain approval from others. Eventually, they see that each rule is consistently adhered to by members of their culture, and they come to understand its value as a generally accepted standard for expressive behavior (Meerum Terwogt & Olthof, 1989; Saarni, 1989).

BRIEF REVIEW

Although a set of basic emotions may be present in the newborn infant, the development of emotional expression is a gradual process that continues into adolescence. Changes in the expression of happiness, anger, fear, and sadness over the first year reflect infants' developing cognitive capacities and serve social as well as survival functions. At the end of the second year, self-development supports the emergence of complex emotions, which become increasingly refined into middle childhood. Self-regulation of emotional experience develops gradually and is supported by central nervous system maturation, cognitive and linguistic capacities, and sensitive child-rearing practices. During the preschool years, children start to conform to the emotional display rules of their culture; in middle childhood, they become consciously aware of these rules.

Recognizing and Responding to the Emotions of Others

Children's emotional expressiveness is intimately tied to their ability to recognize and respond to the affective signals of other people. In the following sections, we turn to the development of this receptive side of emotional communication.

Emotional Recognition in Infancy. The ability to respond to the facial expressions of others is evident in early infancy. Habituation studies show that during the first 6 months, babies discriminate some aspects of static facial configurations (see Chapter 4). Moreover, earlier we noted that infants as young as 3 months of age respond in a discriminating way to maternal expressions of emotion, spontaneously matching them in affective tone and becoming upset when confronted with the depressed, immobile faces of their mothers (Haviland & Lewica, 1987; Tronick, 1989). These findings suggest that young infants recognize and interpret emotional signals in meaningful ways, a capacity that improves markedly over the second half of the first year (Termine & Izard, 1988). By 8 to 10 months of age, babies actively seek information about other people's feelings, since social referencing begins at this time.

Social Referencing. <u>Social referencing</u> involves <u>relying on another person's</u> <u>emotional reaction to appraise an uncertain situation.</u> Two cognitive prerequisites permit infants to engage in it. First, as we indicated above, by the end of the first year, <u>babies are competent interpreters of others' basic emotional signals.</u> Second, older <u>infants start to *evaluate* events and objects in the environment with regard to their</u> <u>safety and security.</u> For example, they pause longer to study a new object or person than they did at a younger age.

Research indicates that the mother's emotional expression (e.g., happiness, fear, or anger) influences whether a 1-year-old baby will exhibit wariness toward strangers, play with an unfamiliar toy, or cross an uncertain drop-off on the visual cliff (Hornik, Risenhoover, & Gunnar, 1987; Sorce et al., 1985; Walden & Ogan, 1988). In fact, the <u>mother's provision of affective cues during moments of uncertainty may be a</u> <u>major reason that she serves as a secure base for exploration.</u> In a strange playroom, babies show a strong desire to remain within "eyeshot" of their mother. If she turns away, they abandon exploration of an attractive set of toys to reposition themselves within her visual field, thereby retaining access to her facial and gestural cues (Carr, Dabbs, & Carr, 1975). Infants can also be seen looking toward a familiar caregiver after a fall or other mildly threatening event. Many parents are aware that, depending on their own emotional reaction, the baby's tears can be prevented or encouraged in these situations. Consequently, social referencing provides yet another example of how socialization agents help children regulate their emotional experiences.

Although there is little research on social referencing beyond infancy, sensitivity to other people's emotional evaluations undoubtedly becomes more finely tuned as cognitive and language development proceeds. An expanding social world leads older children to use a variety of significant individuals, such as siblings, teachers, and peers, as influential sources of affective appraisal (Feinman, 1982). Moreover, through social referencing, children observe how mature members of society react emotionally to a great many everyday events.

Further Changes in Emotional Recognition During Childhood. Children emerge from infancy with a sophisticated capacity to discriminate and respond to the affective cues of others. Additional advances in the ability to interpret other people's emotions take place over the childhood years.

Inferences about how people feel can be made on the basis of a variety of situational as well as expressive cues. By age 4, children are quite accurate in judging the situational determinants of a playmate's happy, sad, angry, or distressed reactions (Fabes et al., 1988). During the school years, children become proficient at considering multiple sources of information when appraising others' emotions. In a study by Gnepp (1983), children were given conflicting cues about a person's feelings. One cue was situational, and the other was a facial expression. For example, children were shown a picture of a happy-faced child with a broken bicycle. When asked how the child in the picture felt, preschoolers tended to rely on the facial cue alone. By sixth grade, children showed no preference for one cue over the other. This finding suggests that older children consider neither type of information sufficient by itself for making inferences about another's feelings.

Elementary school children also recognize that a person can experience more than one emotion at a time — in other words, that they can have "mixed feelings" (Donaldson & Westerman, 1986; Gnepp, McKee, & Domanic, 1987). Four- and 5-year-olds staunchly deny that two feelings can occur at once, in much the same way that they do not integrate two variables (height and width) in a Piagetian conservation of liquid task. Between ages 6 and 8, children describe feelings occurring in close temporal proximity ("If you were in a haunted house, you'd be scared, but then you'd be happy after you got out of it"). Then, between ages 8 and 12, children start to describe the simultaneous occurrence of two emotions, at first making reference to different targets for their feelings ("I was sitting in school worrying about my dog, but

I was happy I got straight As on my report card"). Only gradually do they recognize that it is possible to have two conflicting feelings about the same person or situation ("I'd be happy that I got a present but mad that it wasn't exactly what I wanted"). This advanced appreciation of affective states is a function of cognitive-developmental achievements of the middle childhood years, but opportunities to observe and talk about mixed emotional reactions are also important (Harter & Buddin, 1987).

Finally, as children achieve these advanced emotional understandings, they use them to reflect on their own affective states as well as those of others. Consequently, these developments provide older youngsters with an additional set of inner resources in their efforts to anticipate and regulate everyday emotional experiences.

The Development of Empathy. In **empathy,** recognition and expression of emotions are intimately interwoven, since both awareness of the feeling states of others and a vicarious affective response to those feelings are required to experience empathy. Current theorists agree that empathy involves a complex interaction of cognition and affect. The cognitive ability to distinguish among different emotions, perspective-taking capacity to comprehend another person's emotional experience, and congruent feelings aroused within the self all combine to produce a mature empathic response (Hoffman, 1984). Beginning in the preschool years, empathy is an important motivator of prosocial and altruistic behavior, a relationship that strengthens with age (Eisenberg & Miller, 1987).

Empathy has roots early in development. As we mentioned in Chapter 4, newborn babies cry in response to the cry of another baby. This reaction is only a primitive precursor of empathic behavior, since babies cannot yet put themselves in another individual's place and imagine what the other person is feeling. Nevertheless, human beings seem to come into the world predisposed to resonate with the emotional states of others.

Like the complex emotions we discussed earlier, empathy requires a cognitive appreciation of the self as separate and distinct from other people. As children become aware of this distinction during the second year of life, they experience empathic distress for the first time (Thompson, 1987). This is illustrated by the fact that toddlers no longer cry vigorously and seek comfort for themselves in reaction to another

An increase in empathic responding occurs over the elementary school years, due to the older child's improved ability to accurately detect the emotions of others and imagine the self in another's place.

child's tears. Instead, they start to give to others what they themselves would find most comforting. For example, Hoffman (1984) describes a 13-month-old child who responded with a distressed look to an adult who appeared sad and then gave the adult her favorite doll.

Preschool children recognize and respond empathically to emotions of others in simple situations. For example, they laugh in response to another child's joy and offer comfort and reassurance when another child is sad or hurt (Strayer, 1980). Empathic responding increases over the elementary school years (Bryant, 1982a; Marcus, Telleen, & Roke, 1979). Older children's understanding of a wider range of emotions, as well as their ability to take multiple cues into account in accurately discerning what another person feels, contributes to advances in empathic ability. In addition, elementary school children are better able to imagine themselves in another person's place. Experimental instructions to do so increase the intensity of emotional reactions in older children and adults but have little effect on preschoolers (Cantor & Wilson, 1984; Stotland, 1969; Thompson & Hoffman, 1980).

Hoffman (1984) suggests that advances in perspective-taking during late childhood and early adolescence permit an empathic response not just to other people's immediate distress, but also to their general life condition. He regards the ability to empathize with the plight of the poor, oppressed, or sick as the most mature form of empathic distress. It requires an advanced form of perspective-taking in which the child understands that people lead continuous affective lives beyond the immediate situation.

The development of empathy is molded by cognitive development in general and perspective-taking in particular, but it is also affected by early experience. Parents who are nurturant and encouraging and who show a sensitive, empathic concern for their youngsters have children who are more likely to react in a concerned way to the distress of others (Radke-Yarrow & Zahn-Waxler, 1984). In one study, Main and George (1985) observed a group of severely physically abused toddlers to see how they responded to naturally occurring incidents of other children's distress in a day care center. Unlike their nonabused counterparts, not one showed any evidence of empathy. Instead, they responded with fear, anger, and physical attacks. These findings indicate that by the second year of life, the reactions of abused children already resemble the behavior of their parents, since both respond with anger and aversion to others' distress. Harsh, punitive parenting seems to be related to disruptions in the normal course of empathic development at a very early age.

BRIEF REVIEW

The ability to recognize and meaningfully interpret emotional reactions improves markedly during infancy. By the end of the first year, babies engage in social referencing, actively seeking emotional information from others. During childhood, emotional recognition skills continue to expand. By the end of elementary school, children rely on both personal and situational cues to appraise the feelings of others, and they recognize that people can experience conflicting feelings at the same time. Finally, the ability to respond empathically undergoes gradual improvement from early infancy into adolescence and is influenced by cognitive development and social experience.

TEMPERAMENT AND DEVELOPMENT

While virtually all individuals manifest joy, anger, sadness, fear, interest, and increased or diminished activity levels in certain situations, as we get to know people well, the way their emotional responsiveness is unique becomes increasingly apparent. We take note of these individual differences when we describe one person as particularly cheerful and "upbeat" in personality, another as especially cautious and hesitant when faced with uncertain situations, a third as prone to angry outbursts, and a fourth as having a calm and quiet disposition. The term **temperament** encompasses this potpourri of ~~stable individual differences among people in quality and intensity of emotional reaction~~ (Goldsmith, 1987). Child development specialists have become increasingly interested in the causes and consequences of temperamental differences among infants and children, since the child's style of emotional responding is believed to form the cornerstone of the adult personality.

Research on temperament was inspired by findings of the classic Berkeley and Fels longitudinal studies (see Chapter 2), which were the first to identify continuities in personality development from infancy into the adult years (Kagan & Moss, 1962; Schaefer & Bayley, 1963). In addition, interest in temperament was sparked by practical concerns of child guidance professionals who worked with problem children. They quickly realized that a one-sided emphasis on the environment as responsible for children's adjustment difficulties could not account for what they saw. Sometimes children with psychological problems experienced family environments that differed very little from the environments of those who did not develop problems. Moreover, a few children appeared to be relatively free of adjustment difficulties even after experiencing family disorganization and poor parental care.

These observations provided the impetus for the New York Longitudinal Study, initiated in 1956 by Alexander Thomas and Stella Chess. To chart the impact of temperament on the course of development, they followed 141 children over a period that now extends into adulthood. The findings indicated that temperamental characteristics were major factors in predisposing children to vulnerability or buffering them from stress. When negative factors piled up in childhood, especially difficult temperament combined with insensitive child rearing and high parental conflict, an increased likelihood of poor psychological adjustment occurred. However, temperamental characteristics were not fixed and immutable. Some children were not constant, and environmental circumstances seemed to modify their reactions and behavior.

The findings of the New York Longitudinal Study inspired a growing body of research on temperament and development, including new studies of the stability of temperament, its biological roots, its relationship to social and cognitive functioning, and its interaction with child-rearing practices. Before we review what is known about these issues, let's look at some current models of temperament and at how temperament is measured.

Models of Temperament

A variety of classification systems of temperament currently exist, with Thomas and Chess's (1977) dimensions serving as the first systematic model from which all others have been derived. Analyzing detailed descriptions of infants' and children's behavior obtained from parental interviews, Thomas and Chess identified nine dimensions of temperament, which are summarized in Table 10.1. When these dimensions were used to rate the behavior of children in their longitudinal sample, certain characteristics clustered together, yielding three temperamentally different types of children:

The **easy child** (40 percent of the sample). This child quickly establishes regular routines in infancy, is generally cheerful, and adapts easily to new experiences.

The **difficult child** (10 percent of the sample). This child is irregular in daily routines, is slow to accept new experiences, and tends to react negatively and intensely.

The **slow-to-warm-up child** (15 percent of the sample). This child is inactive, is somewhat negative, and exhibits mild, low-key reactions to environmental stimuli.

Note that a large minority of children in the New York Longitudinal Study (35 percent) did not fit any one of these patterns. Instead, they showed diverse mixtures of temperamental traits that did not add up to a clear characterization.

Table 10.1. Two Models of Temperament

THOMAS AND CHESS		ROTHBART	
DIMENSION	DESCRIPTION	DIMENSION	DESCRIPTION
Activity level	Proportion of active periods to inactive ones	Activity level	Level of gross motor activity
Rhythmicity	Regularity of functions, such as hunger, excretion, sleep, and wakefulness	Smiling and laughter	Frequency of expression of happiness and pleasure
Distractibility	Degree to which extraneous stimuli alter behavior	Undisturbed persistence	Duration of orienting and interest
Approach/withdrawal	Response to a new object or person, in terms of whether the child accepts the new experience or withdraws from it	Fear	Wariness and distress in response to intense or novel stimuli
Adaptability	Ease with which the child adapts to changes in the environment	Soothability	Reduction of fussing, crying, or distress when soothing techniques are used by the caregiver or child
Attention span and persistence	Amount of time devoted to an activity and the effect of distraction on the activity	Distress to limitations	Fussing, crying, and showing distress when desires are frustrated
Intensity of reaction	Intensity or energy level of response		
Threshold of responsiveness	Intensity of stimulation required to evoke a response		
Quality of mood	Amount of friendly, pleasant, joyful behavior as contrasted with unpleasant, unfriendly behavior		

Sources: A. Thomas, S. Chess, & H. G. Birch, 1970, "The Origins of Personality," *Scientific American*, 223(2), 102–109. © August 1970 by Scientific American, Inc. All rights reserved. M. K. Rothbart, 1981, "Measurement of Temperament in Infancy," *Child Development*. 52, 569–578. © The Society for Research in Child Development, Inc. Reprinted by permission.

The difficult temperament type has been of special interest because it places children at greater risk for adjustment problems than any other set of temperamental characteristics. In the New York Longitudinal Study, 70 percent of young preschoolers classified as difficult developed behavior problems by school age, whereas only 18 percent of the easy children did (Thomas, Chess, & Birch, 1968). Despite these findings, the temperamentally difficult pattern has been questioned by some investigators, who suggest that it is too global and that there may be more than one kind of difficult child (Bates, 1987; Campos et al. 1983). In addition, critics have noted that what is difficult to some parents may not be difficult to others, especially when temperament is viewed in cross-cultural context. Nevertheless, for a great many American parents, a young child who reacts with fussing and turmoil when faced with new foods, new people, and new places and whose hunger, sleep, and elimination patterns are unpredictable is harder to raise than others, a finding that has been confirmed in many investigations (Thomas, Chess, & Korn, 1982). Interestingly, unlike difficult youngsters, slow-to-warm-up children do not present many problems in the early years. Their difficulties emerge later, after they enter school and peer group settings in which they are expected to respond actively and quickly. Chess and

Thomas (1984) reported that 50 percent of these children began to show adjustment difficulties during middle childhood.

A second model of temperament, devised by Rothbart (1981), is also shown in Table 10.1. Rothbart's typology was stimulated by Thomas and Chess's model, but it has fewer dimensions because it combines those of Thomas and Chess that overlap with one another (e.g., "distractibility" and "attention span" are merged into "undisturbed persistence"). It also includes temperamental characteristics not represented by Thomas and Chess that place special emphasis on individual differences in emotional self-regulation, such as soothability and distress to limitations. Other models of temperament also exist (e.g., Buss & Plomin, 1984), but the dimensions displayed in Table 10.1 provide a fairly comprehensive representation of those most often studied.

Measuring Temperament

Temperament is usually assessed in one of three ways: through interviews or questionnaires given to parents; through behavior ratings by pediatricians, nurses, teachers, or other individuals familiar with the child; or through direct observation in either the home or the laboratory (Bates, 1987). Occasionally, physiological indices are also used to supplement these measures. For example, heart rate and stress hormone levels distinguish highly inhibited, shy youngsters from their very sociable counterparts (Kagan, 1988; Kagan, Reznick, & Snidman, 1987).

The most common assessment technique is to rely on parental reports because parents have a depth of knowledge about the child that cannot be matched by any other source of information. A widely used assessment tool is the Carey Infant Temperament Questionnaire (Carey & McDevitt, 1978), which asks parents to indicate their degree of agreement with 70 statements about their baby's specific behaviors, such as "The infant lies quietly in the bath" (an item that assesses activity level). In addition, the questionnaire also asks parents to describe in their own words their impressions of the baby's temperament. Parental perceptions, even though they include subjective elements, are regarded as useful for understanding the way parents view and respond to their child (Hubert et al., 1982; Sirignano & Lachman, 1985). Moreover, parental reports often do converge with aspects of children's temperament. For example, when parents describe a baby as irritable and difficult, independent observations confirm somewhat higher levels of fussing and crying (Bates, 1987; Worobey & Blajda, 1989).

Most measures, whether parental report or observational, can assess temperament only across a very narrow age range because the way temperamental traits are expressed changes considerably with development (Lerner et al., 1982). For example, a child who is high in fearfulness and withdrawal may vehemently reject his first spoonfuls of cereal at 3 months of age, cry vigorously in response to unfamiliar people at 8 months, refuse to sleep in a strange bed at a year of age, avoid new children on the playground as a preschooler, and hide behind his mother when first entering kindergarten.

The Stability of Temperament

We have already mentioned the Fels, Berkeley, and New York longitudinal studies, all of which provided evidence for the long-term stability of temperament. Their findings are supported by other investigations, which report moderate stability for measures of attentiveness, activity level, and irritability over the period of infancy and into the childhood and adult years (Caspi, Elder, & Bem, 1987, 1988; Korner et al., 1981; Matheny, Riese, & Wilson, 1985; Riese, 1987; Ruff et al., 1990; Worobey & Blajda, 1989).

Evidence for temperamental stability is crucially important. Without it, temperament cannot be regarded as an enduring disposition of the individual. Nevertheless, the findings as a whole indicate that the stability of temperament is not high. In fact, on some dimensions, such as shyness-sociability, long-term stability occurs only for children at the extremes — that is, those who are very inhibited or very gregarious in behavioral style (Kagan, Reznick, & Gibbons, 1989). These findings indicate that temperament is a malleable aspect of the individual that can be modified substantially by child-rearing experiences. Furthermore, no study has shown that children maintain early temperamental characteristics in the absence of environmental supports. Instead, environmental factors contribute to stability, since as we discussed in Chapter 3, behavioral tendencies shape experience by evoking, controlling, and modifying the impact of environmental events.

Biological Foundations of Temperament and Personality

The very term "temperament" implies a biological foundation for individual differences in personality. Some theorists believe that a valid measure of temperament not only must be stable but also must be heritable (Bates, 1987; Buss & Plomin, 1984).

In recent years, many kinship studies have compared individuals of differing degrees of genetic relationship to determine the extent to which temperament and personality are heritable. As with the heritability of intelligence, the most common approach has been to compare identical and fraternal twins. The findings reveal that across a wide range of temperamental traits (activity level, sociability, distress to limitations, intensity of emotional reaction, attention span, and persistence) as well as childhood and adult personality measures (introversion, extroversion, anxiety, and impulsivity), identical twins are more similar than fraternals at just about any age they are assessed (Campos et al., 1983; Plomin, 1989; Scarr & Kidd, 1983).

The degree of resemblance between twins is fairly similar across different temperamental and personality dimensions. Representative average correlations are given in Table 10.2, and it can easily be seen that they are considerably lower than those obtained for intelligence. When heritability estimates (reflecting the proportion of variation among individuals in temperament and personality that can be attributed to genetic factors) are computed from twin studies, they are moderate, around .40 to .50 (Scarr & Kidd, 1983).

However, as we indicated in earlier chapters, the twin method of arriving at heritabilities is suspect; it may lead to an overestimation of the importance of heredity. Cross-fostering studies, in which the characteristics of children reared in adoptive families are compared to both their biological relatives (with whom they share genes) and adoptive relatives (with whom they share a common rearing environment) provide a more powerful approach to the study of genetic influences on behavior

Table 10.2. Twin Correlations for Temperament, Personality, and Intelligence

	INFANT TEMPERAMENT[a]	PERSONALITY MEASURED IN CHILDHOOD AND ADULTHOOD[b]	INTELLIGENCE[c]
Identical twins reared together	.46	.52	.86
Fraternal twins reared together	.30	.25	.60

Note: Correlations presented are averages across a variety of temperamental and personality characteristics.
[a] From Goldsmith and Gottesman (1981).
[b] From Nichols (1978). Correlations reported are averages over published studies.
[c] From Bouchard & McGue (1981). Correlations reported are averages over published studies.

Table 10.3. Kinship Correlations for Personality from Scarr et al.'s (1981) Cross-Fostering Study

	KINSHIP CORRELATION
Biological parent-child	.20
Adoptive parent-child	.06
Biological siblings	.20
Unrelated siblings	.07

Note: Correlations presented are averages across a variety of personality characteristics.

Source: Scarr et al., 1981.

(Scarr & Kidd, 1983).[6] The few such studies that are available for personality report correlations that are strikingly low for both biological and adoptive pairs. For example, Scarr and her collaborators (1981) gave a battery of personality tests to almost 200 adolescents who had been adopted in infancy as well as to their adoptive relatives. A sample of adolescents reared by their biological parents was also tested. The correlations obtained are reported in Table 10.3. Comparisons between adoptive parent-child correlations and biological parent-child correlations produced heritabilities that were only around .20. This finding suggests a very modest role for genetic factors in the development of personality.

An intriguing finding of adoption studies is the light they shed on the role of environment in the development of personality. Look at Table 10.3 again, and you will see that there is an almost total lack of correlation between biological or adoptive children reared together in the same family. How can this be explained when their resemblance is considerably higher for intelligence? Recall from Chapter 8 that there are two broad classes of environmental influences: *between-family* influences, factors that make one home environment different from another and affect all children in a family to same extent, and *within-family* influences, those that act to make children growing up in the same household different from each other.[7] The fact that siblings reared in the same household show no consistent resemblance in personality suggests that between-family influences, such as the overall climate of the home, are not very influential in explaining individual differences in personality traits. This conclusion is also supported by the finding that rearing identical twins apart in separate families (instead of together) does not affect their resemblance in personality (Bouchard, 1984; Rowe, 1987).

These results have led behavioral geneticists to conclude that the environmental factors most salient in personality development are within-family influences that bring out each child's uniqueness (Plomin, 1989). In other words, when it comes to children's personalities, parents may look for and emphasize differences. This is reflected in the comments many parents make after the birth of a second child: "She's nothing like the first one," "He's so much calmer," "She's a lot more active," or "He's more sociable." Schachter and Stone (1985) found that parents' descriptions of their offspring as temperamentally easy or difficult are governed by a sharp contrast effect. To the extent that one child is perceived as easy, another is regarded as difficult. Children, in turn, evoke reactions from caregivers that are consistent both with parental views and with their actual temperamental dispositions. Furthermore, as

[6] Return to Chapter 8, pages 322–323, to review the reasons that cross-fostering investigations are generally regarded as more useful and valid than twin comparisons.

[7] If you need to review the concepts of between- and within-family environmental influences, return to Chapter 8, page 330.

they get older, children may actively seek ways in which they can be different from their siblings. This is especially true when children are of the same sex or come from large families. Under these conditions, the child's need to stand out as someone special is particularly great (Huston, 1983).

However, not everyone agrees with behavioral geneticists that within-family influences are supreme in personality development. In Chapter 14, we will see that investigators who have assessed between-family influences directly (such as parents' overall child-rearing styles) report that they have a powerful impact on children's personalities. As Hoffman (1985) points out, we must think of personality as resulting from many different inputs. For some qualities, child-specific experiences may be important; for others, the general family environment may be important; and perhaps for most, both within- and between-family factors are involved.

Finally, consistent racial/ethnic differences in infant temperament exist. For example, Chinese and Japanese babies are calmer, more easily soothed when upset, and better at self-quieting than Caucasian infants (Caudill & Frost, 1975; Freedman, 1976). Again, however, cultural variations in caregiving appear to reflect as well as support these differences. For example, Japanese mothers interact gently, soothingly, and gesturally with their babies, while Caucasian mothers use a more active, stimulating, verbal approach (Fogel, Toda, & Kawai, 1988). Determining how these early temperamental variations combine further with aspects of the environment to produce significant ethnic group differences in personality remains a task for future research.

Taken together, research on the nature-nurture issue in the realm of temperament and personality indicates that the importance of heredity cannot be ignored. At the same time, individual differences in personality functioning can only be understood in terms of complex transactions and interdependencies between genetic and environmental factors.

Beginning at birth, Chinese-American infants are calmer than Caucasian-American babies. This finding suggests the existence of biologically based racial/ethnic differences in early temperament.

*Temperament as a Predictor of Individual Differences
in Children's Behavior*

Throughout this chapter we have discussed many examples of how emotions serve as powerful determinants of cognitive and social behavior. Since temperament refers to a person's characteristic style of emotional responding, it should be an effective predictor of those behaviors that emotions are thought to organize (Campos, et al., 1983). A rapidly accumulating body of research reveals that this is indeed the case.

Temperament and Cognitive Performance. Temperamental dispositions play an important role in cognitive performance, with interest and persistence showing strong relationships with learning and cognitive functioning almost as soon as they can be reliably measured. For example, 2- to 3-month-old infants rated high in persistence show faster operant conditioning rates than their less persistent counterparts (Dunst & Linderfelt, 1985). Infant persistence also correlates with concurrent infant mental test scores as well as preschool IQ (Goldsmith & Gottesman, 1981; Matheny, Dolan, & Wilson, 1974). During the school years, persistence, in the form of teacher-perceived task orientation, continues to predict IQ, grades in school, and teacher estimates of children's academic ability. In contrast, distractibility, avoidance of new situations, and lack of adaptability are related to poor school performance (Keogh, 1985).

Temperamental characteristics grouped under the rubric of **cognitive style** — an individual's general manner of perceiving and reacting to cognitive problems — have a particular bearing on intellectual performance. One cognitive style dimension that has been studied extensively during the past two decades is **reflection-impulsivity.** It refers to the degree to which a child will pause to reflect about a solution to a problem when a number of possible answers are available and there is uncertainty as to which one is correct.

The instrument most often used to measure reflection-impulsivity is Kagan's *Matching Familiar Figures Test* (Kagan, 1965). It presents children with a series of items in which they must select from an array of complex stimuli the one that exactly matches a standard (see the sample item in Figure 10.5). Reflective children search the alternatives carefully, taking a long time to respond, and they generally perform more accurately. In contrast, impulsives dash headlong toward an answer, and they tend to make more errors. Research on children in a variety of cultures reveals a general developmental trend toward greater reflectivity over the middle childhood years. With age, children's accuracy improves as they take more time to respond, up to a point at which response time starts to decrease as children perform the task more efficiently (Smith & Caplan, 1988). Nevertheless, at all ages, stable individual differences in reflection-impulsivity exist that predict performance on a wide variety of cognitive tasks (Messer & Schacht, 1983).

Most children who are impulsive on the *Matching Familiar Figures Test* are not "hyperactive" in a general behavioral sense, although children diagnosed as hyperactive do score toward the impulsive extreme on Kagan's measure (Campbell, 1973). For the majority of children, measures of reflection-impulsivity predict behavior only when they are working on cognitive tasks in which a solution is not immediately apparent (Kagan & Messer, 1975). Emotional factors underlying the fast-inaccurate responding of impulsives are anxious self-doubting and intense fear of making mistakes, feelings that seem to be translated into an urge to escape the task by responding as quickly as possible (Yap & Peters, 1985). In view of this, it is not surprising that impulsive children achieve less well in school and show particular deficits in reading skills when compared to their reflective counterparts (Barrett, 1977).

The foundations of the impulsive child's poorer cognitive performance may also be rooted in the information-processing strategies they use to solve problems. Impulsive children focus more on the stimulus as a whole, doing better on tasks that require global analysis, whereas reflective children pay more attention to fine details, a

Figure 10.5. Sample item from the *Matching Familiar Figures Test*. The child is asked to point to the picture in the array that matches the standard at the top. Impulsive children dash quickly toward an answer, frequently making mistakes, while reflective children take more time and are more accurate. *(From J. Kagan, 1965,* Matching Familiar Figures Test. *Cambridge, Mass.: Harvard University. Reprinted by permission.)*

strategy that leads them to search stimuli more exhaustively and places them at an advantage in academic situations (Kemler Nelson & Smith, 1989; Zelnicker et al., 1972). However, one underlying difference between a detailed versus global information-processing strategy is degree of persistence and effort, and we have already seen how this temperamental characteristic predicts cognitive performance from the earliest ages (Kogan, 1983).

Techniques used to promote reflectivity in elementary school children include training in the use of more efficient stimulus-scanning strategies, insistence by an adult that the child take more time to respond, and teaching the child to use verbal self-instruction as a means of self-control (Egeland, 1974; Meichenbaum & Goodman, 1971; Zelniker, Cochavi, & Yered, 1974). These procedures lead the high error rates of impulsive children to be modified successfully on a short-term basis. However, interventions that produce lasting gains in reflectivity among these youngsters have yet to be discovered.

Although reflective children are advantaged in cognitive performance, some investigators believe that extremes at either end of the impulsivity-reflectivity dimension may be maladaptive. Children who delay responding for a very long period of time may also feel self-doubt in learning situations. In agreement with this interpretation, Kagan (as reported by Asher, 1987) found that temperamentally fearful, inhibited children tend to score at both extremes on the *Matching Familiar Figures Test*. In view of these findings, intervention strategies might fruitfully be implemented with both kinds of youngsters, although to date they have focused only on children who fall at the impulsive extreme.

Temperament and Social Interaction. Temperament is associated with important variations in social interaction. For example, highly active preschoolers are very sociable with their peers, but they also become involved in more conflict situations than their less active counterparts. Emotionally sensitive preschoolers with a low threshold of reaction tend to interact physically by hitting, touching, and taking things away from agemates. Shy, withdrawn children do more watching of their classmates and engage in behaviors that discourage social interaction, such as pushing other children away and speaking to them less often (Billman & McDevitt, 1980; Hinde, Stevenson-Hinde, & Tamplin, 1985). Temperament even influences children's prosocial behavior; shy preschoolers are less likely help an unfamiliar adult who, for example, spills a box of gold stars (Stanhope, Bell, & Parker-Cohen, 1987).

In some cases, the social behavior seems to be a direct outcome of the temperamental characteristic in question, as is the case with shy children. In other cases, it results from the response of other people to the child's temperamental trait. For example, highly assertive and active children evoke more negative communications from others and therefore become embroiled in more arguments and disagreements. This is nicely illustrated by research on sibling relationships; sibling conflict increases when one member of a sibling pair is emotionally intense or highly active (Brody, Stoneman, & Burke, 1987; Stocker, Dunn, & Plomin, 1989). Early high activity level and emotional reactivity also predict aggression in adolescence, but the connection seems to result from the inclination of many mothers to be permissive of antisocial behavior in children with these characteristics (Olweus, 1980b). Thus, individual differences in temperament lead to differences in the reactions of others toward children, which, in turn, regulate their social development.

Temperament and Child Rearing: The "Goodness-of-Fit" Model

The evidence reviewed so far shows that only a bidirectional relationship between temperamental and environmental factors can explain healthy or maladaptive development. The nature of this transaction determines whether a child's initial behavioral tendencies will be maintained, modified, or changed over time, and this outcome, in turn, affects the nature of future organism-environment interactions. Thomas and Chess (1977; Chess & Thomas, 1984) propose a **"goodness-of-fit" model** as a useful summary of how temperamental style and environmental pressures act in concert to determine the course of later development. The model states that when the organism's style of behaving and environmental pressures are in harmony or achieve "good fit" with one another, then optimum development results. When there is dissonance or a "poor fit" between temperamental dispositions and environmental demands, then the outcome is maladaptive functioning and distorted development.

The goodness-of-fit model helps explain why children with difficult temperaments are at risk for later psychological disturbance. Such children, at least in American middle-class society, frequently experience child-rearing environments that fit poorly with their behavioral styles. Many studies indicate that difficult babies experience less responsive caregiving in infancy (Crockenberg, 1986). By the second year of life, mothers of difficult children are likely to use more intrusive and punitive discipline. In response, temperamentally difficult children react with recalcitrance and disobedience, and then their mothers often behave inconsistently, rewarding the child's noncompliant behavior by giving in to it, although they initially resisted (Lee & Bates, 1985). The difficult child's temperament combined with the mother's intrusive and inconsistent child-rearing techniques form a "poor fit" that serves to maintain and even increase the child's irritable, reactive, conflict-ridden style.

In the goodness-of-fit model, caregiving is not just responsive to the child's temperament. It also depends on characteristics of parents and the social and cultural context in which they live. In some cultures and socioeconomic strata, difficult temperament does not evoke demanding and inconsistent parental reactions. For example, difficult children from working-class Puerto Rican families are not more

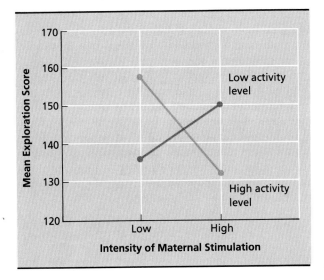

Figure 10.6. Relationship of intensity of maternal stimulation to exploratory behavior in the Gandour (1989) study. Intense parenting increased independent exploration of novel toys among inactive children but decreased it among active children. *(From M. J. Gandour, 1989, "Activity Levels as a Dimension of Temperament in Toddlers: Its Relevance for the Organismic Specificity Hypothesis," Child Development, 60, 1096. © The Society for Research in Child Development, Inc. Reprinted by permission.)*

likely be maladjusted, presumably because they are exposed to more accepting child-rearing attitudes and practices (Gannon & Korn, 1983).

Even in cultures in which difficult temperament and maladjustment are connected, the outcome is not inevitable. Change is possible when dissonant organism-environment connections are replaced with child-rearing practices that are more consonant with the child's disposition. Thomas and Chess (1977; Chess & Thomas, 1984) advocate interventions that encourage parents to provide environments that are warm and accepting and that make firm, reasonable, and consistent demands for mastering new experiences and situations.

Congruence between socialization practices and child temperament is best accomplished in early childhood, before unfavorable temperament-environment relationships have had a chance to solidify maladaptive behavior patterns. In a recent study, Gandour (1989) showed how compatibility between early parenting and toddlers' activity level influences independent exploration, which is crucial for cognitive mastery. As shown in Figure 10.6, mothers' provision of intense stimulation (continually instructing, questioning, and pointing out objects to the child) promoted exploration in less active 15-month-olds. Yet under the same conditions, the exploratory behavior of highly active children was inhibited. Perhaps highly active babies are better able to provide their own stimulation, and extensive maternal intervention interferes with their resourcefulness. Gandour's findings reveal once again that optimal child rearing must adapt to children's temperamental characteristics.

BRIEF REVIEW

Beginning in infancy, children show substantial individual differences in temperament, or quality and intensity of emotional responding. Temperament is modestly heritable. Nevertheless, its stability is not strong; children's behavioral styles can be modified substantially by environmental factors. Temperamental dispositions predict a wide range of characteristics and behaviors. For example, difficult temperament predisposes children to adjustment problems; reflection-impulsivity is associated with cognitive performance; and shyness-sociability affects peer relationships. A "good fit" between parenting style and child temperament promotes optimum development.

THE DEVELOPMENT OF ATTACHMENT

Attachment is the strong affectional tie we feel for special people in our lives that leads us to feel pleasure and joy when we interact with them and to be comforted by their nearness during times of stress. Its first manifestation is in the baby's tendency to send positive emotional signals and seek physical closeness to the primary caregiver (generally the mother) in preference to other individuals — behaviors that are clearly evident by the middle to end of the first year of life.

Freud first suggested that the infant's emotional tie to the mother serves as the prototype for all later social relationships and continues to exert its influence throughout the life span. Research on children deprived of an early attachment bond indicates that Freud's conjecture about the importance of attachment was correct. However, attachment has also been the focal point of intense debate for decades. Behaviorist and psychoanalytic theories were early views that vied with one another to explain how attachment developed and the reasons for its significance. The deficiencies of each of these perspectives eventually led to the emergence of a new view of infant-mother attachment, ethological theory, which is most popular today.

Early Views

Behaviorism. In the history of research on the infant-mother relationship, the concept of *dependency* preceded the term attachment and was linked to behaviorism and social learning theory. A number of behaviorists adopted a **drive reduction model** that accorded central importance to the role of feeding in the infant-mother relationship. The baby's dependency behaviors — seeking closeness by clinging, following the mother about, and crying and calling in her absence — were viewed as a secondary or learned drive, acquired as a result of the mother's repeated association with satisfaction of infant hunger. However, the drive reduction model was soon overturned by both animal and human evidence. A famous study of rhesus monkeys by Harlow and Zimmerman (1959) played a major role in its demise. Baby monkeys separated from their mothers at birth and reared with terry cloth and wire mesh surrogates preferred to cling to a terry cloth substitute, even though the wire mesh "mother" held the bottle and infants had to climb on it to be fed. "Contact comfort," not feeding, was shown to be a central component of dependency behavior, a finding that was completely at odds with the drive reduction model.

Observations of human infants soon revealed that they became attached to a variety of people who did not feed them. For example, in a study of 60 Scottish family-reared infants, Schaffer and Emerson (1964) reported that although the babies showed a special preference for their mothers, they frequently directed attachment behaviors toward other familiar people, such as fathers, grandparents, and siblings, who did not participate in routine caregiving. Moreover, perhaps you have observed that many toddlers develop strong emotional ties to soft, cuddly objects, such as blankets and teddy bears (see Box 10.2). Obviously, such objects have never played an active role in infant feeding!

Another variant of behaviorist theory is an **operant conditioning model** of infant social responsiveness (Gewirtz, 1969). According to this view, babies look, smile, and seek proximity because their mothers reciprocate with contingent smiles, vocalizations, pats, and hugs, thereby reinforcing the infant's social engagement. The greater the number of infant behaviors that have been consistently reinforced by and have therefore come under the stimulus control of a particular person, the stronger the attachment relationship is said to be. While a mechanism like this undoubtedly plays a role in the development of pleasurable and satisfying exchanges between mother and baby, by itself it cannot serve as a satisfactory explanation for the attachment bond. One reason is that attachment behaviors emerge even under conditions of serious infant maltreatment. Harlow and his collaborators reported that socially deprived mother monkeys (who had themselves been isolated in infancy) behaved violently toward their babies, but the infants continued to seek physical contact (Seay, Alexander, & Harlow, 1964). Similar attempts to approach nonreinforcing, abusive mothers have been observed in human children.

A major deficiency of drive reduction and operant conditioning explanations is that neither can explain why an attachment relationship, once formed, tends to persist over long periods of time in which attachment figures are absent and do not satisfy primary drives or provide social reinforcement. Think about your own feelings of attachment for a loved one whom you have not seen (and been reinforced by) in many months. Behaviorist theory would predict that the attachment relationship should be extinguished, yet it clearly is not. Because behaviorism ignores the child's growing capacity to form a stable, internal representation of the attachment figure that persists despite extended absences of the person, it cannot account for the remarkable persistence of human attachments over time and space (Ainsworth, 1969).

Psychoanalytic Theory. Like the drive reduction model, **psychoanalytic theory** emphasizes that the infant becomes attached to the mother through dependency on her for satisfying hunger and sucking needs, since the oral zone of the body is regarded as the locus of instinctual gratification during the first year of life. Also like behaviorism, the psychoanalytic perspective views the infant as initially passive in the establishment of this bond. When the mother consistently satisfies the baby's urgent pangs of hunger and her feeding practices are accompanied by sensitive, loving care, the baby gains a sense of trust, or confident expectation, that his needs will be satisfied (Erikson, 1950). This feeling of trust and security provides an emotional shelter that frees the baby from total preoccupation with biological tensions and, instead, enables the infant to turn his attention outward toward the environment. This process supports the development of the baby's *ego*, or self-system, and eventually the infant develops a sense of self that is separate from the mother and the surrounding world. At the same time, a more mature form of attachment emerges in which a permanent, positive internal representation of the mother is maintained, independent of the baby's momentary need state. Now if the mother leaves, she is not forgotten, and babies begin to show considerable distress at her departure and in her absence.

In general, psychoanalytic theory offers a richer view of attachment than behaviorism. It emphasizes that the quality of mother-infant interaction has a profound effect on later personality development and that it also provides the necessary emotional security for exploration of the environment and cognitive mastery. Nevertheless, in viewing attachment as originating in relief of the baby's hunger, the psychoanalytic position suffers from some of the same problems as behaviorism. In addition, because the newborn baby is incorrectly regarded as passive, psychoanalysts place too much emphasis on faulty maternal behavior as the cause of developmental problems and too little on what the infant brings to the relationship in the way of temperamental dispositions and readiness to respond.

Bowlby's Ethological Theory

Today, **ethological theory** is the most widely accepted view of the attachment relationship. The influence of ethology on attachment theory was initially inspired by Konrad Lorenz's studies of *imprinting* among baby birds.[8] Lorenz's view of imprinting as an instinctive behavior that helps ensure survival influenced John Bowlby (1969), originally a psychoanalyst, to formulate an approach to human attachment in which the infant's emotional tie to the mother is viewed in adaptive terms. In developing the theory, Bowlby updated the psychoanalytic perspective by emphasizing that the newborn baby is biologically prepared to contribute actively to the attachment relationship. At the same time, he retained a number of psychoanalytic contributions, such as the importance of attachment in providing emotional support for exploration

---

[8] Return to Chapter 1, page 20, if you need to review the phenomenon of imprinting.

of the environment and the vital role of cognitive development in the emergence of a mature attachment relationship.

The central feature of Bowlby's theory is that the human infant, like the young of other animal species, is endowed with a set of built-in behaviors that elicit parental care and, as a result, increase the baby's chances of survival. This repertoire of attachment-related behaviors — sucking, clinging, crying, smiling, gazing at the mother's face, and eventually following her when the infant can move about independently — bring the baby into close proximity to the mother and thereby provide protection from danger. Contact with the mother also ensures that the infant will be fed, but Bowlby was careful to point out that hunger satisfaction is not the basis for attachment. Instead, the attachment bond itself has strong biological roots; it can be understood only within an evolutionary framework in which survival of the species is of paramount importance.

Although ethological theory was stimulated by evidence on imprinting, it is important to note that imprinting cannot serve as an adequate account of human attachment. In contrast to the imprinted bird, whose time for development is short

---

◆　　　　THEORY, RESEARCH, AND APPLICATIONS　　　　◆

Blankets and Teddies: Young Children's Attachment to Soft Objects　　　Box 10.2

Theory. The importance to small children of special objects, such as blankets, teddy bears, and other cuddly toys, has long been recognized by parents. Such attachments are highly frequent, occurring in more than 50 percent of children in Western cultures (e.g., Passman & Halonen, 1979). Children especially appreciate the presence of their favorite soft object when exposed to unfamiliar situations, when going to sleep, or when tired or ill. In fact, almost half the children who form such attachments during the first or second year still display them during middle childhood (Sherman et al., 1981).

One interpretation of the significance of attachments to soft objects is that they help children manage the stress and anxiety of maternal separation and serve as substitutes for special people when they are not available. Richard Passman and Paul Weisberg (1975) decided to test this conjecture by investigating whether blanket-attached children would use their special object as a secure base of exploration in the same way that they depend on their mothers when exposed to unfamiliar environments.

Research. Two- and 3-year-old children were assigned to one of four conditions in which they were accompanied by either their mother, a familiar blanket, a favorite hard toy, or no object to a strange playroom. Half the children were blanket-attached and half were not. As shown in the adjacent figure, children attached to a blanket who had it with them played longer without becoming distressed than nonattached children who were provided with a blanket, and also longer than children in the toy-present and no-object conditions. Also, the extent of their play and exploration was comparable

to that of blanket-attached children who had their mother (but not their object of attachment) with them. These findings indicate that distress can be alleviated and play promoted by favorite objects that offer young children clinging and contact comfort. However, blankets are not always as comforting as mothers. In another study, Passman (1976) showed that when a strange playroom is made more fear-arousing by dimming the lights and piping strange clicking noises through a loudspeaker, "security blankets" become ineffective, and only the mother's presence is successful in promoting exploration and alleviating distress.

Passman and Weisberg's research provides insight into the functions of attachment objects, but it does not tell us why some children become attached to them and others do not. The phenomenon is more frequent among higher socioeconomic groups in many countries and is absent in non-Western societies in which caregivers are continuously available to infants (Gaddini & Gaddini, 1970; Hong & Townes, 1976). These findings suggest that parental accessibility, the provision of soft toys, and adult encouragement may have something to do with these attachments. In addition, temperamental characteristics may be involved. One study found that college students who reported having had an attachment object in early childhood were high in restlessness and excitability; they may have experienced more difficulty calming down when highly aroused than their nonattached counterparts (Cohen & Clark, 1984). Finally, there is no evidence that object-attached children experience unsatisfactory parental affectional ties or are less well adjusted than other children (Mahalski, Silva, & Spears, 1985; Passman, 1987).

and who must acquire only a narrow range of behaviors, human infants have a long period of immaturity and an extraordinary capacity for learning. As a result, the infant's relationship to the mother is not fixed but changes considerably over the course of infancy. It evolves from a set of instinctive behaviors that summon the mother to the neonate's side into a true attachment relationship, which is highly selective in having the mother as the preferred target of physical closeness and social interaction. Then it moves toward increasing independence from the caregiver, a process that is supported by a history of warm, responsive caregiving as well as by cognitive development. Bowlby divides this developmental progression into four phases, which are summarized below.

The Developmental Course of Attachment

1. **The preattachment phase** (birth–6 weeks). During this phase, the behavior of the infant consists largely of genetically determined reflexes with survival value. By grasping, smiling, crying, and tracking with the eyes, infants orient toward and signal

Applications. Objects of attachment are normal and effective sources of security during a developmental period in which children start to increase their physical and psychological separateness from parents. Such objects help children recapture the soft, tactile comfort of physical closeness to the mother and provide emotional support when children are tired, frustrated, or exposed to strange, fear-arousing situations. No harm results from allowing a child who so chooses to become dependent on a cuddly comforter.

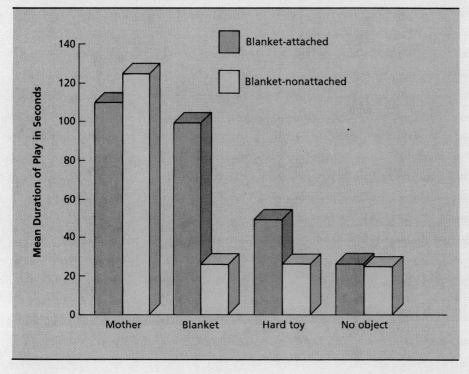

Effects of presence of mother versus different familiar objects on duration of play in an unfamiliar room in the Passman and Weisberg (1975) study. The blanket was as effective a source of emotional support as the mother among blanket-attached children. (Adapted from Passman & Weisberg, 1975.)

other human beings. They are also biased to respond to stimuli that come from other people, since they are comforted when picked up, stroked, and talked to softly. Infant signals are especially important in promoting physical contact during this period. In their study of Scottish family-reared babies, Schaffer and Emerson (1964) found that the situation that most often evoked protest from very young babies was being put down from the arms of an adult (see Figure 10.7).

Rudimentary sensory recognition of the mother appears during this phase. As we noted in Chapter 4, even neonates prefer their own mother's voice to that of another adult, although as yet they show no specific attachment to her. However, the process of beginning to distinguish mother from stranger is facilitated by maternal emotional cues. When the mother deliberately speaks in a monotone, infants fail to make this distinction (Fernald, 1984).

2. **The "attachment-in-the-making" phase** (6 weeks – 6 to 8 months). Infants in this phase orient toward and respond in more marked preference to the mother than they did before. For example, the baby smiles and vocalizes more freely to the mother, quiets more quickly when she picks him up, and keeps track of her whereabouts more consistently than that of a stranger. However, infants do not yet protest when separated from the mother, despite the fact that they can distinguish her perceptually from an unfamiliar individual. During this period, it is not separation from the mother per se, but rather separation from other human beings, that causes babies to become especially anxious and upset. As shown in Figure 10.7, responding with distress to being left alone in a room begins during this phase and rises steadily over the the course of the first year.

Figure 10.7. Age changes in infant protest in response to being put down, left alone in a room, and left with people other than the mother in the Schaffer and Emerson (1964) study. *(From H. R. Schaffer & P. E. Emerson, 1964,* The Development of Social Attachments in Infancy. *Monographs of the Society for Research in Child Development, 29 (3, Serial No. 94), 35 – 36 © The Society for Research in Child Development, Inc. Adapted by permission.)*

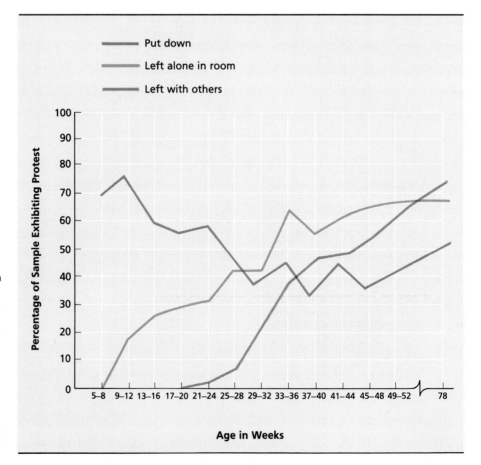

3. **The phase of "clearcut" attachment** (6 to 8 months – 18 months to 2 years). Now attachment to the mother is clearly evident. Babies of this period show **separation anxiety** in that they become very upset when the mother leaves. As Schaffer and Emerson (1964) report, until about 7 months of age, departure of the mother is the least likely situation to arouse protest. After this age, reactions to it rise dramatically until, at 18 months, more infants become upset in this situation than in any other (see Figure 10.7). With their new-found powers of crawling and walking, babies of this period also act more deliberately to maintain the mother's presence. They approach, follow, climb on her in preference to others, and use her as a secure base from which to explore.

It is no accident that the period of "clearcut" attachment coincides with the emergence of Piagetian object permanence. Infants cannot display a discriminating attachment to the mother without a cognitive appreciation of her as a permanent object and the ability to search for her when she is not in view. In fact, babies who have not yet mastered object permanence usually do not protest when separated from their mothers (Lester et al., 1974).

4. **Formation of a reciprocal relationship** (18 months – 2 years and on). Rapid growth in language and mental representation permit children to appreciate factors that influence the mother's coming and going and to predict her return. As a result, separation anxiety declines over the third year. In addition, children start to engage in active efforts to alter the mother's goals, using request and persuasion, rather than merely adjusting their own behaviors to suit hers (by clinging and crawling after the mother). Understanding and attempting to modify the mother's goals require considerable cognitive competence, including a beginning ability to see things from another person's perspective. Children start to develop these capacities during the early preschool years, but they can be facilitated or hampered by the extent to which parents clarify their goals to children. Weinraub and Lewis (1977) found that mothers who "slipped out" without giving the child advance warning had 2-year-olds who were most likely to cry during separation. In contrast, mothers who explained that they were leaving and would return soon and who also gave the child an explicit instruction about what to do in the interim (e.g., "Build me a house with Tinkertoys while I'm gone") had youngsters who accepted the mother's departure far more easily. Explanations that match the child's level of understanding work best. Short descriptions of where the mother is going and when she will return are most effective. Lengthy, repetitive explanations delivered long in advance of the departure actually heighten the young child's separation anxiety (Adams & Passman, 1981).

Bowlby's four phases show that a positive, enduring affectional tie to the caregiver emerges from the experiences of the first two years of life. Once firmly established, the attachment bond bridges time and distance, and children no longer need to engage in proximity-seeking behaviors as insistently as they did before. Ethological theory is also bidirectional; secure attachment depends on the baby's equipment for evoking responsive caregiving as well as on a history of sensitive maternal behavior. Therefore, deviations in the development of attachment can result from problems on the infant's side, when the behavioral system responsible for infant signaling is not intact, or problems on the environmental side, when responsive caregiving is either infrequent or entirely absent. Also, each side — the infant's as well as the mother's — can modify the adequacy of the other.

Now that we have traced the developmental course of attachment, let's turn to a consideration of individual differences in the quality of this formative emotional bond.

Measuring the Security of Attachment: Ainsworth's Strange Situation

The **Strange Situation** is the most widely used technique for assessing the quality of attachment to the caregiver between 1 and 2 years of age. In designing it, Mary

Ainsworth and her colleagues (Ainsworth & Wittig, 1969; Ainsworth, et al., 1978) reasoned that if the development of attachment has gone along as it should, the baby should show feelings of security in the presence of the mother. In addition, the quality of the baby's attachment ought to be most evident when fear and distress are activated, first by introducing a stranger into the situation and then by the departure of the mother as well as the unfamiliar person so that the infant is left alone. Therefore, as summarized in Table 10.4, the Strange Situation takes the baby through eight short episodes that simulate brief separations and reunions commonly experienced by infants in our culture.

Observing the responses of infants to these episodes, Ainsworth identified a secure attachment pattern along with two insecure patterns — avoidant and resistant — that describe the quality of the parent-child relationship. A new insecure pattern — disorganized/disoriented — was recently discovered by Main and her colleagues

Table 10.4. Episodes in Ainsworth's Strange Situation

EPISODE	PERSONS PRESENT	DURATION	EVENTS AND PROCEDURES	ATTACHMENT BEHAVIORS ACTIVATED
1	Mother and baby	30 seconds	Experimenter introduces mother and baby to room and then leaves.	
2	Mother and baby	3 minutes	Mother is seated while baby plays with toys for exploration.	Mother as a "secure base"
3	Mother, baby, and stranger	3 minutes	Stranger enters, is seated, and talks to mother.	Reaction to unfamiliar adult Mother as a "haven of safety"
4	Stranger and baby	3 minutes or less[a]	Mother leaves room. Stranger responds to baby's initiations and offers comfort if baby is upset.	Separation anxiety
5	Mother and baby	3 minutes or more[b]	Mother returns, greets baby, and if necessary offers comfort.	Reaction to reunion
6	Baby alone	3 minutes or less[a]	Mother leaves room.	Separation anxiety
7	Stranger and baby	3 minutes or less[a]	Stranger enters room and offers comfort.	Ability to be soothed by stranger
8	Mother and baby	3 minutes	Mother returns, greets baby, if necessary offers comfort, and tries to reinterest baby in toys.	Reaction to reunion

[a] Episode is cut short if the baby becomes very distressed.
[b] Episode is extended if more time is needed for the baby to become reinvolved in play.

Source: From M. D. S. Ainsworth, M. Blehar, E. Waters, & S. Wall, 1978. *Patterns of Attachment*. Hillsdale, N.J.: Lawrence Erlbaum Associates, p. 37. Adapted by permission.

After a short separation, this securely attached infant seeks physical contact with his mother and is easily comforted by her presence.

(Main, Kaplan, & Cassidy, 1985; Main & Solomon, 1986). The four attachment classifications are summarized below:

Secure attachment. These infants may or may not cry on separation, but if they do, it is due to the mother's absence, since they show a marked preference for the mother over the stranger. When the mother returns, they actively seek contact with her, and their crying is reduced immediately. About two thirds of American middle-class babies show this pattern.

Avoidant attachment. These babies are usually not distressed during separation, but when they are, it seems to be due to being left alone rather than to the mother's absence, since they react to the stranger in much the same way as to the mother. During reunion, these infants typically avoid or are slow to greet the mother. When picked up, they often fail to cling, although they do not resist physical contact. About 20 percent of American middle-class infants show this pattern.

Resistant attachment. Before separation, these infants seek proximity to the mother, but after she returns, they display conspicuously angry, resistive behavior, sometimes hitting and pushing. In addition, many continue to cry for a period of time after being picked up and cannot easily be comforted by the mother. This pattern is found in approximately 10 to 12 percent of American middle-class infants.

Disorganized/disoriented attachment. This classification seems to reflect the greatest insecurity. In response to reunion, these babies display a variety of confused behaviors. Disorganization is evident in contradictory responses — for example, gazing away while being held by the mother or approaching her with flat or depressed affect. Also, most of these infants communicate their disorientation and apprehension through a dazed facial expression. A few cry out unexpectedly after having calmed down and exhibit odd, frozen postures. A small percentage of American middle-class infants conform to this pattern — about 5 percent.

Since reactions in the Strange Situation are clearly related to the way infants respond to parental separations and reunions in everyday life, the procedure has proved to be a powerful tool for assessing attachment security (Ainsworth, Bell, & Stayton, 1971; Blanchard & Main, 1979). Moreover, for middle-class samples experiencing stable life conditions, quality of attachment to a particular caregiver is highly stable over the course of infancy (Waters, 1978; Owen et al., 1984). In fact, recent evidence indicates that such children continue to respond to the parent in a similar fashion when reobserved in a laboratory reunion episode several years later, at age 6 (Main & Cassidy, 1988). Stability is not as great for children whose families have experienced major life changes, such as a shift in employment or marital status (Thompson, Lamb, & Estes, 1982; Vaughn et al., 1979). This is an expected outcome, since family transitions are likely to affect the parent-child relationship and, in turn, the attachment bond.

Nevertheless, new cross-cultural evidence reveals that Strange Situation behavior may need to be interpreted differently for children of different cultures. For example, German babies show a higher incidence of avoidant attachment than American infants. However, German parents deliberately encourage their babies to be non-clinging and independent, so the baby's response is probably an intended outcome of parental training (Grossmann et al., 1985). An unusually high proportion of Japanese babies display a resistant response, but infants in Japan are rarely separated from their mothers and left in the care of strange people. Therefore, the Strange Situation may create far greater stress in Japanese babies than it does in infants residing in countries where brief mother-infant separations are common (Miyake, Chen, & Campos, 1985). Despite these cultural variations, it is still the case that the secure attachment pattern is the most frequent Strange Situation response in all societies studied to date (van Ijzendoorn & Kroonenberg, 1988).

Factors That Affect the Development of Attachment

Maternal Deprivation and Institutionalization. Research has consistently shown that early experience that prevents the formation of a secure attachment relationship to one or a very few caregivers leads to seriously impaired development. In a series of landmark studies, Spitz (1945, 1946) observed the development of institutionalized babies who had been given up by their mothers between the third month and end of the first year of life. The infants were placed on a general ward in unstimulating cubicles where they shared a nurse with at least seven other babies. From the time of separation, they showed extreme susceptibility to infection as well as marked delays in development.

In addition, infants who experienced prolonged maternal separation during the second half of the first year displayed a severe depressive disorder that Spitz (1946) called **anaclitic depression.** In contrast to the happy, outgoing behavior that they exhibited before separation, these babies wept and withdrew from their surroundings, lost weight, and suffered from insomnia. If the mother was not restored or an adequate caregiving relationship supplied, the depression deepened rapidly. Spitz concluded that anaclitic depression was caused by the combined effects of separation from a warm, familiar caregiver and placement in an environment that did not provide an adequate mother substitute.

In agreement with Spitz's observations, subsequent research on institutionalized infants reveals that lasting developmental disruptions are not the result of separation from the parent per se. Instead, they occur when babies are prevented from forming an emotional bond with one or a few adults. Longitudinal studies show that when large numbers of staff care for institutionalized children and close personal relationships are discouraged, social and emotional adjustment is impaired. In the most recent of these investigations, Tizard observed children reared in an institution that offered a good caregiver/child ratio and a rich selection of books and toys. However, staff turnover was so rapid that the average child experienced a total of 50 caregivers by the the age of 4½! Although the stimulating physical conditions offset many of the cognitive deficits previously found in institutionalized samples (see Chapter 4), adjustment difficulties persisted into childhood. In comparison to their home-reared counterparts, these youngsters displayed an insatiable desire for attention, indiscrim-

inate friendliness toward strange adults, difficulties with peer relationships, and inability to concentrate (Tizard & Hodges, 1978; Tizard & Rees, 1975).

Many children in Tizard's sample became "late adoptees" who were placed in home environments after age 4. Since most developed deep relationships with their adoptive parents, Tizard's study indicates that a first attachment bond can develop as late as 4 to 6 years of age. However, when followed up in middle childhood and adolescence, these children continued to show the same social and attentional problems as those who remained in the institution (Hodges & Tizard, 1989). This finding suggests that fully normal development depends on establishing attachment bonds in infancy. The evidence is consistent with a possible sensitive period for optimal attachment in the early years of life.

The research reviewed above should not be taken as a blanket indictment of institutional upbringing. Neither Bowlby nor Spitz claimed that all institutions are harmful or that all children separated from their mothers suffer permanent damage. The *conditions* of institutional rearing are of central importance. For example, in special agricultural settlements in Israel called *kibbutzim*, children are deliberately reared in institutional environments to free both parents for full participation in the work life of the community. Between 6 and 12 weeks of age, kibbutz babies enter a children's house, where they spend most of the day and sleep at night (although for several hours each evening they visit their parents). Since kibbutz infants spend most of their time in the group care setting, it is not surprising that their early development is better predicted by quality of attachment to the metapelet (communal caregiver) than to parents (Oppenheim, Sagi, & Lamb, 1988). Overall, communally reared kibbutz children do not experience more adjustment problems than family-reared Israeli youngsters (Beit-Hallahmi & Rabin, 1977).

Quality of Caregiving. Ethological theory predicts that even when infants are raised in families, those who experience caregiving that is insensitive to their signals and needs will develop insecure attachments. While virtually everyone agrees that good parenting is a matter of warmth and responsiveness to infant cues, there is controversy over how crucial these factors are for the emergence of a satisfactory attachment relationship (Campos et al., 1983; Sroufe, 1985). Some investigators believe that the nuances of early caregiving have a limited impact on attachment security and that what infants bring to the caregiving circumstances in the way of temperamental dispositions is of central importance (e.g., Kagan, 1982). However, recent research on the antecedents of attachment behavior has moved this controversy toward a clearer resolution. As we will see in this section and the one that follows, *both* maternal and infant contributions are important, just as Bowlby's original theoretical formulation assumes, since the quality of infant-mother attachment is the result of a *relationship* that builds over the first year of life (Belsky & Rovine, 1987; Thompson, 1986).

Extremely inadequate maternal care is a powerful predictor of disruptions in attachment. Child abuse and neglect are associated with all three forms of attachment insecurity, with the incidence of the most worrisome classification—disorganized/disoriented—being especially high (Carlson et al., 1989; Main & Solomon, 1986). Infants of severely depressed mothers also display the uncertain and conflicted behaviors of this pattern, exhibiting mixtures of high proximity-seeking, resistance, and avoidance, along with stiff body postures and sad affect (Radke-Yarrow et al., 1985).

Caregiving need not consist of extreme abuse and neglect or parental psychopathology to affect the attachment relationship. Ainsworth and her collaborators (1978) reviewed the findings of studies in which direct observations as well as ratings of maternal behavior in the home were related to Strange Situation classification at one year of age. Securely attached infants had mothers who, during the first three months, responded promptly to infant crying, handled their babies tenderly and carefully, and paced their behavior to fit the tempo of the baby's behavior. In contrast, insecurely attached babies had mothers who disliked physical contact, handled them ineptly, and behaved in a "routine" manner when face to face with the infants. These differences in maternal sensitivity persisted over the first year. Ainsworth's conclusion—that securely attached infants have mothers who are more sensitive and psychologically available—is supported by many recent studies involving highly diverse samples, including low-income and middle-income mother-infant pairs (Bates, Maslin, & Frankel, 1985; Belsky, Rovine, & Taylor, 1985; Egeland & Farber, 1984; Kiser et al., 1986). In fact, new evidence suggests that overstimulating and intrusive maternal behavior is associated with avoidant attachment, while underinvolved, preoccupied caregiving is linked to infant resistance (Isabella, Belsky, & von Eye, 1989).

As we have already indicated in this and previous chapters, quality of caregiving can only be fully understood in relation to the larger social and environmental context in which mother and infant are situated. In this regard, a number of factors exert an important influence on maternal contributions to attachment security. In families where there is stress and instability, insensitive parenting and insecure attachment are especially high. However, the availability of social supports, especially a good marital relationship and the father's assistance in caregiving, reduces stress and predicts more effective caregiving as well as greater attachment security (Durrett, Otaki, & Richards, 1984; Howes & Markman, 1989; Pianta, Sroufe, & Egeland, 1989).

Moreover, several studies indicate that parents' recollections of their own childhood histories are related to the quality of infant attachment (Main, Kaplan, & Cassidy, 1985; Morris, 1981; Ricks, 1985). In these investigations, parents who described their own mothers as warm and competent were far more likely to have securely attached babies of their own. However, parents who remembered unsatisfactory attachment-related experiences but who looked back on them in a forgiving, understanding way also had securely attached infants. These findings indicate that not all people who experience an unhappy and disturbed upbringing are destined to become insensitive parents themselves. Instead, the way adults reconstruct their early experiences—in particular, their ability to come to terms with negative events and to place them in context—is at least as important as the actual history of care they received.

Infant Characteristics. Recall from Chapter 3 that prematurity, birth complications, and neonatal illness make caregiving more taxing for new parents. Moreover, there is good evidence that many children who will later be abused begin life as difficult newborns (Sameroff & Chandler, 1975). However, as long as parents have the personal resources to care for a baby with special needs and the infant is not very ill, an at-risk newborn is likely to fare quite well in the development of attachment (Easterbrooks, 1989). Nevertheless, some infants are likely to challenge the resources of just about any parent. For example, a substantial number of preterm babies born with severe respiratory distress syndrome[9] later develop resistant attachments, probably because the illness demands such extraordinary attention and creates sufficient parental anxiety to interfere with optimal caregiving (Meisels et al., 1984).

Although normal infants do not strain parental resources to the same degree as sick babies, as we mentioned earlier, the precise role that temperament plays in the unfolding of the infant-caregiver relationship has been a matter of dispute. Some investigators believe that temperament fully accounts for individual differences in the Strange Situation. They believe, for example, that babies who are prone to irritability, fearfulness, and anxiety may simply react to transient separations from the mother with undue alarm, regardless of the parent's sensitivity to the baby.

Currently, most experts reject this view as far too simplistic (Crockenberg, 1986; Sroufe, 1985; Thompson, 1986). Evidence arguing against it is that quality of attachment to the mother is often different from attachment to the father and substitute caregiver (Bridges, Connell, & Belsky, 1988; Lamb et al., 1984; Sagi et al., 1985; Oppenheim, Sagi, & Lamb, 1988). If infant characteristics were the only important influence, we would expect attachment to be constant across all attachment figures.

Furthermore, although irritable neonates are somewhat more likely to develop insecure (resistant) attachments than their more even-tempered counterparts, the association is not a direct one. Instead, temperamental characteristics influence attachment by affecting subtle nuances of the caregiver-infant relationship (Goldsmith & Alansky, 1987). For example, Crockenberg (1981) found that neonatal irritability does not predict insecure attachment for all infants. It only predicts for babies whose mothers report few social supports in the form of help from husbands, extended family, and friends. Moreover, recent fine-grained analyses of Strange Situation behavior reveal that although difficult, irritable, and fearful temperamental styles are related to high levels of distress at parental departure, temperament is a far less effective predictor of infant reactions to the parent at reunion (Bridges, Connell, & Belsky, 1988; Thompson, Connell, & Bridges, 1988; Vaughn et al., 1989). These findings offer added support to the conclusion that quality of attachment is not simply a function of infant behavioral tendencies.

One reason that many temperamental characteristics have not shown a straightforward relationship with attachment security may be that temperament largely exerts its effect on attachment through "goodness of fit." From this perspective, *many* temperamental characteristics may be associated with secure attachment as long as the caregiver is able to harmoniously adjust her behavior to accommodate the infant. In fact, as Sroufe (1985) suggests, the reason that maternal sensitivity is an especially effective predictor of attachment security is that the very concept of sensitive caregiving implies a mother who adjusts her behavior to suit the unique characteristics of her baby.

Multiple Attachments: The Father's Special Role

We have already seen that most infants develop a number of attachment relationships that include fathers, grandparents, siblings, and substitute caregivers. Although

---

[9] Return to Chapter 3, page 104, if you need to refresh your memory about this condition.

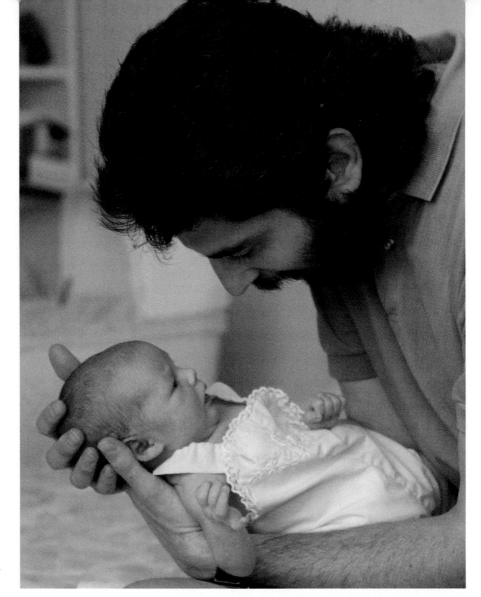

Elated by the birth of his baby, this father displays the absorbed interest in his newborn known as engrossment.

Bowlby (1969) made room for such subsidiary attachments in his theory, he believed that infants were biologically predisposed to direct their attachment behaviors toward a single preferred figure, especially when they were distressed. Observations of family-reared babies lend support to Bowlby's assumption. When an anxious, unhappy 1-year-old is permitted to choose between the mother and father as a source of comfort and security, the infant generally chooses the mother (Lamb, 1976). However, this preference diminishes over time until, at about 18 months, it is no longer present (Schaffer & Emerson, 1964). Moreover, when babies are not distressed, they approach, touch, ask to be held, vocalize, and smile equally to both parents, and they sometimes prefer their fathers (Clarke-Stewart, 1978; Kotelchuck, 1976).

Fathers are salient figures in the lives of babies, beginning to build relationships with them shortly after birth. Interviews with fathers of newborn infants reveal that most are elated by the birth of their baby and experience a feeling state that Greenberg and Morris (1974) called **engrossment,** a term that captures the sense of absorption and interest that fathers display toward their newborn child. Regardless of their social class or whether they participated in childbirth classes, fathers touch, look at, vocalize to, and kiss their newborn infants just as much as mothers. When they hold the baby, they sometimes exceed mothers in stimulation and affection (Parke & Tinsley, 1981).

As infancy progresses, mothers and fathers start to relate to infants in different ways. Mothers devote more time to caregiving, such as changing, bathing, and feeding. In contrast, fathers spend more time in playful interactions (Kotelchuk, 1976). In addition, the play initiations of mothers and fathers tend to be different. Mothers offer toys and verbal stimulation and initiate more conventional games like pat-a-cake and peekaboo. In contrast, fathers engage in more unconventional, highly physical bouncing and lifting games, especially with boys (Yogman, 1981). In view of these differences, it is not surprising that babies tend to look to their mothers when distressed and to their fathers for playful stimulation (Clarke-Stewart, 1980; Lamb, 1976). In fact, fathers' playful engagement may provide infants with special preparation for the social and emotional give and take that will later be required for successful participation in play with peers (Parke et al., 1988).

Even in the eyes of parents, the view of "mother as caregiver" and "father as playmate" is widely held (Parke & Tinsley, 1981). However, this picture is changing in some families as a result of the revised work status of women. Working mothers engage in more playful stimulation of their babies than nonworking mothers, while their husbands engage in less play (Pedersen et al., 1980). Perhaps mothers who spend the day away from their infants return in the evening with a heightened desire to interact with them, thereby reducing the father's opportunity for playful engagement. In families in which the father is the primary caregiver and the mother assumes a secondary role, fathers retain their arousing play style while increasing their attentiveness to the baby's physical well-being (Hwang, 1986). Such highly involved fathers are less stereotypical in their sex role orientations and regard parenthood as an especially enriching experience (Levy-Shiff & Israelashvili, 1988; Palkovitz, 1984).

Research on fathers as attachment figures helps us appreciate the complex, multidimensional nature of the infant's social world. Both mothers and fathers are emotionally important to infants and are equally capable of behaving sensitively and responsively. No evidence exists to support the commonly held assumption that women are biologically constituted to be more effective caregivers than are men.

Quality of Attachment and Later Development

Both psychoanalytic and ethological theories predict that the inner feelings of security and affection that emanate from a healthy attachment relationship provide the foundation for virtually all aspects of later psychological functioning. Consistent with this view, in several studies assessments of attachment between 12 and 18 months of age predicted aspects of cognitive and social development during the preschool years.

In one longitudinal investigation, securely attached infants showed more sophisticated make-believe play and greater enthusiasm, flexibility, and persistence on problem-solving tasks by 2 years of age (Matas, Arend, & Sroufe, 1978). Secure attachment is also related to more harmonious and responsive interaction with peers during the preschool years (Jacobson & Wille, 1986; Park & Waters, 1989). In line with these observations, Sroufe and his colleagues reported that 4-year-olds who had been securely attached as infants were rated by preschool teachers as high in self-esteem, socially competent, cooperative, autonomous, popular, and empathic. In contrast, their avoidantly attached peers were viewed as isolated, disconnected, and elusive, while those who were resistantly attached were regarded as disruptive, difficult, and prone to tantrums (Sroufe, 1983; Sroufe, Fox, & Pancake, 1983).

These correlational findings have been taken by some as evidence that secure attachment in infancy *causes* increased autonomy and competence during the preschool years (e.g., Sroufe, 1983). However, a cautious approach to this conclusion is warranted. Lamb and his colleagues (1985) believe that later differences in adjustment may not result from the early attachment relationship per se, but rather from continuity in parenting throughout the early childhood years. From this perspective, current patterns of parent-child interaction, not just the formative attachment bond, could be responsible for the results described above. Consistent with this view, among samples of children who have experienced major changes in family and caregiving circumstances, correlations between early attachment security and later functioning have not been found (Erickson, Sroufe, & Egeland, 1985; Sroufe, 1978). Moreover, two recent investigations could not replicate the connection between insecure attachment and preschool adjustment difficulties obtained in earlier studies (Bates & Bayles, 1988; Fagot & Kavanagh, 1990). Clearly, more research is needed to determine whether early secure attachment is critical for a variety of aspects of later development among family-reared youngsters.

BRIEF REVIEW   In the sections above, we considered three theoretical perspectives on the development of attachment — behaviorist, psychoanalytic, and ethological. Currently, ethological theory, which views infants' formative affectional tie to the caregiver in evolutionary, adaptive terms, is the dominant point of view. According to this perspective, maternal caregiving and infant readiness to respond combine to produce the attachment relationship, which evolves through four phases of development. Ainsworth's Strange Situation is designed to assess individual differences in the quality of the attachment bond; infants are classified as secure, avoidant, resistant, or disorganized/disoriented. Sensitive, responsive caregiving is the most powerful predictor of secure attachment. Infant temperament affects attachment indirectly, by influencing parental responsiveness. In some studies quality of attachment predicts cognitive and social development during the preschool years. However, continuity of caregiving rather than the infant-mother relationship may account for this association.

ATTACHMENT AND SOCIETAL CHANGE: MATERNAL EMPLOYMENT AND DAY CARE

With the tremendous rise in the number of women entering the labor force during the last several decades, routine substitute care has become common for infants and very young children. By the mid-1980s, 54 percent of American mothers with children under the age of 3 were employed (U.S. Department of Labor, 1987). Today, the proportion of working mothers with babies 1 year of age and younger is increasing faster than that of any other age sector. In response to this trend, child development specialists as well as concerned laypeople have raised questions about the impact of day care and repeated daily separations of infant from mother on the attachment bond.

The current controversy over whether day care threatens infants' emotional security is reviewed in Box 10.3. Although research is still in its early stages, the evidence suggests that quality of substitute care and family conditions, rather than day care itself, may be the important variables. The findings as a whole underline the importance of ensuring that all infants receive substitute care that safeguards their emotional needs while their mothers are at work. What are the components of such care? Day care that is supportive of early development harmoniously integrates the four levels of Bronfenbrenner's ecological model, discussed in Chapter 1, in the following ways:

At the level of the *microsystem* — the provision of stable care in which frequent changes are not made in children's placement nor in the staff within a placement, a generous caregiver/child ratio,[10] and caregivers who engage in sensitive, one-to-one interaction and provide age-appropriate learning experiences.

[10] Kagan, Kearsley, and Zelazo (1978) reported a caregiver/child ratio of 1 to 3 for infants and 1 to 5 for toddlers in a model day care center of very high quality.

At the level of the *mesosystem* — frequent communication between parents and care-givers so that each is cognizant of the infant's life at home and in the substitute care environment.

At the level of the *exosystem* — supervisory agencies that license and oversee the day care environment to ensure high-quality care, and employers who permit parents to arrange work schedules that are compatible with good early caregiving experiences.

◆ CONTEMPORARY ISSUES: SOCIAL POLICY ◆

Infant Day Care and Attachment

Box 10.3

Are infants who experience daily separations from their employed mothers and early placement in day care at risk for insecure attachments? Child development specialists disagree sharply on answers to this question. Some believe that substitute care puts infants at serious risk for emotional insecurities (Belsky, 1988; Sroufe, 1988). Others think that there is too little evidence to support this claim (Clarke-Stewart, 1989; Phillips et al., 1987). Let's examine the research and consider how it should be interpreted.

Recent studies indicate that American infants placed in full-time day care (more than 20 hours per week) before age 1 are more likely than home-reared controls to display insecure attachment in the Strange Situation (see reviews by Belsky, 1988; Clarke-Stewart, 1989). Yet extreme caution should be exercised before concluding from these correlational findings that day care is harmful to babies.

First, the incidence of attachment insecurity among day care infants is only slightly higher than that of control subjects (34 versus 29 percent), and it is identical to the overall figure reported for children in industrialized countries around the world (van IJzendoorn & Kroonenberg, 1988). In fact, most infants of employed mothers (6 percent) are securely attached. These findings indicate that the early emotional development of day care youngsters is probably within normal range (Thompson, 1988).

Second, reactions in the Strange Situation may not mean the same thing for day care and home-reared babies. Infants who go to day care may find short separations from their mothers less stressful because they experience maternal departure and reunion every day. Consequently, day care infants may feel less need to seek maternal proximity in the Strange Situation.

Third, family conditions are known to affect the attachment security of home-reared babies, and they do so for infants of working mothers as well, but often in quite different ways. Employed women often find the pressures of handling two full-time jobs (work and motherhood) stressful; some respond less sensitively to their babies because they are fatigued and harried, thereby risking the infant's security (Owen & Cox,

1988). Other working mothers probably value and encourage their infant's independence. In these cases, avoidance in the Strange Situation could signify healthy autonomy rather than maladaptive development (Clarke-Stewart, 1989).

Finally, quality of day care may contribute to the slightly higher incidence of attachment insecurity in infants of employed mothers. In support of this conclusion, most studies carried out during the 1970s in university-based centers with generous caregiver/infant ratios and exceptionally well-trained staffs did not find that infants of working mothers experienced attachment difficulties (Belsky & Steinberg, 1978). Recent research focuses on infants who are not fortunate enough to be enrolled in such high-quality programs. In one investigation, babies classified as insecurely attached to both mother and caregiver tended to be placed in day care environments with large numbers of children and few adults, where their bids for attention were frequently ignored (Howes et al., 1988). Infants exposed to the poorest-quality day care are usually those who experience the greatest family disorganization (Howes & Olenick, 1986; Vaughn, Gove, & Egeland, 1980). Highly stressed parents generally have little time and energy to monitor the quality of their children's daily lives. Consequently, these youngsters experience a double dose of vulnerability, both at home and in the substitute care setting.

In summary, the research to date suggests that inadequate day care combined with the pressures of full-time work and raising a baby may place a small number of infants at risk for insecure attachments. However, using this evidence to justify a reduction in infant day care services is inappropriate. When family incomes are limited and mothers who want to work are forced to stay at home, children's emotional security is not promoted (Hock & DeMeis, 1987). Instead, it makes sense to increase the availability of high-quality infant day care, to educate parents about early emotional development, and to conduct more research so that better assistance can be offered to employed mothers and their young children.

At the level of the *macrosystem* — a national social policy that embodies respect for the complex, sophisticated, and vital role of the substitute caregiver and that places a high value on quality day care to meet the formative developmental needs of young children while their parents are at work (Belsky, 1984; Clarke-Stewart, 1989; Thompson, 1988).

In Chapter 14, we will return to the topics of maternal employment and day care and consider their consequences for development during the preschool, school-age, and adolescent years. In Chapter 16, we will discuss current efforts to build a day care policy in the United States that safeguards the development of its youngest citizens.

CHAPTER SUMMARY

The Course of Emotional Development

■ The field of child development is experiencing a rebirth of interest in emotions, stimulated in part by the discovery of new methods for assessing young children's emotional reactions. Behaviorism, cognitive-developmental **discrepancy theory,** and the new **organizational approach** have each enhanced our understanding of emotional development. Currently, the organizational perspective has the broadest explanatory power. Campos's organizational theory regards emotions as adaptive forces in human behavior, as interdependent with cognition, and as facilitating exploration, self-awareness, and social interaction.

■ A diverse array of **basic emotions** may already be present in the newborn baby. However, the frequency and circumstances under which they are expressed change with age. Smiling and laughter serve vital social functions, and their development reflects as well as supports infant perceptual and cognitive development. Anger and fear increase substantially after 7 months of age, along with infants' improved ability to cognitively appraise objects and events. These emotions also have adaptive significance. Anger motivates babies to defend themselves or overcome obstacles, while fear holds in check the baby's compelling explorative drive.

■ At the end of infancy, self-awareness and socialization experiences lead to the emergence of **complex emotions,** such as shame, embarrassment, guilt, envy, and pride. Complex emotions become less outcome-related and more internally governed with age.

■ **Emotional self-regulation** — the ability to modulate emotional arousal adaptively — emerges from the early caregiver-infant relationship. As motor, language, and cognitive development proceed, children gradually acquire a diverse array of self-regulatory strategies. During the preschool years, children start to conform to the **emotional display rules** of their culture; older children develop a conscious awareness and understanding of them.

■ The ability to recognize and interpret facial expressions improves markedly during the first year. By 8 to 10 months of age, infants engage in **social referencing,** actively seeking emotional information from others. During middle childhood, children can take multiple cues into account in appraising the feelings of others, and they understand that people can experience mixed emotions.

■ **Empathy** evolves from a rudimentary ability to experience the feeling states of others to an advanced capacity to respond to another's general life condition. Advances in perspective-taking, the ability to comprehend others' emotions, and sensitive parenting contribute to empathic development.

Temperament and Development

■ Measures of **temperament** — individual differences in quality and intensity of emotional responding — are modestly stable and heritable characteristics. Nevertheless, complex genetic-environmental transactions are necessary to explain individual differences in temperament and personality functioning. Within-family environmental factors are especially influential in personality development, although between-family factors are also important.

■ Temperament affects both cognitive and social development. Persistence and **reflection-impulsivity** are related to cognitive functioning. A wide array of temperamental characteristics are linked to social behavior. The **goodness-of-fit model** summarizes the varied ways in which temperamental style and child-rearing practices combine to yield positive or negative child outcomes.

The Development of Attachment

■ Infant-caregiver attachment has been the focal point of intense theoretical debate for decades. **Drive reduction, operant conditioning,** and **psychoanalytic** accounts of its development exist. Currently, the most widely accepted perspective is **ethological theory,** which views attachment as an adaptive system that ensures infant survival.

■ Attachment begins as a set of built-in behaviors and evolves into a true affectional relationship around 8 months of age. At about this time, the mother becomes the preferred target of physical closeness and social interaction. The emergence of a positive inner image of the parent permits the child to become increasingly independent over the preschool years.

- Ainsworth's **Strange Situation** is the preferred procedure for assessing individual differences in the attachment bond. The baby's reactions to a series of brief separations from and reunions with the mother yield four attachment classifications: **secure, avoidant, resistant** and **disorganized/disoriented**.

- Institutionalized babies deprived of affectional ties with one or a few adults show social and emotional deficits that extend into the adolescent years. However, family rearing does not ensure a healthy attachment bond. Children who experience early caregiving that is not sensitive and responsive develop anxious, insecure attachments. Infant characteristics, such as neonatal illness and temperament, affect attachment through their impact on the caregiver-infant relationship.

- Besides attachments to mothers, infants develop strong emotional ties to their fathers, usually through stimulating, playful interaction. Several studies indicate that attachment quality predicts cognitive and social functioning into the preschool years. However, a causal association has not yet been established.

Attachment and Societal Change: Maternal Employment and Day Care

- Maternal employment and day care during the first year of life may be a "risk" factor for insecure attachment. However, research suggests that this association is mediated by quality of day care and family conditions.

IMPORTANT TERMS AND CONCEPTS

discrepancy theory   (p. 385)
organizational approach to emotional
  development   (p. 387)
basic emotions   (p. 391)
endogenous smile   (p. 392)
social smile   (p. 392)
stranger distress   (p. 394)
secure base   (p. 394)
complex emotions   (p. 395)
emotional self-regulation   (p. 396)
emotional display rules   (p. 397)
social referencing   (p. 399)
empathy   (p. 400)
temperament   (p. 401)

easy child   (p. 402)
difficult child   (p. 402)
slow-to-warm-up child   (p. 402)
cognitive style   (p. 408)
reflection-impulsivity   (p. 408)
goodness-of-fit model   (p. 410)
attachment   (p. 411)
drive reduction model   (p. 412)
operant conditioning model   (p. 412)
psychoanalytic theory   (p. 413)
ethological theory   (p. 413)
preattachment phase   (p. 415)
"attachment-in-the-making"
  phase   (p. 416)

phase of "clearcut" attachment   (p. 417)
separation anxiety   (p. 417)
formation of a reciprocal relationship   (p. 417)
Strange Situation   (p. 417)
secure attachment   (p. 419)
avoidant attachment   (p. 419)
resistant attachment   (p. 419)
disorganized/disoriented attachment   (p. 419)
anaclitic depression   (p. 420)
engrossment   (p. 424)

Robert Henri: *Indian Girl in White Ceremonial Blanket*.
In the collection of The Corcoran Galley of Art.

11

The Self and Social Understanding

Conceptualizing the Self
Conceptualizing Other People
Conceptualizing Relations between People
Social Cognition in Context

This chapter addresses the development of **social cognition,** or how children come to understand their multifaceted social world. Like our consideration of cognitive development in Chapters 6 and 7, the changes to which we now turn are concerned with matters of perceiving, thinking, and interpreting experience. However, the experience of interest is no longer the child's physical, inanimate surroundings. Instead, social cognition has a unique content: the behavior and inner characteristics of the self and other people. Social-cognitive investigators want to know how children and adults conceptualize themselves and others as psychological beings and how they understand relationships between people. Although historically, social and cognitive development were studied separately, in the last two decades, efforts have been made to put them together. Today, child development specialists recognize that children are active social thinkers who bring cognitive skills to social interactions and take meaning from them according to their current cognitive capacities (Youniss, 1975).

In this chapter, you will see that many of the same developmental trends that we identified for nonsocial thinking apply to social cognition as well. Like nonsocial cognition, the development of social understanding proceeds from *concrete to abstract.* Children first appreciate the immediately observable aspects of their social world, such as people's physical appearance and overt behavior. Soon after, they start to grasp internal processes, such as perceptions, beliefs, intentions, motivations, abilities, and attitudes. Social thinking also becomes *better organized and integrated* with age, as children gather together their observations of separate behaviors into coherent, socially relevant concepts, such as personalities and identities. In addition, children revise their conceptions of the causes of people's behavior, from *simple, one-sided explanations to complex interacting relationships* that take into account both person and situational variables. Finally, social cognition *moves toward a metacognitive level of understanding.* As children get older, they not only think about social reality, but also *think about the social thoughts* of themselves and others.

Although nonsocial and social understanding share many features in common, they are also different. The world of physical objects is far more predictable than the realm of social experience. Movements of things can be fully understood on the basis of the physical forces that act on them. In contrast, the behavior of people is not simply the result of others' actions toward them; it is also mediated by inner psychological states not directly observable to others. This makes people more complex than physical objects, since people's behavior is determined by an interplay of observable and unobservable forces.

In view of this complexity, we might expect the development of social cognition to always lag behind nonsocial thinking. Yet, surprisingly, it does not (Hoffman, 1981). In this chapter, we will return to a theme that has already appeared in many parts of this book: Children demonstrate some sophisticated understandings at early ages, even though many others require an extensive time period to attain.

The rather surprising rapidity of social-cognitive development is facilitated by special features of social experience that help children make early sense out of its complexity. First, the fact that people are animated beings as well as objects of deep emotional investment leads them to be particularly attractive objects of contemplation, for children as well as adults. Second, social interaction is an ideal context for promoting *cognitive disequilibrium.* Social experience continually presents children with discrepancies between the behaviors they expect and the behaviors that occur, motivating *accommodation,* or reassessments of their thoughts about social concerns. Finally, children and the people with whom they interact are all human beings, with the same basic nervous system and a shared background of similar experiences. As a result, assessing another's behavior from the self's point of view often leads to correct inferences and helps make the behavior of other people more understandable (Flavell, 1985; Hoffman, 1981; Shantz, 1983). In situations in which our own perspective leads to incorrect predictions, human beings are equipped with a unique capacity — *perspective-taking* — that permits them to imagine what another's thoughts and feelings might be. Perspective-taking is so important for many aspects of psychological functioning that we have already made frequent reference to it in earlier parts of this book. We will devote considerable attention to its development in this chapter.

Our discussion is organized around the following three facets of social-cognitive development: the child's conception of self, of other people, and of relationships between people. Before we begin, perhaps you have already noticed on the basis of this introduction that we considered some social-cognitive topics in previous chapters. Good examples are children's referential communication skills (Chapter 9) and recognition and understanding of others' emotions (Chapter 10). In addition, children's developing sense of morality — how people *ought to* behave toward each other as opposed to how they *do* behave — is another important social-cognitive topic. However, research on the development of moral reasoning is so extensive that it merits a chapter of its own. We will consider it in Chapter 12.

CONCEPTUALIZING THE SELF

Infancy: The Emergence of Self-Recognition

Infancy is a rich, formative period for the development of social understanding. As we showed in Chapter 10, by the middle to end of the first year, infants demonstrate a complex set of social cognitions, including the capacity to recognize and respond appropriately to others' emotions and the ability to identify familiar people. Moreover, this same period brings with it landmark achievements in nonsocial cognition, as the work of Piaget and his followers has revealed (see Chapter 6). The fact that both objects and people achieve an independent, stable existence in infancy implies that knowledge of the self as a separate, permanent entity also emerges around this time.

Researchers rely on clever laboratory observations in which they expose babies to images of themselves in mirrors, on videotapes, and in still photos to illuminate the infant's developing sense of self. As early as the first few months, infants smile and return friendly social behaviors to their own image in a mirror. At what age do they realize that the charming baby gazing and grinning back at them is really the self?

To find out, Lewis and Brooks-Gunn (1979) brought 9- to 24-month-old infants into a laboratory, where each was placed in front of a large mirror. Then, under pretext of wiping the baby's nose, each mother was asked to rub red dye on her infant's face. The researchers watched to see how the babies reacted to their trans-formed images. Younger infants smiled, vocalized, and touched the mirror as if the red marks had little to do with any aspect of the self. By 15 months of age, "mark-di-rected" behavior began to appear, and it rose steadily until age 2, when the majority of infants touched and rubbed their strange-looking little red noses. As age increased, so did the probability that infants would entertain themselves by acting silly or coy in front of the mirror—responses that also reflect the beginnings of self-recognition.

Mirrors offer two kinds of cues that can be used to recognize the self: *contingency cues*, which provide a perfect correspondence between one's own bodily movements and the movements of the image in the mirror, and *featural cues*, which have to do with the unique visual appearance of the self. Research using videotapes of infant behavior permits the separation and exploration of each of these cues and, conse-quently, provides important insights into how the baby's first awareness of self develops.

When Lewis and Brooks-Gunn (1979) showed infants a "live" video playback of their ongoing behavior, babies as young as 9 to 12 months of age engaged in "contin-gent play" with the image. They initiated a kind of peek-a-boo game in which they moved their head, eyes, body, or hand in and out of the camera's view, a pattern of behavior that rose steadily throughout the second year of life. When videotapes of noncontingent behavior were shown, even young infants "tested" the image by trying to play contingently. When it did not respond, they immediately stopped trying.

Between 15 and 18 months, infants start to respond to specific perceptual features of the self in videotaped sequences. At this age, they react differently to a film of a strange infant than to one of the self—smiling, moving toward, and attending more closely to the unfamiliar baby but imitating and trying contingent play in response to

The perfect correspondence between a baby's own move-ments and the movements of the image in the mirror is a cue that infants use to recog-nize the self at an early age.

the self. By the end of infancy, recognition of the self's perceptual features is well established. Two-year-olds look and smile more at a still photo of themselves than at one of a same-age peer, and almost all of them will use their own name or a personal pronoun to label a picture of themselves (Lewis & Brooks-Gunn, 1979).

The research reviewed above indicates that contingency information provides babies with their first cues regarding the self's existence. Featural information becomes salient only later on, at the end of the second year of life. As young infants act on the environment, different contingencies between behavior and aspects of the external world probably help them sort out self, social, and nonsocial facets of experience. For example, batting a mobile and seeing it swing in a pattern and rhythm different from the infant's own actions informs the baby about the nature of the physical world, whereas smiling and vocalizing at a caregiver who reciprocally smiles and vocalizes back help specify the nature of the social world (Bahrick & Watson, 1985). But all types of contingency cues are necessary for understanding each facet of experience because it is the contrast among them that enables infants to build a clear image of the self versus external reality (Lewis, Brooks-Gunn, & Jaskir, 1985).

Once awareness of the self's existence is well established, it quickly becomes an integral part of children's social and cognitive lives. As we saw in Chapter 10, complex emotions and empathy cannot occur until a sense of self emerges. The capacity to form plans and recognize the consequences of one's own actions also requires an active, independently existing self. Self-recognition is also the first step toward developing a differentiated psychological self-concept, a major social-cognitive achievement of the childhood years.

From Childhood to Adolescence: The Development of Self-Concept

From the preschool period through adolescence, children work on constructing a **self-concept,** or "personal theory" of what the self is like as an experiencing, functioning individual. Like any theory, the self-concept is subject to continual change as it is exposed to new information and as the child becomes a more sophisticated thinker about the self and the social world (Epstein, 1973; Harter, 1983).

The Categorical Self. As soon as representational thought and language appear at the end of infancy, children start to construct a **categorical self.** They use a number of concrete descriptors that refer to salient dimensions on which people differ, such as sex ("boy" or "girl," "lady" or "man") and age (e.g., "baby," "boy," or "man"). Young children apply these terms appropriately, indicating that they categorize the self and the social world on the basis of these dimensions almost as early as they can talk (Lewis & Brooks-Gunn, 1979). However, as we indicated in Chapter 6, several characteristics of the self that are permanent and unchangeable, such as the child's sex and humanness, have not yet attained *constancy* for most preschool children. For example, while the 2- to 4-year-old may say today that she is a girl and a person, she is also likely to indicate that by dressing up, wearing a mask, or playing with her brother's cars and trucks she can change gender or species in the future (Carey, 1985; DeVries, 1969; Emmerich, 1982; Guardo & Bohan, 1971; Kohlberg, 1966).

These unstable self-descriptions are thought to be due to the preschool child's cognitive limitations, but growth of the young child's body and feedback from the social environment may also contribute to them. After all, many aspects of the child's physical self *do* change, including height, weight, strength, and hair length. In addition, adults often emphasize change when they make such comments as "My, how big and tall you're getting!" or "You're getting smarter all the time — you know your ABCs!" Young children may make the mistake of generalizing these prominent dimensions of change to stable self-attributes, only gradually accomplishing the task of sorting out constant from changing characteristics around the late preschool and early school years (Harter, 1983).

Even after constancy the categorical self is established, many children still think that they would not be the same person if their name were changed. By age 8, children recognize that names are arbitrary and have nothing to do with continuity of the self (Guardo & Bohan, 1971).

The Inner Self. Children's responses to Piagetian clinical interviews suggest that below age 7 or 8, they regard mental entities, such as ideas and dreams, as physical things. On the basis of this evidence, Piaget (1926/1930) concluded that preschoolers cannot distinguish internal and external phenomena. However, recent research indicates that this is not the case.[1] Early in the preschool years, children become aware of an **inner self** made up of private thoughts and imaginings accessible only to themselves and not to others (Miller & Aloise, 1989; Pillow, 1988). In one study, Wellman and Estes (1986) described pairs of mental and real entities (e.g., a dreamed-about dog versus a real dog) and asked children to indicate which had a sensory and physical existence (could be seen or touched), had a public existence (could be seen or touched by others), and had a continuous existence (could be seen and touched tomorrow). Children as young as age 3 could answer these questions correctly.

As further evidence for an early grasp of the distinction between an inner mental and outer physical world, young preschoolers already understand that beliefs and reality can differ — in other words, that people can hold *false beliefs*. For example, when given a story depicting a character engaged in an unexpected action (e.g., "Jane is looking for her kitten. The kitten is hiding under the chair. But Jane is looking under the piano"), 3-year-olds frequently attribute a false belief to the actor ("She thinks the kitten is under the piano") (Bartsch & Wellman, 1989). Similarly, when asked to trick an adult in an object-hiding game, 2½-year-olds spontaneously generate deceptive strategies, such as misleading clues, that are aimed at instilling false beliefs in others (Chandler, Fritz, & Hala, 1989). These remarkable findings, along with research indicating that preschoolers use such words as "think," "remember," and "pretend" appropriately in everyday conversation (see Chapter 7), indicate that awareness of an inner self is present at a very early age.

The Psychological Self. In line with their grasp of an inner self, by age 3½, children can describe themselves in terms of momentary internal states — beliefs, emotions, and attitudes, such as "I wasn't happy about school today" — that all people experience from time to time. However, their descriptions do not yet make reference to stable psychological traits that distinguish the self as an individual (Eder, 1989). In fact, before middle childhood, self-concepts are largely based on concrete, observable characteristics such as names, physical appearance, possessions, and typical behaviors. For example, Keller, Ford, and Meacham (1978) asked 3- to 5-year-olds to tell about themselves. The most frequently mentioned responses were actions in which children typically engage (e.g., "I go to school." "I can wash my hair by myself." "I help mommy."). These findings indicate, in agreement with Piaget and other theorists, that acting on the environment and finding out *what one can do* are an especially important early basis for self-definition (Cooley, 1902; Erikson, 1950; Piaget, 1954).

During the elementary school years, children's descriptions of themselves evolve from a catalogue of observable characteristics to an emphasis on psychological dispositions, with a major shift occurring between ages 8 and 11. The following self-descriptions reflect this change:

---

[1] Return to Chapter 1, page 23, to review an example of a Piagetian clinical interview that explores a young child's understanding of dreams. Compared to the research described in the section above, clinical interviewing seems to underestimate preschoolers' appreciation of the inner self, perhaps because it depends so heavily on children's ability to give complete verbal explanations.

A *boy age 7*: I am 7 and I have hazel brown hair and my hobby is stamp collecting. I am good at football and I am quite good at sums and my favourite game is football and I love school and I like reading books and my favourite car is an Austin. (Livesley & Bromley, 1973, p. 237)

A *girl age 11½*: My name is A. I'm a human being. I'm a girl. I'm a truthful person. I'm not pretty. I do so-so in my studies. I'm a very good cellist. I'm a very good pianist. I'm a little bit tall for my age. I like several boys. I like several girls. I'm old-fashioned. I play tennis. I am a *very* good swimmer. I try to be helpful. I'm always ready to be friends with anybody. Mostly I'm good, but I lose my temper. I'm not well-liked by some girls and boys. I don't know if I'm liked by boys or not. (Montemayor & Eisen, 1977, pp. 317–318)

A *girl almost age 13*: I have a fairly quick temper and it doesn't take much to rouse me. I can be a little bit sympathetic to the people I like, but to the poor people I dislike my temper can be shown quite easily. I'm not thoroughly honest, I can tell a white lie here and there when it's nessersary, but I am trying my hardest to redeem myself, as after experience I've found it's not worth it. If I cannot get my way with various people I walk away and most likely never talk to that person again. I take an interest in other people and I like to hear about their problems as more than likley they can help mesolve my own. My friends are used to me now and I don't realy worry them. I worry a bit after I have just yelled somebody out and more than likely I am the first to appologise. (Livesley & Bromley, 1973, p. 239)

If you look carefully at these descriptions, you will see that the number of psychological characteristics mentioned about the self increases with age. In addition, when traits first appear, they focus on overall qualities of character (e.g., "smart," "honest," "helpful," "friendly," "truthful") and emotional dispositions ("happy," "cheerful," "able to control my temper") as the child forms general ideas about the self. A developmental shift occurs during early adolescence from these global evaluative terms to the use of qualifiers ("I have a *fairly* quick temper," "I'm *not thoroughly* honest"), along with indicators of how psychological characteristics are manifested in different situations. This trend reflects the adolescent's increasing understanding that the behavior of the self is best understood as a complex interaction of psychological traits and situational influences (Barenboim, 1977; Livesley & Bromley, 1973). In addition, during adolescence, a greater emphasis on interpersonal virtues, such as being sociable, considerate, and cooperative, appears in self-descriptions, a change that reflects increasing concern with being liked and viewed in a positive light by others (Rosenberg, 1979).

What factors are responsible for these revisions in the self-concept? Cognitive development contributes to the changing *structural organization* of the self, from an array of isolated behavioral attributes during the preschool years to consolidation of typical behaviors into stable psychological dispositions during late childhood and adolescence (Harter, 1983; Paget & Kritt, 1986). But the *content* of the developing self is largely gleaned from interaction with others, although feedback from acting directly on the environment also plays an important role (Shavelson, Hubner, & Stanton, 1976; Shavelson & Bolus, 1982).

Early in this century, sociologist C. H. Cooley (1902) proposed that the role of other people in the child's emerging self-definition resembles a social mirror, since the self is the synthesis of what we imagine significant others think of us. Cooley called this reflected or social self *the looking glass self*. Several decades later, George Herbert Mead (1934) elaborated on Cooley's idea with his concept of the **generalized other,** indicating that a coherent, psychological self truly emerges when the child is able to assume the attitude that others take toward the self. Mead theorized that in stepping outside the self, assuming this role of a generalized other, and then looking back at the self, "we appear as social objects, as selves" to ourselves (p. 270).

Cooley's and Mead's ideas indicate that perspective-taking skills emerging during middle childhood and adolescence — in particular, the ability to imagine what other people are thinking—play a crucial role in the development of a psychological self. These skills permit the child to construct the generalized other, consisting of descriptions of how the self appears to others as well as evaluative statements about how others judge that appearance. The shift during adolescence, noted earlier, toward interpersonal virtues as part of the self-concept is a clear indication of the operation of the generalized other. These traits reveal that adolescents place increasing emphasis on psychological attributes that have to do with their attractiveness as people and personalities in the eyes of others. In addition, the existence of the generalized other has been repeatedly supported by research (Rosenberg, 1979). In one study, adolescents in grades 6 to 12 were asked to describe the impressions that parents and peers formed of them. An increase with age was found in their tendency to think that others perceived them as individuals with stable psychological dispositions and personalities, rather than solely in terms of surface characteristics (Herzberger et al., 1981).

The work of Cooley and Mead suggests that the contents of people's self-concepts differ because sources of the generalized other vary from person to person. Parents and teachers send different messages to different children, and as a result, children incorporate a particular constellation of psychological qualities into their sense of self. In addition, significant others to whom children look as sources for the self-concept —the people whose opinions they care about and value—initially expand and then come to be selected more deliberately with age. Consequently, the older child's self-concept depends not only on the attitudes of others toward the child, but also on the child's attitude toward others with whom he comes in contact. Between 8 and 15 years of age, peer evaluations become more important as sources of self-definition. A related change is that, during adolescence, the self-concept starts to become increasingly vested in the reactions of close friends (Rosenberg, 1979).

However, parental influences do not, as commonly believed, decline during this period. In a survey of over 3,000 American adolescents, Douvan and Adelson (1966) found that of all people, 14- to 16-year-olds admired their parents most and, in general, felt they had honest and trusting relationships with them. In a British study, adolescent alienation from parents was also uncommon. Although an increase in petty disputes about clothes, hair, and going out did occur, few teenagers reported being overly critical and rejecting of their parents, and most continued to share parental values (Rutter et al., 1976).

Self-Esteem: The Evaluative Side of Self-Concept

In the discussion above, we focused on the general structure and content of the self-concept and how it changes with age. An additional component of self-concept is **self-esteem,** the judgments we make about the worth of ourselves (Coopersmith, 1967; Harter, 1983; Rosenberg, 1979). According to Rosenberg (1979), "a person with high self-esteem is fundamentally satisfied with the type of person he is, yet he may acknowledge his faults while hoping to overcome them" (p. 31). Thus, high self-esteem implies a realistic appraisal of the self's characteristics and competencies, coupled with an attitude of self-acceptance, self-respect, and self-worth.

Self-esteem is such a conspicuous part of people's reflections about themselves that many investigators who study it make no distinction between self-esteem and the broader idea of self-concept. In fact, the great majority of studies of self-concept are really studies of self-esteem. The interest of child development specialists in this evaluative side of the self has been so great that it has generated a virtual mountain of research.

One Self-Esteem or Many? Although the first studies of self-esteem emphasized a single global self-evaluation, new evidence indicates that as early as the preschool period, children make distinctions about how they feel about various aspects of the self. In fact, recent research indicates that children develop an array of separate self-esteems first, only later integrating them into an overall impression. Therefore,

During adolescence, peer evaluations become more important as sources of self-definition.

the course of self-esteem development involves *differentation* of a number of separate self-evaluations, followed by their eventual *integration* into an overall sense of self-worth, producing a hierarchically organized system of self-appraisal. Harter (1983, 1990) believes that before middle childhood, children cannot verbalize a general self-esteem, since they have not yet constructed a coherent psychological picture of themselves. They only evaluate specific behaviors as good or bad.

Researchers have investigated the multidimensional nature of self-esteem in the same way that they have explored the question of whether there is only one intelligence or many: by applying the technique of *factor analysis*[2] to children's ratings of themselves on many characteristics. Results reveal that during the preschool and early elementary school years, children already distinguish between two separate self-esteems: social acceptance and competence (being "good" at doing things). However, 4- to 7-year-olds do not yet discriminate among competence in different activity domains. Perceiving the self as good at one activity (e.g., schoolwork) is fused with perceptions of competence at others (e.g, sports and games) (Harter, 1983, 1990). By age 7 to 8, children differentiate among a variety of self-esteems. Three independent dimensions—cognitive or academic competence, physical prowess, and social self-worth—appear in many studies. Shavelson's hierarchical model, shown in Figure 11.1, depicts how self-esteem is organized by the mid-elementary school years (Marsh et al., 1984; Marsh, 1989; Shavelson & Bolus, 1982). By this time, in addition to a set of independent self-evaluations, children have begun to build an overall view of how they feel about themselves. As children move toward adolescence, several dimensions of self-esteem are added—close friendship, romantic appeal, and job competence—that reflect salient concerns of this new period (Harter, 1990). In addition, the hierarchical structure of self-esteem is reflected even more

---

[2] You may find it helpful to reread the description of factor analysis on page 30 of Chapter 8.

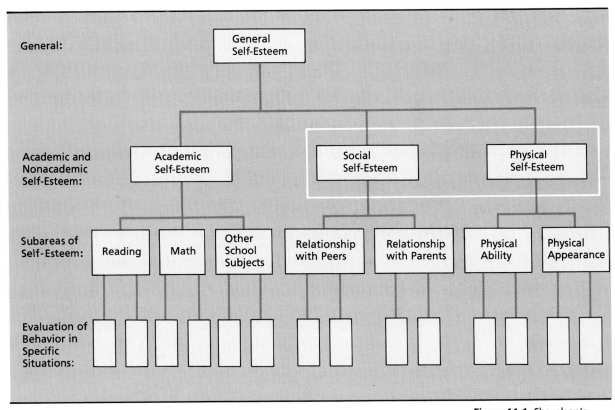

General: **General Self-Esteem**

Academic and Nonacademic Self-Esteem: **Academic Self-Esteem** **Social Self-Esteem** **Physical Self-Esteem**

Subareas of Self-Esteem: **Reading** **Math** **Other School Subjects** **Relationship with Peers** **Relationship with Parents** **Physical Ability** **Physical Appearance**

Evaluation of Behavior in Specific Situations:

Figure 11.1. Shavelson's model of the hierarchical organization of self-esteem. *(From R. J. Shavelson, J. J. Hubner, & J. C. Stanton, 1976, "Self-Concept: Validation of Construct Interpretations,"* Review of Educational Research, 46, 407–441. *Adapted by permission.)*

clearly in factor-analytic studies, and it appears among socioeconomically and ethnically diverse samples of youngsters (Cauce, 1987; Marsh et al., 1984; Marsh & Gouvernet, 1989).

✓**Developmental Changes in the Level of Self-Esteem.** Once the child formulates a sense of self-esteem, does it remain stable over childhood or does it fluctuate a great deal? The results of cross-sectional studies suggest that self-esteem drops over the early elementary school years (Eshel & Klein, 1981; Marsh et al., 1984; Nicholls, 1979; Ruble et al., 1980; Stipek, 1981). This decline can be explained by the fact that young children's self-judgments are at first inordinately high and do not match the opinions of others or objective performance. In one study, Stipek (1981) had kindergartners through third graders rate their own and each of their classmate's "smartness" at school. Pupils in all grades could provide assessments of classmates' abilities that correlated with teacher perceptions. However, self-ratings of kindergartners and first graders were overly favorable and showed no relationship with teacher or peer judgments. Not until second grade did pupil self-ratings reflect the opinions of those around them. Similarly, Ruble and her colleagues (1980) reported that second graders could make use of social comparison information (their own score along with the scores of several peers) in judging how well they themselves did on a task, but younger pupils could not. As children become better able to incorporate information from the environment regarding their own performance, self-esteem adjusts to a more realistic level and gradually becomes more strongly correlated with teacher ratings, test scores, and direct observations of children's behavior.

Both longitudinal and cross-sectional findings indicate that from fourth grade on and continuing throughout the adolescent years, self-esteem, based on global assessments as well as the separate areas of social and physical self-worth, is on the rise for most youngsters (Nottelmann, 1987; O'Malley & Bachman, 1983; Savin-Williams & Demo, 1984; Wallace, Cunningham, & Del Monte, 1984). However, one exception to this trend is a temporary decline in self-esteem associated with the transition from elementary to junior high school (Marsh, 1989; Rosenberg, 1979; Simmons et al., 1979). Entry into a new school, accompanied by new expectations on the part of teachers and peers, may lead adolescents to have difficulty making realistic judgments about their behavior and performance for a period of time.

Aside from this exception, the fact that self-esteem shows a steady increase beginning in late childhood is one reason that researchers now question the long-held assumption that the transition to adolescence is a time of serious emotional turmoil (Nottelmann, 1987). To the contrary, improved self-evaluations suggest that for a great many young people, becoming an adolescent is relatively free from disturbance and, on the whole, fosters feelings of pride and self-confidence (Powers, Hauser, & Kilner, 1989). This is true not just in the United States, but also around the world. In a comparative study of adolescent self-images in ten industrialized countries, Offer (1988) reported that the large majority of teenagers expressed common feelings — a generally optimistic outlook on life, a positive valuing of school and work, and faith in their own ability to cope with life's problems. Most adolescents feel good about growing up, look forward to greater freedom and independence, and reap personal benefits from new responsibilities and expectations, not just in terms of what they learn, but also in terms of a growing sense of competence, self-worth, and self-respect.

The Antecedents of Self-Esteem

From middle childhood on, strong relationships exist between children's self-evaluations and their everyday behavior and performance. For example, academic self-esteem predicts children's school achievement as well as their curiosity and motivation to engage in challenging tasks (Harter, 1981; Marsh et al., 1984; Marsh, Smith, & Barnes, 1985). Children with high social self-esteem are consistently rated as better liked by their peers (Cauley & Tyler, 1989; Harter, 1982). Large sex differences in self-esteem, for physical skills favoring boys and reading favoring girls, parallel clear behavioral differences between the sexes (Marsh, Relich, & Smith, 1983; Marsh et al., 1984). The fact that self-esteem is so powerfully related to individual differences in behavior is the major reason that child development specialists have been interested in studying its origins. If ways can be found to improve children's sense of self-worth, then many aspects of children's development may be enhanced as well.

Child-Rearing Practices. Investigators interested in the antecedents of self-esteem have focused on the importance of a nurturant home environment that provides children with firm but reasonable expectations for behavior. Warm, positive parenting is believed to provide children with confirmation that they are accepted as competent and worthwhile human beings. Firm expectations, backed up with rational explanations, are thought to encourage children to make sensible choices, evaluate their own behavior against reasonable standards, and feel confident about the decisions they make. In contrast, repeated use of coercion communicates a sense of inadequacy to children. It suggests that their behavior needs to be controlled by adults because they are ineffective in managing it themselves.

Although research relating child-rearing practices to self-esteem is limited, it is consistent with the predictions described above (Bishop & Ingersoll, 1989; Coopersmith, 1967; Openshaw, Thomas, & Rollins, 1984). However, we must be cautious in interpreting these relationships, since they are merely correlational. Although parental acceptance is probably an important prerequisite for a positive sense of self-worth, we cannot separate the extent to which child-rearing styles are causes of or reactions to children's characteristics and behavior (Wylie, 1979).

Research that has been far more successful at isolating the antecedents of self-esteem is based on *attribution theory,* which focuses on how children interpret the multiple environmental cues that provide them with information about themselves. Unlike the correlational findings reported above, attribution research has identified powerful adult communication styles that cause changes in children's sense of self-worth. In the next section, we look at how one set of influential attributions develops: children's explanations for their successes and failures in academic learning situations.

Making Attributions: Speculating about the Causes of Success and Failure. **Attributions** are our common everyday speculations about the causes of behavior—the answers we provide to the question, "Why did he (or I) do that?" to make behavior meaningful and understandable. Adults group the causes of their own and others' behavior into two general categories: external, environmental causes and internal, psychological causes. Then they subdivide the category of psychological causes into ability (what a person is able to do) and effort (what a person is trying to do). When explaining behavior, they apply the cause most closely associated with people's actions. For example, if a behavior occurs for a great many people, but only in a single situation (e.g., the whole class gets A's on Ms. Apple's French test), it is seen as caused by the situation (an easy test). However, if an individual exhibits a behavior in many situations (e.g., Johnny always gets A's on French tests), it is seen as caused by some aspect of the person (ability, effort, or both).

In Chapter 8, we showed that although intelligence predicts school achievement, it is imperfectly correlated with it. Differences among children in **achievement motivation**—the tendency to display initiative and persistence when faced with challenging tasks—account for the fact that some less intelligent children do better in school than their brighter counterparts and that children who are equally endowed intellectually often respond quite differently in achievement situations (Dweck & Elliott, 1983). Because achievement motivation is the characteristic that spurs us on to acquire new knowledge and skills, to master the unknown, and to increase the self's competence, it is highly valued in all human societies and worthy of encouragement at an early age (Fyans et al., 1983). Today, child development specialists regard children's achievement-related attributions as the major reason that some children are competent learners who are oriented toward mastery in the face of obstacles to success, while others treat failure as insurmountable and readily give up when task goals are not immediately achieved.

The Development of Achievement-Related Attributions. Children begin to engage in competence-increasing activities almost as soon as they enter the world. In Chapter 10, we showed that infants derive great pleasure from engaging in physical and mental activity. When mastery is attained as a consequence of their own actions (e.g., pulling a lever to produce an interesting sight or sound), the satisfaction they experience reinforces their behavior, motivating them to engage in similar activities in the future. Infants cannot yet cognitively evaluate the outcomes of their actions against internally or externally imposed standards. Nor do they take the results of their actions as an indication of the worth or goodness of the self. Instead, they are naturally driven toward mastery of activities that foster their own development. Achievement motivation is believed to have roots in this early drive (White, 1959).

Around age 3, children begin to cognitively appraise their own performance by making attributions about their successes and failures. These attributions affect children's *expectancies of success*, and expectancies, in turn, influence the extent to which children are motivated to persist when confronted with similar tasks in the future.

Children age 6 and below view their own ability as extremely high, often underestimate task difficulty, and as a result, hold very high expectancies of success. Even in the face of repeated failure, 5-year-olds, in comparison to older grade-school children, will keep on working for a longer period of time (Rholes et al., 1980). When asked to react to a situation in which one person does worse on a task than another, young children indicate that the lower-scoring person can still succeed if he keeps trying, and they believe that a smart person is one who expends more effort (Nicholls, 1978). In short, preschoolers and early elementary school children are "learning optimists" (Dweck & Elliott, 1983). They develop naive explanations for their successes and failures that support a continuation of the mastery-oriented behavior they freely displayed as infants. As evidence for this optimism, when kindergartners and first graders are asked to indicate how well they think they are doing in school, most rank themselves at the top of the class (Nicholls, 1979; Stipek, 1981).

Part of the reason that young children arrive at these positive attributional conclusions is that they are not yet capable of the complex reasoning that older grade-school children use to explain their successes and failures. Recall from Chapters 6 and 7 that young children do not notice and separate relevant variables in the sphere of physical cognition; neither do they do so in the realm of social cognition. Several studies report that preschool and early elementary school youngsters fail to isolate and coordinate effort and ability in making achievement-related attributions. Instead, they view all good things as going together: a person who tries hard is also a smart person who is going to succeed (Kun, 1977; Nicholls, 1978).

During middle childhood, children can separate the attributional variables of ability and effort, and they take a wider array of information into account in explaining why they succeed and fail (Chapman & Skinner, 1989; Dweck & Leggett, 1988). Elementary school pupils who are high in academic self-esteem develop **mastery-oriented attributions** that are adaptive in sustaining achievement motivation on the more intellectually demanding tasks of the school years. These children attribute their successes to high ability, and since they understand ability to be a characteristic of the self that can be depended on in the future to help them succeed, their causal attribution engenders high expectancies of success. When failure occurs, mastery-oriented children attribute it to factors about the self or the environment that can be changed and controlled, such as insufficient effort or an especially difficult task. Consequently, regardless of whether they succeed or fail, their attributions result in a willingness to approach challenging tasks with vigor, and they retain the enthusiasm for learning that characterized them during their earlier years (Nicholls, 1976).

Learned Helplessness. Unfortunately, some elementary school children use their new-found capacities for social reasoning to arrive at far less flattering explanations for task outcomes. Dweck and her collaborators (Dweck & Elliott, 1983; Dweck et al., 1978) refer to a phenomenon called **learned helplessness** that characterizes children who believe that failure is insurmountable. The achievement strivings of these youngsters are seriously disrupted when they encounter obstacles to success or receive negative feedback from parents and teachers. Under these circumstances, their performance quickly deteriorates, and they show decreased persistence and signs of giving up.

Learned helpless children construct a very different pattern of attributions than their mastery-oriented counterparts. They explain their failures (and not their successes) as due to ability, and since they have come to regard ability as a fixed characteristic of the self that is difficult to change, they have little confidence in themselves and develop low expectancies of success. Consequently, when failure hits, they regard themselves as hopelessly inadequate in the face of it (Diener & Dweck, 1978, 1980).

Because learned helplessness engenders disrupted performance along with feelings of anxious lack of control, it acts to sustain itself, providing children with repeated confirmation of their failure-related explanations. A recent longitudinal study of third-grade learned helpless pupils indicated that many maintained their self-defeating attitudes over time and, by fifth grade, were doing less well in school than their classmates (Fincham, Hokoda, & Sanders, 1989). Moreover, to protect themselves from the debilitating psychological consequences of failure, these youngsters begin to select less challenging tasks and, over the long term, less challenging courses and even less demanding careers (Parsons, 1983). Thus, learned helplessness prevents children from pursuing tasks that they are capable of mastering because their attributions lead to low expectancies of success.

What accounts for the very different attributions of learned helpless and mastery-oriented pupils? Children pick up some information about how capable they are from their actual performance and how well it compares to that of their peers. But the kind of feedback they receive from adults also plays a significant role. In one study Parsons, Adler, and Kaczala (1982) found that among children of equivalent performance in mathematics, those with low expectancies of success had parents who believed that they were less able and had to work harder to succeed, and the children shared these beliefs. In another, Dweck and her colleagues (1978) experimentally manipulated the feedback fourth and fifth graders received after they failed at a task. Those receiving negative evaluations consistently implicating their ability were far more likely to attribute their poor performance to lack of ability than children receiving feedback suggesting insufficient effort was involved. Dweck's research shows that the evaluative messages adults send to children are a strong determinant of how they interpret failure experiences. According to the chain of events depicted in Figure 11.2, once such attributions are formed, they affect children's self-evaluations and future expectancies of success, which, in turn, moderate their achievement motivation and performance in learning situations.

At this point, it is important to note that girls are far more likely than boys to exhibit the helpless pattern of attributions and low expectancies of success described above (Dweck, Goetz, & Strauss, 1980; Stipek & Hoffman, 1980). Girls more often than boys blame their ability for poor performance, and they are also more likely to show decreased persistence and impaired performance following failure (Dweck & Gilliard, 1975; Dweck & Repucci, 1973; Nicholls, 1975; Weisz & McGuire, 1980). Girls also tend to receive evaluative feedback from adults (both teachers and parents) that credits their effort when they succeed but denigrates their ability when they fail, whereas the reverse is true for boys (Dweck et al., 1978; Parsons, Adler, and Kaczala, 1982). Although the greater learned helplessness of girls is not related to poorer achievement in the grade-school years, the low sense of self-esteem and expectancies for success engendered by it may pave the way for future diminished achievement and an increased likelihood of falling short of realizing their intellectual potential during adolescence and adulthood (Dweck & Licht, 1980; Parsons, 1983).

Finally, cultural values affect the probability that children will develop learned helpless orientations. Compared to American mothers, Chinese and Japanese mothers believe that success in school is far more dependent on effort than on innate ability. These attitudes affect parental encouragement of academic performance,

Repeated negative evaluations from adults can cause children to develop learned helplessness — low expectancies for success and debilitating anxiety when faced with challenging academic tasks.

Figure 11.2. The attributional approach to explaining children's achievement motivation.

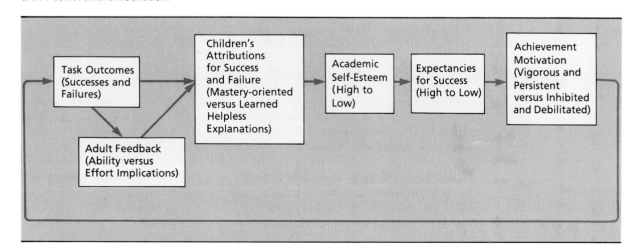

carry over to children, and are believed to be partly responsible for the higher academic achievement of Asian than American youngsters in recent cross-national studies (Stevenson & Lee, 1990). We will return to these intriguing cultural differences when we consider the topic of schooling in Chapter 15.

Attribution Retraining. **Attribution retraining** involves methods that try to get children who have been identified as low achievers or who exhibit learned helplessness to view failure as surmountable if additional effort is exerted. Most often, children are asked to work on tasks that are hard enough that some failure experiences are bound to occur. Then they are provided with repeated feedback from an adult that helps them revise their failure-related attributions, such as "You can do it if you try harder" (e.g., Dweck, 1975). In addition to reinterpreting failures, many programs encourage children to ascribe their successes to both ability and effort instead of chance factors like good luck, by giving them additional feedback after they succeed, such as "You're really good at this" or "You really tried hard on that one" (Fowler & Peterson, 1981; Medway & Venino, 1982; Schunk, 1983). Other helpful techniques are exposure to models who demonstrate self-effort statements (e.g., "I tried hard and found out I could do it") and persistence in the face of obstacles to task success (Cecil & Medway, 1986; Schunk, Hanson, & Cox, 1987). These easy-to-implement procedures are remarkably effective at enhancing children's judgments of their own ability, increasing task persistence, and improving ultimate task success. In addition, the greater task persistence that accrues from attribution retraining generalizes to new tasks and endures over long periods of time (Chapin & Dyck, 1976).

According to Dweck and Leggett (1988), when children replace learned helpless with mastery-oriented attributions, their motivational style changes from a *fixed* to an *incremental* view of their ability. Even if ability is low to begin with, it can be improved by trying hard. Attribution retraining is a simple, practical tool for helping teachers and parents replace destructive feedback (criticisms for errors, negative comparisons with peers, and unreasonably high expectations) with communication that fosters the fullest possible development of children's intellectual potential.

Adolescence: Constructing an Identity

The following self-searching statement was written by a 17-year-old girl asked to compose a short essay to answer the question, "Who am I?" As you read it, consider how it differs from the sample self-descriptions of younger children given on page 436:

> I am a human being. I am a girl. I am an individual. I don't know who I am. I am a Pisces. I am a moody person. I am an indecisive person. I am an ambitious person. I am a very curious person. I am not an individual. I am a loner. I am an American (God help me). I am a Democrat. I am a liberal person. I am a radical. I am a conservative. I am a pseudoliberal. I am an atheist. I am not a classifiable person (i.e., I don't want to be). (Montemayor & Eisen, 1977, p. 318)

This response exemplifies the direction of self-development during adolescence: toward a sense of **identity,** a coherent conception of the self composed of an integrated set of goals, values, and beliefs to which the individual is solidly committed. The young person who wrote this statement is still formulating her identity, since we see her reviewing, reflecting, and vacillating about a large number of ideological beliefs. As she gradually builds a well-developed self-structure, various elements will be added and discarded until she patterns the various parts into a consistent, organized self-system worthy of giving direction and meaning to her life (Erikson, 1950; Marcia, 1980; Waterman, 1984).

Erikson's (1950, 1968) theory, summarized in Chapter 1, has inspired virtually all current research on identity development. According to Erikson, establishing an identity involves a search for *continuity* of the self's attributes over time. As adolescents move toward adulthood, they must sort through the characteristics that defined the self during childhood and mold them into a mature self-conception that provides a sense of sameness and consistency. Another component of identity formation involves *unity*. Adolescents must construct a unified self that integrates the new roles they will assume — occupational, sexual, and ideological (e.g., religious, political, and moral) — into an organized configuration. Thus, attaining an identity is a matter of synthesizing childhood self-definitions into more mature commitments having to do with getting a job, establishing new relationships, and becoming a citizen.

Is Adolescence an Inevitable Period of Storm and Stress? In a complex society that confronts young people with many possible directions and choices, each adolescent who successfully formulates an identity experiences an **identity crisis** — a temporary period of heightened self-consciousness and self-focusing as the individual experiments with a variety of alternatives before settling on a set of goals and values. Erikson believes that adolescent commitments arrived at without a period of inner "soul searching" are not true identity formations, since a secure identity results from sifting through many choices and assuming the formidable responsibility of choosing goals and values that fit with the self's strengths and weaknesses. As part of this process, adolescents must not only affirm a set of commitments, but also relinquish some fantasized, glamorous possibilities of what they once thought they would become as unrealistic, impractical, and unattainable.

A few adolescents experience identity crises that are traumatic and totally preoccupying. However, Erikson recognized that for most, identity formation proceeds in a very gradual, uneventful way. The many daily decisions that adolescents make — "whom to date, whether or not to break up, having intercourse, taking drugs, going to college or working, which college, what major, studying or playing, being politically active" — and the bases on which these decisions are made eventually are integrated into a unified self-structure (Marcia, 1980, p. 161). As we indicated earlier, for most young people, adolescence is not a period of intense emotional upheaval that brings with it an increased risk of adjustment difficulties, although it has often been thought of in this way. In fact, the incidence of serious psychological disturbance increases only slightly from childhood to adolescence (by about 2 percent), at which time the rate is about the same as it is in the adult population (Powers, Hauser, & Kliner, 1989; Rutter et al., 1976). Among the mild rise during the teenage years, depression and suicide are common occurrences (see Box 11.1). However, it is important to keep in mind that an identity crisis is a normal and necessary experience during adolescence, not a cataclysmic and seriously disruptive event that predisposes young people to high rates of psychopathology. In this regard, perhaps the term "exploration" provides a better description of the typical adolescent identity experience than Erikson's choice of the word "crisis," which is prevalent in the literature.

Paths to Identity Formation. Because Erikson's account of identity was originally intended for clinical purposes, its initial impact rested on its usefulness in the psychoanalytic interpretation of case histories. As a result, some of his ideas appeared vague to child development specialists (Waterman, 1982). Recently, Erikson's theory has been tested and extended by using social-cognitive research methods that clarify the course of identity development and the various means that adolescents use to arrive at a coherent, integrated sense of self.

Marcia (1966, 1980) used a semistructured interviewing technique to evaluate the extent to which young people are in a period of crisis or have made commitments to occupational choices and religious and political values. He found evidence for four identity statuses that indicate the degree of progress adolescents have made toward formulating a mature personal identity. Marcia's four identity statuses are a clear outgrowth of Erikson's theory, but they also add to it by making the various paths toward identity formation explicit, measurable, and testable:

Identity achievement. These individuals have already experienced a period of crisis and decision making and now manifest a secure sense of commitment to an occupation or ideology.

Moratorium. The word moratorium refers to a temporary delay or holding pattern. These individuals have suspended definite commitments while they go through an identity crisis, searching for an appropriate occupation and ideology in which to make a positive self-investment.

Identity foreclosure. Like identity-achieved individuals, foreclosed young people have committed themselves to occupational and ideological positions. However, they have avoided a period of crisis and have, instead, reached a premature commitment to a ready-made identity that authority figures (usually parents) have formulated for them.

Identity diffusion. These individuals differ from the three identity statuses described above in that they do not have firm occupational or ideological commitments and are not actively trying to reach them. Diffused adolescents are characterized by a lack of direction. They may have never experienced an identity crisis, or they may have had a period of crisis that they could not resolve.

In the process of forming an identity, adolescents often shift from one status to another until an identity is finally achieved. In a cross-sectional study of college-

---

◆ CONTEMPORARY ISSUES: SOCIAL POLICY ◆

Adolescent Suicide: Annihilation of the Self

Box 11.1

Over the last 30 years, the suicide rate has tripled among young people between 15 and 24 years of age. Suicide currently ranks as the third most common form of death (following accidents and homicides) among this sector of the population. More than 5,000 youths die from it each year (Pfeffer, 1986).

Marked sex differences in suicidal behavior exist. The number of boys who kill themselves exceeds the number of girls by 4 or 5 to 1. Girls more often make unsuccessful suicide attempts and use methods with a likelihood of resuscitation, such as a sleeping pill overdose. In contrast, boys select more active and instantaneously lethal methods, such as firearms or hanging (Holden, 1986; Shaffer, 1985). These differences may be partly the result of societal sex-role expectations, since there is less tolerance for feelings of helplessness and failed efforts in males than in females (Smith, 1981).

Many studies point to a common set of internal and external forces that predispose young people to suicidal actions. Suicidal adolescents often show signs of severe depression during the period preceding the suicidal act; many verbalize the wish to die, lose interest in school or hobbies, and manifest a pervasive sense of gloom and hopelessness (Shafii et al., 1985; Triolo et al., 1984). These depressive symptoms appear in two different types of suicidal youngsters. In one group are adolescents of superior intelligence who lead a solitary, withdrawn existence, hold themselves to inordinately high standards of performance, and are very self-critical. A second, larger group is characterized by antisocial tendencies. These adolescents engage in bullying, fighting, and stealing, and many have a history of school truancy and drug and alcohol abuse. These behavior patterns indicate that many suicidal young people do not just turn aggression inward; they are also hostile and destructive in their actions toward others (Holden, 1986; Shaffer, 1985).

Family turmoil, parental emotional problems, and marital breakups are prevalent in the backgrounds of suicidal adolescents (Curran, 1987; Shaffer, 1985). However, since these factors, as well as the behavior constellations noted above, can be found in young people who do not commit suicide, other precipitating events are also involved. Common circumstances just before a suicide

bound males between the ages of 12 and 24, Meilman (1979) found that young adolescents often start out as identity diffused and foreclosed but gradually shift toward the moratorium and identity-achieved statuses between 18 and 21 years of age (see Figure 11.3). This trend has been documented for both males and females in a more representative sample of both college- and non-college-oriented adolescents (Archer, 1982). Late adolescence seems to be an especially important time for identity achievement, and longitudinal research on college youths confirms this, since many undergraduates show shifts from a moratorium to an identity-achieved status between their freshman and senior years (Adams & Fitch, 1982; Waterman & Waterman, 1971; Waterman, Geary, & Waterman, 1974). The diversity of experiences provided by college environments undoubtedly triggers considerable self-searching and suggests various resolutions for identity concerns. However, young people who go to work following high school are not handicapped in formulating a sense of identity. They are not more foreclosed or diffused; in fact they are less so. They simply move toward identity achievement sooner than their college-bound counterparts (Munro & Adams, 1977).

As you have probably surmised, identity achievement and moratorium are regarded as healthy and adaptive avenues to identity formation, whereas foreclosure and diffusion are considered maladaptive. In general, research supports this idea. Young people who are either identity-achieved or experiencing a moratorium tend to "do better and feel better about themselves" than their less well-developed counterparts (Marcia, 1980, p. 181). They have a higher sense of self-esteem, report greater similarity between their ideal self (what they had hoped to become) and their real self, are more advanced in moral reasoning, and are more likely to assume personal responsibility for their decisions and the direction of their lives (Marcia, 1980; Waterman & Goldman, 1976). In addition, identity-achieved individuals, more than those in the other three statuses, have moved beyond the preoccupation with an

include the breakup of an important peer relationship or learning that parents will be informed about the adolescent's antisocial behavior. Such experiences trigger shame and humiliation in a young person whose sense of self is already extremely precarious. Also, exposure to the suicidal behavior of relatives and friends seems to be important, since one third to two thirds of suicide victims have known someone who has attempted or completed suicide (Holden, 1986; Shafii et al., 1985).

Why is suicide extremely rare in childhood but on the rise thereafter? Investigators believe that the adolescents' improved ability to engage in planning and foresight and greater awareness of the self as seen by others play significant roles. Many who succeed in their suicidal intent plan it out purposefully and secretively; few adolescent suicides are sudden and impulsive. In addition, cognitive advances may cause depression to be experienced differently during adolescence than it is during the childhood years. Depressed teenagers are believed to be extremely self-preoccupied and self-focused, a circumstance that may lead them to the exaggerated conclusion that no one could possibly understand them or could ever experience the intense psychological pain they feel. Thus, cognitive maturity is an added factor that may contribute to the hopelessness, isolation, and despair of an already vulnerable adolescent (Pfeffer, 1986; Shaffer, 1985).

Prevention and treatment of suicide are multidimensional activities. Young people who show warning signs, such as suicidal threats and comments, a sense of hopelessness and gloom, and declining interest in activities, need professional help and the understanding of significant adults who take their despair seriously. Telephone hotlines through which emergency assistance can be sought, knowledgeable and sympathetic counselors in school systems, and the availability of effective treatment programs are crucial. Family and peer survivors of suicide victims also need help, to assist them in emotionally integrating the event and as a means for preventing additional suicides in the future (Smith, 1980).

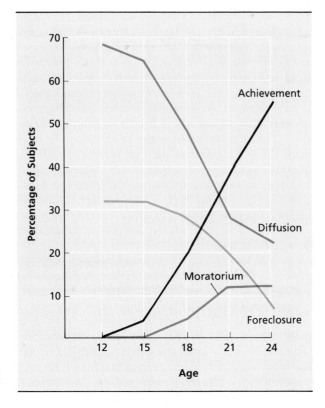

Figure 11.3. Percentages of individuals between 12 and 24 in each of the four identity statuses in Meilman's (1979) study. *(Adapted from P. W. Meilman, 1979.)*

imaginary audience[3] that characterizes adolescents upon entry into the formal operational stage. They are less self-focused and preoccupied with how others regard them and more self-assured and outer-directed than their same-age counterparts (Adams, Abraham, & Markstrom, 1987).

What factors facilitate adolescent identity achievement? Waterman (1982) speculates that exposure to a wide range of identity alternatives and opportunities to observe productive and successful models are important. In addition, parenting styles that grant adolescents individuality in ideas and beliefs and that are involved but democratic as opposed to dominating (likely to yield foreclosure) or uninvolved (likely to promote diffusion) are thought to play a role (Grotevant & Cooper, 1986).

Identity achievement is especially problematic for minority youths. Often they must grapple with value conflicts between their subculture and the culture of the majority. In addition, they must integrate a positive sense of ethnic belonging into their self-constructions in midst of a larger society that devalues and stereotypes their culture of origin. Special efforts to enhance ethnic pride at home, at school, and in the larger community are particularly important for these youngsters (Gibbs & Huang, 1989; Spencer & Markstrom-Adams, 1990). A profitable direction for future research will be to isolate the antecedents of identity development among diverse populations of adolescents. Then interventions that facilitate identity consolidation can be initiated, thereby maximizing opportunities for young people to lead socially responsible as well as personally satisfying adult lives.

BRIEF REVIEW

In the sections above, we have seen that vast changes in the sense of self occur from infancy through adolescence. The first step in self-development is self-recognition, which is attained by the second year of life. To this, the preschooler adds concrete categorical descriptors of the self and awareness of a private, inner self. In middle

[3] Return to Chapter 6, page 240, to review the concept of the *imaginary audience*.

childhood, psychological dispositions appear in children's self-descriptions. In addition, a differentiated, hierarchically organized self-esteem develops that is strongly influenced by feedback from others. Self-development culminates during the adolescent years in the formation of an identity — a coherent, integrated conception of the self consisting of self-chosen goals and values.

CONCEPTUALIZING OTHER PEOPLE

Children's developing cognitions about other people — their descriptions of others as personalities and the inferences they make about others' behavior and internal thoughts — constitute the largest area of social-cognitive research. As we examine how children's understanding of others develops, you will see that it has much in common with their developing conceptions of themselves, becoming more psychologically based and increasingly differentiated, well-organized, and integrated with age.

Person Perception: Understanding Others as Personalities

Person perception deals with how we conceptualize the personalities of people with whom we are familiar. To study its development, investigators use methods much like those used to illuminate how children think about themselves: asking them to give descriptions of people they know, such as "Can you tell me what kind of person _____ is?"

Like their self-descriptions, below age 8, children's descriptions of others focus on commonly experienced inner states and concrete, observable characteristics such as appearance, possessions, and routine activities. Around third grade, children discover consistencies and regularities in the overt behavior of people they know. As a result, they begin to describe others in terms of psychological traits (Barenboim, 1977; Eder, 1989; Livesley & Bromley, 1973; Peevers & Secord, 1973). However, the sophistication of children's descriptions of others as unique, differentiated personalities builds slowly and gradually. The first mention of these attributes is closely tied to behavior and consists only of *implied* dispositions, such as "He is always fighting with people" or "he steals and he lies" (Peevers & Secord, 1973). Later, children mention psychological characteristics directly, but they are global and stereotyped descriptors, such as "good," "nice," or "acts smart," that reflect little in the way of differentiation of the other person's character. Eventually, these broad, amorphous impressions evolve into sharper descriptions, and adjectives like "honest," "trustworthy," "generous," "polite," "likeable," and "selfish" appear (Livesley & Bromley, 1973; Scarlett, Press, & Crockett, 1971).

Children start to make comparisons among people at about the same time they begin to compare themselves to others. These comparisons also follow the concrete-to-abstract progression noted above. In the early elementary school years comparisons are cast in behavioral terms (e.g., "Billy runs a lot faster than Jason"). Only between the ages of 10 and 12, after children have had sufficient experience in inferring psychological attributes from regularities in others' behavior, do they use newly created psychological constructs to make comparisons between people (e.g., "Paul's a lot more considerate than thick-heated Del.") (Barenboim, 1981, p. 133).

Throughout middle childhood, children's character sketches remain poorly organized, with different descriptors strung together in a fairly random, unintegrated way. Between the ages of 14 and 16, person perception undergoes a major change in this regard. As Piagetian formal operations become better established, adolescents begin to formulate integrated descriptions of other people (Livesley & Bromley, 1973; O'Mahoney, 1989). To do so, they present much richer accounts of people they know that operate on several levels, simultaneously referring to external attributes, overt behavior, inner dispositions, and their complex interconnections. In addition, adolescents recognize that their own experiences with a particular person, and therefore their constructed impressions of them, may differ from the opinions of other people (Barenboim, 1977; Livesley & Bromley, 1973).

The research described above indicates that young people become capable amateur "personality theorists" by the midadolescent years, an accomplishment that is facilitated by improved abstract reasoning and perspective-taking abilities as well as a broader range of social experiences. Adolescents' capacity to synthesize unique combinations of behavior and inner characteristics into complex, integrated conceptualizations of others is useful and adaptive. It permits them to understand as well as predict the actions of people they know more effectively than they could at an earlier age.

Understanding Others' Intentions

Besides coming to know others as unique personalities, children, like adults, must observe and interpret the ongoing behavioral stream of other people to know how to react to it. Making behavior meaningful and responding to it appropriately often depend on being able to separate deliberate and intentional actions from those that are accidental and fortuitous. By two years of age, children already have intentionality on their minds, since they use "gonna," "hafta," and "wanna" to announce actions they are about to perform (Brown, 1973). In a number of studies, children have been shown filmed sequences of behavior and asked to describe what is happening. Even 4- and 5-year-olds spontaneously infer intentions, making such statements as "He wants to know . . . ," "He's trying to . . . ," and "He needs . . . ," a tendency that increases over the school years (Flapan, 1968; Livesley & Bromley, 1973).

Children have the capacity to infer intentions at a very early age, but how good are they at distinguishing people's accidental from intentional acts? Parents' and teachers' anecdotal reports indicate that very young preschoolers clearly distinguish between their own unintentional and intended acts when it is in their own best interests to do so. After being reproached by an adult for bumping into a playmate or spilling a glass of milk, they defend themselves by exclaiming, "It was an accident!" or "I didn't do it on purpose!" (Shultz, 1980). Some evidence suggests that preschoolers separate the accidental from the intended at a somewhat earlier age for themselves than they do for others (Keasey, 1977). Adults help them make this distinction by providing relevant feedback — assigning blame for intentional behaviors and excusing or ascribing less blame for unintended ones. In addition, children are aided in making the discrimination by noticing how they themselves are thinking and feeling while they act. The cognitive experience of doing something that one wants to do is very different from the experience of finding oneself doing something that one did not try to do (Flavell, 1985; Shultz, 1980). Once children appreciate this difference for themselves, they may generalize it to the behavior of others.

Children's ability to diagnose the intended and accidental behavior of others must follow quickly after self-understanding, since some ingenious laboratory studies reveal that even 3-year-olds separate intended actions from unintentional behaviors such as mistakes and reflexes. Shultz, Wells, and Sarda (1980) had children repeat an easy-to-pronounce sentence ("She lives in a house") or a tongue-twister ("She sells sea shells by the sea shore") in which they invariably made mistakes. Then an adult asked them, "Did you mean to say it that way?" Three-years-olds knew that an incorrectly repeated tongue-twister was not intended to be spoken with errors, regardless of whether they did the speaking or watched another child make the mistake. In a second study, an experimenter elicited a knee-jerk reflex by tapping the child's knee and also had the child imitate a similar voluntary leg movement. Three- and 4-year-olds showed some tendency to distinguish these voluntary from involuntary movements in themselves and others, an ability that improved markedly by age 5.

In the above instances, the researcher stated ahead of time exactly what the child's purposeful action was to be (e.g., repeating a sentence or moving one's leg like

When this child explains to her older sister, "I didn't spill it on purpose!" she displays her ability to separate intentional from unintentional acts at an early age.

the experimenter). Shultz and Wells (1985) showed that children between the ages of 2½ and 12 rely heavily on a *matching rule* to separate intended from unintended behavior. If the self's or another person's prior stated intention matches the subsequent behavioral result, then the behavior must have been deliberate, but if it does not match, then the behavior was not intended.

The matching rule always works for judging the self's behavior. However, it cannot always be relied on to infer the intentions of others because people do not always announce what they will do before they do it. Therefore, in many instances, children must notice environmental cues to figure out whether an actor's behavior was purposeful or not. Important cues have to do with whether an action leads to a positive or negative outcome (e.g., if you drop an empty milk carton in a garbage pail, the behavior was probably intended, but if you drop it on the floor, it probably was not); whether or not the actor is monitoring his own actions (concentrating on what one is doing implies intentionality, whereas not paying attention suggests unintentionality); and whether an external cause can account for the person's behavior (e.g., stumbling over a box in the middle of a room is very likely an accidental behavior). Smith (1978) showed 4- to 6-year-old children films in which these cues were varied. Four-year-olds failed to notice them, but 5-year-olds clearly did. By the late preschool years, children have at their command a rich set of cognitive tools for separating others' behaviors into deliberate and unintended actions.

The range of intentional behaviors of which people are capable extends beyond the ones examined in the studies above. We can intentionally simulate unintentional acts like falling over an object or bumping into someone. We can also deliberately refrain from acting but pretend that our lack of response was unintentional (e.g., "I forgot all about it!"). Investigators are just beginning to find out how children come to appreciate these deceptive forms of intentional behavior. One recent study showed that between 5 and 9 years of age, children rely increasingly on a *verbal-nonverbal consistency rule* to evaluate the sincerity of others' stated intentions. For example, older children understand quite well that telling another person you like something when you look neutral or unhappy probably means that you are not telling the truth (Rotenberg, Simourd, & Moore, 1989). The ability to detect more subtle efforts to conceal intentions clearly involves sophisticated perspective-taking skills, a topic to which we turn in the next section.

Finally, because of their unique personalities and history of social experiences, children differ from one another in how accurately they interpret other people's streams of behavior. As Box 11.2 indicates, highly aggressive children exhibit striking biases in inferring intentions; they often see hostility where it does not exist. Children's ability to observe and reason about the human behavioral stream is also of great applied significance. It is especially important when children are asked to provide eyewitness testimony in court proceedings, a topic we address in Box 11.3.

Understanding Another's Viewpoint: The Development of Perspective-Taking Skills

In this and other chapters, we have repeatedly emphasized that **perspective-taking** — the ability to imagine what other people may be thinking and feeling[4] — is important for a wide variety of social-cognitive achievements, including referential communication skills (Chapter 9), empathic responding (Chapter 10), self-concept and self-esteem, conceptualizing other people as unique personalities, and understanding others' intentions. Recall from Chapter 6 that Piaget regarded egocentrism — an inability to differentiate between the self's perspective and that of others — as the overriding feature responsible for the immaturity of young children's thought in both social and nonsocial domains. We now know that preschoolers are not as egocentric

---

[4] Sometimes an alternative term — *role-taking* — is used to refer to this phenomenon in the research literature.

as Piaget believed. Nevertheless, Piaget's ideas about egocentrism inspired new work on children's ability to take the perspective of others, which improves steadily over childhood and adolescence.

Selman's Stages of Perspective-Taking. Robert Selman developed a five-stage model that describes major changes in children's understanding of others' perspectives in relation to their own. Selman's stages, like Piaget's, are assumed to mark qualitatively distinct ways of thinking, to develop in an invariant sequence, and to apply universally to all children. The stages were originally formulated from clinical interviews in which children were asked to respond to social dilemmas like this one:

> Holly is an 8-year-old girl who likes to climb trees. She is the best tree climber in the neighborhood. One day while climbing down from a tall tree she falls off the bottom branch but does not hurt herself. Her father sees her fall. He is upset and asks her to promise not to climb the trees any more. Holly promises.
>
> Later that day, Holly and her friends meet Sean. Sean's kitten is caught up in a tree and cannot get down. Something has to be done right away or the kitten may fall. Holly is the only one who climbs trees well enough to reach the kitten and get it down, but she remembers her promise to her father. (Selman & Byrne, 1974, p. 805)

Questions are then asked that focus on the characters' perspectives, such as "Does Sean know why Holly cannot decide whether or not to climb the tree? What will Holly's father think? Will he understand why if she climbs the tree?"

Selman's five stages are as follows:

Level 0: Undifferentiated and egocentric perspective-taking (about 3–6 years). At this stage, the existence of self and others' inner thoughts and feelings is recognized, but there is frequent confusion between the two. Children seldom ac-

---

◆   THEORY, RESEARCH, AND APPLICATIONS   ◆

I*nferring* Intentions: *The Special Case of the Aggressive Child*   Box 11.2

Theory. The inferences that children make about the intentions of others are major determinants of how they respond in social situations. For example, if Bobby's knocking down the block tower is seen as deliberate and hostilely motivated, his classmates are likely to retaliate with verbal or physical aggression. If his destroying the tower is seen as prosocially motivated (carried out while helping to clean up the room) or purely accidental, his peers are likely to refrain from seeking revenge.

Since children often respond with aggression when they regard others' behavior as hostile and threatening, Kenneth Dodge hypothesized that highly aggressive and socially rejected children may behave as they do because they perceive hostile intentions in social situations where, in fact, they do not exist. To find out whether such children suffer from serious social-cognitive deficits in their ability to use behavioral cues to interpret others' intentions, Dodge examined aggressive-rejected and nonaggressive boys' interpretations of peer behavior in which cues about the peer's intentions were systematically varied.

Research. Aggressive and nonaggressive boys in grades 2, 4, and 6 were told that they could win a prize for putting together a puzzle and that another (fictitious) boy was working on a similar puzzle in an adjoining room. When each subject was partly finished, the experimenter borrowed his puzzle, ostensibly to show it to the other boy. Moments later, the subject heard his puzzle crashing apart, along with one of three taped messages providing different cues about the peer's intentions: a *hostile condition*, in which the other boy said he did not want the subject to win a prize; *a prosocial condition*, in which the boy said he would help the subject get more done, but as he put another piece in, he accidentally knocked the puzzle over; and an *ambiguous condition*, in which the puzzle could be heard breaking apart, but the intentions of the boy were not made clear. Then the experimenter returned with the subject's destroyed puzzle as well as the other child's partly finished one. The subject was told to look over the puzzles while the adult was out of the room, and the researchers filmed his response. Both groups of subjects responded

knowledge that another person can respond to and interpret the same situation differently from the self.

Typical response to the "Holly" dilemma: The child predicts that Holly will save the kitten because she does not want it to get hurt and believes that Holly's father will feel just as she does about her climbing the tree: "Happy, he likes kittens." (Selman, 1976, p. 303)

Level 1: Differentiated and subjective perspective-taking (about 5–9 years). Children of this stage clearly understand that interpretations of social situations by the self and others may be the same or different, and they recognize that different perspectives may result because different people have access to different information. However, a Level 1 child is not yet capable of coordinating perspectives. He cannot put himself in the place of another person to judge that person's actions or reflect upon himself, and he also cannot appreciate that his own view of the other person is influenced by what he imagines the other's view of himself to be.

Typical response to the "Holly" dilemma: When asked how Holly's father will react when he finds out that she climbed the tree, the child responds, "If he didn't know anything about the kitten, he would be angry. But if Holly shows him the kitten, he might change his mind." The child clearly recognizes that depending on the information Holly's father has available for interpreting the situation, he may or may not be angry and his perspective may or may not be the same as Holly's.

Level 2: Self-reflective or reciprocal perspective-taking (about 7–12 years). Level 2 children can see their own thoughts, feelings, and behavior from another person's perspective and recognize that others can do the same. Therefore, Level 2 children are better able to anticipate others' reactions to their behavior than they

to the hostile condition with retaliatory aggression (messing up the other boy's puzzle) and to the prosocial condition with restraint and helping behavior. However, in the ambiguous condition, aggressive and nonaggressive boys differed sharply, with the aggressive boys reacting much more hostilely. The results indicated that when the intentions of a peer are unclear, the social inferences of aggressive boys are distorted in the direction of hostile intentions, and they react accordingly (Dodge, 1980).

Another study showed that when aggressive boys feel personally threatened (for example, when they are led to expect an imminent conflict with a peer), their processing of intentional cues deteriorates further. Under these conditions, they interpret both ambiguous and accidental cues as hostile (Dodge & Somberg, 1987).

Dodge's research reveals that aggressive-rejected children have difficulty appraising intentions accurately. Primed to interpret the actions of others in a hostile fashion, they react with aggressive behavior that leads peers to respond in kind, creating an escalating spiral of peer-directed aggressive interaction. By the end of the elementary school years, normal peers have become biased in the way they view the intentions of highly aggressive boys, perceiving malice in instances in which their intent is benign, because of the aggressive child's long history of belligerent behavior (Dodge and Frame, 1983).

Applications. Dodge's work suggests that social-cognitive interventions aimed at teaching aggressive boys to accurately interpret the intentional cues of others may help reduce their aggressive behavior. Once aggressive children's appraisal of others begins to change, peers need to be taught to view them differently, so that past reputations of aggressive children do not continue to provoke antagonistic reactions that serve to perpetuate their overly hostile view of the world.

could at earlier stages. However, they cannot move outside a two-person situation and view it from a third-party perspective.

> *Typical response to the "Holly" dilemma*: When asked what punishment Holly might regard as fair if she climbs the tree, the child responds, "None. (Holly) knows that her father will understand why she climbed the tree, so she knows that he won't punish her at all" (Selman, 1976, p. 305). This response indicates that Holly's point of view is influenced by her assumption that her father will be able to "step in her shoes" and understand her motives for saving the kitten.

Level 3: Third-party or mutual perspective-taking (about 10–15 years). This individual can step outside a two-person situation and imagine how the self and other are viewed from a third-party "generalized other" position. The third party can be a typical member of a group or class of people (e.g., other children or parents) or simply a disinterested spectator. Assuming a third-party position enables the Level 3 youngster to engage in mutual perspective-taking, which involves looking at the relationship between two perspectives simultaneously. Mutual perspective-taking is *recursive*, in that the person's viewpoint can take itself as an object of thought. For example, the individual can imagine that "Holly thinks that her father thinks that she thinks. . . ."

> *Typical response to the "Holly" dilemma*: To the question of whether Holly should be punished by her father, a Level 3 youngster says: "No, because Holly thought it was important to save the kitten. But she also knows that her father told her not to climb the tree and that he didn't know about the kitten, so she'd only think that she shouldn't be punished if she could get her father to understand why she thought it was important to climb the tree." This response steps outside the immediate situation to view both Holly's and her father's perspectives simultaneously. In addition, it has a recursive quality, in that Holly's viewpoint takes itself as an object of thought.

◆　　　　CONTEMPORARY ISSUES: SOCIAL POLICY　　　　◆

Children's Eyewitness Testimony in Court Proceedings　　　　Box 11.3

Increasingly, children are being called on to testify in court cases involving child abuse and neglect, child custody, adoption, and other civil and criminal matters. Having to provide such testimony can be difficult and traumatic. Children are confronted with a strange and unfamiliar situation—at the very least an interview in the judge's chambers and at most an open courtroom with an audience of judge, jury, and spectators and the possibility of unsympathetic cross-examination. Moreover, they may be asked to give testimony against a parent or other relative toward whom they have strong feelings of loyalty. For these reasons, when children's eyewitness accounts are not absolutely necessary, it is best to protect them from having to testify. Nevertheless, their testimony is often essential. For example, in allegations of child abuse, the child is not only the victim, but often the only witness to the crime.

Once a child's testimony is deemed important, judgments must be made concerning whether the child is mature enough to provide reliable and accurate information. Although some states have legal rules that exclude very young children from testifying, in others the court makes a judgment about each child's competence (Bulkley, 1989; Ross, Miller, & Moran, 1987). Nevertheless, it is rare for children under age 5 to be asked to testify, while those 6 years of age and older often are, and children between the ages of 10 and 14 are generally assumed sufficiently mature to appear in court (Saywitz, 1987). These guidelines make good sense in view of what we know about the development of children's social-cognitive capacities. Compared to preschoolers, school-age children are better able to give detailed descriptions of past experiences, make accurate inferences about others' motives and intentions, and base their judgments on many different pieces of information instead of just a single event. Also, older children are more resistant to misleading and suggestive questions of the sort asked by attorneys when they probe for more information or, in cross-examination, try to influence the content of the child's response (Goodman, Aman, & Hirschman, 1987; Wells et al., 1989).

Still, each child's competence to testify should be reviewed on an individual basis. When children are under stress, as is the case after a traumatic experience

Level 4: In-depth and societal perspective-taking (about 14 years–adult). This stage is marked by an appreciation that mutual coordination of perspectives can take place at progressively deeper levels of understanding, from shared information to common interests and expectations to unverbalized feelings and values. However, each of these levels is understood as influenced by one of a number of possible societal perspectives, such as "the American viewpoint," "the democratic viewpoint," or "the Judeo-Christian perspective." Thus, a distinguishing feature of this stage is the capacity to view mutual perspective-taking as shaped by one or more systems of larger societal values:

> *Response to the "Holly" dilemma:* At this level, the individual can make reference to societal values in deciding whether Holly should save the kitten, how her father should view her action, and whether he should punish her. For example, a Level 4 adolescent might suggest that the value of humane treatment of animals justifies Holly's retrieval of the kitten and that her father's appreciation of this value will lead him not to punish her.

Research Confirming Selman's Developmental Sequence. As shown in Table 11.1, responses of cross-sectional samples to Selman's dilemmas indicate that maturity of perspective-taking rises steadily with age. In addition, longitudinal research reveals gradual movement to the next higher stage over a period of two to five years, with no subjects skipping stages and practically none regressing to a previous stage (Gurucharri & Selman, 1982; Selman, 1980). These findings provide strong support for Selman's assumption that perspective-taking skills develop in an age-related, invariant sequence.

In addition, advances in perspective-taking are related to nonsocial-cognitive capacities. Maturity of perspective-taking is moderately correlated with general intelligence (Rubin, 1973, 1978). It is also associated with Piagetian cognitive perform-

or separation from abusive, neglectful, or divorcing parents, they may experience distortions in social-cognitive processes. Misperceptions, misidentifications, overgeneralizations, and other errors in thinking can occur, seriously diminishing the child's accuracy as a witness (Peters, 1987). However, when properly questioned and protected against memory-distorting experiences, even preschoolers can recount episodes they have witnessed with considerable accuracy (although they provide less complete descriptions than older youngsters). To ease the stress of providing information, some legal representatives use alternative interviewing methods, such as puppets who ask questions and through which the child answers. Courts have also made efforts to reduce the incidence of repeated questioning (which can confuse children and lead to distorted renditions) by arranging joint interviews with several professionals or videotaping a single session (Bulkley, 1989; Raskin & Yuille, 1989).

Children judged competent as witnesses need to be prepared so that they understand the courtroom process and know what to expect. Below age 8, children exhibit considerable misunderstanding of the legal process and

how it works. The roles of judge, attorney, and police are yet not clearly differentiated, and many regard the court negatively, as "a room you pass through on your way to jail" (Saywitz, 1989, p. 149; Warren-Leubecker et al., 1989). In some places, "court schools" exist where children are prepared for trial through exposure to the physical setting and court personnel and opportunities to role-play courtroom activities. As part of this process children can be encouraged to admit not knowing an answer rather than guessing or going along with what an adult appears to expect of them (Cole & Loftus, 1987). If the child is likely to experience emotional trauma or later retribution (e.g., in a family dispute) as a result of appearing in court, then mechanisms exist for adapting typical courtroom procedures. Children may testify over closed circuit TV or behind a screen where they do not have visual access to the defendant. When it is not wise for the child to participate directly, expert witnesses can provide testimony that reports on the child's psychological condition and that contains important elements of the child's story (Bulkley, 1989).

Table 11.1. Percentage of Subjects Reaching Each of Selman's Perspective-Taking Levels Between 4 Years of Age and Adulthood

LEVEL	AGE 4	AGE 6	AGE 8	AGE 10	AGE 13	AGE 16	ADULT
0	80	10	0	0	0	0	0
1	20	90	40	20	7	0	0
2	0	0	50	60	50	21	0
3	0	0	10	20	36	58	0
4	—	—	—	—	7	21	100

Source: From R. L. Selman & D. F. Byrne, 1974, "A Structural-Developmental Analysis of Levels of Role Taking in Middle Childhood," *Child Development, 45,* 803–806. © The Society for Research in Child Development, Inc. Additional data from D. F. Byrne, 1973, "The Development of Role Taking in Adolescence," unpublished doctoral dissertation, Harvard University.

ance. Individuals who fail Piaget's concrete operational tasks tend to be at Selman's Level 0, those who pass concrete but not formal operational tasks tend to be at Levels 1 and 2, and those who are increasingly formal operational tend to be at Levels 3 and 4 (Keating & Clark, 1980; Krebs & Gillmore, 1982). These findings offer additional support for Selman's developmental sequence as a stage-wise progression. Research also indicates that attainment of each Piagetian cognitive stage tends to occur somewhat earlier than its related perspective-taking level (Krebs & Gillmore, 1982; Walker, 1980). Because Piagetian milestones are reached first and are not a perfect guarantee of parallel perspective-taking competence, they are regarded as *necessary but not sufficient conditions* for the attainment of Selman's perspective-taking stages. Investigators believe that additional (as yet unidentified) social-cognitive competencies are also required. As Shantz (1983) points out, we still do not know much about the precise processes that underlie and facilitate perspective-taking skills.

Besides responses to social dilemmas, "games and the delights of deception" offer ideal opportunities to study children's perspective-taking (Selman, 1980, p. 49). For example, Taylor (1988) played a clever "privileged information" game with 3- to 8-year-old children, who were given three facts about animals depicted in line drawings: the animal's identity (e.g., giraffe), what the animal was doing (the giraffe was sitting down), and personal information about the animal (the giraffe's name was George). Then the drawing was covered up, and the children were asked what a naive puppet who saw only a small, nondescript part of the animal knew about it. Much like the change between Selman's Level 0 and Level 1, a steady age-related increase in children's ability to take the perspective of the puppet occurred. Below age 6, most children thought that seeing an unidentifiable part of an animal permitted the puppet to discern the animal's identity. Nevertheless, younger children demonstrated some subjective perspective-taking skill, in that they did not attribute everything they knew to an uninformed observer. Only some of the preschoolers believed that after seeing a small part of the animal, the puppet knew what the animal was doing and had access to personal information about it.[5]

A large number of gamelike tasks have focused on the development of **recursive thought,** the reflective, self-embedded cognitive endeavor that involves thinking about what another person is thinking. Selman's theory suggests that the ability to think recursively undergoes rapid improvement during the early to midadolescent years, a trend that has been confirmed in numerous studies. For example, Miller, Kessel, and Flavell (1970) asked first- through sixth-grade children to verbally de-

[5] Recall from an earlier section of this chapter that very young preschoolers realize that another person can hold false beliefs. This finding also indicates that Level 1 (subjective) perspective-taking starts to emerge earlier than Selman anticipated, although preschoolers' understanding of it is not yet complete (Pillow, 1988).

scribe cartoon drawings depicting one- and two-loop recursive thinking (see Figure 11.4). As expected, one-loop recursions were achieved before two-loop recursions. However, at sixth grade, only 50 percent of the children displayed simple recursive thought, and two-loop recursions were rare. By midadolescence, young people have mastered the complexities of recursive understanding (Flavell et al., 1968).

The recursive thought that grows out of advances in perspective-taking has been of particular interest to child development specialists, since it is one feature of human social interaction that makes it truly reciprocal and interactive (Shultz, 1980). In everyday conversations, people depend on recursive thinking to clear up misunderstandings, as when they say, "I thought you would think I was just kidding when I said that." Recursive thought is also involved in our attempts to disguise our real feelings and cognitions (e.g., "He'll think I'm jealous if I tell him I don't like his new car, so I'll pretend I do") (Perner, 1988). Finally, recursive reflection is an integral part of the intense self-focusing and preoccupation with an imaginary audience that is typical of early adolescence. As Miller, Kessel, and Flavell (1970) point out, "Often to their pain, adolescents are much more gifted at this sort of wondering than first graders are" (p. 623).

Perspective-Taking and Social Behavior. Children's developing ability to understand the perspectives of others provides an important basis for effective interpersonal behavior. As early as the preschool years, children's budding recognition that others may have momentary needs different from their own underlies their altruistic attempts to share, help, and comfort others. Eisenberg-Berg and Neal (1979) waited in a nursery school until 4- and 5-year-old children engaged in a spontaneous altruistic act and then immediately asked them, "Why did you do that?" Nearly a quarter of the answers referred to the needs of others (e.g., "He's hungry." "He can't carry it by himself"). Stereotypical and approval-oriented reasons for behaving prosocially (e.g., "It's nice to help." "My teacher wants us to") were rare.

In studies using laboratory tasks and games, perspective-taking is also related to effective interpersonal behavior, including altruism and *social problem solving,* or the ability to think of effective ways of handling difficult social situations (Barnett, King, & Howard, 1979; Buckley, Siegel, & Ness, 1979; Cutrona & Feshbach, 1979; Eisen-

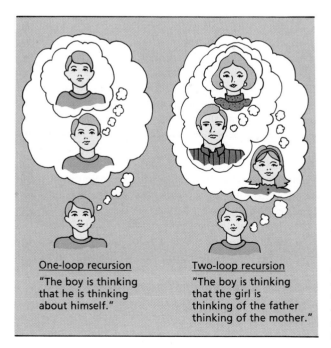

Figure 11.4. Cartoon drawings depicting recursive thinking in the Miller, Kessel, and Flavell (1970) study. *(From P. H. Miller, F. S. Kessel, & J. H. Flavell, 1970, "Thinking about People Thinking about People Thinking about . . . . : A Study of Social Cognitive Development," 41, 613–623. © The Society for Research in Child Development, Inc. Reprinted by permission.)*

One-loop recursion
"The boy is thinking that he is thinking about himself."

Two-loop recursion
"The boy is thinking that the girl is thinking of the father thinking of the mother."

berg-Berg & Hand, 1979; Marsh, Serafica, & Barenboim, 1981). Also, good perspective-takers tend to be sociable and especially well liked by their peers (Deutsch, 1974; LeMare & Rubin, 1987; Rubin & Maioni, 1975). Nevertheless, some contradictory relationships between perspective-taking and interpersonal functioning have emerged, indicating that the relationship of perspective-taking to social behavior is, in reality, quite complex and moderated by other factors.

A careful examination of the research reveals that a wide array of tasks and social situations have been used to relate perspective-taking to social functioning, only some of which produce positive results. In those that do, the recipients of the child's helpfulness, generosity, comfort, and cooperation tend to be hypothetical peers or peers actually known to the subject child rather than strange adults. Perhaps at first children are better at taking the perspective of another person with whom they share common experiences; only later do they become adept at putting themselves in the place of people whose backgrounds differ from their own (Chandler & Helm, 1984).

In addition, perspective-taking tasks that are good predictors of positive interpersonal behavior frequently require children to comprehend another person's feeling state (Iannotti, 1985). When children appreciate the affective states of others, this increases the likelihood that they will empathize, a response that makes the other's needs and feelings even more salient and increases the chances that children will act on their awareness. In contrast, other perspective-taking tasks — ones that require the child to imagine what an opponent is thinking in a competitive game or describe how different characters view a scene in a story — often show no relationship to prosocial behavior or, on occasion, even evoke responses that are incompatible with it. In one study, elementary school pupils who did well on these kinds of tasks were actually rated by their teachers as *more* disruptive in the classroom (Kurdek, 1978). These results indicate that, depending on the context in which perspective-taking and social behavior are assessed, skilled perspective-takers may be as adept at defending and supporting their own viewpoints as they are at cooperating with and helping other people. In fact, a few mildly antisocial behaviors, such as knowing how to needle your sister in order to triumphantly "get her goat," sometimes make use of masterful perspective-taking capacities.

Even the ability to appreciate other people's feelings does not uniformly lead to altruistic behavior, partly because additional factors, such as temperament and personality, affect the extent to which children will act on their social cognitions. Barrett and Yarrow (1977) found that among 5- to 8-year-old children who scored high in affective perspective-taking, assertiveness was the crucial factor in determining whether they spontaneously helped their peers. In another study, shy, withdrawn preschoolers less often lent a helping hand to a strange adult in need than their more gregarious counterparts (Stanhope, Bell, & Parker-Cohen, 1987). Thus, although perspective-taking is evident in a great many prosocial acts, being skilled at it does not guarantee altruistic responding, since social behavior is multiply determined — by social-cognitive functioning, personality characteristics, and situational conditions.

Nevertheless, among youngsters who display extremes of antisocial behavior, substantial developmental delays in perspective-taking have been found. Chronic delinquents have a limited capacity to imagine the thoughts and feelings of others (Chandler, 1973; Lee & Prentice, 1988), a social-cognitive deficit that could be responsible for the fact that they mistreat and manipulate others for their own ends without experiencing guilt and remorse. In one investigation, delinquents between the ages of 11 and 15 achieved perspective-taking scores that were so immature that they resembled the performance of children only half their age (Chandler, 1973). Because severe deficits in perspective-taking may help to sustain antisocial activity in aggressive and delinquent youths, investigators have experimented with techniques that induce perspective-taking as a way to lessen antisocial behavior and facilitate prosocial responding.

Research shows that children who display extremes of antisocial behavior have a limited capacity to imagine the thoughts and feelings of others.

Training Perspective-Taking Skills. Interventions that encourage children and adolescents to set aside their own egocentric vantage points and assume either real-world or fantasy-type roles can improve perspective-taking. Chandler (1973) had delinquent boys make up, act out, and videotape brief skits about people their own age. At the end of a 10-session training period, delinquent boys showed significant gains in perspective-taking when compared to a control group participating in a film-making activity that did not offer role-taking practice. Furthermore, improved perspective-taking was associated with a substantial reduction in delinquent behavior over a subsequent 18-month period. Recently, these findings were replicated with a sample of delinquent girls (Chalmers & Townsend, 1990).

In Chapter 6, we showed that sociodramatic play involving role enactment leads to advances in perspective-taking among preschoolers. The same seems to be true for older children and adolescents who are very poor perspective-takers. That perspective-taking and everyday social functioning undergo simultaneous improvement after a relatively short-term intervention provides additional support for the central role of this social-cognitive skill in effective human interaction.

BRIEF REVIEW

A number of important changes in children's understanding of other people occur over childhood and adolescence. Like self-concept, person perception shifts from a focus on concrete, observable characteristics to descriptions of unique psychological dispositions during the elementary school years. The ability to infer others' intentions from their ongoing stream of behavior emerges during the preschool period and is refined in middle childhood. Children's understanding of others' viewpoints undergoes vast changes from early childhood into adolescence. It begins with rudimentary awareness that others have thoughts and feelings different from those of the self and evolves into advanced societal and recursive perspective-taking capacities. Advances in perspective-taking build on Piagetian cognitive-developmental milestones and are related to a wide variety of social skills.

As children develop, they apply their capacity to appreciate the inner psychological worlds of themselves and others to an understanding of relations between people. A relatively recent focus in social cognition has to do with how children reason about dyadic relationships, including friendship and conflict, and how their increasingly sophisticated insights affect their social behavior.

Understanding Friendship

Stages of Friendship Relations. To an adult, friendship is not a one-sided relationship. It is not enough to just like or be attracted to another person. You can like someone without being a friend to that person, since your liking may not be reciprocated. Instead, friendship is a mutually satisfying psychological relationship involving companionship, sharing, understanding of thoughts and feelings, and caring for and comforting one another in times of need. In addition, a friendship is a relationship that endures over time and transcends occasional conflicts.

Children's ideas about friendship do not start out this way. Several investigators have conducted interviews with preschool through adolescent youngsters, generally by asking them to name a best friend, explain why that child is a friend, and indicate what they expect of a close friend. Another technique is to present children with story dilemmas about friendship that tap such issues as motives for friendship formation, characteristics of friendships, ways in which good friends resolve conflicts, and how and why friendships break up. From children's responses, several theories of children's conceptions of friendship have emerged (Damon, 1977; Selman, 1980, 1981; Youniss, 1975; Youniss & Volpe, 1978). All emphasize that an understanding of friendship evolves from a concrete, behavioral relationship based on sharing material goods and pleasurable activity to a more abstract conception based on mutual consideration and psychological satisfaction. Damon (1977) has synthesized the developmental progressions of other investigators into a three-stage sequence, as follows:

Level 1: Friendship as a handy playmate[6] (about 5–7 years). During this stage, friendship is concrete and activity-based. Friends are regarded as associates with whom one frequently plays, and friendship is affirmed by giving or sharing material goods. As yet, there is no sense of liking or disliking the personality traits of the other person, since (as we saw earlier) young children have little appreciation of the unique psychological characteristics of self and other. Because friendship is merely pleasurable play association and material exchange, young children regard it as easily begun—for example, simply by meeting in the neighborhood and saying, "Hi." However, it does not yet have a long-term, enduring quality. Level 1 children indicate that a friendship is easily terminated by refusing to share, hitting, or not being available to meet and play. The following response from a 5-year-old boy to the question "What makes a good friend?" sums up the Level 1 child's view of friendship: "Boys play with boys, trucks play with trucks, dogs play with dogs." When the interviewer probed, "Why does that make them good friends?" the child answered, "Because they do the same things" (Selman, 1980, p. 136).

Level 2: Friendship as mutual trust and assistance (about 8–10 years). During middle childhood, friendship becomes a consensual relationship in which both parties respond to each other's needs and desires. Since friendship is now a matter of mutual consent, getting it started is not as simple as it was at an earlier age. Older children regard it as important to *offer* to get together or *invite* another child to play, an action that assumes willing participation by both individuals. As in the previous

---

[6] Titles for each of the stages have been provided by this author to help you remember them.

stage, friendship can be affirmed by gift-giving and other material offers. However, it goes beyond these concrete exchanges to include help-giving and other acts of kindness that signify that each person can be counted on to support and not harm or take advantage of the other. Thus, mutual trust becomes a central defining element of friendship, and older elementary school children regard violations of trust, such as not helping when the other needs help, breaking promises, or gossiping behind the other's back, as serious breaches of friendship expectations. At younger ages, friendships simply resume after squabbles over activities and material possessions dissipate. In contrast, at this level, friendship violations require some acknowledgment that trust has been broken, in the form of apologies and explanations, to reinstate the former relationship. Finally, Level 2 respondents recognize that friendship involves psychological and not just concrete elements, and they like or dislike others on the basis of their inferred dispositions. The following response of an 8-year-old child to queries about her best friend illustrates some of the qualities of a Level 2 friendship:

> Who is your best friend? *Shelly.* Why is Shelly your best friend? *Because she helps when I'm getting beaten up, she cheers me when I'm sad, and she shares.* Do you share with Shelly? *Yes. I share so she'll share. . . .* How come you like Shelly better than anyone else? *She's done the most for me. She never disagrees, she never eats in front of me, she never walks away when I'm crying, and she helps me on my schoolwork.* (Damon, 1977, pp. 159–160)

Level 3: Friendship as intimacy and mutual understanding (11–15 years and older). By early adolescence, conceptions of friendship take on greater depth. Friends are now regarded as people who understand and accept one another as individuals and who share their innermost thoughts and feelings. Because friendship has this depth dimension to it, adolescents regard it as a stable relationship that is established and affirmed over a long period of time by "getting to know someone," and a good friendship rests on impressions of one another that promote feelings of compatibility and closeness. Since each party knows the other well, friendships are regarded as important in alleviating psychological problems, such as loneliness, sadness, and fear. Also, because true mutual understanding implies forgiveness, only serious disaffection and breaches of the relationship can lead Level 3 friendships to dissolve. One Level 3 early adolescent characterized his best friendship as follows:

> *Well, you need someone you can tell anything to, all kinds of things that you don't want spread around. That's why you're someone's friend.* Is that why Jimmy is your friend? Because he can keep a secret? *Yes, and we like the same kinds of things. We speak the same language. My mother says we're two peas in a pod. . . .* Do you ever get mad at Jimmy? *Not really.* What if he did something that got you really mad? *He'd still be my best friend. I'd tell him what he did wrong and maybe he'd understand. I could be wrong too, it depends.* (Damon, 1977, p. 163)

Many studies report findings that are in remarkable agreement with this developmental progression. For example, Bigelow (1977; Bigelow & LaGaipa, 1975) analyzed first through eighth graders' essays about expectations of a best friend and found three clusters of friendship expectations, each emerging at successive ages and showing close agreement with the stages described above (see Table 11.2). Longitudinal research yields similar developmental trends (Keller & Wood, 1989). Moreover, virtually every study shows that while more psychological conceptions of friendship emerge with age, earlier concepts, such as engaging in common activities, are not relinquished (e.g., Furman & Bierman, 1983). Instead, they are reconceptualized and integrated into successively higher levels. As additional support for a stage-wise progression of friendship understanding, Selman (1981) found that friendship reasoning is related to advances in perspective-taking. We would certainly expect this to be the case, since attainment of the higher perspective-taking levels implies consciousness of others' thoughts, motives, and feelings. Finally, reference to the intimacy and faithfulness of friends is more common among girls than boys (Furman &

Table 11.2. Children's Changing Expectations of Their Friends from First through Eighth Grade

GRADES 1–3 SITUATIONAL EXPECTATIONS	GRADES 4–5 NORMATIVE EXPECTATIONS	GRADES 6–8 INTERNAL PSYCHOLOGICAL EXPECTATIONS
Propinquity (physical nearness)	Character admiration	Acceptance
Common activities		Loyalty and commitment
Evaluation		Genuineness
		Common interests
		Intimacy potential

Source: Bigelow, 1977.

Buhrmester, 1985; Hunter & Youniss, 1982). This finding is probably explained by societal sex-role standards that permit girls to be more open and expressive of their inner feelings.

Are Children's Developing Conceptions of Friendship Related to Features of Their Real Friendships? If social understanding plays a vital role in everyday relationships and behavior, then children's changing ideas about friendship should predict a number of age-related changes in the qualities of their real friendships.

First, we would expect friendships to show greater stability as mutual trust and loyalty become more important in what one expects of a friend. In general, research bears out this prediction. In a study in which mutual friendship choices of first, fourth, and eighth graders were assessed in both the fall and spring of the school year, friendships did become more stable from first to fourth grade, although the number of stable friendships showed no change from fourth to eighth grade. However, the researchers discovered that eighth graders permitted a larger number of friendships to dissolve than younger children and were reluctant to add new people to their friendship repertoire. As adolescents place a higher premium on friendships with psychological depth and intimacy, they seem to restrict their friendships to people with whom they feel comfortable sharing their innermost thoughts. An eighth grader expressed this idea when he explained why one of his friendships ended, saying, "[name of friend] is trying to single out his friends now. At the beginning of the year, he was friends with almost everybody because he wanted to be friends over [during] the school year with a lot of kids. Now he's singling out best friends" (Berndt & Hoyle, 1985, p. 1013).

Although changes in friendship stability do occur, it is important to note that children's friendships are actually remarkably stable at all ages. Even during the preschool years, two thirds of children who identify one another as friends do so again four to six months later (Gershman & Hayes, 1983). However, lasting friendships at younger ages are more a function of the constancy of social environments—the preschool and the neighborhood—than of social-cognitive processes. In one study, preschoolers maintained friendships across a summer vacation period only if parents made special arrangements for mutual home visits and periods of interaction (Schaivo & Solomon, 1981).

In addition to stability, mature conceptions of friendship should lead older children to behave with more mutual responsiveness, sympathetic understanding, and altruism toward friends. Actually, positive social exchange and mutuality occur more among friends than nonfriends at all ages (Hartup, 1983). Masters and Furman (1981) observed 4- and 5-year-olds at play and found that children gave twice as much positive reinforcement, in the form of greetings, praise, and compliance, to friends than nonfriends, and they also received more from them. In addition, when friends participate in joint activities, they are more interactive and emotionally expressive, talking, laughing, and looking at each other to a greater extent than in nonfriendship interactions. Similarly, the conversational strategies of friends are more mutually directed (e.g., "Let's do it this way") as opposed to being aimed at the other person as an individual (e.g., "Put your piece over there") (Newcomb, Brady, & Hartup, 1979). In several studies in which friends and nonfriends worked on challenging tasks together, the greater social responsiveness and harmonious interaction of friends led to more extensive exploration of materials and improved problem-solving performance (Nelson & Aboud, 1985; Newcomb, Brady, & Hartup, 1979; Schwartz, 1972). Apparently, sensitivity, spontaneity, and intimacy characterize friendship relations very early, although verbalizing that these qualities are essential to a good friendship does not occur until later ages.

Altruism among friends does increase over middle childhood. When pairs of children worked on a task that allowed them to help and share with each other, fourth graders helped more than first graders did (Berndt, 1981). Generosity and helpfulness toward friends undergo additional increments from middle childhood into adolescence (Berndt, 1985). In fact, one study showed that fifth- and sixth-grade children who had close friendships, in contrast to ones who did not, performed better on an affective perspective-taking task, and when observed at school, they behaved more altruistically toward others in general (McGuire & Weisz, 1982). Many altruistic behaviors may emerge first in the context of friendship and then generalize to other people.

Elementary school children do not just behave more prosocially with their friends; when paired with one another in competitive games, they freely compete with each other to a greater extent than nonfriends. Since children regard friendship as based on equality, they seem especially concerned about losing a contest to a friend (Berndt, 1988). Moreover, school-age friends openly express disagreement on topics about which they hold differing opinions (Nelson & Aboud, 1985). As early as middle

In schools and neighborhoods where interracial contact is common, many children form close cross-race friendships.

childhood, friends seem to be secure enough in their mutual approval of one another to risk being direct and open about their different points of view. As a result, friendship probably provides an important context in which children learn to tolerate argument, criticism, and disagreement.

The value that adolescents accord to feeling especially "in sync" with their close associates would lead us to expect friends to increasingly resemble one another in attitudes and values at older ages. In line with this expectation, during adolescence, stable friendship pairs, in contrast to those that dissolve, are more alike in educational aspirations, political values, and tendency to use drugs and engage in minor delinquent acts. Friendships may also have a socializing influence on attitudes and values, since adolescents who choose to continue their friendship become even more similar in these psychological characteristics over time (Kandel, 1978a).

Nevertheless, research reveals that the attributes on which friends are most alike throughout childhood and adolescence are not psychological characteristics, but age, race, and sex (Duck, 1975; Kandel, 1978b; Singleton & Asher, 1979).[7] These findings indicate that an inclination to make friends with children who are like the self in observable characteristics is present at an early age. However, the association of these factors with friendship choice is, to some extent, the result of school and neighborhood contexts as well as adult influence and social pressures. In a recent investigation of junior high school pupils attending an integrated school, DuBois and Hirsch (1990) found that over 50 percent of seventh to ninth graders reported at least one close cross-race school friendship — that is, with a child different from the self. But cross-race friendship interaction seldom extended to out-of-school contexts unless children lived in integrated neighborhoods where interracial contact was common.

Do adolescent friends, because of the greater intimacy of their relationship, "know" each other better as individuals than their younger grade school counterparts? It appears that they do. In a study in which fourth and eighth graders were asked about their best friend's personality, preferences, and typical behavioral and emotional reactions, accuracy of knowledge (determined by comparing the child's responses with the friend's self-reports) increased with age. No age changes occurred in knowledge of external characteristics, such as birth date and phone number (Diaz & Berndt, 1982).

Taken together, the research described above indicates that as children get older, greater stability, prosocial responding, psychological similarity, and intimate personal knowledge characterize their friendship relations. These developmental trends fit with children's changing understanding of friendship. Because friendships are based on emotional sensitivity and social reciprocity between individuals who meet on an equal footing, they provide children with invaluable contexts in which they can learn to resolve social conflicts, form new attachments, and get to know another person as a unique individual. In fact, friendships may be as vital for development as early family attachments. Several decades ago, noted psychiatrist Harry Stack Sullivan (1953) wrote about the significance of friendship:

> if you will look very closely at one of your children when he finally finds a chum — somewhere between eight-and-a-half and ten — you will discover something very different in the relationship — namely, that your child begins to develop a real sensitivity to what matters to another person. And this is not in the sense of "what should I do to get what I want," but instead "what should I do to contribute to the happiness or to support the prestige and feeling of worthwhileness of my chum." So far as I have been

---

[7] Although opposite-sex peer associations increase during early adolescence, stable friendships continue to be limited to members of the same sex throughout the adolescent years. In a survey of 1,879 high school students between the ages of 13 and 18, a total of 91 percent reported best-friend choices that were restricted to members of the same sex (Kandel, 1978b).

able to discover, nothing remotely like this appears before. . . . Thus the developmental epoch of preadolescence is marked by the coming of integrating tendencies which, when they are completely developed, we call love. . . . (pp. 245–246)

Research on the development of children's friendship relations bears out Sullivan's vision.

Understanding Social Conflict: Social Problem Solving

Children, even when they are best friends, come into conflict with one another. Recall from Chapter 6 that social conflict was accorded an important role in development by Piaget, who believed that peer interactions involving arguments and disagreements help children overcome their egocentrism. According to Piaget, social conflict prods children to scrutinize their own viewpoints and the merits of their own reasoning. This, in turn, facilitates their cognitive development as well as their ability to engage in effective, mutually satisfying social discourse (Piaget, 1923/1926).

As Shantz (1987) points out, adults often equate children's conflicts with aggression and socially disruptive behavior. Although conflicts occasionally resolve into aggression, intensely hostile reactions among children are rare. Instead, arguments, disagreements, refusals, denials, and opposition are far more typical. Furthermore, conflicts are not very frequent when compared to children's harmonious interactions (Hay, 1984). When conflicts do occur, most are brief in duration and settled by children themselves (Bakeman & Brownlee, 1982; O'Keefe & Benoit, 1982).

Despite their infrequency and brevity, peer conflicts are not unimportant. Watch children work out their disputes over possession and use of play objects ("That's mine!" "I had it first!"), entry into and control over the social environment ("I'm on your team, Jerry." "No you're not!"), and disagreements over ideas, facts, and beliefs ("I'm taller than he is." "No you aren't!"). You will see that children take these matters quite seriously. Recent research reveals that social conflicts offer children invaluable learning opportunities in **social problem solving.** In their efforts to resolve conflict effectively — in ways that are socially acceptable but at the same time achieve results that are beneficial to the self — children must bring together a variety of social-cognitive skills. These include encoding and interpreting social information pertaining to a social goal, generating alternative strategies for reaching the goal, and evaluating the effectiveness of these strategies as a prelude to selecting one and translating it into a behavioral response. Dodge (1986) regards social problem solving as a special, interpersonal form of the more general problem-solving process. He organizes the steps of social problem solving into the temporal sequence depicted in Figure 11.5.

With age, children become more proficient social problem solvers in both hypothetical and real-life situations. But at all ages, substantial individual differences exist, and social problem solving is currently regarded as one of the most important dimensions of social competence (Rubin & Krasnor, 1985; Shantz, 1983).

The Development of Social Problem Solving. Spivack and Shure (1974) initiated the large body of research that now exists on social problem solving. They focused on the strategy generation part of the process by asking young children to think of as many possible ways as they could for dealing with hypothetical conflicts, such as wanting to play with a toy someone else has. Spivack and Shure's work, along with more recent findings, indicates that the ability to flexibly generate a variety of solutions to hypothetical social conflicts increases over the preschool and early school years. Also, children's repertoire of problem-solving strategies is moderately related to friendly, sociable peer interaction and teacher ratings of social adjustment (Dubow & Tisak, 1989; Rubin & Krasnor, 1985; Spivack & Shure, 1974).

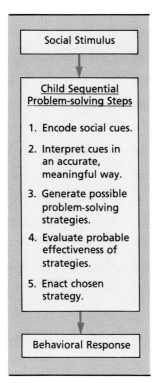

Figure 11.5. A social problem-solving flowchart. *(Adapted from Dodge, 1986.)*

Besides quantity of strategies, the quality of strategies generated by children changes with age. During elementary school, younger children, as well as children with especially poor peer relations, describe strategies that impulsively meet their own needs, such as grabbing, physically pushing away another child, or ordering another to do what one wants. Older children and those with good peer relations assert the self's needs in ways that take into account the needs of others, such as friendly persuasion and compromise (Downey & Walker, 1989; Renshaw & Asher, 1983; Rubin & Daniels-Beirness, 1983; Selman et al., 1983; Selman & Demorest, 1984).

Recently, investigators have expanded their study of social problem solving in an effort to find out at what other points, besides strategy generation, things may go awry for children who have difficulty getting along with peers. In one study, Dodge and his collaborators (1986) assessed grade-school children's skillfulness at each of the five problem-solving steps depicted in Figure 11.5. A videotape presented children with a dramatized problem involving how best to gain entry into a play group situation. In the first scene, two children were seated at a table playing a board game, and the investigators assessed each subject's ability to *encode and correctly interpret social cues* about the video characters' willingness to let the subject join the game. Then subjects were asked to *generate strategies* for joining the game, and their responses were coded into one of five categories: competent (polite requests to play and other friendly comments); aggressive (threats, physical violence, or barging in without permission); self-centered (statements about the self, such as "Hey, I know how to play that"); passive (shy, hovering responses, such as waiting or "hanging around"); and authority intervention ("The teacher said I could play"). Next, children viewed five more scenes in which a child tried to enter the game using each of the strategy types noted above, and the subject was asked to engage in *strategy evaluation* by indicating whether or not the particular technique would succeed. Finally, children engaged in *strategy enactment* by demonstrating a way of asking to join the game. In a separate session, Dodge examined children's actual social competence in the laboratory by having them try to gain entry into a real peer group activity. Results showed that all five social problem-solving skills predicted children's performance. In a second investigation, the predictability of the social-cognitive measures generalized to children's group entry effectiveness on their school playground.

Perhaps you have already noticed, on the basis of the flowchart depicted in Figure 11.5, that Dodge takes an *information processing* approach to the study of social problem solving. Information processing research in the social-cognitive arena is aimed at finding out precisely how a child thinks in the process of social negotiations and how a particular set of processing steps results in a social response. Once this is known, specific processing deficits at the heart of the social incompetencies of particular children can be assessed, and individualized treatment programs can be implemented.

Social information processing has just begun to infiltrate research on social development. Nevertheless, research like that of Dodge and his co-workers is an indication that the study of social-cognitive development may follow in the footsteps of its nonsocial-cognitive partner. In our efforts to explain and predict children's social behavior, social information processing may very well be an important wave of the future.

Training Social Problem Solving. Recent evidence indicates that intervening with children who are deficient social problem solvers is especially important. Besides improving peer relations, effective social problem solving reduces the risk of maladjustment among children from distressed family backgrounds (Downey & Walker, 1989; Pettit, Dodge, & Brown, 1988).

A well-known social problem-solving training program has been developed by Spivack and Shure (1974; Shure, 1981). During daily sessions over a number of months, preschool and kindergarten children participate in games involving puppet dramatizations of social problems and discussions about effective and ineffective means of resolving conflicts. In addition, teachers intervene as problems arise to point out consequences and suggest alternatives. After applying the training program in low-income inner city classrooms with children at risk for adjustment difficulties, Spivack and Shure found that trained pupils, in contrast to untrained controls, improved in both social reasoning and teacher-rated social adjustment. These gains were still evident a year after completion of training.

Spivack and Shure's findings have been replicated, and comparable interventions have proved effective with older elementary school children (Feis & Simons, 1985; Ridley & Vaughn, 1982; Stiefvater, Kurdek, & Allik, 1986). At present, investigators are not sure which training ingredients are most effective. Preliminary evidence indicates that practice in strategy enactment may need to accompany cognitive manipulations. Such practice makes new strategies more accessible and automatic, thereby increasing the likelihood that they will take precedence over old, maladaptive procedures (Mize & Ladd, 1988). Also, current programs have not been individually tailored to fit the social-cognitive deficits of particular children. However, it is in precisely these ways that the information processing approach to social problem solving promises to make a unique contribution.

On a final note, social-cognitive programs are not the only means for helping children with deficiencies in social competence. We consider other approaches, including reinforcement, modeling, and direct teaching of social skills, in Chapter 15.

BRIEF REVIEW

In the sections above, we have seen that children's conceptions of friendship evolve from an emphasis on shared activities and material goods to a concern with mutual trust and assistance over the middle childhood years. During adolescence, intimacy and mutual understanding become defining features of friendship. Consistent with these social-cognitive changes, children's real friendships reflect greater stability, altruism, shared values, and mutual knowledge of one another with age. During early and middle childhood, children become more effective negotiators of social conflict. Social problem solving is an important dimension of social competence that can be trained in children at risk for adjustment problems.

SOCIAL COGNITION IN CONTEXT

The vast changes in children's social-cognitive capacities that take place from infancy through adolescence are generally interpreted in terms of revisions in children's underlying mental structures. Throughout this chapter, we have emphasized this *cognitive-developmental approach* to social understanding because it has consumed the lion's share of research attention. As we conclude our discussion, it is only fair to note that a growing number of investigators regard inner cognitive forces as only one side of the social-cognitive story. They believe that age-related shifts in the social life of the child also play a powerful role (Damon & Hart, 1988; Graziano, Moore, & Collins, 1988; Higgins & Parsons, 1983; Lerner & Lerner, 1986).

Try to think of some important changes in children's social lives that could support the social-cognitive changes we have described. Higgins and Parsons (1983) suggest a number of intriguing possibilities. For example, entry into elementary school, where pupils observe agemates working on similar tasks and experience the semipublic evaluative judgments of teachers, probably encourages children to construct achievement-related attributions. During early adolescence, expanding social roles — student, employee, club member, leader, community volunteer, and friend — may augment perspective-taking competence. In addition, new social pressures — to achieve, decide on future goals, and get along with a diversity of people — may motivate adolescents to seek associates with whom they can share their anxieties, aspirations, and beliefs. As a result, intimate friendships are fostered.

As yet, these ideas about the connection between social experience and social understanding remain untested. Nevertheless, their plausibility suggests that in the years to come, social-cognitive theory is likely to become more *ecological* — regarding development as a joint product of children's inner cognitive capacities and the richness and diversity of their social worlds.

CHAPTER SUMMARY

Introduction

■ The development of **social cognition** deals with how children's understanding of themselves, other people, and relationships between people changes with age.

Conceptualizing the Self

■ Infants have completed the task of self-recognition by the end of the second year of life. During the preschool years, children start to construct a **self-concept,** or personal theory of what the self is like as an experiencing, functioning individual. A **categorical self** based on salient individual differences, such as sex and age, emerges with the capacity for representation and language. Young preschoolers are also aware of a private, **inner self** that is not accessible to others.

■ During middle childhood, self-concept changes from a catalogue of internal states and observable characteristics to an emphasis on unique psychological dispositions, a transformation that is facilitated by general cognitive development and perspective-taking skills. In adolescence, the self-concept becomes even more differentiated and subtle. In addition, adolescents emphasize interpersonal virtues in their self-descriptions, a change that reflects their increasing concern with being liked and viewed in a positive light by others.

■ **Self-esteem,** the evaluative side of self-concept, differentiates into a number of separate self-evaluations by 7 to 8 years of age, including academic, social, and physical self-worth. Around this time, children also build a global sense of self-esteem. Level of self-esteem declines over the early grade school years as children become increasingly sensitive to social comparison information. Except for a temporary dip in early adolescence, self-esteem rises from late childhood on. New responsibilities and greater independence that accompany growing up foster feelings of pride, self-confidence, and self-respect.

■ A warm, approving parenting style along with firm but reasonable expectations is positively related to self-esteem. However, the extent to which child-rearing practices cause changes in self-esteem is not clarified by these correlational findings.

■ Studies of children's achievement-related **attributions** have identified adult communication styles that do cause changes in self-esteem. Pupils with **mastery-oriented attri-**

butions credit their successes to high ability and their failures to insufficient effort. As a result, they approach learning tasks with enthusiasm and high expectancies of success. In contrast, children affected by **learned helplessness** attribute their failures to low ability. When faced with obstacles to task success, they show decreased persistence and signs of giving up. Children who consistently receive negative feedback about their ability develop the learned helpless pattern. **Attribution retraining** programs have succeeded in improving the self-evaluations and task performance of low-achieving and learned helpless youngsters.

■ Constructing an **identity** is a major task of the adolescent years. In complex societies, a period of exploration and self-searching is a necessary step before identity is achieved. For most young people, adolescence is not a period of storm and stress that engenders serious emotional turmoil. **Identity achievement** and **moratorium** are healthy approaches to identity formation. In contrast, **identity foreclosure** and **identity diffusion** are associated with less effective psychological functioning.

Conceptualizing Other People

■ Like self-concept, **person perception** places greater emphasis on unique psychological dispositions and becomes more differentiated and organized with age. By the end of the preschool years, children have developed a sophisticated set of rules for distinguishing intentional from unintentional acts. During middle childhood, children become more skilled at identifying efforts by others to conceal their true intentions.

■ **Perspective-taking** undergoes substantial development during childhood and adolescence, as Selman's five-stage theory indicates. Children's ability to understand the viewpoints of others provides an important basis for effective interpersonal functioning. Youngsters who show extremes of antisocial behavior are seriously delayed in the development of perspective-taking. These deficits can be reduced through training programs that encourage children and adolescents to step outside their egocentric vantage points.

Conceptualizing Relations between People

■ Children's understanding of friendship evolves from a concrete relationship based on sharing material goods and pleasurable activities to a more abstract conception based on mutual consideration, intimacy, and psychological satisfaction. In line with this trend, children's real friendships are characterized by more stability, prosocial responding, psychological similarity, and intimate personal knowledge with age.

■ As children get older, they become more effective at handling interpersonal conflict through **social problem solving.** All components of the social problem-solving process—encoding and interpretation of social cues and strategy generation, evaluation, and enactment—predict social competence. Children at risk for adjustment problems can be trained in effective social problem solving.

Social Cognition in Context

■ Besides inner cognitive forces, age-related changes in children's social lives are believed to affect social-cognitive development. However, the importance of children's expanding social worlds has not yet been investigated.

IMPORTANT TERMS AND CONCEPTS

social cognition   (p. 431)
self-concept   (p. 434)
categorical self   (p. 434)
inner self   (p. 435)
generalized other   (p. 436)
self-esteem   (p. 437)
attributions   (p. 441)
achievement motivation   (p. 441)
mastery-oriented
   attributions   (p. 442)

learned helplessness   (p. 442)
attribution retraining   (p. 444)
identity   (p. 444)
identity crisis   (p. 445)
identity achievement   (p. 446)
moratorium   (p. 446)
identity foreclosure   (p. 446)
identity diffusion   (p. 446)

person perception   (p. 449)
perspective-taking   (p. 451)
stages of perspective-taking
   skill   (p. 452–455)
recursive thought   (p. 456)
stages of friendship relations
   (p. 460–461)
social problem solving   (p. 465)

Boys Netting Crabs, by John Bulloch Souter.
Roy Miles Fine Paintings, London/Bridgeman Art Library.

12

The Development of Morality and Self-Control

Moral development has been of intense interest to child development specialists since the early part of this century. Today, the empirical literature on the topic is so vast that it exceeds research on all other topics in the field of social development (Flavell, 1985). The understanding of human morality and the related practical matter of how to motivate children to behave morally are not just twentieth century research concerns; they are age-old preoccupations. It has long been recognized that behavior aimed at benefiting others is essential for the continued existence of human groups (Radke-Yarrow, Zahn-Waxler, & Chapman, 1983; Rest, 1986).

. The determinants of human morality exist on multiple levels. In all societies, morality is protected by an overarching social organization that specifies rules for human interaction. At the same time, morality has roots in each major facet of the human psyche. First, as we indicated in Chapter 10, morality has an *emotional component,* since powerful affective reactions cause us to empathize when we witness another's distress or feel guilty when we are the cause of it. Second, morality has an important *cognitive component.* As we showed in Chapter 11, human beings actively think about their social experiences, and children's developing social understanding permits them to make increasingly sophisticated moral judgments about actions they believe to be right or wrong. Third, morality has a vital *behavioral component,* since experiencing morally relevant thoughts and feelings only increases the probability, but does not guarantee, that people will act in accord with them.

Traditionally, these three facets of morality were investigated separately: psychoanalytic theorists focused on emotions, cognitive-developmental theorists on moral thought, and behaviorists on moral behavior. But even though major theorists have emphasized very different aspects of morality, there is one point on which there is fairly common agreement. At first, the child's morality is *externally imposed and controlled* by direct instruction, supervision, and rewards and punishments of authority figures. Eventually, children *internalize* moral rules and principles, taking over the responsibility for regulating their own moral conduct. **Internalization** — the shift from externally controlled responses to behavior that is governed by internal standards and principles — permits children to behave in a moral fashion in the absence of adult monitoring and vigilance. The concept of internalization underscores a quality that most of us regard as indispensable to moral functioning. Truly moral individuals do not just comply with the momentary social influences of others. Instead, they have adopted relatively permanent, general standards of conduct that govern their behavior with many people, across many settings, and over a wide variety of occasions.

We begin our consideration of moral development with a brief overview of the philosophical foundations of major theories. Then we discuss biological, psychoanalytic, behaviorist, and cognitive-developmental perspectives, highlighting the strengths and shortcomings of each view. Finally, we conclude with a consideration of the child's capacity for *self-control,* or the ability to inhibit the expression of spontaneous impulses. The development of an inner resolve to keep the self from doing anything it feels like doing — from painting on the walls and playing with matches in the young preschooler to ignoring one's chores, insulting an agemate, or breaking a promise in the older child — is a major determinant of the extent to which inner moral commitments actually become translated into moral action.

THEORIES OF MORALITY

For centuries preceding modern scientific study of the child, philosophers mused about what morality is and how it develops. Many of their views anticipated present-day perspectives and found their way into modern theories. Recall from Chapter 1 that the sixteenth century Protestant doctrine of original sin held that only through severe disciplinary practices could children learn to subordinate their innate, self-centered depravity to behavior in the service of the public good. This philosophical position resembles Freud's idea of a harsh, punitive conscience as the inner force ensuring moral behavior. Jean Jacques Rousseau's (1762/1955) natural philosophy of childhood, with its vision of the child as innately good and naturally motivated by sympathy, compassion, and caring for others, is similar to the modern-day biological perspective on the origins of morality. The philosophy of John Locke (1690/1892), with its image of the child as a "blank slate" — born neither good nor bad but molded into a moral being by wise, consistent adult tutoring — finds its modern parallel in the behaviorist principles of modeling and reinforcement as determinants of moral action.[1] Finally, the German philosopher Immanuel Kant (1785/1952) regarded human beings as motivated by *both* selfish and benevolent passions and concluded that only reason could resolve the conflicting tendencies between the two. To Kant, the essence of morality was acting according to rational principles of justice, fairness, and respect for other people. Kant's philosophy foreshadows the modern cognitive-developmental approach to moral development, as exemplified by Piaget's theory and its more recent extension by Lawrence Kohlberg.

The diverse theoretical orientations mentioned above can be organized into three fundamental positions on the origins of morality: (1) morality as rooted in human nature, or the biological perspective; (2) morality as the adoption of externally imposed societal norms, which includes both the Freudian and behaviorist perspectives;

---

[1] You may wish to return to Chapter 1, pages 4–6, to review these basic philosophical preludes to modern developmental theory in greater detail.

and (3) morality as rational understanding of concepts of social justice, or the cognitive-developmental perspective. As we will see below, no single theory provides a complete account of the foundations of morality and the essence of moral development (Rest, 1983). Rather, by highlighting different facets, each adds to our appreciation of the complex, interacting factors that contribute to the emergence of moral functioning in children and adolescents.

MORALITY AS ROOTED IN HUMAN NATURE: THE BIOLOGICAL PERSPECTIVE

During the 1960s and 1970s, biological theories of human social behavior became prominent, spurred by a controversial new field called **sociobiology.** Sociobiology advanced the idea that morally relevant human behaviors, including cooperation, helping, and other self-sacrificing and prosocial responses, were rooted in the genetic heritage of the species (Wilson, 1975). This view was supported by the observations of ethologists, who reported cases of animals helping other members of their species, often at considerable risk to their own survival. For example, some small birds, including robins, thrushes, and titmice, emit a warning call that lets others know of an approaching predator, even though the sound itself may betray the caller's presence. Certain species of insects, such as bees, ants, and termites, show extremes of self-sacrificial behavior. Large numbers of them will viciously sting or bite an animal that threatens the hive, a defensive response that often results in death to the attackers. Among primates, chimpanzees can be seen sharing meat after a cooperative hunt and practicing adoption when a baby loses its mother. On the basis of such animal evidence, sociobiologists reasoned that evolution must have made similar provisions for prosocial behavior in humans, perhaps in the form of genetically prewired emotions such as empathy that serve to motivate altruistic behavior (Trivers, 1971).

It is likely that human prosocial behavior does have some biological roots, although the evidence for this hypothesis remains sparse. As we pointed out in earlier chapters, even neonates show a rudimentary empathic response, since they cry when they hear the cry of another baby. But like most other human behaviors, morality is only partly accounted for by its biological foundations. As we showed in Chapter 10, the development of empathy requires strong environmental supports to be realized. Recall that it hinges on experiences with adults who respond in a sensitive, caring way to the child, and its mature expression depends on cognitive development, especially advances in perspective-taking skill. Finally, although affective motivation is one basis for moral action, it is not a complete explanation, since there are instances in which blindly following our empathic feelings is not necessarily moral. For example, most of us would question the morality of a parent who decides not to take a sick child to the doctor because she empathizes with the youngster's fear and anxiety (Rest, 1983). Still, the biological perspective is a useful one because it reminds us of the adaptive significance of moral behavior and suggests some intriguing ideas about its evolutionary foundations.

MORALITY AS THE ADOPTION OF SOCIETAL NORMS: THE PSYCHOANALYTIC AND BEHAVIORIST PERSPECTIVES

Although psychoanalytic and behaviorist theories emphasize vastly different mechanisms of development, both approaches regard moral development as the adoption of standards for behavior that conform to societal prescriptions for good conduct, or norms.

The Psychoanalytic Perspective

According to Freud, the seat of morality rests in a portion of the personality called the **superego,** which is the end product of the young boy's Oedipal conflict during the phallic or early childhood stage of development (a comparable Electra conflict exists for girls). In the Oedipal conflict, the young boy desires to have his mother all to himself and feels hostile and rivalrous toward his father. These feelings soon lead to intense anxiety, since the boy fears he will lose his parents' love and be punished for his unacceptable desires. To master the anxiety, avoid punishment, and maintain the continued affection of parents, the child forms a superego by **identifying** with the same-sex parent and emulating that parent's characteristics, thereby internalizing parental standards and prohibitions that reflect society's norms. In addition, the child turns inward the hostility previously aimed at the same-sex parent, which results in the self-punitive affect of guilt. These events lead to the formation of the superego, which is made up of two basic components: an *ego ideal,* or set of ideal standards (derived from parental identification) against which the worth of the self is measured, and a *conscience,* or judging and punishing agency that leads the child to experience guilt each time the standards of the ego ideal are violated. According to Freud's theory, children are motivated to act in accord with societal prescriptions in order to avoid guilt. Freud regarded moral development as largely complete by 5 or 6 years of age, with some strengthening of the superego taking place during middle childhood (Freud, 1925/1961b; Freud, 1933).

Is Psychoanalytic Theory of Morality Supported by Current Research?

Although Freud's theory of conscience development is still widely accepted by psychoanalytic writers, most child development specialists disagree with it on a number of grounds. For example, few current researchers accept Freud's view of guilt as a hostile impulse redirected toward the self. Instead, they regard guilt as a complex emotion arising from experiences in which a person intentionally engages in a morally unacceptable behavior and feels personally responsible for the outcome. From this perspective, young children cannot experience guilt in mature form without first having attained certain cognitive prerequisites. These include awareness of themselves as autonomous beings who make choices about their own actions and the capacity to distinguish between intentional and unintentional acts (Campos et al., 1983; Hoffman, 1988). If you return to our discussion of complex emotions in Chapter 10 and our consideration of children's self-development and understanding of intentions in Chapter 11, you will see that the cognitive capacities that support the guilt response emerge during the preschool years and undergo refinement into middle childhood. Although this is the same period that Freud assigned to conscience formation, the basis of the guilt response is very different from what Freud described in his Oedipal theory.

Although Freud was not very explicit about the child-rearing practices he thought would promote strong conscience formation, the dynamics of the Oedipal conflict suggest that discipline promoting fear of punishment and loss of parental love should motivate children to behave morally. However, research does not support this conclusion. Childen whose parents frequently use power assertion (threats, commands, or physical force) generally experience low levels of guilt after acting harmfully toward others (Hoffman, 1988). In the case of love withdrawal (refusing to speak and listen to or explicitly stating a dislike for the child), children often react with abnormally high levels of self-blame after a transgression. Eventually, these youngsters may protect themselves from overwhelming feelings of guilt by denying the emotion and distancing themselves from the distress of others (Zahn-Waxler et al., 1990).

In contrast to power assertion and love withdrawal, **induction** is a rational form of discipline that facilitates conscience formation. Induction points out the effects of

When parents use threats, commands, and other coercive disciplinary techniques, children experience high levels of fear and anxiety that interfere with conscience formation.

the child's behavior on others, either directly, by using such statements as "If you keep pushing him, he'll fall down and cry," or indirectly, by saying something like "Don't yell at him. He was only trying to help" (Hoffman, 1988, p. 524). Induction may also include suggestions for making amends, such as apologies or ways of compensating for the wrongs done to others. As long as the reasoning given matches the child's capacity to understand, induction is effective in motivating morally relevant behavior as early as 2 years of age. Zahn-Waxler, Radke-Yarrow, and King (1979) found that mothers who delivered explanations about the unhappiness their young preschoolers caused in others had children who were more likely to make up for their misbehavior. Such children were also more altruistic, in that they spontaneously gave hugs, toys, and verbal sympathy to others in distress.

Virtually all parents resort to coercive discipline at one time or another. An occasional power assertion administered by parents who normally use induction may actually foster conscience development because it lets children know that the parent feels strongly about an issue. Also, it may get the child to stop doing something long enough to pay attention to the parent's inductive communication. Why is induction such an effective disciplinary technique? According to Hoffman (1988), it provides children with a verbal prohibition against harming others and reasons that particular actions are right or wrong so they can store this information in memory as a moral norm. Then, in future situations in which the child is tempted to act in a harmful manner, cues from the situation activate the norm along with unpleasant feelings of guilt for having hurt another person. Disciplinary techniques that rely too heavily on power assertion or love withdrawal may produce such high levels of fear and anxiety that they interfere with effective processing of the moral norm. As a result, although these methods may suppress unacceptable behavior temporarily, in the long run they are ineffective in motivating moral internalization.

Although there is little empirical support for psychoanalytic mechanisms of conscience development, Freud was still correct in regarding guilt as an important motivator of moral action. Recently, Chapman and his colleagues (1987) gave 4- to 11-year-olds ambiguous stories in which a child like themselves could have caused another person's distress. Subjects completed the stories by describing how the child felt. Youngsters who made reference to guilt reactions (expressions of personal responsibility, such as "She's sorry she pushed him down") were far more likely than their agemates to help an adult in need when given the opportunity to do so in a laboratory. In a similar study, 10- to 12-year-olds often portrayed story characters who had transgressed as resolving to become less selfish and more considerate in the future. This finding suggests that guilt may contribute to moral behavior in older children by triggering a generalized motive to behave morally that goes beyond immediate restitution to a victim (Hoffman, 1980).

Despite the effectiveness of guilt as a moral motive, it is not the only force that propels us to act morally, and Freud's theory suffers from one-sidedness in regarding it as such. Furthermore, a wealth of evidence that we will review later in this chapter indicates that, contrary to what Freud believed, moral development is not an abrupt event that is virtually complete by 5 or 6 years of age. Instead, it is a far more gradual process, beginning in early childhood and extending into the adult years.[2]

BRIEF REVIEW

In the sections above, we have seen that Freud's Oedipal theory falls short as an adequate account of moral development. Although guilt is an important motivator of moral action, Freud's view of it as hostility redirected toward the self is no longer widely accepted. In contrast to predictions drawn from Freudian theory, disciplinary practices that engender fear of punishment and loss of parental love are not effective in promoting moral internalization. Instead, induction is far more successful. Finally, although Freud regarded the preschool years as crucial for conscience formation, morality develops over a much longer period than he anticipated.

The Behaviorist Perspective

Unlike psychoanalytic theory, behaviorist approaches to moral development do not consider moral functioning to be a special form of human activity that is subject to a unique course of development. Rather, moral behavior is seen as acquired just like any other set of responses: through the learning mechanisms of reinforcement and modeling.

Reinforcement. According to the traditional operant conditioning view, behavior in conformity with societal norms increases with age because adults follow it up with positive reinforcement in the form of approval, affection, and other rewards. Similarly, behavior that violates normative standards is punished by reproof, loss of privileges, or other outcomes that make it less likely to occur in the future. Most behaviorists regard positive reinforcement as a far more effective means than punishment for promoting socially desirable behavior. However, one social learning theory modification of the operant conditioning paradigm regards punishment as a prime motivator of moral action. According to this view, when children experience punishment for deviant acts, painful anxiety becomes associated with the unacceptable

---

[2] Contemporary descendents of Freudian theory, while accepting the punitive, restrictive dimension of the superego, place greater emphasis on its positive, constructive side. For example, Erikson (1950) describes the psychological outcome of the Oedipal period as a *sense of initiative,* which provides the foundation for a realistic sense of ambition and purpose in life. Children develop initiative by identifying with heroic and idealized representatives of their society, whose roles they act out in play. Unlike Freud, Erikson (1968) views conscience development as extending from early childhood into adulthood. Recall from Chapter 11 that an important component of identity development is the adolescent's search for an ideology, or a set of ethical values, to have faith in. These values are selected during late adolescence as identity is achieved, and they undergo further refinement during the adult years.

behavior. Since anxiety is reexperienced each time the child starts to deviate again, it is best avoided by not engaging in the act (Aronfreed, 1968; Mowrer, 1960). However, we have already seen in our discussion of Freud's theory that coercive parental tactics are less effective in motivating resistance to transgression than rational, inductive techniques. Box 12.1 will tell you more about why punishment works so poorly as a method for inducing socially acceptable behavior, when its use is justified, and how adults can apply it so that its adverse consequences are reduced to a minimum.

Other social learning theorists point out that it is probably unlikely that very many prosocial behaviors are initially acquired through operant conditioning. For a behavior to be reinforced, it must first occur spontaneously. Most morally relevant behaviors, like sharing, helping, or comforting a distressed playmate, do not occur often enough by chance for reinforcement to account for their rapid acquisition in early childhood. Consequently, these social learning theorists believe that children learn to act morally largely through observation and imitation of models who demonstrate appropriate behavior (Bandura, 1977, 1989; Grusec, 1988). However, once children acquire a prosocial response, reinforcement in the form of praise, along with the presence of adults who remind children of the rules for moral behavior, are factors that increase its frequency (Gelfand et al., 1975; Mills & Grusec, 1989; Zarbatany, Hartmann, & Gelfand, 1985). However, we might question whether responses that are maintained in this way are truly "moral." As we noted in the introduction to this chapter, becoming increasingly independent of the pressures of the immediate situation and governed by internalized standards is generally regarded as an essential

When adults provide examples of altruistic behavior, they encourage children to act prosocially as well.

feature of moral development. However, traditional behaviorists differ from other theorists in that they do not look upon morality in this fashion.

Modeling. Laboratory evidence indicates that exposure to models who behave in a helpful or generous fashion is very effective in encouraging children to act more prosocially themselves (Bryan & London, 1970; Canale, 1977; Elliott & Vasta, 1970; Gray & Pirot, 1984). In fact, an altruistic behavioral example will continue to affect children's behavior from several hours to several weeks after original exposure to the model (Midlarsky & Bryan, 1972; Yarrow, Scott, & Waxler, 1973).

Altruistic models exert their most powerful effects on children below the age of 7 or 8. Older children who have a history of consistent exposure to caring, giving adults tend to behave altruistically regardless of whether a nearby adult's behavior is charitable or selfish (Lipscomb et al., 1982, 1985). By middle childhood, altruism is based on cognitive mediators, or *internalized normative prescriptions* abstracted from repeated experiences in which children have seen others help and give, heard them state the importance of doing so, and been encouraged to behave in a similar fashion themselves (Mussen & Eisenberg-Berg, 1977). In fact, by 7 to 9 years of age, children can spontaneously verbalize the norm of helping people in need (Bryan & Walbek, 1970). As a result, they are more apt to follow this internalized standard whether behavior consistent with it is modeled for them or not. In contrast, younger children are still formulating the norm and finding out the conditions under which to apply it.

◆ THEORY, RESEARCH, AND APPLICATIONS ◆

Punishment and the Socialization of Moral Behavior

Box 12.1

Punishment is a form of discipline that presents children with noxious stimulation aimed at inhibiting undesirable behavior. All parents rely on it sometimes, and the use of sharp verbal reprimands and physical force to restrain or move a child from one place to another is warranted when a behavior needs to be stopped immediately because it can result in serious harm to the child or others. But unpleasant pokes, taps, and spankings or verbal rebukes that denigrate the child's worth as a person are never justified. Research highlights several important reasons for avoiding these types of punishments:

1. Punishment promotes temporary suppression of a response, not long-term internalization of a prohibition. Frequently punished children will inhibit an undesirable behavior while the punishing agent is present, but they will revert back to engaging in the act as soon as the adult leaves the scene and they can "get away with it." In fact, children of highly punitive parents are known to be especially aggressive and defiant in settings outside the home (Eron et al., 1974).

2. Punishment involving physical or verbal injury provides children with models of adult-instigated aggression. Both naturalistic and experimental studies indicate that children adopt the punitive tactics used by adults in their own interactions with others (Parke & Slaby, 1983). Aggressive behaviors displayed by abused children are especially extreme. Both at home and in school, they verbally threaten and physically assault peers and adults far more often than do their nonabused counterparts (Emery, 1989; George & Main, 1979; Reid et al., 1981).

3. Frequently punished children soon learn to protect themselves by avoiding punitive agents (Redd, Morris, & Martin, 1975). When children refrain from approaching and interacting with those responsible for their upbringing, adults have fewer opportunities to teach desirable behaviors, and their power as socializing agents is severely reduced.

4. As punishment "works" to temporarily suppress children's unacceptable behavior, it offers immediate relief to adults, and they are reinforced for applying the punitive techniques. Consequently, a punitive adult is likely to punish with greater frequency over time, a course of action that can spiral into serious abuse (Parke & Collmer, 1975).

For obvious ethical reasons, investigators cannot study highly punitive methods of discipline in the laboratory. Instead, they are limited to the use of loud buzzers or verbal reprimands that do not cover the full range of noxious consequences to which children are exposed in natural environments. Nevertheless, experimentation with these techniques has identified several ways in which sharp warnings and admonitions can be combined with other disciplinary tactics to increase children's behavioral inhibition.

Thus, they look to adult models for information about where, when, and what kinds of altruistic behaviors are appropriate (Peterson, 1982).

Research indicates that children do not imitate the behavior of just any model. The model's characteristics—especially warmth and responsiveness—have a profound impact on children's prosocial inclinations. In an experiment by Yarrow, Scott, and Waxler (1973), a caregiver interacted with two groups of preschoolers. In one condition, the caregiver behaved warmly and nurturantly while she demonstrated a wide variety of prosocial behaviors. In the other condition, the caregiver was equally altruistic, but her mood was cold and aloof. Children in the first group were far more likely to behave like the model. Warmth and nurturance may facilitate prosocial behavior by making children more receptive to the model and therefore more attentive to the model's behavior. In addition, warm, affectionate responding is itself an example of altruism, and part of what children may be imitating is this aspect of the model's behavior.

Other influential characteristics of models are power and competence, dimensions believed to be especially important in the father's impact on children's moral development. Research indicates that the types of disciplinary strategies used by fathers have far less influence on children's moral behavior than those used by mothers, perhaps because in most families the mother is the primary caregiver and therefore the child's chief disciplinarian (Brody & Shaffer, 1982). Instead, the father's impact seems to derive primarily from his portrayal of an instrumentally competent

Timing. Punishment delivered early, soon after the child initiates a prohibited act, is most effective. Delaying punishment for several hours after a transgression occurs markedly reduces the inhibition of undesirable behavior (Parke, 1977).

Consistency. Punishment that is erratic and intermittent is related to especially high rates of disobedience in children. When parents react to a violation with laxity on some occasions and disapproval on others, children cannot discern what is expected of them, and the unacceptable behavior persists (Parke & Deur, 1972).

Characteristics of Punitive Agents. Punishment administered by an adult who has a warm relationship with the child produces more immediate behavioral inhibition (Parke & Walters, 1967). Children of involved and caring parents find the disruption of parental affection that accompanies an occasional punishment to be especially unpleasant. As a result, they are motivated to regain the positive attentions of their parents as quickly as possible.

Verbal Rationales. The most successful way to improve the effectiveness of punishment is to accompany it with a verbal rationale (Harter, 1983). Such reasoning can take the form of inductions that tell children how their behavior affects others, instructions about how to behave in a particular situation, or explanations of the adult's motives for punishing the child. The addition of a rationale permits children to internalize the adult's rea-

soning and call on it when they are tempted to transgress again. Reasoning also increases the effectiveness of late-timed punishment because it helps children recall an earlier transgression and relate it to expectations for future behavior (Walters & Andres, 1967).

On a final note, several alternatives to physical and verbal punishment exist that help adults discipline children effectively and, at the same time, avoid the undesirable side effects of punishment. One is a procedure called *time out,* in which children are removed from the immediate setting and the opportunities it offers for positive reinforcement until they are ready to behave acceptably. For most children, time out requires only a few minutes to change behavior, and it also offers a "cooling off" period for parents, who may be highly angered by a child's unacceptable actions. Another commonly used technique is withdrawal of privileges, such as loss of allowance or deprivation of a special experience like going to the movies. Removing privileges may generate some anger and resentment in children, but at least parents are not engaging in punitive behaviors that could easily escalate into abuse and violence. Finally, parental practices that do not wait for children to misbehave but that encourage and reward children for good conduct are, in the long run, the most effective forms of discipline. When adults help children acquire acceptable behaviors that they can use to replace prohibited acts, the need to use punishment in the socialization of children is greatly reduced (Parke, 1977).

role model.[3] Social learning theorists believe that powerful individuals serve as effective models because children want to acquire their prestige, mastery, and other resources. Acting like the model is rewarding to children because it signifies that they, too, may be able to attain the model's desirable goal states in the future (Bandura, 1977).

An additional characteristic of models that affects children's emulation of their behavior is whether the models "practice what they preach"—that is, demonstrate consistency between what they say and what they actually do. One study found that grade-school children were more likely to place money that they had won in a jar for the needy if a model who played the game first made a charitable statement (e.g., "It's a good thing to give, especially when you know it will make others happy") and also behaved charitably than if the model's statement and behavior contradicted one another (Midlarsky & Bryan, 1972). When adults say one thing and do another, in choosing between their words and actions, children generally opt for the most lenient standard of adult-demonstrated behavior (Mischel & Liebert, 1966).

The evidence reviewed above indicates that children pick up many positive, prosocial behaviors by observing parents and other adults. Social learning theorists have also been interested in whether modeling facilitates children's self-control and restraint — the *inhibition* of behaviors that violate normative prescriptions. Research is not as clear on this issue. Laboratory studies reveal that the impact of watching a model who shows lapses in self-control far exceeds that of watching a model who resists temptation (Fry, 1975; Rosenkoetter, 1973; Stein, 1967). These findings suggest that models can easily encourage deviant behavior, but they are far less effective in helping children overcome their self-centered, egoistic impulses.

However, under certain conditions, models *can* foster children's resistance to temptation. Grusec and her colleagues (1979) had a person first try to lure a model and then 5- to 8-year-old subjects away from a boring task to play with toys that the experimenter had forbidden them to touch. A model who verbalized that she was resisting temptation and clearly stated her reason for doing so (e.g., "I can't come play with the toys because I'm here to sort cards and I always try to do what's right") was more effective in promoting children's resistance to temptation than a model who merely demonstrated resistance. Grusec's findings indicate that the behavior of a self-controlled model is more likely to rub off on children when the model makes her own efforts at behavioral inhibition obvious by verbalizing them. In addition, the verbalization provides children with a cognitive rationale that they can internalize and rely on at a later time to facilitate resistance to temptation.

BRIEF REVIEW

Adult modeling of moral behavior combined with positive reinforcement of children's prosocial responding is highly successful in encouraging children to behave helpfully and generously toward others, especially at younger ages. Several characteristics of models increase children's willingness to imitate their behavior, including warmth, power, competence, and consistency between words and deeds. Resistance to temptation is less likely to be imitated by children than a model's lapses in self-control. However, imitation of self-controlled behavior is enhanced when adult models make the nature of their behavior explicit by describing and explaining it to children.

Consistency across Situations in Moral Behavior

Once children are old enough to have internalized normative standards, we would expect them to show a reasonable degree of consistency in moral conduct from one

---

[3] It is important to keep in mind that the parental differences described here may not be operative in nontraditional families in which mothers provide examples of competent, mastery-oriented behavior and fathers participate in household and child care responsibilities.

occasion to another. To what extent do children develop *traits of character*, such as honesty, generosity, and helpfulness (or their opposites — deceitfulness, selfishness, and inconsiderateness) that predict how they will behave across a wide variety of situations?

Six decades ago, in a study that examined the consistency of moral conduct among 11,000 children between the ages of 8 and 16 who were tempted to steal, lie, or cheat in a variety of contexts, Hartshorne and May (1928) found that children's moral behavior varied substantially from one situation to another. Knowing that a child behaved honestly or dishonestly on one occasion was not a good clue as to whether the child would behave that way on another occasion. Instead, expediency seemed to account for children's behavior. When circumstances made it safe and easy to cheat and when other children approved of the cheating, a child was likely to do so. Hartshorne and May concluded that morality was entirely specific to the situation; there was no such thing as a moral character guaranteeing that a person would behave honorably under all or even most conditions.

However, follow-up research indicated that Hartshorne and May's conclusion was too extreme. Using more sophisticated techniques, Burton (1963, 1976) reanalyzed Hartshorne and May's data and found that children do have a moderate tendency to behave in a morally consistent fashion across situations. These results reveal that moral behavior is neither completely situation-specific nor entirely stable and predictable. Instead, its consistency lies somewhere in between these two extremes, a conclusion that has been confirmed by other investigations (Nelson, Grinder & Mutterer, 1969; Rushton, 1980).

A moderate level of individual consistency in moral conduct does not rule out the possibility that situational factors affect moral behavior to some degree. In fact, a long history of research on children's classroom cheating behavior reveals that situational variables play an important role. For example, the level of honesty of peer associates affects children's tendency to cheat. Cheaters generally sit close to one another in the classroom, and students who happen to sit near or next to a cheater are more likely to cheat themselves (Sherrill et al., 1970). Moreover, circumstances that increase children's anxieties about not doing well in school augment their tendency to cheat. When teachers tell pupils about the superior performance of classmates, place a high premium on doing well on a particular task, or give children assignments beyond their ability, the incidence of cheating rises (Taylor & Lewit, 1966; Vitro, 1969). Although strong parental pressure to succeed predicts better academic performance, it is also related to cheating. This is especially true in low-income families in which the disparity between educational goals and financial resources is very great. Under these conditions, parents may try to overcome the gap by making achievement demands of their youngsters that are extreme (Pearlin, Yarrow, & Scarr, 1967).

Taken together, the research reviewed above indicates that there is variability across situations in moral behavior, but there is also a counterbalancing picture of consistency. A morally well-socialized child is less likely to succumb to a ready opportunity to copy from a neighbor, use crib notes in class, or change a test score. At the same time, the importance of situational factors suggests that honest conduct can be enhanced by arranging environments in ways that minimize children's temptation to cheat. One way of doing so might be to reduce extreme parental and school pressures placed on children for competitive success.

Critique of the "Morality as Social Conformity" Perspective

Learning to behave in conformity with societal norms is, without question, an important dimension of moral development. Nevertheless, a major criticism of psychoanalytic and behaviorist theories, which treat morality as entirely a matter of social

Susan B. Anthony's (1820–1906) leadership in the campaign for women's suffrage illustrates how behavior at odds with prevailing societal norms is sometimes highly moral and courageous.

conformity, is that normative prescriptions sometimes conflict with important ethical principles and social goals. Under these conditions, deliberate violation of norms is not immoral; it is justifiable and often very courageous. Cases of famous nonconformists whose actions dramatized the inadequacy of societal norms at great personal sacrifice illustrate the difficulty of equating morality with social conformity. Few of us would place Susan B. Anthony, Mahatma Gandhi, or Martin Luther King in the same moral class as Al Capone or Jack the Ripper. Yet all have in common the fact that they were nonconformists who were seriously at odds with prevailing societal standards (Rest, 1983).

Furthermore, many normative matters are not primarily moral matters. Instead, they involve arbitrary **social conventions,** such as dress styles, table manners, and customs of social interaction. At an early age, children growing up in the United States as well as in a variety of non-Western cultures understand the difference between social conventions and moral rules (Hollis, Leis, & Turiel, 1986; Song, Smetana, & Kim, 1987). For example, Nucci (1981) asked individuals between 7 and 19 years of age which would be more wrong — engaging in behaviors like eating lunch with one's fingers (breaking with social convention) or committing such acts as lying, stealing, or hitting another person (violating moral rules). Subjects of all ages consistently indicated that moral violations were more serious, giving as reasons that they result in harm to others, deprive people of what is rightfully theirs, or simply should not be committed. In contrast, violations of social conventions were regarded as merely unmannerly, disruptive, or unpleasantly messy. In fact, even 4- to 6-year-olds seem to grasp the distinction between moral and social conventional matters. When asked, young children indicate that moral (but not social conventional) transgressions would still be wrong if no rules existed to prohibit them (Nucci & Turiel, 1978; Turiel, 1983).

On the basis of these findings, Turiel (1983) has proposed that social conventions and morality are distinct domains of social understanding and behavior that undergo separate lines of development. How do young children learn to differentiate between the two? According to Turiel, not through direct teaching, modeling, and reinforcement, but by *actively thinking about* their experiences in social-conventional and moral situations. Although adults insist on conformity to social conventions at least as often as they press for obedience to moral norms, the way in which they respond to children's transgressions in the two areas is markedly different. When a moral violation occurs, parents and teachers more often comment on the rights and feelings of others, whereas they refer to institutional rules and disorderliness in the case of social conventional infractions. Furthermore, children themselves respond quite differently to moral and social conventional violations. When a moral offense occurs, nursery school children react emotionally, verbalize their own injury or loss, tell another child to stop, or retaliate. In contrast, they seldom react to social conventional disobedience, leaving this for teachers to handle (Nucci & Turiel, 1978).

Turiel's research, as well as the work of others, indicates that children strive to *make sense* out of social rules. They make moral judgments, deciding what is right or wrong on the basis of underlying concepts they have about justice and fairness. As Rest (1983) indicates, "Children do not just learn lists of prescriptions and prohibitions; they also come to understand the nature and function of social arrangements," including promises, bargains, divisions of labor, and fair principles and procedures for regulating human relationships (p. 616). The cognitive-developmental position on morality is unique in its view of the child as a thinking moral being who wonders about right and wrong and actively searches for moral truth. We will see in the following sections that Piaget's and Kohlberg's theories, which comprise the major cognitive-developmental research tradition in moral development, do not make the same distinction between moral and social conventional matters to which Turiel adheres. However, all of these theorists are in full agreement that children *reason* about the rightness and wrongness of social acts and that changes in their reasoning are at the heart of moral development.

MORALITY AS SOCIAL UNDERSTANDING: THE
COGNITIVE-DEVELOPMENTAL PERSPECTIVE

483

CHAPTER 12
THE DEVELOPMENT OF
MORALITY AND
SELF-CONTROL

Cognitive-developmental theorists study how moral reasoning changes with age. They believe that increasing cognitive maturity and social experience gradually lead children to gain a better understanding of cooperative social arrangements that regulate moral responsibilities. Children's understanding of social arrangements evolves from a simple, concrete grasp of obligations between people to a more abstract, comprehensive appreciation of societywide institutions and law-making systems. As the understanding of society and social structures changes, children's moral ideals — their conceptions of what ought to be done when the needs and desires of people are in conflict with one another — also undergo revision, toward increasingly just, fair, and balanced solutions to moral problems (Rest, 1983).

Piaget's Theory of Moral Development

Piaget's book *The Moral Judgment of the Child* (1932/1965) served as the original inspiration for the cognitive-developmental perspective on morality and continues to be influential in contemporary research. According to Piaget's theory, as children's understanding of social arrangements changes, their moral reasoning undergoes revision, from a rigid view of moral rules as sacred, unalterable dictates of authority figures to an appreciation of them as flexible instruments of human purposes that can be changed in response to human needs.

Piaget's Stages of Moral Understanding. To study children's ideas about morality, Piaget relied on his open-ended clinical interviewing procedure, questioning scores of Swiss children between 5 and 13 years of age about their understanding of rules in the game of marbles. In addition, he gave children pairs of stories in which characters' intentions to engage in right or wrong action and the outcomes resulting from their behavior were varied. In the best known of these stories, children were asked to judge which of the following two boys, well-intentioned John who causes much damage or ill-intentioned Henry who does little damage, is naughtier and why:

> Story A: A little boy who is called John is in his room. He is called to dinner. He goes into the dining room. But behind the door there was a chair, and on the chair there was a tray with fifteen cups on it. John couldn't have known that there was all this behind the door. He goes in, the door knocks against the tray, bang go the fifteen cups, and they all get broken!

> Story B: Once there was a litle boy whose name was Henry. One day when his mother was out he tried to get some jam out of the cupboard. He climbed up on to a chair and stretched out his arm. But the jam was too high up and he couldn't reach it and have any. But while he was trying to get it he knocked over a cup. The cup fell down and broke. (Piaget, 1932/1965, p. 122)

On the basis of children's responses, Piaget identified two broad stages of moral development:

1. **The stage of heteronomous morality,**[4] **or moral realism** (about 5–10 years): During the early preschool years and before the beginning of this stage, children show little understanding of social rules. When they play rule-oriented games like marbles, they do so for the sheer pleasure of exploring and manipulating the materials and are generally unconcerned about winning, losing, or systematically coordinating their actions with those of other players. Around 5 or 6 years of age, as

---

[4] *Heteronomous* means under the authority of another.

According to Piaget, 5- to 10-year-olds view the rules of games as fixed, external regularities handed down by authorities. At older ages, children regard rules as flexible instruments of human purposes that can be changed to suit the will of the majority.

children enter the period of heteronomous morality, they start to show great concern and respect for rules. However, they view rules as fixed, external regularities that are created and handed down by adult authorities. For example, young children state that the rules of the game of marbles cannot be changed, explaining that "God didn't teach (the new rules)," "you couldn't play any other way," or "it would be cheating. . . . A fair rule is one that is in the game" (pp. 58, 59, 63). Many of Piaget's younger subjects claimed that rules originate with God or their fathers or that the rules have existed in their current form since the beginning of time.

Piaget believed that the heteronomous child's view of rules as sacred and unchangeable results from two factors that limit the young child's moral understanding: (1) the coercive constraint of adult authority, which promotes unquestioning respect for rules and the adults who enforce them, and (2) cognitive immaturity, particularly the young child's egocentrism. Because young children make the egocentric assumption that everyone else's thoughts are identical to their own, their moral understanding is characterized by **realism.** That is, they externalize rules and treat them as permanent fixtures in reality, like gravity and other physical laws, instead of viewing them as subjective, internal principles that can be modified at will.

Together, egocentrism and realism lead to other deficiencies in children's moral judgments. For example, the heteronomous child bases an action's wrongness on *objective consequences,* not on people's subjective intent to do harm. In the stories about John and Henry given above, John is regarded as the naughtier of the two boys because he broke the greatest number of cups, despite the fact that he did not do so on purpose. Also, since young childen do not distinguish between violating a social rule and violating a physical law, they believe in *immanent justice,* that wrongdoing inevitably leads to punishment. Inescapable punishment for bad acts is regarded as the way in which the physical world maintains moral order, and it may do so through a variety of unfortunate experiences and accidents, such as making children fall off their bikes, break treasured toys, or have bad dreams during the night.

2. **The stage of autonomous morality, or the morality of cooperation** (about 10 years and older). As the result of cognitive development, gradual release from adult vigilance and constraint, and interaction with peers, children eventually shift from heteronomous to autonomous morality. Social experience with peers was regarded as particularly important in this transition. Recall from Chapter 6 that Piaget believed that arguments and disagreements between agemates lead to a decline in egocentrism. Consequently, children recognize that people can have different perspectives

about moral action and that the subjective intentions of others, not the objective consequences of their actions, serve as the basis for judging behavior.

In addition, as children participate as co-equals in social exchanges with peers, they learn to settle conflicts in mutually beneficial ways. Gradually, they become aware of **reciprocity** as the organizing principle of cooperative social relations. By reciprocity, Piaget meant a rational ideal of fairness, a concern for the welfare of others in the same way that each person is concerned about the welfare of the self, or, phrased in a very familiar form: "Do unto others as you would have them do unto you."

Piaget believed that an appreciation of reciprocity was at the heart of the transition from heteronomous to autonomous moral functioning. For example, autonomous children no longer view rules as fixed and immutable. They see them as flexible, socially agreed upon principles of cooperation that can be changed to suit the will of the majority. Therefore, not all rules enunciated by adults need to be upheld. At times, there may be good reason to break a rule, and unquestioning obedience to authority is no longer regarded as a sound basis for moral action.

Furthermore, an understanding of reciprocity leads to a new perspective on punishment. Bad acts are no longer seen as inevitably punished. Instead, the autonomous child believes that punishment should be reciprocity-based, or rationally related to the offense. That is, the severity of punishment should fit the seriousness of the transgression as well as the intentions of the transgressor. Also, whenever possible, punishment should be a logical consequence of the crime. It should require offenders to make active restitution or allow them to suffer the natural consequences of their actions (e.g., a cheater whom no one will play with; a liar whom no one will believe anymore, even when he tells the truth). Finally, punishment should be meted out in an even-handed, nonarbitrary fashion to all participants in a situation, guaranteeing "equal justice for all."

Critique of Piaget's Theory. Follow-up research on Piaget's theory has upheld his general vision of moral development. In a large number of studies, some conducted in different cultures, the diverse moral attributes that distinguish heteronomous from autonomous morality show the expected differences between younger and older subjects (Lickona, 1976). Moreover, considerable evidence supports Piaget's conclusion that moral reasoning is facilitated by release from the coercive constraint of adult authority, intellectual growth, and peer interaction. A well-documented relationship exists between parental power assertion and immaturity of moral judgment (Hoffman, 1976; Hoffman & Saltzstein, 1967). In addition, IQ, perspective-taking skill, and performance on Piagetian logical tasks are all positively related to the development of moral thought (Kurdek, 1980; Lickona, 1976). As we will see later on, extensions of Piaget's work by Kohlberg and his followers have led to a more refined analysis of the connection between cognitive development and moral reasoning. They also provide support for the role of peer associations in stimulating moral growth.

Nevertheless, certain aspects of Piaget's theory have been the subject of considerable criticism. Recall that earlier in this chapter, we summarized work by Turiel and his co-workers indicating that as early as the preschool years, children do not regard all rules with equal reverence and respect. They make cognitive distinctions between social-conventional and moral rules and regard the former as far less permanent and immutable than the latter.

Furthermore, it is now known that Piaget's story vignettes underestimated young children's moral understanding. Look again at the stories about John and Henry on page 483. Because they confound character intentions with objective consequences (e.g., bad intentions are always coupled with minor consequences and good intentions with serious consequences), the stories yield a biased picture of young children's ability to consider intentions in making moral judgments. In Chapter 11, we showed that preschoolers are quite sensitive to social cues regarding people's intentions.

When Piagetian stories are modified to make intentions salient — either by holding consequences constant and varying only intentions, giving character intentions last in the story sequence, or making story events very salient by acting them out on film — preschool and early elementary school children are quite capable of judging ill-intentioned characters as naughtier than well-intentioned ones (Chandler, Greenspan, & Barenboim, 1973; Grueneich, 1982; Nelson-Le Gall, 1985; Yuill & Perner, 1988). Many researchers now believe that Piaget's younger subjects responded to his interviews immaturely because his stories accentuated the prominence of consequences while minimizing character intentions.

Although the capacity to consider intentions appears much earlier than Piaget believed, an advanced understanding of the morality of intentions does await the reciprocal orientation of Piaget's autonomous stage. Recent evidence indicates that 5- and 6-year-olds interpret statements of intention in a rigid, heteronomous fashion. They believe that once you say you will do something, you are obligated to follow through, even if uncontrollable circumstances (such as an accident) make it difficult or impossible for you to do so. By 9 to 10 years of age, children appreciate that not keeping your word is much worse in some situations than others — in particular, when you are able to do so and permit another person to count on your actions (Astington, 1988; Mant & Perner, 1988). Thus, Piaget was partly right and partly wrong in his analysis of this aspect of moral reasoning.

A final reservation about the validity of Piaget's theory is that the characteristics of his stages do not correlate very highly with one another, as one would expect if each stage represented a general, unifying organization of moral judgment. As Lickona (1976) puts it, "The child's moral thought, as it unfolds in Piagetian interviews, is not all of a piece but more of a patchwork of diverse parts" (p. 240). Consequently, the various features of heteronomous and autonomous reasoning are best viewed as separate dimensions of moral understanding, not as manifestations of closely knit stages.

Moral development is now regarded as a more extended process than Piaget believed. In fact, Kohlberg's theory, to which we now turn, identifies three stages beyond Piaget's autonomous morality. Over the past two decades, Piaget's groundbreaking work has been supplanted by Kohlberg's more comprehensive six-stage sequence. Nevertheless, it is clear that Kohlberg's theory is a direct continuation of the research that Piaget began — the search for universal stages of moral development and the study of how children's moral understanding is intimately tied to the course of cognitive growth (Lickona, 1976).

Kohlberg's Extension of Piaget's Theory

Kohlberg based his stage sequence on responses to situations quite different from Piaget's stories. Whereas Piaget asked children to judge the naughtiness of a character who had already decided on a moral course of action, Kohlberg gave his subjects hypothetical **moral dilemmas** in which competing courses of action were possible and asked them to indicate what an actor should do and why. Because he had subjects both decide on and justify a course of action, Kohlberg was able to obtain a clearer idea of the reasoning on which moral decisions were based.

Lawrence Kohlberg's (1927–1987) stage sequence of moral development extends Piaget's theory by providing a more complete description of qualitative changes in moral reasoning from childhood into adulthood.

Methods of Assessment. Before we summarize Kohlberg's theory, let's look at the dilemmas he used to assess moral understanding, his extensive interviewing procedure, as well as another "objective" approach to assessing moral reasoning that is more efficient than the clinical interviewing technique.

The Clinical Interview. Like Piaget, Kohlberg regarded the clinical interview as the preferred method for studying children's moral development. Each moral dilemma that serves as the basis for an interview presents a genuine crisis situation that pits one moral value against another. The best-known of these dilemmas, the "Heinz dilemma," asks individuals to choose between the value of upholding the law (not stealing) and the value of human life (saving a dying person):

> In Europe a woman was near death from a very special kind of cancer. There was one drug that the doctors thought might save her. It was a form of radium that a druggist in the same town had recently discovered. The drug was expensive to make, but the druggist was charging ten times what the drug cost him to make. He paid $200 for the radium and charged $2,000 for a small dose of the drug. The sick woman's husband, Heinz, went to everyone he knew to borrow the money, but he could only get together about $1,000, which is half of what it cost. He told the druggist that his wife was dying, and asked him to sell it cheaper or let him pay later. But the druggist said, "No, I discovered the drug and I'm going to make money from it." So Heinz got desperate and broke into the man's store to steal the drug for his wife. Should Heinz have done that? Why? (Colby et al., 1983, p. 77)

Kohlberg emphasized that it is the *structure* of the subject's answer — how the individual *reasons* about a course of action — that is paramount in determining its level of moral maturity. Consequently, if a person responds to the Heinz dilemma by saying, "Heinz shouldn't steal the drug because it would be against the law," the interviewer must find out how the subject thinks about the law — in terms of simple fear of punishment or as a system that is worthy of respect in its own right. Similarly, if the subject indicates, "Heinz should steal the drug to save his wife's life," it is necessary to find out why her life is so important — because Heinz feels gratitude toward her for doing things for him, because it is a husband's duty to protect his wife, or because life is among the highest of human values. As we will see shortly, each of these justifications implies a qualitatively distinct organization of moral thought and a different stage of moral development (Kohlberg, 1969, 1976).

To bring out the structure of the subject's moral reasoning, Kohlberg's interviewing procedure is lengthy and free-ranging. After a dilemma is presented, a series of follow-up questions elicits the individual's views on such issues as obedience to laws and authority figures and understanding of higher moral values like respect for human life. In the case of the Heinz dilemma, the interviewer would ask, "If Heinz does not love his wife, should he still steal the drug for her?", "Is it important for people to do everything they can to save another's life?", "It is against the law for Heinz to steal. Does that make it morally wrong?", and "Why or why not?" (Colby et al., 1983, p. 77). After the answers are obtained, they are subjected to an elaborate scoring procedure through which the structure of the response is evaluated.

Although moral structure is the primary criterion for determining the subject's developmental progress, it is important to note that at the highest two stages, moral *content* — the course of action the subject chooses — is also relevant. That is, mature moral reasoners not only agree on *why an action is justified* but also on *what one ought to do* in a moral dilemma situation. Given a choice between obedience to authority on the one hand and preserving individual rights on the other, the most advanced subjects prefer the autonomous course of action (in the Heinz dilemma, stealing the drug to save a life rather than obeying the law). In contrast, subjects at the lower stages choose either alternative. Thus, in Kohlberg's scheme, structure and content are initially independent, but as development proceeds, these two facets of morality become integrated into a coherent ethical system (Kohlberg, Levine, & Hewer, 1983). This is an important point to which we will return as we consider Kohlberg's theory in greater detail.

An Objective Instrument: The Defining Issues Test. Once the characteristics of Kohlberg's stages were well known, some investigators worked on developing less time-consuming methods for assessing moral maturity. Rest's **Defining Issues Test (DIT)** is the most widely used objective measure. It asks individuals to read a series of dilemmas, among them the familiar Heinz problem, and then rate the importance of "moral issue" statements for deciding on a course of action. Each statement captures the crux of moral reasoning associated with a particular stage. By scoring the ratings, the investigator can identify a stage of reasoning as well as the relative importance that the subject attaches to "principled morality," or Kohlberg's highest two stages. Several DIT issue statements associated with the Heinz dilemma are given in Table 12.1. Which ones seem most important to you in making a decision about what Heinz should do? (Look at the fine print at the bottom of the table to find the stage of reasoning represented by each statement.)

Subjects generally appear more advanced in moral development on the DIT than Kohlberg's clinical interview (Rest, 1979a). This finding is not surprising, in view of the fact that Kohlberg's method asks subjects to *produce* a rationale for a course of action, whereas the DIT requires only that they *recognize* and indicate their preferences for stage-linked responses. Recall from Chapter 7 that recognition is a far less demanding cognitive process than active production of a response.

Nevertheless, both DIT and clinical interviewing scores produce similar longitudinal developmental trends, correlate similarly with other cognitive measures, and show similar changes in response to interventions designed to facilitate moral reasoning (Rest, 1983). Because of its efficiency of administration and impressive reliability and validity, the DIT has been used more often than any other single measure in moral reasoning research, including Kohlberg's method (Rest, 1986).

Kohlberg's Stages of Moral Understanding. Kohlberg intended his stage sequence to describe very closely and accurately the qualitative changes in moral thinking that take place from childhood into adulthood. Consequently, he made strong statements about the properties of his stages. First, the stages were assumed to form an *invariant* sequence, or fixed series of steps that people traverse sequentially, without skipping any stages. Second, each new stage was regarded as a more *equilibrated* way of making and justifying moral judgments. In other words, each successive step integrates and builds on the reasoning of the previous stage, resulting in a more broadly applicable, logically consistent, and morally adequate notion of justice than its predecessor. Finally, each stage was believed to form a tightly structured, *organized* whole — that is, a qualitatively distinct pattern of moral reasoning that a person applies across a wide range of moral situations (Walker, 1988). Note that these are strict stage characteristics in the Piagetian sense of the word.[5]

Furthermore, Kohlberg regarded change in moral reasoning as motivated by the same basic factors that Piaget thought were important for cognitive growth: (1) *cognitive disequilibrium,* or actively noticing inadequacies in one's current moral reasoning and revising it accordingly, and (2) *advances in perspective-taking*. As you read the descriptions of Kohlberg's stages below, look for qualitative changes in the nature of thought and in perspective-taking that each of the stages assumes.

Kohlberg organized his six stages into three general levels of moral progress. To illustrate the initial independence of moral structure and content that we discussed earlier, two examples of typical thinking for each of the first four stages are presented: one a "pro-stealing" and the other an "anti-stealing" response. At the highest level of development, structure and content become integrated; Stage 5 subjects usually believe that Heinz should steal the drug and Stage 6 individuals always do. Consequently, for these two stages only "pro-stealing" examples are given. Kohlberg's developmental progression is as follows:

I. The preconventional level. At this level, morality is still externally governed. Preconventional children justify actions as right or wrong on the basis of whether they lead to pleasurable or punitive consequences. Behaviors that result in punishment are

[5] You may wish to review the various concepts that Kohlberg borrowed from Piaget to formulate the characteristics of his moral stages. They can be found on pages 211–212 of Chapter 6.

Table 12.1. "Heinz Dilemma" Issue Statements from the Defining Issues Test (DIT)

WHICH ISSUES ARE MOST IMPORTANT IN MAKING A DECISION ABOUT WHAT HEINZ SHOULD DO?[a]

1. Whether a community's laws are going to be upheld.

2. Is Heinz willing to risk getting shot as a burglar or going to jail for the chance that stealing the drug might help?

3. Isn't it only natural for a loving husband to care so much for his wife that he'd steal?

4. What values are going to be the basis for governing how people act toward each other?

5. Whether the law in this case is getting in the way of the most basic claim of any member of society.

[a] 1. Stage 4. 2. Stage 2. 3. Stage 3. 4. Stage 6. 5. Stage 5.

Source: J. R. Rest, 1979b, *Revised Manual for the Defining Issues Test.* Minneapolis: Moral Research Projects. (Reprinted by permission.)

regarded as bad, while those that result in rewards or concrete exchanges of favors are thought of as good. As in Piaget's heteronomous stage, morality is governed by the constraint of authority, and children frequently make reference to the power of adults who enforce the rules. The preconventional level is subdivided into the following two stages:

Stage 1: The punishment and obedience orientation. Children at this stage find it difficult to consider two points of view in a moral dilemma. Unaware that people's interests and perspectives may differ, they ignore the motives and intentions of others in judging the goodness or badness of an action. Instead, they unquestioningly accept an authority's perspective as their own and focus on avoidance of punishment and deference to superior power as reasons for behaving morally. The following responses to the Heinz dilemma reflect the Stage 1 child's orientation toward obedience and fear of punishment:

Pro-stealing: "If you let your wife die, you will get in trouble. You'll be blamed for not spending the money to help her and there'll be an investigation of you and the druggist for your wife's death." (Kohlberg, 1969, p. 381)

Anti-stealing: "You shouldn't steal the drug because you'll be caught and sent to jail if you do. If you do get away, your conscience would bother you thinking how the police would catch up with you any minute." (Kohlberg, 1969, p. 381)

Stage 2: The naive hedonistic orientation. Awareness that people can have different points of view in a moral dilemma appears at this stage, but this understanding is initially very concrete. Right action is regarded as what satisfies one's own needs in a very physical, pragmatic way, and others are also viewed as acting out of self-interest. If some sacrifice for another person is to be made, Stage 2 individuals base it on a need for the services of that person, a desire for something the other person has, or the expectation that the other person will do the same for them someday. Reciprocity is understood as equal exchange of favors — "you do this for me and I'll do that for you." This hedonistic, self-gratifying morality is reflected in the following two interview responses:

Pro-stealing: "The druggist can do what he wants and Heinz can do what he wants to do. It's up to each individual to do what he wants with what he has. But if Heinz decides to risk jail to save his wife, it's his life he's risking; he can do what he wants with it. And the same goes for the druggist; it's up to him to decide what he wants to do." (Rest, 1979a, p. 26)

Anti-stealing: "(Heinz) is running more risk than it's worth unless he's so crazy about her he can't live without her. Neither of them will enjoy life if she's an invalid." (Rest, 1979a, p. 27)

II. The conventional level. At this level, the individual continues to regard conformity to social norms as the basis for morality. However, upholding them is no longer motivated by the immediate consequences of one's actions. Instead, active maintenance of the social order is regarded as important in its own right. The conventional individual believes strongly in supporting and preserving the laws and rules of the existing social system.

Stage 3: The "good boy – good girl" orientation, or the morality of interpersonal concordance. Belief in the importance of adhering to social prescriptions for their own sake makes its first appearance in relationships with people one knows well. The Stage 3 individual is oriented toward maintaining the continued affection and approval of relatives and friends by being a "good person" — trustworthy, loyal, respectful, helpful, and nice. Newly acquired capacities for mutual perspective-taking and the understanding of reciprocity support this revised conception of morality. The Stage 3 individual can anticipate what another person is thinking and feeling and knows that the other person can do the same, as the following responses to the Heinz dilemma indicate:

> *Pro-stealing*: "No one will think you're bad if you steal the drug, but your family will think you're an inhuman husband if you don't. If you let your wife die, you'll never be able to look anyone in the face again." (Kohlberg, 1969, p. 381)

> *Anti-stealing*: "It isn't just the druggist who will think you're a criminal, everyone else will too. After you steal it, you'll feel bad thinking how you've brought dishonor on your family and yourself; you won't be able to face anyone again." (Kohlberg, 1969, p. 381)

Stage 4: The social order-maintaining orientation. At this stage the individual is able to step outside a two-person, mutual relationship and take into account a third perspective of societal laws in deciding on a course of action. As a result, morality is no longer restricted to those with whom one has personal ties. Instead, rules must be uniformly enforced in an even-handed fashion for everyone, and each member of society has a personal duty to uphold them. When asked, the Stage 4 individual responds that laws cannot be disobeyed under any circumstances because they are indispensable for ensuring societal order. The following are typical Stage 4 answers to the Heinz dilemma:

At Kohlberg's Stage 3, this youngster helps his grandfather to earn approval and respect, not (as he did at Stage 2) to have a favor returned.

Pro-stealing: "He should steal it. Heinz has a duty to protect his wife's life; it's a vow he took in marriage. But it's wrong to steal, so he would have to take the drug with the idea of paying the druggist for it and accepting the penalty breaking the law later."

Anti-stealing: "It's a natural thing for Heinz to want to save his wife, but it's still always wrong to steal. You have to follow the rules regardless of how you feel or regardless of the special circumstances. Even if his wife is dying, it's still his duty as a citizen to obey the law. No one else is allowed to steal, why should he be? If everyone starts breaking the law in a jam, there'd be no civilization, just crime and violence." (Rest, 1979a, p. 30)

III. The postconventional or principled level. Postconventional individuals move beyond unquestioning adherence to the moral dictates of their own society. They make an effort to define morality in terms of abstract principles and values that are valid in all situations and all societies.

Stage 5: The social contract, legalistic orientation. At Stage 5, individuals become aware that any single rule system is only one of many possible rule systems, and they can envision alternatives to their own social order. Consequently, they no longer regard rules as established givens, but as flexible instruments for furthering human values. At this stage, there is an emphasis on fair procedures for interpreting and changing the law when there is an ethically valid reason to do so. When laws are consistent with individual rights and with the interests of the majority, each person's obligation to abide by them stems from a *social contract orientation* — free and willing participation in the system because it brings about more good for the self and others than if no such arrangement existed. This rational approach to the validity of rules and laws appears in the following statement:

Pro-stealing: "Although there is a law against stealing, the law wasn't meant to violate a person's right to life. Taking the drug does violate the law, but Heinz is justified in stealing in this instance. If Heinz is prosecuted for stealing, the law needs to be reinterpreted to take into account situations in which it goes against people's natural right to keep on living."

Stage 6: The universal ethical principle orientation. At this highest stage, right action is defined by self-chosen ethical principles that are comprehensive and universally applicable. These principles transcend legal formulations; there is recognition at Stage 6 that some moral obligations and values are valid for all humanity, regardless of law and social agreement. Typical principles referred to are equal consideration of the claims of all human beings and respect for the worth and dignity of each individual. These values are abstract and ethical, not concrete moral rules like the Ten Commandments, and they are justified by an appeal to one's inner private conscience. According to Kohlberg, a very abstract form of perspective-taking underlies moral reasoning at this stage. Stage 6 individuals make moral decisions by simultaneously considering the perspectives of all parties in a moral dilemma and then choosing an action that they could endorse if they did not know ahead of time which role (e.g., Heinz, his wife, or the druggist) they would play. The following response reflects Stage 6 moral reasoning:

Pro-stealing: "If Heinz does not do everything he can to save his wife, then he is putting some value higher than the value of life. It doesn't make sense to put respect for property above respect for life itself. Men could live together without private property at all. Respect for human life and personality is absolute and accordingly men have a mutual duty to save one another from dying." (Rest, 1979a, p. 37)

Research Aimed at Verifying Kohlberg's Stage Theory

Since its original construction, a large body of research has been directed at verifying Kohlberg's stage-wise progression. If Kohlberg's theory is correct, movement through his stages should be related to age, cognitive growth, and improvements in perspective-taking. In addition, changes in moral reasoning should be consistent with strict Piagetian stage characteristics. We consider the evidence on these issues in the following sections.

Age-Related Changes and an Invariant Developmental Sequence. A wealth of research reveals that maturity of moral reasoning is strongly related to age. Thoma (as reported by Rest, 1986) combined data from many cross-sectional studies, arriving at a sample size of approximately 6,000 subjects, and found that age correlated with moral maturity at .72. Similarly powerful relationships have been identified in other large-scale cross-sectional investigations (Gibbs & Widaman, 1982; Rest, Davison, & Robbins, 1978).

Longitudinal studies provide the most convincing evidence for Kohlberg's developmental sequence. The most extensive of these is a 20-year continuation of Kohlberg's initial study of adolescent boys in which 58 of the 84 original subjects were retested at regular 3- to 4-year intervals. Like cross-sectional findings, the correlation between age and moral maturity was strong, at .78. In addition, the results supported Kohlberg's assumption that the stages form an invariant developmental sequence. With few exceptions, subjects proceeded through the stages in the prescribed order, without skipping a stage or regressing to an earlier level once a stage had been attained (Colby et al., 1983). Other longitudinal findings also confirm the invariance of the stages (Nisan & Kohlberg, 1982; Rest, 1986; Snarey, Reimer, & Kohlberg, 1985; Walker, 1989).

Age trends provide information about when, on the average, individuals move from one moral stage to another and how long it takes them to achieve each major transformation. Figure 12.1 shows the extent to which subjects between 10 and 36 years of age used each stage of moral reasoning in the 20-year longitudinal study conducted by Kohlberg and his collaborators. The age trends reveal that development is extremely gradual. Stages 1 and 2 decrease from age 10 on, Stage 3 rises until about 16 to 18 and then declines, and Stage 4 increases steadily from early adolescence into adulthood, when it becomes the typical response; few subjects move beyond it to Stage 5 (Colby et al., 1983). Additional research attests to this very gradual development of moral thought (Gibbs & Widaman, 1982; Nisan & Kohlberg, 1982; Snarey, Reimer, & Kohlberg, 1985). In fact, principled morality is such a rarity in most samples studied that there is no clear evidence to date that Kohlberg's Stage 6 actually

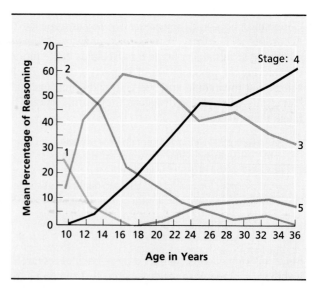

Figure 12.1. Mean percentage of moral reasoning at each stage for each age level in the Colby et al. (1983) 20-year longitudinal study. *(From A. Colby et al., 1983,* A Longitudinal Study of Moral Judgment. *Monographs of the Society for Research in Child Development, 48, (1– 2, Serial No. 200), 46. © The Society for Research in Child Development, Inc. Reprinted by permission.)*

follows Stage 5. The distinctiveness of the highest stage of moral development is still a matter of speculation.

Do Kohlberg's Stages Form Tightly Knit, Organized Wholes? If each of Kohlberg's moral stages forms an organized whole, then individuals should apply the same level of moral reasoning consistently across many tasks and situations. Research shows that when Kohlberg's interviewing procedure is used, most subjects do display fairly uniform reasoning from one moral dilemma to another (Walker, 1988). However, Kohlberg's scoring procedure tends to minimize variability in subjects' responses. When alternative scoring approaches are applied, people show greater diversity in the types of reasoning they produce (Rest, 1983).

Furthermore, when the procedures used to elicit moral thinking are systematically varied, moral reasoning changes as well. We have already mentioned that using an objective assessment procedure like the DIT produces more advanced moral judgments than Kohlberg's clinical interview. Changing aspects of the dilemmas has a profound effect as well. In one study, Sobesky (1983) gave high school and college students the Heinz dilemma, presenting the original version in addition to several new ones. In one rendition, the consequences Heinz would experience for stealing were dire; he would "be caught for sure and sent to prison." In another they were minimal; Heinz could "take the drug and the druggist [would] never miss it" (p. 578). When consequences were severe, students were less certain that stealing the drug was appropriate, and they gave fewer principled answers and more preconventional responses. Sobesky believes that highlighting the possibility of punishment for Heinz increased subjects' concern with self-interest, a major preconventional basis of morality. Other investigations indicate that when subjects are given moral dilemmas set in practical, familiar contexts, their reasoning changes, sometimes in an upward and sometimes in a downward direction (Gilligan & Belenky, 1980; Leming, 1978).

Earlier in this chapter we indicated that situational factors reduce the consistency of children's moral behavior; the findings summarized above indicate that they produce variability in moral judgments as well. Consequently, Kohlberg's stages do not look like the tightly knit entities he originally envisioned. Subjects do not seem to be completely "in" one stage or another. Instead, they manifest a number of different moral structures that depend on the type of task. Rest (1979a) suggests that Kohlberg's sequence be viewed in terms of a much looser stage conception, in much the same way that (as we indicated in Chapter 6) Flavell regards Piaget's stages of cognitive development. While retaining the idea of qualitatively distinct organizations of moral thought, Rest believes that change does not proceed one step at a time. Instead, it consists of shifting distributions of moral responses in which less mature reasoning declines as more mature thinking gradually becomes prominent. From this perspective, developmental periods vary in the *range of possible types of reasoning* that are evident, not in a single stage response.

Cognitive Prerequisites for Moral Reasoning. Like Piagetian moral judgment scores, assessments of moral maturity based on Kohlberg's theory are positively correlated with IQ, Piagetian cognitive performance, and perspective-taking skill (Rest, 1979a). However, these correlations do not tell us how cognitive maturity is related to moral thought. Do cognitive and moral development undergo separate but fairly similar lines of development, or does moral understanding actually depend on the acquisition of certain cognitive and perspective-taking structures?

Kohlberg (1969, 1976) and other cognitive-developmental theorists (Damon, 1977, Selman, 1977) have argued that moral development depends on cognitive and perspective-taking skills in a very specific way. As shown in Table 12.2, each moral stage is assumed to require the attainment of certain cognitive and perspective-taking stages, based on Piaget's and Selman's developmental sequences. However, cognitive-developmental theorists also believe that moral development cannot be entirely reduced to these other facets of cognitive growth. Moral understanding is assumed to

Table 12.2. Hypothesized Parallel Stages in Cognitive, Perspective-Taking, and Moral Development

PIAGET'S COGNITIVE STAGE	SELMAN'S PERSPECTIVE-TAKING STAGE	KOHLBERG'S MORAL STAGE
Preoperational	0 Undifferentiated and egocentric perspective-taking	0 Premoral
Transitional preoperational and concrete operational	1 Differentiated and subjective perspective-taking	1 Punishment and obedience orientation
Concrete operational	2 Self-reflective or reciprocal perspective-taking	2 Naive hedonistic orientation
Early formal operational	3 Third party or mutual perspective-taking	3 "Good boy–good girl" orientation
Consolidated formal operational	4 In-depth and societal perspective-taking	4 Social-order-maintaining perspective
		5 Social contract, legalistic orientation
		6 Universal ethical principle orientation

Source: Selman, 1976.

involve additional cognitive reorganizations that are entirely unique to the moral domain. Consequently, Kohlberg and others have hypothesized that cognitive and perspective-taking stages are *necessary but not sufficient conditions* for each of the moral stages.

Recall from Chapter 11 that the necessary but not sufficient condition applies to the relationship between Piaget's cognitive and Selman's perspective-taking stages, since Piagetian competencies are generally achieved before their respective perspective-taking counterparts. If Kohlberg is correct that the necessary but not sufficient assumption also applies to moral development, then moral maturity should either keep pace with or lag behind the attainment of corresponding cognitive and perspective-taking stages, but never be ahead of them. To what extent does research bear out this prediction?

Although no single study has examined the entire continuum of stage relationships shown in Table 12.2, several have focused on portions of it, and their findings are remarkably consistent with Kohlberg's predictions (Krebs & Gillmore, 1982; Selman, 1976; Walker, 1980). For example, in Walker's study of fourth through seventh graders, with only one exception, all children who demonstrated Stage 3 moral reasoning scored at either a higher stage or the equivalent stage of cognitive development and perspective-taking skill. Furthermore, intervention research indicates that moral development cannot be stimulated beyond the stage for which an individual possesses the appropriate cognitive prerequisites (Arbuthnot et al., 1983; Walker & Richards, 1979).

The research summarized above indicates that both nonsocial-cognitive and perspective-taking achievements are crucial building blocks of moral reasoning but that they are not enough by themselves. What other factors besides the achievement of Piaget's and Selman's stages might promote moral maturity? Earlier we mentioned Kohlberg's belief that cognitive disequilibrium is vital for moral change. That is, exposing people to conflicting information just ahead of their present moral level challenges them to move in the direction of more advanced moral thinking. A number of investigators believe that cognitive conflict is fundamental to moral change (Berkowitz, 1985; Haan, Aerts, & Cooper, 1985; Kohlberg, 1984; Turiel, 1977; Walker, 1983). Perhaps it is the critical factor that bridges the gap between children's cognitive attainments and their moral stage. As we will see in the following sections, the development of moral structures is related to many environmental factors, including peer interaction, child-rearing practices, formal education, and cultural variations. When environmental influences facilitate moral reasoning, it is conceivable that an important way in which they do so is by inducing disequilibrium — providing children and adolescents with just those cognitive challenges deemed essential for moral growth.

Environmental Influences on Moral Reasoning

Experiences that foster the development of moral reasoning have been investigated through a wealth of correlational studies. The weakness of this research literature is one we have mentioned a great many times before: Correlational investigations cannot guarantee that an important experiential cause of moral reasoning has been isolated. Fortunately, in a few instances, correlational studies have been supplemented with experiments that manipulate the environmental variable in question, providing more convincing evidence of its role in moral development.

Peer Interaction. Studies relating peer experiences to progress through Kohlberg's moral stages are consistent with Piaget's belief (discussed earlier) that interaction with agemates promotes moral understanding. Maturity of moral reasoning is correlated with peer popularity, participation in social organizations, and service in leadership roles (Enright & Sutterfield, 1980; Harris, Mussen, & Rutherford, 1976; Keasey, 1971). Research conducted in Africa underlines the importance of exposure to differing peer value systems for stimulating moral thought. Kenyan and Nigerian students who attended culturally heterogeneous high schools and colleges were advanced in moral judgment in comparison to those who were enrolled in homogeneous settings (Edwards, 1978; Maqsud, 1977). Culturally diverse educational environments may confront students with opposing moral perspectives that are especially challenging. In fact, the African college students attributed the greatest change in their personal values to encountering ethnic and racial diversity at school (Edwards, 1981).

Peer experiences have provided the framework for a number of interventions aimed at improving moral understanding. A major feature of most of them is peer discussion and role-playing of moral problems. A study by Blatt and Kohlberg (1975) is one of the most impressive in terms of its findings. After participating in teacher-led classroom discussions of moral dilemmas for one semester, many sixth and tenth graders moved partially or totally to the next stage, a change that was not found in subjects who had no opportunity for moral discussion. A year later, these differences were still evident. Other peer discussion interventions have also produced upward changes in moral reasoning, although in most instances, stage gains are slight (Arbuthnot, 1975; Berkowitz, Gibbs, & Broughton, 1980; Colby et al., 1977; Crockenberg & Nicolayev, 1979).

A major shortcoming of the studies noted above is that we cannot tell exactly what aspects of peer discussion serve as catalysts for moral change. Yet it is precisely this kind of information that is needed to design more effective moral education programs. Some researchers have begun to tackle this question by conducting fine-grained analyses of ongoing peer dialogues, comparing the features of those that produce greater stage change with those that lead to little or no change. Berkowitz and Gibbs (1983) found that college students who gained in moral maturity as the result of a discussion experience spent a great deal of time confronting, critiquing, and attempting to clarify one another's statements. In contrast, nongainers made independent assertions, gave personal anecdotes, or expressed confusion about the task. In another study, Haan, Aerts, and Cooper (1985) had small friendship groups of university students participate in weekly interaction sessions. Some groups discussed hypothet-

Membership in social organizations is positively related to children's maturity of moral reasoning.

ical moral dilemmas, while others played games designed to stir up actual moral problems among friends (e.g., a game called "Ghetto" in which citizens confront a corrupt staff person who represents "the system"). In the games, students engaged in more emotionally intense expressions of disagreement, while during discussions, the interchanges tended to be emotionally controlled, intellectual responses to conflict. Games facilitated the development of moral reasoning far more effectively than discussions. Taken together, these investigations indicate that discussions in which peers merely express disagreement are less effective in stimulating moral development than cognitively penetrating, emotionally involved exchanges in which participants experience one another's moral indignation.

Child-Rearing Practices. Family influences that are associated with mature moral reasoning are those that reflect rational, democratic processes. Adolescents who are at the conventional as opposed to the preconventional level have parents who are more advanced in moral understanding themselves and who encourage their youngsters to contribute actively to family discussions (Holstein, 1972; Parikh, 1980). These parents also rely on disciplinary methods that facilitate modeling and internalization of parental beliefs and practices, including low levels of power assertion and high levels of warmth, involvement, and inductive control techniques (Saltzstein, 1976). Edwards (1981) sums up the kind of parent who facilitates children's moral reasoning as one who is verbal, rational, and affectionate and who promotes a cooperative style of family life.

Formal Education. Since children and adolescents at higher levels of education are also older, it is difficult to separate the impact of schooling on moral reasoning from other age-related variables in youthful samples. However, studies of adults provide an opportunity to disentangle the effects of age and education. Among adult samples, older subjects need not have completed more formal education than younger subjects. The results of many such investigations indicate that formal schooling is one of the most powerful predictors of moral change. For example, Dortzbach (1975) examined the relationship of age and education to moral judgment scores on the DIT among adults between 25 and 74 years of age. As shown in Figure 12.2, mature reasoning increased dramatically with education, whereas it declined slightly when the subjects were grouped by age. Even the decline among older adults could be accounted for by education, since most 65- to 74-year-olds had attained only a grade-school education, while younger adults in the sample tended to be college educated.

Additional research indicates that individuals do not show much advance in moral reasoning beyond that accounted for by their level of education. Rest and Thoma (1985) conducted a six-year longitudinal study of young people who did not differ from each other in moral reasoning when they graduated from high school. Those who went to college continued to show gains in moral judgment maturity, whereas those who did not leveled off in development. Moral reasoning seems to advance regularly as long as a person remains in school, but when formal education is discontinued, moral reasoning tends to stabilize (Rest, 1979a).

Why is formal education such an important contributor to the development of moral understanding? Its impact could be due to many factors, including extracurricular participation, classroom exposure to morally relevant subject matter, and other elements of the school milieu. As yet, the precise mechanisms of school influence have not been identified, and further research is needed to clarify them.

Culture. Cross-cultural research on Kohlberg's stages indicates that the rate and end point of moral development vary substantially from one society to another. A great many studies indicate that individuals in technologically advanced cultures move through the stages more rapidly and advance to higher levels than do individuals in less industrialized and more rural environments. Stages 4 and above are not

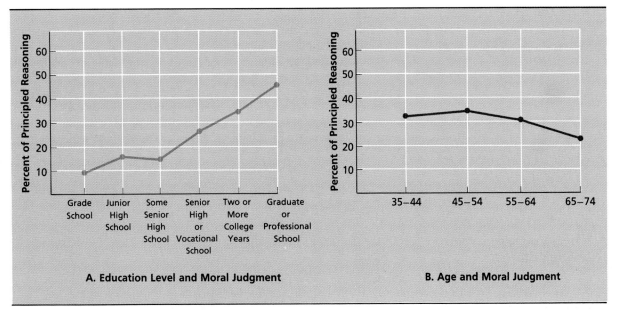

A. Education Level and Moral Judgment

B. Age and Moral Judgment

Figure 12.2. Relationship of education and age to moral judgment in the Dortzbach (1975) study. *(Adapted from J. R. Dortzbach, 1975.)*

reached by members of isolated peasant and tribal communities, whereas they are achieved by high school- and college-educated adolescents and adults in a variety of Western and non-Western samples (Boyes & Walker, 1988; Snarey, 1985).

Why these cultural differences exist remains a matter of considerable debate. One possibility is that Kohlberg's dilemmas are inappropriate for eliciting moral reasoning in some cultures and, in these cases, underestimate moral understanding. Countering this argument are the reports of several investigators that people from quite different cultures easily comprehend the dilemmas and regard the issues that they raise as familiar and important (Walker, 1988). A second explanation addresses the role of societal institutions in stimulating moral development. Kohlberg (1969) argued that greater societal complexity in terms of governmental institutions and legal systems is necessary for a culture to foster the highest stages. In traditional peasant and tribal communities, participation in village life, with its emphasis on interpersonal expectations as the primary basis for cooperation, fosters reasoning as high as Stage 3. More advanced reasoning is not needed to carry out the activities of the social group. The existence of formalized systems of government and law as well as opportunities to participate in them is believed to be necessary for Stage 4 and above. In support of this interpretation, Snarey, Reimer, and Kohlberg (1985) found that the moral stage scores of Israeli kibbutz-reared adolescents and young adults, who receive participatory training in the cooperative institutions of their society from an early age, were unusually high. When compared to Americans, kibbutz-reared young people were advanced at all ages between 13 and 26, and a greater proportion of them eventually reached Stage 5. In fact, by third grade, children growing up on a kibbutz already verbalize more concerns about societal laws and norms when discussing moral conflicts than do Israeli city-reared or American children (Fuchs et al., 1986).

The fact that the highest stages are absent in traditional village societies raises the question of whether Kohlberg's principled reasoning represents a culturally specific rather than universal form of moral understanding. Some critics believe that Kohlberg's highest level is limited to Western European societies that emphasize moral values based on individual rights and appeal to an inner, private conscience (e.g.,

Shweder, 1982). One way to find out would be to examine the development of moral reasoning in societies that are just as complex as Western industrialized nations but guided by very different philosophical traditions. Recently, one such study was conducted in India. Its findings shed new light on the cross-cultural validity of Kohlberg's theory and are summarized in Box 12.2.

Taken together, research reviewed in the sections above suggests a powerful role for environmental contexts in the development of moral understanding. Higher stages are not realized unless appropriate environmental supports exist on multiple levels, including family, peer group, schooling, and institutions of the wider society.

◆ CONTEMPORARY ISSUES: CULTURAL DIFFERENCES ◆

Moral Reasoning in India: A Test of the Cultural Universality of Kohlberg's Stages

Box 12.2

Cross-cultural research has supported Kohlberg's claim of a universal sequence of moral development through the preconventional and conventional levels. However, the absence of postconventional reasoning in non-Western village societies has raised doubts about whether Kohlberg was correct that there is a higher conception of justice that human beings everywhere would attain if they were exposed to adequate educational and social opportunities.

To investigate this issue, Jyotsna Vasudev and Raymond Hummel (1987) studied the development of moral reasoning in India—a country that is as structurally complex as any Western society and that has a class of adults sufficiently well educated to progress to Kohlberg's principled level. At the same time, India's traditions, religions, and philosophies are based on unique conceptions of morality not found in Western nations. Consequently, the study of moral development among Indian subjects provides an ideal opportunity to test the universality of Kohlberg's scheme.

Moral reasoning interviews were conducted with urban middle-class and upper-middle-class subjects from 11 to over 50 years of age whose religious affiliation was either Hindu, Jain, or Sikh—a homogeneous group of theologies emphasizing nonviolence and the interrelatedness of all forms of life as fundamental moral values. Consistent with research on Western samples, the Indian subjects displayed an age-related pattern of moral understanding, with all three levels represented and 20 percent of adults giving postconventional responses. These findings support Kohlberg's claim that principled thinking is not simply a Western phenomenon.

At the same time, themes emerged in the Indian subjects' reasoning that were difficult to classify according to Kohlberg's scheme. For example, an emphasis on collective solutions to moral dilemmas, rather than appeals to private conscience, appeared among the most mature members of the sample. In fact, the Heinz dilemma seemed especially meaningful to these respondents, who were quick to relate it to pressing problems of the Indian population. Yet they resisted choosing a particular course of action, explaining that a moral solution should not be the burden of a single individual, but of the entire society. As one woman explained:

> The problems that Heinz is up against are not individual problems that are afflicting 1 or 2 Heinzes of the world. These are social problems. Forget Heinz in Europe, just come to India and you are speaking of the same thing with 60% of the people living below the poverty line. In fact, Heinz's story is being repeated all around us all the time with wives dying, with children dying, and there is no money to save them. . . . So Heinz in his individual capacity—yes, okay, steal the drug, but it's not going to make any difference on a larger scale; and if his wife dies it is not going to make any difference on a larger scale. I don't think in the final analysis a solution can be worked out on an individual basis. . . . It will probably have to be tackled on a macro level. (p. 110)

The collective solutions adhered to by the Indian interviewees are similar to responses obtained from Israeli kibbutz and Chinese subjects—also not easily reconciled with Kohlberg's system (Hwang, 1986; Snarey et al., 1985). Vasudev and Hummer concluded that Kohlberg's justice morality taps an important universal dimension of human moral reasoning. Yet it does not describe the whole domain of morality in every culture. From a cross-cultural perspective, there appear to be both commonalities and diversity in principled moral thought.

Are There Sex Differences in Moral Reasoning?

499

CHAPTER 12
THE DEVELOPMENT OF
MORALITY AND
SELF-CONTROL

One of the most controversial questions about Kohlberg's theory concerns whether it fails to tap important aspects of moral thought that are uniquely feminine. Carol Gilligan (1977, 1982) is the most prominent figure among those who have argued that Kohlberg's theory is sex-biased. Gilligan noticed that the findings of a handful of early studies indicated that the moral reasoning of females lagged behind that of males. Girls appeared to advance to Stage 3 and then remain there, while boys moved beyond, reaching Stages 4 and 5 by late adolescence and adulthood (e.g., Haan, Smith, & Block, 1968; Holstein, 1976). If these findings are accurate, they support a widely held stereotype that men develop an abstract, rational commitment to moral ideals, whereas women embed their morality in a less mature, concrete concern for interpersonal approval and maintenance of harmonious relationships.

Gilligan accepts the idea that female morality is embedded in human relationships, but she believes that a feminine commitment to an "ethic of care" is not a mark of moral inferiority. Instead, she argues that Kohlberg's stages are limited to a description of how individuals arrive at *abstract justice reasoning* and do not adequately incorporate other valid bases of morality, such as a *concern for others*. Gilligan has proposed an alternative sequence of development in which a "morality of care" moves from an egoistic, self-centered emphasis to a concrete commitment to people with whom one has close affectional ties (a Stage 3–like conception), and finally to an abstract understanding of care as a universal obligation (a principle of postconventional judgment).

Recent comprehensive reviews of research do not support Gilligan's claim that Kohlberg's approach underestimates the moral maturity of females. Walker and de Vries (1985) examined the results of 80 studies that, taken together, included responses from over 10,000 subjects to Kohlberg's interviews. In the vast majority of investigations, no sex differences were found. In another comprehensive review, this time of 56 samples involving 6,000 subjects who responded to the DIT, females scored *higher* than males at every age and level of education examined, although the size of the discrepancy was small (Thoma, 1986). In both of these summary analyses, the investigators concluded that females do not score lower than males on justice-oriented measures of moral development.

However, it is still possible that important sex differences in moral understanding would emerge if researchers focused on subjects' reasoning about issues of interpersonal commitment and care. Responding to Gilligan's suggestion that everyday moral problems might better evoke this kind of reasoning than Kohlberg's moral dilemmas, Walker, de Vries, and Trevethan (1987; Walker, 1989) asked first-, fourth-, seventh-, and tenth-grade youngsters as well as adults to recall a personal moral conflict that they had actually experienced. In addition, the subjects responded to standard hypothetical dilemmas. In both problem situations, the investigators looked at how each subject oriented to the moral problem — that is, whether they defined it as a matter of personal relationship concerns or impersonal rights and fairness concerns. Contrary to Gilligan's claim that females orient toward interpersonal issues more often than males, for the majority of subjects, both caring and justice orientations emerged in response to everyday as well as hypothetical dilemmas. Furthermore, when females did raise interpersonal issues, they were not down-scored by Kohlberg's assessment system. In fact, there was a slight tendency for subjects who had a stronger caring orientation to be at higher moral stages.

These findings suggest that although Kohlberg emphasized fairness and justice rather than interpersonal commitment and caring as the highest of moral ideals, his theory and methods may, in actuality, tap both sets of values. For example, the Stage 6 person's appeal to universal moral principles, such as the dignity and worth of each individual, may combine abstract notions of justice with a deep, abiding concern for other human beings. Although current evidence indicates that justice and caring are not sex-specific moralities, Gilligan's work has had the effect of broadening cognitive-developmental conceptions of the highly moral person. As Brabeck (1983) indicates:

> [Gilligan's] major contribution rests in a redefinition of what constitutes an adequate description of the moral ideal. When Gilligan's and Kohlberg's theories are taken together, the moral person is seen as one whose moral choices reflect reasoned and deliberate judgments that ensure justice be accorded each person while maintaining a passionate concern for the well-being and care of each individual. Justice and care are then joined . . . and the need for autonomy and for interconnection are united in an enlarged and more adequate conception of morality. (p. 289)

Moral Reasoning and Behavior

An integral part of the cognitive-developmental approach is that moral understanding should affect moral motivation. Cognitive-developmental theorists believe that as children come to understand the purpose and function of cooperative social arrangements, they develop increased respect for the arrangements themselves and for the people who work to uphold and protect them. As a result, children gradually realize that behaving in line with the way one thinks is an important part of creating and maintaining a just social world (Rest, 1983). On the basis of this idea, the cognitive-developmental approach predicts a very specific relationship between moral thought and behavior: the two should come closer together as individuals advance toward the higher levels of moral understanding.

Consistent with this prediction, research indicates that progress through the moral stages is associated with many facets of moral behavior (Blasi, 1980). For example, maturity of moral reasoning is related to altruism, including helping, sharing, and defending victims of injustice (e.g., Harris, Mussen, & Rutherford, 1976; Staub, 1974). It also predicts honesty, as measured by cheating in school and resistance to temptation in laboratory tasks that require children not to touch forbidden toys or return money that does not belong to them (e.g., Harris, Mussen, & Rutherford, 1976; Nelson, Grinder, & Biaggio, 1969).

Moral understanding is also related to student protest behavior in colleges and universities. In a well-known study, Haan, Smith, and Block (1968) interviewed university students during a period of frequent campus demonstrations over free speech and other human rights issues in the 1960s. In general, postconventional students were more involved in political-social matters and were more likely to protest than the conventionally moral. Some preconventional students were also politically active. However, their reasons for participation reflected reactive and rebellious motivations. In contrast, postconventional students appeared to be acting on higher moral principles, since they described a deep personal commitment to civil liberties and the rights of students as citizens in a university community. Other studies also report that advanced moral reasoning is related to value stances on controversial public issues. For example, Kohlberg's principled morality is associated with a firm belief in the right to free speech, due process, and opposition to capital punishment (de Vries & Walker, 1986; Rest, 1986). Commitment to such values may be an important intermediate link between postconventional moral structures and political behavior.

Despite a clear connection between moral reasoning and behavior, the strength of this association is, in all instances, only moderate. In fact, Kohlberg acknowledged that the relationship would be imperfect. As we indicated earlier, moral behavior is influenced by a great many factors besides moral thinking, including emotional reactions such as empathy and guilt and social background and experiences that affect moral choices and decision making. Once investigators discover how all these aspects of moral motivation work together as parts of a complex, functioning whole, prediction of moral behavior will undoubtedly improve (Blasi, 1983).

In 1988, students protested the appointment of a nondeaf president at Gallaudet University, a campus with an all-deaf student body. Participants in campus demonstrations are often morally mature individuals with deep commitments to civil liberties.

BRIEF REVIEW

In the sections above, we have seen that Kohlberg's extension of Piaget's original work has amassed substantial research support. Although moral reasoning seems to fit a looser stage conception than Kohlberg originally envisioned, the stages conform to an orderly, invariant developmental sequence. From late childhood into adulthood, morality gradually evolves from concrete, externally governed reasoning toward increasingly abstract, comprehensive, and ethically adequate justifications for moral choices and actions. Each moral stage builds on cognitive and perspective-taking capacities. In addition, a broad range of experiences promotes development, including moral discussions with peers and family members, formal education, and citizenship activities in the wider political and economic arena of society. Recent evidence indicates that Kohlberg's theory is not sex-biased. However, cross-cultural research suggests that Kohlberg's principled morality does not capture all aspects of mature moral reasoning in non-Western cultures.

Unresolved Questions about Kohlberg's Theory

Despite considerable support for Kohlberg's stage sequence, several unresolved questions about his theory remain. These concern the relationship of moral structure to content, Kohlberg's ideas on moral education, and the appropriateness of his dilemmas for studying the moral reasoning of young children. To conclude our consideration of Kohlberg's work, let's examine each of these issues in turn.

Kohlberg's emphasis on moral structure rather than content to assess moral maturity has been troubling to many investigators. Although he acknowledged that these two aspects of moral functioning merge at the postconventional level into a more broadly applicable and effective form of moral reflection, the relationship between structure and content at the first four stages of development is less clear. Movement through the lower stages would hardly seem to be of much consequence unless it could be argued that these increments in reasoning are also accompanied by more valid moral commitments. To fully verify Kohlberg's theory, current investigators recognize the need to specify how each advance in quality of moral structures implies improvements in moral content, or particular kinds of moral choice (Lapsley, Enright, & Serlin, 1989; Snarey, 1985; Vasudev, 1988; Walker, 1989).

A related controversy has to do with Kohlberg's ideas regarding moral education. Look back at the kinds of experiences that Kohlberg regarded as important for facilitating moral growth. They do not focus on teaching moral rules. Instead, they emphasize cognitive challenges that are likely to induce disequilibrium and consequent revision of moral structures. In fact, for many years, Kohlberg opposed approaches to moral education that taught children prescriptions for good behavior, regarding them as a form of indoctrination that prevented children from building their own rational moral structures. However, others disagreed with this assumption, arguing that direct teaching of moral content is not only necessary but compatible with Kohlberg's theory and that it can be fruitfully combined with efforts to foster moral reasoning (Hamm, 1977; Watson et al., 1989). According to this view, teaching particular rules and behaviors that constitute specific instances of higher moral principles provides children with concrete examples that they can reflect on and organize into abstract moral ideals. When adults encourage children not to cause pain to others, to keep promises and abide by contracts, and not to lie or cheat, they actually support the cause of justice rather than interfere with it. Kohlberg (1978, 1980; Power, 1989) later revised his conception of moral education to include direct teaching of moral attitudes and behavior, acknowledging that it could facilitate moral understanding if accompanied by rational appeals to fairness and community welfare. However, he continued to regard social interaction that encourages young people to question the validity of existing rules and laws as essential for the attainment of postconventional moral thought.

Finally, Kohlberg's stages focus on broad transformations in moral understanding that take place between late childhood and adulthood. Since most research on his theory concentrates on children age 10 and older, it tells us little about changes in moral reasoning that take place during early and middle childhood. Moreover, Kohlberg's moral dilemmas are remote from the experiences of young children and may not be clearly understood by them. Consequently, the dilemmas are inappropriate for gathering information about moral understanding during the preschool and early elementary school years. Investigations in which young children have been provided with moral problems related to their everyday experience indicate that Kohlberg's Stage 1, much like Piaget's heteronomous morality, underestimates the moral reasoning of the younger child. We turn to a consideration of this evidence in the following sections.

THE MORAL REASONING OF YOUNG CHILDREN

Two bodies of research have used moral dilemmas specifically designed for children age 12 and below: (1) studies of children's **distributive justice,** or how they think rewards should be allocated among group members, and (2) investigations of children's responses to *prosocial moral dilemmas* in which they must choose between satisfying their own needs and those of others. Besides being relevant to children's real-life experiences, the moral problems used in these studies differ from Kohlberg's in that the importance of laws and the possibility of punishment are de-emphasized and there are few obvious rules on which to base a course of action. When dilemmas are formulated in this way, young children reveal some surprisingly sophisticated moral judgments.

Young Children's Understanding of Distributive Justice

In everyday life, children are frequently the recipients of adults' and peers' distributive decisions, and they dispense rewards to others as well. How much weekly allowance is to be given to siblings of different ages, who has to sit where in the family car on an extended vacation, and in what way an eight-slice pizza is to be shared by six hungry playmates are all questions of distributive justice.

William Damon (1977) gave children between 4 and 9 years of age a distributive justice interview in which they were asked to react to dilemmas like this one:

> All of these boys and girls are in the same class together. One day their teacher lets them spend the whole afternoon making paintings and crayon drawings. The teacher thought that these pictures were so good that the class could sell them at the fair. They sold the pictures to their parents, and together the class made a whole lot of money. Now all the children gathered the next day and tried to decide how to split up the money. What do you think they should do with it? Why? (p. 66)

On the basis of children's responses, Damon identified a six-level sequence of distributive justice reasoning. As shown in Table 12.3, preschool children's ideas about how rewards should be allocated start out as egocentric; fairness is equated with self-interest. By middle childhood, children consider a variety of claims to rewards, including work accomplished and special needs of participants. Eight-year-olds also believe that the distribution of rewards should serve some higher social goal, such as helping the group do better next time or promoting positive feelings among group members.

Damon's levels of distributive justice reasoning are supported by both cross-sectional and longitudinal evidence (Blotner & Bearison, 1984; Damon, 1977; Enright, Franklin, & Manheim, 1980; Enright et al., 1980). Furthermore, like Piaget's and Kohlberg's stages, distributive justice concepts are related to cognitive development. For example, Damon's Level 1-B (refer to Table 12.3) is associated with the attainment of concrete operations and subjective perspective-taking skill (Enright, Franklin, & Manheim, 1980; McNamee & Peterson, 1986).

Table 12.3. Damon's Levels of Distributive Justice Reasoning

LEVEL	APPROXIMATE AGE	DESCRIPTION
0-A	4	Fair allocation of rewards is confused with the child's momentary desires. Children of this level believe that they themselves should get more simply because they want more.
0-B	4–5	Children cite an objective attribute as a fair basis for distribution, but it is arbitrary and irrelevant to the situation. A child should get more for being the oldest, a fast runner, or having the most friends.
1-A	5	There is recognition that each participant has a stake in the rewards, but children of this level think that the only way competing claims can be resolved is by strictly equal distribution. Special considerations like merit or need are not taken into account.
1-B	6–7	Fair distribution is equated with deservingness. There is recognition that some people may have a greater claim to rewards for having worked harder.
2-A	8	Children recognize a variety of conflicting claims to justice, including equal treatment, merit, and need. Each claim is weighed, and parties with special needs, such as a younger child who cannot produce as much or a child who does not get any allowance, are given consideration.
2-B	8 and older	As in 2-A, all claims are considered. In addition, a fair distribution of rewards is seen as one that furthers the social goals of the group — for example, by encouraging future productivity or promoting friendship and group solidarity.

Source: Damon, 1977.

A mature understanding of distributive justice also predicts everyday social behavior. Children who reason at advanced levels are better social problem solvers (see Chapter 11), more altruistic when given opportunities to share or help another child, and rated as more popular and fair-minded by classmates than their less mature counterparts (Blotner & Bearison, 1984; Damon, 1977; Enright & Sutterfield, 1980; McNamee & Peterson, 1986).

Research on children's ideas of distributive justice suggests that complex, internalized concepts of fairness emerge much earlier than Kohlberg's punishment-oriented Stage 1 would have us believe.[6] In fact, fear of punishment and deference to authority do not even appear as themes in children's distributive justice rationales. Because Damon's dilemmas minimize the relevance of these factors to moral choice, they permit some impressively mature reasoning by children to rise to the surface.

Young Children's Prosocial and Altruistic Reasoning

Earlier, when we considered Gilligan's challenge to Kohlberg's theory, we showed that Kohlberg's stages and dilemmas do tap a caring orientation, in addition to a morality of fairness and justice. Nevertheless, prosocial choices in Kohlberg's dilemmas are always pitted against legal prohibitions or an authority's dictates (Eisenberg, 1982; Eisenberg, Lennon, & Pasternack, 1986). For example, in the Heinz dilemma, to help his wife, Heinz has no choice but to break the law and steal. In most everyday situations in which children must decide whether or not to do something for another person, the primary cost is not disobeying a law or an authority figure. Instead, the cost is a personal one of not satisfying one's own wants or needs. Nancy Eisenberg has constructed a set of prosocial moral dilemmas that make the primary sacrifice in aiding another person a matter of giving up personal desires. Here is a typical prosocial dilemma that Eisenberg gives to younger children:

> One day a girl named Mary was going to a friend's birthday party. On her way she saw a girl who had fallen down and hurt her leg. The girl asked Mary to go to her house and get her parents so the parents could come and take her to the doctor. But if Mary did run and get the child's parents, she would be late for the birthday party and miss the ice cream, cake, and all the games. What should Mary do? Why? (Eisenberg, 1982, p. 231)

Interviewing children from preschool through twelfth grade, Eisenberg found that their responses to prosocial moral problems fell into five age-related levels, which are summarized in Table 12.4. Both cross-sectional and longitudinal evidence supports this developmental pattern (Eisenberg, Lennon, & Roth, 1983; Eisenberg et al., 1987; Eisenberg-Berg, 1979; Eisenberg-Berg & Roth, 1980).

Perhaps you have already noticed that Eisenberg's developmental sequence bears considerable similarity to Kohlberg's stages. Her hedonistic, pragmatic orientation is like Kohlberg's Stage 2, her "needs of others" and approval-focused orientations are like Kohlberg's Stage 3, and her internalized values orientation includes forms of reasoning that match Kohlberg's Stages 4 through 6. But several features of Eisenberg's research differ from Kohlberg's. First, like the distributive justice findings noted above, authority- and punishment-oriented reasoning is completely absent from the prosocial dilemma responses of children at all ages. Second, children's prosocial understanding is clearly accelerated when compared to the timing of Kohlberg's stages. For example, Kohlberg reported that approval-focused (Stage 3) rea-

---

[6] Note that this very same conclusion is supported by Turiel and Nucci's research on children's moral versus social conventional understanding, described earlier in this chapter. By the early elementary school years, children are aware that a distinguishing feature of moral transgressions is that they violate another person's right to be treated fairly and humanely.

Table 12.4. Eisenberg's Levels of Prosocial Moral Reasoning

LEVEL	APPROXIMATE AGE	DESCRIPTION
1. Hedonistic, pragmatic orientation	Preschool, early elementary school	Right behavior satisfies one's own needs. Reasons for helping or not helping another refer to gains for the self, e.g., "I wouldn't help because I might be hungry."
2. "Needs of others" orientation	Preschool, elementary school	Concern for the physical, material, and psychological needs of others is expressed in simple terms, without clear evidence of perspective-taking or empathic feeling, e.g., "He needs it."
3. Stereotyped, approval-focused orientation	Elementary school and high school	Stereotyped images of good and bad persons and concern for approval justify behavior, e.g., "He'd like him more if he helped."
4. Empathic orientation	Older elementary school and high school	Reasoning reflects an emphasis on perspective-taking and empathic feeling for the other person. e.g., "I'd feel bad if I didn't help because he'd be in pain."
5. Internalized values orientation	Small minority of high school students, no elementary school pupils	Justifications for moral choice are based on internalized values, norms, desire to maintain contractual obligations, and belief in the dignity, rights, and equality of all individuals, e.g., "I would feel bad if I didn't help because I'd know that I didn't live up to my values."

Source: Eisenberg, 1982.

soning is rare before adolescence. In Eisenberg's system, it occurs often during middle childhood. Finally, Eisenberg's dilemmas bring out a new form of moral reasoning that she calls "empathic." By the late elementary school years, children realize that empathy is an important motivator of behavior aimed at benefiting others. The appearance of empathic reasoning also indicates that children's prosocial understanding has become truly altruistic, since empathic justifications include a clear willingness to help others without expecting concrete rewards or social approval in return.

In a recent longitudinal study, Eisenberg and her colleagues found that 9- and 10-year-olds who empathized easily with others advanced to higher levels of prosocial reasoning during early adolescence than their less empathic counterparts (Eisenberg et al., 1987). Eisenberg believes that the ability to react empathically may encourage advanced prosocial reasoning and strengthen its realization in everyday behavior. In line with this idea, children who score at the higher stages of prosocial reasoning do behave in a more prosocial and altruistic fashion than those who show less advanced prosocial judgments (Eisenberg-Berg, 1979; Eisenberg-Berg & Hand, 1979). Eisenberg is one investigator who has made an important start at putting the cognitive, affective, and behavioral components of morality together.

Viewed together with Kohlberg's theory, Damon's and Eisenberg's research reveals that moral understanding is a rich and multifaceted phenomenon. Its dimensions are not exhaustively described by any single theory or set of moral dilemmas. Children's responses to a wide range of moral problems, including ones that focus on justice, fair distribution of material goods, and prosocial behavior, are needed to comprehensively describe the development of moral thought.

The study of moral reasoning tells us what people think they would do and why when faced with a moral problem, but we have already indicated that people's good intentions often fall short. Whether children and adults actually follow through on what they believe partly depends on characteristics that we call iron will, firm resolve, strong character, or, put more simply, **self-control.** Self-control in the moral arena involves inhibiting behaviors that conflict with a moral course of action. Sometimes it is referred to as resistance to transgression or resistance to temptation. You are already familiar with these terms, since we made reference to them in the first part of this chapter. Recall that children's self-control is enhanced by inductive discipline, as well as by models who demonstrate and explicitly verbalize self-controlled behavior. Thus we have already seen that the practices of socialization agents play an important role in the development of self-control. However, children cannot be affected by these practices until they have developed the ability to internalize parental prohibitions and resist temptation. When and how does the child's own capacity for self-control develop?

The Beginnings of Self-Control: Late Infancy and Early Childhood

The beginnings of self-control are supported by several cognitive achievements of the second year of life that we discussed in earlier chapters. Children cannot deliberately resist temptation until they are aware of themselves as separate, autonomous beings and understand that their actions have consequences that are controllable by the self (Chapters 6 and 11). Self-control also requires representational and memory capacities (Chapters 6 and 7) that permit children to internalize a caregiver's directives and apply them to their own behavior (Kopp, 1982, 1987). As these abilities mature and consolidate, the first glimmerings of self-control appear in the form of **compliance.** Between 12 and 18 months of age, children start to show clear awareness of caregivers' wishes and expectations and can voluntarily obey their commands and requests (Kopp, 1982; Luria, 1961; Vygotsky, 1934/1987).

Also, toddlers can decide to do just the opposite! One way they assert their emerging sense of autonomy is by resisting adult demands — a phenomenon called early childhood negativism or, as parents commonly refer to it, "the terrible twos." Fortunately, among children who experience warm, rational child rearing, oppositional behavior is far less common than compliance. Moreover, toddler resistance is gradually transformed over the preschool years into polite refusals and socially skilled negotiation strategies in which children try to effect compromises with their parents. These are far more acceptable expressions of the child's growing autonomy than outright defiance and resistance (Kuczynski et al., 1987; Kuczynski & Kochanska, 1990).

Parents are generally delighted at their toddler's new-found ability to comply, since it signals that the child is ready to learn the rules of social life. In addition, adults can moderate the child's behavior more easily and from a greater distance than was possible at an earlier age. Nevertheless, control of the child's actions during the second year is still tied to the here and now of caregiver prompts and commands, and adults must repeatedly call the young child's attention to expectations for acceptable behavior (Kopp, 1987). According to the Soviet theorist Vygotsky (1934/1987), children cannot control their own behavior until they are able to incorporate adult directives into their own speech and use it to instruct the self. You may remember from Chapter 6 that this self-directed form of language is often referred to as *private speech.*

The first investigations of very young children's ability to use speech to control their own actions were conducted by one of Vygotsky's followers, Alexander Luria (1961). Luria was interested in how early children could *initiate* as well as *inhibit* a behavior when they told themselves to do so. The ability to voluntarily inhibit action tendencies is especially important for morally relevant self-control, since without it, young children clearly cannot resist temptation. In Luria's research, 1½- to 5-year-olds were given a bulb-squeezing task in which each child was requested to say "press" and squeeze a rubber bulb, following which the child was told to say "don't press" and release the bulb. Children below age 3 could respond to their own verbal instructions to initiate behavior, but curiously, they could not use a verbal command to inhibit an ongoing action. Upon giving themselves the directive "don't press," they squeezed the bulb even harder! On the basis of this finding, Luria concluded that before age 3, children cannot use self-directed speech to control their own behavior. According to Luria, 2-year-olds simply react to the energizing, motor quality of speech rather than to its meaningful content. Therefore, regardless of whether they tell themselves to press or not press the bulb, they continue to engage in bulb-squeezing behavior.

Follow-up investigations reveal that Luria's conclusion regarding the 2-year-old's lack of self-control was only partly correct (Pressley, 1979). The bulb-squeezing task requires children to stop a behavior that is already in progress, and in line with Luria's findings, 2-year-olds do find this kind of problem to be quite difficult. For example, when asked to stop playing with a very attractive toy, they inhibit their own behavior far less effectively than do 3- and 4-year-olds (Masters & Binger, 1976). However, the 2-year-old *can* make use of language to inhibit behavior in situations that call for **delay of gratification.** In a delay of gratification task, children must hold an impulse to respond in check that has not yet been initiated. Many everyday problems in self-control are of this kind—waiting to eat a piece of candy until after dinner, refraining from taking another child's attractive toy, or not turning on the TV set until homework and household chores are finished, to name just a few.

In a study aimed at investigating 2-year-olds' capacity to delay gratification, Vaughn, Kopp, and Krakow (1984) gave 18-, 24-, and 30-month-old children a series of three tasks. In the first task, the child was instructed not to touch an interesting toy telephone that was within arm's reach. In the second, raisins were hidden under cups, and the child was told to wait until the experimenter said it was all right to pick up a cup and eat a raisin. In the third task, the child was told not to open an attractively wrapped gift until the experimenter had finished her work. As shown in Figure 12.3,

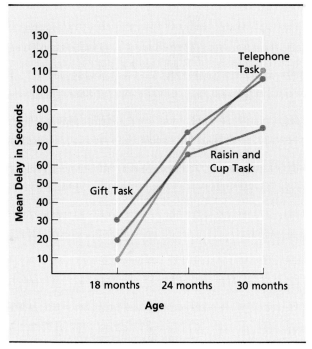

Figure 12.3. Age changes in delay of gratification in the Vaughn, Kopp, and Krakow (1984) study. *(Adapted from Vaughn, Kopp, and Krakow, 1984.)*

on all three problems, the ability to delay gratification increased dramatically from 18 months to 2½ years of age. Furthermore, by age 2½, clear individual differences in the ability to exercise self-control were evident, and the single best predictor of them was language development.

These findings reveal that self-control undergoes an important period of development and consolidation around 2 to 2½ years of age, considerably earlier than Luria's bulb-pressing research indicated. However, Vaughn, Kopp, and Krakow's results are clearly supportive of Luria and Vygotsky's view that speech and language are intimately tied to children's ability to control their own behavior. In fact, the investigators informally noted that 2-year-olds used a number of verbal techniques to help themselves wait, including singing and talking out loud to themselves.

The Development of Self-Control from the Late Preschool through Adolescent Years

The capacity for self-control is in place by the third year of life, but it is not completely developed. Improved cognitive abilities permit older children to use a variety of effective *self-instructional strategies* for resisting temptation. As a result, delay of gratification undergoes steady improvement during childhood and adolescence (Mischel & Metzner, 1962; Weisz, 1978).

Strategies for Self-Control. Walter Mischel has studied exactly what older children think and say to themselves that enables them to resist temptation more effectively than their younger counterparts. His research was initially inspired by Freud's (1925/1961a) suggestion that thinking about a desired object can substitute for real satisfaction, reduce the feeling of need, and help children to delay. However, an early study by Mischel and Ebbesen (1970) indicated that Freud's belief was incorrect. Preschoolers were given a delay of gratification problem in which they could choose between a highly desirable food reward that they would have to wait to eat and a less desirable food reward that they could eat anytime during the waiting period. Informal observations of the most self-controlled preschoolers indicated that rather than focusing their attention on the reward, they did just the opposite. They used any technique they could think of to *distract* themselves from the desired object, including covering their eyes and inventing games with their hands and feet.

In everyday situations, preschoolers find it extremely difficult to keep their minds off tempting activities and objects for very long. When children's thoughts do turn to an enticing but prohibited object, instructions that get them to engage in *cognitive transformations* of the mental stimulus are highly effective in promoting delay of gratification. In one study, Mischel and Baker (1975) had some preschoolers think about marshmallows imaginatively as "white and puffy clouds" and others focus on their realistic, "sweet and chewy" properties. In the realistic condition, children had much more difficulty waiting to eat the reward. These results show that not all mental images containing the desired object interfere with response inhibition. Instead, the nature of the cognitive representation is the critical feature that influences a child's capacity to delay. When diverting attention from rewards is difficult, thinking about them in stimulus-transforming ways that de-emphasize their arousing qualities improves children's self-control.

In the study described above, an experimenter taught preschool children to use delay-enhancing strategies. How good are preschoolers at thinking up these techniques on their own? Toner and Smith (1977) found that when an adult refrained from giving preschool children explicit instructions in how to resist temptation, their ability to wait in a delay of gratification task declined considerably. In contrast, early elementary school children did just as well whether an adult provided them with strategies or not. These findings indicate that not until first and second grade are children good at applying their own strategies for resisting temptation. Of course, even very young preschoolers can generate some effective self-control techniques (as the examples given earlier indicate), but the ability to do so improves markedly during middle childhood.

Knowledge of Strategies. In Chapter 7, we indicated that *metacognition,* or conscious awareness of strategies, plays a role in how effectively children apply them. Mischel and Mischel (1983) interviewed 3- to 11-year-olds to find out how much they knew about situational conditions and self-instructions likely to facilitate performance on a delay of gratification task. A few preschoolers were aware that diverting their attention from the reward would be helpful, since they gave such suggestions as "Close two eyes" and "Talk to the wall." However, most of the younger children had considerable difficulty describing the strategies they would use. As children moved through the elementary school grades, they suggested an increasingly broad array of delay tactics. In addition, older children described why certain techniques worked by referring to their arousal-reducing properties. Finally, not until the late elementary school years did children mention strategies involving cognitive transformations of rewards or their own arousal states. For example, one creative 11-year-old recommended saying, "the marshmallows are filled with an evil spell." Another indicated that he would tell himself, "I hate marshmallows, I can't stand them. But when the grown-up gets back, I'll tell myself 'I love marshmallows' and eat it" (p. 609). Perhaps awareness of transforming ideation appears so late in development because it requires the abstract hypothetical reasoning processes of formal operational thought.

Do the findings of Mischel and his co-workers enhance your understanding of why disciplinary practices that include inductions and explanations (discussed earlier in this chapter) are so effective in promoting children's capacity for behavioral inhibition? Such practices fit with the child's natural inclination to use self-guiding and self-inhibiting instructions to control their own behavior. They also provide children with examples of successful techniques for resisting temptation, and they offer rationales that promote metacognitive awareness of which strategies work best and why.

From Self-Control to Responsibility. There is one final factor that contributes to the older child's improved capacity for self-control. During late childhood and adolescence, self-control starts to become an important part of the young person's self-concept. In one study, children between 6 and 12 years of age were asked to explain why they did chores that they did not like to do, such as cleaning their rooms, going to bed on time, and doing what their parents asked without talking back or arguing. Younger respondents focused on pleasing authority figures, whereas older children mentioned the achievement of goals they had set for themselves (Chandler, 1981). In another study, nearly a thousand students between 8 and 19 years of age were asked to describe themselves. In telling what they liked best about themselves, older subjects were more likely to mention matters of self-control, such as "The way I apply myself," "I don't lose my temper easily," and "My attitude — if I don't like something, I won't get nasty about it." Also, nearly a third of the adolescents mentioned a concern about some self-control problem, such as "Sometimes I get mad at my sister over nothing" or "It's hard for me to force myself to do homework or whatever I'm supposed to do." In contrast, only 15 percent of the elementary school pupils mentioned such issues (Rosenberg, 1979, pp. 210, 213). As young people make the transition from childhood to adolescence, self-control starts to become an internalized value of considerable importance — a matter of *personal commitment and responsibility.*

Recall from Chapter 11 that children construct their self-concepts — in this case, a picture of the self as more or less in command of one's own actions — largely on the basis of feedback they get from others. In a study of how adults' statements affect children's self-control, Toner, Moore, and Emmons (1980) exposed kindergarten through second-grade girls to a delay of gratification task. Before it began, half the children were given a task-relevant personal label. The experimenter commented in the course of a short conversation, "I hear you are very patient because you can wait for nice things when you can't get them right away." The other half received a task-irrelevant label—"I hear that you have some very nice friends at school." The results revealed that adult feedback to children about their capacity to wait was an extremely effective motivator of self-control. Children labeled as patient were able to delay gratification far longer than those who were told they had nice friends.

These findings indicate that besides suggesting effective self-instructional strategies, adults can facilitate resistance to temptation by bolstering children's images of themselves as patient, self-disciplined personalities. Once self-control becomes a valued dimension of the self-concept, it is sustained not just by children's understanding that it is the sensible thing to do, but also by a firm inner resolve that it is what they want and ought to do.

CHAPTER SUMMARY

Theories of Morality

■ Moral development is concerned with how individuals come to resolve discrepancies between their self-centered, egoistic needs and obligations to act in favor of the needs of others. Four theoretical perspectives, each with roots in Western philosophical tradition, provide different accounts of moral growth. Most theories agree that a basic feature of moral development is **internalization.** At first the child's morality is externally imposed and controlled by adults. Eventually, children develop internalized moral rules and principles, taking over the responsibility for regulating their own moral conduct.

Morality as Rooted in Human Nature: The Biological Perspective

■ The biological perspective on moral development, represented by a controversial new field called **sociobiology,** assumes that the motivation to behave morally is grounded in the genetic heritage of the species. Although human prosocial behavior may have genetic roots, considerable evidence indicates that it requires strong environmental supports to be realized.

Morality as the Adoption of Societal Norms: The Psychoanalytic and Behaviorist Perspectives

■ Although psychoanalytic and behaviorist theories propose different mechanisms of development, both regard morality as the adoption of societal prescriptions for good conduct, or norms.

■ According to Freud, morality resides in a portion of the personality called the **superego,** which results from resolution of the Oedipal and Electra conflicts during early childhood. Fear of punishment and loss of parental love lead children to **identify** with the same-sex parent, internalize adult rules and prohibitions, and redirect hostile impulses toward the self in the form of guilt. Although guilt is an important motivator of moral action, Freud's interpretation of it is no

longer widely accepted. In contrast to predictions drawn from Freudian theory, power assertion and love withdrawal do not foster conscience development. Instead **induction** is far more effective.

■ Behaviorists regard morality as learned in the same way as all other responses: according to the principles of reinforcement and modeling. Positive reinforcement is a far more effective means than punishment for promoting socially desirable behavior. Young children readily imitate the morally relevant behaviors of those around them, especially when models are warm and affectionate, are powerful and competent, and demonstrate consistency between words and deeds.

■ Even after children internalize moral prescriptions, consistency in moral conduct from one occasion to another is only moderate. Situational conditions influence children's tendency to behave honestly or dishonestly. For example, the level of honesty of peer associates and adult achievement pressures affect children's tendency to cheat on assignments and examinations in school.

Morality as Social Understanding: The Cognitive-Developmental Perspective

■ In contrast to the psychoanalytic and behaviorist traditions, the cognitive-developmental perspective does not regard morality as a matter of conforming to societal norms. Instead, it emphasizes that children actively reason about moral issues. Cognitive maturity and broadening social experience lead children's conceptions of justice and fairness to become more abstract and morally adequate with age.

■ Piaget's work served as the original inspiration for the cognitive-developmental perspective. He identified two broad stages of moral development: (1) **heteronomous morality,** in which moral rules are viewed as unalterable dictates of authority figures, and (2) **autonomous morality,** in which rules are regarded as flexible procedures established through cooperative social agreement. Research has confirmed Piaget's general vision of moral development, although it has failed to support a number of specific aspects of his theory.

■ Kohlberg's six-stage sequence, which follows in the tradition of Piaget, has supplanted his two-stage theory. According to Kohlberg, moral reasoning advances through three levels, each of which contains two stages: (1) the **preconventional level,** in which morality is externally governed by rewards and punishments; (2) the **conventional level,** in which conformity to laws and rules is regarded as necessary to preserve the social system; and (3) the **postconventional level,** in which individuals develop abstract, universally applicable principles of justice.

■ Kohlberg's stages are strongly related to age and form an invariant developmental sequence. However, moral development requires a less tightly organized stage conception than Kohlberg originally envisioned. Piaget's cognitive and Selman's perspective-taking stages are necessary but not sufficient conditions for each advance in moral reasoning. Many experiences also contribute to moral maturity, including peer interaction; warm, rational child-rearing practices; and higher education.

■ Cross-cultural research indicates that a certain level of societal complexity is required for Kohlberg's highest stages. At the same time, his theory may not encompass the full range of principled reasoning in all cultures. Recent evidence does not support the claim that Kohlberg's theory is sex-biased. In line with cognitive-developmental predictions, maturity of moral reasoning is moderately related to a wide variety of moral behaviors.

The Moral Reasoning of Young Children

■ Kohlberg's theory, like Piaget's, underestimates the young child's moral understanding. Damon's research on young children's concepts of **distributive justice** and Eisenberg's levels of prosocial moral reasoning indicate that elementary school children are capable of some surprisingly sophisticated moral judgments.

The Development of Self-Control

■ The capacity for **self-control** is supported by the development of cognitive and representational capacities during the second year of life. Self-control makes its initial appearance in the form of **compliance.** By age 2, children use self-directed speech to **delay gratification,** and they begin to profit from adult-provided self-control strategies. In middle childhood, children produce a variety of strategies themselves, and they become consciously aware of which ones work best and why. By late childhood and early adolescence, self-control becomes a vital component of the self-concept—a matter of personal commitment and responsibility.

IMPORTANT TERMS AND CONCEPTS

internalization (p. 472)
sociobiology (p. 473)
superego (p. 474)
identification (p. 474)
induction (p. 474)
social conventions (p. 482)
heteronomous morality (p. 483)

realism (p. 484)
autonomous morality (p. 484)
reciprocity (p. 485)
moral dilemma (p. 486)
Defining Issues Test (DIT) (p. 487)
preconventional level (p. 488)
conventional level (p. 490)

postconventional level (p. 491)
distributive justice (p. 502)
self-control (p. 506)
compliance (p. 506)
delay of gratification (p. 507)

The Hilltop, by Frank W. Benson.
Courtesy of the Malden (MA) Public Library.

13
The Development of Sex Differences and Sex Roles

Sex Stereotypes and Sex Roles
Biological and Environmental Influences on Sex Stereotyping and Sex-Role Adoption
Sex-Role Identity
To What Extent Do Boys and Girls *Really* Differ in Cognitive Abilities and Personality
Attributes?
Raising Non-Sex-Stereotyped Children

Four-year-old Jenny arrives at her preschool classroom and enters the housekeeping corner, where she dons a frilly long dress and grown-up-looking high heels. Karen, while setting the table, produces whimpering sound effects for the swaddled baby doll in the crib. Jenny lifts the baby and gently whispers, "You need milk and a new diaper." She picks up a bottle, sits down in the rocker, and pretends to feed the doll. In a few moments, Jenny says to Karen, "I think the baby's sick. Ask Rachel if she'll be the nurse." Karen goes off to find Rachel, who is coloring at the art table.

In the same classroom, Nathan hurriedly hangs up his jacket and calls to Tommy, "Wanna play traffic?" Both boys dash energetically toward the cars and trucks in the block corner. Soon David joins them. "I'll be policeman first!" says Nathan, who pulls a chair into the block area and stands on it. "Green light, go!" shouts the young police officer. With this signal, Tommy and David scurry on all fours around the chair as fast as possible, each pushing a large wooden truck. "Red light," exclaims Nathan, and the trucks screech to a halt.

"My truck beat yours," says Tommy to David.

"Only 'cause I need gas," retorts David, who pulls off to the side and pretends to fill the tank.

"Let's build a runway for the trucks," suggests Nathan. The three construction engineers begin to gather large blocks and boards for the task.

The activity preferences and behaviors of these young preschoolers indicate that at a tender age, they have begun to adopt the sex-typed standards of their cultural community. Jenny and Karen gravitate to play with dresses, dolls, and household

513

props; act out a stereotypically feminine scene of nurturance and caregiving; and summon Rachel to assume the occupational role of nurse, not doctor. The play of Nathan, Tommy, and David, with its traffic scene turned racecourse, is active, competitive, and thematically masculine. Already, all of these 4-year-olds interact more often with children of their own sex than of the opposite sex. In addition, the boys seldom enter the housekeeping area, and rarely do the girls choose to build with large blocks or use the cars and trucks.

What causes play preferences and social orientations to become so rigidly sex-typed at an early age, and how do children's sex-typed knowledge and behavior change over time? Do societal expectations limit the way children *think about themselves* as masculine and feminine beings, with implications for the development of their self-concepts, personal attributes, and behavior? Finally, to what extent do widely held beliefs about the characteristics of males and females reflect reality? Is it the case that the average man is fairly aggressive, assertive, competitive, and good at spatial and mathematical skills, while the average woman is passive, conforming, nurturant, socially responsive, and better at verbal skills? How large are the differences that exist between the sexes, and what are their origins in childhood socialization and the biology of the organism? These are the central questions asked by investigators who study the development of sex typing, and we consider evidence that responds to them in this chapter.

The acquisition of sex-typed characteristics has been of central concern to child development specialists for decades, and interest in the topic has grown in recent years. The wealth of accumulated studies is vast; there are comparisons of the sexes on virtually every form of behavior imaginable (Deaux, 1985). The research is also highly controversial. Like investigations into children's intelligence, the study of sex typing has become embroiled in the nature-nurture debate and has taken on a political flavor because of its implications for gender equality.

Perhaps more than any other area of child development, the study of sex typing has responded to the winds of societal change. Largely as a consequence of social and political progress in the area of women's rights, during the past two decades there have been major shifts in how sex differences are regarded. Until the early 1970s, the adoption of sex-typed behavior was viewed as a desirable goal of socialization and as crucial for optimal psychological adjustment. Today, it is recognized that some extremely sex-typed characteristics are actually threats to mental health. Unrelenting aggressiveness and competitiveness on the part of men and dependency, conformity, and passivity on the part of women are maladaptive behavior patterns for any person. This realization has led modern research to be guided by the new assumption that the adoption of some sex-typed behaviors may not be good because it limits developmental possibilities for both sexes (Huston, 1983; Ruble, 1988).

Like other aspects of child development, theoretical revision marks the study of sex differences and sex roles. Psychoanalytic theory at one time offered a prominent and persuasive account of how children, like Jenny and Nathan described earlier, acquired masculine and feminine characteristics. According to Freud, sex-typed attitudes and behavior were adopted in the same way as other societal norms (see Chapter 12). Both resulted from identification with the same-sex parent during the late preschool years (Freud, 1925/1961). However, recent evidence indicates that same-sex parental identification is only one of many socializing influences on sex typing. Interactions with peers, teachers, and opposite-sex parents also make a difference, as do examples of sex-appropriate behavior in the broader social environment. Furthermore, investigators now know that the age range during which sex-typed learning takes place begins earlier and extends beyond the time frame Freud assigned to it, continuing into the middle childhood, adolescent, and even adulthood years (Huston, 1983). Finally, Freudian theory and subsequent extensions of it (e.g., Erikson, 1950) view sex typing as a natural and normal outcome of biological differences between males and females. Although debate continues about the truth of this assumption, firm adherence to it by psychoanalytic theorists has not been helpful in the quest to discover how people might become free of the constraints of gender-based definitions of appropriate behavior. Consequently, child development specialists have, for the most part, abandoned the psychoanalytic framework and turned toward other theoretical perspectives.

Social learning theory, with its emphasis on modeling and reinforcement, and cognitive-developmental theory, with its focus on children as active thinkers about their social world, are the major contemporary approaches to the development of sex typing. Neither has proved entirely adequate by itself. We will see later that a new, integrative perspective called *gender schema theory* combines elements of both these perspectives to explain the acquisition of sex-typed knowledge and behavior.

Along with new research and theories have come a proliferation of new terms. *Sex* and *gender* are labels that have distinct meanings to some investigators (e.g., Deaux, 1985) but are used interchangeably by others (Huston, 1983; Maccoby, 1988; Ruble, 1988). We will adopt the second convention in this chapter.[1] Other important terms are sex stereotypes, sex roles, and sex-role identity. Sex stereotypes and sex roles are the public face of gender in society, and they support and influence one another. **Sex stereotypes** refer to widely held beliefs about the characteristics associated with one sex as opposed to the other (Ruble & Ruble, 1982). **Sex roles** are the reflection of these stereotypes in behaviors regarded as culturally appropriate for males and females (Rosen & Rekers, 1980). In the first portion of this chapter, we discuss the content of current stereotypes and sex-role expectations and how children's knowledge and understanding of them change with age. The term **sex-role identity** has a private connotation. It refers to perception of the self as relatively masculine or feminine in characteristics, capabilities, and behaviors. In the second part of this chapter, we consider how children's images of themselves as masculine or feminine beings develop and the relationship of sex-role identity to sex-typed behavior. Finally, the last portion of this chapter addresses the question of how different males and females really are in cognitive abilities and personality attributes, along with the biological versus environmental roots of these differences.

SEX STEREOTYPES AND SEX ROLES

Beliefs about sex differences have appeared in religious, philosophical, and literary writings for centuries, and they have been closely linked to the roles of the sexes in society. For example, in ancient times, Aristotle wrote:

> Woman is more compassionate than man and has a greater propensity to tears. She is, also, more envious, more querulous, more slanderous, and more contentious. Farther still, the female is more dispirited, more despondent, more impudent and more given to falsehood than the male. . . . But the male . . . is more disposed to give assistance in danger, and is more courageous than the female. (cited in Miles, 1935, p. 700)

Although the latter part of the twentieth century has brought a new level of awareness about the wide range of role possibilities for each sex, strong beliefs about differences between males and females continue to exist. Systematic research on sex stereotyping did not begin until the latter part of the 1960s. Using a variety of techniques, including open-ended responses, checklists, and rating scales, investigators asked people what characteristics they regarded as typical of men and women. Despite the diversity of methods employed and samples studied, considerable consensus emerged in adults' beliefs about sex-related attributes (Ruble & Ruble, 1982).

---

[1] The term *sex* is often taken to refer to biologically based differences between males and females, whereas *gender* invokes explanations based on social influences. However, differences can be due to both biological and environmental factors. In this chapter, use of the terms sex and gender does not imply specific assumptions about the determinants of differences being discussed.

For example, in 1968, Rosenkrantz and his colleagues asked college students to rate the extent to which they thought a large number of characteristics were typical of males and females. Masculine-rated traits reflected competence, rationality, and self-assertion — personality characteristics termed **instrumental** in the research literature. Feminine-associated traits were warm, caring, and emotional — characteristics labeled as **expressive** in nature. During the 1970s and early 1980s, a period of intense political activism with respect to women's rights, these stereotypes remained essentially the same (Broverman et al, 1972; Ruble, 1983; Spence, Helmreich, & Stapp, 1975). A list of attributes that college students of the 1980s regarded as associated with males and females is provided in Table 13.1. It bears a strong resemblance to the findings of Rosenkrantz obtained a decade and a half earlier. Furthermore, in a cross-cultural study that included respondents from 30 nations, Williams and Best (1982) reported that the instrumental-expressive dichotomy is a widely held sex-stereotypic viewpoint around the world.

In addition to the personal attributes listed in Table 13.1, other components of sex stereotypes exist, including physical characteristics (e.g., tall, strong, and sturdy for men; soft, dainty, and graceful for women) and occupations (e.g., truck driver, insurance agent, and chemist for men; telephone operator, elementary school teacher, and nurse's aide for women) (Deaux & Lewis, 1984). The variety of attributes that are sex stereotypic, their constancy over time, and their generality across samples suggests that sex stereotypes are salient, deeply ingrained patterns of thinking. In the following sections, we consider when children become aware of sex stereotypes and the implications of stereotyping for the development of sex-role behavior.

Table 13.1. Some Characteristics Regarded as Stereotypically Masculine and Feminine by College Students in the 1980s

MASCULINE CHARACTERISTICS	FEMININE CHARACTERISTICS
Independent	Emotional
Aggressive	Home-oriented
Skilled in business	Kind
Mechanical aptitude	Cries easily
Outspoken	Creative
Acts as a leader	Considerate
Self-confident	Devotes self to others
Takes a stand	Needs approval
Ambitious	Gentle
Not easily influenced	Aware of others' feelings
Dominant	Excitable in a major crisis
Active	Expresses tender feelings
Makes decisions easily	Enjoys art and music
Doesn't give up easily	Tactful
Stands up under pressure	Feelings hurt
Likes math and science	Neat
Competitive	Likes children
Adventurous	Understanding

Source: Ruble, 1983.

How Early Do Children Display Sex-Stereotyped Knowledge?

Recall from our discussion of social cognition in Chapter 11 that as early as age 2, children apply common gender-linked labels, such as boy, girl, mommy, daddy, lady, and man, to categorize themselves and other people (Lewis & Brooks-Gunn, 1979; Weinraub et al., 1984). As soon as basic gender categories are established, children start to sort out what they mean in terms of activities and behaviors, and a wide variety of sex stereotypes are quickly mastered. Young preschoolers associate many toys, articles of clothing, tools, household objects, games, and occupations with one sex as opposed to the other (Blakemore, LaRue, & Olejnik, 1979; Edelbrock & Sugawara, 1978; Nemerowicz, 1979; Thompson, 1975; Weinraub et al., 1984). In one study, children as young as 2½ were shown a series of pictures. As each was presented, the experimenter described it by making a statement about a sex-typed behavior (e.g., "I can hit you"), a physical characteristic (e.g., "I am strong"), an activity (e.g., "I like to play ball"), or a future role (e.g., "When I grow up, I'll fly an airplane"). Both boys and girls at this young age indicated that girls "like to play with dolls," "talk a lot," "never hit," say "I need some help," and later on as grown-ups will "clean the house" and "be a nurse." They also believed that boys "like to help father," say "I can hit you," and as future adults will "be boss" and "mow the grass" (Kuhn, Nash, & Brucken, 1978).

Even before children can verbalize their own gender and match up statements and objects with a male or female stimulus figure, their play behavior suggests that they have acquired some implicit knowledge about "sex-appropriate" activities. This is particularly evident in sex-typed game and toy choices, which are present by 1½ years of age (Fagot, Leinbach, & Hagan, 1986). The tendency of toddlers and young 2-year-olds to select and play in a more involved way with "same-sex" than "opposite-sex" toys has been found in both naturalistic and laboratory research (Fagot, 1978; Fein et al., 1975; Caldera, Huston, & O'Brien, 1989). Between 1 and 3 years of age, sex-typed toy and game choices become highly consistent for both sexes (O'Brien & Huston, 1985).

A notable feature of preschoolers' sex stereotypes is that they operate like blanket rules rather than flexible guidelines (Martin, 1989). Shown a picture of a Scottish bagpiper wearing a kilt, a 4-year-old is likely to state emphatically, "Men don't wear skirts!" At nursery school, children can be heard exclaiming that girls don't drive fire engines and can't be police officers and boys don't take care of babies and can't be the teacher. These rigid gender categories are a joint product of the salience of sex-typed information in the environment, preschoolers' cognitive tendency to exaggerate differences they observe, and their limited appreciation of the biological basis of male and female. As we will see in greater detail when we discuss the development of sex-role identity, prominent observable characteristics — play activities, toy choices, occupational roles, hairstyles, and clothing — are the defining features of gender for the majority of 3- to 5-year-olds. Most have not yet learned that genital characteristics take precedence over social cues in determining a person's sex.

Changes in Sex Stereotyping During Middle Childhood and Adolescence

During middle childhood and adolescence, awareness of sex stereotypes increases, particularly in the less obvious areas of personality attributes and achievement. At the same time, older children recognize that activities and behavior are *associated,* not *defining* features of a person's sex (Ullian, 1976). Consequently, some notions about gender-related characteristics actually become more flexible with age.

Sex Stereotyping of Personality Attributes. In Chapter 11, we showed that before age 8, children's descriptions of themselves and others largely consist of concrete activities, possessions, and behaviors. Not until middle childhood do children think about people in terms of psychological dispositions. This same developmental trend appears in research on children's awareness of sex stereotypes.

An instrument called the *Sex Stereotype Questionnaire* is frequently used to assess stereotyping of personality dispositions. Children are given masculine adjectives (e.g., tough, aggressive, rational, dominant) and feminine adjectives (gentle, appreciative, excitable, affectionate) and asked to assign them to either a male or a female stimulus figure. Best and her colleagues (1977) administered this measure to 5-year-olds, 8-year-olds, 11-year-olds, and college students. As shown in Figure 13.1, the kindergartners responded at better than chance, but the tendency to stereotype increased markedly over the elementary school years and into adolescence. In addition, masculine-stereotyped traits were learned at an earlier age than feminine ones by children of both sexes. Perhaps male stereotypes are acquired sooner because boys are permitted far less freedom than girls to engage in ''cross-sex'' activities. Boys' earlier and more complete conformity to sex-stereotypic behaviors may lead children to abstract the inner dispositions typically associated with the male role at an earlier age (Williams, Bennett, & Best, 1975).

Several cautions should be kept in mind about the developmental trends described above. Virtually all the work on children's knowledge of personality stereotypes has used forced-choice techniques in which children have had to assign a characteristic to either one gender or the other. Only a handful of investigations have asked subjects whether a personality attribute might be appropriate for *both* genders. The results of these studies suggest that the forced-choice procedure overestimates children's stereotyping of personality attributes (Etaugh, Levine, & Mennella, 1984; Kelly & Smail, 1986; Marantz & Mansfield, 1977). Furthermore, awareness of sex-stereotyped characteristics is not the same as endorsement of them. Preliminary evidence suggests that although older children recognize many personality attributes as associated with one gender rather than the other, they do not necessarily approve of these distinctions (Kelly and Smail, 1986).

Sex Stereotyping of Achievement Areas. Not long after children enter elementary school, they figure out which academic subjects and skill areas are considered

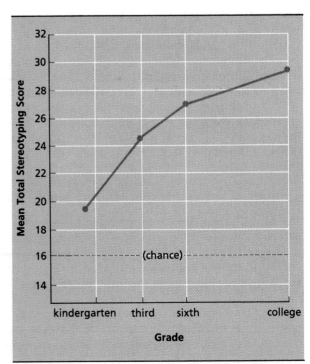

Figure 13.1. Age changes in sex stereotyping of personality attributes in the Best et al. (1977) study. *(From D. L. Best et al., 1977, "Development of Sex-Trait Stereotypes among Young Children in the United States, England, and Ireland,"* Child Development, *48, 1357–1384. © The Society for Research in Child Development, Inc. Reprinted by permission.)*

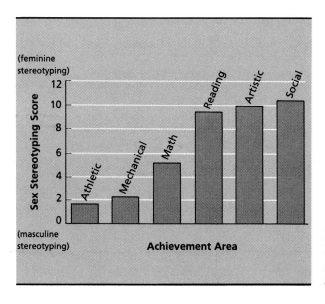

Figure 13.2. Sex stereotyping of achievement areas in the Stein and Smithells (1969) study. *(Adapted from Stein & Smithells, 1969.)*

masculine and which are feminine. Stein and Smithells (1969; Stein, 1971) asked second, sixth, and twelfth graders whether they thought activities in six achievement areas were more for boys or more for girls. As shown in Figure 13.2, children of all ages thought that reading, artistic (art and music), and social skills were feminine and athletics, mechanical skills, and mathematics were masculine. In a more recent study, elementary school pupils in the United States, Japan, and Taiwan were asked to name the school subject they liked best. Girls were more likely to choose reading and boys mathematics in all three countries. Moreover, when asked to predict how well they would do in the two subject matter areas once they reached high school, boys indicated they would do better in mathematics than did girls. In contrast, no sex difference in favor of girls emerged in predictions about reading (Lummis & Stevenson, 1990).

Other more subtle forms of achievement stereotyping also appear during middle childhood. Recall our discussion of achievement-related attributions in Chapter 11. We reviewed evidence indicating that attributing failure to ability as opposed to effort has an undermining effect on achievement motivation.[2] Research indicates that elementary school children explain the failures of females, particularly in "cross-sex" activities, as due to ability. In contrast, they interpret comparable male failures more generously, in terms of insufficient effort or learning opportunities (Nemerowicz, 1979).

When females do succeed at an important activity, adolescents tend to devalue their accomplishments. In one study, seventh, ninth, and eleventh graders were shown short articles that had appeared in magazines for teenagers. Some were on feminine subjects like child care and grocery shopping, some were on masculine subjects such as car racing and space exploration, and others were sex-neutral. A fictitious author's name followed each of the articles, which were described as entries in a writing contest. The subjects were asked to evaluate the merits of the writing and the ability of the author. The work of male authors was judged better than that of female authors, especially when the article was on a masculine topic (Etaugh & Rose, 1975). This pattern of results occurred at all age levels and among both male and female participants, and it duplicates the findings of similar research on adults (Mischel, 1974).

[2] Turn back to Chapter 11, pages 441–444, if you need to review the research on the development of children's achievement-related attributions.

Furthermore, by the mid-elementary school years, children have acquired a more general stereotype of achievement as a "masculine" norm. Hawkins and Pingree (1978) told third through twelfth graders stories about a woman (Anne) and a man (John) who either succeeded or failed in medical school and had them rate how nice each was under both conditions. For male and female subjects of all ages, Anne was somewhat less nice than John when they both succeeded, but John was much less nice than Anne when they both failed. Although children and adolescents are biased in favor of males who succeed, they seem to evaluate a male who fails to reach an important achievement goal especially negatively.

Sex Stereotyping of Activities and Occupations. Unlike research on personality attributes and achievement areas, in studies of children's stereotyping of activities and occupations, researchers have gone beyond asking children whether a particular endeavor is appropriate for males or females. They have also asked whether members of each sex *can* or *should* engage in the activity. Results indicate that although awareness of stereotypes increases with age, a more flexible and varied appreciation of what males and females can and should do emerges as well (Archer, 1984; Cummings & Taebel, 1980; Garrett, Ein, & Tremaine, 1977; Meyer, 1980). In one study, children's flexible appreciation of activity and occupational stereotypes paralleled the development of their understanding of social conventions, a topic we discussed in Chapter 12. In other words, children's grasp of the idea that sex-stereotyped activities are arbitrary, socially defined matters went hand-in-hand with their appreciation that social conventions (e.g., eating with a knife and fork instead of with one's hands) are not fixed, immutable laws, but relative practices arrived at by group consensus (Carter & Patterson, 1982).

These findings suggest that children's judgments about the appropriateness of activities for males and females gradually become less rigid as their understanding of the social origins of certain rules improves over the course of middle childhood. In agreement with this interpretation, between 6 and 18 years of age, children's answers to the question "Why do you think boys and girls are different/do different things?" focus less on biological and physical explanations (e.g., "Boys have different things in their innards than girls") and more on different socialization experiences (e.g., "We do different things because it is the way we have been brought up") (Smith & Russell, 1984; Ullian, 1976).

Group Differences in Sex Stereotyping

Besides the developmental trends noted above, group differences exist in children's sex stereotyping. The strongest and most consistent of these is between boys and girls. In many investigations, boys have been found to hold more sex-typed views. In toddlerhood, boys play more often with toys stereotyped for their own gender, a difference that persists throughout the preschool years (O'Brien & Huston, 1985; O'Brien, Huston, & Risley, 1983). By middle childhood and adolescence, boys make more stereotyped judgments on all the dimensions discussed above — personality attributes, achievement areas, occupations, and activities (e.g., Archer, 1984; Cummings, & Taebel, 1980; Fennema & Sherman, 1977; Kleinke & Nicholson, 1979; Raymond & Benbow, 1986). In addition, boys are less flexible in their view of occupational stereotypes than girls, and they are more likely to devalue feminine achievement and to attribute gender differences to biological rather than social causes (Etaugh & Rose, 1975; Nemerowicz, 1979; Smith & Russell, 1984).

Studies that have included American minority children in their samples report that black children hold less stereotyped views of women than white children (Bardwell, Cochran, & Walker, 1986; Kleinke & Nicholson, 1979). This finding may be linked to differences in black and white family life. For example, more black than white women with children under 18 are employed (U.S. Department of Labor,

1988). This means that black children are more likely to have mothers whose lives reflect less traditional sex roles.

Although lower social-class groups are more rigidly stereotyped than members of the middle class during adolescence and adulthood (e.g., Bayer, 1975; Canter & Ageton, 1984; Tomeh, 1979), research on children has failed to confirm this same finding. In several studies, no socioeconomic differences were found in children's stereotyping of activities, achievement areas, and occupations (Cummings & Taebel, 1980; Nemerowicz, 1979; Stein, 1971). In one investigation, low-income kindergarten children actually appeared less stereotyped than their middle-class agemates (Bardwell, Cochran, & Walker, 1986).

Cross-national research on children's stereotyping of personality attributes has also been conducted. Like the findings on adults described earlier, the instrumental-expressive dichotomy has held up in a variety of countries (Best et al., 1977; Williams et al., 1979). But as yet, a great many cultural groups, especially non-Western societies, remain unstudied. Therefore, the extent of cross-cultural variation in children's sex-stereotyped beliefs is not fully known.

Does Sex Stereotyping Affect Sex-Role Adoption?

If we were to find that sex stereotyping affects only children's patterns of thinking and not their actual behavior, there would be little reason to be concerned that stereotypes restrict children's developmental potential. However, research, especially in the area of achievement, indicates that children's stereotyped knowledge *is* related to their behavior. An impressive number of correlational studies report that children and adolescents show greater motivation and mastery when they regard an achievement area as consistent with their own sex role and less motivation and mastery when they view it as an opposite-sex endeavor (Dwyer, 1974; Kelly & Smail, 1986; Paulsen & Johnson, 1983; Sherman & Fennema, 1977; Sherman, 1980; Stein, 1971).

More conclusive evidence on the power of stereotypes to affect sex-typed interests and behavior comes from experimental research in which investigators take gender-neutral tasks and artificially label them as appropriate for one sex or the other. In one such study, 6- to 8-year-olds played a game in which they had to toss as many marbles as possible into a clown's body within a short time limit. In one condition, the game was labeled as an activity for girls, in another as an activity for boys, and in a third it was not given a gender label. Children of both sexes judged the game as more attractive and also performed better when it was labeled as sex-appropriate or not labeled at all than when they were told that it was an opposite-sex activity (Montemayor, 1974).

Experimental findings in combination with correlation evidence provide strong support for the influence of sex stereotypes on children's attraction to tasks, effortful behavior, and performance. The impact of stereotypes on behavior is likely to be even more potent as children take their sex-typed knowledge and integrate it into their sex-role identities — self-perceptions about what they can and should do at play, in school, and as future participants in society. But the emergence of sex-role identity is a topic that we treat at a later point in this chapter. For now, let's turn to a consideration of various influences that may promote children's sex-stereotyped view of the world.

<hr>

During the preschool years, children develop well-defined sex stereotypes about activities, playthings, and occupations. More abstract stereotypes, including personality and achievement attributes, emerge in middle childhood and undergo further refinement during adolescence. At the same time, a more flexible view of sex-typed activities and occupations appears. As children grasp the arbitrary nature of social rules, they come to understand that people can engage in "cross-sex" activities. Group differences in sex stereotyping exist; boys hold more stereotyped views than

BRIEF REVIEW

girls, and white children more than black children. Finally, children's sex-stereo-typed thinking fosters the acquisition of sex-typed preferences and behavior.

BIOLOGICAL AND ENVIRONMENTAL INFLUENCES ON SEX STEREOTYPING AND SEX-ROLE ADOPTION

Social learning theorists emphasize direct teaching, modeling, and reinforcement of sex-typed knowledge and behavior as the major mechanisms through which sex-role standards are transmitted to children. We will see shortly that a great deal of research is consistent with this point of view. Nevertheless, some theorists argue that biological variations lead each sex to be uniquely suited to fill particular roles and that the great majority of societies merely promote sex differences that are grounded in the biological makeup of the organism. What evidence, if any, exists to support this idea?

Are Sex Stereotypes and Traditional Sex Roles Grounded in Biological Differences between the Sexes?

While practically no modern theorist would argue that "biology is destiny" — that women are constitutionally ordained to stay home and care for children and men to serve as economic providers, warriors, and protectors — serious questions about the influence of biological factors on sex-role development remain (Ruble, 1988). Cross-cultural similarities in stereotypes and sex-role behavior are sometimes taken as evidence for the importance of biology. Earlier in this chapter we indicated that the instrumental-expressive dichotomy is represented in the sex stereotyping of a great many national groups. Although this appears to support the argument that socialization practices simply adapt to genetically determined sex differences, it must be interpreted with caution. A careful examination of the anthropological literature reveals that although most societies encourage instrumental traits in boys and ex-pressive traits in girls, substantial diversity exists in the *magnitude* of this difference (Hendrix & Johnson, 1985). Furthermore, reversals of traditional roles do exist, as Margaret Mead's (1935/1963) classic study of three tribal societies in New Guinea revealed over half a century ago. Among the Arapesh, both men and women were cooperative and nurturant; among the Mundugumore, both sexes were ruthless and aggressive; and among the Tchambuli, women were dominant and assertive while men were docile and emotionally dependent.

Mead's cross-cultural comparisons indicate that sex-role behavior is enormously malleable, but it can still be argued that cultural deviations from sex-stereotypic expectations are more the exception than the rule. Biological pressures may still be operating, manifesting themselves in behavior as long as cultural pressures against them are not extreme. Because cross-cultural research is inconclusive, scientists have turned to a direct examination of biological mechanisms that might be involved in the development of sex-role behavior.

It is well known that genetic makeup and associated hormones have a direct effect on anatomical development of the sexes. Between the ninth and twelfth weeks of prenatal life, the presence of androgen hormones causes differentiation of the male genitalia in the fetus. In the absence of androgens, physical characteristics of the fetus are feminized (Moore, 1989). Again during puberty, an upsurge of sex hormones in varying balances regulates maturation of male and female sexual characteristics (see Chapter 5). In addition, sex hormones are known to affect central nervous system development and neural activity in many animal species, and they probably do so in humans as well (McEwen, 1981). Can sex hormones, which so pervasively affect the development of body structures, be said to influence sex-role behavior as well?

Animal research, in which hormone levels can be experimentally manipulated, indicates that exposure to sex hormones during certain critical periods, such as the prenatal phase and puberty, does affect behavioral development. For example, prenatally administered androgens increase the incidence of rough-and-tumble play in both male and female nonhuman mammals. Androgens also promote male-typical sexual behavior, higher activity levels, greater aggression, and reduced maternal behavior in a wide variety of animal species (Bardin & Catterall, 1981; Meany, Stewart, & Beatty, 1985; Parsons, 1982; Quadagno, Briscoe, & Quadagno, 1977).

Ethical considerations preclude manipulating hormone levels in human subjects. Instead, human research is limited to circumstances in which hormone levels vary inadvertently or are modified for medical reasons. A classic series of investigations by John Money, Anke Ehrhardt, and their collaborators involved such cases. They studied children afflicted with **adrenogenital syndrome (AGS),** a disorder in which prenatal exposure to unusually high levels of androgens or androgenlike hormones occurred. In some of the AGS subjects, a genetic defect caused the unborn child's adrenal system to malfunction. In others, the mother had been given a synthetic hormone during pregnancy to prevent miscarriage that had androgenizing consequences for the fetus. All of the girls were born with masculinized external genitalia. Most underwent surgical correction in infancy or childhood; a few experienced it in later life. In addition, those with genetic AGS were placed on continuous drug therapy to correct the hormonal imbalance (Ehrhardt & Baker, 1974; Ehrhardt, Epstein, & Money, 1968; Money & Ehrhardt, 1972).

Assessing gender-related behaviors by interviewing subjects and family members, the investigators found that AGS girls exhibited masculinized sex-role behavior. They preferred boys over girls as playmates; liked cars, trucks, and blocks better than dolls; showed little interest in fantasizing about traditional feminine roles such as bride and mother, and were less concerned about matters of appearance, such as clothing, jewelry, and hairstyle, than normal controls. In addition, both boys and girls with AGS displayed heightened physical activity levels, as manifested by greater participation in active sports and outdoor games.

Money and Ehrhardt concluded from this evidence that prenatal androgen exposure is a biological factor that supports the development of masculine sex-role behavior. However, their findings do not rule out the possibility that subtle environmental pressures contributed to the differences found. For example, genital abnormalities, which in some cases were not corrected until well beyond infancy, may have caused family members to perceive afflicted girls as boyish and unfeminine and to treat them accordingly (Huston, 1983; Quadagno, Briscoe & Quadagno, 1977). In addition, genetic AGS girls required prolonged medical contact in order to treat their condition. In the course of clinic visits, they were probably informed that menarche would be delayed and that as adults they might have difficulty conceiving a child. These girls may have shown little interest in fantasizing about the maternal role because they had reason to be unsure of their futures as women and mothers, not because of prenatal androgen exposure. In fact, a careful examination of Money and Ehrhardt's (1972) data indicates that girls with nongenetic AGS, who after surgical intervention required no further medical treatment, did not show the same degree of disinterest in fantasizing about marriage and motherhood as did the more severely affected genetic AGS subjects.[3]

[3] Long-term follow-ups of genetic AGS girls in adolescence indicate that they are reluctant to date and prefer to postpone romantic interests until a later age. Among 30 cases studied as young adults, a disproportionate number (37 percent) described themselves as homosexual or bisexual in orientation (Money, Schwartz, & Lewis, 1984). However, Money (1985) cautions against attributing these psychosexual outcomes entirely to prenatal androgens, for precisely the reasons described above. Moreover, longitudinal evidence on children reared as members of the opposite sex because they had abnormal or ambiguous genitalia indicates that in the large majority of these cases, sexual orientation is consistent with sex of rearing, irrespective of genetic sex (Baker, 1980; Money, 1985).

Studies of individuals exposed to abnormal levels of prenatal androgens, but without the consequence of genital abnormalities, eliminate some of the problems that plague the Money and Ehrhardt research. Although most of these investigations report no behavioral effects (Hines, 1982), a few lend support to Money and Ehrhardt's conclusions. For example, one study of children whose mothers took progesterone during pregnancy (which has androgenlike consequences) reported increases for both males and females in self-reported hostility and preference for aggressive solutions to problems (Reinisch, 1981). Another study reported a rise in activity level and participation in active sports (Ehrhardt, 1975), and a third found increases in stereotypically masculine personality characteristics such as independence, self-sufficiency, and self-assurance (Reinisch & Karow, 1977).

Taken together, research on hormonal variations suggests that biological differences between the sexes may influence the emergence of some aspects of sex-role functioning. However, since none of the behavioral differences described above were very large, biological predispositions appear to be modest influences that combine in complex ways with environmental factors to shape sex-role development. In addition, it is important to keep in mind that even biological factors are subject to environmental modification. For example, in animals, environmental stress and social dominance have been found to increase androgen production (Macrides, Bartke, & Dalterio, 1975; Rose, Holaday, & Bernstein, 1976).

Environmental Influences on Children's Sex Stereotyping and Sex-Role Adoption

A large body of evidence indicates that environmental factors provide powerful support for children's acquisition of sex-typed attitudes and behavior. As we will see in the following sections, adults view boys and girls differently, and they treat them differently. In addition, the social environments to which children are exposed on a daily basis provide them with plenty of opportunity to observe people behaving in ways consistent with widely held stereotypes. Finally, as soon as young children enter the world of the peer group, their playmates teach and reinforce conformity to sex-role standards of the larger cultural community.

Perceptions and Expectations of Adults. Sex-stereotyped perceptions of children exist in the "eye of the beholder," even when cues that could evoke them are absent from children's behavior. In a variety of studies, researchers have asked adults to observe infants dressed neutrally who are artificially labeled as boys or girls. When all else is held constant, people "see" qualities that fit with a child's artificially assigned sex. In these investigations, adults rated infants' physical features and (to a lesser extent) their personality attributes in a sex-typed fashion (Stern & Karraker, 1989).

The tendency to interpret infant characteristics in terms of prevailing sex stereotypes is even stronger among real parents. Rubin, Provenzano, and Luria (1974) interviewed mothers and fathers within 24 hours after the birth of their first child. Although male and female newborns did not differ in weight, length, or Apgar scores, parents clearly perceived them differently. Sons were rated as firmer, larger-featured, better-coordinated, more alert, stronger, and hardier, while daughters were regarded as softer, finer-featured, more awkward, more inattentive, weaker, and more delicate.

During childhood and adolescence, parents continue to hold different perceptions and expectations of their sons and daughters. They persist in interpreting the behaviors of boys and girls in stereotypical ways (Fagot, 1981), want their preschoolers to play with "sex-appropriate" toys (Schau et al, 1980), and voice beliefs that boys and girls should be raised differently. For example, when asked about their child-rearing values, parents describe achievement, competitiveness, and control of emotional expression as important for boys. In contrast, warmth, "ladylike" behavior, and close supervision of activities are regarded as important for girls (Block, 1983). Despite increased attention given to women's rights, parental expectations for boys and girls have changed very little during the last several decades (Brooks-Gunn, 1986; Emihovich, Gaier, & Cronin, 1984; McGuire, 1988). Furthermore, in several studies, men's stereotyped perceptions and expectations of children were found to be more extreme than those of women (Fagot, 1981; Rubin, Provenzano, & Luria, 1974).

Differential Treatment by Parents. Do adults actually treat children in accord with their stereotypical beliefs? Using the same basic procedure described earlier in which a child's gender is artificially assigned — only this time, the adult is asked to interact with the baby in a laboratory playroom — investigators have found that differential treatment *does* emanate from adults' stereotypical views of boys and girls. In general, adults play in a ''masculine'' way with a baby they think is a boy and in a ''feminine'' way with one they think is a girl (Stern & Karraker, 1989). For example, the toys offered are influenced by the infant's gender label (Sidorowicz & Lunney, 1980), and adults encourage girl babies to engage in more ''nurturance play'' with dolls and puppets than boys (Frisch, 1977).

Similar findings appear when parents' interaction with their own children is studied. Parents more often encourage gross motor activity in boy than girl babies (Smith & Lloyd, 1978), and they are more likely to respond contingently to the smiles, babbles, and reaches of infant sons than daughters (Parke & Sawin, 1976; Yarrow, 1975). By the second year of life, parents react favorably to sex-stereotypic and negatively to ''cross-sex'' play and behavior. In one study, parents and their young

Observations of parents interacting with their own children indicate that toys offered are strongly influenced by the baby's sex.

toddlers were observed as they went about their daily activities at home. Mothers and fathers differentially reinforced boys and girls in a sex-stereotypic fashion for a great many behaviors, including block play, doll play, large motor activities of running and jumping, assisting with household tasks, and seeking help and physical closeness (Fagot, 1978).

During the preschool and elementary school years, differential treatment of sons and daughters increases as children's skills expand and issues of achievement and independence become more salient (Block, 1978). Observations of parents interacting with their youngsters in teaching situations show that higher levels of independent task performance are demanded from boys than from girls. For example, parents are more likely to respond quickly to girls' requests for help on cognitive tasks, while they more often ignore or actively refuse to respond to similar requests from boys (Rothbart & Rothbart, 1976). When parents do provide help in achievement situations to children of both sexes, they do so in different ways. They behave in a more task-oriented, mastery-emphasizing fashion with sons, setting higher standards and pointing out important cognitive elements of the task. In contrast, parents tend to use a teaching situation with a girl to cement a positive but dependent interpersonal relationship. For example, they will digress from a task-oriented agenda to joke and play with a daughter more often than they will with a son (Block, Block, & Harrington, 1975). In addition, parents frequently interrupt the conversational initiatives of daughters, subtly delivering the message that what a girl has to say is of little consequence. They tend to permit sons to finish their statements before responding (Greif, 1979).

In middle childhood, boys are allowed to range farther from home without adult supervision. In a study of over 700 English children, girls were more often picked up after school or required to go home directly and less often permitted to be at home in the absence of an adult. In addition, girls more often brought friends into the house instead of playing in the neighborhood (Newson & Newson, 1976). In many cultures, girls are assigned chores, such as food preparation, cleaning, and babysitting, that keep them close to home, while boys are given responsibilities that take them into the surrounding world, such as yard work and running errands (Whiting & Edwards, 1988a).

Earlier we noted that fathers more than mothers view children in sex-stereotypic ways. Similarly, in most aspects of parental behavior in which differential treatment of boys and girls occurs, fathers are the ones who discriminate the most. For example, fathers engage in far more active, physically stimulating play with boy than with girl babies; mothers play in a quieter way with infants of both sexes (Parke & Suomi, 1980; Yogman, 1981). By the time infants are 15 months of age, fathers vocalize twice as much to their sons as to their daughters, and fathers are twice as interactive with their sons as mothers are (Lamb, 1977). In childhood, there is greater sex differentiation in encouragement for cognitive performance by fathers than mothers. In addition, when physical punishment is meted out by a parent, boys are targets of it more often than girls, and fathers generally deliver it (Jacklin & Maccoby, 1983). The greater pressure exerted by fathers to get children to conform to sex-role expectations is dramatically illustrated by the findings of a study reported in Box 13.1.

Parents also seem especially committed to ensuring the sex-role socialization of the child of their own gender. While mothers go on shopping excursions and bake cookies with their daughters, fathers play catch, help coach the Saturday morning soccer game, and take fishing trips with their sons. The special significance of the same-sex parent-child relationship may be partly responsible for the finding that among children of divorced parents, boys in father-absent homes and girls in mother-absent homes show fewer sex-typed play preferences and behaviors (Hetherington, Cox, & Cox, 1979; Santrock & Warshak, 1979). Furthermore, this same-sex child bias is another aspect of sex-role socialization that is more pronounced for fathers than mothers. When asked whether certain aspects of child rearing are the province of one parent rather than the other, parents of boys indicated that fathers have a special responsibility to serve as a role model and play companion to their sons (Fagot, 1974).

What are the developmental implications of parents' differential treatment of boys and girls? Block (1983) suggests that sex differences in cognitive abilities may accrue from the fact that boys' toys (e.g., blocks, chemistry sets, and model airplanes) encourage manipulation, inventive possibilities, and feedback from the physical world, whereas girls' toys (e.g., dolls, dress-up clothing, and tea sets) emphasize imitation and offer fewer opportunities for discovery and innovation. In addition, parental help-giving and patterns of communication may convey subtle messages to girls that they are less competent and that their achievement is less important than that of boys. Finally, parents' more intense surveillance of their daughters' whereabouts may lead girls to miss important opportunities for developing feelings of self-reliance and confidence about venturing beyond the family setting into the wider world.

◆ THEORY, RESEARCH, AND APPLICATIONS ◆

The Special Place of Fathers in Sex-Role Socialization

Box 13.1

Theory. Theorists of sex role socialization have suggested that fathers serve as the primary tutors of sex-typed behavior during the childhood years. Mothers, because of their expressive orientation, are thought to treat children of both sexes nurturantly and supportively. In contrast, fathers are believed to differentiate at an early age, assuming the special responsibility of pushing sons in the direction of an instrumental role to ensure their successful fit into the larger society. To test these assumptions, Judith Langlois and Chris Downs (1980) watched closely to see how mothers and fathers reacted when their 3- to 5-year-old sons and daughters played with "sex-appropriate" as well as "sex-inappropriate" toys.

Fathers exert more pressure than mothers to get children to conform to sex-role expectations, especially with their sons.

Research. Preschool children came to a laboratory, some with their mothers and others with their fathers. Each child and parent participated in two short play sessions. In one, children were asked by the experimenter to play with a set of masculine toys as boys would. In a second, they were given a set of feminine toys and asked to play with them as girls would. After each child had begun to play, the mother or father was permitted to enter the room. Play behavior and parental reactions to it were recorded.

Results revealed that mothers were warm, expressive, and nurturant to children of both sexes, regardless of the type of toys with which they played. In contrast, fathers' reactions varied sharply between the two play sessions. When children engaged in "sex-appropriate" play, the fathers were rewarding—smiling, praising, talking pleasantly, and joining in the child's activity. When "sex-inappropriate" play occurred, fathers reacted punitively by taking toys away, shaking their

heads "no," frowning in disgust, or directing other negative verbal communications to the child. These differential reactions were especially pronounced among fathers who participated in play sessions with their sons.

Applications. Langlois and Downs' research suggests that fathers play a more decisive role in the socialization of traditionally sex-typed behaviors than do mothers (however, evidence reviewed elsewhere in this chapter indicates that the role of mothers cannot be discounted). In an era of transition away from sex-stereotypic values and behavior, modification of paternal treatment of sons and daughters could be especially important for opening up a wider array of role possibilities for boys and girls.

Differential Treatment by Teachers. Parents are not the only agents of socialization who encourage sex-stereotypic behaviors in children. Teachers do so as well, but to some extent they do so in different ways than parents. Schools are often thought of as feminine-oriented environments in which quiet, passive obedience is rewarded and assertiveness is discouraged. This "feminine bias" is believed to promote discomfort for boys in elementary school classrooms. However, it may be equally or even more harmful for girls, who willingly comply with typical classroom demands for passivity and conformity, with possible long-term negative consequences for their sense of independence and self-esteem (Huston, 1983). In support of the feminine bias of school environments, the findings of many studies indicate that preschool and elementary school teachers positively reinforce children of both sexes for "feminine" rather than "masculine" instructional and play activities (Brophy & Good, 1974; Etaugh, Collins, & Gerson, 1975; Fagot & Patterson, 1969; Oettingen, 1985). Surprisingly, experienced male teachers do so as strenuously as female teachers (Fagot, 1985a; Robinson & Canaday, 1978).

At the same time, teachers also act in ways that serve to maintain or even increase the sex-typed behaviors that have already been fostered at home. For example, when introducing new materials, preschool teachers call on boys rather than girls to demonstrate how to use a masculine-stereotyped item, thereby contributing to sex-typed activity preferences (Serbin, Connor, & Iler, 1979).

Teachers also differentially reinforce social behaviors in male and female pupils. Fagot and her colleagues (1985) observed the interaction of teachers with very young children who were participants in toddler play groups. The teachers reacted to the children's social initiatives in terms of sex stereotypes. They attended to boys' assertive behaviors (e.g., pushing another child, grabbing a toy, crying or whining for attention) by talking to them, giving them a new toy, or physically moving them. Comparable behaviors were ignored in girls. In contrast, girls' less intense social initiatives, such as gestures, gentle touches, and talking, were responded to more often than the same behaviors of boys. Although the children in this study did not differ in their use of communicative acts at the start of the play groups, when they were observed nine months later, there were clear sex differences in behavior. The boys were more assertive, and the girls talked to teachers more.

During the preschool and elementary school years, teachers discourage aggressive actions and other forms of misbehavior in children of both sexes, but they do so more loudly, emphatically, and frequently for boys (Etaugh & Harlow, 1975; Serbin et al., 1973). Teachers' greater scolding and disapproval of boys seems to result from their expectation that boys will misbehave more often than girls, a belief based partly on real behavioral differences that have emerged during the early childhood years and partly on stereotypical beliefs about the sexes (Huston, 1983).

A series of natural experiments conducted in preschool classrooms by Serbin and her colleagues reveals that changing teacher reinforcement contingencies and cues about the sex-appropriateness of play activities can quickly modify the way boys and girls respond at school. For example, when teachers introduce new play materials nonstereotypically and compliment pupils when they show independence and persistence while ignoring attention-seeking and dependency, children's behavior changes accordingly (Serbin, Connor, & Citron, 1978; Serbin, Connor, & Iler, 1979). Also, when teachers move out of "feminine" activity areas, such as fine motor skills and arts and crafts (where they tend to spend most of their time) and locate themselves in male-preferred contexts such as the block and transportation toy centers, children follow their lead (Serbin, Connor, & Citron, 1981). However, girls are consistently more responsive to teacher-delivered contingencies than boys. Furthermore, changes in children's behavior as a result of teacher interventions are transient and short-lived; as soon as the usual reinforcement patterns are permitted to reassert themselves in the classroom, children's activity choices and behavior rapidly return to their former patterns. Sex-typed behaviors of young children, once acquired, are extremely tenacious and difficult to modify in any lasting fashion, especially among boys.

Observational Learning. In addition to direct pressures from adults, a wide variety of models of sex-stereotypic behavior are readily available in children's everyday social environments. As Huston (1983) points out:

> Although American society has changed to some degree, most adults continue to manifest sex-stereotyped patterns of household responsibility, occupational activity, recreational interests, and achievement. The average child sees women cooking, cleaning, and sewing; working in "female" jobs such as clerical, secretarial, sales, teaching, nursing; choosing to dance, sew, or play bridge for recreation; and achieving in artistic or literary areas more often than in science and engineering. That same child sees men mowing the lawn, washing the car, or doing household repairs; working in "male" occupations . . . choosing team sports, fishing, and nights with "the boys" for recreation; and achieving in math, science, and technical areas more often than in poetry or art. In school, the teachers of young children are women; the teachers of older students and the administrators with power are usually men. Peers and siblings pursue sex-stereotyped activities, games, and interests more often than they engage in cross-sex activity. Hence, although there are some individual differences, most children are exposed continually in their own environments to models of sex-stereotyped activities, interests, and roles. (pp. 420–421)

Not only do many real people with whom the child comes in contact conform to traditional sex-role expectations, but media portrayal, as we will see in Chapter 15, is highly sex-stereotypic as well. Little overall change in the way males and females are represented in television programs has taken place in recent years (Signiorelli, 1989). Moreover, content analyses of children's storybooks and textbooks reveal that they commonly portray males and females in traditional roles. In the majority of books, boys and men far outnumber girls and women as main characters, and males take center stage in most of the exciting and adventurous plot activities. Females, when they do appear as important characters, are generally engaged in such "feminine" pursuits as housekeeping and caring for children. Although the availability of sex-equitable reading materials for children is increasing, school texts have been particularly slow to change (Scott & Schau, 1985).

Modeling not only encourages conformity to sex stereotypes, but promotes nonstereotypic behavior as well. Children who see their parents behaving in a nonstereotypic fashion on a day-to-day basis — mothers who work and fathers who take over household and child care responsibilities — are less sex-typed in their views of men and women (Carlson, 1984; Selkow, 1984; Weinraub et al., 1984). Furthermore, girls who have career-oriented mothers show a number of changes in sex-role behavior. They more often engage in typically masculine pursuits such as physically active play, and they report higher educational aspirations as well as more nontraditional career choices (Hoffman, 1984, 1989; Tauber, 1979).

Peer Influences. Children's peer relations are another major context in which the development of sex typing occurs. Sex segregation — the tendency of boys to play with boys and girls to play with girls — is one of the most conspicuous features of children's peer associations, and it emerges surprising early in development. The preference for same-sex peers is already evident at age 2, when children are just beginning to play socially with one another (Jacklin & Maccoby, 1978; La Freniere, Strayer, & Gauthier, 1984). It rises dramatically over the preschool and elementary school years, reaching a peak in early adolescence, at which time it declines as interest in members of the opposite sex accompanies the physical changes of puberty (Hartup, 1983).

Research on sex-segregated peer relations provides a clear illustration of the way biological and environmental factors may combine to promote sex-typed behavior. A number of investigators believe that children's attraction to same-sex playmates has biological roots (Maccoby, 1988; Meany, Stewart, & Beatty, 1985). In line with this hypothesis, we indicated earlier that AGS girls prefer boys as social partners as well as physically active play. These findings suggest that prenatal androgen programming may underlie same-sex peer associations. As additional support for the role of biology, children's preference for sex-segregated play has been observed in a wide variety of cultures (Edwards & Whiting, 1988), and it also characterizes the peer interaction of nonhuman juvenile primates (Meany, Stewart, & Beatty, 1985).

Exactly why is sex segregation among peers so widespread and persistent? According to Maccoby (1988, 1990), hormonal influences differentially affect boys' and girls' play styles; this causes members of each sex to seek partners with compatible play behaviors. From an early age, girls appear overwhelmed by boys' rambunctious behavior. When paired with boys in a laboratory play session, 2-year-old girls show signs of withdrawal; the girl stands quietly by while the boy explores the toys (Jacklin & Maccoby, 1978).[4] Similarly, boys may gravitate to same-sex peers because they prefer playmates who respond positively to their rough and noisy initiatives.

Once formed, sex-segregated peer groups serve as powerful environments for strengthening sex-typed beliefs and behavior. Observations of preschoolers reveal that by age 3, same-sex peers positively reinforce one another for sex-typed play by praising, approving, imitating, or joining in the activity of an agemate who exhibits the "gender-appropriate" response (Fagot & Patterson, 1969; Langlois & Downs, 1980). Similarly, when preschoolers display "sex-inappropriate" play — for example, when boys play with dolls or girls with woodworking tools — they receive criticism and social ostracism from peers. Social rejection is greater for boys who frequently cross gender lines. Their male peers ignore them even when they enter masculine activities (Fagot, 1977a).

Children also develop different modes of social influence within sex-segregated peer groups. To get their way with male peers, boys come to rely heavily on commands, threats, and physical coercion. In contrast, girls learn to use polite persuasion, which succeeds with their female agemates but is ineffective with males, who start to ignore girls' polite requests by school entry (Charlesworth & Dzur, 1987; Maltz & Borker, 1983; Serbin et al., 1984). Consequently, an additional reason that girls may avoid interacting with boys during the elementary school years is that they do not find it very rewarding to try to communicate with an unresponsive social partner (Maccoby, 1988, 1990).

Although children prefer playmates of the same sex, cross-sex interaction does occur, and adults can promote it. This can be done on a short-term basis by having teachers comment approvingly when mixed-sex pairs or groups of children do come together (Serbin, Tonick, & Sternglanz, 1977). Cross-sex interaction is sustained on a long-term basis in nontraditional classrooms in which transmission of nonstereotyped values to children is an important part of the school curriculum (Berk & Lewis, 1977; Bianchi & Bakeman, 1978; Lockheed, 1986).[5] Mixed-sex play can also be promoted by changing the design of preschool environments. In one study, a wall of shelves separating the housekeeping and block area was removed so that these two sex-typed play contexts were joined. In response to the change, boys and girls interacted much more often with one another (Kinsman & Berk, 1979).

---

[4] A similar pattern of response occurs in nonhuman primates. When a male juvenile initiates an episode of rough physical play, male peers join in; nearby females withdraw (Meany, Stewart, & Beatty, 1985).

[5] You may wish to turn back to Chapter 2, Box 2.2, to reread the summary of Bianchi and Bakeman's (1978) study of same- and mixed-sex play in a traditional and an open school.

Some investigators believe that encouraging cross-sex interaction at school is a vital means for broadening the developmental possibilities of both genders (Lloyd & Smith, 1985). However, to be successful, such interventions may need to modify the social influence techniques acquired by children in their same-sex peer associations. Otherwise, boys' dominative style is likely to prevail, and girls' passivity may be encouraged, thereby strengthening traditional sex roles and the stereotypes each sex holds about the other (Lockheed & Harris, 1984).

Sibling Influences. Growing up with siblings of the same or the opposite gender also affects sex typing. However, sibling effects are more varied than peer influences because their impact is affected by family configurational variables such as birth order and family size.

If sibling effects operated just like peer influences, we might expect a family of same-sex siblings to promote stereotyped behavior and a family of mixed-sex siblings to do just the opposite. Some evidence exists to support this prediction. In a classic study of sibling influences on sex typing, Brim (1958) analyzed teacher ratings of several hundred 5- and 6-year-olds on a great many masculine and feminine attributes. Children with same-sex siblings were viewed as having more "sex-appropriate" traits than those with opposite-sex siblings. Similar results emerged in a recent observational study of the play behaviors of 4- to 9-year-olds in their homes. Activities selected by same-sex siblings were highly sex-typed. However, among opposite-sex sibling pairs, play choices were determined by the gender of the older child. In fact, this effect was so strong that boys with older sisters actually played "house" and "dolls" as much as pairs of sisters did. In contrast, boys with older brothers never engaged in such pursuits (Stoneman, Brody, & MacKinnon, 1986).

Curiously, other research directly contradicts these findings. For example, Tauber (1979) videotaped 8- and 9-year-olds while each played with toys in a laboratory. In her study, play with "opposite-sex" toys was more common among children who came from families in which all siblings were of the same gender. Similarly, several other studies report that individuals with same-sex siblings have less sex-typed interests and personality characteristics than those from mixed-gender families (Grotevant, 1978; Leventhal, 1970). How can such conflicting results be explained?

Recall from Chapter 10 that an important *within-family* environmental influence on children's personality development is that siblings often strive to be different from one another.[6] This effect is most pronounced when children are of the same sex and when they come from large families. An analysis of the studies reviewed above reveals that investigations reporting a *modeling and reinforcement effect* (an increase in sex-typing among same-sex siblings) were limited to children from small, two-child families. In contrast, those reporting a *differentiation effect* included children from large families. In the latter studies, an older sibling of the same sex may have provided an effective sex-typed model, but the younger child may not have responded to it out of a need to be different or a reluctance to compete with an older sibling in an area in which that child was already quite competent.

It is also possible that parents may relax pressures toward sex typing among offspring of the same sex. Consistent with this idea, in a study in which mothers were asked to choose toys that they wanted their younger children to receive as gifts, they more often selected "opposite-sex" toys if the child's older sibling was of the same sex (Stoneman, Brody, & MacKinnon, 1986). Furthermore, in all-girl and all-boy families, children are more likely to be given "cross-sex" household responsibilities. In such families, girls may be asked to mow the lawn and take out the garbage and boys to cook and wash the dishes because no "gender-appropriate" child is available to do

[6] Return to Chapter 10, pages 406–407, to refresh your memory about within-family environmental influences on personality development.

When siblings are all of the same sex, they are more likely to be assigned "cross-sex" chores. This father encourages his daughters to help with yard work—a responsibility typically reserved for boys.

the job. Thus, families in which siblings are all of the same sex may provide some special opportunities for expansion of traditional sex roles.

BRIEF REVIEW Research reveals that prenatally administered androgens influence a variety of masculine sex-typed behaviors in nonhuman animal species. Studies of human children with adrenogenital syndrome (AGS) suggest similar (but more limited) effects that are difficult to separate from the wide variety of environmental influences on sex-role development. Beginning in infancy, adults view and treat boys and girls differently. Parents encourage children to engage in sex-stereotypic play activities, and they promote independence, assertiveness, and cognitive mastery among boys and nurturant, dependent behavior among girls. Fathers make these distinctions to a greater degree than do mothers, although each parent plays a special role in the sex-typed socialization of the same-sex child. Traditional sex-role learning receives further support from teachers and same-sex peers. Sibling effects on sex typing vary considerably, depending on gender mixture, birth order, and family size.

SEX-ROLE IDENTITY

Besides biological predispositions and environmental pressures, an additional variable that eventually comes to influence children's sex typing is *sex-role identity,* a person's perception of the self as relatively masculine or feminine in characteristics. In the sections that follow, we consider how children's sex-role identity develops. In addition, we look at the implications of individual differences in the content of children's self-perceptions for their psychological adjustment and behavior.

Masculinity, Femininity, and Androgyny

The first studies of sex-role identity assumed that all normally developing, well-adjusted individuals view themselves as either masculine or feminine in attributes—whichever happened to be congruent with their biological gender. By the 1970s, it became apparent that this assumption was incorrect. First, not all traditionally sex-typed individuals turned out to be pictures of psychological health. In 1970, Broverman and her colleagues asked psychologists experienced in treating people for adjustment problems to rate a series of stereotypically masculine and feminine attributes in terms of how well they represented the characteristics of a "mature, healthy, socially competent" individual. The masculine items were regarded as far healthier than the feminine ones. Furthermore, most people regarded masculine instrumental traits as more desirable than feminine ones, probably because masculine attributes are essential for positions of power and prestige in society (e.g., Rosenkrantz et al., 1968).

Research also revealed that many men and women did not view themselves in a traditionally sex-typed fashion. In 1974, Sandra Bem presented evidence that around 30 to 40 percent of people have an **androgynous** sex-role identity. When given a list of masculine and feminine attributes and asked to indicate how well each describes themselves, androgynous people score high on both sets of characteristics (Bem, 1974, 1977). Bem hypothesized that a person with an androgynous identity would be particularly advantaged in psychological adjustment. An androgynous orientation, she reasoned, should permit greater behavioral adaptability—masculine independence as well as feminine nurturance, depending on what the situation calls for. In contrast, a traditional sex-role orientation is, by definition, narrower and more inhibiting in its behavioral possibilities.

The first studies to examine the behavioral correlates of androgyny were consistent with Bem's predictions. Androgynous subjects comfortably displayed "cross-sex" behavior, had a higher sense of self-esteem, and showed greater maturity of moral judgment than individuals with other sex-role orientations (Bem, 1975, 1977; Block, 1973; Spence, Helmreich, & Stapp, 1975). However, Bem's ideas were soon challenged. When a large number of investigations reporting on a diverse array of adjustment measures were carefully examined, masculine-oriented individuals again appeared advantaged. Furthermore, the masculine component of androgyny turned out to be largely responsible for the superior psychological health of androgynous females over those with traditional sex-role identities (Taylor & Hall, 1982; Whitley, 1983, 1985).

Nevertheless, the studies of androgyny demonstrated that individuals vary considerably in their sex-role orientations. Possessing masculine attributes does not preclude adopting feminine ones; being independent, forceful, and interested in baseball and science does not mean that a person cannot be affectionate, compassionate, and interested in cooking and poetry as well. Moreover, in a future society in which feminine characteristics are socially rewarded to the same degree as masculine ones, androgynous individuals may very well excel in psychological health. Perhaps a blend of masculine and feminine attributes does represent the ideal personality, even though the feminine side is not valued as much as the masculine one in our present culture.

The Development of Sex-Role Identity

How do children develop identities that consist of varying mixtures of traditionally masculine and feminine characteristics? Both social learning and cognitive-developmental answers to this question exist. Social learning theory stresses that *behavior is primary*. Modeling and reinforcement of sex-typed responses cause children to learn society's rules for gender-related behavior, which are accepted as appropriate for the self. In contrast, cognitive-developmental theory emphasizes that *behavior is secondary to thought*. Children actively organize their experiences into gender-linked self-perceptions. Then children strive to behave in ways that are consistent with these cognitive structures.

According to cognitive-developmental theory, the development of sex-role identity begins with **gender constancy,** an appreciation of the fact that gender is a permanent characteristic of the self that does not change with superficial variations in appearance or behavior. Cognitive-developmental theory assumes that before children understand that their gender is permanent, they display very little sex-typed behavior because no consistent cognitive structure is available to guide and sustain it. But once children attain gender constancy, they are believed to use this knowledge as the basis for a sex-role identity. From the vast array of alternatives in the environment, they actively select attitudes and values that fit with their own gender, and they start to pattern their behavior after same-sex models whom they judge to be similar to the self.

Cognitive-developmental and social learning theory lead to different predictions about sex-role development. The cognitive-developmental approach assumes that sex-typed behavior follows after gender constancy, while social learning theory states that the behavior is there first. Before we look at what research has to say about the accuracy of these two hypotheses, let's trace the emergence of gender constancy during the early childhood years.

The Emergence of Gender Constancy. On the basis of Piaget's description of the preoperational stage, Lawrence Kohlberg (1966) first proposed that before age 6 or 7, children are not capable of conserving the constancy of their own gender. Only gradually do they attain this understanding, by moving through three stages of development:

1. **Gender labeling.** During the early preschool years, children learn such sex-linked verbal labels as man, boy, lady, and girl and apply them systematically to the self and others. However, their first gender categories are not based on biologically permanent features of sex. When asked such questions as "When you (a girl) grow up, could you ever be a daddy?" or "Could you be a boy if you wanted to?", young children freely answer yes (Slaby & Frey, 1975). In addition, when shown a doll whose hairstyle and clothing are transformed before their eyes and asked, "Now is (doll's name) a girl or a boy?", children of this stage indicate that the doll's sex is no longer the same (McConaghy, 1979; Marcus & Overton, 1978).

2. **Gender stability.** During this intermediate stage, children have a partial understanding of the permanence of their own gender. They grasp the constancy of gender across time — its temporal stability. However, although they know that male and female babies eventually become boys and girls and men and women, they continue to assert, as they did at younger ages, that changing hairstyle, clothing, and "sex-appropriate" activities will lead a person to switch genders as well (Coker, 1984; Fagot, 1985b; Slaby & Frey, 1975).

3. **Gender consistency.** During the late preschool and early school years, children become certain of the *situational consistency* of their sex (Marcus & Overton, 1978; Siegal & Robinson, 1987). They know that gender remains constant, even if on a particular occasion a person decides to dress in an "opposite-sex" fashion or engage in "cross-sex" activities, and that sex is determined by genital characteristics (McConaghy, 1979; Emmerich, 1981).

As the studies cited above suggest, considerable evidence lends support to this developmental progression. However, new research indicates that preschoolers' poor performance on gender constancy tasks is not a function of preoperational cognitive immaturity, as Kohlberg believed it to be. Instead, it is due to an absence of knowledge about genital differences between the sexes and faulty assessment procedures that lead young children to misinterpret the experimenter's questions. For example, when preschoolers are asked whether a doll is a boy or a girl after its clothes have been changed, they may think the experimenter means, "Does the doll *look like* a boy or a girl?" or "Is the doll *pretending to be* a boy or a girl?" Also, perhaps children regard dolls as toy objects whose sex *can* be changed at will rather than as symbols for real human beings (as the investigator intends them to be).

In a recent gender constancy study, Bem (1989) corrected these methodological problems. First, she used realistic stimuli — color photos of nude boy and girl toddlers who were subsequently depicted in "same-sex" and "opposite-sex" clothing. Second, she rephrased the gender constancy question by asking, "What is (child in photo) *really*, a boy or a girl?" Under these conditions, 40 percent of 3- to 5-year-olds conserved sex across perceptual transformations — considerably more than in previous research. In addition, Bem assessed children's awareness of the genital features associated with each sex. As shown in Figure 13.3, the large majority of preschoolers who knew about genital characteristics also understood gender constancy. In contrast, those who had not yet acquired genital information typically failed the gender constancy task. In many households in Western societies, young children do not see members of the opposite sex naked. Bem's findings reveal that *lack of opportunity* to learn about genital differences (not perception-bound preoperational thought) accounts for the fact that most preschoolers rely on superficial appearance and behavior as the primary basis for classifying gender.

How Well Does Gender Constancy Predict Sex-Role Behavior. Is cognitive-developmental theory correct that gender constancy is the major determinant of children's sex-role behavior? From findings we discussed earlier in this chapter, perhaps you have already concluded that the evidence for this assertion is weak. Long before most preschoolers appreciate the permanence of their gender, they show a wide variety of sex-typed responses and are especially attentive to same-sex models (Bussey & Bandura, 1984). In fact, "gender-appropriate" behaviors appear so early in development that direct reinforcement and modeling must be of formative importance. In addition, once gender constancy is achieved, it does not augment preschoolers' already well-developed sex-typed preferences (Carter & Levy, 1988; Downs & Langlois, 1988; Levy & Carter, 1989).

Even though gender constancy is not a prerequisite for sex typing, some of the cognitive acquisitions that precede it may facilitate children's tendency to respond to the world in sex-linked terms. In a recent longitudinal study, Fagot and Leinbach (1989) found that children who attained the stage of gender labeling early (before 27

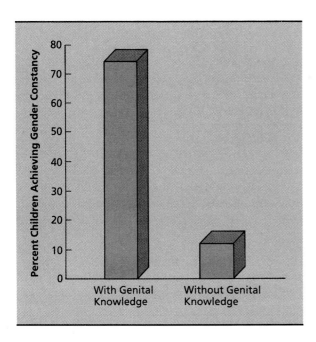

Figure 13.3. Percentage of preschoolers with and without genital knowledge who understood gender constancy in the Bem (1989) study. (*Adapted from Bem, 1989.*)

months) showed especially rapid acquisition of sex-typed behaviors between 1½ and 2½ years of age. Moreover, by age 4, they were more knowledgeable about sex stereotypes than their late-labeling counterparts. These findings suggest that as soon as children acquire basic gender categories, they use them as the basis for assimilating gender-relevant information and modifying their own behavior.

If a complete understanding of gender constancy is not necessary for the adoption of sex-typed responses, then just what role, if any, does it play in children's sex-role development? One speculation is that instead of increasing conformity to societal standards, gender constancy may free children to experiment with "opposite-sex" choices (Bem, 1989; Huston, 1983). Before attaining gender constancy, children may be motivated to engage in "same-sex" behaviors because they believe that doing so is what makes them a boy or a girl. Once gender constancy is achieved, children understand that their gender will remain the same regardless of their sex-role preferences. As a result, nonstereotypic behaviors become less threatening. There is some research to support this idea. In the early elementary school years, children's understanding of gender constancy is positively related to the number of sex-typed attributes they rate as appropriate for both sexes (Urberg, 1979). In addition, gender-constant youngsters understand that the adoption of sex-typed behaviors is ultimately a matter of individual choice, whereas non-gender-constant children tend to view it as a rigid necessity (Ullian, 1976).

The Development of Sex-Role Identity during Middle Childhood and Adolescence. Once children enter elementary school, researchers use questionnaires much like those given to adults to find out how their masculine, feminine, and androgynous self-perceptions change with age. A finding that appears repeatedly in such studies is that boys' and girls' sex-role identities follow different paths of development. From third to sixth grade, boys strengthen their identification with a same-sex, masculine role. In contrast, girls' identification with feminine traits declines over this period, and they begin to adopt some "opposite-sex," masculine characteristics. Although girls' overall orientation still leans toward the feminine side, they are clearly the more androgynous of the sexes (Hall & Halberstadt, 1980). In early adolescence, an upsurge in same-sex orientation occurs for both sexes. This diminishes by the college years, although it does so to a greater extent for females than for males (Leahy & Eiter, 1980).

Children's activity preferences and behaviors show similar developmental patterns. Unlike boys, girls do not increase their preference for sex-typed activities in middle childhood. Instead, they experiment with some "opposite-sex" pursuits—participating in organized sports, taking up science projects, and building forts in the backyard (Huston-Stein & Higgins-Trenk, 1978). Then a temporary return to "same-sex" interests emerges during early adolescence that becomes less pronounced in the late adolescent years (Leahy & Eiter, 1980; Stoddart & Turiel, 1985; Ullian, 1976).

These developmental trends can be accounted for by a mixture of social and cognitive forces. We have already seen that society attaches greater prestige to "masculine" attributes and to the male role in general. Girls undoubtedly become aware of this as they grow older. As a result, they start to identify with "masculine" traits and are attracted to some typically masculine activities. The heightened same-sex orientation during early adolescence may be a function of new perspective-taking competencies that emerge during the teenage years. Because adolescents are often preoccupied with what others think of them, they have a greater need to adhere to social conventions and to avoid being seen as different than they did at an earlier age. As they move toward establishing a mature personal identity (see Chapter 11), they become less concerned with others' evaluations of their behavior and more involved in finding meaningful attributes to incorporate into their self-definitions. As a result, highly stereotypic self-perceptions decline by late adolescence (Leahy & Eiter, 1980; Ullian, 1976).

During middle childhood, girls feel freer than boys to engage in "opposite-sex" pursuits. These preadolescent girls participate in a team sport typically reserved for boys and men.

Although sex-role identity follows the general path of development described above, individual differences exist at all ages, and they are moderately predictive of sex-typed behavior. A more masculine and less feminine identity is associated with better performance on spatial and mathematical tasks (Signorella & Jamison, 1986; Signorella, Jamison, & Krupa, 1989). In the personal-social domain, adolescent girls with feminine orientations are more popular with agemates, but masculine-oriented youngsters of both sexes are more assertive, less dependent, and have a higher sense of self-esteem (Hall & Halberstadt, 1980). At the present time, androgynous children, much like their adult counterparts, are not especially advantaged either intellectually or socially. Instead, it is the masculine sex-role orientation that is the key factor in predicting positive behavioral outcomes for children of both sexes.

Since these relationships are correlational in nature, the perennial "chicken-and-egg" question emerges as soon as we try to explain them. We do not know the extent to which masculine and feminine self-perceptions *arise* from particular activities and behaviors (as social learning theory assumes) or serve as *determinants* of behavior (as cognitive-developmental theory would predict). According to a new perspective on the origins and consequences of sex role identity—gender schema theory—the answer is *both,* as we will see in the following section.

Gender Schema Theory: A New Approach to Sex-Role Identity. Gender schema theory is an integrative approach to the development of sex typing that contains both social learning and cognitive-developmental features. It also combines a number of separate elements of the sex-typing process—stereotyping, sex-role identity, and sex-role preferences and behavior—into a unified picture of how and why sex-typed orientations emerge and are often tenaciously maintained (Bem, 1981, 1983; Martin & Halverson, 1981, 1987).

Schema theory states that children learn from the environment stereotypical definitions of maleness and femaleness and incorporate them into masculine and feminine cognitive categories, or *gender schemas,* which they actively use to interpret their world. Once these basic schemas are formed, children select the contents associated with their own sex and construct a sex-role identity, or set of attributes appropriate for and characteristic of the self. As a result, children's self-perceptions become sex-typed, and they also function as gender schemas that children use to process incoming information and to guide their own behavior.

Figure 13.4 shows exactly how this network of gender schemas works to organize and regulate sex-typed preferences and behavior. Let's take the example of a child

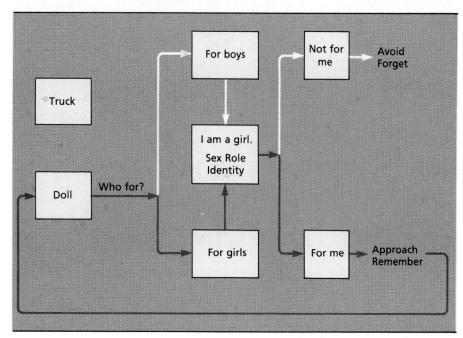

Figure 13.4. Model of how gender-relevant stimuli are encoded into sex-role identity and used to organize sex-role preferences and behavior. *(From C. L. Martin & C. F. Halverson, 1981, "A Schematic Processing Model of Sex-typing and Stereotyping in Children,"* Child Development, 52, 1119–1134. © The Society for Research in Child Development, Inc. Adapted by permission.)

who has been taught that "dolls are for girls" and who also knows that she is a girl. Our young-child uses this schematic information to interpret the environment and make decisions about how to behave. Because her schemas lead her to conclude that "dolls are for me," she approaches the doll, explores it, and learns more about it. In contrast, on seeing a truck, she uses her gender schemas to conclude that "trucks are not for me" and responds by avoiding the "sex-inappropriate" toy (Martin & Halverson, 1981).[7]

Gender schema theory explains why stereotypes and sex-role orientations are self-perpetuating and difficult to modify and exactly how they restrict behavioral alternatives. The reason is that schemas structure experience so that schema-consistent information is attended to and approached, while schema-inconsistent information is ignored, misinterpreted, or actively rejected. In fact, investigators have found that when children see others behaving in gender-inconsistent ways, either they have difficulty remembering what they have seen, or they change the sex of the actor or distort the nature of the activity to make the two elements fit with one another. For example, when shown a picture of a boy cooking at a stove, many children recall the picture as a girl rather than a boy, and when shown a film that includes a male nurse, they remember him as a doctor instead of a nurse (Cordua, McGraw, & Drabman, 1979; Martin & Halverson, 1983; Signorella & Liben, 1984). The result of this schematic processing is that over time, children begin to increase their detailed knowledge of "things for me" that are consistent with their own gender schemas, while they learn much less about "opposite-sex" activities and behaviors.

Among children who have strong stereotypical beliefs, activity preferences, and self-perceptions, gender-schematic thinking is especially extreme (Carter & Levy, 1988; Levy & Carter, 1989; Signorella & Liben, 1984). But gender-schematic thinking could not operate at all to restrict behavior and learning opportunities if society

---

[7] Does this flowchart of how gender schemas work make you think of an information processing approach to children's cognition? Gender schema theory is one of the few examples of the application of information processing to children's understanding of themselves and their social world. Recall that the topic of social problem solving, which was discussed in Chapter 11, is another.

did not teach children an extensive network of gender-linked associations. Thus, schema theory tells us that children would not view themselves and others in such a gender-biased fashion if their social environments did not exaggerate distinctions between the sexes (Bem, 1983).

Social learning theory regards sex-typed behavior as the basis for sex-role identity. In contrast, cognitive-developmental theory assumes that gender constancy precedes sex-typed self-perceptions, which serve to promote and sustain sex-role behavior. Contrary to cognitive-developmental predictions, lack of genital knowledge rather than preoperational cognitive immaturity accounts for preschoolers' poor performance on gender constancy tasks. Moreover, sex typing appears so early in development that gender constancy cannot have preceded it; modeling and reinforcement must govern its initial acquisition. However, once gender constancy is achieved, it may contribute to the development of more flexible sex-role orientations. During middle childhood, boys' masculine sex-role identities strengthen, while girls become more androgynous. An increase in same-sex identification occurs for both sexes during early adolescence that subsequently diminishes.

Gender schema theory is a new, integrative approach that combines social learning with cognitive-developmental features and puts the various pieces of sex-typed functioning together. Culturally transmitted stereotypes lead children to construct gender schemas, or cognitive representations of the environment and of themselves, that perpetuate sex-typed preferences and behavior.

TO WHAT EXTENT DO BOYS AND GIRLS *REALLY* DIFFER IN COGNITIVE ABILITIES AND PERSONALITY ATTRIBUTES?

So far in this chapter, we have looked at the relationship of biological, environmental, and cognitive-developmental factors to children's sex-stereotypic preferences and behaviors. At the same time, we have said little about the extent to which boys and girls are measurably different in cognitive and personality attributes on which we might expect them to vary, given the pervasive stereotypes available in our culture. Over the past three decades, there have been thousands of efforts to measure sex differences in these characteristics. At the heart of all of these studies is the age-old nature-nurture debate, couched in gender-related terms. Investigators have looked for stable differences between males and females and, from there, have searched for the biological and environmental roots of each variation.

In 1974, Eleanor Maccoby and Carol Jacklin published *The Psychology of Sex Differences,* a monumental review of the sex differences literature. Examining 1,600 studies conducted between 1966 and 1973 and comparing the number that reported sex differences to the number that did not, they concluded that actual sex differences were far less prevalent than commonly believed. Convincing evidence, they indicated, could be found in only four areas: verbal abilities (in favor of girls) and spatial abilities, mathematical abilities, and aggression (all in favor of boys).

Careful scrutiny of Maccoby and Jacklin's procedures quickly produced criticisms of their overall findings (Block, 1976). A major shortcoming was that many studies included in their review were based on such small and potentially biased samples that some sex differences could have gone undetected. Since 1974, many new literature reviews have been conducted. Instead of tabulating the results of individual studies, researchers now reanalyze the data of many investigations together, thereby avoiding the pitfall of giving too much weight to those with limited numbers of subjects. This approach has another advantage. Besides telling us whether a sex difference exists, it provides an estimate of how large the difference is between males and females.

New findings, summarized in Table 13.2, indicate that Maccoby and Jacklin's synthesis of research *did* underestimate sex differences, particularly in the realm of personality. However, even though more sex differences have since been confirmed, many common assumptions about gender variations continue to be unfounded. For example, contrary to popular belief, girls are not more sociable, suggestible, kinder, and more giving and helpful to others. Also, boys are not "smarter." They do not excel at complex, analytical thinking, and girls are not better at rote, repetitive tasks.

Furthermore, a repeated conclusion of new research is that the disparities between boys and girls are quite small—surprisingly so, in view of pervasive societal stereotypes. Gender accounts for no more than 5 percent of individual differences among children in any characteristic, leaving most to be explained by other factors (Deaux, 1985).[8] Also, some sex differences have changed over time. For example, over the last several decades, sex differences have narrowed in all areas of intellectual abilities in which they have been identified, except for upper-level mathematics, where boys' advantage has remained constant (Feingold, 1988; Friedman, 1989; Linn & Hyde, 1989). This trend is a reminder that currently established sex differences are not settled for all time. The general picture of how boys and girls differ may not be the same in the twenty-first century as it is today.

Sex Differences in Cognitive Abilities

Sex differences in the intellectual domain continue to be consistent with the findings of Maccoby and Jacklin—favoring girls in verbal skills and boys in spatial and mathematical skills. There is considerable agreement that heredity is involved in the verbal and spatial disparities. In recent years, scientists have turned their attention toward unraveling the specific biological mechanisms responsible for these differences, and we will see that a diverse array of speculative hypotheses exists. But no biological factor ever operates in a cultural or experiential vacuum. In the case of each type of mental ability, environment has been shown to play a crucial role.

Verbal Abilities. In infancy and early childhood, girls are the more verbal of the two sexes. Between 6 and 12 months of age, girls are more responsive to their mothers' verbalizations and initiate more interactions; by age 2, they speak in longer sentences (Gunnar & Donahue, 1980; Schachter et al., 1978). At school entry, girls learn to read earlier, achieve higher scores on standardized reading measures, and account for a lower percentage of children referred for remedial reading instruction (Halpern, 1986; Lummis & Stevenson, 1990). However, the sex disparity on tests of general verbal ability given during the school years has declined considerably since the 1970s; at present, it is so small that researchers judge it to be negligible (Feingold, 1988; Hyde & Linn, 1988).

Girls' more rapid language acquisition is difficult to explain in purely environmental terms; the most common biological explanation is their faster rate of physiological maturation. However, sex differences in early reading progress may very well be accounted for by experience. For example, conflict between the masculine sex role and the demands of the typical classroom environment place limits on boys' initial reading performance. Earlier in this chapter, we indicated that children think of reading as a "feminine" subject and that schools are feminine-biased settings in which boys' greater activity level and noncompliance lead them to experience more scolding

---

[8] Although this estimate is quite small and means that the distributions of boys' and girls' scores on every ability and personality characteristic overlap considerably, psychologists still regard a difference of this size as meaningful. For example, even if sex accounted for only 4 to 5 percent of individual differences, this would still amount to 60 percent of one group but only 40 percent of the other scoring above the mean on the attribute in question.

Table 13.2. Current Differences Between Boys and Girls

CHARACTERISTIC	SEX DIFFERENCE
Physical and motor development	Boys are slightly larger than girls at birth, but they lag behind girls in physiological and skeletal maturation throughout childhood. Sex differences in body size and strength are small during infancy and childhood. Boys surpass girls in size and muscle strength at adolescence (see Chapter 5).
Verbal abilities	Girls show faster early language development and are advantaged in reading achievement during the first few years of school. During middle childhood and adolescence, sex differences on measures of general verbal ability are negligible.
Spatial abilities	Boys outperform girls in spatial abilities by the mid-elementary school years, a difference that persists into adulthood. However, the sex difference is small and evident only on certain types of spatial tasks.
Mathematical abilities	Beginning in adolescence, boys do better than girls on tests of mathematical reasoning. The difference is especially pronounced at the high end of the distribution; more boys than girls are exceptionally talented in math.
School achievement	From kindergarten through third grade, girls outperform boys in all areas of school achievement. Beyond this age, sex differences are no longer evident, and boys start to show an advantage in some areas, such as mathematics, by junior high and high school.
Achievement motivation	Sex differences in achievement motivation are linked to type of task. Boys perceive themselves as more competent and have higher expectancies of success in ''masculine'' achievement areas, such as mathematics, athletics, and mechanical skills. Girls have higher expectancies and set higher standards for themselves in ''feminine'' areas, such as English and art.
Emotional sensitivity	As early as the preschool years, girls are more effective senders and receivers of emotional information. They also score higher on self-report measures of empathy, although it is not clear that they are more empathic in real life situations.
Fear, timidity, and anxiety	Girls are more fearful, timid, and anxious than boys. These differences may be present as early as the first year of life. In school, girls are more anxious about failure and expend more energy trying to avoid it than boys. In contrast, boys are more daring and greater risk-takers than girls. This difference is reflected in boys' higher accident rates at every age between 4 and 18.
Compliance and dependency	Beginning in the early preschool years, girls are more compliant than boys in response to directives from either adults or peers. They also engage in more help-seeking from adults and score higher on measures of dependency. In contrast, boys are the more dominant and socially assertive of the two sexes.
Activity level	Although some studies report no sex difference, those that do consistently find boys to be more active than girls.
Aggression	Beginning in the preschool years, boys are more aggressive than girls, but the difference is small during childhood. In adolescence, boys are far more likely than girls to become involved in antisocial behavior and violent crime.
Developmental difficulties	Boys are overrepresented among children with many types of developmental problems, including speech and language disorders, reading disabilities, and behavior problems such as hyperactivity, hostile acting-out behavior, and social and emotional immaturity. More boys than girls are born with genetic defects, physical impairments, and mental retardation. Overall, boys are the more vulnerable of the two sexes.

Based on: Benbow & Stanley, 1980; Feingold, 1988; Friedman, 1989; Hall, 1978; Hall & Halberstadt, 1981; Hyde, 1984; Hyde & Linn, 1988; Jacklin & Maccoby, 1983; Linn & Hyde, 1989; Richardson, Koller, & Katz, 1986; U.S. Department of Justice, 1990.

from teachers than girls. Consistent with this idea, research indicates that girls' initial advantage in reading development is reduced or eliminated in countries where reading and early school learning are regarded as well suited to the male sex role (e.g., Preston, 1962).

Spatial Abilities. Spatial skills involve the ability to mentally manipulate non-verbal, pictorial information. The male advantage in spatial performance is not large (Linn & Hyde, 1989). However, since gender variation in spatial skills has implications for math and science education and later entry into scientific careers, it has commanded considerable research attention.

The study of sex differences in spatial ability is complicated by the fact that a variety of spatial tasks exist, and sex differences appear on some but not all of them (see Figure 13.5). The gender gap is strongest for *mental rotation tasks* in which subjects must rotate a three-dimensional figure rapidly and accurately inside their heads. Sex differences also occur on *spatial perception tasks* in which people must determine spatial relationships based on the orientation of their own bodies. Interestingly, no systematic sex differences appear on *spatial visualization tasks* that involve complex, multistep manipulations of spatially presented material. Many mental strategies can be used to solve these problems. While males may solve them with spatial

Figure 13.5. Types of spatial tasks on which the performance of males and females has been compared. *(From M. C. Linn & A. C. Petersen, 1985, "Emergence and Characteristics of Sex Differences in Spatial Ability: A Meta-Analysis."* Child Development, 56, *1479–1498.* © The Society for Research in Child Development, Inc. Reprinted by permission.)

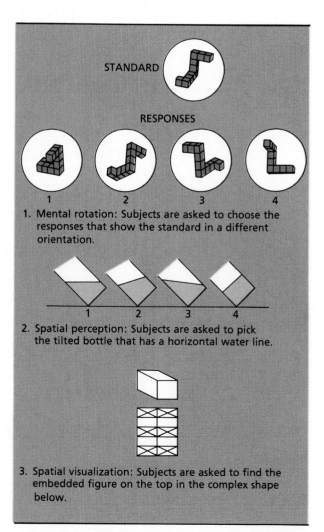

STANDARD

RESPONSES

1 2 3 4

1. Mental rotation: Subjects are asked to choose the responses that show the standard in a different orientation.

1 2 3 4

2. Spatial perception: Subjects are asked to pick the tilted bottle that has a horizontal water line.

3. Spatial visualization: Subjects are asked to find the embedded figure on the top in the complex shape below.

manipulations, perhaps females come up with other equally effective cognitive strategies and, for this reason, perform just as well (Linn & Petersen, 1985).

Until the 1980s, investigators thought that sex differences in spatial skills did not appear until the adolescent years, but recent evidence indicates that they are clearly evident in middle childhood and persist throughout the life span (Johnson & Meade, 1987; Linn & Petersen, 1985). The pattern is consistent enough to suggest the operation of a biological mediator. Three controversial hypotheses about the specific biological mechanisms involved exist.

1. *The brain lateralization/maturation rate hypothesis.* Waber's (1976) theory of how brain lateralization and maturation rate work together to produce sex differences in mental abilities has been the subject of intense research scrutiny in recent years. Waber hypothesized that girls' faster rate of physiological maturation leads to earlier but less strong brain lateralization[9] than that of boys. Early hemispheric specialization in girls is thought to enhance verbal skills, which develop quickly during the first few years of life. In contrast, boys' slower maturation rate is believed to promote stronger lateralization during adolescence, a pattern of development thought to enhance later-emerging spatial functions.

Research testing Waber's theory has not provided clear support for it. When the verbal and spatial scores of early- and late-maturing adolescents from a variety of investigations are compared, the expected association between speed of maturation and cognitive abilities holds only for spatial skills, and it is marginal at best (Newcombe & Dubas, 1987). Moreover, even when late maturers outperform early maturers on spatial tasks, they do not show evidence of stronger lateralization (Bruder et al., 1987; Meyer-Bahlburg et al., 1985).

2. *The X-linked recessive gene hypothesis.* This explanation suggests that a recessive gene for spatial abilities is carried on the X chromosome. Since girls have two X chromosomes, they must inherit two recessive genes for the "spatial trait" to be manifest. In contrast, boys need only one, and as a result, they are advantaged. To test this hypothesis, investigators study relationships among the spatial scores of family members. For example, since boys get their X chromosome from their mothers, their spatial scores should be more strongly correlated with the scores of mothers than fathers. This prediction has been examined in a great many studies, which, taken together, yield contradictory findings (Parsons, 1982).

3. *The androgen hormone hypothesis.* A third hypothesis is that prenatal and/or pubertal exposure to androgen hormones accounts for the male advantage in spatial abilities. Of all biological mechanisms, this one has received the least support. Studies of adrenogenital syndrome girls provide no evidence of an association between prenatal androgens and later cognitive functioning (Parsons, 1982). Moreover, if pubertal hormones do play a role, their effects are not simple. Although high levels of pubertal androgens do predict better spatial scores in females, the reverse has been reported for males (Broverman, Klaiber, & Vogel, 1980; Petersen, 1979). A number of investigators believe that hormonal influences, if they exist, may exert their effects by interacting with other biological mechanisms, such as brain lateralization and maturation rate, but a great deal of work needs to be done to sort out these complex relationships.

Although less attention has been devoted to the environmental bases of sex differences in spatial abilities, several studies suggest that experience can widen or reduce the gender gap. Boys' early play activities may contribute to their spatial

[9] Recall from Chapter 5 that lateralization refers to specialization of functions between the hemispheres of the brain. For most individuals, verbal skills tend to localize in the left hemisphere and spatial skills in the right hemisphere. You may wish to return to Chapter 5, pages 192–195, to review what is known about the development of brain lateralization in childhood.

advantage, since children of both sexes who play with highly manipulative, "masculine" toys do better on spatial problems (Fagot & Littman, 1976). In addition, girls' more limited awareness of certain scientific principles may sometimes prevent them from demonstrating their true spatial competencies. Liben and Golbeck (1984) found that when female college students were given information about a relevant physical rule before solving the spatial perception problem shown in Figure 13.5, their performance equaled that of males. Finally, on spatial rotation tasks for which sex differences are largest, females differ only in speed, not accuracy, and training substantially improves their scores (Linn & Petersen, 1985; Lohman, 1988). Perhaps females' greater anxiety about failing in achievement situations contributes to their slower performance, although use of less efficient cognitive strategies may also play a role.

Mathematical Abilities. The male advantage in mathematics is clearly evident by high school, although among highly intellectually gifted youngsters, it is present earlier — by age 13. Although the magnitude of sex difference is small, it is greater at the upper end of the ability distribution. In a series of studies, Benbow and Stanley (1980, 1983) examined the mathematical performance of thousands of high-achieving seventh- and eighth-grade youngsters who were invited to take the Scholastic Aptitude Test long before they were required to do so for college admission. Year after year, the boys outscored the girls on the mathematics subtest. Twice as many boys as girls had scores above 500; 13 times as many scored over 700. Sex differences in mathematics do not occur on all kinds of test items. Boys and girls perform equally well on tests of basic math knowledge, and girls do better in computational skills. The difference occurs on tests of mathematical reasoning, primarily in solving complex word problems (Friedman, 1989; Hyde, Fennema, & Lamon, 1990).

Some researchers believe that the gender gap in mathematical performance, particularly at the high end of the distribution, is biologically based. A variety of hypotheses about the biological mechanisms involved have been advanced, including hormonal influences and brain lateralization (Benbow, 1988), but none have been verified. One common assumption is that sex differences in mathematical abilities are rooted in boys' superior spatial skills. If this is the case, then children's spatial and mathematical scores should be positively correlated. However, the literature as a

Are sex differences in mathematical abilities biologically or environmentally determined? This controversial question has become the subject of intense research scrutiny.

whole shows inconsistent patterns of relationships. In some studies, verbal skills are as effective as spatial skills in predicting math achievement (Linn & Petersen, 1985; Parsons, 1982). However, even if we could be sure that spatial and mathematical performance were consistently related, we would not be able to tell from the correlation whether boys' spatial advantage actually caused them to excel in mathematics.

Mathematics achievement is also related to a wide variety of experiential variables, including the number of math courses taken in high school (boys take more than girls) and the extent to which math is regarded as a "sex-appropriate" subject (both boys and girls think of math as a "male domain") (Fennema & Sherman, 1977; Paulsen & Johnson, 1983; Sherman, 1980). Furthermore, girls' inclination to attribute their academic failures to insufficient ability (rather than effort) is known to undermine self-confidence and promote debilitating anxiety in achievement situations. Girls exhibit this style of attributional reasoning particularly strongly in mathematics (Stipek, 1984). Girls' self-derogating attributions may be partly responsible for the fact that they are more likely than boys to stop taking math courses when they are not mandatory and, ultimately, to achieve less well during the high school years. In Chapter 11, we showed that children develop their attributional biases largely from the evaluative messages they get from others. As soon as children enter school, teachers and parents expect girls to do less well in math and subtly communicate this message to children (Lummis and Stevenson, 1990; Meece et al., 1982; Parsons, Adler, & Kaczala, 1982). These findings indicate that girls' lack of confidence in themselves as learners is just as plausible a reason for their poorer math performance as any biologically based difference between the sexes.

Sex Differences in Personality Attributes

In the following sections, we consider the origins of sex differences in several personality attributes — emotional sensitivity, compliance and dependency, and aggression.

Emotional Sensitivity. Females are stereotyped as the more emotionally sensitive of the two sexes. Recent reviews of many studies indicate that, in fact, females send and receive emotional messages more effectively than males. The difference, although small, appears quite early. When subjects are asked to make judgments of others' emotional states using nonverbal cues, girls perform better than boys beginning in the preschool years (Hall, 1978). Girls also express feelings more freely through facial and bodily gestures (Hall & Halberstadt, 1981). Moreover, as early as age 2, they use more emotion words in their conversations with others. However, mothers also talk more about feelings with their daughters than their sons (Dunn, Bretherton, & Munn, 1987).

It would be reasonable to expect these differences to carry over to empathic responding, but to date the evidence is mixed. On self-report measures of empathic arousal, girls consistently score higher than boys. However, when children are observed for behavioral signs that they are responding to the distress of a nearby person, boys and girls show no difference (Eisenberg & Lennon, 1983).

As with other attributes, both biological and environmental explanations for sex differences in emotional sensitivity exist. One speculation is that females are genetically prewired to be especially sensitive to nonverbal cues so that as mothers they will be able to detect and respond quickly to the distress signals of their offspring. Against this interpretation is a growing body of evidence that girls are not "naturally" more nurturant than boys. Before age 5, boys and girls spend equal amounts of time talking to and playing with a baby during interaction sessions arranged in either laboratory or natural environments (Berman, 1986; Fogel et al., 1987). In middle childhood, boys' willingness to relate to infants declines, although they continue to respond with just as much care and affection to other targets of nurturance, such as pets and elderly relatives (Melson & Fogel, 1988). Moreover, sex differences in emotional sensitivity are not apparent in adulthood when parents interact with their own babies. In Chapter 10 we showed that fathers respond very affectionately to their infants, and they are just as competent caregivers as mothers. In Chapter 4, we noted that men and women react in a similar fashion to the sound of a crying baby.

Taken together, these findings indicate that the gender gap in emotional sensitivity is a function of social expectations that girls be warm and expressive and boys be emotionally distant and controlled. However, when males enter contexts in which the expression of tenderness and nurturance is permitted, they are quite capable of manifesting these behaviors, a conclusion that is strengthened by the cross-cultural findings described in Box 13.2.

Compliance and Dependency. Beginning in the preschool years, girls are the more passive and compliant of the two sexes in the face of both adult and peer demands. In addition, girls more often seek help and information from adults and score higher in dependency on personality inventories (Block, 1976; Jacklin & Maccoby, 1978). There is widespread agreement that these patterns of behavior are learned. As with emotional sensitivity, they have much to do with the activity environments in which boys and girls spend their time.

Research by Carpenter (1983) indicates that from an early age, girls are encouraged to participate in adult-structured activities at home and in preschool. In contrast,

◆ CONTEMPORARY ISSUES: CULTURAL DIFFERENCES ◆

"Feminine" Task Assignment and the Social Behaviors of Boys and Girls   Box 13.2

Between 1950 and 1980, anthropologists Beatrice Whiting and Carolyn Edwards (1988a, 1988b) carried out extensive cross-cultural research on children's social development in 12 communities around the world. At each site, field workers collected detailed information on the daily activities and interaction patterns of 2- to 10-year-olds in an effort to clarify the process by which cultures shape sex-differentiated behavior. The findings revealed that in most societies, boys were dominant and aggressive and girls were dependent, compliant, and nurturant. However, striking exceptions emerged in communities in which children were assigned "cross-sex" tasks as part of their daily responsibilities.

Nyansongo, a small agricultural settlement in Kenya, is one such community. In many East African societies, boys are categorized with girls and women until they approach puberty, at which time initiation into manhood and associated "masculine" activities takes place. Nyansongo mothers, who work four to five hours a day in the gardens, assign the care of young children, the tending of the cooking fire, and the washing of utensils to older siblings in the family. Although girl caregivers are preferred, child care is delegated to boys if there are no females to assume it. In Nyansongo, half the boys between the ages of 5 and 8 take care of infants, and half help with domestic chores. As a result, girls are relieved of total responsibility for "feminine" tasks and have more idle time for casual interaction with agemates. Moreover,

Nyansongo men spent much of the day away from the compound herding livestock, and at night, they sleep in different buildings than their families. Consequently, fathers rarely interact with young children and have little direct impact on their development.

Compared to children of other cultures, Nyansongo youngsters display considerably less conformity to traditional sex roles. Whiting and Edwards reported that girls scored high in dominance and playful roughhousing, boys in offering help and emotional support. The contexts in which Nyansongo children spend their days, rather than deliberate adult tutoring in sex-appropriate behavior, account for these findings. Frequent responsibility for small children pressures boys into nurturance; holding, feeding, and comforting are readily evoked by the needs of their young charges. In contrast, increased opportunities for unsupervised play engender autonomy and assertiveness in Nyansongo girls. Once children acquire these interaction patterns in particular contexts, they generalize them to new circumstances and a wider array of social partners.

Whiting and Edwards's research broadens our conception of environmental factors impinging on children's sex-typed socialization. Culture influences the daily settings to which children are assigned and the individuals with whom they come in contact. These, in turn, affect the interpersonal skills they practice and the range of behaviors mastered by boys and girls.

boys gravitate to activities in which adults are either minimally involved or entirely absent. The result of this process is that boys and girls engage in very different social behaviors. Compliance and bids for help and attention appear more often in adult-structured contexts, whereas assertiveness, leadership, and creative use of materials occur more often in unstructured pursuits. Since optimal development involves the ability to lead and assert as well as to comply and fit into structures imposed by others, Carpenter recommends that children be encouraged to participate in a balanced array of structurally different activities. In one study, she showed that the compliant and assertive tendencies of preschoolers of both sexes could easily be modified by assigning them to classroom activities that differed in degree of adult structure (Carpenter, Huston, & Holt, 1986).

Aggression. Sex differences in aggression have attracted more attention from researchers than any other gender variation. The findings are the same in study after study: Beginning in the preschool years, boys engage in more physical and verbal aggression, and by adolescence they are ten times more likely than girls to be involved in antisocial behavior and violent crime (U.S. Department of Justice, 1990). Although the sex difference in aggression appears very reliably, it is small in childhood, accounting for only 5 percent of individual variability (Hyde, 1984). In fact, because most research has focused on highly visible aggressive acts, such as physical assaults and verbal insults, it underestimates girls' aggressiveness in early adolescence. We will see that around this time, girls start to display less obvious forms of hostility, such as malicious gossip and social exclusion, that are just as harmful to a victim as boys' overt aggressive outbursts.

Sex Similarities and Differences in the Development of Aggression. The seeds of aggressive behavior are already apparent by the end of the first year of life. In Chapter 10, we showed that angry emotional reactions to frustration and blocked goals increase after 7 months of age. As infants develop the cognitive capacity to isolate sources of frustration and the motor skills to lash out at them, two basic forms of aggression appear. The first is **instrumental aggression,** in which the child tries to gain access to an object, privilege, or space and, in doing so, pushes, shouts at, or otherwise attacks an individual who is in the way. In this type of aggression, there is little or no malicious intent toward the victim. Instead, the child is merely trying to reach a desired goal. The second form is **hostile aggression.** It is person-oriented and meant to hurt, as when the child hits or insults a playmate with no other aim in mind but to injure the other individual.

In children of both sexes, the form of aggression and the avenue through which it is expressed (physical or verbal) change with age. In a classic study of the development of early aggressive behavior, Goodenough (1931) asked mothers to keep records of their children's angry outbursts. Physical aggression was gradually replaced by verbal aggression over the preschool years. This change parallels young children's rapid language acquisition, but it is also the result of negative reactions on the part of adults and peers to instances of physical aggression (Parke & Slaby, 1983). In another study, Hartup (1974) recorded the aggressive displays of 4- to 7-year-old children at school and reported a decline over this age period in instrumental aggression and a gradual increase in hostile, person-oriented outbursts. An interesting finding was that tattling, criticism, and ridicule frequently provoked hostile reactions in 6- and 7-year-olds but seldom did so in 4- and 5-year-olds. The rise in hostile aggression occurs during the same period in which children become better able to assess the intentions of other people (see Chapter 11). As a result, when the behavior of another child is deliberately hostile, older children are more likely to "read" it as such and respond with an aggressive retaliation.

Although there are similarities, differences between boys and girls in the development of aggression also exist. Between 1½ and 2½ years of age, as children first

*As early as the preschool
years, physically aggressive
interchanges occur more
often in boy-boy interactions
than in boy-girl and girl-girl
pairs.*

become aware of sex-role expectations, aggression begins to decline in girls but is maintained in boys (Fagot, Leinbach, & Hagen, 1986; Fagot & Leinbach, 1989). During the preschool and elementary school years, boys display more overt peer aggression of all kinds (Barrett, 1979; Maccoby & Jacklin, 1980), and cross-cultural observations in many nations reveal a similar picture (Omark, Omark, & Edelman, 1975; Whiting & Edwards, 1988a). In addition, analyses of the circumstances in which aggressive encounters occur show that physically aggressive interchanges are especially frequent in boy-boy interactions and less so in boy-girl and girl-girl pairs (Barrett, 1979; Maccoby & Jacklin, 1980; Strauss, Gelles, & Steinmetz, 1980). Boys are also far more likely than girls to respond with retaliatory aggression when they are physically attacked (Darvill & Cheyne, 1981).

In early adolescence, boys continue to rely on direct confrontation when provoked by a peer. In contrast, girls' aggressive encounters become increasingly indirect and concealed. Cairns and his collaborators (1989) followed a group of children from fourth grade through junior high school, asking them at yearly intervals to report two recent conflicts with agemates, one same-sex and one opposite-sex. As shown in Figure 13.6, by seventh grade, a dramatic rise occurred in the proportion of girls who described same-sex disputes involving social alienation—malicious gossip, rumor spreading, and exclusion. Boys never mentioned these kinds of conflicts. Unlike direct assaults, these hidden social cruelties make it difficult for victims to identify the precise perpetrator of an act and retaliate. Thus, they permit girls to vent their anger while avoiding overt conflict, which violates the "feminine" sex role. Because girls' aggression goes underground in this way, it becomes difficult to observe and study at older ages. Yet more needs to be known about these subtle forms of female hostility if we are to fully understand the nature and extent of sex differences in aggressive behavior.

From middle childhood on, aggression is a highly stable personality characteristic, especially among males (Cairns et al., 1989; Huesmann et al., 1984; Olweus, 1982). In a longitudinal investigation that spanned 22 years, very aggressive 8-year-

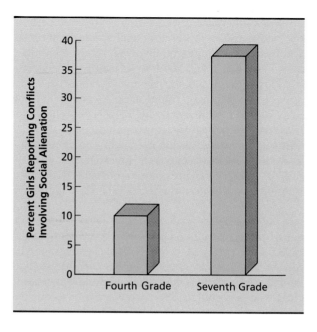

Figure 13.6. Percentage of girls in fourth and seventh grade reporting themes of social alienation in conflicts with same-sex peers in the Cairns et al. (1989) study. *(Adapted from Cairns et al., 1989.)*

olds became 30-year-olds who were more likely to score high in aggressive inclinations on a personality inventory, use severe punishment with their children, and be convicted of serious criminal offenses (see Figure 13.7). In this study, the researchers also tracked the aggressive tendencies of the subjects' family members. Strong continuity across multiple generations emerged. Highly aggressive children were more likely to have parents and grandparents who were antisocial themselves and whose behavioral difficulties were apparent in their own childhoods (Huesmann et al., 1984).

Recently, investigators have made considerable progress in unraveling the complex ways in which biological and environmental factors work together to promote and sustain aggressive behavior. We turn to a consideration of this evidence in the following sections.

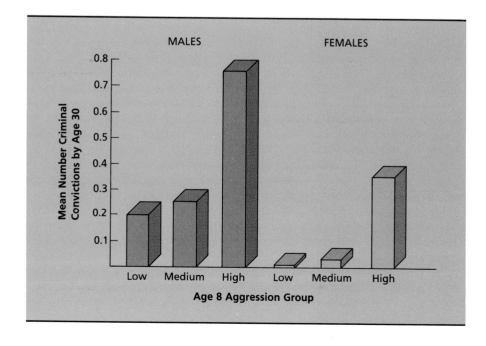

Figure 13.7. Relationship of childhood aggression to criminal behavior in adulthood in the Huesmann et al. (1984) study. *(From L. R. Huesmann, L. D. Eron, M. M. Lefkowitz, & L. O. Walder, 1984, "Stability of Aggression over Time and Generations," Developmental Psychology, 20, 1120–1134. Copyright 1984 by the American Psychological Association. Reprinted by permission of the author.)*

Biological Influences. Since the sex difference in aggression is apparent early in life, generalizes across cultures, and is found in many animal species, almost all researchers agree that biological mechanisms must be involved. As we mentioned earlier in this chapter, androgen hormones are related to aggressive behavior in animals, and they are also believed to play a role in human beings. But think back for a moment to our discussion of sex-role development among adrenogenital syndrome children. These youngsters were exposed to abnormally high levels of prenatal androgens, but they showed no evidence of increased aggression (although they did exhibit higher activity levels). This finding suggests that in humans, no more than a *predisposition* for aggression results from androgen exposure. Investigators currently believe that androgen hormones affect intervening response tendencies that, when combined with environmental influences, lead to a higher likelihood of aggressive outcomes in males.

One speculation is that prenatal androgens promote higher levels of physical activity, which may or may not be translated into aggression, depending on child-rearing conditions (Parsons, 1982). For example, a highly active youngster who participates in aggressive-conducive activities as an outlet for his energies, such as water fights, boxing matches, and tackle football, is more likely to display aggressive behavior than a comparable child who is encouraged to participate in vigorous but nonaggressive pursuits, such as running track, playing baseball, or working out in the gym. The findings of one study lend support to this idea. Bullock and Merrill (1980) had third and fourth graders indicate their own activity preferences as well as nominate the most aggressive youngsters in their class in the fall of the school year and one year later. Girls showed little attraction to aggressive-conducive activities, and their activity choices had no predictive value as far as aggression was concerned. But for boys who were neither high nor low in aggression at the beginning of the study, activity preferences had a strong impact on behavior. Those who found aggressive-conducive pursuits attractive were regarded by their peers as much higher in aggressive attributes the following year.

Another biological hypothesis is that prenatal hormone levels influence the basic organization of the nervous system in ways that affect children's later emotional reactions and mood states. According to this theory, hormone levels induce more frequent displays of certain feelings, such as excitement, anger, or anxiety, and these have an increased likelihood of culminating in aggression in the presence of certain environmental conditions. In support of this idea, Marcus and her collaborators (1985) found that early hormone levels (measured at birth from umbilical cord blood samples) predicted excited as opposed to calm emotional states during the first two years of life for boys, although no relationships appeared for girls.

Besides the prenatal period, adolescence is a second phase during which hormone levels have important implications for aggressive responding. Adolescent boys who are high in androgens experience more sad and anxious emotional reactions, and they also display more aggressive behavioral attributes, such as hostile retaliations to threatening provocations, low frustration tolerance, and delinquent and rebellious behavior (Nottelmann et al., 1987; Olweus et al., 1980; Susman et al., 1987). In a recent investigation, higher estrogen and androgen levels were associated with an increase in expressions of anger on the part of adolescent girls when interacting with their parents in a laboratory discussion session (Inoff-Germain et al., 1988).

These intriguing findings require replication and extension; there is still much to be learned about the link between hormonal processes and aggressive behavior. However, from the evidence that currently exists, it is apparent that there are multiple pathways between hormones and aggression, that each involves a complex series of steps, and that each may vary with the sex and age of the child. It is also clear that whether hormonally induced intervening responses, such as activity level or emotional state, are eventually channeled into aggressive outbursts or other forms of

behavior is heavily dependent on child-rearing conditions. Next we turn to the environmental side of children's aggressive behavior.

Environmental Influences: The Family as Training Ground for Aggressive Behavior. A wealth of evidence exists on environmental provocations of aggressive behavior. Child-rearing practices; strife, anger, and discord in the family; and television violence have been the most commonly studied sources. In this section, we focus on familial factors, reserving our consideration of television influences for Chapter 15.

Many studies reveal that the same child-rearing dimensions that undermine the development of moral internalization and self-control (see Chapter 12) are also correlated with aggressive behavior. Parental love withdrawal and rejection, power-assertive and physically punitive discipline, and inconsistent punishment are associated with higher levels of aggression from the preschool through the adolescent years in children of both sexes (Parke & Slaby, 1983). When parents repeatedly discipline children with anger and hostility, they provide examples of aggressive behavior, fail to teach youngsters acceptable behavioral alternatives, and frustrate children's needs for nurturance so that that they are likely to lash out toward others in return. Unfortunately, a variety of ineffective and destructive child-rearing techniques are often found together in the same family, compounding their harmful consequences for some children. Questioning parents of 13- to 16-year-old boys, Olweus (1980) reported that mothers who had highly aggressive sons recalled not only being negative, rejecting, and indifferent to their youngsters at an early age, but also relying on power-assertive discipline.

The use of coercive tactics within the family is likely to spread from one member to another and become part of a self-perpetuating cycle that serves to elicit and maintain aggression among all family members. Making detailed home observations of typical sequences of interaction that occur in aggressive families, Patterson (1981, 1982) discovered how this happens. As indicated in Figure 13.8, the pattern begins with dominative and forceful disciplinary practices, which are made more likely by parental personality characteristics, stressful life experiences, or a temperamentally difficult child (see Chapter 10). Once the parent acts coercively, the child responds in kind by whining, yelling, and refusing until the parent eventually finds the child's behavior too much to take and "gives in." This pattern is likely to repeat itself in the future, since at the end of the interchange, both parent and child experience immediate relief and reinforcement for stopping the negative, unpleasant behavior of the other. The next time the child misbehaves, the parent is likely to react even more coercively and the child more recalcitrantly until one member of the pair again experiences the behavior of the other as unbearable and "begs off." Coercive tactics soon generalize to other family members, creating a conflict-ridden family atmosphere in which communication and successful problem solving are seriously disrupted and children become "out of control," unmanageable youngsters.

Aggressive children who are products of these family processes soon learn to approach the world from a hostile and violent perspective. Because they expect others to behave coercively, they begin to "see" malicious intent in the actions of other people even when it does not exist. As a result, they engage in a large number of unprovoked aggressive attacks, which stimulate additional hostile reactions among family members and peers, contributing further to the spiraling aggressive cycle. You may recall our discussion of Dodge's work, presented in Chapter 11, which showed that highly aggressive youngsters are especially prone to misinterpret the innocent behaviors of others as hostilely motivated.

For a variety of reasons, boys are more likely than girls to become embroiled in family interaction patterns that serve as training ground for aggressive behavior. Parents more often use physical punishment with boys, which encourages them to adopt the same tactics in their own interactions with others. In contrast, inductive

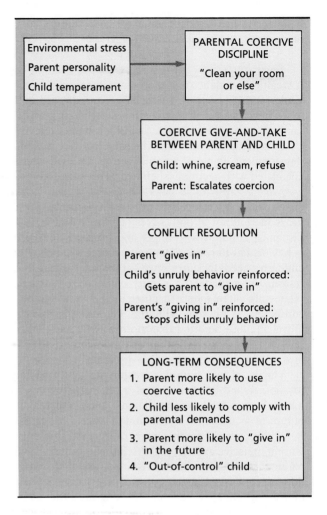

Figure 13.8. Coercive interaction pattern that induces and perpetuates aggression among family members.

discipline, which promotes self-control and empathy for a victim (see Chapter 12), is used more often with girls (Block, 1978). Also, parents are less likely to interpret peer fighting as aggressive when it occurs among boys (Condry & Ross, 1985). The stereotype embodied in the familiar adage "Boys will be boys" may lead many adults to overlook male hostility except when it is extreme, thereby setting up conditions in which it is encouraged, or at least tolerated, to a greater extent than hostility among girls. In view of these findings, it is not surprising that by middle childhood, boys expect less parental disapproval and report feeling less guilty for aggressive acts than do girls (Perry, Perry, & Weiss, 1989). By adolescence, males are more likely than females to believe that aggression enhances self-esteem (Slaby & Guerra, 1988).

Furthermore, arguing and bickering between husband and wife, while stimulating aggression among all family members, does so to a greater extent among boys. Cummings, Iannotti, and Zahn-Waxler (1985) exposed 2-year-old children to backgrounds of warm and angry verbal exchanges between adults while the children played with familiar peers. Friendly adult interactions had the effect of slightly dampening peer aggression in children of both sexes. In contrast, angry interactions led to changes in the way children behaved that were different for boys and girls. Girls tended to show fearful, withdrawing reactions (e.g., tensely freezing in place, covering or hiding their faces), while boys engaged in more interpersonal aggression. In line with our earlier discussion of emotional mediators of aggressive behavior, these findings suggest that boys may be "primed" to react to familial hostility and discord with feelings that are easily translated into aggressive impulses. Additional evidence indicates that living in a strife-ridden family magnifies children's distress reactions to adult background anger (Cummings et al., 1989).

Finally, parents do not just teach aggressive behavior directly through communication and disciplinary practices in the home. They also influence children's aggression indirectly, as "managers" of their youngsters' environments (Parke & Slaby, 1983; Patterson, DeBaryshe, & Ramsey, 1989). Poor parental supervision over children's whereabouts and peer associates is strongly linked to aggressive behavior. Unfortunately, children from conflict-ridden homes who already manifest serious antisocial tendencies are the ones most likely to experience inadequate parental monitoring. Eventually, their hostile style of responding and poor self-control lead to school failure, rejection by nonaggressive classmates, and association with deviant peer groups, which provide further encouragement for antisocial acts (Cantrell & Prinz, 1985; Hawkins & Lishner, 1987; Snyder, Dishion, & Patterson, 1986). Research indicates that the path to chronic delinquency unfolds through this series of steps, which are summarized in Figure 13.9. Putting together all the evidence we have reviewed so far, we can see that boys have a considerably higher likelihood of completing this developmental progression than do girls.

Helping Children and Parents Control Aggression. Help for aggressive children and their parents must break the bidirectional exchange of hostilities between family members and equip each party with effective techniques for interacting with one another. Interventions with preadolescent youngsters have been most successful. Once antisocial patterns persist into adolescence, so many factors converge to sustain them that treatment generally leads to disappointing outcomes (Kazdin, 1987). Over the past several decades, a variety of procedures for reducing childhood aggression have been investigated. Among them are the cathartic approach; coaching, modeling, and reinforcing alternative parent and child behaviors; and training in empathy and perspective-taking skills.

The Cathartic Approach. Catharsis is the oldest treatment technique. It was originally inspired by psychoanalytic theory, which assumed that aggressive urges gradually accumulate and, unless drained off, inevitably result in hostile outbursts. Cathartic treatment is aimed at discharging pent-up anger and frustration by offering

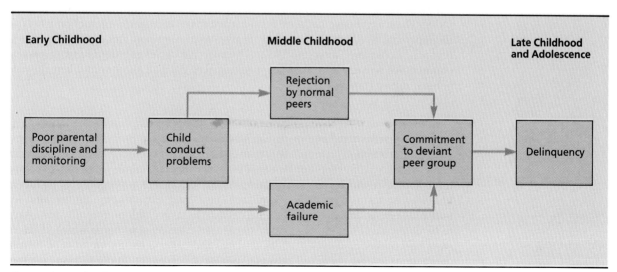

Figure 13.9. A developmental progression for antisocial behavior. *(From G. R. Patterson, B. D. DeBaryshe, & E. Ramsey, 1989, "A Developmental Perspective on Antisocial Behavior,"* American Psychologist, 44, *331. Copyright 1989 by the American Psychological Association. Reprinted by permission of the author.)*

children "safe" opportunities to behave aggressively, such as a session with a punching bag or a violent videogame. Another approach is to provide passive exposure to the aggression of others. Violent television programs and reading materials are assumed to reduce hostility as children identify with aggressive characters and experience their behavior vicariously.

On the basis of what we have said about modeling in this and other chapters, are you skeptical about the effectiveness of cathartic treatment? If so, you are correct. It has received very little research support. In fact, there is considerable evidence that aggression can be stimulated by such experiences (e.g., Mallick & McCandless, 1966; Parke et al., 1977).

Coaching, Modeling, and Reinforcing Alternative Parent and Child Behaviors. The most effective way to treat aggression among preadolescent youngsters is to interrupt the destructive family processes that led to it (Kazdin, 1987; Patterson, DeBaryshe, & Ramsey, 1989). Techniques based on social learning theory have been developed that teach both parents and children new ways of interacting with one another.

On the parent's side, modeling and coaching in child discipline have been successfully applied by Patterson (1976). A therapist carefully observes the parent's inept practices, describes and demonstrates alternative techniques, and has the parent practice them. Parents learn not to give in to a hostile, acting-out child and not to escalate their coercive efforts to control misbehavior. In addition, they are taught to pair commands with reasons and to replace verbal insults and spankings with more effective punishments, such as time out and withdrawal of privileges (see Chapter 12). Patterson's (1981) research shows that ineffective discipline contributes significantly to parents' anger, anxiety, and doubt about their own competence, further limiting their ability to control their children. Although parents of aggressive youngsters often need help with marital conflicts and other problems, one way to help them make their own lives less stressful is to teach them to manage their children more successfully.

On the child's side, aggressive youngsters benefit from programs in which they are taught alternative techniques for resolving conflict, such as cooperation and sharing, that are incompatible with aggressive behavior. Sessions in which these nonaggressive alternatives are explained, modeled, and role-played and children have opportunities to see that they result in rewarding social outcomes have been shown to reduce aggression and increase positive social behavior (Zahavi & Asher, 1978). Once aggressive children demonstrate more acceptable interaction patterns, their parents need to be reminded to give them attention and approval for their prosocial behavior (Patterson, 1982). The coercive cycles of parents and aggressive children are so pervasive that these youngsters get punished even when they do behave appropriately!

Empathy and Perspective-Taking Training. Aggression is known to be inhibited by empathic reactions to another person's pain and suffering. However, highly aggressive children express little pain or remorse after injuring another individual (Boldizar, Perry, & Perry, 1989; Perry & Bussey, 1977). Because aggressive children often come from homes in which they have had few opportunities to witness family members behaving in a sensitive, caring way, they miss early experiences that are vital for nurturing empathic reactions (see Chapter 10). In such children, empathy may have to be deliberately taught. One study found that training sessions in which children were encouraged to identify others' feelings and express their own reduced hostile interactions among peers and increased prosocial behaviors of cooperation, helping, and generosity (Feshbach & Feshbach, 1982). Empathy training necessarily involves practice in perceiving situations from the perspective of others. In Chapter 11, we showed that the antisocial behaviors of delinquent youths could be substantially reduced through an intervention program that improved perspective-taking skills through dramatic role-playing. Perhaps the reason this program worked so well was that it promoted empathic responding, which then served as a deterrent to antisocial behavior.

In the sections above, we have seen that boys and girls differ in a variety of intellectual and personality characteristics. Girls show more rapid early verbal development and are more emotionally sensitive, dependent, and compliant, while boys are advantaged in spatial and mathematical abilities and are more aggressive. However, these disparities are small and, in the case of intellectual abilities, have declined considerably over the last several decades. Biological factors operate in some sex differences, but biology only makes it slightly easier for one sex rather than the other to acquire certain attributes. Both boys and girls can learn all of them, and socialization experiences in the family, school, and peer group determine whether each sex difference is minimized or maximized. Finally, given the myriad of ways in which it is possible for human beings to vary, our overall conclusion must be that males and females are really much more alike in developmental potential than they are different from one another.

RAISING NON-SEX-STEREOTYPED CHILDREN

A comparison of the roles and achievements of men and women in our society with the actual sex differences discussed above indicates that the developmental horizons of many children are seriously limited by pervasive sex stereotyping in our culture. Although child development specialists recognize the importance of raising children who feel free to express their human qualities without fear of violating gender-related expectations, no easy recipe exists for accomplishing this difficult task. It undoubtedly needs to be tackled on many fronts—in the home, at school, and at the level of the wider society.

Throughout this chapter we have mentioned ways in which sex stereotyping and sex-role adoption in childhood can be minimized. But even children who are fortunate enough to grow up in family, school, and peer settings that minimize stereotyping will eventually encounter it in the media and in their observations of what men and women typically do in the surrounding community. Until societal values change, children need early experiences with astute caregivers who repeatedly counteract their readiness to absorb our culture's extensive network of gender-linked associations.

Bem (1983, 1984) suggests that parents make a concerted effort to delay young children's absorption of sex-stereotyped messages from the surrounding culture as long as possible. Parents can begin by eliminating sex stereotyping from their own behavior and from the alternatives they provide for their children. For example, mothers and fathers can take turns making dinner, bathing children, and driving the family car, and they can ensure that all children have trucks and dolls to play with and pink and blue clothing. In addition, adults can deliberately shield young children from media presentations indicating that the sexes differ in what they can and should do.

At the same time, parents can teach young children that anatomy and reproduction are the only characteristics that determine a person's gender. We have seen that many youngsters do not learn to view sex in terms of genital characteristics during the preschool years. Instead, they mistakenly assume that the cultural correlates of maleness and femaleness are defining features of gender. By encouraging children to construct their first gender-linked associations on the basis of biology, parents can capitalize in a favorable way on preschoolers' tendency to interpret rules and categories rigidly and inflexibly. If children grasp at an early age that sex is narrowly defined in terms of anatomy and reproduction, then they should be less likely to view it in terms of arbitrary social conventions that must be strictly obeyed (Bem, 1984).

Once children begin to notice the vast array of sex-typed associations that prevail in our culture, parents and teachers can take steps to prevent these stereotypes from being absorbed into the child's gender schemas. For example, arrangements can be made for children to see males and females pursuing nontraditional activities and careers. In addition, older children can be informed directly about the historical roots and current consequences of gender inequalities in our society — why, for example, there has never been a female president, why few fathers stay home with their children, and why stereotypical views of men and women in the larger community are so pervasive and hard to change (Bem, 1984). As such efforts help children of the next generation build conceptions of themselves and their social world that are not limited by the male-female dichotomy, they contribute to the transformation of societal values, and they bring us closer to a time when individuals will be released from the constraints of conformity to traditional sex roles.

CHAPTER SUMMARY

Sex Stereotypes and Sex Roles

■ Children begin to acquire **sex stereotypes** and notice distinctions in **sex roles** in the early preschool years. By middle childhood, children are aware of a broad array of stereotypes, including those associated with personality attributes, achievement areas, activities, and occupations. Preschoolers' understanding of sex roles is rigid and inflexible. Elementary school children recognize that many gender-linked activities and behaviors are socially defined and can vary from one culture to another.

■ Boys hold more sex-stereotyped views than girls, and white children more than black children. The belief that **instrumental traits** are typical of males and **expressive traits** of females is present in many countries. Moreover, sex-stereotyped attitudes are important determinants of sex-typed preferences and behavior.

Biological and Environmental Influences on Sex Stereotyping and Sex-Role Adoption

■ Cross-cultural similarities in sex stereotyping and sex-role adoption have been taken as evidence for biological influences on traditional sex roles. However, cultural diversity does exist, including some instances of traditional sex-role reversal, as Margaret Mead's study of New Guinean tribal societies illustrates.

■ Research on **adrenogenital syndrome (AGS)** children suggests that prenatal hormone levels may influence some aspects of sex-role adoption. At the same time, a variety of environmental factors provide powerful support for sex-stereotyped attitudes and behavior.

■ Beginning in infancy, parents hold sex-typed perceptions and expectations of their children. By the preschool years, they reinforce their sons and daughters for a great many "sex-appropriate" activities and behaviors. Fathers differen-

tiate more than mothers, although each parent takes special responsibility for the sex-role development of the same-sex child.

■ Teachers also reinforce sex-typed behaviors and activity preferences, and children have ample opportunity to observe traditional sex roles in their everyday social environments. Children's preference for same-sex peer associates may be biologically based. Once formed, sex-segregated peer groups serve as powerful environments for strengthening sex-typed beliefs and behavior. Sibling influences on sex-role development are affected by family configurational variables. In small, two-child families, children are more likely to imitate the sex-typed behavior of an older, same-sex sibling.

Sex-Role Identity

■ According to cognitive-developmental theory, sex-role identity — one's perception of the self as relatively masculine or feminine in characteristics — begins with **gender constancy,** an understanding of the permanence of one's own gender. Gender constancy develops through three stages: **gender labeling, gender stability,** and **gender consistency.** However, in contrast to cognitive-developmental predictions, gender constancy depends on genital knowledge, not preoperational cognitive immaturity. Moreover, sex-typed behavior is acquired before gender constancy and is not augmented by it. Nevertheless, the attainment of gender constancy may free children to experiment with "opposite-sex" choices during middle childhood.

■ During the elementary school years, boys strengthen their identification with the same-sex masculine role, while girls become more **androgynous.** Same-sex identification increases in early adolescence for both sexes and declines thereafter. Although androgynous individuals were at one time thought to be better adjusted, masculine-oriented children and adults are consistently advantaged, probably because of the greater societal value attached to the male sex role.

■ **Gender schema theory** combines features of social learning and cognitive-developmental theory to explain the development of sex-role identity. On the basis of their experiences, children derive masculine and feminine cognitive categories, or gender schemas, which they incorporate into sex-typed self-definitions and use to interpret their world. Schema-consistent information is attended to and explored, while schema-conflicting information is ignored, rejected, or distorted to fit the schema. As a result, children learn much more about "same-sex" than "opposite-sex" activities and behavior.

To What Extent Do Boys and Girls *Really* Differ in Cognitive Abilities and Personality Attributes?

■ Girls excel in early verbal development and are more emotionally sensitive, compliant, and dependent, while boys are advantaged in spatial and mathematical abilities and are more aggressive than girls. In all instances, the variations are small, and there are many more ways in which boys and girls are alike than different from one another.

■ Genetic factors may underlie sex differences in verbal development and spatial abilities, although the precise biological mechanisms responsible have not yet been identified. At the same time, adult encouragement and learning opportunities contribute importantly to each sex difference in intellectual performance. Girls' advantage in emotional sensitivity, compliance, and dependency results from sex-stereotyped expectations and assignment to everyday activities that evoke these behaviors.

■ Aggression first appears in children of both sexes during late infancy. Changes in the way aggression is expressed (from physical to verbal) and its form (from **instrumental** to **hostile aggression**) take place during early childhood. While boys display more physical and verbal assaults at all ages, by early adolescence girls engage in more indirect forms of aggression, such as malicious gossip, rumor spreading, and social exclusion. Beginning in middle childhood, aggression is a highly stable characteristic, particularly among boys.

■ Prenatal and pubertal androgens appear to contribute to aggressive behavior. However, hormones seem to exert their effects indirectly, through intervening response tendencies that, when combined with environmental factors, lead to a higher likelihood of aggression in boys than in girls. Ineffective parental discipline and strife-ridden family environments promote self-perpetuating cycles of aggressive behavior between parents and children. Boys are more likely to become embroiled in these coercive family processes than are girls.

■ Among treatments designed to reduce aggression, the cathartic approach has been shown to be ineffective. Interventions based on social learning theory that teach parents and children new ways of interacting with one another work well during middle childhood. Empathy and perspective-taking training is also effective.

Raising Non-Sex-Stereotyped Children

■ Parents can minimize preschoolers' acquisition of sex-stereotyped attitudes and behaviors by delaying access to sex-typed information and teaching children that anatomy and reproduction are the defining features of gender. Once children are exposed to sex stereotypes, adults can counteract their absorption into gender schemas by providing examples of non-sex-stereotyped behavior and discussing the arbitrariness of gender inequalities in society.

IMPORTANT TERMS AND CONCEPTS

sex stereotypes (p. 515)
sex roles (p. 515)
sex-role identity (p. 515)
instrumental traits (p. 516)
expressive traits (p. 516)

adrenogenital syndrome (AGS) (p. 523)
androgyny (p. 533)
gender constancy (p. 533)
gender labeling (p. 534)

gender stability (p. 534)
gender consistency (p. 534)
gender schema theory (p. 537)
instrumental aggression (p. 547)
hostile aggression (p. 547)

Theodore Earl Butler: *The Card Players*, 1938. Oil on canvas
3. 1982 Daniel J. Terra Collection. Terra Museum of American Art, Chicago.

14

The Family

Evolutionary Origins
Functions of the Family
The Family as a Social System
Socialization within the Family
The Changing American Family
The Vulnerable Family: Child Maltreatment

In this chapter we consider the child's first and formative context for development — the family. Other social settings also have important consequences for development, but the impact of the family is, without a doubt, the most profound. In Chapter 10, we showed that the family is the source of ties to other people that are unique. The attachments formed with parents and siblings generally endure over the life span, and they serve as prototypes for social relationships in the wider world of neighborhood and school. Within the family, children also experience their first social conflicts. As we saw in Chapters 11 and 12, disciplinary encounters with parents and arguments between siblings provide children with valuable lessons in compliance and cooperation, as well as early opportunities to learn how to influence the behavior of others. Finally, in several previous chapters, we showed that the parent-child relationship serves as the child's first context for the development of cognition, language, and social and moral values. Thus, the family provides the foundation for an impressively diverse array of characteristics that make each of us human.

Research on the family has a long history in the social sciences. However, for many years, it was studied primarily by sociologists and anthropologists. They paid less attention to its impact on child development than to describing its *structure* — the roles and relationships of its members — and *functions* — the purposes it serves in people's everyday lives in comparison to other institutions of society (Hareven, 1984). When child development specialists first turned to family-related issues, they did so in a very restricted way. From the 1940s to the 1970s, most research was limited to the mother-child dyad and emphasized one-way effects of parental treatment on children's behavior. You already know from earlier sections of this book that modern investigators are intensely interested in bidirectional influences between parents and children. In addition, they want to know how parent-child interaction is affected by other family members as well as by forces outside the family situation.

Today, child development specialists conceive of the family as a complex system of multiple interacting relationships. To understand it, they have moved beyond their original focus on the mother-child dyad to the study of fathers, siblings, and extended family members. In addition, they have joined forces with researchers in other disciplines. New trends include an interest in looking at the family from an *ethological* perspective — in terms of its evolutionary origins and adaptive significance. The family is currently being studied from an *ecological* standpoint as well. Modern investigators believe that the impact of the family on child development can be understood only when it is viewed in terms of its connections with other social institutions and as embedded in a larger context of cultural customs, attitudes, and values.

We begin our discussion of the family by examining the reasons that this formative social unit came into being and has survived over thousands of years. Then we describe the current view of the family as a *social system* of complex, interacting relationships with multiple sources of influence on the child. Next we take a close look at the family as the core socializing agency of society. We consider how to conceptualize the diverse child-rearing styles used by parents and their consequences for children's development.

In the last part of this chapter, we take up the significance of major changes in the American family over the last several decades — the trend toward fewer births per family unit, the high rates of divorce and remarriage, and the increase in maternal employment and use of alternative child care arrangements. Finally, the modern family appears especially vulnerable to a breakdown in protective, emotionally supportive relationships between parent and child. We conclude this chapter by considering the origins and consequences of child abuse and neglect, which rank among America's most serious national problems.

EVOLUTIONARY ORIGINS

The structure of the human family as it exists in its most common form — a lifelong commitment between a man and woman who feed, shelter, and nurture their children until they reach maturity — had its origins tens of thousands of years ago among our hunting-and-gathering ancestors. Nonhuman primates also live in social groups and give birth to offspring who are protected by adult members of their species. But apes and monkeys do not organize themselves into family units in which food is shared and both parents invest in the rearing of offspring. Instead, their young cling to and are nursed by the mother until they are able to move about themselves. After that time, they travel with the larger group and are protected from predators, but they must forage to feed themselves (Lancaster & Whitten, 1980).

Anthropologists believe that *bipedalism* — the ability of humans to walk upright on two legs — was an important evolutionary development that led to the formation of the family unit. Bipedalism permitted division of labor among adults. Once arms were freed to carry things, our evolutionary ancestors could cooperate and share, especially in providing food for the young. Men traveled to hunt for game and brought it back to women and children, while women gathered fruit and berries that provided a temporary food supply when game was scarce. The human family pattern in which a specific male assumed special responsibility for a single female and their joint offspring soon appeared because it enhanced survival. It ensured a relatively even balance of male hunters and female gatherers within a social group, thereby guaranteeing the maximum possible protection against starvation in times when game was scarce. Also, it led to the emergence of the "husband-father" role, one with no true counterpart among nonhuman primates. Furthermore, the economic and social obligations of parents to each other and to their children were so important to the survival of early humans that they could not be entrusted to rational thinking alone. The capacity for strong emotional bonds evolved to ensure long-term commitment among family members (Lancaster & Whitten, 1980; Lovejoy, 1981; Mitchell & Shively, 1984).

Ninety-nine percent of the cumulative history of our species was spent in the hunting-and-gathering stage. Although a hunting-and-gathering economy no longer sustains the family ties of the vast majority of living humans, the special demands of this lifestyle appear to have left a lasting imprint on modern familial behavior (Lancaster & Whitten, 1980).

FUNCTIONS OF THE FAMILY

The family unit of our evolutionary ancestors not only promoted the survival of its own members, but also performed vital services for the larger society of which it was a part. Winch (1971) describes five functions that must be performed for society as a whole to survive:

1. *Reproduction:* replacements for dying members of society must be provided.
2. *Economic services:* goods and services must be produced and distributed to support members of society.
3. *Societal order:* procedures must exist for reducing conflict and maintaining orderly relationships among members of society.
4. *Socialization:* the young must be trained by mature members to become competent, participating members of society.
5. *Emotional support:* there must be procedures for binding individuals together, harmonizing their goals with those of other members of society, dealing with emotional crises, and fostering a sense of commitment, direction, and purpose in each individual.

In preindustrial society, the family was the basic unit of economic activity, and parents and children worked together to produce goods and services for society. Today, children are liabilities rather than contributors to the family's economic well-being.

In the early history of our species, families probably served all or most of these functions. But as the environments in which human beings lived became increasingly complex, the demands placed on the family became too much for it to sustain alone. Consequently, other institutions took over or shared in certain functions, and families became linked to larger social structures of society and culture (Lerner, Spanier, & Belsky, 1982). For example, political and law-making institutions assumed responsibility for ensuring societal order, and schools built on the family's socialization function by educating children for participation in an increasingly complex social world. Religious institutions supplemented both socialization and emotional support functions by providing educational services and offering family members a set of common beliefs that enhanced their sense of purposefulness and shared goals.

Finally, although the family was the basic unit of economic activity in preindustrial society, today this is no longer true (Hareven, 1984). Although members of some families still carry out economic tasks together (as in family-run farms and businesses), economic productivity has, for the most part, been taken over by institutions that make up the world of work (Winch, 1971). The economic role of the modern family is largely limited to consumption of goods and services, not to production. Consequently, whereas children used to be important contributors to the family's economic well-being, today they are "economic liabilities." The cost of raising an American child born in the early 1990s from birth through four years of college will be about $83,000 to $123,000.[1] The money required to give children the care and education necessary to prepare them for the roles they will assume as adults is one factor, among others, that has contributed to the declining birth rate in modern industrialized nations (Espenshade, 1980).

While important functions have been taken over by or are now shared with other institutions, three of the functions mentioned above — reproduction, socialization, and emotional support — remain primarily the province of the family. Interestingly, these are the ones especially related to children, since they include the tasks of giving birth to, rearing, and nurturing the young. Researchers interested in finding out how modern families go about fulfilling these functions take a social systems approach, viewing the family as a set of mutually influencing relationships affected by the larger social context of which the family is a part.

THE FAMILY AS A SOCIAL SYSTEM

The **social systems perspective** on the family grew out of the efforts of family researchers and therapists to describe and explain the complex patterns of social behavior they observed among family members (Kantor & Lehr, 1975). As we review its fundamental features, you will see that it has much in common with Bronfenbrenner's (1989) ecological model, which we discussed in Chapter 1.[2] According to the systems view, the family is not a unidirectional social mold in which the child is shaped by parental (largely maternal) treatment. Instead, it consists of a complex interplay of interdependent parts that, together, form a network of reciprocal causal effects. Thus, basic to the social systems perspective is that children and parents influence each other. Furthermore, the bidirectional quality of familial interaction is affected by the quality of other relationships in the setting, or what Bronfenbrenner calls the effect of *third parties*. For example, research indicates that when parents'

---

[1] These figures are based on a 1980 estimate, corrected for subsequent inflation (U. S. Department of Labor, 1990). The estimate includes basic expenses related to food, housing, clothing, medical care, and education.

[2] You may wish to return to Chapter 1, pages 16–20, to review Bronfenbrenner's ecological model at this time.

marital relationship is warm and supportive, mothers and fathers praise and stimulate their children more and nag and scold them less—practices associated with more effective child functioning (Belsky, 1984; Cox et al., 1989; Howes & Markman, 1989). In contrast, high marital hostility is linked to frequent use of coercion and punishment, techniques that often lead children to respond noncompliantly and aggressively in return. Take a moment to think about other examples of third-party influences—for example, the impact of sibling relationships on parent-child communication and vice versa. Have you conjured up an image of family interaction that looks much like a web of intricately crossed fibers in which pulling any single thread bends and shapes others nearby?

To make matters more complicated, the social systems approach views the interplay of forces within the family as dynamic, progressive, and ever-changing (Kantor & Lehr, 1975). Individuals continue to grow and change throughout the life span. As a result, the interactive nature of the family is not static; it shifts across time. For example, as children develop, so does parental participation in child rearing, and changes in parents' behavior toward their physically, cognitively, and socially more competent youngsters pave the way for new competencies and further adjustments in family relationships. In fact, no other social unit is required to accommodate to such vast developmental changes in its members as is the family.

Finally, the social systems approach, as we indicated earlier, regards relationships among mothers, fathers, and children as situated in larger social contexts. Connections to the community—in terms of both *formal organizations,* such as the school, workplace, day care center, church or synagogue, and *informal social networks* of relatives, friends, and neighbors—are regarded as significant for family well-being, and a wealth of research supports this view (Bronfenbrenner, Moen, & Garbarino, 1984). For example, high rates of psychopathology, particularly disturbances that appear early in development, last a long time, and are accompanied by severe parental discord, are more prevalent in urban than rural communities (Rutter, 1981). Although population density and poverty contribute to this finding, additional factors are also responsible. Psychological disturbance is greatest in metropolitan areas characterized by fragmented communication networks—high population mobility, weak community leadership, lack of organized leisure time activities, and few telephones and visits among friends and neighbors (Hughes et al., 1960). In addition,

The social systems approach views formal and informal ties to the community as essential for optimal family functioning.

child abuse and neglect are greatest in urban neighborhoods where unemployment is high and residents report dissatisfaction with the community, describing it as a socially isolated place in which to live (Garbarino & Sherman, 1980; Steinberg, Catalano, & Dooley, 1981). In contrast, when family ties to the community are strong—as reflected in regular church attendance and participation in informal networks of friends and relatives—family stress and child adjustment problems are reduced (Werner & Smith, 1982). Moreover, links established between family and community enhance children's development. In one study, support from relatives and membership in social and religious organizations predicted the extent to which mothers of high-risk newborns provided their children with a stimulating home environment during the preschool years (Pascoe et al., 1981). In another study, parents who were more involved in school organizations and activities had children who showed superior academic achievement (Stevenson & Baker, 1987).

Why do social ties to the community serve as an effective buffer against family stress and facilitate child development? There are several reasons. First, social supports provide parents with interpersonal acceptance. A neighbor or relative who listens sympathetically and tries to allay a parent's doubts and concerns enhances the parent's self-esteem. The parent, in turn, is likely to behave more sensitively toward her children. Second, social networks provide parents with opportunities to exchange valuable information, goods, and services. A friend who offers useful advice about where a parent might find a job, better living arrangements, or a good doctor or who looks after children while the parent attends to other pressing needs helps make the multiple roles of spouse, economic provider, and caregiver easier to fulfill. As a result, benefits return to the parent-child relationship. Third, informal social networks and links to formal community organizations provide parents with child-rearing controls and role models. In giving advice, friends and relatives may encourage or discourage particular patterns of parent-child interaction; during mutual visits, they may demonstrate effective ways of interacting with children. Finally, as children participate in the informal social networks of their parents, other adults can influence the children's development directly by providing warmth, encouragement, and exposure to a wider array of competent adult models (Cochran & Brassard, 1979; Mitchell & Trickett, 1980).

BRIEF REVIEW

In the sections above, we have seen that the origins of the family date back to our hunting-and-gathering ancestors, for whom it was uniquely suited to ensure survival. Salient functions carried out by the modern family include reproduction, socialization, and emotional support. The social systems perspective regards family functioning as the product of a complex network of bidirectional relationships that constantly readjust as family members change over time. The quality of these relationships and therefore children's development depend partly on links established between the family and formal and informal social supports in the larger community.

No investigator could possibly study all facets of family functioning encompassed by the social systems perspective at the same time. However, as we address each piece of the larger family puzzle in the course of this chapter, it is important to keep in mind the many interlocking parts that simultaneously influence children's development.

SOCIALIZATION WITHIN THE FAMILY

Socialization—the process by which mature members of society shape the behaviors of immature individuals so that they grow into competent, contributing participants—has been of greatest interest to child development specialists who study the family. In previous chapters, we discussed numerous ways in which parents can foster children's development—by being sensitively responsive to infants' momentary behaviors and needs (Chapter 10); by serving as models and reinforcers of children's socially acceptable behavior (Chapter 12); by relying on reasoning, explanation, and inductive discipline to promote moral internalization and self-control (Chapter 12); and by communicating causal attributions that implicate children's effort rather than ability when they fail, thereby encouraging a mastery-oriented approach to challenging tasks (Chapter 11).

Socialization pressures begin in earnest during the second year of life, when children first display an ability to comply with parental directives (see Chapter 12). Effective caregivers pace their demands in accord with children's capacity to control their own actions. For example, parents who are in tune with their child's development do not impose a range of "don'ts" on a small infant. Instead, they put away breakable objects, place barriers across steep staircases, and remove babies physically when they start to behave in ways that are dangerous to themselves or bothersome to others. As soon as parents place greater emphasis on socialization toward the end of the infancy period, they vary considerably in how they go about the task. Researchers have been interested in describing the overall quality of communication that distinguishes parents who are especially effective at socializing the child from those who are less effective.

Dimensions of Child Rearing

In a series of influential studies, Diana Baumrind gathered information on child-rearing practices by making home and laboratory observations of parents interacting with their preschool children. Two broad dimensions of parenting behavior emerged from the data (Baumrind, 1967, 1971; Baumrind & Black, 1967). The first is **control** or demandingness. Some parents establish high standards for what they expect of their children and insist that their youngsters meet those standards. Other parents demand very little and rarely redirect or inhibit their children's behavior. The second dimension is **responsiveness** or child-centeredness. Some parents are highly accepting of and responsive to their children; they frequently engage in open discussion and verbal give-and-take. Others are aloof, rejecting, and unresponsive to their youngster's social initiatives.

When looked at together, these two parenting dimensions sum up basic differences in how parents go about the task of socialization. As shown in Table 14.1, the various combinations of control and responsiveness yield four types of parents. Baumrind's research focused on three of them: the authoritative, the authoritarian, and the permissive parent. The fourth type—the indifferent parent—has been studied by other investigators. Each parenting pattern predicts important aspects of child

Table 14.1. A Two-Dimensional Classification of Parenting Styles

	RESPONSIVE, CHILD-CENTERED	UNRESPONSIVE, PARENT-CENTERED
CONTROLLING, DEMANDING	Authoritative parent	Authoritarian parent
LOW IN CONTROL, UNDEMANDING	Permissive parent	Uninvolved parent

Source: Adapted from E. E. Maccoby & J. A. Martin, 1983, "Socialization in the Context of the Family: Parent-Child Interaction," in E. M. Hetherington, (ed.), *Handbook of Child Psychology: Vol. 4. Socialization, Personality, and Social Development* (4th ed., pp. 1–101). New York: Wiley. Copyright 1983 by John Wiley & Sons. Reprinted by permission.

development. Overall, research indicates that authoritative parents have socially active, responsible, and cognitively competent children, whereas parents who rely on the other three approaches have youngsters who develop less optimally in a number of ways. Let's take a closer look at each of these child-rearing styles in the following sections.

The Authoritative Parent. In Baumrind's (1967) first study, preschool children were separated into categories based on ratings by psychologists who observed them over several months at nursery school. As shown in Figure 14.1, one group, the "mature" preschoolers, differed sharply from the others in that their parents used a set of child-rearing tactics that were clearly **authoritative** in style. Parents of these youngsters were controlling and demanding; they had high expectations for mature behavior and firmly enforced them by using commands and consequences for disobedience when necessary. At the same time, they were warm and nurturant, listened patiently and sensitively to their youngster's point of view, and encouraged children's input into family decision making. These authoritative parents used a rational, democratic approach to child rearing in which the rights of both parents and children were recognized and respected.

Ratings by psychologists of the children of authoritative parents indicated that they were buoyant, zestful, and content in mood; self-reliant in their mastery of new tasks; and self-controlled in their ability to show sustained effort and refrain from engaging in disruptive behavior (Baumrind, 1967). Subsequent studies by Baumrind replicated this finding and also revealed that independent, achievement-oriented

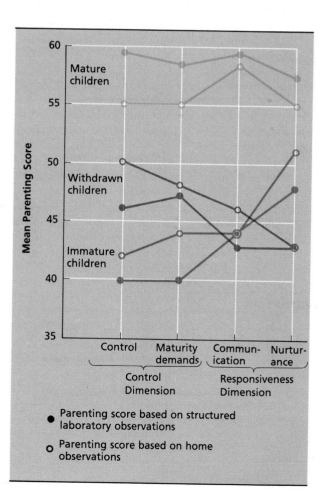

Figure 14.1. Relationship of parental control and responsiveness to children's competence in the Baumrind (1967) study. Assessments of parenting were based on observations of parent-child interaction in the home and in a structured laboratory situation in which parents were given an opportunity to teach and play with their preschool child. *(From D. Baumrind, "Child Care Practices Anteceding Three Patterns of Preschool Behavior,"* Genetic Psychology Monographs, 75, *p. 73, 1967. Reprinted with permission of the Helen Dwight Reid Educational Foundation. Published by Heldref Publications, 4000 Albermarle Street N.W., Washington, DC 20016 © 1967.)*

behavior among girls and friendly, cooperative social behavior among boys showed especially strong associations with authoritative parenting (Baumrind, 1971; Baumrind & Black, 1967). Furthermore, follow-up research by other investigators indicated that the authoritative style continues to predict a variety of dimensions of competence during middle childhood and adolescence, including high self-esteem, internalized moral standards, and superior academic performance in high school (Dornbusch et al., 1987; Hoffman, 1970; Loeb, Horst, & Horton, 1980; Steinberg, Elmen, & Mounts, 1989).

The Authoritarian Parent. Authoritarian parents are also demanding and controlling, but they place such a high value on conformity and obedience that they are unresponsive—even outright rejecting—when children assert opposing opinions and beliefs. Consequently, little communicative give-and-take takes place between these parents and their youngsters. Rather, children are expected to accept their parent's word for what is right in an unquestioning manner. If they do not, authoritarian parents resort to forceful, punitive measures to curb the child's will. The authoritarian style is clearly biased in favor of parents' needs, with little room accorded to the child's independent self-expression.

In Baumrind's (1967) early research, preschoolers with authoritarian parents were withdrawn and unhappy (see Figure 14.1). They appeared anxious and insecure when interacting with peers and tended to react hostilely when frustrated. In subsequent research, girls who were products of authoritarian child rearing were especially dependent and lacking in exploration and achievement motivation, while some boys showed high rates of anger and defiance (Baumrind, 1971). Furthermore, you may remember from Chapter 12 that authoritarian, power-assertive discipline is negatively related to internalization of moral prohibitions and self-esteem (Coopersmith, 1967; Hoffman, 1970).

The Permissive Parent. Permissive parents are nurturant, communicative, and accepting, but they avoid asserting their authority or imposing controls of any kind. They are overly tolerant and permit children to make virtually all of their own decisions. Children of permissive parents eat meals and go to bed when they feel like it, watch as much television as they want, do not have to learn good manners or be responsible for household chores, and are allowed to interrupt and annoy others without parental intervention. While some permissive parents consciously believe that a lax style of child rearing is good for children, many others lack confidence in their ability to influence their youngster's behavior and are disorganized and ineffective in running their households.

Baumrind (1967) found it difficult to identify many parents who were extremely permissive among her research participants, but some leaned in that direction. As indicated in Figure 14.1, their children were highly "immature" youngsters. They had difficulty controlling their impulses, were overly dependent and demanding of adults, and showed less sustained involvement in classroom activities than children of parents who exerted more control. In addition, they were disobedient, explosive, and reactive when asked to do something that conflicted with their momentary desires. Later findings indicated that the link between permissive parenting and passive, dependent, nonachieving behavior held for boys but not for girls (Baumrind, 1971).

The Uninvolved Parent. When undemanding parenting is combined with indifferent or rejecting behavior, it falls within the **uninvolved** cell in Table 14.1. Uninvolved parents display little commitment to their role as caregivers and socialization agents beyond the minimum effort required to maintain the child as a member of the household. Often these parents are overwhelmed by many daily pressures and stresses in their lives, and they have little time and energy to spare for children. As a result, they cope with the requirements of parenting by keeping the child at a distance and are strongly oriented toward avoiding inconvenience. They may respond to the child's immediate demands for food and easily accessible objects. However, any efforts that have to do with long-term goals, such as establishing and enforcing rules about homework or setting standards for acceptable social behavior, amount to little more than fleeting, feeble attempts to get the child to conform (Maccoby & Martin, 1983).

At its extreme, uninvolved parenting ranks as a form of child maltreatment called neglect. Especially when it begins early, it leads to disruptions in a great many aspects of development. Detached, emotionally uninvolved, depressed mothers who show little interest in their babies have children who by two years of age show deficits in virtually all aspects of psychological functioning, including substantial intellectual declines; attachment difficulties; lack of participation in play and feeding situations; and a rise in angry, noncompliant, and dependent behavior (Egeland & Sroufe, 1981; Radke-Yarrow et al., 1985).

Even when parental disinterest and detachment are less pronounced, child development is far from optimal. In a longitudinal investigation of the relationship between early parent-child interaction and children's behavior, Martin (1981) reported that uninvolved as opposed to responsive mothers had preschoolers who were noncompliant, demanding, and interfering in their behavior. Required to wait while the mother filled out a questionnaire, the child tugged and pulled at her clothing, grabbed her pencil, and sometimes kicked and hit her. Other studies have examined the correlates of an uninvolved, parent-centered approach at older ages. In longitudinal research carried out in Finland, Pulkkinen (1982) found that parents who rarely had conversations with their adolescents, took little interest in their life at school, and were seldom aware of their whereabouts and activities had youngsters who were low in frustration tolerance and emotional control, lacked long-term goals, and more often had records of delinquent acts than adolescents of involved parents. These differences persisted when the sample was followed up at 20 years of age. Other longitudinal findings support an association between a distant, indifferent, and unconcerned parenting style and impulsive, undercontrolled behavior throughout the childhood and adolescent years (Block, 1971).

As children get older, effective parents adjust their level of involvement to fit with the child's changing capacity for independent, autonomous functioning. While too little parental involvement is associated with serious developmental difficulties, too much can be overbearing and intrusive. A gradual lessening of parental monitoring and vigilance as children get older supports their movement toward mature, responsible behavior, as long as it continues to be built on high parental commitment and a warm, openly communicative relationship (Maccoby & Martin, 1983).

What Makes Authoritative Child Rearing So Effective?

The repeated association of authoritative parenting with social, emotional, and intellectual maturity led Baumrind to conclude that the authoritative style plays a causal role in children's superior development. But like other correlational findings discussed throughout this book, these results are open to different interpretations. Lewis (1981) suggested that authoritative child rearing is largely a reaction to children's personality dispositions rather than the cause of them. According to Lewis, parents of well-socialized children use firm, demanding tactics because their youngsters happen to have cooperative, obedient dispositions, not because firm control is an essential ingredient of effective parenting. Baumrind (1983) has countered Lewis's challenge by pointing out that many children of authoritative parents do not submit willingly to adult authority. Disciplinary conflict occurred often in the authoritative homes she studied, but parents handled it firmly, patiently, and rationally. They neither gave in to children's unreasonable demands nor responded in a harsh, arbitrary fashion. Baumrind emphasizes that it is not the exercise of firm control per se, but rather the rational and reasonable use of firm control, that has positive consequences for children's development.

Nevertheless, children's characteristics contribute to the ease with which parents are able to implement an authoritative pattern. We saw in earlier chapters that temperamentally difficult youngsters are more likely than other children to receive highly coercive discipline. When children react recalcitrantly and disobediently, some parents respond inconsistently by giving in to the child's unruly behavior, thereby rewarding it and increasing the chances that it will occur again. Children of parents who go back and forth between authoritarian and passive, indifferent child-rearing styles have especially impulsive, aggressive, and irresponsible youngsters who do very poorly in school (Dornbusch et al., 1987; Olweus, 1980; Patterson, 1982). As Maccoby and Martin (1983) point out, the direction of influence between parenting practices and children's characteristics goes both ways. Impulsive and difficult children make it harder for parents to remain firm as well as democratically involved, but parenting practices can either sustain or reduce children's difficult behavior.

Why do authoritative practices support such a wide array of positive developmental outcomes and help to bring the demanding, unruly behavior of poorly socialized children under control? There are a number of reasons. First, as we saw in Chapter 12, control exercised in a way that appears fair and reasonable to the child, not impetuous and arbitrary, is far more likely to be complied with and internalized. Second, nurturant, nonpermissive parents who are secure in the standards they hold for their youngsters provide children with models of caring concern for others as well as confident, assertive behavior (Kuczynski, Zahn-Waxler, & Radke-Yarrow, 1987). In addition, such parents are likely to be more effective reinforcing agents, praising the child for behaviors that meet their expectations and making more successful use of disapproval, which works best when applied by a nurturant parent who can withstand counterpressures from the child. Finally, parents who rely on authoritative techniques make demands that are sensitive and responsive to their children's developing capacities. By adjusting expectations so they fit with children's ability to take responsibility for their own behavior, these parents communicate to children a sense that they are competent beings who can do things successfully for themselves. As a result, high self-esteem and mature, autonomous functioning are fostered (Kuczynski et al., 1987; Steinberg, Elmen, & Mounts, 1989).

Cultural, Social-Class, and Ethnic Variations in Child Rearing

The same dimensions of parenting that underlie the child-rearing styles described above apply to a wide range of cultures around the world. Rohner and Rohner (1981) rated descriptions of parental behavior from anthropological records collected in 186 societies and found that children everywhere seem to experience differing degrees of control and nurturant involvement from parents and other major caregivers. Although cross-cultural variability does exist, the most common pattern of child rearing in the cultures studied by the Rohners was a style that is warm and controlling but neither very lax nor very restrictive, much like Baumrind's authoritative pattern. As the investigators put it, "the majority of (cultures) . . . have discovered for themselves over the centuries a 'truth' that has only recently emerged from empirical research in the Western world—healthy psychosocial development of children is promoted most effectively by love with at least moderate parental control" (p. 257).

In the United States and other Western nations, consistent social-class differences in child-rearing patterns exist (Duvall, 1946; Gecas, 1979; Hoffman, 1984; Kohn, 1977). When asked about qualities they would like to encourage in their children, parents who work in semiskilled and skilled manual occupations (e.g., machinists, truck drivers, and custodians) place a high value on external characteristics, such as obedience, neatness, and cleanliness. In contrast, white-collar and professional parents more often emphasize internal psychological dispositions, such as curiosity, happiness, and self-control. These differences in child-rearing values are reflected in social-class variations in parenting behaviors. Middle-class parents use more explanations, verbal praise, and inductive disciplinary techniques. In contrast, commands, such as "You'll do that because I told you to," as well as criticism and physical punishment occur more often in low-income and working-class households (Kohn, 1977; Laosa, 1981). These coercive practices are verbally restricted, and they do not encourage children to compare and evaluate alternative courses of action. Consequently, they contribute to the cognitively less enriching home environments experienced by many low-income children (Bernstein, 1964; Hess & Shipman, 1965).

Social-class variations in child-rearing practices can be understood in terms of a number of differences in life conditions that exist between low-income and middle-income families. First, low-income parents often feel a sense of powerlessness and lack of influence in their relationships with institutions beyond the family, a factor that has consequences for the way they rear their children. For example, several theorists suggest that because lower-class parents are continually subjected to the rules and authorities of others in the workplace, their parent-child interaction duplicates their own experiences, only with them in the authority roles. Working-class occupations generally require the employee to follow the explicit rules of a supervisor, whereas middle-class occupations allow more room for self-direction and place greater emphasis on the manipulation of ideas and symbols. The values and behaviors required for success in the world of work are thought to affect parents' ideas about characteristics important to train in their children, who are expected to enter similar work roles in the future. Social-class differences in educational attainment may also affect these child-rearing variations. Middle-class parents' concern with nurturing their children's internal psychological characteristics is probably facilitated by years of higher education, during which the parents learned to think about abstract, subjective ideas. Furthermore, the greater economic security of middle-class parents frees them from the burden of having to worry about making ends meet on a daily basis. As a result, they can devote more energy and attention to thinking about and encouraging the inner characteristics of themselves and their children (Hoffman, 1984; Kohn, 1977, 1979).

The constant stresses that affect many low-income families constitute an additional factor that contributes to social-class differences in child-rearing patterns. Families of poverty experience an extraordinarily high frequency of daily crises and hassles — bills to pay, arguments with one's spouse, the car breaking down, termination of welfare and unemployment payments, something stolen from the house, a family member arrested, school reports of child misbehavior or truancy, to name just a few (Brown, Bhrolchain, & Harris, 1976; Tonge, James, & Hillam, 1975). When daily crises arise, parental irritability, child behavior problems, and coercive interactions within the household increase (Compas et al., 1989; Patterson, 1988). These outcomes are especially severe in families experiencing chronically depressed living conditions, such as poor housing and dangerous neighborhoods, that make day-to-day existence even more difficult (McLoyd, 1990).

Nevertheless, within a single social class, there is considerable variation in factors that affect child rearing. The family structure and customs of some ethnic groups buffer the stress and disorganization that result from living in poverty. A case in point is the American black family, which has been studied extensively to find out how its members have managed to endure generations of severe economic deprivation and racism. A far greater proportion of American black than white children live in poverty, and a greater percentage experience the stresses associated with marital breakup and widowhood as well as out-of-wedlock and teenage pregnancy (Reid, 1982; Wilson, 1986). As Box 14.1 indicates, the black cultural tradition of **extended family households,** in which one or several grandparents, uncles, aunts, siblings, or cousins live with the parent-child **nuclear family unit,** is a vital feature of the black family that has enabled its members to survive and, in some instances, surmount highly adverse social conditions. Active and involved extended families also characterize other poor American minorities (Harrison et al., 1990). The study of such families increases our appreciation of the ability of the family unit to mobilize its cultural traditions to support its members under conditions of high life stress.

Parenting behavior can be organized along two dimensions — control and responsiveness — that, when combined, yield four parenting styles: authoritative, authoritarian, permissive, and uninvolved. Children of authoritative parents are the most socially and cognitively competent; those of uninvolved parents fare least well. Authoritative parenting is the most common pattern of child rearing in cultures around the world. At the same time, consistent social-class differences in Western nations exist; low-income parents tend to be more coercive, while middle-income parents use more explanations and inductive discipline. The practices of some ethnic minority groups, such as the black extended family, protect children from the debilitating effects of poverty and high life stress.

◆ CONTEMPORARY ISSUES: CULTURAL DIFFERENCES ◆

The Black Extended Family

Box 14.1

The salience of the black extended family can be traced to the African heritage of the large majority of black Americans. In many African societies, newly married couples do not move away from kin and start their own households. Instead, individuals marry into a large extended family that assists its members with essential family functions. The tradition of a broad network of highly committed kinship ties was transferred to the United States during the period of slavery. Since then, it has served as a protective mechanism against the destructive impact of poverty and racial prejudice on black family life (Harrison et al., 1990; McLoyd, 1990; Wilson, 1989). Today, more black than white adults have relatives other than their own children living in the same household. Black parents also see more kin during the week and perceive them as more important figures in their lives, respecting the advice of relatives and caring deeply about what they think is important (Wilson, 1986).

Research has consistently shown that the black extended family structure helps reduce the stress of poverty and single parenthood by providing emotional support and reciprocal sharing of income and essential resources. In addition, extended family members often act as effective surrogate parents in the rearing of children (Pearson et al. 1990). The presence of grandmothers in the households of many black teenagers and their infants protects babies from the negative influence of an overwhelmed and inexperienced young mother. In one study, black grandmothers exhibited more responsive interaction with the babies of their teenage daughters than did the teenage mothers themselves and transmitted to the young mother basic information about infant development (Stevens, 1984). In another investigation, the grandmother's presence reduced the teenage mother's tendency to behave punitively toward her baby (King & Fullard, 1982). Moreover, black adolescent mothers who live in extended families are released from child care long enough to engage in self-improvement activities. Consequently, they are more likely to complete high school and get a job and less likely to receive welfare than mothers living on their own — factors that return to benefit children's well-being (Furstenberg & Crawford, 1978).

Among older children, extended family living arrangements are associated with more give-and-take in adult-child interaction, better school achievement, and improved psychological adjustment (Kellam, Ensminger, & Turner, 1977; Wilson & Tolson, 1985). During adolescence, the presence of additional adults in the home promotes parental control and lessens children's tendency to become involved in deviant behavior (Dornbusch et al., 1985).

Finally, black extended families play an important role in transmitting black cultural values to children. Compared to black nuclear families, extended family arrangements are associated with a greater emphasis on cooperation and moral-religious values (Bowman & Howard, 1985; Tolson & Wilson, 1990). These factors strengthen family cohesion, protect children's development, and foster the transmission of the extended family life style to the next generation.

THE CHANGING AMERICAN FAMILY

Over the last several decades, rapid changes in family life have pervaded all sectors of the American population, challenging the once widely held assumption of stability in the American family. A shrinking family size due to a declining birth rate, a rise in marital dissolution and single-parent households, and increasing participation in the labor market by mothers with children of all ages have reshaped modern family functioning. Today, the traditional family form in which the father earns a livelihood while the mother stays home and assumes primary responsibility for household tasks and the rearing of two or more children characterizes only a small minority of family units. In 1955, 60 percent of families fit this traditional pattern; by the mid-1980s, only 7 percent did (Hodgkinson, 1985). In the following sections, we take up these changes in the American family, placing special emphasis on how each affects the roles and relationships of family members and, ultimately, children's development.

From Large to Small Families

Birth rate statistics indicate that although the size of the American family was on the decline from the early to middle part of this century, childbearing increased dramatically from 1945 to 1957, a period known as the post–World War II baby boom.

◆　　　　　THEORY, RESEARCH, AND APPLICATIONS　　　　　◆

Bearing Children Past 30: *Consequences for Caregiving Attitudes and Behavior*　　　Box 14.2

Theory. Although the overall birth rate declined during the 1970s, first births to women in their 30s more than doubled, and they have continued to rise during the past decade (Ventura, 1989). In years past, delayed childbearing depended largely on marriage opportunities and fertility. Today, it is largely the result of career commitments and finances.

Waiting to have a baby until a later period in the life course is likely to affect a mother's attitudes and behavior as a parent and, in turn, her children's development. Popular wisdom has it that giving birth during the 20s is optimal, not only because the risk of having a baby with abnormalities is reduced (see Chapter 3), but also because younger parents are better equipped with the energy levels needed to keep up with active youngsters over the long years of childhood. Alternatively, since older mothers are economically better off and have had more experience in nonparenting roles, they may be better able to invest in parenting. As a result, they may perform child care tasks more effectively. Arlene Ragozin and her colleagues (1982) examined the child care attitudes and behaviors of 17- to 38-year-old mothers of preterm and full-term newborns to find out how they compared in child-rearing enthusiasm and competence.

Research. One month after discharge from the hospital, over 100 mothers were asked about their perceptions of and satisfactions with parenting, and their interactions with their infants were observed in a laboratory playroom. After background variables such as family income and maternal education were controlled, age con-

Today, more women are delaying childbirth until their careers are well-established. The emotional maturity and secure life circumstances of the older mother promotes especially effective early parenting.

tinued to predict both parenting attitudes and behavior. The more stable life circumstances and emotional maturity of older mothers seemed to help them cope with the stress of caring for a preterm baby. These mothers reported greater pleasure in the maternal role, more involvement in caregiving responsibilities, and less social time away from their infants than their younger counterparts. Among mothers with full-term babies, maternal age showed strong relationships with several aspects of mother-infant interaction. However, as indicated in the adjacent figure, the nature of these associations depended on the number of prior births. For mothers having their first child, the older the mother the more she

During that time, many couples were making up for births they had postponed during wartime, and the average family size was greater than three children. However, birth rates dropped steadily thereafter. Today there are many more one- and two-child families than there were in earlier decades, as well as more couples opting to have no children at all. This trend is likely to continue into the 1990s. When women between 18 and 39 years of age were asked in 1988 to indicate how many offspring they expected to have, their projections averaged 2.1 children, in comparison to 3.1 in 1960 (U.S. Bureau of the Census, 1990). Fertility rates are expected to drop even further by the early part of the twenty-first century, to a record low of 1.5 births per woman of childbearing age (Westoff, 1978).

The declining family size among all sectors of the population is the result of a number of broad social changes in the United States. Improved contraceptive effectiveness as well as the 1972 Supreme Court decision legalizing abortion make the current period one of greater choice with respect to whether or not to have children. In addition, increased entry into the labor market and career advancement among women has meant that many have chosen to divide their energies between work and family. A smaller family size is certainly more compatible with this dual commitment to career and child rearing. Furthermore, more couples are now delaying the birth of their first child until they are well established professionally and secure economically, a trend that has repercussions for family size (see Box 14.2). Women who postpone

vocalized and was sensitively responsive to her baby's cues. These positive maternal age–behavior associations declined in strength until they became negative for mothers who had more than two children. Ragozin and her colleagues speculated that older mothers with several children, having already experienced parenthood a number of times, may have been less interested in the new baby and eager to turn to extrafamilial roles, while those giving birth to their first child were probably especially committed to the parenting experience.

Applications. Ragozin's research challenges the common assumption of less optimal parenting on the part of older mothers, at least during early infancy. While little is known about the consequences of parents' age for their relationships with older children and adolescents, the findings reported above suggest that positive developmental outcomes may accrue for first-born and at-risk babies from delaying parenthood until a later age.

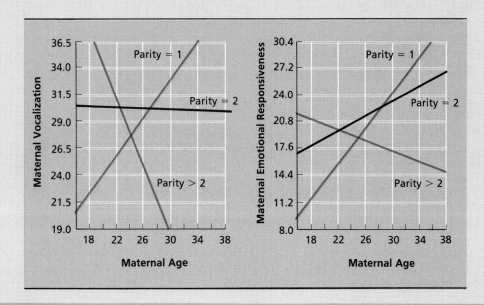

Relationship of mothers' age and parity (number of births) to their vocalization and emotional responsiveness to full-term babies in the Ragozin et al. (1982) study. *(Adapted from A. S. Ragozin, R. B. Basham, K. A. Crnic, M. T. Greenberg, & N. M. Robinson (1982), "Effects of Maternal Age on Parenting Role," Developmental Psychology, 18, 627–634. Copyright 1982 by the American Psychological Association. Adapted by permission of the author.)*

childbirth are likely to have fewer children than those who begin their families at an earlier age (David & Baldwin, 1979; Hofferth, 1984). Finally, greater marital instability is another reason that families are smaller. More couples today get divorced before their childbearing plans are complete (Falbo, 1984).

Family size has consequences for parent-child interaction as well as children's opportunities to grow up with siblings. In the following sections, we consider the implications of the smaller American family for child development by looking at its impact on relationships among nuclear family members.

Family Size and Parent-Child Interaction. In general, the trend toward a smaller family has favorable consequences for parent-child interaction and, in turn, for a variety of aspects of child development. Many studies show that parental attitudes and treatment of children change systematically as more youngsters are added to the household. More children mean less time that husband and wife have to devote to one another as well as to each youngster's activities, school work, and other concerns. As a result, parents of large families tend to feel less satisfied with their marital relationships and parenting roles (Hurley & Palonen, 1967; Rutter & Madge, 1976). Furthermore, disciplinary practices become more authoritarian and punitive as family size increases and parents try to keep large numbers of youngsters "in line." Crowding and lack of a special place each child can call his own promote additional tensions in households with many children, with further repercussions for parent-child relationships (Blau, 1981). Investigators believe that together, these factors account for the fact that children who grow up in larger families have somewhat lower intelligence test scores, poorer school achievement, and lower self-esteem. Forms of child maladjustment also vary with family size. A smaller number of children provides some parents with ample opportunity to pressure their youngsters too much, leading anxiety to be somewhat more common among children from small families. In contrast, antisocial behavior and delinquency appear more often among children and adolescents with many siblings (Wagner, Schubert, & Schubert, 1985).

However, an important qualification regarding the above findings is in order, since family size is strongly correlated with socioeconomic status. Larger families are less well off economically than smaller ones. In fact, the birth of additional children contributes to the family size – socioeconomic status relationship, given the cost mentioned earlier in this chapter of rearing a child to maturity. Rutter and Madge (1976) believe that the negative impact of increasing family size on children's development is largely due to insufficient financial and material resources, which result in less adequate housing, poorer nutrition, greater parental stress, and consequent deterioration in the quality of the parent-child relationship. Consistent with this interpretation, research indicates that unfavorable outcomes associated with growing up in a large family are substantially reduced in economically well-off households with many children (Kennett & Cropley, 1970; Page & Grandon, 1979).

Growing Up with Siblings. Despite the shrinking family size, the two-child family is still very common in the United States, accounting for 42 percent of families who have children. Most American children still grow up with at least one sibling. In a survey in which married individuals were asked to explain why they desired more than one child, the most frequently mentioned reason was sibling companionship, cited by nearly half the respondents (Bulatao & Arnold, 1977). The consequences of growing up with brothers and sisters have received relatively little research attention until recently, given the historical focus of investigators on the mother-child dyad. However, new research indicates that siblings exert important influences on development, both directly, through the relationships that siblings establish with one another, and indirectly, through the effects that the presence of an additional child has on the attitudes and behaviors of parents. In previous chapters, we looked at some developmental consequences of having brothers and sisters, including birth order effects on intelligence (Chapter 8) and the impact of siblings on language acquisition (Chapter 9), personality development (Chapter 10), and sex typing (Chapter 13). In this chapter, we focus more directly on the quality of the sibling relationship itself and its implications for childhood socialization and development.

Among adults, sibling associations generally conjure up images of rivalry and competition — thoughts of brothers and sisters competing for a fair share of parental attention, approval, and material resources. The common assumption that jealousy and rivalry are key elements in sibling interactions originated with psychoanalytic theory, which stressed that sibling relationships are mediated by each youngster's desire to monopolize the attention and love of the parent (Levy, 1937). Although some siblings are highly conflictual and rivalrous, we now know that this dimension of sibling interaction is only one element in a complex array of feelings and social exchanges that take place among youngsters growing up in the same family.

In a longitudinal study of the early development of sibling relationships, Dunn and Kendrick (1982) conducted parent interviews and made home observations of 40 preschoolers from a point late in their mother's second pregnancy through the infancy of the younger child. A drop in maternal involvement with the first-born child occurred immediately after the birth of the infant. As a result, jealousy was an element in the older child's feelings toward the new arrival. Many preschoolers responded by becoming demanding and clingy and engaging in instances of "deliberate naughtiness" while the mother was preoccupied with caring for the baby. But resentment about being displaced by the new infant was only one of a wide range of emotions displayed by the older youngster. Positive social approaches and expressions of affection and concern for the baby also occurred. By the time the infant was 8 months old, the two siblings had become salient social partners for each other. A high frequency of interaction occurred, with the preschoolers comforting, sharing toys with, imitating, and expressing friendliness toward the baby in addition to signs of anger and ambivalence. By 14 months of age, imitations by the baby of the first-born child became frequent. Older children were already serving as influential models and agents of socialization for their younger brothers and sisters.

Substantial individual differences in the quality of relationships established by first-born preschoolers with their siblings appear in the first few weeks after the second child's birth that remain remarkably stable over the early childhood years (Dunn, 1989). As we indicated in Chapter 10, children's temperamental characteristics have some bearing on how positive or conflictual sibling interactions will be. But sibling relationships are also affected by the mother's manner of responding to her youngsters. Dunn and Kendrick (1982) found that when mothers were positive and playful in their style of interaction, feelings of rivalry emerged in older children, who were slightly less friendly toward the babies than older siblings with less playful mothers. In contrast, for first-borns who experienced tense maternal relationships or whose mothers were especially tired and depressed after the second birth, a warm and caring relationship with the sibling often developed that relieved the stressful impact of the parent's behavior. Additional research indicates that mothers who frequently discuss their baby's feelings and intentions have preschoolers who are more likely to comment on the baby as a person with special wants and needs. Moreover, such children display substantially more friendly and considerate behavior toward their younger brothers and sisters than do children whose mothers do not discuss the baby in this way (Dunn & Kendrick, 1982; Howe & Ross, 1990).

During middle childhood, when children begin to participate in sports, music, and school activities, parental comparisons of each child's abilities and accomplishments occur more frequently. When these evaluations are communicated to children, they accentuate sibling rivalry. The child who gets less parental attention, more disapproval, and the "short end of the stick" in terms of rewards and material resources is likely to express resentment and ill will toward a sibling who receives preferential treatment (Bryant & Crockenberg, 1980; Pfouts, 1976). Social comparisons are prob-

Although rivalry is one dimension of sibling relationships, positive interactions are also prevalent. Siblings often provide one another with companionship and assistance with everyday tasks.

ably an important source of conflict for all siblings during the middle childhood years. The common tendency of many siblings to strive to be different from one another in activities, talents, and interests (see Chapter 10) may be a major way in which children try to minimize this aspect of sibling rivalry.

Despite some increased potential for sibling conflict during the elementary school years, many preadolescent youngsters rely on siblings as important sources of social support. Siblings provide companionship, assistance with everyday tasks, and comfort during times of emotional stress, and they generally continue to do so throughout adolescence and adulthood (Bryant, 1982b; Furman et al., 1989). Warm, enduring bonds among brothers and sisters occur especially often in large families. Having more offspring dilutes the attention each child receives from parents, a circumstance that appears to intensify children's rapport with one another (Bossard & Boll, 1956).

The research summarized above suggests that sibling associations offer a rich interactional context in which children learn and practice a wide range of social skills, including affectionate caring, conflict resolution, and control of competitive and hostile feelings. Child development specialists actually know very little about how experiences with siblings influence social relationships outside the family. In general, later-born children are more popular with agemates than first-born children (Miller & Maruyama, 1976). Perhaps as the result of learning to get along with larger, more powerful brothers and sisters, younger siblings become especially adept at negotiating, accommodating, and accepting less favorable outcomes, and they transfer these skills to their peer associations. However, much more evidence is needed to establish causal connections between children's sibling relationships and their social competencies in the wider world of neighborhood and school.

The Only Child. Without opportunities to experience the closeness and conflicts inherent in sibling relationships, are children born into one-child families disadvantaged in social and emotional development? Many Americans think so. Parents of only children frequently report that relatives pressure them to have a second, believing that an only child is destined to become a spoiled, self-centered, dependent, socially inadequate adult (Falbo, 1984). This popular belief has been reinforced by the pessimistic pronouncements of many child development specialists, which can be traced at least as far back as 1907, when the eminent American psychologist G. Stanley Hall remarked, "Being an only child is a disease in itself" (Fenton, 1928, p. 547).

A great deal of research now indicates that the stereotypical view that siblings are indispensable for normal development is incorrect. In fact, during the preschool years, there is some evidence that only youngsters are advanced in sociability. Snow, Jacklin, and Maccoby (1981) observed 2-year-olds with an unfamiliar peer in a laboratory playroom. Only children, when compared to youngsters from two-child families, showed more social behavior of all kinds, including positive as well as assertive-aggressive interactions, while second-borns showed the least. Later in development, only as well as first-born children are more willing than later borns to lean on others in times of stress (Hoyt & Raven, 1973; Schachter, 1959). Perhaps they do so because their parents were able to respond especially promptly to their signs of discomfort when they were infants and young children. This circumstance may have led them to develop a high expectation that other people will be comforting when they are anxious and worried. By college age, only children do report a smaller circle of friends and membership in fewer organizations than individuals with siblings. But they do not appear to suffer socially or emotionally because of this, since they have just as many close friends as non-only children and do not describe themselves as lonelier. Furthermore, as adults, they report a level of life satisfaction and general happiness that is equal to that of other people (Blake, 1981; Falbo, 1978).

On the average, only children do better in school and attain higher educational levels than children with siblings (Claudy, 1984; Falbo & Polit, 1986). This difference is also thought to result from special parent-child relationships experienced by only youngsters. Research indicates that onlies as well as first-borns receive greater pressure for mature behavior than do later-born children (Clausen, 1966; Kammeyer, 1967). A single child means that parents have only one chance to confirm a view of themselves as "successful parents," and as a result, greater pressure may be placed on only youngsters for mastery and accomplishment. In addition, the achievement of singletons may be enhanced by the fact that they have only adult models in the home, a circumstance that may accelerate their acquisition of adultlike behavior. Only children also experience more parent-child interaction (Lewis & Kreitzberg, 1979), and their relationships with parents are more positive and affectionate than those of non-only youngsters (Falbo & Polit, 1986). We have already seen that the combination of high parental standards and warm, nurturant involvement — namely, authoritative parenting — is especially conducive to competent, mastery-oriented behavior.

The evidence reviewed above indicates that negative developmental consequences do not accrue from being raised as an only child. Instead, both advantages and disadvantages are associated with family constellations that have just one or more than one youngster. In a survey in which only children and their parents were questioned about what they liked and disliked about living in a single-child family, the overwhelming majority of respondents depicted their lifestyles in positive terms (Hawke & Knox, 1978). However, they did mention a set of pros and cons, which are summarized in Table 14.2. Prospective parents might consider this list when deciding on how many children would best fit their personal and family life plans, rather than basing their decision on the erroneous assumption that only children are destined to grow up as selfish, lonely, and maladjusted.

Divorce and Remarriage

Parental separation and divorce have become extremely common in the lives of American children. The incidence of marital breakup in the United States is the highest in the world, nearly doubling that of the second-ranked country, Sweden

Table 14.2. Advantages and Disadvantages of Living in a One-Child Family

ADVANTAGES		DISADVANTAGES	
MENTIONED BY CHILDREN	MENTIONED BY PARENTS	MENTIONED BY CHILDREN	MENTIONED BY PARENTS
Avoiding sibling rivalry	Having time to pursue one's own interests and career	Not getting to experience the closeness of a sibling relationship	Walking a "tightrope" between healthy attention and overindulgence
Having more privacy	Less financial pressure	Feeling too much pressure from parents to succeed	Having only one chance to "make good" as a parent
Enjoying greater affluence	Not having to worry about "playing favorites" among children	Having no one to help care for parents when they get old	Being left childless in case of the child's death
Closer parent-child relationship			

Source: Hawke & Knox, 1978.

(Bronfenbrenner, 1986). Between 1960 and 1980, the American divorce rate tripled and then stabilized. Currently, over one million children experience the separation or divorce of their parents each year, and recent census figures indicate that a total of 15 million children under age 18 (24 percent of all America's youngsters) live in single-parent households. While the great majority (89 percent) live with their mothers, the number residing in father-headed households increased slightly over the past decade, from 9 to 11 percent (U.S. Bureau of the Census, 1990).

The average period of time that children whose parents divorce spend in a single-parent home is 5 years, amounting to almost one third of their total childhood. But for many children, divorce eventually leads to new family relationships, since remarriage among divorced adults is on the rise. Approximately two thirds of divorced parents marry a second time (Glick & Lin, 1987), merging parent, stepparent, and children into a new family structure called the **reconstituted family.** Half of these children eventually experience a third major change in their family lives — the dissolution of their parent's second marriage (Bumpass, 1984).

These figures reveal that divorce is not a single event in the lives of parents and children. Instead, it is a transition that leads to a range of new familial arrangements that are often accompanied by changes in residence, financial resources, and familial roles and responsibilities. Since the 1960s, many studies have reported that the stress of marital breakup is associated with negative social, emotional, and cognitive consequences for children. But the research has also revealed considerable variability in how children respond. Some youngsters adjust with comparative ease, while others suffer prolonged psychological difficulties.

Recently, investigators have begun to understand these different outcomes in terms of a complex array of variables that affect how well the family unit is able to adapt to stress and sustain a pattern of interaction that is supportive of children's development. Factors that make a difference in children's adjustment include adult psychological functioning; children's characteristics such as sex, age, and temperament; and the availability of social supports in the surrounding community.

Effects of Divorce on Children's Development. In the following sections, we consider what is known about how well children take the series of major life changes associated with parental divorce. Our knowledge is enhanced by the results of several major longitudinal studies that have tracked children's development over extended time periods as well as a large number of short-term investigations.

Immediate Consequences. The period surrounding divorce is almost always ac-companied by an escalation of family conflict as parents separate and try to settle disputes over personal belongings, finances, and child custody and visitation. Once one parent moves out, a cluster of additional, highly stressful events generally ensues that further threatens the adaptive functioning of the custodial parent and children. Mother-headed households typically experience a dramatic drop in income, since many divorced women lack the necessary education and experience to obtain well-paid jobs and the majority of ex-husbands fail to meet their child support obligations (Children's Defense Fund, 1990). Often the family must relocate for economic rea-sons, generally to poorer-quality housing and neighborhoods, a circumstance that reduces supportive ties to neighbors and friends. Many single mothers who pre-viously did not work must find immediate employment. As a result, young children are likely to experience inadequate child care while the mother is at work and an overburdened, distracted, and unavailable caregiver when she is at home (Hethering-ton, Stanley-Hagan, & Anderson, 1989).

The life circumstances of many newly divorced mothers often promote a highly disorganized family situation that Wallerstein and Kelly (1980) characterize as "min-imal parenting." Predictable household events and routines—scheduled mealtimes and bedtimes, regular completion of household chores, and joint parent-child recre-ational activities—usually disintegrate. Disciplining of children vacillates between detachment and highly authoritarian, restrictive practices as mothers try to recapture control of youngsters who are distressed, confused, and angry about their less secure home lives. Divorced fathers generally spend more time with their youngsters imme-diately after divorce, but for many children this contact diminishes over time. Infre-quent paternal visitation often brings with it indulgent and permissive parenting that conflicts with the mother's style of discipline and increases her difficulties in manag-ing the youngster on a day-to-day basis (Furstenberg & Nord, 1985; Furstenberg, Spanier, & Rothschild, 1982; Hetherington, Cox, & Cox, 1982; Weitzman, 1985).

In view of these changes in living conditions and family relationships, it is not surprising that many studies report that children experience painful emotional reac-tions and a rise in behavior problems during the period surrounding parental divorce. Common initial responses of preschool through adolescent-age youngsters are anger, fear, depression, divided parental loyalty, and guilt (Wallerstein & Kelly, 1980). However, the intensity of these feelings and the manner in which they are translated into behavior vary considerably from child to child.

In mother-custody families, boys show more severe behavioral disorganization than girls, typically reacting with noncompliance, demandingness, and hostility. The coercive interaction cycles that boys establish with their mothers soon spread to sibling relations as well (Baldwin & Skinner, 1989; Hetherington, 1989; MacKinnon, 1989; Zaslow, 1989). Recall from Chapter 13 that boys are somewhat more assertive and noncompliant than girls to begin with. They seem to engage in these behaviors even more strongly when they encounter high parental conflict and unpredictable disciplinary tactics. In fact, a recent longitudinal study revealed that many sons of parents who eventually divorce exhibit impulsive and undercontrolled behavior long before the marital dissolution occurs. Consequently, they enter the period of turmoil surrounding divorce with a reduced capacity to cope with family stress (Block, Block, & Gjerde, 1988). Boys also receive less nurturance and are viewed more negatively by custodial mothers, teachers, and peers, perhaps because their behavior is especially difficult to manage. In addition, some mothers may respond more negatively to their sons because the male child serves as a reminder of the divorcee's ex-husband. These unsympathetic reactions increase the frustration that boys experience and further magnify their unmanageable behavior (Hetherington, Stanley-Hagan, & Anderson, 1989).

Girls are also intensely affected by parental separation. Sometimes they show internalizing reactions, such as crying, self-criticism, withdrawal, and passivity, that are easier for parents to deal with in a patient, sympathetic manner (Emery, 1982; Wallerstein, Corbin, & Lewis, 1988). More often, girls display some demanding, attention-getting behavior, but their responses are considerably less intense than those of their male counterparts (Hetherington, Cox, & Cox, 1982; Hetherington, Stanley-Hagan, & Anderson, 1989). Although children of both sexes show declines in school achievement during the aftermath of divorce, once again, school difficulties are far more prevalent among boys (Guidubaldi & Cleminshaw, 1985; Guidubaldi & Perry, 1985; Wallerstein & Kelly, 1980).

Besides children's sex, developmental maturity influences how they respond to divorce. The more limited cognitive competencies of preschool and early elementary school children make it difficult for them to accurately appraise the reasons behind their parents' separation. These youngsters often blame themselves, imagine that they must have done something wrong to cause the departure of one parent from the household, and take the marital rupture as a sign that they could be abandoned by both of their parents. Consequently, younger children are often profoundly upset, revert to more immature behaviors, and display intense separation anxiety (Wallerstein, Corbin, & Lewis, 1988).

In contrast, older children and adolescents are better able to understand their parents' divorce in terms of irreconcilable differences of opinion, incompatible personalities, and lack of caring for one another (Neal, 1983). Older youngsters' ability to appropriately assign responsibility may moderate some of the pain that they feel. Nevertheless, many adolescents do react strongly to the dissolution of their parents' marriage, although the way they respond is qualitatively different from the reactions of younger children. Some enter into a variety of undesirable peer activities that provide an escape from their unpleasant home lives, and truancy, running away from home, smoking, school discipline problems, and delinquent behavior increase (Dornbusch et al., 1985). Girls in particular show a rise in sexual activity that often coincides with the discovery of parental sexual infidelities (Wallerstein & Kelly, 1980).

However, not all older youngsters react in this fashion. For some — especially the oldest children in the family — divorce can be a catalyst for mature behavior. These children may respond by taking on greater responsibility for household tasks, care and protection of younger siblings, and emotional support of a depressed, anxious mother. Nevertheless, some investigators speculate that too much responsibility can lead some older youngsters to feel overburdened and resentful, eventually causing them to withdraw from the family into some of the more destructive behavior patterns described above (Wallerstein & Kelly, 1980).

Long-Term Outcomes. The majority of children show markedly improved adjustment by two years after the divorce. However, a considerable number continue to display difficulties for years after the marital disruption (Hetherington, Stanley-Hagan, & Anderson, 1989). Parental adjustment — in particular, the capacity of the custodial parent to cope with adversity, shield the child from divorce-related stresses, and engage in authoritative parenting — facilitates healthy child development. But when poor parent-child relationships continue for an extended period of time, long-term negative outcomes accrue, especially for children whose characteristics limit their resilience when they are confronted with stressful life conditions (Hetherington, 1989; Kalter et al., 1989).

Children with difficult temperaments are especially likely to show lasting emotional problems (Hetherington, Stanley-Hagan, & Anderson, 1989). Recall from Chapter 10 that difficult youngsters are more likely to be exposed to ineffective parenting, which further undermines their coping skills. In addition, boys who remain in mother-custody households are more vulnerable in the long run than are girls. Many show continued problems with school performance as well as heightened dependency, poor self-control, and increases in aggressive behavior (Hetherington,

Cox, & Cox, 1985; Guidubaldi & Perry, 1985). However, contact with fathers is particularly important in affecting how well boys do. Regular paternal visitation and a good father-son relationship are associated with improved long-term outcomes (Hetherington, Cox, & Cox, 1982; Wallerstein & Kelly, 1980).

Moreover, the limited evidence available on paternal custody suggests that sons who live with their fathers show special benefits in terms of psychological adjustment, including less demanding and more mature behavior than that of their mother-custody counterparts (Camara & Resnick, 1988; Santrock & Warshak, 1986). Fathers seem to be able to evoke more compliance and cooperation from their male children than mothers, perhaps because of the way they interact with and discipline boys. One study reported that divorced fathers do less ignoring of their sons' disruptive behavior and offer more praise for following directions than do mothers (Hetherington, Cox, & Cox, 1982). The father's image of greater power and authority may be an added reason that he is able to engender more obedience in sons (Hetherington, 1979). In addition, sons whose fathers maintain frequent contact have more opportunities to identify with and adopt their father's self-controlled behavior.

Girls experience far fewer lasting problems than boys, particularly when they reside in mother-headed households. Their long-term difficulties are concentrated in the sphere of heterosexual adjustment. A disproportionate number display precocious sexual activity at adolescence, short-lived sexual relationships in early adulthood, and diminished self-confidence in their associations with men (Hetherington, Stanley-Hagan, & Anderson, 1989; Kalter et al., 1985; Wallerstein & Corbin, 1989). These findings indicate that a good father-daughter relationship appears to be important for the girl's eventual heterosexual development, even though it is less crucial for her overall social and emotional well-being during childhood than a supportive maternal relationship (Santrock & Warshak, 1979; Wallerstein & Kelly, 1980).

The research described above underlines the importance of positive relationships with both parents for optimal child development, with the same-sex parent appearing to be especially important for many aspects of psychological adjustment during early and middle childhood. In fact, the ability of divorcing couples to put aside their conflicts and support one another in their respective parenting roles is the most important factor in ensuring that a single-parent family will serve as an effective context for the development of competent, stable, and happy children (Camara & Resnick, 1988; Hetherington, Stanley-Hagan, & Anderson, 1989).

Where parental cooperation is not possible, the assistance of extended family members and friends can lead to improved child outcomes. In fact, following divorce, 25 to 33 percent of custodial mothers move in with a relative, usually their own mother, who provides economic and child-rearing support (Hernandez, 1988). If an involved, caring grandfather is available in these households, boys show fewer difficulties (Hetherington, 1989).

School environments also make a difference. Hetherington, Cox, & Cox (1982) found that during the two years following divorce, the social and cognitive development of preschoolers was enhanced if they attended schools in which teachers provided consistent structure, used warm but firm disciplinary techniques, and made reasonable demands for mature behavior. Note that these are the same characteristics of authoritative parenting associated with competent social and intellectual development among children raised in intact families. Young children clearly benefit from a safe, predictable, and nurturant classroom environment when comparable experiences are not available at home.

Changing Societal Attitudes toward Divorce. Several decades ago, the prevalent view of divorce in American society was that children were doomed to maladjustment if they were raised in a single-parent household. Professionals and laypeople alike believed that unhappily married couples should avoid separation at almost any cost, and many remained together for the sake of their children. Today, divorce carries little of the social stigma that it did a generation or two ago, and child rearing has become an activity governed less by constraint and obligation and more by voluntary choice (Furstenberg & Nord, 1985). As a result, children figure less importantly into parents' decision to dissolve a marriage than they did in decades past. Some people wonder whether these changes are for the better, or whether most youngsters would benefit if their parents returned to the practice of tolerating a conflict-ridden, unfulfilling relationship to safeguard their children's development.

A growing body of evidence indicates that children from stressed intact families are more poorly adjusted than youngsters who have weathered the stormy transition to a single-parent family and are living in low-conflict households (Block, Block, & Gjerde, 1988; Hetherington, Cox, & Cox, 1982; Long & Forehand, 1987; Stolberg et al., 1987). These findings suggest that in the long run, it is probably not a good idea for parents to remain in a strife-ridden marriage for the sake of children if they can work toward a harmonious single-parent arrangement.

Nevertheless, when we look at the research on divorce as a whole, it is abundantly clear that children suffer deeply from experiencing their parents' divorce. An overwhelming majority of youngsters from divorced families are much less content with the quality of their family relationships than children who live in intact homes, and they report that they do not get all the affection and attention that they need. They would much rather be together with both of their parents than in their current living arrangements. Although an involved, noncustodial parent can ease the strain that children feel, shared parenting among formerly married couples takes place in only a minority of cases. Many children of divorce indicate that they no longer feel close to both their mother and father, miss the nonresidential parent deeply, and are grateful for the small amount of contact that they have (Furstenberg & Nord, 1985). Whereas school performance and psychological adjustment ratings improve over time for many youngsters, deep-seated inner feelings remain. Conducting interviews with adolescents and young adults who had experienced their parents' marital breakup ten years earlier, Wallerstein (1984, 1985) found that those old enough to recall the circumstances surrounding the divorce retained vivid, emotionally painful memories of their own suffering at the time. Even among those who remembered little, the dissolution of their parents' marriage remained a salient aspect of their lives and often evoked tears and sadness as they spoke of it. Most of these young people had resolved to avoid the unhappiness associated with divorce in their own adulthoods. As a group, they were strongly committed to the traditional ideal of a lasting marriage for the sake of their own as yet unborn children.

So the question of whether divorce is best for children if their parents' marriage is unhappy really has no simple, satisfactory answer. We must conclude, overall, that the dissolution of a strife-ridden marital relationship has significant costs, as well as benefits, for the youngsters who experience it.

The Reconstituted Family. For many children whose parents divorce, life in a single-parent household is a temporary condition. Their parents marry again before the children become young adults. Remarriage often leads to many improvements in the life circumstances of single-parent families — a better standard of living, another adult to share the household tasks and responsibilities, and an end to the loneliness and isolation that many divorced parents experience. As a result, it is often associated with improved life satisfaction for the remarried adult (Hetherington, Cox, & Cox, 1982).

But remarriage also creates a complex set of new relationships for all family members, as stepparents, stepchildren, stepsiblings, stepgrandparents, and others begin to play roles in family life. For some children, this expanded network of family ties is a gratifying turn of events that compensates for the loss in parental attention associated with divorce. But for most youngsters, it presents difficult adjustments. Stepparents and children must define a relationship in the absence of clear guidelines like those that exist for biological parents and their offspring. Many stepparents wonder how and whether to discipline their spouse's child. When they do, they often use different practices than the child was used to in the "old" family. Having to switch to a new set of rules and expectations is stressful for many youngsters (Lutz, 1983). Moreover, some children view the entry of steprelatives into the household as an intrusion into their relationship with the custodial parent (Cherlin, 1981). Remarriage also leads to changes in children's opportunities to interact with the noncustodial parent. For example, remarried noncustodial fathers visit their children far less often, especially daughters (Hetherington, Cox, & Cox, 1982; Furstenberg, Spanier, & Rothschild, 1982).

Evidence on children's adaptation to reconstituted family arrangements indicates that many go through a trying period during which they display more behavior problems than children in nondivorced families (Bray, 1988; Hetherington, Cox, & Cox, 1985). Nevertheless, how well children fare varies with the sex of parent and child. Children accommodate best to mother/stepfather families, the most frequent form of reconstituted arrangement (since mothers generally retain custody of the child). When custodial mothers remarry, boys in particular acclimate fairly quickly, accepting a relationship with a stepfather who is warm and responsive and who offers relief from the coercive cycles of interaction that tend to build between divorced mothers and their sons (Hetherington, Stanley-Hagan, & Anderson, 1989). One study indicated that less than two years after remarriage, boys living in mother/stepfather households were functioning almost as well as those living in nondivorced families (Hetherington, Cox, & Cox, 1985). In contrast, girls adapt less favorably to a mother/ stepfather arrangement. Their behavior problems last longer than those of boys, perhaps because of disruption in the close ties many girls established with their mothers while living in a single-parent family (Brand, Clingempeel, & Bowen-Woodward, 1988; Bray, 1988; Zaslow, 1989).

Although only a few studies have focused on father/stepmother remarriages, the evidence is consistent in revealing more confusion and problematic interaction in these homes (Ihinger-Tallman & Pasley, 1987). However, this outcome may be due to the fact that stepmother families generally start out with more problems. In instances in which biological fathers obtain custody of their children, the arrangement is often not a matter of choice, but of necessity. The biological mother can no longer handle the difficult, unruly child (usually a boy), and the father and his new wife are faced with a youngster who has experienced an especially troubled mother-child relationship. In other cases, the father assumes custody because of a close relationship with the child, but his remarriage jeopardizes this bond (Brand, Clingempeel, & Bowen-Woodward, 1988).

Girls, especially, have a difficult time getting along with their stepmothers (Brand, Clingempeel, & Bowen-Woodward, 1988; Clingempeel, Brand, & Ievoli, 1984; Clingempeel, Ievoli, & Brand, 1985; Hobart & Brown, 1988). Paternal custody of girls is a rare arrangement that may occur in instances of a vary warm father-daughter relationship, which (as indicated above) is threatened by the entry of a stepmother. Other evidence suggests that noncustodial mothers (unlike their paternal counterparts) maintain regular contact with their children, but frequent visits by the nonresident mother are associated with less positive stepmother-stepdaughter relationships. Perhaps girls are especially likely to become embroiled in loyalty conflicts between their two mother figures, a circumstance that promotes an ambivalent and strained relationship with the stepmother. However, the longer girls live in father/stepmother households, the more positive stepmother-daughter relationships become. Over time, the relative child-rearing roles of biological mothers and stepmothers seem to be negotiated, and girls eventually benefit from the support of a second mother figure (Brand, Clingempeel, & Bowen-Woodward, 1988).

These findings indicate that children in father/stepmother families, and daughters in particular, have the most difficult time adjusting to parental remarriage. However, the quality of the stepparent-child relationship is probably much more important than the precise makeup of the reconstituted family in moderating the consequences of remarriage for children (Clingempeel & Segal, 1986). To date, research has only scratched the surface with regard to how children feel about and interact with their remarried parents and new steprelatives. Furthermore, most of the evidence summarized above is based on preadolescent and early adolescent youngsters, who may find it harder to adjust to their parents' remarriage than their younger counterparts (Hetherington & Anderson, 1987; Hobart, 1987). Older children are more perceptive about the implications of remarriage for their own life circumstances. As a result, they may initially challenge some aspects of the reconstituted family that younger children simply accept, thereby creating more relationship issues with their steprelatives. Finally, it is important to note that the impact of reconstituted families, as well as repeated divorce in instances of failed remarriage, on the long-term trajectory of development is still unknown.

Helping Children and Families Adjust to Divorce and Remarriage. The stressful events that surround divorce and remarriage leave many parents and children in need of supportive services during these times of family transition. A wide variety of resource and intervention programs have been initiated by local community agencies as well as single-parent and stepparent associations. The largest of these organizations is *Parents Without Partners*, with a national membership of 180,000. It provides informative publications, telephone referrals, and programs through local chapters that are designed to alleviate the problems of single parents in relation to the upbringing of their children (Koek & Martin, 1988). The aim of most of these efforts is prevention — working with parents and children before serious maladjustment develops. Some offer informal self-help sessions in which small groups of single parents or stepparents meet together on a regular basis to share experiences, discuss problems, and provide one another with social support. Formal psychological services also exist, consisting of individual, family, or group counseling in which health professionals teach parents communication and child discipline skills and offer specific information about what to expect after entry into a single-parent or reconstituted family arrangement. Support groups are also available for children, often sponsored by schools, churches, synagogues, and mental health agencies, in which youngsters can share fears and concerns and learn anger control and other coping skills. The limited evidence available on the effectiveness of such interventions suggests that they can reduce stress and promote improved communication among family members (Emery, 1988).

Another recently developed service is **divorce mediation.** It consists of a series of meetings between the divorcing parents and a trained professional who tries to facilitate agreement on disputed issues, such as child custody and property settlement. Its purpose is to permit divorcing parties to remain involved in important decisions, rather than turning them over to the court entirely, and to avoid extended courtroom battles that lead to an escalation of conflict within the family. In some states, divorce mediation is voluntary, while in others it is mandatory and must be attempted before a case is heard by a judge. Research indicates that divorce mediation increases out-of-court settlements, voluntary compliance with these agreements, and feelings of well-being among divorcing adults (Emery & Wyer, 1987). Little is known about its consequences for children's adjustment, although by reducing parental conflict, divorce mediation may ease the stress that children experience once their parents decide to divorce.

Joint Custody. Child custody arrangements condoned by the American legal system are far more flexible today than they were several decades ago. In addition to the traditional **sole custody** arrangement in which one parent assumes responsibility for the education and welfare of the child, **joint custody,** which grants both parents an equal right to be involved in important decisions about the child's upbringing, is now possible in most states. Joint custody may promote increased contact on the part of each parent with the child and reduce the stress of perpetual caregiving that often comes with single parenthood. In addition, it eliminates a "winner" and "loser" resolution to child custody disputes, a circumstance that sometimes diminishes the "loser's" willingness to spend time with the children. All of these factors may lead joint custody to be beneficial for children's adjustment (Emery, Hetherington, & DiLalla, 1984).

Nevertheless, joint custody is a controversial practice, and not all psychologists and legal professionals advocate it. *Joint legal custody* is not synonymous with *joint physical custody*—a shared parenting arrangement in which both mother and father participate equally in the care and upbringing of the child (Emery, 1988). In fact, practically speaking, joint legal custody translates into a multitude of different child living arrangements. In most instances, children reside primarily with one parent and see the other on a fixed visitation schedule, much like the typical sole custody arrangement. In other cases, parents do share in the physical custody of their children, who must alternate between parental homes, sometimes on a daily and other times on a weekly, monthly, or even yearly basis. Some of these transitions require a shift not just in residence, but also in school and peer group. As a result, they introduce a new kind of instability into children's lives that may be especially difficult for some youngsters to handle. The success of joint physical custody requires a reasonably cooperative relationship between divorcing parents (Steinman, Zemmelman, & Knoblauch, 1985). When parental interaction following separation continues to be argumentative and destructive, shared custody may prolong children's immersion in a conflict-ridden family atmosphere.

Unfortunately, there is not much research on the advantages and disadvantages of joint custody. While some evidence suggests that children who experience joint physical custody have fewer emotional and behavioral problems than those in sole custody families (Shiller, 1986), other studies find no difference (Johnston, Kline, & Tschann, 1989; Kline et al., 1989; Wolchik, Braver, & Sandler, 1985). As is the case with other child-rearing arrangements, the consequences of joint physical custody are probably mediated by a variety of factors. These include the quality of the divorcing parents' relationship, the child's characteristics, and the proximity of the two parents' homes to one another. Also, attitudes of extended family members and friends toward the shared custody arrangement, as well as support from formal organizations (e.g., schools that permit flexible busing arrangements so that children can alternate easily between parents' homes), may be important. Some investigators speculate that joint custody may ease children's adjustment to parental remarriage, since living arrangements and interaction patterns with at least one parent remain unchanged (Clingempeel & Reppucci, 1982). However, the moderating effect of joint custody on children's adaptation to reconstituted family environments has not been studied.

Maternal Employment and Day Care

For many years, divorce has been associated with a high rate of maternal employment, due to the financial strains experienced by women who are responsible for maintaining their own families. However, over the last several decades, women of all sectors of the population—not just those who are single and poor—have gone to work in increasing numbers. The most dramatic change in labor force participation has occurred among mothers in two-parent families. The percentage of employed married women with children under age 18 has more than doubled since 1960, from about 30 to 63 percent (Hayghe, 1990). The greatest rise has been among mothers of infants, but impressive increases have occurred for those with preschoolers, elementary school children, and adolescents as well. In fact, maternal employment is no longer the exception; it is the modal pattern. Today, single and married mothers are in the labor market in nearly equal proportions, and when children in both types of families are considered together, at any given age, more than 50 percent of their mothers work (U.S. Department of Labor, 1987).

In Chapter 10, we discussed the impact of maternal employment and day care on the development of infant-mother attachment and concluded that for babies, the consequences depend on the quality of substitute care as well as the nature of the continuing parent-child relationship. Research that examines the relationship of maternal employment to children's development during the childhood and adolescent years reveals much the same overall conclusion. Moreover, a growing body of evidence indicates that a host of additional moderating variables — the sex of the child, the social class of the family, the mother's satisfaction with her work, the support she receives from her husband, and her daily work schedule — have a bearing on whether children show benefits or problems from growing up in an employed-mother family. We consider the implications of maternal employment, and the related topic of day care, for children's intellectual, social, and emotional development in the following two sections.

Effects of Maternal Employment on Child Development. Much like societal attitudes toward divorce, the popular view of the employed mother has changed considerably in recent years. Before the 1960s, most people frowned on mothers who worked outside the home. Many were under pressure to demonstrate to family and friends that their employment was not having adverse consequences for children (Bronfenbrenner & Crouter, 1982; Hoffman, 1984). Today, this public censure is much diminished. During a time period in which the cost of living has soared, maternal employment has come to be regarded as an economic necessity. In addition, families are now smaller, marriages less stable, and life expectancies longer, and modern technology has reduced the time needed for housework and food preparation. As a result, the traditional expectation that a woman must derive most or all of her personal satisfactions from home, hearth, and children is no longer widely accepted. Women's expectations for accomplishment and fulfillment have expanded, and work is recognized as a major way in which these needs can be met (Hoffman, 1989). Consistent with this new positive perspective, research indicates that maternal employment can bring many benefits to women and also to their preschool- through adolescent-age youngsters.

As long as mothers want to work, like their jobs, and have found satisfactory child care arrangements, employment is associated with greater life satisfaction for both low-income and middle-income mothers (Gold & Andres, 1978a, 1978b, 1978c; Goldberg & Easterbrooks, 1988; Gove & Zeiss, 1987). How a mother feels about her life circumstances affects the way she interacts with her children and, in turn, their psychological well-being. Overall, children of employed mothers show indications of better social and emotional adjustment — a higher sense of self-esteem and better family and peer relations (Cherry & Eaton, 1977; Gold & Andres, 1978a, 1978b; Gold, Andres, & Glorieux, 1979). In addition, both sons and daughters of working women are less sex-stereotyped in their beliefs and attitudes. They have more flexible ideas regarding appropriate roles and activities for males and females, regard women as more competent and effective, and view men as warmer than do children whose mothers are not employed (Gold & Andres, 1978c; Gold, Andres, & Glorieux, 1979; Hoffman, 1989).

These positive outcomes undoubtedly result from a variety of child-rearing factors associated with maternal employment. When compared to full-time mothers, employed mothers seem willing to grant their children greater independence when they are ready for it — a likely reason that many children of employed women display such mature social behavior (Hoffman, 1989). Also, as long as employed mothers retain a high commitment to parenting, they are particularly likely to use an authoritative child-rearing style (Greenberger & Goldberg, 1989). Maternal employment often leads to a conscious decision on the part of mothers to compensate for their absence by scheduling special, uninterrupted times to devote to their children (Hoffman, 1984). Moreover, to have the household function smoothly, employed women often find it necessary to lay down firm rules for their children's behavior. As a result, there is greater consistency between child-rearing theory and practice in the homes of working than nonworking mothers. Furthermore, during middle childhood and adolescence, children of employed mothers are more often given regular household responsibilities (Hoffman, 1974, 1977). As long as these assignments are reasonable, they are positively associated with children's self-esteem and intellectual performance (Medrich, 1981; Smokler, 1975).

Finally, a modest increase in fathers' involvement in household and child-care tasks accompanies maternal employment (Hoffman, 1986). Greater paternal participation in domestic activities appears to have a facilitating impact on a variety of aspects of children's development. In a recent longitudinal study of maternal employment, fathers' early involvement in child care was positively associated with later measures of intelligence, achievement, and mature social behavior for both sons and daughters (Gottfried, Gottfried, & Bathurst, 1988). Moreover, fathers' participation serves as one of the routes through which children of employed mothers develop more flexible sex-role attitudes (Baruch & Barnett, 1986).

Nevertheless, there are a number of qualifiers to the encouraging findings described above. First, outcomes associated with maternal employment are more favorable for daughters than for sons. Girls of employed mothers more often have higher educational aspirations and voice plans to work in adulthood (Hoffman, 1974); at the college level, they are more likely to choose nontraditional careers, such as law, medicine, and physics (Tangri, 1972). In contrast, the relaxation of traditional sex stereotypes is less pronounced for boys, especially in low-income families. In fact, several studies indicate that lower-class boys whose mothers are employed experience strain in the father-son relationship and tend to be less admiring of their fathers (Gold & Andres, 1978a; Hoffman, 1974, 1980). These outcomes appear to be mediated by a lingering belief in many lower-class homes that when a mother works outside the home, the father has failed in his traditional provider role (Hoffman, 1989).

Additional evidence suggests that maternal employment, when it introduces heavy demands into the mother's schedule, may place young boys at risk for ineffective socialization. Two studies report that in families in which both parents work full time, parent-child interaction is more positive for daughters than it is for sons (Stuckey, McGhee, & Bell, 1982; Zaslow et al., 1983). In another investigation, highly educated full-time employed mothers, compared to their part-time employed and nonemployed counterparts, described their 3-year-old sons in especially negative terms (Bronfenbrenner, Alvarez, & Henderson, 1984). Perhaps these findings result from the fact that boys' more active behavior requires greater parental monitoring than is necessary for girls. Full-time employed mothers simply have less time and energy to provide this structure. In support of this interpretation, mothers who work full time mention their sons' activity level as especially bothersome, and they also remark that their boys seem demanding and noncompliant (Alvarez, 1985).

Beyond the sex and social-class differences noted above, several other factors make a difference in how children adjust to maternal employment. As we mentioned earlier, a mother's feelings of life satisfaction are important, and many mothers do derive a special sense of challenge, stimulation, and achievement from their work. Nevertheless, women continue to have less prestigious jobs than men, and they also earn less money than men in comparable occupations. Because these factors influence financial status and morale, they are likely to affect how mothers feel and behave when they arrive home at the end of the working day (Mortimer & Sorensen, 1984). Furthermore, issues surrounding work time and scheduling are often highly problematic for mothers who are employed full-time or in very demanding careers. Several

Employed mothers face special challenges in juggling the multiple responsibilities of job, household tasks, and child rearing.

studies indicate that part-time maternal employment has benefits for children across the entire age range, probably because it provides a flexible enough time schedule for mothers to meet the needs of youngsters with a wide variety of characteristics (Alvarez, 1985; Douvan, 1963; Kappel & Lambert, 1972).

Finally, when a mother works, her husband's support is especially crucial. If he does not assist with family responsibilities, she experiences a double load, at home and at work, a circumstance that leads to fatigue, distress, and reduced time and energy to interact with children in an optimal fashion. Recent evidence indicates that although husbands of employed women participate in household and child care tasks to a greater extent than husbands of nonemployed women, working mothers continue to shoulder most of this burden (Baruch & Barnett, 1986; Hoffman, 1984). Employed mothers' psychological well-being is known to increase when husbands provide at least some child care assistance (Kessler & McRae, 1981, 1982).

Research on maternal employment suggests a variety of ways in which work settings can support parents in their child-rearing roles and, at the same time, increase their effectiveness as employees. More opportunities for part-time employment, permission to bring suitable work home during normal working hours, and liberal maternity and paternity leaves (including time off when children are ill) would help many parents juggle the multiple demands of jobs, household maintenance, and child rearing more successfully. Moreover, the availability of high-quality substitute child care is a vital component of parents' peace of mind during the working day (Baruch & Barnett, 1987), and, as we will see shortly, it has major implications for children's development.

Effects of Day Care on Child Development. Although research on the consequences of day care for children's development has increased over the past several decades, our knowledge continues to be limited because of the wide variety of child care arrangements utilized by working mothers in the United States. A recent national survey indicated that at all ages, most children are placed in home-based care (see

Table 14.3. Who's Minding America's Children?

	PERCENTAGE OF CHILDREN WITH EMPLOYED MOTHERS IN DIFFERENT TYPES OF CHILD CARE ARRANGEMENTS			
AGE OF CHILD	HOME-BASED CARE *(See breakdown below)*	ORGANIZED CHILD CARE FACILITIES (DAY CARE CENTERS)	PARENT CARES FOR CHILD WHILE ON THE JOB	CHILD "SELF-CARE"
2 years and under	75.5	16.3	8.2	—
3–4 years	58.0	33.9	8.1	—
5–14 years	66.6	7.6	5.8	20.0

	PERCENTAGE OF CHILDREN IN DIFFERENT TYPES OF HOME-BASED CARE			
	CARE IN CHILD'S OWN HOME		CARE IN ANOTHER HOME	
AGE OF CHILD	BY RELATIVE	BY NONRELATIVE	BY RELATIVE	BY NONRELATIVE
2 years and under	27.5	6.5	15.8	25.7
3–4 years	22.1	5.0	13.2	17.7
5–14 years	37.8	3.8	12.1	12.8

Note: Many children experience more than one type of child care arrangement in the course of a single day. The figures for children 4 years of age and younger refer to settings in which children spend *most* time while their mothers are at work. Since the majority of children between 5 and 14 are in school during their mother's employment hours, these figures reflect the child care arrangements in which children spend most time during out-of-school hours.
Source: U.S. Bureau of the Census, 1987.

Table 14.3). Home care is an especially common arrangement for infants and school-age children; a greater proportion of 3- and 4-year olds attend day care centers. These trends are due to the fact that center facilities generally specialize in preschool care; very few accommodate infants or offer before- and after-school services. Therefore, most working mothers with non-preschool-age youngsters must seek other options. In fact, a close look at the figures in Table 14.3 reveals an alarming statistic: 20 percent of school-age children whose mothers work receive no supervised care at all (U.S. Bureau of the Census, 1987).

Since organized child care facilities are easiest for researchers to study, most investigations have focused on center-based care for preschoolers. In recent years, more research has reported on children's experiences in *family day care homes,* a form of care in which a neighborhood woman looks after a small group of youngsters in her own household. However, these studies are still very few in number. Moreover, at present, we know practically nothing about how the millions of children watched by relatives or baby sitters in their own or someone else's home respond to these types of care. And only in the last few years have researchers started to look into the consequences of releasing large numbers of children to "self-care" during after-school hours (see Box 14.3).

The very first investigations of day care, carried out in the 1960s and 1970s, compared preschool children enrolled in high-quality, university-sponsored centers with children of the same social class who were being reared at home. Although the environments sampled were limited to model programs, the research responded to the concerns of many people that the development of preschool children would suffer from long hours spent in group care arrangements. The findings were reassuring and encouraging. With respect to intellectual development, test scores of middle-class day care children did not differ from those of their home-reared counterparts. And in some studies of low-income children, enriched day care experiences actually predicted better intellectual performance. For these youngsters, good day care seemed to serve as effective early intervention, offsetting the negative impact of growing up in an impoverished family environment. Several early studies also indicated that group care could lead to social benefits for children. When compared to home-reared youngsters, children who attended high-quality day care programs during their early years were advantaged in sociability, although a rise in negative as well as positive peer interactions appeared (Belsky & Steinberg, 1978).

Once research had established that day care need not be harmful and could be beneficial for children's development, investigators turned to the study of child care programs available in ordinary communities. These new studies improved on the first wave of day care research by comparing children's experiences and development in day care environments that differed widely on dimensions of quality. Their aim was to identify specific conditions of care that support healthy psychological development, as well as those that were likely to undermine it. Once the precise ingredients of good care were known, parents could be encouraged to rely on them as guides in choosing a child care setting. And government officials could use the information in devising day care licensing standards that safeguard children's development.

The *National Day Care Study,* which included over 60 day care centers serving low-income children in three large cities, and *The National Day Care Home Study,*

◆   CONTEMPORARY ISSUES: SOCIAL POLICY   ◆

Latchkey Children

Box 14.3

Latchkey children are youngsters who regularly care for themselves after school with no adult supervision. Over the last two decades their numbers have risen dramatically, along with maternal employment. One recent estimate indicated that just over 1 million children between 5 and 14 years of age look after themselves when they are not in school (U.S. Bureau of the Census, 1987). Other projections are considerably higher, some as great as 5 to 7 million (Simons & Bohen, 1982; U.S. Department of Labor, 1982). While many latchkey children return home to an empty house, others "hang out" with peers in the neighborhood or in nearby shopping malls in the late afternoon and evening hours.

Widespread public concern exists about the dangers to which latchkey children are exposed, as well as the possibility that in the absence of adult supervision, many will engage in undesirable, antisocial behavior. However, research reveals contradictory findings. Some investigators report that latchkey children have problems that adult-supervised children do not, including low self-esteem, poor academic achievement, inadequate social skills, and an increase in anxiety and fearfulness. In contrast, other researchers report no detrimental consequences as the result of after-school "self-care" (Robin-

son, Rowland, & Coleman, 1986). But much of the research has failed to take into account the type of latchkey arrangement. In a recent study, Laurence Steinberg (1986, 1988b) showed that the way latchkey youngsters spend their time and whether or not parents supervise them "in absentia" make a difference in one important aspect of their adjustment: susceptibility to peer antisocial activity.

Steinberg asked a large number of fifth- through eighth-grade children residing in a small Midwestern city to answer a series of questions about how they spend their afternoons, what their parents' child-rearing practices are like, and whether or not they would join in the activities of a best friend who had decided to engage in antisocial behavior, such as vandalism and stealing. The findings showed that the more removed children's after-school care was from an adult-related environment, the more susceptible they were to peer pressure. Youngsters who frequently hung out with agemates described themselves as willing to participate in a peer's antisocial activities more often than those who spent time at friends' homes after school. Both of these groups were, in turn, more susceptible to peer influence than children who returned to their own homes once the school day was

involving several hundred family day care homes serving a diverse urban population, are the largest comparative investigations of day care conducted to date (Divine-Hawkins, 1981; Ruopp et al., 1979). The goal of both investigations was to determine the impact on children of such dimensions of quality as group size (number of children accommodated in a single classroom or well-defined physical space), caregiver/child ratio, and staff educational preparation. In each study, systematic observations of caregiver and child behavior were collected. The center study also included standardized tests of intellectual and language development administered in the fall and spring of the year.

The findings were remarkably consistent. In both center and home environments, group size and the related variable of adult/child ratio influenced caregivers' style of interaction. As the number of children decreased (to around 2 to 4 in day care homes and to about 14 preschoolers accompanied by at least 2 caregivers in day care centers), management of children became easier. Under these conditions, caregivers spent less time commanding and correcting and more time in positive, stimulating verbal interaction. Furthermore, training in early childhood education, child development, or a related field showed widespread relationships with caregiver behavior. Caregivers knowledgeable about children were more verbally stimulating as well as responsive to children's needs, helping and comforting them more than their untrained counterparts. Finally, in the center study, both smaller group size and caregiver training predicted large gains in intelligence and language test scores over a year's period of time.

Other comparative studies have replicated as well as extended these findings. In one series of investigations, day care centers serving low-income families on the

The safety and psychological adjustment of large numbers of latchkey children is a major concern in the United States.

over. Moreover, whether or not parents knew their child's whereabouts had a substantial impact on the child's willingness to be persuaded by peers. Latchkey children who were monitored from a distance by telephone calls or given regular after-school chores differed very little from those who experienced direct adult supervision. In contrast, youngsters left entirely to their own devices were particularly susceptible to peer influence. Finally, authoritative child rearing greatly increased latchkey children's resistance to undesirable peer pressures. The social responsibility and internalized moral standards encouraged by warm but firm parental control appeared to serve as a powerful buffer against peer antisocial tendencies.

Steinberg's research suggests that when parents can find no alternative to after-school self-care, distant supervision of their youngster's whereabouts and activities, along with authoritative parenting, reduces the chances that latchkey children will become problems to themselves, their peers, and the community. Parents are wise to try to arrange appropriate after-school supervision of children while they finish the working day. And communities need to provide more after-school care alternatives, to prevent the many American school-age youngsters whose mothers are employed from being exposed to the risks of unsupervised after-school hours.

island of Bermuda, where approximately 85 percent of children enter substitute care by age 2, were studied. Adult stimulating verbal interaction along with a global rating of center quality (based on a wide variety of characteristics, from physical facilities to program activities) predicted a broad array of positive outcomes for children, including cognitive, language, and social skills (McCartney, 1984; McCartney et al., 1985; Phillips, McCartney, & Scarr, 1987). Additional evidence indicates that these dimensions of quality are associated with enhanced social and intellectual development among middle-class children as well (Clarke-Stewart & Gruber, 1984; Howes, 1988; Vandell & Powers, 1983).

At the same time, low-quality day care is a serious risk to children's development. In a recent longitudinal investigation, Howes (1990) found that kindergarten children exposed to inadequate center care during their preschool years displayed a variety of undesirable behaviors, including distractibility, low task involvement, and inconsiderate behavior toward peers. Moreover, parents who enrolled their children in low-quality care tended to lead stressful lives and use inappropriate child-rearing techniques. These findings suggest that quality of substitute care combined with parental child-rearing practices mediates the link between day care and undesirable social behavior reported in some investigations (Haskins, 1985; Schwarz, Strickland, & Krolick, 1974).

Investigators still have much to learn about the wide variety of child care arrangements that America's children experience. But even though our knowledge is limited, the evidence available to date has established that not all day care has identical implications for development. High-quality settings in which group size is small, caregiver/child ratios are low, staff training is high, and adults communicate in stimulating, responsive, and affectionate ways contribute positively to many aspects of children's psychological functioning. At the same time, poor-quality care interferes with children's optimal development.

BRIEF REVIEW

In the sections above, we considered a variety of contemporary changes in the American family. The trend toward a smaller family size is associated with positive intellectual and adjustment outcomes for children. Most youngsters continue to grow up with siblings. Although inequities in parental attention promote sibling rivalry, sibling relationships serve as an important context in which children acquire a wide range of social skills. At the same time, siblings are not essential for healthy adjustment, since only children fare quite well in all aspects of development.

Today, large numbers of American children experience the divorce of their parents. Boys and temperamentally difficult children living in mother-custody homes are especially likely to display lasting adjustment problems. However, negative consequences are lessened by effective parenting and a continuing positive relationship with noncustodial fathers. When custodial parents remarry, children residing in father/stepmother families, and daughters especially, display more adjustment difficulties, although these subside over time.

Maternal employment, which has risen dramatically over the past several decades, is associated with children's sex-role flexibility and social and emotional maturity. However, these outcomes are moderated by a variety of factors, including children's sex and social class, demands of the mother's job, and fathers' participation in child rearing. Finally, high-quality day care promotes children's intellectual and social development, while low-quality care undermines it.

THE VULNERABLE FAMILY: CHILD MALTREATMENT

Families, as we indicated in the first part of this chapter, contribute in essential ways to the maintenance of society by serving as contexts in which children are loved, protected, and encouraged to develop into competent, productive adults. Throughout our discussion of the changing American family, we highlighted conditions under which family functioning is strained and parent-child relationships are likely to be less than optimal. When these circumstances become extreme, the family can be transformed from a supportive child-rearing context into a dangerous environment for children.

Incidence and Definitions

Child maltreatment is as old as the history of humankind. However, only in the latter half of the twentieth century has there been widespread public and professional acceptance that the problem exists, research aimed at understanding its psychological and social roots, and programs directed at helping maltreated children and their families (Oates, 1982). Perhaps the recent upsurge in professional and public concern is due to the fact that child maltreatment is especially common in large, industrialized nations like the United States (Gelles & Cornell, 1983). Although estimates of how often it occurs vary considerably from study to study, all of them are high. On the basis of data supplied by a nationwide sample of community professionals, a recent government-sponsored investigation estimated that in 1986, approximately 1 million American children were victims of child maltreatment severe enough to result in demonstrable harm (U.S. Department of Health and Human Services, 1988). Yet this estimate is undoubtedly very conservative, since it is based on a very stringent definition of maltreatment. Moreover, the majority of cases, including those in which children experience serious physical injury, go unreported (Emery, 1989).

Child maltreatment assumes a wide variety of forms. The following types of maltreatment are included in legal statutes and professional definitions:

1. *Physical abuse:* assaults on children that produce pain, cuts, welts, bruises, burns, broken bones, and other injuries
2. *Sexual abuse:* sexual molestation, intercourse, and exploitation of children
3. *Physical neglect:* living conditions in which children receive insufficient food, clothing, shelter, medical attention, or supervision
4. *Emotional neglect:* failure of caregivers to meet children's needs for nurturance and emotional support
5. *Psychological abuse:* actions that seriously damage children's emotional, social, or intellectual functioning

Although mental health and legal professionals agree that these five forms exist, they do not agree on the range of adult behaviors that actually constitute mistreatment. Definitions vary in the frequency and intensity of behaviors regarded as abusive, their impact on the victim, consideration of extenuating situational influences, and the emphasis they place on intentionality — whether or not the harm is deliberately inflicted by an adult (Emery, 1989). Consensus on a definition of child maltreatment is important, since if we cannot define it, we are hampered in studying its origins and impact on children and in designing effective intervention programs (Starr, 1979). The greatest definitional problems arise in the case of subtle, interpretable behaviors. For example, some investigators regard psychological abuse, in which children are rejected, scapegoated, ridiculed, humiliated, or terrorized by adults, as the most prevalent and potentially destructive form (Garbarino, Guttman, & Seeley, 1986; Hart & Brassard, 1987). But definitions of psychological abuse are especially complex and serious in their consequences for children and families. If they are too narrow and include only the most severe instances of mental cruelty, they allow many harmful actions toward children to continue unchecked and untreated. If they are too lenient, they can result in arbitrary, disruptive legal intrusions into family life (Melton & Davidson, 1987; Melton & Thompson, 1987).

The Origins of Child Maltreatment

When child maltreatment first became a topic of research in the early 1960s (Kempe et al., 1962), most child development specialists viewed it as rooted in adult psychopathology. The first studies indicated that adults who physically abused or neglected their offspring usually had one or more of the following characteristics: a history of abuse or neglect during their own childhoods, unrealistic expectations that children satisfy their own unmet psychological needs, and poor control of aggressive impulses (Spinetta & Rigler, 1972). (See Box 14.4 for a special discussion of child sexual abuse, which until the 1970s was not recognized as a serious social problem.)

These early findings suggested that only particular kinds of people mistreated children. However, it soon became apparent that many adults who had been abused as children did not repeat the cycle with their own offspring, that a single "abusive personality syndrome" did not exist, and that even "normal" parents were capable of abusive behavior (Emery, 1989). A more comprehensive explanation was needed to account for the widespread occurrence of child abuse and neglect in the United States. Child development specialists turned for help to the social systems perspective on family functioning, which views child maltreatment as multiply determined — not just by forces within the individual but also by characteristics of the family, community, and culture of which parent and child are a part.

At the level of the individual, in addition to parental characteristics, attributes of children increase the chances that child maltreatment will occur. A premature or very sick baby, or a child with a difficult temperament, a hyperactive behavioral style, or other developmental difficulties, has an increased likelihood of becoming the target of

---

◆   CONTEMPORARY ISSUES: SOCIAL POLICY   ◆

Child Sexual Abuse

Box 14.4

Throughout the first half of this century, child sexual abuse was regarded as a rare phenomenon. Cases that came to the attention of professionals were usually not taken seriously; the popularity of Freudian theory led many of them to be attributed to children's sexual fantasies. In the 1970s, the efforts of child advocates and researchers along with widespread media attention caused child sexual abuse to be recognized as a serious national problem. Recent estimates indicate that it accounts for over 13 percent of reported instances of child maltreatment — about 137,000 cases per year (U.S. Department of Health and Human Services, 1988). However, this figure represents only a small portion of the actual rate. Retrospective accounts of adult women indicate that from 12 to 38 percent were sexually molested as children (Finkelhor, 1986).

Unlike other forms of maltreatment, which do not differ as a function of children's sex, sexual abuse is committed against girls four times more often than it is against boys (U.S. Department of Health and Human Services, 1988). In the majority of instances (51 to 94 percent across a variety of studies), perpetrators are parents or close parental associates — frequently a stepfa-

ther or a mother's live-in boyfriend, less often the child's natural father, an uncle, or an older teenage brother (Alter-Reid et al., 1986). In cases involving nonrelatives, offenders tend to be adults whom children have come to know and trust (Bulkley, 1990).

Reported cases are strongly associated with poverty, unstable family structure, social isolation, and resulting weakening of family ties. Children who have spent substantial periods of their childhood living away from parents and who reside in homes where there is a history of constantly changing characters — repeated marriages, separations, and introduction of new partners into the household — are especially vulnerable. However, anonymous community surveys reveal that middle-class children in relatively stable households are also susceptible; families with greater economic resources are simply more likely to escape detection (Gomes-Schwartz, Horowitz, & Cardarelli, 1990). Intense pressure toward secrecy from the offender and feelings of confusion and guilt on the part of child victims prevent most youngsters from seeking help.

Adjustment difficulties experienced by many child sexual abuse victims are severe. Depression, low self-es-

abuse. Moreover, a passive, lethargic youngster can also engender mistreatment, especially in the form of neglect, simply by not demanding care and attention from parents (Belsky, 1980; Parke & Collmer, 1975). However, whether such children are maltreated depends on parental characteristics. In one recent investigation, temperamentally difficult youngsters who were physically abused had mothers who believed that they could do very little to control the child's irritating behavior. Instead, they attributed the child's unruliness to a stubborn or bad disposition — an interpretation that led the mothers to accelerate quickly to coercive strategies when disciplining the child (Bugental, Blue, & Cruzcosa, 1989). Once both the parent's and child's role in maltreatment are appreciated, our understanding of it moves beyond the level of the individual to a problem that is embedded in a family relationship.

In many instances, child abuse begins with small interactive discrepancies that are magnified and multiplied over time until maladaptive parent-child interaction becomes acute (Garbarino, 1977). Research shows that asynchronous interactions between abusive mothers and their infants sometimes appear as early as the first few weeks of life (Kennell, Voos, & Klaus, 1976). By the preschool years, abusive and neglectful families are characterized by low levels of parent-child interaction. When parental communication does occur, it tends to be negative (Burgess & Conger, 1978; Patterson, 1976; Trickett & Kuczynski, 1986). Maltreated children, in turn, display especially high rates of misbehavior, aggressing against peers and caregivers and reacting with defiance to parental intervention (George & Main, 1979; Howes & Eldredge, 1985; Trickett & Kuczynski, 1986). Maladaptive parenting and child recalcitrance feed on one another and escalate until maltreatment becomes a chronic family pattern. Children who consistently experience abuse or neglect quickly de-

teem, poor social skills, repressed anger and hostility, impaired ability to trust others, difficulties with self-control, precocious interest in sex, and seductive behavior are among the reported consequences. Younger children often react with sleep difficulties and generalized fearfulness; adolescents sometimes exhibit runaway and suicidal reactions. Children who were victimized by relatives rather than acquaintances or strangers, who were physically injured in the course of the abuse, and whose prior emotional health was poor are least likely to be functioning adequately (Alter-Reid et al., 1986; Haugaard & Reppucci, 1988).

Treatment of child sexual abuse is difficult. Once the abuse is revealed, reactions of family members — anxiety about permanent harm to child, anger toward the perpetrator, and sometimes hostility toward the child — often increase the victim's distress. Consequently, sensitive work with parents is critical to helping the child. Since sexual abuse is generally embedded in a variety of serious family problems, long-term intervention is usually necessary (Gomes-Schwartz, Horowitz, & Cardarelli, 1990).

Efforts at prevention are probably the best way to reduce the suffering of child sexual abuse victims. Prosecution of perpetrators, especially nonfamily members, is now more common (Bulkley, 1990). Currently, public education programs caution parents to take children's allegations of sexual abuse seriously and alert school officials and physicians to signs that a child may have been victimized. Educational efforts are also directed at children to help them recognize inappropriate sexual advances and encourage them to report these overtures (Finkelhor, 1986).

Knowledge about causes, consequences, and effective intervention in child sexual abuse is still at a rudimentary level. The topic is especially hard to investigate because of difficulties in obtaining parental consent for children's research participation and ethical concerns surrounding repeated questioning of children about sexual molestation (Haugaard & Reppucci, 1988). At the same time, more information is desperately needed to help professionals predict, prevent, and treat this widespread problem.

velop very serious adjustment and learning problems (Brassard, Germain, & Hart, 1987; Egelund & Sroufe, 1981; Kempe & Kempe, 1984; Lamphear, 1985). These outcomes contribute to the continuation of their mistreatment.

Nevertheless, most parents have sufficient self-control not to respond to their children's misbehavior with abuse, and not all children with developmental difficulties are mistreated. Other factors must combine with these conditions to precipitate an extreme parental response. Research indicates that unmanageable parental stress is almost invariably associated with child maltreatment. Unemployment, marital conflict, large and closely spaced families, overcrowded living conditions, and extreme household disorganization are common in abusive homes — factors that increase the chances that tolerable levels of stress will be passed and that parents will discharge their frustration by lashing out at their children (Emery, 1989).

Furthermore, many studies show that the overwhelming majority of abusive parents are isolated from formal and informal social supports in their communities (Belsky, 1980; Garbarino, 1977). The causes of this social isolation are multiple. Because of their own life histories, many abusive and neglectful parents have learned to mistrust and avoid other people and have failed to develop the skills that are necessary for establishing positive interpersonal relationships. At the same time, these parents are often rejected by extended family and neighbors because they are seen as deviant and unlikely to reciprocate when assistance is offered (Polansky et al., 1985). In addition, maltreating parents are more likely to live in neighborhoods that provide little in the way of supportive links between family and community (Garbarino & Sherman, 1980). Consequently, during particularly stressful times, they lack "lifelines" to other people and have no one to turn to for help. In fact, recent evidence suggests that social support is the major distinguishing variable between mothers who repeat their own childhood histories of abuse with their offspring and those who do not. Mothers who break the intergenerational cycle are far more likely to have received affection and comfort from a nonabusive adult as children, to have participated in therapy sometime during their lives, and to have established a satisfying relationship with a mate (Egeland, Jacobvitz, & Sroufe, 1988).

One final factor — the broad ideology and customs of our culture — profoundly affects the chances that child maltreatment will occur when parents feel stressed and overburdened. In societies in which force and violence are viewed as appropriate techniques for solving problems, including those that arise in the rearing of children, the stage is set for child abuse. These conditions exist in the United States (Belsky, 1980; Garbarino, 1977; Hart & Brassard, 1987). Although all 50 states as well as the federal government have enacted child abuse legislation, there is still strong societal support for the use of physical force in American caregiver-child relations. For example, during the past two decades, the United States Supreme Court has twice upheld the legal right of school officials to use corporal punishment to discipline children. Moreover, high crime rates permeate American cities, and television sets beam graphic displays of violence into family livingrooms. In view of the widespread acceptance of violent behavior in American culture, it is not surprising that most American parents employ physical punishment at one time or another to discipline their children. In countries where corporal punishment is not condoned, such as China and Sweden, child abuse is rare (Belsky, 1980).

Preventing Child Maltreatment

Because child maltreatment is embedded in families, communities, and society as a whole, efforts to prevent it must be directed at each of these levels. Techniques that have been suggested include interventions that teach high-risk parents effective caregiving and disciplinary practices; efforts to make child development knowledge and experience with children a regular part of the high school curriculum; and broad social programs that have as their goal full employment and improved economic conditions for low-income families (Belsky, 1978; Rosenberg & Reppucci, 1985; Zigler, 1978).

We have already seen in earlier parts of this chapter that providing social supports to families is extraordinarily effective in minimizing parental stress. Consequently, it is not surprising that it sharply reduces the incidence of child maltreatment as well (Garbarino, 1977). *Parents Anonymous,* a national organization consisting of 10,000 members that has as its main goal the rehabilitation of child-abusing parents, does so largely through providing social supports to abuse-prone families. Each of its 1,500 local chapters offers self-help group meetings, daily phone calls, and regular home visits to relieve social isolation and encourage the use of effective parenting techniques (Koek & Martin, 1988). Crisis intervention services also exist in many communities. Nurseries provide temporary child care when parents feel they are about to lose control, and telephone hotlines offer immediate help to parents under stress and refer them to appropriate community agencies when long-term assistance is warranted.

Other preventive approaches include media campaigns, such as public service announcements in newspapers, magazines, and on television and radio, that are designed to educate laypeople about child maltreatment and inform them of where and how to seek help (Rosenberg & Reppucci, 1985). In addition to these efforts, substantial changes in the overall attitudes, practices, and priorities of American culture are needed. Many child development specialists believe that child maltreatment cannot be eradicated as long as parents must rear their children in a society in which violence is commonplace and corporal punishment continues to be regarded as an acceptable child-rearing alternative (Belsky, 1980; Garbarino, Guttman, & Seeley, 1986; Gil, 1987; Hyman, 1987; Melton & Thompson, 1987).

Although more cases reach the courtroom today than in decades past, child maltreatment remains a crime that is very difficult to prove. Most of the time, the only witnesses are the child victims themselves or other loyal family members. Even in court cases in which the evidence is strong, judges hesitate to impose the ultimate

Public service announcements help prevent child abuse by educating people about the problem and informing them of how and where to seek help.

preventive to further mistreatment—permanent removal of the child from the family. There are several reasons for this reluctant posture. First, in American society, state intervention into family life is viewed as a last resort, to be imposed only when there is near certainty that a child will be denied basic care and protection by parents. Second, despite destructive family relationships, maltreated children and their parents are usually attached to one another, and most of the time, neither desires separation. Finally, the tendency of the American legal system to regard children as parental property, rather than as human beings in their own right, also serves to impede court-ordered protection (Hart & Brassard, 1987). Yet despite intensive intervention and therapy, some adults persist in their abusive acts. Approximately 1,100 abused children end up as fatalities each year (U.S. Department of Health and Human Services, 1988). In cases in which parental rehabilitation is unlikely, society's obligation to ensure safe and healthy rearing environments for children should be paramount, even if this requires the drastic steps of separating parent from child and legally terminating parental rights.

Child maltreatment is a distressing and horrifying topic. When we consider how often it occurs in a society such as our own that claims to place a high value on the dignity and worth of the individual, it is all the more shocking. Nevertheless, there is reason to be optimistic, since considerable progress has been made in understanding and preventing child maltreatment over the last several decades. Although we still have a long way to go, the situation for abused and neglected children is far better now than it has been at any time in history (Kempe & Kempe, 1984).

CHAPTER SUMMARY

Evolutionary Origins

■ The origins of the human family can be traced to our hunting-and-gathering ancestors. Bipedalism enabled adults to cooperate and share, especially in providing food for the young. A single male became committed to a female and their joint offspring—a pattern of social organization that enhanced survival.

Functions of the Family

■ In addition to safeguarding its own members, the family performs essential functions for society. In modern industrialized nations, these are largely restricted to reproduction, socialization, and emotional support.

The Family as a Social System

■ Currently, investigators view the family from a **social systems perspective**—as a complex network of mutually influencing relationships affected by the larger social context of which it is a part. Connections to the community—through formal organizations and informal social networks—promote effective family interaction and optimal child development.

Socialization within the Family

■ Two broad dimensions, **control** and **responsiveness,** describe individual differences in the way parents go about the task of **socialization.** When combined, these dimensions yield four parenting types.

■ **Authoritative** parents, who are both controlling and responsive, are especially effective agents of socialization. Their rational, democratic style promotes socially active, responsible, and cognitively competent children. **Authoritarian** parents, who are high in control but low in responsiveness, tend to have anxious, withdrawn, dependent children who react hostilely when frustrated. **Permissive parents** are warm and responsive but lacking in control; their youngsters are often dependent, demanding, and impulsive. Finally, **uninvolved parents** are low in both responsiveness and control. Their indifferent, rejecting behavior is associated with deficits in virtually all aspects of psychological functioning.

■ Authoritative parenting has emerged as the most common form of child rearing in many cultures around the world. Nevertheless, systematic social-class differences in parenting styles exist in modern industrialized nations. Low-income, working-class families place a high value on children's obedience and are more authoritarian and punitive than their middle-class counterparts. In contrast, middle-class parents emphasize children's psychological characteristics; they more often use explanations, verbal praise, and inductive techniques. These differences can be understood in terms of the life conditions of lower- and middle-class parents, including variations in work roles, education, and stress impinging on the family. The cultural traditions of some low-income minorities, such as the black **extended family household,** help protect children from the stresses of living in poverty.

The Changing American Family

■ Over the last several decades, substantial changes in American family life have occurred. The current trend toward smaller families has had consequences for parent-child interaction. In households with large numbers of children, parents tend to be more authoritarian and punitive, and children score somewhat lower in intelligence, school achievement, and self-esteem. However, these unfavorable outcomes are substantially reduced in economically well-off households with many youngsters.

■ Sibling relationships offer children practice in a wide range of social skills. Nevertheless, contrary to popular belief, siblings are not essential for normal development. Only children are not lonelier than other youngsters. Moreover, they are more likely to experience authoritative parenting, and their school achievement and educational attainment are somewhat higher than those of children with siblings.

■ Divorce is extremely common in the lives of American children. Although most youngsters experience painful emotional reactions in the period surrounding divorce, there are substantial individual differences in the way they respond. Boys typically show more severe behavioral disorganization than girls, reacting to parental conflict and inconsistent discipline with noncompliant, hostile behavior and a marked increase in school difficulties. Preschool and early school-age children have difficulty understanding their parents' estrangement and therefore may exhibit more extreme behavioral reactions than many older youngsters.

■ By two years after the divorce, most children show improved adjustment. Nevertheless, boys in mother-custody homes remain vulnerable to lasting academic, social, and emotional problems, although a continuing positive father-son relationship reduces these negative outcomes. The most consistent long-term negative consequences for girls are concentrated in adolescent and early adult heterosexual behavior. Children who live in tranquil divorced families are better adjusted in the long run than those who continue to reside in strife-ridden intact homes. However, the research as a whole indicates that children suffer deeply from their parents' divorce and, even many years later, continue to wish that they could have grown up in a happy intact family.

■ Many divorced parents eventually remarry; their children must adjust to a **reconstituted family** arrangement that includes a complex array of new figures and relationships. Like the period surrounding divorce, this transition is difficult and stressful for most children. How well they fare in the long run varies with sex of parent and child. Boys adjust well in mother/stepfather families. In contrast, children in father/stepmother families, and girls especially, display the greatest adjustment difficulties.

■ Over the last several decades, women have entered the labor force in rising numbers. A variety of positive outcomes for children are associated with maternal employment, including a higher sense of self-esteem, better family and peer relations, and less sex-stereotyped views of males and females. In general, girls benefit more than boys. Some studies indicate that children of all ages fare best under conditions of part-time maternal employment. A flexible work schedule and assistance by fathers with household responsibilities help mothers balance the multiple demands of work and child rearing effectively.

■ American children experience a diverse array of child care arrangements while their mothers are at work. Although most children are placed in home-based care, organized child care facilities have been most frequently studied. Research comparing child care settings on dimensions of quality indicates that when group size is small, caregiver/child ratios are generous, staff training is high, and adults communicate in stimulating, responsive ways, many aspects of child development are fostered.

The Vulnerable Family: Child Maltreatment

■ Child maltreatment is especially common in the United States and other modern industrialized nations. Although early investigators viewed child abuse and neglect as rooted in adult psychopathology, recent research indicates that it is multiply determined — by characteristics of individuals, families, communities, and the larger culture of which parent and child are a part. Certain child attributes, such as prematurity and difficult temperament, combined with unmanageable parental stress and isolation from supportive ties to the community increase the chances that maltreatment will occur. When societies sanction force and violence as an appropriate means for solving problems, child abuse is fostered.

IMPORTANT TERMS AND CONCEPTS

social systems perspective   (p. 562)
socialization   (p. 564)
control   (p. 565)
responsiveness   (p. 565)
authoritative parenting   (p. 566)

authoritarian parenting   (p. 567)
permissive parenting   (p. 567)
uninvolved parenting   (p. 567)
extended family household   (p. 570)
nuclear family unit   (p. 570)

reconstituted family   (p. 578)
divorce mediation   (p. 584)
sole custody   (p. 584)
joint custody   (p. 584)
latchkey children   (p. 590)

Charles Clarence Dawson, *The Last Marble,* watercolor on paper, 29¼ × 27¾ in.
DuSable Museum of African-American History.

15

Beyond the Family

Peer Relations
Media
Schooling

Beginning at an early age, socialization in the family is supplemented by experiences in the wider world of peers, media, and school. In this chapter, we take up the significance of these three major extrafamilial contexts for development.

We begin by considering children's peer relations. In all human societies, children receive extensive informal exposure to other children during their daily lives. In no culture are they reared entirely by adults. From our discussion of social cognition in Chapter 11, you already know that one special type of peer relationship, friendship, changes substantially during childhood and contributes uniquely to social, emotional, and cognitive development. In this chapter, we take a broader look at how peer sociability changes with age. Then we turn to the topic of *peer acceptance*. Perhaps you remember from your own childhood years that some of your classmates were especially well liked by peers, while others were actively rejected. We consider the origins of peer acceptance in children's personal characteristics and social behaviors, along with its long-term significance for psychological adjustment. Next we discuss children's *peer groups*—self-generated informal associations that become increasingly common during middle childhood and adolescence. We trace how peer groups form, factors that affect their functioning, and their impact on children's development. We conclude our discussion of peer influences by taking a close look at the processes through which children serve as socialization agents for one another—peer reinforcement and modeling during childhood and conformity to the peer group during the adolescent years.

Children are profoundly affected by major technological advances in their culture. In this chapter, we concentrate on two prevalent innovations of this century: television and computers. We review what is known about the effects of these captivating electronic devices on children's cognitive and social development. We also discuss how best to ensure that these media serve as constructive forces in the lives of children, helping them to acquire new cognitive skills and prosocial values and behaviors.

Finally, our discussion turns to the school, an institution established by society to assist the family in transmitting culturally valued knowledge and skills to the next generation. We consider how schools accomplish their socializing goal. We begin with the physical setting—the implications of such factors as physical layout and school size for children's academic and social learning. Next we take up the basic philosophical orientation of the classroom, focusing on the implications of traditional versus open schooling for classroom experiences and academic outcomes. Then we turn to the teacher's role as mediator of classroom learning. We place special emphasis on *teacher expectations* for pupil performance—how these expectations form, their effects on teacher-pupil interaction, and their motivational and achievement consequences. Problems faced by schools in accommodating pupils with special needs—the child with learning difficulties as well as the intellectually gifted youngster—are considered next. Our chapter concludes with a discussion of the success of schools in contributing to two major societal goals—improving the life chances of racial/ethnic minorities and equipping young people to keep pace with their increasingly well-educated counterparts in other industrialized nations around the world.

PEER RELATIONS

Research on children's peer relations began early in this century, sparked by the interest of social scientists in effects of group processes on individual behavior. A lull occurred around World War II, a period in which child development specialists were intensely preoccupied with the study of parent-child relations. The past two decades have brought renewed interest in peer associations, stimulated by the discovery of more effective techniques for observing child-child interaction and provocative speculations about the vital role of peers in social and cognitive development.

Much like the study of the family, contemporary research on peers has been heavily influenced by the field of *ethology*. In the 1960s, ethologists moved beyond the classic motherless monkey studies to investigate the consequences of early peer deprivation. Maternally reared rhesus monkeys with no peer contact displayed a broad array of behavioral disturbances, including immature play, excessive aggression and fearfulness, and less effective cooperation among group members at maturity (Harlow, 1969). However, additional primate studies revealed that optimal development depended on *both* parental and peer rearing. Maternally deprived peer-raised monkeys also showed behavior problems, including heightened dominant and submissive (as opposed to friendly) interaction and deficient sexual behavior (Goy & Goldfoot, 1974). The complementary socialization roles of parents and peers suggested by these findings have become a major current emphasis in human peer research. Moreover, social behaviors observed among a wide variety of mammalian species, such as dominance hierarchies and rough-and-tumble play, have led researchers to search for similar qualities in children's peer relations and to study their adaptive function.

Also like research into family relations, an *ecological* perspective has become increasingly common in studies of peers. We will see that the peer network is an organized, structured system that functions in concert with other social systems, such as the family and school. Moreover, child-child interactions are molded in part by situational influences, such as the number, age range, and familiarity of peer participants and the type of play materials available. We will return to the role of environmental contexts in children's peer associations many times in the course of our discussion.

Before we begin, a word of caution about the limitations of contemporary research on peers is appropriate. Strictly speaking, the term *peer* means "equal in rank or standing." Most research bears the mark of this definition, since it focuses on children who are close in age. However, this one-sided emphasis on agemates is not just an outgrowth of the meaning of the word. Children are most accessible to researchers in age-graded settings, such as schools, clubs, and summer camps. Yet in the neighborhood, where children's activities are harder to track, more than half their contacts are with children who differ by a year or more from their own age (Barker & Wright, 1955; Ellis, Rogoff, & Cromer, 1981). Moreover, in cultures in which children are not segregated by age for schooling and recreation, cross-age interaction is even more common (Weisner & Gallimore, 1977; Whiting & Edwards, 1988a). We will point out what is known about the importance of mixed-age peer associations as our discussion proceeds. But it is important to note that the heavy research focus on same-age relationships limits what we currently know about the breadth and significance of children's peer experiences (Hartup, 1983).

The Development of Peer Sociability

Child-child interaction appears early in cultures in which children experience regular contact with peers during the first year of life. Mothers' anecdotal reports indicate that about 60 percent of American 6- to 12-month-olds see other babies at least once a week (Vandell & Mueller, 1980). Observations of these infant playmates reveal that peer interaction begins with isolated, nonreciprocated social contacts. Gradually, these evolve into the complex, coordinated interaction sequences typical of the childhood and adolescent years. The development of peer sociability parallels the acquisition of important cognitive and linguistic capacities that we discussed in earlier chapters. Changes in each domain occur in tandem and support one another (Brownell, 1986).

Infant Beginnings. How skilled a peer social partner is the infant during the first two years of life? Early claims that babies fail to interact socially (e.g., Parten, 1932) have recently been challenged. Investigators mark the occurrence of a true social act when an infant looks at another person's face while engaging in an attention-getting behavior. When pairs of babies are brought together in a laboratory, looking accompanied by touching occurs at 3 to 4 months, and peer-directed smiles and babbles are evident by 6 months (Vandell & Mueller, 1980). These social acts increase in fre-

The beginnings of peer sociability emerge in infancy, in the form of looks, touches, and gestures that increase in frequency and complexity over the second year of life.

quency during the second half of the first year, and occasional reciprocal exchanges occur in which babies smile, laugh, gesture, or otherwise duplicate each other's behavior (Eckerman & Whatley, 1977; Vandell, Wilson, & Buchanan, 1980).

Between 1 and 2 years, infant social behavior develops further. Isolated social initiations recede, and coordinated interaction occurs more often. Also, older toddlers combine more behaviors into a single social act — for example, they look, vocalize, gesture, and smile simultaneously at a nearby peer (Bronson, 1981; Mueller & Brenner, 1977). By age 2, when both the mother and a peer are present, attempts to engage the peer in play occur more often than initiations to the mother (Eckerman, Whatley, & Kutz, 1975).

Nevertheless, it is important not to exaggerate the baby's social capacities. Even in highly focused playroom situations where infants have little else to capture their attention besides one another, social contacts are not very frequent, and sustained interaction is rare (Eckerman & Stein, 1982). Moreover, the increase in reciprocal exchanges that occurs around the end of the second year consists largely of toddlers' imitations of a nearby peer's actions, such as jumping, chasing, or banging a toy. Not until age 2½ do children flexibly alter their playful gestures to suggest new bases for interaction and use words to regulate a peer's behavior (Eckerman, Davis, & Didow, 1989). You may recall from Chapter 9 that the ability of toddlers and very young preschoolers to actively participate in reciprocal turn-taking with adults is also limited. Therefore, it is not surprising that the same skill is tenuous in their encounters with peers, who are far less optimal social partners than most adults.

But rudimentary peer sociability is present during infancy, and researchers have been interested in how it grows out of the baby's earliest experiences. One hypothesis is that infants' animated play with objects captures the attention of other babies, who soon want to join in their activities (Mueller & Lucas, 1975). This idea may have some validity, but it cannot serve as a complete explanation. Social development does not proceed from an initial focus on toys to a focus on peers during the first two years of life. In fact, babies as young as 6 months of age are much more responsive to each other when toys are absent than when they are present in a laboratory playroom (Eckerman & Whatley, 1977; Vandell, Wilson, & Buchanan, 1980).

A second idea is that early peer social skills are supported by the infant's growing attachment to the caregiver. By the end of the first year, the attachment bond creates a secure base that frees the baby to venture away from the adult and approach other children (see Chapter 10). Also, from interacting with sensitive, responsive adults, babies learn how to send and interpret emotional signals in their first peer associations (Bronson, 1981; Jacobson et al., 1986; Parke et al., 1988). In support of this explanation, research indicates that the looks, touches, smiles, and vocalizations that characterize infant-infant responsiveness resemble salient qualities of mother-infant interaction (Eckerman, Whatley, & Kutz, 1975; Vandell, 1980). Furthermore, babies who experience a sensitive, warm parental relationship engage in more extended peer social exchanges (Howes & Stewart, 1987; Vandell & Wilson, 1987). These children, in turn, display more socially competent behavior during the preschool years (Howes, 1988; Sroufe, 1983).

The Preschool Years. During the preschool period, the frequency and quality of child-child interaction change substantially. Both positive and negative social behaviors become more prevalent, although friendly social acts are more common (Hay, 1984; Lougee, Grueneich, & Hartup, 1977; Walters, Pearce, & Dahms, 1957). In addition, preschoolers gradually abandon immature social responses in favor of more mature and effective ones. For example, when observed in nursery school, 2-year-olds often stand and watch their peers, retreat from conflict, cry, and orient toward the teacher. In contrast, 4- and 5-year-olds come closer together in play, and they engage in longer verbal exchanges while smiling, maintaining eye contact, and using

Table 15.1. Changes in Occurrence of Parten's Social Play Types from Preschool to Kindergarten Age

	PRESCHOOL 3–4 YEARS	KINDERGARTEN 5–6 YEARS
Total nonsocial activity	41%	34%
Uninvolved and onlooker behavior	19%	14%
Solitary play	22%	20%
Parallel play	22%	23%
Cooperative play	37%	43%

Sources: Preschool figures are averages of those reported by Barnes (1971); Rubin, Maioni, and Hornung (1976); Rubin, Watson, and Jambor (1978); and Smith (1978). Kindergarten figures are averages of those reported by Barnes (1971) and Rubin, Watson, and Jambor (1978).

such attention-getting devices as touching and calling a play partner by name (Mueller, 1972; Smith & Connolly, 1972).

These findings suggest that a major change in peer sociability — a dramatic rise in reciprocal, coordinated interaction — takes place over the preschool years. In a classic study of preschool social behavior, Parten (1932) observed nursery school children at play and concluded that social development proceeds in a three-step sequence. It begins with nonsocial activity — unoccupied, onlooker behavior and solitary play — and then shifts to a limited degree of social participation called **parallel play,** in which the child plays near other children with similar materials but does not interact with them. Toward the middle of the preschool years, truly social, **cooperative play,** in which children converse, share toys, and act out complementary roles, predominates as the other play forms decline.

However, recent efforts to replicate Parten's findings (see Table 15.1) reveal that preschool social behavior does not conform to this straightforward developmental progression. Although nonsocial activity does decrease with age, it is still the most frequent form of behavior among preschoolers, and among kindergartners it continues to consume as much as a third of children's free-play time. Moreover, solitary and parallel play remain fairly stable from 3 to 6 years of age, and together, these categories account for as much of the young child's play activity as highly social, cooperative interaction. Social development during the preschool years is not simply a matter of eliminating nonsocial and partially social activity from the young child's behavioral repertoire.

We now know that it is the *type,* rather than the amount, of solitary and parallel play that undergoes important developmental changes during the early years. In a detailed study of preschool children's play behavior, Rubin, Watson, and Jambor (1978) looked at the cognitive maturity of nonsocial, parallel, and cooperative play among 4- and 5-year-old children by applying Smilansky's (1968) cognitive play categories, shown in Table 15.2. Within each of Parten's social play types, 5-year-olds engaged in more cognitively mature behavior than 4-year-olds. At the same time, cooperative make-believe play — a form we called *sociodramatic*[1] in Chapter 6 — became increasingly prevalent with age.

Parents and teachers often voice concerns about children who frequently play in a solitary fashion and engage in low rates of interaction with peers. In line with the

[1] In Chapter 6, we discussed the emergence of sociodramatic play during the preschool years along with its significance for children's social and cognitive development. You may wish to return to pages 222–223 to review these findings.

Table 15.2. Smilansky's (1968) Developmental Sequence of Cognitive Play

PLAY TYPE	DEFINITION	EXAMPLES	AGES AT WHICH ESPECIALLY COMMON
Functional play	Simple, repetitive muscle movements with or without objects	Running around a room, rolling a car back and forth, kneading clay with no intent to construct with it	1–2
Constructive play	Creating or constructing something	Making a house out of toy blocks, drawing a picture, putting together a puzzle	3–6
Make-believe play	Acting out everyday and imaginary roles in play	Playing house, school, or police officer. Acting out fairy tales or television characters	3–7
Play and games with rules	Understanding and conforming to rules in play activities	Playing board games, cards, hopscotch, baseball	6–11

Sources: Rubin, Fein, & Vandenberg (1983); Smilansky (1968).

findings described above, current evidence indicates that only certain kinds of nonsocial activity — aimless wandering and functional play involving immature, repetitive motor actions — are predictive of lags in cognitive development and early difficulties in relating to peers. Most nonsocial play of preschoolers is not of this kind. Instead, it is positive and constructive, and preschool teachers encourage it when they set out art materials, puzzles, and construction toys for children to choose during free play. Contrary to popular belief, children who spend much of their play time in these activities are not maladjusted. Instead, they are bright, socially competent youngsters who enjoy and do especially well at complex problem-solving tasks (Rubin, 1982).

In the preschool years, contact with agemates provides children with opportunities to practice a wide variety of social skills. But young children, who are limited in mobility and independence, depend largely on parents to help them establish rewarding peer associations. Parents influence children's peer relationships in many ways. One is through the neighborhood in which they choose to live. Neighborhoods differ in the extent to which they permit easy contact and play among young children. Berg and Medrich (1980) examined the impact of different residential areas in Oakland, California, on peer interaction. Monterrey, an affluent hilly subdivision in which secluded homes were set back from busy roads with no sidewalks, constricted children's opportunities to move about freely and congregate with peers. In contrast, the flat, densely populated inner city neighborhood of Yuba offered easy access to a rich and varied neighborhood social life. Children played often in large, mixed-age groups, made use of the streets for spontaneous games, built secret hideaways in empty lots, and traveled together to make small purchases in nearby shops.

Parents also act as social planners and ''booking agents'' for young children, scheduling visits between playmates and enrolling them in preschool and other organized activities that offer contact with agemates. Older children arrange more peer experiences for themselves, but preschoolers must rely on their parents' efforts, especially if the neighborhood prevents them from gathering spontaneously. Parents also influence their children's social behavior by offering advice and guidance about how to interact with playmates. Finally, adult social relationships provide children with influential examples of how to act toward peers. As we saw in earlier chapters, young children quickly integrate parental styles of interaction into their own social behaviors (Rubin & Sloman, 1984).

Children's opportunities to interact with peers are influenced by the physical and social characteristics of their neighborhood. The flat terrain of this inner-city area permits these children to move about freely and gather together spontaneously.

Neighborhood play life and parental support, guidance, and modeling of social skills continue to be influential beyond the preschool years. Throughout childhood, the social worlds of family and peers are linked in fundamental ways.

Middle Childhood and Adolescence. With the beginning of formal schooling, contact with a diversity of peers increases substantially. The school's emphasis on intellectual tasks soon makes it apparent that agemates vary in achievement-related characteristics, and children also learn that peers differ in many other ways, including ethnicity, religion, interests, and personality. Greater breadth of peer contact probably contributes to heightened awareness by elementary school children that others have viewpoints that differ from their own (see Chapter 11). Peer interaction, in turn, profits from children's enhanced perspective-taking capacity. Communication skills with agemates undergo marked improvement during middle childhood. For example, children become better at accurately interpreting the intentions of others and taking them into account in peer dialogues (Hartup, 1983).

In middle childhood, peer interaction also becomes increasingly governed by social norms that promote courteous, prosocial behavior. Recall from Chapter 12 that sharing, helping, and other forms of altruism are more common in middle childhood than during the preschool years. Also, older children differ from their younger counterparts in the way they go about helping others. Kindergartners move right in and give assistance, regardless of whether it is desired or not. Older children offer to help and wait for a peer to accept it before they behave altruistically (Hartup, 1983). During adolescence, agemates work more cooperatively in groups — staying on task, interacting more, interrupting each other less, asking for opinions, and acknowledging one another's contributions (Smith, 1960; Smith, 1973).

In line with children's increasing adherence to prosocial expectations, the overall incidence of quarreling and aggressive interchanges decreases over the late preschool and middle childhood years, although, as we indicated in Chapter 13, the form of aggression makes a difference. Verbal insults among boys and social ostracism among girls continue into adolescence, while physical attacks decline.

Another form of peer interaction becomes common in the late preschool and middle childhood years. Watch children at play in a public park or school yard, and you will see them wrestle, roll, jump, hit, and run after one another while smiling and

*During the late preschool
and middle childhood years,
children engage in friendly
chasing and play-fighting
known as rough-and-tumble
play.*

laughing. This friendly chasing and play-fighting is called **rough-and-tumble play.**
Research indicates that it is a good-natured, sociable activity that is quite distinct from
aggressive fighting. Children initiate it with peers whom they like especially well, and
they continue interacting after a rough-and-tumble episode, rather than separating
(as they do at the end of an aggressive encounter). The resemblance of rough-and-
tumble play to the juvenile social behavior of a wide variety of mammalian species
raises questions about its adaptive significance. By age 11, children choose rough-
and-tumble partners who are not only likable, but also similar in strength to themselves. In our evolutionary past, this form of interaction may have been important for
the development of dominance and fighting skill. Rough-and-tumble play occurs
more often among boys, but girls also engage in it. However, girls' rough-and-tumble
behaviors largely consist of running and chasing, while boys engage in more playful
wrestling and hitting (Blurton Jones, 1972; Humphreys & Smith, 1987; Smith &
Connolly, 1972).

Over the course of middle childhood, children interact increasingly often with
peers, until at adolescence, more time is spent in peer associations than with any
other agent of socialization (Medrich et al., 1982). Why do children choose to spend
so much time with agemates? Common interests, novel play activities, comparable
social skills, and opportunities to interact with others on a relatively equal footing
make peer relationships especially satisfying. As childhood draws to a close, the
average young person emerges from these frequent and intense social encounters
with a great many sensitive and sophisticated social behaviors (Hartup, 1983).

Situational Influences on Peer Interaction

At all ages, peer interaction is highly subject to situational influences. In the following
sections, we consider several important ones: the play materials available, and the
group size, age mixture, and familiarity of peer participants.

Play Materials. The quantity and kind of play materials available have an important bearing on the nature of peer interaction. Play with small objects—especially
when there are too few to go around—is the most common setting for fights and

quarrels among young children (DeStefano & Mueller, 1982; McGrew, 1969). In preschool classrooms, certain play areas, such as art and reading, promote solitary and parallel play, while others, such as the housekeeping and block areas, stimulate cooperative social behavior (Rubin, 1977). Active play spaces — school playgrounds or indoor slides and jungle gyms — also encourage high levels of coordinated interaction as well as rough-and-tumble play (Hartup, 1983; Humphreys & Smith, 1984).

Providing children with toys that have highly specific functions (e.g., trucks, dolls, stove) as opposed to materials with ambiguous functions (e.g., pipe cleaners, cardboard cylinders, paper bags) also influences peer sociability. In one study, small groups of preschoolers came together for two play sessions — one with specific and the other with ambiguous play objects. Children used the specific toys to enact realistic roles, such as mother, doctor, and baby. In contrast, the ambiguous materials encouraged fantastic role play, such as pirate and creature from outer space. Fantastic roles, in turn, led to more social interaction, especially planning statements, such as "I'll be the pirate and you be the prisoner" or "Watch out! Now I'm going to jump ship!" Since fantastic role play is not governed by familiar, everyday scripts, children devoted more time to planning each episode and explaining what they were doing to peer companions (McLoyd, Warren, & Thomas, 1984).

Group Size. A smaller group size encourages more intense and cooperative social behavior at all ages. Interacting in twosomes seems to be especially conducive to the development of early social skills. Tracking the development of peer sociability among toddlers over a 6-month period, Vandell and Mueller (1977) reported that the number and complexity of exchanges increased under conditions of dyadic (but not group) interaction. Similarly, in family day care homes with only two or three youngsters, children are more likely to talk and play among themselves (Howes & Rubenstein, 1985). When day care homes have more than five children, preschoolers perform poorly on perspective-taking tasks, and their behavior is less socially competent (Clarke-Stewart & Gruber, 1984). This same trend carries over into the middle childhood years. In elementary school classrooms, small discussion and study groups of about five members promote more involved and cooperative peer interaction than larger group sizes (Hare, 1953; Hertz-Lazarowitz, Sharan, & Steinberg, 1980).

Age Mix of Child Participants. The theories of Piaget and Vygotsky, which we reviewed in Chapter 6, suggest that children derive different benefits from interacting with same-age as opposed to different-age peers. Piaget (1932/1965) emphasized the importance of experiences with children of equivalent status who challenge the young child's egocentric viewpoint, thereby fostering cognitive, social, and moral growth. In contrast, Vygotsky (1933–1935/1978) believed that children derive unique advantages from interacting with older, more capable peers, who encourage more mature behavior in their younger counterparts.

Research reveals that children accommodate quite differently to the presence of same-age and different-age youngsters. In several studies, preschool and early elementary school children were brought together in laboratories to play or work on problem-solving tasks. Mixed-age conditions evoked more social interaction from younger children, along with special accommodations by older youngsters, who reduced their rate of social communication and assumed more responsibility for task performance than they did with same-age partners (Brody, Graziano, & Musser, 1983; Graziano et al., 1976; Lougee, Grueneich, & Hartup, 1977). Even toddlers display a rudimentary capacity to adjust their social behavior to the age of their partners. In one study, 24-month-olds engaged in longer and more complex social initiations when paired with an 18-month-old than with a same-age playmate. They seemed to try to compensate for the younger child's less skilled social behavior by behaving in ways likely to attract the partner's attention. In response, 18-month-olds were more interactive with older than with same-age peers (Brownell, 1990).

Moreover, children freely imitate behaviors of same-age and older youngsters, but they rarely imitate a younger child (Brody & Stoneman, 1981; Thelen & Kirkland, 1976). Similarly, observations of child-child interaction in classrooms that combine preschool and early school-age children reveal that younger children cross age boundaries more often than older children, who are more likely to initiate to same-age partners. However, for children of both age levels, same-age interaction is more positive, more verbal, and more likely to evoke cooperative play (Day & Hunt, 1975; Lederberg et al., 1986; Roopnarine & Johnson, 1984). Children in mixed-age settings seem to gravitate to same-age companions because play interests are more compatible and social engagement is more reinforcing. Younger children also turn toward older classmates because of their superior knowledge and power and because their play appears especially stimulating and exciting.

By the beginning of elementary school, children are consciously aware of the different social functions of older, younger, and same-age peers. When asked, they indicate that they prefer to establish friendships with agemates; to seek help, comfort, and instruction from older children; and to give help and sympathy to younger ones (French, 1984). Although more needs to be learned about the unique developmental consequences of same-age and mixed-age relationships, children seem to profit cognitively and socially from both types of associations. As we indicated in Chapters 11 and 12, from interacting with coequals, children learn to cooperate and resolve conflicts, and they develop important moral notions of justice and reciprocity. In addition, younger children acquire new competencies from older companions, and when more mature children teach their less mature counterparts, they practice nurturance, guidance, and other prosocial behaviors (Whiting & Edwards, 1988a; Hartup, 1983).

Finally, age is not the only child characteristic that affects peer sociability. Recall from Chapter 13 that children often choose companions of the same sex and that same-sex and mixed-sex peer associates differ substantially in the activities they pursue and their style of interaction. Later on, when we take up the topic of school desegregation, we will see that children also prefer to interact with members of their own racial/ethnic group. However, peer relations do not change in quality when children of different racial/ethnic origins choose to associate with one another (Finkelstein & Haskins, 1983; Lederberg et al., 1986).

Familiarity of Peer Associates. "Familiarity breeds sociability" in the case of peer companions. As children get to know each other better, they interact more frequently, intensely, and competently. Gestures, imitation, and reciprocal exchanges among infants; maturity of play among preschoolers; and verbal interaction and group problem-solving among elementary school children are all enhanced when peers are acquaintances rather than strangers (Becker, 1977; Brody, Graziano, & Musser, 1983; Doyle, Connolly, & Rivest, 1980; Harper & Huie, 1985; Young & Lewis, 1979). Peer familiarity may augment sociability for at least two reasons. First, much like adults, when children get to know each other better, their social behaviors probably achieve a "better fit" as smooth, comfortable interaction replaces the stilted, awkward exchanges of strangers. Second, among infants and young children, well-known peers (much like familiar caregivers) provide a secure base for exploration, thereby promoting vigorous, competent behavior toward social as well as inanimate surroundings (Ipsa, 1981). In line with this idea, one recent study found that children who entered kindergarten classes with a large number of peers whom they had known in nursery school the previous year liked school better and showed fewer anxious symptoms than children who had few familiar companions (Ladd & Price, 1987).

BRIEF REVIEW

Peer sociability begins in infancy as isolated smiles, gestures, and vocalizations evolve into reciprocal social exchanges over the first two years of life. During the preschool years, cooperative social play becomes common, although solitary and parallel play are also frequent. In middle childhood and adolescence, children develop a variety of subtle social skills that increase their effectiveness as peer companions.

Situational factors have a major bearing on the quantity and quality of child-child interaction. Flat, densely populated neighborhoods encourage peer sociability. Liberally equipped play environments; nonspecific toys; small group sizes; and same-age, familiar associates promote positive, highly verbal, cooperative child-child interaction. Cross-age contact provides older children with opportunities to practice important prosocial skills, and it permits younger children to benefit from the expertise of older companions.

Peer Acceptance and Popularity

Although the quantity and complexity of social behavior increase with age for all children, not all youngsters are equally sought after as peer companions. The term popularity refers to likability — the extent to which a child is regarded by others as a worthy social partner. Investigators generally measure it with **sociometric techniques.** These are self-report measures that ask peers in the same classroom to evaluate one another's likability. A variety of sociometric methods have been developed to assess peer opinion. Children may be asked to nominate several peers in their class whom they especially like or dislike; to indicate for all possible pairs of classmates which one they prefer to play with; or to rate each peer on a scale from "like very much" to "like very little" (Asher & Hymel, 1981). Pupils as young as 4 years of age can answer sociometric questions reliably (Hymel, 1983).

Currently, sociometric methods are used to distinguish among four types of social acceptance: (1) **popular children,** who receive many positive votes; (2) **rejected children,** who are actively disliked; (3) **controversial children,** who receive a large number of positive and negative votes; and (4) **neglected children,** who are seldom chosen, either positively or negatively. Together, these four kinds of youngsters comprise about two thirds of pupils in a typical elementary school classroom. The remaining one third are *average* in peer acceptance; they do not receive extreme scores on sociometric measures (Coie, Dodge, & Coppotelli, 1982; Gottman, 1977).

Assessments of peer acceptance remain reasonably stable over childhood and adolescence. At any given year from preschool on, those children who are liked most and liked least tend to retain their status the following year (Bukowski & Newcomb, 1984; Howes, 1988; Ladd & Price, 1987; Rubin & Daniels-Bierness, 1983). Although the stability of sociometric choices declines as the interval between assessments lengthens, even over a 5-year period there is moderate consistency in peer opinion, with the rejected category remaining the most stable over time (Coie & Dodge, 1983). Moreover, by first grade, children have formed a fairly accurate notion of how well liked each of their classmates is, and by third grade they can accurately appraise their own peer reputation (Krantz & Burton, 1986). Popularity is a salient social attribute in children's minds by the early school years.

Peer acceptance is a powerful predictor of current as well as later psychological well-being. Rejected children, especially, are unhappy, alienated, poorly achieving youngsters who have a low sense of self-esteem. Both parents and teachers view them as having a wide range of social and emotional difficulties (Achenbach & Edelbrock, 1981; French & Waas, 1985; Green et al., 1981). Moreover, peer rejection in middle childhood is associated with dropping out of school, delinquency and criminality, and, to a lesser extent, serious psychological difficulties in adolescence and young adulthood (Parker & Asher, 1987). In contrast, neglected children, at one time assumed to be at risk for adjustment problems, are indistinguishable from youngsters of average social status in mental health assessments.

Although peer acceptance predicts a wide variety of later life problems and certainly may contribute to them, it is important to keep in mind that the evidence described above is correlational, and peer relations may not be a major causal factor.

Peer acceptance could be linked to psychological adjustment through other prior influences, such as children's personality characteristics, parental child-rearing practices, or some combination of the two. In fact, the combined results of several recent studies suggest that factors in the home environment — in particular, high life stress and ineffective, power-assertive discipline — increase the probability of behavioral and academic problems in children, which, in turn, promote peer rejection (Dishion, 1990; Hart, Ladd, & Burleson, 1990; Pettit, Dodge, & Brown, 1988; Putallaz, 1987). Clearly, more research is needed to sort out the precise linkages between peer acceptance and the wide variety of additional factors known to be associated with later life adjustment.

Correlates and Causes of Acceptance in the Peer Situation. To better understand how peer acceptance emerges in the context of child-child relations, researchers have correlated a great many child characteristics and social behaviors with sociometric scores. These investigations have led to provocative speculations about what leads some children to be liked and others to be rejected by their classmates, but most cannot tell us for sure what engenders these different reactions. However, in several studies, investigators have successfully made use of the longitudinal research design to isolate causal connections between children's social behavior and peer acceptance. In each case, initially unacquainted children were brought together for repeated sessions in a laboratory, and behaviors that eventually turned them on or off to one another were tracked over time. We will discuss the findings of these groundbreaking investigations shortly. But first, let's look at the significance of some nonbehavioral characteristics for children's popularity — their names and physical appearance.

Names. Do offbeat names like Bertha and Horatio reduce a child's chances of being accepted by peers, and do common ones like Karen and Michael enhance it? McDavid and Harari (1966) asked 10- to 12-year-olds to rate the attractiveness of a large number of first names and then provide sociometric ratings of children in their classrooms. A positive relationship emerged between children's name preferences and the likability of children who bore the names.

It is unlikely that children's attitudes toward classmates simply generalize to their names, since the name preferences of peers who do not know each other also predict popularity. McDavid and Harari believe that children and adults are prone to judge others by their labels. Common, socially desirable names are associated with positive personal qualities, while rare and unusual ones produce negative personal images. However, the connection between names and peer likability may be more complex than this interpretation suggests. Perhaps parents who give their children offbeat names are nonconformists who place little value on peer popularity and raise their children in ways that limit the acquisition of social skills needed for peer acceptance. At present, information that would permit us to choose between these different explanations is not available.

Physical Appearance. In Chapter 5, we indicated that physical attractiveness has an important bearing on peer acceptance. Recall that children who deviate from society's ideal standards of physical beauty are less well accepted by peers. As early as age 4, children have different social expectations of attractive and unattractive agemates. When asked to guess the characteristics of unfamiliar peers from their photographs, preschool and elementary school pupils attributed friendliness, smartness, and niceness to good-looking peers and aggressiveness and other negative social behaviors to physically unattractive youngsters (Adams & Crane, 1980; Langlois & Stephan, 1977). Attractiveness also predicts popularity and behavior ratings among children who know each other well, although these relationships are stronger among girls than boys (Langlois & Styczynski, 1979).

Do children derive their opinions about attractive and unattractive youngsters from the way these children behave or from stereotypes associated with physical appearance? In one study, good-looking children did behave differently from their less handsome counterparts. Langlois and Downs (1979) paired same-age and same-sex 3- and 5-year-olds with one another to form three types of dyads: two attractive children, two unattractive children, and one attractive and one unattractive child. Then the social behaviors of each pair were observed in a laboratory playroom. No behavioral differences based on attractiveness were found among the 3-year-olds, but 5-year-old unattractive children more often aggressed against their partners than attractive youngsters did. These findings indicate that unattractive children actually display some of the negative behaviors attributed to them by their peers. But the fact that behavioral differences did not appear until the end of the preschool years leaves open the possibility that unattractive youngsters responded as they did because of others' prior reactions to their physical appearance.

Parents and teachers hold the same "beauty is best" bias exhibited by peers in their behavioral expectations of children (Adams, 1978). In one study, the stronger the bias held by a mother against unattractive children, the more likely her child was to prefer the handsomer of two agemates as a play partner (Adams & Crane, 1980). When combined with the research summarized above, these results suggest that the physical attractiveness–peer popularity connection is multiply determined. Parents may respond differently to their own children on the basis of physical appearance, and along with the media, they teach children a variety of stereotypes about physical beauty. Over time, the reactions of adults and children may promote different behaviors in attractive and unattractive youngsters. These, in turn, sustain the social preferences of agemates with whom the child comes in contact.

Interpersonal Behavior. Although names and physical appearance are related to popularity, their importance pales in comparison to children's social behavior (Dodge, 1983; Reaves & Roberts, 1983). Popular, rejected, controversial, and neglected youngsters interact with agemates in distinct ways that serve to evoke as well as sustain peer opinion.

Popularity is consistently associated with cooperative, friendly social behavior (Coie, Dodge, & Coppotelli, 1982; Hartup, Glazer, & Charlesworth, 1967; Ladd & Price, 1987). Moreover, well-liked youngsters are especially effective social problem solvers who communicate with peers in a mature and sensitive fashion. When they do not understand another child's reaction, they are likely to ask for an explanation (Gottman, Gonso, & Rasmussen, 1975; Rubin, 1972). If they disagree with a play partner in a game, they go beyond voicing their displeasure; they suggest what the other child could do instead (Putallaz & Gottman, 1981). In addition, popular children gain entry into ongoing play groups by adapting their behavior to the flow of peer activity, offering relevant comments about the game instead of hovering around the outskirts of the group (as neglected children often do) or barging in and disrupting the ongoing activity (approaches that are typical of rejected youngsters) (Black & Hazen, 1990; Dodge et al., 1983; Hazen & Black, 1989; Putallaz, 1983). In view of these findings, it is not surprising that popular children are judged by classmates as especially willing and helpful companions who possess leadership qualities (Carlson, Lahey, & Neeper, 1984).

Rejected social status is associated with a wide range of negative social behaviors — high rates of conflict, aggression, hyperactive-distractible behavior, and immature forms of play (Carlson, Lahey, & Neeper, 1984; Coie, Dodge, & Coppotelli, 1982; Dodge, Coie, & Brakke, 1982; Ladd & Price, 1987; Shantz, 1986). Peer-rejected children also show deficits in a number of social-cognitive skills that we discussed in Chapter 11. For example, they are more likely than other children to misinterpret ambiguous acts of peers as hostile (Waas, 1988), and they generate few prosocial solutions to hypothetical social problems (Rubin & Daniels-Bierness, 1983). These social-cognitive deficits contribute to rejected children's inept and hostile style of relating to agemates.

Controversial children display a blend of positive and negative social behaviors that is consistent with the mixed peer opinion they engender. Like rejected youngsters, they are active and disruptive, yet they also engage in high rates of positive, prosocial acts. As a result, they are salient individuals to their classmates and, much like popular children, are regarded as leaders (Coie, Dodge, & Coppotelli, 1982; Milich & Landau, 1984). As yet, controversial children are an understudied group. We do not know whether their antisocial tendencies eventually lead to adjustment problems or whether their positive social skills reduce the chances that they will experience long-term developmental difficulties.

Neglected children fall at the opposite extreme of controversial children, engaging in low rates of peer interaction of all kinds. These youngsters often choose to play alone; classmates regard them as shy children who seldom call attention to themselves (Carlson, Lahey, & Neeper, 1984; Dodge, Coie, & Brakke, 1982; Gottman, 1977). Nevertheless, neglected children are not less socially skilled than their average counterparts. Instead, these are the youngsters we discussed earlier who have a repertoire of effective social behaviors but are simply content to pursue their solitary interests. Despite their low rates of social interaction, they do not report feeling especially lonely (Asher & Wheeler, 1985). However, it is still possible that some neglected children — those who are extremely withdrawn — are at risk for psychological problems. In fact, recent research suggests that very withdrawn children who deliberately avoid peers and display inappropriate behavior in their presence eventually become rejected, rather than neglected, at older ages (French, 1988; Howes, 1988; Hymel & Rubin, 1985; Rubin, LeMare, & Lollis, 1990).

The findings summarized above are based on correlational studies of already acquainted agemates. As mentioned earlier, they do not tell us for sure whether social behavior is actually responsible for variations in peer acceptance. However, by making creative use of the longitudinal research design, several investigators have established that behavioral styles *do* play a causal role in peer opinion. Dodge (1983) brought groups of unacquainted second-grade boys together for a series of play sessions in a laboratory and looked at how their interaction patterns predicted sociometric assessments at the end of the study. Much like the constellations of findings reported above, boys who came to be popular engaged in friendly conversation and cooperative play; those who became rejected engaged in high frequencies of antisocial acts; while those who developed a controversial status displayed both prosocial and antisocial behaviors. Neglected boys showed some inappropriate social responses, but they were noticeably low in aggressive behavior. In a similar study, Coie & Kupersmidt (1983) reported much the same findings, except for the fact that many youngsters who were neglected by familiar classmates showed highly competent social behavior when brought together with unfamiliar agemates in a laboratory. Under these conditions, they broke away from their usual pattern of playing by themselves and became more sociable. The fact that neglected children can behave in a positive, socially outgoing manner when they enter new situations may be one reason that, as a group, they do not experience adjustment difficulties.

Helping Unpopular Children. A variety of intervention programs aimed at helping unpopular children achieve more satisfactory peer relations have been developed. Most are based on social learning theory principles and include coaching, modeling, and reinforcement of positive social skills, such as how to initiate peer interaction, cooperate in play, and respond to another child with friendly emotion and approval. Several of these efforts have produced impressive gains in social competence and peer acceptance that last from several weeks to a year after the treatment (Bierman, 1986; Ladd, 1981; Mize & Ladd, 1990; Oden & Asher, 1977).

Despite the success of some interventions, others have shown mixed or negative outcomes, and a great deal remains to be learned about how to help children who are not accepted by their peers. In many studies, rejected and neglected pupils have been combined into a global category of unpopular children and then subjected to the same treatment. Yet we have already seen that the majority of neglected children are socially competent and not in need of intervention (Asher, Markell, & Hymel, 1981). Only a few programs have targeted rejected children, who are most in need of help. In one that did, intensive academic tutoring proved to be more effective in increasing social acceptance than coaching in social skills (Coie & Krehbiel, 1984). These findings suggest that satisfactory school achievement may be a vital indirect link to successful social relations in the classroom.

Because many rejected children display high levels of aggressive and disruptive behavior, techniques designed to reduce these antisocial acts may need to be combined with coaching in social skills and academic remediation (Coie & Koeppl, 1990; Krehbiel & Milich, 1986). In one study, including verbal prohibitions against antisocial behaviors and negative consequences for engaging in them in a coaching program led to better social acceptance among rejected elementary school boys than a program that focused only on teaching positive social skills (Bierman, Miller, & Stabb, 1987).

Finally, some investigators recommend combining instruction in social skills with social-cognitive interventions, such as training in perspective-taking and modifying expectancies for social success (Ladd & Mize, 1983). Recently, Rabiner and Coie (1989) prompted rejected children (who, after many rebuffs, become pessimistic about their ability to be liked by peers) to anticipate social success before joining a group of unfamiliar agemates. Children who received the induction were better liked, and girls actually behaved more competently. These findings suggest that rejected youngsters can make better use of the positive social skills they do have when they believe peers will accept them.

BRIEF REVIEW

Peer acceptance is a powerful predictor of current and future psychological well-being. Rejected children, especially, display serious academic and behavior problems and are at risk for lasting adjustment difficulties. Children's styles of relating to agemates are a major determinant of peer opinion. Popular children interact positively, rejected children behave ineptly and antisocially, and controversial children display a mixture of these behaviors. Although neglected youngsters engage in low rates of peer interaction, most are socially competent, well-adjusted children who enjoy solitary endeavors. Interventions that coach children in effective social skills are commonly used to treat youngsters with poor peer acceptance.

Peer Groups

In the sections above, our major focus has been on developmental changes and individual differences in dyadic peer interaction. Beginning in the preschool years, collectives of three to a dozen or more children assemble on a regular basis in the neighborhood or school yard. Younger children, when gathered together in this fashion, "behave simply as a number of independent persons, each mainly concerned with his own immediate ends." By middle childhood, an important change occurs. Aggregates of older youngsters give the impression of greater interdependence — "more developed and reciprocal social relationships, with a settled organization" (Isaacs, 1933, p. 213). When peer participants feel a strong desire to belong to a social unit, generate shared rules or norms of conduct beyond those maintained by society at large, and develop a hierarchical social structure of roles and relationships that govern their interaction, a **peer group** is formed (Hartup, 1983).

In Chapter 11, we showed that close, one-to-one friendships in middle childhood and adolescence contribute uniquely to the development of interpersonal trust and sensitivity. During the same period, experiences in multimember social groups also provide a unique context for social learning. The group teaches children how to engage in cooperative activity aimed at collective rather than individual goals. In addition, through group membership, children experience social structures firsthand, practice the skills associated with leadership and followership, master control of hostile impulses toward fellow members, and learn to mobilize aggression in the service of group loyalty by directing it toward "outsiders" (Fine, 1980).

A classic study by Sherif and his colleagues (1961) called the *Robbers Cave experiment* illustrates how peer groups form, their essential features, and the functions they serve in the social life of the child.

Peer Group Formation. Fifth-grade boys selected on the basis of being well-adjusted in school and in peer group relations were brought to a summer campground known as Robbers Cave, divided into two clusters of 11 members each, and removed to separate campsites. Friendships developed as the boys in each collective mingled with one another. However, a strong, cohesive group structure did not emerge until the camp staff arranged circumstances that required cooperation and interdependent activity. Backpacking excursions into the woods and opportunities to improve swimming and athletic areas led the campers to create a division of labor. Soon, several individuals with superior skills took on greater status—one boy for his cooking, another for his athletic prowess, and a third for his entertaining personality and ability to "horse around." Over time, shifting patterns of leaders and followers from one activity to the next began to stabilize. One boy in each group ranked highest, followed by several other prestigious associates, while a few members sifted toward the bottom of the emerging hierarchy.

As group structures coalesced, the boys at each campsite developed distinct notions of appropriate behavior and ways of doing things. For example, one group generated a "norm of toughness" adhered to so strongly that members suppressed any signs of hurt when injured and refused treatment for cuts and scratches. In the other group, a very different "norm of good behavior" emerged. In contrast to the swearing and rowdiness of the "tough" group, these boys used "clean" language and were polite and considerate. At each campsite, group members coined nicknames for one another, and special jargon, jokes, and ways of performing tasks developed. Eventually, the groups took names for themselves—the Rattlers and the Eagles. Boys in both groups displayed considerable pride in their collective accomplishments and a strong group identity.

The next phase of Sherif's study showed that group norms and social structures evolve further, on the basis of the group's relationship with "outsiders." The camp counselors arranged for the Rattlers and Eagles to "discover" one another, and a tournament of competitive activities was initiated. Although the games began in an atmosphere of good sportsmanship, these conditions quickly deteriorated. The consequences of losing for the solidarity of each group were striking. Members became angry and vindictive, blaming each other for defeat, and disintegration of established group structures ensued. The leader of the Eagles was deposed when he proved reluctant to confront the hostilities of the out-group. Among the Rattlers, a large bully whose aggressiveness had been squelched during the early period of group formation emerged as a hero. Revised group structures and new normative behaviors based on intergroup rivalry started to develop. Members devoted themselves to hurling animosities and retaliating against the out-group, with each successful attack increasing intragroup solidarity. Over time, both the Rattlers and the Eagles showed a strong tendency to stereotype each other as nasty and sneaky, reactions that further magnified the social distance between the groups.

In the final phase of Sherif's study, the camp staff faced the challenging task of how to bring the two groups into harmonious interaction. Joint recreational activities, such as a trip to the movies and Fourth of July fireworks, were tried, but these were disasters. Far from reducing conflict, they provided opportunities for each group to renew its berating of the other. But once the staff arranged activities with *superordinate goals* that each group desired but that neither could achieve without the cooperation of the other, intergroup hostility began to subside. In one instance, the camp water supply "broke down," and in another, a truck preparing to get food for the hungry campers "stalled"—circumstances that required interdependent action among all the boys to solve a common problem. After a series of these experiences, negative stereotyping of the out-group diminished, and new friendship choices emerged that cut across group lines.

The Robbers Cave study reveals that peer groups form when individuals perceive that others share common goals. Norms and social structures gradually emerge in the service of shared motivations. As goals change, these basic determinants of group cohesion are modified as well. Group functioning is affected by situational factors external to the group. Although differences in ethnicity and skin color are known to promote prejudice and negative stereotyping, Sherif's study reveals that hatred by an in-group of an out-group can be generated without them. Competition for scarce but highly desired resources is sufficient to produce deep-seated intergroup animosities. Activities with superordinate goals that one group cannot reach without the help of the other gradually reduce intergroup hostilities and foster positive feelings and attitudes.

In the following sections, we take a closer look at two processes that Sherif's study showed to be essential for peer group cohesion: the emergence of group norms and group social structures.

Group Norms. Group norms are responsible for the existence of "peer cultures" —unique systems of knowledge, beliefs, and customs that bind group members together, creating a sense of joint commitment and solidarity. In earlier chapters, we indicated that societal norms, such as sex-role stereotypes and moral standards, begin to affect child-child interaction as early as the preschool years. But these norms are derived from adults. Self-generated norms in the peer group, such as a specialized language, unique codes of dress, musical preferences, and a place to "hang out" during leisure hours—are not evident until late childhood and adolescence. Once they do appear, different peer groups generate quite distinct normative prescriptions. Hartup (1983) describes the array of peer group norms that emerged in one Minnesota high school:

> *Sporties* . . . are adolescents of both sexes who engage in sports, who attend sports activities, and who drink beer. *Workers* are students who have jobs, who are motivated to accumulate money, who own cars, and whose social lives revolve mostly around the automobile. *Crispies* are students who use drugs on other than a one-time basis, who are the best football players, and who do not work very hard at school. *Musicians* are students who spend much time in the music room, who attend or assist with performance activities of one type or another, and who drink alcoholic beverages. *Debaters* are those who read a lot, get good grades, participate in clubs focused on intellectual activities and who drink Pepsi-Cola at their parties. (p. 146)

What governs the assortment of peers into separate groups with unique normative standards? Recent longitudinal studies in which adolescent values and peer associates have been tracked over time show that selection of group companions and the norms generated by them are a blend of family and peer group influences (Britt & Campbell, 1977; Chassin et al., 1986; Downs, 1985). In other words, when young people join a group, they select associates who are likely to create norms compatible with their current values. Then the new norms generated modify group members' original beliefs and behaviors. A study by Chassin and her co-workers (1986) illustrates this process. Nearly 4,000 sixth through eleventh graders were surveyed about their own smoking behavior and that of their parents and peers. The same questions were asked again one year later. Adolescents who took up smoking on a regular basis during the year of the study, when compared to their nonsmoking counterparts, were more likely to have both parents and peer associates who smoked. You may recall from our discussion of identity development in Chapter 11 that contrary to popular belief, adolescence is not a period in which a radical break with parental values occurs. Chassin's findings support this conclusion; many norms generated by the peer group are an extension of those acquired at home.

Nevertheless, the onset of peer group ties during preadolescence coincides with a period in which some of the "nicest children begin to behave in the most awful way" (Redl, 1966, p. 395). Prank-playing, such as egging a house, making a funny phone call, or ringing a door bell and running away, is usually performed with agemates, who provide temporary social support for breaking the normative traditions of society. Interviewing a sample of 48 middle-class 12-year-old boys, Fine (1980) reported that 70 percent had participated in such activities at one time or another. At school, peer groups may become status conscious with respect to other rival groups with whom they jockey for power, influence, and visibility. These conditions intensify the exclusive, condescending behavior of some cliques toward outsiders (Savin-Williams, 1980b).

◆ CONTEMPORARY ISSUES: SOCIAL POLICY ◆

Adolescent Substance Abuse

Box 15.1

Drug and alcohol experimentation among American youth is pervasive, with the United States ranking first among industrialized nations (Newcomb & Bentler, 1989). Recent surveys of junior high and high school students reveal that by 13 to 14 years of age, 45 percent have already tried smoking, 56 percent drinking, and 30 percent at least one illicit drug (usually marijuana). By the end of the high school years, 20 percent are regular cigarette users, 37 percent have succumbed to heavy drinking on at least one occasion, and over 57 percent have tried illicit drugs. Of these, one third report experimenting with at least one highly addictive and toxic substance, such as amphetamines, cocaine, phencyclidine (PCP), or heroin (National Institute on Drug Abuse, 1987).

The prevalence of drug use by American young people is partly a function of growing up in a drug-dependent society. Many adults use caffeine to wake up in the morning, cigarettes to cope with daily hassles, alcohol to calm down in the evening, and other remedies to alleviate stress, headaches, depression, and physical illness. Consequently, for most adolescents, drug experimentation is a manifestation of their intense curiosity about "adultlike" behaviors in general; interest subsides after minimal involvement. But a growing minority are making the transition from drug use to *abuse*—engaging in regular consumption, requiring increasing amounts to achieve the same effect, and finding themselves unable to stop using the drug (Newcomb & Bentler, 1989; Rahdert, 1988). Five percent of high school seniors are daily drinkers, and almost as many indicate that they took an illicit drug on a daily basis over the past month (Cólon & Cólon, 1989; National Institute on Drug Abuse, 1987; Rahdert, 1988).

Adolescent substance abuse is associated with a wide variety of risk factors and additional problem behaviors. Peer influences, including modeling, encouragement, and access to drugs, are the most consistent predictors of serious involvement, but they do not occur in isolation. Other predisposing factors include low socioeconomic status, family mental health problems, parental drug use, poor school performance, and such psychological variables as low self-esteem, anxiety, depression, a high need for excitement, and attraction to deviant behaviors. Moreover, as shown in the adjacent figure, the more of these risk factors experienced by adolescents, the greater the incidence of heavy drug use (Newcomb, Maddahian, & Bentler, 1986).

Longitudinal research reveals that drug addiction during the teenage years can affect many areas of life because it interferes with successful accomplishment of adolescent developmental tasks. When adolescents use drugs to deal with daily stresses, they fail to learn responsible decision-making skills and alternative coping techniques—crucial lessons during this time of transition to adulthood. Affected young people enter into marriage, family, and work force responsibilities prematurely and fail at them readily, displaying high rates of divorce and job instability (Newcomb & Bentler, 1988).

Although a wide variety of treatment programs for drug-abusing adolescents are available, relapse rates are high, ranging from 35 to 70 percent. As yet, little is known about effective treatment approaches, and adolescent substance abuse is an area in which research is urgently needed to guide the development of successful interventions (Newcomb & Bentler, 1989).

Pranks and petty antagonisms are mild forms of antisocial behavior when compared to the delinquent acts perpetrated by a small number of juvenile gangs. Do children and adolescents learn behaviors and attitudes conducive to delinquency within the peer group? At present, investigators continue to debate the question of whether most delinquents are highly social individuals with strong bonds to agemates who share their antisocial norms or are social misfits who fail to establish effective peer relations. Currently, evidence in favor of both these positions exists. The home lives of most delinquent youths are characterized by stress, disorganization, and poverty, leading them to be poorly equipped to succeed in the mainstream world of peers and school. Gradually, these youngsters come to view conventional routes to achievement and self-esteem as unreachable, and these goals are replaced by their very opposite — antisocial and destructive behavior — through which the adolescent gains acceptance in the eyes of like-minded peers (Campbell, 1980). As Box 15.1 indicates, adolescent substance abuse, a serious problem in the United States, is associated with precisely this constellation of risk factors.

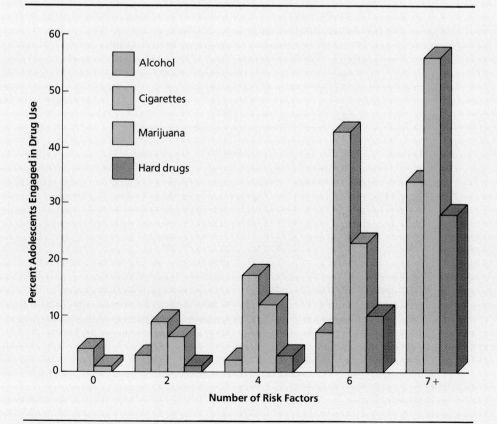

Relationship of number of risk factors experienced by adolescents and heavy drug use. As risk factors rise, heavy use increases, and adolescents shift from licit (alcohol and cigarettes) to illicit substances (marijuana and hard drugs). *(Adapted from Newcomb, Maddahian, & Bentler, 1986.)*

For most youngsters, peer cultures do not constitute a strongly antisocial force. Instead, they promote important dimensions of personal development during the adolescent years. The unique normative structure of the peer group fosters security, belongingness, and opportunities to experiment with new commitments in a supportive social context. In fact, the intensification of peer group loyalties during early adolescence can be viewed as one means by which young people establish a temporary, interim sense of identity as they separate from the family and begin to build a personally meaningful identity of their own (Erikson, 1950).

Group Social Structures. In all groups, members differ in power or status, an arrangement that facilitates division of responsibility and smooth coordination among group participants. Some children become leaders who direct the group's activities; others end up as followers who cooperate with leader-set objectives. Group norms and group social structures are interdependent. Leaders are usually the major norm-setters, and high-status children's ideas are often sufficient to alter the group's opinion (Fine, 1980). On what basis do status hierarchies emerge in children's groups?

Research by ethologists demonstrates that group social structures are sometimes based on toughness and assertiveness. A **dominance hierarchy** is a stable ordering of individuals that predicts who will win under conditions of conflict between group members. Dominance hierarchies exist in the social organization of many animal species, and they are a basic feature of human group cohesion as well. Observations of physical attacks, threats, and struggles over objects between children reveal a consistent lineup of winners and losers as early as the preschool years. This hierarchy becomes increasingly stable during middle childhood and adolescence, especially for boys (Savin-Williams, 1979; Strayer & Strayer, 1976).

Dominance hierarchies among humans, like those among other primates, serve the adaptive function of limiting aggression between group members. Once dominance relations are clearly established, intragroup hostility rarely occurs. When it does, it is very restrained, often taking the form of verbal insults delivered in a playful manner that can be accepted with equanimity by the target (Fine, 1980; Savin-Williams, 1980a). The gradual substitution of friendly insults for more direct hostility between group members may be functional in helping youngsters learn how to control their aggressive impulses.

Think back to the findings of the Robbers Cave study once more, and you will see that group structures are not always a matter of the largest and strongest children rising to the top. When the goals of the group involve the conquest of "outsiders," then a group organization based on dominance is likely to emerge, as it did when the Rattlers and Eagles confronted one another in competitive games. Under other conditions, many personal qualities may become relevant. During adolescence, group structures become less dependent on physical size and strength and more dependent on characteristics that support a group's current normative activities, such as knowing what to do on a camp-out, being a skilled athlete, or behaving in a friendly and sociable manner (Savin-Williams, 1980a). Effective group leaders are not always tough and coercive. Rather, individuals who possess a combination of attributes that best facilitate the group's current objectives are likely to rise to the top of the status hierarchy. Since groups vary in their normative orientations, social power often accrues to different children in different social situations (Hartup, 1983).

Peer Relations and the Socialization of the Child

We have seen that peer interaction contributes in important ways to the acquisition of a wide variety of skills that help children adapt successfully to their social world. In the sections below, we consider the precise mechanisms by which peers socialize one another. Peers use some of the same techniques that parents do to influence each other's behavior. Reinforcement, modeling, and direct pressures to conform to peer expectations[2] are among the mechanisms that have been studied.

Peer Reinforcement and Modeling. Children's social responses to one another operate as reinforcers, modifying the extent to which they display certain behaviors. Peer reinforcement increases over the course of childhood, and children often employ this socialization mechanism to positive ends. Preschoolers value the positive, prosocial behaviors of their peer associates. Children who engage in attentive, approving, and affectionate social acts are likely to be the recipients of similar behaviors in return (Charlesworth & Hartup, 1967; Leiter, 1977).

However, children are just as receptive to peer reinforcement for aggressive, antisocial responses as they are for prosocial behavior. A well-known study by Patterson, Littman, and Bricker (1967) shows how peer reactions to aggressive initiations modify the future occurrence of aggressive behavior among preschoolers. The investigators recorded instances in which a child insulted, hit, kicked, or grabbed a toy from a classmate, the reaction of the target child, and the subsequent behavior of the attacker. When the target cried, did nothing, or withdrew, the initiator was more likely to perform the same aggressive act in the future. In other words, these responses served as positive reinforcers for aggressive behavior. In contrast, successful retaliations by the target—for example, hitting back or hanging on to the desired toy—served as punishments. Under these conditions, the aggressor either moved on to a new victim or tried a new form of assertive behavior.

If you study these contingencies carefully, you will see that they quickly lead to conditions in which the least aggressive children in a classroom are victimized the most. But after many instances of being the target of others' aggression, even a very passive child is likely to retaliate, a response that is reinforced when the attacker retreats. A striking finding of this study was a steady increase in aggressive behavior on the part of initially nonaggressive youngsters who counterattacked after being victimized. Peer feedback is an important means through which children's aggression is enhanced as well as controlled, and even mild-mannered children can learn to behave aggressively if they are frequently the targets of hostile attacks.

Besides dispensing social reinforcement, peers provide each other with models of a wide variety of social behaviors. Peer imitation is a common occurrence from infancy through the preschool years, but by middle childhood, imitation of both peer and adult models declines (Grusec & Abramovitch, 1982). As we indicated in Chapter 12, once children grasp and internalize the rules of social life, there is less need to rely on observations of others for information about how to behave. Although peers will copy each other's negative behaviors, children who have been guided by adults toward socially acceptable standards of conduct are able to resist these influences, and they provide effective models of prosocial behavior for other youngsters (Toner, Parke, & Yussen, 1978).

The powerful effects of peer reinforcement and modeling have led child development specialists to experiment with peers as behavior change agents in remediating a wide variety of problematic behaviors in children. Socially adept children can be taught to encourage socially competent acts in less skilled youngsters, and both trainers and targets show gains in social maturity as a result (Strain, 1977). Peers can also serve as effective tutors for less knowledgeable children at school, teaching, modeling, and reinforcing academic skills. Carefully planned peer tutoring programs in which tutors are trained and supervised by adult teachers have been found to

[2] You may recall from our discussion of sex-role development in Chapter 13 that peer reinforcement and modeling in early childhood and conformity in early adolescence are important mechanisms through which children acquire sex-typed behaviors. Turn back to page 530 and page 536 to review this evidence.

promote self-esteem and academic progress in both tutor and tutee (Bargh & Schul, 1980; Devin-Sheehan, Feldman, & Allen, 1976).

Peer Conformity. The adolescent period is noted for a special mechanism of peer socialization—conformity, or acting in concert with the pressures of a particular social group. We have already seen in our discussion of group norms that parental influences are not relinquished during the teenage years. Nevertheless, it is widely believed that adolescence is a period in which young people slavishly ''follow the crowd.'' Many parents are concerned that when conflicts between parent and peer values do arise, young people will turn toward their peers.

In actuality, peer conformity is a complex process that fluctuates with the adolescent's age and need for social approval and the situation (Hartup, 1983). Several studies report a rise in peer conformity between 11 and 14 years of age, especially in the area of peer-sponsored misconduct, that diminishes during the late adolescent years (Berndt, 1979; Bixenstine, DeCorte, & Bixenstine, 1976; Devereux, 1970). You may recall from our discussion of self-esteem in Chapter 11 that early adolescence is a period during which young people are especially concerned about what their age-mates think of them. However, compared to other spheres of influence, peer pressures toward antisocial behavior are not strong.

In a recent study, Brown, Lohr, and McClenahan (1986) asked nearly 400 junior and senior high school students how much pressure they felt from peers to engage in various behaviors. In addition, they were questioned about their adoption of peer values—how important they thought it was to engage in the behaviors and the frequency with which they actually performed them. As shown in Figure 15.1, adolescents perceived greatest pressure to conform to the most visible aspects of the peer culture—dressing and grooming like everyone else and engaging in peer-condoned social activities (having a boyfriend or girlfriend and going to parties, school functions, or the local teenage hangout). Furthermore, they reported that peer pressure to engage in pro-adult behavior (achieving good grades, getting along with parents) was also strong. Although peer pressure toward misconduct rose in early adolescence, compared to all other areas it was low, and a substantial number of respondents indicated that peers actively discouraged these activities. Moreover, peer pressures were only moderately related to adolescent values and behavior. These young people did not blindly follow the dictates of their peers.

Figure 15.1. Grade differences in perceived peer pressure for four areas of behavior in the Brown, Lohr, and McClenahan (1986) study. *(From B. B. Brown, M. J. Lohr, and E. L. McClenahan, 1986, "Early Adolescents' Perceptions of Peer Pressure," Journal of Early Adolescence, 6, 147. Reprinted by permission.)*

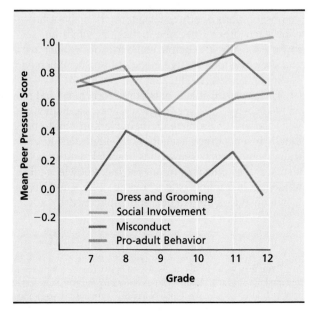

In instances in which parent and peer pressures are in opposition, adolescents do not always lean toward peers as a means of rebelling against the family. Instead, parents and peers are likely to differ in their spheres of greatest influence. Parents usually exceed peers in the areas of educational aspirations and job expectations (Kandel & Lesser, 1972), whereas peers exceed parents in matters of grooming, preferred music, and choice of friends. With respect to less desirable behaviors—smoking, alcohol use, delinquency, and early sexual activity—we have already seen that what an adolescent does is a joint product of parental and peer influences. Moreover, personal characteristics make a difference. Adolescents who view themselves as competent, worthwhile individuals are less likely to feel a need to fall in line with their peers (Landsbaum & Willis, 1971). Finally, you may recall from Chapter 14 that an effective deterrent to participation in peer antisocial behavior is authoritative child rearing, a warm but demanding parent-child relationship that fosters high self-esteem and social and moral maturity.

BRIEF REVIEW

In the sections above, we considered the formation of peer groups—contexts in which older children and adolescents learn to engage in joint activity in the service of common goals. The unique norms generated by peer groups foster a sense of group cohesion and permit adolescents to experiment with new commitments in a supportive social context. Group social structures facilitate a division of labor and offer practice in leader and follower roles.

Our discussion of peer relations concluded with a consideration of the mechanisms by which peers socialize one another. The powerful effects of peer reinforcement and modeling have inspired investigators to experiment with interventions in which peers promote social and academic competence in one another. Pressures toward peer conformity become stronger during early adolescence, but for most youngsters they do not supplant the impact of parental values.

MEDIA

Television

Television is pervasive in American society and in many other countries of the Western world. Ninety-eight percent of American homes have at least one television set, over 50 percent have two or more, and a TV set is switched on in a typical household for a total of 7.1 hours per day. Television's popularity is nearly universal, but for some, the set conjures up images of passive, vegetating individuals mesmerized by a "plug-in drug" that diverts them from other worthwhile pursuits and teaches antisocial lessons, stereotyped social attitudes, and materialistic values. In fact, there is good reason to be concerned about the effects of television on children and youth. In an unusual investigation, residents of a small Canadian town were studied just before TV reception became available in their community and then two years later. Grade school children showed a decline in reading fluency and creative thinking, a rise in sex-stereotyped attitudes, and increases in verbal and physical aggression during spontaneous play. Moreover, the advent of television was associated with a marked drop in community participation by adolescents and adults (Williams, 1986).

Disturbing findings like these have surfaced in hundreds of studies conducted over the last four decades. But the negative consequences of television are not an inherent part of the medium itself. Instead, they result from the way it is used in our society (Greenfield, 1984). As our discussion proceeds, you will see that television has as much potential for good as it does for ill. If the content of TV programming were substantially changed and adults capitalized on it to enhance children's interest and participation in their physical and social surroundings, television could serve as a powerful, cost-effective means of strengthening the intellectual and social development of millions of American youngsters.

How Much Television Do Children View? The amount of time American children spend in front of TV is extraordinary. The average child between 2 and 18 years of age watches over 3 hours a day, clocking in a total of 25 hours in a single week (Nielsen Television Services, 1985). Considering the time the set is on during weekends, school holidays, and summer vacations, children spend more time watching television than they do in any other waking activity, including going to school, interacting with family members, and getting together with peers. Even babies are surprisingly committed viewers. In one study in which the activities of a small sample of toddlers were tracked at home, the average time spent attending to the set was 1.1 hours per day, a very long time in the life of an 18-month-old (Nelson, 1973).

Individual differences exist in television viewing; some children gravitate to the set much more than others. As shown in Figure 15.2, age makes a difference. Viewing time rises steadily over the preschool years, shows a slight dip around the time of school entry, and then increases steadily into early adolescence, at which point it levels off and declines slightly. Boys watch slightly more TV than girls from the preschool years on (Huston et al., 1990; Nielsen Television Services, 1985). But at all ages, children who have lower IQs, who come from low-income family backgrounds, and who are members of America's poor minorities tend to watch the most (Huston, Watkins, & Kunkel, 1989; Liebert & Sprafkin, 1988). Excessive TV viewing is often associated with other problems, such as family and peer difficulties and less trusting perceptions of other people (Liebert, 1986; Singer, Singer, & Rapaczynski, 1984).

The Development of "Television Literacy." The young child, confronted with the television medium for the first time, faces a formidable problem in making sense of its complexity. The television stimulus presents a rapid stream of people, objects, places, words, and sounds. Only gradually do children learn to interpret this flow of perceptual events in a coherent, undistorted fashion.

Television, or film, has its own specialized symbolic code of conveying information. Investigators liken the task of cracking this code to that of learning to read and therefore refer to it as **television literacy** (Anderson & Smith, 1984; Greenfield,

The average American child spends more time watching television than in any other waking activity, including going to school, interacting with family members, and getting together with peers.

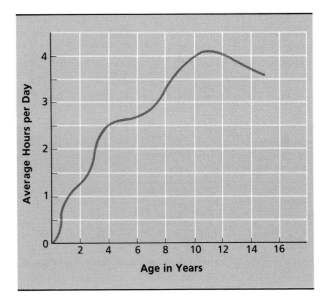

Figure 15.2. Estimated average hours of television viewing by age, based on research conducted over the past 20 years. *(Reprinted with permission from R. M. Liebert and J. Sprafkin,* The Early Window: Effects of Television on Children and Youth *(3rd ed.), 1988, Pergamon Books Ltd. P. 5.)*

1984). The symbolic learning required to understand television is not as great as that demanded by reading, but it is still considerable. Television literacy has two basic parts. The first involves making sense of the *form* of the message. Children must master the meaning of a wide variety of visual and auditory effects, such as camera zooms, panoramic views, scene switches, fadeouts, split screens, instant replays, and sound effects. Second, children must process the *content* of the message, deriving an accurate story line by integrating scenes, character behavior, and dialogue into a meaningful whole. These two parts are really interdependent because television form provides essential cues for interpreting a program's meaning. For example, young children will come to the wrong conclusion about television content if they do not understand that a scene switch from the exterior of a house to a family dinner means that the family is in that house or that an instant replay is a repeated rendition of a single event, not two identical events occurring in succession.

Throughout early and middle childhood, children are captivated by television's most salient perceptual features, such as quickly paced character movement, special effects not seen in the real world, loud music, sound effects, nonhuman speech, and children's voices. At other times, they look away, play with toys, or talk to others in the same room (Rice, Huston, & Wright, 1982; Wright et al., 1984). While involved in other activities, preschoolers quickly learn to follow the TV sound track. They turn back to the set when they hear cartoon character and puppet voices and certain words such as "Big Bird" and "cookie" — features that signal that the content is likely to be child-oriented and related to their own experience (Alwitt et al., 1980).

These findings indicate that young children are selective and strategic processors of televised information, but how much do they really understand when they watch a television show? Not a great deal, according to current research. Before age 8, children have difficulty integrating separate scenes into a continuous story line. Instead, they treat each scene as an isolated incident (Collins et al., 1978). Because they do so, children have difficulty relating a TV character's behavior to its prior motives and eventual consequences (Collins, 1973; Collins, Berndt, & Hess, 1974). Other TV forms are confusing as well, such as fades that signal the passage of time and instant replays, which preschoolers take as repeated events (Anderson & Smith, 1984; Rice, Huston, & Wright, 1986). In addition, young children have difficulty distinguishing between true-to-life and fantasized televised material. They assume that the medium reflects their world unless extraordinary violations of physical reality occur, such as Superman shooting across the sky (Kelly, 1981). Moreover, most 5- to 7-year-olds, who have little knowledge of the mechanics of television, think that TV puppets and cartoon figures are alive and real rather than make-believe characters (Quarfoth, 1979).

Cognitive development, growth in the child's general storehouse of information, and specific experience with the TV medium itself are responsible for gradual improvement in television literacy during middle childhood and adolescence (Greenfield, 1984; Salomon, 1979). Understanding of cinematic forms and memory for information important to plot comprehension increase dramatically from grade school into high school. Older children also go beyond concrete televised data to make inferences about implicit content (Collins, 1983; Newcomb & Collins, 1979). For example, fifth to eighth graders recognize that a character who seems like a "good guy" at first but who unexpectedly behaves callously and aggressively toward others is really a double-dealing "bad guy" in the end. In this kind of episode, younger children have a harder time reconciling their initial positive expectations with the character's eventual bad behavior, and they end up evaluating the character and his actions much more positively (Collins, 1983).

The research summarized above indicates that preschool and early school-age children misunderstand a great deal of televised material. Piecemeal assimilation, realistic appraisal, and inability to evaluate televised content are factors that increase young children's willingness to indiscriminately mimic what they see on the screen. For example, televised violence that seems real and justified is more likely to be imitated than violence that a child can associate with negative consequences to the aggressor (Hearold, 1986).

Steps can be taken to improve children's television literacy. One way is through special programming adjusted to children's cognitive capacities. When the rapid pace of televised material is reduced, young children recall its content far more accurately (Wright et al., 1984). When the events displayed are familiar, preschoolers grasp the implications of many more cinematic forms (Anderson & Smith, 1984). But children spend long hours watching adult-oriented entertainment that is not suited for young viewers. In these instances, parents can limit children's TV consumption, and when children do watch, parents can help them understand what they see. When adults make comments about how scenes in a show fit together, children comprehend the meaning of a program much better than they otherwise would (Watkins et al., 1980). Also, when adult co-viewers express disapproval of on-screen behavior, raise questions about the realism of a portrayal, and encourage children to talk about televised events that are troubling to them, they teach children to evaluate TV content rather than absorb it uncritically (Collins, 1983). Through efforts like these, it is possible to counteract the adverse effects of television viewing on children's development that we take up in the following sections.

Television and Social Learning. Since the 1950s, scientists and public citizens have been concerned about the social attitudes and behaviors that TV cultivates in child and adolescent viewers. The largest number of studies focus on the implications of high levels of TV violence for the development of antisocial conduct, but research exists on television's power to teach undesirable sex-role and racial/ethnic attitudes as well. In addition, a growing body of evidence illustrates television's as yet untapped potential to contribute to children's positive, prosocial behavior.

Aggression. Most American television—in fact, 82 percent of all programs broadcast—contain at least some violence, with particularly high levels appearing in material specifically designed for children. Cartoons contain more acts of aggression than any other type of programming—21 violent acts per hour, a rate over four times greater than that of prime-time adult-oriented and family programming (Gerbner et al., 1986).

Many reviewers of a now massive research literature have concluded that TV violence increases aggressive behavior in children and adolescents (Dorr & Kovaric, 1980; Friedrich-Cofer & Huston, 1986; Hearold, 1986; Liebert & Sprafkin, 1988; Parke & Slaby, 1983). A few studies have not produced consistent findings, and there are critics who believe that a causal association has not yet been proven (Freedman, 1984). But most experts think that the cumulative weight of the evidence argues in favor of a causal relationship. The case is strengthened by the fact that similar results emerge in studies employing a wide variety of research designs, methodological procedures, and subjects. In addition, the relationship between TV violence and aggression remains the same even after many factors that might otherwise account for it are controlled, such as social class, IQ, school achievement, and child-rearing practices (Friedrich-Cofer & Huston, 1986; Parke & Slaby, 1983).

In Chapter 2, we provided examples of important correlational and experimental findings that support a short-term link between televised violence and antisocial conduct.[3] Longitudinal studies, lasting from 1 to as many as 22 years, suggest that the effects are long-lasting and that TV violence is one factor (among others) that contributes to the development of a hostile, undercontrolled personality disposition. In the most extensive longitudinal study conducted to date, boys who watched a great many violent programs at age 8 were more likely to be rated by peers as highly aggressive at age 19 (Lefkowitz et al., 1972). A second follow-up at age 30 revealed a continuing association between early violent TV viewing and adult aggressiveness, measured this time in terms of serious criminal activity (see Figure 15.3) (Huesmann, 1986b).

In our discussion of the development of aggression in Chapter 13, we indicated that childhood aggressiveness also predicts adult criminal behavior. In fact, highly aggressive children (who are generally boys) show a greater appetite for violent TV, and they are more profoundly affected by it as well (Greenberg, 1975; Friedrich & Stein, 1973; Huesmann, 1986a; Huesmann, Lagerspetz, & Eron, 1984; Parke et al., 1977; Singer & Singer, 1981). These findings suggest that television violence and aggressive behavior feed on one another in a bidirectional fashion. Violent TV instructs children in aggressive modes of solving problems, and greater knowledge of and familiarity with hostile interpersonal tactics promote attraction to media violence. These reciprocal influences lead to a spiraling pattern of learning that, if left unchecked, results in enduring patterns of antisocial responding by early adulthood (Friedrich-Cofer & Huston, 1986; Huesmann, 1986b).

Television violence does not just augment children's aggression; it also "hardens" them so they are more likely to tolerate aggressive behavior in others. Drabman and Thomas (1976) had fifth graders view either an aggressive detective show or a nonaggressive excerpt from an exciting baseball game. Afterward, each subject was left "in charge" of two younger children (who were allegedly playing in an adjacent room and could be watched through a video monitor) and told to notify the experimenter if anything went wrong. A prepared film showed the younger children becoming increasingly hostile toward one another and destructive toward physical property. Subjects who had seen the aggressive film took much longer to seek help; many were willing to tolerate all but the most violent acts among their charges.

Other research indicates that heavy viewers of violent TV, in comparison to light viewers, overestimate violence and danger in society (Gerbner et al., 1979; Singer, Singer, & Rapaczynski, 1984). These findings suggest that violent television modifies children's attitudes toward social reality so they increasingly match the world reflected on TV. Children who watch a great deal of violent television begin to think of their social world as a mean and scary place in which aggressive acts are a widespread and appropriate means for solving problems.

[3] Return to Chapter 2, pages 49–51 to review this research.

Figure 15.3. Relationship between boys' violent television viewing at age 8 and seriousness of criminal convictions at age 30 in the Huesmann (1986b) study. *(From R. L. Huesmann, 1986, "Psychological Processes Promoting the Relation between Exposure to Media Violence and Aggressive Behavior by the Viewer," Journal of Social Issues, 42, 129. Reprinted by permission.)*

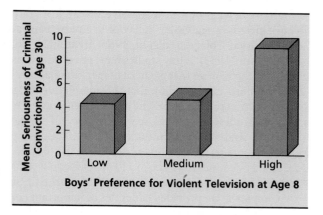

Sex-Role and Racial/Ethnic Stereotypes. Television conveys sex-role and racial/ethnic stereotypes that are common in American society. Women are underrepresented as characters, and when they do appear, their marital and child-rearing roles are emphasized. If they work, they generally perform "feminine" jobs, such as nurse, teacher, or secretary, while most professional and law enforcement roles are given over to men. The personalities of TV characters also conform to a sex-stereotyped pattern. Women are deferent, passive, and emotional, while men are active, dominant, and rational (Barcus, 1983; Macklin & Kolbe, 1984). Even formal features of television reflect sex-stereotypic views. In an analysis of TV toy commercials, Welch and her colleagues (1979) found that those aimed at boys had more variability of scenes, rapid cuts, loud music, and sound effects, conveying a masculine image of "fast, sharp, and loud." Those directed at girls had camera fades and background music, communicating a feminine message of "gradual, soft, and fuzzy." By first grade, children interpret these subtle features as an indication that an ad is aimed at one sex rather than the other (Huston et al., 1984).

In the early days of television, blacks rarely appeared on TV, and when they did, they were portrayed in subservient roles. The civil rights movement of the 1960s led to an increase in black television figures, and their social and occupational status rose as well (Clark, 1972; Roberts, 1970). Although blacks appear more often than they once did, they are largely segregated from whites in child- and adult-oriented programs (Barcus, 1983). Other racial/ethnic minorities continue to be underrepresented on television. When they do appear, they are usually depicted negatively, as villains or victims of violence (Gerbner et al., 1986).

Are children's sex-role and racial attitudes affected by these stereotyped portrayals? Much like the reciprocal relationship between TV violence and aggressive behavior, a bidirectional association between TV viewing and sex stereotyping may exist. Research suggests that highly sex-typed adolescents are especially attracted to TV and select programs with sex-stereotypic characters because they approve of their behavior (Friedrich-Cofer et al., 1978). At the same time, longitudinal findings reveal that television viewing is associated with increments in sex-stereotyped beliefs over time (Kimball, 1986; Morgan, 1982).

Studies of television's impact on children's racial attitudes are scarce. In one investigation, black and white children were shown cartoons that portrayed blacks in either a positive light (as competent, hardworking, and trustworthy) or a negative light (as inept, destructive, lazy, and powerless). The attitudes of black children toward their own race became more favorable regardless of which films they saw. Apparently, the mere presence of black TV characters was enough to make their attitudes more positive. Among white children, attitudes toward blacks conformed to the content of the film. Moreover, white children shown a negative portrayal changed more than any other group in the study (Graves, 1975). An impressive finding of this investigation was that substantial changes in children's racial attitudes occurred after only a single viewing session.

Consumerism. Television commercials directed at children "work" by increasing product sales. In the aisles of grocery and toy stores, young children can be seen asking for advertised products, and adult refusals often result in arguments between parents and children (Atkin, 1978). Although children can distinguish a TV program from a commercial as early as 3 years of age, below age 8 they seldom understand the selling purpose of the ad (Gaines & Esserman, 1981; Levin, Petros, & Petrella, 1982; Ward, Reale, & Levinson, 1972). When asked, "What are commercials for?", one typical 5-year-old replied, "So people know how to buy things. So if somebody washes their clothes, they'll know what to use" (Blatt, Spencer, & Ward, 1972, p. 457). This child thought that TV ads were simply well-intentioned efforts by film makers to be helpful to viewers. Around age 8 or 9, most children understand that commercials are meant to persuade, and by age 11, they realize that advertisers will resort to clever techniques to achieve their objectives. During this period, children also become increasingly skeptical of the truthfulness of commercial messages (Ward, Wackman, & Wartella, 1977).

Despite increased awareness of the advertising agenda, even older children find many commercials alluring and convincing. In one study of 8- to 14-year-old boys, celebrity endorsement of a racing toy made the product more attractive; inclusion of live race track footage led to exaggerated estimates of the toy's positive features as well as decreased awareness that the ad was staged (Ross et al., 1984). Commercials for heavily sugared food products comprise about 80 percent of advertising aimed at children, and heavy viewers come to prefer these foods and believe they are highly nutritious (Atkin, Reeves, & Gibson, 1979; Barcus, 1978; Gorn & Goldberg, 1982). Moreover, pronutrition messages are not very effective in counteracting the effects of such ads. Children absorb the pronutrition content, but their actual choice of snack foods does not change (Jeffrey, McLellarn, & Fox, 1982; Peterson et al., 1984). Apparently, long-term exposure to commercials for sugared products is not easily reversed by short-term interventions. The ease with which television advertising can manipulate the beliefs and preferences of children, especially young children who do not grasp the selling intent of the ads, has raised questions about the extent to which child-directed commercials constitute fair and ethical practice by the broadcasting industry (Huston, Watkins, & Kunkel, 1989; Singer & Singer, 1983).

Prosocial Behavior. Many programs on television include acts of altruism, cooperation, and sympathetic understanding of others (Liebert & Poulos, 1975). A recent large-scale review of research on prosocial television leaves little doubt that it can have socially desirable consequences, increasing children's willingness to share, help, and cooperate (Hearold, 1986). But research also reveals some important qualifications with regard to television's prosocial impact. First, virtually all of the demonstrated effects are short-term and limited to circumstances quite similar to those shown on the program. Longitudinal studies that examine the effects of exposure to prosocial TV over extended periods of time have not been conducted (Liebert & Sprafkin, 1988). Second, television programs often mix prosocial intentions and behavior with antisocial acts. Recall from our earlier discussion of television literacy that young children process TV material piecemeal; they have difficulty integrating televised information about motives, behavior, and consequences. When prosocial and antisocial content are combined, preschool and elementary school children usually attend to the hero's aggressions and miss the prosocial message, and their antisocial behavior rises accordingly (Collins, Berndt, & Hess, 1974; Liss, Reinhardt, & Fredriksen, 1983). These findings indicate that prosocial TV has positive consequences only when it is unencumbered by violent content. Finally, parents who discipline their children authoritatively with warmth and reasoning rather than commands and physical force have children who watch more prosocial programs (Abelman, 1985). Consequently, children from families that already promote social and moral maturity probably benefit most from prosocial television fare.

Television, Academic Learning, and Imagination. Since the early days of television, educators have been captivated by the potential of TV to support and supplement the school's curriculum, especially for low-income youngsters who enter kindergarten academically behind their middle-class peers. *"Sesame Street,"* the best known and most popular of children's educational programs, was created for public television with this goal in mind. Today, it is seen by almost half of America's 2- to 5-year-olds on a regular basis, and it is broadcast in more than 40 countries around the world (Liebert & Sprafkin, 1988). Combining the expertise of child development and media specialists, the designers of "Sesame Street" capitalized on the attention-grabbing power of fast-paced action, lively sound effects and music, and humorous puppet characters to foster basic academic skills, including letter and number recognition, counting, vocabulary, and conceptual understanding.

How well does "Sesame Street" work as an academic tutor? During the first year of the program, researchers conducted an evaluation of its effectiveness on a socioeconomically diverse sample of about 950 preschoolers. Participants were divided into four groups on the basis of how much they viewed over a 6-month period, and gains on tests designed to measure the learning goals of the program were compared. As shown in Figure 15.4, children did acquire academic skills from "Sesame Street," and the more they watched, the more they learned (Ball & Bogatz, 1970). Moreover, a second, similarly designed study that included only urban disadvantaged preschoolers replicated these findings. It also showed that when regular "Sesame Street" viewers from low-income families entered first grade, they were rated by teachers as better prepared for school than their light-viewing counterparts (Bogatz & Ball, 1972). In a recent investigation, Rice and her colleagues (1990) reported findings in

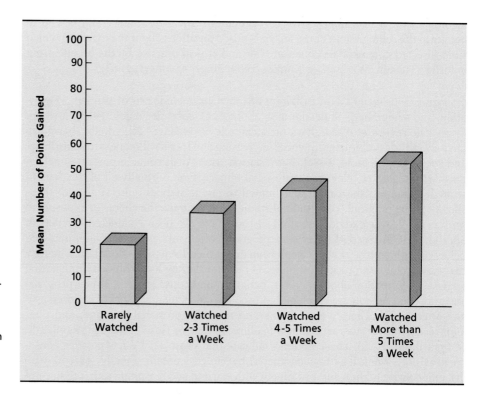

Figure 15.4. Relationship between amount of "Sesame Street" viewing and preschoolers' gains on tests of basic academic knowledge in the Ball and Bogatz (1970) evaluation. *(From Ball and Bogatz, 1970.)*

agreement with these early evaluations. "Sesame Street" viewing was positively related to vocabulary development among preschoolers of a wide range of socioeconomic backgrounds.

Although "Sesame Street" facilitates school readiness skills, the rapid-paced, densely packed information format on which it and other children's programs are based has not earned high marks in the area of imagination and creativity. Longitudinal research reveals that more TV viewing at age 3 and 4 is associated with less elaborate make-believe play in older preschoolers and lower creativity scores in elementary school children (Singer & Singer, 1981, 1983). In experimental studies in which TV treatments have facilitated young children's imaginative play, gains occurred only for slow-paced, nonviolent material that provides high continuity of story line, not for programs that offer rapid-paced, disconnected bits of information (Huston-Stein et al., 1981; Tower et al., 1979).

Some experts argue that because television presents more complete data to the senses than other media, such as radio or the printed page, in heavy doses it promotes reduced mental effort and shallow information processing, circumstances that undermine children's thoughtfulness and constructive learning. In addition, too much television subtracts from the time children devote to other activities, such as reading, playing, and conversing, that require more sustained concentration and active thinking skills (Peterson, Peterson, & Carroll, 1986). However, television can have positive intellectual consequences as long as children's viewing is not excessive and programs are specially designed to take into account children's cognitive-developmental needs.

Improving Children's Television. Evidence that television is a major socializer of undesirable attitudes and behavior has led to efforts to improve its content by major professional organizations and by citizen's groups, such as *Action for Children's Television,* a 20,000-member organization aimed at encouraging quality programming for children. However, the First Amendment right to freedom of speech has made the federal government reluctant to place limits on the content of television broadcasting. Although government monies have helped to finance many excellent educational programs (which cost more to produce than typical commercial fare), funding has been insufficient to produce major changes in the availability of high-quality children's programming (Huston, Watkins, & Kunkel, 1989).

The combined result of these factors is that the heavy doses of violence and commercialism beamed at children have not declined in recent years (Liebert & Sprafkin, 1988). Until children's television does improve, creating a discriminating audience by educating parents about the dangers of excessive TV viewing and providing children with instruction in critical viewing skills (e.g., Dorr, Graves, & Phelps, 1980; Singer, Zuckerman, & Singer, 1980) are probably the most expedient approaches to reducing the harmful impact of television on children's social development.

Computers

Invention of the microcomputer chip in the 1970s sharply reduced the cost and cumbersomeness of computer circuitry and made it possible for the general public to have ready access to computer technology. Today, microcomputers are a familiar fixture in many schools and homes, bringing a wide range of new entertainment and learning tools within easy reach of preschool through adolescent youngsters. Children are fascinated by this new technology. They generally prefer it to television, perhaps because computers combine the visual and auditory dynamism of TV with an active, participatory role for the child. As one youngster commented, "It's fun because you get to control it. TV controls itself" (Greenfield, 1984, p. 128). What is the impact of this new interactive medium on the human mind and the world in which we live? Many researchers believe that a good way to answer this question is to study how microcomputers affect children — their impact on intellectual development, every-day activities, and social behavior.

Research on computers and child development has proliferated in the last few years. Most studies have been carried out in classrooms, where computers are used as learning aids and children's reactions to them can easily be observed. Findings reveal that computers can have rich educational and social benefits. Children as young as 3 years of age like computer activities and can type in simple commands on a standard keyboard. At the same time, they do not find the computer so captivating that it diverts them from other worthwhile play activities (Campbell & Schwartz, 1986). Moreover, preschool and elementary school pupils generally use computers socially. Small groups often gather around the machine, and children take turns as well as help each other figure out next steps (Hawkins et al., 1982; Kull, 1986). Therefore the common fear that computers channel children into solitary, mechanistic pursuits is unfounded, although exactly what children learn from computers depends on how teachers use them in the classroom.

Three major uses of computer technology in schools are computer-assisted instruction, word processing, and programming. In *computer-assisted instruction,* children acquire new knowledge and practice academic skills with the help of learning software. The unique properties of many instructional programs make them effective and absorbing ways to learn. For example, pupils can begin at points that fit with their current level of mastery; programs are often written to intervene when children's responses indicate that special help is needed; and multiple communication modes of text, graphics, animation, voice, and music enhance children's attention and interest. While some programs provide drill and practice on basic academic skills, others involve gamelike activities that encourage more indirect and experiential learning. For example, in one, children operate a lemonade stand and learn about economic principles of cost, profit, supply, and demand in a familiar context. Many studies report significant gains in achievement when computer-assisted instruction is integrated into the curriculum, with elementary school students benefiting most from this highly responsive teaching medium (Kulik, 1986).

In *word processing,* the computer does not instruct; instead, it serves as a tool for writing and editing text material. Children can use word processing programs as soon as they have acquired minimal reading and writing skills. When word processing becomes part of the language arts curriculum, it permits children to write freely and to experiment with letters and words without being encumbered by the fine motor task of handwriting. As a result, children produce material that is longer and of higher

In classrooms, computers provide learning environments that are stimulating and socially interactive. However, boys spend much more time with computers than do girls.

Sex Differences and Computers

Box 15.2

Child development specialists have been especially concerned about the impact of microcomputer technology on equality of access to computer literacy for children of both sexes. Observations in classrooms indicate that boys and girls do not differ in their attraction to computer activities during the preschool years (Campbell & Schwartz, 1986). But girls' involvement decreases with age, while boys' increases. Parents with sons are twice as likely as those with daughters to install a microcomputer in the home, and by late childhood, participation in special computer programming courses and summer camps shows large sex differences in favor of boys, especially at the more advanced and costly levels of activity (Hess & Miura, 1985). In addition, because it emphasizes themes of war, violence, and male sex-typed sports such as baseball, basketball, and football, much computer game software is unappealing to girls, and it may even have the unfortunate consequence of turning them off to computers in general (Lepper, 1985).

Girls' decreasing attraction to computers is not a matter of any deficiency in basic skills required for computer literacy. When girls do enroll in computer courses, they perform as well as or better than boys (Linn, 1985), and the cognitive benefits of learning to program are similar for both sexes (Lockheed, 1985). But girls' reduced interest in computers may compound existing sex differences in spatial and mathematical performance (see Chapter 13). This is especially unfortunate because computers could do just the opposite. Non-sex-biased computer environments are needed in which software programs appeal to girls as well as boys and in which all children are encouraged to explore the new medium. Early exposure to and mastery of the microcomputer could be especially important for girls as a means of reducing male domination of the new technology and ensuring that females realize their developmental potential in mathematical and scientific fields.

quality, since they are less worried about making mistakes and find it easy to revise and polish their work (Levin, Boruta, & Vasconellos, 1983).

Finally, *programming* offers children the highest degree of control over the computer, since they must tell it just what to do. Specially designed computer languages are available to introduce children to programming skills. Research shows that when teachers encourage and support children's efforts, computer programming increases kindergartners' problem-solving performance (Degelman et al., 1986), and it helps 9- to 11-year-olds master formal operational concepts in mathematics once thought beyond their level of understanding (Pea & Kurland, 1984). In addition, because children must detect errors in their programs to get them to work, computer programming helps them reflect on their own thought processes. Several studies report gains in the metacognitive skill of comprehension monitoring[4] as a result of programming experience (Clements, 1986; Miller & Emihovich, 1986). Increases in general *computer literacy* also accrue from learning to program. Children know more about the uses of computers and how they function (Pea & Kurland, 1984). As a result, they are better prepared to participate in a society in which computers are becoming increasingly important in daily life.

Although computers provide children with many learning advantages, they raise serious concerns as well. Computers appear most often in the homes and classrooms of economically well-off children. Moreover, high-achieving youngsters have been found to acclimate more quickly to computer-based tasks at school and to progress at a much more rapid pace through them (Hativa, 1988). These circumstances could widen the intellectual performance gap that already exists between lower- and middle-class youngsters. Furthermore, by the end of elementary school, boys spend much more time with computers than do girls. Consequently, certain gender differences in cognitive abilities may also be exaggerated by computer usage (see Box 15.2).

---

[4] Recall from Chapter 7 that comprehension monitoring refers to continuous assessment of the degree to which information in a text passage that one is reading or listening to can be understood.

Finally, video games consume a large proportion of the out-of-school recreational use of computers by children and adolescents, especially boys. Many parents are seriously concerned about the allure of these fast-paced electronic amusements, fearing that their youngsters will become overly involved as well as more aggressive because of the games' highly violent themes. However, as yet, little research exists on this aspect of children's computer-related activities.

BRIEF REVIEW

American children spend more time watching television than they do in any other waking state activity. Before age 8, children have difficulty processing fast-paced, adult-oriented TV content in an undistorted fashion. Heavy TV viewing promotes aggressive behavior, sex-stereotyped beliefs, and indiscriminate consumerism. In addition, television can modify children's attitudes toward racial/ethnic minorities in a single viewing session. Although the right kinds of program content can promote prosocial behavior, academic skills, and imaginative thinking, the television medium seldom capitalizes on its positive potential.

Computers have become increasingly common in the lives of American children. Substantial educational benefits accrue when children have access to computer-assisted instruction, word processing, and programming experiences at school. However, computer-based learning may be magnifying intellectual performance gaps between economically advantaged and disadvantaged youngsters and between boys and girls.

SCHOOLING

Unlike the informal world of peer relations, school is a formal institution designed to transmit knowledge and skills required of children to become productive members of society. Children spend many long hours in school — 6 hours a day, 5 days a week, 36 weeks of the year — totaling, altogether, about 15,000 hours by graduation from high school. Do schools make a difference in the lives of children? This question was explored in the 1960s and 1970s by investigators who compared family and school variables as predictors of intellectual and occupational attainment (Coleman et al., 1966; Jencks, 1972). They reached the startling conclusion that quality of schooling is relatively unimportant and that the attitudes, abilities, and family support systems children bring to the classroom are primarily responsible for their academic and vocational success.

However, these studies focused on only a very narrow range of school variables and pupil outcomes, such as expenditures per child, teacher/pupil ratio, and achievement test scores. They did not look at what happens inside schools or at the implications of schooling for social as well as academic development. Research examining the characteristics of schools as complex social systems — their physical environments, educational philosophies, teacher-pupil interaction patterns, and the larger societal context in which they are embedded — indicates that schools exert powerful influences on many aspects of child development (Minuchin & Shapiro, 1983).

The Physical Environment

Although the physical plants of all schools bear similarities — each has classrooms, hallways, a lunchroom, and a play yard — they are also different. Schools vary in how many children are enrolled, how much space is available for work and play, and how classrooms are furnished and arranged. Crowding and room arrangements make an important difference in children's life at school.

In a series of careful studies, Smith and Connolly (1980) examined the effects of classroom crowding by systematically varying group size, amount of space, and quantity of material resources in preschools. Extreme social density — less than 15 feet per child (the size of a 3×5 throw rug) — led to a rise in aggressive behavior. Moreover, when greater social density was not accompanied by more plentiful materials, aggression was further magnified. However, teachers can reduce these negative outcomes through effective management of children's behavior. In one study of a Dutch nursery school that was very crowded by American standards, pupils did not react aggressively; instead, many positive and friendly interactions occurred. The teachers at this school reduced children's opportunities to fight over toys and space by assigning pupils to particular play areas. The program sacrificed free choice of activities for an arrangement that permitted large numbers of children to coexist amicably in a small classroom space (Fagot, 1977b). Although research on classroom crowding focuses on preschool children, similar effects may occur at the elementary school level as well.

Is there an optimal class size that fosters smooth classroom functioning and effective pupil learning? As classes are reduced below 15 or 20 pupils, elementary school children show improved academic achievement, but above this threshold, class size has little consequence for learning outcomes (Cooper, 1989; Educational Research Service, 1980; Glass et al., 1982). Also, teachers in classrooms with fewer children spend less time disciplining and more time providing their pupils with individualized attention, factors that may be responsible for the achievement gains noted above (Cahan et al., 1983). Moreover, when class size is small, both teachers and pupils report greater satisfaction with their life at school (Smith & Glass, 1980).

Room arrangements also affect children's school experiences. Teachers' seating plans are often a reflection of their educational philosophies. The familiar row-and-column configuration is generally associated with a traditional approach to classroom learning, while desks arranged in circles or clusters reflect a more open orientation (we will take up the significance of these two educational philosophies shortly). Therefore, it is difficult to study the impact of room arrangements separately from the teacher's instructional program, but a few researchers have isolated the effects of physical setting alone. As shown in Figure 15.5, in the row-and-column seating plan, pupil location is a strong determinant of classroom participation, with pupils located "front and center" interacting with teachers the most (Adams, 1969). Although children who are gregarious tend to choose central desks and those who are shy avoid them, the seating effect is not just a function of pupil personality. When very sociable youngsters sit away from the center, they consistently show a drop in participation (Koneya, 1976).

Do these findings mean that teachers should locate noninteractive pupils "front and center," where they will be forced to participate in class discussion? Doing so could produce considerable psychological discomfort in shy youngsters, thereby undermining their learning rather than enhancing it. A better approach might be to rearrange the seating configuration as a whole so that participation of all pupils is encouraged. In an experiment in which three seating plans — row-and-column, a large circle, and small clusters of adjoining desks — were compared, the circular configuration was the most effective in facilitating participation and attentiveness during class discussion. The cluster arrangement ranked second, while the row-and-column configuration produced more pupil withdrawal and off-task behavior than either of the other conditions (Rosenfield, Lambert, & Black, 1985).

By the time students reach junior high and high school, they no longer spend most of their time in a single, self-contained classroom. Instead, older students come into contact with a wider range of teachers and peers, and they are offered many activities outside of academic classes. As a result, the relevant physical context becomes the school as a whole. One feature of the general school environment that shows consistent relationships with high school students' behavior is student body size. You may recall from our discussion of ecological research in Chapter 1 that a greater proportion of students in small high schools than in large ones are actively involved in the

Figure 15.5. Area associated with highest pupil participation rates in Adams's (1969) study of row-and-column classroom seating arrangements. *(Adapted from Adams, 1969.)*

extracurricular life of their schools. Schools of 500 students or less promote personalized conditions because there are fewer people to ensure that clubs, sports events, and social activities will continue to function. As a result, a greater percentage of students are pressed into participation and hold positions of responsibility and leadership. In contrast, plenty of people are available to fill activity slots in large schools, and only a small elite can be genuinely active (Barker & Gump, 1964).

In view of these findings, it is not surprising that students in small schools report a greater sense of personal responsibility, competence, and challenge from their extracurricular experiences. This is true even for "marginal" students—those with academic difficulties, low IQs, and impoverished backgrounds—who, under other conditions, display little commitment to school life (Willems, 1967). Some evidence indicates that the incidence of truancy and delinquency is lower in small schools (McPartland & McDill, 1977; Reynolds et al., 1980). Perhaps this occurs because participation in extracurricular activities prevents the otherwise alienated youngster from retreating to the fringes of the environment and becoming involved in socially deviant peer groups (Garbarino, 1980). Small schools are not associated with better academic achievement, but the experience they offer in productive social roles is an equally important gain, increasing students' feelings of satisfaction and promoting a sense of social obligation that transfers to community participation in adult life (Berk, 1991).

The Educational Philosophy: Traditional versus Open Classrooms

Each teacher brings an educational ideology to the classroom that plays a major role in determining the structure and organization of children's school experiences. Two philosophical orientations have been studied in American education: traditional and open. They differ in what children are taught, how they are believed to learn, the extent to which decision making is vested in teacher or child, and how pupil progress is evaluated.

In **traditional classrooms,** which represent the dominant approach to education in the United States today, the goal of instruction is to transmit culturally valued knowledge and standards of conduct. Children are relatively passive in the learning process; they acquire information presented by the teacher, who serves as the sole authority for knowledge, rules, and decision making. A traditional classroom is easily recognized by the fact that the teacher is the center of attention and does most of the talking; children spend much time seated at their desks — listening, responding when called on, and completing teacher-assigned tasks. Pupil progress is determined by how well children keep pace with a common set of expectations for all pupils in their grade; children are compared to one another and to age-related, normative standards of performance.

In **open classrooms,** acquisition of culturally valued knowledge is deemed important, but not to the exclusion of other goals. Greater emphasis is placed on nurturing social and emotional development, in addition to academic progress. The open philosophy regards children as active agents in their own development. Consequently, the teacher assumes a flexible authority role, sharing decision making with children in accord with their developing capacity to formulate classroom rules and select appropriate learning activities. Evaluation is based on children's progress in relation to their own prior development and only secondarily to classmates' performance and normative standards. A glance inside the door of an open classroom reveals richly equipped learning centers, small groups of pupils conversing and collaborating on learning tasks, and a teacher who moves about from one area to another, guiding, supporting, and instructing in response to children's individual needs (Minuchin & Shapiro, 1983).

The aims of open education include the development of autonomous learners who feel positively about themselves, are respectful of individual differences, and respond to learning with pleasure and enthusiasm. The combined results of many studies suggest that open environments are successful in achieving these goals. Open classroom pupils are more independent; they express less need for social approval

In open classrooms, teachers assume a flexible authority role. Pupils take more responsibility for their own learning, and teachers move about the classroom, guiding and instructing in response to children's individual needs.

and explicit direction than traditionally instructed youngsters. Although most studies report no differences in self-esteem, when differences do appear, they favor children in open classrooms. Moreover, children exposed to open education cooperate more effectively when working on common tasks. Sociometric measures also reveal fewer extremes of peer popularity and rejection in open classrooms. In these environments, pupils with a wide range of characteristics are liked, and children more often select peer associates who differ from themselves in sex and race. Finally, children in open environments like school better than those in traditional classrooms, and their attitudes toward school become increasingly positive as they spend more time in the setting (Hedges, Giaconia, & Gage, 1981; Horwitz, 1979; Peterson, 1979; Walberg, 1986).

Although open classrooms are associated with social and attitudinal advantages, they do not lead to better academic achievement. Most investigations show no difference on this score; when differences do appear, open education pupils perform slightly below their traditionally educated counterparts. One careful synthesis of research revealed that open programs placing greatest emphasis on child-directed learning and individualized assessment of pupil progress were especially effective in promoting self-esteem and positive attitudes toward school, but they sacrificed achievement gains to some degree. Perhaps children in these settings did less well on conventional achievement tests because their classroom experiences seldom presented them with testlike situations (Giaconia & Hedges, 1982).

An additional complicating factor in assessing the learning outcomes of traditional and open education is that some children may perform better under one approach than the other. However, as yet, research is not conclusive about which pupils fare best in each type of classroom. Some findings suggest that it is best to place children in classrooms that are consistent with their personality dispositions—for example, anxious and conforming pupils in highly structured, traditional environments and autonomous, self-directed learners in open settings (Grimes & Allinsmith, 1961; Peterson, 1977). However, other results suggest just the opposite — that children fare best when they are placed in classrooms that emphasize a mode of learning they might otherwise avoid (Solomon & Kendall, 1979).

Furthermore, the dichotomous traditional-open distinction appears to oversimplify the real world of classroom philosophical differences. In several studies, some classrooms could not be classified as either traditional or open; instead, they fell somewhere in between (Aitken, Bennett, & Hesketh, 1981; Minuchin et al., 1969; Thomas & Berk, 1981). In the future, more precise distinctions among educational philosophies may be needed to improve our understanding of how classroom environments affect children's development. Perhaps a balanced mixture of traditional and open education will turn out to be the optimal kind of learning environment because it can accommodate the needs of many types of children.

Finally, even teachers who have very similar ideologies differ substantially in how they interact with their pupils on a day-to-day basis (Carew & Lightfoot, 1979). In the following sections, we consider the implications of this finer level of classroom experience for children's learning and development.

Teacher-Pupil Interaction

The classroom is a complex social system in which a myriad of interactions between teachers and children take place on a daily basis. Teachers play a central role in this highly social environment, engaging in as many as 1,000 interpersonal exchanges with pupils each day (Jackson, 1968). While most teacher talk centers on communicating academic content and some on managing the complex flow of classroom events (Jackson & Lahaderne, 1968), a substantial portion is evaluative in nature. Children get feedback from teachers about whether their ideas and answers are right or wrong and whether their behavior fits with what is expected of them in the student role. A large body of research exists on teacher-pupil interaction, the bulk of which deals with its significance for the most salient goal of schooling — academic achievement.

Classroom time devoted to academic instruction and pupil involvement in academic work show consistent positive associations with achievement (Brophy & Good, 1986; Minuchin & Shapiro, 1983). But for children to learn effectively in an environment as crowded and potentially distracting as an elementary school classroom, teachers must arrange conditions that make work possible. Teacher behaviors that show the strongest relationships with pupil achievement involve classroom management skills (Brophy & Evertson, 1976; Gage, 1978; Good & Power, 1976). Effective classroom managers establish learning environments in which activities flow easily from one to the next. Little time is devoted to transitions between lessons, and there are few disruptions and discipline problems. As a result, pupils spend more time learning, which is reflected in higher achievement test scores.

In addition to management skills, the quality of teachers' instructional messages affects children's task involvement and consequent learning. Disappointingly, American elementary schools place greater emphasis on rote repetitive drill than on cognitively challenging tasks, such as applying concepts and skills and analyzing and synthesizing ideas and information (Dossey et al., 1988; Goodlad, 1984; McKnight et al., 1987; Sirotnik, 1983). However, individual differences among teachers do exist, and both cognitively simple and complex instruction occurs in all classrooms to some degree. In a recent study, Stodolsky (1988) found that fifth-grade teachers' instructional style varied across the school day in accord with the subject matter being taught. Math lessons were heavily laden with lower-level intellectual activity — memorization of number facts and computational routines. In contrast, the mental processes encouraged by social studies lessons included both fact acquisition and higher-level processes. Within each subject, students were far more attentive when given complex tasks than simple memory exercises, and overall, their level of engagement was greater in social studies than in math. These findings suggest that introducing more cognitively complex activities (as long as they have a good fit with pupil capabilities) is likely to increase children's involvement in classroom learning and their academic achievement as well.

So far, we have emphasized one-way effects of teacher communication on pupil behavior and performance, but as you already know from earlier parts of this book, social relationships are bidirectional, with each participant influencing the behavior of the other. Teacher-pupil relationships are not equivalent for all children; over time, some receive more attention, praise, and criticism than others. Teachers' differential reactions to pupils are a function of the extent to which children's behavior fits with the academic and conduct expectations of the school. Research indicates that teachers prefer children who are high-achieving, well-motivated, and conforming. These youngsters are frequently called on to share ideas with the class and receive more praise than other pupils. In contrast, teachers especially dislike children who combine low achievement with active, disruptive behavior. These pupils receive high levels of criticism for their classroom work and conduct and are rarely asked to contribute to class discussion. Moreover, when they seek special help or permission, their requests are usually denied (Brophy & Good, 1974; Feshbach, 1969; Silberman, 1969).

Unfortunately, once established, teacher attitudes are in danger of becoming more extreme and stereotyped than is warranted by children's behavior. If teachers rigidly and inflexibly treat pupils in ways that fit with their impressions, they may engage in discriminatory practices that have long-term consequences for children's motivation and academic progress. Child development specialists have been especially interested in whether teachers harbor unfair biases about the intellectual capabilities of

The quality of teachers' instructional messages affects children's involvement in classroom activities and consequent learning.

some pupils based on their classroom behavior, racial/ethnic backgrounds, and social class. We take up this issue in the following two sections.

Teacher Expectations of Children's Academic Performance. The idea that teacher expectations for pupils' academic performance may become realities, causing some children to do better and others to do worse than they otherwise would, is known as the educational **self-fulfilling prophecy.** In the early 1960s, psychologist Robert Rosenthal found that the maze performance of rats could be modified by experimenter beliefs about an animal's "brightness" or "dullness" (Rosenthal & Fode, 1963). Rosenthal reasoned that if rats learn more effectively when expected to, the same might be true for children whose teachers believe in their ability to learn.

With Lenore Jacobson, Rosenthal conducted a famous experiment in which he tested this hypothesis.[5] First, children in an elementary school were administered an IQ test, and teachers were given erroneous information that the test results could identify pupils expected to "bloom," or show an intellectual growth spurt, during the ensuing months. Each teacher was provided with a list of "bloomers" in her classroom (children who were actually randomly chosen by the researchers). Then the IQ test was readministered at the end of the school year. Results indicated that first and second graders for whom teachers expected gains actually showed them. However, self-fulfilling prophecy effects did not emerge in the third through sixth grades (Rosenthal & Jacobson, 1968).

[5] Although most research on self-fulfilling prophecies focuses on the teacher-pupil relationship, the phenomenon can occur in other social contexts, such as parent-child and peer associations, as well. Try to think of other findings we have discussed, in this and earlier chapters, that can be viewed as self-fulfilling prophecies.

Rosenthal and Jacobson's study was soon criticized on methodological grounds, and numerous attempts to replicate it failed to produce the same findings. Later, it became clear that many teachers, especially those who are self-confident and experienced, will reject experimenter-provided expectancy information if it disagrees with their firsthand observations (Carter et al., 1987). Research that has done the most to advance our understanding of how self-fulfilling prophecies operate in classrooms focuses on teachers' *naturally formed* expectations for children, the quality of their interaction with individual pupils (through which expectations are communicated), and children's consequent learning. Findings reveal that for the great majority of teachers, self-fulfilling prophecies are minimal. Although teachers do interact differently with high-achieving and low-achieving youngsters, in most cases their behavior is a reality-based response to pupils' learning needs and does not cause children to do well or poorly in school. But in a few instances, teachers *have* been found to harbor unfair pupil expectations. Unfortunately, they are usually biased in a negative rather than a positive direction, leading to more unfavorable classroom experiences and learning outcomes than would otherwise occur (Brophy, 1983).

Research suggests that these self-fulfilling prophecies interact in complex ways with teacher and pupil characteristics. In other words, certain teachers are more likely to promote these effects, and some pupils are especially susceptible targets. Teachers who regard low-achieving pupils as limited by ability rather than effort or opportunity to learn are likely to provide them with little encouragement for mastering new and difficult tasks. In addition, teachers who have a strong fear of losing control of their class more often initiate negative self-fulfilling prophecies. They do so by avoiding public communication with low-achieving pupils (who often present behavior problems and are threats to teacher control) and giving them feedback that is abrupt, inconsistent, and not contingent on the quality of their work. When this happens, children attribute their classroom performance to external forces beyond their control. This lowers their expectancies for success, their motivation to achieve, and, ultimately, academic achievement itself (Cooper, 1979).

Note that this explanation of how teachers' self-fulfilling prophecies are realized is drawn from *attribution theory* of achievement motivation, which we considered in Chapter 11. Moreover, it suggests that certain children are especially likely to experience negative self-fulfilling prophecies — namely, low achievers who cause serious behavior problems in the classroom. There is good evidence to support this view. Recall from our earlier discussion that children who display this combination of characteristics are seldom called on publicly and receive especially high levels of criticism from teachers. Brophy (1983) believes that quiet, noninteractive youngsters, to whom many teachers react with indifference, may also be candidates for negative self-fulfilling prophecies. Because these children approach teachers infrequently, they provide little evidence about what they are like as learners, a circumstance that makes it easier for teachers who hold inappropriate expectations to sustain them.

Finally, in many classrooms and schools, children are *ability grouped* or *tracked* into classes in which children of similar achievement levels are taught together, a practice designed to ease the teacher's task of having to accommodate a wide range of academic needs in the same learning environment. Some investigators believe that differential teacher treatment of these intact groups and classes may be an especially powerful mediator of self-fulfilling prophecies (Brophy, 1983; Corno & Snow, 1986). In low ability groups, pupils receive more drill on basic facts and skills, are exposed to a slower learning pace, and spend less time engaged in academic pursuits than do high-ability-group youngsters (Borko, Shavelson, & Stern, 1981; Brookover et al., 1979; Evertson, 1982). Over time, children in low groups display a drop in self-esteem and achievement motivation, are socially stigmatized as "not smart," and limit their friendship choices to children within their own group. In view of these findings, it is not surprising that ability grouping is associated with a widening of the school performance gap between high and low achievers (Calfee & Brown, 1979; Good & Stipek, 1983; Rosenholtz & Wilson, 1980).

Teacher Reactions to Children's Racial/Ethnic and Social Class Backgrounds. The American school has often been characterized as a white, middle-class institution in which the social attitudes of the larger society prevail (Minuchin & Shapiro, 1983). There is good evidence that teachers often respond in stereotyped ways to children from poor and minority backgrounds, making them especially susceptible to negative self-fulfilling prophecies. In most (but not all) studies examining differential treatment of black and white pupils, black pupils received less favorable communication from teachers (Aaron & Powell, 1982; Byers & Byers, 1972; Hillman & Davenport, 1978; Irvine, 1986). One investigation reported that as early as the preschool years, teachers provide less verbal stimulation when they teach classes of low-income than middle-income children (Quay & Jarrett, 1986).

In Chapter 8, we indicated that ethnic minority children often have unique customs of social interaction that are not well understood at school. Teachers who are unaware of this fact may interpret the minority child's behavior as an indication of uncooperativeness when, in fact, it is not. For this reason, it is vitally important that teachers understand the communication practices that culturally different children bring to school. Then they can adjust classroom expectations to take into account the child's prior experiences, and negative self-fulfilling prophecies with serious consequences for the minority child's future academic performance can be avoided.

BRIEF REVIEW

In the sections above, we have seen that both the physical context and philosophical orientation of the school can powerfully affect pupil behavior. By reducing class size, rearranging classroom seating arrangements, and (at the junior high and high school levels) manipulating the size of the student body as a whole, educators can promote many aspects of student development. Open classrooms are more effective than traditional classrooms in fostering autonomous learning, tolerance of individual differences, and positive attitudes toward school. However, pupils in open classrooms are not advantaged in academic achievement.

When teachers are skilled classroom managers and provide children with cognitively challenging tasks, involvement in learning and academic achievement are enhanced. Most teachers respond in reasonable ways to individual differences in children's personal characteristics and learning needs. However, when teachers believe that low-achieving youngsters are limited by ability, doubt their own capacity to control the class, and do not understand the cultural backgrounds of ethnic minority pupils, negative self-fulfilling prophecies are likely to be initiated.

Teaching Children with Special Needs

Effective teachers flexibly adjust their curriculum to meet the needs of the majority of children, accommodating pupils with a wide range of aptitudes for learning. But making such adjustments becomes increasingly difficult at the very low and high ends of the ability distribution. How do schools serve youngsters with special learning needs?

Mainstreaming Children with Learning Difficulties. In 1975, Congress passed *Public Law (PL) 94-142, The Education for All Handicapped Children Act.* It mandated that schools grant handicapped children an *appropriate* public education and place them in the *least restrictive environments* able to meet their educational needs. The intent of the legislation was to better prepare handicapped children to participate in a nonhandicapped world by providing educational experiences as similar as possible to those of nonhandicapped pupils.

PL 94-142 requires school districts to offer an array of alternative placements to meet the varied needs of handicapped pupils. Among the options, ranging from most to least restrictive, are special schools, self-contained classrooms in regular school buildings, and integration into classrooms serving nonhandicapped children for part or all of the school day. **Mainstreaming** is a term that refers to this last alternative. PL 94-142 recognizes that regular classroom placement is not appropriate for all handicapped children and does not require it. But since passage of the law, the "least restrictive environment" concept has been translated into a nationwide reduction in self-contained classes and an increase in mainstreaming for pupils with mild handicapping conditions (MacMillan, Keogh, & Jones, 1986). Research has focused on the academic and social consequences of regular classroom instruction for mildly retarded and learning-disabled children, since they are the most likely candidates for mainstreaming.[6]

Does mainstreaming accomplish the dual goal of providing more appropriate academic experiences for mildly handicapped children and integrated participation in the nonhandicapped social world? At present, the weight of the evidence is not positive on either of these points. Achievement differences between mainstreamed pupils and those instructed in self-contained classrooms have not been dramatic (MacMillan, Keogh, & Jones, 1986). Furthermore, a large number of studies indicate that mildly retarded children are consistently rejected by their nonhandicapped schoolmates (Hartup, 1983; MacMillan & Morrison, 1984). Overwhelmed by the social competence of normal agemates, many mainstreamed retarded youngsters exhibit high levels of avoidant and withdrawn behavior. When asked, they report considerable dissatisfaction and anxiety about their peer experiences as well as intense feelings of loneliness (Taylor, Asher, & Williams, 1987).

Do these findings indicate that mainstreaming is not a good way to meet the educational needs of mildly handicapped children? This extreme conclusion is not warranted. Educators agree that successful mainstreaming requires a carefully individualized instructional program that takes into account each pupil's strengths and weaknesses and that minimizes comparisons between handicapped children and their higher-achieving peers. In a handful of well-designed studies in which mainstreamed youngsters were placed in classrooms with these characteristics, they showed gains in self-esteem and achievement over their nonmainstreamed counterparts (Madden & Slavin, 1983; Wang & Baker, 1985–1986). Furthermore, as we saw earlier in this chapter, children seek out peer companions who, in comparison to themselves, are either equivalent or more advanced in social maturity. Therefore, without special encouragement, interaction between handicapped and nonhandicapped pupils is unlikely to occur. Bender (1986–1987) recommends that before being mainstreamed, handicapped children receive intensive social skills training to develop an effective set of peer interaction skills.

Once children enter the regular classroom, cooperative learning projects in which a handicapped child and several nonhandicapped peers work together on the same task have been found to promote friendly interaction and improved social acceptance of mainstreamed pupils (Ballard et al., 1977; Johnson, Johnson, & Maruyama, 1984; Slavin, Madden, & Leavey, 1984). Finally, teachers can prepare children for the arrival of a handicapped youngster and encourage them to welcome and assist the

[6] Mildly retarded children are those whose IQ scores fall between 55 and 70 (Grossman, 1983). Learning-disabled children have specific learning difficulties in verbal or mathematical areas that are not attributable to general intellectual impairment, physical handicaps, or emotional problems.

new pupil. Under these conditions, mainstreaming may lead to valuable gains in emotional sensitivity, perspective-taking, and altruistic behavior among nonhandicapped peers. When better ways are devised to achieve mainstreaming, it may very well break down social barriers and foster early integration of individuals with disabilities into the mainstream of American life.

Teaching the Gifted. Since the early part of this century, the term *gifted* has been used to designate individuals who have superior mental abilities. Terman's longitudinal study of high-IQ children, to which you were introduced in Chapter 1, initiated a widespread identification of giftedness with superior intelligence test performance. However, you may recall from Chapter 8 that intelligence tests do not sample the entire range of human mental skills. Only within the last two decades have conceptions of giftedness not based on IQ gained acceptance in public schools. Today, definitions of giftedness encompass high general intelligence, creativity, and talent in a specific field of endeavor. In Chapter 8, we discussed the development of highly intelligent, creative, and talented youngsters. Here we focus on how schools meet the challenge of nurturing their exceptional abilities.

Enrichment activities provided in regular classrooms and pull-out programs in which bright youngsters are gathered together for special instruction have been common ways of serving gifted children for decades. These approaches are limited in effectiveness, since the same enrichment experience is generally provided to all pupils without consideration for each child's unique talents and skills. Current trends in gifted education place greater emphasis on experiences that build on each child's special abilities. These include mentorship programs in which a highly skilled adult tutors the gifted youngster in a relevant field and accelerated learning programs in which gifted pupils are provided with fast-paced instruction in a particular subject or permitted to advance to a higher grade (Torrance, 1986).

Acceleration is among the most controversial practices in gifted education because of concerns that intellectually precocious children will suffer socially if they are placed with older pupils. Yet when applied selectively to mature and able youngsters, it is highly successful. Longitudinal studies of accelerated students indicate that they continue to be socially well-adjusted and demonstrate exceptional academic attainments (Brody & Benbow, 1987).

Another controversial practice involves identifying gifted children during the preschool years and providing very early educational programming. However, gifted preschool programs pose the danger of premature academic training during a period in which children need relaxed opportunities to explore their surroundings through play. Furthermore, assessment of giftedness is difficult during the preschool years. IQ is not yet very stable, and young children are not yet mature enough to display many talents that will become apparent at older ages. As an alternative to early gifted education, Johnson (1983) recommends child-responsive preschool environments that serve the educational needs of all children, including gifted children who can be identified early as well as those whose exceptional talents are not yet apparent.

The School and American Society

Society often turns to its schools for solutions to pressing social problems. In the following sections, we review the accomplishments of American education in two areas relevant to concerns of the larger society. First, we discuss how well schools have fared in promoting increased contact among children of diverse racial/ethnic backgrounds and in bringing us closer to the goal of equal educational opportunity for all American children. Second, we evaluate the overall quality of American education. We consider the extent to which it produces a well-educated populace and how well it measures up to the educational preparation of young citizens in other technologically advanced nations around the world.

Desegregation. In 1954, an historic Supreme Court decision, *Brown* v. *Board of Education of Topeka*, affirmed the injustice of separate educational facilities for racially different children growing up in an egalitarian society. The law gradually resulted in the desegregation of many American schools, but not without substantial community polarization in many areas of the country. Racial prejudice, fierce defense of the neighborhood school, and strong objections to mandatory busing led many white parents to oppose the practice, if not the principle, of school desegregation. Even in school districts where desegregation took place with relative calm, placing white and black children in the same school did not guarantee equitable educational services. In many instances, blacks were resegregated inside the building. Rigid ability grouping practices and prejudicial teacher attitudes led to the continuation of inferior instruction for black pupils, and little positive contact took place that permitted black and white children to get to know each other as individuals.

In view of these conditions, it is not surprising that, by 1975, a large literature on the impact of school desegregation revealed no improvement in black children's self-esteem and school achievement (St. John, 1975). But an additional decade of research in which investigators looked closely at classroom social arrangements and instructional methods produced findings much like those on mainstreaming, discussed earlier in this chapter. School desegregation results in clear benefits for children when active efforts are made to change educational practices in racially mixed classrooms.

Many studies reveal that cooperative learning experiences in which small, racially mixed groups of pupils help one another work toward common academic goals are highly successful in producing cross-race peer acceptance, and they lead to gains in black children's self-esteem and school achievement as well (Johnson, Johnson, & Maruyama, 1984). In addition, multiethnic curricula and projects that focus on racial issues are beneficial (Genova & Walberg, 1984). When teachers help pupils understand the customs of different ethnic groups and inform them of the destructive impact of racial discrimination, children can internalize this information and call on it in their future peer associations. Teachers' educational philosophies are also important. In classrooms where competitive success is de-emphasized, peer status hierarchies in which whites fall at the top and blacks at the bottom are less likely to develop. Finally, small class size promotes cross-race sociability. In large classes, students usually have a sufficient number of same-race peers from whom to choose their companions, and they do not need to cross racial barriers to establish satisfying peer relationships (Hallinan & Teixeira, 1987).

As yet, the constructive potential of mixed-race classrooms for providing minority children with a better education and promoting interracial acceptance has been realized in only a few American schools. But enough research has accumulated to show that when they are carefully planned and implemented, mixed-race learning environments can foster harmonious intergroup relations and bring us closer to the goal of equality of educational opportunity for all American children.

How Well Are Schools Educating America's Children? *A Nation at Risk* was the 1983 conclusion of the National Commission on Excellence in Education, a group of scholars, educators, and citizens appointed by the federal government to examine the quality of American education and report back to the nation. Serious concerns about American schools were raised on the basis of a variety of indicators, including steadily plummeting Scholastic Aptitude Test (SAT) scores of high school students from 1963 to 1980; severe deficiencies in basic academic skills among

America's poor minorities; and a population of gifted youngsters who, as a group, were not achieving up to their potential. Similar trends were documented in a recent Nation's Report Card, which summarized the academic competence of America's youth.

The Nation's Report Card: Academic Skills of Young Americans. In response to a mandate from Congress for continuous monitoring of the performance of young Americans in various learning areas, several national assessments of the reading, writing, and mathematical achievement of schoolchildren were conducted from the early 1970s into the mid-1980s. Large representative samples of 9-, 13-, and 17-year-olds were tested every 4 to 5 years during this time period, and achievement trends were carefully examined. Although the findings pointed to some hopeful signs, they revealed a worrisome overall picture.

On the positive side, the Nation's Report Card showed that the majority of American children master basic literacy skills by 9 years of age. In addition, gains in reading and mathematics performance occurred during the late 1970s and 1980s, partially offsetting an earlier decline. However, this recovery was largely confined to low-level academic skills. The average performance of 17-year-olds in the mid-1980s did not reach a level in reading that permitted them to understand and explain moderately complicated information. In math, it did not move beyond an intermediate level of skill required to read simple graphs and solve basic algebraic equations (Dossey et al., 1988; National Assessment of Educational Progress, 1985). Finally, the findings on writing ability were least encouraging. Only 41 percent of 9-year-olds could write a description of a series of simple pictures, and only 65 percent of 17-year-olds could prepare a clear paragraph for a job application. Tasks requiring students to write a well-reasoned paper on a particular subject were very difficult at all ages (Applebee, Langer, & Mullis, 1986).

Supplementary information collected by the investigators suggested several probable causes of these disappointing findings. Consistent with results discussed in several earlier chapters, a stimulating home environment predicted better academic performance. But quality of schooling also played a major role, since classroom instructional emphases were clearly associated with student achievement. For example, the amount of homework assigned was positively correlated with performance. By 1986, teachers were giving more homework than in previous years, but as many as 30 percent of high school students still reported less than one hour per night; 6 percent had none. In mathematics, the cognitive level of most classroom teaching matched the mediocre level of pupil performance. As we reported earlier in this chapter, math instruction that moved beyond basic fact and rule memorization was rare (Dossey et al., 1988).

Cross-National Research on School Achievement. Comparisons of the academic achievement of American youngsters with that of children in other industrialized nations reveal a similarly discouraging picture. In every cross-national study conducted to date, Asian youngsters have been among the top performers, especially in mathematics and science, while Americans have scored no better than at the mean and often at the bottom of the pack (Husén, 1967; IEA, 1988; McKnight et al., 1987; Stevenson, Lee, & Stigler, 1986).

For example, a recent comprehensive survey of the mathematics achievement of eighth- and twelfth-grade students in countries around the world showed American junior high pupils to be at about the international average in computational skills but well below it in higher-order problem solving. Among students about to complete high school, the most talented American performers—those enrolled in the most advanced high school math courses—scored substantially below the average of 15 participating countries. When all college-bound high school seniors were considered, the United States ranked among the poorest-performing nations (see Table 15.3) (McKnight et al., 1987).

These differences are apparent early in development. In a comparison of the achievement of elementary school children in Japan, Taiwan, and the United States, large differences in mathematics were already present in kindergarten and became progressively greater with increasing grade. Furthermore, achievement differences were not limited to math. Less extreme disparities emerged in reading, in which Taiwanese children scored highest, Japanese children lowest, and American children in between (Stevenson & Lee, 1990; Stevenson, Lee, & Stigler, 1986).

An analysis of home and school influences in top-scoring Asian countries and the United States adds to our appreciation of the achievement disparities described above. Asian pupils are not "smarter" when they begin school; they do not score higher than American children on intelligence tests (Stevenson et al., 1985). Also, Asian parents do not hurry their youngsters into academic work during the preschool years (Leetsma et al., 1987; Song & Ginsburg, 1987). Instead, as indicated by Box 15.3, stronger parental pressures to perform well after school entry and a more intensive process of education appear to underlie their extraordinary performance.

Our discussion ends on a note of concern mixed with hopefulness about the quality of America's schools. Education defines a society's ability to compete in a complex world economy, make new discoveries, transmit a common cultural identity to each new generation, and enjoy an enriched quality of life. Success in improving American education is crucial for the optimal development of children and the future

Table 15.3. Mathematics Achievement of College-Bound Graduating High School Students in Fifteen Nations

COUNTRY (IN RANK ORDER OF PERFORMANCE)	MEAN PERCENT CORRECT ON ACHIEVEMENT TESTS[a]
Hong Kong	74
Japan	70
Finland	61
England and Wales	60
Sweden	58
New Zealand	55
Belgium (Flemish)	52
Canada (Ontario)	51
Belgium (French)	48
Israel	46
Scotland	43
United States	40
Canada (British Columbia)	38
Thailand	35
Hungary	32

Source: McKnight et al. (1987).

[a] The percentage given is an average of each nation's performance on the following six achievement tests: sets and relations, number systems, algebra, geometry, elementary functions and calculus, and probability and statistics.

of the nation as a whole. America's educational system has risen to challenges before; today it provides basic education to a greater proportion of its citizenry than any other country in the world. Already, every state has responded to the current educational crisis with some needed reforms. In many areas of the country, school curricula are being strengthened, high school graduation requirements raised, and teacher certification standards upgraded. These are encouraging signs that reflect the firm desire of many educators and concerned citizens to rebuild an educational system capable of nurturing American children toward a prosperous and civilized adulthood in a rapidly changing world.

CHAPTER SUMMARY

Peer Relations

- Peer sociability begins in infancy with isolated touches, smiles, and vocalizations that increase in frequency and complexity during the second year of life. During the preschool years, coordinated peer interaction becomes more prevalent, and both nonsocial and **cooperative play** become more cognitively mature. In middle childhood and adolescence, children's interactions become more sensitively tuned to the

---

◆ CONTEMPORARY ISSUES: CULTURAL DIFFERENCES ◆

Education in Japan and Taiwan   Box 15.3

Repeated findings that American pupils score poorly in mathematics and science achievement when compared to their counterparts in many other industrialized nations has led investigators to search for the roots of this disparity in children's learning environments. Recent research has centered on Asian children because they are consistently among the top performers in international studies. Findings reveal substantial differences in parental socialization and school practices that parallel the achievement gap between the United States and Japan and Taiwan.

For example, Japanese and Taiwanese parents and teachers believe that all children have the potential to master a challenging academic curriculum if they work hard enough; in contrast, many more of their American counterparts regard native ability as the key to academic success. These attitudinal differences may contribute to the fact that American parents are less likely to encourage cognitive activities at home that might augment school success. Japanese and Taiwanese children spend larger amounts of free time engaged in academic pursuits, such as reading and playing academic-related games, than do children in the United States (Stevenson & Lee, 1990).

Moreover, Asian parents devote many hours to helping their children with homework. American parents spend comparatively little and, at least in elementary school, do not regard homework as an especially important activity. Overall, American parents hold much lower standards for their children's academic performance and are far more complacent about how well their youngsters are doing in school than their Asian counterparts (Chen & Stevenson, 1989; McKnight et al., 1987; Stevenson & Lee, 1990; Stevenson et al., 1986).

In the United States, the school year is over 50 days shorter than that in Japan or Taiwan, and much less class time is devoted to academic instruction, particularly in mathematics (see the accompanying figure) (Stevenson et al., 1986). Instructional time is also used differently in the United States. For example, a recent comparison of American and Japanese mathematics curricula revealed more superficial treatment of topics and much more time devoted to repetition of material taught the previous year in American schools (McKnight et al., 1987). Moreover, as the figure reveals, American children are assigned considerably less homework than are Asian youngsters (Stevenson & Lee, 1990).

Unlike teachers in the United States, Japanese and Taiwanese teachers do not make early educational decisions about pupils on the basis of their achievement. There are no separate ability groups or tracks in grade schools; instead, all pupils receive the same high-quality education. Although classes are generally larger than in American schools, Japanese and Taiwanese teachers

viewpoints of peer partners and increasingly governed by prosocial norms.

■ At all ages, child-child interaction is heavily influenced by situational factors. The quantity and quality of play materials affect the extent to which young children quarrel and fight, engage in cooperative play, or spend time in solitary pursuits. Smaller group sizes, same-age peers, and familiar companions encourage more intense and cooperative peer exchanges. Mixed-age peer experiences provide older children with practice in helping, comforting, and instructing others, and younger children benefit from the superior knowledge and skill of their older companions.

■ Children differ in peer acceptance or popularity—the extent to which agemates regard them as likable social partners. **Sociometric techniques** are used to distinguish among four types of peer acceptance: (1) **popular children,** who are liked by many agemates; (2) **rejected children,** who are actively disliked; (3) **controversial children,** who are both liked and disliked; and (4) **neglected children,** who are seldom chosen, either positively or negatively.

■ The most powerful predictor of peer acceptance is social behavior. Popular children are socially skilled youngsters who interact in a mature and sensitive fashion with agemates. In contrast, rejected children engage in negative, antisocial acts and are seriously at risk for lasting adjustment problems. Controversial youngsters display a blend of positive and negative peer behaviors, while neglected children have a repertoire of effective social skills but prefer to play alone. Coaching in social skills and intensive academic remediation have improved the peer acceptance of rejected children.

■ Beginning in middle childhood, children spontaneously organize themselves into **peer groups,** cohesive social units

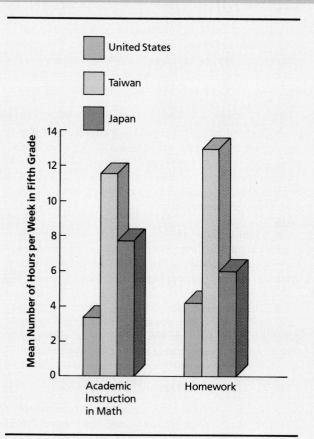

come to know their pupils well because they teach the same youngsters for two or three years and make annual or semiannual visits to their students' homes. Continuous communication between teachers and parents takes place with the aid of small notebooks that children carry back and forth every day and in which messages about their assignments, academic performance, and behavior are written. No such formalized system of frequent teacher-parent communication exists in the United States (Stevenson & Lee, 1990).

The findings summarized above suggest that the superior academic achievement of Asian over American pupils can be attributed to a variety of family and school variables. Among these are greater quantities of time devoted to academic pursuits, high-quality experiences to fill that time, and especially dedicated efforts by parents to encourage children's expenditure of effort and to assist with their learning.

Hours per week of academic instruction in mathematics and of homework in all subjects for fifth graders in the Stevenson and Lee (1990) study. The estimates for classroom instruction were obtained from teachers and those for homework from parents on comparable samples of over 200 fifth graders in each of the three countries. *(Adapted from Stevenson & Lee, 1990.)*

that generate unique norms and hierarchical social structures. Peer groups form when members perceive that they share common goals. Selection of group companions and generation of group norms result from a blend of family and peer influences. Group social structures are sometimes based on **dominance hierarchies.** During adolescence, dominance becomes less important, and group structures are often based on special talents that further the group's objectives.

■ Peers serve as socialization agents by reinforcing and modeling a wide variety of social behaviors. Peer pressures toward conformity are strongest during early adolescence. At the same time, peers seldom demand total conformity, and most peer pressures are not in conflict with important adult values.

Media

■ Children spend more time watching television than in any other waking activity. The heaviest child viewers have low IQs, come from low-income families, and experience family and peer difficulties. Only gradually do children acquire **television literacy,** the ability to process the form and content of TV messages in an accurate fashion.

■ Violent TV fare has been linked to both short- and long-term increments in aggressive behavior. In addition, much televised material conveys sex-role and racial/ethnic stereotypes that children readily incorporate into their belief systems. TV commercials successfully manipulate toy and food preferences, especially among young children who do not comprehend the selling purpose of the ads. At the same time, appropriately designed TV programs can foster positive social and intellectual outcomes.

■ Computers can have rich educational and social benefits for children. In classrooms, children use them collaboratively and cooperatively. Gains in academic performance result from computer-assisted instruction and word processing programs. Specialized programming languages teach children how computers function and promote advanced cognitive skills. Nevertheless, computers may widen existing intellectual gaps between the social classes and sexes.

Schooling

■ Children's experiences in school affect many aspects of their development. The physical characteristics of the school setting make an important difference. Crowded classrooms and scarcity of materials promote conflict among children, while class sizes below 15 to 20 pupils are related to better achievement. In the traditional row-and-column seating arrangement, children placed "front-and-center" interact with

teachers the most. In circular and clustered seating plans, pupil participation is more evenly distributed. Small high schools provide students with an enhanced extracurricular experience; in large high schools, active involvement is restricted to an elite few.

■ Two broad educational philosophies have been studied in American schools. Compared to children in **traditional classrooms,** pupils in **open classrooms** are autonomous learners who are especially tolerant of individual differences and who have more positive attitudes toward school. However, children in open classrooms are not advantaged in achievement.

■ Patterns of teacher-pupil interaction affect children's engagement in classroom activities and academic progress. Teachers who are effective classroom managers have attentive pupils who achieve especially well. Instruction that focuses on rote repetitive drill rather than cognitively challenging tasks reduces children's interest and involvement.

■ Teachers do not interact with all pupils in the same way. In most instances, teachers' behaviors are reasonable reactions to the characteristics of different children. However, negative **self-fulfilling prophecies** sometimes occur in which children display poorer school progress than would otherwise occur. Disruptive, low-achieving youngsters; children assigned to low ability tracks; and racial/ethnic minority pupils are especially susceptible to negative teacher expectation effects.

■ The legal mandate that handicapped children be placed in least restrictive environments has led to widespread **mainstreaming** of mildly retarded and learning-disabled children. The success of mainstreaming depends on efforts by teachers to promote positive peer relations and provide individualized educational programming.

■ Gifted children are best served by educational programs that build on their special strengths. Academic acceleration is a controversial practice in gifted education, but when carefully implemented, it is highly successful.

■ School desegregation depends on practices that promote positive interaction among racially different children. Cooperative learning experiences, multiethnic curricula, efforts to minimize comparisons among pupils, and small class sizes help break down social barriers between black and white youngsters.

■ National assessments of the academic performance of American pupils, along with cross-national comparisons of school achievement, reveal the United States to be a seriously underachieving nation. Recent concern about the academic preparation of American children has stimulated educational reforms in every state in the nation.

IMPORTANT TERMS AND CONCEPTS

parallel play   (p. 605)
cooperative play   (p. 605)
rough-and-tumble play   (p. 608)
sociometric techniques   (p. 611)
popular children   (p. 611)

rejected children   (p. 611)
controversial children   (p. 611)
neglected children   (p. 611)
peer group   (p. 615)
dominance hierarchy   (p. 620)

television literacy   (p. 624)
traditional classroom   (p. 637)
open classroom   (p. 637)
self-fulfilling prophecy   (p. 640)
mainstreaming   (p. 643)

Kept In by Edaward Lamson Henry (1841–1919), oil on canvas, 1988, 12½″ × 17″.
New York State Historical Association, Cooperstown.

16

Child Development and Social Policy

What Is Social Policy?
Components of the Public Policymaking Process
Contemporary Progress on Problems Facing America's Children
Worldwide Status of Children and Youth
Looking toward the Future

This chapter describes the general condition of children in the United States and around the world, along with examples of how government agencies, organizations, and individuals have responded to their needs. Despite the wide variety of success stories portrayed, we will see that the overall status of American children as we enter the final decade of the twentieth century is much less than satisfactory. Many child development specialists have concluded that the United States, among the wealthiest and most powerful of nations, could do much more to ensure the welfare of its youngest citizens (Horowitz & O'Brien, 1989a; Hymes, 1990; Macchiarola & Gartner, 1989). We certainly do not lack sufficient knowledge to help our children grow into successful, contributing adults. To the contrary, the wealth of research we have explored throughout this book attests to the fact that our understanding of child development has expanded considerably over the last several decades. Although there are still many questions to be answered, we have learned a great deal about family, school, and community contexts that foster the development of physically healthy, cognitively competent, and socially mature children.

Like many other citizens who care about children, you may be deeply disturbed by this conclusion—that the United States has not yet succeeded in creating wide-spread social conditions through which its storehouse of knowledge about child development is successfully applied. Cross-national comparisons reveal that the United States lags behind other Western nations in the creation of policies that support children and families. Consequently, large numbers of children are beset with problems that severely limit their developmental potential. We have already seen in earlier chapters that the American family is strained by inadequate supports for single parents and employed mothers; that many abused and neglected children do not receive the help they need from legal and social service institutions; that each year hundreds of thousands of babies are born to teenagers who are ill-equipped for the responsibilities of parenthood; and that the United States needs to upgrade the overall quality of education that it offers its future work force and family providers.

Later in this chapter, it will become clear that the general condition of American children has not improved over the last decade. Today, more children are vulnerable as the result of rising rates of poverty, homelessness, and family disintegration among the economically disadvantaged—a trend that is expected to continue through the 1990s (Hymes, 1990). In fact, not since the Great Depression of the 1930s have so many American children faced the future with such diminished life chances (Edelman, 1989; Rosewater, 1989).

Recall Bronfenbrenner's (1979, 1989) ecological model of human development, presented in Chapter 1, which describes nested layers of the environment that influence children's development. The outermost level, the one that encompasses and affects all others, is the *macrosystem*—the overarching values, laws, regulations, rules, and customs of a particular culture. Bronfenbrenner's analysis indicates that the plight of large numbers of children in the United States and elsewhere around the world cannot be blamed on their own inadequacies or the personal weaknesses of their parents. Instead, it can be traced to the broad social climate of society. Many child development experts believe that government policies promoting positive, nurturant child-rearing contexts are the most effective way to improve the lives of children (Goffin, 1983).

This chapter explores the reasons behind America's difficulty in ensuring the well-being of its youngest citizens. We begin by examining the policymaking process—the complex social, political, and economic forces that contribute to a nation's responsiveness to child and family concerns. Next, we take up a variety of pressing problems experienced by American children and adolescents, and we look at examples of progress toward solutions that suggest what might be done on a larger scale to

Today, more American children are affected by poverty, homelessness, and family disintegration than at any time since the Great Depression.

protect and foster children's development. Then we turn to a consideration of the status of children in Third World countries afflicted by economic crisis, war, and deteriorated health and welfare services. We will see that although the condition of children is considerably worse in many places than it is in the United States, the principles that govern inadequate attention to children's needs are much the same around the globe.

WHAT IS SOCIAL POLICY?

Social policy is any planful set of actions directed at solving a social problem or attaining a social goal. The breadth of this definition indicates that social policies favoring children can take place at many levels. Policies can be proposed by individuals; by small groups or large, formal organizations; by private or public institutions, such as schools, businesses, and social service agencies; and by governing bodies, such as the United States Congress, state legislatures, the courts, and city councils. Each of the following interventions falls under the broad rubric of social policy:

A large insurance firm offers on-site child care for employees with young children.

A local hospital provides a day nursery for sick youngsters so that parents can meet their work responsibilities.

A professional teachers' organization develops brochures for parents and day care providers addressing such topics as age-appropriate toys, child safety, and health and nutrition.

A university and inner-city school district work together to improve the education of poor and minority pupils. University faculty members guide teachers in refocusing the school curriculum, assessing children's academic strengths and weaknesses, and enlisting parents' involvement in children's learning.

In each of these examples, the efforts of individuals and groups make important differences in the lives of children. While extremely worthwhile in their own right and generating enthusiasm and motivation for larger reforms, notice that all of these policies have a fairly circumscribed impact. They help children whose parents are employed by a particular business, who reside in a certain community, or whose caregivers receive and read information about child health and safety. Enacted independently of one another and allowed to accumulate over time, these policies may eventually reach large numbers of children, but it will be many years before they do so.

Consider Bronfenbrenner's ecological model once more, and notice how the concept of the macrosystem suggests that a special type of social policy effort, called **public policy,** is required to pervasively affect the welfare of children and families. Public policies are prescriptions for action codified into law or standards and guidelines developed by government agencies that have the force of law. Consider the following examples:

A legislative committee develops a bill mandating paid employment leaves for expectant parents. It is subsequently passed by Congress.

The President presents Congress with a plan for a national system of guaranteed health insurance for all its citizens. Congress responds by approving the bill.

A national administrative agency for children, youth, and families develops and implements licensing standards for publicly funded child care facilities. The new regulations require liberal caregiver/child ratios, adequate space, nutritious meals, and a well-rounded educational program.

The nation's highest court rules that because corporal punishment violates children's constitutional right to protection from cruel and unusual punishment, it can no longer be used by school officials to discipline children.

When policies like these are authorized by government bodies and officials, they constitute broad societal plans for action. Consequently, they protect all or a great many children and their families over an extended period of time, not just a select few on a one-time or unpredictable basis.

Each of the examples of public policies given above has already been implemented in one or more European countries. In contrast, none is yet available in the United States, although dedicated individuals and organizations are working toward these goals. This does not mean that the United States has no child-related public policies. There are, to be sure, a wide variety of government-sponsored programs that do provide help to parents and children. For example, we will see that income assistance, medical care, supplementary food programs for pregnant women and young children, and day care subsidies are currently in place for low-income families. But analyses of these programs reveal that the majority have been enacted piecemeal, over a long period of time, with little attention given to their interrelatedness. Moreover, they are largely crisis-oriented, aimed at handling the most severe of America's family difficulties rather than preventing problems before they happen. In addition, funding for these efforts has waxed and waned and has been seriously threatened at various times. In most cases, only a minority of needy individuals have been helped (Hayes, 1982; Takanishi, DeLeon, & Pallak, 1983; Zigler & Finn-Stevenson, 1988).

To appreciate why attempts to help children on a national scale have been difficult to realize in the United States, we must have some understanding of the complex factors that affect the policymaking process. This is a topic to which we turn in the following sections.

COMPONENTS OF THE PUBLIC POLICYMAKING PROCESS

Since demands for change are generated in social contexts, the characteristics of a society place constraints on what can be done to develop and implement public policies. A wide variety of variables — a nation's dominant value orientations, the diversity of its population, its economic resources, its scientific knowledge base, and the attitudes and allegiances of individuals involved in the policymaking process — make an important difference in the kinds of policies that are proposed and the efficiency with which policymaking proceeds (Anderson, 1984).

Societal Values

The *political culture* of nation — widely held beliefs about the relationship that should exist between citizen and government — has a major impact on the policymaking process. In fact, differences among industrialized countries in government-sponsored social programs can largely be accounted for by variations in their political cultures. For example, publicly sponsored health insurance and medical care are broadly available in Europe because many Europeans approve of government control and ownership of such services. In the United States, very few people do.

A common belief in the United States is that parents should assume total responsibility for the care and rearing of children — an ideology that reflects the historical emphasis American society has placed on individualism, self-sufficiency, and the privacy of family life. The prevalence of these values has led government to be reluctant to become heavily involved in family matters (Goffin, 1988; Steiner, 1976, 1981). Moreover, America's deep faith in self-reliance and hard work as the way to get ahead has tended to foster a victim-blaming ideology with regard to the poor and underprivileged. When carried to an extreme, the belief in rugged individualism causes people to minimize the importance of external circumstances impinging on troubled children and families and to assume that parents are largely at fault for their own and their children's condition. Notice how this perspective can encourage the general approach to child and family policy that we mentioned earlier — that is, reacting only when problems become severe instead of providing continuous social and economic supports that prevent family dysfunction (Melton, 1987).

Special Interests

In complex societies, considerable variation exists among different geographic regions and population groups, producing a series of distinct subcultures that stand alongside a nation's overall political values. In the United States, for example, there are differences between North and South, blacks and whites, and young and old. The pluralism of American society has led *special interest groups* to exert a particularly strong impact on the policymaking process. In fact, policies generally arise out of conflicts and compromises between groups of people who have distinct beliefs and desires. In this clash of special interests from which policies emerge, groups that are well-organized, have a skilled leadership, contribute to the economic welfare of the nation, and amass a large constituency are likely to fare much better than groups that are poorly organized, a drain on economic reserves, and small in number.

Notice how particular problems arise out of this process of jockeying for public influence when it comes to children's needs. Children can easily remain unrecognized because they do not make immediate contributions to the economic welfare of their nation; instead, their care and development are a costly drain on economic resources that people with quite different special interests want for their own pressing needs. Moreover, children are not capable of organizing and speaking out to protect their own priorities, as adult citizens do. Because they must rely on the good will of others for becoming an important governmental priority, children are constantly in danger of becoming a "forgotten constituency" in the policymaking process (Takanishi, DeLeon, & Pallak, 1983).

Economic Conditions

Besides dominant national values and the demands of powerful special interest groups, the current state of a nation's economy affects what it does to improve the welfare of its populace. The scarcity of public resources is very limiting in less developed countries of the world, which depend on economic aid from affluent nations like the United States to feed, clothe, educate, and provide medical care for many citizens. But even in large industrialized nations, the government does not always have adequate resources to do everything that needs to be done to solve its social problems. In times of economic crisis, governments are less likely to initiate new social programs, and they may cut back or even eliminate those that exist. For example, the early 1970s marked a period of unusual receptivity to a national health insurance plan in the United States. However, efforts to get such legislation passed into law quickly lost momentum because of the high estimated cost of universal health subsidies in an era of growing federal budget deficits (Anderson, 1984). During the 1980s, the United States federal deficit nearly tripled, rising from 914 billion dollars to an astronomical 2.6 trillion dollars (U.S. Office of Management and Budget, 1989), a circumstance that made competition for economic resources by various interest groups especially severe. It is not surprising that federal support for children's needs became particularly difficult to secure during this period, and funding of many child-related services declined considerably (Garwood et al., 1989).

Official Participants: Policymakers

Policymakers are individuals directly involved in drawing up and implementing public policy. A large cast of individuals from all branches of government is involved, each with unique personal priorities and allegiances to special interest groups. Legislators play a central role in all democratic countries. In the United States, the President asserts leadership by submitting legislation to Congress, and he may consult with his cabinet and appoint special commissions and committees to help with this task. Moreover, because of his veto power, the President can make or break policies initiated by others.

Lack of time and expertise on the part of the President and legislators has led authority for implementing policies to be delegated to administrative agencies. In the United States, the federal Departments of Agriculture, Health and Human Services, Housing and Urban Development, Labor, and Education contain agencies charged with overseeing a wide variety of policies relevant to children and families. For example, the Department of Agriculture administers child nutrition programs; the Department of Health and Human Services monitors Project Head Start, child abuse prevention and treatment, and public health programs for the poor; and the Department of Labor oversees youth employment and training programs (Garwood et al., 1989). Agencies are also a major source of policy proposals. Since administrators know a great deal about problems with existing programs in relation to current national needs, they often suggest legislation and press for its adoption.

Finally, the courts play an important role in policy formation, particularly when laws and the manner in which they are implemented are challenged. For example, in 1954, the Supreme Court contributed to the shaping of American educational policy by holding that separate schools for youngsters of different racial and ethnic backgrounds violated the equal protection clause of the Constitution (*Brown* v. *Board of Education of Topeka,* 1954). While this decision was a landmark achievement in the area of civil rights, we must keep in mind that the courts, like other policymaking bodies, are influenced by the complex mix of contradictory values and special interests that make up the political culture in which they are embedded. Consequently, court decisions are not always consistent with one another or uniformly responsive to children's needs as developing citizens in a democratic society (Melton, 1987). For example, children's rights to privacy (to be free of unreasonable searches and seizures by school officials), to due process (to be entitled to a hearing before commitment to a mental institution), and to protection against cruel and unusual punishment (to be safe from paddlings at school) have not been upheld in recent Supreme Court decisions (see *New Jersey* v. *T.L.O.,* 1985; *Parham* v. *J.R.,* 1979; *Ingraham* v. *Wright,* 1977).

Unofficial Participants

In addition to government officials, the activities of many others can affect public policy. However, the remaining participants are "unofficial" in that they do not possess legal authority to make binding policy decisions. Instead, they attempt to influence the decisions of official policymakers (Anderson, 1984). Special interest groups are examples of unofficial participants that we have already mentioned in our discussion of political values. Additional important ones include the media, scientific researchers, and the individual citizen.

The Media. An unsolved problem can be converted into a salient national issue through media presentations that attract broad public attention, thereby compelling lawmakers to respond. For example, in the early 1960s, media revelations that Americans had narrowly missed mass marketing of the drug thalidomide[1] triggered widespread public outrage, a response that resulted in quick passage of stringent consumer protection laws in the area of drug safety (Nadel, 1971). In recent years,

---

[1] Return to Chapter 3, page 90, to review the teratogenic impact of thalidomide on the developing embryo.

television documentaries, newspaper stories, and magazine articles on such issues as hunger, drug abuse, child sexual abuse, teenage pregnancy, and infant mortality have helped to define these issues as serious national problems and to mobilize public opinion in support of policy formation. The effect of the media on the policy process can be direct; it can influence policymakers who happen to see a program or read an article themselves. However, in most instances, its influence is indirect. It inspires citizens to communicate with lawmakers or support organizations and interest groups lobbying for greater attention to child-related concerns. The power of the media lies in its dramatic images and arresting anecdotes. By presenting an issue in graphic form to millions of viewers and readers, a once invisible social problem can be transformed into an emotionally charged national issue (Hayes, 1982; Kelman, 1987; McCall, 1987).

Scientific Researchers. For the policy process to be optimally effective in serving social needs, research should guide it at every major step along the way — during initiation, design, and implementation of new programs. However, much to the disappointment of many investigators, scientific knowledge does not invariably affect policymaking. The impact of research depends heavily on its interactions with other components of the policy process, such as prevailing societal values and pressures exerted by special interest groups. Recall from your reading of many parts of this book that research evidence is often not consistent enough to point to clear solutions; investigators themselves participate in fervent debates over the scientific interpretation of new results. Consequently, proponents and opponents of particular policies can be very selective in the research on which they choose to rely, discounting findings that contradict their beliefs and ignoring reservations about results that support their point of view (Lindblom, 1986).

Nevertheless, when research findings are consistent and effectively communicated, they can have a substantial impact on policy formation. For example, research on the importance of early experience for children's intellectual development played a major role in the initiation of Project Head Start in 1965 (Hunt, 1961), and findings on the long-term benefits of preschool intervention helped Head Start survive when its funding was threatened.[2] In another instance, evidence addressing the severe impact of malnutrition on early brain development was instrumental in passage by Congress of the *Special Supplemental Food Program for Women, Infants, and Children.* Since the early 1970s, it has supplied food packages to many poverty-stricken pregnant women and young children. However, we have already suggested that the impact of research on the policy process is determined by much more than its scientific credibility. For both Head Start and the Special Supplemental Food Program, if public sentiments had not been so receptive to helping poor children at the time these policies were proposed, compelling findings on the importance of early stimulation and nutrition might have been less influential (Hayes, 1982).

Although the effect of research on policy is often not as great as it should be, modern scientists are engaging in activities that promise to increase its impact. Today, child development specialists are actively contributing to and promoting a research literature related to policy, and they are making a greater effort than ever before to disseminate important results so they can be easily understood by policymakers and the general public. In this regard, a number of investigators have pointed out that it is just as important to help policymakers understand what is not known as it is to make them aware of conclusive research on a critical social issue (McCall, 1987; Melton, 1987; Mnookin, 1978; Thompson et al., 1989). When scientists make clear what we do not yet know about child development, they help policymakers resist the tempta-

---

[2] Return to Chapter 8, page 335, to review how research had a substantial impact on the survival of Head Start.

tion to use selective evidence to support a particular position and encourage them to think harder about the possible consequences of each course of action.

Finally, a closer partnership between scientific research and public policy promises not just to increase the impact of research on government programs, but also to advance our understanding of child development. See Box 16.1 for an example of how the generation of new policies in response to changing social conditions helps identify important aspects of development that merit further research scrutiny.

The Individual Citizen. In analyses of policymaking, the individual citizen often gets lost in discussions of legislators, interest groups, research findings, and other prominent policy components. This is unfortunate because the actions of individuals are crucial. The power of many special interest groups, particularly those that support children's needs, rests in the hands of committed citizens. Moreover, in many locales, bond issues and tax increases that support schools, parks, recreational facilities, and other services of benefit to children and families must be authorized directly by the voters. Unfortunately, a great many citizens do not take advantage of opportunities they have to shape public policy, perhaps because they believe that their actions will not make a difference. For example, in the most recent national election, only 50 percent of citizens eligible to vote went to the polls.

Interactions among Components. Although each component of the policymaking process has its own identifiable impact, we have already alluded to the idea that it

---

◆　　　　CONTEMPORARY ISSUES: SOCIAL POLICY　　　　◆

Grandparent Visitation Rights: A Policy Dilemma

Box 16.1

Before the 1970s, no state laws existed that explicitly gave grandparents the opportunity to petition the court for visitation privileges with their grandchildren after parental separation and divorce. The right to request a legally mediated schedule of continued contact with a child was reserved for parents, and grandparents' privileges remained largely a function of parental discretion. Although grandparent visitation cases occasionally reached the courts in past decades, judges were extremely wary about authorizing these requests. They recognized that intense conflict between parents and grandparents prompted most legal petitions and that it was not in the best interests of children to embroil them in intergenerational disputes, especially during stressful times of family change (Derdeyn, 1985).

During the last two decades, a rising population of older Americans has resulted in a dramatic broadening of grandparents' rights. Currently, citizens over age 65 constitute approximately 11 percent of the American population, a figure that is expected to increase to 16 percent within the next 30 years (Organization for Economic Cooperation and Development, 1988a). Interest groups representing senior citizens have successfully convinced state legislators to support the grandparent-grandchild relationship during an era in which the high incidence of marital breakup has threatened extended

family ties. Today, all 50 states permit grandparents to seek visitation decrees through the legal system (Thompson et al., 1989).

Policymakers' responsiveness to grandparents' claims is not just a matter of bending to the demands of a large, politically powerful constituency of older Americans. It is also motivated by a well-intentioned effort to foster children's access to social supports within the family system as well as widespread public belief in the specialness of the grandparent-grandchild relationship. Indeed, as we saw in Chapter 14, grandparents can promote children's social and cognitive development in many ways—both directly, through cultivating a warm, responsive relationship with the child, and indirectly, by providing supports to parents in the form of child-rearing advice, models of child-rearing skill, and even financial assistance.

Nevertheless, on the basis of what we currently know about family functioning and children's adjustment, child development specialists have begun to raise serious questions about the advisability of the current trend to legalize children's ties to their grandparents. Research indicates that the most significant mediator of how children's development is affected by frequent interaction with grandparents is the quality of the relationship between the grandparents and the child's own paris the relations among components, rather than the isolated roles of each one, that explain policy outcomes. Consequently, public policy must be understood as the cumulative product of many decisions by a large number of participants, each with quite different motivations and goals (Garwood et al., 1989; Hayes, 1982; Maccoby, Kahn, & Everett, 1983; Marmor, 1983). The nature of this process is a major reason that changes are difficult to achieve in the United States and that adjustments in existing programs have been the typical response to problems of children and families. Major restructuring of a nation's policy priorities requires that a variety of conditions converge to create a more favorable climate. These include greater congressional commitment to children, a concerned President, hospitable economic conditions, increased pressure for change by supportive special interest groups, and research that highlights children's needs and indicates that they are being harmed by current conditions. In the following sections, we will see that although progress is being made on many fronts, a variety of factors have conspired against the creation of this broad national climate in the United States.

CONTEMPORARY PROGRESS ON PROBLEMS FACING AMERICA'S CHILDREN

Until very recently, America's child and youth population was relatively plentiful, allowing society to survive and its economy to flourish, despite the sacrifice of many

In all fifty states, grandparents have the right to petition the court for visitation privileges with their grandchildren after parental separation and divorce. However, very little is known about the impact of this new policy on grandparent-grandchild relations.

ents. If it is positive, children are likely to profit from the extended family association. But courtroom battles that turn parents and grandparents into adversaries may close the door to both direct and indirect benefits that would otherwise accrue from grandparent visitation (Thompson et al., 1989).

Although available evidence suggests that courts should exercise considerable restraint in awarding visitation privileges to grandparents, the new social policy has highlighted a variety of issues that merit additional study. Whereas research on divorcing families indicates that children almost always benefit from a continuing relationship with their noncustodial parent (see Chapter 14), we have little comparable information on grandparents. We do not know, for example, how often grandparents exercise visitation rights, how children react to such visits, how children view their continuing relationships with parents and grandparents under these circumstances, and the extent to which children are drawn into intergenerational conflict when grandparent visitation occurs. Answers to these questions will help policymakers devise guidelines ensuring that children's best interests are paramount in grandparent visitation decisions (Thompson et al., 1989). They also promise to enhance our understanding of how well children and families accommodate to rapidly changing social conditions.

young lives to tragic social conditions (Edelman, 1989). But the number of children and youths in the United States is beginning to shrink rapidly. From 1975 to 1987, the population under 18 years of age decreased by over 3 ½ million, a trend anticipated to continue into the twenty-first century (Organization for Economic Cooperation and Development, 1988a; U.S. Bureau of the Census, 1989b). Consequently, the problems affecting children today take on even greater significance as they threaten to affect larger proportions of future generations of citizens (Wetzel, 1987).

Pressing Problems Facing Children of All Ages

Poverty. For 25 years following World War II, the United States experienced a period of unparalleled economic expansion, accompanied by a steady rise in the average family's income and standard of living. But beginning in 1973, the United States suffered three recessions. These periods of reduced economic activity prompted many industries either to close down or to move production out of major American cities to cheaper labor sites, often out of the country. Consequently, millions of workers with families lost their jobs. Although new employment opportunities were created over this period, they were not sufficient to replace jobs that disappeared, and most were in retail trade and service occupations that paid less than half as much as the manufacturing positions that had evaporated. In addition, motivated by a need to reduce costs, many businesses began to hire temporary and part-time workers who could be paid less and who did not require expensive fringe benefits, such as health insurance, sick leave, and retirement. As a result, low-income parents who managed to locate work frequently found themselves *underemployed* — forced to accept part-time jobs because full-time employment was not available. Moreover, even full-time work has not kept very many low-income families out of poverty. Despite continuing inflation, the minimum wage did not change between 1981 and 1990. Consequently, during the 1980s, the pay check taken home by a minimum-wage earner supporting a family of three people dropped considerably below the **poverty line** — the income level judged by the federal government to be necessary for bare subsistence (see Figure 16.1). Recently, Congress augmented the minimum wage by 27 percent, an action that reduced (but did not eliminate) the distance between a base-level income and the poverty line. The gap remains substan-

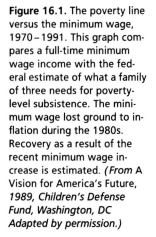

Figure 16.1. The poverty line versus the minimum wage, 1970–1991. This graph compares a full-time minimum wage income with the federal estimate of what a family of three needs for poverty-level subsistence. The minimum wage lost ground to inflation during the 1980s. Recovery as a result of the recent minimum wage increase is estimated. *(From* A Vision for America's Future, *1989, Children's Defense Fund, Washington, DC Adapted by permission.)*

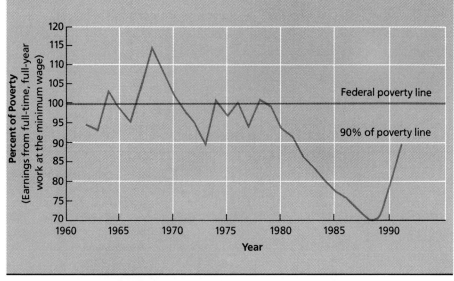

tial for low-income families with large numbers of children (Children's Defense Fund, 1990b; Rosewater, 1989).

The economic shifts described above caused the poverty rate among children to climb from 15 to 19 percent between the early 1970s and 1990. Today, more than 12 million youngsters are affected. In fact, children are the poorest of any age sector of the American population, and (as shown in Figure 16.2) they are in more dire straits than young citizens in many other industrialized nations. Families hit hardest by poverty include parents under 25 years of age with preschool children, the growing number of mother-only families (children of teenage mothers are especially vulnerable), and racial/ethnic minorities. Current estimates indicate that the poverty rate is as high as 38 percent among Hispanic children and 44 percent among black children (Children's Defense Fund, 1990b; Edelman, 1989).

In fact, poverty has become so extreme in inner-city neighborhoods with high concentrations of disadvantaged racial/ethnic minorities that residents of these areas are no longer referred to as low-income or lower-class, but rather as *underclass*. Underclass citizens are the long-term poor of American society — those deprived of the manufacturing employment that was once plentiful in inner cities and whose poor educational preparation and completion levels make them ineligible for the jobs that are currently available. In ghetto areas where they live, behavior contrasts sharply with that of the mainstream occupational community. Family instability, crime, drug addiction, alcoholism, frequent illness, and early death are common. Moreover, a dramatic rise in the youth population of such neighborhoods has led the incidence of school dropout, delinquency, out-of-wedlock pregnancy, and mother-headed single-parent families to reach crisis proportions (Wilson, 1987).

Homelessness. An additional problem — one that was quite uncommon a decade ago — has further jeopardized the life chances of poor children in the United States. By the end of the 1980s, approximately 3 million Americans had no place to live. Currently, families make up over one third of the nation's homeless population, and

Figure 16.2. Prevalence of poverty among children in eight industrialized nations, based on the most recent cross-national data (obtained between 1979 and 1982). Poverty rates can be computed in a number of different ways. In this case, the percentage of children in families with earnings below one half of the national median income serves as the basis of comparison. *(Adapted from Smeeding, Torrey, & Rein, 1988.)*

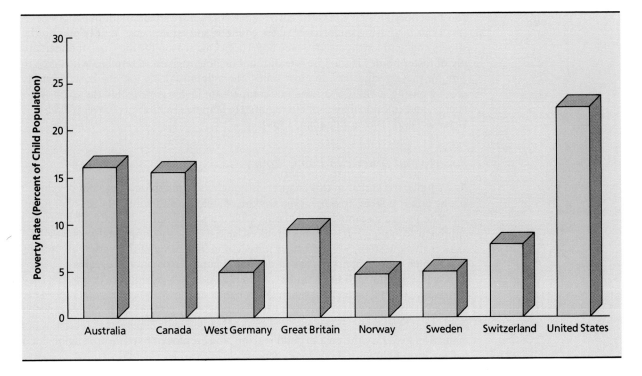

one in every four homeless individuals is believed to be a child (Children's Defense Fund, 1990b).

The rapid increase in homelessness over the last decade is the combined result of several factors that have conspired to reduce the availability of low-cost housing. Beginning in 1975, the median price of a family home began to inflate dramatically; since then, it has risen more than 92 percent (Edelman, 1989). At the same time, affluent suburban Americans were reattracted to city life, and slum clearance projects converted many inner-city neighborhoods into urban villages for the well-to-do. Moreover, federal programs directed at maintaining a plentiful supply of housing for the poor were precipitously curtailed during the 1980s; by the end of the decade, their funding had been reduced by more than 80 percent. In response to these trends, waiting lists for public housing vacancies in most large cities climbed to unmanageable proportions, and many families with children were consigned to the streets (Children's Defense Fund, 1990b; Hayes, 1989).

The largest proportion of homeless families consists of women on their own with young children — usually under the age of 5 (Hayes, 1989; Solarz, 1988). Research indicates that these youngsters suffer from serious developmental delays and emotional stress (Bassuk & Rosenberg, 1988; Bassuk & Rubin, 1987). Homeless children are also poorly nourished and experience more health problems than the child population in general. Respiratory infections, gastrointestinal illnesses, and lice infestations from exposure to the elements or to crowded, unsanitary living conditions in public shelters are especially common. Many such children are prone to childhood diseases because they have not received regular medical attention or a program of childhood immunizations (Miller & Lin, 1988). Moreover, an estimated 40 percent of homeless youngsters who are eligible do not attend school (Egan, 1988).

The number of homeless children actually extends beyond those without a permanent roof over their heads but who are still with at least one parent. As a result of abuse and neglect or because their poverty-stricken parents cannot care for them, several hundred thousand American children live in group homes, residential treatment centers, and other institutions. Currently, there is a shortage of foster placements for these youngsters. Many experience frequent transfers from one temporary care facility to another, remaining wards of the state for years because the developmental consequences of their deprived early experiences have made them unadoptable. A small but increasing minority of older children and adolescents simply take to the streets and fend for themselves (see Box 16.2). One reason for the current undersupply of foster homes is the low rate of reimbursement given to families who agree to care for these youngsters. In most states, the amount falls below the basic monthly cost of raising a child and does not compensate foster parents for the extra time, energy, and emotional investment required to help these children recover (Children's Defense Fund, 1989a; Edelman, 1989).

Poverty and American Public Policy

As we indicated earlier in this chapter, although the United States has not developed strong public policies to protect the welfare of children and youth, it does offer many separate programs aimed at alleviating children's difficulties. Exactly why has this approach to policy left so many children at risk for developmental problems? To answer this question, we must have a basic understanding of the variety of options from which governments choose in designing family assistance programs.

One way is through **tax benefits.** As long as a child's parents are taxpayers, they can receive federal financial assistance through deductions and credits that reduce the amount of taxes they must pay. At present, many family policies are available through the United States tax system. For example, families with dependents receive a tax deduction to defray the cost of child rearing, and employed parents are eligible for a tax credit to help with day care expenses.

But notice that parents whose wages are very meager cannot take full advantage of tax benefits; their tax liability is so low that there is little to charge family-related deductions against. Moreover, unemployed parents, who have no taxable income, do not profit from policies available through the tax system at all. Instead, poor families depend for financial assistance on another type of government policy called **income transfers.** In this case, money is taken from the public treasury and *transferred,* in the form of income, directly to citizens judged to need it on the basis of government guidelines for dispersal of the funds. **Aid to Families with Dependent Children**

◆ CONTEMPORARY ISSUES: SOCIAL POLICY ◆

S*treet Kids*

Box 16.2

Recent estimates indicate that as many as 1.5 million teenagers run away from home each year. Although the large majority return after no more than a few days, about one fourth are *street kids*—long-term runaway or homeless youths who fend for themselves, generally through illegal activities. Some of these adolescents are "throwaway" youths, pushed from their homes because they are no longer wanted by parents. Others leave by mutual agreement because of limited economic and emotional resources at home. Still others, mainly boys, separate from already homeless parents and siblings because many government-sponsored family shelters do not accept male youths over 12 or 13 years of age (Children's Defense Fund, 1989a).

Although little is known about street kids who do not use shelter and runaway services, the information we do have indicates that the majority come from seriously troubled families. Histories of physical and sexual abuse are common, as is parental alcoholism, which contributes further to family violence and conflict (Adams, Gullotta, & Clancy, 1985; Janus et al., 1987). In addition, most of these young people have had unsuccessful school lives in which behavior problems and learning difficulties resulted in peer rejection, grade retention, frequent suspension, and eventual dropping out (Price, 1987; Shaffer & Caton, 1984; Yates et al., 1988).

Street kids suffer from serious health problems, both physically and emotionally. In one study of homeless adolescents in Hollywood, California, over 57 percent reported at least one day in the past month with nothing to eat (Robertson, 1989). Stressful conditions of living without shelter lower resistance to disease and leave these youngsters at risk for a wide variety of medical conditions. In a New York City sample, one fourth of drifting youths were engaged in street prostitution for survival, and 85 percent used drugs and alcohol (Yates et al., 1988). Unprotected sexual activity and sharing of needles during intravenous drug injection make street kids highly vulnerable to teenage pregnancy and AIDS. Moreover, many are seriously depressed, have attempted suicide, or have some other serious mental health prob-

Long-term runaway and homeless youths come from troubled families and suffer from serious physical and emotional health problems.

lem (Robertson, 1989; Shaffer & Caton, 1984; Yates et al., 1988).

Most street kids recognize that they need help and indicate that they would come for it if it were readily available (Crystal, 1986; Solarz, 1988). The *Runaway and Homeless Youth Act,* passed by Congress in 1980, assists local communities in meeting the needs of these young people. Federally funded centers provide temporary housing, counseling, and recreational, educational, and employment services, along with assistance in finding permanent living arrangements. The Act also funds the *National Runaway Switchboard,* which offers crisis counseling and puts many runaways in touch with their families; its *Adolescent Suicide Hotline* has prevented many tragedies. Nevertheless, more needs to be done. Because of inadequate facilities and staff, youth shelters serve only about one fifth of adolescents in need (Children's Defense Fund, 1989a).

(AFDC), the nation's key income program for poor families, is an example of an income transfer policy. Parents with children under 18 living at home and whose incomes fall below a state-defined level receive a monthly check. Another example is *Food Stamps,* the largest American food program for the poor. On the basis of income level, needy families are given coupons that can be exchanged for food items at grocery stores.

Tax benefits and income transfers fall within a category of public policies called **entitlements.** In other words, the benefit is available to any person who meets eligibility requirements for the program—that is, anyone who is *entitled* to it, according to government regulations. The largest number of federal programs for American children and families are **discretionary programs** rather than entitlements. In this kind of policy, only a limited amount of government funding is authorized. Program benefits are available as long as these last, but no effort is made to reach all people who are eligible. Unlike AFDC and Food Stamps, discretionary programs usually do not offer direct financial assistance to families. Instead, they provide goods and services. Head Start, the nation's preschool intervention program for poor children, is an example of a discretionary program. Although it serves approximately 450,000 children annually, its federal allocation is limited. As a result, it reaches only 16 percent of eligible youngsters (Children's Defense Fund, 1989a). Other important discretionary programs include child abuse prevention and treatment, foster care services, and the Special Supplemental Food Program for Women, Infants, and Children, which we mentioned earlier in this chapter.

Finally, children require more than financial assistance, goods, and services to ensure their well-being. They also need to be protected from adverse circumstances and treatment. **Protective regulations** serve this purpose. Child labor laws, compulsory education laws, and government standards for day care services are examples of regulations directed at safeguarding children's development. The stringency of protective regulations has implications for the cost of programs serving children. For example, making day care standards tough—requiring high standards for caregiver preparation, generous staff/child ratios, and well-equipped facilities—means that greater public subsidies will be required to operate programs for children whose parents cannot afford such high-quality care.

Now that we understand the various avenues through which governments can support children's needs, let's take a look at the nature of America's investment in child-related services. We have already indicated in our discussion of childhood poverty that as unemployment rose during the 1980s, the federal government reduced its funding of many social programs. As shown in the first column of Table 16.1, the United States currently provides fewer cash benefits to poor families than do other industrialized nations that have lower child poverty rates (O'Higgins, 1988; Smeeding & Torrey, 1988; Smeeding, Torrey, & Rein, 1988), and noncash benefits are less generous as well (Smeeding & Torrey, 1988). The availability of AFDC is a case in point. The federal government pays more than half the cost of the AFDC program, but each state sets its own eligibility requirements and benefit levels. To help a family survive, the amount provided must be equivalent to a minimum standard of living. Yet in most areas of the country, the benefits available are significantly less than required for bare subsistence. One recent estimate indicated that even when the maximum AFDC grant is combined with the maximum food stamp benefit, a family of three will be left below the poverty line (usually far below it) in 48 of the 50 states (Children's Defense Fund, 1989a).

In addition to its overall economic commitment to children, the way in which a country balances the availability of different kinds of social programs makes an important difference in the extent to which it serves children's needs. To support children and families, the United States relies to a greater degree on the tax system than do most industrialized countries. Recall that tax benefits only help families who earn incomes large enough to qualify them for tax credits. Families with limited

Table 16.1. How Much Do Income Transfers Reduce Child Poverty in Eight Industrialized Nations?

COUNTRY	POVERTY GAP REDUCTION RATE (%)	PERCENTAGE OF POVERTY RATE REDUCTION BY TYPE OF INCOME TRANSFER	
		SOCIAL INSURANCE	INCOME-LINKED (WELFARE) PROGRAMS
Australia	71	13	87
Canada	85	52	48
Great Britain	117	62	38
West Germany	106	89	11
Norway	105	97	3
Sweden	176	63	37
Switzerland	91	93	7
United States	65	29	71

Note: *Poverty gap reduction rate* refers to the average income of poor citizens as a percentage of the national poverty line after receipt of government-supported income transfers. The table shows that certain countries (Great Britain, West Germany, Norway, and Sweden) completely eliminate the poverty gap through their income transfer programs. In fact, the 100+ percentage values indicate that cash benefits in these countries actually raise poor families *above* the poverty line. Other countries (Australia and the United States) are less successful in reducing poverty. The United States does least well. Notice that the most successful nations distribute a greater proportion of income transfer funds through social insurance (available to all citizens) rather than through income-linked programs (targeted at the poor).

Source: Smeeding, Torrey, & Rein, 1988.

earnings benefit only partially, and the unemployed are totally excluded. Moreover, income transfers in the United States are entirely welfare-oriented — that is, based on economic need — and restrictions on program eligibility in many states prevent poor families with some income from receiving support (Wilson, 1987).

In many European nations, income transfers are granted to poor families on a very different basis — through **social insurance** (Kamerman & Kahn, 1989; Smeeding & Torrey, 1988; Smeeding, Torrey, & Rein, 1988). In this approach, standard government benefits are either linked to employment or (more often) granted to all members of society. Examples are paid parental leave for childbirth and child illness, health care, child allowances (which provide a standard yearly payment for each youngster in a family), and housing subsidies. The unique feature of the social insurance strategy is that services are available to all citizens, regardless of the size of their incomes. In the few instances in which these benefits are scaled according to earnings (as is the case with housing allowances in Great Britain, France, Sweden, and West Germany), the largest shares go to low-income families (Erikson & Fritzell, 1988). Consequently, the policy not only serves the entire citizenry, but also offers a meaningful income supplement to its poorest members. In fact, the availability of comprehensive social insurance programs that supplement family income has greatly reduced the need for public aid in many European countries (Kamerman & Kahn, 1982, 1989).

Several policy analysts believe that implementing universal social insurance programs like those described above is the most promising route to solving the poverty crisis in the United States (Kamerman & Kahn, 1982; Wilson, 1987). As indicated in Table 16.1, cross-national evidence reveals that the social insurance strategy reduces poverty more successfully than the American income-linked approach. You may be wondering, at this point, why social insurance programs are so prevalent in European countries but are not widely available in the United States. According to Wilensky (1983), one reason is that powerful, well-organized special interest groups exist to support such policies in Europe. In contrast, the goals of American constituencies on issues of family policy are far less unified and often act in direct opposition to one another.

However, over the past two decades, two influential interest groups with children's well-being as their central purpose have emerged in the United States. One of them is government-based — the **Select Committee on Children, Youth, and Families** of the House of Representatives. Select committees, unlike standing congressional committees, cannot write legislation or recommend appropriation of funds. Instead, they provide forums for ongoing review of national problems. Established in 1982 at a time when the overall condition of American children was rapidly deteriorating, the Select Committee on Children, Youth, and Families devotes its energies to highlighting children's needs and assessing the effectiveness of existing federal programs. Recently, the committee helped to focus the attention of Congress on the devastating impact of unemployment and homelessness on children's development and the pressing need for high-quality child care to serve employed mothers and their children. The other vigorous champion of children's cause is a private, nonprofit organization, the **Children's Defense Fund,** founded in 1973. To learn more about it, refer to Box 16.3.

BRIEF REVIEW

High unemployment combined with substantial reductions in government-sponsored social programs caused the incidence of child poverty and homelessness to rise substantially over the past decade, especially among racial/ethnic minority sectors of the population. The American reliance on tax benefits and welfare-oriented income transfers has been less successful than the European emphasis on social insurance in reducing family poverty. Lack of public consensus on appropriate government intervention has impeded the development of stronger child- and family-related policies in the United States.

In the following sections, we turn from an analysis of pervasive problems affecting children of all ages to a selection of equally serious ones associated with particular times of development. As our discussion proceeds, you will see that many threats to children's well-being are a function of the recent upsurge in poverty discussed above combined with limited public programs to protect the well-being of children and youth.

Problems of Infancy and Early Childhood

Infant Mortality and Health Care. As shown in Table 16.2, **infant mortality,** the number of deaths in the first year of life per 1,000 live births, declined rapidly in

Table 16.2. Infant Mortality Rates per 1,000 Live Births in the United States, 1940–1986

YEAR	ALL RACES	WHITE	BLACK	TOTAL NONWHITE	RATIO OF BLACK TO WHITE
1940	47.0	43.2	72.9	73.8	1.7
1950	29.2	26.8	43.9	44.5	1.6
1960	26.0	22.9	44.3	43.2	1.9
1970	20.0	17.8	32.6	30.9	1.8
1975	16.1	14.2	26.2	24.2	1.9
1980	12.6	11.0	21.4	19.1	2.0
1982	11.5	10.1	19.6	17.3	1.9
1984	10.8	9.4	18.4	16.1	2.0
1986	10.4	8.9	18.0	15.7	2.0

Source: U. S. Bureau of the Census (1989).

the United States from 1940 to 1980, at which point progress slowed. Despite its advanced health care technology, the United States has made less progress than other industrialized nations in reducing infant deaths, actually slipping down in the international rankings over the past three decades, from seventh in the 1950s to twentieth at the end of the 1980s. Moreover, as the statistics summarized in Table 16.2 indicate,

---

◆ CONTEMPORARY ISSUES: SOCIAL POLICY ◆

The Children's Defense Fund

Box 16.3

Five Questions about the Status of American Children

1. How many American children live in poverty?
2. Which of these countries has the highest infant mortality rate: Spain, Austria, Ireland, Hong Kong, the United States?
3. How effectively are American children immunized against childhood diseases?
4. How many American youths drop out of school each year?
5. What is the average American welfare payment to a destitute family with children?

Answers

1. Slightly over 12 million. 2. The United States. 3. An estimated 35 to 50 percent of low-income urban 2-year-olds are not fully immunized. 4. Approximately 500,000. 5. $4.16 per person per day.

Many people are not aware of the problems experienced by large numbers of children in the United States. To sensitize the public, the Children's Defense Fund conducts nationwide mailings in which it asks citizens to think about questions and answers like these. Besides promoting public awareness, the Children's Defense Fund provides policymakers with a steady stream of facts about the status of American children and encourages them to develop and support legislation responsive to children's needs.

The Children's Defense Fund is the most avid interest group for children in the United States. To accomplish its goals, it engages in research, public education, legal action, drafting of legislation, congressional testimony, and community organizing. Each year, it publishes its annual *Children's Defense Budget,* which provides a comprehensive analysis of the current status of children, government-sponsored programs serving them, and proposals for improving America's child and family programs. The Children's Defense Fund also supports an extensive network of state and local organizations that have children's needs as their central purpose. Two of its most significant projects are an adolescent pregnancy prevention program and a prenatal care campaign designed to reduce the high incidence of mortality, illness, and developmental disabilities among poverty-stricken infants in the United States. Dissemination of

A public service poster distributed to American communities by the Children's Defense Fund. *(Reprinted by permission of the Children's Defense Fund.)*

information on how communities can develop more effective child and family services, preparation of a monthly newsletter on what people across the nation are doing to solve children's problems, and public service announcements (see adjacent example) are among its many activities.

The Children's Defense Fund is supported by foundations, corporate grants, and individual donations. To inquire about its publications and efforts on children's behalf, contact: The Children's Defense Fund, 122 C Street N.W., Washington, DC 20001. Phone (202) 628-8787.

members of America's racial/ethnic minorities (especially black infants) are at greatest risk.

Research reveals that babies born to mothers who do not receive comprehensive prenatal services beginning in the first trimester are two to four times more likely to be born with low birth weights and three times more likely to die during the first year than babies born to mothers who receive such care. Many child development and medical experts attribute the high infant death rate in the United States to deficient public health services to meet the needs of pregnant women and young children (Children's Defense Fund, 1989a; Cólon & Cólon, 1989; Miller, 1985; National Commission to Prevent Infant Mortality, 1988).

In the United States, health insurance is an employment-related fringe benefit, not a government-sponsored program available to all citizens (as it is in most industrialized nations around the world). Yet many businesses that rely on low-wage and part-time help do not insure their employees. If they do, they often do not subsidize coverage for other family members, including children (Renner & Navarro, 1989). Research indicates that low-income children see a doctor only half as often as economically advantaged youngsters with similar illnesses because of the high cost of medical treatment (Newacheck & Starfield, 1988).

Public health benefits are available in the United States, but they are accessible only to the most needy individuals. For example, **Medicaid,** the nation's largest medical insurance program, has recently been expanded to provide excellent preventive and primary health services for children (Children's Defense Fund, 1990c). However, Medicaid mainly covers individuals whose severely impoverished circumstances also qualify them for AFDC. Linking Medicaid to AFDC restricts the number of families covered, since (as we indicated earlier) many states have permitted AFDC eligibility to fall considerably below the poverty line. In 1986, Congress permitted the states to extend Medicaid coverage to pregnant women and preschool children whose family incomes fell below 185 percent of the poverty level. However, many states do not exercise this option (Children's Defense Fund, 1989a; 1989c; Oberg, 1988).

Several other federally funded public health programs provide grants to the states to support health and family planning clinics. Policies like these are highly effective in

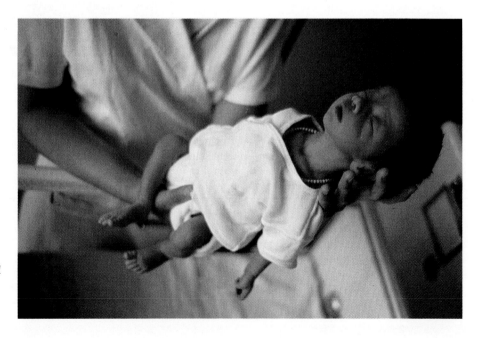

The mother of this drug-addicted, low-birth-weight newborn received no prenatal care. Infant mortality is especially high among such babies.

reducing infant mortality and improving maternal and child health. For example, between 1970 and 1980, when these programs were more liberally funded, infant mortality fell by 37 percent. But during the first half of the 1980s, when federal support was cut substantially, infant mortality declined by only 16 percent, less than half the improvement of the previous decade (refer to Table 16.2). Although some funding has recently been restored, it has not been sufficient to meet the need for medical services caused by widespread poverty and loss of insurance by many employed citizens (Rosewater, 1989). Today, America's low-income families face a serious health crisis. As shown in Figure 16.3, children constitute the largest segment of America's medically uninsured population. Besides those below the poverty line, children of low-income working parents with incomes up to 200 percent of the poverty threshold have the greatest likelihood of being affected (Oberg, 1988).

Infants and Young Children at Risk: The Need for Early Intervention. Early childhood programs providing comprehensive intervention — educational, nutritional, medical, and parental support services — are especially crucial for poverty-stricken infants and preschoolers to help compensate for the adverse effects of their everyday lives. Head Start, targeted at preschoolers from the most impoverished families, is a pioneer in the field of early intervention. Since its inception in 1965, it has served over 11 million children. Yet, as we mentioned earlier, Head Start serves only a minority of eligible youngsters, and it reaches very few who are under 3 years of age. Insufficient funding has also prevented most Head Start centers from lengthening their daily hours and offering services through the summer months to better meet the needs of low-income working parents (Children's Defense Fund, 1989a).

However, a recent federal initiative promises to dramatically improve the nation's intervention services for infants and young children. *Public Law (PL) 99-457, The*

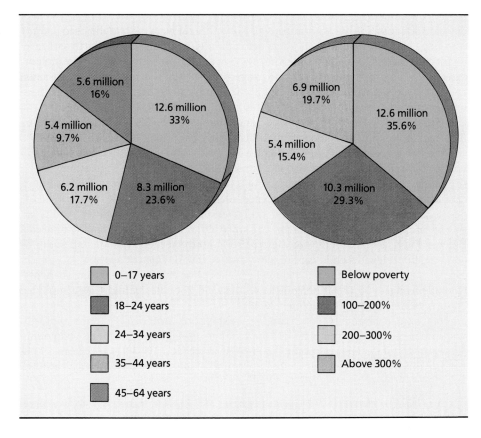

Figure 16.3. Age and income distribution of America's uninsured population. The chart on the left shows that children represent the largest age segment (one third) of the uninsured. The chart on the right reveals that the majority (65 percent) of the uninsured live in families with incomes below 200 percent of the poverty threshold. *(From Oberg, 1988, pp. 2–3.)*

Education of the Handicapped Amendments of 1986, is an extension downward of PL 94-142, *The Education for All Handicapped Children Act,* which we discussed in Chapter 15. According to the new law, all states will be required by the early 1990s to offer a free and appropriate education, along with other support services, not just for school-age children with handicapping conditions, but for 3- to 5-year-olds as well (Gallagher, 1989; Hauser-Cram et al., 1988). In addition, PL 99-457 addresses the need for much earlier intervention by providing modest funding to the states to serve children from birth through age 2. A unique feature of the law is that eligibility for program benefits is based on an unusually flexible set of criteria. Services can be extended to youngsters who either display serious developmental delays or are at risk for such delays in addition to children with clearly diagnosable handicapping conditions. Also, a special part of the legislation mandates that parents join in educational planning for their youngsters, a requirement aimed at enhancing the capacity of each participating family to raise a child with special needs (Gallagher, 1989; Hauser-Cram et al., 1988).

Policy experts recognize that PL 99-457 will have to weather many storms before its goals become realities. The federally mandated expansion of services is very great, while the funding provided to initiate them is limited. Nevertheless, the law represents a new policy that is highly sensitive to the needs of young children at risk for developmental problems and with established disabilities. Moreover, it was initiated at a time of little expanded federal investment in family programs because the right ingredients combined to make it possible — powerful advocates within Congress, intensive lobbying efforts by energetic child-oriented organizations, and convincing research on the effectiveness of early intervention (Gallagher, 1989).

Employed Parents and Their Children: The Need for Quality Day Care and Workplace Policies. Unlike most European nations, which provide free publicly sponsored preschool care to all families regardless of whether the mother is employed, the United States has only recently begun to move toward a national system of day care services. European countries also offer liberal workplace policies to parents of young children. Typically, mothers may take 5 to 6 months of childbirth and early infant care leave. During that time, they receive full job protection and a government-subsidized benefit equal to their full wage or a substantial portion of it. In some countries, the time a mother spends with her baby can be extended further with an unpaid employment-protected leave (Kammerman & Kahn, 1989).[3] At present, the United States is the only industrialized nation that has no policy guaranteeing parents time with a new infant while safeguarding their jobs (Stipek & McCroskey, 1989).

America's reluctance to implement a national child care policy has left many young children exposed to inadequate substitute care. Child care regulations, set by the states, vary widely in stringency. For example, some states permit one adult to care for as many as 8 infants or 20 preschoolers; some have no age, educational, or on-the-job training requirements for caregivers; and the large majority require no special preparation before a person can open a family day care home (Children's Defense Fund, 1989a; Phillips & Zigler, 1987). Minimal regulation of staff and program quality relegates child care to a low-status, low-paying occupation. Most child care workers earn incomes well below the poverty line and receive no fringe benefits. Not surprisingly, 35 to 40 percent leave the field annually (Child Care Employee Project, 1990; Kagan, 1989; Willer, 1988).

Day care — especially good care — is expensive. American parents typically spend about $3,500 per year per child for less than optimal care, a figure that amounts to 10 percent of an average family income. For poor families, an expenditure of this size is exhorbitant. For example, the proportion of annual minimum wage earnings

---

[3] Workplace policies are especially progressive in Sweden, a country that places a high priority on gender equality. Swedish mothers and fathers can choose to share parental leave benefits.

that would be consumed ranges from 45 percent for one child to 90 percent for two. *Title XX of the Social Securities Block Grant,* which provides states with federal monies to cover a wide range of social services, can be used to subsidize day care for low-income families. However, since child care is in constant competition with other state programs for these funds, the supply of Title XX day care is far less than the need. Waiting lists have swelled into the thousands in many states (Children's Defense Fund, 1990c).

However, public receptivity to an expanded day care policy has increased in recent years — in fact, so much so that the United States seems to be on the brink of a major transformation in its approach to child care services (Kagan, 1989). The change is the result of a number of factors. First, many businesses now recognize that inadequate child care is a major cause of employee absenteeism and unproductive work time. Consequently, some large corporations have begun to provide parental assistance plans, including flexible work schedules, parental leave, child care subsidies and referral services, and (in a few instances) on-site center care (Hymes, 1990). Currently, approximately 3,000 businesses offer their employees some kind of child care assistance (Kagan, 1989). Although this is a small number when one considers that six million companies are located in the United States, recognition of the importance of high-quality day care services from the business community is continuing to grow (Stipek & McCroskey, 1989).

Second, organizations with an interest in children's needs have vigorously pressed for better child care services. A leader in this effort is the *National Association for the Education of Young Children,* a 70,000-member organization of early childhood educators. In 1985, it launched an initiative designed to substitute for the current lack of federal child care regulations and the inadequacy of standards in many states. The project, called the *National Academy of Early Childhood Programs,* is a voluntary accreditation system for center-based child care facilities. Each day care center that desires to become accredited must comply with a rigorous set of criteria shown by research to be indicative of good care. By the end of the 1980s, over 1,000 centers across the country had received accreditation, and more than 3,500 had initiated the process (Hymes, 1990). The new system grants recognition to exemplary programs, provides others with an incentive to upgrade their services, and offers parents a ready means of discriminating good from poor facilities.

Perhaps the most significant recent achievement of child-related organizations has been the formation of the *Alliance for Better Child Care (ABC).* It brought together 130 diverse groups, including child welfare and educational associations, labor unions, religious organizations, and ethnic minority and women's associations, in a powerful lobbying effort aimed at making high-quality, affordable child care available to all American families. The keystone of ABC's work has been the development and introduction of a comprehensive federal child care bill into Congress. In 1990, the Senate and House of Representatives each passed legislation responsive to ABC recommendations and began to move toward a final compromise bill. Thus, both legislative bodies have demonstrated a commitment to substantial federal investments in helping parents pay for child care and in upgrading its quality and availability (Children's Defense Fund, 1990b).

America's high infant mortality rate and incidence of young children at risk for developmental problems are a consequence of escalating family poverty and the need for expanded public health and early intervention programs. In comparison to European nations, high-quality, affordable child care and family-oriented workplace policies have been slow to develop in the United States. However, encouraging signs include Public Law 99-457, which has opened the door to widespread early intervention services, and increased congressional receptivity to comprehensive child care legislation.

BRIEF REVIEW

Children's Mental Health. When environments are permitted to undermine children's development during the early years, the most vulnerable children enter middle childhood and adolescence with serious mental health problems. Approximately 6 to 9 million American children suffer from emotional and behavioral difficulties severe enough to warrant treatment (Inouye, 1988; Saxe, Cross, & Silverman, 1988). Antisocial behavior, attention-deficit hyperactivity disorder, pervasive anxiety, depression, suicide, and eating disorders such as anorexia nervosa and bulimia are among the most common mental health afflictions of childhood and adolescence to which you were introduced in earlier chapters. All respond to intervention, and there is clear evidence that children who receive treatment fare much better than those who do not (Tuma, 1989).

At the same time, current estimates indicate that only about 20 percent of troubled children have access to the mental health services they need (Children's Defense Fund, 1989a). Research indicates that agencies delegated to provide intervention — schools, public health facilities, the juvenile justice system, and foster home care — are usually not well coordinated. Yet integrated treatment approaches are crucial because children's mental health problems are especially complex. We have already seen that risk factors such as family disorganization, child maltreatment, poor school achievement, teenage pregnancy, and poverty rarely occur in isolation. Instead, they pile up to produce even more serious consequences. When treatment is provided, too often it is through residential and hospital care, since these modes of delivery are the ones most likely to be covered by private and public health insurance. Highly restrictive services like these are necessary in extreme cases. But they do not work well in other instances because children are temporarily removed from homes, neighborhoods, and peer groups that contributed to their problems, and these remain unchanged when the child returns. At present, community-based programs that treat troubled children and adolescents in their everyday environments are especially scarce (Children's Defense Fund, 1989a; Tuma, 1989).

Recent encouraging signs include a new federal program designed to provide the states with assistance in developing integrated systems of child and adolescent mental health services. Although funding for this initiative is still limited, some highly successful interventions have already been designed and implemented (Children's Defense Fund, 1989a). For example, in several states, networks of therapeutic foster homes with intensively trained parents provide special help to emotionally disturbed youngsters. In California, a number of counties have succeeded in developing multiagency collaborations that offer troubled children a range of in-home, day treatment, and special education services (Children's Defense Fund, 1990c). However, as long as child mental health programming remains scant and poorly coordinated on a larger scale, developmental outcomes that seriously threaten the future of American youth — such as school dropout (to which we turn in the following section) — will continue to be pervasive.

High School Dropouts. Although school attrition rates declined considerably over the first half of this century, during the past two decades the proportion of 18- and 19-year-olds without a high school diploma has remained relatively stable, at an alarmingly high 23 percent. For low-income racial/ethnic minorities, the figures are substantially greater — 65 percent for black youths and 55 percent for Hispanic youths (Bennett, 1988; Hentoff, 1989).

Most high school dropouts are severely disadvantaged long before they leave school. Poverty, low educational achievement, grade retention, antisocial behavior, adolescent pregnancy, and drug and alcohol dependence are strongly predictive of high school attrition (Cairns, Cairns, & Neckerman, 1989; Rosewater, 1989; Wilcox & Vincent, 1987). Although one third of all high school dropouts return to finish their education within the next few years, minority youths are far less likely to do so than their white counterparts (U.S. General Accounting Office, 1986). The consequences of early school leaving are far more serious today than they were in decades past because the number of jobs requiring minimal academic skills has fallen off sharply while those necessitating post-high school education have increased. As a result, high school dropouts are generally condemned to a life of low earnings and reduced labor market participation.

Education in America is largely a state and local obligation; the federal government contributes less than 10 percent of total monies spent. Nevertheless, the federal role has been a crucial one for children experiencing learning difficulties because federal funding is generally targeted at the most pressing of America's educational problems. During the last decade, the federal government's share of educational expenditures declined from 9 to 6 percent. This meant that poor and minority children lost ground, since many reduced programs were aimed at serving their needs. For example, the *Education of the Disadvantaged* component of the *Education Consolidation and Improvement Act of 1981,* initiated to address the dropout problem and currently the largest of America's federal educational initiatives, provides remediation in basic skills to children attending schools in low-income neighborhoods. It experienced a 27 percent decrease in federal appropriations adjusted for inflation over the last decade. The *Migrant High School Equivalency Program* helps migrant youths, who do not go to school regularly because they assist their parents with farm work, to obtain a high school diploma and find employment or go to college. Despite the fact that the program is highly successful (over 80 percent of participating students earn high school certificates), support for it has diminished in recent years (Children's Defense Fund, 1989a, 1990c).

The dropout problem is expected to become especially acute in the next few years as school districts tighten high school graduation requirements in reaction to recent unfavorable reports about the achievement of American youths on an international basis (see Chapter 15). When demands for competency are increased but preventive and remedial programs for poorly achieving youngsters are not upgraded, marginal students are likely to leave school at earlier ages (Wilcox & Vincent, 1987).

Concern over the high rate of early school leaving has stimulated some school districts to implement new techniques aimed at reaching these youngsters more effectively. These include establishing alternative reward systems that take into account effort and achievement by less competitive students; encouraging extracurricular participation so that at-risk adolescents are integrated into the community life of the school; and upgrading family life, sex education, and substance abuse programs that focus on problems associated with school attrition. Moreover, federal legislative activity is currently addressing the dropout problem, although as yet very little has been signed into law (Children's Defense Fund, 1990c).

Youth in the Workplace. About 25 percent of American young people who complete high school terminate their education with a high school diploma. Although substantially better off than those who drop out, non-college-bound youths have fewer work opportunities available than they did several decades ago. More than one fourth of all high school graduates younger than 20 who do not continue in school are unemployed. When they do find work, low wages and scarcity of full-time employment make it increasingly difficult for them to support themselves. Research reveals that too many of these young people are ill-equipped with applied skills that make them attractive as employees. In addition, they have few alternatives to turn to for vocational counseling and job placement as they make the transition from high school to the world of work (Children's Defense Fund, 1989b, 1989d; Hamilton, 1990).

Educators have long recognized that providing work experiences as a complement to high school classes can facilitate the integration of non-college-bound adolescents into the labor market. However, most part-time jobs available to high school students are not dovetailed with high school vocational education. Instead, students seek them out in the private sector, where they find work in retail businesses, fast food chains, and other establishments that depend on low-cost teenage help for covering afternoon and evening shifts. Most of these jobs consist of low-level repetitive tasks, offer little in the way of close contact with and instruction from supervising adults, and do not prepare young people for a well-paid career. Moreover, research suggests that heavy involvement in them (more than 15 hours a week) is associated with poorer academic performance and reduced commitment to school life (Berk, 1991; Steinberg et al., 1982).

However, work experiences designed to supplement formal vocational education show quite different outcomes. Enrollment in work-study programs predicts favorable school and work attitudes, improved achievement, and increased school retention rates among students whose low-income backgrounds and poor academic skills make them highly vulnerable to subsequent unemployment (Barton & Frazer, 1980; Owens, 1982; Steinberg, 1984). In other industrialized nations, work-study apprenticeships that help high school graduates make a smooth transition from secondary school into occupations requiring highly specialized skills are broadly available. For example, in West Germany, over 60 percent of 16- to 18-year-olds are apprenticed in employment settings while they attend part-time vocational schools. West German businesses are highly committed to the preparation of young workers, often employ professional training staffs, and immerse young people in complex and challenging business functions while they study them in school. Upon graduation, West German youths immediately move into well-paid employment positions. In contrast, the United States has no widespread training system to prepare its non-college-bound youths for entry into skilled industrial occupations and manual trades (Hamilton, 1990; William T. Grant Foundation, 1988).

The federal government does support some job training programs, but their funding is limited. The most extensive services are available through the *Job Training Partnership Act of 1982.* However, most of this funding is directed toward relatively immediate job placement. The average training program lasts only 18 weeks, a period too short to make a difference in the lives of many poorly skilled adolescents who need intensive remediation in basic skills as well as vocational training before they are ready to enter the job market (Children's Defense Fund, 1989c; William T. Grant Foundation, 1988). One special federal initiative that provides more comprehensive services is the *Job Corps.* Its participants come from very poor homes, typically enter with no more than a sixth-grade reading level, and often have prior arrest records. The program combines remedial education, vocational training, and counseling within a residential setting offering housing, food, and medical attention. Most centers are operated as government/business partnerships to ensure that training is closely tied to job opportunities in the surrounding community. Although the Job Corps has been highly successful in increasing employment, earnings, and school completion rates and reducing crime and welfare costs, it serves only 3 percent of unemployed teenagers (Children's Defense Fund, 1989b).

Recently, the *William T. Grant Foundation,* a private nonprofit organization established to promote a better future for children and youth, proposed legislation to meet the job training needs of non-college-bound adolescents. Among the important features of the plan is an integrated approach to basic education, vocational training, and work experience, with participation guaranteed to all non-college-bound young people who need assistance (William T. Grant Foundation, 1988).

Most work experiences available to American teenagers consist of low-level repetitive tasks. They do not help prepare non-college-bound youths for highly skilled, well-paid occupations.

BRIEF REVIEW

In the sections above, we have seen that increased community-based treatment programs and improved agency coordination are needed to serve the millions of American children who suffer from serious mental health problems. Poverty combined with persistent learning, emotional, and behavioral difficulties has contributed to a national high school dropout rate of nearly one in four students. While better off than those who leave school early, non-college-bound high school graduates also face an increased likelihood of unemployment and are largely limited to low-paid jobs because they are not well prepared for vocational careers. Successful programs addressing each of these problems currently exist, although the large majority of children and adolescents who need assistance have not yet been reached.

WORLDWIDE STATUS OF CHILDREN AND YOUTH

At the end of the 1970s, after an extended period of economic growth and accompanying improvements in the health and welfare of children around the world, an international recession began to undermine the accomplishments of prior decades. Although largely invisible to citizens of industrialized nations, poverty in developing nations is greater today than it has been at any time during the last half century (Cornia, Jolly, & Stewart, 1988; Grant, 1989).

Two elements have dominated recent declining economic conditions in much of the Third World: rising national debts requiring large repayments to lending countries and falling prices of raw commodities, such as rubber, coffee, and timber, which have caused the flow of money from industrialized into developing nations to drop substantially. When economic progress plummets in countries where resources are in short supply to begin with, governments have little choice but to decrease social expenditures. As a result, family-related services decline, and poverty rises, along with infant mortality, low birth weight, hunger, disease, and serious physical and mental disabilities. Two thirds of the Third World has been affected by these trends; worldwide, 40,000 children die each day because of them. African and Latin American nations have been hit hardest, followed by countries in the Middle East and South and East Asia (Grant, 1989; Jupp, 1989).

Research reveals that the single most important factor that protects poverty-stricken Third World children is the literacy level of their mothers. Better education of women is correlated with fertility practices that favor children's survival, such as smaller families and wider spacing of children. It is also related to knowledge of child-rearing techniques that safeguard children's health under adverse circumstances—for example, appreciation of the importance of infant breast feeding,[4] immunization against disease, clean drinking water, and effective methods of caring for youngsters afflicted with dehydration caused by diarrhea, which takes the lives of four million Third World children each year. Yet educational expenditures, like other social services, have fallen steeply in developing nations (Grant, 1989; Jupp, 1989).

In addition to economic conditions, war, internal armed conflict, and the foreign policies of superpowers play a major role in the status of children in developing nations. For example, hunger plagues many children not because of an undersupply of worldwide food or, sometimes, even a shortage in their own land. Intense civil strife may lead to destruction of transport routes that carry food and supplies to certain areas of the country. As civilian areas are devastated, large numbers of children become orphaned and homeless or lose their lives. More than 70 percent of the population of refugee camps in war-torn developing nations are children. Moreover, under extreme circumstances like these, some poor countries may not receive the foreign aid they need because of the nature of their relationships with a superpower's friends or enemies (Green et al., 1989).

With increasing awareness of the condition of many children around the globe, diplomats, religious leaders, organizations, professionals, and concerned citizens recently drew up a United Nations–sponsored treaty called the **International Convention on the Rights of the Child.** Passed by the U.N. General Assembly in the fall

---

[4] Return to Chapter 5, page 200, to review how breast feeding promotes infant survival and healthy early growth in developing countries.

Declining economic conditions in much of the Third World threaten the survival and development of millions of children.

of 1989, the International Convention is written in the form of a legal agreement that is binding on all countries whose legislative bodies ratify it. The document is designed to ensure each child's right to a name and nationality; to adequate health care, nutrition, and education; and to be shielded from abuse, neglect, and involvement in warfare. The treaty is a first step toward widespread recognition that policies protecting the development of children must be built, first and foremost, on an international ethic in which children's welfare is paramount and on a foundation of worldwide peace.

LOOKING TOWARD THE FUTURE

In this chapter, we examined a wide variety of problems that threaten the survival and development of children in the United States and around the world. We have seen that the design and implementation of solutions to children's difficulties are complicated tasks; they challenge government, community agencies, child welfare organizations, researchers, and the public to work together in the creation of improved rearing environments for children.

The fact that many successful small-scale social programs do exist and that several important large-scale initiatives are on the horizon in the United States is a hopeful message. It demonstrates that progress in alleviating the worrisome condition of many children is an attainable goal. At the same time, the arduous path that must be traversed from identification of a social need to an effective solution reminds us to be patient, since change is difficult to accomplish. Not only are there many different perspectives on how best to deal with child and family problems, but families and children change rapidly over time. Thus, added to an already complex policymaking process is the special difficulty of fashioning flexible programs that serve children with a great diversity of needs (Steiner, 1981).

Today, child development specialists are more involved than ever before in conducting policy-relevant research and disseminating their findings to government officials and the country as a whole. In addition, growing awareness of the imbalance between our vast knowledge base and its application to children's everyday lives has led many investigators to become advocates for children's cause — participating in lobbying efforts and collaborating with policymakers in identifying solutions that are both feasible and responsive to research evidence (Zigler & Finn-Stevenson, 1988). Thus, the modern field of child development is playing a significant role in spurring the policy process forward. As these efforts continue, there is every reason to anticipate increased societal responsiveness to children's needs in the years to come.

CHAPTER SUMMARY

What Is Social Policy?

■ **Social policy** is any planful set of actions directed at solving a social problem or reaching a social goal. A special kind of social policy called **public policy,** which involves prescriptions for action codified into law, offers the greatest promise for promoting children's welfare.

Components of the Public Policymaking Process

■ Dominant political values, competing claims of special interest groups, and the state of the nation's economy affect child-related public policies. In addition, many individuals play important roles in the policymaking process. Legislators, the President, administrators in government agencies, and the courts are official **policymakers** with authority to make binding policy decisions. Their actions are influenced by a wide array of unofficial participants, including the media, scientific researchers, powerful special interest groups, and committed citizens. Complex interactions among these components rather than any single factor alone determine policy outcomes.

Contemporary Progress on Problems Facing America's Children

■ A series of recessions accompanied by reduced federal support for programs serving low-income sectors of the population prompted the rate of poverty and homelessness to rise precipitously during the 1980s. Currently, the United States delivers many important child-related subsidies through **tax benefits.** These do not reach poverty-stricken families, who depend on **income transfers** and **discretionary programs** to serve their needs. The European **social insurance** approach has been more successful than American income-linked policies in lifting families above the **poverty line.**

■ Recent impaired progress in reducing **infant mortality** in the United States has been linked to rising poverty combined with limited government investments in public health care for low-income families. Public Law 99-457 is an optimistic sign that widespread early intervention services will

soon be available to help the large number of infants and young children at risk for developmental difficulties. The United States lags behind most European nations in developing a system of high-quality, affordable day care and providing workplace policies that assist employed parents in their child-rearing role. However, support from the business community and powerful lobbying by the Alliance for Better Child Care (ABC) have brought the United States close to a comprehensive child care program.

■ Well-coordinated community-based treatment programs are needed to help millions of American children with serious emotional and behavioral difficulties who receive either no treatment or inappropriate services. Expansion of educational services for poor and minority youngsters is essential for combating the high rate of school dropout in the United States. Non-college-bound high school graduates require better vocational preparation and job placement services to increase their chances of entering well-paid, skilled occupations. Although a variety of efforts have been made to address each of these problems, most children and adolescents who need assistance have not yet been reached.

Worldwide Status of Children and Youth

■ International recession, war, and internal armed conflict have jeopardized the survival and development of many children in the Third World. The United Nations–sponsored **International Convention on the Rights of the Child** is designed to foster global cooperation in improving the worldwide status of children and youth.

Looking toward the Future

■ The design and implementation of solutions to the wide variety of problems faced by children are complex tasks. Currently, child development specialists are helping to spur the policy process forward by conducting policy-relevant research, engaging in lobbying efforts, and collaborating with policymakers in devising feasible programs that are responsive to research evidence.

IMPORTANT TERMS AND CONCEPTS

social policy   (p. 655)
public policy   (p. 655)
policymakers   (p. 657)
poverty line   (p. 662)
tax benefits   (p. 664)
income transfers   (p. 665)
Aid to Families with Dependent
   Children (AFDC)   (p. 665)

entitlements   (p. 666)
discretionary programs   (p. 666)
protective regulations   (p. 666)
social insurance   (p. 667)
Select Committee on Children,
   Youth, and Families   (p. 668)
Children's Defense Fund   (p. 668)

infant mortality   (p. 668)
Medicaid   (p. 670)
International Convention on the
   Rights of the Child   (p. 677)

Glossary

Accommodation. A form of Piagetian cognitive adaptation in which schemes are revised and adjusted to take into account newly apprehended properties of the environment. Distinguished from *assimilation*.

Achievement Motivation. The tendency to display initiative and persistence when faced with challenging tasks.

Acquired Immune Deficiency Syndrome (AIDS). A deadly viral disease that affects the body's immune system.

Action-Consequence Learning. The active efforts of infants to explore and control events around them and to repeat those behaviors that lead to interesting effects. Distinguished from the behaviorist view that the infant passively responds to environmental contingencies.

Active Genetic-Environmental Correlation. A type of genetic-environmental correlation in which children actively select environments that are compatible with their genetic predispositions. Also called *niche-picking*. Distinguished from *passive* and *evocative correlations*.

Adaptation. A central principle of Piagetian theory which suggests that mental structures achieve a better fit with external reality through the complementary processes of assimilation and accommodation.

Adrenocorticotropic Hormone (ACTH). A hormone released by the pituitary gland that stimulates the adrenal cortex to produce corticoids and androgens.

Adrenogenital Syndrome (AGS). A congenital disorder caused by prenatal androgen exposure. AGS-affected girls are born with masculinized external genitalia.

Aid to Families with Dependent Children (AFDC). America's key income transfer program for poor families. Supplies parents with a monthly check, provided they have children under age 18 living at home and their income falls below a state-defined level.

Allele. Each of the two forms of a gene located at identical places on the autosomes.

Alliance for Better Child Care (ABC). A child-related special interest group that brought together over 130 organizations in a powerful lobbying effort aimed at making high quality, affordable child care available to all American families.

Amniocentesis. A medical test for chromosomal abnormalities in which a sample of amniotic fluid is extracted through a needle inserted into the maternal abdominal wall. Cannot be performed prior to 11 to 14 weeks' gestation.

Amnion. The thin inner fetal membrane that forms a protective sac around the embryo and contains fluid in which the embryo is suspended.

Anaclitic Depression. An infant depressive reaction that occurs when there is no adequate mother substitute to replace a familiar caregiver from whom the infant is permanently separated and to whom the infant had previously formed an affectional tie.

Androgens. A group of hormones produced by the adrenal cortex and testes, high levels of which are evident at puberty. Androgens play an important role in the adolescent growth spurt, appearance of body hair, and development of male sexual characteristics.

Androgyny. A type of sex-role identity characterized by both masculine and feminine characteristics.

Animistic Thinking. Young children's belief that inanimate objects have thoughts, wishes, feelings and other lifelike qualities. Believed by Piaget to result from preoperational egocentrism.

Anorexia Nervosa. A severe emotional and physical disorder prevalent among adolescent females involving self-induced starvation.

Anoxia. A harmful condition in which insufficient oxygen reaches the brain of the infant during labor and delivery; can cause brain damage.

Apgar Scale. A rating scale used by physicians to assess the newborn infant's physical condition immediately after birth.

Aphasia. Difficulty in either comprehending or producing speech caused by brain damage in areas of the cerebral cortex that control verbal functions.

Apnea. Prolonged suspension of breathing.

Assimilation. A form of Piagetian cognitive adaptation in which the external world is interpreted in terms of currently available schemes. Distinguished from *accommodation*.

Attachment. The strong affectional tie that humans feel toward special people in their lives. Its first behavioral manifestation is the infant's tendency to send positive emotional signals and seek physical closeness to the primary caregiver.

Attention Deficit-Hyperactivity Disorder (ADHD). A childhood disorder involving inattentiveness, impulsive responding, and hyperactivity. Often leads to social problems, academic failure, and low self-esteem.

Attribution Retraining. Modifying the self-deprecating beliefs of low-achieving and/or learned helpless children through feedback that encourages them to view failure as surmountable if additional effort is exerted.

Attributions. Common, everyday speculations about the causes of one's own and others' behavior.

Authoritarian Parenting. A parenting style that is high in control and demandingness but low in responsiveness to children's rights or needs. Conformity and obedience are valued over open communication between parent and child, and punitive, coercive discipline is used to curb the child's will. Distinguished from *authoritative, permissive,* and *uninvolved parenting.*

Authoritative Parenting. A parenting style that is controlling and demanding but also warm and responsive. A rational, democratic approach in which both parents' and children's rights are recognized and respected. Distinguished from *authoritarian, permissive,* and *uninvolved parenting.*

Autonomous Morality. The highest Piagetian stage of moral development in which rules are viewed as flexible instruments of human purposes established through cooperative social agreement. Usually characteristic of children 10 years and older.

Autosomes. The 22 homologous pairs of chromosomes. Distinguished from the nonhomologous 23rd pair, called *sex chromosomes.*

Autostimulation Theory. The theory that REM sleep provides spontaneous stimulation necessary for central nervous system development in the immature organism.

Avoidant Attachment. The pattern of insecure attachment characterizing infants who are usually not distressed during separation from the mother and who, upon reunion, avoid her. Distinguished from *disorganized/disoriented, resistant,* and *secure attachment.*

Axon. A long fiber extending from the cell body of a neuron that sends impulses to other neurons.

Babbling. The repetition of extended strings of consonant-vowel combinations first appearing around 6 months of age.

Basic Emotions. The set of discrete emotions believed by some investigators to be present during the early weeks of life. Includes happiness, interest, surprise, fear, anger, sadness, and disgust.

Behavioral Genetics. A field devoted to discovering the genetic and environmental roots of individual differences in behavior and characteristics.

Behaviorism. A theoretical approach that regards directly observable events—stimuli and responses—as the important focus of psychological study. This position views the child as a passive entity shaped from without and development as a quantitative increase in learned responses.

Behavior Modification. A set of practical procedures derived from behaviorism and social learning theory, including reinforcement, modeling, and the manipulation of situational cues; these procedures are used to replace children's undesirable behaviors with socially acceptable responses.

Between-Family Environmental Influences. Factors related to the general climate of the home that affect all children within a family to the same extent. Distinguished from *within-family environmental influences.*

Biased Sampling. Failure to select subjects who are representative of the population of interest in study.

Binocular Depth Cues. Cues for depth that rely on each eye receiving a slightly different view of the visual field. Also called *stereopsis.* Distinguished from *kinetic* and *pictorial depth cues.*

Black Box Model. The traditional behaviorist view that only the environmental stimuli impinging on the organism and the overt responses that emerge are proper objects of psychological study. Investigation of inner mental processes is rejected.

Blastocyst. The zygote 4 days after fertilization, after numerous cell divisions have yielded a hollow cluster of 60 to 70 cells.

Bulimia. An eating disorder involving eating binges followed by intestinal purges in which the individual vomits or ingests large doses of laxatives. Sometimes accompanies anorexia nervosa.

Canalization. The tendency for growth to return to a genetically predetermined path in spite of environmental influences that may temporarily deflect it.

Catch-Up Growth. Physical growth that returns to its genetically predetermined growth path after being deflected off course by environmental factors.

Categorical Self. Early classification of the self according to observable, concrete characteristics on which people differ, such as sex and age.

Categorical Speech Perception. The tendency to perceive a range of sounds that belong to the same phonemic class as identical to one another.

Centration. Young children's tendency to focus attention on one detail of a situation at a time, to the neglect of other important features. A quality of Piagetian preoperational thought.

Cephalo-Caudal Trend. A principle of growth in which certain maturationally determined aspects of development proceed in a head-to-foot direction.

Cerebral Cortex. The deeply enfolded gray matter making up the surface layer of the brain that houses the "higher brain centers" and accounts for the highly developed intelligence of the human species.

Child Development. The field of study devoted to understanding all facets of human growth and change from conception through adolescence.

Children's Defense Fund. A private, nonprofit organization that promotes awareness of the condition of American children among official policymakers and the general public. The most active interest group for children in the United States.

Chorion. The outer membrane that encases the embryo and subsequently develops into the fetal portion of the placenta.

Chorionic Villi Biopsy. A relatively new prenatal diagnostic method that permits analysis of fetal tissue for chromosomal abnormalities. Can be used as early as 6 to 8 weeks gestation.

Chromosomes. Rodlike structures within the cell nucleus that store and transmit genetic information.

Chunking. Grouping pieces of information into meaningful units or chunks, thereby expanding the capacity of short-term memory.

Circular Reaction. A Piagetian sensorimotor learning mechanism in which the infant repeats a chance behavior that leads to an interesting or satisfying result, until eventually the response becomes consolidated into a new scheme.

Classical Conditioning. A learning paradigm that involves a new association between a neutral stimulus (CS) and a stimulus (UCS) that reliably elicits a reflexive response (UCR). After repeated pairings of the CS and UCS, the CS presented by itself produces the reflexive response (now called the CR), and learning has occurred. Distinguished from *operant conditioning.*

Clinical Interview. A research method that employs flexible, open-ended questions to probe for the subject's point of view.

Clinical Method. A method that collects information on the unique functioning of the individual child by synthesizing interview material, psychological test results, and observations of the child's behavior.

Co-Dominance. The pattern of autosomal inheritance in which both alleles in a heterozygous combination are expressed phenotypically.

Cognitive-Developmental Theory. Perspective originating with Piaget that regards the child as an active, constructive being and cognitive development as taking place through a series of qualitatively distinct stages.

Cognitive Maps. Mental representations of environmental space.

Cognitive Style. An individual's general manner of perceiving and reacting to the environment.

Cohort Effects. See *cultural-historical change.*

Complex Emotions. Emotions involving either injury to or enhancement of the sense of self. Examples are shame, guilt, envy, and pride.

Compliance. Voluntary obedience to adult commands and requests. In young children, a beginning form of self-control.

Componential Analysis. A research procedure in which performance on intelligence test items is correlated with laboratory measures designed to reveal the speed and effectiveness of information processing skills.

Comprehension. In language development, the language children can understand. Distinguished from *production.*

Comprehension Monitoring. Continuous assessment of the degree to which one understands a passage being read or listened to.

Concrete Operational Stage. The third Piagetian stage of development in which reasoning becomes logical, systematic, and rational in its application to concrete objects but abstract thinking is still lacking. Characteristic of children between about 7 and 11 years of age.

Conditioned Response (CR). In classical conditioning, an originally unconditioned, reflexive response that is produced by a conditioned stimulus (CS).

Conditioned Stimulus (CS). In classical conditioning, an orig-inally neutral stimulus that, through repeated pairings with an unconditioned stimulus (UCS), evokes a new response (CR).

Confluence Model. The view that children's mental growth is a function of family size, birth order, and spacing between children — variables that affect the quality of the intellectual environment in the home.

Congenital Rubella Syndrome. A range of abnormalities appearing in the offspring of mothers who have been infected with rubella during pregnancy. The type and severity of abnormalities depend on the timing of prenatal infection.

Consanguinity. The extent to which a couple is genetically related through descent from a common ancestor in the last few generations. Used in genetic counseling to help predict the odds that parents may bear an abnormal child.

Conservation. The Piagetian term for knowledge that certain physical attributes of objects, such as their mass and weight, do not vary when the object changes shape.

Contents. A Piagetian concept that refers to the specific intellectual acts that infants and children exhibit from which structures and functions are inferred.

Continuum of Caretaking Casualty. The range of risk factors associated with caretaking environments in which children develop.

Continuum of Reproductive Casualty. The range in severity of biological insults to the organism during the prenatal and perinatal phases of development.

Control Deficiency. In information processing, the inability to skillfully implement a mental strategy. Distinguished from *production deficiency.*

Control Processes. In information processing, procedures that individuals use to increase the efficiency and capacity of the cognitive system. Examples include rehearsal, organization, and elaboration. Also called *strategies.*

Controversial Children. Children who receive a large number of positive and negative votes on sociometric measures of peer acceptance. Distinguished from *popular, rejected,* and *neglected children.*

Conventional Level of Morality. Kohlberg's intermediate level of moral development in which a desire to conform to social norms and preserve the social order underlies moral judgments. Distinguished from *preconventional* and *postconventional levels of morality.*

Convergent Thinking. Seeking a single correct answer to a problem or task. Distinguished from *divergent thinking.*

Cooperative Play. A form of social participation in which children converse, share toys, and act out complementary roles.

Corpus Callosum. The large bundle of myelinated neural fibers that connects the two hemispheres of the brain and transmits information from one side of the brain to the other.

Corpus Luteum. A ruptured ovarian follicle that secretes hormones that ready the uterine lining for implantation of the ovum.

Correlation Coefficient. A numerical estimate of the relationship between two variables that indicates the strength, as well as the direction, of the relationship.

Correlational Design. A type of research design that indicates whether two or more variables are related to one another. In contrast to experimental designs, a correlational design cannot determine cause and effect because there is no manipulation of an independent variable.

Corticoids. A type of hormone released by the adrenal cortex that regulates the body's protein-carbohydrate balance.

Critical Period. A period of development in which harmful environmental influences can result in permanent damage to a bodily structure or behavior that is developing rapidly.

Cross-Fostering Study. An investigation of the development of children reared in environments that differ from their family of origin.

Cross-Sectional Design. A developmental research design in which subjects of different ages are observed at a single point in time. Distinguished from *longitudinal design*.

Cross-Validation Study. A type of study in which the investigator tries to replicate results in new situations and with different samples of children. Used to establish external validity.

Crossing Over. Exchange of segments between a pair of homologous chromosomes during meiosis so that genes from one chromosome are replaced by genes from another. Increases genetic variability among offspring.

Crystallized Intelligence. A form of intelligence that is culturally loaded and fact-oriented. Distinguished from *fluid intelligence*.

Cultural-Historical Change. Shifts in cultural conditions that may compromise the validity of longitudinal and cross-sectional studies. Also called *cohort effects*.

Cumulative Deficit Hypothesis. The view that attributes the progressive decline in IQ scores to the compounding effect of depressed environmental conditions.

Debriefing. Providing a full account and justification of research activities to subjects who participated in a study in which deception was used. Raises special ethical concerns in research with children.

Decoding. In information processing, interpreting the meaning of information by comparing and combining it with other previously stored information.

Deferred Imitation. The ability to replicate the behaviors of models no longer present in the immediate perceptual field.

Defining Issues Test (DIT). A widely used objective instrument for assessing moral maturity in which subjects rate the importance of statements that represent different stages of moral reasoning.

Delay of Gratification. A form of self-control that involves the capacity to wait before acting on an impulse.

Dendrite. A branchlike extension of a neuron that receives impulses from other neurons.

Deoxyribonucleic Acid (DNA). Long, double-stranded molecules that make up chromosomes, segments of which are genes containing the blueprint for the individual's characteristics and capacities.

Dependent Variable. In an experiment, behaviors that an investigator expects to be influenced by an independent or manipulated variable.

Deprivation Dwarfism. A growth disorder characterized by short stature and by weight that is proportionate to height. Believed to be caused by the negative impact of emotional deprivation on growth hormone production.

Developmental Pediatrics. A relatively new branch of pediatrics that integrates physical and psychological assessment of children, traditional health care, and parental guidance.

Developmental Psychology. The field of study devoted to understanding all changes that human beings experience throughout the life span. In its interdisciplinary sense, called *human development*.

Developmental Quotient (DQ). An index of infant intelligence, based primarily on perceptual and motor performances. Computed in the same manner as an IQ.

Deviation IQ. An IQ score based on the extent to which a child's performance deviates from the mean of his or her particular age group.

Dialectical Theory. The Vygotskian perspective that considers cooperative dialogues between children and more mature members of their culture as essential for developmental progress. As knowledgeable members of society help children master culturally meaningful activities, the communication between them is internalized and used to accomplish tasks independently.

Differentiation Theory. The view that developmental changes in sensory processing reflect the ability to detect increasingly fine-grained and subtle differences among objects and patterns.

Difficult Child. A child whose temperament is such that he or she is irregular in daily routines, is slow to accept new experiences, and tends to react negatively and intensely. Distinguished from *easy child* and *slow-to-warm-up child*.

Discrepancy Theory. The view that a child's emotional response to a novel stimulus is determined by the degree of similarity between the stimulus and an internal representation of a familiar object to which the new stimulus is compared.

Discretionary Programs. Public policies in which only a limited amount of government funding is authorized. Usually provide citizens with goods and services rather than direct financial assistance. Head Start is an example. Distinguished from *entitlements*.

Dishabituation. Recovery of a habituated response after stimulation changes.

Disorganized/Disoriented Attachment. The pattern of insecure attachment characterizing infants who, upon reunion with their mothers, display a variety of confused behaviors, such as gazing away while being held or exhibiting flat, depressed affect. Of all attachment classifications, reflects the greatest insecurity. Distinguished from *avoidant, resistant,* and *secure attachment*.

Distance Curve. A growth curve that records the height and weight of an individual child, or the average height and weight of a group of children, for each age level. Shows degree of progress toward mature size.

Distributive Justice. A concept of fairness concerning the allocation of rewards among group members.

Divergent Thinking. Fluency in generating ideas and a ready ability to think of wide variety of alternatives to meet a particular need. Associated with creativity. Distinguished from *convergent thinking*.

Divorce Mediation. A series of meetings between divorcing parents and a trained professional who tries to facilitate agreement on disputed issues, such as child custody and property settlement. Aimed at reducing family conflict during the period surrounding divorce.

Dizygotic Twins. See *fraternal twins*.

Domain-Specific Knowledge. Knowledge of a specific content area that makes new information in that area more familiar and meaningful, thereby facilitating its storage in and retrieval from memory.

Dominance Hierarchy. A stable ordering of group members

that predicts who will win under conditions of conflict. Serves the adaptive function of limiting aggression between group members.

Dominant-Recessive Mode of Inheritance. A common pattern of autosomal inheritance in which, under heterozygous conditions, the influence of only the dominant allele becomes phenotypically apparent.

Donor Insemination. Artificial insemination of a woman with sperm donated from an anonymous man.

Down Syndrome. A disorder caused by abnormalities in the twenty-first pair of chromosomes. Associated with physical defects, slow motor development, and mental retardation.

Drive Reduction Theory. The view that stimuli associated with reduction of primary drives, such as hunger, thirst, and sex, become secondary, or learned drives. Used by some behaviorists to explain infant-mother attachment.

Easy Child. A child whose temperament is such that he or she quickly establishes regular routines in infancy, is generally cheerful, and adapts easily to new experiences. Distinguished from *difficult child* and *slow-to-warm-up child.*

Ecology of Human Development. A perspective that views layers of the natural environment—*microsystem, mesosystem, exosystem,* and *macrosystem*—as major sources of influence on development.

Ectoderm. One of three layers of cells formed by the embryonic disc from which will emerge the nervous system, outer skin, hair, and sweat glands.

Ego. In Freud's theory, the part of personality that moderates and redirects the id's impulses so that they are satisfied in accordance with reality.

Egocentric Speech. The name given by Piaget to children's verbal utterances that are not directly addressed to others or not expressed in ways that can easily be understood by others.

Egocentrism. A Piagetian term for the inability to distinguish one's own cognitive perspective from the perspectives of others.

Elaboration. A memory strategy in which a relationship, or shared meaning, is created between two or more pieces of information that do not bear any natural categorical relationship to one another.

Embryo. The prenatal organism from implantation to 8 weeks gestation, during which time the groundwork for all body structures and systems is established.

Embryonic Disk. The inner cell mass projecting into the blastocyst cavity, from which will develop the future individual.

Emotional Display Rules. Cultural rules specifying the circumstances under which it is acceptable to express emotions.

Emotional Self-Regulation. Strategies used to adjust one's emotional state to a suitable level of intensity. Allows one to remain productively engaged with the environment.

Empathy. The perception and vicarious experience of others' emotions. Plays an important role in motivating prosocial and altruistic behavior.

Encoding. In information processing, entering information from the environment into the mental system and storing it in symbolic, representational form.

Endoderm. One of three layers of cells formed by the embryonic disc from which will emerge the digestive system, lungs, urinary tract, and internal glands.

Endogenous Smiles. The earliest neonatal smiles that occur in the absence of external stimulation, most commonly during REM sleep. Distinguished from *exogenous smiles.*

Engrossment. The father's experience of elation and positive emotional involvement following the birth of his child.

Enrichment Theory. The view that sensory processing involves using internal mental schemes to interpret incoming stimulus information. As schemes are refined with development, perceptual intake is elaborated and enriched.

Entitlements. A type of public policy available to any person who meets eligibility requirements for the program. Examples include *tax benefits* and *income transfers.* Distinguished from *discretionary programs.*

Epiphyses. Centers of bone ossification.

Episodic Memory. Memory for specific, personally experienced events, people, and objects. Distinguished from *semantic memory.*

Epistemology. A subdiscipline within the field of philosophy concerned with the study of knowledge and various forms of knowing.

Equilibration. A Piagetian concept referring to continuous movement between states of cognitive equilibrium and disequilibrium. Describes how assimilation and accommodation work together to produce cognitive change.

Erythroblastosis. A condition stemming from Rh blood incompatibility in which fetal and maternal bloodstreams mix, causing the mother's antibodies to destroy fetal red blood cells and reduce fetal oxygen supply.

Estrogens. Hormones produced by the ovaries; they influence maturation of the breasts, uterus, and vagina at adolescence and, during the menstrual cycle, help ready the uterus for implantation in the event of fertilization of an ovum.

Ethological Theory of Attachment. A theory of attachment formulated by Bowlby that views the infant's emotional tie to the mother in adaptive, evolutionary terms. Regards the infant as an active, biologically prepared contributor to the attachment relationship.

Ethology. An theoretical approach concerned with understanding the adaptive or survival value of behavior and its evolutionary origins.

Event Sampling. An observational procedure in which an observer records every occurrence of a particular event or behavior during a specified time period.

Evocative Genetic-Environmental Correlation. A type of genetic-environmental correlation in which the child's genotype influences the responses the child receives from others. Distinguished from *passive* and *active correlations.*

Exogenous Smiles. Smiles elicited by external stimulation that initially appear during the first to second weeks of life. Distinguished from *endogenous smiles.*

Exosystem. In Bronfenbrenner's ecological model of human development, settings that do not actually contain children but that affect children's experiences in their immediate settings. Examples are the parents' workplace and health and welfare services in the community.

Expansions. Parental responses that incorporate and elaborate on young children's speech in ways that facilitate their language acquisition.

Experimental Design. A type of research design in which an independent variable is manipulated to determine its effect on a dependent variable, while other factors are controlled. Unlike a correlational design, experimental designs enable researchers to determine cause-and-effect relationships between variables.

Expressive Style. A style of early language learning characterizing children who use language to express feelings, needs, and social forms. Initial vocabularies emphasize pronouns and social formulas.

Expressive Traits. Feminine sex-typed personality characteristics that reflect warmth, caring, and emotion. Distinguished from *instrumental traits*.

Extended Family Household. A household in which parents and children plus other nonnuclear family members, such as grandparents, uncles, aunts, and cousins, live together.

External Validity. The accuracy with which research results can be generalized to other groups of children and situations where the same findings are expected to prevail.

Extinction. Elimination of a response as the result of repeated nonreinforcement.

Factor Analysis. A statistical procedure that combines scores from many separate test items into just a few factors, which substitute for the separate scores.

Failure to Thrive. Growth retardation accompanied by psychological apathy during infancy for which there are no apparent organic or nutritional causes. Believed to be the result of inadequate maternal attention and affection.

Fallopian Tubes. The long, thin structures that convey the ovum from the ovaries to the uterus.

Fast Mapping. The process by which children map a new word onto an underlying concept after just one encounter with the word. Accounts for the speed with which children build their early vocabularies.

Fetal Alcohol Syndrome (FAS). A cluster of abnormalities appearing in the offspring of mothers who ingest large quantities of alcohol during pregnancy. Includes facial abnormalities, defects of the skeleton and internal organs, small body stature, and mental retardation.

Fetoscopy. A method of prenatal diagnosis that permits visual inspection of the fetus to detect limb and facial malformations. Also permits sampling of fetal blood to detect certain genetic disorders.

Fetus. The prenatal organism from the beginning of the third month until the end of pregnancy, during which time organ systems are elaborated and refined and dramatic growth in body size takes place.

Field Experiment. An experiment in which investigators assign subjects to different treatments in the natural environment as opposed to an artificial laboratory setting.

Fluid Intelligence. A form of intelligence that demands little specific informational content and that involves the ability to see complex relationships and solve problems. Distinguished from *crystallized intelligence*.

Follicle Stimulating Hormone (FSH). A pituitary hormone that causes the gonads to release hormones affecting growth and sexual changes during adolescence. In females, FSH initiates the production of estrogens and is involved in regulating the menstrual cycle. In males, FSH causes the testes to produce sperm.

Fontanels. A group of six soft spots of fibrous tissue that separate the bones of the cranial vault at birth.

Formal Operational Egocentrism. The form of egocentrism that appears during Piaget's formal operational stage in which adolescents rigidly insist that reality submit itself completely to their grand idealistic visions.

Formal Operational Stage. The fourth Piagetian stage of development in which the individual acquires the capacity for abstract, scientific thinking. Begins around 11 years of age.

Fovea. The area at the center of the retina where images are focused most sharply.

Fragile X Syndrome. A sex chromosome abnormality in which a gap or break in a certain place on the X chromosome is present. Associated with mild facial deformities and mental retardation.

Fraternal Twins. Pairs of siblings resulting from two separately released and fertilized ova and who are not genetically identical; also called *dizygotic twins*. Distinguished from *identical*, or *monozygotic twins*.

Functions. A Piagetian concept that includes the mental phenomena of organization and adaptation, which explain how cognitive change takes place.

Gametes. Human sperm and ova, formed through meiosis, that contain half as many chromosomes as a body cell.

Gender Constancy. The understanding that one's own gender is permanent despite superficial variations in appearance or characteristics.

Gender Schema Theory. A theory that integrates aspects of social learning and cognitive-developmental theory to explain how sex-stereotyped knowledge and behavior are acquired.

Gene. A segment of a DNA molecule that contains hereditary instructions for the individual's characteristics and capacities.

General Factor ("g"). In Spearman's theory of intelligence, a single, common factor representing abstract reasoning power that underlies a wide variety of separate mental abilities. Distinguished from *specific* and *group factors*.

Generalized Other. A synthesis of what we imagine significant others think of us; determines self-concept.

Genetic Counseling. Counseling that helps couples who want to have a child assess the likelihood of giving birth to a baby with a genetic disorder.

Genotype. The genetic makeup of the individual, which, in combination with environmental factors, determines physical and behavioral characteristics (phenotype).

Glial Cells. Brain cells serving the function of myelinization and regulation of neuronal metabolism.

Goal-Directed Behavior. See *intentional behavior*.

Goodness-of-Fit Model. Thomas and Chess's theory of how temperament and environmental pressures act together to determine the course of development. Optimal development is most likely when environmental demands are in harmony, or achieve a "good fit," with temperament.

Grammar. An area of language skill concerned with syntax, the rules by which words are arranged into comprehensible sentences, and morphology, the application of grammatical markers that denote number, tense, case, person, gender, and other meanings.

Group Factors. Mental ability factors of moderate degrees of generality, such as verbal, visual, and numerical ability. Distinguished from *general factor ("g")* and *specific factors*.

Growth Hormone (GH). A pituitary hormone that affects growth of almost all body tissues except the central nervous system and possibly the adrenal glands and gonads.

Habituation. Gradual reduction in the strength of a response as the result of repetitive stimulation.

Hemophilia. An X-linked recessive disorder involving deficiencies in blood coagulation factors that cause blood to fail to clot normally.

Heritability Estimate. An index of the extent to which variation among individuals in complex behaviors can be attributed to genetic factors. Derived from *kinship studies*.

Heteronomous Morality. The initial Piagetian stage of moral development in which rules are regarded as fixed, externally imposed absolutes. Characteristic of children between about 5 and 10 years of age.

Heterozygous. Having two different alleles at a corresponding site on a pair of chromosomes. Often results in the dominant allele becoming phenotypically apparent, but codominance is also possible. Distinguished from *homozygous*.

Hierarchical Classification. A Piagetian logical operation involving the organization of objects into hierarchies of classes and subclasses, based on similarities and differences between the groups.

Holophrases. The name given young children's one-word utterances by investigators who believe these utterances function like sentences and stand for complete thoughts.

Home Observation for Measurement of the Environment (HOME). A technique employing direct observation of mother-child interaction in the home plus parental interviews to assess the relationship of between-family environmental influences to intelligence.

Homologous. Having two chromosomes that correspond to one another in size, shape, and genetic function.

Homozygous. Having two identical alleles at a corresponding site on a pair of chromosomes, resulting in phenotypic appearance of the inherited trait. Distinguished from *heterozygous*.

Horizontal Décalage. A Piagetian term referring to the sequential mastery of concepts in different content areas within a single stage of development. For example, during the concrete operational stage, conservation of number is acquired prior to conservation of length, mass, and liquid.

Hormones. Chemical substances secreted into the bloodstream by specialized cells in one part of the body that pass to and influence cells in other parts of the body.

Hostile Aggression. Aggressive behavior intended to harm another individual. Distinguished from *instrumental aggression*.

Human Development. The interdisciplinary field of study devoted to understanding all changes that human beings experience throughout the life span.

Hyaline Membrane Disease. See *respiratory distress syndrome*.

Hypothalamus. A structure located at the base of the brain that initiates and regulates pituitary gland secretions.

Hypothesis. A testable prediction about behavior drawn from a theory.

Hypothetico-Deductive Reasoning. A Piagetian formal operational problem-solving strategy. The adolescent begins with a general theory of all possible factors that could affect an outcome in a problem and deduces specific hypotheses, which are systematically tested.

Id. According to Freud, the portion of personality present at birth that is the source of basic biological needs and desires.

Identical Twins. Pairs of siblings who develop from a single fertilized egg and have identical genetic makeup; also called *monozygotic twins*. Distinguished from *dizygotic*, or *fraternal twins*.

Identification. In Freudian theory, a process that leads to conscience formation in which the child emulates the same-sex parent and internalizes the parent's rules and prohibitions.

Identity. A coherent conception of the self composed of an integrated set of goals, values, and beliefs; develops during adolescence.

Identity Achievement. The identity status that characterizes adolescents who have experienced a period of crisis and who manifest a secure sense of commitment to an occupation or ideology. Distinguished from *moratorium, identity diffusion,* and *identity foreclosure*.

Identity Constancy. The knowledge that some qualitative characteristics of individuals, such as their sex and species, are permanent despite superficial changes in appearance.

Identity Crisis. A normal, temporary period of inner struggle that precedes successful formulation of an identity during adolescence.

Identity Diffusion. The identity status that characterizes adolescents who lack firm occupational or ideological commitments and who are not actively seeking them. Distinguished from *identity achievement, moratorium,* and *identity foreclosure*.

Identity Foreclosure. The identity status that characterizes adolescents who have made a premature commitment to occupational and ideological choices that others (usually parents) have chosen for them. Distinguished from *identity achievement, moratorium,* and *identity diffusion*.

Illocutionary Intent. What a speaker means to say, regardless of whether that meaning is perfectly consistent with the linguistic form actually uttered.

Imaginary Audience. A kind of Piagetian formal operational egocentrism in which the adolescent believes that others are as concerned with and critical of the adolescent's behavior as adolescents are themselves.

Imitation. Learning in which the individual observes and then replicates the behavior of others.

Immanent Justice. The belief that wrongdoing inevitably leads to punishment. Characterizes children in Piaget's stage of heteronomous morality.

Imprinting. The early following behavior of certain baby birds that assures that the young will stay close to the mother and be fed and protected from predators. Appears during an early, restricted time period of development.

Income Transfers. Public policies that authorize money to be transferred from the public treasury in the form of income to citizens who need it. Aid to Families with Dependent Children (AFDC) is an example.

Incidental Learning. Learning of irrelevant aspects of a task. With age, attention to irrelevant stimuli is replaced by increased attentional control.

Independent Variable. An event or condition in an experiment that the investigator manipulates and expects to cause changes in a dependent variable.

Induction. A disciplinary technique in which the effect of the child's own behavior on others is communicated to the child.

Infantile Amnesia. The inability to remember specific autobiographical events that happened during the first few years of life.

Infant Mortality. The number of infant deaths in the first year of life per 1000 live births.

Information Processing. A general theoretical approach to the study of cognition that views the human mind as a complex, symbol-manipulating system through which information flows, operating much like a digital computer. Focuses on the operation of distinct, sequential mental processes and emphasizes the commonalities between child and adult thinking.

Informed Consent. An ethical procedure that entails explaining the nature of the research to prospective subjects to ensure that they have the freedom to make choices regarding their participation. When subjects are children, parental permission must be obtained. Children's consent should be sought as soon as they are capable of making reasoned judgments about participation.

Inner Self. Aspects of the self, such as inner thoughts and imaginings, that are accessible only to the self and not to others.

Institutional Review Board. A panel of individuals established in research-oriented institutions and organizations to independently evaluate the ethical advisability of proposed research studies.

Instrumental Aggression. Aggressive acts aimed at gaining access to an object, privilege, or space and in which there is no direct intent to harm another person. Distinguished from *hostile aggression.*

Instrumental Traits. Masculine sex-typed personality characteristics that reflect competence, rationality, and self-assertion. Distinguished from *expressive traits.*

Intelligence Quotient (IQ). An index that permits an individual's performance on an intelligence test to be readily compared to the scores of other individuals.

Intentional, or Goal-Directed, Behavior. In Piaget's sensorimotor stage, a new action sequence deliberately aimed at attaining a goal.

Intermodal Coordination. Perceiving information offered to more than one sensory modality at a time as an integrated unit.

Internal Validity. The accuracy of a study's cause-and-effect conclusions. Present when there are no competing, uncontrolled factors internal to the design that serve as plausible alternative explanations of the results. Distinguished from *external validity.*

Internalization. The developmental shift from behavior that is externally controlled to behavior that is controlled by internal standards and principles.

International Convention on the Rights of the Child. A United Nations-sponsored treaty protecting children's welfare around the world.

Invariant. Unchanging or constant; applied to stages of development emerging in a maturationally determined, fixed sequence that is universal for all children.

Invariant Features. According to differentiation theory, any stable, discriminable aspect of a stimulus that distinguishes it from its background or from other stimulus objects in the environment.

In Vitro Fertilization. A method of assisted conception in which an ovum is extracted from a woman, fertilized in a laboratory dish, and then injected into the mother's uterus where, hopefully, it will implant and develop.

Jargon Stretches. Sequences of infant babbling that contain real words and are spoken with communicative intent and eye contact.

Joint Custody. A child custody arrangement following divorce in which the court grants both parents equal power over and participation in child rearing. Distinguished from *sole custody.*

Kinetic Depth Cues. Depth cues that result from changes in the size of an object's retinal image. Created by movements of the head or body or by movement of objects in the environment. Distinguished from *binocular* and *pictorial depth cues.*

Kinship Study. Research comparing individuals of differing degrees of genetic relationship to one another. Used to infer the influence of heredity on behavior when knowledge of specific gene pathways is unavailable.

Klinefelter's Syndrome (XXY). A sex chromosome disorder in males due to the presence of an extra X chromosome. Associated with depressed verbal intelligence, incomplete development of secondary sex characteristics, tallness, and sterility.

Kwashiorkor. A dietary disease caused by extreme protein deficiency that commonly appears between 1 and 3 years of age. Leads to a wasted condition of the body, skin rash, and swelling of the face, limbs, and abdomen.

Laboratory Experiment. An experiment in which the investigator assigns subjects to different treatments under controlled laboratory conditions.

Language Acquisition Device (LAD). According to Chomsky, an innate grammatical representation underlying all human languages that enables children to combine words into novel but grammatically consistent utterances and to understand the meaning of the language they hear.

Language-Making Capacity (LMC). A hypothetical set of innate cognitive procedures for analyzing linguistic input that supports children's discovery of grammatical rules.

Lanugo. White, downy hair covering the fetus, nearly all of which is shed prior to birth. Helps keep vernix on the skin.

Latchkey Children. Children who regularly care for themselves during after-school hours with no adult supervision.

Lateralization. Specialization of functions between the two hemispheres of the brain. For example, verbal processing is typically localized in the left hemisphere and spatial processing in the right hemisphere.

Learned Helplessness. The attributional pattern in which failures are ascribed to lack of ability. Contributes to low expectancies of success, decreased persistence when faced with challenging tasks, and impaired performance following failure.

Level I – Level II Theory. Jensen's controversial theory that racial and social-class variations in intelligence are due to genetic differences in complex cognitive processing (Level II) abilities rather than basic rote memory (Level I) skills.

Levels-of-Processing Model. An information processing model that suggests that retention of information is a function of the depth to which an incoming stimulus is analyzed. Allocation of attention determines the individual's information processing capacity.

Lexical Contrast Theory. A theory of semantic development that describes how children acquire a new word by contrasting it with those they already know and attending to the word's conventional usage in their linguistic community.

Long-Term Memory Store. In Atkinson and Shiffrin's store model, that part of the information processing system in which information is retained and filed permanently. The capacity of long-term memory is assumed to be limitless. Distinguished from *short-term memory store*.

Longitudinal Design. A developmental research design in which repeated observations of a group of subjects are made at different ages. Distinguished from *cross-sectional design*.

Longitudinal-Sequential Design. A research design with both longitudinal and cross-sectional components in which several different samples born in different years are repeatedly tested over the same time span.

Luteinizing Hormone (LH). A pituitary hormone that, in females, causes the ovaries to release ova and produce progesterone. In males, LH stimulates testicular production of androgens.

M-Space. Mental space; in Case's information processing version of Piaget's theory, the maximum number of schemes an individual can apply simultaneously. M-space increases in each successive Piagetian stage.

Macrosystem. In Bronfenbrenner's ecological model of human development, the overarching ideology, values, laws, regulations, rules, and customs of a culture that influence experiences and interactions at lower levels of the model.

Mainstreaming. The integration of handicapped pupils into classrooms serving nonhandicapped children for part or all of the school day.

Make-Believe Play. A type of play in which children reenact familiar activities. Emerges during the preschool years.

Marasmus. A dietary disease resulting from general starvation that appears in the first year of life and leads to severe weight loss, muscular atrophy, and reduction in subcutaneous fat.

Mastery-Oriented Attributions. The attribution of success to high ability, and of failure to insufficient effort. Associated with high academic self-esteem and a willingness to undertake challenging tasks.

Matching. A research procedure in which subjects with comparable characteristics are matched and then assigned in equal numbers to different treatment groups.

Maturation. A naturally unfolding, genetically predetermined pattern of growth.

Mean. The average score in a distribution of scores.

Mean Length of Utterance (MLU). An index of grammatical development based on the average number of morphemes per utterance. Derived from a large sample of utterances made by a child.

Mechanistic Model. A view that regards the child as a passive recipient of environmental inputs. Represented by behaviorism and social learning theory.

Mediational Theory. Modern behaviorist position that recognizes the limitations of a black box model and acknowledges the need to study covert mental processes.

Medicaid. The largest public health insurance program in the United States. Serves poor children and families.

Meiosis. The process of cell division through which gametes are formed and in which the number of chromosomes in each cell is reduced by half.

Memory Span. The number of items an individual can hold in short-term memory.

Menarche. The first menstrual period.

Mental Age (MA). A measure of a child's performance on an intelligence test in terms of the chronological age at which children, on the average, obtain that score.

Mesoderm. One of three layers of cells formed by the embryonic disc from which will develop the deeper layers of skin, muscles, skeleton, circulatory system, and a variety of internal organs.

Mesosystem. In Bronfenbrenner's ecological model of human development, the interconnections among children's immediate settings.

Metacognition. Awareness and understanding of one's own cognitive processes; thinking about thought.

Metacognitive Training. Training children to use self-guiding verbalizations to improve their task performance.

Metalinguistic Awareness. The ability to think about language as a system.

Microsystem. In Bronfenbrenner's ecological model of human development, the activities, roles, and relationships in the child's immediate surroundings.

Mismatch. A form of early vocabulary error in which the child applies a newly acquired label to an inappropriate set of events.

Mitosis. The process of cell duplication in which each new cell receives an exact copy of the original chromosomes and, therefore, the identical genetic material.

Modeling. Learning acquired through mere exposure to the behavior of others; also known as observational learning.

Modifier Gene. A gene that modifies the phenotypic expression of another gene by either enhancing or diluting its effects.

Monozygotic Twins. See *identical twins*.

Moral Dilemma. A hypothetical conflict situation in which the subject is asked to choose and justify a moral course of action. Used to assess the development of moral reasoning.

Moratorium. The identity status that characterizes adolescents who have suspended definite commitments while they search for an appropriate occupation and ideology in which to make a positive self-investment. Distinguished from *identity achievement, identity diffusion,* and *identity foreclosure*.

Morpheme. The smallest meaningful unit of adult speech.

Motherese. The altered language adopted by adults when speaking to young children; includes simple sentences, exaggerated intonation, and very clear pronunciation.

Mutation. A sudden but permanent change in genetic material. Can occur spontaneously or in response to hazardous environmental agents.

Myelinization. The process whereby axons in the developing brain become coated with the insulating fatty sheath necessary for efficient conduction of nerve impulses.

National Academy of Early Childhood Programs. A voluntary national accreditation system for center-based child care facilities designed to substitute for the lack of federal child care regulations. Sponsored by the National Association for the Education of Young Children.

Natural Childbirth. An approach designed to make childbirth as comfortable and rewarding to mothers as possible in the context of hospital delivery. Includes educational classes about what to expect during childbirth, instruction in breathing exercises, and the availability of a supportive companion during labor and delivery. Also called *prepared childbirth*.

Natural Experiment. A research design in which investigators study the effects of naturally occurring treatments.

Naturalistic Observation. A research method in which the investigator goes into the natural environment to observe behaviors of interest.

Natural Kind Categories. Richly structured categories found in nature (such as various types of plants and animals) whose members share both observable and unobservable characteristics.

Natural Selection. A principle of evolution stating that those members of a species who best meet the survival requirements of their environment will live long enough to reproduce and pass on their more favorable characteristics to future generations. Others with less favorable traits will die out.

Neglected Children. Children who are seldom chosen, either positively or negatively, on sociometric measures of peer acceptance. Distinguished from *popular, rejected,* and *controversial children.*

Neonatal Behavioral Assessment Scale (NBAS). An instrument developed by Brazelton for assessing the overall behavioral status of newborn infants, including neonatal reflexes, environmental responsiveness, state changes, and soothability.

Neurons. Cells in the central nervous system that transmit neural impulses.

Niche-Picking. See *active genetic-environmental correlation.*

Noble Savage. Rousseau's view of the child as naturally endowed with a sense of right and wrong and with an innate plan for orderly, healthy growth.

Non-Rapid Eye Movement Sleep (NREM Sleep). A sleep state in which heart rate, respiration, and brain wave activity are slow and regular and body movements are essentially absent. Also called *regular sleep.* Distinguished from *rapid eye movement (REM) sleep.*

Nonreversal Learning. A type of discrimination learning in which subjects who have learned to respond to an aspect of one stimulus dimension (e.g., large size) must switch to an aspect of another stimulus dimension (e.g., black color). Distinguished from *reversal learning.*

Normal Curve. A bell-shaped frequency distribution that denotes the variability of certain characteristics in a population. Most individuals cluster near the mean, while only a few people achieve very high or very low scores.

Normative Approach. An approach in which quantitative measurements of behavior are taken and age-related averages are computed to chart the course of development.

Nuclear Family Unit. The portion of the family that consists of parents and their children. Excludes extended family members.

Obesity. A nutritional disorder involving intake of excess nutrients that results in a greater than 20 percent increment over average body weight. Associated with heart disease, hypertension, and diabetes as well as psychological and social consequences.

Object Permanence. The knowledge that objects in the environment have a permanent existence independent of one's interaction with them. According to Piaget, a developmental achievement of the sensorimotor period.

Observational Learning. See *modeling.*

Oedipal Conflict. A series of events of Freud's phallic stage that results in the emergence of the superego, or conscience. The boy feels a sexual desire for his mother but represses this urge out of fear of punishment. To gain his parents' approval, the boy identifies with his father's characteristics and social values. in a similar Electra conflict, girls form a conscience by identifying with their mothers.

Open Classroom. Classroom with a philosophical orientation that emphasizes nurturing social and emotional development in addition to academic progress. Decision making is shared between teacher and children, evaluation is based on children's progress in relation to their own prior development, and learning activities are responsive to children's individual needs. Distinguished from *traditional classroom.*

Operant Conditioning. A form of learning in which a spontaneously emitted behavior is followed by an outcome that either increases the probability that a response will occur again (reinforcement) or decreases it (punishment). Distinguished from *classical conditioning.*

Operations. A Piagetian term for internalized mental actions that are logical. According to Piaget, operations are not present during the sensorimotor or preoperational stages of development.

Organismic Model. A view that assumes the existence of organizing structures internal to the child that underlie and exert control over development. Represented by maturational, psychoanalytic, and cognitive-developmental theories.

Organization. In Piaget's theory, a cognitive function involving constant internal rearrangement of schemes so that they form organized, integrated totalities. In information processing, a memory strategy that recodes new information into a more tightly knit, efficient form, increasing the probability that it will be transferred from short-term to long-term memory.

Organizational Approach to Emotional Development. An approach that regards emotions as centrally important in all facets of human functioning and that emphasizes the adaptive role of emotions in promoting the survival of the organism.

Ossification. The process by which cartilage hardens into bone.

Overextension. A form of early vocabulary error that involves applying a word to a wider collection of events than is appropriate. Distinguished from *underextension.*

Overregularization. In language development, the inappropriate extension of a regular morphological rule to irregular instances. For example, saying "mouses" instead of "mice."

Paired-Associate Learning Task. A laboratory task used in memory studies in which subjects learn pairs of stimulus-response items (e.g., fish-pipe) so that when the stimulus is presented (fish), the response is recalled (pipe).

Parallel Play. A form of social participation in which the child plays near other children with similar materials but does not interact with them.

Parity. The number of children to whom a mother has given birth.

Passive Genetic-Environmental Correlation. A type of genetic-environmental correlation in which the rearing environments provided by parents are congruent with their own genotypes and therefore happen to fit well with their children's. Distinguished from *evocative* and *active genetic-environmental correlation*.

Pedigree. A pictorial representation of the occurrence of genetic disorders in a family's history that is prepared by a genetic counselor.

Peer Group. Peers who form a social unit by generating shared rules or norms of conduct and a hierarchical social structure of roles and relationships.

Perception-Bound. In Piaget's theory, a characteristic of the preoperational stage in which children are easily distracted by the concrete, perceptual appearance of objects in a logical problem.

Permissive Parenting. A parenting style that is responsive and nurturant, but low in control and demandingness. Permissive parents are overly tolerant and rarely restrict their child's behavior. Distinguished from *authoritative, authoritarian,* and *uninvolved parenting*.

Personal Fable. A type of formal operational egocentrism in which adolescents believe that their ideas and feelings are so unique that no one else could experience anything like them.

Person Perception. The way individuals conceptualize the personalities of people they know in their everyday lives.

Perspective-Taking. The capacity to understand what another person is thinking and feeling.

Phenotype. An individual's physical and behavioral characteristics, which are determined by both genetic makeup (genotype) and environmental influences.

Phenylketonuria (PKU). A disease resulting from inheritance of a pair of recessive genes that adversely affects protein metabolism and central nervous system development, leading to severe mental retardation. Treated through dietary intervention.

Phoneme. The smallest unit of speech sound that can be distinguished acoustically.

Phonology. The area of language skill concerned with understanding and producing speech sounds.

Pictorial Depth Cues. Monocular (i.e., visually discernable even if one eye is closed) depth cues, including linear perspective, texture gradients, shading, and interposition of objects. Distinguished from *kinetic* and *binocular depth cues*.

Pincer Grasp. The well-coordinated grasp involving thumb and forefinger opposition that emerges at the end of the first year. Distinguished from *ulnar grasp*.

Pituitary Gland. A major endocrine gland located at the base of the brain near the hypothalamus that releases hormones affecting physical maturation.

Placenta. The organ that separates the fetal and maternal bloodstreams but permits exchange of nutrients and waste products.

Plasticity. The ability of different areas of the brain to take over the functioning of damaged regions.

Play. Pleasurable, spontaneous, self-expressive activity carried out for its own sake. Play involving simple, sensorimotor repetition appears during infancy; constructive and make-believe forms emerge during the preschool years; and games with rules develop during middle childhood.

Pleiotropism. In genetic terminology, the determination of more than one characteristic by a single gene.

Policymakers. Individuals from all branches of government who are directly involved in drawing up and implementing public policy.

Polygenic Inheritance. Genetic inheritance in which multiple genes determine a particular characteristic. Associated with traits such as height, weight, intelligence, and personality.

Popular Children. Children who receive many positive votes from peers on sociometric measures of peer acceptance. Distinguished from *rejected, controversial,* and *neglected children*.

Postconventional Level of Morality. Kohlberg's highest level of moral development in which moral understanding is based on abstract, universal principles of justice. Distinguished from *preconventional* and *conventional levels of morality*.

Poverty Line. The income level judged by the federal government to be necessary for bare subsistence.

Practice Effects. Alteration of subjects' natural responses as a consequence of repeated testing. A factor that threatens the validity of longitudinal studies.

Pragmatics. The communicative side of language skill concerned with how to engage in effective and appropriate discourse with others.

Preconventional Level of Morality. Kohlberg's first level of moral development in which moral understanding is based on rewards, punishments, and the power of authority figures. Distinguished from *conventional* and *postconventional levels of morality*.

Preformationism. Medieval view of the child as a miniature, preformed adult.

Prenatal Diagnostic Methods. Methods that permit detection of some fetal problems prior to birth.

Preoperational Egocentrism. The form of egocentrism that appears during Piaget's preoperational stage; involves an inability to consider points of view other than one's own.

Preoperational Stage. The second Piagetian stage of development characterized by rapid growth in symbolic activity. However, reasoning is prelogical and intuitive rather than rational. Characteristic of children between about 2 and 7 years of age.

Prepared Childbirth. See *natural childbirth*.

Prereaching. The uncoordinated, primitive reaching movements of neonates.

Preterm. Premature infants who are born several weeks or more before the end of a full gestational period. The birth weight of preterm infants is low but may be appropriate for gestational age. Distinguished from *small for dates*.

Primacy Effect. In a memory task, better recall of items at the beginning of a list than in the middle. Distinguished from *recency effect*.

Primary Mental Abilities. Thurstone's set of seven distinct mental ability factors (verbal meaning, perceptual speed, reasoning, number, rote memory, word fluency, spatial visualization), which led him to conclude that intelligence is a multidimensional construct.

Private Speech. Children's verbal utterances that serve a self-guiding function and that are eventually internalized as silent, inner speech.

Production. In language development, the language children can say. Distinguished from *comprehension*.

Production Deficiency. In information processing, the failure to spontaneously use an already available mental strategy. Distinguished from *control deficiency*.

Progesterone. A hormone produced by the ovaries that helps prepare the uterus in the event of fertilization of an ovum.

Propositional Reasoning. Thought that evaluates the logic of verbal assertions without making reference to concrete, real-world circumstances. Characteristic of Piaget's formal operational stage.

Protective Regulations. Public policies aimed at protecting children from adverse circumstances and treatment. Examples include child labor laws, compulsory education laws, and state and federal standards for day care centers.

Protodeclarative. A preverbal communicative act through which infants make an assertion about an object by touching it, holding it up, and pointing to it.

Protoimperative. A preverbal communicative act in which infants point, reach, and make sounds to get another person to do something.

Proximo-distal Trend. A principle of growth in which certain maturationally determined aspects of development proceed in direction from the center of the body outward.

Pseudodialogues. Sequences of infant and maternal vocalizations that mimic the form but do not yet serve the function of information exchange. Provide opportunities for infants to learn conversational turn-taking.

Psychoanalytic Theory. The body of psychosexual and psychosocial theories of personality development, including those of Freud and Erikson, that emphasize the role of biological instincts and unconscious motivations in determining behavior and the formative importance of early experience in development.

Puberty. A period of rapid physical change leading to an adult-sized body and sexual maturity at adolescence.

Public Law 94-142. The federal law that requires schools to grant all handicapped children an appropriate public education in the least restrictive environment possible.

Public Policy. A special form of social policy involving prescriptions for action codified into law, or standards and guidelines developed by government agencies that have the force of law.

Punishment. Any outcome following an organism's spontaneously emitted behavior that decreases the probability that the behavior will be repeated.

Questionnaire. A self-report instrument in which each subject is asked the same question in the same way. Permits easy comparison of subjects' responses and efficient administration and scoring.

Random Assignment. A research procedure in which subjects are assigned to different treatment groups in such a way that any subject has an equal chance of being assigned to any group; examples include drawing numbers out of a hat or flipping a coin.

Range of Reaction. Each genotype's unique response to a range of environmental conditions.

Rapid Eye Movement Sleep (REM Sleep). An active sleep state associated with the presence of rapid eye movements, brain wave activity similar to that of the waking state, and heart rate, blood pressure, and respiration that are uneven and slightly accelerated. Also called *irregular sleep.* Distinguished from *non-rapid eye movement (NREM) sleep.*

Realism. According to Piaget, the young child's inability to separate subjective and objective aspects of experience.

Recall. The form of productive memory involving the ability to remember a stimulus that is not present.

Recasts. Parental feedback that restructures the child's speech into a more mature form.

Recency Effect. In memory tasks, better recall of items at the end of a list than items in the middle. Distinguished from *primacy effect.*

Recessive. In dominant-recessive relationships, the allele that, under heterozygous conditions, is not phenotypically apparent.

Reciprocity. A rational ideal of fairness involving a concern for the welfare of others in the same way that each person is concerned about the welfare of the self. Develops in Piaget's stage of autonomous morality.

Recoding. In information processing, internal revision of the symbolic structure of information when its form proves inadequate for further processing.

Recognition. Memory that involves noticing that a stimulus is identical or similar to one previously experienced.

Reconstituted Family. A family structure resulting from the remarriage of a divorced parent; includes parent, child, and new steprelatives.

Reconstruction. A constructive memory process in which previously stored information is reinterpreted and embellished, based on its correspondence with the individual's existing knowledge base. Upon retrieval, the information is a transformed version of the originally encoded stimulus.

Recursive Thought. The reflective, self-embedded cognitive activity that involves thinking about what another person is thinking. Grows out of advances in perspective-taking skill.

Referential Communication Skills. The ability to produce clear verbal messages and to recognize when the meaning of others' verbal messages is not clear.

Referential Style. A style of early language learning characterizing children who use language to talk about things. First words are mostly nouns.

Reflection-Impulsivity. A cognitive style dimension involving the degree to which a child will pause to consider a solution to a problem when a number of possible answers are available and there is uncertainty about which is correct.

Rehearsal. The strategy of repeating information that is to be remembered; increases the probability that information will be transferred from short-term to long-term memory.

Reinforcer. An outcome or reward following an organism's spontaneously emitted behavior that increases the occurrence of the behavior.

Rejected Children. Children who receive many negative votes from peers on sociometric measures of peer acceptance. Distinguished from *popular, controversial,* and *neglected children.*

Reliability. The extent to which a research method, when applied again within a short period of time, yields the same results. Distinguished from *validity.*

Replication. Repetition of an investigation that leads to results similar to those of a prior study.

Resistant Attachment. The pattern of insecure attachment characterizing infants who are distressed upon separation from the mother but who, upon reunion, display angry, resistive behavior. Distinguished from *avoidant, disorganized/disoriented,* and *secure attachment.*

Respiratory Distress Syndrome. A condition afflicting preterm infants in which the lungs are so underdeveloped that the air sacs collapse, causing serious breathing difficulties and, in some cases, death by suffocation. Also called *hyaline membrane disease.*

Retrieval. In information processing, recovery of information from long-term memory.

Reversal Learning. A type of discrimination learning in which subjects who have learned to respond to one aspect of a stimulus dimension (e.g., large size) must switch to another aspect of the same dimension (e.g., small size). Distinguished from *nonreversal learning.*

Reversibility. A Piagetian characteristic of logical operations; involves the ability to mentally go through a series of steps in a problem and then reverse direction, returning to the starting point.

Risks Versus Benefits Ratio. A comparison of the costs of research to the individual participant against its value for advancing knowledge and bettering children's conditions of life. Used in assessing the ethics of research.

Rough-and-Tumble Play. A form of peer interaction involving friendly chasing and play-fighting. In our evolutionary past, it may have been important for the development of dominance and fighting skill.

Rule-Assessment Approach. Siegler's information processing view that changes in children's thinking stem from the acquisition of more broadly applicable rules for solving problems.

Saccades. Sudden, swift eye movements that bring objects from the periphery to the center of the field of vision. Used to explore the visual field.

Schemes. A Piagetian term for cognitive structures that change with development.

Script. An organized representation that provides a general description of what occurs and when it occurs in a familiar situation. A basic means through which children organize and interpret their world.

Secular Trend. A progressive pattern of change over successive generations in the average age at which physical or behavioral milestones are achieved.

Secure Attachment. The pattern of attachment characterizing infants who are distressed upon separation from the mother and who, upon reunion, actively seek contact and are easily comforted by her presence. Distinguished from *avoidant, disorganized/disoriented,* and *resistant attachment.*

Secure Base. The adaptive function of the familiar caregiver as a base from which the infant confidently explores the environment and as a haven of safety when distress occurs.

Select Committee on Children, Youth, and Families. The influential interest group affiliated with the United States House of Representatives that highlights children's needs and assesses the effectiveness of existing child-related federal programs.

Self-Concept. A personal theory of what the self is like as an experiencing, functioning individual.

Self-Control. The capacity to inhibit behavioral responses that conflict with a moral course of action; resistance to temptation.

Self-Esteem. The evaluative side of self-concept that includes judgments about the extent to which the self is good, capable, significant, and praiseworthy.

Self-Fulfilling Prophecy. The idea that teacher expectations for pupil performance may become realities, causing some children to do better and others to do worse than they otherwise would.

Self-Regulation. In information processing, continuous, conscious monitoring and evaluation of one's progress toward a goal, including checking outcomes and redirecting unsuccessful efforts.

Semantic Memory. The organized store of general information in long-term memory. Distinguished from *episodic memory.*

Semantics. The area of language skill concerned with the understanding of word meaning.

Sensitive Phase. A particular time period during which an organism is biologically prepared to acquire certain new behaviors, provided it is supported by the presence of an appropriately stimulating environment. Weaker form of the critical period concept.

Sensorimotor Egocentrism. The form of egocentrism characteristic of Piaget's sensorimotor stage that involves an absence of the understanding that objects exist independently of one's own actions and that the self is an object in a world of objects.

Sensorimotor Stage. The first Piagetian stage of cognitive development, during which cognitive structures consist of perceptual and motor adjustments to the environment and internalized thinking is largely absent. Object permanence and intentional, goal-directed behavior are major achievements of this stage. Characteristic of infants from birth to about 2 years of age.

Sensory Store. In Atkinson and Shiffrin's store model of the information processing system, the initial way station in which auditory and visual stimulation is held briefly before it decays or is transferred to short-term memory.

Separation Anxiety. An infant distress reaction to the departure of the primary caregiver. Typically appears during the latter half of the first year and declines during the third year.

Sequential Processing. The capacity of the information processing system to solve problems in a stepwise fashion.

Serial Position Effect. In memory tasks involving lists of items, the tendency to remember those located at the beginning and end of the list better than those in the middle.

Sex Chromosomes. The twenty-third pair of chromosomes, which determine the sex of the future individual; in females called XX and in males called XY.

Sex-Role Identity. An individual's perception of the self as relatively masculine or feminine in characteristics, abilities, and behavior.

Sex Roles. Sex-stereotyped sets of behaviors deemed culturally appropriate for males and females in particular situations.

Sex Stereotypes. Widely held beliefs about the characteristics associated with one sex as opposed to the other.

Shading. A conversational strategy in which a change of topic is initiated by gradually modifying the focus of the conversation, rather than through an abrupt change of topic.

Shape Constancy. The ability to perceive the shape of an object as stable, despite changes in the shape projected on the retina.

Short-Term Memory Store. The central processing portion of Atkinson and Shiffrin's store model of the information processing system, where information from the environment is consciously operated on and combined with additional information from long-term memory. Distinguished from *long-term memory store*.

Sickle-Cell Anemia. A genetic blood disorder resulting from the inheritance of a recessive pair of genes, which results in the production of defective red blood cells that clog the blood vessels and interrupt the flow of oxygen to body tissues.

Simultaneous Processing. The capacity of the information processing system to grasp the overall configuration among several related elements and meaningfully integrate a variety of stimuli at the same time.

Size Constancy. The ability to perceive the size of an object as constant, despite changes in its retinal image size.

Skeletal Age. An estimate of progress toward physical maturity based on skeletal maturation.

Skill Theory. Theory proposed by Fischer that reinterprets Piaget's stages in information processing terms. Each stage is regarded as an extended period of skill acquisition in which children acquire new competencies in specific contexts, integrate them with others, and gradually transform them into more efficient, broadly generalizable, higher-order skills.

Slow-to-Warm-Up Child. A child whose temperament is such that he or she is inactive, is somewhat negative, and exhibits mild, low-key reactions to environmental stimuli. Distinguished from *easy child* and *difficult child*.

Small for Dates. An infant whose birth weight is lower than that expected for his or her gestional age. A small-for-dates infant may be full term or preterm.

Smooth Pursuit Eye Movements. Visual fixation on a moving target that permits an object's motion to be tracked.

Social Cognition. Thinking and reasoning about the self, other people, and social relationships.

Social Conventions. Normative matters that are not primarily moral, such as dress styles, table manners, and customs of social interaction.

Social Insurance. A type of public policy in which benefits are either linked to employment or (more often) granted to all members of society. Examples are paid parental leave for childbirth and child illness, publicly supported health care, and housing subsidies. Prevalent in European countries, but rare in the United States.

Social Learning Theory. The theoretical approach that emphasizes the role of modeling, reinforcement, and, more recently, intervening cognitive variables as determinants of human behavior.

Social Policy. Any planful set of actions on the part of an individual or group directed at solving a social problem or attaining a social goal.

Social Problem Solving. A process involving a combination of social-cognitive skills through which social conflicts are resolved in ways that are mutually acceptable to the self and others.

Social Referencing. Relying on another person's emotional reaction to form one's own appraisal of an uncertain situation.

Social Smile. A smile that occurs in response to the human face; first appears during the second month of life.

Social Systems Perspective. The view of the family, peer group, school, or any other social aggregate as a complex set of mutually influencing relationships affected by the larger social context in which it is embedded.

Socialization. The process by which members of society shape the behaviors of immature individuals so they develop into competent, contributing participants.

Sociobiology. The theory that complex social behaviors have a genetic basis and have evolved because of their survival value.

Sociodramatic Play. The make-believe play with others that first appears around 2 1/2 years of age.

Sociometric Techniques. Self-report measures that ask peers to evaluate one another's likability.

Sole Custody. A child custody arrangement following divorce in which the court grants one parent primary responsibility for the care and upbringing of the child. Distinguished from *joint custody*.

Sound Play. Playful repetition of early words through which infants and young children expand their phonological capacities.

Specific Factors ("s"). In Spearman's theory of intelligence, mental ability factors that are unique to particular tasks. Distinguished from *general factor ("g")* and *group factors*.

Specimen Record. An observational procedure in which a description of the subject's entire stream of behavior for a specified time period is recorded.

Speech Registers. Speech variations that are adapted to changes in social expectations.

Spermarche. The first spontaneous ejaculation of seminal fluid.

Stage. A qualitatively distinct organization of thought, feeling, and behavior at a particular period of development.

Stereopsis. See *binocular depth cues*.

Standard Deviation. A measure of the average variability or "spread-outness" of scores from the mean of a distribution.

States versus Transformations. In Piaget's theory, a characteristic of the preoperational stage in which children treat the initial and final state of a sequence of events as completely unrelated events.

Store Model. Atkinson and Shiffrin's information processing model that views information as moving sequentially through three finite-capacity stores: the sensory register, the short-term memory store, and the long-term memory store. Deployment of control processes, or strategies, increases the efficiency and capacity of each part of the system.

Strange Situation. A structured laboratory procedure devised by Ainsworth to study the quality of infant-mother attachment between 1 and 2 years of age.

Stranger Distress. The infant's expression of fear in response to unfamiliar adults. Generally emerges during the second half of the first year and wanes by the beginning of the third year.

Strategies. See *control processes*.

Structure-of-Intellect Model. Guilford's 150-factor model of intelligence that classifies mental activity according to three dimensions: mental operations, contents, and products.

Structured Interview. An interviewing technique in which each subject is asked the same questions in the same way. Permits convenient comparison of subjects' responses and efficient administration.

Structured Observation. An Observational method in which the investigator sets up a cue for the behavior of interest and observes it in the laboratory.

Structures. A Piagetian concept that refers to organized properties of intelligence that change with age.

Subject Attrition. Selective loss of subjects in the course of an investigation.

Subject Reactivity. Revisions in a subject's natural responses that stem from the subject's awareness of the experimental procedures employed in a study.

Sudden Infant Death Syndrome (SIDS). Death of a seemingly healthy baby who stops breathing, usually during the night, without apparent cause. Responsible for more deaths of infants between 10 days and 1 year of age than any other factor.

Superego. In Freud's theory, the part of personality that is the seat of conscience and that is often in conflict with the id's desires.

Surrogate Motherhood. A form of medically assisted conception in which sperm from a man, whose wife is infertile, is used to artificially inseminate a woman. She agrees to relinquish her parental rights and turn the baby over to the man (who is the natural father). The child is subsequently adopted by his wife.

Synapse. The gap between the axon of one neuron and the dendrites of another, across which chemical transmission of neural messages takes place.

Tabula Rasa. Locke's conception of the child as a blank slate whose character is shaped by experience.

Tax Benefits. A form of public policy granting families financial assistance through deductions and credits that reduce the amount of taxes they must pay.

Telegraphic Speech. Children's early word combinations, which emphasize high-content words and omit smaller and less important words, such as auxiliary verbs, prepositions, and articles.

Television Literacy. The task of learning television's specialized symbolic code of conveying information.

Temperament. Stable individual differences in quality and intensity of emotional responding. Thought to provide the biological foundation for individual differences in personality.

Teratogen. Any environmental agent that causes damage during the prenatal period.

Testosterone. A type of androgen secreted from the testes that influences male skeletal growth and appearance of secondary sex characteristics.

Theory. An orderly, integrated set of statements that explains and predicts behavior.

Thyroid Stimulating Hormone (TSH). A pituitary hormone that stimulates the release of thyroxin, produced by the thyroid gland, into the bloodstream.

Thyroxine. A hormone produced by the thyroid gland that plays an important role in development of the fetal brain, skeletal growth, and sexual maturation.

Time-Lag Comparison. The comparison of samples born in different years when they have reached the same age; allows the investigator to assess cultural-historical change.

Time Sampling. An observational procedure in which the investigator records whether or not certain behaviors occur during a sample of short time intervals.

Traditional Classroom. Classroom with a philosophical orientation that emphasizes acquisition of culturally valued knowledge and standards of conduct. Decision making is vested in the teacher, children are relatively passive in the learning process, and evaluation is based on comparisons of children to one another and to age-related, normative standards of performance. Distinguished from *open classroom*.

Transductive Reasoning. In Piaget's theory, a characteristic of the preoperational stage in which two events that are close in time and space are linked together as if one caused the other.

Transitivity. A Piagetian logical operation involving mental arrangement of a set of objects according to some quantitative characteristic.

Triarchic Theory of Intelligence. Sternberg's theory, which states that information processing skills, prior experience with tasks, and contextual factors interact to determine intellectual performance.

Triple X Syndrome (XXX). A sex chromosome abnormality in which an extra X chromosome is present in the female, leading to tallness, low verbal intelligence, and delayed speech and language development.

Turnabout. A conversational strategy that sustains verbal interaction. The speaker not only comments on what has just been said, but also adds some other kind of request to get the partner to respond again.

Turner Syndrome (XO). A sex chromosome abnormality in which a second X chromosome or a part of it is missing. Affected individuals are phenotypic females. In most cases, ovaries do not develop prenatally and secondary sexual characteristics and menstruation do not appear at puberty. Associated with intellectual deficits in spatial perception and orientation.

Type A Personality. A personality disposition characterized by excessive competitiveness, impatience, anger, and irritation. Linked to increased risk of heart disease.

Ulnar Grasp. The clumsy grasp of the young infant, in which the fingers close against the palm. Distinguished from *pincer grasp*.

Ultrasound. A method of prenatal diagnosis in which high-frequency sound waves are beamed at the uterus to reflect the size and shape of the fetus. Used to estimate gestational age and detect gross structural abnormalities.

Umbilical Cord. A prenatal structure that delivers nutrients to and removes waste products from the fetus.

Unconditioned Response (UCR). In classical conditioning, a reflexive response that is reliably elicited by an unconditioned stimulus (UCS).

Unconditioned Stimulus (UCS). In classical conditioning, a stimulus that reliably elicits a reflexive response (UCR).

Underextension. An early vocabulary error in which a word is applied to a smaller collection of events than is acceptable in conventional usage. Distinguished from *overextension*.

Uninvolved Parenting. A parenting style that is low in control as well as responsiveness. Uninvolved parents display minimal commitment to the caregiver role and are indifferent or rejecting in their behavior toward children. Distinguished from *authoritative, authoritarian,* and *permissive parenting.*

Validity. The extent to which measures taken in a research study accurately reflect what the investigator intended to measure. Distinguished from *reliability.*

Velocity Curve. A growth curve that shows the absolute amount of growth at each yearly interval. Clarifies the timing of growth spurts.

Vernix. A white, cheeselike substance covering the fetus during the second trimester. Prevents chapping and hardening of skin from constant immersion in the amniotic fluid.

Vestibular Sensitivity. The awareness of body orientation and motion governed by displacement of fluid in the semicircular canals of the inner ear. Becomes integrated with visual cues in the control of postural stability during the second half of the first year.

Visual Acuity. Fineness of visual discrimination.

Visual Cliff. An experimental apparatus used to study depth perception in infants. Consists of a glass-covered table beneath which are patterns designed to create the perception of a shallow and a deep side.

Wash-Out Effect. The tendency for intellectual gains resulting from early intervention to last for only a few years following program termination.

Within-Family Environmental Influences. Factors in the home that make children in the same family different from one another, such as differential treatment of siblings by parents. Distinguished from *between-family environmental influences*.

Working Memory. The general attentional resource pool from which information processing activities draw.

X-Linked Inheritance. A hereditary pattern in which a phenotypic characteristic is caused by a recessive gene on the X chromosome. Males are more likely to be affected than females because male sex chromosomes are not homologous and there are no complementary alleles on the Y to suppress the effects of those on the X.

XYY Syndrome. A sex chromosome abnormality involving an extra Y chromosome in males. The belief that it leads to increases in aggressive and antisocial behavior has been refuted. Associated with tallness, large teeth, and in some cases severe acne.

Yolk Sac. The sac attached to the embryo that produces blood cells until the liver, spleen, and bone marrow are mature enough to take over this process during the second month of gestation.

Zone of Proximal Development. Vygotsky's term for the range of tasks that are too difficult for the child to accomplish alone, but that can be mastered with the verbal guidance and assistance of adults or more skilled children.

Zygote. The prenatal organism during the 2-week period of development between fertilization and implantation.

References

AARON, R., & POWELL, G. (1982). Feedback practices as a function of teacher and pupil race during reading groups instruction. *Journal of Negro Education, 51,* 50–59.

AARONSON, L. S., & MACNEE, C. L. (1989). Tobacco, alcohol, and caffeine use during pregnancy. *Journal of Obstetrics, Gynecology, and Neonatal Nursing, 18,* 279–287.

ABEL, E. L. (1988). Fetal alcohol syndrome in families. *Neurotoxicology and Teratology, 10,* 1–2.

ABELMAN, R. (1985). Styles of parental disciplinary practices as a mediator of children's learning from prosocial television portrayals. *Child Study Journal, 15,* 131–145.

ABRAHAM, S., COLLINS, G., & NORDSIECK, M. (1971). Relationship of childhood weight status to morbidity in adults. *HSMHA Health Reports, 86,* 273–284.

ABRAMOV, I., GORDON, J., HENDRICKSON, A., HAINLINE, L., DOBSON, V., & LABOSSIERE, E. (1982). The retina of the newborn infant. *Science, 217,* 265–267.

ABRAVANEL, E., & SIGAFOOS, A. D. (1984). Exploring the presence of imitation during early infancy. *Child Development, 55,* 381–392.

ACHENBACH, T. M. (1978). *Research in developmental psychology: Concepts, strategies, methods.* New York: The Free Press.

ACHENBACH, T. M., & EDELBROCK, C. S. (1981). Behavioral problems and competencies reported by parents of normal and disturbed children aged 4 through 16. *Monographs of the Society of Research in Child Development, 46*(1, Serial No. 188).

ACHENBACH, T. M., & WEISZ, J. R. (1975). A longitudinal study of developmental synchrony between conceptual identity, seriation, and transitivity of color, number, and length. *Child Development, 46,* 840–848.

ACKERMAN, B. P. (1986). The relation between attention to the incidental context and memory for words in children and adults. *Journal of Experimental Child Psychology, 41,* 149–183.

ACREDOLO, C., ADAMS, A., & SCHMID, J. (1984). On the understanding of the relationships between speed, duration, and distance. *Child Development, 55,* 2151–2159.

ACREDOLO, L. P., & HAKE, J. L. (1982). Infant perception. In B. B. Wolman (Ed.), *Handbook of development psychology* (pp. 244–283). Englewood Cliffs, NJ: Prentice-Hall.

ADAMS, G. R. (1978). Racial membership and physical attractiveness effects on preschool teachers' expectations. *Child Study Journal, 8,* 29–41.

ADAMS, G. R., ABRAHAM, K. G., & MARKSTROM, C. A. (1987). The relations among identity development, self-consciousness, and self-focusing during middle- and late-adolescence. *Developmental Psychology, 23,* 292–297.

ADAMS, G. R., & CRANE, P. (1980). An assessment of parents' and teachers' expectations of preschool children's social preference for attractive or unattractive children and adults. *Child Development, 51,* 224–231.

ADAMS, G. R., & FITCH, S. A. (1982). Ego stage and identity status development: A cross-sequential analysis. *Journal of Personality and Social Psychology, 43,* 574–583.

ADAMS, G. R., GULLOTTA, T., & CLANCY, M. (1985). Homeless adolescents: A descriptive study of similarities and differences between runaways and throwaways. *Adolescence, 20,* 715–724.

ADAMS, R. E., & PASSMAN, R. H. (1981). The effects of preparing two-year-olds for brief separations from their mothers. *Child Development, 52,* 1068–1070.

ADAMS, R. J. (1987). An evaluation of color preference in early infancy. *Infant Behavior and Development, 10,* 143–150.

ADAMS, R. J., MAURER, D., & DAVIS, M. (1986). Newborns' discrimination of chromatic from achromatic stimuli. *Journal of Experimental Child Psychology, 41,* 267–281.

ADAMS, R. S. (1969). Location as a feature of instructional interaction. *Merrill-Palmer Quarterly, 15,* 309–321.

AFFLECK, G., TENNEN, H., ROWE, J., ROSCHER, B., & WALKER, L. (1989). Effects of formal support on mothers' adaptation to the hospital-to-home transition of high-risk infants: The benefits and costs of helping. *Child Development, 60,* 488–501.

AFFLECK, G., TENNEN, H., ROWE, J., WALKER, L., & HIGGINS, P. (in press). Mothers' interpersonal relationships and adaptation to hospital and home care of high risk infants. In R. Antonak & J. Mulick (Eds.), *Transitions in mental retardation,* Norwood, NJ: Ablex.

AINSWORTH, M. D. S. (1969). Object relations, dependency, and attachment: A theoretical review of the infant–mother relationship. *Child Development, 40,* 969–1025.

AINSWORTH, M. D. S. (1973). The development of infant–mother attachment. In B. M. Caldwell & H. R. Riccuiti (Eds.), *Review of child development research* (Vol. 3, pp. 1–94). Chicago: University of Chicago Press.

AINSWORTH, M. D. S., BELL, S., & STAYTON, D. (1971). Individual differences in strange situation behavior of one-year-olds. In H. Schaffer (Ed.), *The origins of human social relations* (pp. 17–52). London: Academic Press.

AINSWORTH, M. D. S., BLEHAR, M. C., WATERS, E., & WALL, S. (1978). *Patterns of attachment.* Hillsdale, NJ: Erlbaum.

AINSWORTH, M. D. S., & WITTIG, B. (1969). Attachment and exploratory behavior of one-year-olds in a strange situation. In B. Foss (Ed.), *Determinants of infant behavior* (Vol. 4, pp. 111–136). New York: Wiley.

AITKEN, M., BENNETT, S. N., & HESKETH, J. (1981). Teaching styles and pupil progress: A re-analysis. *British Journal of Educational Psychology, 51,* 187–196.

ALBERT, R. S., & RUNCO, M. A. (1986). The achievement of eminence: A model based on a longitudinal study of exceptionally gifted boys and their families. In R. J. Sternberg & J. E. Davidson (Eds.), *Conceptions of giftedness* (pp. 332–357). New York: Cambridge University Press.

ALEXANDER, K. L., & ENTWISLE, D. R. (1988). Achievement in the first 2 years of school: Patterns and processes. *Monographs of the Society for Research in Child Development, 53*(2, Serial No. 218).

ALI, F., & COSTELLO, J. (1971). Modification of the Peabody Picture Vocabulary Test. *Developmental Psychology, 5,* 86–91.

ALS, H., LESTER, B. M., TRONICK, E., & BRAZELTON, T. B. (1980). Toward a research instrument for the assessment of preterm infants' behavior (APIB). In H. E. Fitzgerald, B. M. Lester, & M. W. Yogman (Eds.), *Theory and research in behavioral pediatrics* (Vol. 1, pp. 35–63). New York: Plenum.

ALTEMEIER, W. A., O'CONNOR, S. M., SHERROD, K. B., & VIETZE, P. M. (1984). Prospective study of antecedents for nonorganic failure to thrive. *Journal of Pediatrics, 106,* 360–365.

ALTER-REID, K., GIBBS, M. S., LACHENMEYER, J. R., SIGAL, J., & MASSOTH, N. A. (1986). Sexual abuse of children: A review of empirical findings. *Clinical Psychology Review, 6,* 249–266.

ALTSHULER, J. L., & RUBLE, D. N. (1989). Developmental changes in children's awareness of strategies for coping with uncontrollable stress. *Child Development, 60,* 1337–1349.

ALVAREZ, W. F. (1985). The meaning of maternal employment for mothers and their perceptions of their three-year-old. *Child Development, 56,* 350–360.

ALWITT, L. F., ANDERSON, D. R., LORCH, E. P., & LEVIN, S. R. (1980). Preschool children's visual attention to attributes of television. *Human Communication Research, 7,* 52–67.

AMERICAN PSYCHIATRIC ASSOCIATION (1987). *Diagnostic and statistical manual of mental disorders* (3rd ed., rev.). Washington, DC: Author.

AMERICAN PSYCHOLOGICAL ASSOCIATION, DIVISION ON DEVELOPMENTAL PSYCHOLOGY (1968). Ethical standards for research with children. *Newsletter,* 1–3.

AMIEL-TISON, C. (1985). Pediatric contribution to the present knowledge on the neurobehavioral status of infants at birth. In J. Mehler & R. Fox (Eds.), *Neonate cognition: Beyond the blooming buzzing confusion* (pp. 365–380). Hillsdale, NJ: Erlbaum.

ANASTASI, A. (1958). Heredity, environment and the question how? *Psychological Review, 65,* 197–208.

ANASTASI, A. (1988). *Psychological testing* (6th ed.). New York: Macmillan.

ANDERS, T. F., & ROFFWARG, H. P. (1973). The effects of selective interruption and deprivation of sleep in the human newborn. *Developmental Psychobiology, 6,* 77–89.

ANDERSON, D. R., & SMITH, R. (1984). Young children's TV viewing: The problem of cognitive continuity. In F. J. Morrison, C. Lord, & D. P. Keating (Eds.), *Applied developmental psychology* (Vol. 1, pp. 115–163). Orlando, FL: Academic Press.

ANDERSON, E. S. (1984). The acquisition of sociolinguistic knowledge. Some evidence from children's verbal role play. *Western Journal of Speech Communication, 48,* 125–144.

ANDERSON, J. E. (1984). *Public policy-making* (2nd ed.). New York: Holt, Rinehart and Winston.

ANDERSON, N. H., & CUNEO, D. O. (1978). The height + width rule in children's judgment of quantity. *Journal of Experimental Psychology: General, 107,* 335–378.

ANDREWS, L. B. (1987). Ethical and legal aspects of in-vitro fertilization and artificial insemination by donor. *Urologic Clinics of North America, 14,* 633–643.

ANDREWS, S. R., BLUMENTHAL, J. B., JOHNSON, D. L., KAHN, A. J., FERGUSON, C. J., LASATER, T. M., MALONE, P. E., & WALLACE, D. B. (1982). The skills of mothering: A study of parent child development centers. *Monographs of the Society of Research in Child Development, 47*(6, Serial No. 198).

ANOOSHIAN, L. J., HARMAN, S. R., & SCHARF, J. S. (1982). Determinants of young children's search strategies in a large-scale environment. *Developmental Psychology, 18,* 608–616.

APGAR, V. (1953). A proposal for a new method of evaluation in the newborn infant. *Current Research in Anesthesia and Analgesia, 32,* 260–267.

APPLEBEE, A., LANGER, J., & MULLIS, I. V. S. (1986). *The Writing Report Card: Writing achievement in American Schools.* Princeton, NJ: Educational Testing Service.

APPLETON, T., CLIFTON, R., & GOLDBERG, S. (1975). The development of behavioral competence in infancy. In F. D. Horowitz (Ed.), *Review of child development research* (Vol. 4, pp. 101–186). Chicago: University of Chicago Press.

ARBUTHNOT, J. (1975). Modification of moral judgment through role playing. *Developmental Psychology, 11,* 319–324.

ARBUTHNOT, J., SPARLING, Y., FAUST, D., & KEE, W. (1983). Logical and moral development in preadolescent children. *Psychological Reports, 52,* 209–210.

ARCHER, C. J. (1984). Children's attitudes toward sex-role division in adult occupational roles. *Sex Roles, 10,* 1–10.

ARCHER, S. L. (1982). The lower age boundaries of identity development. *Child Development, 53,* 1551–1556.

ARIES, P. (1962). *Centuries of childhood.* New York: Random House.

ARLIN, P. K. (1975). Cognitive development in adulthood: A fifth stage? *Developmental Psychology, 11,* 602–606.

ARONFREED, J. (1968). *Conduct and conscience.* New York: Academic Press.

ARTERBERRY, M. E., & YONAS, A. (1988). Infants' sensitivity to kinetic information for three-dimensional object shape. *Perception and Psychophysics, 44,* 1–6.

ARTERBERRY, M., YONAS, A., & BENSEN, A. S. (1989). Self-produced locomotion and the development of responsiveness to linear perspective and texture gradients. *Developmental Psychology, 25,* 976–982.

ASCH, P. A. S., GLESER, G. C., & STEICHEN, J. J. (1986). Dependability of Brazelton Neonatal Behavioral Assessment Cluster Scales. *Infant Behavior and Development, 9,* 291–306.

ASHER, J. (1987, April). Born to be shy? *Psychology Today, 21*(4), 56–64.

ASHER, S. R. (1983). Social competence and peer status: Recent advances and future directions. *Child Development, 54,* 1427–1434.

ASHER, S. R., & HYMEL, S. (1981). Children's social competence in peer relations: Sociometric and behavioral assessment. In J. D. Wine & M. D. Smye (Eds.), *Social competence* (pp. 125–157). New York: Guilford Press.

ASHER, S. R., MARKELL, R. A., & HYMEL, S. (1981). Identifying children at risk in peer relations: A critique of the rate of interaction approach to assessment. *Child Development, 52,* 1239–1245.

ASHER, S. R., & RENSHAW, P. D. (1981). Children without friends: Social knowledge and social skills training. In S. R. Asher & J. Gottman (Eds.), *The development of children's friendships* (pp. 273–296). New York: Cambridge University Press.

ASHER, S. R., & WHEELER, V. A. (1985). Children's loneliness: A comparison of rejected and neglected peer status. *Journal of Consulting and Clinical Psychology, 53,* 500–505.

ASHMEAD, D. H., & PERLMUTTER, M. (1980). Infant memory in everyday life. In M. Perlmutter (Ed.), *New directions for child development* (Vol. 10, pp. 1–16). San Francisco: Jossey-Bass.

ASLIN, R. N. (1987). Visual and auditory development in infancy. In J. D. Osofsky (Ed.), *Handbook of infant development* (2nd ed., pp. 5–97). New York: Wiley.

ASLIN, R. N., PISONI, D. B., & JUSCZYK, P. W. (1983). Auditory development and speech perception in infancy. In M. M. Haith & J. J. Campos (Eds.), M. M. Haith, & J. J. Campos (Eds.), *Handbook of* child psychology: Vol. 2, Infancy and developmental psychobiology (4th ed., pp. 573–687). New York: Wiley.

ASTINGTON, J. W. (1988). Children's understanding of the speech act of promising. Journal of Child Language, 15, 157–173.

ATKIN, C. (1978). Observation of parent–child interaction in supermarket decision making. Journal of Marketing, 42, 41–45.

ATKIN, C., REEVES, B., & GIBSON, W. (1979). Effects of television food advertising on children. Paper presented at the annual meeting of the Association for Education in Journalism, Houston, TX.

ATKINSON, R. C., & SHIFFRIN, R. M. (1968). Human memory: A proposed system and its control processes. In K. W. Spence & J. T. Spence (Eds.), Advances in the psychology of learning and motivation (Vol. 2, pp. 90–195). New York: Academic Press.

ATKINSON-KING, K. (1973). Children's acquisition of phonological stress contrasts (UCLA Working Papers in Phonetics, No. 25). University of California, Los Angeles.

ATTIE, I., & BROOKS-GUNN, J. (1989). Development of eating problems in adolescent girls: A longitudinal study. Developmental Psychology, 25, 70–79.

AUGUST, D., & GARCIA, E. E. (1988). Language minority education in the United States. Springfield, IL: Charles C. Thomas.

AZMITIA, M. (1988). Peer interaction and problem solving: When are two heads better than one? Child Development, 59, 87–96.

BADDELEY, A. D. (1986). Working memory. London: Oxford University Press.

BAHRICK, L. E. (1983). Infants' perception of substance and temporal synchrony in multimodal events. Infant Behavior and Development, 6, 429–451.

BAHRICK, L. E. (1988). Intermodal learning in infancy: Learning on the basis of two kinds of invariant relations in audible and visible events. Child Development, 59, 197–209.

BAHRICK, L. E., & WATSON, (1985). Detection of intermodal proprioceptive-visual contingency as a potential basis of self-perception in infancy. Developmental Psychology, 21, 963–973.

BAILLARGEON, R. (1987). Object permanence in 3½- and 4½-month-old infants. Developmental Psychology, 23, 655–664.

BAILLARGEON, R., & GRABER, M. (1988). Evidence of location memory in 8-month-old infants in a nonsearch AB task. Developmental Psychology, 24, 502–511.

BAILLARGEON, R., SPELKE, E. S., & WASSERMAN, S. (1985). Object permanence in five-month-old infants. Cognition, 20, 191–208.

BAIRD, P., & SADOVNICK, A. D. (1987). Life expectancy in Down syndrome. Journal of Pediatrics, 110, 849–854.

BAIRD, P. A., & SADOVNICK, A. D. (1988). Maternal age-specific rates for Down syndrome: Changes over time. American Journal of Medical Genetics, 29, 917–927.

BAKEMAN, R., & BROWNLEE, J. R. (1982). Social rules governing object conflicts in toddlers and preschoolers. In K. H. Rubin & H. S. Ross (Eds.), Peer relationships and social skills in childhood (pp. 99–111). New York: Springer-Verlag.

BAKER, L., & BROWN, A. L. (1984). Metacognitive skills of reading. In D. Pearson (Ed.), Handbook of reading research (pp. 353–394). New York: Longman.

BAKER, S. W. (1980). Biological influences on human sex and gender. Signs: Journal of Women in Culture and Society, 6, 80–96.

BAKER-WARD, L., ORNSTEIN, P. A., & HOLDEN, D. J. (1984). The expression of memorization in early childhood. Journal of Experimental Child Psychology, 37, 555–575.

BALDWIN, D. V., & SKINNER, M. L. (1989). Structural model for antisocial behavior: Generalization to single-mother families. Developmental Psychology, 25, 45–50.

BALDWIN, W. (1983). Trends in adolescent contraception, pregnancy and sexual activity. In E. R. McAnarney (Ed.), Premature adolescent pregnancy and parenthood (pp. 3–19). New York: Grune & Stratton.

BALL, S., & BOGATZ, G. (1970). The first year of Sesame Street: An evaluation. Princeton, NJ: Educational Testing Service.

BALLARD, B. D., GIPSON, M. T., GUTTENBERG, W., & RAMSEY, K. (1980). Palatability of food as a factor influencing obese and normal-weight children's eating habits. Behavior Research and Therapy, 18, 598–600.

BALLARD, M., COREMAN, L., GOTTLIEB, J., & KAUFMAN, M. (1977). Improving the social status of mainstreamed retarded children. Journal of Educational Psychology, 69, 605–611.

BANCROFT, J., AXWORTHY, D., & RATCLIFFE, S. (1982). The personality and psycho-sexual development of boys with 47 XXY chromosome constitution. Journal of Child Psychology and Psychiatry, 23, 169–180.

BAND, E. B., & WEISZ, J. R. (1988). How to feel better when it feels bad: Children's perspectives on coping with everyday stress. Developmental Psychology, 24, 247–253.

BANDURA, A. (1967). Behavioral psychotherapy. Scientific American, 216, 78–86.

BANDURA, A. (1977). Social learning theory. Englewood Cliffs, NJ: Prentice-Hall.

BANDURA, A. (1986). Social foundations of thought and action: A social cognitive theory. Englewood Cliffs, NJ: Prentice-Hall.

BANDURA, A. (1989). Social cognitive theory. In R. Vasta (Ed.), Annals of child development (Vol. 6, pp. 1–60). Greenwich, CT: JAI Press.

BANDURA, A., ROSS, D., & ROSS, S. A. (1963). Imitation of film-mediated aggressive models. Journal of Abnormal and Social Psychology, 66, 3–11.

BANIS, H. T., VARNI, J. W., WALLANDER, J. L., KORSCH, B. M., JAY, S. M., ADLER, R., GARCIA-TEMPLE, E., & NEGRETE, V. (1988). Psychological and social adjustment of obese children and their families. Child: Care, Health and Development, 14, 157–173.

BANKS, M. S. (1980). The development of visual accommodation during early infancy. Child Development, 51, 646–666.

BANKS, M. S., & GINSBURG, A. P. (1985). Early visual preferences: A review and new theoretical treatment. In H. W. Reese (Ed.), Advances in child development and behavior (Vol. 19, pp. 207–246). New York: Academic Press.

BANKS, M. S., & SALAPATEK, P. (1981). Infant pattern vision: A new approach based on the contrast sensitivity function. Journal of Experimental Child Psychology, 31, 1–45.

BANKS, M. S., & SALAPATEK, P. (1983). Infant visual perception. In M. S. Banks & P. Salapatek (Eds.), Handbook of child psychology: Vol. 2. Infancy and developmental psychobiology (4th ed., pp. 436–571). New York: Wiley.

BARCLAY, J. R., & REID, M. (1974). Semantic integration in children's recall of discourse. Developmental Psychology, 10, 277–281.

BARCUS, F. E. (1978). Food advertising on children's television: An analysis of appeals and nutritional content. Newtonville, MA: Action for Children's Television.

BARCUS, F. E. (1983). Images of life on children's television. New York: Praeger.

BARDIN, C. W., & CATTERALL, J. F. (1981). Testosterone: A major determinant of extragenital sexual dimorphism. Science, 211, 1285–1293.

BARDWELL, J. R., COCHRAN, S. W., & WALKER, S. (1986). Relationship of parental education, race, and gender to sex role stereotyping in five-year-old kindergartners. Sex Roles, 15, 275–281.

BARENBOIM, C. (1977). Developmental changes in the interpersonal cognitive system from middle childhood to adolescence. Child Development, 48, 1467–1474.

BARENBOIM, C. (1981). The development of person perception in childhood and adolescence: From behavioral comparisons to psychological constructs to psychological comparisons. Child Development, 52, 129–144.

BARGH, J. A., & SCHUL, Y. (1980). On the cognitive benefits of peer teaching. Journal of Educational Psychology, 72, 593–604.

BARKER, R. G., & GUMP, P. V. (1964). Big school, small school: High school size and student behavior. Stanford, CA: Stanford University Press.

BARKER, R. G., & WRIGHT, H. F. (1955). Midwest and its children. New York: Harper & Row.

BARNES, K. E. (1971). Preschool play norms: A replication. Developmental Psychology, 5, 99–103.

BARNET, A. B., WEISS, I. P., SOTILLO, M. V., & OHLRICH, E. S. (1978). Abnormal auditory evoked potential in early infancy malnutrition. *Science, 201,* 450–452.

BARNETT, M. A., KING, L. M., & HOWARD, J. A. (1979). Inducing affect about self or other: Effects on generosity in children. *Developmental Psychology, 15,* 164–167.

BARRERA, M. E., & MAURER, D. (1981a). Discrimination of strangers by the three-month-old. *Child Development, 52,* 559–563.

BARRERA, M. E., & MAURER, D. (1981b). Recognition of mother's photographed face by the three-month-old infant. *Child Development, 52,* 714–716.

BARRETT, D. E. (1977). Reflection-impulsivity as a predictor of children's academic achievement. *Child Development, 48,* 1443–1447.

BARRETT, D. E. (1979). A naturalistic study of sex differences in children's aggression. *Merrill-Palmer Quarterly, 25,* 193–203.

BARRETT, D. E., RADKE-YARROW, M., & KLEIN, R. E. (1982). Chronic malnutrition and child behavior. Effects of early caloric supplementation on social and emotional functioning at school age. *Developmental Psychology, 18,* 541–556.

BARRETT, D. E., & YARROW, M. R. (1977). Prosocial behavior, social inferential ability, and assertiveness in children. *Child Development, 48,* 475–481.

BARRETT, K. C., & CAMPOS, J. J. (1987). Perspectives on emotional development: II. A functionalist approach to emotion. In J. D. Osofsky (Ed.), *Handbook of infant development* (2nd ed., pp. 1101–1149). New York: Wiley.

BARRON, F. (1963). *Creativity and psychological health.* Princeton, NJ: Van Nostrand.

BARRON, F. (1983). Creative writers. In R. S. Albert (Ed.), *Genius and eminence* (pp. 302–310). Oxford, England: Pergamon Press.

BARRON, R., & HARRINGTON, D. (1981). Creativity, intelligence, and personality. *Annual review of psychology, 32,* 439–476.

BARTLETT, F. C. (1932). *Remembering.* Cambridge, England: Cambridge University Press.

BARTON, D. P. (1980). Phonemic perception in children. In G. Yeni-Komshian, J. F. Kavanagh, & C. A. Ferguson (Eds.), *Child phonology: Vol. 2. Perception* (pp. 97–116). New York: Academic Press.

BARTON, P., & FRAZER, B. (1980). *Between two worlds: Youth transition from school to work* (Youth Knowledge Development Report 2.3). Washington, DC: U.S. Government Printing Office.

BARTSCH, K., & WELLMAN, H. (1989). Young children's attribution of action to beliefs and desires. *Child Development, 60,* 946–964.

BARUCH, G. K., & BARNETT, R. C. (1986). Fathers' participation in family work and children's sex-role attitudes. *Child Development, 57,* 1210–1223.

BARUCH, G. K., & BARNETT, R. C. (1987). Role quality and psychological well-being. In F. Crosby (Ed.), *Spouse, parent, worker* (pp. 63–84). New Haven, CT: Yale University Press.

BASSUK, E., & ROSENBERG, L. (1988). Why does family homelessness occur? A case-control study. *American Journal of Public Health, 78,* 783–788.

BASSUK, E., & RUBIN, L. (1987). Homeless children: A neglected population. *American Journal of Orthopsychiatry, 57,* 279–286.

BATES, E. (1979). *The emergence of symbols: Cognition and communication in infancy.* New York: Academic Press.

BATES, E., BRETHERTON, I., & SNYDER, L. (1988). *From first words to grammar.* Cambridge, England: Cambridge University Press.

BATES, E., CAMAIONI, L., & VOLTERRA, V. (1975). The acquisition of performatives prior to speech. *Merrill-Palmer Quarterly, 21,* 205–226.

BATES, E., & MACWHINNEY, B. A. (1982). Functionalist approaches to grammar. In L. Gleitman & H. E. Wanner (Ed.), *Language acquisition: The state of the art* (pp. 173–218). Cambridge, England: Cambridge University Press.

BATES, E., & MACWHINNEY, B. (1987). Competition, variation, and language learning. In B. MacWhinney (Ed.), *Mechanisms of language acquisition* (pp. 157–194). Hillsdale, NJ: Erlbaum.

BATES, J. E. (1987). Temperament in infancy. In J. D. Osofsky (Ed.), *Handbook of infant development* (2nd ed., pp. 1101–1149). New York: Wiley.

BATES, J. E., & BAYLES, K. (1988). Attachment and the development of behavior problems. In J. Belsky & T. Nezworski (Eds.), *Clinical implications of attachment* (pp. 253–294). Hillsdale, NJ: Erlbaum.

BATES, J. E., MASLIN, C. A., & FRANKEL, K. A. (1985). Attachment security, mother-child interaction, and temperament as predictors of behavior-problem ratings at age three years. In I. Bretherton & E. Waters (Eds.), *Growing points of attachment theory and research: Monographs of the Society for Research in Child Development, 50*(1-2, Serial No. 209).

BATESON, M. C. (1975). Mother-infant exchanges: The epigenesis of conversational interaction. In D. Aaronson & R. W. Rieber (Eds.), *Annals of the New York Academy of Sciences: Vol. 263. Developmental psycholinguistics and communication disorders* (pp. 101–113). New York: New York Academy of Sciences.

BAUER, P. J., & MANDLER, J. M. (1989). One thing follows another: Effects of temporal structure on 1- to 2-year-olds' recall of events. *Developmental Psychology, 25,* 197–206.

BAUMRIND, D. (1967). Child care practices anteceding three patterns of preschool behavior. *Genetic Psychology Monographs, 75,* 43–88.

BAUMRIND, D. (1971). Current patterns of parental authority. *Developmental Psychology Monograph, 4*(No. 1, Pt. 2).

BAUMRIND, D. (1983). Rejoinder to Lewis's reinterpretation of parental firm control effects: Are authoritative families really harmonious? *Psychological Bulletin, 94,* 132–142.

BAUMRIND, D., & BLACK, A. E. (1967). Socialization practices associated with dimensions of competence in preschool boys and girls. *Child Development, 38,* 291–327.

BAYER, A. E. (1975). Sexist students in American colleges: A descriptive note. *Journal of Marriage and the Family, 37,* 391–397.

BAYLEY, N. (1949). Consistency and variability in the growth of intelligence from birth to eighteen years. *Journal of Genetic Psychology, 75,* 165–196.

BAYLEY, N. (1969). *Bayley Scales of Infant Development.* New York: Psychological Corporation.

BAYLEY, N. (1970). The development of mental abilities. In P. Mussen (Ed.), *Carmichael's manual of child psychology* (3rd ed., Vol. 1, pp. 1163–1209). New York: Wiley.

BECKER, J. M. T. (1977). A learning analysis of the development of peer-oriented behavior in nine-month-old infants. *Developmental Psychology, 13,* 481–491.

BECKER, J. (1989). Preschoolers' use of number words to denote one-to-one correspondence. *Child Development, 60,* 1147–1157.

BECKER, W. C., & GERSTEN, R. (1982). A follow-up of Follow Through: The later effects of the direct instruction model on children in the fifth and sixth grades. *American Educational Research Journal, 19,* 75–92.

BECKWITH, L., & COHEN, S. E. (1980). Interactions of preterm infants with their caregivers and test performance at age 2. In T. F. Field (Ed.), *High-risk infants and children* (pp. 155–178). New York: Academic Press.

BEE, H. L., BARNARD, K. E., EYRES, S. J., GRAY, C. A., HAMMOND, M. A., SPIETZ, A. L., SNYDER, C., & CLARK, B. (1982). Prediction of IQ and language skill from perinatal status, child performance, family characteristics, and mother-infant interaction. *Child Development, 53,* 1134–1156.

BEHREND, D. A. (1988). Overextensions in early language comprehension: Evidence from a signal detection approach. *Journal of Child Language, 15,* 63–75.

BEHREND, D. A., ROSENGREN, K. S., & PERLMUTTER, M. (1988, April). *Parental style and children's private speech: Relations between two sources of regulation.* Paper presented at the biennial meeting of the Society for Research in Child Development, Kansas City.

BEILIN, H. (1978). Inducing conservation through training. In G. Steiner (Ed.), *Psychology of the twentieth century* (Vol. 7, pp. 260–289). Munich: Kindler.

BEILIN, H. (1980). Piaget's theory: Refinement, revision, or rejection? In R. Kluwe & H. Spada (Eds.), *Developmental models of thinking* (pp. 245–261). New York: Academic Press.

BEILIN, H. (1989). Piagetian theory. In R. Vasta (Ed.), *Annals of child development* (Vol. 6, pp. 85–131). Greenwich, CN: JAI Press.

BEIT-HALLAHMI, B., & RABIN, A. I. (1977). The kibbutz as a social experiment and as a child-rearing laboratory. *American Psychologist, 32,* 532–541.

BELCHER, T. L. (1975). Modeling original divergent responses: An initial investigation. *Journal of Educational Psychology, 67,* 351–358.

BELL, S. M., & AINSWORTH, M. D. S. (1972). Infant crying and maternal responsiveness. *Child Development, 43,* 1171–1190.

BELL-DOLAN, D. J., FOSTER, S. L., & SIKORA, D. M. (1989). Effects of sociometric testing on children's behavior and loneliness in school. *Developmental Psychology, 25,* 306–311.

BELLINGER, D. C., NEEDLEMAN, H. L., LEVITON, A., WATERNAUX, C., RABINOWITZ, M. B., & NICHOLS, M. L. (1984). Early sensory-motor development and prenatal lead exposure. *Neurobehavioral Toxicology and Teratology, 6,* 387–402.

BELMONT, L., & MAROLLA, F. A. (1973). Birth order, family size, and intelligence. *Science, 182,* 1096–1101.

BELSKY, J. (1978). A theoretical analysis of child abuse remediation strategies. *Journal of Clinical Child Psychology, 7,* 113–117.

BELSKY, J. (1980). Child maltreatment: An ecological integration. *American Psychologist, 35,* 320–335.

BELSKY, J. (1984a). The determinants of parenting: A process model. *Child Development, 55,* 83–96.

BELSKY, J. (1984b). Two waves of day-care research: Developmental effects and conditions of quality. In R. Ainslie (Ed.), *The child and the day care setting* (pp. 37–53). New York: Praeger.

BELSKY, J. (1988). The "effects" of infant day care reconsidered. *Early Childhood Research Quarterly, 3,* 235–272.

BELSKY, J., GOODE, M., & MOST, R. (1980). Maternal stimulation and infant exploratory competence: Cross-sectional, correlational and experimental analyses. *Child Development, 51,* 1168–1178.

BELSKY, J., & MOST, R. K. (1981). From exploration to play: A cross-sectional study of infant free play behavior. *Developmental Psychology, 17,* 630–639.

BELSKY, J., & ROVINE, M. (1987). Temperament and attachment security in the Strange Situation: An empirical rapprochement. *Child Development, 58* 787–795.

BELSKY, J., ROVINE, M., & TAYLOR, D. G. (1984). The Pennsylvania infant and family development project: III. The origins of individual differences in infant–mother attachment: Maternal and infant contributions. *Child Development, 55,* 718–728.

BELSKY, J., & STEINBERG, L. D. (1978). The effects of day care: A critical review. *Child Development, 49,* 929–949.

BEM, S. L. (1974). The measurement of psychological androgyny. *Journal of Consulting and Clinical Psychology, 42,* 155–162.

BEM, S. L. (1975). Sex role adaptability: One consequence of psychological androgyny. *Journal of Personality and Social Psychology, 31,* 634–643.

BEM, S. L. (1977). On the utility of alternative procedures for assessing psychological androgyny. *Journal of Consulting and Clinical Psychology, 45,* 196–205.

BEM, S. L. (1981). Gender schema theory: A cognitive account of sex typing. *Psychological Review, 88,* 354–364.

BEM, S. L. (1983). Gender schema theory and its implications for child development: Raising gender aschematic children in a gender-schematic society. *Signs: Journal of Women in Culture and Society, 8,* 598–616.

BEM, S. L. (1984). Androgyny and gender schema theory: A conceptual and empirical integration. In R. A. Dienstbier & T. B. Sonderegger (Eds.), *Nebraska Symposium on Motivation* (Vol. 34, pp. 179–226). Lincoln, NB: University of Nebraska Press.

BEM, S. L. (1989). Genital knowledge and gender constancy in preschool children. *Child Development, 60,* 649–662.

BEMIS, K. (1978). Current approaches to the etiology and treatment of anorexia nervosa. *Psychological Bulletin, 85,* 593–617.

BENACERRAF, B. R., GREEN, M. F., SSALTZMAN, D. H., BARSS, V. A., PENSO, C. A., NADEL, A. S., HEFFNER, L. J., STRYKER, J. M., SANDSTROM, M. M., & FRIGOLETTO, F. D., JR. (1988). Early amniocentesis for prenatal cytogenetic evaluation. *Radiology, 169,* 709–710.

BENBOW, C. P. (1986). Physiological correlates of extreme intellectual precocity. *Neuropsychologia, 24,* 719–725.

BENBOW, C. P. (1988). Sex differences in mathematical reasoning ability in intellectually talented preadolescents: Their nature, effects, and possible causes. *Behavioral and Brain Sciences, 11,* 169–232.

BENBOW, C. P., & STANLEY, J. C. (1980). Sex differences in mathematical ability: Fact or artifact? *Science, 210,* 1262–1264.

BENBOW, C. P., & STANLEY, J. C. (1983). Sex differences in mathematical reasoning. More facts. *Science, 222,* 1029–1031.

BENCH, R. J., COLLYER, Y., MENTZ, L., & WILSON, I. (1976). Studies in infant behavioural audiometry: I. Neonates. *Audiology, 15,* 85–105.

BENDER, W. H. (1986-1987). Effective educational practices in the mainstream setting: Recommended model for evaluation of mainstream teacher classes. *Journal of Special Education, 20,* 475–487.

BENEDICT, R. (1934). Anthropology and the abnormal. *Journal of Genetic Psychology, 10,* 59–82.

BENNETT, E. L., DIAMOND, M. C., KRECH, D., & ROSENZWEIG, M. R. (1964). Chemical and anatomical plasticity of the brain. *Science, 146,* 610–619.

BENNETT, W. (1988). *American education: Making it work.* Washington, DC: U.S. Government Printing Office.

BEN-ZEEV, S. (1977). The influence of bilingualism on cognitive strategy and cognitive development. *Child Development, 48,* 1009–1018.

BERBAUM, M. L., & MORELAND, R. L. (1985). Intellectual development within transracial adoptive families: Retesting the confluence model. *Child Development, 56,* 207–216.

BERG, M., & MEDRICH, E. A. (1980). Children in four neighborhoods: The physical environment and its effects on play and play patterns. *Environment and Behavior, 12,* 320–348.

BERG, W. K., & BERG, K. M. (1987). Psychophysiological development in infancy: State, startle, and attention. In J. Osofsky (Ed.), *Handbook of infant development* (2nd ed., pp. 238–317). New York: Wiley.

BERGMAN, L. R., & MAGNUSSON, D. (1986). Type A behavior: A longitudinal study from childhood to adulthood. *Psychosomatic Medicine, 48,* 134–142.

BERK, L. (1985). Relationship of caregiver education to child-oriented attitudes, job satisfaction, and behaviors toward children. *Child Care Quarterly, 14,* 103–129.

BERK, L. E. (1986). Relationship of elementary school children's private speech to behavioral accompaniment to task, attention, and task performance. *Developmental Psychology, 22,* 671–680.

BERK, L. E. (1991). The extracurriculum. In P. W. Jackson (Ed.), *Handbook of research on curriculum.* New York: Macmillan.

BERK, L. E., & GARVIN, R. A. (1984). Development of private speech among low-income Appalachian children. *Developmental Psychology, 20,* 271–286.

BERK, L. E., & LEWIS, N. G. (1977). Sex role and social behavior in four school environments. *Elementary School Journal, 77,* 205–217.

BERKO, J. (1958). The child's learning of English morphology. *Word, 14,* 150–177.

BERKO GLEASON, J. (1989). Studying language development. In J. Berko Gleason (Ed.), *The development of language* (pp. 1–34). Columbus, OH: Merrill.

BERKOWITZ, M. (1985). The role of discussion in moral education. In M. Berkowitz & F. Oser (Eds.), *Moral education: Theory and application* (pp. 197–218). Hillsdale, NJ: Erlbaum.

BERKOWITZ, M. W., & GIBBS, J. C. (1983). Measuring the developmental features of moral discussion. *Merrill-Palmer Quarterly, 29,* 399–410.

BERKOWITZ, M. W., GIBBS, J. C., & BROUGHTON, J. M. (1980). The relation of moral judgment stage disparity to developmental effects of peer dialogues. *Merrill-Palmer Quarterly, 26,* 341–357.

BERMAN, P. W. (1986). Young children's responses to babies: Do they foreshadow differences between maternal and paternal styles? In A. Fogel & G. F. Melson (Eds.), *Origins of nurturance* (pp. 25–51). Hillsdale, NJ: Erlbaum.

BERNDT, T. J. (1979). Developmental changes in conformity to peers and parents. *Developmental Psychology, 15,* 608–616.

BERNDT, T. J. (1981). The effects of friendship on prosocial intentions and behavior between friends. *Developmental Psychology, 17,* 408–416.

BERNDT, T. J. (1985). Prosocial behavior between friends in middle childhood and early adolescence. *Journal of Adolescence, 5,* 307–313.

BERNDT, T. J. (1988). The nature and significance of children's friendships. In R. Vasta (Ed.), *Annals of child development* (Vol. 5, pp. 155–186). Greenwich, CT: JAI Press.

BERNDT, T. J., & HOYLE, S. G. (1985). Stability and change in childhood and adolescent friendships. *Developmental Psychology, 21,* 1007–1015.

BERNSTEIN, B. (1964). Elaborated and restricted codes: The social origins and some consequences. *The Ethnography of Communication: American Anthropologist Special Publication, 66,* 55–69.

BERRUETA-CLEMENT, J. R., SCHWEINHART, L. J., BARNETT, W. S., EPSTEIN, A. S., & WEIKART, D. P. (1984). Changed lives: The effects of the Perry Preschool Program on youths through age 19: *Monographs of the High/Scope Research Foundation, 8.*

BERTENTHAL, B. I., & BAI, D. L. (1989). Infants' sensitivity to optical flow for controlling posture. *Developmental Psychology, 25,* 936–945.

BERTENTHAL, B. I., & CAMPOS, J. J. (1987). New directions in the study of early experience. *Child Development, 58,* 560–567.

BERTENTHAL, B. I., CAMPOS, J., & BARRETT, K. (1984). Self-produced locomotion: An organizer of emotional, cognitive, and social development in infancy. In R. Emde & R. Harmon (Eds.), *Continuities and discontinuities in development* (pp. 174–210). New York: Plenum.

BERTENTHAL, B. I., CAMPOS, J. J., & HAITH, M. (1980). Development of visual organization: The perception of subjective contours. *Child Development, 51,* 1077–1080.

BERTENTHAL, B. I., PROFFITT, D. R., & CUTTING, J. E. (1984). Infant sensitivity to figural coherence in biomechanical motions. *Journal of Experimental Child Psychology, 37,* 213–230.

BERTENTHAL, B. I., PROFFITT, D. R., KRAMER, S. J., & SPETNER, N. B. (1987). Infants' encoding of kinetic displays varying in relative coherence. *Developmental Psychology, 23,* 171–178.

BERTENTHAL, B. I., PROFFITT, D. R., SPETNER, N. B., & THOMAS, M. A. (1985). The development of infant sensitivity to biomechanical motions. *Child Development, 56,* 531–543.

BEST, D. L., & ORNSTEIN, P. A. (1986). Children's generation and communication of mnemonic organizational strategies. *Developmental Psychology, 22,* 845–853.

BEST, D. L., WILLIAMS, J. E., CLOUD, J. M., DAVIS, S. W., ROBERTSON, L. S., EDWARDS, J. R., GILES, H., & FOWLES, J. (1977). Development of sex-trait stereotypes among young children in the United States, England, and Ireland. *Child Development, 48,* 1375–1384.

BEVER, T. G. (1982). Some implications of the nonspecific bases of language. In E. Wanner & L. R. Gleitman (Ed.), *Language acquisition: The state of the art* (pp. 429–449). Cambridge, England: Cambridge University Press.

BIALYSTOK, E. (1986). Factors in the growth of linguistic awareness. *Child Development, 57,* 498–510.

BIANCHI, B. D., & BAKEMAN, R. (1978). Sex-typed affiliation preferences observed in preschoolers: Traditional and open school differences. *Child Development, 49,* 910–912.

BICKERTON, D. (1981). *Roots of language.* Ann Arbor, MI: Karoma.

BICKERTON, D. (1984). The language bioprogram hypothesis. *Behavioral and Brain Sciences, 7,* 178–188.

BIERMAN, K. L. (1986). Process of change during social skills training with preadolescents and its relation to treatment outcome. *Child Development, 57,* 230–240.

BIERMAN, K. L., MILLER, C. L., & STABB, S. D. (1987). Improving the social behavior and peer acceptance of rejected boys: Effects of social skill training with instructions and prohibitions. *Journal of Consulting and Clinical Psychology, 55,* 194–200.

BIGELOW, B. J. (1977). Children's friendship expectations: A cognitive-developmental study. *Child Development, 48,* 246–253.

BIGELOW, B. J., & LAGAIPA, J. J. (1975). Children's written descriptions of friendship: A multidimensional analysis. *Developmental Psychology, 11,* 857–858.

BILLMAN, J., & MCDEVITT, S. C. (1980). Convergence of parent and observer ratings of temperament with observations of peer interaction in nursery school. *Child Development, 51,* 395–400.

BIRCH, L. L. (1981). Generalization of a modified food preference. *Child Development, 52,* 755–758.

BIRCH, L. L., ZIMMERMAN, S., & HIND, H. (1980). The influence of social-affective context on preschool children's food preferences. *Child Development, 51,* 856–861.

BIRNS, B., & NOYES, D. (1984). Child nutrition: The role of theory in the world of politics. *International Journal of Mental Health, 12,* 22–42.

BISCHOFSHAUSEN, S. (1985). Developmental differences in schema dependency for temporally ordered story events. *Journal of Psycholinguistic Research, 14,* 543–556.

BISHOP, S. M., & INGERSOLL, G. M. (1989). Effects of marital conflict and family structure on the self-concepts of pre- and early adolescents. *Journal of Youth and Adolescence, 18,* 25–38.

BIVENS, J. A., & BERK, L. E. (1990). A longitudinal study of the development of elementary school children's private speech. *Merrill-Palmer Quarterly, 36,* 000–000.

BIXENSTINE, V. E., DECORTE, M. S., & BIXENSTINE, B. A. (1976). Conformity to peer-sponsored misconduct at four age levels. *Developmental Psychology, 12,* 226–236.

BJORK, E. L., & CUMMINGS, E. M. (1984). Infant search errors: Stage of concept development or stage of memory development. *Memory and Cognition, 12,* 1–19.

BJORKLUND, D. F. (1987). How age changes in knowledge base contribute to the development of children's memory: An interpretive review. *Developmental Review, 7,* 93–130.

BJORKLUND, D. F., & DE MARCHENA, M. R. (1984). Developmental shifts in the basis of organization memory: The role of associative versus categorical relatedness in children's free recall. *Child Development, 55,* 952–962.

BJORKLUND, D. F., & HARNISHFEGER, K. K. (1987). Developmental differences in the mental effort requirements for the use of an organizational strategy in free recall. *Journal of Experimental Child Psychology, 44,* 109–125.

BJORKLUND, D. F., & HOCK, H. S. (1982). Age differences in the temporal locus of memory organization in children's recall. *Journal of Experimental Child Psychology, 32,* 347–362.

BJORKLUND, D. F., & JACOBS, J. W. (1985). Associative and categorical processes in children's memory: The role of automaticity in the development of organization in free recall. *Journal of Experimental Child Psychology, 39,* 599–617.

BJORKLUND, D. F., & MUIR, J. E. (1988). Children's development of free recall memory: Remembering on their own. In R. Vasta (Ed.), *Annals of child development* (Vol. 5, pp. 79–123). Greenwich, CT: JAI Press.

BJORKLUND, D. F., & ZEMAN, B. R. (1983). The development of organizational strategies in children's recall of familiar information: Using social organization to recall the names of classmates. *International Journal of Behavioral Development, 6,* 341–353.

BLACK, B., & HAZEN, N. L. (1990). Social status and patterns of communication in acquainted and unacquainted preschool children. *Developmental Psychology, 26,* 379–387.

BLAKE, J. (1981). The only child in America: Prejudice versus performance. *Population and Development Review, 1,* 43–54.

BLAKEMORE, J. E. O., LARUE, A. A., & OLEJNIK, A. B. (1979). Sex-appropriate toy preference and the ability to conceptualize toys as sex-role related. *Developmental Psychology, 15,* 339–340.

BLANCHARD, M., & MAIN, M. (1979). Avoidance of the attachment figure and social-emotional adjustment in day-care infants. *Developmental Psychology, 15,* 445–446.

BLASI, A. (1980). Bridging moral cognition and moral action: A critical review of the literature. *Psychological Bulletin, 88,* 593–637.

BLASI, A. (1983). Moral cognition and moral action: A theoretical perspective. *Developmental Review, 3,* 178–210.

BLASS, E. M., GANCHROW, J. R., & STEINER, J. E. (1984). Classical conditioning in newborn humans 2–48 hours of age. *Infant Behavior and Development, 7*, 223–235.

BLATT, M., & KOHLBERG, L. (1975). The effects of classroom moral discussion upon children's level of moral judgment. *Journal of Moral Education, 4*, 129–161.

BLATT, J., SPENCER, L., & WARD, S. (1972). A cognitive developmental study of children's reactions to television advertising. In E. A. Rubinstein, G. A. Combstock, & J. P. Murray (Eds.), *Television and social behavior* (Vol. 4, pp. 452–467). Washington, DC: U.S. Government Printing Office.

BLAU, Z. S. (1981). *Black children, white children: Competence, socialization and social structure.* New York: The Free Press.

BLOCK, J. (1971). *Lives through time.* Berkeley, CA: Bancroft Books.

BLOCK, J., BLOCK, J. H., & GJERDE, P. F. (1988). Parental functioning and home environment in families of divorce: Prospective and concurrent analyses. *Journal of the American Academy of Child and Adolescent Psychiatry, 27*, 207–213.

BLOCK, J. H. (1973). Conceptions of sex role: Some cross-cultural and longitudinal perspectives. *American Psychologist, 28*, 512–526.

BLOCK, J. H. (1976). Issues, problems, and pitfalls in assessing sex differences: A critical review of "The Psychology of Sex Differences." *Merrill-Palmer Quarterly, 22*, 283–308.

BLOCK, J. H. (1978). Another look at sex differentiation in the socialization behavior of mothers and fathers. In J. Sherman & F. L. Denmark (Eds.), *Psychology of women: Future directions of research* (pp. 29–87). New York: Psychological Dimensions.

BLOCK, J. H. (1983). Differential premises arising from differential socialization of the sexes: Some conjectures. *Child Development, 54*, 1335–1354.

BLOCK, J. H., BLOCK, J., & HARRINGTON, D. (1975). *Sex role typing and instrumental behavior: A developmental study.* Paper presented at the annual meeting of the Society for Research in Child Development, Denver.

BLOOM, B. S. (1982). The role of gifts and markers in the development of talent. *Exceptional Children, 48*, 510–522.

BLOOM, B. S., & SOSNIAK, L. A. (1981). Talent development vs. schooling. *Educational Leadership, 39*, 86–94.

BLOOM, L. (1970). *Language development: Form and function in emerging grammars,* Cambridge, MA: MIT Press.

BLOOM, L. (1973). *One word at a time: The use of single word utterance before syntax.* The Hague: Mouton.

BLOOM, L., LAHEY, M., LIFTEN, K., & FIESS, K. (1980). Complex sentences: Acquisition of syntactic connections and the semantic relations they encode. *Journal of Child Language, 7*, 235–256.

BLOTNER, R., & BEARISON, D. J. (1984). Developmental consistencies in socio-moral knowledge: Justice reasoning and altruistic behavior. *Merrill-Palmer Quarterly, 30*, 349–367.

BLUEBOND-LANGER, M. (1977). Meanings of death to children. In H. Feifel (Ed.), *New meanings of death* (pp. 47–66). New York: McGraw-Hill.

BLURTON JONES, N. (1972). Categories of child-child interaction. In N. Blurton Jones (Ed.), *Ethological studies of child behaviour* (pp. 97–127). Cambridge, England: Cambridge University Press.

BLYTH, D. A., SIMMONS, R. G., BULCROFT, R., FELT, D., VAN CLEAVE, E. F., & BUSH, D. M. (1981). The effects of physical development on self-image and satisfaction with body-image for early adolescent males. In R. Simmons (Ed.), *Research in community mental health* (Vol. 2, pp. 43–73). Greenwich, CN: JAI Press.

BLYTH, D. A., SIMMONS, R. G., & ZAKIN, D. F. (1985). Satisfaction with body image for early adolescent females: The impact of pubertal timing within different school environments. *Journal of Youth and Adolescence, 14*, 207–225.

BOGATZ, G. A., & BALL, S. (1972). *The second year of Sesame Street: A continuing evaluation.* Princeton, NJ: Educational Testing Service.

BOHANNON, J. N., III, MACWHINNEY, B., & SNOW, C. (1990). No negative evidence revisited: Beyond learnability or who has to prove what to whom. *Developmental Psychology, 26*, 221–226.

BOHANNON, J. N., III, & STANOWICZ, L. (1988). The issue of negative evidence: Adult responses to children's language errors. *Developmental Psychology, 24*, 684–689.

BOHANNON, J. N., III, & WARREN-LEUBECKER, A. (1988). Recent developments in child-directed speech: We've come a long way, baby-talk. *Language Sciences, 10*, 89–110.

BOHANNON, J. N., III, & WARREN-LEUBECKER, A. (1989). Theoretical approaches to language acquisition. In J. Berko Gleason (Ed.), *The development of language* (pp. 167–223). Columbus, OH: Merrill.

BOISMIER, J. D. (1977). Visual stimulation and wake-sleep behavior in human neonates. *Developmental Psychobiology, 10*, 219–227.

BOLDIZAR, J. P., PERRY, D. G., & PERRY, L. C. (1989). Outcome values and aggression. *Child Development, 60*, 571–579.

BONVILLIAN, J., NELSON, K. E., & CHARROW, V. (1976). Language and language-related skills in deaf and hearing children. *Sign Language Studies, 12*, 211–250.

BORGHGRAEF, M., FRYNS, J. P., DIELKENS, A., PYCK, K., & VAN DEN BERGHE, H. (1987). Fragile (X) syndrome: A study of the psychological profile in 23 prepubertal patients. *Clinical Genetics, 32*, 179–186.

BORKE, H. (1975). Piaget's mountains revisited: Changes in the egocentric landscape. *Developmental Psychology, 11*, 240–243.

BORKO, H., SHAVELSON, R., & STERN, P. (1981). Teachers' decisions in the planning of reading instruction. *Reading Research Quarterly, 16*, 449–466.

BORKOWSKI, J. G., & MAXWELL, S. E. (1985). Looking for Mr. Good-g: General intelligence and processing speed. *Behavioral and Brain Sciences, 8*, 221–222.

BORNSTEIN, M. H., & SIGMAN, M. D. (1986). Continuity in mental development from infancy. *Child Development, 57*, 251–274.

BORSTELMANN, L. J. (1983). Children before psychology: Ideas about children from antiquity to the late 1800s. In W. Kessen (Ed.), *Handbook of child psychology: Vol. 1. History, theory, and methods* (pp. 1–40). New York: Wiley.

BOSSARD, J. S. S., & BOLL, E. S. (1956). *The large family system.* Philadelphia: University of Pennsylvania Press.

BOUCHARD, T. J., JR. (1981). *The Minnesota study of twins reared apart: Description and preliminary findings.* Paper presented at the annual meeting of the American Psychological Association.

BOUCHARD, T. J., JR. (1984). Twins reared together and apart: What they tell us about human diversity. In S. W. Fox (Ed.), *Individuality and determinism: Chemical and biological bases* (pp. 147–184). New York: Plenum.

BOUCHARD, T. J., JR., & McGUE, M. (1981). Familial studies of intelligence: A review. *Science, 212*, 1055–1058.

BOUCHARD, T. J., JR., & SEGAL, N. L. (1985). Environment and IQ. In B. B. Wolman (Eds.), *Handbook of intelligence* (pp. 391–464). New York: Wiley.

BOUKYDIS, C. F. Z. (1985). Perception of infant crying as an interpersonal event. In B. M. Lester & C. F. Z. Boukydis (Eds.), *Infant crying* (pp. 187–215). New York: Plenum.

BOUKYDIS, C. F. Z., & BURGESS, R. L. (1982). Adult physiological response to infant cries: Effects of temperament of infant, parental status and gender. *Child Development, 53*, 1291–1298.

BOWER, G. (1981). Mood and memory. *American Psychologist, 36*, 128–148.

BOWER, T. G. R. (1982). *Development in infancy* (2nd ed.). San Francisco: Freeman.

BOWERMAN, M. (1973). *Early syntactic development: A cross-linguistic study with special reference to Finnish.* Cambridge, England: Cambridge University Press.

BOWERMAN, M. (1985). What shapes children's grammars? In D. I. Slobin (Ed.), *The crosslinguistic study of language acquisition: Vol. 2. Theoretical issues* (pp. 1257–1319). Hillsdale, NJ: Erlbaum.

BOWLBY, J. (1969). *Attachment and loss: Vol. 1. Attachment.* New York: Basic Books.

BOWLBY, J. (1980). *Attachment and loss: Vol. 3. Loss.* New York: Basic Books.

BOWMAN, P. J., & HOWARD, C. (1985). Race-related socialization, motivation, and academic achievement: A study of black youth in three generation families. *Journal of the American Academy of Child Psychiatry, 24,* 134–141.

BOYES, M. C., & WALKER, L. J. (1988). Implications of cultural diversity for the universality claims of Kohlberg's theory of moral reasoning. *Human Development, 31,* 44–59.

BOYSSON-BARDIES, B., DESAGART, L., & DURAND, C. (1984). Discernable differences in the babbling of infants according to target language. *Journal of Child Language, 11,* 1–15.

BRABECK, M. (1983). Moral judgment: Theory and research on differences between males and females. *Developmental Review, 3,* 274–291.

BRACHT, G. H., & GLASS, G. V. (1968). The external validity of experiments. *American Educational Research Journal, 5,* 437–474.

BRACKBILL, Y., MCMANUS, K., & WOODWARD, L. (1985). *Medication in maternity: Infant exposure and maternal information.* Ann Arbor: University of Michigan Press.

BRACKBILL, Y., & NICHOLS, P. L. (1982). A test of the confluence model of intellectual development. *Developmental Psychology, 18,* 192–198.

BRADLEY, R. H., & CALDWELL, B. M. (1976). The relation of infants' home environments to mental test performance at fifty-four months: A follow-up study. *Child Development, 47,* 1172–1174.

BRADLEY, R. H., & CALDWELL, B. M. (1979). Home Observation for Measurement of the Environment: A revision of the preschool scale. *American Journal of Mental Deficiency, 84,* 235–244.

BRADLEY, R. H., & CALDWELL, B. M. (1981). The HOME Inventory: A validation of the preschool scale for black children. *Child Development, 52,* 708–710.

BRADLEY, R. H., & CALDWELL, B. M. (1982). The consistency of the home environment and its relation to child development. *International Journal of Behavioral Development, 5,* 445–465.

BRADLEY, R. H., CALDWELL, B. M., & ROCK, S. L. (1988). Home environment and school performance: A ten-year follow-up and examination of three models of environmental action. *Child Development, 59,* 852–867.

BRADLEY, R. H., CALDWELL, B. M., ROCK, S. L., HAMRICK, H. M., & HARRIS, P. (1988). Home Observation for Measurement of the Environment: Development of a home inventory for use with families having children 6 to 10 years old. *Contemporary Educational Psychology, 13,* 58–71.

BRADLEY, R. H., CALDWELL, B. M., ROCK, S. L., RAMEY, C. T., BARNARD, K. E., GRAY, C., HAMMOND, M. A., MITCHELL, S., GOTTFRIED, A., SIEGEL, L., & JOHNSON, D. L. (1989). Home environment and cognitive development in the first 3 years of life: A collaborative study involving six sites and three ethnic groups in North America. *Developmental Psychology, 25,* 217–235.

BRADLEY, R. M. (1972). Development of the taste bud and gustatory papillae in human fetuses. In J. F. Bosma (Ed.), *The third symposium on oral sensation and perception: The mouth of the infant* (pp. 137–162). Springfield, IL: Thomas.

BRAINE, M. D. S. (1976). Children's first word combinations. *Monographs for the Society for Research in Child Development, 41*(1, Serial No. 164).

BRAINE, M. D. S. (1987). What is learned in acquiring word classes—A step toward an acquisition theory. In B. MacWhinney (Ed.), *Mechanisms of language acquisition* (pp. 65–87). Hillsdale, NJ: Erlbaum.

BRAINERD, C. J. (1974). Inducing ordinal and cardinal representations of the first five natural numbers. *Journal of Experimental Child Psychology, 18,* 520–534.

BRAINERD, C. J. (1978). *Piaget's theory of intelligence.* Englewood Cliffs, NJ: Prentice-Hall.

BRAINERD, C. J., & ALLEN, T. W. (1971). Training and generalization of density conservation: Effects of feedback and consecutive similar stimuli. *Child Development, 42,* 693–704.

BRAINERD, C. J., & BRAINERD, S. H. (1972). Order of acquisition of number and liquid quantity conservation. *Child Development, 43,* 1401–1405.

BRAINERD, C. J., KINGMA, J., & HOWE, M. L. (1985). On the development of forgetting. *Child Development, 56,* 1103–1119.

BRAINERD, C. J., & REYNA, V. F. (1988). Generic resources, reconstruc-

tive processing, and children's mental arithmetic. *Developmental Psychology, 24,* 324–334.

BRAND, E., CLINGEMPEEL, W. E., & BOWEN-WOODWARD, K. (1988). Family relationships and children's psychological adjustment in stepmother and stepfather families: Findings and conclusions from the Philadelphia Stepfamily Research Project. In E. M. Hetherington & J. D. Arasteh (Eds.), *Impact of divorce, single-parenting, and stepparenting on children* (pp. 299–324). Hillsdale, NJ: Erlbaum.

BRANSFORD, J. D., STEIN, B. S., SHELTON, T. S., & OWINGS, R. A. (1981). Cognition and adaptation: The importance of learning to learn. In J. Harvey (Ed.), *Cognition, social behavior, and the environment* (pp. 93–110). Hillsdale, NJ: Erlbaum.

BRASSARD, M. R., GERMAIN, R., & HART, S. N. (EDS.). (1987). *Psychological maltreatment of children and youth.* New York: Pergamon Press.

BRAY, J. H. (1988). Children's development during early remarriage. In E. M. Hetherington & J. D. Arasteh (Ed.), *Impact of divorce, single parenting, and stepparenting on children* (pp. 279–298). Hillsdale, NJ: Erlbaum.

BRAZELTON, T. B. (1983). *Infants and mothers.* New York: Delacorte Press.

BRAZELTON, T. B. (1984). *Neonatal Behavioral Assessment Scale.* Philadelphia: Lippincott.

BRAZELTON, T. B. (1989a). Culture and newborn behavior: Uses of the NBAS in different cultural settings. In J. K. Nugent, B. M. Lester, & T. B. Brazelton (Eds.), *Biology, culture, and development* (Vol. 1, pp. 367–381). Norwood, NJ: Ablex.

BRAZELTON, T. B. (1989b). *Toddlers and parents* (rev. ed.). New York: Delacorte Press.

BRAZELTON, T. B., & CRAMER, B. (1990). *The earliest relationship: Parents, infants, and the drama of early attachments.* New York: Delacorte Press.

BRAZELTON, T. B., KOSLOWSKI, B., & TRONICK, E. (1976). Neonatal behavior among urban Zambians and Americans. *Journal of the American Academy of Child Psychiatry, 15,* 97–107.

BRAZELTON, T. B., NUGENT, J. K., & LESTER, B. M. (1987). Neonatal Behavioral Assessment Scale. In J. D. Osofsky (Ed.), *Handbook of infant development* (2nd ed., pp. 780–817). New York: Wiley.

BRAZELTON, T. B., ROBEY, J. S., & COLLIER, G. A. (1969). Infant development in the Zinacanteco Indians of southern Mexico. *Pediatrics, 44,* 274–290.

BRENNAN, W. M., AMES, E. W., & MOORE, R. W. (1966). Age differences in infants' attention to patterns of different complexities. *Science, 151,* 354–356.

BRENNER, D., & HINSDALE, G. (1978). Body build stereotypes and self-identification in three age groups of females. *Adolescence, 13,* 551–562.

BRETHERTON, I., FRITZ, J., ZAHN-WAXLER, C., & RIDGEWAY, D. (1986). Learning to talk about emotions: A functionalist perspective. *Child Development, 57,* 529–548.

BRETHERTON, I., O'CONNELL, B., SHORE, C., & BATES, E. (1984). The effect of contextual variation on symbolic play: Development from 20 to 28 months. In I. Bretherton (Ed.), *Symbolic play and the development of social understanding* (pp. 271–298). New York: Academic Press.

BRICE-HEATH, S. (1982). Questioning at home and at school: A comparative study. In G. Spindler (Ed.), *Doing the ethnography of schooling: Educational anthropology in action* (pp. 102–127). New York: Holt.

BRICE-HEATH, S. (1989). Oral and literate traditions among black Americans living in poverty. *American Psychologist, 44,* 367–373.

BRIDGES, A. (1985). Actions and things: What adults talk about to 1-year-olds. In S. A. Kuczaj, II, & M. D. Barrett (Eds.), *The development of word meaning* (pp. 225–255). New York: Springer-Verlag.

BRIDGES, F. A., & CICCHETTI, D. (1982). Mothers' ratings of the temperament characteristics of Down syndrome infants. *Developmental Psychology, 18,* 238–244.

BRIDGES, L. J., CONNELL, J. P., & BELSKY, J. (1988). Similarities and differences in infant-mother and infant-father interaction in the Strange Situation: A component process analysis. *Developmental Psychology, 24,* 92–100.

BRIM, O. G. (1958). Family structure and sex role learning by children: A further analysis of Helen Koch's data. *Sociometry, 21,* 1–16.

BRITT, D. W., & CAMPBELL, E. Q. (1977). Assessing the linkage of norms, environments, and deviance. *Social Forces, 56,* 532–550

BRODY, G. H., GRAZIANO, W. G., & MUSSER, L. M. (1983). Familiarity and children's behavior in same-age and mixed-age peer groups. *Developmental Psychology, 19,* 568–576.

BRODY, G. H., & SHAFFER, D. R. (1982). Contributions of parents and peers to children's moral socialization. *Developmental Review, 2,* 31–75.

BRODY, G. H., & STONEMAN, Z. (1981). Selective imitation of same-age, older, and younger peer models. *Child Development, 52,* 717–720.

BRODY, G. H., STONEMAN, Z., & BURKE, M. (1987). Child temperaments, maternal differential behavior, and sibling relationships. *Developmental Psychology, 23,* 354–362.

BRODY, L. E., & BENBOW, C. P. (1987). Accelerative strategies: How effective are they for the gifted? *Gifted Child Quarterly, 3,* 105–110.

BRODY, N. (1985). The validity of tests of intelligence. In B. B. Wolman (Ed.), *Handbook of intelligence* (pp. 353–389). New York: Wiley.

BRODZINSKY, D. M., & RIGHTMYER, J. (1980). Individual differences in children's humour development. In P. E. McGee & A. J. Chapman (Eds.), *Children's humour* (pp. 181–212). Chichester, England: Wiley.

BROMAN, S. H. (1983). Obstetric medications. In C. C. Brown (Ed.), *Childhood learning disabilities and prenatal risk* (pp. 56–64). New York: Johnson & Johnson.

BRONFENBRENNER, U. (1972). Is 80% of intelligence genetically determined? In U. Bronfenbrenner (Ed.), *Influences on human development* (pp. 118–130). Hinsdale, IL: Dryden Press.

BRONFENBRENNER, U. (1975). Is early intervention effective? In M. Guttentag & E. L. Struening (Eds.), *Handbook of evaluation research* (Vol. 2, pp. 519–603). Beverly Hills, CA: Sage.

BRONFENBRENNER, U. (1979). *The ecology of human development: Experiments by nature and design.* Cambridge, MA: Harvard University Press.

BRONFENBRENNER, U. (1986). Alienation and four worlds of childhood. *Phi Delta Kappan, 67,* 430–436.

BRONFENBRENNER, U. (1989). Ecological systems theory. In R. Vasta (Ed.), *Annals of child development* (Vol. 6, pp. 187–251). Greenwich, CN: JAI Press.

BRONFENBRENNER, U., ALVAREZ, W. F., & HENDERSON, C. R., JR. (1984). Working and watching: Maternal employment status and parents' perceptions of their three-year-old children. *Child Development, 55,* 1362–1378.

BRONFENBRENNER, U., & CROUTER, A. C. (1982). Work and family through time and space. In S. B. Kamerman & C. D. Hayes (Eds.), *Families that work: Children in a changing world* (pp. 39–83). Washington, DC: National Academy Press.

BRONFENBRENNER, U., MOEN, P., & GARBARINO, J. (1984). Child, family, and community. In R. D. Parke (Ed.), *Review of child development research* (Vol. 7, pp. 283–328). Chicago: University of Chicago Press.

BRONSON, W. C. (1981). *Toddlers' behaviors with agemates: Issues of interaction, cognition, and affect.* Norwood, NJ: Ablex.

BROOKE, O. G., ANDERSON, H. R., BLAND, J. M., PEACOCK, J. L., & STEWART, C. M. (1989). Effects on birth weight of smoking, alcohol, caffeine, socioeconomic factors, and psychosocial stress. *British Medical Journal, 298,* 795–801.

BROOKOVER, W., BEADY, C., FLOOD, P., SCHWEITZER, J., & WISENBAKER, J. (1979). *School social systems and student achievement: Schools can make a difference.* New York: Bergin.

BROOKS, J., & LEWIS, M. (1976). Infants' responses to strangers: Midget, adult, and child. *Child Development, 47,* 323–332.

BROOKS-GUNN, J. (1984). The psychological significance of different pubertal events to young girls. *Journal of Early Adolescence, 4,* 315–327.

BROOKS-GUNN, J. (1986). The relationship of maternal beliefs about sex typing to maternal and young children's behavior. *Sex Roles, 14,* 21–35.

BROOKS-GUNN, J. (1988). Antecedents and consequences of variations in girls' maturational timing. *Journal of Adolescent Health Care, 9,* 1–9.

BROOKS-GUNN, J., & FURSTENBERG, F. F., JR. (1989). Adolescent sexual behavior. *American Psychologist, 44,* 249–257.

BROOKS-GUNN, J., & RUBLE, D. N. (1980). Menarche: The interaction of physiology, cultural, and social factors. In A. J. Dan, E. A. Graham, & C. P. Beecher (Eds.), *The menstrual cycle: A synthesis of interdisciplinary research* (pp. 141–159). New York: Springer-Verlag.

BROOKS-GUNN, J., & RUBLE, D. N. (1983). The experience of menarche from a developmental perspective. In J. Brooks-Gunn & A. C. Petersen (Eds), *Girls at puberty* (pp. 155–177). New York: Plenum.

BROOKS-GUNN, J., & WARREN, M. P. (1985). The effects of delayed menarche in different contexts: Dance and nondance students. *Journal of Youth and Adolescence, 14,* 285–300.

BROOKS-GUNN, J., & WARREN, M. P. (1988). The psychological significance of secondary sexual characteristics in nine- to eleven-year-old girls. *Child Development, 59,* 1061–1069.

BROOKS-GUNN, J., WARREN, M. P., SAMELSON, M., & FOX, R. (1986). Physical similarity of and disclosure of menarcheal status to friends: Effects of grade and pubertal status. *Journal of Early Adolescence, 6,* 3–14.

BROPHY, J. E. (1983). Research on the self-fulfilling prophecy and teacher expectations. *Journal of Educational Psychology, 75,* 631–661.

BROPHY, J. E., & EVERTSON, C. (1976). *Learning from teaching: A developmental perspective.* Boston: Allyn and Bacon.

BROPHY, J. E., & GOOD, T. L. (1974). *Teacher–student relationships: Causes and consequences.* New York: Holt, Rinehart and Winston.

BROPHY, J. E., & GOOD, T. L. (1986). Teacher behavior and student achievement. In M. C. Wittrock (Ed.), *Handbook of research on teaching* (3rd ed., pp. 328–375). New York: Macmillan.

BROVERMAN, D. M., KLAIBER, E. L., & VOGEL, W. (1980). Gonadal hormones and cognitive functioning. In J. E. Parsons (Ed.), *The psychology of sex differences and sex roles* (pp. 57–80). Washington, DC: Hemisphere Publishing.

BROVERMAN, I. K., BROVERMAN, D. M., CLARKSON, F. E., ROSENKRANTZ, P. S., & VOGEL, S. R. (1970). Sex-role stereotypes and clinical judgments of mental health. *Journal of Consulting and Clinical Psychology, 34,* 1–7.

BROVERMAN, I. K., VOGEL, S. R., BROVERMAN, D. M., CLARKSON, F. E., & ROSENKRANTZ, P. S. (1972). Sex-role stereotypes: A current appraisal. *Journal of Social Issues, 28,* 59–78.

BROWN, A. L., BRANSFORD, J. D., FERRARA, R. A., & CAMPIONE, J. C. (1983). Learning, remembering and understanding. In J. H. Flavell & E. M. Markman (Eds.), *Handbook of child psychology: Vol. 3. Cognitive development* (4th ed., pp. 77–166). New York: Wiley.

BROWN, A. L., & CAMPIONE, J. C. (1972). Recognition memory for perceptually similar pictures in preschool children. *Journal of Experimental Psychology, 95,* 55–62.

BROWN, A. L., SMILEY, S. S., DAY, J. D., TOWNSEND, M., & LAWTON, S. Q. C. (1977). Intrusion of a thematic idea in children's recall of prose. *Child Development, 48,* 1454–1466.

BROWN, A. L., SMILEY, S. S., & LAWTON, S. Q. C. (1978). The effects of experience on the selection of suitable retrieval cues for studying texts. *Child Development, 49,* 829–835.

BROWN, B. B., LOHR, M. J., & McCLENAHAN, E. L. (1986). Early adolescents' perceptions of peer pressure. *Journal of Early Adolescence, 6,* 139–154.

BROWN, G. W., BHROLCHAIN, M., & HARRIS, T. O. (1976). Social class and psychiatric disturbance among women in an urban population. *Sociology, 9,* 225–254.

BROWN, R. (1957). Linguistic determinism and the part of speech. *Journal of Abnormal and Social Psychology, 55,* 1–5.

BROWN, R. W. (1973). *A first language: The early stages.* Cambridge, MA: Harvard University Press.

BROWN. R., & HANLON, C. (1970). Derivational complexity and order of acquisition in child speech. In J. R. Hayes (Ed.), *Cognition and the development of language* (pp. 11–53). New York: Wiley.

BROWN V. BOARD OF EDUCATION OF TOPEKA, 349 U.S. 294 (1954).

BROWNELL, C. A. (1986). Convergent developments: Cognitive-developmental correlates of growth in infant/toddler peer skills. *Child Development, 57*, 275–286.

BROWNELL, C. A. (1990). Peer social skills in toddlers: Competencies and constraints illustrated by same-age and mixed-age interaction. *Child Development, 61*, 838–848.

BRUCH, H. (1970). Juvenile obesity: Its courses and outcome. In C. V. Rowlan (Ed.), *Anorexia and obesity* (pp. 231–254). Boston: Little Brown.

BRUCH, H. (1978). *The golden cage: The enigma of anorexia nervosa.* Cambridge, MA: Harvard University Press.

BRUDER, G. E., MEYER-BAHLBURG, H. F. L., SQUIRE, J. M., & EHRHARDT, A. A. (1987). Dichotic listening following idiopathic precocious puberty: Speech processing capacity and temporal efficiency. *Brain and Language, 31*, 267–275.

BRUMBERG, J. J. (1988). *Fasting girls.* Cambridge, MA: Harvard University Press.

BRUNER, J. S. (1974). The ontogenesis of speech acts. *Journal of Child Language, 2*, 1–19.

BRUNER, J. S. (1977). Early social interaction and language acquisition. In H. R. Schaffer (Ed.), *Studies in mother–infant interaction* (pp. 271–289). London: Academic Press.

BRYAN, J., & LONDON, P. (1970). Altruistic behavior by children. *Psychological Bulletin, 73*, 200–211.

BRYAN, J. H., & WALBEK, N. (1970). Preaching and practicing self-sacrifice: Children's actions and reactions. *Child Development, 41*, 329–353.

BRYANT, B., & CROCKENBERG, S. (1980). Correlates and dimensions of prosocial behavior: A study of female siblings with their mothers. *Child Development, 51*, 529–544.

BRYANT, B. K. (1982a). An index of empathy for children and adolescents. *Child Development, 53*, 413–425.

BRYANT, B. K. (1982b). Sibling relationships in middle childhood. In M. E. Lamb & B. Sutton-Smith (Eds.), *Sibling relationships: Their nature and significance across the life span* (pp. 87–121). Hillsdale, NJ: Erlbaum.

BRYANT, B. K. (1985). The neighborhood walk: Sources of support in middle childhood. *Monographs for the Society for Research in Child Development, 50*(3, Serial No. 210).

BRYANT, P. E., & TRABASSO, T. (1971). Transitive inferences and memory in young children. *Nature, 232*, 456–458.

BUCK, G. M., COOKFAIR, D. L., MICHALEK, A. M., NASCA, P. C., STANDFAST, S. J., SEVER, L. E., & KRAMER, A. A. (1989). Intrauterine growth retardation and risk of sudden infant death syndrome (SIDS). *American Journal of Epidemiology, 129*, 874–884.

BUCKLEY, N., SIEGEL, L. S., & NESS, S. (1979). Egocentrism, empathy, and altruistic behavior in young children. *Developmental Psychology, 15*, 329–330.

BUGENTAL, D. B., BLUE, J., & CRUZCOSA, M. (1989). Perceived control over caregiving outcomes: Implications for child abuse. *Developmental Psychology, 25*, 532–539.

BUKOWSKI, W. M., & NEWCOMB, A. F. (1984). Stability and determinants of sociometric status and friendship choice: A longitudinal perspective. *Developmental Psychology, 20*, 941–952.

BULATAO, R. A., & ARNOLD, F. (1977). *Relationships between the value and cost of children and fertility: Cross-cultural evidence.* Paper presented at the General Conference of the International Union for the Scientific Study of Population, Mexico City.

BULKLEY, J. A. (1989). The impact of new child witness research on sexual abuse prosecutions. In S. J. Ceci, D. F. Ross, & M. P. Toglia (Eds.), *Perspectives on children's testimony* (pp. 208–229). New York: Springer-Verlag.

BULLOCK, D., & MERRILL, L. (1980). The impact of personal preference on consistency through time: The case of childhood aggression. *Child Development, 51*, 808–814.

BUMPASS, L. L. (1984). Children and marital disruption: A replication and update. *Demography, 21*, 71–82.

BURGESS, R. L., & CONGER, R. (1978). Family interaction in abusive, neglectful, and normal families. *Child Development, 49*, 163–173.

BURKE, B. S., BEAL, V. A., KIRKWOOD, S. B., & STUART, H. C. (1943). The influence of nutrition during pregnancy upon the conditions of the infant at birth. *Journal of Nutrition, 26*, 569–583.

BURNS, S. M., & BRAINERD, C. J. (1979). Effects of constructive and dramatic play on perspective taking in very young children. *Developmental Psychology, 15*, 512–521.

BURTON, R. V. (1963). Generality of honesty reconsidered. *Psychological Review, 70*, 481–499.

BURTON, R. V. (1976). Honesty and dishonesty. In T. Lickona (Ed.), *Moral development and behavior: Theory, research, and social issues* (pp. 173–197). New York: Holt, Rinehart and Winston.

BUSHNELL, E. W. (1985). The decline of visually guided reaching during infancy. *Infant Behavior and Development, 8*, 139–155.

BUSHNELL, I. W. R., GERRY, G., & BURT, K. (1983). The externality effect in neonates. *Infant Behavior and Development, 6*, 151–156.

BUSS, A. H., & PLOMIN, R. (1984). *Temperament: Early developing personality traits.* Hillsdale, NJ: Erlbaum.

BUSSEY, K., & BANDURA, A. (1984). Influence of gender constancy and social power on sex-linked modeling. *Journal of Personality and Social Psychology, 47*, 1292–1302.

BUTLER, N. R., & GOLDSTEIN, H. (1973). Smoking in pregnancy and subsequent child development. *British Medical Journal, 4*, 573–575.

BYERS, P., & BYERS, H. (1972). Non-verbal communication in the education of children. In C. Cazden, V. John, & D. Hymes (Eds.), *Functions of language in the classroom* (pp. 3–31). New York: Teachers College Press.

BYRD, D. M., & GHOLSON, B. (1985). Reading, memory, and metacognition. *Journal of Educational Psychology, 77*, 428–436.

BYRNE, D. F. (1973). The development of role taking in adolescence. *Dissertation Abstracts International, 34*, 5647B. (University Microfilms No. 74-11, 314).

BYRNE, M. C., & HAYDEN, E. (1980). *Topic maintenance and topic establishment in mother–child dialogue.* Paper presented at the meeting of the American Speech and Hearing Association, Detroit, MI.

BYRNES, J. P., & OVERTON, W. F. (1986). Reasoning about certainty and uncertainty in concrete, causal, and propositional contexts. *Developmental Psychology, 22*, 793–799.

CAHAN, L. S., FILBY, N. N., McCUTCHEON, G., & KYLE, D. W. (1983). *Class size and instruction.* New York: Longman.

CAHAN, S., & COHEN, N. (1989). Age versus schooling effects on intelligence development. *Child Development, 60*, 1239–1249.

CAINE, N. (1986). Behavior during puberty and adolescence. In G. Mitchell & J. Erwin (Eds.), *Comparative primate biology: Vol. 2A. Behavior, conservation, and ecology* (pp. 327–361). New York: Alan R. Liss.

CAIRNS, R. B., CAIRNS, B. D., & NECKERMAN, H. J. (1989). Early school dropout: Configurations and determinants. *Child Development, 60*, 1437–1452.

CAIRNS, R. B., CAIRNS, B. D., NECKERMAN, H. J., FERGUSON, L. L., & GARIÉPY, J-L. (1989). Growth and aggression: 1. Childhood to early adolescence. *Developmental Psychology, 25*, 320–330.

CALDERA, Y. M., HUSTON, A. C., & O'BRIEN, M. (1989). Social interactions and play patterns of parents and toddlers with feminine, masculine, and neutral toys. *Child Development, 60*, 70–76.

CALFEE, R., & BROWN, R. (1979). Grouping students for instruction. In D. L. Duke (Ed.), *Classroom management* (78th yearbook of the National Society for the Study of Education, pp. 144–182). Chicago: University of Chicago Press.

CAMAIONI, L., & LAICARDI, C. (1985). Early social games and the acquisition of language. *British Journal of Developmental Psychology, 3*, 31–39.

CAMARA, K. A., & RESNICK, G. (1988). Interparental conflict and cooperation: Factors moderating children's post-divorce adjustment. In E. M. Hetherington & J. D. Arasteh (Ed.), *Impact of divorce, single parenting, and stepparenting on children* (pp. 169–195). Hillsdale, NJ: Erlbaum.

CAMARATA, S., & LEONARD, L. B. (1986). Young children pronounce object words more accurately than action words. *Journal of Child Language, 13,* 51–65.

CAMPBELL, A. C. (1980). Friendship as a factor in male and female delinquency. In H. C. Foot, A. J. Chapman, & J. R. Smith (Eds.), *Friendship and social relations in children* (pp. 365–389). Chichester, England: Wiley.

CAMPBELL, D. T., & STANLEY, J. C. (1966). *Experimental and quasi-experimental designs for research.* Chicago: Rand McNally.

CAMPBELL, P. F., & SCHWARTZ, S. S. (1986). Microcomputers in the preschool: Children, parents, and teachers. In P. Campbell & G. Fein (Eds.), *Young children and microcomputers* (pp. 45–60). Englewood Cliffs, NJ: Prentice-Hall.

CAMPBELL, S. B. (1973). Cognitive styles in reflective, impulsive and hyperactive boys and their mothers. *Perceptual and Motor Skills, 36,* 747–752.

CAMPOS, J., & BERTENTHAL, B. (1989). Locomotion and psychological development. In F. Morrison, K. Lord, & D. Keating (Eds.), *Applied developmental psychology* (Vol. 3, pp. 229–258). New York: Academic Press.

CAMPOS, J. J., CAPLOVITZ, K. B., LAMB, M. E., GOLDSMITH, H. H., & STENBERG, C. (1983). Socioemotional development. In M. M. Haith & J. J. Campos (Eds.), *Handbook of child psychology: Vol. 2. Infancy and developmental psychobiology* (4th ed., pp. 783–915). New York: Wiley.

CAMPOS, J. J., & STENBERG, C. (1981). Perception, appraisal, and emotion: The onset of social referencing. In M. E. Lamb & L. R. Sherrod (Eds.), *Infant social cognition: Empirical and theoretical considerations* (pp. 273–314). Hillsdale, NJ: Erlbaum.

CAMPOS, R. G. (1989). Soothing pain-elicited distress in infants with swaddling and pacifiers. *Child Development, 60,* 781–792.

CANALE, J. R. (1977). The effect of modeling and length of ownership on sharing behavior of children. *Social Behavior and Personality, 5,* 187–191.

CANTER, R. J., & AGETON, S. S. (1984). The epidemiology of adolescent sex-role attitudes. *Sex Roles, 11,* 657–676.

CANTOR, J., & WILSON, B. J. (1984). Modifying fear responses to mass media in preschool and elementary school children. *Journal of Broadcasting, 28,* 431–443.

CANTRELL, V. L., & PRINZ, R. J. (1985). Multiple predictors of rejected, neglected, and accepted children: Relation between sociometric status and behavioral characteristics. *Journal of Consulting and Clinical Psychology, 53,* 884–889.

CAPELLI, C. A., & MARKMAN, E. M. (1980). *Children's sensitivity to incomprehensible material in written texts.* Unpublished manuscript, Stanford University.

CAPUTE, A. J., SHAPIRO, B. K., PALMER, F. B., ROSS, A., & WACHTEL, R. C. (1985). Normal gross motor development: The influence of race, sex, and socio-economic status. *Developmental Medicine & Child Neurology, 27,* 635–643.

CARDOSO-MARTINS, C., & MERVIS, C. (1985). Maternal speech to prelinguistic children with Down syndrome. *American Journal of Mental Deficiency, 89,* 451–458.

CAREW, J. V., & LIGHTFOOT, S. L. (1979). *Beyond bias: Perspectives on classrooms.* Cambridge, MA: Harvard University Press.

CAREY, S. (1978). The child as a word learner. In M. Halle, J. Bresnan, & G. Miller (Eds.), *Linguistic theory and psychological reality* (pp. 264–293). Cambridge, MA: MIT Press.

CAREY, S. (1985). *Conceptual change in childhood.* Cambridge, MA: MIT Press.

CAREY, W. B., & McDEVITT, S. C. (1978). Revision of the Infant Temperament Questionnaire. *Pediatrics, 61,* 735–739.

CARLSON, B. E. (1984). The father's contribution to child care: Effects on children's perceptions of parental roles. *American Journal of Orthopsychiatry, 54,* 123–136.

CARLSON, C. L., LAHEY, B. B., & NEEPER, R. (1984). Peer assessment of the social behavior of accepted, rejected, and neglected children. *Journal of Abnormal Child Psychology, 12,* 189–198.

CARLSON, V., CICCHETTI, D., BARNETT, D., & BRAUNWALD, K. (1989). Disorganized/disoriented attachment relationship in maltreated infants. *Child Development, 25,* 525–531.

CARON, R. F., CARON, A. J., & MYERS, R. S. (1982). Abstraction of invariant face expressions in infancy. *Child Development, 53,* 1008–1015.

CARPENTER, C. J. (1983). Activity structure and play: Implications for socialization. In M. Liss (Eds.), *Social and cognitive skills: Sex roles and children's play* (pp. 117–145). New York: Academic Press.

CARPENTER, C. J., HUSTON, A. C., & HOLT, W. (1986). Modification of preschool sex-typed behaviors by participation in adult-structured activities. *Sex Roles, 14,* 603–615.

CARR, M., KURTZ, B. E., SCHNEIDER, W., TURNER, L. A., & BORKOWSKI, J. G. (1989). Strategy acquisition and transfer among American and German children: Environmental influences on metacognitive development. *Developmental Psychology, 25,* 765–771.

CARR, S., DABBS, J., & CARR, T. (1975). Mother–infant attachment: The importance of the mother's visual field. *Child Development, 46,* 331–338.

CARROLL, J. B. (1981). Ability and task difficulty in cognitive psychology. *Educational Researcher, 10,* 11–21.

CARROLL, J. B. (1982). The measurement of intelligence. In R. J. Sternberg (Ed.), *Handbook of human intelligence* (pp. 29–120). Cambridge, England: Cambridge University Press.

CARROLL, J. B., & MAXWELL, S. E. (1979). Individual differences in cognitive abilities. *Annual Review of Psychology, 30,* 603–640.

CARTER, D. B., & LEVY, G. D. (1988). Cognitive aspects of early sex-role development: The influence of gender schemas on preschoolers' memories and preferences for sex-typed toys and activities. *Child Development, 59,* 782–792.

CARTER, D. B., & PATTERSON, C. J. (1982). Sex roles as social conventions: The development of children's conceptions of sex-role stereotypes. *Developmental Psychology, 18,* 812–824.

CARTER, K., SABERS, D., CUSHING, K., PINNEGAR, S., & BERLINER, D. C. (1987). Processing and using information about students: A study of expert, novice, and postulant teachers. *Teaching & Teacher Education, 3,* 147–157.

CARTER-SALTZMAN, L. (1980). Biological and socio-cultural effects on handedness: Comparison between biological and adoptive families. *Science, 209,* 1263–1265.

CASE, R. (1977). Responsiveness to conservation training as a function of induced subjective uncertainty, M-space, and cognitive style. *Canadian Journal of Behavioral Sciences, 9,* 12–25.

CASE, R. (1978). Intellectual development from birth to adulthood: A neo-Piagetian approach. In R. S. Siegler (Ed.), *Children's thinking: What develops?* (pp. 37–71). Hillsdale, NJ: Erlbaum.

CASE, R. (1985). *Intellectual development: A systematic reinterpretation.* New York: Academic Press.

CASE, R., KURLAND, D. M., & GOLDBERG, J. (1982). Operational efficiency and growth of short-term memory span. *Journal of Experimental Child Psychology, 33,* 386–404.

CASEY, M. B. (1986). Individual differences in selective attention among prereaders: A key to mirror-image confusions. *Developmental Psychology, 22,* 58–66.

CASPI, A., ELDER, G. H., JR., & BEM, D. J. (1987). Moving against the world: Life-course patterns of explosive children. *Developmental Psychology, 23,* 308–313.

CASPI, A., ELDER, G. H., JR., & BEM, D. J. (1988). Moving away from the world: Life-course patterns of shy children. *Developmental Psychology, 24,* 824–831.

CATTELL, J. M. (1890). Mental tests and measurements. *Mind, 15,* 373–381.

CATTELL, R. B. (1963). Theory of fluid and crystallized intelligence: A critical experiment. *Journal of Educational Psychology, 54,* 1–22.

CATTELL, R. B. (1971). *Abilities: Their structure, growth and action.* Boston: Houghton Mifflin.

CAUCE, A. M. (1987). School and peer competence in early adolescence: A test of domain-specific self-perceived competence. *Developmental Psychology, 23,* 287–291.

CAUDILL, W., & FROST, L. (1975). A comparison of maternal care and infant behavior in Japanese-American, American, and Japanese families. In U. Bronfenbrenner & M. A. Mahoney (Eds.), *Influences* on human development (2nd ed., pp. 329–342). Hinsdale, IL: Dryden.

CAULEY, K., & TYLER, B. (1989). The relationship of self-concept to prosocial behavior in children. *Early Childhood Research Quarterly, 4,* 51–60.

CAVIOR, N., & LOMBARDI, D. A. (1973). Developmental aspects of judgment of physical attractiveness of children. *Developmental Psychology, 8,* 67–71.

CAZDEN, C. (1984). *Effective instructional practices in bilingual education.* Washington, DC: National Institute of Education.

CECI, S. J., & BRONFENBRENNER, U. (1985). "Don't forget to take the cupcakes out of the oven": Prospective memory, strategic time-monitoring, and context. *Child Development, 56,* 152–164.

CECIL, M. A., & MEDWAY, F. J. (1986). Attribution retraining with low-achieving and learned helpless children. *Techniques: A Journal of Remedial Education and Counseling, 2,* 173–181.

CERNOCH, J. M., & PORTER, R. H. (1985). Recognition of maternal axillary odors by infants. *Child Development, 56,* 1593–1598.

CHALMERS, J. B., & TOWNSEND, M. A. R. (1990). The effects of training in social perspective taking on socially maladjusted girls. *Child Development, 61,* 178–190.

CHANDLER, C. (1981). *The effects of parenting techniques on the development of motivational orientations in children.* Dissertation Abstracts International, 42, 4594B. (University Microfilms No. 82-09, 943).

CHANDLER, M. J. (1973). Egocentrism and antisocial behavior: The assessment and training of social perspective-taking skills. *Developmental Psychology, 9,* 326–332.

CHANDLER, M., FRITZ, A. S., & HALA, S. (1989). Young children's attribution of action to beliefs and desires. *Child Development, 60,* 946–964.

CHANDLER, M. J., GREENSPAN, S., & BARENBOIM, C. (1973). Judgments of intentionality in response to videotaped and verbally presented moral dilemmas: The medium is the message. *Child Development, 44,* 315–320.

CHANDLER, M. J., & HELM, D. (1984). Developmental changes in the contribution of shared experience to social role-taking competence. *International Journal of Behavioral Development, 7,* 145–156.

CHAPIN, M., & DYCK, D. G. (1976). Persistence in children's reading behavior as a function of n length and attribution retraining. *Journal of Abnormal Psychology, 85,* 511–515.

CHAPMAN, K. L., LEONARD, L. B., & MERVIS, C. B. (1986). The effect of feedback on young children's inappropriate word usage. *Journal of Child Language, 13,* 101–117.

CHAPMAN, M., & SKINNER, E. A. (1989). Children's agency beliefs, cognitive performance, and conceptions of effort and ability: Individual and developmental differences. *Child Development, 60,* 1229–1238.

CHAPMAN, M., ZAHN-WAXLER, C., IANNOTTI, R., & COOPERMAN, G. (1987). Empathy and responsibility in the motivation of children's helping. *Developmental Psychology, 23,* 140–145.

CHARLESWORTH, R., & HARTUP, W. W. (1967). Positive social reinforcement in the nursery school peer group. *Child Development, 38,* 993–1002.

CHARLESWORTH, W. R., & DZUR, C. (1987). Gender comparisons of preschoolers' behavior and resource utilization in group problem-solving. *Child Development, 58,* 191–200.

CHARNEY, E., GOODMAN, H. C., McBRIDE, M., BARBRO, L., & PRATT, R. (1976). Childhood antecedents of adult obesity: Do chubby infants become obese adults? *New England Journal of Medicine, 295,* 6–9.

CHASNOFF, I. J., GRIFFITH, D. R., MacGREGOR, S., DIRKES, K., & BURNS, K. A. (1989). Temporal patterns of cocaine use in pregnancy: Perinatal outcome. *Journal of the American Medical Association, 261,* 1741–1744.

CHASSIN, L., PRESSON, C. C., MONTELLO, D., SHERMAN, S. J., & McGREW, J. (1986). Changes in peer and parent influence during adolescence: Longitudinal versus cross-sectional perspectives on smoking initiation. *Developmental Psychology, 22,* 327–334.

CHEN, C., & STEVENSON, H. W. (1989). Homework: A cross-cultural examination. *Child Development, 60,* 551–561.

CHERLIN, A. J. (1981). *Marriage, divorce and remarriage.* Cambridge, MA: Harvard University Press.

CHERRY, R. R., & EATON, E. L. (1977). Physical and cognitive development in children of low-income mothers working in the child's early years. *Child Development, 48,* 158–166.

CHESS, S., & THOMAS, A. (1984). *Origins and evolution of behavior disorders.* New York: Brunner/Mazel.

CHI, M. T. H. (1978). Knowledge structures and memory development. In R. S. Siegler (Ed.), *Children's thinking: What develops?* (pp. 73–96). Hillsdale, NJ: Erlbaum.

CHI, M. T. H. (1982). Knowledge development and memory performance. In M. Friedman, J. P. Das, & N. O'Connor (Eds.), *Intelligence and learning* (pp. 221–229). New York: Plenum.

CHI, M. T. H., & KOESKE, R. D. (1983). Network representation of a child's dinosaur knowledge. *Developmental Psychology, 19,* 29–39.

CHILD CARE EMPLOYEE PROJECT (1990). *Who cares? Child care teachers and the quality of care in America: Report of the National Child Care Staffing Study.* Oakland, CA: Author.

CHILDREN'S DEFENSE FUND (1987). *Child care: The time is now.* Washington, DC: Author.

CHILDREN'S DEFENSE FUND (1989a). *A children's defense budget.* Washington, DC: Author.

CHILDREN'S DEFENSE FUND (1989b, September). *Fundraising letter.* Washington, DC: Author.

CHILDREN'S DEFENSE FUND (1989c, November). Maternal and child health. *CDF Reports, 11*(4), 4.

CHILDREN'S DEFENSE FUND (1989d). *A vision for America's future.* Washington, DC: Author.

CHILDREN'S DEFENSE FUND (1990a). *Children 1990.* Washington, DC: Author.

CHILDREN'S DEFENSE FUND (1990b, April). Improving the health of Medicaid-eligible children. *CDF Reports, 11*(8), 1–2.

CHILDREN'S DEFENSE FUND (1990c). *S.O.S. America! A children's defense budget.* Washington, DC: Author.

CHILDS, C. P., & GREENFIELD, P. M. (1982). Informal modes of learning and teaching: The case of Zinacanteco weaving. In N. Warren (Ed.), *Advances in cross-cultural psychology* (Vol. 2, pp. 269–316). London: Academic Press.

CHISHOLM, J. S. (1989). Biology, culture, and the development of temperament: A Navajo example. In J. K. Nugent, B. M. Lester, & T. B. Brazelton (Eds.), *Biology, culture, and development* (Vol. 1, pp. 341–364). Norwood, NJ: Ablex.

CHOMSKY, C. (1969). *The acquisition of syntax in children from five to ten.* Cambridge, MA: MIT Press.

CHOMSKY, N. (1957). *Syntactic structures.* The Hague: Mouton.

CHOMSKY, N. (1959). Review of B. F. Skinner's "Verbal Behavior." *Language, 35,* 26–129.

CHOMSKY, N. (1982). *Lectures on government and binding.* New York: Foris.

CHRISTIE, D. J., & SCHUMACHER, G. M. (1975). Developmental trends in the abstraction and recall of relevant versus irrelevant thematic information from connected verbal materials. *Child Development, 46,* 598–602.

CICCHETTI, D., & ABER, J. L. (1986). Early precursors of later depression: An organizational perspective. In L. P. Lipsitt & C. Rovee-Collier (Eds.), *Advances in infancy research* (Vol. 4, pp. 87–137). Norwood, NJ: Ablex.

CICERELLI, V. G., EVANS, J. W., & SCHILLER, J. S. (1969). *The impact of Head Start: An evaluation of the effects of Head Start on children's cognitive and affective development* (Vols. 1–2). Athens, OH: Westinghouse Learning Corporation and Ohio University.

CLANCY, P. (1985). Acquisition of Japanese. In D. I. Slobin (Ed.), *The crosslinguistic study of language acquisition: Vol. 1. The data* (pp. 323–524). Hillsdale, NJ: Erlbaum.

CLARK, C. C. (1972). Race, identification, and television violence. In G. A. Comstock, E. A. Rubinstein, & J. B. Murray (Eds.), *Television and social behavior* (Vol. 5, pp. 120–184). Washington, DC: U.S. Government Printing Office.

CLARK, E. V. (1973). Nonlinguistic strategies and the acquisition of word meanings. *Cognition, 2,* 161–182.

CLARK, E. V. (1978). Strategies for communicating. *Child Development, 49,* 977–987.

CLARK, E. V. (1980). Here's the top: Nonlinguistic strategies in the acquisition of orientational terms. *Child Development, 51,* 329–338.

CLARK, E. V. (1983). Meanings and concepts. In J. H. Flavell & E. M. Markman (Eds.), *Handbook of child psychology: Vol. 3. Cognitive development* (pp. 787–840). New York: Wiley.

CLARK, E. V. (1987). The principle of contrast: A constraint on language acquisition. In B. MacWhinney (Ed.), *Mechanisms of language acquisition* (pp. 1–33). Hillsdale, NJ: Erlbaum.

CLARK, E. V., & HECHT, B. F. (1982). Learning to coin agent and instrument nouns. *Cognition, 12,* 1–24.

CLARKE-STEWART, K. A. (1973). Interactions between mothers and their young children. Characteristics and consequences. *Monographs of the Society for Research in Child Development, 38*(6–7, Serial No. 153).

CLARKE-STEWART, K. A. (1978). Recasting the lone stranger. In J. Glick & K. A. Clarke-Stewart (Eds.), *The development of social understanding* (pp. 109–176). New York: Gardner Press.

CLARKE-STEWART, K. A. (1980). The father's contribution to children's cognitive and social development in early childhood. In F. A. Pedersen (Ed.), *The father–infant relationship: Observational studies in a family setting* (pp. 111–146). New York: Praeger.

CLARKE-STEWART, K. A. (1989). Infant day care: Maligned or malignant? *American Psychologist, 44,* 266–273.

CLARKE-STEWART, K. A., & GRUBER, C. P. (1984). Day care forms and features. In R. C. Ainslie (Ed.), *The child and the day care setting* (pp. 35–62). New York: Praeger.

CLAUDY, J. G. (1984). The only child as a young adult: Results from Project Talent. In T. Falbo (Ed.), *The single–child family* (pp. 211–252). New York: Guilford Press.

CLAUSEN, J. A. (1966). Family structure, socialization, and personality. In L. W. Hoffman & M. L. Hoffman (Eds.), *Review of child development research* (Vol. 2, pp. 1–53). New York: Russell Sage Foundation.

CLAUSEN, J. A. (1975). The social meaning of differential physical and sexual maturation. In S. E. Dragastin & G. H. Elder (Eds.), *Adolescence in the life cycle: Psychological change and the social context* (pp. 25–47). New York: Halsted.

CLAY, P. (1987). *At risk of loss: The endangered future of low-income rental housing resources.* Cambridge, MA: MIT Press.

CLEARY, T. A., HUMPHREYS, L. G., KENDRICK, S. A., & WESMAN, A. (1975). Educational uses of tests with disadvantaged students. *American Psychologist, 30,* 15–41.

CLEMENTS, D. H. (1986). Effects of Logo and CAI environments on cognition and creativity. *Journal of Educational Psychology, 78,* 309–318.

CLIATT, M. J. P., SHAW, J. M., & SHERWOOD, J. M. (1980). Effects of training on the divergent-thinking abilities of kindergarten children. *Child Development, 51,* 1061–1064.

CLIFTON, R. K., MORRONGIELLO, B. A., KULIG, J. W., & DOWD, J. M. (1981). Developmental changes in auditory localization in infancy. In R. N. Aslin, J. R. Alberts, & M. R. Petersen (Eds.), *Development of perception: Psychobiological perspectives: Vol. 1. Audition, somatic perception and the chemical senses* (pp. 141–160). New York: Academic Press.

CLINGEMPEEL, W. G., BRAND, E., & IEVOLI, R. (1984). Stepparent–stepchild relationships in stepmother and stepfather families: A multimethod study. *Family Relations, 33,* 465–473.

CLINGEMPEEL, W. G., IEVOLI, R., & BRAND, E. (1985). Structural complexity and the quality of stepfather–stepchild relationships. *Family Process, 23,* 547–560.

CLINGEMPEEL, W. G., & REPPUCCI, N. D. (1982). Joint custody after divorce: Major issues and goals for research. *Psychological Bulletin, 91,* 102–127.

CLINGEMPEEL, W. G., & SEGAL, S. (1986). Stepparent–stepchild relationships and the psychological adjustment of children in stepmother and stepfather families. *Child Development, 57,* 474–484.

COCHI, S. L., EDMONDS, L. E., DYER, K., GREAVES, W. L., MARKS, J. S., ROVIRA, E. Z., PREBLUD, S. R., & ORENSTEIN, W. A. (1989). Congenital rubella syndrome in the United States, 1970–1985: On the verge of elimination. *American Journal of Epidemiology, 129,* 349–361.

COCHRAN, M. M., & BRASSARD, J. A. (1979). Child development and personal social networks. *Child Development, 50,* 601–616.

COHEN, F. L. (1984). *Clinical genetics in nursing practice.* Philadelphia: Lippincott.

COHEN, K. N., & CLARK, J. A. (1984). Transitional object attachments in early childhood and personality characteristics in later life. *Journal of Personality and Social Psychology, 46,* 106–111.

COHEN, S. E., & PARMELEE, A. H. (1983). Prediction of five-year Stanford-Binet scores in preterm infants. *Child Development, 54,* 1242–1253.

COHEN, S., GLASS, D. C., & SINGER, J. E. (1973). Apartment noise, auditory discrimination and reading ability. *Journal of Experimental Social Psychology, 9,* 407–422.

COHEN, Y. (1964). *The transition from childhood into adolescence.* Chicago: Aldine.

COHN, J. F., & TRONICK, E. Z. (1983). Three-month-old infants' reaction to simulated maternal depression. *Child Development, 54,* 185–193.

COHN, J. F., MATIAS, R., TRONICK, E. Z., LYONS-RUTH, K., & CONNELL, D. (1986). Face-to-face interactions, spontaneous and structured, of mothers with depressive symptoms. In T. Field & E. Z. Tronick (Eds.), *New directions for child development* (Vol. 34, pp. 31–46). San Francisco: Jossey-Bass.

COHN, J. F., & TRONICK, E. Z. (1988). Mother-infant face-to-face interaction: Influence is bidirectional and unrelated to periodic cycles in either partner's behavior. *Developmental Psychology, 24,* 386–392.

COIE, J. D., & DODGE, K. A. (1983). Continuities and changes in children's social status: A five-year longitudinal study. *Merrill-Palmer Quarterly, 29,* 261–282.

COIE, J. D., DODGE, K. A., & COPPOTELLI, H. (1982). Dimensions and types of social status: A cross-age perspective. *Developmental Psychology, 18,* 557–570.

COIE, J. D., & KOEPPL, G. K. (1990). Adapting intervention to the problems of aggressive and disruptive rejected children. In S. R. Asher & J. D. Coie (Eds.), *Peer rejection in childhood* (pp. 309–337). New York: Cambridge University Press.

COIE, J. D., & KREHBIEL, G. (1984). Effects of academic tutoring on the social status of low-achieving, socially rejected children. *Child Development, 55,* 1465–1478.

COIE, J. D., & KUPERSMIDT, J. B. (1983). A behavioral analysis of emerging social status in boys' groups. *Child Development, 54,* 1400–1416.

COKER, D. R. (1984). The relationships among gender concepts and cognitive maturity in preschool children. *Sex Roles, 10,* 19–31.

COLBY, A., KOHLBERG, L., FENTON, E., SPEICHER-DUBIN, B., & LIEBERMAN, M. (1977). Secondary school moral discussion programmes led by social studies teachers. *Journal of Moral Education, 6,* 90–111.

COLBY, A., KOHLBERG, L., GIBBS, J., & LIEBERMAN, M. (1983). A longitudinal study of moral judgment. *Monographs of the Society for Research in Child Development, 48*(1–2, Serial No. 200).

COLE, C. B., & LOFTUS, E. F. (1987). The memory of children. In S. J. Ceci, M. P. Toglia, & D. F. Ross (Eds.), *Children's eyewitness memory* (pp. 178–208). New York: Springer-Verlag.

COLE, M., & SCRIBNER, S. (1977). Cross-cultural studies of memory and cognition. In R. V. Kail & J. W. Hagen (Eds.), *Perspectives on the development of memory and cognition* (pp. 239–271). Hillsdale, NJ: Erlbaum.

COLEMAN, J. S., CAMPBELL, E. Q., HOBSON, C. J., McPARTLAND, J., MOOD, A. M., WEINFELD, F. D., & YORK, R. L. (1966). *Equality of educational opportunity.* Washington, DC: U.S. Government Printing Office.

COLES, R. (1977). *Children of crisis: Vol. 4. Eskimos, Chicanos, Indians.* Boston: Little, Brown.

COLLARD, R. (1971). Exploratory and play behaviors of infants reared in an institution and in lower and middle class homes. *Child Development, 42,* 1003–1015.

COLLINS, W. A. (1973). Effect of temporal separation between motivation, aggression, and consequences: A developmental study. *Developmental Psychology, 8,* 215–221.

COLLINS, W. A. (1983). Children's processing of television content: Implications for prevention of negative effects. *Prevention in Human Services, 2,* 53–66.

COLLINS, W. A., BERNDT, T. V., & HESS, V. L. (1974). Observational learning of motives and consequences for television aggression: A developmental study. *Child Development, 45,* 799–802.

COLLINS, W. A., WELLMAN, H., KENISTON, A. H., & WESTBY, S. D. (1978). Age-related aspects of comprehension and inference from a televised dramatic narrative. *Child Development, 49,* 389–399.

CÓLON, P. A., & CÓLON, A. R. (1989). The health of America's children. In F. J. Macchiarola & A. Gartner (Eds.), *Caring for America's children* (pp. 45–57). New York: The Academy of Political Science.

COMPAS, B. E., HOWELL, D. C., PHARES, V., WILLIAMS, R. A., & LEDOUX, N. (1989). Parent and child stress symptoms: An integrative analysis. *Developmental Psychology, 25,* 550–559.

CONDRY, J. C., & ROSS, D. F. (1985). Sex and aggression: The influence of gender label on the perception of aggression in children. *Child Development, 56,* 225–233.

CONNOLLY, J., & DOYLE, A. B. (1984). Relations of social fantasy play to social competence in preschoolers. *Developmental Psychology, 20,* 797–806.

CONNOLLY, J. A., DOYLE, A. B., & REZNICK, E. (1988). Social pretend play and social interaction in preschoolers. *Journal of Applied Developmental Psychology, 9,* 301–313.

CONNOLLY, K., & DALGLEISH, M. (1989). The emergence of a tool-using skill in infancy. *Developmental Psychology, 25,* 894–912.

CONSTANZO, P. R., & WOODY, E. Z. (1979). Externality as a function of obesity in children: Pervasive style or eating-specific attribute? *Journal of Personality and Social Psychology, 37,* 2286–2296.

COOKE, R. A. (1982). The ethics and regulation of research involving children. In B. B. Wolman (Ed.), *Handbook of developmental psychology* (pp. 149–172). Englewood Cliffs, NJ: Prentice-Hall.

COOLEY, C. H. (1902). *Human nature and the social order.* New York: Scribner.

COOPER, H. M. (1979). Pygmalion grows up: A model for teacher expectation communication and performance. *Review of Educational Research, 49,* 389–410.

COOPER, H. M. (1989). Does reducing student-to-instructor ratios affect achievement? *Educational Psychologist, 24,* 79–98.

COOPERSMITH, S. (1967). *The antecedents of self-esteem.* San Francisco: W. H. Freeman.

CORAH, N. L., ANTHONY, E. J., PAINTER, P., STERN, J. A., & THURSTON, D. L. (1965). Effects of perinatal anoxia after seven years. *Psychological Monographs, 79*(3, Whole No. 596).

CORDUA, G. D., McGRAW, K. O., & DRABMAN, R. S. (1979). Doctor or nurse: Children's perceptions of sex types occupations. *Child Development, 50,* 590–593.

CORMAN, H. H., & ESCALONA, S. K. (1969). Stages of sensorimotor development: A replication study. *Merrill-Palmer Quarterly, 15,* 351–360.

CORNELL, E. H., & BERGSTROM, L. I. (1983). Serial-position effects in infants' recognition memory. *Memory and Cognition, 11,* 494–499.

CORNELL, E. H., & GOTTFRIED, A. W. (1976). Intervention with premature human infants. *Child Development, 47,* 32–39.

CORNELL, E. H., HETH, C. D., & BRODA, L. S. (1989). Children's wayfinding: Response to instructions to use environmental landmarks. *Developmental Psychology, 25,* 755–764.

CORNIA, A., JOLLY, R., & STEWART, F. (EDS.) (1988). *Adjustment with a human face: Protecting the vulnerable and promoting growth* (Vols. 1 & 2). Oxford, England: Clarendon Press.

CORNO, L., & SNOW, R. E. (1986). Adapting teaching to individual differences among learners. In M. C. Wittrock (Ed.), *Handbook of research on teaching* (3rd ed., pp. 214–229). New York: Macmillan.

CORRIGAN, R. (1987). A developmental sequence of actor-object pretend play in young children. *Merrill-Palmer Quarterly, 33,* 87–106.

COUTURIER, L. C., MANSFIELD, R. S., & GALLAGHER, J. M. (1981). Relationships between humor, formal operational ability, and creativity in eighth graders. *Journal of Genetic Psychology, 139,* 221–226.

COWAN, C. P., & COWAN, P. A. (1988). Changes in marriage during the transition to parenthood: Must we blame the baby? In G. Y. Michaels & W. A. Goldberg (Eds.), *The transition to parenthood* (pp. 114–154). New York: Cambridge University Press.

COX, M. J., OWEN, M., LEWIS, J. M., & HENDERSON, V. K. (1989). Marriage, adult adjustment, and early parenting. *Child Development, 60,* 1015–1024.

COX, T. (1983). Cumulative deficit in culturally disadvantaged children. *British Journal of Educational Psychology, 53,* 317–376.

CRAIK, F. I. M., & LOCKHART, R. S. (1972). Levels of processing: A framework for memory research. *Journal of Verbal Learning and Verbal Behavior, 11,* 671–684.

CRAIK, F. I. M., & TULVING, E. (1975). Depth of processing and the retention of words in episodic memory. *Journal of Experimental Psychology: General, 104,* 268–294.

CRAIN, W. C. (1980). *Theories of development.* Englewood Cliffs, NJ: Prentice-Hall.

CRAWLEY, S. B., & SPIKER D. (1983). Mother–child interactions involving two-year-olds with Down syndrome: A look at individual differences. *Child Development, 54,* 1312–1323.

CROCKENBERG, S. B. (1981). Infant irritability, mother responsiveness, and social support influences on the security of mother-infant attachment. *Child Development, 52,* 857–865.

CROCKENBERG, S. B. (1986). Are temperamental differences in babies associated with predictable differences in care-giving? In J. V. Lerner & R. M. Lerner (Eds.), *New directions for child development.* (No. 30, pp. 75–88). San Francisco: Jossey-Bass.

CROCKENBERG, S. B., & NICOLAYEV, J. (1979). Stage transition in moral reasoning as related to conflict experienced in naturalistic settings. *Merrill-Palmer Quarterly, 25,* 185–192.

CROOK, C. K. (1978). Taste perception in the newborn infant. *Infant Behavior and Development, 1,* 52–69.

CROOK, C. K., & LIPSITT, L. P. (1976). Neonatal nutritive sucking: Effects of taste stimulation upon sucking rhythm and heart rate. *Child Development, 47,* 518–522.

CROSS, T. G. (1978). Mothers' speech and its association with rate of linguistic development in young children. In N. Waterson & C. E. Snow (Eds.), *The development of communication* (pp. 199–216). New York: Wiley.

CROVITZ, H. F., & ZENER, K. (1962). A group test for assessing hand and eye-dominance. *American Journal of Psychology, 75,* 271–276.

CROWELL, D. J., JONES, R. H., KAPUNIAI, L. E., & NAKAGAWA, J. K. (1973). Unilateral cortical activity in newborn humans: An early index of cerebral dominance? *Science, 142,* 1480–1481.

CRYSTAL, S. (1986). Psychosocial rehabilitation and homeless youth. *Psychosocial Rehabilitation Journal, 10,* 15–21.

CUMMINGS, E. M., IANNOTTI, R. J., & ZAHN-WAXLER, C. (1985). Influence of conflict between adults on the emotions and aggression of young children. *Development Psychology, 21,* 495–507.

CUMMINGS, J. S., PELLEGRINI, D. S., NOTARIUS, C. I., & CUMMINGS, E. M. (1989). Children's responses to angry adult behavior as a function of marital distress and history of interparent hostility. *Child Development, 60,* 1035–1043.

CUMMINGS, S. & TAEBEL, D. (1980). Sexual inequality and the reproduction of consciousness: An analysis of sex-role stereotyping among children. *Sex Roles, 6,* 631–644.

CUNEO, D. O. (1980). A general strategy for quantity judgments: The height and width rule. *Child Development, 50,* 170–179.

CURRAN, D. K. (1987). *Adolescent suicidal behavior.* Washington, DC: Hemisphere.

CURTISS, S. (1977). *Genie: A psycholinguistic study of a modern-day "wild child."* New York: Academic Press.

CURTISS, S. (1985). The development of human cerebral lateralization. In D. F. Benson & E. Zaidel (Eds.), *The dual brain* (pp. 97–116). New York: Guilford Press.

CUSHNER, I. M. (1981). Maternal behavior and perinatal risks: Alcohol, smoking, and drugs. *Annual Review of Public Health, 2,* 201–218.

CUTRONA, C. E., & FESHBACH, S. (1979). Cognitive and behavioral correlates of children's differential use of social information. *Child Development, 50,* 1036–1042.

DAEHLER, M. W., & BUKATKO, D. (1977). Recognition memory for pictures in very young children: Evidence from attentional preferences using a continuous presentation procedure. *Child Development, 48,* 693–696.

DAMON, W. (1977). *The social world of the child.* San Francisco: Jossey-Bass.

DAMON, W., & HART, D. (1988). *Self-understanding in childhood and adolescence.* New York: Cambridge University Press.

DANNEMILLER, J. L., & STEPHENS, B. R. (1988). A critical test of infant pattern preference models. *Child Development, 59,* 210–216.

DANSKY, J. L. (1980). Make-believe: A mediator of the relationship between play and associative fluency. *Child Development, 51,* 576–579.

DANZA, R. (1983). Menarche: Its effects on mother–daughter and father–daughter interactions. In S. Golub (Ed.), *Menarche* (pp. 99–104). Lexington, MA: Lexington Books.

DARVILL, D., & CHEYNE, J. A. (1981). *Sequential analysis of responses to aggression: Age and sex effects.* Paper presented at the biennial meeting of the Society of Research in Child Development, Boston.

DARWIN, C. (1936). *The descent of man.* New York: Modern Library. (Original work published 1871).

DARWIN, C. (1936). *On the origin of species by means of natural selection.* New York: Modern Library. (Original work published 1859).

DAS GUPTA, P., & BRYANT, P. E. (1989). Young children's causal inferences. *Child Development, 60,* 1138–1146.

DAVID, H. P., & BALDWIN, W. P. (1979). Childbearing and child development: Demographic and psychosocial trends. *American Psychologist, 34,* 866–871.

DAVIS, K. (1947). A final note on a case of extreme deprivation. *American Journal of Sociology, 45,* 554–565.

DAY, B., & HUNT, G. H. (1975). Multiage classrooms: An analysis of verbal communication. *Elementary School Journal, 75,* 458–466.

DAY, R. H., & McKENZIE, B. E. (1981). Infant perception of the invariant size of approaching and receding objects. *Developmental Psychology, 17,* 670–677.

DEAUX, K. (1985). Sex and gender. In M. R. Rosenzweig & L. W. Porter (Eds.), *Annual review of psychology* (Vol. 36, pp. 49–81). Palo Alto, CA: Annual Reviews.

DEAUX, K., & LEWIS, L. L. (1984). Structure of gender stereotypes: Interrelationships among components and gender label. *Journal of Personality and Social Psychology, 46,* 991–1004.

DeCASPER, A. J., & FIFER, W. P. (1980). Of human bonding. Newborns prefer their mothers' voices. *Science, 208,* 1174–1176.

DeCASPER, A. J., & SPENCE, M. J. (1986). Prenatal maternal speech influences newborns' perception of speech sounds. *Infant Behavior and Development, 9,* 133–150.

DeFRIES, J. C., PLOMIN, R., & LABUDA, M. C. (1987). Genetic stability of cognitive development from childhood to adulthood. *Developmental Psychology, 23,* 4–12.

DEGELMAN, D., FREE, J. U., SCARLATO, M., BLACKBURN, J. M., & GOLDEN, T. (1986). Concept learning in preschool children: Effects of a short-term Logo experience. *Journal of Educational Computing Research, 2,* 199–205.

DE JONGE, G. A., ENGELBERTS, A. C., KOOMEN-LIEFTING, A. J. M., & KOSTENSE, P. J. (1989). Cot death and prone sleeping position in the Netherlands. *British Medical Journal, 298,* 722.

DELECKI, J. (1985). Principles of growth and development. In P. M. Hill (Ed.), *Human growth and development throughout life* (pp. 33–48). New York: Wiley.

DeLISI, R., & STAUDT, J. (1980). Individual differences in college students' performance on formal operational tasks. *Journal of Applied Developmental Psychology, 1,* 201–208.

DeLOACHE, J. (1987). Rapid change in the symbolic ability of very young children. *Science, 238,* 1556–1557.

DeLOACHE, J. S., & TODD, C. M. (1988). Young children's use of spatial categorization as a mnemonic strategy. *Journal of Experimental Child Psychology, 46,* 1–20.

DEMBROSKI, T. M., MacDOUGALL, J. M., HERD, J. A., & SHIELDS, J. L. (1979). Effect of level of challenge on pressor and heart rate responses in Type A and Type B subjects. *Journal of Applied Social Psychology, 9,* 209–228.

DENNIS, M., & WHITAKER, H. A. (1976). Language acquisition following hemidecortication: Linguistic superiority of the left over the right hemisphere. *Brain and Language, 3,* 404–433.

DENNIS, W. (1960). Causes of retardation among institutionalized children: Iran. *Journal of Genetic Psychology, 96,* 47–59.

DENNIS, W. (1973). *Children of the Creche.* New York: Appleton-Century-Crofts.

DENNIS, W., & DENNIS, M. G. (1940). The effect of cradling practices upon the onset of walking in Hopi children. *Journal of Genetic Psychology, 56,* 77–86.

DENNIS, W., & NAJARIAN, P. (1957). Infant development under environmental handicap. *Psychological Monographs, 71,* 1–13.

D'ERCOLE, A. J., & UNDERWOOD, L. E. (1986). Regulation of fetal growth by hormones and growth factors. In F. Falkner & J. M. Tanner (Eds.), *Human Growth* (2nd ed., Vol. 1, pp. 327–338). New York: Plenum.

DERDEYN, A. P. (1985). Grandparent visitation rights: Rendering family dissension more pronounced? *American Journal of Orthopsychiatry, 55,* 277–287.

DeSTEFANO, C. T., & MUELLER, E. (1982). Environmental determinants of peer social activity in 18-month-old males. *Infant Behavior and Development, 5,* 175–183.

DEUTSCH, F. (1974). Observational and sociometric measures of peer popularity and their relationship to egocentric communication in female preschoolers. *Developmental Psychology, 10,* 745–747.

DEUTSCH, R., & STEIN, A. (1972). The effects of personal responsibility and task interruption on the private speech of preschoolers. *Human Development, 15,* 310–324.

DEUTSCH, W., & PECHMANN, T. (1982). Social interaction and the development of definite descriptions. *Cognition, 11,* 159–184.

DEVEREUX, E. C. (1970). The role of the peer group experience in moral development. In J. P. Hill (Ed.), *Minnesota Symposia on Child Psychology* (Vol. 4, pp. 94–140). Minneapolis: University of Minnesota Press.

DE VILLIERS, J. G., & DE VILLIERS, P. A. (1973a). Development of the use of word order in comprehension. *Journal of Psycholinguistic Research, 2,* 331–341.

DE VILLIERS, J. G., & DE VILLIERS, P. A. (1973b). A cross-sectional study of the acquisition of grammatical morphemes in child speech. *Journal of Psycholinguistic Research, 2,* 267–278.

DE VILLIERS, J. G., & DE VILLIERS, P. A. (1978). *Language acquisition.* Cambridge, MA: Harvard University Press.

DE VILLIERS, P. A., & DE VILLIERS, J. G. (1979). Form and function in the development of sentence negation. *Papers and Reports on Child Language Development, 13,* 118–125.

DEVIN-SHEEHAN, L., FELDMAN, R. S., & ALLEN, V. L. (1976). Research on children tutoring children: A critical review. *Review of Educational Research, 46,* 355–385.

DE VRIES, B., & WALKER, L. J. (1986). Moral reasoning and attitudes toward capital punishment. *Developmental Psychology, 22,* 509–513.

DeVRIES, R. (1969). Constancy of gender identify in the years three to six. *Monographs of the Society for Research in Child Development, 34*(3, Serial No. 127).

DIAZ, R. M. (1983). Thought and two languages: The impact of bilingualism on cognitive development. *Review of Research in Education, 10,* 23–54.

DIAZ, R. M. (1985). Bilingual cognitive development: Addressing three gaps in current research. *Child Development, 56,* 1376–1388.

DIAZ, R. M., & BERNDT, T. J. (1982). Children's knowledge of a best friend: Fact or fancy. *Developmental Psychology, 18,* 787–794.

DICK-READ, G. (1959). *Childbirth without fear*. New York: Harper & Brothers.

DICKINSON, D. K. (1984). First impressions: Children's knowledge of words gained from a single exposure. *Applied Psycholinguistics, 5,* 359–373.

DIENER, C. I., & DWECK, C. S. (1978). An analysis of learned helplessness: Continuous changes in performance, strategy, and achievement cognitions following failure. *Journal of Personality and Social Psychology, 36,* 451–462.

DIENER, C. I., & DWECK, C. S. (1980). An analysis of learned helplessness: II. The processing of success. *Journal of Personality and Social Psychology, 39,* 940–952.

DIETZ, W. H., JR., & GORTMAKER, S. L. (1985). Do we fatten our children at the television set? Obesity and television viewing in children and adolescents. *Pediatrics, 75,* 807–812.

DiLALLA, L. F., & WATSON, M. W. (1988). Differentiation of fantasy and reality: Preschoolers' reactions to interruptions in their play. *Developmental Psychology, 24,* 286–291.

DIRKS, J. (1982). The effect of a commercial game on children's Block Design scores on the WISC-R test. *Intelligence, 6,* 109–123.

DIRKS, J., & GIBSON, E. (1977). Infants' perception of similarity between live people and their photographs. *Child Development, 48,* 124–130.

DISHION, T. J. (1990). The family ecology of boys' peer relations in middle childhood. *Child Development, 61,* 874–892.

DITTRICHOVA, J., BRICHACEK, V., PAUL, K., & TAUTERMANNOVA, M. (1982). The structure of infant behavior: An analysis of sleep and waking in the first months of life. In W. W. Hartup (Ed.), *Review of child development research* (Vol. 6, pp. 73–100). Chicago: University of Chicago Press.

DIVINE-HAWKINS, P. (1981). *Family day care in the United States: National Day Care Home Study final report, executive summary.* Washington, DC: U.S. Government Printing Office.

DIXON, R. A., & LERNER, R. M. (1988). A history of systems in developmental psychology. In M. Bornstein & M. Lamb (Eds.), *Developmental psychology: An advanced textbook* (2nd ed., pp. 3–50). Hillsdale, NJ: Erlbaum.

DODD, B. J. (1972). Effects of social and vocal stimulation on infant babbling. *Developmental Psychology, 7,* 80–83.

DODGE, K. A. (1980). Social cognition and children's aggressive behavior. *Child Development, 51,* 162–170.

DODGE, K. A. (1983). Behavioral antecedents of peer social status. *Child Development, 54,* 1386–1399.

DODGE, K. A. (1986). A social information processing model of social competence in children. In M. Perlmutter (Ed.), *Minnesota Symposia on Child Psychology* (Vol. 18, pp. 77–125). Hillsdale, NJ: Erlbaum.

DODGE, K. A. (1989). Coordinating responses to aversive stimuli: Introduction to a special section on the development of emotional regulation. *Developmental Psychology, 25,* 339–342.

DODGE, K. A., COIE, J. D., & BRAKKE, N. P. (1982). Behavior patterns of socially rejected and neglected preadolescents: The roles of social approach and aggression. *Journal of Abnormal Child Psychology, 10,* 389–410.

DODGE, K. A., & FRAME, C. L. (1983). Social cognitive biases and deficits in aggressive boys. *Child Development, 53,* 620–635.

DODGE, K. A., PETTIT, G. S., McCLASKEY, C. L., & BROWN, M. M. (1986). Social competence in children. *Monographs of the Society for Research in Child Development, 51*(2, Serial No. 213).

DODGE, K. A., SCHLUNDT, D. C., SCHOCKEN, L., & DELUGACH, J. D. (1983). Social competence and children's sociometric status: The role of peer group entry strategies. *Merrill-Palmer Quarterly, 29,* 309–336.

DODGE, K. A., & SOMBERG, D. R. (1987). Hostile attributional biases among aggressive boys are exacerbated under conditions of threats to the self. *Child Development, 58,* 213–224.

DODWELL, P. C., HUMPHREY, G. K., & MUIR, D. W. (1987). Shape and pattern perception. In P. Salapatek & L. Cohen (Eds.), *Handbook of infant perception* (Vol. 2, pp. 1–77). Orlando, FL: Academic Press.

DOLLAGHAN, C. (1985). Child meets word: "Fast mapping" in preschool children. *Journal of Speech and Hearing Research, 28,* 449–454.

DOLLARD, J., DOOB, L. W., MILLER, N. E., MOWRER, O. H., & SEARS, R. R. (1939). *Frustration and aggression.* New Haven, CT: Yale University Press.

DONALDSON, S. K., & WESTERMAN, M. A. (1986). Development of children's understanding of ambivalence and causal theories of emotion. *Developmental Psychology, 22,* 655–662.

DORE, J. (1974). A pragmatic description of early language development. *Journal of Psycholinguistic Research, 4,* 423–430.

DORE, J. (1985). Holophrases revisited: Their logical development from dialog. In M. D. Barrett (Ed.), *Children's single-word speech* (pp. 23–58). Chichester, England: Wiley.

DORNBUSCH, S. M., CARLSMITH, J. M., BUSHWALL, S. J., RITTER, P. L., LEIDERMAN, H., HASTORF, A. H., & GROSS, R. T. (1985). Single, parents, extended households, and the control of adolescents. *Child Development, 56,* 326–341.

DORNBUSCH, S. M., RITTER, P. L., LEIDERMAN, P. H., ROBERTS, D. F., & FRALEIGH, M. J. (1987). The relation of parenting style to adolescent school performance. *Child Development, 58,* 1244–1257.

DORR, A., GRAVES, S. B., & PHELPS, E. (1980). Television literacy for young children. *Journal of Communication, 30*(3), 71–83.

DORR, A., & KOVARIC, P. (1980). Some of the people some of the time—But which people? Televised violence and its effects. In E. L. Palmer & A. Dorr (Eds.), *Children and the faces of television: Teaching, violence, selling* (pp. 183–199). New York: Academic Press.

DORTZBACH, J. R. (1975). *Moral judgment and perceived locus of control: A cross-sectional developmental study of adults, aged 25–74.* Dissertation Abstracts International, 36, 4662B. (University Microfilms No. 76-05, 160).

DOSSEY, J. A., MULLIS, I. V. S., LINDQUIST, M. M., & CHAMBERS, D. L. (1988). *The Mathematics Report Card: Are we measuring up?* Princeton, NJ: Educational Testing Service.

DOTY, R. L., SHAMAN, P., APPLEBAUM, S. L., GIBERSON, R., SIKORSKI, L., & ROSENBERG, L. (1984). Smell identification ability: Changes with age. *Science, 226,* 141–143.

DOUGLAS, V. I. (1980). Treatment and training approaches to hyperactivity: Establishing internal or external control? In C. K. Whalen & B. Henker (Eds.), *Hyperactive children: The social ecology of identification and treatment* (pp. 238–317). New York: Academic Press.

DOUVAN, E. (1963). Employment and the adolescent. In F. I. Nye & L. W. Hoffman (Eds.), *The employed mother in America* (pp. 142–164). Chicago: Rand McNally.

DOUVAN, E., & ADELSON, J. (1966). *The adolescent experience.* New York: Wiley.

DOWNEY, G., & WALKER, E. (1989). Social cognition and adjustment in children at risk for psychopathology. *Developmental Psychology, 25,* 835–845.

DOWNS, A. C., & LANGLOIS, J. H. (1988). Sex typing: Construct and measurement issues. *Sex Roles, 18,* 87–100.

DOWNS, W. R. (1985). Using panel data to examine sex differences in causal relationships among adolescent alcohol use, norms, and peer alcohol use. *Journal of Youth and Adolescence, 14,* 469–486.

DOYLE, A., CONNOLLY, J., & RIVEST, L. (1980). The effects of playmate familiarity on the social interactions of young children. *Child Development, 51,* 217–223.

DRABMAN, R. S., CORDUA, G. D., HAMMER, D., JARVIE, G. J., & HORTON, W. (1979). Developmental trends in eating rates of normal and overweight preschool children. *Child Development, 50,* 211–216.

DRABMAN, R. S., & THOMAS, M. H. (1976). Does watching violence on television cause apathy? *Pediatrics, 57,* 329–331.

DRAPER, P., & CASHDAN, E. (1988). Technological change and child behavior among the !Kung. *Ethnology, 27,* 339–365.

DREYFUS-BRISAC, C. (1970). Ontogenesis of sleep in human prematures after 32 weeks of conceptional age. *Developmental Psychobiology, 3,* 91–121.

DROTAR, D. (ED.) (1985). *New directions in failure to thrive: Implications for research and practice.* New York: Plenum.

DROTAR, D., & STURM, L. (1988). Prediction of intellectual development in young children with early histories of nonorganic failure-to-thrive. *Journal of Pediatric Psychology, 13,* 281–296.

DUBOIS, D. L., & HIRSCH, B. J. (1990). School and neighborhood friendship patterns of black and whites in early adolescence. *Child Development, 61,* 524–536.

DUBOW, E. R., & TISAK, J. (1989). The relation between stressful life events and adjustment in elementary school children: The role of social support and social problem-solving skills. *Child Development, 60,* 1412–1423.

DUCK, S. W. (1975). Personality similarity and friendship choices by adolescents. *European Journal of Social Psychology, 5,* 351–365.

DUNN, J. (1989). Siblings and the development of social understanding in early childhood. In P. G. Zukow (Ed.), *Sibling interaction across cultures* (pp. 106–116). New York: Springer-Verlag.

DUNN, J., BRETHERTON, L., & MUNN, P. (1987). Conversations about feeling states between mothers and their young children. *Developmental Psychology, 23,* 132–139.

DUNN, J., & KENDRICK, C. (1980). The arrival of a sibling: Changes in patterns of interaction between mothers and first-born child. *Journal of Child Psychology and Psychiatry, 21,* 119–132.

DUNN, J., & KENDRICK, C. (1982). *Siblings: Love, envy and understanding.* Cambridge, MA: Harvard University Press.

DUNN, J., & SHATZ, M. (1989). Becoming a conversationalist despite (or because of) having an older sibling. *Child Development, 60,* 399–410.

DUNST, C. J., & LINDERFELT, B. (1985). Maternal ratings of temperament and operant learning in two- to three-month-old infants. *Child Development, 56,* 555–563.

DURRETT, M. E., OTAKI, M., & RICHARDS, P. (1984). Attachment and the mother's perception of support from the father. *International Journal of Behavioral Development, 7,* 167–176.

DUVALL, E. M. (1946). Conceptions of parenthood. *American Journal of Sociology, 57,* 193–203.

DWECK, C. S. (1975). The role of expectations and attributions in the alleviation of learned helplessness. *Journal of Personality and Social Pyschology, 31,* 674–685.

DWECK, C. S. (1983). Achievement motivation. In E. M. Hetherington (Ed.), *Handbook of child psychology: Vol. 4. Socialization, personality, and social development* (4th ed., pp. 643–691). New York: Wiley.

DWECK, C. S. (1986). Motivational processes affecting learning. *American Psychologist, 41,* 1040–1048.

DWECK, C. S., DAVIDSON, W., NELSON, S., & ENNA, B. (1978a). Sex differences in learned helplessness: II. The contingencies of evaluative feedback in the classroom. *Developmental Psychology, 14,* 268–276.

DWECK, C. S., DAVIDSON, W., NELSON, S., & ENNA, B. (1978b). Sex differences in learned helplessness: III. An experimental analysis. *Developmental Psychology, 14,* 268–276.

DWECK, C. S., & ELLIOTT, E. S. (1983). Achievement motivation. In E. M. Hetherington (Ed.), *Handbook of child psychology: Vol. 4. Socialization, personality, and social development* (pp. 643–691). New York: Wiley.

DWECK, C. S., & GILLIARD, D. (1975). Expectancy statements as determinants of reactions to failure: Sex differences in persistence and expectancy change. *Journal of Personality and Social Psychology, 32,* 1077–1084.

DWECK, C. S., GOETZ, T. E., & STRAUSS, N. L. (1980). Sex differences in learned helplessness: IV. An experimental and naturalistic study of failure generalization and its mediators. *Journal of Personality and Social Psychology, 38,* 441–452.

DWECK, C. S., & LEGGETT, E. L. (1988). A social–cognitive approach to motivation and personality. *Psychological Review, 95,* 256–273.

DWECK, C. S., & LICHT, B. G. (1980). Learned helplessness and intellectual achievement. In J. Garber & M. E. P. Seligman (Eds.), *Human helplessness: Theory and applications* (pp. 197–221). New York: Academic Press.

DWECK, C. S., & REPUCCI, N. D. (1973). Learned helplessness and reinforcement responsibility in children. *Journal of Personality and Social Psychology, 25,* 109–116.

DWYER, C. A. (1974). Influence of children's sex role standards on reading and arithmetic achievement. *Journal of Educational Psychology, 66,* 811–816.

DYE-WHITE, E. (1986). Environmental hazards in the work setting: Their effect on women of child-bearing age. *American Association of Occupational Health and Nursing Journal, 34,* 76–78.

EAST, M. C., & STEELE, P. R. M. (1987). Inhaling heroin during pregnancy: Effects on the baby. *British Medical Journal, 296,* 754.

EASTERBROOKS, M. A. (1989). Quality of attachment to mother and to father. Effects of perinatal risk status. *Child Development, 60,* 831–837.

EBEL, R. L. (1975). Educational tests: Valid? Biased? Useful? *Phi Delta Kappan, 57,* 83–89.

EBELING, K. S., & GELMAN, S. A. (1988). Coordination of size standards by young children. *Child Development, 59,* 888–896.

ECKERMAN, C. O., DAVIS, C. C., & DIDOW, S. M. (1989). Toddlers' emerging ways of achieving social coordination with a peer. *Child Development, 60,* 440–453.

ECKERMAN, C. O., & STEIN, M. R. (1982). The toddler's emerging interactive skills. In K. H. Rubin & H. S. Ross (Eds.), *Peer relationships and social skills in childhood* (pp. 41–71). New York: Springer-Verlag.

ECKERMAN, C. O., & WHATLEY, J. L. (1977). Toys and social interaction between infant peers. *Child Development, 48,* 1645–1656.

ECKERMAN, C. O., WHATLEY, J. L., & KUTZ, S. L. (1975). Growth of social play with peers during the second year of life. *Developmental Psychology, 11,* 42–49.

EDELBROCK, C., & SUGAWARA, A. I. (1978). Acquisition of sex-typed preferences in preschool-aged children. *Developmental Psychology, 14,* 614–623.

EDELMAN, M. W. (1989). Children at risk. In F. J. Macchiarola & A. Gartner (Eds.), *Caring for America's children.* New York: The Academy of Political Science. (pp. 20–30).

EDER, R. A. (1989). The emergent personologist: The structure and content of 3½-, 5½-, and 7½-year-olds' concepts of themselves and other persons. *Child Development, 60,* 1218–1228.

EDUCATIONAL RESEARCH SERVICE (1980). *Class size: A critique of recent meta-analyses.* Arlington, VA: Educational Research Service.

EDWARDS, C. P. (1978). Social experiences and moral judgment in Kenyan young adults. *Journal of Genetic Psychology, 133,* 19–30.

EDWARDS, C. P. (1981). The comparative study of the development of moral judgment and reasoning. In R. L. Munroe, R. Munroe, & B. B. Whiting (Eds.), *Handbook of cross-cultural human development* (pp. 501–528). New York: Garland.

EDWARDS, C. P., & WHITING, B. B. (1988). *Children of different worlds.* Cambridge, MA: Harvard University Press.

EGAN, T. (1988, November 17). School for homeless children: A rare experience. *New York Times,* p. A20.

EGELAND, B. (1974). Training impulsive children in the use of more efficient scanning techniques. *Child Development, 45,* 165–171.

EGELAND, B., & FARBER, E. (1984). Infant–mother attachment: Factors related to its development and changes over time. *Child Development, 55,* 753–771.

EGELAND, B., JACOBVITZ, D., & SROUFE, L. A. (1988). Breaking the cycle of abuse. *Child Development, 59,* 1080–1088.

EGELAND, B., & SROUFE, L. A. (1981). Developmental sequelae of maltreatment in infancy. In R. Rizley & D. Cicchetti (Ed.), *New directions for child development* (No. 11, pp. 77–92). San Francisco: Jossey-Bass.

EHRHARDT, A. A. (1975). Prenatal hormone exposure and psychosexual differentiation. In E. J. Sachar (Ed.), *Topics in psychoendocrinology* (pp. 67–82). New York: Grune & Stratton.

EHRHARDT, A. A., & BAKER, S. W. (1974). Fetal androgens, human central nervous system differentiation, and behavior sex differences. In R. C. Friedman, R. M. Richart, & R. L. VandeWiele (Eds.), *Sex differences in behavior* (pp. 33–51). New York: Wiley.

EHRHARDT, A. A., EPSTEIN, R., & MONEY, J. (1968). Fetal androgens and female gender identity in the early treated adrenogenital syndrome. *Johns Hopkins Medical Journal, 122,* 160–167.

EHRI, L. C. (1979). Linguistic insight: Threshold of reading acquisition. In T. G. Waller & G. E. MacKinnon (Eds.), *Reading research: Advances in theory and practice* (Vol. 1, pp. 63–114). New York: Harcourt Brace Jovanovich.

EID, E. E. (1970). Follow up study of physical growth of children who had excessive weight gain in first six months of life. *British Medical Journal, 2,* 74–76.

EISENBERG, N. (1982). The development of reasoning regarding prosocial behavior. In N. Eisenberg (Ed.), *The development of prosocial behavior* (pp. 219–249). New York: Academic Press.

EISENBERG, N., & LENNON, R. (1983). Sex differences in empathy and related capacities. *Psychological Bulletin, 94,* 100–131.

EISENBERG, N., LENNON, R., & PASTERNACK, J. F. (1986). Altruistic values and moral judgment. In N. Eisenberg (Ed.), *Altruistic emotion, cognition, and behavior* (pp. 115–159). Hillsdale, NJ: Erlbaum.

EISENBERG, N., LENNON, R., & ROTH, K. (1983). Prosocial development: A longitudinal study. *Developmental Psychology, 19,* 846–855.

EISENBERG, N., & MILLER, P. A. (1987). The relation of empathy to prosocial and related behaviors. *Psychological Bulletin, 101,* 91–119.

EISENBERG, N., SHELL, R., PASTERNACK, J., LENNON, R., BELLER, R., & MATHY, R. M. (1987). Prosocial development in middle childhood: A longitudinal study. *Developmental Psychology, 23,* 712–718.

EISENBERG-BERG, N. (1979). Development of children's prosocial moral judgment. *Developmental Psychology, 15,* 128–137.

EISENBERG-BERG, N., & HAND, M. (1979). The relationship of preschoolers' reasoning about prosocial moral conflicts to prosocial behavior. *Child Development, 50,* 356–363.

EISENBERG-BERG, N., & NEAL, C. (1979). Children's moral reasoning about their own spontaneous prosocial behavior. *Developmental Psychology, 15,* 228–229.

EISENBERG-BERG, N., & ROTH, K. (1980). The development of children's prosocial moral judgment: A longitudinal follow-up. *Developmental Psychology, 16,* 375–376.

EKMAN, P., & FRIESEN, W. (1972). Constants across culture in the face and emotion. *Journal of Personality and Social Psychology, 17,* 124–129.

EKMAN, P., & OSTER, H. (1979). Facial expressions of emotion. *Annual Review of Psychology, 30,* 527–554.

ELARDO, R., BRADLEY, R., & CALDWELL, B. M. (1975). The relation of infants' home environments to mental test performance from six to thirty-six months: A longitudinal analysis. *Child Development, 46,* 71–76.

ELARDO, R., BRADLEY, R., & CALDWELL, B. M. (1977). A longitudinal study of the relation of infants' home environments to language development at age 3. *Child Development, 48,* 595–603.

ELBERS, L., & TON, J. (1985). Play pen monologues: The interplay of words and babbles in the first words period. *Journal of Child Language, 12,* 551–565.

ELDER, G. H., JR. (1974). *Children of the Great Depression.* Chicago: University of Chicago Press.

ELDER, G. H., JR., & CASPI, A. (1988). Human development and social change: An emerging perspective on the life course. In N. Bolger, A. Caspi, G. Downey, & M. Moorehouse (Eds.), *Persons in context: Developmental processes* (pp. 77–113). Cambridge, England: Cambridge University Press.

ELDER, G. H., JR., CASPI, A., & VAN NGUYEN, T. (1986). Resourceful and vulnerable children: Family influences in hard times. In R. K. Silbereisen, K. Eysferth, & G. Rodinger (Eds), *Development as action in context: Problem behavior and normal youth development* (pp. 167–186). New York: Springer-Verlag.

ELDER, G. H., JR., LIKER, J. K., & CROSS, C. E. (1984). Parent-child behavior in the Great Depression: Life course and intergenerational influences. In P. B. Baltes & O. G. Brim (Eds.), *Life-span development and behavior* (Vol. 6, pp. 109–158). New York: Academic Press.

ELDER, G. H., JR., VAN NGUYEN, T., & CASPI, A. (1985). Linking family hardship to children's lives. *Child Development, 56,* 361–375.

ELDREDGE, L., & SALAMY, A. (1988). Neurobehavioral and neurophysiological assessment of healthy and "at-risk" full-term infants. *Child Development, 59,* 186–192.

ELKIND, D. (1971). Two approaches to intelligence: Piagetian and psychometric. In D. R. Green, M. P. Ford, & G. B. Flamer (Eds.), *Measurement and Piaget* (pp. 12–28). New York: McGraw-Hill.

ELKIND, D. (1976). *Child development and education.* New York: Oxford.

ELKIND, D. (1981). *Children and adolescents: Interpretive essays on Jean Piaget* (3rd ed.). New York: Oxford.

ELLIOT, R., & VASTA, R. (1970). The modeling of sharing: Effects associated with vicarious reinforcement, symbolization, age, and generalization. *Journal of Experimental Child Psychology, 10,* 8–15.

ELLIS, S., ROGOFF, B., & CROMER, C. (1981). Age segregation in children's social interactions. *Developmental Psychology, 17,* 399–407.

ELLISON, P. T. (1982). Skeletal growth, fatness, and menarcheal age: A comparison of two hypotheses. *Human Biology, 54,* 269–281.

ELSTER, A. B., & PANZARINE, S. (1983). Adolescent fathers. In E. R. McAnarney (Ed.), *Premature adolescent pregnancy and parenthood* (pp. 231–252). New York: Grune & Stratton.

EMDE, R. N. (1983). The prepresentational self and its affective core. *The Psychoanalytic Study of the Child, 38,* 165–192.

EMDE, R. N., GAENSBAUER, T. J., & HARMON, R. J. (1976). Emotional expression in infancy: A biobehavioral study. *Psychological Issues, 10*(No. 37). New York: International Universities Press.

EMDE, R. N., & KOENIG, K. L. (1969). Neonatal smiling and rapid eye movement states. *American Academy of Child Psychiatry, 8,* 57–67.

EMERY, R. E. (1982). Marital turmoil: Interparental conflict and the children of discord and divorce. *Psychological Bulletin, 92,* 310–330.

EMERY, R. E. (1988). *Marriage, divorce, and children's adjustment.* Newbury Park, CA: Sage.

EMERY, R. E. (1989). Family violence. *American Psychologist, 44,* 321–328.

EMERY, R. E., HETHERINGTON, E. M., & DILALLA, L. F. (1984). Divorce, children, and social policy. In H. W. Stevenson & A. E. Siegel (Eds.), *Child development research and social policy* (Vol. 1, pp. 189–266). Chicago: University of Chicago Press.

EMERY, R. E., & WYER, M. M. (1987). Divorce mediation. *American Psychologist, 42,* 472–480.

EMIHOVICH, C. A., GAIER, E. L., & CRONIN, N. C. (1984). Sex-role expectations changes by fathers and their sons. *Sex Roles, 11,* 861–868.

EMMERICH, W. (1982). Nonmonotonic developmental trends in social cognition: The case of gender constancy. In S. Strauss (Ed.), *U-shaped behavioral growth* (pp. 249–269). New York: Academic Press.

EMORY, E. K., & TOOMEY, K. A. (1988). Environmental stimulation and human fetal responsibility in late pregnancy. In W. P. Smotherman & S. R. Robinson (Eds.), *Behavior of the fetus* (pp. 141–161). Caldwell, NJ: The Telford Press.

ENGSNER, G., & WOLDEMARIAM, T. (1974). Motor nerve conduction velocity in marasmus and kwashiorkor. *Neuropadiatrie, 5,* 34–48.

ENRIGHT, R. D., ENRIGHT, W. F., MANHEIM, L. A., & HARRIS, B. E. (1980). Distributive justice development and social class. *Developmental Psychology, 16,* 555–563.

ENRIGHT, R. D., FRANKLIN, C. C., & MANHEIM, L. A. (1980). Children's distributive justice reasoning: A standardized and objective scale. *Developmental Psychology, 16,* 193–202.

ENRIGHT, R. D., & SUTTERFIELD, S. J. (1980). An ecological validation of social cognitive development. *Child Development, 51,* 156–161.

EPSTEIN, H. T. (1974a). Phrenoblysis: Special brain and mind growth periods. I. Human brain and skull development. *Developmental Psychobiology, 7,* 207–216.

EPSTEIN, H. T. (1974b). Phrenoblysis: Special brain and mind growth periods. II. Human mental development. *Developmental Psychobiology, 7,* 217–224.

EPSTEIN, H. T. (1980). EEG developmental stages. *Developmental Psychobiology, 13,* 629–631.

EPSTEIN, L. H., & WING, R. R. (1987). Behavioral treatment of childhood obesity. *Psychological Bulletin, 101,* 331–342.

EPSTEIN, S. (1973). The self-concept revisited, or a theory of a theory. *American Psychologist, 28,* 405–416.

ERICKSON, M. F., SROUFE, L. A., & EGELAND, B. (1985). The relationship between quality of attachment and behavior problems in preschool in a high-risk sample. In I. Bretherton & E. Waters (Eds.), Growing points of attachment theory and research. *Monographs of the Society for Research in Child Development, 50*(1–2, Serial No. 209).

ERIKSON, E. H. (1950). *Childhood and society.* New York: Norton.

ERIKSON, E. (1968). *Identity, youth, and crisis.* New York: Norton.

ERIKSON, R., & FRITZELL, J. (1988). The effects of the social welfare system in Sweden on the well-being of children and the elderly. In J. L. Palmer, T. Smeeding, & B. B. Torrey (Eds.), *The vulnerable* (pp. 309–330). Washington, DC: Urban Institute Press.

ERNHART, C. B., WOLF, A. W., FILIPOVICH, H. F., KENNARD, M. J., ERHARD, P., & SOKOL, R. J. (1985). Intrauterine lead exposure. *Teratology, 31,* 7B–8B.

ERON, L. D., WALDER, L. O., HUESMANN, L. R., & LEFKOWITZ, N. M. (1974). The convergence of laboratory and field studies of the development of aggression. In J. deWit & W. W. Hartup (Eds.), *Determinants and origins of aggressive behavior* (pp. 347–380). The Hague: Mouton.

ERVIN-TRIPP, S., O'CONNOR, S., & ROSENBERG, J. (1984). Language and power in the family. In M. Schulz & C. Kramerae (Eds.), *Language and power* (pp. 116–135). Belmont, CA: Sage Press.

ESCALONA, S. K., & CORMAN, H. (1969). *Albert Einstein Scales of Sensorimotor Development.* New York: Albert Einstein College of Medicine, Yeshiva University.

ESHEL, Y., & KLEIN, Z. (1981). Development of academic self-concept of lower-class and middle-class primary school children. *Journal of Educational Psychology, 73,* 287–293.

ESPENSCHADE, A. (1971). Motor performance in adolescence. In M. C. Jones, N. Bayley, J. W. Macfarlane, & M. P. Honzik (Eds.), *The course of human development* (pp. 86–90). Waltham, MA: Xerox Publishing.

ESPENSHADE, T. J. (1980). Raising a child can now cost $85,000. *Intercom, 8*(9), 10–12.

ETAUGH, C., COLLINS, G., & GERSON, A. (1975). Reinforcement of sex-typed behaviors of two-year-old children in a nursery school setting. *Developmental Psychology, 11,* 255.

ETAUGH, C., & HARLOW, H. (1975). Behaviors of male and female teachers as related to behaviors and attitudes of elementary school children. *Journal of Genetic Psychology, 127,* 163–170.

ETAUGH, C., LEVINE, D., & MENNELLA, A. (1984). Development of sex biases in children: 40 years later. *Sex Roles, 10,* 913–924.

ETAUGH, C., & ROSE, S. (1975). Adolescents' sex bias in the evaluation of performance. *Developmental Psychology, 11,* 663–664.

ETZEL, B., & GEWIRTZ, J. (1967). Experimental modification of caretaker-maintained high rate operant crying in a 6- and a 20-week-old infant (Infans tyrannotearus): Extinction of crying with reinforcement of eye contact and smiling. *Journal of Experimental Child Psychology, 5,* 303–317.

EVANS, D., HANSEN, J. D. L., MOODIE, A. D., & SPUY, H. I. J. (1980). Intellectual development and nutrition. *The Journal of Pediatrics, 97,* 358–363.

EVELETH, P. B., & TANNER, J. M. (1976). *Worldwide variation in human growth.* Cambridge, England: Cambridge University Press.

EVERTSON, C. (1982). Differences in instructional activities in higher- and lower-achieving junior high English and math classes. *Elementary School Journal, 82,* 329–350.

FABES, R. A., EISENBERG, N., McCORMICK, S. E., & WILSON, M. S. (1988). Preschoolers' attributions of the situational determinants of others' naturally occurring emotions. *Developmental Psychology, 24,* 376–385.

FAGAN, J. F., III. (1971). Infants' recognition memory for a series of visual stimuli. *Journal of Experimental Child Psychology, 11,* 244–250.

FAGAN, J. F., III. (1973). Infants' delayed recognition memory and forgetting. *Journal of Experimental Child Psychology, 16,* 424–450.

FAGAN, J. F., III. (1976). Infants' recognition of invariant features of faces. *Child Development, 47,* 627–638.

FAGAN, J. F., III. (1977). Infant recognition memory: Studies in forgetting. *Child Development, 45,* 351–356.

FAGAN, J. F., III. (1984). Infant memory. In M. Moscovitch (Ed.), *Infant memory* (pp. 1–27). New York: Plenum.

FAGAN, J. F., III, & SINGER, L. T. (1979). The role of simple feature differences in infants' recognition of faces. *Infant Behavior and Development, 2,* 39–45.

FAGOT, B. I. (1974). Sex differences in toddlers' behavior and parental reaction. *Developmental Psychology, 10,* 554–558.

FAGOT, B. I. (1977a). Consequences of moderate cross-gender behavior in preschool children. *Child Development, 48,* 902–907.

FAGOT, B. I. (1977b). Variations in density: Effect on task and social behaviors of pre-school children. *Developmental Psychology, 13,* 166–167.

FAGOT, B. I. (1978). The influence of sex of child on parental reactions to toddler children. *Child Development, 49,* 459–465.

FAGOT, B. I. (1981). Stereotypes versus behavioral judgments of sex differences in young children. *Sex Roles, 7,* 1093–1096.

FAGOT, B. I. (1985a). Beyond the reinforcement principle: Another step toward understanding sex role development. *Developmental Psychology, 21,* 1097–1104.

FAGOT, B. I. (1985b). Changes in thinking about early sex role development. *Developmental Review, 5,* 83–98.

FAGOT, B. I., HAGAN, R., LEINBACH, M. D., & KRONSBERG, S. (1985). Differential reactions to assertive and communicative acts of toddler boys and girls. *Child Development, 56,* 1499–1505.

FAGOT, B. I., & KAVANAGH, K. (1990). The prediction of antisocial behavior from avoidant attachment classifications. *Child Development, 61,* 864–873.

FAGOT, B. I., & LEINBACH, M. D. (1989). The young child's gender schema: Environmental input, internal organization. *Child Development, 60,* 663–672.

FAGOT, B. I., LEINBACH, M. D., & HAGEN, R. (1986). Gender labeling and the adoption of sex-typed behaviors. *Developmental Psychology, 22,* 440–443.

FAGOT, B. I., & LITTMAN, I. (1976). Relation of pre-school sex-typing to intellectual performance in elementary school. *Psychological Reports, 39,* 699–704.

FAGOT, B. I., & PATTERSON, G. R. (1969). An in vivo analysis of reinforcing contingencies for sex-role behaviors in the preschool child. *Developmental Psychology, 1,* 563–568.

FALBO, T. (1978). Only children and interpersonal behavior: An experimental and survey study. *Journal of Applied Social Psychology, 8,* 244–253.

FALBO, T. (1984). Only children: A review. In T. Falbo (Ed.), *The single-child family* (pp. 1–24). New York: Guilford Press.

FALBO, T., & POLIT, D. (1986). A quantitative review of the only child literature: Research evidence and theory development. *Psychological Bulletin, 100,* 176–189.

FANTZ, R. L. (1961, May). The origin of form perception. *Scientific American, 204*(5), 66–72.

FANTZ, R. L. (1963). Pattern vision in newborn infants. *Science, 140,* 296–297.

FANTZ, R. L., ORDY, J. M., & UDELF, M. S. (1962). Maturation of pattern vision in infants during the first six months. *Journal of Comparative Physiological Psychology, 55,* 907–917.

FAUST, M. S. (1960). Developmental maturity as a determinant in prestige of adolescent girls. *Child Development, 31,* 173–186.

FAUST, M. S. (1983). Alternative constructions of adolescent growth. In J. Brooks-Gunn & A. C., Petersen (Eds.), *Girls at puberty: Biological and psychosocial perspectives* (pp. 105–125). New York: Plenum.

FEIN, G. G. (1979). Play and the acquisition of symbols. In L. Katz

(Ed.), *Current topics in early childhood education* (pp. 195–225). Norwood, NJ: Ablex.

FEIN, G., JOHNSON, D., KOSSON, N., STORK, L., & WASSERMAN, L. (1975). Sex stereotypes and preferences in the toy choices of 20-month-old boys and girls. *Developmental Psychology, 11,* 527–528.

FEINGOLD, A. (1988). Cognitive gender differences are disappearing. *American Psychologist, 43,* 95–103.

FEINMAN, S. (1982). Social referencing in infancy. *Merrill-Palmer Quarterly, 28,* 445–470.

FEIS, C. L., & SIMONS, C. (1985). Training preschool children in interpersonal cognitive problem-solving skills: A replication. *Prevention in Human Services, 3,* 59–70.

FENNEMA, E., & SHERMAN, J. (1977). Sex-related differences in mathematics achievement, spatial visualization, and affective factors. *American Educational Research Journal, 14,* 51–71.

FENTON, N. (1928). The only child. *Journal of Genetic Psychology, 35,* 546–556.

FERGUSON, L. R. (1978). The competence and freedom of children to make choices regarding participation in research: A statement. *Journal of Social Issues, 34,* 114–121.

FERNALD, A. (1984). The perceptual and affective salience of mothers' speech to infants. In L. Feagans, C. Garvey, & R. Golinkoff (Eds.), *The origins of growth in communication* (pp. 5–29). Norwood, NJ: Ablex.

FERNALD, A., & KUHL, P. (1987). Acoustic determinants of infant preference for motherese speech. *Infant Behavior and Development, 10,* 279–293.

FERNALD, A., TAESCHNER, T., DUNN, J., PAPOUSEK, M., BOYSSEN-BARDIES, B., & FUKUI, I. (1989). A cross-language study of prosodic modifications in mothers' and fathers' speech to preverbal infants. *Journal of Child Language, 16,* 477–502.

FESHBACH, N. D. (1969). Student teacher preferences for elementary school pupils varying in personality characteristics. *Journal of Educational Psychology, 60,* 126–132.

FESHBACH, N. D., & FESHBACH, S. (1982). Empathy training and the regulation of aggression: Potentialities and limitations. *Academic Psychology Bulletin, 4,* 399–413.

FIELD, D. (1981). Can preschool children really learn to conserve? *Child Development, 52,* 326–334.

FIELD, J. (1977). Coordination of vision and prehension in young infants. *Child Development, 48,* 97–103.

FIELD, J., MUIR, D., PILON, R., SINCLAIR, M., & DODWELL, P. (1980). Infants' orientation to lateral sounds from birth to three months. *Child Development, 51,* 295–298.

FIELD, T. M., SCHANBERG, S. M., SCAFIDI, F., BAUER, C. R., VEGA-LAHR, N., GARCIA, R., NYSTROM, J., & KUHN, C. M. (1986). Effects of tactile/kinesthetic stimulation on preterm neonates. *Pediatrics, 77,* 654–658.

FIELD, T. M., WIDMAYER, S. M., STRINGER, S., & IGNATOFF, E. (1980). Teenage, lower-class, black mothers and their preterm infants: An intervention and developmental follow-up. *Child Development, 51,* 426–436.

FIELD, T. M., WOODSON, R., GREENBERG, R., & COHEN, D. (1982). Discrimination and imitation of facial expressions by neonates. *Science, 218,* 179–181.

FINCHAM, F. D., HOKODA, A., & SANDERS, R., JR. (1989). Learned helplessness, test anxiety, and academic achievement: A longitudinal analysis. *Child Development, 60,* 138–145.

FINE, G. A. (1980). The natural history of preadolescent male friendship groups. In H. C. Foot, A. J. Chapman, & J. R. Smith (Eds.), *Friendship and social relations in children* (pp. 293–320). Chichester, England: Wiley.

FINKELHOR, D. (1986). *A sourcebook on child sexual abuse.* Beverly Hills, CA: Sage.

FINKELSTEIN, N., & HASKINS, R. (1983). Kindergarten children prefer same-color peers. *Child Development, 54,* 502–508.

FISCHER, K. W. (1980). A theory of cognitive development: The control and construction of hierarchies of skills. *Psychological Review, 87,* 477–531.

FISCHER, K. W. (1987). Commentary—Relations between brain and cognitive development. *Child Development, 58,* 623–632.

FISCHER, K. W., & PIPP, S. L. (1984). Processes of cognitive development: Optimal level and skill acquisition. In R. J. Sternberg (Ed.), *Mechanisms of cognitive development* (pp. 45–80). New York: W. H. Freeman.

FIVUSH, R. (1984). Learning about school: The development of kindergartners' school scripts. *Child Development, 55,* 1697–1709.

FLAPAN, D. (1968). *Children's understanding of social interaction.* New York: Teachers College Press.

FLAVELL, J. H. (1963). *The developmental psychology of Jean Piaget.* New York: Van Nostrand.

FLAVELL, J. H. (1976). Metacognitive aspects of problem solving. In L. B. Resnick (Ed.), *The nature of intelligence* (pp. 231–235). Hillsdale, NJ: Erlbaum.

FLAVELL, J. H. (1981). Cognitive monitoring. In W. P. Dickson (Ed.), *Children's oral communication skills* (pp. 35–60). New York: Academic Press.

FLAVELL, J. H. (1982a). On cognitive development. *Child Development, 53,* 1–10.

FLAVELL, J. H. (1982b). Structures, stages and sequences in cognitive development. In W. A. Collins (Ed.), *Minnesota Symposia on Child Psychology* (Vol. 15, pp. 1–28). Hillsdale, NJ: Erlbaum.

FLAVELL, J. H. (1985). *Cognitive development* (2nd ed.). Englewood Cliffs, NJ: Prentice-Hall.

FLAVELL, J. H., BOTKIN, P. T., FRY, C. L., JR., WRIGHT, J. W., & JARVIS, P. E. (1968). *The development of role-taking and communication skills in children.* New York: Wiley.

FLAVELL, J. H., FLAVELL, E. R., & GREEN, F. L. (1987). Young children's knowledge about the apparent–real and pretend–real distinctions. *Developmental Psychology, 23,* 816–822.

FLAVELL, J. H., GREEN, F. L., & FLAVELL, E. R. (1987). Development of knowledge about the appearance–reality distinction. *Monographs of the Society for Research in Child Development, 51*(1, Serial No. 212).

FLAVELL, J. H., GREEN, F. L., & FLAVELL, E. R. (1989). Young children's ability to differentiate appearance–reality and level 2 perspectives in the tactile modality. *Child Development, 60,* 201–213.

FLAVELL, J. H., SPEER, J. R., GREEN, F. L., & AUGUST, D. L. (1981). The development of comprehension monitoring and knowledge about communication. *Monographs of the Society for Research in Child Development, 46*(5, Serial No. 192).

FLAVELL, J. H., & WELLMAN, H. M. (1977). Metamemory. In R. V. Kail, Jr., & J. W. Hagen (Eds.), *Perspectives on the development of memory and cognition* (pp. 3–33). Hillsdale, NJ: Erlbaum.

FODOR, J. (1977). *Semantics: Theories of meaning in generative grammar.* New York: Thomas Y. Crowell.

FOGEL, A., MELSON, G. F., TODA, S., & MISTRY, T. (1987). Young children's responses to unfamiliar infants. *International Journal of Behavioral Development, 10,* 1071–1077.

FOGEL, A., TODA, S., & KAWAI, M. (1988). Mother–infant face-to-face interaction in Japan and the United States: A laboratory comparison using 3-month-old infants. *Devlopmental Psychology, 24,* 398–406.

FORD, M. E., & KEATING, D. P. (1981). Development and individual differences in long-term memory retrieval: Process and organization. *Child Development, 52,* 234–241.

FORMAN, D., COOK-MOZAFFARI, P., DARBY, S., DAVEY, G., STRATTON, G., DOLL, R., & PIKE, M. (1987). Cancer near nuclear installations. *Nature, 329,* 499–505.

FORMAN, E., & MCPHAIL, J. (1989). *What have we learned about the cognitive benefits of peer interaction? A Vygotskian critique.* Paper presented at the annual meeting of the American Educational Research Association, San Francisco.

FOWLER, J., & PETERSON, P. (1981). Increasing reading persistence and altering attributional style of learned helpless children. *Journal of Educational Psychology, 73,* 251–260.

FOX, N. A., & DAVIDSON, R. J. (1986). Taste-elicited changes in facial signs of emotion and the asymmetry of brain electrical activity in newborn infants. *Neuropsychologia, 24* 417–422.

FOX, R., ASLIN, R. N., SHEA, S. L., & DUAIS, S. T. (1979). Stereopsis in human infants. *Science, 207,* 323–324.

FRANCIS, P. L., & MCCROY, G. (1983). *Bimodal recognition of hu-*

man stimulus configurations. Paper presented at the biennial meeting of the Society for Research in Child Development, Detroit.

FRANCIS, P. L., SELF, P. A., & HOROWITZ, F. D. (1987). The behavioral assessment of the neonate: An overview. In J. D. Osofsky (Ed.), *Handbook of infant development* (2nd ed., pp. 723–779). New York: Wiley.

FRANK, L. K. (1943). Research in child psychology: History and prospect. In R. Barker, J. Kounin, & H. Wright (Eds.), *Child behavior and development* (pp. 1–15). New York: McGraw Hill.

FRANKEL, M. T., & ROLLINS, H. A. (1985). Associative and categorical hypotheses of organization in the free recall of adults and children. *Journal of Experimental Child Psychology, 40,* 304–318.

FRANKLIN, B. S., & RICHARDS, P. N. (1977). Effects on children's divergent thinking abilities of a period of direct teaching for divergent production. *British Journal of Educational Psychology, 47,* 66–70.

FRAUENGLASS, M. H., & DIAZ, R. M. (1985). Self-regulatory functions of children's private speech: A critical analysis of recent challenges to Vygotsky's theory. *Developmental Psychology, 21,* 357–364.

FREDERIKSEN, J. R., & WARREN, B. M. (1987). A cognitive framework for developing expertise in reading. In R. Glaser (Ed.), *Advances in instructional psychology* (Vol. 3, pp. 1–39). Hillsdale, NJ: Erlbaum.

FREEDMAN, D. G. (1976). *Developmental psychobiology: The significance of infancy.* Hillsdale, NJ: Erlbaum.

FREEDMAN, D. G., & FREEDMAN, N. (1969). Behavioral differences between Chinese-American and European-American newborns. *Nature, 224,* 1227.

FREEDMAN, J. L. (1984). Effect of television violence on aggressiveness. *Pyschological Bulletin, 96,* 227–246.

FRENCH, D. C. (1984). Children's knowledge of the social functions of younger, older, and same-age peers. *Child Development, 55,* 1429–1433.

FRENCH, D. C. (1988). Heterogeneity of peer-rejected boys: Aggressive and nonaggressive subtypes. *Child Development, 59,* 976–985.

FRENCH, D. C., & WAAS, G. A. (1985). Behavior problems of peer-neglected and peer-rejected elementary age children: Parent and teacher perspectives. *Child Development, 56,* 246–252.

FRENCH, L. A., & NELSON, K. (1985). *Young children's knowledge of relational terms: Some ifs, ors, and buts.* New York: Springer-Verlag.

FREUD, A., & DANN, S. (1951). An experiment in group upbringing. *Psychoanalytic Study of the Child, 6,* 127–168.

FREUD, S. (1933). *New introductory lectures on psychoanalysis.* New York: Norton.

FREUD, S. (1961a). Formulations regarding the two principles of mental functioning. In J. Strachey (Ed.), *Standard edition of the complete psychological works of Sigmund Freud* (Vol. 12, pp. 215–226). London: Hogarth Press. (Original work published 1925)

FREUD, S. (1961b). Some psychological consequences of the anatomical distinction between the sexes. In J. Strachey (Ed.), *Standard edition of the complete pyschological works of Sigmund Freud* (Vol. 19, pp. 248–258). London: Hogarth Press. (Original work published 1925)

FREUD, S. (1973). *An outline of psychoanalysis.* London: Hogarth. (Original work published 1938)

FREUD, S. (1974). *The ego and the id.* London: Hogarth. (Original work published 1923)

FREUDENBERG, R. P., DRISCOLL, J. W., & STERN, G. S. (1978). Reactions of adult humans to cries of normal and abnormal infants. *Infant Behavior and Development, 1,* 224–227.

FRIED, P. A., WATKINSON, B., DILLON, R. F., & DULBERG, C. S. (1987). Neonatal neurological status in a low-risk population after prenatal exposure to cigarettes, marijuana, and alcohol. *Journal of Developmental and Behavioral Pediatrics, 8,* 318–326.

FRIEDMAN, L. (1989). Mathematics and the gender gap: A meta-analysis of recent studies on sex differences in mathematical tasks. *Review of Educational Research, 59,* 185–214.

FRIEDMAN, M., & ROSENMAN, R. H. (1959). Association of specific overt behavior patterns with blood and cardiovascular findings. *Journal of the American Medical Association, 169,* 1286–1296.

FRIEDRICH, L. K., & STEIN, A. H. (1973). Aggressive and prosocial television programs and the natural behavior of preschool children.

Monographs of the Society for Research in Child Development, 38(4, Serial No. 151).

FRIEDRICH-COFER, L., & HUSTON, A. C. (1986). Television violence and aggression: The debate continues. *Psychological Bulletin, 100,* 364–371.

FRIEDRICH-COFER, L. K., TUCKER, C. J., NORRIS-BAKER, C., FARNSWORTH, J. B., FISHER, D. P., HANNINGTON, C. M., & HOXIE, K. (1978). *Perceptions by adolescents of television heroines.* Paper presented at the annual meeting of the Southwestern Psychological Association, New Orleans.

FRISCH, H. L. (1977). Sex stereotypes in adult–infant play. *Child Development, 48,* 1671–1675.

FRISCH, R. E. (1983). Fatness, puberty, and fertility. In J. Brooks-Gunn & A. C. Petersen (Eds.), *Girls at puberty: Biological and psychosocial perspectives* (pp. 29–49). New York: Plenum.

FRISCH, R. E., GOTZ-WELBERGEN, A., MCARTHUR, J. W., ALBRIGHT, T. WITSCHI, J., BULLEN, B., BIRNHOLZ, J., REED, R. B., & HERMANN, H. (1981). Delayed menarche and amenorrhea of college athletes in relation to age of onset of training. *Journal of the American Medical Association, 246,* 1559–1563.

FRISCH, R. E., WYSHAK, G., & VINCENT, L. (1980). Delayed menarche and amenorrhea of ballet dancers. *New England Journal of Medicine, 303,* 17–19.

FRODI, A. (1985). When empathy fails: Aversive infant crying and child abuse. In B. M. Lester & C. F. Z. Boukydis (Eds.), *Infant crying: Theoretical and research perspectives* (pp. 263–277). New York: Plenum.

FRODI, A. M., LAMB, M. E., LEAVITT, L. A., BONOVAN, W. L., NEFF, C., & SHERRY, D. (1978). Fathers' and mothers' responses to the faces and cries of normal and premature infants. *Developmental Psychology, 14,* 490–498.

FRY, P. S. (1975). The resistance of temptation: Inhibitory and disinhibitory effects of models in children from India and the United States. *Journal of Cross-Cultural Psychology, 6,* 189–202.

FUCHS, I., EISENBERG, N., HERTZ-LAZAROWITZ, R., & SHARABANY, R. (1986). Kibbutz, Israeli city, and American children's moral reasoning about prosocial moral conflicts. *Merrill-Palmer Quarterly, 32,* 37–50.

FURMAN, W., & BIERMAN, K. L. (1983). Developmental changes in young children's conceptions of friendship. *Child Development, 54,* 549–556.

FURMAN, W., & BUHRMESTER, D. (1985). Children's perceptions of the personal relationships in their social networks. *Developmental Psychology, 21,* 1016–1024.

FURMAN, W., JONES, L., BUHRMESTER, D., & ADLER, T. (1989). Children's, parents', and observers' perspectives on sibling relationships. In P. G. Zukow (Ed.), *Sibling interaction across cultures* (pp. 165–183). New York: Springer-Verlag.

FURROW, D., & NELSON, K. (1984). Environmental correlates of individual differences in language acquisition. *Journal of Child Language, 11,* 523–534.

FURSTENBERG, F. F., JR., BROOKS-GUNN, J., & CHASE-LANSDALE, L. (1989). Teenaged pregnancy and childbearing. *American Psychologist, 44,* 313–320.

FURSTENBERG, F. F., JR., BROOKS-GUNN, J., & MORGAN, S. P. (1987). *Adolescent mothers in later life.* New York: Cambridge University Press.

FURSTENBERG, F. F., JR., & CRAWFORD, D. B. (1978). Family support: Helping teenagers to cope. *Family Planning Perspectives, 10,* 322–333.

FURSTENBERG, F. F., JR., & NORD, C. W. (1985). Parenting apart: Patterns of childrearing after marital disruption. *Journal of Marriage and the Family, 47,* 893–904.

FURSTENBERG, F. F., JR., SPANIER, G. V., & ROTHSCHILD, N. (1982). Patterns of parenting in the transition from divorce to remarriage. In P. W. Berman & E. R. Ramey (Eds.), *Women: A developmental perspective* (NIH Publication No. 82-2298, pp. 325–343). Bethesda, MD: National Institutes of Health.

FUSON, K. C. (1988). *Children's counting and concepts of number.* New York: Springer-Verlag.

FUSON, K. C., SECADA, W. G., & HALL, J. W. (1983). Matching, counting, and conservation of numerical equivalence. *Child Development,* 54, 91–97.

FYANS, L. J., JR., SALILI, F., MAEHR, M. L., & DESAI, K. A. (1983). A cross-cultural exploration into the meaining of achievement. *Journal of Personality and Social Psychology, 44,* 1000–1013.

GADDINI, R., & GADDINI, E. (1970). Transitional objects and the process of individuation: A study in three different social groups. *Journal of the American Academy of Child Psychiatry, 9,* 347–365.

GADDIS, A., & BROOKS-GUNN, J. (1985). The male experience of pubertal change. *Journal of Youth and Adolescence, 14,* 62–62.

GAENSBAUER, T. J. (1980). Anaclitic depression in a three-and-one-half month-old child. *American Journal of Psychiatry, 137,* 841–842.

GAENSBAUER, T. J., EMDE, R. J., & CAMPOS, J. J. (1976). Stranger distress: A confirmation of a developmental shift in a longitudinal sample. *Perceptual and Motor Skills, 12,* 99–106.

GAGAN, R. J. (1984). The families of children who fail to thrive: Preliminary investigations of parental deprivation among organic and non-organic cases. *Child Abuse and Neglect, 8,* 93–103.

GAGE, N. (1978). The yield of research on teaching. *Phi Delta Kappan, 59,* 229–235.

GAINES, L., & ESSERMAN, J. (1981). A quantitative study of young children's comprehension of television programs and commercials. In J. F. Esserman (Ed.), *Television advertising and children: Issues, research and findings* (pp. 96–105). New York: Child Research Service.

GALAMBOS, S. J., & GOLDIN-MEADOW, S. (1990). The effects of learning two languages on levels of metalinguistic awareness. *Cognition, 34,* 1–56.

GALBRAITH, R. C. (1982). Sibling spacing and intellectual development: A closer look at the confluence model. *Developmental Psychology, 18,* 151–173.

GALIN, D., JOHNSTONE, J., NAKELL, L., & HERRON, J. (1979). Development of the capacity for tactile information transfer between hemispheres in normal children. *Science, 204,* 1330–1332.

GALLAGHER, J. J. (1989). A new policy initiative: Infants and toddlers with handicapping conditions. *American Psychologist, 44,* 387–392.

GALLAGHER, T. M. (1981). Contingent query sequences within adult–child discourse. *Journal of Child Language, 8,* 51–62.

GALLER, J. R., RAMSEY, F., & SOLIMANO, G. (1985a). A follow-up study of the effects of early malnutrition on subsequent development: I. Physical growth and sexual maturation during adolescence. *Pediatric Research, 19,* 524–527.

GALLER, J. R., RAMSEY, F., & SOLIMANO, G. (1985b). A follow-up study of effects of early malnutrition on subsequent development: II. Fine motor skills in adolescence. *Pediatric Research, 19,* 524–527.

GALLER, J. R., RAMSEY, F., SOLIMANO, G., KUCHARSKI, L. T., & HARRISON, R. (1984). The influence of early malnutrition on subsequent behavioral development: IV. Soft neurological signs. *Pediatric Research, 18,* 826–832.

GALTON, R. (1883). *Inquiries into human faculty and its development.* London: Macmillan.

GANDOUR, M. J. (1989). Activity level as a dimension of temperament in toddlers: Its relevance for the organismic specificity hypothesis. *Child Development, 60,* 1092–1098.

GANNON, S., & KORN, S. J. (1983). Temperament, cultural variation, and behavior disorder in preschool children. *Child Psychiatry and Human Development, 13,* 203–212.

GANON, E. C., & SWARTZ, K. B. (1980). Perception of internal elements of compound figures by one-month-old infants. *Journal of Experimental Child Psychology, 30,* 159–170.

GARBARINO, J. (1977). The human ecology of child maltreatment: A conceptual model for research. *Journal of Marriage and the Family, 39,* 721–736.

GARBARINO, J. (1980). Some thoughts on school size and its effects on adolescent development. *Journal of Youth and Adolescence, 9,* 19–31.

GARBARINO, J., GUTTMAN, E., & SEELEY, J. (1986). *The psychologically battered child: Strategies for identification, assessment and intervention.* San Francisco: Jossey-Bass.

GARBARINO, J., & SHERMAN, D. (1980). High-risk neighborhoods and high-risk families: The human ecology of child maltreatment. *Child Development, 51,* 188–198.

GARDNER, H. (1980). *Artful scribbles: The significance of children's drawings.* New York: Basic Books.

GARDNER, J. M., KARMEL, B. Z., & DOWD, J. M. (1985). Relationship of infant psychobiological development to infant intervention programs. In M. Frank (Ed.), *Infant intervention programs: Truths and untruths* (pp. 93–108). New York: Haworth.

GARDNER, L. I. (1972, July). Deprivation dwarfism. *Scientific American, 227,* 76–82.

GARRETT, C. S., EIN, P. L., & TREMAINE, L. (1977). The development of gender stereotyping of adult occupations in elementary school children. *Child Development, 48,* 507–512.

GARVEY, C. (1974). Requests and responses in children's speech. *Journal of Child Language, 2,* 41–60.

GARVEY, C. (1977). Play with language and speech. In S. Ervin-Tripp & C. Mitchell-Kernan (Eds.), *Child discourse* (pp. 27–47). New York: Academic Press.

GARWOOD, S. G., PHILLIPS, D., HARTMAN, A., & ZIGLER, E. F. (1989). As the pendulum swings: Federal agency programs for children. *American Psychologist, 44,* 434–440.

GATHERCOLE, V. C. (1987). The contrastive hypothesis for the acquisition of word meaning: A reconsideration of the theory. *Journal of Child Language, 14,* 493–531.

GAUVAIN, M., & ROGOFF, B. (1989). Collaborative problem solving and children's planning skills. *Developmental Psychology, 25,* 139–151.

GECAS, V. (1979). The influence of social class in socialization. In W. Burr, R. Hill, I. Reiss, & F. I. Nye (Eds.), *Comtemporary theories about the family* (Vol. 1, pp. 365–404). New York: Free Press.

GEKOSKI, M. J., ROVEE-COLLIER, C. K., & CARULLI-RABINOWITZ, V. (1983). A longitudinal analysis of inhibition of infant distress: The origins of social expectations? *Infant Behavior and Development, 6,* 339–351.

GELFAND, D. M., HARTMANN, D. P., CROMER, C. C., SMITH, C. L., & PAGE, B. C. (1975). The effects of instructional prompts and praise on children's donation rates. *Child Development, 46,* 980–983.

GELLATLY, A. R. H. (1987). Acquisition of a concept of logical necessity. *Human Development, 30,* 32–47.

GELLES, R. (1978). Violence toward children in the United States. *American Journal of Orthopsychiatry, 48,* 580–592.

GELLES, R. J., & CORNELL, C. P. (1983). International perspectives on child abuse. *Child Abuse & Neglect, 7,* 375–386.

GELMAN, M., & SHATZ, M. (1978). Appropriate speech adjustments: The operation of conversational constraints on talk to two-year-olds. In M. Lewis & L. A. Rosenblum (Eds.), *Interaction, conversation, and the development of language* (pp. 27–61). New York: Wiley.

GELMAN, R. (1972). Logical capacity of very young children: Number invariance rules. *Child Development, 43,* 75–90.

GELMAN, R., & BAILLARGEON, R. (1983). A review of some Piagetian concepts. In J. H. Flavell & E. M. Markman (Eds.), *Handbook of child psychology: Vol. 3. Cognitive development* (4th ed., pp. 167–230). New York: Wiley.

GELMAN, R., & GALLISTEL, C. R. (1986). *The child's understanding of number.* Cambridge, MA: Harvard University Press.

GELMAN, S. A., & EBELING, K. S. (1989). Children's use of nonegocentric standards in judgments of functional size. *Child Development, 60,* 920–932.

GELMAN, S. A., & MARKMAN, E. M. (1987). Young children's inductions from natural common names for unfamiliar objects. *Child Development, 55,* 1535–1540.

GENOVA, W. J., & WALBERG, H. J. (1984). Enhancing integration in urban high schools. In D. E. Bartz & M. L. Maehr (Eds.), *Advances in motivation and achievement* (Vol. 1, pp. 243–283). Greenwich, CT: JAI Press.

GENTNER, D. (1982). Why nouns are learned before verbs: Linguistic relativity versus natural partitioning. In S. A. Kuczaj, II (Ed.), *Lan-*

guage development: Vol. 2. Language, thought, and culture (pp. 301–322). Hillsdale, NJ: Erlbaum.

GENTNER, D., & STUART, P. (1983). Metaphor as structure mapping: What develops? Paper presented at the biennial meeting of the Society for Research in Child Development, Detroit.

GEORGE, C., & MAIN, M. (1979). Social interactions of young abused children: Approach, avoidance and aggression. Child Development, 50, 306–318.

GERBNER, G., GROSS, L., SIGNORIELLI, N., & MORGAN, M. (1986). Television's mean world: Violence Profile No. 14–15. Philadelphia, PA: Annenberg School of Communications, University of Pennsylvania.

GERBNER, G., GROSS, L., SIGNORIELLI, N., MORGAN, M., & JACKSON-BEECK, M. (1979). The demonstration of power: Violence Profile No. 10. Journal of Communications, 29(3), 177–195.

GERKEN, L. A., LANDAU, B., & REMEZ, R. (1990). Function morphemes in young children's speech perception and production. Developmental Psychology, 26, 204–216.

GERSHMAN, E. S., & HAYES, D. S. (1983). Differential stability of reciprocal friendships and unilateral relationships among preschool children. Merrill-Palmer Quarterly, 29, 169–177.

GESELL, A. (1929). Maturation and infant behavior pattern. Psychological Review, 36, 307–319.

GESELL, A. (1933). Maturation and the patterning of behavior. In C. Murchison (Ed.), A handbook of child psychology. Worcester, MA: Clark University Press.

GESELL, A., & ILG, F. L. (1949). The infant and child in the culture of today. In A. Gesell & F. Ilg (Eds.), Child development (pp. 1–393). New York: Harper & Row. (Original work published 1943)

GETZELS, J. W., & JACKSON, P. W. (1962). Creativity and intelligence: Explorations with gifted students. New York: Wiley.

GEWIRTZ, J. (1969). Mechanisms of social learning: some roles of stimulation and behavior in early human development. In D. A. Goslin (Eds.), Handbook of socialization theory and research (pp. 57–212). Skokie, IL: Rand McNally.

GEWIRTZ, J. L., & BOYD, E. F. (1977a). Does maternal responding imply reduced infant crying? A critique of the 1972 Bell and Ainsworth report. Child Development, 48, 1200–1207.

GEWIRTZ, J. L., & BOYD, E. F. (1977b). In reply to the rejoinder to our critique of the 1972 Bell and Ainsworth report. Child Development, 48, 1217–1218.

GIACONIA, R. M., & HEDGES, L. V. (1982). Identifying features of open education. Stanford, CA: Stanford University Press.

GIBBS, J. C., & WIDAMAN, K. F. (1982). Social intelligence: Measuring the development of sociomoral reflection. Englewood Cliffs, NJ: Prentice-Hall.

GIBBS, J. T., & HUANG, L. N. (EDS.). (1989). Children of color. San Francisco: Jossey-Bass.

GIBSON, D., & HARRIS, A. (1988). Aggregated early intervention effects for Down's syndrome persons: Patterning and longevity of benefits. Journal of Mental Deficiency Research, 32, 1–7.

GIBSON, E. J. (1970). The development of perception as an adaptive process. American Scientist, 58, 98–107.

GIBSON, E. J. (1984). Perceptual development from the ecological approach. In M. E. Lamb, A. L. Brown, & B. Russell (Eds.), Advances in developmental psychology (Vol. 3, pp. 243–286). Hillsdale, NJ: Erlbaum.

GIBSON, E., & RADER, N. (1979). Attention: The perceiver as performer. In G. Hale & M. Lewis (Eds.), Attention and cognitive development (pp. 1–21). New York: Plenum.

GIBSON, E. J., SCHAPIRO, F., & YONAS, A. (1968). Confusion matrices for graphic patterns obtained with a latency measure (Final report, Cornell University and U.S. Office of Education Project No. 5-1213, Contract No. OE6-10-156).

GIBSON, E. J., & SPELKE, E. S. (1983). The development of perception. In J. H. Flavell & E. M. Markman (Eds.), Handbook of child psychology: Vol. 3. Cognitive development (4th ed., pp. 1–76). New York: Wiley.

GIBSON, E. J., & WALK, R. D. (1960). The "visual cliff." Scientific American, 202, 64–71.

GIBSON, J. J. (1979). The ecological approach to visual perception. Boston: Houghton-Mifflin.

GIBSON, K. (1977). Brain structure and intelligence. In S. Chevalier-Skolnikoff and F. Porter (Eds.), Primate bio-social development (pp. 113–157). New York: Garland Press.

GIL, D. G. (1987). Maltreatment as a function of the structure of social systems. In M. R. Brassard, R. Germain, & S. N. Hart (Eds.), Psychological maltreatment of children and youth (pp. 159–170). New York: Pergamon Press.

GILBERT, E. H., & DeBLASSIE, R. R. (1984). Anorexia nervosa: Adolescent starvation by choice. Adolescence, 76, 839–846.

GILLIGAN, C. F. (1977). In a different voice: Women's conceptions of self and morality. Harvard Educational Review, 47, 481–517.

GILLIGAN, C. F. (1982). In a different voice. Cambridge, MA: Harvard University Press.

GILLIGAN, C. F., & BELENKY, M. F. (1980). A naturalistic study of abortion decisions. In R. L. Selman & R. Yando (Eds.), New directions for child development (Vol. 7, pp. 69–90). San Francisco: Jossey-Bass.

GINSBURG, H., & OPPER, S. (1979). Piaget's theory of intellectual development (2nd ed.). Englewood Cliffs, NJ: Prentice-Hall.

GLASER, R. (1988). Introduction: Further notes toward a psychology of instruction. In R. Glaser (Ed.), Advances in instructional psychology (Vol. 3, pp. vii–xxv). Hillsdale, NJ: Erlbaum.

GLASS, D. C., KRAKOFF, L. R., CONTRADA, R., HILTON, W. F., KEHOE, K., MANNUCCI, E. G., COLLINS, C., SNOW, B., & ELTING, E. (1980). Effect of harassment and competition upon cardiovascular and plasma catecholamine responses in Type A and Type B individuals. Psychophysiology, 17, 453–463.

GLASS, G. V., CAHEN, L. S., SMITH, M. L., & FILBY, N. N. (1982). School class size. Beverly Hills, CA: Sage.

GLEITMAN, L., NEWPORT, E. L., & GLEITMAN, H. (1984). The current status of the motherese hypothesis. Journal of Child Language, 11, 43–80.

GLICK, P. C., & LIN, S. (1987). Remarriage after divorce: Recent changes and demographic variations. Sociological Perspectives, 30, 162–179.

GNEPP, J. (1983). Children's social sensitivity: Inferring emotions from conflicting cues. Developmental Psychology, 19, 805–814.

GNEPP, J., McKEE, E., & DOMANIC, J. A. (1987). Children's use of situational information to infer emotion: Understanding emotionally equivocal situations. Developmental Psychology, 23, 114–123.

GOELMAN, H. (1986). The language environments of family day care. In S. Kilmer (Ed.), Advances in early education and day care (Vol. 4, pp. 153–179). Greenwich, CT: JAI Press.

GOETZ, E. T., & HALL, R. J. (1984). A critical analysis of the psychometric properties of the K-ABC. Journal of Special Education, 18, 281–296.

GOFFIN, S. G. (1983). A framework for conceptualizing children's services. American Journal of Orthopsychiatry, 53, 282–290.

GOFFIN, S. G. (1988, March). Putting our advocacy efforts into a new context. Young Children, 43(3), 52–56.

GOLD, D., & ANDRES, D. (1978a). Developmental comparisons between 10-year-old children with employed and nonemployed mothers. Child Development, 49, 75–84.

GOLD, D., & ANDRES, D. (1978b). Developmental comparisons between adolescent children with employed and nonemployed mothers. Merrill-Palmer Quarterly, 24, 243–254.

GOLD, D., & ANDRES, D. (1978c). Relations between maternal employment and development of nursery school children. Canadian Journal of Behavioural Science, 10, 116–129.

GOLD, D., ANDRES, D., & GLORIEUX, J. (1979). The development of Francophone nursery school children with employed and nonemployed mothers. Canadian Journal of Behavioural Science, 11, 169–173.

GOLDBERG, S., BRACHFELD, S., & DiVITTO, B. (1980). Feeding, fussing, and play: Parent–infant interaction in the first year as a function of prematurity and perinatal medical problems. In T. M. Field (Ed.), High-risk infants and children (pp. 133–153). New York: Academic Press.

GOLDBERG, W. A., & EASTERBROOKS, M. A. (1988). Maternal employment when children are toddlers and kindergartners. In A. E. Gottfried & A. W. Gottfried (Eds.), *Maternal employment and children's development: Longitudinal research*. New York: Plenum.

GOLBFARB, W. (1945). Effects of psychological deprivation in infancy and subsequent stimulation. *American Journal of Psychiatry, 102,* 18–33.

GOLDFIELD, B. A. (1987). The contributions of child and caregiver to referential and expressive language. *Applied Psycholinguistics, 8,* 267–280.

GOLDFIELD, B. A., & SNOW, C. E. (1989). Individual differences in language acquisition. In J. Berko Gleason (Ed.), *The development of language* (pp. 303–325). Columbus, OH: Merrill.

GOLDFIELD, E. C. (1989). Transition from rocking to crawling: Postural constraints on infant movement. *Developmental Psychology, 25,* 913–919.

GOLDIN-MEADOW, S. (1979). Structure in a manual communication system developed without a conventional language model: Language without a helping hand. In H. Whitaker & H. A. Whitaker (Eds.), *Studies in neurolinguistics* (Vol. 4, pp. 125–209). New York: Academic Press.

GOLDIN-MEADOW, S., & MORFORD, M. (1985). Gesture in early language: Studies of deaf and hearing children. *Merrill-Palmer Quarterly, 31,* 145–176.

GOLDIN-MEADOW, S., & MYLANDER, C. (1983). Gestural communication in deaf children: Noneffect of parental input on language development. *Science, 221,* 372–374.

GOLDIN-MEADOW, S., SELIGMAN, M. E. P., & GELMAN, R. (1976). Language in the two-year-old. *Cognition, 4,* 189–202.

GOLDMAN, P. S., & RAKIC, P. T. (1979). Impact of the outside world upon the developing primate brain. *Bulletin of the Menninger Clinic, 43,* 20–28.

GOLDMAN-RAKIC, P. S. (1987). Development of cortical circuitry and cognitive function. *Child Development, 58,* 601–622.

GOLDSCHMID, M. L., & BENTLER, P. M. (1968). *Manual: Concept Assessment Kit—Conservation.* San Diego, CA: Educational and Industrial Testing Service.

GOLDSMITH, H. H. (1987). Roundtable: What is temperament? Four approaches. *Child Development, 58,* 505–529.

GOLDSMITH, H. H., & ALANSKY, J. A. (1987). Maternal and infant temperamental predictors of attachment: A meta-analytic review. *Journal of Consulting and Clinical Psychology, 55,* 805–816.

GOLDSMITH, H. H., & GOTTESMAN, I. I. (1981). Origins of variation in behavioral style: A longitudinal study of temperament in young twins. *Child Development, 52,* 91–103.

GOLEMAN, D. (1980, February). 1,528 little geniuses and how they grew. *Psychology Today, 13*(9), 28–53.

GOLINKOFF, R. M. (1983). The preverbal negotiation of failed messages: Insights into the transition period. In R. M. Golinkoff (Ed.), *The transition of prelinguistic to linguistic communication* (pp. 57–78). Hillsdale, NJ: Erlbaum.

GOMES-SCHWARTZ, B., HOROWITZ, J. M., & CARDARELLI, A. P. (1990). *Child sexual abuse: Initial effects.* Newbury Park, CA: Sage.

GOOD, T. L., & POWER, C. (1976). Designing successful classroom environments for different types of students. *Journal of Curriculum Studies, 8,* 45–69.

GOOD, T. L., & STIPEK, D. J. (1983). Individual differences in the classroom: A psychological perspective. In G. D. Fenstermacher & J. I. Goodlad (Eds.), *Individual differences and the common curriculum* (82nd yearbook of the National Society for the Study of Education, Part 1, pp. 9–44). Chicago: University of Chicago Press.

GOODENOUGH, F. L. (1931). *Anger in young children.* Minneapolis: University of Minnesota Press.

GOODLAD, J. I. (1984). *A place called school.* New York: McGraw-Hill.

GOODMAN, G. S., AMAN, C., & HIRSCHMAN, J. (1987). Child sexual and physical abuse: Children's testimony. In S. J. Ceci, M. P. Toglia, & D. F. Ross (Eds.), *Children's eyewitness memory* (pp. 1–23). New York: Springer-Verlag.

GOODMAN, J. F. (1979). Is tissue the issue? A critique of SOMPA's models and tests. *School Psychology Digest, 8,* 47–62.

GOODMAN, R. A., & WHITAKER, H. A. (1985). Hemispherectomy: A review (1928–1981) with special reference to the linguistic abilities and disabilities of the residual right hemisphere. In R. A. Goodman & H. A. Whitaker (Eds.), *Hemispheric function and collaboration in the child* (pp. 121–155). New York: Academic Press.

GOPNIK, A., & MELTZOFF, A. N. (1986). Relations between semantic and cognitive development in the one-word stage: The specificity hypothesis. *Child Development, 57,* 1040–1053.

GOPNIK, A., & MELTZOFF, A. N. (1987a). The development of categorization in the second year and its relation to other cognitive and linguistic developments. *Child Development, 58,* 1523–1531.

GOPNIK, A., & MELTZOFF, A. N. (1987b). Language and thought in the young child: Early semantic developments and their relationships to object permanence, means–ends understanding, and categorization. In K. Nelson & A. Van Kleeck (Eds.), *Children's language* (Vol. 6, pp. 191–212). Hillsdale, NJ: Erlbaum.

GORDON, D., COHEN, R. J., KELLY, D., AKSELROD, S., & SHANNON, D. C. (1984). Sudden infant death syndrome: Abnormalities in short term fluctuations in heart rate and respiratory activity. *Pediatric Research, 18,* 921–926.

GORN, G. J., & GOLDBERG, M. E. (1982). Behavioral evidence of the effects of televised food messages on children. *Journal of Consumer Research, 9,* 200–205.

GOTTESMAN, I. I. (1963). Genetic aspects of intelligent behavior. In N. Ellis (Ed.), *Handbook of mental deficiency* (pp. 253–296). New York: McGraw-Hill.

GOTTFRIED, A. E., GOTTFRIED, A. W., & BATHURST, K. (1988). Maternal employment, family environment, and children's development: Infancy through the school years. In A. E. Gottfried & A. W. Gottfried (Eds.), *Maternal employment and children's development: Longitudinal research* (pp. 11–58). New York: Plenum.

GOTTMAN, J. M. (1977). Toward a definition of social isolation in children. *Child Development, 48,* 513–517.

GOTTMAN, J. M., GONSO, J., & RASMUSSEN, B. (1975). Social interaction, social competence, and friendship in children. *Child Development, 46,* 709–718.

GOTTMAN, J. M., & KATZ, L. F. (1989). Effects of marital discord on young children's peer interaction and health. *Developmental Psychology, 25,* 373–381.

GOVE, W. R., & ZEISS, C. (1987). Multiple roles and happiness. In F. Crosby (Ed.), *Spouse, parent, worker* (pp. 125–137). New Haven, CT: Yale University Press.

GOY, R. W., & GOLDFOOT, D. A. (1974). Experiential and hormonal factors influencing development of sexual behavior in the male rhesus monkey. In R. O. Schmitt & F. G. Worden (Eds.), *The neurosciences* (pp. 571–581). Cambridge, MA: MIT Press.

GRAHAM, F. K., ERNHART, C. B., THURSTON, D. L., & CRAFT, M. (1962). Development three years after perinatal anoxia and other potentially damaging newborn experiences. *Psychological Monographs, 76*(3, Whole No. 522).

GRAHAM, F. K., PENNOYER, M. M., CALDWELL, B. M., GREENMAN, M., & HARTMAN, A. F. (1957). Relationship between clinical status and behavior test performance in a newborn group with histories suggesting anoxia. *Journal of Pediatrics, 50,* 177–189.

GRAHAM, P. (1979). Epidemiological studies. In H. C. Quay & J. S. Werry (Eds.), *Psychopathological disorders of childhood* (pp. 185–246). New York: Wiley.

GRAHAM, S., DOUBLEDAY, C., & GUARINO, P. A. (1984). The development of relations between perceived controllability and the emotions of pity, anger, and guilt. *Child Development, 55,* 561–565.

GRANRUD, C. E., & YONAS, A. (1984). Infants' perception of pictorially specified interposition. *Journal of Experimental Child Psychology, 37,* 500–511.

GRANRUD, C. E., YONAS, A., & OPLAND, E. A. (1985). Infants' sensitivity to the depth cue of shading. *Perception and Psychophysics, 37,* 415–419.

GRANT, J. P. (1989). *The state of the world's children.* New York: Oxford University Press.

GRANTHAM-MCGREGOR, S., SCHOFIELD, W., & POWELL, C. (1987). Development of severely malnourished children who received psychosocial stimulation: Six-year follow-up. *Pediatrics, 79,* 247–254.

GRAVES, S. N. (1975). *How to encourage positive racial attitudes.* Paper presented at the biennial meeting of the Society for Research in Child Development, Denver, CO.

GRAY, R., & PIROT, M. (1984). The effects of prosocial modeling on young children's nurturing of a "sick" child. *Psychology and Human Development, 1,* 41–46.

GRAY, S. W., & WANDERSMAN, L. P. (1980). The methodology of home-based intervention studies: Problems and promising strategies. *Child Development, 51,* 993–1009.

GRAY, W. M. (1978). A comparison of Piagetian theory and criterion-referenced measurement. *Review of Educational Research, 48,* 223–250.

GRAY, W. M., & HUDSON, L. M. (1984). Formal operations and the imaginary audience. *Developmental Psychology, 20,* 619–627.

GRAZIANO, W. G., FRENCH, D., BROWNELL, C. A., & HARTUP, W. W. (1976). Peer interaction in same- and mixed-age triads in relation to chronological age and incentive condition. *Child Development, 47,* 707–714.

GRAZIANO, W. G., MOORE, J. S., & COLLINS, J. E., II (1988). Social cognition as segmentation of the stream of behavior. *Developmental Psychology, 24,* 568–573.

GREEN, J. A., GUSTAFSON, G. E., & WEST, M. J. (1980). Effects of infant development on mother–infant interactions. *Child Development, 51,* 199–207.

GREEN, J. A., JONES, L. E., & GUSTAFSON, G. E. (1987). Perception of cries by parents and nonparents: Relation to cry acoustics. *Developmental Psychology, 23,* 370–382.

GREEN, K. D., VOSK, R., FOREHAND, R., & BECK, S. J. (1981). An examination of the differences among sociometrically identified accepted, rejected, and neglected children. *Child Study Journal, 11,* 117–124.

GREEN, R. H., ASRAT, D., MAURS, M., & MORGAN, R. (1989). Children in southern Africa. In United Nations Children's Fund (Ed.), *Children on the front line* (pp. 9–42). New York: United Nations.

GREENBERG, B. S. (1975). British children and televised violence. *Public Opinion Quarterly, 38,* 531–547.

GREENBERG, M., & MORRIS, N. (1974). Engrossment: The newborn's impact upon the father. *American Journal of Orthopsychiatry, 44,* 520–531.

GREENBERGER, E., & GOLDBERG, W. A. (1989). Work, parenting, and the socialization of children. *Developmental Psychology, 25,* 22–35.

GREENBOWE, T., HERRON, J. D., LUCAS, C., NURRENBERN, S., STAVER, J. R., & WARD, C. R. (1981). Teaching preadolescents to act as scientists: Replication and extension of an earlier study. *Journal of Educational Psychology, 73,* 705–711.

GREENFIELD, P. M. (1984). *Mind and media: The effects of television, video games, and computers.* Cambridge, MA: Harvard University Press.

GREENFIELD, P. M., & SMITH, J. H. (1976). *The structure of communication in early language development.* New York: Academic Press.

GREENO, J. G. (1989). A perspective on thinking. *American Psychologist, 44,* 134–141.

GREENOUGH, W. T., BLACK J. E., & WALLACE, C. S. (1987). Experience and brain development. *Child Development, 58,* 539–559.

GREIF, E. B. (1979). *Sex differences in parent–child conversations: Who interrupts who?* Paper presented at the biennial meeting of the Society for Research in Child Development, Boston.

GREIF, E. B., & BERKO GLEASON, J. (1980). Hi, thanks, and goodbye: More routine information. *Language in Society, 9,* 159–166.

GREIF, E. B., & ULMAN, K. (1982). The psychological impact of menarche on early adolescent females: A review. *Child Development, 53,* 1413–1430.

GRIMES, D. A., & MISHELL, D. R., JR. (1988). Congenital limb reduction deformities and oral contraceptives [letter]. *American Journal of Obstetrics and Gynecology, 158,* 439–440.

GRIMES, S. W., & ALLINSMITH, W. (1961). Compulsivity, anxiety, and school achievement. *Merrill-Palmer Quarterly, 7,* 247–271.

GROSSMAN, H. J. (ED.) (1983). *Classification in mental retardation.* Washington, DC: American Association on Mental Deficiency.

GROSSMAN, K., GROSSMANN, K. E., SPANGLER, G., SUESS, G., & UNZNER, L. (1985). Maternal sensitivity and newborns' orientation responses as related to quality of attachment in Northern Germany. In I. Bretherton & E. Waters (Eds.), Growing points of attachment theory and research. *Monographs of the Society for Research in Child Development, 50*(1–2, Serial No. 209).

GROTEVANT, H. D. (1978). Sibling constellations and sex-typing of interests in adolescence. *Child Development, 49,* 540–542.

GROTEVANT, H. D., & COOPER, C. R. (1986). Individuation in family relationships. *Human Development, 29,* 82–100.

GRUEN, G. E., & VORE, D. A. (1972). Development of conservation in normal and retarded children. *Developmental Psychology, 6,* 146–157.

GRUENEICH, R. (1982). Issues in the developmental study of how children use intention and consequence information to make moral evaluations. *Child Development, 53,* 29–43.

GRUSEC, J. E. (1988). *Social development: History, theory, and research.* New York: Springer-Verlag.

GRUSEC, J. E., & ABRAMOVITCH, R. (1982). Imitation of peers and adults in a natural setting: A functional analysis. *Child Development, 53,* 636–642.

GRUSEC, J. E., KUCZYNSKI, L., RUSHTON, J., & SIMUTIS, Z. (1979). Learning resistance to temptation through observation. *Developmental Psychology, 15,* 233–240.

GUARDO, C. J., & BOHAN, J. B. (1971). Development of a sense of self-identity in children. *Child Development, 42,* 1909–1921.

GUIDUBALDI, J., & CLEMINSHAW, H. K. (1985). Divorce, family health and child adjustment. *Family Relations, 34,* 35–41.

GUIDUBALDI, J., & PERRY, J. D. (1985). Divorce and mental health sequelae for children: A two-year follow-up of a nationwide sample. *Journal of the American Academy of Child Psychiatry, 24,* 531–537.

GUILFORD, J. P. (1950). Creativity. *American Psychologist, 4,* 444–454.

GUILFORD, J. P. (1967). *The nature of human intelligence.* New York: McGraw-Hill.

GUILFORD, J. P. (1985). The structure-of-intellect model. In B. B. Wolman (Ed.), *Handbook of intelligence* (pp. 225–266). New York: Wiley.

GUNN, P., & BERRY, P. (1985). Down's syndrome temperament and maternal response to descriptions of child behavior. *Developmental Psychology, 21,* 842–847.

GUNNAR, M., & DONAHUE, M. (1980). Sex differences in social responsiveness between six months and twelve months. *Child Development, 51,* 262–265.

GURUCHARRI, C., & SELMAN, F. L. (1982). The development of interpersonal understanding during childhood, preadolescence, and adolescence: A longitudinal follow-up study. *Child Development, 53,* 924–927.

GUSTAFSON, G. E., & HARRIS, K. L. (1990). Women's responses to young infants' cries. *Developmental Psychology, 26,* 144–152.

HAAKE, R. J., SOMERVILLE, S. C., & WELLMAN, H. M. (1980). Logical ability of young children in searching a large-scale environment. *Child Development, 51,* 1299–1302.

HAAN, N., AERTS, E., & COOPER, B. (1985). *On moral grounds: The search for practical morality.* New York: New York University Press.

HAAN, N., SMITH, M. B., & BLOCK, J. (1968). Moral reasoning of young adults: Political–social behavior, family background, and personality correlates. *Journal of Personality and Social Psychology, 10,* 183–201.

HAGEN, J. W., & HALE, G. A. (1973). The development of attention in children. In A. D. Pick (Ed.), *Minnesota symposium on child psychology* (Vol. 7, pp. 117–140). Minneapolis: University of Minnesota Press.

HAGEN, J. W., HARGROVE, S., & ROSS, W. (1973). Prompting and rehearsal in short-term memory. *Child Development, 44,* 201–204.

HAGEN, J. W., & STANOVICH, K. G. (1977). Memory: Strategies of acquisition. In R. V. Kail & J. W. Hagen (Eds.), *Perspectives on the development of memory and cognition* (pp. 89–111). Hillsdale, NJ: Erlbaum.

HAHN, W. K. (1987). Cerebral lateralization of function: From infancy through childhood. *Psychological Bulletin, 101,* 376–392.

HAINLINE, L. (1985). Oculomotor control in human infants. In R. Groner, G. W. McConkie, & C. Menz (Eds.), *Eye movements and human information processing* (pp. 71–84). Amsterdam: Elsevier.

HAITH, M. M. (1986). Sensory and perceptual processes in early infancy. *Journal of Pediatrics, 109,* 158–171.

HAKUTA, K. (1986). *Mirror of language.* New York: Basic Books.

HAKUTA, K., & GARCIA, E. E. (1989). Bilingualism and education. *American Psychologist, 44,* 374–379.

HALE, J. E. (1982). *Black children: Their roots, culture, and learning styles.* Provo, UT: Brigham Young University Press.

HALFORD, G. S., & BOYLE, F. M. (1985). Do young children understand conservation of number? *Child Development, 56,* 165–176.

HALL, G. S. (1904). *Adolescence* (Vols. 1–2). New York: Appleton-Century-Crofts.

HALL, J. A. (1978). Gender effects in decoding nonverbal cues. *Psychological Bulletin, 85,* 845–857.

HALL, J. A., & HALBERSTADT, A. G. (1980). Masculinity and femininity in children: Development of the Children's Attributes Questionnaire. *Developmental Psychology, 16,* 270–280.

HALL, J. A., & HALBERSTADT, A. G. (1981). Sex roles and nonverbal communication skills. *Sex Roles, 7,* 273–287.

HALL, J. G., SYBERT, V. P., WILLIAMSON, R. A., FISHER, N. L., & REED, S. D. (1982). Turner's syndrome. *West Journal of Medicine, 137,* 32–44.

HALL, W. S. (1989). Reading comprehension. *American Psychologist, 44,* 157–161.

HALLINAN, M. T., & TEIXEIRA, R. A. (1987). Opportunities and constraints: Black–white differences in the formation of interracial friendships. *Child Development, 58,* 1358–1371.

HALPERN, D. F. (1986). *Sex differences in cognitive abilities.* Hillsdale, NJ: Erlbaum.

HALVERSON, H. M. (1931). An experimental study of prehension in infants by means of systematic cinema records. *Genetic Psychology Monographs, 10,* 107–286.

HAMBURG, B. A. (1985). *Comments on the relationship of child development to modern child health care.* Historical selections from the 50th anniversary meeting of the Society for Research in Child Development, Topeka, KS.

HAMILTON, S. F. (1990). *Apprenticeship for adulthood.* New York: The Free Press.

HAMM, C. M. (1977). The content of moral education, or in defense of the "bag of virtues." *School Review, 85,* 218–228.

HARDY-BROWN, K. (1983). Universals and individual differences: Disentangling two approaches to the study of language acquisition. *Developmental Psychology, 19,* 610–624.

HARE, A. P. (1953). Small group discussions with participatory and supervisory leadership. *Journal of Abnormal and Social Psychology, 48,* 273–275.

HAREVEN, T. K. (1984). Themes in the historical development of the family. In R. D. Parke (Ed.), *Review of child development research* (Vol. 7, pp. 137–178). Chicago: University of Chicago Press.

HARLOW, H. F. (1969). Age-mate or peer affectional system. In D. S. Lehrman, R. A. Hinde, & E. Shaw (Eds.), *Advances in the study of behavior* (Vol. 2, pp. 333–383). New York: Academic Press.

HARLOW, H. F., & ZIMMERMAN, R. (1959). Affectional responses in the infant monkey. *Science, 130,* 421–432.

HARMON, R. J., MORGAN, G. A., & KLEIN, R. P. (1977). Determinants of normal variation in infants' negative reactions to unfamiliar adults. *Journal of the American Academy of Child Psychiatry, 16,* 670–683.

HARPER, L. V., & HUIE, K. S. (1985). The effects of prior group experience, age, and familiarity in the quality and organization of preschoolers' social relationships. *Child Development, 56,* 704–717.

HARPER, R. M., LEAKE, B., HOFFMAN, H., WALTER, D. O., HOPPENBROUWERS, T., HODGMAN, J., & STERMAN, M. B. (1981). Periodicity of sleep is altered in infants with sudden infant death syndrome. *Science, 213,* 1030–1032.

HARRELL, R. F., WOODYARD, E., & GATES, A. I. (1955). *The effects of mothers' diets on the intelligence of offspring.* New York: Teachers College.

HARRIS, P. L. (in press). Object permanence in infants. In A. Slater & J. G. Bremner (Eds.), *The psychology of infancy.* Hillsdale, NJ: Erlbaum.

HARRIS, P. L., KRUITHOF, A., TERWOGT, M. M., & VISSER, P. (1981). Children's detection and awareness of textual anomaly. *Journal of Experimental Child Psychology, 31,* 212–230.

HARRIS, S., MUSSEN, P. H., & RUTHERFORD, E. (1976). Some cognitive, behavioral, and personality correlates of maturity of moral judgment. *Journal of Genetic Psychology, 128,* 123–135.

HARRISON, A. O., WILSON, M. N., PINE, C. J., CHAN, S. Q., & BURIEL, R. (1990). Family ecologies of ethnic minority children. *Child Development, 61,* 347–362.

HART, C. H., LADD, G. W., & BURLESON, B. R. (1990). Children's expectations of the outcomes of social strategies: Relations with sociometric status and maternal disciplinary styles. *Child Development, 61,* 127–137.

HART, S. N., & BRASSARD, M. R. (1987). A major threat to children's mental health. *American Psychologist, 42,* 160–165.

HARTER, S. (1981). A new self-report scale of intrinsic versus extrinsic orientation in the classroom: Motivational and informational components. *Developmental Psychology, 17,* 300–312.

HARTER, S. (1982). The perceived competence scale for children. *Child Development, 53,* 87–97.

HARTER, S. (1983). Developmental perspectives on the self-system. In E. M. Hetherington (Ed.), *Handbook of child psychology: Vol. 4. Socialization, personality, and social development* (4th ed., pp. 275–385). New York: Wiley.

HARTER, S. (1990). Issues in the assessment of the self-concept of children and adolescents. In A. LaGreca (Ed.), *Through the eyes of a child* (pp. 292–325). Boston: Allyn and Bacon.

HARTER, S., & BUDDIN, B. J. (1987). Children's understanding of the simultaneity of two emotions: A five-stage developmental acquisition sequence. *Developmental Psychology, 23,* 388–399.

HARTER, S., WRIGHT, K., & BRESNICK, S. (1987). *A developmental sequence of the emergence of self affects: The understanding of pride and shame.* Paper presented at the biennial meeting of the Society for Research in Child Development, Baltimore.

HARTSHORNE, H., & MAY, M. A. (1928). *Studies in the nature of character. Vol. I: Studies in deceit.* New York: Macmillan.

HARTUP, W. W. (1974). Aggression in childhood: Developmental perspectives. *American Psychologist, 29,* 336–341.

HARTUP, W. W. (1983). Peer relations. In E. M. Hetherington (Ed.), *Handbook of child psychology: Vol. 4. Socialization, personality, and social development* (4th ed., pp. 103–196). New York: Wiley.

HARTUP, W. W., GLAZER, J. A., & CHARLESWORTH, K. (1967). Peer reinforcement and sociometric status. *Child Development, 38,* 1017–1024.

HASKINS, R. (1985). Public school aggression among children with varying day care experience. *Child Development, 56,* 689–703.

HASKINS, R. (1989). Beyond metaphor: The efficacy of early childhood education. *American Psychologist, 44,* 274–282.

HATIVA, N. (1988). Computer-based drill and practice in arithmetic: Widening the gap between high- and low-achieving students. *American Educational Research Journal, 25,* 366–397.

HAUGAARD, J. J., & REPPUCCI, N. D. (1988). *The sexual abuse of children.* San Francisco: Jossey-Bass.

HAUSER-CRAM, P., UPSHUR, C. C., KRAUSS, M. W., & SHONKOFF, J. P. (1988). Implications of Public Law 99-457 for early intervention services for infants and toddlers with disabilities. *Social Policy Report of the Society for Research in Child Development, 3*(No. 3).

HAVIGHURST, R. J. (1976). The relative importance of social class and ethnicity in human development. *Human Development, 19,* 56–64.

HAVILAND, J., & LELWICA, M. (1987). The induced affect response: 10-week-old infants' responses to three emotion expressions. *Developmental Psychology, 23,* 97–104.

HAWKE, S., & KNOX, D. (1978). The one-child family: A new life-style. *The Family Coordinator, 27,* 215–219.

HAWKINS, J., PEA, R. D., GLICK, J., & SCRIBNER, S. (1984). "Merds that laugh don't like mushrooms": Evidence for deductive reasoning by preschoolers. *Developmental Psychology, 20,* 584–594.

HAWKINS, J., SHEINGOLD, K., GEARHART, M., & BERGER, C. (1982). Microcomputers in schools: Impact on the social life of elementary school classrooms. *Journal of Applied Developmental Psychology, 3,* 361–373.

HAWKINS, J. D., & LISHNER, D. M. (1987). Schooling and delinquency. In E. H. Johnson (Ed.), *Handbook on crime and delinquency prevention* (pp. 179–221). New York: Greenwood Press.

HAWKINS, R. P., & PINGREE, S. (1978). A developmental exploration of the fear of success phenomenon as cultural stereotype. *Sex Roles, 4,* 539–547.

HAWORTH, J. C., ELLESTAD-SAYED, J. J., KING, J., & DILLING, L. A. (1980). Relation of maternal cigarette smoking, obesity, and energy consumption to infant size. *American Journal of Obstetrics and Gynecology, 138,* 1185–1189.

HAY, D. F. (1984). Social conflict in early childhood. In G. Whitehurst (Ed.), *Annals of child development* (Vol. 1, pp. 1–44). Greenwich, CT: JAI Press.

HAYES, C. D. (1982). *Making policies for children: A study of the federal process.* Washington, DC: National Academy Press.

HAYES, L. A., & WATSON, J. S. (1981). Neonatal imitation: Fact or artifact. *Developmental Psychology, 17,* 655–660.

HAYES, R. M. (1989). Homeless children. In F. J. Macchiarola & A. Gartner (Eds.), *Caring for America's children* (pp. 58–69). New York: The Academy of Political Science.

HAYGHE, H. V. (1990, March). Family members in the work force. *Monthly Labor Review,* Washington, DC: U.S. Government Printing Office.

HAYNES, C. F., CUTLER, C., GRAY, J., O'KEEFE, K., & KEMPE, R. S. (1983). Nonorganic failure to thrive: Implications of placement through analysis of videotaped interactions. *Child Abuse and Neglect, 7,* 321–328.

HAZEN, N. L., & BLACK, B. (1989). Preschool peer communication skills: The role of social status and interaction context. *Child Development, 60,* 867–876.

HEALD, F. P., & HOLLANDER, R. J. (1965). The relationship between obesity in adolescence and early growth. *Journal of Pediatrics, 67,* 35–38.

HEAROLD, S. (1986). A synthesis of 1043 effects of television on social behavior. In G. Comstock (Ed.), *Public communications and behavior* (Vol. 1, pp. 65–133). New York: Academic Press.

HEBB, D. O. (1946). On the nature of fear. *Psychological Review, 53,* 259–276.

HEBB, D. O. (1949). *The organization of behavior.* New York: Wiley.

HEDGES, L. V., GIACONIA, R. M., & GAGE, N. L. (1981). *Meta-analysis of the effects of open and traditional instruction.* Stanford, CA: Stanford University, Program on Teaching Effectiveness.

HEINONEN, O. P., SLONE, D., & SHAPIRO, S. (1977). *Birth defects and drugs in pregnancy.* Littleton, MA: PSG Publishing Company.

HELSON, R., & CRUTCHFIELD, R. S. (1970). Mathematicians: The creative researcher and the average Ph.D. *Journal of Consulting and Clinical Psychology, 34,* 250–257.

HENDRIX, L., & JOHNSON, G. D. (1985). Instrumental and expressive socialization: A false dichotomy. *Sex Roles, 13,* 581–595.

HENTOFF, N. (1989). Anonymous children/diminished adults. In F. J. Macchiarola & A. Gartner (Eds.), *Caring for America's children* (pp. 137–148). New York: The Academy of Political Science.

HERBST, A. L. (1981). Diethylstilbestrol and other sex hormones during pregnancy. *Obstetrics and Gynecology, 58,* 35S–40S.

HERNANDEZ, D. J. (1988). Demographic trends and the living arrangements of children. In E. M. Hetherington & J. D. Arasteh (Eds.), *Impact of divorce, single-parenting, and stepparenting on children* (pp. 3–22). Hillsdale, NJ: Erlbaum.

HERON, A., & KROEGER, E. (1981). Introduction to developmental psychology. In H. C. Triandis & A. Heron (Eds.), *Handbook of cross-cultural psychology: Vol. 4. Developmental psychology* (pp. 1–15). Boston: Allyn & Bacon.

HERRERA, M. G., MORA, J. O., CHRISTIANSEN, N., ORTIZ, N., CLEMENT, J., VUORI, L., WABER, D., DE PAREDES, B., & WAGNER, M. (1980). Effects of nutritional supplementation and early education on physical and cognitive development. In R. R. Turner & H. W. Reese (Eds.), *Lifespan psychology: Intervention* (pp. 149–184). New York: Academic Press.

HERSHENSON, M. (1964). Visual discrimination in the human newborn. *Journal of Comparative and Physiological Psychology, 58,* 270–276.

HERTZ-LAZAROWITZ, R., SHARAN, S., Steinberg, R. (1980). Classroom learning style and cooperative behavior of elementary school children. *Journal of Educational Psychology, 72,* 99–106.

HERZBERGER, S. D., DIX, T., ERLEBACHER, A., GINSBURG, M. (1981). A developmental study of social self-conceptions in adolescence: Impressions and misimpressions. *Merrill-Palmer Quarterly, 27,* 15–29.

HESS, R. D., & MIURA, I. T. (1985). Gender differences in enrollment in computer camps and classes. *Sex Roles, 13,* 193–203.

HESS, R. D., & SHIPMAN, V. C. (1965). Early experience and the socialization of cognitive modes in children. *Child Development, 34,* 869–886.

HETHERINGTON, E. M. (1972). Effects of father absence on personality development in adolescent daughters. *Developmental Psychology, 7,* 313–326.

HETHERINGTON, E. M. (1979). Divorce: A child's perspective. *American Psychologist, 34,* 851–858.

HETHERINGTON, E. M. (1989). Coping with family transitions: Winners, losers, and survivors. *Child Development, 60,* 1–14.

HETHERINGTON, E. M., & ANDERSON, E. R. (1987). The effects of divorce and remarriage on early adolescents and their families. In M. D. Levine & E. R. McArney (Eds.), *Early adolescent transitions* (pp. 49–67). Lexington, MA: Heath.

HETHERINGTON, E. M., COX, M., & COX, R. (1979). Play and social interaction in children following divorce. *Journal of Social Issues, 35,* 26–49.

HETHERINGTON, E. M., COX, M., & COX, R. (1982). Effects of divorce on parents and children. In M. E. Lamb (Ed.), *Nontraditional families: Parenting and child development* (pp. 233–288). Hillsdale, NJ: Erlbaum.

HETHERINGTON, E. M., COX, M., & COX, R. (1985). Long-term effects of divorce and remarriage on the adjustment of children. *Journal of the American Academy of Child Psychiatry, 24,* 518–530.

HETHERINGTON, E. M., STANLEY-HAGAN, M., & ANDERSON, E. R. (1989). Marital transitions: A child's perspective. *American Psychologist, 44,* 303–312.

HIER, D. B., & KAPLAN, J. (1980). Are sex differences in cerebral organization clinically significant? *Behavioral and Brain Sciences, 3,* 215–263.

HIGGINS, A. T., & TURNURE, J. E. (1984). Distractibility and concentration of attention in children's development. *Child Development, 55,* 1799–1810.

HIGGINS, E. T., & PARSONS, J. E. (1983). Social cognition and the social life of the child: Stages as subcultures. In E. T. Higgins, D. N. Ruble, & W. W. Hartup (Eds.), *Social cognition and social development* (pp. 15–62). Cambridge, England: Cambridge University Press.

HILL, J. P. (1988). Adapting to menarche: Family control and conflict. In M. Gunnar (Ed.), *Minnesota Symposia on Child Psychology* (Vol. 21, pp. 43–77). Hillsdale, NJ: Erlbaum.

HILL, R. M. (1973). Drugs ingested by pregnant women. *Clinical Pharmacology and Therapeutics, 14,* 654–659.

HILLMAN, S. B., & DAVENPORT, G. G. (1978). Teacher–student interactions in desegregated schools. *Journal of Educational Psychology, 70,* 545–553.

HINDE, R. A. (1989). Ethological and relationships approaches. In R. Vasta (Ed.), *Annals of child development* (Vol. 6, pp. 251–285). Greenwich, CT: JAI Press.

HINDE, R. A., STEVENSON-HINDE, J., & TAMPLIN, A. (1985). Characteristics of 3- to 4-year-olds assessed at home and their interactions in preschool. *Developmental Psychology, 21,* 130–140.

HINES, M. (1982). Prenatal gonadal hormones and sex differences in human behavior. *Psychological Bulletin, 92,* 56–80.

HIRSCHI, T., & HINDELANG, M. J. (1977). Intelligence and delinquency: A revisionist view. *American Sociological Review, 42,* 571–587.

HIRSH-PASEK, KEMLER NELSON, D. G., JUSCZYK, P. W., CASSIDY, K. W., DRUSS, B., & KENNEDY, L. (1987). Clauses are perceptual units for young infants. *Cognition, 26,* 269–286.

HISCOCK, M., & KINSBOURNE, M. (1987). Specialization of the cerebral hemispheres: Implications for learning. *Journal of Learning Disabilities, 20,* 130–143.

HO, H., GLAHN, T. J., & HO, J. (1988). The fragile-X syndrome. *Developmental Medicine and Child Neurology, 30,* 257–261.

HOBART, C. (1987). Parent–child relations in remarried families. *Journal of Family Issues, 8,* 259–277.

HOBART, C., & BROWN, D. (1988). Effects of prior marriage children on adjustment in remarriages: A Canadian study. *Journal of Comparative Family Studies, 19,* 381–396.

HOCK, E., & DeMEIS, D. (1987). *Depression in mothers of infants: The role of maternal employment.* Paper presented at the biennial meeting of the Society for Research in Child Development, Baltimore.

HODGES, J., & TIZARD, B. (1989). Social and family relationships of ex-institutional adolescents. *Journal of Child Psychology and Psychiatry, 30,* 77–97.

HODGES, R. M., & FRENCH, L. A. (1988). The effect of class and collection labels on cardinality, class-inclusion, and number conservation tasks. *Child Development, 59,* 1387–1396.

HODGKINSON, H. L. (1985). *All one system: Demographics of education, kindergarten through graduate school.* Washington, DC: Institute of Educational Leadership.

HOFFERTH, S. L. (1984). Long-term economic consequences for women of delayed childbearing and reduced family size. *Demography, 21,* 141–155.

HOFFMAN, C. D., & DICK, S. A. (1976). A developmental investigation of recognition memory. *Child Development, 47,* 794–799.

HOFFMAN, L. W. (1974). Effects of maternal employment on the child—A review of the research. *Developmental Psychology, 10,* 204–228.

HOFFMAN, L. W. (1977). Changes in family roles, socialization, and sex differences. *American Psychologist, 32,* 644–657.

HOFFMAN, L. W. (1980). The effects of maternal employment on the academic attitudes and performance of school-aged children. *School Psychology Review, 9,* 319–336.

HOFFMAN, L. W. (1984). Work, family and the socialization of the child. In R. D. Parke (Ed.), *Review of child development research* (Vol. 7, pp. 223–282). Chicago: University of Chicago Press.

HOFFMAN, L. W. (1985). The changing genetics/socialization balance. *Journal of Social Issues, 41,* 127–148.

HOFFMAN, L. W. (1986). Work, family, and the child. In M. S. Pallak & R. O. Perloff (Eds.), *Psychology and work: Productivity, change, and employment* (pp. 173–220). Washington, DC: American Psychological Association.

HOFFMAN, L. W. (1989). Effects of maternal employment in the two-parent family. *American Psychologist, 44,* 283–292.

HOFFMAN, M. L. (1970). Moral development. In P. H. Mussen (Ed.), *Carmichael's manual of child psychology* (Vol. 2, pp. 261–359). New York: Wiley.

HOFFMAN, M. L. (1976). Empathy, role taking, guilt, and development of altruistic motives. In T. Lickona (Ed.), *Moral development and behavior: Theory, research, and social issues* (pp. 124–143). New York: Holt, Rinehart and Winston.

HOFFMAN, M. L. (1980). Moral development in adolescence. In J. Adelson (Ed.), *Handbook of adolescent psychology* (pp. 295–343). New York: Wiley.

HOFFMAN, M. L. (1981). Perspectives on the difference between understanding people and understanding things: The role of affect. In J. H. Flavell & L. Ross (Eds.), *Social cognitive development: Frontiers and possible futures* (pp. 67–81). New York: Cambridge University Press.

HOFFMAN, M. L. (1984). Interaction of affect and cognition in empathy. In C. E. Izard, J. Kagan, & R. B. Zajonc (Eds.), *Emotions, cognition, and behavior* (pp. 103–131). Cambridge, England: Cambridge University Press.

HOFFMAN, M. L. (1988). Moral development. In M. H. Bornstein &

M. E. Lamb (Eds.), *Developmental psychology: An advanced textbook* (2nd ed., pp. 497–548). Hillsdale, NJ: Erlbaum.

HOFFMAN, M. L., & SALTZSTEIN, H. D. (1967). Parent discipline and the child's moral development. *Journal of Personality and Social Psychology, 5,* 45–47.

HOFSTEN, C. VON. (1982). Eye–hand coordination in the newborn. *Developmental Psychology, 18,* 450–461.

HOFSTEN, C. VON. (1984). Developmental changes in the organization of prereaching movements. *Developmental Psychology, 20,* 378–388.

HOFSTEN, C. VON. (1989). Motor development as the development of systems: Comments on the special section. *Developmental Psychology, 25,* 950–953.

HOFSTEN, C. VON, & RÖNNQVIST, L. (1988). Preparation for grasping an object: A developmental study. *Journal of Experimental Psychology: Human Perception and Performance, 14,* 610–621.

HOFSTEN, C. VON, & SPELKE, E. S. (1985). Object perception and object-directed reaching in infancy. *Journal of Experimental Psychology: General, 114,* 198–212.

HOLDEN, C. (1986). Youth suicide: New research focuses on a growing social problem. *Science, 233,* 839–841.

HOLLENBECK, A. R., GEWIRTZ, J. L., & SEBRIS, S. L. (1984). Labor and delivery medication influences parent–infant interaction in the first post-partum month. *Infant Behavior and Development, 7,* 201–209.

HOLLIS, M., LEIS, P., & TURIEL, E. (1986). Social reasoning in Nigerian children and adolescents. *Journal of Cross-Cultural Psychology, 17,* 352–374.

HOLSTEIN, C. B. (1972). The relation of children's moral judgment level to that of their parents and to communication patterns in the family. In R. Smart & M. Smart (Eds.), *Readings in child development and relationships* (pp. 484–494). New York: Macmillan.

HOLSTEIN, C. B. (1976). Irreversible, stepwise sequence in the development of moral judgment: A longitudinal study of males and females. *Child Development, 47,* 51–61.

HONG, K., & TOWNES, B. (1976). Infants' attachment to inanimate objects. *Journal of the American Academy of Child Psychiatry, 15,* 49–61.

HONZIK, M. P. (1967). Environmental correlates of mental growth: Prediction from the family setting at 21 months. *Child Development, 38,* 337–364.

HONZIK, M. P. (1983). Measuring mental abilities in infancy: The value and limitations. In M. Lewis (Ed.), *Origins of intelligence* (2nd ed., pp. 67–105). New York: Plenum.

HONZIK, M. P., MACFARLANE, J. W., & ALLEN, L. (1948). The stability of mental test performance between two and eighteen years. *Journal of Experimental Education, 17,* 309–329.

HOOK, E. B. (1973). Behavioral implications of the human XYY genotype. *Science, 179,* 131–150.

HOOK, E. B. (1980). Genetic counseling dilemmas: Down syndrome, paternal age, and recurrence risk after remarriage. *American Journal of Medical Genetics, 5,* 145.

HOOK, E. B. (1988). Evaluation and projection of rates of chromosome abnormalities in chorionic villus studies (c.v.s.). *American Journal of Human Genetics Supplement, 43,* A108.

HOOPER, F. H., & DeFRAIN, J. D. (1980). On delineating distinctly Piagetian contributions to education. *Genetic Psychology Monographs, 101,* 151–181.

HOPKINS, B., & WESTRA, T. (1988). Maternal handling and motor development: An intracultural study. *Genetic, Social and General Psychology Monographs, 14,* 377–420.

HORGAN, D. (1978). The development of the full passive. *Journal of Child Language, 5,* 65–80.

HORGAN, D. (1980). Nouns: Love 'em or leave 'em. In V. Teller & S. White (Eds.), *Studies in child language and multilingualism* (Annals of the New York Academy of Sciences, Vol. 345, pp. 5–25). New York: New York Academy of Sciences.

HORGAN, D. (1981). Rate of language acquisition and noun emphasis. *Journal of Psycholinguisitic Research, 10,* 629–640.

HORN, J. L. (1985). Remodeling old models of intelligence. In B. B.

Wolman (Ed.), *Handbook of intelligence* (pp. 267–300). New York: Wiley.

HORN, J. L., & KNAPP, J. R. (1974). Thirty wrongs do not make a right: A reply to Guilford. *Psychological Bulletin, 81,* 502–504.

HORN, J. M. (1983). The Texas Adoption Project: Adopted children and their intellectual resemblance to biological and adoptive parents. *Child Development, 54,* 268–275.

HORN, J. M., LOEHLIN, J. C., & WILLERMAN, L. (1979). Intellectual resemblance among adoptive and biological relatives: The Texas Adoption Project. *Behavior Genetics, 9,* 177–201.

HORNER, T. M. (1980). Two methods of studying stranger reactivity in infants: A review. *Journal of Child Psychology and Psychiatry, 21,* 203–219.

HORNIK, R., RISENHOOVER, N., & GUNNAR, M. (1987). The effects of maternal positive, neutral, and negative affective communications on infant responses to new toys. *Child Development, 58,* 937–944.

HOROWITZ, F. D. (1987). *Exploring developmental theories: Toward a structural/behavioral model of development.* Hillsdale, NJ: Erlbaum.

HOROWITZ, F. D., & O'BRIEN, M. (1989a). In the interest of the nation: A reflective essay on the state of our knowledge and the challenges before us. *American Psychologist, 44,* 441–445.

HOROWITZ, F. D., & O'BRIEN, M. (1989b). Children and their development: Knowledge base, research agenda, and social policy application [Introduction to the special issue]. *American Psychologist, 44,* 95.

HORWITZ, R. A. (1979). Psychological effects of the open classroom. *Review of Educational Research, 49,* 71–86.

HOWE, N., & ROSS, H. S. (1990). Socialization, perspective-taking, and the sibling relationship. *Developmental Psychology, 26,* 160–165.

HOWES, C. (1988). Peer interaction of young children. *Monographs of the Society for Research in Child Development, 53*(1, Serial No. 217).

HOWES, C. (1988). Relations between early child care and schooling. *Developmental Psychology, 24,* 53–57.

HOWES, C. (1990). Can the age of entry into child care and the quality of child care predict adjustment in kindergarten? *Developmental Psychology, 26,* 292–303.

HOWES, C., RODNING, C., GALLUZZO, D. C., & MYERS, L. (1988). Attachment and child care: Relationships with mother and caregiver. *Early Childhood Research Quarterly, 3,* 403–416.

HOWES, C., & ELDREDGE, R. (1985). Responses of abused, neglected, and non-maltreated children to the behaviors of their peers. *Journal of Applied Developmental Psychology, 6,* 261–270.

HOWES, C., & OLENICK, M. (1986). Family and child care influences on toddler's compliance. *Child Development, 57,* 202–206.

HOWES, C., & RUBENSTEIN, J. (1985). Determinants of toddlers experience in day care: Age of entry and quality of setting. *Child Care Quarterly, 14,* 140–151.

HOWES, C., & STEWART, P. (1987). Child's play with adults, toys, and peers: An examination of family and child-care influences. *Developmental Psychology, 23,* 423–430.

HOWES, P., & MARKMAN, H. J. (1989). Marital quality and child functioning: A longitudinal investigation. *Child Development, 60,* 1044–1051.

HOY, E. A., BILL, J. M., & SYKES, D. H. (1988). Very low birthweight: A long-term developmental impairment? *International Journal of Behavioral Development, 11,* 37–67.

HOYSETH, K. S., & JONES, P. J. H. (1989). Ethanol induced teratogenesis: Characterization, mechanisms, and diagnostic approaches. *Life Sciences, 44,* 643–649.

HOYT, M. P., & RAVEN, B. H. (1973). Birth order and the 1971 Los Angeles earthquake. *Journal of Personality and Social Psychology, 28,* 123–128.

HUBEL, D. H., & WIESEL, T. N. (1970). The period of susceptibility to the physiological effects of unilateral eye closure in kittens. *Journal of Physiology, 206,* 419–436.

HUBERT, N., WACHS, T. D., PETERS-MARTIN, P., & GANDOUR, M. (1982). The study of early temperament: Measurement and conceptual issues. *Child Development, 53,* 571–600.

HUDSON, J., & NELSON, K. (1983). Effects of script structure on children's story recall. *Developmental Psychology, 19,* 625–635.

HUDSON, J. A. (1988). Children's memory for atypical actions in script-based stories: Evidence for a disruption effect. *Journal of Experimental Child Psychology, 46,* 159–173.

HUESMANN, L. R. (1986a). Commonalities in learning of aggression. In L. R. Huesmann & L. D. Eron (Eds.), *Television and the aggressive child: A cross-national comparison* (pp. 239–257). Hillsdale, NJ: Erlbaum.

HUESMANN, L. R. (1986b). Psychological processes promoting the relation between exposure to media violence and aggressive behavior by the viewer. *Journal of Social Issues, 42,* 125–139.

HUESMANN, L. R., ERON, L. D., LEFKOWITZ, M. M., & WALDER, L. O. (1984). Stability of aggression over time and generations. *Developmental Psychology, 20,* 1120–1134.

HUESMANN, L. R., LAGERSPETZ, K., & ERON, L. D. (1984). Intervening variables in the TV violence-aggression relation: Evidence from two countries. *Developmental Psychology, 20,* 746–775.

HUGHES, C. C., TREMBLAY, M-A., RAPOPORT, R. N., & LEIGHTON, A. H. (1960). *People of cove and woodlot.* New York: Basic Books.

HULME, C., THOMSON, N., MUIR, C., & LAWRENCE, A. (1984). Speech rate and the development of short-term memory span. *Journal of Experimental Child Psychology, 38,* 241–253.

HUMPHREY, T. (1978). Function of the nervous system during prenatal life. In U. Stave (Ed.), *Perinatal physiology* (pp. 651–683). New York: Plenum.

HUMPHREYS, A. P., & SMITH, P. K. (1984). Rough and tumble in preschool and playground. In P. K. Smith (Ed.), *Play in animals and humans* (pp. 241–266). Oxford, England: Basil Blackwell.

HUMPHREYS, A. P., & SMITH P. K. (1987). Rough and tumble, friendship, and dominance in schoolchildren: Evidence for continuity and change with age. *Child Development, 58,* 201–212.

HUMPHREYS, L. G., RICH, S. A., & DAVEY, T. C. (1985). A Piagetian test of general intelligence. *Developmental Psychology, 21,* 871–877.

HUNT, J. McV. (1961). *Intelligence and experience.* New York: Ronald Press.

HUNT, J. McV., MOHANDESSI, K., GHODESSI, M., & AKEYAMA, M. (1976). The psychological development of orphanage-reared infants: Interventions with outcomes (Tehran). *Genetic Psychology Monographs, 94,* 177–226.

HUNTER, F. T., & YOUNISS, J. (1982). Changes in functions of three relations during adolescence. *Developmental Psychology, 18,* 806–811.

HUNTER, J. E., & HUNTER, R. F. (1984). Validity and utility of alternative predictors of job performance. *Psychological Bulletin, 96,* 72–98.

HUNTINGTON, G. S., & SIMEONSSON, R. J. (1987). Down's syndrome and toddler temperament. *Child: Care, health, and development, 13,* 1–11.

HURLEY, J., & PALONEN, D. (1967). Marital satisfaction and child density among university student parents. *Journal of Marriage and the Family, 29,* 483–484.

HUSÉN, T. (1967). *International study of achievement in mathematics: A comparison of twelve countries.* New York: Wiley.

HUSTON, A. C. (1983). Sex-typing. In E. M. Hetherington (Ed.), *Handbook of child psychology: Vol. 4. Socialization, personality, and social development* (4th ed., pp. 387–467). New York: Wiley.

HUSTON, A. C., GREER, D., WRIGHT, J. C. WELCH, R., & ROSS, R. (1984). Children's comprehension of televised formal features with masculine and feminine connotations. *Developmental Psychology, 20,* 707–716.

HUSTON, A. C., WATKINS, B. A., & KUNKEL, D. (1989). Public policy and children's television. *American Psychologist, 44,* 424–433.

HUSTON, A. C., WRIGHT, J. C., RICE, M. L., KERKMAN, D., & ST. PETERS, M. (1990). Development of television viewing patterns in early childhood: A longitudinal investigation. *Developmental Psychology, 26,* 409–420.

HUSTON-STEIN, A., FOX, S., GREER, D., WATKINS, B. A., & WHITAKER, J.

(1981). The effects of TV action and violence on children's social behavior. *Journal of Genetic Psychology, 138,* 183–191.

HUSTON-STEIN, A., & HIGGINS-TRENK, A. (1978). Development of females from childhood through adulthood: Career and feminine role orientations. In P. B. Baltes (Ed.), *Life-span development and behavior* (Vol. 1, pp. 257–296). New York: Academic Press.

HUTCHINGS, D. E., & FIFER, W. P. (1986). Behavioral teratology: A new frontier in neurobehavioral research. In E. M. Johnson & D. M. Kochhar (Eds.), *Handbook of experimental pharmacology: Vol 65. Teratogenesis and reproductive toxicology.* Berlin: Springer-Verlag.

HUTTENLOCHER, J., & LUI, F. (1979). The semantic organization of some simple nouns and verbs. *Journal of Verbal Learning and Verbal Behavior, 18,* 141–162.

HUTTUNEN, M. O., & NISKANEN, P. (1978). Prenatal loss of father and psychiatric disorders. *Archives of General Psychiatry, 35,* 429–431.

HWANG, C. P. (1986). Behavior of Swedish primary and secondary caretaking fathers in relation to mother's presence. *Developmental Psychology, 22,* 749–751.

HWANG, K. (1986). A psychological perspective of Chinese interpersonal morality. In M. H. Bond (Ed.), *The psychology of the Chinese people.* New York: Oxford University Press.

HYDE, J. S. (1984). How large are gender differences in aggression? A developmental meta-analysis. *Developmental Psychology, 20,* 722–736.

HYDE, J. S., FENEMA, E., & LAMON, S. J. (1990). Gender differences in mathematics performance: A meta-analysis. *Psychological Bulletin, 107,* 139–155.

HYDE, J. S., & LINN, M. C. (1988). Gender differences in verbal ability: A meta-analysis. *Psychological Bulletin, 104,* 53–69.

HYMAN, I. A. (1987). Psychological correlates of corporal punishment. In M. R. Brassard, R. Germain, & S. N. Hart (Eds.), *Psychological maltreatment of children and youth* (pp. 59–68). New York: Pergamon Press.

HYMEL, S. (1983). Preschool children's peer relations: Issues in sociometric assessment. *Merrill-Palmer Quarterly, 19,* 237–260.

HYMEL, S., & RUBIN, K. H. (1985). Children with peer relationship and social skills problems: Conceptual, methodological, and developmental issues. In G. J. Whitehurst (Ed.), *Annuals of child development* (Vol. 2, pp. 251–297). Greenwich, CT: JAI Press.

HYMES, J. L., JR. (1990). *The year in review: A look at 1989.* Washington, DC: National Association for the Education of Young Children.

HYSON, M. C., & IZARD, C. E. (1983). Continuities and changes in emotion expressions during brief separations at 13 and 18 months. *Developmental Psychology, 21,* 1165–1170.

IANCO-WORRALL, A. (1972). Bilingualism and cognitive development. *Child Development, 43,* 1390–1400.

IANNOTTI, R. J. (1985). Naturalistic assessment of prosocial behavior in preschool children: The influence of empathy and perspective taking. *Developmental Psychology, 21,* 46–55.

IHINGER-TALLMAN, M., & PASLEY, K. (1987). *Remarriage.* Newbury Park, CA: Sage.

INGRAHAM V. WRIGHT, 430 U.S. 651 (1977).

INGRAM, D. (1986). Phonological development: Production. In P. Fletcher & M. Garman (Eds.), *Language acquisition* (2nd ed., pp. 223–239). Cambridge, England: Cambridge University Press.

INHELDER, B., & PIAGET, J. (1958). *The growth of logical thinking from childhood to adolescence: An essay on the construction of formal operational structures.* New York: Basic Books. (Original work published 1955)

INHELDER, B., SINCLAIR, H., & BOVET, M. (1974). *Learning and the development of cognition.* Cambridge, MA: Harvard University Press.

INOFF-GERMAIN, G., ARNOLD, G. S., NOTTELMAN, E. D., SUSMAN, E. J., CUTLER, G. B. JR., & CROUSOS, G. P. (1988). Relations between hormone levels and observational measures of aggressive behavior of young adolescents in family interactions. *Developmental Psychology, 24,* 129–139.

INOUYE, D. K. (1988). Children's mental health issues. *American Psychologist, 43,* 813–816.

INTERNATIONAL EDUCATION ASSOCIATION (1988). *Science achievement in seventeen countries: A preliminary report.* Oxford, England: Pergamon Press.

IPSA, J. (1981). Peer support among Soviet day care toddlers. *International Journal of Behavioral Development, 4,* 255–269.

IRVINE, J. J. (1986). Teacher–student interactions: Effects of student race, sex, and grade level. *Journal of Educational Psychology, 78,* 14–21.

ISAACS, S. (1933). *Social development in young children: A study of beginnings.* London: Routledge.

ISABELLA, R. A., BELSKY, J., & VON EYE, A. (1989). Origins of infant–mother attachment: An examination of interactional synchrony during the infant's first year. *Developmental Psychology, 25,* 12–21.

ISTOMINA, Z. M. (1975). The development of voluntary memory in preschool-age children. *Soviet Psychology, 13,* 5–64.

IZARD, C. E. (1979). *The maximally discriminative facial movement scoring system.* Unpublished manuscript, University of Delaware.

IZARD, C. E., HEMBREE, E. A., & HUEBNER, R. R. (1987). Infant's emotion expressions to acute pain. *Developmental Psychology, 23,* 105–113.

IZARD, C. E., & MALATESTA, C. Z. (1987). Perspectives on emotional development: I. Differential emotions theory of early emotional development. In J. D. Osofsky (Ed.), *Handbook of infant development* (2nd ed., pp. 494–554). New York: Wiley.

JACKLIN, C. N., & MACCOBY, E. E. (1978). Social behavior at thirty-three months in same-sex and mixed-sex dyads. *Child Development, 49,* 557–569.

JACKLIN, C. N., & MACCOBY, E. E. (1983). Issues of gender differentiation in normal development. In M. D. Levine, W. B. Carey, A. C. Crocker, & R. T. Gross (Eds.), *Developmental-behavioral pediatrics* (pp. 175–184). Philadelphia: Saunders.

JACKSON, P. W. (1968). *Life in classrooms.* New York: Holt, Rinehart and Winston.

JACKSON, P. W., & LAHADERNE, H. M. (1968). Inequalities of teacher–pupil contacts. *Psychology in the Schools, 4,* 201–211.

JACOBSON, J. L., JACOBSON, S. W., FEIN, G., SCHWARTZ, P. M., & DOWLER, J. (1984). Prenatal exposure to an environmental toxin: A test of the multiple effects model. *Developmental Psychology, 20,* 523–532.

JACOBSON, J. L., TIANEN, R. L., WILLE, D. E., & AYTCH, D. M. (1986). Infant-mother attachment and early peer relations: The assessment of behavior in an interactive context. In E. Mueller & C. Cooper (Eds.), *Process and outcome in peer relations* (pp. 57–78). New York: Academic Press.

JACOBSON, J. L., & WILLE, D. E. (1986). The influence of attachment pattern on developmental changes in peer interaction from the toddler to the preschool period. *Child Development, 57,* 338–347.

JACOBSON, S. W., FEIN, G. G., JACOBSON, J. L., SCHWARTZ, P. M., & DOWLER, J. (1985). The effect of intrauterine PCB exposure on visual recognition memory. *Child Development, 56,* 853–860.

JANUS, M., MCCORMACK, A., BURGESS, A., & HARMAN, C. (1987). *Adolescent runaways: Causes and consequences.* Lexington, MA: Lexington Books.

JARVIK, L. F., KLODIN, V., & MATSUYAMA, S. S. (1973). Human aggression and the extra Y chromosome: Fact or fantasy? *American Psychologist, 28,* 674–682.

JEANS, P. C., SMITH, M. B., & STEARNS, G. (1955). Incidence of prematurity in relation to maternal nutrition. *Journal of the American Dietetic Association, 31,* 576–581.

JEFFREY, D. P., MCLELLARN, R. W., & FOX, D. T. (1982). The development of children's eating habits: The role of television commercials. *Health Education Quarterly, 9,* 78–93.

JENCKS, C. (1972). *Inequality: A reassessment of the effect of family and schooling in America.* New York: Basic Books.

JENSEN, A. R. (1969). How much can we boost IQ and scholastic achievement? *Harvard Educational Review, 39,* 1–123.

JENSEN, A. R. (1973). *Educability and group differences.* New York: Harper & Row.

JENSEN, A. R. (1974). Cumulative deficit: A testable hypothesis. *Developmental Psychology, 10,* 996–1019.

JENSEN, A. R. (1977). Cumulative deficit in IQ of blacks in the rural South. *Developmental Psychology, 13,* 184–191.

JENSEN, A. R. (1980). *Bias in mental testing.* New York: Free Press.

JENSEN, A. R. (1985a). Methodological and statistical techniques for the chronometric study of mental abilities. In C. R. Reynolds & V. L. Willson (Eds.), *Methodological and statistical advances in the study of individual difference* (pp. 51–116). New York: Plenum.

JENSEN, A. R. (1985b). The nature of the black-white difference on various psychometric tests: Spearman's hypothesis. *Behavioral and Brain Sciences, 8,* 193–219.

JENSEN, A. R. (1988). Speed of information processing and population differences. In S. H. Irvine & J. W. Berry (Eds.), *Human abilities in cultural context* (pp. 105–145). New York: Cambridge University Press.

JENSEN, A. R., & FIGUEROA, R. A. (1975). Forward and backward digit-span interaction with race and IQ: Predictions from Jensen's theory. *Journal of Educational Psychology, 67,* 882–893.

JOHNSON, D. W., JOHNSON, R. T., & MARUYAMA, G. (1984). Goal interdependence and interpersonal attraction in heterogeneous classrooms: A meta-analysis. In N. Miller & M. B. Brewer (Eds.), *Groups in contact: The psychology of desegregation* (pp. 187–212). New York: Academic Press.

JOHNSON, E. S., & MEADE, A. C. (1987). Developmental patterns of spatial ability: An early sex difference. *Child Development, 58,* 725–740.

JOHNSON, J. E., & HOOPER, F. E. (1982). Piagetian structuralism and learning: Two decades of educational application. *Contemporary Educational Psychology, 7,* 217–237.

JOHNSON, L. G. (1983). Giftedness in preschool: A better time for development than identification. *Roeper Review, 5*(4), 13–15.

JOHNSON, W., EMDE, R. N., PANNABECKER, B., STENBERG, C., & DAVIS, M. (1982). Maternal perception of infant emotion from birth through 18 months. *Infant Behavior and Development, 5,* 313–322.

JOHNSTON, F. E. (1980). The causes of malnutrition. In L. S. Greene & F. E. Johnston (Eds.), *Social and biological predictors of nutritional status, physical growth, and neurological development* (pp. 1–6). New York: Academic Press.

JOHNSTON, J. R., KLINE, M., & TSCHANN, J. M. (1989). Ongoing postdivorce conflict: Effects on children of joint custody and frequent access. *American Journal of Orthopsychiatry, 59,* 576–592.

JOHNSTON, J. R., & SLOBIN, D. I. (1979). The development of locative expressions in English, Italian, Serbo-Croatian, and Turkish. *Journal of Child Language, 16,* 531–547.

JONES, C. P., & ADAMSON, L. B. (1987). Language use in mother-child and mother-child-sibling interactions. *Child Development, 58,* 356–366.

JONES, E. F., FORREST, J. D., GOLDMAN, N., HENSHAW, S. K., LINCOLN, R., ROSOFF, J. I., WESTOFF, C. F., & WULF, D. (1985). Teenage pregnancy in developed countries: Determinants and policy implications. *Family Planning Perspectives, 17,* 53–63.

JONES, K. L., SMITH, D. W., ULLELAND, C. N., & STREISSGUTH, A. P. (1973). Patterns of malformation in offspring of chronic alcoholic mothers. *Lancet, 1,* 1267–1271.

JONES, M. C. (1965). Psychological correlates of somatic development. *Child Development, 36,* 899–911.

JONES, M. C., & BAYLEY, N. (1950). Physical maturing among boys as related to behavior. *Journal of Educational Psychology, 41,* 129–148.

JONES, M. C., & MUSSEN, P. H. (1958). Self-conceptions, motivations, and interpersonal attitudes of early- and late-maturing girls. *Child Development, 29,* 491–501.

JONES, S. S., & RAAG, T. (1989). Smile production in older infants: The importance of a social recipient for the facial signal. *Child Development, 60,* 811–818.

JONES, W. H., & BRIGGS, S. R. (1984). The self–other discrepancy in social shyness. In R. Schwarzer (Ed.), *The self in anxiety, stress, and depression* (pp. 93–108). Amsterdam: North Holland.

JOOS, S. K., POLLITT, K. E., MUELLER, W. H., & ALBRIGHT, D. L. (1983). The Bacon Chow study: Maternal nutritional supplementation and infant behavioral development. *Child Development, 54,* 669–676.

JUPP, M. (1989). The International Year of the Child: Ten years later. In F. J. Macchiarola & A. Gartner (Eds.), *Caring for America's children* (pp. 31–44). New York: The Academy of Political Science.

JUSCZYK, P. W. (1985). On characterizing the development of speech perception. In J. Mehler & R. Fox (Eds.), *Neonate cognition: Beyond the blooming, buzzing confusion* (pp. 199–230). Hillsdale, NJ: Erlbaum.

KAGAN, J. (1964). American longitudinal research on psychological development. *Child Development, 35,* 1–32.

KAGAN, J. (1965). *Matching familiar figures test.* Cambridge, MA: Harvard University.

KAGAN, J. (1971). *Change and continuity in infancy.* New York: Wiley.

KAGAN, J. (1974). Discrepancy, temperament and infant distress. In M. Lewis & L. Rosenblum (Eds.), *The origins of fear* (pp. 229–248). New York: Wiley.

KAGAN, J. (1982). *Psychological research on the human infant: An evaluative summary.* New York: W. T. Grant Foundation.

KAGAN, J. (1988). Temperamental contributions to social behavior. *American Psychologist, 44,* 668–674.

KAGAN, J., KEARSLEY, R. B., & ZELAZO, P. R. (1978). *Infancy: Its place in human development.* Cambridge, MA: Harvard University Press.

KAGAN, J., KLEIN, R. E., FINLEY, G. E., ROGOFF, B., & NOLAN, E. (1979). A cross-cultural study of cognitive development. *Monographs of the Society for Research in Child Development, 44*(5, Serial No. 180).

KAGAN, J., & MESSER, S. B. (1975). A reply to "Some misgivings about the Matching Familiar Figures Test as a measure of reflection–impulsivity." *Developmental Psychology, 11,* 244–248.

KAGAN, J., & MOSS, H. A. (1962). *Birth to maturity.* New York: Wiley.

KAGAN, J., REZNICK, J. S., & GIBBONS, J. (1989). Inhibited and uninhibited types of children. *Child Development, 60,* 838–845.

KAGAN, J. S., REZNICK, J. S., & SNIDMAN, N. (1987). The physiology and psychology of behavioral inhibition in children. *Child Development, 58,* 1459–1473.

KAGAN, S. L. (1989). The care and education of America's young children: At the brink of a paradigm shift? In F. J. Macchiarola & A. Gartner (Eds.), *Caring for America's children* (pp. 70–83). New York: The Academy of Political Science.

KAIL, R. (1990). *The development of memory in children* (3rd ed.). New York: Freeman.

KAITZ, M., MESCHULACH-SARFATY, O., AUERBACH, J., & EIDELMAN, A. (1988). A reexamination of newborns' ability to imitate facial expressions. *Developmental Psychology, 24,* 3–7.

KALTER, N., KLONER, A., SCHREIER, S., & OKLA, K. (1989). Predictors of children's postdivorce adjustment. *American Journal of Orthopsychiatry, 59,* 605–618.

KALTER, N., RIEMER, B., BRICKMAN, A., & CHEN, J. W. (1985). Implications of parental divorce for female development. *Journal of the American Academy of Child Psychiatry, 24,* 538–544.

KAMERMAN, S. B., & KAHN, A. J. (1982). Income transfers, work and the economic well-being of families with children. *International Social Security Review, 35,* 345–382.

KAMERMAN, S. B., & KAHN, A. J. (1989). The possibilities for child and family policy: A cross-national perspective. In F. J. Macchiarola & A. Gartner (Eds.), *Caring for America's children* (pp. 84–98). New York: The Academy of Political Science.

KAMII, C. (ED.) (1990). *Achievement testing in the early grades.* Washington, DC: National Association for the Education of Young Children.

KAMMEYER, K. (1967). Birth order as a research variable. *Social Forces, 46,* 71–80.

KANDEL, D., & LESSER, G. S. (1972). *Youth in two worlds.* San Francisco: Jossey-Bass.

KANDEL, D. B. (1978a). Homophily, selection, and socialization in adolescent friendships. *American Journal of Sociology, 84,* 427–436.

KANDEL, D. B. (1978b). Similarity in real-life adolescent friendship pairs. *Journal of Personality and Social Psychology, 36,* 306–312.

KANT, I. (1952). Fundamental principles of the metaphysics of morals. In C. W. Elliot (Ed.), *The Harvard classics: Vol 32. Literary and philosophical essays* (pp. 305–373). New York: P. F. Collier & Son Corporation. (Original work published 1785)

KANTOR, D., & LEHR, W. (1975). *Inside the family.* San Francisco: Jossey-Bass.

KAPLAN, B. J. (1972). Malnutrition and mental deficiency. *Psychological Bulletin, 78,* 321–334.

KAPLAN, R. M. (1985). The controversy related to the use of psychological tests. In B. B. Wolman (Ed.), *Handbook of intelligence* (pp. 465–504). New York: Wiley.

KAPPEL, B. E., & LAMBERT, R. D. (1972). *Self-worth among the children of working mothers.* Unpublished manuscript, University of Waterloo, Ontario, Canada.

KARMILOFF-SMITH, A. (1979). Language development after five. In P. Fletcher & M. Garman (Ed.), *Language acquisition* (pp. 307–323). New York: Cambridge University Press.

KATO, S., & ISHIKO, T. (1966). Obstructed growth of children's bones due to excessive labor in remote corners. In K. Kato (Ed.), *Proceedings of International Congress of Sports Sciences.* Tokyo: Japanese Union of Sports Sciences.

KAUFMAN, A. S. (1979). *Intelligence testing with the WISC-R.* New York: Wiley.

KAUFMAN, A. S., & KAUFMAN, N. L. (1983a). *Kaufman Assessment Battery for Children: Interpretive manual.* Circle Pines, MN: American Guidance Service.

KAUFMAN, A. S., KAMPHAUS, R. W., & KAUFMAN, N. L. (1985). New directions in intelligence testing: The Kaufman Assessment Battery for Children (K-ABC). In B. B. Wolman (Ed.), *Handbook of intelligence* (pp. 663–698). New York: Wiley.

KAUFMAN, A. S., & KAUFMAN, N. L. (1983b). *Kaufman Assessment Battery for Children: Administration and scoring manual.* Circle Pines, MN: American Guidance Service.

KAUFMANN, F., STUCKI, M., & KAUFMANN-HAYOZ, R. (1985). Development of infants' sensitivity for slow and rapid motions. *Infant Behavior and Development, 8,* 89–98.

KAYE, K., & CHARNEY, R. (1980). How mothers maintain "dialogue" with two-year-olds. In D. Olson (Ed.), *The social foundations of language and thought* (pp. 211–230). New York: Norton.

KAYE, K., ELKIND, L., GOLDBERG, D., & TYTUN, A. (1989). Birth outcomes for infants of drug abusing mothers. *New York State Journal of Medicine, 89,* 256–261.

KAYE, K., & MARCUS, J. (1981). Infant imitation: The sensory-motor agenda. *Developmental Psychology, 17,* 258–265.

KAYE, K., & WELLS, A. J. (1980). Mothers' jiggling and the burst-pause pattern in neonatal feeding. *Infant Behavior and Development, 3,* 29–46.

KAZDIN, A. E. (1987). Treatment of antisocial behavior in children: Current status and future directions. *Psychological Bulletin, 102,* 187–203.

KEARINS, J. M. (1981). Visual spatial memory in Australian aboriginal children of desert regions. *Cognitive Psychology, 13,* 434–460.

KEASEY, C. B. (1971). Social participation as a factor in the moral development of preadolescents. *Developmental Psychology, 5,* 216–220.

KEASEY, C. B. (1977). Young children's attribution of intentionality to themselves and others. *Child Development, 48,* 261–264.

KEATING, D. (1979). Adolescent thinking. In J. Adelson (Ed.), *Handbook of adolescent psychology* (pp. 211–246). New York: Wiley.

KEATING, D. P., & BOBBITT, B. L. (1978). Individual and developmental differences in cognitive-processing components of mental ability. *Child Development, 49,* 155–167.

KEATING, D., & CLARK, L. V. (1980). Development of physical and social reasoning in adolescence. *Developmental Psychology, 16,* 23–30.

KEENEY, T. J., CANIZZO, S. R., & FLAVELL, J. H. (1967). Spontaneous and induced verbal rehearsal in a recall task. *Child Development, 38,* 953–966.

KEIL, F. (1985). Conceptual domains and the acquisition of metaphor. *Cognitive Development, 1,* 73–96.

KELLAM, S. G., ENSMINGER, M. A., & TURNER, J. T. (1977). Family structure and the mental health of children. *Archives of General Psychology, 34,* 1012–1022.

KELLER, A., FORD, L. H., & MEACHAM, J. A. (1978). Dimensions of self-concept in preschool children. *Developmental Psychology, 14,* 483–489.

KELLER, M., & WOOD, P. (1989). Development of friendship reasoning: A study of interindividual differences and intraindividual change. *Developmental Psychology, 25,* 820–826.

KELLMAN, P. J., & SPELKE, E. S. (1983). Perception of partly occluded objects in infancy. *Cognitive Psychology, 15,* 483–524.

KELLMAN, P. J., SPELKE, E. S., & SHORT, K. (1986). Infant perception of object unity from transitory motion in depth and vertical translation. *Child Development, 57,* 72–86.

KELLY, A., & SMAIL, B. (1986). Sex stereotypes and attitudes to science among eleven-year-old children. *British Journal of Educational Psychology, 56,* 158–168.

KELLY, H. (1981). Viewing children through television. In H. Kelly & H. Gardner (Eds.), *New directions for child development* (No. 13, pp. 59–71). San Francisco: Jossey-Bass.

KELMAN, S. (1987). *Making public policy: A hopeful view of American government.* New York: Basic Books.

KEMLER NELSON, D. G., & SMITH, J. D. (1989). Analytic and holistic processing in reflection–impulsivity and cognitive development. In T. Globerson & T. Zelnicker (Eds.), *Cognitive development and cognitive style* (pp. 116–140). Norwood, NJ: Ablex.

KEMPE, C. H., SILVERMAN, B. F., STEELE, P. W., DROEGMUELLER, P. W., & SILVER, H. K. (1962). The battered-child syndrome. *Journal of the American Medical Association, 181,* 17–24.

KEMPE, R. S., & KEMPE, C. H. (1984). *The common secret: Sexual abuse of children and adolescents.* New York: Freeman.

KENDLER, H. H., & KENDLER, T. S. (1962). Vertical and horizontal processes in problem-solving. *Psychological Review, 69,* 1–16.

KENDLER, H. H., & KENDLER, T. S. (1975). From discrimination learning to cognitive development: A neobehaviorist odyssey. In W. K. Estes (Ed.), *Handbook of learning and cognitive processes* (Vol. 1, pp. 191–247). Hillsdale, NJ: Erlbaum.

KENNELL, J., VOOS, D., & KLAUS, M. (1976). Parent–infant bonding. In R. Helfer & C. H. Kempe (Eds.), *Child abuse and neglect: The family and the community* (pp. 25–54). Cambridge, MA: Ballinger.

KENNELL, J. H., VOOS, D. K., & KLAUS, M. H. (1979). Parent–infant bonding. In J. Osofsky (Ed.), *Handbook of infant development* (pp. 786–798). New York: Wiley.

KENNETT, K. F., & CROPLEY, A. J. (1970). Intelligence, family size and socioeconomic status. *Journal of Biosocial Science, 2,* 227–236.

KEOGH, B. (1985). Temperament and schooling: Meaning of "goodness of fit?" In J. V. Lerner & R. M. Lerner (Eds.), *New directions for child development* (No. 31, pp. 89–108). San Francisco: Jossey-Bass.

KESSEN, W. (1967). Sucking and looking: Two organized congenital patterns of behavior in the human newborn. In H. W. Stevenson, E. H. Hess, & H. L. Rheingold (Eds.), *Early behavior: Comparative and developmental approaches* (pp. 147–179). New York: Wiley.

KESSEN, W. (1983). Preface to Volume 1. In W. Kessen (Ed.), *Handbook of child psychology: Vol. 1. History, theory, and methods* (pp. iix–x). New York: Wiley.

KESSEN, W., HAITH, M. M., & SALAPATEK, P. H. (1970). Human infancy: A bibliography and guide. In P. H. Mussen (Ed.), *Carmichael's manual of child psychology* (3rd ed., pp. 287–445). New York: Wiley.

KESSLER, R. C., & McRAE, J. A., JR. (1981). Trends in the relationship between sex and psychological distress: 1957–1976. *American Sociological Review, 46,* 443–452.

KESSLER, R. C., & McRAE, J. A., JR. (1982). The effects of wives' employment on the mental health of married men and women. *American Sociological Review, 47,* 216–227.

KIELMAN, A. A. (1977). Weight fluctuations after immunization in a rural preschool child community. *American Journal of Clinical Nutrition, 30,* 592–598.

KIMBALL, M. M. (1986). Television and sex-role attitudes. In T. M. Williams (Ed.), *The impact of television* (pp. 265–301). New York: Academic Press.

KINARD, E. M., & KLERMAN, L. V. (1983). Effects of early parenthood on the cognitive development of children. In E. R. McAnarney (Ed.), *Premature adolescent pregnancy and parenthood* (pp. 253–266). New York: Grune & Stratton.

KING, T., & FULLARD, W. (1982). Teenage mothers and their infants: New findings on the home environment. *Journal of Adolescence, 5,* 333–346.

KINGMA, J. (1987). Training of seriation in young kindergartners. *Journal of Genetic Psychology, 148,* 167–181.

KINSMAN, C. A., & BERK, L. E. (1979). Joining the block and housekeeping areas: Changes in play and social behavior. *Young Children, 35,* 66–75.

KISER, L. J., BATES, J. E., MASLIN, C. A., & BAYLES, K. (1986). Mother–infant play at six months as a predictor of attachment security at thirteen months. *Journal of the American Academy of Child Psychiatry, 25,* 68–75.

KISILEVSKY, B. S., & MUIR, W. (1984). Neonatal habituation and dishabituation to tactile stimulation during sleep. *Developmental Psychology, 20,* 367–373.

KLAHR, D. (1989). Information-processing approaches. In R. Vasta (Ed.), *Annals of child development* (Vol. 6, pp. 133–185). Greenwich, CT: JAI Press.

KLAHR, D., & WALLACE, J. G. (1976). *Cognitive development: An information processing view.* Hillsdale, NJ: Erlbaum.

KLATZKY, R. L. (1984). *Memory and awareness: An information processing perspective.* New York: Freeman.

KLEINER, K. A., & BANKS, M. S. (1987). Stimulus energy does not account for 2-month-olds' face preferences. *Journal of Experimental Psychology: Human Perception and Performance, 13,* 594–600.

KLEINKE, C. L., & NICHOLSON, T. A. (1979). Black and white children's awareness of de facto race and sex differences. *Developmental Psychology, 15,* 84–86.

KLINE, M., TSCHANN, J. M., JOHNSTON, J. R., & WALLERSTEIN, J. S. (1989). Children's adjustment in joint and sole physical custody families. *Developmental Psychology, 25,* 430–438.

KLINNERT, M., SORCE, J., EMDE, R. N., STENBERG, C., & GAENSBAUER, T. J. (1984). Continuities and change in early affective life: Maternal perceptions of surprise, fear, and anger. In R. N. Emde & R. J. Harmon (Eds.), *Continuities and discontinuities in development* (pp. 339–354). New York: Plenum.

KNITTLE, J. L. (1972). Obesity in childhood: A problem of adipose tissue cellular development. *Pediatrics, 81,* 1048.

KNOBLOCH, H., & PASAMANICK, B. (EDS.). (1974). *Gesell and Amatruda's Developmental Diagnosis.* Hagerstown, MD: Harper & Row.

KNOBLOCH, H., STEVENS, F., & MALONE, A. (1980). *A manual for Developmental Diagnosis.* New York: Harper & Row.

KOCHANSKA, G., KUCZYNSKI, L., & RADKE-YARROW, M. (1989). Correspondence between mothers' self-reported and observed child-rearing practices. *Child Development, 60,* 56–63.

KODROFF, J. K., & ROBERGE, J. J. (1975). Developmental analysis of the conditional reasoning abilities of primary-grade children. *Developmental Psychology, 11,* 21–28.

KOEK, K. E., & MARTIN, S. B. (EDS.). (1988). *Encyclopedia of associations* (2nd ed.). Detroit: Gale Research Company.

KOFF, E., RIERDAN, J., & SHEINGOLD, K. (1982). Memories of menarche: Age, preparation, and prior knowledge as determinants of initial menstrual experience. *Journal of Youth and Adolescence, 11,* 1–9.

KOGAN, N. (1983). Stylistic variation in childhood and adolescence: Creativity, metaphor, and cognitive style. In J. H. Flavell, & E. M. Markman (Eds.), *Handbook of child psychology: Vol. 3. Cognitive development* (pp. 630–708). New York: Wiley.

KOHLBERG, L. (1966). A cognitive-developmental analysis of children's sex-role concepts and attitudes. In E. E. Maccoby (Ed.), *The development of sex differences* (pp. 82–173). Stanford, CA: Stanford University Press.

KOHLBERG, L. (1969). Stage and sequence: The cognitive-developmental approach to socialization. In D. A. Goslin (Ed.), *Handbook of socialization theory and research* (pp. 347–480). Chicago: Rand McNally.

KOHLBERG, L. (1976). Moral stages and moralization: The cognitive-developmental point of view. In T. Lickona (Ed.), *Moral development and behavior: Theory, research, and social issues* (pp. 31–53). New York: Holt.

KOHLBERG, L. (1978). Revisions in the theory and practice of moral development. In W. Damon (Ed.), *New directions for child development* (No. 2, pp. 83–87). San Francisco: Jossey-Bass.

KOHLBERG, L. (1980). High school democracy and educating for a just society. In R. L. Mosher (Ed.), *Moral education* (pp. 20–57). New York: Praeger.

KOHLBERG, L. (1984). *Essays on moral development. Vol. 2: The psychology of moral development.* San Francisco: Harper & Row.

KOHLBERG, L., LEVINE, C., & HEWER, A. (1983). *Moral stages: A current formulation and a response to critics.* Basel, Switzerland: Karger.

KOHLBERG, L., YAEGER, J., & HJERTHOLM, E. (1968). Private speech: Four studies and a review of theories. *Child Development, 39,* 691–736.

KOHN, B., & DENNIS, M. (1974). Selective impairments of visuo-spatial abilities in infantile hemiplegics after right cerebral hemidecortication. *Neuropsychologia, 12,* 505–512.

KOHN, M. L. (1977). *Class and conformity: A study in values* (rev. ed.). Chicago: University of Chicago Press.

KOHN, M. L. (1979). The effects of social class on parental values and practices. In D. Reiss & H. A. Hoffman (Eds.), *The American family: Dying or developing* (pp. 45–68). New York: Plenum.

KOLATA, G. B. (1989, May 14). Operating on the unborn. *The New York Times Magazine,* pp. 34–35, 46–48.

KOLUCHOVA, J. (1972). Severe deprivation in twins: A case study. *Journal of Child Psychology and Psychiatry, 13,* 107–114.

KONEYA, M. (1976). Location and interaction in row-and-column seating arrangements. *Environment and Behavior, 8,* 265–282.

KONNER, M. J. (1972). Aspects of the developmental ethology of a foraging people. In N. Blurton Jones (Ed.), *Ethological studies of child behaviour* (pp. 285–304). Cambridge, England: Cambridge University Press.

KOOCHER, G. (1981). Children's conceptions of death. In R. Bibace & M. E. Walsh (Eds.), *New directions for child development* (No. 14, pp. 85–99). San Francisco: Jossey-Bass.

KOPP, C. (1983). Risk factors in development. In M. M. Haith & J. J. Campos (Eds.), *Handbook of child psychology: Vol. 2. Infancy and developmental psychobiology* (pp. 1081–1188). New York: Wiley.

KOPP, C., & KALER, S. R. (1989). Risk in infancy. *American Psychologist, 44,* 224–230.

KOPP, C. B. (1982). Antecedents of self-regulation: A developmental perspective. *Developmental Psychology, 18,* 199–214.

KOPP, C. B. (1987). The growth of self-regulation: Caregivers and children. In N. Eisenberg (Ed.), *Contemporary topics in developmental psychology* (pp. 34–55). New York: Wiley.

KOPP, C. B. (1989). Regulation of distress and negative emotions: A developmental view. *Developmental Psychology, 25,* 343–354.

KORNER, A. F. (1987). Infant stimulation: Issues of theory and research. In N. Gunzenhauser (Ed.), *Infant stimulation: For whom, what kind, when, and how much?* (pp. 88–97). New York: Johnson & Johnson.

KORNER, A. F., HUTCHINSON, C. A., KOPERSKI, J. A., KRAEMER, H. C., & SCHNEIDER, P. A. (1981). Stability of individual differences of neonatal motor and crying pattern. *Child Development, 52,* 83–90.

KOTELCHUK, M. (1976). The infant's relationship to the father: Experimental evidence. In M. E. Lamb (Ed.), *The role of the father in child development* (pp. 329–344). New York: Wiley.

KRAMER, M. S., BARR, R. G., LEDUC, D. G., BIOSJOLY, C., & PLESS, I. B. (1985). Infant determinants of childhood weight and adiposity. *Journal of Pediatrics, 107,* 104–107.

R-33

KRANTZ, M., & BURTON, C. (1986). The development of the social cognition of social status. *Journal of Genetic Psychology, 147,* 89–95.

KREBS, D., & GILLMORE, J. (1982). The relationship among the first stages of cognitive development, role-taking abilities, and moral development. *Child Development, 53,* 877–886.

KREHBIEL, G., & MILICH, R. (1986). Issues in the assessment and treatment of socially rejected children. In R. J. Prinz (Ed.), *Advances in behavioral assessment of children and families* (pp. 249–270). Greenwood, CT: JAI Press.

KREMENITZER, J. P., VAUGHAN, H. G., KURTZBERG, D., & DOWLING, K. (1979). Smooth-pursuit eye movements in the newborn infant. *Child Development, 50,* 441–448.

KREUTZER, M. A., LEONARD, C., & FLAVELL, J. H. (1975). An interview study of children's knowledge about memory. *Monographs of the Society for Research in Child Development, 40*(1, Serial No. 159).

KRICKER, A., ELLIOTT, J. W., FORREST, J. M., & MCCREDIE, J. (1986). Congenital limb reduction deformities and use of oral contraceptives. *American Journal of Obstetrics and Gynecology, 155,* 1072–1078.

KROLL, J. (1977). The concept of childhood in the Middle Ages. *Journal of the History of the Behavioral Sciences, 13,* 384–393.

KUCZAJ, S. A., II. (1977a). The acquisition of regular and irregular past tense forms. *Journal of Verbal Learning and Verbal Behavior, 16,* 589–600.

KUCZAJ, S. A., II. (1977b). *Old and new forms, old and new meanings: The form–function hypothesis revisited.* Paper presented at the biennial meeting of the Society for Research in Child Development, New Orleans.

KUCZAJ, S. A., II. (1979). Evidence for a language learning strategy: On the relative ease of acquisition of prefixes and suffixes. *Child Development, 50,* 1–13.

KUCZAJ, S. A., II. (1986). Thoughts on the intentional basis of early object word extension: Evidence from comprehension and production. In S. A. Kuczaj, II, & M. D. Barrett (Eds.), *The development of word meaning* (pp. 99–120). New York: Springer-Verlag.

KUCZYNSKI, L., & KOCHANSKA, G. (1990). Development of children's noncompliance strategies from toddlerhood to age 5. *Developmental Psychology, 26,* 398–408.

KUCZYNSKI, L., KOCHANSKA, G., RADKE-YARROW, M., & GIRNIUS-BROWN, O. (1987). A developmental interpretation of young children's noncompliance. *Developmental Psychology, 23,* 799–806.

KUCZYNSKI, L., ZAHN-WAXLER, C., & RADKE-YARROW, M. R. (1987). Development and content of imitation in the second and third year of life: A socialization perspective. *Developmental Psychology, 23,* 276–282.

KUHN, D. (1979). The significance of Piaget's formal operations stage in education. *Journal of Education, 161,* 34–50.

KUHN, D. (1988). Cognitive development. In M. H. Bornstein & M. E. Lamb (Eds.), *Developmental psychology: An advanced textbook* (2nd ed., pp. 205–260). Hillsdale, NJ: Erlbaum.

KUHN, D., HO, V., & ADAMS, C. (1979). Formal reasoning among pre- and late adolescents. *Child Development, 50,* 1128–1135.

KUHN, D., NASH, S. C., & BRUCKEN, L. (1978). Sex role concepts of two- and three-year olds. *Child Development, 49,* 445–451.

KULIK, J. A. (1986). Evaluating the effects of teaching with computers. In P. F. Campbell & G. G. Fein (Eds.), *Young children and microcomputers* (pp. 159–169). Englewood Cliffs, NJ: Prentice-Hall.

KULL, J. A. (1986). Learning and Logo. In P. F. Campbell & G. G. Fein (Eds.), *Young children and microcomputers* (pp. 103–128). Englewood Cliffs, NJ: Prentice-Hall.

KUN, A. (1977). Development of the magnitude-covariation and compensation schemata in ability and effort attributions of performance. *Child Development, 48,* 862–872.

KUNZINGER, E. L., III (1985). A short-term longitudinal study of memorial development during early grade school. *Developmental Psychology, 21,* 642–646.

KURDEK, L. A. (1978). Relationship between cognitive perspective-taking and teachers' ratings of children's classroom behavior in grades one through four. *Journal of Genetic Psychology, 132,* 21–27.

KURDEK, L. A. (1980). Developmental relations among children's perspective-taking, moral judgment, and parent-rated behavior. *Merrill-Palmer Quarterly, 26,* 103–121.

LA BARRE, W. (1954). *The human animal.* Chicago: University of Chicago Press.

LA FRENIERE, P., STRAYER, F. F., & GAUTHIER, R. (1984). The emergence of same-sex affiliative preferences among preschool peers: A developmental/ethological perspective. *Child Development, 55,* 1958–1965.

LABORATORY OF COMPARATIVE HUMAN COGNITION (1983). Culture and cognitive development. In W. Kessen (Ed.), *Handbook of child psychology: Vol. 1. History, theory, and methods* (pp. 295–356). New York: Wiley.

LADD, G. W. (1981). Effectiveness of a social learning method for enhancing children's social interaction and peer acceptance. *Child Development, 52,* 171–178.

LADD, G. W., & MIZE, J. (1983). A cognitive–social learning model of social-skill training. *Psychological Review, 90,* 127–157.

LADD, G. W., & PRICE, J. M. (1987). Predicting children's social and school adjustment following the transition from preschool to kindergarten. *Child Development, 58,* 1168–1189.

LAGERCRANTZ, H., & SLOTKIN, T. A. (1986). The "stress" of being born. *Scientific American, 254,* 100–107.

LAMAZE, F. (1958). *Painless childbirth.* London: Burke.

LAMB, M. E. (1976). Interaction between eight-month-old children and their fathers and mothers. In M. E. Lamb (Ed.), *The role of the father in child development* (pp. 307–327). New York: Wiley.

LAMB, M. E. (1977). The development of parental preferences in the first two years of life. *Sex Roles, 3,* 445–451.

LAMB, M. E., THOMPSON, R. A., GARDNER, W., CHARNOV, E. L., & CONNELL, J. P. (1985). *Infant–mother attachment: The origins and developmental significance of individual differences in Strange Situation behavior.* Hillsdale, NJ: Erlbaum.

LAMB, M. E., THOMPSON, R. A., GARDNER, W., CHARNOV, E. L., & ESTES, C. (1984). Security of attachment as assessed in the Strange Situation: Its study and biological interpretation. *Behavioral and Brain Sciences, 7,* 127–147.

LAMPHEAR, V. S. (1985). The impact of maltreatment of children's psychosocial adjustment: A review of the research. *Child Abuse & Neglect, 9,* 251–263.

LANCASTER, J. B., WHITTEN, P. (1980). Family matters. *The Sciences, 20,* 10–15.

LANDAU, R. (1982). Infant crying and fussing. *Journal of Cross-Cultural Psychology, 13,* 427–443.

LANDAU, S., MILICH, R., & LORCH, E. P. (in press). Visual attention to and comprehension of television in attention-deficit hyperactivity disordered and normal boys. *Child Development.*

LANDESMAN, S., & RAMEY, C. (1989). Developmental psychology and mental retardation: Integrating scientific principles with treatment practices. *American Psychologist, 44,* 409–415.

LANDSBAUM, J. B., & WILLIS, R. H. (1971). Conformity in early and late adolescence. *Developmental Psychology, 4,* 334–337.

LANE, D. M., & PEARSON, D. A. (1982). The development of selective attention. *Merrill-Palmer Quarterly, 28,* 317–337.

LANGLOIS, J. H., & DOWNS, A. C. (1979). Peer relations as a function of physical attractiveness: The eye of the beholder or behavioral reality? *Child Development, 50,* 409–418.

LANGLOIS, J. H., & DOWNS, A. C. (1980). Mothers, fathers, and peers as socialization agents of sex-typed play behaviors in young children. *Child Development, 51,* 1237–1247.

LANGLOIS, J. H., ROGGMAN, L. A., CASEY, R. J., RITTER, J. M., REISER-DANNER, L. A., & JENKINS, V. Y. (1987). Infant preferences for attractive faces: Rudiments of a stereotype? *Developmental Psychology, 23,* 363–369.

LANGLOIS, J. H., ROGGMAN, L. A., & REISSER-DANNER, L. A. (1990). Infants' differential social responses to attractive and unattractive faces. *Developmental Psychology, 26,* 153–159.

LANGLOIS, J. H., & STEPHAN, C. W. (1981). Beauty and the beast: The role of physical attraction in peer relationships and social behavior. In S. S. Brehm, S. M. Kassin, & S. X. Gibbons (Eds), *Developmental social psychology: Theory and research* (pp. 152–168). New York: Oxford University Press.

LANGLOIS, J. H., & STYCZYNSKI, L. E. (1979). The effects of physical attractiveness on the behavioral attributions and peer preferences of acquainted children. *International Journal of Behavioral Development, 2,* 325–342.

LAOSA, L. M. (1981). Maternal behavior. Sociocultural diversity in modes of family interaction. In R. W. Henderson (Ed.), *Parent–child interaction: Theory, research, and prospects* (pp. 125–167). New York: Academic Press.

LAPSLEY, D. K. (1985). Elkind on egocentrism. *Developmental Review, 5,* 227–236.

LAPSLEY, D. K., ENRIGHT, R. D., & SERLIN, R. C. (1989). Moral and social education. In J. Worell & F. Danner (Eds), *The adolescent as decision-maker. Applications to development and education* (pp. 111–141). New York: Academic Press.

LAPSLEY, D. K., MILSTEAD, M., QUINTANA, S. M., FLANNERY, D., & BUSS, R. R. (1986). Adolescent egocentrism and formal operations: Tests of a theoretical assumption. *Developmental Psychology, 22,* 800–807.

LAWLER, K. A., ALLEN, M. T., CRITCHER, E. C., & STANDARD, B. A. (1981). The relationship of physiological responses to the coronary-prone behavior pattern in children. *Journal of Behavioral Medicine, 4,* 203–216.

LAWRENCE, R. A. (1983). Early mothering by adolescents. In E. R. McAnarney (Ed.), *Premature adolescent pregnancy and parenthood* (pp. 207–218). New York: Grune & Stratton.

LAWRENCE, R. A., McANARNEY, E. R., ATEN, M. J., IKER, H. P., BALDWIN, C. P., & BALDWIN, A. L. (1981). Aggressive behaviors in young mothers: Markers of future morbidity? *Pediatric Research, 15,* 443.

LAZAR, I., & DARLINGTON, R. (1982). Lasting effects of early education: A report from the Consortium for Longitudinal Studies. *Monographs of the Society for Research in Child Development, 47*(2–3, Serial No. 195).

LEAHY, R. L., & EITER, M. (1980). Moral judgment and the development of real and ideal androgynous self-image during adolescence and young adulthood. *Developmental Psychology, 16,* 362–370.

LEDERBERG, A. R., CHAPIN, S. L., ROSENBLATT, V., & VANDELL, D. L. (1986). Ethnic, gender, and age preferences among deaf and hearing preschool peers. *Child Development, 57,* 375–386.

LEE, C. L., & BATES, J. E. (1985). Mother–child interaction at age two years and perceived difficult temperament. *Child Development, 56,* 1314–1325.

LEE, D. N., & ARONSON, E. (1974). Visual proprioceptive control of standing in human infants. *Perception and Psychophysics, 15,* 529–532.

LEE, M., & PRENTICE, N. M. (1988). Interrelations of empathy, cognition, and moral reasoning with dimensions of juvenile delinquency. *Journal of Abnormal Child Psychology, 16,* 127–139.

LEE, N. N. Y., CHAN, Y. F., DAVIES, D. P., LAU, E., & YIP, D. C. P. (1989). Sudden infant death syndrome in Hong Kong: Confirmation of low incidence. *British Medical Journal, 298,* 721.

LEE, V. E., BROOKS-GUNN, J., & SCHNUR, E. (1988). Does Head Start work: A 1-year follow-up comparison of disadvantaged children attending Head Start, no preschool, and other preschool programs. *Developmental Psychology, 24,* 210–222.

LEETSMA, R., AUGUST, R. L., GEORGE, B., & PEAK, L. (1987). *Japanese education today: A report from the U.S. Study of Education in Japan.* Washington, DC: U.S. Government Printing Office.

LEFKOWITZ, M. M., ERON, L. D., WALDER, L. O., & HUESMANN, L. R. (1972). Television violence and child aggression: A follow-up study. In G. A. Cornstock & E. A. Rubinstein (Eds.), *Television and social behavior* (Vol. 3, pp. 35–135). Washington, DC: U.S. Government Printing Office.

LEGENDRE-BERGERON, M. F., & LAVEAULT, D. (1983). Is formal thought the final stage of cognitive development: An internal criticism of Piagetian theory. *Genetic Epistemologist, 11,* 15–20.

LEITER, M. P. (1977). A study of reciprocity in preschool play groups. *Child Development, 48,* 1288–1295.

LEMARE, L. J., & RUBIN, K. H. (1987). Perspective taking and peer interaction: Structural and developmental analyses. *Child Development, 58,* 306–315.

LEMING, J. (1978). Intrapersonal variations in stage of moral reasoning among adolescents as a function of situational context. *Journal of Youth and Adolescence, 7,* 405–416.

LEMPERERS, J. D., FLAVELL, E. R., & FLAVELL, J. H. (1977). The development in very young children of tacit knowledge concerning visual perception. *Genetic Psychology Monographs, 95,* 3–53.

LEMPERT, H. (1989). Animacy constraints on preschoolers' acquisition of syntax. *Child Development, 60,* 237–245.

LENNEBERG, E. H. (1967). *Biological foundations of language.* New York: Wiley.

LENNEBERG, E. H., REBELSKY, F. G., & NICHOLS, I. A. (1965). The vocalizations of infants born to deaf and hearing parents. *Human Development, 8,* 23–37.

LENNON, R. T. (1985). Group tests of intelligence. In B. B. Wolman (Ed.), *Handbook of intelligence* (pp. 825–845). New York: Wiley.

LEON, G. R., LUCAS, A. R., COLLIGAN, R. C., FERDINANCE, R. J., & KAMP, J. (1985). Sexual, body-image, and personality attitudes in anorexia nervosa. *Journal of Abnormal Child Psychology, 13,* 245–258.

LEONARD, M. F., RHYMES, J. P., & SOLNIT, A. J. (1986). Failure to thrive in infants: A family problem. *American Journal of Diseases of Children, 111,* 600–612.

LEPPER, M. R. (1985). Microcomputers in education: Motivational and social issues. *American Psychologist, 40,* 1–18.

LERNER, R. M. (1985). Adolescent maturational changes and psychosocial development: A dynamic interactional perspective. *Journal of Youth and Adolescence, 14,* 355–372.

LERNER, R. M. (1986). *Concepts and theories of human development* (2nd ed.). New York: Random House.

LERNER, R. M., & BRACKNEY, B. (1978). The importance of inner and outer body parts attitudes in the self-concept of late adolescents. *Sex Roles, 4,* 225–238.

LERNER, R. M., KARABENICK, S. A., & MEISELS, M. (1975). Effects of age and sex on the development of personal space schemata towards body build. *Journal of Genetic Psychology, 127,* 151–152.

LERNER, R. M., & KORN, S. J. (1972). The development of body build stereotypes in males. *Child Development, 43,* 908–920.

LERNER, R. M., & LERNER, J. V. (1986). Contextualism and the study of child effects in development. In R. L. Rosnow & M. Georgoudi (Eds.), *Contextualism and understanding in behavioral science* (pp. 89–104). New York: Praeger.

LERNER, R. M., PALERMO, M., SPIRO, A., & NESSELROADE, J. (1982). Assessing the dimensions of temperamental individuality across the life-span: The Dimension of Temperament Survey (DOTS). *Child Development, 53,* 149–160.

LERNER, R. M., & SCHROEDER, C. (1971). Physique Identification, preference, and aversion in kindergarten children. *Developmental Psychology, 5,* 538.

LERNER, R. M., SPANIER, G. B., & BELSKY, J. (1982). The child in the family. In C. B. Kopp & J. B. Krakow (Eds.), *The child: Development in a social context* (pp. 393–455). Reading, MA: Addison-Wesley.

LERNER, R. M., VENNING, J., & KNAPP, J. R. (1975). Age and sex effects on personal space schemata towards body build in late childhood. *Developmental Psychology, 11,* 855–856.

LESSER, G. S., FIFER, G., & CLARK, D. H. (1965). Mental abilities of children from different social-class and cultural groups. *Monographs of the Society for Research in Child Development, 30*(4, Serial No. 102).

LESTER, B. M. (1985). Introduction: There's more to crying than meets the ear. In B. M. Lester & C. F. Z. Boukydis (Eds.), *Infant crying* (pp. 1–27). New York: Plenum.

LESTER, B. M. (1987). Developmental outcome prediction from acoustic cry analysis in term and preterm infants. *Pediatrics, 80,* 529–534.

LESTER, B. M., & DREHER, M. (1989). Effects of marijuana use during pregnancy on newborn cry. *Child Development, 60,* 765–771.

LESTER, B. M., KOTELCHUCK, M., SPELKE, E., SELLERS, M. J., & KLEIN, R. E. (1974). Separation protest in Guatemalan infants: Cross-cultural and cognitive findings. *Developmental Psychology, 10,* 79–85.

LEVENTHAL, G. S. (1970). Influence of brothers and sisters on sex role behavior. *Journal of Personality and Social Psychology, 16,* 452–465.

LEVIN, J. A., BORUTA, M. J., & VASCONELLOS, M. T. (1983). Microcomputer-based environments for writing: A writer's assistant. In A. C. Wilkinson (Ed.), *Classroom computers and cognitive science* (pp. 219–232). New York, Academic Press.

LEVIN, S. R., PETROS, T. V., & PETRELLA, F. W. (1982). Preschoolers' awareness of television advertising. *Child Development, 53,* 933–937.

LEVY, D. M. (1937). Sibling rivalry. *American Orthopsychiatric Association Research Monographs* (No. 2).

LEVY, G. D., & CARTER, D. B. (1989). Gender schema, gender constancy, and gender-role knowledge. The roles of cognitive factors in preschoolers' gender-role stereotype attributions. *Developmental Psychology, 25,* 444–449.

LEVY-SHIFF, R., & ISRAELASHVILI, R. (1988). Antecedents of fathering: Some further exploration. *Developmental Psychology, 24,* 434–440.

LEWIS, C. C. (1981). The effects of parental firm control: A reinterpretation of findings. *Psychological Bulletin, 90,* 547–563.

LEWIS, M., & BROOKS, J. (1978). Self-knowledge and emotional development. In M. Lewis & L. A. Rosenblum (Ed.), *The development of affect* (pp. 205–226). New York: Plenum.

LEWIS, M., & BROOKS-GUNN, J. (1979). *Social cognition and the acquisition of self.* New York: Plenum.

LEWIS, M., BROOKS-GUNN, J., & JASKIR, J. (1985). Individual differences in visual self-recognition as a function of mother–infant attachment relationship. *Developmental Psychology, 21,* 1181–1187.

LEWIS, M., & KREITZBERG, V. S. (1979). Effects of birth order and spacing on mother-infant interactions. *Developmental Psychology, 15,* 617–625.

LEWIS, M., & MCGURK, H. (1972). Evaluation of infant intelligence. *Science, 178,* 1174–1177.

LEWIS, M., & MICHALSON, L. (1982). The socialization of emotions. In T. Field & A. Fogel (Eds.), *Emotion and early interaction* (pp. 189–212). Hillsdale, NJ: Erlbaum.

LEWIS, M., & MICHALSON, L. (1983). *Children's emotions and moods.* New York: Plenum.

LEWIS, M., & SULLIVAN, M. W. (1985). Infant intelligence and its assessment. In B. B. Wolman (Ed.), *Handbook of infant intelligence* (pp. 505–599). New York: Wiley.

LEWIS, M., SULLIVAN, M., & MICHALSON, L. (1984). The cognitive-emotional fugue. In C. E. Izard, J. Kagan, & R. Zajonc (Eds.), *Emotions, cognition, and behavior* (pp. 264–288). New York: Cambridge University Press.

LEWIS, M., SULLIVAN, M. W., STANGER, C., & WEISS, M. (1989). Self development and self-conscious emotions. *Child Development, 60,* 146–156.

LEWIS, M., SULLIVAN, M. W., & VASEN, A. (1987). Making faces: Age and emotion differences in the posing of emotional expressions. *Developmental Psychology, 23,* 690–697.

LEWONTIN, R. C. (1976). Race and intelligence. In N. J. Block & G. Dworkin (Eds.), *The IQ controversy* (pp. 78–92). New York: Pantheon Books.

LIBEN, L. S., & DOWNS, R. M. (1986). *Children's production and comprehension of maps: Increasing graphic literacy,* Washington, DC: National Institute of Education.

LIBEN, L. S., & GOLBECK, S. L. (1984). Performance on Piagetian horizontality and verticality tasks: Sex-related differences in knowledge of relevant physical phenomena. *Developmental Psychology, 20,* 595–606.

LIBERTY, C., & ORNSTEIN, P. A. (1973). Age differences in organization and recall: The effects of training in categorization. *Journal of Experimental Child Psychology, 15,* 169–186.

LICKONA, T. (1976). Research on Piaget's theory of moral development. In T. Lickona (Ed.), *Moral development and behavior* (pp. 219–240). New York: Holt, Rinehart and Winston.

LIEBERT, R. M. (1986). Effects of television on children and adolescents. *Developmental and Behavioral Pediatrics, 7,* 43–48.

LIEBERT, R. M., & POULOS, R. W. (1975). Television and personality development: The socializing effects of an entertainment medium. In A. Davids (Ed.), *Child personality and psychopathology: Current topics* (Vol. 2, pp. 61–97). New York: Wiley.

LIEBERT, R. M., & SPRAFKIN, J. (1988). *The early window: Effects of television on children and youth* (3rd edition). New York: Pergamon Press.

LIEVEN, E. (1978). Conversations between mothers and young children: Individual differences and their possible implications for the study of language learning. In N. Waterson & C. Snow (Eds.), *The development of communication* (pp. 173–187). Chichester, England: Wiley.

LINDBLOM, C. E. (1986). Who needs what social research for policy-making? *Knowledge: Creation, Diffusion, Utilization, 7,* 345–366.

LINDE, E. V., MORRONGIELLO, B. A., & ROVEE-COLLIER, C. (1985). Determinants of retention in 8-week-old infants. *Developmental Psychology, 21,* 601–613.

LINDELL, S. G. (1988). Education for childbirth: A time for change. *Journal of Obstetrics, Gynecology, and Neonatal Nursing, 17,* 108–112.

LINN, M. C. (1985). Fostering equitable consequences from computer learning environments. *Sex Roles, 13,* 229–240.

LINN, M. C., & HYDE, J. S. (1989). Gender, mathematics, and science. *Educational Researcher, 18,* 17–27.

LINN, M. C., & PETERSEN, A. C. (1985). Emergence and characterization of sex differences in spatial ability: A meta-analysis. *Child Development, 56,* 1479–1498.

LINN, S., LIEBERMAN, E., SCHOENBAUM, S. C., MONSON, R. R., STUBBLEFIELD, P. G., & RYAN, K. J. (1988). Adverse outcomes of pregnancy in women exposed to diethylstilbestrol in utero. *Journal of Reproductive Medicine, 33,* 3–7.

LIPSCOMB, T. J., LARRIEU, J. A., MCALLISTER, H. A., & BREGMAN, N. J. (1982). Modeling and children's generosity: A developmental perspective. *Merrill-Palmer Quarterly, 28,* 275–282.

LIPSCOMB, T. J., MCALLISTER, H. A., & BREGMAN, N. J. (1985). A developmental inquiry into the effects of multiple models on children's generosity. *Merrill-Palmer Quarterly, 31,* 335–344.

LIPSITT, L. P. (1982). Infant learning. In T. M. Field, A. Huston, H. C., Quay, L. Troll, & G. E. Finley (Eds.), *Review of human development* (pp. 62–78). New York: Wiley.

LIPSITT, L. P., ENGEN, T., & KAYE, H. (1963). Developmental changes in the olfactory threshold of the neonate. *Child Development, 34,* 371–376.

LIPSITT, L. P., STURNER, W. Q., & BURKE, P. (1979). Perinatal indicators and subsequent crib death. *Infant Behavior and Development, 2,* 325–328.

LIPSITT, L. P., & WERNER, J. S. (1981). The infancy of human learning processes. In E. S. Gollin (Ed.), *Developmental plasticity* (pp. 101–133). New York: Academic Press.

LISS, M. B., REINHARDT, L. C., & FREDRIKSEN, S. (1983). TV heroes: The impact of rhetoric and deeds. *Journal of Applied Developmental Psychology, 4,* 175–187.

LITOWITZ, B. (1977). Learning to make definitions. *Journal of Child Language, 8,* 165–175.

LITTLE, B. B., SNELL, L. M., KLEIN, V. R., & GILSTRAP, L. C., III (1989). Cocaine abuse during pregnancy: Maternal and fetal implications. *Obstetrics and Gynecology, 73,* 157–160.

LIVESLEY, W. J., & BROMLEY, D. B. (1973). *Person perception in childhood and adolescence.* London: Wiley.

LLOYD, B., & SMITH, C. (1985). The social representation of gender and young children's play. *British Journal of Developmental Psychology, 3,* 65–73.

LOCKE, J. (1892). Some thoughts concerning education. In R. H. Quick (Ed.), *Locke on education* (pp. 1–236). Cambridge, England: Cambridge University Press. (Original work published 1690)

LOCKHEED, M. E. (1985). Women, girls, and computers: A first look at the evidence. *Sex Roles, 13,* 115–122.

LOCKHEED, M. E. (1986). Reshaping the social order: The case of gender segregation. *Sex Roles, 14,* 617–628.

LOCKHEED, M. E., & HARRIS, A. M. (1984). Cross-sex collaborative learning in elementary classrooms. *American Educational Research Journal, 21,* 275–294.

LOEB, R. C., HORST, L., & HORTON, P. J. (1980). Family interaction patterns associated with self-esteem in preadolescent girls and boys. *Merrill-Palmer Quarterly, 26,* 203–217.

LOEHLIN, J. C., HORN, J. M., & WILLERMAN, L. (1989). Modeling IQ change: Evidence from the Texas Adoption Project. *Child Development, 60,* 993–1004.

LOEHLIN, J. C., LINDZEY, G., & SPUHLER, J. N. (1975). *Raw differences in intelligence.* San Francisco: Freeman.

LOHMAN, D. F. (1988). Spatial abilities as traits, processes, and knowledge. In R. J. Sternberg (Ed.), *Advances in the psychology of human intelligence* (Vol. 4, pp. 181–248). Hillsdale, NJ: Erlbaum.

LONEY, J. (1974). Intellectual functioning of hyperactive elementary school boys: A cross-sectional investigation. *American Journal of Orthopsychiatry, 44,* 754–762.

LONG, N., & FOREHAND, R. (1987). The effects of parental divorce and marital conflict on children: An overview. *Journal of Developmental and Behavioral Pediatrics, 8,* 292–296.

LONGSTRETH, L. E. (1981). Revisiting Skeels' final study: A critique. *Developmental Psychology, 17,* 620–625.

LONGSTRETH, L. E., DAVIS, B., CARTER, L., FLINT, D., OWEN, J., RICKERT, M., & TAYLOR, E. (1981). Separation of home intellectual environment and maternal IQ as determinants of child IQ. *Developmental Psychology, 17,* 532–541.

LORENZ, K. (1952). *King Solomon's ring.* New York: Thomas Y. Crowell.

LOUGEE, M. D., GRUENEICH, R., & HARTUP, W. W. (1977). Social interaction in same- and mixed-age dyads of preschool children. *Child Development, 48,* 1353–1361.

LOVEJOY, C. O. (1981). The origin of man. *Science, 211,* 341–350.

LOVELAND, K. A. (1987). Behavior of young children with Down syndrome before the mirror: Exploration. *Child Development, 58,* 768–778.

LOWITZER, A. C. (1987). Maternal phenylketonuria: Cause for concern among women with PKU. *Research on Developmental Disabilities, 8,* 1–14.

LOZOFF, B. (1989). Nutrition and behavior. *American Psychologist, 44,* 231–236.

LUCARIELLO, J., & NELSON, K. (1985). Slot-filler categories as memory organizers for young children. *Developmental Psychology, 21,* 272–282.

LUMMIS, M., & STEVENSON, H. W. (1990). Gender differences in beliefs about achievement: A cross-cultural study. *Developmental Psychology, 26,* 254–263.

LUNDBERG, U. (1983). Note on Type A behavior and cardiovascular responses to challenge in 3–6-yr-old children. *Journal of Psychosomatic Research, 27,* 39–42.

LURIA, A. R. (1961). *The role of speech in the regulation of normal and abnormal behavior.* New York: Pergamon Press.

LUTZ, P. (1983). The stepfamily: An adolescent perspective. *Family Relations, 32,* 367–375.

LYTTON, H. (1977). Do parents create, or respond to, differences in twins. *Developmental Psychology, 13,* 456–459.

MACCHIAROLA, F. J., & GARTNER, A. (EDS.) (1989). *Caring for America's children.* New York: The Academy of Political Science.

MACCOBY, E. E. (1988). Gender as a social category. *Developmental Psychology, 24,* 755–765.

MACCOBY, E. E. (1990). Gender and relationships. *American Psychologist, 45,* 513–520.

MACCOBY, E. E., & HAGEN, J. W. (1965). Effects of distraction upon central versus incidental recall: Developmental trends. *Journal of Experimental Child Psychology, 3,* 113–122.

MACCOBY, E. E., & JACKLIN, C. N. (1974). *The psychology of sex differences.* Stanford, CA: Stanford University Press.

MACCOBY, E. E., & JACKLIN, C. N. (1980). Sex differences in aggression: A rejoinder and reprise. *Child Development, 51,* 964–980.

MACCOBY, E. E., & JACKLIN, C. N. (1987). Gender segregation in childhood. In E. H. Reese (Ed.), *Advances in child development and behavior* (Vol. 20, pp. 239–287). New York: Academic Press.

MACCOBY, E. E., KAHN, A. J., & EVERETT, B. A. (1983). The role of psychological research in the formation of policies affecting children. *American Psychologist, 38,* 80–84.

MACCOBY, E. E., & MARTIN, J. A. (1983). Socialization in the context of the family: Parent–child interaction. In E. M. Hetherington (Ed.), *Handbook of child psychology: Vol. 4. Socialization, personality, and social development* (4th ed., pp. 1–101). New York: Wiley.

MACFARLANE, A. (1975). Olfaction in the development of social preferences in the human neonate. In *Parent–infant interaction: Ciba Foundation Symposium 33* (pp. 103–117). Amsterdam: Elsevier.

MACKINNON, C. E. (1989). An observational investigation of sibling interactions in married and divorced families. *Developmental Psychology, 25,* 36–44.

MACKINNON, D. W. (1968). Selecting students with creative potential. In P. Heist (Ed.), *The creative college student: An unmet challenge* (pp. 101–116). San Francisco: Jossey-Bass.

MACKINNON, D. W., & HALL, W. B. (1973). Intelligence and creativity. In B. T. Eiduson & L. Beckman (Eds.), *Science as a career choice: Theoretical and empirical studies* (pp. 148–152). New York: Russell Sage Foundation.

MACKLIN, M. C., & KOLBE, R. H. (1984). Sex role stereotyping in children's advertising: Current and past trends. *Journal of Advertising, 13,* 34–42.

MACMILLAN, D. L., KEOGH, B. K., & JONES, R. L. (1986). Special educational research on mildly handicapped learners. In M. C. Wittrock (Ed.), *Handbook of research on teaching* (3rd ed., pp. 686–724). New York: Macmillan.

MACMILLAN, D. L., & MORRISON, G. M. (1984). Sociometric research in special education. In R. L. Jones (Ed.), *Attitudes and attitude change in special education: Theory and practice* (pp. 93–117). Reston, VA: Council for Exceptional Children.

MACRIDES, R., BARTKE, A., & DALTERIO, S. (1975). Strange females increase plasma testosterone levels in male mice. *Science, 189,* 1104–1105.

MACTURK, R., VIETZE, P., McCARTHY, M., McQUISTON, S., & YARROW, L. (1985). The organization of exploratory behavior in Down syndrome and nondelayed infants. *Child Development, 56,* 573–581.

MADDEN, N., & SLAVIN, R. (1983). Mainstreaming students with mild handicaps: Academic and social outcomes. *Review of Educational Research, 53,* 519–659.

MAGNUSSON, D., STATTIN, H., & ALLEN, V. L. (1985). Biological maturation and social development: A longitudinal study of some adjustment processes from mid-adolescence to adulthood. *Journal of Youth and Adolescence, 14,* 267–283.

MAGNUSSON, D., STATTIN, H., & ALLEN, V. L. (1986). Differential maturation among girls and its relation to social adjustment: A longitudinal perspective. In P. B. Baltes, D. L. Featherman, & R. M. Lerner (Eds.), *Life span development* (Vol. 7, pp. 136–172). New York: Academic Press.

MAHALSKI, P. A., SILVA, P. A., & SPEARS, G. F. S. (1985). Children's attachment to soft objects at bedtime, child rearing, and child development. *Journal of the American Academy of Child Psychiatry, 24,* 442–446.

MAIER, R. A., HOLMES, D. L., SLAYMAKER, F. L., & REICH, J. N. (1984). The perceived attractiveness of preterm infants. *Infant Behavior and Development, 7,* 403–414.

MAIN, M., & CASSIDY, J. (1988). Categories of response to reunion with the parent at age 6: Predictable from infant attachment classifications and stable over a 1-month period. *Developmental Psychology, 24,* 415–426.

MAIN, M., & GEORGE, C. (1985). Responses of abused and disadvantaged toddlers to distress in agemates: A study in the day care setting. *Developmental Psychology, 21,* 407–412.

MAIN, M., KAPLAN, N., & CASSIDY, J. (1985). Security in infancy, childhood, and adulthood: A move to the level of representation. *Monographs of the Society for Research in Child Development, 50*(1–2, Serial No. 209).

MAIN, M., & SOLOMON, J. (1986). Discovery of an insecure-disorganized/disoriented attachment pattern. In T. B. Brazelton & M. W. Yogman (Eds.), *Affective development in infancy* (pp. 95–124). Norwood, NJ: Ablex.

MAKIN, J. W., & PORTER, R. H. (1989). Attractiveness of lactating females' breast odors to neonates. *Child Development, 60,* 803–810.

MALATESTA, C. Z., GRIGORYEV, P., LAMB, C., ALBIN, M., & CULVER, C. (1986). Emotion socialization and expressive development in preterm and full-term infants. *Child Development, 57,* 316–330.

MALATESTA, C. Z., & HAVILAND, J. M. (1982). Learning display rules: The socialization of emotion expression in infancy. *Child Development, 53,* 991–1003.

MALINA, R. M. (1975). *Growth and development: The first twenty years in man.* Minneapolis: Burgess.

MALINA, R. M. (1979). Secular changes in size and maturity: Causes and effects. In A. F. Roche (Ed.), Secular trends in human growth, maturation, and development. *Monographs of the Society for Research in Child Development, 44*(3–4, Serial No. 179).

MALINA, R. M. (1980). Biosocial correlates of motor development during infancy and early childhood. In L. S. Greene & F. E. Johnston (Eds.), *Social and biological predictors of nutritional status, physical growth, and neurological development* (pp. 143–171). New York: Academic Press.

MALINA, R. M., HARPER, A. B., & HOLMAN, J. D. (1970). Growth status and performance relative to parental size. *Research Quarterly, 41,* 503–509.

MALLICK, S. K., & MCCANDLESS, B. R. (1966). A study of catharsis of aggression. *Journal of Personality and Social Psychology, 4,* 591–596.

MALTZ, D. N., & BORKER, R. A. (1983). A cultural approach to male–female miscommunication. In J. A. Gumperz (Ed.), *Language and social identity* (pp. 195–216). New York: Cambridge University Press.

MANCHESTER, D. (1988). Prehensile development: A contrast of mature and immature patterns. In J. E. Clark & J. H. Humphrey (Eds.), *Advances in motor development research* (pp. 165–199). New York: AMS Press.

MANDLER, J. M. (1983). Representation. In J. H. Flavell & E. M. Markman (Eds.), *Handbook of child psychology: Vol. 3. Cognitive development* (4th ed., pp. 420–494). New York: Wiley.

MANDLER, J. M., & JOHNSON, N. S. (1977). Remembrance of things parsed: Story structure and recall. *Cognitive Psychology, 9,* 111–151.

MANDLER, J. M., & ROBINSON, C. A. (1978). Developmental changes in picture recognition. *Journal of Experimental Child Psychology, 26,* 122–136.

MANT, C. M., & PERNER, J. (1988). The child's understanding of commitment. *Developmental Psychology, 24,* 343–351.

MAQSUD, M. (1977). The influence of social heterogeneity and sentimental credibility on moral judgments of Nigerian Muslim adolescents. *Journal of Cross-Cultural Psychology, 8,* 113–122.

MARANTZ, S. A., & MANSFIELD, A. F. (1977). Maternal employment and the development of sex-role stereotyping in five- to eleven-year-old girls. *Child Development, 48,* 668–673.

MARATSOS, M. (1983). Some current issues in the study of the acquisition of grammar. In J. H. Flavell & E. M. Markman (Eds.), *Handbook of child psychology: Vol. 3. Cognitive development* (4th ed., pp. 707–786). New York: Wiley.

MARATSOS, M. P., & CHALKLEY, M. A. (1980). The internal language of children's syntax: The ontogenesis and representation of syntactic categories. In K. Nelson (Ed.), *Children's language* (Vol. 2, pp. 127–214). New York: Gardner Press.

MARCH OF DIMES (1983). *PKU* (Genetic Series: Public Information Health Sheet). White Plains, NY: March of Dimes Birth Defects Foundation.

MARCIA, J. E. (1966). Development and validation of ego identity status. *Journal of Personality and Social Psychology, 3,* 551–558.

MARCIA, J. E. (1980). Identity in adolescence. In J. Adelson (Ed.), *Handbook of adolescent psychology* (pp. 159–187). New York: Wiley.

MARCUS, D. E., & OVERTON, W. F. (1978). The development of cognitive gender constancy and sex role preferences. *Child Development, 49,* 434–444.

MARCUS, J., MACCOBY, E. E., JACKLIN, C. N., & DOERING, C. H. (1985). Individual differences in mood in early childhood: Their relation to gender and neonatal sex steroids. *Developmental Psychobiology, 18,* 327–340.

MARCUS, L. C. (1983). Preventing and treating toxoplasmosis. *Drug Therapy, 13,* 129–144.

MARCUS, R. F., TELLEEN, S., & ROKE, E. J. (1979). Relation between cooperation and empathy in young children. *Developmental Psychology, 15,* 346–347.

MARION, R. W., WIZNIA, A. A., HUTCHEON, R. G., & RUBINSTEIN, A. (1986). Human T-cell lymphotropic virus Type III (HTLV-III) embryopathy. *American Journal of Diseases of Children, 140,* 638–640.

MARKMAN, E. M. (1979a). Classes and collections: Conceptual organization and numerical abilities. *Cognitive Psychology, 11,* 395–411.

MARKMAN, E. M. (1979b). Realizing that you don't understand: Elementary school children's awareness of inconsistencies. *Child Development, 50,* 643–655.

MARKMAN, E. M. (1989). *Categorization and naming in children.* Cambridge, MA: MIT Press.

MARKMAN, E. M., & HUTCHINSON, J. E. (1984). Children's sensitivity to constraints on word meaning: Taxonomic vs. thematic relations. *Cognitive Psychology, 16,* 1–27.

MARKMAN, E. M., & WACHTEL, G. A. (1988). Children's use of mutual exclusivity to constrain the meanings of words. *Cognitive Psychology, 20,* 121–157.

MARKMAN, H. J., & KADUSHIN, F. S. (1986). Preventive effects of Lamaze training for first-time parents: A short-term longitudinal study. *Journal of Consulting and Clinical Psychology, 54,* 872–874.

MARKOVITS, H., SCHLEIFER, M., & FORTIER, L. (1989). Development of elementary deductive reasoning in young children. *Developmental Psychology, 25,* 787–793.

MARMOR, T. (1983). Competing perspectives on social policy. In E. F. Zigler, S. L. Kagan, & E. Klugman (Eds.), *Children, families, and government: Perspectives on American social policy* (pp. 35–56). New York: Cambridge University Press.

MARSH, D. T., SERAFICA, F. C., & BARENBOIM, C. (1981). Interrelationships among perspective taking, interpersonal problem solving, and interpersonal functioning. *Journal of Genetic Psychology, 138,* 37–48.

MARSH, H. W. (1989). Age and sex effects in multiple dimensions of self-concept: Preadolescence to early adulthood. *Journal of Educational Psychology, 81,* 417–430.

MARSH, H. W., BARNES, J., CAIRNS, L., & TIDMAN, M. (1984). Self-description questionnaire: Age and sex effects in the structure and level of self-concept for preadolescent children. *Journal of Educational Psychology, 76,* 940–956.

MARSH, H. W., & GOUVERNET, P. J. (1989). Multidimensional self-concepts and perceptions of control: Construct validation of responses by children. *Journal of Educational Psychology, 81,* 57–69.

MARSH, H. W., RELICH, J. D., & SMITH, I. D. (1983). Self-concept: The construct validity of interpretations based upon the SDQ. *Journal of Personality and Social Psychology, 45,* 173–187.

MARSH, H. W., SMITH, I. D., & BARNES, J. (1985). Multidimensional self-concepts: Relations with sex and academic achievement. *Journal of Educational Psychology, 77,* 581–596.

MARSH, R. W. (1985). Phrenoblysis: Real or chimera? *Child Development, 56,* 1059–1061.

MARSHALL, W. A., & TANNER, J. M. (1969). Variations in the pattern of pubertal changes in girls. *Archives of Disease in Childhood, 44,* 291–303.

MARTIN, C. L. (1989). Children's use of gender-related information in making social judgments. *Developmental Psychology, 25,* 80–88.

MARTIN, C. L., & HALVERSON, C. F., JR. (1981). A schematic processing model of sex typing and stereotyping in children. *Child Development, 52,* 1119–1134.

MARTIN, C. L., & HALVERSON, C. F., JR. (1983). The effects of sex-typing schemas on young children's memory. *Child Development, 54,* 563–574.

MARTIN, C. L., & HALVERSON, C. F. (1987). The role of cognition in sex role acquisition. In D. B. Carter (Ed.), *Current conceptions of sex roles and sex typing: Theory and research* (pp. 123–137). New York: Praeger.

MARTIN, G. B., & CLARK, R. D., III (1982). Distress crying in neonates: Species and peer specificity. *Developmental Psychology, 18,* 3–9.

MARTIN, J. A. (1981). A longitudinal study of the consequences of early mother–infant interaction: A microanalytic approach. *Monographs of the Society for Research in Child Development, 46*(3, Serial No. 190).

MARTIN, J. B. (1987). Molecular genetics: Applications to the clinical neurosciences. *Science, 298,* 765–772.

MARTIN, R. M. (1975). Effects of familiar and complex stimuli on infant attention. *Developmental Psychology, 11,* 178–185.

MARTORELL, R. (1980). Interrelationships between diet, infectious disease, and nutritional status. In L. S. Greene & F. E. Johnston (Eds.), *Social and biological predictors of nutritional status, physical growth, and neurological development* (pp. 81–106). New York: Academic Press.

MASSEY, C. M., & GELMAN, R. (1988). Preschoolers' ability to decide whether a photographed unfamiliar object can move itself. *Developmental Psychology, 24,* 307–317.

MASSACHUSETTS SABBATH SCHOOL SOCIETY. (1836). *New England primer: Or an easy and pleasant guide to the art of reading.* Boston: Author.

MASTERS, J. C., & BINGER, C. G. (1976). *Inhibitive capability in young children: Stability and development.* Minneapolis: University of Minnesota Press.

MASTERS, J. C., & FURMAN, W. (1981). Popularity, individual friendship selections, and specific peer interaction among children. *Developmental Psychology, 17,* 344–350.

MASUR, E. F., McINTYRE, C. W., & FLAVELL, J. H. (1973). Developmental changes in apportionment of study time among items in a multi-trial free recall task. *Journal of Experimental Child Psychology, 15,* 237–246.

MATAS, L., AREND, R., & SROUFE, L. A. (1978). Continuity of adaptation in the second year. The relationship between quality of attachment and later competence. *Child Development, 49,* 547–556.

MATHENY, A. P., DOLAN, A., & WILSON, R. S. (1974). Bayley's Infant Behavior Record: Relations between behavior and mental test scores. *Developmental Psychology, 10,* 696–702.

MATHENY, A. P., RIESE, M. L., & WILSON, R. S. (1985). Rudiments of infant temperament: Newborn to 9 months. *Developmental Psychology, 21,* 486–494.

MATIAS, R., COHN, J. F., & ROSS, S. (1989). A comparison of two systems that code infant affective expression. *Developmental Psychology, 25,* 483–489.

MATTHEWS, K. A., & ANGULO, J. (1980). Measurement of the Type A behavior pattern in children: Assessment of children's competitiveness, impatience, anger, and aggression. *Child Development, 51,* 466–475.

MAURER, D. (1985). Infants' perception of facedness. In T. Fields & N. Fox (Eds.), *Social perception in infants* (pp. 73–100). Norwood, NJ: Ablex.

MAURO, R. J., & FEINS, R. P. (1977). *Kids, food and television: The compelling case for state action.* Albany, NY: New York State Assembly.

McANARNEY, E. R., LAWRENCE, R. A., & ATEN, M. J. (1979). Premature parenthood: A preliminary report of adolescent mother–infant interaction. *Pediatric Research, 13,* 328.

McCABE, A. E., EVELY, S., ABRAMOVITCH, R., CORTER, C. M., & PEPLER, D. J. (1983). Conditional statements in children's spontaneous speech. *Journal of Child Language, 10,* 253–258.

McCABE, A., & PETERSON, C. (1988). A comparison of adults' versus children's spontaneous use of *because* and *so*. *Journal of Genetic Psychology, 149,* 257–268.

McCABE, A. E., & SIEGEL, L. S. (1987). The stability of training effects in young children's class inclusion reasoning. *Merrill-Palmer Quarterly, 33,* 187–194.

McCALL, R., & McGHEE, P. (1977). The discrepancy hypothesis of attention and affect. In F. Weizmann & I. Užgiris (Eds.), *The structuring of experience* (pp. 179–210). New York: Plenum.

McCALL, R. B. (1977). Childhood IQs as predictors of adult educational and occupational status. *Science, 197,* 482–483.

McCALL, R. B. (1983). Environmental effects on intelligence: The forgotten realm of discontinuous nonshared within-family factors. *Child Development, 54,* 408–415.

McCALL, R. B. (1984). Developmental changes in mental performance: The effect of birth of a sibling. *Child Development, 55,* 1317–1321.

McCALL, R. B. (1985). The confluence model and theory. *Child Development, 56,* 217–218.

McCALL, R. B. (1987). The media, society, and child development research. In J. D. Osofsky (Ed.), *Handbook of infant development* (pp. 1199–1255). New York: Wiley.

McCALL, R. B., APPELBAUM, M. I., & HOGARTY, P. S. (1973). Developmental changes in mental performance. *Monographs of the Society for Research in Child Development, 38*(3, Serial No. 150).

McCALL, R. B., EICHORN, D. H., & HOGARTY, P. S. (1977). Transitions in early mental development. *Monographs of the Society for Research in Child Development, 42*(3, Serial No. 171).

McCALL, R. B., & HOGARTY, P. S., & HURLBURT, N. (1972). Transitions in sensorimotor development and the prediction of childhood IQ. *American Psychologist, 27,* 728–748.

McCALL, R. B., KENNEDY, C. B., & APPELBAUM, M. I. (1977). Magnitude of discrepancy and the distribution of attention in infants. *Child Development, 48,* 772–785.

McCARTHY, D. A. (1954). Language development in children. In L. Carmichael (Ed.), *Manual of child psychology* (2nd ed., pp. 476–581). New York: Wiley.

McCARTHY, K. A., & NELSON, K. (1981). Children's use of scripts in story recall. *Discourse Processes, 4,* 59–70.

McCARTNEY, K. (1984). The effect of quality of day care environment upon children's language development. *Developmental Psychology, 20,* 244–260.

McCARTNEY, K., SCARR, S., PHILLIPS, D., & GRAJEK, S. (1985). Day care as intervention: Comparisons of varying quality programs. *Journal of Applied Developmental Psychology, 6,* 247–260.

McCAULEY, E., ITO, J., & KAY, T. (1986). Psychosocial functioning in girls with Turner syndrome and short stature. *Journal of the American Academy of Child Psychiatry, 25,* 105–112.

McCAULEY, E., KAY, T., ITO, J., & TREDER, R. (1987). The Turner syndrome: Cognitive deficits, affective discrimination, and behavior problems. *Child Development, 58,* 464–473.

McCLAIN, C. S. (1987). Some social network differences between women choosing home and hospital birth. *Human Organization, 46,* 146–152.

McCONAGHY, M. J. (1979). Gender permanence and the genital basis of gender. Stages in the development of constancy of gender identity. *Child Development, 50,* 1223–1226.

McCORMICK, C. M., & MAURER, D. M. (1988). Unimanual hand preferences in 6-month-olds: Consistency and relation to familial-handedness. *Infant Behavior and Development, 11,* 21–29.

McCUNE-NICHOLICH, L., & FENSON, L. (1984). Methodological issues in studying early pretend play. In T. Yawkey & A. Pelligrini (Eds.), *Child's play: Developmental and applied* (pp. 81–104). Hillsdale, NJ: Erlbaum.

McDavid, J. W., & Harari, H. (1966). Stereotyping of names and popularity in grade-school children. *Child Development, 37,* 453–459.

McDonald, L., & Pien, D. (1982). Mother conversational behavior as a function of interactional intent. *Journal of Child Language, 9,* 337–358.

McEwen, B. S. (1981). Neural gonadal steroid actions. *Science, 211,* 1303–1311.

McGhee, P. E. (1974). Development of children's ability to create the joking relationship. *Child Development, 45,* 552–556.

McGhee, P. E. (1979). *Humor: Its origin and development.* San Francisco: Freeman.

McGinty, M. J., & Zafran, E. I. (1988). *Surrogacy: Constitutional and legal issues.* Cleveland, OH: The Ohio Academy of Trial Lawyers.

McGivern, J. E., Levin, J. R., Ghatala, E. S., & Pressley, M. (1986). Can selection of an effective memory strategy by induced vicariously? *Contemporary Educational Psychology, 11,* 170–186.

McGowan, J. D., Altman, R. E., & Kanto, W. P., Jr. (1988). Neonatal withdrawal symptoms after chronic maternal ingestion of caffeine. *Southern Medical Journal, 81,* 1092–1094.

McGowan, R. J., & Johnson, D. L. (1984). The mother–child relationship and other antecedents of childhood intelligence: A causal analysis. *Child Development, 55,* 810–820.

McGrew, W. (1969). An ethological study of agonistic behavior in preschool children. In C. R. Carpenter (Ed.), *Proceedings of the International Congress of Primatology* (Vol. 1, pp. 149–159). Basel: Karger.

McGuire, J. (1988). Gender stereotypes of parents with two-year-olds and beliefs about gender differences in behavior. *Sex Roles, 19,* 233–240.

McGuire, K. D., & Weisz, J. R. (1982). Social cognition and behavior correlates of preadolescent chumship. *Child Development, 53,* 1483–1484.

McKenzie, B., & Over, R. (1983). Young infants fail to imitate facial and manual gestures. *Infant Behavior and Development, 6,* 85–95.

McKenzie, B. E., Tootell, H. E., & Day, R. H. (1980). Development of visual size constancy during the 1st year of human infancy. *Developmental Psychology, 16,* 163–174.

McKey, R. H., Condelli, L., Ganson, H. Barrett, B. J., McConkey, C., & Plantz, M. C. (1985). *The impact of Head Start on children, families, and communities.* Washington, DC: U.S. Government Printing Office.

McKnight, C. C., Crosswhite, F. J., Dossey, J. A., Kifer, E., Swafford, J. O., Travers, K. J., & Cooney, T. J. (1987). *The underachieving curriculum: Assessing U.S. school mathematics from an international perspective.* Champaign, IL: Stipes.

McKusick, V. A. (1988). *Mendelian inheritance in man: Catalogs of autosomal dominant, autosomal recessive, and X-linked phenotypes* (7th ed.). Baltimore: The Johns Hopkins University Press.

McLoyd, V. C. (1990). The impact of economic hardship on black families and children: Psychological distress, parenting, and socioemotional development. *Child Development, 61,* 311–346.

McLoyd, V. C., Warren, D., & Thomas, E. A. C. (1984). Anticipatory and fantastic role enactment in preschool triads. *Developmental Psychology, 20,* 807–814.

McManus, I. C., Sik, G., Cole, D. R., Mellon, A. F., Wong, J., & Kloss, J. (1988). The development of handedness in children. *British Journal of Developmental Psychology, 6,* 257–273.

McNamee, S., & Peterson, J. (1986). Young children's distributive justice reasoning, behavior, and role taking: Their consistency and relationship. *Journal of Genetic Psychology, 146,* 399–404.

McNeill, D. (1970). The development of language. In P. H. Mussen (Ed.), *Carmichael's manual of child psychology* (3rd ed., pp. 1061–1161). New York: Wiley.

McPartland, J. M., & McDill, E. L. (1977). Research on crime in schools. In J. M. McPartland & E. L. McDill (Eds.), *Violence in schools* (pp. 3–22). Lexington, MA: Lexington Books.

Mead, G. H. (1934). *Mind, self, and society,* Chicago University of Chicago Press.

Mead, M. (1963). *Sex and temperament in three primitive societies.* New York: Morrow. (Original work published 1935)

Mead, M., & Newton, N. (1967). Cultural patterning of perinatal behavior. In S. Richardson & A. Guttmacher (Eds.), *Childbearing: Its social and psychological aspects* (pp. 142–244). Baltimore: Williams & Wilkins.

Meany, M. J., Stewart, J., & Beatty, W. W. (1985). Sex differences in social play: The socialization of sex roles. In J. S. Rosenblatt, C. Bear, C. M. Busnell, & P. Slater (Eds.), *Advances in the study of behavior* (Vol. 15, pp. 1–58). New York: Academic Press.

Mednick, B. R., Baker, R. L., & Sutton-Smith, B. (1979). Teenage pregnancy and perinatal mortality. *Journal of Youth and Adolescence, 8,* 343–357.

Medrich, E. A., Rosen, J., Rubin, V., & Buckley, S. (1982). *The serious business of growing up.* Berkeley: University of California Press.

Medway, F. J., & Venino, G. R. (1982). The effects of effort feedback and performance patterns on children's attributions and task persistence. *Contemporary Educational Psychology, 7,* 26–34.

Meece, J. L., Parsons, J. E., Kaczala, C. M., Goff, S. B., & Futterman, R. (1982). Sex differences in math achievement: Toward a model of academic choice. *Psychological Bulletin, 91,* 324–348.

Meerum Terwogt, M., & Olthof, T. (1989). Awareness and self-regulation of emotion in young children. In C. Saarni & P. L. Harris (Eds.), *Children's understanding of emotion.* New York: Cambridge University Press.

Mehler, J., Jusczyk, P., Lambertz, G., Halsted, N., Bertoncini, J., & Amiel-Tison, C. (1988). A precursor of language acquisition in young infants. *Cognition, 29,* 143–178.

Meichenbaum, D. H., & Goodman, J. (1971). Training impulsive children to talk to themselves: A means of developing self-control. *Journal of Abnormal Psychology, 77,* 115–126.

Meilman, P. W. (1979). Cross-sectional age changes in ego identity status during adolescence. *Developmental Psychology, 15,* 230–231.

Meisels, S., Plunkett, J. Stiefel, G., Pasick, P., & Roloff, D. (1984). *Patterns of attachment among preterm infants of differing biological risk.* Paper presented at the biennial meeting of the International Conference on Infant Studies, New York.

Melson, G. F., & Fogel, A. (1988, January). Learning to care. *Psychology Today, 22*(1), 39–45.

Melton, G. B. (1987). The clashing of symbols: Preclude to child and family policy. *American Psychologist, 42,* 345–354.

Melton, G. B., & Davidson, H. A. (1987). Child protection and society: When should the state intervene? *American Psychologist, 42,* 172–175.

Melton, G. B., & Thompson, R. A. (1987). Legislative approaches to psychological maltreatment: A social policy analysis. In M. R. Brassard, R. Germain, & S. N. Hart (Eds), *Psychological maltreatment of children and youth* (pp. 203–216). New York: Pergamon Press.

Melzoff, A. N. (1988a). Infant imitation after a 1-week delay: Long-term memory for novel acts and multiple stimuli. *Developmental Psychology, 24,* 470–476.

Meltzoff, A. N. (1988b). Infant imitation and memory: Nine-month-olds in immediate and deferred tests. *Child Development, 56,* 62–72.

Meltzoff, A. N., & Borton, R. W. (1979). Intermodal matching by human neonates. *Nature, 282,* 403–404.

Meltzoff, A. N., & Moore, M. K. (1977). Imitation of facial and manual gestures by human neonates. *Science, 198,* 75–78.

Meltzoff, A. N., & Moore, M. K. (1989). Imitation in newborn infants: Exploring the range of gestures imitated and the underlying mechanisms. *Developmental Psychology, 25,* 954–962.

Menig-Peterson, C. L. (1975). The modification of communicative behavior in preschool-aged children as a function of the listener's perspective. *Child Development, 46,* 1015–1018.

Menn, L. (1976). *Pattern, control, and contrast in beginning speech: A case study in the acquisition of word form and function.* Dissertation Abstracts International, 37, 2833A. (University Microfilms No. 76-24, 139).

Menn, L. (1989). Phonological development: Learning sounds and sound patterns. In J. Berko Gleason (Ed.), *The development of language* (2nd ed. pp. 59–100). Columbus, OH: Merrill.

MENYUK, P. (1977). *Language and maturation.* Cambridge, MA: MIT Press.

MENYUK, P., MENN, L., & SILBER, R. (1986). Early strategies for the perception and production of words and sounds. In P. Fletcher & M. Garman (Ed.), *Language acquisition* (2nd ed., pp. 198–222). Cambridge, England: Cambridge University Press.

MERCER, J. R. (1972, September). IQ: The lethal label. *Psychology Today, 6*(4), 44–47, 95–97.

MERCER, J. R. (1975). Psycological assessment and the rights of children. In N. Hobbs (Ed.), *Issues in the classification of children* (Vol. 1, pp. 130–158). San Francisco: Jossey-Bass.

MERCER, J. R. (1979a). In defense of racially and culturally nondiscriminatory assessment. *School Psychology Digest, 8,* 89–115.

MERCER, J. R. (1979b). *System of Multicultural Pluralistic Assessment: Technical Manual.* New York: Psychological Corporation.

MERCER, J. R., & LEWIS, J. F. (1978). *System of Multicultural Pluralistic Assessment.* New York: Psychological Corporation.

MERVIS, C. B., & CRISAFI, M. A. (1982). Order of acquisition of subordinate-, basic-, and superodinate-level categories. *Child Development, 53,* 258–266.

MESSER, S. B., & SCHACHT, T. (1983). A cognitive–dynamic theory of reflection-impulsivity. In J. Masling (Ed.), *Empirical studies of psychoanalytic theory* (Vol. 2, pp. 151–195). Hillsdale, NJ: Erlbaum.

MEYER, B. (1980). The development of girls' sex-role attitudes. *Child Development, 48,* 507–512.

MEYER-BAHLBURG, H. F. L., BRUDER, G. E., FELDMAN, J. R., EHRHARDT, A. A., HEALEY, J. M., & BELL, J. (1985). Cognitive abilities and hemispheric lateralization in females following idiopathic precocious puberty. *Developmental Psychology, 21,* 878–887.

MICHAELS, S. (1980). *Sharing time: An oral preparation for literacy,* Paper presented at the Ethnography in Education Research Forum, University of Pennsylvania, Philadelphia.

MICHALS, K., AZEN, C., ACOSTA, P., KOCH, R., & MATALON, R. (1988). Blood phenylalanine levels and intelligence of 10-year-old children with PKU in the National Collaborative Study. *Journal of the American Dietetic Association, 88,* 1226–1229.

MICHEL, C. (1989). Radiation embryology. *Experientia, 45,* 69–77.

MIDLARSKY, E., & BRYAN, J. H. (1972). Affect expressions and children's imitative altruism. *Journal of Experimental Research in Personality, 6,* 195–203.

MILES, C. (1935). Sex in social psychology. In C. Murchison (Ed.), *Handbook of social psychology* (pp. 699–704). Worcester, MA: Clark University Press.

MILICH, R., & PELHAM, W. E. (1986). The effects of sugar ingestion on the classroom and play group behavior of attention deficit disordered boys. *Journal of Consulting and Clinical Psychology, 54,* 714–718.

MILLER, C. A. (1985, July). Infant mortality in the U.S. *Scientific American, 253*(1), 31–37.

MILLER, D. S., & LIN, E. H. (1988). Children in sheltered homeless families: Reported health status and use of health services. *Pediatrics, 81,* 668–673.

MILLER, G. E., & EMIHOVICH, C. (1986). The effects of mediated programming instruction on preschool children's self-monitoring. *Journal of Educational Computing Research, 2,* 283–297.

MILLER, G. E., & PRESSLEY, M. (1987). Partial picture effects on children's memory for sentences containing implicit information. *Journal of Experimental Child Psychology, 43,* 300–310.

MILLER, K. F., & BAILLARGEON, R. (1990). Length and distance: Do preschoolers think that occlusion brings things together? *Developmental Psychology, 26,* 103–114.

MILLER, N., & MARUYAMA, G. (1976). Ordinal position and peer popularity. *Journal of Personality and Social Psychology, 33,* 123–131.

MILLER, P., & SPERRY, L. L. (1987). The socialization of anger and aggression. *Merrill-Palmer Quarterly, 33,* 1–31.

MILLER, P. H. (1989). *Theories of developmental psychology* (2nd ed.). San Francisco, CA: Freeman.

MILLER, P. H., & ALOISE, P. A. (1989). Young children's understanding of the psychological causes of behavior: A review. *Child Development, 60,* 257–285.

MILLER, P. H., & BIGI, L. (1979). The development of children's understanding of attention. *Merrill-Palmer Quarterly, 25,* 235–250.

MILLER, P. H., KESSEL, F. S., & FLAVELL, J. H. (1970). Thinking about people thinking about people thinking about . . .: A study of social cognitive development. *Child Development, 41,* 613–623.

MILLER, P. H., & ZALENSKI, R. (1982). Preschoolers' knowledge about attention. *Developmental Psychology, 18,* 871–875.

MILLER, S. A. (1987). *Developmental research methods.* Englewood Cliffs, NJ: Prentice-Hall.

MILLS, R., & GRUSEC, J. (1989). Cognitive, affective, and behavioral consequences of praising altruism. *Merrill-Palmer Quarterly, 35,* 299–326.

MINKOFF, H., DEEPAK, N., MENEZ, R., & FIKRIG, S. (1987). Pregnancies resulting in infants with acquired immunodeficiency syndrome of AIDS-related complex: Follow-up of mothers, children, and subsequently born siblings. *Obstetrics, and Gynecology, 69,* 288–291.

MINUCHIN, P., BIBER, B., SHAPIRO, E., & ZIMILES, H. (1969). *The psychological impact of school experience.* New York: Basic Books.

MINUCHIN, P. P., & SHAPIRO, E. K. (1983). The school as a context for social development. In E. M. Hetherington (Ed.), *Handbook of child psychology: Vol. 4, Socialization, personality, and social development* (4th ed., pp. 197–274). New York: Wiley.

MINUCHIN, S., ROSMAN, B. L., & BAKER, L. (1978). *Psychosomatic families.* Cambridge, MA: Harvard University Press.

MISCHEL, H. N. (1974). Sex bias in the evaluation of professional achievements. *Journal of Educational Psychology, 66,* 157–166.

MISCHEL, H. N., & MISCHEL, W. (1983). The development of children's knowledge of self-control strategies. *Child Development, 54,* 603–619.

MISCHEL, W., & BAKER, N. (1975). Cognitive appraisals and transformations in delay behavior. *Journal of Personality and Social Psychology, 31,* 254–261.

MISCHEL, W., & EBBESEN, E. B. (1970). Attention in delay of gratification. *Journal of Personality and Social Psychology, 16,* 329–337.

MISCHEL, W., & LIEBERT, R. M. (1966). Effects of discrepancies between observed and imposed reward criteria on their acquisition and transmission. *Journal of Personality and Social Psychology, 3,* 45–53.

MISCHEL, W., & METZNER, R. (1962). Preference for delayed reward as a function of age, intelligence, and length of delay interval. *Journal of Abnormal and Social Psychology, 64,* 425–431.

MISCIONE, J. L., MARVIN, R. S., O'BRIEN, R. G., & GREENBURG, M. T. (1978). A developmental study of preschool children's understanding of the words "know" and "guess." *Child Development, 48,* 1107–1113.

MITCHELL, G., & SHIVELY, C. (1984). Natural and experimental studies of nonhuman primate and other animal families. In R. D. Parke (Ed.), *Review of child development research* (Vol. 7, pp. 20–41). Chicago: University of Chicago Press.

MITCHELL, R. E., & TRICKETT, E. J. (1980). An analysis of the effects and determinants of social networks. *Community Mental Health Journal, 16,* 27–44.

MIYAKE, K., CHEN, S., & CAMPOS, J. J. (1985). Infant temperament, mother's mode of interaction, and attachment in Japan: An interim report. In I. Bretherton & E. Waters (Eds.), Growing points of attachment theory and research. *Monographs of the Society for Research in Child Development, 50*(1–2, Serial No. 209).

MIYAWAKI, K., STRANGE, W., VERBRUGGE, R., LIBERMAN, A. M., JENKINS, J. J., & FUJIMURA, O. (1975). An effect of linguistic experience: The discrimination of [r] and [l] by native speakers of Japanese and English. *Perception and Psychophysics, 18,* 331–340.

MIZE, J., & LADD, G. W. (1988). Predicting preschoolers' peer behavior and status from their interpersonal strategies. A comparison of verbal and enactive responses to hypothetical social dilemmas. *Developmental Psychology, 24,* 782–788.

MIZE, J., & LADD, G. W. (1990). A cognitive–social learning approach to social skill training with low-status preschool children. *Developmental Psychology, 26*, 388–397.

MNOOKIN, R. H. (1978). Children's rights: Beyond kiddie libbers and child savers. *Journal of Clinical Child Psychology, 7*, 163–167.

MOELY, B. E. (1977). Organizational factors in the development of memory. In R. V. Kail & J. W. Hagen (Eds.), *Perspectives on the development of memory and cognition* (pp. 203–236). Hillsdale, NJ: Erlbaum.

MOELY, B. E., HART, S. S., LEAL, L., JOHNSON, T., RAO, N., & BURNEY, L. (1986). How do teachers teach memory skills? *Educational Psychologist, 21*, 55–71.

MOERK, E. L. (1983). A behavioral analysis of controversial topics in first language acquisition: Reinforcements, corrections, modeling, input frequencies, and the three-term contingency pattern. *Journal of Psycholinguistic Research, 12*, 129–155.

MOERK, E. L. (1989). The LAD was a lady and the tasks were ill-defined. *Developmental Review, 9*, 21–57.

MOLFESE, D. L. (1977). Infant cerebral asymmetry. In S. J. Segalowitz & F. A. Gruber (Eds.), *Language development and neurological theory* (pp. 22–35). New York: Academic Press.

MOLFESE, D. L., & MOLFESE, V. J. (1979). Hemispheric and stimulus differences as reflected in the cortical responses of newborn infants to speech stimuli. *Developmental Psychology, 15*, 505–511.

MOLFESE, D. L., & MOLFESE, V. J. (1980). Cortical response of preterm infants to phonetic and nonphonetic speech stimuli. *Developmental Psychology, 16*, 574–581.

MONEY, J. (1985). Pediatric sexology and hermaphroditism. *Journal of Sex and Marital Therapy, 11*, 139–156.

MONEY J., & EHRHARDT, A. A. (1972). *Man and woman, boy and girl.* Baltimore: Johns Hopkins University Press.

MONEY, J., SCHWARTZ, M., & LEWIS, V. G. (1984). Adult erotosexual status and fetal hormonal masculinization and demasculinization: 46,XX congenital virilizing adrenal hyperplasia (CVAH) and 46,XY androgen-insensitivity syndrome (AIS) compared. *Psychoneuroendocrinology, 9*, 405–414.

MONTEMAYOR, R. (1974). Children's performance in a game and their attraction to it as a function of sex-typed labels. *Child Development, 45*, 152–156.

MONTEMAYOR, R., & EISEN, M. (1977). The development of self-conceptions from childhood to adolescence. *Developmental Psychology, 13*, 314–319.

MOORE, C., BRYANT, D., & FURROW, D. (1989). Mental terms and the development of certainty. *Child Development, 60*, 167–171.

MOORE, E. G. J. (1986). Family socialization and the IQ test performance of traditionally and transracially adopted black children. *Developmental Psychology, 22*, 317–326.

MOORE, K. L. (1989). *Before we are born* (3rd ed.). Philadelphia: Saunders.

MOORE, T. (1968). Language and intelligence: A longitudinal study of the first eight years: II. Environmental correlates of mental growth. *Human Development, 10*, 88–106.

MORAN, G. F., & VINOVSKIS, M. A. (1986). The great care of godly parents: Early childhood in Puritan New England. *Monographs of the Society for Research in Child Development, 50*(4–5, Serial No. 211).

MORAN, J. D., MILGRAM, R. M., SAWYERS, J. K., & FU, V. R. (1983). Original thinking in preschool children. *Child Development, 54*, 921–926.

MORGAN, M. (1982). Television and adolescents' sex stereotypes: A longitudinal study. *Journal of Personality and Social Psychology, 43*, 947–955.

MORRIS, D. (1981). Attachment and intimacy. In G. Stricker (Ed.), *Intimacy* (pp. 305–323). New York: Plenum.

MORRIS, J. A. (1989). Sudden infant death syndrome [letter]. *British Medical Journal, 298*, 958.

MORRONGIELLO, B. A. (1986). Infants' perception of multiple-group auditory patterns. *Infant Behavior and Development, 9*, 307–319.

MORRONGIELLO, B. A., & CLIFTON, R. K. (1984). Effects of sound frequency on behavioral and cardiac orienting in newborn and five-month-old infants. *Journal of Experimental Child Psychology, 38*, 429–446.

MORRONGIELLO, B. A., & ROCCA, P. T. (1988). Infants' localization of sounds in the median vertical plane: Estimates of minimum audible angle. *Journal of Experimental Child Psychology, 43*, 181–193.

MORTIMER, J. T., & SORENSEN, G. (1984). Men, women, work, and family. In K. M. Borman, D. Quarm, & S. Gideonse (Ed.), *Women in the workplace: Effects on families* (pp. 139–167). Norwood, NJ: Ablex.

MOSS, M., COLOMBO, J., MITCHELL, D. W., & HOROWITZ, F. D. (1988). Neonatal behavioral organization and visual discrimination at 3 months of age. *Child Development, 59*, 1211–1220.

MOSSBERG, N. (1948). Obesity in children: A clinical–prognostical investigation. *Acta Paediatrica, 35*(Suppl. 2), 1.

MOWRER, O. H. (1960). *Learning theory and behavior.* New York: Wiley.

MOYNAHAN, E. D. (1973). The development of knowledge concerning the effect of categorization upon free recall. *Child Development, 44*, 238–246.

MUELLER, E. (1972). The maintenance of verbal exchanges between young children. *Child Development, 43*, 930–938.

MUELLER, E., & BRENNER, J. (1977). The origins of social skills and interaction among playgroup toddlers. *Child Development, 48*, 854–861.

MUELLER, E., & LUCAS, T. A. (1975). Developmental analysis of peer interaction among toddlers. In M. Lewis & L. A. Rosenblum (Eds.), *Friendship and peer relations* (pp. 223–257). New York: Wiley.

MUNDY, P., SIGMAN, M., KASARI, C., & YIRMIYA, N. (1988). Nonverbal communication skills in Down syndrome children. *Child Development, 59*, 235–249.

MUNRO, G., & ADAMS, G. R. (1977). Ego identity formation in college students and working youth. *Developmental Psychology, 13*, 523–524.

MURETT-WAGSTAFF, S., & MOORE, S. G. (1989). The Hmong in America: Infant behavior and rearing practices. In J. K. Nugent, B. M. Lester, & T. B. Brazelton (Eds.), *Biology, culture, and development* (Vol. 1, pp. 319–339). Norwood, NJ: Ablex.

MURPHY, G. L., & SMITH, E. E. (1982). Basic-level superiority in picture categorization. *Journal of Verbal Learning and Verbal Behavior, 21*, 1–20.

MURRAY, A. D. (1985). Aversiveness is in the mind of the beholder. In B. M. Lester & C. F. Z. Boukydis (Eds.), *Infant crying* (pp. 217–239). New York: Plenum.

MURRAY, C. (1984). *Losing ground: American social policy, 1950–1980.* New York: Basic Books.

MURRAY, F. B. (1978). Teaching strategies and conservation training. In A. M. Lesgold, J. W. Pellegrino, S. D. Fekkema, & R. Glaser (Eds.), *Cognitive psychology and instruction* (Vol. 1, pp. 419–428). New York: Plenum.

MUSSEN, P., & EISENBERG-BERG, N. (1977). *Roots of caring, sharing, and helping.* San Francisco: Freeman.

NADEL, M. V. (1971). *The politics of consumer protection.* Indianapolis: Bobbs-Merrill.

NAEYE, R. L., BLANC, W., & PAUL, C. (1973). Effects of maternal nutrition on the human fetus. *Pediatrics, 52*, 494–503.

NAEYE, R. L., & PETERS, E. C. (1984). Mental development of children whose mothers smoked during pregnancy. *Obstetrics and Gynecology, 64*, 601–607.

NAGEL, E. (1959). Methodological issues in psychoanalytic theory. In S. Hook (Ed.), *Psychoanalysis, scientific method, and philosophy* (pp. 38–56). New York: New York University Press.

NANEZ, J. (1987). Perception of impending collision in 3- to 6-week-old infants. *Infant Behavior and Development, 11*, 447–463.

NAPIER, J. (1970). *The roots of mankind.* Washington, DC: Smithsonian Institution Press.

NASH, J. E., & PERSAUD, T. V. N. (1988). Embryopathic risks of cigarette smoking. *Experimental Pathology, 33*, 65–73.

NASTASI, B. K., CLEMENTS, D. H., & BATTISTA, M. T. (1990). Social–

cognitive interactions, motivation, and cognitive growth in Logo programming and CAI problem-solving environments. *Journal of Educational Psychology, 82,* 1–9.

NATIONAL ASSESSMENT OF EDUCATIONAL PROGRESS (1985). *The Reading Report Card: Progress toward excellence in our schools.* Princeton, NJ: Educational Testing Service.

NATIONAL COMMISSION FOR THE PROTECTION OF HUMAN SUBJECTS (1977). *Report and recommendations: Research involving children.* Washington, DC: U.S. Government Printing Office.

NATIONAL COMMISSION ON EXCELLENCE IN EDUCATION (1983). *A nation at risk: The imperative for educational reform.* Washington, DC: U.S. Government Printing Office.

NATIONAL COMMISSION TO PREVENT INFANT MORTALITY (1988). *Death before life: The tragedy of infant mortality,* Washington DC: Author.

NATIONAL INSTITUTE ON DRUG ABUSE, U.S. DEPARTMENT OF HEALTH AND HUMAN SERVICES (1987). *National trends in drug use and related factors among American high school students and young adults.* Rockville, MD: Author.

NEAL, J. H. (1983). Children's understanding of their parents' divorces. In L. A. Kurdek (Ed.), *New directions for child development* (Vol. 19, pp. 3–14). San Francisco: Jossey-Bass.

NEEDLEMAN, H. L., SCHELL, A., BELLINGER, D., LEVITON, A., & ALLRED, E. N. (1990). The long-term effects of exposure to low doses of lead in childhood. *New England Journal of Medicine, 322,* 83–88.

NEIMARK, E. (1975). Intellectual development during adolescence. In F. Horowitz (Ed.), *Review of child development research* (Vol. 4, pp. 541–594). Chicago: University of Chicago Press.

NEISSER, U. (1967). *Cognitive psychology,* Englewood Cliffs, NJ: Prentice-Hall.

NELSON, E. A., GRINDER, R. E., & BIAGGIO, A. M. (1969). Relationships among behavioral, cognitive-developmental, and self-support measures of morality and personality. *Multivariate Behavioral Research, 4,* 483–500.

NELSON, E. A., GRINDER, R. E., & MUTTERER, M. L. (1969). Sources of variance in behavioral measures of honesty in temptation situations: Methodological analyses. *Developmental Psychology, 1,* 265–279.

NELSON, J., & ABOUD, F. E. (1985). The resolution of social conflict between friends. *Child Development, 56,* 1009–1017.

NELSON, K. (1973). Structure and strategy in learning to talk. *Monographs of the Society for Research in Child Development, 38*(1–2, Serial No. 149).

NELSON, K. (1975). The nominal shift in semantic–syntactic development. *Cognitive Psychology, 7,* 461–479.

NELSON, K. (1976). Some attributes of adjectives used by young children. *Cognition, 4,* 13–30.

NELSON, K. (1981). Individual differences in language development: Implications for development and language. *Developmental Psychology, 17,* 170–187.

NELSON, K. (1984). The transition from infant to child memory. In M. Moscovitch (Ed.), *Infant memory* (pp. 103–130). New York: Plenum.

NELSON, K. (1986). *Event knowledge.* Hillsdale, NJ: Erlbaum.

NELSON, K. (1989). Strategies for first language teaching. In M. L. Rice & R. L. Schiefelbusch (Eds.), *The teachability of language.* Baltimore: Brookes.

NELSON, K., & BROWN, A. L. (1978). The semantic–episodic distinction in memory development. In P. A. Ornstein (Ed.), *Memory development in children* (pp. 233–241). Hillsdale, NJ: Erlbaum.

NELSON, K., & GRUENDEL, J. (1981). Generalized event representations: Basic building blocks of cognitive development. In M. Lamb & A. Brown (Eds.), *Advances in developmental psychology,* (Vol. 1, pp. 131–158). Hillsdale, NJ: Erlbaum.

NELSON, K., & ROSS, G. (1980). The generalities and specifics of long-term memory in infants and young children. In M. Perlmutter (Ed.), *Children's memory* (pp. 87–101). San Francisco: Jossey-Bass.

NELSON, K., RESCORLA, L., GRUENDEL, J. M., & BENEDICT, H. (1978). Early lexicons: What do they mean? *Child Development, 49,* 960–968.

NELSON, K. E., DENNINGER, M., BONVILLIAN, J., KAPLAN, B., & BAKER, N. (1984). Maternal adjustments and non-adjustments as related to children's linguistic advances and language acquisition theories. In A. Pellegrini & T. Yawkey (Eds.), *The development of oral and written languages: Readings in developmental and applied linguistics* (pp. 31–56). Norwood, NJ: Ablex.

NELSON, K. E., & KOSSLYN, S. M. (1976). Recognition of previously labeled or unlabeled pictures by 5-year-olds and adults. *Journal of Experimental Child Psychology, 21,* 40–45.

NELSON-LE GALL, S. A. (1985). Motive–outcome matching and outcome foreseeability: Effects on attribution of intentionality and moral judgments. *Developmental Psychology, 21,* 332–337.

NEMEROWICZ, G. M. (1979). *Children's perceptions of gender and work roles.* New York: Praeger.

NESHER, P. (1988). Multiplicative school and word problems: Theoretical approaches and empirical findings. In M. J. Behr & J. Hiebert (Eds.), *Research agenda in mathematical education: Number concepts and operations in the middle grades* (pp. 19–40). Reston, VA: National Council of Teachers of Mathematics.

NETLEY, C. T. (1986). Summary overview of behavioural development in individuals with neonatally identified X and Y aneuploidy. *Birth Defects, 22,* 293–306.

NEVIN, M. M. (1988, March). Dormant dangers of DES. *The Canadian Nurse, 84*(3), 17–19.

NEW JERSEY V. T.L.O., 469 U.S. 325 (1985).

NEWACHECK, P. W., & STARFIELD, B. (1988). Morbidity and use of ambulatory care services among poor and nonpoor children. *American Journal of Public Health, 78,* 927–933.

NEWCOMB, A. F., BRADY, J. E., & HARTUP, W.W. (1979). Friendship and incentive condition as determinants of children's task-oriented social behavior. *Child Development, 50,* 878–881.

NEWCOMB, A. F., & COLLINS, W. A. (1979). Children's comprehension of family role portrayals in televised dramas: Effects of socioeconomic status, ethnicity, and age. *Developmental Psychology, 15,* 417–423.

NEWCOMB, M. D., & BENTLER, P. M. (1988). Consequences of adolescent substance use on young adult health status and utilization of health services: A structural equation model over four years. *Social Science and Medicine, 24,* 71–82.

NEWCOMB, M. D., & BENTLER, P. M. (1989). Substance use and abuse among children and teenagers. *American Psychologist, 44,* 242–248.

NEWCOMB, M. D., MADDAHIAN, E., & BENTLER, P. M. (1986). Risk factors for drug use among adolescents: Concurrent and longitudinal analyses. *American Journal of Public Health, 76,* 525–531.

NEWCOMBE, N. (1982). Development of spatial cognition and cognitive development. In R. Cohen (Ed.), *Children's conceptions of spatial relationships* (pp. 65–81). San Francisco: Jossey-Bass.

NEWCOMBE, N., & DUBAS, J. S. (1987). Individual differences in cognitive ability: Are they related to timing of puberty? In R. M. Lerner & T. T. Foch (Eds.), *Biological–psychosocial interactions in early adolescence: A life-span perspective* (pp. 249–302). Hillsdale, NJ: Erlbaum.

NEWPORT, E. L., GLEITMAN, H., & GLEITMAN, L. R. (1977). Mother, I'd rather do it myself: Some effects and non-effects of maternal speech style. In C. A. Ferguson & C. E. Snow (Eds.), *Talking to children* (pp. 109–149). New York: Cambridge University Press.

NEWELL, A., & SIMON, H. A. (1972). *Human problem solving.* Englewood Cliffs, NJ: Prentice-Hall.

NEWSON, J., & NEWSON, E. (1976). *Seven years old in the home environment.* London: Allen & Unwin.

NICHOLLS, J. G. (1975). Causal attributions and other achievement related cognitions: Effects of task outcome, attainment value, and sex. *Journal of Personality and Social Psychology, 31,* 379–389.

NICHOLLS, J. G. (1976). Effort is virtuous but it's better to have ability: Evaluative responses to perceptions of effort and ability. *Journal of Research in Personality, 10,* 306–315.

NICHOLLS, J. G. (1978). The development of concepts of effort and ability, perception of academic attainment, and the understanding that difficult tasks require more ability. *Child Development, 49,* 800–814.

NICHOLLS, J. G. (1979). Development of perceptions of own attainment and causal attributions for success and failure in reading. *Journal of Educational Psychology, 71,* 94–99.

NICHOLS, R. C. (1978). Heredity and environment: Major findings from twin studies of ability, personality, and interests. *Home, 29,* 158–173.

NIELSEN, J., NYBORG, M., & DAHL, G. (1977). Turner's syndrome. *Acta Jut Landiei, 45*(Medicare Series No. 21).

NIELSEN TELEVISION SERVICES (1985). *Nielsen report on television.* Northbrook, IL: A.C. Nielsen.

NILSSON, L. (1986). *A child is born.* New York: Delacorte.

NISAN, M., & KOHLBERG, L. (1982). Universality and cross-cultural variation in moral development: A longitudinal and cross-sectional study in Turkey. *Child Development, 53,* 865–876.

NORBECK, J. S., & TILDEN, V. P. (1983). Life stress, social support, and emotional disequilibrium in complications of pregnancy: A prospective, multivariate study. *Journal of Health and Social Behavior, 24,* 30–46.

NOTTELMANN, E. D. (1987). Competence and self-esteem during transition from childhood to adolescence. *Developmental Psychology, 23,* 441–450.

NOTTELMANN, E. D., SUSMAN, E. J., BLUE, J. H., INOFF-GERMAIN, G., DORN, L. D., LORIAUX, D. L., CUTLER, G. B., JR., & CHROUSOS, G. P. (1987). Gonadal and adrenal hormone correlates of adjustment in early adolescence. In R. M. Lerner & T. T. Foch (Eds.), *Biological–psychosocial interactions in early adolescence: A life-span perspective* (pp. 303–323). Hillsdale, NJ: Erlbaum.

NOVICK, B. (in press). Pediatric AIDS: A medical overview. In J. M. Seibert & R. A. Olson (Eds.), *Children adolescents, and AIDS.* Lincoln, NE: University of Nebraska Press.

NOWAKOWSKI, R. S. (1987). Basic concepts of CNS development. *Child Development, 58,* 568–595.

NUCCI, L. (1981). Conceptions of personal issues: A domain distinct from moral or societal concepts. *Child Development, 52,* 114–121.

NUCCI, L. P., & TURIEL, E. (1978). Social interactions and the development of social concepts in preschool children. *Child Development, 49,* 400–407.

NUCKOLLS, K. B., CASSEL, J., & KAPLAN, B. H. (1972). Psychosocial assets, life crisis, and the prognosis of pregnancy. *American Journal of Epidemiology, 95,* 431–441.

NUNNALLY, J. C. (1982). The study of human change: Measurement, research strategies, and methods of analysis. In B. B. Wolman (Ed.), *Handbook of developmental psychology* (pp. 133–148). Englewood Cliffs, NJ: Prentice-Hall.

OAKLAND, T. D. (1978). Predictive validity of readiness tests of middle and lower socio-economic status Anglo, Black, and Mexican American children. *Journal of Educational Psychology, 70,* 574–582.

OAKLAND, T. D. (1979). Research on the Adaptive Behavior Inventory for Children and the Estimated Learning Potential. *School Psychology Digest, 8,* 209–213.

OAKLAND, T., & PARMELEE, R. (1985). Mental measurement of minority-group children. In B. B. Wolman (Ed.), *Handbook of intelligence* (pp. 699–736). New York: Wiley.

OATES, R. K. (1982). Child abuse — A community concern. In R. K. Oates (Ed.), *Child abuse: A community concern* (pp. 1–12). New York: Brunner/Mazel.

OATES, R. K. (1984). Similarities and differences between nonorganic failure to thrive and deprivation dwarfism. *Child Abuse and Neglect, 8,* 438–445.

OATES, R. K., PEACOCK, A., & FORREST, D. (1985). Long-term effects of nonorganic failure to thrive. *Pediatrics, 75,* 36–40.

OBERG, C. N. (1988, Spring). Children and the uninsured. *Social Policy Report of the Society for Research in Child Development, 3*(No. 1).

O'BRIEN, M., & HUSTON, A. C. (1985). Development of sex-typed play behavior in toddlers. *Developmental Psychology, 21,* 866–871.

O'BRIEN, M., HUSTON, A. C., & RISLEY, T. R. (1981). *Emergence and stability of sex-typed toy preferences in toddlers.* Paper presented at the annual meeting of the Association for Behavior Analysis, Milwaukee.

O'BRIEN, M., HUSTON, A. C., & RISLEY, T. R. (1983). Sex-typed play of toddlers in a day care center. *Journal of Applied Developmental Psychology, 4,* 1–9.

O'CONNOR, M., FOCH, T., SHERRY, T., & PLOMIN, R. (1980). A twin study of specific behavioral problems of socialization as viewed by parents. *Journal of Abnormal Child Psychology, 8,* 189–199.

ODEN, S. L., & ASHER, S. R. (1977). Coaching children in social skills for friendship making. *Child Development, 48,* 495–506.

OETTINGEN, G. (1985). The influence of kindergarten teacher on sex differences in behavior. *International Journal of Behavioral Development, 8,* 3–13.

OFFER, D. (1988). *The teenage world: Adolescents' self-image in ten countries.* New York: Plenum.

O'HIGGINS, M. (1988). The allocation of public resources to children and the elderly in OECD countries. In J. L. Palmer & I. V. Sawhill (Eds.), *The vulnerable* (pp. 201–228). Washington, DC: The Urban Institute Press.

O'KEEFE, B. J., & BENOIT, P. J. (1982). Children's arguments. In J. R. Cox & C. A. Willard (Eds.), *Advances in argumentation theory and research* (pp. 154–183). Carbondale, IL: Southern Illinois University Press.

OLLER, D. K., & EILERS, R. E. (1988). The role of audition in infant babbling. *Child Development, 59,* 441–449.

OLSHO, L. W. (1984). Infant frequency discrimination. *Infant Behavior and Development, 7,* 27–35.

OLSON, C. F., & WOROBEY, J. (1984). Perceived mother–daughter relations in a pregnant and nonpregnant adolescent sample. *Adolescence, 12,* 781–794.

OLWEUS, D. (1980). Familial and temperamental determinants of aggressive behavior in adolescent boys: A causal analysis. *Developmental Psychology, 16,* 644–666.

OLWEUS, D., MATTSSON, A., SCHALLING, D., & LOW, H. (1980). Testosterone, aggression, physical, and personality dimensions in normal adolescent males. *Psychosomatic Medicine, 33,* 265–277.

O'MAHONEY, J. F. (1989). Development of thinking about things and people: Social and nonsocial cognition during adolescence. *Journal of Genetic Psychology, 150,* 217–224.

O'MALLEY, P. M., & BACHMAN, J. G. (1983). Self-esteem: Change and stability between ages 13 and 23. *Developmental Psychology, 19,* 257–268.

OMARK, D. R., OMARK, M., & EDELMAN, M. S. (1975). Formation of dominance hierarchies in young children: Attention and perception. In T. Williams (Ed.), *Psychological anthropology* (pp. 289–315). The Hague: Mouton.

OMER, H., & EVERLY, G. S. (1988). Psychological factors in preterm labor. Critical review and theoretical synthesis. *American Journal of Psychiatry, 145,* 1507–1513.

OPENSHAW, D. K., THOMAS, D. L., & ROLLINS, B. C. (1984). Parental influences of adolescent self-esteem. *Journal of Early Adolescence, 4,* 259–274.

OPPENHEIM, D., SAGI, A., & LAMB, M. E. (1988). Infant–adult attachments on the kibbutz and their relation to socioemotional development 4 years later. *Developmental Psychology, 24,* 427–433.

ORGANIZATION FOR ECONOMIC COOPERATION AND DEVELOPMENT (1988a). *Aging populations: The social policy implications.* Paris: Author.

ORGANIZATION FOR ECONOMIC COOPERATION AND DEVELOPMENT (1988b). *Development cooperation: 1988 review.* Paris: Author.

ORNSTEIN, P. A., MEDLIN, R. G., STONE, B. P., & NAUS, M. J. (1985). Retrieving for rehearsal: An analysis of active rehearsal in children's memory. *Developmental Psychology, 21,* 633–641.

ORNSTEIN, P. A., NAUS, M. J., & LIBERTY, C. (1975). Rehearsal and organizational processes in children's memory. *Child Development, 46,* 818–830.

ORNSTEIN, P. A., NAUS, M. J., & STONE, B. P. (1977). Rehearsal training and developmental differences in memory. *Developmental Psychology, 13,* 15–24.

OSHERSON, D. N., & MARKMAN, E. M. (1975). Language and the ability to evaluate contradictions and tautologies. *Cognition, 2,* 213–226.

OSOFSKY, H. J., & OSOFSKY, J. D. (1983). Adolescent adaptation to pregnancy and parenthood. In E. R. McAnarney (Ed.), *Premature adolescent pregnancy and parenthood* (pp. 195–206). New York: Grune & Stratton.

OWEN, M. T., & COX, M. (1988). Maternal employment and the transition to parenthood. In A. E. Gottfried & A. W. Gottfried (Eds.), *Maternal employment and children's development: Longitudinal research* (pp. 85–119). New York: Plenum.

OWEN, M. T., EASTERBROOKS, M. A., CHASE-LANSDALE, L. & GOLDBERG, W. A. (1984). The relation between maternal employment status and the stability of attachments to mother and father. *Child Development, 55,* 1894–1901.

OWENS, T. (1982). Experience-based career education: Summary and implications of research and evaluation findings. *Child and Youth Services Journal, 4,* 77–91.

PAGE, D. C., MOSHER, R., SIMPSON, E. M., FISHER, E. M. C., MARDON, G., POLLACK, J., McGILLIVRAY, B., DE LA CHAPELLE, A., & BROWN, L. G. (1987). The sex-determining region of the human Y chromosome encodes a finger protein. *Cell, 51,* 1091–1104.

PAGE, E. B., & GRANDON, G. M. (1979). Family configuration and mental ability: Two theories contrasted with U.S. data. *American Educational Research Journal, 16,* 257–272.

PAGET, K. F., & KRITT, D. (1986). The development of the conceptual organization of self. *Journal of Genetic Psychology, 146,* 333–341.

PALKOVITZ, R. (1984). Parental attitudes and fathers' interactions with their 5-month-old infants. *Developmental Psychology, 20,* 1054–1060.

PAPINI, D., & SEBBY, R. (1987). Adolescent pubertal status and affective family relationships: A multivariate assessment. *Journal of Youth and Adolescence, 16,* 1–15.

PAPOUSEK, M., & PAPOUSEK, H. (in press). Melodic units in maternal speech in tonal and nontonal languages: Evidence of a universal parental support for prelinguistic communication. *Infant Behavior and Development.*

PAREKH, U. C., PHERWANI, A., UDANI, P. M., & MUKHERJEE, S. (1970). Brain weight and head circumference in fetus, infant and children of different nutritional and socio-economic groups. *Indian Pediatrics, 7,* 347–358.

PARHAM, V. J. R., 442 U.S. 584 (1979).

PARIKH, B. (1980). Development of moral judgment and its relation to family environmental factors in Indian and American families. *Child Development, 51,* 1030–1039.

PARIS, S. G., & LINDAUER, B. K. (1977). Constructive processes in children's comprehension and memory. In R. V. Kail & J. W. Hagen (Eds.), *Perspectives on the development of memory and cognition* (pp. 35–60). Hillsdale, NJ: Erlbaum.

PARIS, S. G., & LINDAUER, B. K. (1982). The development of cognitive skills during childhood. In B. Wolman (Ed.), *Handbook of developmental psychology* (pp. 333–349). Englewood Cliffs, NJ: Prentice-Hall.

PARIS, S. G., SAARNIO, D. A., & CROSS, D. R. (1986). A metacognitive curriculum to promote children's reading and learning. *Australian Journal of Psychology, 38,* 107–123.

PARK, K. A., & WATERS, E. (1989). Security of attachment and preschool friendships. *Child Development, 60,* 1076–1081.

PARKE, R. D. (1977). Punishment in children: Effects, side effects, and alternative control strategies. In H. Hom, Jr., & A. Robinson (Eds.), *Early childhood education: A psychological perspective* (pp. 71–97). New York: Academic Press.

PARKE, R. D., BERKOWITZ, L., LEYENS, J. P., WEST, S. G., & SEBASTIAN, R. J. (1977). Some effects of violent and nonviolent movies on the behavior of juvenile delinquents. In L. Berkowitz (Ed.), *Advances in experimental social psychology* (Vol. 10, pp. 135–172). New York: Academic Press.

PARKE, R. D., & COLLMER, C. W. (1975). Child abuse: An interdisci-

plinary analysis. In E. M. Hetherington (Ed), *Review of child development research* (Vol. 5, pp. 264–283). Chicago: University of Chicago Press.

PARKE, R. D., & DEUR, J. L. (1972). Schedule of punishment and inhibition of aggression in children. *Developmental Psychology, 7,* 266–269.

PARKE, R. D., MacDONALD, K. B., BEITEL, A., & BHAVNAGRI, N. (1988). The role of the family in the development of peer relationships. In R. DeV. Peters & R. J. McMahan (Eds.), *Marriages and families: Behavioral treatment and processes.* New York: Brunner/Mazel.

PARKE, R. D., & SAWIN, D. B. (1976). The father's role in infancy. *Family Coordinator, 25,* 265–371.

PARKE, R. D., & SLABY, R. G. (1983). The development of aggression. In E. M. Hetherington (Ed.), *Handbook of child psychology: Vol. 4, Socialization, personality, and social development* (Vol. 4, pp. 547–641). New York: Wiley.

PARKE, R. D., & SUOMI, S. J. (1980). Adult male–infant relationships: Human and nonprimate evidence. In K. Immelmann, G. Barlow, M. Main, & L. Petrinovitch (Eds.), *Behavioral development: The Bielefeld interdisciplinary project* (pp. 700–725). New York: Cambridge University Press.

PARKE, R. D., & TINSLEY, B. R. (1981). The father's role in infancy: Determinants of involvement in caregiving and play. In M. E. Lamb (Ed.), *The role of the father in child development* (pp. 429–458). New York: Wiley.

PARKE, R. D., & WALTERS, R. H. (1967). Some factors determining the efficacy of punishment for inducing response inhibition. *Monographs of the Society for Research in Child Development, 32*(1, Serial No. 109).

PARKER, J. G., & ASHER, S. R. (1987). Peer relations and later personal adjustment: Are low-accepted children at risk? *Psychological Bulletin, 102,* 357–389.

PARMELEE, A., WENNER, W., AKIYAMA, Y., STERN, E., & FLESCHER, J. (1967). Electroencephalography and brain maturation. In A. Minkowski (Ed.), *Symposium on regional development of the brain in early life.* Philadelphia: Davis.

PARSONS, J. E. (1982). Biology, experience, and sex-dimorphic behaviors. In W. R. Gove & G. R. Carpenter (Eds.), *The fundamental connection between nature and nurture* (pp. 137–170). Lexington, MA: Lexington Books.

PARSONS, J. E. (1983). Expectancies, values and academic behaviors. In J. T. Spence (Ed.), *Achievement and achievement motives: Psychological and sociological approaches* (pp. 75–146). San Francisco: Freeman.

PARSONS, J. E., ADLER, T. F., & KACZALA, C. M. (1982). Socialization of achievement attitudes and beliefs: Parental influences. *Child Development. 53,* 310–321.

PARTEN, M. (1932). Social participation among preschool children. *Journal of Abnormal and Social Psychology, 27,* 243–269.

PASAMANICK, B., & KNOBLOCH, H. (1966). Retrospective studies on the epidemiology of reproductive casualty: Old and new. *Merrill-Palmer Quarterly, 12,* 7–26.

PASCOE, J. M., LODA, F. A., JEFFRIES, V., & EASP, J. A. (1981). The association between mother's social support and provision of stimulation to their children. *Developmental and Behavioral Pediatrics, 2,* 15–19.

PASSMAN, R. H. (1976). Arousal reducing properties of attachment objects: Testing the functional limits of the security blanket relative to the mother. *Developmental Psychology, 12,* 468–469.

PASSMAN, R. H. (1987). Attachments to inanimate objects: Are children who have security blankets insecure? *Journal of Consulting and Clinical Psychology, 55,* 825–830.

PASSMAN, R. H., & HALONEN, J. S. (1979). A developmental survey of young children's attachment to inanimate objects. *Journal of Genetic Psychology, 134,* 165–178.

PASSMAN, R. H., & WEISBERG, P. (1975). Mothers and blankets as agents for promoting play and exploration by young children in a novel environment: The effects of social and nonsocial attachment objects. *Developmental Psychology, 11,* 170–177.

PATTERSON, G. R. (1976). The aggressive child: Victim and architect of a coercive system. In L. Hammerlyck, E. Marsh, & L. Handy (Eds.),

Behavior modification and families (pp. 267–316). New York: Brunner/Mazel.

PATTERSON, G. R. (1981). Mothers: The unacknowledged victims. *Monographs of the Society for Research in Child Development, 45*(5, Serial No. 186).

PATTERSON, G. R. (1982). *Coercive family processes.* Eugene, OR: Castilia Press.

PATTERSON, G. R. (1988). Stress: A change agent for family process. In N. Garmezy & M. Rutter (Eds.), *Stress, coping, and development in children* (pp. 235–264). Baltimore: Johns Hopkins University Press.

PATTERSON, G. R., DEBARYSHE, B. D., & RAMSEY, E. (1989). A developmental perspective on antisocial behavior. *American Psychologist, 44,* 329–335.

PATTERSON, G. R., LITTMAN, R. A., & BRICKER, W. (1967). Assertive behavior in children: A step toward a theory of aggression. *Monographs of the Society for Research in Child Development, 32*(5, Serial No. 113).

PAULSEN, K., & JOHNSON, M. (1983). Sex-role attitudes and mathematical ability in 4th, 8th, and 11th grade students from a high socioeconomic area. *Developmental Psychology, 19,* 210–214.

PEA, R. D., & KURLAND, D. M. (1984). On the cognitive effects of learning computer programming. *New Ideas in Psychology, 2,* 137–168.

PEAL, E., & LAMBERT, W. (1962). The relation of bilingualism to intelligence. *Psychological Monographs, 76,* 1–23.

PEARLIN, L. I., YARROW, M. R., & SCARR, H. A. (1967). Unintended consequences of parental aspirations: The case of children's cheating. *American Journal of Sociology, 73,* 73–83.

PEARSON, J. L., HUNTER, A. G., ENSMINGER, M. E., & KELLAM, S. G. (1990). Black grandmothers in multigenerational households: Diversity in family structure and parenting involvement in the Woodlawn community. *Child Development, 61,* 434–442.

PECHMANN, T., & DEUTSCH, W. (1982). The development of verbal and nonverbal devices for reference. *Journal of Experimental Child Psychology, 34,* 330–341.

PEDERSEN, F. A. (1976). *Mother, father and infant as an interaction system.* Paper presented at the annual meeting of the American Psychological Association, Washington, DC.

PEDERSEN, F. A., CAIN, R., ZAZLOW, M., & ANDERSON, B. (1980). *Variation in infant experience associated with alternative family role organization.* Paper presented at the International Conference on Infant Studies, New Haven, CT.

PEDERSON, D., BENTO, S., CHANCE, G., & EVANS, B. (1987). Maternal emotional responses to preterm birth. *American Journal of Orthopsychiatry, 57,* 15–21.

PEEPLES, D. R., & TELLER, D. Y. (1975). Color vision and brightness discrimination in two month old human infants. *Science, 189,* 1102–1103.

PEEVERS, B. H., & SECORD, P. F. (1973). Developmental changes in attribution of descriptive concepts and to persons. *Journal of Personality and Social Psychology, 27,* 120–128.

PELHAM, W. E. JR., & MURPHY, D. A. (in press). Attention deficit disorder. In D. Byrne & G. Caddy (Eds.), *International perspectives in behavioral medicine.* Norwood, NJ: Ablex.

PENNER, S. G. (1987). Parental responses to grammatical and ungrammatical utterances. *Child Development, 58,* 376–384.

PENNINGTON, B. F., BENDER, B., PUCK, M., SALBENBLATT, J., & ROBINSON, A. (1982). Learning disabilities in children with sex chromosome anomalies. *Child Development, 53,* 1182–1192.

PEPLER, D. J., & ROSS, H. S. (1981). The effects of play on convergent and divergent problem solving. *Child Development, 52,* 1202–1210.

PERFETTI, C. A. (1988). Verbal efficiency in reading ability. In M. Daneman, G. E. MacKinnon, & T. G. Waller (Eds.), *Reading research: Advances in theory and practice* (Vol. 6, pp. 109–143). San Diego, CA: Academic Press.

PERLMUTTER, M. (1984). Continuities and discontinuities in early human memory: Paradigms, processes, and performances. In R. V. Kail, Jr., & N. R. Spear (Eds.), *Comparative perspectives on the development of memory* (pp. 253–287). Hillsdale, NJ: Erlbaum.

PERLMUTTER, M., BEHREND, S. D., KUO, F., & MULLER, A. (1989). Social influences on children's problem solving. *Developmental Psychology, 25,* 744–754.

PERLMUTTER, M., & LANGE, G. (1978). A developmental analysis of recall–recognition distinctions. In P. A. Ornstein (Ed.), *Memory development in children* (pp. 243–258). Hillsdale, NJ: Erlbaum.

PERNER, J. (1988). Higher-order beliefs and intentions in children's understanding of social interaction. In J. W. Astington, P. L. Harris, & D. R. Olson (Eds.), *Developing theories of mind* (pp. 271–294). Cambridge, England: Cambridge University Press.

PERRY, D. G., & BUSSEY, K. (1977). Self-reinforcement in high- and low-aggressive boys following acts of aggression. *Child Development, 48,* 653–657.

PERRY, D. G., PERRY, L. C., & WEISS, R. J. (1989). Sex differences in the consequences children anticipate for aggression. *Developmental Psychology, 25,* 171–184.

PESKIN, H. (1973). Influence of the developmental schedule of puberty on learning and ego functioning. *Journal of Youth and Adolescence, 2,* 273–290.

PETERS, D. P. (1987). The impact of naturally occurring stress on children's memory. In S. J. Ceci, M. P. Toglia, & D. F. Ross (Eds.), *Children's eyewitness memory* (pp. 122–141). New York: Springer-Verlag.

PETERSEN, A. C. (1979). Hormones and cognitive functioning in normal development. In M. A. Wittig & A. C. Petersen (Eds.), *Sex differences in cognitive functioning* (pp. 189–214). New York: Academic Press.

PETERSEN, A. C. (1983). Menarche: Meaning of measures and measuring meaning. In S. Golub (Ed.), *Menarche* (pp. 63–76). Lexington, MA: Lexington Books.

PETERSON, C. C., PETERSON, J. L., & CARROLL, J. (1986). Television viewing and imaginative problem solving during preadolescence. *Journal of Genetic Psychology, 147,* 61–67.

PETERSON, L. (1982). An alternative perspective to norm-based explanations of modeling and children's generosity: A reply to Lipscomb, Larrieu, McAllister, and Bregman. *Merrill-Palmer Quarterly, 28,* 283–290.

PETERSON, P. E., JEFFREY, D. B., BRIDGWATER, C. A., & DAWSON, B. (1984). How pronutrition television programming affects children's dietary habits. *Developmental Psychology, 20,* 55–63.

PETERSON, P. L. (1977). Interactive effects of student anxiety, achievement orientation, and teacher behavior on student achievement and attitude. *Journal of Educational Psychology, 69,* 779–792.

PETERSON, P. L. (1979). Direct instruction reconsidered. In P. L. Peterson & H. J. Walberg (Eds.), *Research on teaching: Concepts, findings, and implications.* Berkeley, CA: McCutchan.

PETTIT, G. S., DODGE, K. A., & BROWN, M. M. (1988). Early family experience, social problem solving patterns, and children's social competence. *Child Development, 59,* 107–120.

PEZZULLO, T. R., THORSEN, E. E., & MADAUS, G. F. (1972). The heritability of Jensen's Level I and II and divergent thinking. *American Educational Research Journal, 9,* 539–546.

PFEFFER, C. R. (1986). *The suicidal child.* New York: Guilford Press.

PFOUTS, J. H. (1976). The sibling relationship: A forgotten dimension. *Social Work, 21,* 200–204.

PHILIPPS, C., & JOHNSON, N. E. (1977). The impact of quality of diet and other factors on birth weight of infants. *American Journal of Clinical Nutrition, 30,* 215–225.

PHILLIPS, D., & McCARTNEY, K., & SCARR, S. (1987). Child-care quality and children's social development. *Developmental Psychology, 23,* 537–543.

PHILLIPS, D. A., McCARTNEY, K., SCARR, S., & HOWES, C. (1987). Selective review of infant day care research: A cause for concern. *Zero to Three, 7,* 18–21.

PHILLIPS, D., & ZIGLER, E. (1987). The checkered history of federal child care regulation. In E. Z. Rothkopf (Ed.), *Review of research in education* (Vol., 14, pp. 3–41). Washington, DC: American Educational Research Association.

PHILLIPS, J. C., & KELLY, D. H. (1979). School failure and delinquency: What causes which? *Criminology, 17,* 194–207.

PIAGET, J. (1926). *The language and thought of the child*. New York: Harcourt, Brace & World. (Original work published 1923)

PIAGET, J. (1928). *Judgment and reasoning in the child*. New York: Harcourt, Brace & World. (Original work published 1926)

PIAGET, J. (1929). *The child's conception of physical causality*. New York: Harcourt, Brace & World. (Original work published 1927)

PIAGET, J. (1930). *The child's conception of the world*. New York: Harcourt, Brace & World. (Original work published 1926)

PIAGET, J. (1950). *The psychology of intelligence*. New York: International Universities Press.

PIAGET, J. (1951). *Play, dreams and imitation in childhood*. New York: Norton. (Original work published 1945)

PIAGET, J. (1952a). Jean Piaget (autobiographical sketch). In E. G. Boring, H. S. Langfeld, H. Werner, & R. M. Yerkes (Eds.), *A history of psychology in autobiography* (pp. 237–256). Worcester, MA: Clark University Press.

PIAGET, J. (1952b). *The origins of intelligence in children*. New York: International Universities Press. (Original work published 1936)

PIAGET, J. (1954). *The construction of reality in the child*. New York: Basic Books. (Original work published 1937)

PIAGET, J. (1965). *The moral judgment of the child*. New York: Free Press. (Original work published 1932)

PIAGET, J. (1966). Nécessité et signification des recherches comparatives en psychologie génétique. *Journal International de Psychologie, 1,* 1–13.

PIAGET, J. (1969). *The child's conception of time*. London: Routledge & Kegan Paul. (Original work published 1946)

PIAGET, J. (1970). *The child's conception of movement and speed*. London: Routledge & Kegan Paul. (Original work published 1946)

PIAGET, J. (1971). *Biology and knowledge*. Chicago: University of Chicago Press.

PIAGET, J. (1978). *Success and understanding*. Cambridge, MA: Harvard University Press.

PIAGET, J. (1985). *The equilibration of cognitive structures: The central problem of intellectual development*. Chicago: University of Chicago Press.

PIAGET, J., & INHELDER, B. (1956). *The child's conception of space*. London: Routledge & Kegan Paul. (Original work published 1948)

PIAGET, J., & INHELDER, B. (1969). *The psychology of the child*. London: Routledge & Kegan Paul. (Original work published 1967)

PIAGET, J., & INHELDER, B. (1973). *Memory and intelligence*. New York: Basic Books.

PIAGET, J., INHELDER, B., & SZEMINSKA, A. (1960). *The child's conception of geometry*. New York: Basic Books. (Original work published 1948)

PIANTA, R. C., SROUFE, L. A., & EGELAND, B. (1989). Continuity and discontinuity in maternal sensitivity at 6, 24, and 42 months in a high-risk sample. *Child Development, 60,* 481–487.

PICK, H. L., JR. (1989). Motor development: The control of action. *Developmental Psychology, 25,* 867–870.

PICONE, T. A., ALLEN, L. H., OLSEN, P. N., & FERRIS, M. E. (1982a). Pregnancy outcome in North American women: II. Effects of diet, cigarette smoking, stress, and weight gain on placentas, and on neonatal physical and behavioral characteristics. *American Journal of Clinical Nutrition, 36,* 1214–1224.

PICONE, T. A., ALLEN, L. H., SCHRAMM, M. M., & OLSEN, P. N. (1982b). Pregnancy outcome in North American women: I. Effects of diet, cigarette smoking, and psychological stress on maternal weight gain. *American Journal of Clinical Nutrition, 36,* 1205–1213.

PIETZ, J., BENNINGER, C., SCHMIDT, H., SCHEFFNER, D., & BICKEL, H. (1988). Long-term development of intelligence (IQ) and EEG in 34 children with phenylketonuria treated early. *European Journal of Pediatrics, 147,* 361–367.

PILLOW, B. H. (1988). The development of children's beliefs about the mental world. *Merrill-Palmer Quarterly, 34,* 1–32.

PINKER, S. (1981). On the acquisition of grammatical morphemes. *Journal of Child Language, 8,* 477–484.

PINKER, S. (1984). *Language learnability and language development*. Cambridge, MA: Harvard University Press.

PINKER, S., LEBEAUX, D. S., & FROST, L. A. (1987). Productivity and constraints in the acquisition of the passive. *Cognition, 26,* 195–267.

PIPP, S., & HAITH, M. M. (1984). Infant visual responses to pattern: Which metric predicts best? *Journal of Experimental Child Psychology, 38,* 373–379.

PLOMIN, R. (1986). *Development, genetics and psychology*. Hillsdale, NJ: Erlbaum.

PLOMIN, R. (1989). Environment and genes: Determinants of behavior. *American Psychologist, 44,* 105–111.

PLOMIN, R, & DEFRIES, J. C. (1983). The Colorado Adoption Project. *Child Development, 54,* 276–289.

PLOMIN, R., DEFRIES, J. C., & LOEHLIN, J. C. (1977). Genotype–environment interaction and correlation in the analysis of human behavior. *Psychological Bulletin, 84,* 309–322.

POLANSKY, N. A., GAUDIN, J. M., AMMONS, P. W., & DAVIS, K. B. (1985). The psychological ecology of the neglectful mother. *Child Abuse & Neglect, 9,* 265–275.

PORTER, F. L., PORGES, S. W., & MARSHALL, R. E. (1988). Newborn pain cries and vagal tone: Parallel changes in response to circumcision. *Child Development, 59,* 495–505.

POSNER, M. I., & WARREN, R. E. (1972). Traces, concepts and conscious constructions. In A. W. Melton & E. Martin (Eds.), *Coding processes in human memory* (pp. 25–43). New York: Winston.

POWER, F. C. (1989). *Lawrence Kohlberg's approach to moral education*. New York: Columbia University Press.

POWERS, S. I., HAUSER, S. T., & KILNER, L. A. (1989). Adolescent mental health. *American Psychologist, 44,* 200–208.

PRECHTL, H. F. R. (1958). Problems of behavioral studies in the newborn infant. In D. S. Lehrmann, R. A. Hinde, & E. Shaw (Eds.), *Advances in the study of behavior* (Vol. 1, pp. 75–98). New York: Academic Press.

PRECHTL, H. F. R., & BEINTEMA, D. (1965). *The neurological examination of the full-term newborn infant*. London: William Heinemann Medical Books.

PRECHTL, H. F. R., THEORELL, K., & BLAIR, A. (1973). Behavioral state cycles in abnormal infants. *Developmental Medicine and Child Neurology, 15,* 606–615.

PREISSER, D. A., HODSON, B. W., & PADEN, E. P. (1988). Developmental phonology: 18–29 months. *Journal of Speech and Hearing Disorders, 53,* 125–130.

PRESSLEY, G. M. (1979). Increasing children's self-control through cognitive interventions. *Review of Educational Research, 49,* 319–370.

PRESSLEY, M. (1982). Elaboration and memory development. *Child Development, 53,* 296–309.

PRESSLEY, M., CARIGLIA-BULL, T., DEANE, S., & SCHNEIDER, W. (1987). Short-term memory, verbal competence, and age as predictors of imagery instructional effectiveness. *Journal of Experimental Child Psychology, 43,* 194–211.

PRESSLEY, M., & LEVIN, J. R. (1977). Developmental differences in subjects' associative-learning strategies and performance: Assessing a hypothesis. *Journal of Experimental Child Psychology, 24,* 431–439.

PRESSLEY, M., & MILLER, G. E. (1987). Effects of illustrations on children's listening comprehension and oral prose memory. In D. M. Willows & A. H. Houghton (Eds.), *The psychology of illustration: Vol. 1. Basic research* (pp. 87–114). New York: Springer-Verlag.

PRESTON, R. C. (1962). Reading achievement of German and American children. *School and Society, 90,* 350–354.

PRICE, V. (1987). Runaways and homeless street youth. In The Boston Foundation (Ed.), *Homelessness: Critical issues for policy and practice* (pp. 24–28). Boston: Editor.

PROVINE, R. R., & WESTERMAN, J. A. (1979). Crossing the midline: Limits of early eye–hand behavior. *Child Development, 50,* 437–441.

PULKKINEN, L. (1982). Self-control and continuity from childhood to late adolescence. In P. B. Baltes & O. G. Brim, Jr. (Eds.), *Life-span development and behavior* (Vol. 4, pp. 63–105). New York: Academic Press.

PUTALLAZ, M. (1983). Predicting children's sociometric status from their behavior. *Child Development, 54,* 1417–1426.

PUTALLAZ, M. (1987). Maternal behavior and children's sociometric status. *Child Development, 58,* 324–340.

PUTALLAZ, M., & GOTTMAN, J. M. (1981). Social skills and group acceptance. In S. R. Asher & J. M. Gottman (Eds.), *The development of children's friendships* (pp. 116–149). New York: Cambridge University Press.

QUADAGNO, D. M., BRISCOE, R., & QUADAGNO, J. S. (1977). Effect of perinatal gonadal hormones on selected nonsexual behavior patterns: A critical assessment of the nonhuman and human literature. *Psychological Bulletin, 84,* 62–80.

QUARFOTH, J. M. (1979). Children's understanding of the nature of television characters. *Journal of Communication, 29*(2), 210–218.

QUAY, L. C. (1972). Negro dialect and Binet performance in severely disadvantaged black four-year-olds. *Child Development, 43,* 245–250.

QUAY, L. C. (1974). Language dialect, age, and intelligence-test performance in disadvantaged black children. *Child Development, 45,* 463–468.

QUAY, L. C., & JARRETT, O. S. (1986). Teachers' interactions with middle- and lower-SES preschool boys and girls. *Journal of Educational Psychology, 78,* 495–498.

RABINER, D., & COIE, J. (1989). Effect of expectancy inductions on rejected children's acceptance by unfamiliar peers. *Developmental Psychology, 25,* 450–457.

RADER, N., BAUSANO, M., & RICHARDS, J. E. (1980). On the nature of the visual cliff avoidance response in human infants. *Child Development, 51,* 61–68.

RADKE-YARROW, M., CUMMINGS, E. M., KUCZYNSKI, L., & CHAPMAN, M. (1985). Patterns of attachment in two- and three-year-olds in normal families with parental depression. *Child Development, 56,* 884–893.

RADKE-YARROW, M., & ZAHN-WAXLER, C. (1984). Roots, motives and patterns in children's prosocial behavior. In J. Reykowski, J. Karylowski, D. Bar-Tel, & E. Staub (Eds.), *The development and maintenance of prosocial behaviors: International perspectives on positive morality* (pp. 81–99). New York: Plenum.

RADKE-YARROW, M., ZAHN-WAXLER, C., & CHAPMAN, M. (1983). Children's prosocial dispositions and behavior. In E. M. Hetherington (Ed.), *Handbook of child psychology: Vol. 4. Socialization, personality, and social development* (4th ed., pp. 469–545). New York: Wiley.

RADZISZEWSKA, B., & ROGOFF, B. (1988). Influence of adult and peer collaboration on the development of children's planning skills. *Developmental Psychology, 24,* 840–848.

RAGOZIN, A. S., BASHAM, R. B., CRNIC, K. A., GREENBERG, M. T., & ROBINSON, N. M. (1982). Effects of maternal age on parenting role. *Developmental Psychology, 18,* 627–634.

RAHDERT, E. R. (1988). Treatment services for adolescent drug abusers: Introduction and overview. In E. R. Rahdert & J. Grabowski (Eds.), *Adolescent drug abuse: Analyses of treatment research* (pp. 1–3). Rockville, MD: National Institute on Drug Abuse.

RAMSAY, D. S. (1985). Fluctuations in unimanual hand preference in infants following the onset of duplicated babbling. *Developmental Psychology, 21,* 318–324.

RAMSAY, D. S., & MCCUNE, L. (1984). *Fluctuations in bimanual handedness in the second year of life.* Unpublished manuscript, Rutgers University.

RASKIN, D. C., & YUILLE, J. C. (1989). Problems in evaluating interviews of children in sexual abuse cases. In S. J. Ceci, D. F. Ross, & M. P. Toglia (Eds.), *Perspectives on children's testimony* (pp. 184–207). New York: Springer-Verlag.

RATNER, N., & BRUNNER, J. S. (1978). Social exchange and the acquisition of language. *Journal of Child Language, 5,* 391–402.

RAYMOND, C. L., & BENBOW, C. P. (1986). Gender differences in mathematics: A function of parental support and student sex typing? *Developmental Psychology, 22,* 808–819.

READ, B. K., & CHERRY, L. J. (1978). Preschool children's production of directive forms. *Discourse Processes, 1,* 233–245.

REAVES, J. Y., & ROBERTS, A. (1983). The effect of type of information on children's attraction to peers. *Child Development, 54,* 1024–1031.

REDD, W. H., MORRIS, E. K., & MARTIN, J. A. (1975). Effects of positive and negative adult–child interaction on children's social preferences. *Journal of Experimental Child Psychology, 19,* 153–164.

REDL, F. (1966). *When we deal with children.* New York: Free Press.

REED, E. (1975). Genetic anomalies in development. In F. D. Horowitz (Ed.), *Review of child development research* (Vol. 4, pp. 59–99). Chicago: University of Chicago Press.

REEVE, R. A., & BROWN, A. L. (1985). Metacognition reconsidered: Implications for intervention research. *Journal of Abnormal Child Psychology, 13,* 343–356.

REICH, P. A. (1986). *Language development.* Englewood Cliffs, NJ: Prentice-Hall.

REID, J. (1982). Black America in the 1980's. *Population Bulletin, 37*(4), 1–37.

REID, J. B., TAPLIN, P. S., & LORBER, R. (1981). A social interactional approach to the treatment of abusive families. In R. B. Stuart (Ed.), *Violent behavior: Social learning approaches to prediction, management, and treatment* (pp. 83–101). New York: Brunner/Mazel.

REINISCH, J. M. (1981). Prenatal exposure to synthetic progestins increases potential for aggression in humans. *Science, 211,* 1171–1173.

REINISCH, J. M., & KAROW, W. G. (1977). Prenatal exposure to synthetic progestins and estrogens: Effects on human development. *Archives of Sexual Behavior, 6,* 257–288.

REIS, S. M. (1989). Reflections on policy affecting the education of gifted and talented students: Past and future perspectives. *American Psychologist, 44,* 399–408.

REISER, J., YONAS, A., & WIKNER, K. (1976). Radial localization of odors by human neonates. *Child Development, 47,* 856–859.

REISMAN, J. E. (1987). Touch, motion, and proprioception. In P. Salapatek & L. Cohen (Eds.), *Handbook of infant perception: Vol. 1. From sensation to perception* (pp. 265–303). Orlando, FL: Academic Press.

REISSLAND, N. (1988). Neonatal imitation in the first hour of life: Observations in rural Nepal. *Developmental Psychology, 24,* 464–469.

RENNER, C., & NAVARRO, V. (1989). Why is our population of uninsured and underinsured persons growing? In L. Breslow, J. E. Fielding, & L. B. Lave (Eds.), *Annual review of public health* (Vol. 10, pp. 85–94). Palo Alto, CA: Annual Reviews, Inc.

RENSHAW, P. D., & ASHER, S. R. (1983). Children's goals and strategies for social interaction. *Merrill-Palmer Quarterly, 29,* 353–374.

RESCHLY, D. J. (1978). WISC-R factor structures among Anglos, Blacks, Chicanos, and Native American Papagos. *Journal of Consulting and Clinical Psychology, 46,* 417–422.

RESCHLY, D. J. (1981). Psychological testing in educational classification and placement. *American Psychologist, 36,* 1094–1102.

RESCORLA, L. A. (1980). Category development in early language. *Journal of Child Language, 8,* 225–238.

RESNICK, L. B. (1987). Constructing knowledge in school. In L. S. Liben (Ed.), *Development and learning: Conflict or congruence* (pp. 19–50). Hillsdale, NJ: Erlbaum.

RESNICK, L. B. (1989). Developing mathematical knowledge. *American Psychologist, 44,* 162–169.

REST, J. R. (1973). Patterns of preference and comprehension in moral judgment. *Journal of Personality, 41,* 86–109.

REST, J. R. (1979a). *Development in judging moral issues.* Minneapolis: University of Minnesota Press.

REST, J. R. (1979b). *Revised manual for the Defining Issues Test.* Minneapolis: Minnesota Moral Research Projects.

REST, J. R. (1983). Morality. In J. H. Flavell & E. M. Markman (Eds.), *Handbook of child psychology: Vol. 3. Cognitive development* (4th ed., pp. 556–629). New York: Wiley.

REST, J. R. (1986). *Moral development: Advances in research and theory.* New York: Praeger.

REST, J. R., DAVISON, M. L., & ROBBINS, S. (1978). Age trends in judging moral issues: A review of cross-sectional, longitudinal, and sequential studies of the Defining Issues Test. *Child Development, 49,* 263–279.

REST, J. R., & THOMA, S. J. (1985). Relation of moral judgment to formal education. *Developmental Psychology, 21,* 709–714.

REVELLE, G. L., KARABENICK, J. D., & WELLMAN, H. M. (1981). *Comprehension monitoring in preschool children.* Paper presented at the biennial meeting of the Society for Research in Child Development, Boston.

REVILL, S. I., & DODGE, J. A. (1978). Psychological determinants of infantile pyloric stenosis. *Archives of Disease in Childhood, 53,* 66–68.

REYNOLDS, C. R., & JENSEN, A. R. (1983). WISC-R subscale patterns of abilities of blacks and whites matched on Full Scale IQ. *Journal of Educational Psychology, 75,* 207–214.

REYNOLDS, C. R., & NIGL, A. J. (1981). A regression analysis of differential validity of intelligence tests for black and for white inner city children. *Journal of Clinical Child Psychology, 10,* 176–179.

REYNOLDS, D., JONES, D., ST. LEGER, S., & MURGATROYD, S. (1980). School factors and truancy. In L. Hersov & I. Berg (Eds.), *Out of school: Modern perspectives in truancy and school refusal* (pp. 85–110). New York: Wiley.

RHEINGOLD, H., & ECKERMAN, C. O. (1973). Fear of the stranger: A critical examination. In H. W. Reese (Ed.). *Advances in child development and behavior* (Vol. 8, pp. 185–222). New York: Academic Press.

RHEINGOLD, H., GEWIRTZ, J., & ROSS, H. (1959). Social conditioning of vocalizations in the infant. *Journal of Comparative and Physiological Psychology, 52,* 68–72.

RHOADS, G. G., JACKSON, L. G., SCHLESSELMAN, S. E., DE LA CRUZ, F. F., DESNICK, R. J., GOLBUS, M. S., LEDBETTER, D. H., LUBS, H. A., MAHONEY, M. J., & PERGAMENT, E. (1989). The safety and efficacy of chorionic villus sampling for early prenatal diagnosis of cytogenetic abnormalities. *New England Journal of Medicine, 320,* 609–617.

RHOLES, W. S., BLACKWELL, J., JORDAN, C., & WALTERS, C. (1980). A developmental study of learned helplessness. *Developmental Psychology, 16,* 616–624.

RICCO, R. B. (1989). Operational thought and the acquisition of taxonomic relations involving figurative dissimilarity. *Developmental Psychology, 25,* 996–1003.

RICE, M. L. (1989). Children's language acquisition. *American Psychologist, 44,* 149–156.

RICE, M. L., HUSTON, A. C., TRUGLIO, R., & WRIGHT, J. (1990). Words from "Sesame Street": Learning vocabulary while viewing. *Developmental Psychology, 26,* 421–428.

RICE, M. L., HUSTON, A. C., & WRIGHT, J. C. (1982). The forms of television: Effects on children's attention, comprehension, and social behavior. In D. Pearl, L. Bouthilet, & J. Lazar (Eds.), *Television and behavior: Ten years of scientific progress and implications for the eighties* (Vol. 2, pp. 24–38). Washington, DC: U.S. Government Printing Office.

RICE, M. L., HUSTON, A. C., & WRIGHT, J. C. (1986). Replays as repetitions: Young children's interpretation of television forms. *Journal of Applied Developmental Psychology, 7,* 61–76.

RICE, M. L., & WOODSMALL, L. (1988). Lessons from television: Children's word learning when viewing. *Child Development, 59,* 420–429.

RICHARDS, D. D., & SIEGLER, R. S. (1986). Children's understandings of the attributes of life. *Journal of Experimental Child Psychology, 42,* 1–22.

RICHARDS, J. E., & RADER, N. (1981). Crawling-onset age predicts visual cliff avoidance in infants. *Journal of Experimental Psychology, 7,* 382–387.

RICHARDSON, S. A., & BIRCH, H. G. (1973). School performance of children who were severely malnourished in infancy. *American Journal of Mental Deficiency, 77,* 623–632.

RICHARDSON, S. A., HASTORF, A. H., GOODMAN, N., & DORNBUSCH, S. M. (1961). Cultural uniformity in reaction to physical disabilities. *American Sociological Review, 26,* 241–247.

RICHARDSON, S. A., KOLLER, H., & KATZ, M. (1986). Factors leading to differences in the school performance of boys and girls. *Developmental and Behavioral Pediatrics, 7,* 49–55.

RICHMAN, N., STEVENSON, J., & GRAHAM, P. J. (1982). *Preschool to school: A behavioral study.* London: Academic Press.

RICKS, M. (1985). The social inheritance of parenting. In I. Bretherton & E. Waters (Eds.), Growing points of attachment theory and research. *Monographs of the Society for Research in Child Development, 50*(1–2, Serial No. 209).

RIDLEY, C. A., & VAUGHN, R. (1982). Interpersonal problem solving: An intervention program for preschool children. *Journal of Applied Developmental Psychology, 3,* 177–190.

RIESE, M. L. (1987). Temperament stability between the neonatal period and 24 months. *Developmental Psychology, 23,* 216–222.

RILEIGH, K. (1973). Children's selective listening to stories: Familiarity effects involving vocabulary, syntax, and intonation. *Psychological Reports, 33,* 255–266.

RIM, I. J., & RIM, A. A. (1976). Association between juvenile onset obesity and severe adult obesity in 73,532 women. *American Journal of Public Health, 6,* 479.

ROBBINS, L. C. (1963). The accuracy of parental recall of aspects of child development and child rearing practices. *Journal of Abnormal and Social Psychology, 66,* 261–270.

ROBBOY, S. J., NOLLER, K. L., O'BRIEN, P., KAUFMAN, R. H., TOWNSEND, D., BARNES, A. B., GUNDERSEN, J., LAWRENCE, D., BERGSTRAHL, E., MCGORRAY, S., TILLEY, B. C., ANTON, J., & CHAZEN, G. (1984). Increased incidence of cervical and vaginal dysplasia in 3,980 diethylstilbestrol-exposed young women. *Journal of the American Medical Association, 252,* 2979–2983.

ROBERTS, C. (1970). The portrayal of blacks on network television. *Journal of Broadcasting, 15,* 45–53.

ROBERTS, T. (1984). Piagetian theory and the teaching of reading. *Educational Research, 26,* 77–81.

ROBERTSON, M. (1989). *Homeless youth in Hollywood: Patterns of alcohol abuse.* Berkeley: Alcohol Research Group.

ROBINSON, B. E., & CANADAY, H. (1978). Sex-role behaviors and personality traits of male day care teachers. *Sex Roles, 4,* 853–865.

ROBINSON, B. E., ROWLAND, B. H., & COLEMAN, M. (1986). *Latchkey kids: Unlocking doors for children and their families.* Lexington, MA: Heath.

ROBINSON, E. J. (1981). The child's understanding of inadequate messages and communication failure: A problem of ignorance or egocentrism? In W. P. Dickson (Ed.), *Children's oral communication skills* (pp. 167–188). New York: Academic Press.

ROCHAT, P. (1989). Object manipulation and exploration in 2- to 5-month-old infants. *Developmental Psychology, 25,* 871–884.

ROCHE, A. F. (1979). Secular trends in stature, weight, and maturation. In A. F. Roche (Ed.), Secular trends in human growth, maturation, and development. *Monographs of the Society for Research in Child Development, 44*(3–4, Serial No. 179).

RODGERS, J. L. (1984). Confluence effects: Not here, not now! *Developmental Psychology, 20,* 321–331.

ROFFWARG, H. P., MUZIO, J. N., & DEMENT, W. C. (1966). Ontogenetic development of the human sleep–dream cycle. *Science, 152,* 604–619.

ROGOFF, B. (1986). The development of strategic use of context in spatial memory. In M. Perlmutter (Ed.), *Perspectives on intellectual development* (pp. 107–123). Hillsdale, NJ: Erlbaum.

ROGOFF, B. (1990). *Apprenticeship in thinking.* New York: Oxford University Press.

ROHNER, R. P., & ROHNER, E. C. (1981). Parental acceptance–rejection and parental control: Cross-cultural codes. *Ethnology, 20,* 245–260.

ROHWER, W. D., & LITROWNIK, J. (1983). Age and individual differences in the learning of a memorization procedure. *Journal of Educational Psychology, 75*, 799–810.

ROMEO, F. F. (1986). *Understanding anorexia nervosa*. Springfield, IL: Thomas.

ROOPNARINE, J., & JOHNSON, J. (1984). Socialization in a mixed-age experimental program. *Developmental Psychology, 20*, 828–832.

ROOSA, M. W. (1984). Maternal age, social class, and the obstetric performance of teenagers. *Journal of Youth and Adolescence, 13*, 365–374.

ROSCH, E., MERVIS, C. B., GRAY, W. D., JOHNSON, D. M., & BOYES-BRAEM, P. (1976). Basic objects in natural categories. *Cognitive Psychology, 8*, 382–439.

ROSE, R. M., HOLADAY, J. W., & BERNSTEIN, I. S. (1976). Plasma testosterone, dominance rank and aggressive behavior in male rhesus monkeys. *Nature, 231*, 366–368.

ROSE, S. A. (1980). Enhancing visual recognition memory in preterm infants. *Developmental Psychology, 16*, 85–92.

ROSE, S. A., FELDMAN, J. F., & WALLACE, I. F. (1988). Individual differences in infant information processing: Reliability, stability, and prediction. *Child Development, 59*, 1177–1197.

ROSE, S. A., FELDMAN, J. F., WALLACE, I. F., & McCARTON, C. (1989). Infant visual attention: Relation to birth status and developmental outcome during the first 5 years. *Developmental Psychology, 25*, 560–576.

ROSEN, A. C., & REKERS, G. A. (1980). Toward a taxonomic framework for variables of sex and gender. *Genetic Psychology Monographs, 102*, 191–218.

ROSÉN, L. E., BOOTH, S. R., BENDER, M. E., McGRATH, M. L., SORRELL, S., & DRABMAN, R. S. (1988). Effects of sugar (sucrose) on children's behavior. *Journal of Consulting and Clinical Psychology, 56*, 583–589.

ROSENBERG, M. (1979). *Conceiving the self*. New York: Basic Books.

ROSENBERG, M. S., & REPPUCCI, N. D. (1985). Primary prevention of child abuse. *Journal of Consulting and Clinical Psychology, 53*, 576–585.

ROSENBERG, R. N., & PETTEGREW, J. W. (1983). Genetic neurologic diseases. In R. N. Rosenberg (Ed.), *The clinical neurosciences* (pp. 33–165). New York: Churchill Livingstone.

ROSENFIELD, P., LAMBERT, N. M., & BLACK, A. (1985). Desk arrangement effects on pupil classroom behavior. *Journal of Educational Psychology, 77*, 101–108.

ROSENHOLTZ, S. J., & WILSON, B. (1980). The effect of classroom structure on shared perceptions of ability. *American Educational Research Journal, 17*, 75–82.

ROSENKOETTER, L. I. (1973). Resistance to temptation: Inhibitory and disinhibitory effects of models. *Developmental Psychology, 8*, 80–84.

ROSENKRANTZ, P., VOGEL, S., BEE, H., BROVERMAN, I., & BROVERMAN, D. (1968). Sex-role stereotypes and self-concepts in college students. *Journal of Consulting and Clinical Psychology, 32*, 287–295.

ROSENTHAL, R., & FODE, K. L. (1963). The effect of experimenter bias on the performance of the albino rat. *Behavioral Science, 8*, 183–189.

ROSENTHAL, R., & JACOBSON, L. (1968). *Pygmalion in the classroom: Teacher expectation and pupils' intellectual development*. New York: Holt, Rinehart and Winston.

ROSEWATER, A. (1989). Child and family trends: Beyond the numbers. In F. J. Macchiarola & A. Gartner (Eds.), *Caring for America's children*. (pp. 4–19). New York: The Academy of Political Science.

ROSS, D. F., MILLER, B. S., & MORAN, P. B. (1987). The child in the eyes of the jury: Assessing mock jurors' perceptions of the child witness. In S. J. Ceci, M. P. Toglia, & D. F. Ross (Eds.), *Children's eyewitness memory* (pp. 142–154). New York: Springer-Verlag.

ROSS, G. S. (1980). Categorization in 1- to 2-year olds. *Developmental Psychology, 16*, 391–396.

ROSS, H. S., & GOLDMAN, B. D. (1977). Infants' sociability toward strangers. *Child Development, 48*, 638–642.

ROSS, R. P., CAMPBELL, T., HUSTON-STEIN, A., & WRIGHT, J. C. (1984). Nutritional misinformation of children: A developmental and experimental analysis of the effects of televised food commercials. *Journal of Applied Developmental Psychology, 1*, 329–347.

ROTENBERG, K. J., SIMOURD, L., & MOORE, D. (1989). Children's use of a verbal–nonverbal consistency principle to infer truth and lying. *Child Development, 60*, 309–322.

ROTHBART, M. K. (1981). Measurement of temperament in infancy. *Child Development, 52*, 569–578.

ROTHBART, M. K., & ROTHBART, M. (1976). Birth-order, sex of child and maternal help giving. *Sex Roles, 2*, 39–46.

ROTHENBERG, P. B., & VARGA, P. E. (1981). Relationship between age of mother and child health and development. *American Journal of Public Health, 71*, 810–817.

ROUSSEAU, J. J. (1955). *Emile*. New York: Dutton. (Original work published 1762)

ROVEE-COLLIER, C. K. (1984). The ontogeny of learning and memory in human infancy. In R. Kail & N. E. Spear (Eds.), *Comparative perspectives on the development of memory* (pp. 103–134). Hillsdale, NJ: Erlbaum.

ROVEE-COLLIER, C. (1987). Learning and memory. In J. D. Osofsky (Ed.), *Handbook of infant development* (2nd ed., pp. 98–148). New York: Wiley.

ROVEE-COLLIER, C. K., & LIPSITT, L. P. (1982). Learning, adaptation, and memory. In P. M. Stratton (Ed.), *Psychobiology of the human newborn* (pp. 147–190). New York: Wiley.

ROVEE-COLLIER, C., PATTERSON, J., & HAYE, H. (1985). Specificity in the reactivation of infant memory. *Developmental Psychobiology, 18*, 559–574.

ROWE, D. C. (1987). Resolving the person–situation debate: Invitation to an interdisciplinary dialogue. *American Psychologist, 42*, 218–227.

ROWE, D. C., & PLOMIN, R. (1981). The importance of nonshared (E_1) environmental influences on behavioral development. *Developmental Psychology, 17*, 517–531.

ROWE, D. C., RODGERS, J. L., MESECK-BUSHEY, S., & ST. JOHN, C. (1989). Sexual behavior and nonsexual deviance: A sibling study of their relationship. *Developmental Psychology, 25*, 61–69.

ROYCE, J. M., DARLINGTON, R. B., & MURRAY, H. W. (1983). Pooled analyses: Findings across studies. In Consortium for Longitudinal Studies (Ed.), *As the twig is bent: Lasting effects of preschool programs* (pp. 411–459). Hillsdale, NJ: Erlbaum.

RUBENSTEIN, J. L., & HOWES, C. (1976). The effects of peers on toddler interaction with mothers and toys. *Child Development, 47*, 597–605.

RUBIN, J. Z., PROVENZANO, F. J., & LURIA, Z. (1974). The eye of the beholder: Parents' views on sex of newborns. *American Journal of Orthopsychiatry, 44*, 512–519.

RUBIN, K. H. (1972). Relationship between egocentric communication and popularity among peers. *Developmental Psychology, 7*, 364.

RUBIN, K. H. (1973). Egocentrism in childhood: A unitary construct? *Child Development, 44*, 102–110.

RUBIN, K. H. (1977). The social and cognitive value of preschool toys and activities. *Canadian Journal of Behavioural Science/Review of Canadian Science, 9*, 382–385.

RUBIN, K. H. (1978). Role taking in childhood: Some methodological considerations. *Child Development, 49*, 428–433.

RUBIN, K. H. (1982). Nonsocial play in preschoolers: Necessarily evil? *Child Development, 53*, 651–657.

RUBIN, K. H., & DANIELS-BEIRNESS, T. (1983). Concurrent and predictive correlates of sociometric status in kindergarten and grade one children. *Merrill-Palmer Quarterly, 29*, 337–352.

RUBIN, K. H., FEIN, G. G., & VANDENBERG, B. (1983). Play. In E. M. Hetherington (Ed.), *Handbook of child psychology: Vol. 4. Socialization, personality, and social development* (4th ed., pp. 693–744). New York: Wiley.

RUBIN, K. H., & KRASNOR, L. R. (1985). Social-cognitive and social behavioral perspectives on problem solving. In M. Perlmutter (Ed.), *Minnesota Symposia on Child Psychology* (Vol. 18, pp. 1–68). Hillsdale, NJ: Erlbaum.

RUBIN, K. H., LEMARE, L. J., & LOLLIS, S. (1990). Social withdrawal in childhood: Developmental pathways to peer rejection. In S. R. Asher & J. D. Coie (Eds.), *Peer rejection in childhood*. New York: Cambridge University Press.

RUBIN, K. H., & MAIONI, T. (1975). Play preference and its relationship to egocentrism, popularity, and classification skills in preschoolers. *Merrill-Palmer Quarterly, 21*, 171–180.

RUBIN, K. H., MAIONI, T. L., & HORNUNG, M. (1976). Free play behaviors in middle- and lower-class preschoolers: Parten and Piaget revisited. *Child Development, 47*, 414–419.

RUBIN, K. H., WATSON, K. S., & JAMBOR, T. W. (1978). Free-play behaviors in preschool and kindergarten children. *Child Development, 49*, 534–536.

RUBIN, R. T., REINISCH, J. M., & HASKETT, R. F. (1981). Postnatal gonadal steroid effects on human behavior. *Science, 211*, 1318–1324.

RUBIN, Z., & SLOMAN, J. (1984). How parents influence their children's friendship. In M. Lewis (Ed.), *Beyond the dyad* (pp. 223–250). New York: Plenum.

RUBLE, D. N. (1988). Sex-role development. In M. H. Bornstein & M. E. Lamb (Eds.), *Developmental psychology: An advanced textbook* (2nd ed., pp. 411–460). Hillsdale, NJ: Erlbaum.

RUBLE, D. N., BOGGIANO, A. K., FELDMAN, N. S., & LOEBL, J. H. (1980). Developmental analysis of the role of social comparison in self-evaluation. *Developmental Psychology, 16*, 105–115.

RUBLE, D. N., & BROOKS-GUNN, J. (1982). The experience of menarche. *Child Development, 53*, 1557–1566.

RUBLE, D. N., & RUBLE, T. L. (1982). Sex stereotypes. In A. G. Miller (Ed.), *In the eye of the beholder* (pp. 188–252). New York: Praeger.

RUBLE, T. L. (1983). Sex stereotypes: Issues of change in the 1970s. *Sex Roles, 9*, 397–402.

RUDEL, R. G., & TEUBER, H. L. (1963). Discrimination of direction of line in children. *Journal of Comparative and Physiological Psychology, 56*, 892–898.

RUFF, H. A., LAWSON, K. R., PARRINELLO, R., & WEISSBERG, R. (1990). Long-term stability of individual differences in sustained attention in the early years. *Child Development, 61*, 60–75.

RUGH, R., & SHETTLES, L. B. (1971). *From conception to birth: The drama of life's beginnings*. New York: Harper & Row.

RUIZ, R. (1988). Bilingualism and bilingual education in the United States. In C. B. Paulston (Ed.), *International handbook of bilingualism and bilingual education* (pp. 539–560). New York: Greenwood Press.

RUOPP, R., TRAVERS, J., GLANTZ, F., & COELEN, C. (1979). *Children at the center: Final report of the National Day Care Study*. Cambridge, MA: Abt Books.

RUSHTON, J. P. (1980). *Altruism, socialization, and society*. Englewood Cliffs, NJ: Prentice-Hall.

RUTTER, M. (1981). The city and the child. *American Journal of Orthopsychiatry, 51*, 610–625.

RUTTER, M., & GARMEZY, N. (1983). Developmental psychopathology. In E. M. Hetherington (Ed.), *Handbook of child psychology: Vol. 4. Socialization, personality, and social development* (pp. 775–911). New York: Wiley.

RUTTER, M., GRAHAM, P., CHADWICK, O. F. D., & YULE, W. (1976). Adolescent turmoil: Fact or fiction. *Journal of Child Psychology and Psychiatry, 17*, 35–56.

RUTTER, M., & MADGE, N. (1976). *Cycles of disadvantage*. London: Heinemann.

RYAN, K. J. (1989). Ethical issues in reproductive endocrinology and infertility. *American Journal of Obstetrics and Gynecology, 160*, 1415–1417.

SAARNI, C. (1979). Children's understanding of display rules for expressive behavior. *Developmental Psychology, 15*, 424–429.

SAARNI, C. (1989). Children's understanding of strategic control of emotional expression in social transactions. In C. Saarni & P. L. Harris (Eds.), *Children's understanding of emotion*. New York: Cambridge University Press.

SACHS, J. (1985). Prelinguistic development. In J. Berko Gleason (Ed.), *The development of language* (pp. 37–60). Columbus, OH: Merrill.

SADLER, T. W. (1990). *Langman's medical embryology* (6th ed.). Baltimore: Williams & Wilkins.

SAGI, A., LAMB, M. E., LEWKOWICZ, K. S., SHOHAM, R., DVIR, R., & ESTES, D. (1985). Security of infant–mother, –father, and –metapelet attachments among kibbutz-reared Israeli children. In I. Bretherton & E. Waters (Ed.), *Monographs of the Society for Research in Child Development, 50*(1–2, Serial No. 209).

SAHLER, O. J. Z. (1983). Adolescent mothers: How nurturant is their parenting. In E. R. McAnarney (Ed.), *Premature adolescent pregnancy and parenthood* (pp. 219–230). New York: Grune & Stratton.

SALAPATEK, P. (1975). Pattern perception in early infancy. In L. B. Cohen & P. Salapatek (Eds.), *Infant perception: From sensation to cognition* (pp. 133–248). New York: Academic Press.

SALAPATEK, P., & COHEN, L. (EDS.) (1987). *Handbook of infant perception: Vol 2. From perception to cognition*. Orlando, FL: Academic Press.

SALOMON, G. (1979). *Interaction of media, cognition, and learning*. San Francisco, CA: Jossey-Bass.

SALOMON, J. B., MATA, L. J., & GORDON, J. E. (1968). Malnutrition and the common communicable diseases of childhood in rural Guatemala. *American Journal of Health, 58*, 505–516.

SALTZ, E., DIXON, D., & JOHNSON, J. (1977). Training disadvantaged preschoolers on various fantasy activities: Effects on cognitive functioning and impulse control. *Child Development, 48*, 367–380.

SALTZSTEIN, H. D. (1976). Social influence and moral development: A perspective on the role of parents and peers. In T. Lickona (Ed.), *Moral development and behavior: Theory, research and social issues* (pp. 253–265). New York: Holt, Rinehart and Winston.

SAMEROFF, A. J. (1968). The components of sucking in the human newborn. *Journal of Experimental Child Psychology, 6*, 607–623.

SAMEROFF, A. J., & CAVANAUGH, P. J. (1979). Learning in infancy: A developmental perspective. In J. D. Osofsky (Ed.), *Handbook of infant development* (pp. 344–392). New York: Wiley.

SAMEROFF, A. J., & CHANDLER, M. J. (1975). Reproductive risk and the continuum of caretaking casualty. In F. D. Horowitz (Ed.), *Review of child development research* (Vol. 4, pp. 187–244). Chicago: University of Chicago Press.

SAMSON, L. F. (1988). Perinatal viral infections and neonates. *Journal of Perinatal Neonatal Nursing, 1*, 56–65.

SAMUELS, M., & SAMUELS, N. (1986). *The well pregnancy book*. New York: Summit.

SANTROCK, J. W., & WARSHAK, R. A. (1979). Father custody and social development in boys and girls. *Journal of Social Issues, 35*, 112–125.

SANTROCK, J. W., & WARSHAK, R. A. (1986). Development of father custody relationships and legal/clinical considerations in father-custody families. In M. E. Lamb (Ed.), *The father's role: Applied perspectives* (pp. 135–166). New York: Wiley.

SARASON, I. G. (1980). *Test anxiety: Theory, research, and applications*. Hillsdale, NJ: Erlbaum.

SARNAT, H. B. (1978). Olfactory reflexes in the newborn infant. *Journal of Pediatrics, 92*, 624–626.

SATTLER, J. M. (1988). *Assessment of children's intelligence and special abilities* (3rd ed.). San Diego: Author.

SATZ, P., & BULLARD-BATES, C. (1981). Acquired aphasia in children. In M. T. Sarno (Ed.), *Acquired aphasia* (pp. 399–426). New York: Academic Press.

SATZ, P., & FLETCHER, J. M. (1987). Left-handedness and dyslexia: An old myth revisited. *Journal of Pediatric Psychology, 12*, 291–298.

SAVIN-WILLIAMS, R. C. (1979). Dominance hierarchies in groups of early adolescents. *Child Development, 50*, 923–935.

SAVIN-WILLIAMS, R. C. (1980a). Dominance hierarchies in groups of middle to late adolescent males. *Journal of Youth and Adolescence, 9*, 75–85.

SAVIN-WILLIAMS, R. C. (1980b). Social interactions of adolescent females in natural groups. In H. C. Foot, A. J. Chapman, & J. R. Smith

(Eds.), *Friendship and social relations in children* (pp. 343–364. Chichester, England: Wiley.

SAVIN-WILLIAMS, R. C., & DEMO, D. H. (1984). Developmental change and stability in adolescent self-concept. *Developmental Psychology, 20,* 1100–1110.

SAXE, G. B. (1988, August–September). Candy selling and math learning. *Educational Researcher, 17*(6), 14–21.

SAXE, G. B., GUBERMAN, S. R., & GEARHART, M. (1987). Social processes in early number development. *Monographs of the Society for Research in Child Development, 52*(2, Serial No. 216).

SAXE, L., CROSS, T., & SILVERMAN, N. (1988). Children's mental health: The gap between what we know and what we do. *American Psychologist, 43,* 800–807.

SAYWITZ, K. J. (1987). Children's testimony: Age-related patterns of memory errors. In S. J. Ceci, M. P. Toglia, & D. F. Ross (Eds.), *Children's eyewitness memory* (pp. 36–52). New York: Springer-Verlag.

SAYWITZ, K. J. (1989). Children's conceptions of the legal system: "Court is a place to play basketball." In S. J. Ceci, D. F. Ross, & M. P. Toglia (Eds.), *Perspectives on children's testimony* (pp. 131–157). New York: Springer-Verlag.

SCARLETT, H. H., PRESS, A. N., & CROCKETT, W. H. (1971). Children's descriptions of peers: A Wernerian developmental analysis. *Child Development, 42,* 439–453.

SCARR, S. (1968). Environmental bias in twin studies. *Eugenics Quarterly, 15,* 34–40.

SCARR, S. (1985). Constructing psychology: Making facts and fables for our times. *American Psychologist, 40,* 499–512.

SCARR, S. (1988). How genotypes and environments combine: Development and individual differences. In N. Bolger, A. Caspi, G. Downey, & M. Moorehouse (Eds.), *Persons in context: Developmental processes* (pp. 217–244). Cambridge, England: Cambridge University Press.

SCARR, S., & BARKER, W. (1981). The effects of family background: A study of cognitive differences among black and white twins. In S. Scarr (Ed.), *Race, social class, and individual differences in IQ* (pp. 261–315). Hillsdale, NJ: Erlbaum.

SCARR, S., & CARTER-SALTZMAN, L. (1979). Twin method: Defense of a critical assumption. *Behavior Genetics, 9,* 527–542.

SCARR, S., & KIDD, K. K. (1983). Developmental behavior genetics. In M. M. Haith & J. J. Campos (Eds.), *Handbook of child psychology: Vol. 2. Infancy and developmental psychobiology* (pp. 345–433). New York: Wiley.

SCARR, S., & McCARTNEY, K. (1983). How people make their own environments: A theory of genotype → environment effects. *Child Development, 54,* 424–435.

SCARR, S., WEBBER, P. L., WEINBERG, R. A., & WITTIG, M. A. (1981). Personality resemblance among adolescents and their parents in biologically-related and adoptive families. *Journal of Personality and Social Psychology, 40,* 885–898.

SCARR, S., & WEINBERG, R. A. (1976). IQ test performance of black children adopted by white families. *American Psychologist, 31,* 726–739.

SCARR, S., & WEINBERG, R. A. (1978). The influence of "family background" on intellectual attainment. *American Sociological Review, 43,* 674–792.

SCARR, S., & WEINBERG, R. A. (1983). The Minnesota adoption studies: Genetic differences and malleability. *Child Development, 54,* 260–267.

SCARR-SALAPATEK, S. (1975). Genetics and the development of intelligence. In F. D. Horowitz (Ed.), *Review of child development research* (Vol. 4, pp. 1–57). Chicago: University of Chicago Press.

SCHACHTER, F. F., SHORE, E., HODAPP, R., CHALFIN, S., & BUNDY, C. (1978). Do girls talk earlier? Mean length of utterance in toddlers. *Developmental Psychology, 14,* 388–392.

SCHACHTER, F. F., & STONE, R. K. (1985). Difficult sibling, easy sibling: Temperament and the within-family environment. *Child Development, 56,* 1335–1344.

SCHACHTER, S. (1959). *The psychology of affiliation.* Stanford, CA: Stanford University Press.

SCHACHTER, S., & RODIN, J. (EDS.). (1974). *Obese humans and rats.* Washington, DC: Erlbaum/Halsted.

SCHAEFER, E., & BAYLEY, N. (1963). Maternal behavior, child behavior and their intercorrelations from infancy through adolescence. *Monographs of the Society for Research in Child Development, 28*(3, Serial No. 87).

SCHAEFER, M., HATCHER, R. P., & BARGELOW, P. D. (1980). Prematurity and infant stimulation. *Child Psychiatry and Human Development, 10,* 199–212.

SCHAFFER, H. R. (1979). Acquiring the concept of the dialogue. In M. H. Bornstein & W. Kessen (Eds.), *Psychological development from infancy: Image to intention* (pp. 279–305). Hillsdale, NJ: Erlbaum.

SCHAFFER, H. R., & EMERSON, P. E. (1964). The development of social attachments in infancy. *Monographs of the Society for Research in Child Development, 29*(3, Serial No. 94).

SCHAIE, K. W., & HERTZOG, C. (1982). Longitudinal methods. In B. B. Wolman (Ed.), *Handbook of developmental psychology* (pp. 91–115). Englewood Cliffs, NJ: Prentice-Hall.

SCHAIVI, R. C., THEILGAARD, A., OWEN, D., & WHITE, D. (1984). Sex chromosome anomalies, hormones, and aggressivity. *Archives of General Psychiatry, 41,* 93–99.

SCHAIVO, R. S., & SOLOMON, S. K. (1981). *The effect of summer contact on preschoolers' friendships with classmates.* Paper presented at the annual meeting of the Eastern Psychological Association, New York.

SCHANBERG, S., & FIELD, T. M (1987). Sensory deprivation stress and supplemental stimulation in the rat pup and preterm human neonate. *Child Development, 58,* 1431–1447.

SCHANK, R. C., & ABELSON, R. P. (1977). *Scripts, plans, goals, and understanding.* Hillsdale, NJ: Erlbaum.

SCHAU, C. G., KAHN, L., DIEPOLD, J. H., & CHERRY, F. (1980). The relationships of parental expectations and preschool children's verbal sex typing to their sex-typed toy play behavior. *Child Development, 51,* 266–271.

SCHERER, K. R. (1982). The assessment of vocal expression in infants and children. In C. E. Izard (Ed.), *Measuring emotions in infants and children* (pp. 127–163). New York: Cambridge University Press.

SCHIEFFELIN, B. B., & OCHS, E. (1983). A cultural perspective on the transition from prelinguistic to linguistic communication. In R. M. Golinkoff (Ed.), *The transition from prelinguistic to linguistic communication* (pp. 115–131). Hillsdale, NJ: Erlbaum.

SCHIEFFELIN, B. B., & OCHS, E. (1987). *Language socialization across cultures.* New York: Cambridge University Press.

SCHNEIDER, W., & PRESSLEY, M. (1989). *Memory development between 2 and 20.* New York: Springer-Verlag.

SCHNUR, E., & SHATZ, M. (1984). The role of maternal gesturing in conversations with one-year-olds. *Journal of Child Language, 11,* 29–41.

SCHONFELD, I. S. (1990). The child's understanding of correspondence relations. *Developmental Psychology, 26,* 94–102.

SCHRAG, S. G., & DIXON, R. L. (1985). Occupational exposures associated with male reproductive dysfunction. *Annual Review of Pharmacology and Toxicology, 25,* 567–592.

SCHRAMM, W., BARNES, D., & BAKEWELL, J. (1987). Neonatal mortality in Missouri home births. *American Journal of Public Health, 77,* 930–935.

SCHULTZ, D. P. (1975). *A history of modern psychology.* New York: Academic Press.

SCHUNK, D. H. (1983). Ability versus effort attributional feedback: Differential effects on self-efficacy and achievement. *Journal of Educational Psychology, 75,* 848–856.

SCHUNK, D. H., HANSON, A. R., & COX, P. D. (1987). Peer-model attributes and children's achievement behaviors. *Journal of Educational Psychology, 79,* 54–61.

SCHWARTZ, J. C. (1972). Effects of peer familiarity on the behavior of preschoolers in a novel situation. *Journal of Personality and Social Psychology, 24,* 276–284.

SCHWARTZ, R. G., & LEONARD, L. B. (1982). Do children pick and choose? An examination of phonological selection and avoidance in early lexical acquisition. *Journal of Child Language, 9,* 319–336.

SCHWARTZ-BICKENBACH, D., SCHULTE-HOBEIN, B., ABT, S., PLUM, C., & NAU, H. (1987). Smoking and passive smoking during pregnancy and early infancy: Effects on birth weight, lactation period, and cotinine concentrations in mother's milk and infant's urine. *Toxicology Letters, 35,* 73–81.

SCHWARZ, C., STRICKLAND, R., & KROLICK, G. (1974). Infant day care: Behavioral effects at preschool age. *Developmental Psychology, 10,* 502–506.

SCOTT, K. P., & SCHAU, C. G. (1985). Sex equity and sex bias in instructional materials. In S. S. Klein (Ed.), *Handbook for achieving sex equity through education* (pp. 218–232). Baltimore, MD: Johns Hopkins University Press.

SCRIBNER, S. (1977). Modes of thinking and ways of speaking: Culture and logic reconsidered. In P. N. Johnson-Laird & P. C. Wason (Eds.), *Thinking: Readings in cognitive science* (pp. 483–500). London: Cambridge University Press.

SEARS, R. R. (1975). *Your ancients revisited: A history of child development.* Chicago: University of Chicago Press.

SEARS, R. R., MACCOBY, E. E., & LEVIN, H. (1957). *Patterns of child rearing.* New York: Harper & Row.

SEAY, B., ALEXANDER, B. K., & HARLOW, H. F. (1964). Maternal behavior of socially deprived rhesus monkeys. *Journal of abnormal and Social Psychology, 69,* 345–354.

SEITZ, V. (1988). Methodology. In M. H. Bornstein & M. E. Lamb (Eds.), *Developmental psychology* (2nd ed., pp. 37–79). Hillsdale, NJ: Erlbaum.

SEITZ, V., ROSENBAUM, L., & APFEL, N. (1985). Effects of family support intervention: A ten year follow-up. *Child Development, 56,* 376–391.

SELIGMAN, J. (1989, September 4). Cystic fibrosis: Hunting down a killer gene. *Newsweek,* pp. 60–61.

SELIGMAN, M. E. P. (1975). *Helplessness: On depression, development, and death.* San Francisco: Freeman.

SELKOW, P. (1984). Effects of maternal employment on kindergarten and first-grade children's vocational aspirations. *Sex Roles, 11,* 677–690.

SELMAN, R. L. (1976). Social–cognitive understanding: A guide to educational and clinical practice. In T. Likona (Ed.), *Moral development and behavior: Theory, research, and social issues* (pp. 299–316). New York: Holt, Rinehart and Winston.

SELMAN, R. L. (1977). Toward a structural analysis of developing interpersonal relations concepts: Research with normal and disturbed preadolescent boys. In A. D. Pick (Ed.), *Minnesota Symposia on Child Psychology* (Vol. 10, pp. 156–200). Minneapolis: University of Minnesota Press.

SELMAN, R. L. (1980). *The growth of interpersonal understanding.* New York: Academic Press.

SELMAN, R. L. (1981). The child as a friendship philosopher. In S. R. Asher & J. M. Gottman (Eds.), *The development of friendships* (pp. 242–272). New York: Cambridge University Press.

SELMAN, R. L., & BYRNE, D. F. (1974). A structural-developmental analysis of levels of role taking in middle childhood. *Child Development, 45,* 803–806.

SELMAN, R. L., & DEMOREST, A. P. (1984). Observing troubled children's interpersonal negotiational strategies: Implications of and for a developmental model. *Child Development, 55,* 288–304.

SELMAN, R. L., SCHORIN, M. Z., STONE, C., & PHELPS, E. (1983). A naturalistic study of children's social understanding. *Developmental Psychology, 19,* 82–102.

SERBIN, L. A., CONNOR, J. M., & CITRON, C. C. (1978). Environmental control of independent and dependent behaviors in preschool girls and boys: A model for early independence training. *Sex Roles, 4,* 867–875.

SERBIN, L. A., CONNOR, J. M., & CITRON, C. C. (1981). Sex-differentiated free play behavior: Effects of teacher modeling, location, and gender. *Developmental Psychology, 17,* 640–646.

SERBIN, L. A., CONNOR, J. M., & ILER, I. (1979). Sex-stereotyped and nonstereotyped introductions of new toys in the preschool classroom: An observational study of teacher behavior and its effects. *Psychology of Women Quarterly, 4,* 261–265.

SERBIN, L. A., O'LEARY, K. D., KENT, R. N., & TONICK, I. J. (1973). A comparison of teacher response to the preacademic and problem behavior of boys and girls. *Child Development, 44,* 796–804.

SERBIN, L. A., SPRAFKIN, C., ELMAN, M., & DOYLE, A-B. (1984). The early development of sex differentiated patterns of social influence. *Canadian Journal of Social Science, 14,* 350–363.

SERBIN, L. A., TONICK, I. J., & STERNGLANZ, S. H. (1977). Shaping cooperative cross-sex play. *Child Development, 48,* 924–929.

SEVER, J. L. (1983). Maternal infections. In C. C. Brown (Ed.), *Childhood learning disabilities and prenatal risk* (pp. 31–38). New York: Johnson & Johnson.

SEXTON, M., & HEBEL, J. R. (1984). A clinical trial of change in maternal smoking and its effect on birth weight. *Journal of the American Medical Association, 251,* 911–915.

SHAFFER, D. (1985). Depression, mania, and suicidal acts. In M. Rutter & L. Hersov (Eds.), *Child and adolescent psychiatry: Modern approaches* (pp. 698–719). New York: Guilford Press.

SHAFFER, D., & CATON, D. (1984). *Runaway and homeless youth in New York City: A report to the Ittleson Foundation.* New York: The Ittleson Foundation.

SHAFII, M., CARRIGAN, S., WHITTINGHILL, J. R., & DERRICK, A. (1985). Psychological autopsy of completed suicide in children and adolescents. *American Journal of Psychiatry, 142,* 1061–1064.

SHAINESS, N. (1961). A re-evaluation of some aspects of femininity through a study of menstruation: A preliminary report. *Comparative Psychiatry, 2,* 20–26.

SHANNON, D. C., KELLY, D. H., AKSELROD, S., & KILBORN, K. M. (1987). Increased respiratory frequency and variability in high risk babies who die of sudden infant death syndrome. *Pediatric Research, 22,* 158–162.

SHANTZ, C. U. (1983). Social cognition. In J. H. Flavell & E. M. Markman (Eds.), *Handbook of child psychology: Vol 3. Cognitive development* (4th ed., pp. 495–555). New York: Wiley.

SHANTZ, C. U. (1987). Conflicts between children. *Child Development, 58,* 283–305.

SHANTZ, D. W. (1986). Conflict, aggression, and peer status: An observational study. *Child Development, 57,* 1322–1332.

SHATZ, M. (1979). How to do things by asking: Form–function pairings in mothers' questions and their relation to children's responses. *Child Development, 50,* 1093–1099.

SHATZ, M. (1983). Communication. In J. H. Flavell & E. M. Markman (Eds.), *Handbook of child psychology: Vol. 3. Cognitive development* (4th ed., pp. 841–889). New York: Wiley.

SHAVELSON, R. J., & BOLUS, R. (1982). Self-concept: The interplay of theory and methods. *Journal of Educational Psychology, 74,* 3–17.

SHAVELSON, R. J., HUBNER, J. J., & STANTON, G. C. (1976). Self-concept: Validation and construct interpretations. *Review of Educational Research, 46,* 407–441.

SHENNUM, W. A., & BUGENTAL, D. B. (1982). The development of control over affective expression in nonverbal behavior. In R. Feldman (Ed.), *Development of nonverbal behavior in children* (pp. 101–121). New York: Springer-Verlag.

SHEPPARD, J. J., & MYSAK, E. D. (1984). Ontogeny of infantile oral reflexes and emerging chewing. *Child Development, 55,* 831–843.

SHERIF, M., HARVEY, O. J., WHITE, B. J., HOOD, W. R., & SHERIF, C. W. (1961). *Inter-group conflict and cooperation: The Robbers Cave experiment.* Norman: University of Oklahoma Press.

SHERMAN, J. A. (1980). Mathematics, spatial visualization, and related factors: Changes in girls and boys, Grades 8–11. *Journal of Educational Psychology, 72,* 476–482.

SHERMAN, J. A., & FENNEMA, E. (1977). The study of mathematics by high school girls and boys: Related variables. *American Educational Research Journal, 14,* 159–168.

SHERMAN, M., HERTZIG, M., AUSTRIAN, R., & SHAPIRO, T. (1981). Treasured objects in school-aged children. *Pediatrics, 68,* 379–386.

R-53

SHERMAN, T. (1985). Categorization skills in infants. *Child Development, 56*, 1561–1573.

SHERRILL, D., HOROWITZ, B., FRIEDMAN, S. T., & SALISBURY, J. L. (1970). Seating aggregation as an index of contagion. *Educational and Psychological Measurement, 30*, 663–668.

SHIELDS, J. W. (1972). *The trophic function of lymphoid elements.* Springfield, IL: Charles C. Thomas.

SHIFFRIN, R. M., & ATKINSON, R. C. (1969). Storage and retrieval processes in long-term memory. *Psychological Review, 76*, 179–193.

SHILLER, V., IZARD, C. E., & HEMBREE, E. A. (1986). Patterns of emotion expression during separation in the Strange Situation. *Developmental Psychology, 22*, 378–382.

SHILLER, V. M. (1986). Joint versus maternal physical custody for families with latency age boys: Family characteristics and child adjustment. *American Journal of Orthopsychiatry, 56*, 486–489.

SHINN, M. W. (1900). *The biography of a baby.* Boston: Houghton Mifflin.

SHIPMAN, G. (1971). The psychodynamics of sex education. In R. E. Muus (Ed.), *Adolescent behavior and society: A book of readings* (pp. 326–339). New York: Random House.

SHIRLEY, M. M. (1933). *The first two years* (Vol. 2, Institute of Child Welfare Monograph No. 7). Minneapolis: University of Minnesota Press.

SHULTZ, T. R. (1980). Development of the concept of intention. In W. A. Collins (Ed.), *Minnesota Symposia on Child Psychology* (Vol. 13, pp. 131–164). Hillsdale, NJ: Erlbaum.

SHULTZ, T. R., & HORIBE, F. (1974). Development of the appreciation of verbal jokes. *Developmental Psychology, 10*, 13–20.

SHULTZ, T. R., & WELLS, D. (1985). Judging the intentionality of action-outcomes. *Developmental Psychology, 21*, 83–89.

SHULTZ, T. R., WELLS, D., & SARDA, M. (1980). Development of the ability to distinguish intended action from mistakes, reflexes, and passive movements. *British Journal of Social and Clinical Psychology, 19*, 301–310.

SHURE, M. B. (1981). Social competence as a problem-solving skill. In J. D. Wine & M. D. Smye (Eds.), *Social competence* (pp. 158–185). New York: Guilford Press.

SHWEDER, R. (1982). Beyond self-constructed knowledge: The study of culture and morality. *Merrill-Palmer Quarterly, 28*, 41–69.

SIDOROWICZ, L. S., & LUNNEY, G. S. (1980). Baby X revisited. *Sex Roles, 6*, 67–73.

SIEGAL, M., & ROBINSON, J. (1987). Order effects in children's gender-constancy responses. *Developmental Psychology, 23*, 283–286.

SIEGEL, A. W. (1981). The externalization of cognitive maps by children and adults: In search of ways to ask better questions. In L. S. Liben, A. H. Patterson, & N. Newcombe (Eds.), *Spatial representation and behavior across the life span* (pp. 167–194). New York: Academic Press.

SIEGEL, I. E. (1987). Does hothousing rob children of their childhood? *Early Childhood Research Quarterly, 2*, 211–225.

SIEGLER, R. S. (1976). Three aspects of cognitive development. *Cognitive Psychology, 8*, 481–520.

SIEGLER, R. S. (1978). The origins of scientific reasoning. In R. S. Siegler (Ed.), *Children's thinking: What develops?* (pp. 109–149). Hillsdale, NJ: Erlbaum.

SIEGLER, R. S. (1981). Developmental sequences within and between concepts. *Monographs of the Society for Research in Child Development, 46*(2, Serial No. 189).

SIEGLER, R. S. (1983a). Five generalizations about cognitive development. *American Psychologist, 38*, 263–277.

SIEGLER, R. S. (1983b). Information processing approaches to development. In W. Kessen (Ed.), *Handbook of child psychology: Vol. 1. History, theory, and methods* (pp. 129–212). New York: Wiley.

SIEGLER, R. S. (1988). Mechanisms of cognitive development. *Annual Review of Psychology, 40*, 353–379.

SIEGLER, R. S., LIEBERT, D. E., & LIEBERT, R. M. (1973). Inhelder and Piaget's pendulum problem: Teaching preadolescents as scientists. *Developmental Psychology, 9*, 97–101.

SIEGLER, R. S., & RICHARDS, D. D. (1980). *College students' prototypes of children's intelligence.* Paper presented at the annual meeting of the American Psychological Association, New York.

SIEGLER, R. S., & RICHARDS, D. D. (1982). The development of intelligence. In R. J. Sternberg (Ed.), *Handbook of human intelligence* (pp. 897–971). Cambridge, England: Cambridge University Press.

SIEGLER, R. S., & ROBINSON, M. (1982). The development of numerical understandings. In H. W. Reese & L. P. Lipsitt (Eds.), *Advances in child development and behavior* (Vol. 16, pp. 241–312). New York: Academic Press.

SIGNIORELLI, N. (1989). Television and conceptions about sex roles: Maintaining conventionality and the status quo. *Sex Roles, 21*, 341–360.

SIGNORELLA, M. L., & JAMISON, W. (1986). Masculinity, femininity, androgyny, and cognitive performance: A meta-analysis. *Psychological Bulletin, 100*, 207–228.

SIGNORELLA, M. L., JAMISON, W., & KRUPA, M. H. (1989). Predicting spatial performance from gender stereotyping in activity preferences and self-concept. *Developmental Psychology, 25*, 89–95.

SIGNORELLA, M. L., & LIBEN, L. S. (1984). Recall and reconstruction of gender-related pictures: Effects of attitude, task difficulty, and age. *Child Development, 55*, 393–405.

SILBERMAN, M. L. (1969). Behavioral expression of teachers' attitudes toward elementary school students. *Journal of Educational Psychology, 60*, 402–407.

SIMKIN, P., WHALLEY, J., & KEPPLER, A. (1984). *Pregnancy, childbirth, and the newborn.* New York: Meadowbrook.

SIMMONS, R. G., & BLYTH, D. A. (1987). *Moving into adolescence.* New York: Aldine De Gruyter.

SIMMONS, R. G., BLYTH, D. A., & MCKINNEY, K. L. (1983). The social and psychological effects of puberty on white females. In J. Brooks-Gunn & A. C. Petersen (Eds.), *Girls at puberty: Biological and psychosocial perspectives* (pp. 229–272). New York: Plenum.

SIMMONS, R. G., BLYTH, D. A., VAN CLEAVE, E. F., & BUSH, D. M. (1979). Entry into early adolescence: The impact of school structure, puberty and early dating on self-esteem. *American Sociological Review, 44*, 948–967.

SIMMONS, R. G., BURGESON, R., CARLTON-FORD, & BLYTH, D. (1987). The impact of cumulative change in early adolescence. *Child Development, 58*, 1220–1234.

SIMONS, J., & BOHEN, H. (1982). *Employed parents and their children: A data book.* Washington, DC: Children's Defense Fund.

SINGER, D. G., ZUCKERMAN, D. M., & SINGER, J. L. (1980). Helping elementary school children learn about TV. *Journal of Communication, 30*(3), 84–93.

SINGER, J. L., & SINGER, D. G. (1981). *Television, imagination, and aggression: A study of preschoolers.* Hillsdale, NJ: Erlbaum.

SINGER, J. L., & SINGER, D. G. (1983). Psychologists look at television. *American Psychologist, 38*, 826–834.

SINGER, J. L., SINGER, D. G., & RAPACZYNSKI, W. (1984). Family patterns and television viewing as predictors of children's beliefs and aggression. *Journal of Communication, 34*, 73–89.

SINGLETON, L. C., & ASHER, S. R. (1979). Racial integration and children's peer preferences: An investigation of developmental and cohort differences. *Child Development, 50*, 936–941.

SINNOTT, J. M., PISONI, D. B., & ASLIN, R. N. (1983). A comparison of pure tone auditory thresholds in human infants and adults. *Infant Behavior and Development, 6*, 3–17.

SIQUELAND, E. R., & LIPSITT, L. P. (1966). Conditioned head-turning behavior in newborns. *Journal of Experimental Child Psychology, 3*, 356–376.

SIRIGNANO, S. W., & LACHMAN, M. E. (1985). Personality change during the transition to parenthood: The role of perceived infant temperament. *Developmental Psychology, 21*, 558–567.

SIROTNIK, K. A. (1983). What you see is what you get: Consistency, persistency, and mediocrity in classrooms. *Harvard Educational Review, 53*, 16–31.

SKEELS, H. M. (1966). Adult status of children with contrasting early life experiences. *Monographs of the Society for Research in Child Development, 31*(3, Serial No. 105).

SKINNER, B. F. (1957). *Verbal behavior.* New York: Appleton-Century-Crofts.

SKODAK, M., & SKEELS, H. M. (1945). A follow-up study of children in adoptive homes. *Journal of Genetic Psychology, 66,* 21–58.

SKODAK, M., & SKEELS, H. M. (1949). A follow-up study of one hundred adopted children. *Journal of Genetic Psychology, 75,* 85–125.

SLABY, R. G., & FREY, K. S. (1975). Development of gender constancy and selective attention to same-sex models. *Child Development, 46,* 849–856.

SLABY, R. G., & GUERRA, N. G. (1988). Cognitive mediators of aggression in adolescent offenders: I. Assessment. *Developmental Psychology, 24,* 580–588.

SLADE, A. (1987). A longitudinal study of maternal involvement and symbolic play during the toddler period. *Child Development, 58,* 367–375.

SLATER, A., & MORISON, V. (1985). Shape constancy and slant perception at birth. *Perception, 14,* 337–344.

SLAVIC, S. (1980). *How twins learn to talk.* New York: Academic Press.

SLAVIN, R., MADDEN, N., & LEAVEY, M. (1984). Effects of cooperative learning and individualized instruction on mainstreamed students. *Exceptional Children, 50,* 434–443.

SLOBIN, D. I. (1973). Cognitive prerequisites for the development of grammar. In C. A. Ferguson & D. I. Slobin (Eds.), *Studies of child language development* (pp. 175–208). New York: Holt, Rinehart and Winston.

SLOBIN, D. I. (1982). Universal and particular in the acquisition of language. In L. R. Gleitman & H. E. Wanner (Eds.), *Language acquisition: The state of the art* (pp. 128–170). Cambridge, England: Cambridge University Press.

SLOBIN, D. I. (1985). Crosslinguistic evidence for the language-making capacity. In D. I. Slobin (Ed.), *The crosslinguistic study of language acquisition: Vol. 2. Theoretical issues* (pp. 1157–1256). Hillsdale, NJ: Erlbaum.

SMEEDING, T. M., & TORREY, B. B. (1988). Poor children in rich countries. *Science, 242,* 873–877.

SMEEDING, T., TORREY, B. B., & REIN, M. (1988). Patterns of income and poverty: Economic status of children and the elderly in eight countries. In J. L. Palmer & I. V. Sawhill (Eds.), *The vulnerable* (pp. 89–119). Washington, DC: The Urban Institute Press.

SMILANSKY, S. (1968). *The effects of sociodramatic play on disadvantaged children: Preschool children.* New York: Wiley.

SMITH, A. J. (1960). A developmental study of group processes. *Journal of Genetic Psychology, 97,* 29–39.

SMITH, C., & LLOYD, B. (1978). Maternal behavior and perceived sex of infant: Revisited. *Child Development, 49,* 1263–1266.

SMITH, C. L., & TAGER-FLUSBERG, H. (1982). Metalinguistic awareness and language development. *Journal of Experimental Child Psychology, 34,* 449–468.

SMITH, D. F. (1980). Adolescent suicide. In R. E. Muus (Ed.), *Adolescent behavior and society* (3rd ed., pp. 402–409). New York: Random House.

SMITH, E. J. (1981). Adolescent suicide: A growing problem for the school and family. *Urban Education, 16,* 279–296.

SMITH, H. W. (1973). Some developmental interpersonal dynamics through childhood. *American Sociological Review, 38,* 343–352.

SMITH, J., & RUSSELL, G. (1984). Why do males and females differ? Children's beliefs about sex differences. *Sex Roles, 11,* 1111–1119.

SMITH, J. D., & CAPLAN, J. (1988). Cultural differences in cognitive style development. *Developmental Psychology, 24,* 46–52.

SMITH, M. C. (1978). Cognizing the behavior stream: The recognition of intentional action. *Child Development, 49,* 736–743.

SMITH, M. L., & GLASS, G. V. (1980). Meta-analysis of research on class size and its relationship to attitudes and instruction. *American Educational Research Journal, 17,* 419–433.

SMITH, M. S., & BISSELL, J. S. (1970). Report analysis: The impact of Head Start. *Harvard Educational Review, 40,* 51–104.

SMITH, P. K. (1978). A longitudinal study of social participation in preschool children: Solitary and parallel play reexamined. *Developmental Psychology, 14,* 517–523.

SMITH, P. K., & CONNOLLY, K. J. (1972). Patterns of play and social interaction in pre-school children. In N. Blurton Jones (Ed.), *Ethological studies of child behaviour* (pp. 65–95). Cambridge, England: Cambridge University Press.

SMITH, P. K., & CONNOLLY, K. J. (1980). *The ecology of preschool behaviour.* Cambridge, England: Cambridge University Press.

SMITH, T. E. (1984). School grades and responsibility for younger siblings: An empirical study of the "teaching function." *American Sociological Review, 49,* 248–260.

SMOKLER, C. S. (1975). *Self-esteem in pre-adolescent and adolescent females.* Dissertation Abstracts International, 35, 3599B. (University Microfilms No. 75-00, 813).

SMOLUCHA, F. (in press). Mothers' verbal scaffolding of pretend play. In R. M. Diaz & L. E. Berk (Eds.), *Private speech: From social interaction to self-regulation.* Hillsdale, NJ: Erlbaum.

SNAREY, J. R. (1985). Cross-cultural universality of social–moral development: A critical review of Kohlbergian research. *Psychological Bulletin, 97,* 202–232.

SNAREY, J. R., REIMER, J., & KOHLBERG, L. (1985). The development of social–moral reasoning among kibbutz adolescents: A longitudinal cross-cultural study. *Developmental Psychology, 20,* 3–17.

SNOW, C. (1987). Relevance of the notion of a critical period to language acquisition. In M. H. Bornstein (Ed.), *Sensitive periods in development: Interdisciplinary perspectives* (pp. 183–209). Hillsdale, NJ: Erlbaum.

SNOW, C. E., & HOEFNAGEL-HÖHLE, M. (1978). The critical period for language acquisition: Evidence from second language learning. *Child Development, 49,* 1114–1128.

SNOW, M. E., JACKLIN, C. N., & MACCOBY, E. E. (1981). Birth-order differences in peer sociability at thirty-three months. *Child Development, 52,* 589–596.

SNYDER, J. J., DISHION, T. J., & PATTERSON, G. R. (1986). Determinants and consequences of associating with deviant peers during preadolescence and adolescence. *Journal of Early Adolescence, 6,* 20–43.

SOBESKY, W. E. (1983). The effects of situational factors on moral judgments. *Child Development, 54,* 575–584.

SOCIETY FOR RESEARCH IN CHILD DEVELOPMENT, COMMITTEE FOR ETHICAL CONDUCT IN CHILD DEVELOPMENT RESEARCH (1990, Winter). SRCD ethical standards for research with children. *SRCD Newsletter,* Chicago: Author.

SODIAN, B., SCHNEIDER, W., & PERLMUTTER, M. (1986). Recall, clustering, and metamemory in young children. *Journal of Experimental Child Psychology, 41,* 395–410.

SODIAN, B., & WIMMER, H. (1987). Children's understanding of inference as a source of knowledge. *Child Development, 58,* 424–433.

SOKOLOFF, B. Z. (1987). Alternative methods of reproduction: Effects on the child. *Clinical Pediatrics, 26,* 11–17.

SOLAN, L. (1983). *Pronominal reference: Child language and the theory of grammar.* Dordrecht, Holland: Reidel.

SOLARZ, A. L. (1988, Winter). Homelessness: Implications for children and youth. *Social Policy Report of the Society for Research in Child Development,* 2(No. 4).

SOLOMON, D., & KENDALL, A. J. (1979). *Children in classrooms: An investigation of person–environment interaction.* New York: Praeger.

SONG, M.-J., & GINSBURG, H. P. (1987). The development of informal and formal mathematical thinking in Korean and U.S. children. *Child Development, 58,* 1286–1296.

SONG, M.-J., SMETANA, J., & KIM, S. Y. (1987). Korean children's conceptions of moral and conventional transgressions. *Developmental Psychology, 23,* 577–582.

SONNENSCHEIN, S. (1986a). Development of referential communication: Deciding that a message is uninformative. *Developmental Psychology, 22,* 164–168.

SONNENSCHEIN, S. (1986b). Development of referential communication skills: How familiarity with a listener affects a speaker's production of redundant messages. *Developmental Psychology, 22,* 549–552.

SONTAG, C. W., BAKER, C. T., & NELSON, V. L. (1958). Mental growth and personality development: A longitudinal study. *Monographs of the Society for Research in Child Development,* 23(2, Serial No. 68).

SOPHIAN, C. (1988). Early developments in children's understanding of number: Inferences about numerosity and one-to-one correspondence. *Child Development, 59,* 1397–1414.

SORCE, J., EMDE, R., CAMPOS, J., & KLINNERT, M. (1985). Maternal emotional signaling: Its effect on the visual cliff behavior of 1-year-olds. *Developmental Psychology, 21,* 195–200.

SPEARMAN, C. (1927). *The abilities of man: Their nature and measurement.* New York: Macmillan.

SPEECE, M. W., & BRENT, S. B. (1984). Children's understanding of death: A review of three components of a death concept. *Child Development, 55,* 1671–1686.

SPEER, J. R., & FLAVELL, J. H. (1979). Young children's knowledge of the relative difficulty of recognition and recall memory tasks. *Developmental Psychology, 15,* 214–217.

SPEIDEL, G. E., & THARP, R. (1985). Is there a comprehension problem for children who speak nonstandard English? A study of children with Hawaiian–English backgrounds. *Applied Psycholinguistics, 6,* 83–96.

SPELKE, E. S. (1987). The development of intermodal perception. In P. Salapatek & L. Cohen (Eds.), *Handbook of infant perception: Vol 2. From perception to cognition* (pp. 233–273). Orlando, FL: Academic Press.

SPELKE, E., HOFSTEN, C. VON, & KESTENBAUM, R. (1989). Object perception in infancy: Interaction of spatial and kinetic information for object boundaries. *Developmental Psychology, 25,* 185–196.

SPELLACY, W. N., MILLER, S. J., & WINEGAR, A. (1986). Pregnancy after 40 years of age. *Obstetrics and Gynecology, 68,* 452–454.

SPENCE, J. T., HELMREICH, R., & STAPP, J. (1975). Ratings of self and peers on sex role attributes and their relation to self-esteem and conceptions of masculinity and femininity. *Journal of Personality and Social Psychology, 32,* 29–39.

SPENCE, M. J., & DECASPER, A. J. (1987). Prenatal experience with low-frequency maternal voice sounds influences neonatal perception of maternal voice samples. *Infant Behavior and Development, 10,* 133–142.

SPENCER, M. B., & MARKSTROM-ADAMS, C. (1990). Identity processes among racial and ethnic minority children in America. *Child Development, 61,* 290–310.

SPINETTA, J., & RIGLER, D. (1972). The child-abusing parent: A psychological review. *Psychological Bulletin, 77,* 296–304.

SPITZ, R. A. (1945). Hospitalism: An inquiry into the genesis of psychiatric conditions in early childhood. *Psychoanalytic Study of the Child, 1,* 113–117.

SPITZ, R. (1946). Anaclitic depression. *Psychoanalytic Study of the Child, 2,* 313–342.

SPIVACK, G., & SHURE, M. B. (1974). *Social adjustment of young children: A cognitive approach to solving real life problems.* San Francisco: Jossey-Bass.

SPOCK, B. (1946). *Commonsense book of baby and child care.* New York: Duell, Sloan & Pearce.

SPOCK, B., & ROTHENBERG, M. B. (1985). *Dr. Spock's baby and child care.* New York: Dutton.

SPRAGUE, R. L., & SLEATOR, E. K. (1977). Methylphenidate in hyperkinetic children: Differences in dose effects on learning and social behavior. *Science, 198,* 1274–1276.

SPREEN, O., TUPPER, D., RISSER, A., TUOKKO, H., & EDGELL, D. (1984). *Human developmental neuropsychology.* New York: Oxford University Press.

SPRIGLE, J. E., & SCHAEFER, L. (1985). Longitudinal evaluation of the effects of two compensatory preschool programs on fourth-through sixth-grade students. *Developmental Psychology, 21,* 702–708.

SROUFE, L. A. (1977). Wariness of strangers and the study of infant development. *Child Development, 48,* 731–746.

SROUFE, L. A. (1978). Attachment and the roots of competence. *Human Nature, 1*(10), 50–57.

SROUFE, L. A. (1979). Socioemotional development. In J. D. Osofsky (Ed.), *Handbook of infant development* (pp. 462–516). New York: Wiley.

SROUFE, L. A. (1983). Infant–caregiver attachment and patterns of adaptation in preschool: The roots of maladaptation. In M. Perlmutter (Ed.), *Minnesota Symposia on Child Psychology* (Vol. 16, pp. 41–83). Hillsdale, NJ: Erlbaum.

SROUFE, L. A. (1985). Attachment classification from the perspective of infant–caregiver relationships and infant temperament. *Child Development, 56,* 1–14.

SROUFE, L. A. (1988). A developmental perspective on day care. *Early Childhood Research Quarterly, 3,* 293–292.

SROUFE, L. A., FOX, N. E., & PANCAKE, V. R. (1983). Attachment and dependency in developmental perspective. *Child Development, 54,* 1615–1627.

SROUFE, L. A., & WATERS, E. (1976). The ontogenesis of smiling and laughter: A perspective on the organization of development in infancy. *Psychological Review, 83,* 173–189.

SROUFE, L. A. & WUNSCH, J. P. (1972). The development of laughter in the first year of life. *Child Development, 43,* 1324–1344.

ST. JOHN, N. H. (1975). *School desegregation: Outcomes for children.* New York: Wiley.

STAATS, A. (1971). Linguistic–mentalistic theory versus an explanatory S–R learning theory of language development. In D. Slobin (Ed.), *The ontogenesis of grammar* (pp. 103–152). New York: Academic Press.

STAMBROOK, M., & PARKER, K. C. H. (1987). The development of the concept of death in childhood: A review of the literature. *Merrill-Palmer Quarterly, 33,* 133–157.

STANBURY, J. B., WYNGAARDEN, J. B., & FREDERICKSON, D. S. (1983). *The metabolic basis of inherited disease.* New York: McGraw-Hill.

STANHOPE, L., BELL, R. Q., & PARKER-COHEN, N. Y. (1987). Temperament and helping behavior in preschool children. *Developmental Psychology, 23,* 347–353.

STANKOV, L. (1987). Level I/Level II: A theory ready to be archived. In S. Modgil & C. Modgil (Eds.), *Arthur Jensen: Consensus and controversy* (pp. 25–37). New York: Falmer Press.

STANKOV, L., HORN, J. L., & ROY, T. (1980). On the relationship between Gf/Gc theory and Jensen's Level I/Level II theory. *Journal of Educational Psychology, 72,* 796–809.

STARK, L. J., ALLEN, K. D., HURST, M., NASH, D. A., RIGNEY, B., & STOKES, T. F. (1989). Distraction: Its utilization and efficacy with children undergoing dental treatment. *Journal of Applied Behavior Analysis, 22,* 297–307.

STARKEY, P., SPELKE, E. S., & GELMAN, R. (in press). Numerical abstraction by human infants. *Cognition.*

STARR, R. H., JR. (1979). Child abuse. *American Psychologist, 34,* 872–878.

STAUB, E. (1974). Helping a distressed person: Social, personality, and stimulus determinants. In L. Berkowitz (Ed.), *Advances in experimental social psychology* (Vol. 7, pp. 293–341). New York: Academic Press.

STECHLER, G., & HALTON, A. (1982). Prenatal influences on human development. In B. B. Wolman (Ed.), *Handbook of development psychology* (pp. 175–189). Englewood Cliffs, NJ: Prentice-Hall.

STEIN, A. (1983). Pregnancy in gravidas over age 35 years. *Journal of Nurse-Midwifery, 28,* 17–20.

STEIN, A. H. (1967). Imitation of resistance to temptation. *Child Development, 38,* 157–169.

STEIN, A. H. (1971). The effects of sex-role standards for achievement and sex-role preference on three determinants of achievement motivation. *Developmental Psychology, 4,* 219–231.

STEIN, A. H., & SMITHELLS, J. (1969). Age and sex differences in children's sex-role standards about achievement. *Development Psychology, 1,* 252–259

STEIN, Z., SUSSER, M., SAENGER, G., & MAROLLA, F. (1975). *Famine and human development: The Dutch hunger winter of 1944–1945.* New York: Oxford.

STEINBERG, L. (1984). The varieties and effects of work during adolescence. In M. Lamb, A. Brown, & B. Rogoff (Eds.), *Advances in developmental psychology* (pp. 1–37). Hillsdale, NJ: Erlbaum.

STEINBERG, L. (1986). Latchkey children and susceptibility to peer pressure: An ecological analysis. *Developmental Psychology, 22,* 433–439.

STEINBERG, L. (1987). The impact of puberty on family relations: Effects of pubertal status and pubertal timing. *Developmental Psychology, 23,* 451–460.

STEINBERG, L. (1988a). Reciprocal relation between parent–child distance and pubertal maturation. *Developmental Psychology, 24,* 122–128.

STEINBERG, L. (1988b). Simple solutions to a complex problem: A response to Rodman, Pratto, & Nelson. *Developmental Psychology, 24,* 295–296.

STEINBERG, L. (1988c). Stability of Type A behavior from early childhood to young adulthood. In P. B. Baltes, D. L. Featherman, & R. M. Lerner (Eds.), *Life-span development and behavior* (Vol. 8, pp. 129–161). Hillsdale, NJ: Erlbaum.

STEINBERG, L. (1989). Pubertal maturation and parent–adolescent distance: An evolutionary perspective. In G. R. Adams, R. Montemayor, & T. P. Gullotta (Eds.), *Biology of adolescent behavior and development* (pp. 71–97). Newbury Park, CA: Sage.

STEINBERG, L., CATALANO, R., & DOOLEY, D. (1981). Economic antecedents of child abuse and neglect. *Child Development, 52,* 975–985.

STEINBERG, L., ELMAN, J. D., & MOUNTS, N. S. (1989). Authoritative parenting, psychosocial maturity, and academic success among adolescents. *Child Development, 60,* 1424–1436.

STEINBERG, L. D., GREENBERGER, E., GARDUQUE, L., & MCAULIFFE, S. (1982). High school students in the labor force: Some costs and benefits to schooling and learning. *Educational Evaluation and Policy Analysis, 4,* 363–372.

STEINER, G. Y. (1976). *The children's cause.* Washington, DC: The Brookings Institution.

STEINER, G. Y. (1981). *The futility of family policy.* Washington, DC: The Brookings Institution.

STEINER, J. E. (1979). Human facial expression in response to taste and smell stimulation. In H. W. Reese & L. P. Lipsitt (Eds.), *Advances in child development and behavior* (Vol. 13, pp. 257–295). New York: Academic Press.

STEINMAN, S. B., ZEMMELMAN, S. E., & KNOBLAUCH, T. M. (1985). A study of parents who sought joint custody following divorce: Who reaches agreement and sustains joint custody and who returns to court? *Journal of the American Academy of Child and Adolescent Psychiatry, 24,* 554–562.

STENBERG, C., CAMPOS, J., & EMDE, R. (1983). The facial expression of anger in seven-month-old infants. *Child Development, 54,* 178–184.

STENCHEVER, M. A., WILLIAMSON, R. A., LEONARD, J., KARP, L. E., LEY, B., SHY, K., & SMITH, D. (1981). Possible relationship between in utero diethylstilbesterol exposure and male infertility. *American Journal of Obstetrics and Gynecology, 140,* 186–193.

STENE, J., STENE, E., & STENGEL-RUTKOWSKI, S. (1981). Paternal age and Down's syndrome. *Data from prenatal diagnosis (DFG). Human Genetics, 59,* 119–124.

STEPHENSON, M. G., LEVY, A. S., SASS, N. L., & MCGARVEY, W. E. (1987). 1985 NHIS findings: Nutrition knowledge and baseline data for the weight-loss objectives. *Public Health Reports, 102,* 61–67.

STERN, M., & HILDEBRANDT, K. A. (1986). Prematurity stereotyping: Effects on mother–infant interaction. *Child Development, 57,* 308–315.

STERN, M., & KARRAKER, K. H. (1989). Sex stereotyping of infants: A review of gender labeling studies. *Sex Roles, 20,* 501–522.

STERNBERG, R. J. (1977). *Intelligence, information processing, and analogical reasoning: The componential analysis of human abilities.* Hillsdale, NJ: Erlbaum.

STERNBERG, R. J. (1981). Testing and cognitive psychology. *American Psychologist, 36,* 1181–1189.

STERNBERG, R. J. (1982, April). Who's intelligent? *Psychology Today, 16*(4), 30–39.

STERNBERG, R. J. (1984). Evaluation of the Kaufman Assessment Battery for Children from an information processing perspective. *Journal of Special Education, 18,* 269–279.

STERNBERG, R. J. (1985a). *Beyond IQ: A triarchic theory of human intelligence.* New York: Cambridge University Press.

STERNBERG, R. J. (1985b). Cognitive approaches to intelligence. In B. B. Wolman (Ed.), *Handbook of intelligence* (pp. 59–118). New York: Wiley.

STERNBERG, R. J. (1988a). Intellectual development: Psychometric and information-processing approaches. In M. H. Bornstein & M. E. Lamb (Eds.), *Developmental psychology: An advanced textbook* (2nd ed., pp. 261–295). Hillsdale, NJ: Erlbaum.

STERNBERG, R. J. (ED.) (1988b). *The nature of creativity.* New York: Cambridge University Press.

STERNBERG, R. J. (1988c). A triarchic view of intelligence in cross-cultural perspective. In S. H. Irvine & J. W. Berry (Eds.), *Human abilities in cultural context* (pp. 60–85). New York: Cambridge University Press.

STERNBERG, R. J., CONWAY, B. E., KETRON, J. L., & BERNSTEIN, M. (1981). People's conceptions of intelligence. *Journal of Personality and Social Psychology, 41,* 37–55.

STERNBERG, R. J., & DAVIDSON, J. E. (EDS.) (1986). *Conceptions of giftedness.* New York: Cambridge University Press.

STEVENS, J. H. (1984). Black grandmothers' and black adolescent mothers' knowledge about parenting. *Developmental Psychology, 20,* 1017–1025.

STEVENSON, D. L., & BAKER, D. P. (1987). The family–school relation and the child's school performance. *Child Development, 58,* 1348–1357.

STEVENSON, H. W., & LEE, S-Y. (1990). Contexts of achievement: A study of American, Chinese, and Japanese children. *Monographs of the Society for Research in Child Development, 55*(1-2, Serial No. 221).

STEVENSON, H. W., LEE, S-Y., & STIGLER, J. W. (1986). Mathematics achievement of Chinese, Japanese, and American children. *Science, 231,* 693–699.

STEVENSON, H. W., STIGLER, J. W., LEE, S., LUCKER, G. W., LITAMURA, S., & HSU, C. (1985). Cognitive performance and academic achievement of Japanese, Chinese, and American children. *Child Development, 56,* 718–734.

STEVENSON, H. W., STIGLER, J. W., LUCKER, G. W., LEE S. Y., HSU, C. C., & KITAMURA, S. (1986). Classroom behavior and achievement of Japanese, Chinese, and American Children. In R. Glaser (Ed.), *Advances in instructional psychology* (Vol. 3, pp. 153–204). Hillsdale, NJ: Erlbaum.

STEVENSON, R., & POLLITT, C. (1987). The acquisition of temporal terms. *Journal of Child Language, 14,* 533–545.

STEWART, A. J., & HEALY, J. M., JR. (1989). Linking individual development and social changes. *American Psychologist, 44,* 30–42.

STEWART, D. A. (1982). *Children with sex chromosome aneuploidy: Follow-up studies.* New York: Alan R. Liss.

STEWART, R. B., MOBLEY, L. A., VAN TUYL, S. S., & SALVADOR, M. A. (1987). The firstborn's adjustment to the birth of a sibling: A longitudinal assessment. *Child Development, 58,* 341–355.

STIEFVATER, K., KURDEK, L. A., & ALLIK, J. (1986). Effectiveness of a short-term social problem-solving program for popular, rejected, neglected, and average fourth-grade children. *Journal of Applied Developmental Psychology, 7,* 33–43.

STIGLER, J. W., & BARANES, R. (in press). Culture and mathematics learning. In E. Rothkopf (Ed.), *Review of research in education.* Washington, DC: American Educational Research Association.

STIGLER, J. W., LEE, S., & STEVENSON, H. W. (1987). Mathematics classrooms in Japan, Taiwan, and the United States. *Child Development, 58,* 1272–1285.

STILLMAN, R. J. (1982). In utero exposure to diethylstilbesterol: Adverse effects on the reproductive tract and reproductive performance in male and female offspring. *American Journal of Obstetrics and Gynecology, 142,* 905–921.

STINI, W. A., WEBER, C. W., KEMBERLING, S. R., & VAUGHAN, L. A. (1980). Lean tissue growth and disease susceptibility in bottle-fed versus breast-fed infants. In L. S. Greene & R. E. Johnston (Eds.), *Social and biological predictors of nutritional status, physical growth, and neurological development* (pp. 61–79). New York: Academic Press.

STIPEK, D., & McCROSKEY, J. (1989). Investing in children. *American Psychologist, 44,* 416–423.

STIPEK, D. J. (1981). Children's perceptions of their own and their classmates' ability. *Journal of Educational Psychology, 73,* 404–410.

STIPEK, D. J. (1984). Sex differences in children's attributions for success and failure on math and spelling tests. *Sex Roles, 11,* 969–981.

STIPEK, D. J., & HOFFMAN, J. M. (1980). Children's achievement related expectancies as a function of academic performance histories and sex. *Journal of Educational Psychology, 72,* 861–865.

STOCH, M. B., SMYTHE, P. M., MOODIE, A. D., & BRADSHAW, D. (1982). Psychosocial outcome and CT findings after gross undernourishment during infancy: A 20-year developmental study. *Developmental Medicine and Child Neurology, 24,* 419–436.

STOCKER, C., DUNN, J., & PLOMIN, R. (1989). Sibling relationships: Links with child temperament, maternal behavior, and family structure. *Child Development, 60,* 715–727.

STODDART, T., & TURIEL, E. (1985). Children's concepts of cross-gender activities. *Child Development, 56,* 1241–1252.

STODOLSKY, S. S. (1988). *The subject matters.* Chicago: University of Chicago Press.

STODOLSKY, S., & LESSER, G. (1967). Learning patterns in the disadvantaged. *Harvard Educational Review, 37,* 546–593.

STOEL-GAMMON, C., & OTOMO, K. (1986). Babbling development of hearing-impaired and normally hearing subjects. *Journal of Speech and Hearing Disorders, 51,* 33–41.

STOLBERG, A. L., CAMPLAIR, C., CURRIER, K., & WELLS, M. J. (1987). Individual, familial, and environmental determinants of children's post-divorce adjustment and maladjustment. *Journal of Divorce, 11,* 51–70.

STOLZ, H. R., & STOLZ, L. M. (1971). Somatic development of adolescent boys. In M. C. Jones, N. Bayley, J. W. MacFarlane, & M. P. Honzik (Eds.), *The course of human development* (pp. 27–53). Waltham, MA: Xerox Publishing.

STONEMAN, Z., BRODY, G. H., & MACKINNON, C. E. (1986). Same-sex and cross-sex siblings: Activity choices, roles, behavior, and gender stereotypes. *Sex Roles, 15,* 495–511.

STOTLAND, E. (1969). Exploratory investigations of empathy. In L. Berkowitz (Ed.), *Advances in experimental social psychology* (Vol. 4, pp. 271–314). New York: Academic Press.

STRAIN, P. S. (1977). An experimental analysis of peer social initiation on the behavior of withdrawn preschool children: Some training and generalization effects. *Journal of Abnormal Child Psychology, 5,* 445–455.

STRAUSS, C. C., SMITH, K., FRAME, C., & FORCHAND, R. (1985). Personal and interpersonal characteristics associated with childhood obesity. *Journal of Pediatric Psychology, 10,* 337–343.

STRAUSS, M. A., GELLES, R., & STEINMETZ, S. (1980). *Behind closed doors.* New York: Doubleday.

STRAUSS, S., & LEVIN, I. (1981). Commentary on Siegler's "Developmental sequences within and between concepts." *Monographs of the Society for Research in Child Development, 46* (2, Serial No. 189).

STRAYER, F. F., & STRAYER, J. (1976). An ethological analysis of social agonism and dominance relations among preschool children. *Child Development, 47,* 980–989.

STRAYER, J. A. (1980). A naturalistic study of empathic behaviors and their relation to affective states and perspective-taking skills in preschoolers. *Child Development, 51,* 815–822.

STREISSGUTH, A. P., BARR, H. M., SAMPSON, P. D., DARBY, B. L., & MARTIN D. C. (1989). IQ at age 4 in relation to maternal alcohol use and smoking during pregnancy. *Developmental Psychology, 25,* 3–11.

STREISSGUTH, A. P., MARTIN, D. C., BARR, H. M., SANDMAN, B. M., KIRCHNER, G. L., & DARBY, B. L. (1984a). Intrauterine alcohol and nicotine exposure: Attention and reaction time in 4-year-old children. *Developmental Psychology, 20,* 533–541.

STREISSGUTH, A. P., SAMPSON, P. D., & BARR, H. M. (1989). Neurobehavioral dose–response effects of prenatal alcohol exposure in humans from infancy to adulthood. *Annals of the New York Academy of Sciences, 562,* 145–158.

STREISSGUTH, A. P., TREDER, R., BARR, H. M., SHEPARD, T., BLEYER, A., & MARTIN, D. (1984b). Prenatal aspirin and offspring IQ in a large group. *Teratology, 29,* 59A–60A.

STUCKEY, M. R. McGHEE, P. E., & BELL, N. J. (1982). Parent–child interaction: The influence of maternal employment. *Developmental Psychology, 18,* 635–644.

STUNKARD, A. J., d'AQUILI, E., & FILION, R. D. L. (1972). Influence of social class on obesity and thinness in children. *Journal of the American Medical Association, 221,* 579–584.

STUNKARD, A. J., SORENSON, T. I. A., HANIS, C., TEASDALE, T. W., CHAKRABORTY, R., SCHULL, W. J., & SCHULSINGER, F. (1986). An adoption study of human obesity. *New England Journal of Medicine, 314,* 193–198.

STYCZYNSKI, L., & LANGLOIS, J. H. (1977). The effects of familiarity on behavioral stereotypes associated with physical attractiveness in young children. *Child Development, 48,* 1137–1141.

SUDHALTER, V., & BRAINE, M. D. S. (1985). How does comprehension of passives develop? A comparison of actional and experiential verbs. *Journal of Child Language, 12,* 455–470.

SULLIVAN, H. S. (1953). *The interpersonal theory of psychiatry.* New York: Norton.

SULLIVAN, J. W., & HOROWITZ, F. D. (1983). The effects of intonation on infant attention: The role of the rising intonation contour. *Journal of Child Language, 10,* 521–534.

SULLIVAN, L. W. (1987). The risks of the sickle-cell trait: Caution and common sense. *New England Journal of Medicine, 317,* 830–831.

SUOMI, S. (1982). Biological foundations and developmental psychobiology. In C. B. Kopp & J. B. Krakow (Eds.), *The child: Development in a social context* (pp. 42–91). Reading, MA: Addison-Wesley.

SUOMI, S. J., & HARLOW, H. H. (1978). Production and alleviation of depressive behaviors in monkeys. In J. Maser & M. Seligman (Eds.), *Psychopathology: Experimental models* (pp. 131–173). San Francisco: Freeman.

SUPER, C. M. (1980). Cognitive development: Looking across at growing up. In C. Super & M. Harkness (Eds.), *New directions for child development* (Vol. 8, pp. 59–69). San Francisco: Jossey-Bass.

SUPER, C. M., & HARKNESS, S. (1982). The infant's niche in rural Kenya and metropolitan America. In L. L. Adler (Ed.), *Cross-cultural research at issue* (pp. 247–255). New York: Academic Press.

SURANSKY, V. P. (1982). *The erosion of childhood.* Chicago: University of Chicago Press.

SUSANNE, C. (1975). Genetic and environmental influences in morphological characteristics. *Annals of Human Biology, 2,* 279–287.

SUSKIND, R. M. (1977). Characteristics of causation of protein-calorie malnutrition in the infant and preschool child. In L. S. Greene (Ed.), *Malnutrition, behavior, and social organization* (pp. 1–17). New York: Academic Press.

SUSMAN, E. J., INOFF-GERMAIN, G., NOTTELMANN, E. D., LORIAUX, D. L., CUTLER, G. B. JR., & CHROUSOS, G. P. (1987). Hormones, emotional dispositions, and aggressive attributes in young adolescents. *Child Development, 58,* 1114–1134.

SUTTON-SMITH, B. (1975). A developmental structural account of riddles. In B. Kirschenblatt-Gimblett (Ed.), *Speech, play and display* (pp. 111–119). The Hague: Mouton.

TAGER-FLUSBERG, H. (1989). Putting words together: Morphology and syntax in the preschool years. In J. Berko Gleason (Ed.), *The development of language* (pp. 135–165). Columbus, OH: Merrill.

TAITZ, L. S. (1971). Infantile over-nutrition among artificially fed infants in the Sheffield region. *British Medical Journal, 1,* 315.

TAKANISHI, R., DeLEON, P., & PALLAK, M. S. (1983). Psychology and public policy affecting children, youth, and families. *American Psychologist, 38,* 67–69.

TANGRI, S. S. (1972). Determinants of occupational role innovation among college women. *Journal of Social Issues, 28,* 177–199.

TANNER, J. M. (1962). *Growth of adolescence* (2nd ed.). Oxford: Blackwell Scientific Publications.

TANNER, J. M. (1978b). *Education and physical growth.* New York: International Universities Press.

TANNER, J. M. (1978a). *Fetus into man*. Cambridge, MA: Harvard University Press.

TANNER, J. M., & INHELDER, B. (EDS.). (1956). *Discussions on child development* (Vol. 1). London: Tavistock Publications.

TANNER, J. M., & WHITEHOUSE, R. H. (1975). Revised standards for triceps and subscapular skinfolds in British children. *Archives of Disease in Childhood, 50,* 142–145.

TANNER, J. M., WHITEHOUSE, R. H., CAMERON, N., MARSHALL, W. A., HEALEY, M. J. R., & GOLDSTEIN, H. (1983). *Assessment of skeletal maturity and prediction of adult height (TW2 method)* (2nd ed.). New York: Academic Press.

TASK FORCE ON PEDIATRIC AIDS (1989). Pediatric AIDS and human immunodeficiency virus infection. *American Psychologist, 44,* 258–264.

TAUBER, M. A. (1979). Parental socialization techniques and sex differences in children's play. *Child Development, 50,* 225–234.

TAYLOR, A. R., ASHER, S. R., & WILLIAMS, G. A. (1987). The social adaptation of mainstreamed mildly retarded children. *Child Development, 58,* 1321–1334.

TAYLOR, M. (1988). Conceptual perspective taking: Children's ability to distinguish what they know from what they see. *Child Development, 59,* 703–718.

TAYLOR, M., & GELMAN, S. A. (1988). Adjectives and nouns: Children's strategies for learning new words. *Child Development, 59,* 411–419.

TAYLOR, M., & GELMAN, S. A. (1989). Incorporating new words into the lexicon: Preliminary evidence for language hierachies. *Child Development, 60,* 625–636.

TAYLOR, M. C., & HALL, J. A. (1982). Psychological androgyny: Theories, methods, and conclusions. *Psychological Bulletin, 92,* 347–366.

TAYLOR, S. P., & LEWIT, D. W. (1966). Social comparison and deception regarding ability. *Journal of Personality, 34,* 94–104.

TEBERG, A. J., WALTHER, F. J., & PENA, I. C. (1988). Mortality, morbidity, and outcome of the small-for-gestational-age infant. *Seminar in Perinatology, 12,* 84–94.

TELLER, D. Y., & BORNSTEIN, M. H. (1987). Infant color vision and color perception. In P. Salapatek & L. Cohen (Eds.), *Handbook of infant perception* (2nd ed., pp. 185–236). Orlando, FL: Academic Press.

TEMPLIN, M. C. (1957). Certain language skills in children: Their development and interrelationships. *University of Minnesota Institute of Child Welfare Monograph, 26.*

TENNES, K., EMDE, R., KISLEY, A., & METCALF, D. (1972). The stimulus barrier in early infancy: An exploration of some formulations of John Benjamin. In R. Holt and E. Peterfreund (Eds.), *Psychoanalysis and contemporary science* (Vol. 1, pp. 206–234). New York: Macmillan.

TENNEY, Y. J. (1975). The child's conception of organization and recall. *Journal of Experimental Child Psychology, 19,* 100–114.

TERMAN, L. (1925). *Genetic studies of genius: Vol. 1. Mental and physical traits of a thousand gifted children.* Stanford, CA: Stanford University Press.

TERMAN, L., & ODEN, M. H. (1959). *Genetic studies of genius: Vol. 4. The gifted group at midlife.* Stanford, CA: Stanford University Press.

TERMINE, N. T., & IZARD, C. E. (1988). Infants' responses to their mothers' expressions of joy and sadness. *Developmental Psychology, 24,* 223–229.

TERRACE, H. S., PETITTO, L. A., SANDERS, R. J., & BEVER, T. G. (1980). On the grammatical capacity of apes. In K. E. Nelson (Ed.), *Children's language* (Vol. 2, pp. 371–495). New York: Gardner Press.

THARP, R. G., & GALLIMORE R. (1988). *Rousing minds to life.* New York: Cambridge University Press.

THATCHER, R. W., WALKER, R. A., & GIUDICE, S. (1987). Human cerebral hemispheres develop at different rates and ages. *Science, 236,* 1110–1113.

THELEN, E. (1983). Learning to walk is still an "old" problem: A reply to Zelazo. *Journal of Motor Behavior, 15,* 139–161.

THELEN, E. (1989). The (re)discovery of motor development: Learning new things from an old field. *Developmental Psychology, 25,* 946–949.

THELEN, E., FISHER, D. M., & RIDLEY-JOHNSON, R. (1984). The relationship between physical growth and a newborn reflex. *Infant Behavior and Development, 7,* 479–493.

THELEN, M. H., & KIRKLAND, K. D. (1976). On status and being imitated: Effects of reciprocal imitation. *Journal of Personality and Social Psychology, 33,* 691–697.

THEORELL, K., PRECHTL, H., & VOS, J. (1974). A polygraphic study of normal and abnormal newborn infants. *Neuropaediatrie, 5,* 279–317.

THEVENIN, D. M., EILERS, R. E., OLLER, D. K., & LAVOIE, L. (1985). Where's the drift in babbling drift? A cross-linguistic study. *Applied Psycholinguistics, 6,* 3–15.

THOMA, S. J. (1986). Estimating gender differences in the comprehension and preference of moral issues. *Developmental Review, 6,* 165–180.

THOMAS, A., & CHESS, S. (1977). *Temperament and development.* New York: Brunner/Mazel.

THOMAS, A., CHESS, S., & BIRCH, H. G. (1968). *Temperament and behavior disorders in children.* New York: New York University Press.

THOMAS, A., CHESS, S., & KORN, S. J. (1982). The reality of difficult temperament. *Merrill-Palmer Quarterly, 28,* 1–20.

THOMAS, J. R., & FRENCH, K. E. (1985). Gender differences across age in motor performance: A meta-analysis. *Psychological Bulletin, 98,* 260–282.

THOMAS, N. G., & BERK, L. E. (1981). Effects of school environments on the development of young children's creativity. *Child Development, 52,* 1153–1162.

THOMAS, R. M. (1985). *Comparing theories of child development.* Belmont, CA: Wadsworth.

THOMPSON, J. G., & MYERS, N. A. (1985). Inferences and recall at ages four and seven. *Child Development, 56,* 1134–1144.

THOMPSON, R. A. (1986). Temperament, emotionality, and infant social cognition. In J. V. Lerner & R. M. Lerner (Eds.), *New directions for child development* (No. 30, pp. 35–52). San Francisco: Jossey-Bass.

THOMPSON, R. A. (1987). Empathy and emotional understanding: The early development of empathy. In N. Eisenberg & J. Strayer (Eds.), *Empathy and its development* (pp. 119–145). Cambridge, England: Cambridge University Press.

THOMPSON, R. A. (1988). The effects of infant day care through the prism of attachment theory: A critical appraisal. *Early Childhood Research Quarterly, 3,* 273–282.

THOMPSON, R. A. (1990). On emotion and self-regulation. In R. A. Thompson (Ed.), *Nebraska Symposium on Motivation* (Vol. 36, pp. 383–483). Lincoln, NB: University of Nebraska Press.

THOMPSON, R. A. (1990). Vulnerability in research: A developmental perspective on research risk. *Child Development, 61,* 1–16.

THOMPSON, R. A., CONNELL, J. P., & BRIDGES, L. (1988). Temperament, emotion, and social interactive behavior in the Strange Situation: A component process analysis of attachment system functioning. *Child Development, 59,* 1102–1110.

THOMPSON, R. A., & HOFFMAN, M. L. (1980). Empathy and the development of guilt in children. *Developmental Psychology, 16,* 155–156.

THOMPSON, R. A., LAMB, M., & ESTES, D. (1982). Stability of infant–mother attachment and its relationship to changing life circumstances in an unselected middle-class sample. *Child Development, 53,* 144–148.

THOMPSON, R. A., TINSLEY, B. R., SCALORA, M. J., & PARKE, R. D. (1989). Grandparents' visitation rights: Legalizing the ties that bind. *American Psychologist, 44,* 1217–1222.

THOMPSON, S. K. (1975). Gender labels and early sex role development. *Child Development, 46,* 339–347.

THORNDIKE, R. L., HAGEN, E. P., & SATTLER, J. M. (1986). *The Stanford–Binet Intelligence Scale: Guide for administering and scoring* (4th ed.). Chicago: Riverside Publishing.

TIKENOFF, W. J. (1983). *Significant bilingual instructional features study.* San Francisco, CA: Far West Laboratory.

TIZARD, B., CARMICHAEL, H., HUGHES, M., & PINKERTON, G. (1980).

Four-year-olds talking to mothers and teacher. In L. A. Hersov (Ed.), *Language and language disorders in childhood* (pp. 49–76). London: Pergamon Press.

TIZARD, B., & HODGES, J. (1978). The effect of early institutional rearing on the development of eight year old children. *Journal of Child Psychology and Psychiatry, 19,* 99–118.

TIZARD, B., & REES, J. (1975). The effect of early institutional rearing on the behaviour problems and affectional relationships of four-year-old children. *Journal of Child Psychology and Psychiatry, 16,* 61–73.

TOBIAS, P. V. (1975). Anthropometry among disadvantaged people: Studies in Southern Africa. In E. S. Watts, F. E. Johnston, & G. W. Lasker (Eds.), *Biosocial interrelations in population adaptation: World anthropology series* (pp. 287–305). The Hague: Mouton.

TOBIN-RICHARDS, M. H., BOXER, A. M., & PETERSEN, A. C. (1983). The psychological significance of pubertal change: Sex differences in perceptions of self during early adolescence. In J. Brooks-Gunn & A. C. Petersen (Eds.), *Girls at puberty: Biological and psychosocial perspectives* (pp. 127–154). New York: Plenum.

TODD, G., & PALMER, B. (1968). Social reinforcement of infant babbling. *Child Development, 39,* 591–596.

TOLSON, T. F. J., & WILSON, M. N. (1990). The impact of two- and three-generational black family structure on perceived family climate. *Child Development, 61,* 416–428.

TOMASELLO, M. (1990). The role of joint attentional processes in early language development. *Language Sciences, 10,* 69–88.

TOMASELLO, M., MANNIE, S., & KRUGER, A. C. (1986). Linguistic environment of 1- to 2-year-old twins. *Developmental Psychology, 22,* 169–176.

TOMEH, A. K. (1979). Sex role orientation and structural correlates. *Sociological Quarterly, 20,* 333–344.

TONER, I. J., MOORE, L. P., & EMMONS, B. A. (1980). The effect of being labeled on subsequent self control in children. *Child Development, 51,* 618–621.

TONER, I. J., PARKE, R. D., & YUSSEN, S. R. (1978). The effect of observation of model behavior on establishment and stability of resistance to deviation in children. *Journal of Genetic Psychology, 132,* 283–290.

TONER, I. J., & SMITH, R. A. (1977). Age and overt verbalization in delay maintenance behavior in children. *Journal of Experimental Child Psychology, 24,* 123–128.

TONGE, W. L., JAMES, D. S., & HILLAM, S. M. (1975). *Families without hope: A controlled study of 33 problem families.* Ashford, England: Headley Bros.

TORRANCE, E. P. (1966). *The Torrance Tests of Creative Thinking: Technical-norms manual.* Lexington, MA: Personnel Press.

TORRANCE, E. P. (1976). Creativity research in education: Still alive. In I. A. Taylor & J. W. Getzels (Ed.), *Perspectives in creativity* (pp. 278–296). Chicago: Aldine.

TORRANCE, E. P. (1986). Teaching creative and gifted learners. In M. C. Wittrock (Ed.), *Handbook of research on teaching* (3rd ed., pp. 630–647). New York: Macmillan.

TOUWEN, B. (1978). Variability and stereotypy in normal and deviant development. In J. Apley (Ed.), *Care of the handicapped child* (pp. 99–110). Philadelphia: Lippincott.

TOUWEN, B. C. L. (1984). Primitive reflexes—Conceptual or semantic problem? In H. F. R. Prechtl (Ed.), *Continuity of neural functions from prenatal to postnatal life* (Clinics in Developmental Medicine No. 94, pp. 115–125). Philadelphia: Lippincott.

TOVERUD, K. U., STEARNS, G., & MACY, I. G. (1950). *Maternal nutrition and child health: An interpretive review.* Washington, DC: National Research Council.

TOWER, R. B., SINGER, D. G., SINGER, J. L., & BIGGS, A. (1979). Differential effects of television programming on preschoolers' cognition, imagination, and social play. *American Journal of Orthopsychiatry, 49,* 265–281.

TRAUSE, M. A. (1977). Stranger responses: Effects of familiarity, stranger's approach, and sex of infant. *Child Development, 48,* 1657–1661.

TRICKETT, P. K., & KUCZYNSKI, L. (1986). Children's misbehaviors and parental discipline strategies in abusive and nonabusive families. *Developmental Psychology, 22,* 115–123.

TRIOLO, S. J., MCKENRY, P. C., TISHLER, C. L., & BLYTH, D. A. (1984). Social and psychological discriminants of adolescent suicide: Age and sex differences. *Journal of Early Adolescence, 4,* 239–251.

TRIVERS, R. L. (1971). The evolution of reciprocal altruism. *Quarterly Review of Biology, 46,* 35–57.

TRONICK, E. Z. (1989). Emotions and emotional communication in infants. *American Psychologist, 44,* 112–119.

TRONICK, E. Z., & COHN, J. F. (1989). Infant–mother face-to-face interaction: Age and gender differences in coordination and the occurrence of miscoordination. *Child Development, 60,* 85–92.

TRONICK, E. Z., SCANLON, K., & SCANLON, J. (in press). Behavioral organization and its relation to clinical and physiological status of the preterm infant during the newborn period: Apathetic organization may not be abnormal. In B. Lester & E. Z. Tronick (Eds.), *In defense of the premature infant: The limits of plasticity.* Lexington, MA: Lexington Books.

TUDGE, J., & ROGOFF, B. (1989). Peer influences on cognitive development: Piagetian and Vygotskian perspectives. In M. Bornstein & J. Bruner (Eds.), *Interaction in human development* (pp. 17–40). Hillsdale, NJ: Erlbaum.

TULVING, E. (1972). Episodic and semantic memory. In E. Tulving & W. Donaldson (Eds.), *Organization of memory* (pp. 382–403). New York: Academic Press.

TUMA, J. M. (1989). Mental health services for children: The state of the art. *American Psychologist, 44,* 188–199.

TUNMER, W. E., & BOWEY, J. A. (1984). Metalinguistic awareness and reading acquisition. In W. E. Tunmer, C. Pratt, & M. L. Herriman (Eds.), *Metalinguistic awareness in children: Theory, research, and implications* (pp. 144–168). New York: Springer-Verlag.

TUNMER, W. E., & NESDALE, A. R. (1982). The effects of digraphs and pseudo-words on phonemic segmentation in young children. *Journal of Applied Psycholinguistics, 3,* 299–311.

TURIEL, E. (1977). Conflict and transition in adolescent moral development: II. The resolution of disequilibrium through structural reorganization. *Child Development, 48,* 634–637.

TURIEL, E. (1983). *The development of social knowledge: Morality and convention.* New York: Cambridge University Press.

TURNURE, C. (1971). Response to voice of mother and stranger by babies in the first year. *Developmental Psychology, 4,* 182–190.

TVERSKY, B. (1989). Parts, partonomies, and taxonomies. *Developmental Psychology, 25,* 983–995.

TYACK, D., & INGRAM, D. (1977). Children's production and comprehension of questions. *Journal of Child Language, 4,* 211–224.

U.S. BUREAU OF THE CENSUS (1987). *Who's minding the kids? Current population reports, Series P-70.* Washington, DC: U.S. Government Printing Office.

U.S. BUREAU OF THE CENSUS (1989a). *Fertility of American women: June 1988* (Current Population Reports, Series P-20). Washington, DC: U.S. Government Printing Office.

U.S. BUREAU OF THE CENSUS (1989b). *Statistical abstract of the United States* (109th ed.). Washington, DC: U.S. Government Printing Office.

U.S. BUREAU OF THE CENSUS (1990). *Current population reports, Series P-20.* Washington, DC: U.S. Government Printing Office.

U.S. DEPARTMENT OF HEALTH AND HUMAN SERVICES (1988). *Study of national incidence and prevalence of child abuse and neglect.* Washington, DC: U.S. Government Printing Office.

U.S. DEPARTMENT OF JUSTICE (1990). *Crime in the United States.* Washington, DC: U.S. Government Printing Office.

U.S. DEPARTMENT OF LABOR, BUREAU OF LABOR STATISTICS (1987, August 12). *News.* Washington, DC: U.S. Government Printing Office.

U.S. DEPARTMENT OF LABOR, BUREAU OF LABOR STATISTICS (1988, September). *Labor force participation, unchanged among mothers with young children* (Bureau of Labor Statistics press release). Washington, DC: U.S. Government Printing Office.

U.S. Department of Labor, Bureau of Labor Statistics (1990, January). *CPI detailed report*. Washington, DC: U.S. Government Printing Office.

U.S. Department of Labor, Women's Bureau (1982). *Employers and child care: Establishing services through the workplace* (Pamphlet No. 23). Washington, DC: U.S. Government Printing Office.

U.S. General Accounting Office (1986). *School dropouts: The extent and nature of the problem*. Washington, DC: Author.

U.S. Office of Management and Budget (1989). *Historical tables: Budget of the United States*. Washington, DC: U.S. Government Printing Office.

Ullian, D. Z. (1976). The development of conceptions of masculinity and femininity. In B. Loyd & J. Archer (Eds.), *Exploring sex differences* (pp. 25–47). London: Academic Press.

Ungerer, J. A., Zelazo, P. R., Kearsley, R. B., & O'Leary, K. (1981). Developmental changes in the representation of objects in symbolic play from 19–34 months of age. *Child Development, 52,* 186–195.

UNSCEAR (1986). *Genetic and somatic effects of ionizing radiation*. New York: United Nations.

Urberg, K. A. (1979). *The development of androgynous sex-role concepts in young children*. Paper presented at the biennial meeting of the Society for Research in Child Development, San Francisco.

Uttal, D. H., & Wellman, H. M. (1989). Young children's representation of spatial information acquired from maps. *Developmental Psychology, 25,* 128–138.

Užgiris, I. C. (1964). Situational generality of conservation. *Child Development, 35,* 831–841.

Užgiris, I. C. (1973). Patterns of cognitive development in infancy. *Merrill-Palmer Quarterly, 19,* 181–204.

Užgiris, I. C., & Hunt, J. McV. (1975). *Assessment in infancy: Ordinal scales of psychological development*. Urbana: University of Illinois Press.

Valian, V. (1986). Syntactic categories in the speech of young children. *Developmental Psychology, 22,* 562–579.

Valliant, G. (1977). *Adaptation to life*. Boston: Little, Brown.

Vandell, D. L. (1980). Sociability with peer and mother during the first year. *Developmental Psychology, 16,* 355–361.

Vandell, D. L., & Mueller, E. C. (1977). *The effects of group size on toddler social interaction with peers*. Paper presented at the biennial meeting of the Society for Research in Child Development, New Orleans.

Vandell, D. L., & Mueller, E. C. (1980). Peer play and friendships during the first two years. In H. C. Foot, A. J. Chapman, & J. R. Smith (Eds.), *Friendship and social relations in children* (pp. 181–208). New York: Wiley.

Vandell, D., & Powers, C. (1983). Day care quality and children's free play activities. *American Journal of Orthopsychiatry, 53,* 293–300.

Vandell, D. L., & Wilson, K. S. (1987). Infants' interactions with mother, sibling, and peer: Contrasts and relations between interaction systems. *Child Development, 58,* 176–186.

Vandell, D. L., Wilson, K. S., & Buchanan, N. R. (1980). Peer interaction in the first year of life: An examination of its structure, content, and sensitivity to toys. *Child Development, 51,* 481–488.

Van Hekken, S. M. J., Vergerr, M. M., & Harris, P. L. (1980). Ambiguity of reference and listeners' reaction in a naturalistic setting. *Journal of Child Language, 7,* 555–563.

van Ijzendoorn, M. H., & Kroonenberg, P. M. (1988). Cross-cultural patterns of attachment: A meta-analysis of the Strange Situation. *Child Development, 59,* 147–156.

Van Strien, J. W., Bouma, A., & Bakker, D. J. (1987). Birth stress, autoimmune diseases, and handedness. *Journal of Clinical and Experimental Neuropsychology, 9,* 775–780.

Vasudev, J. (1988). Sex differences in morality and moral orientation: A discussion of the Gilligan and Attanucci study. *Merrill-Palmer Quarterly, 34,* 239–244.

Vasudev, J., & Hummel, R. C. (1987). Moral stage sequence and principled reasoning in an Indian sample. *Human Development, 30,* 105–118.

Vaughn, B., Egeland, B., Sroufe, L. A., & Waters, E. (1979). Individual differences in infant–mother attachment at twelve and eighteen months: Stability and change in families under stress. *Child Development, 50,* 971–975.

Vaughn, B., Gove, F., & Egeland, B. (1980). The relationship between out-of-home care and the quality of infant–mother attachment in an economically disadvantaged population. *Child Development, 51,* 1203–1214.

Vaughn, B. E., Kopp, C. B., & Krakow, J. B. (1984). The emergence and consolidation of self-control from eighteen to thirty months of age: Normative trends and individual differences. *Child Development, 55,* 990–1004.

Vaughn, B. E., Lefever, B. G., Seifer, R., & Barglow, P. (1989). Attachment behavior, attachment security, and temperament during infancy. *Child Development, 60,* 728–737.

Vaughn, B., Taraldson, B., Crichton, L., & Egeland, B. (1980). Relationships between neonatal behavior organization and infant behavior during the first year of life. *Infant Behavior and Development, 3,* 78–89.

Vega-Lahr, N., & Field, T. M. (1986). Type A behavior in preschool children. *Child Development, 57,* 1333–1348.

Vega-Lahr, N., Field, T., Goldstein, S., & Carran, D. (1988). Type A behavior in preschool children. In T. M. Field, P. M. McCabe, & N. Schneiderman (Eds.), *Stress and coping across development* (pp. 89–107). Hillsdale, NJ: Erlbaum.

Ventura, S. J. (1989). Trends and variations in first births to older women in the United States, 1970–86. *Public Health and Vital Statistics, 21,* 1–13.

Vernon, P. A. (1981). "Level I and Level II": A review. *Educational Psychologist, 16,* 45–64.

Vernon, P. A. (1987). Level I and Level II revisited. In S. Modgil & C. Modgil (Eds.), *Arthur Jensen: Consensus and controversy* (pp. 17–24). New York: Falmer Press.

Vernon, P. A., Jackson, D. N., & Messick, S. (1988). Cultural influences on patterns of ability in North America. In S. H. Irvine & J. W. Berry (Eds.), *Human abilities in cultural contex* (pp. 208–231). New York: Cambridge University Press.

Vietze, P., Falsey, S., O'Connor, S., Sandler, H., Sherrod, K., & Altemeier, W. (1980). Newborn behavioral and interactional characteristics of nonorganic failure-to-thrive infants. In T. Field, S. Goldberg, D. Stern, & A. Sostek (Eds.), *High-risk infants and children* (pp. 5–23). New York: Academic Press.

Vine, I. (1973). The role of facial visual signalling in early social development. In M. von Cranach & I. Vine (Eds.), *Social communication and movement: Studies of men and chimpanzees* (pp. 195–298). London: Academic Press.

Vitro, F. T. (1969). *The effects of probability of test success, opportunity to cheat and test importance on the incidence of cheating*. Unpublished doctoral dissertation. Iowa State University, Ames.

Vliestra, A. G. (1982). Children's responses to task instructions: Age changes and training effects. *Child Development, 53,* 534–542.

Vohr, B. R., & Garcia-Coll, C. T. (1988). Follow-up studies of high-risk low-birth-weight infants: Changing trends. In H. E. Fitzgerald, B. M. Lester, & M. W. Yogman (Eds.), *Theory and research in behavioral pediatrics* (pp. 1–65). New York: Plenum.

Vorhees, C. V. (1986). Principles of behavioral teratology. In E. P. Riley & C. V. Vorhees (Eds.), *Handbook of behavioral teratology* (pp. 23–48). New York: Plenum.

Vorhees, C. V., & Mollnow, E. (1987). Behavioral teratogenesis: Long-term influences on behavior from early exposure to environmental agents. In J. D. Osofsky (Ed.), *Handbook of infant development* (2nd ed., pp. 913–971). New York: Wiley.

Vurpillot, E. (1968). The development of scanning strategies and their relation to visual differentiation. *Journal of Experimental Child Psychology, 6,* 632–650.

VURPILLOT, E., RUEL, J., & CASTREC, A. (1977). L'organization perceptive chez le nourrisson: Résponse au tout au ses éléments. *Bulletin de Psychologie, 327,* 396–405.

VYGOTSKY, L. S. (1978). *Mind and society: the development of higher mental processes.* Cambridge, MA: Harvard University Press. (Original works published 1930, 1933, and 1935)

VYGOTSKY, L. S. (1987). Thinking and speech. In R. W. Rieber, A. S. Carton (Eds.), & N. Minick (Trans.), *The collected works of L. S. Vygotsky: Vol. 1. Problems of general psychology* (pp. 37–285). New York: Plenum. (Original work published 1934)

WAAS, G. A. (1988). Social attributional biases of peer-rejected and aggressive children. *Child Development, 59,* 969–975.

WABER, D. P. (1976). Sex differences in cognition: A function of maturation rate? *Science, 192,* 572–574.

WACHS, T. D. (1975). Relation of infants' performance on Piaget scales between twelve and twenty-four months and their Stanford–Binet performance at thirty-one months. *Child Development, 46,* 929–935.

WADDINGTON, C. H. (1957). *The strategy of the genes.* London: George Allen and Unwin.

WAGNER, M. E., SCHUBERT, H. J. P., & SCHUBERT, D. S. P. (1985). Family size effects: A review. *Journal of Genetic Psychology, 146,* 65–78.

WALBERG, H. J. (1986). Synthesis of research on teaching. In M. C. Wittrock (Ed.), *Handbook of research on teaching* (3rd ed., pp. 214–229). New York: Macmillan.

WALCZYK, J. J. (1990). The relation between error detection, sentence verification, and low-level reading skills in fourth graders. *Journal of Educational Psychology.*

WALDEN, T. A., & OGAN, T. A. (1988). The development of social referencing. *Child Development, 59,* 1230–1240.

WALK, R. D., & GIBSON, E. J. (1961). A comparative and analytic study of visual depth perception. *Psychological Monographs, 75*(15, Whole No. 519).

WALKER, L. J. (1980). Cognitive and perspective-taking prerequisites for moral development. *Child Development, 51,* 131–159.

WALKER, L. J. (1983). Sources of cognitive conflict for stage transition in moral development. *Developmental Psychology, 19,* 103–110.

WALKER, L. J. (1988). The development of moral reasoning. In R. Vasta (Ed.), *Annals of child development* (Vol. 5, pp. 33–78). Greenwich, CT: JAI Press.

WALKER, L. J. (1989). A longitudinal study of moral reasoning. *Child Development, 60,* 157–166.

WALKER, L. J., & DE VRIES, B. (1985). *Moral stages/moral orientations: Do the sexes really differ?* Paper presented at the annual meeting of the American Psychological Association, Los Angeles.

WALKER, L. J., DE VRIES, B., & TREVETHAN, S. D. (1987). Moral stages and moral orientations in real-life and hypothetical dilemmas. *Child Development, 58,* 842–858.

WALKER, L. J., & RICHARDS, B. S. (1979). Stimulating transitions in moral reasoning as a function of stage of cognitive development. *Developmental Psychology, 15,* 95–103.

WALKER-ANDREWS, A. S., & LENNON, E. M. (1985). Auditory–visual perception of changing distance by human infants. *Child Development, 56,* 544–548.

WALLACE, J. R., CUNNINGHAM, T. F., & DEL MONTE, V. (1984). Change and stability in self-esteem between late childhood and early adolescence. *Journal of Early Adolescence, 4,* 253–257.

WALLACH, G. P. (1984). Later language learning: Syntactic structures and strategies. In G. P. Wallach & K. G. Butler (Eds.), *Language learning disabilities in school age children* (pp. 82–102). Baltimore: Williams and Wilkins.

WALLACH, M. A. (1985). Creativity testing and giftedness. In F. D. Horowitz & M. O'Brien (Eds.), *The gifted and talented: Developmental perspectives* (pp. 99–123). Washington, DC: American Psychological Association.

WALLACH, M. A., & KOGAN, N. (1965). *Modes of thinking in young children.* New York: Holt.

WALLER, J. H. (1971). Achievement and social mobility: Relationships among IQ score, education, and occupation in two generations. *Social Biology, 18,* 252–259.

WALLERSTEIN, J. S. (1984). Children of divorce: Preliminary report of a ten-year follow-up of young children. *American Journal of Orthopsychiatry, 54,* 444–458.

WALLERSTEIN, J. S. (1985). Children of divorce: Preliminary report of a ten-year follow-up of older children and adolescents. *Journal of the American Academy of Child Psychiatry, 24,* 545–553.

WALLERSTEIN, J. S., & CORBIN, S. B. (1989). Daughters of divorce: Report from a ten-year follow-up. *American Journal of Orthopsychiatry, 59,* 593–604.

WALLERSTEIN, J., CORBIN, S. G., & LEWIS, J. M. (1988). Children of divorce: A ten-year study. In E. M. Hetherington & J. Arasteh (Eds.), *Impact of divorce, single parenting, and stepparenting on children* (pp. 198–214). Hillsdale, NJ: Erlbaum.

WALLERSTEIN, J. S., & KELLY, J. B. (1980). *Surviving the break-up: How children and parents cope with divorce.* New York: Basic Books.

WALLIS, C. (1985, December 9). Children having children. *Time, 126,* pp. 78–82.

WALTERS, J., PEARCE, D., & DAHMS, L. (1957). Affectional and aggressive behavior of preschool children. *Child Development, 28,* 15–26.

WALTERS, R. H., & ANDRES, D. (1967). *Punishment procedures and self-control.* Paper presented at the annual meeting of the American Psychological Association, Washington, DC.

WANG, M. C., & BAKER, E. T. (1985–1986). Mainstreaming programs: Design features and effects. *Journal of Special Education, 19,* 503–521.

WANSKA, S. K., & BEDROSIAN, J. L. (1985). Conversational structure and topic performance in mother–child interaction. *Journal of Speech and Hearing Research, 28,* 579–584.

WARD, S., REALE, G., & LEVINSON, D. (1972). Children's perceptions, explanations, and judgements of television advertising: A further exploration. In E. A. Rubinstein, G. A. Comstock, & J. P. Murray (Eds.), *Television and social behavior* (Vol. 4, pp. 468–490). Washington, DC: U.S. Government Printing Office.

WARD, S., WACKMAN, D., & WARTELLA, E. (1977). *How children learn to buy: The development of consumer information-processing skills.* Beverly Hills, CA: Sage.

WARREN-LEUBECKER, A., TATE, C., HINTON, I. D., & OZBEK, I. N. (1989). What do children know about the legal system and when do they know it? First steps down a less traveled path in child witness research. In S. J. Ceci, D. F. Ross, & M. P. Toglia (Eds.), *Perspectives on children's testimony* (pp. 158–183). New York: Springer-Verlag.

WATERMAN, A. S. (1982). Identity development from adolescence to adulthood: An extension of theory and a review of research. *Developmental Psychology, 18,* 341–358.

WATERMAN, A. S. (1984). Identity formation: Discovery or creation? *Journal of Early Adolescence, 4,* 329–341.

WATERMAN, A. S., GEARY, P. S., & WATERMAN, C. K. (1974). Longitudinal study of changes in ego identity status from the freshman to the senior year at college. *Developmental Psychology, 10,* 387–392.

WATERMAN, A. S., & GOLDMAN, J. A. (1976). A longitudinal study of ego identity development at a liberal arts college. *Journal of Youth and Adolescence, 5,* 361–369.

WATERMAN, A. S., & WATERMAN, C. K. (1971). A longitudinal study of changes in ego identity status during the freshman year at college. *Developmental Psychology, 5,* 167–173.

WATERS, E. (1978). The reliability and stability of individual differences in infant–mother attachment. *Child Development, 49,* 483–494.

WATERS, H. S. (1982). Memory development in adolescence: Relationships between metamemory, strategy use, and performance. *Journal of Experimental Child Psychology, 33,* 183–195.

WATKINS, B., CALVERT, S., HUSTON-STEIN, A., & WRIGHT J. C. (1980). Children's recall of television material: Effects of presentation mode and adult labeling. *Developmental Psychology, 16,* 672–674.

WATSON, J. B. (1913). Psychology as the behaviorist views it. *Psychological Review, 20,* 158–177.

WATSON, J. B., & RAYNOR, R. (1920). Conditioned emotional reactions. *Journal of Experimental Psychology, 3,* 1–14.

WATSON, J. D., & CRICK, F. H. C. (1953). Molecular structure of nucleic acids. *Nature, 171,* 737–738.

WATSON, J. S., & RAMEY, C. T. (1972). Reactions to response-contingent stimulation in early infancy. *Merrill-Palmer Quarterly, 18,* 219–229.

WATSON, M., SOLOMON, D., BATTISTICH, V., SCHAPS, E., & SOLOMON, J. (1989). The Child Development Project: Combining traditional and developmental approaches to values education. In L. P. Nucci (Ed.), *Moral development and character education* (pp. 51–92). Berkeley, CA: McCutchan.

WECHSLER, D. (1974). *Manual for the Wechsler Intelligence Scale for Children—Revised.* New York: Psychological Corporation.

WECHSLER, D. (1989). *Manual for the Wechsler Preschool and Primary Scale of Intelligence—Revised.* New York: Psychological Corporation.

WEHREN, A., DELISI, R., & ARNOLD, M. (1981). The development of noun definition. *Journal of Child Language, 8,* 165–175.

WEIDNER, G., SEXTON, G., MATARAZZO, J. D., PEREIRA, C., & FRIEND, R. (1988). Type A behavior in children, adolescents, and their parents. *Developmental Psychology, 24,* 118–121.

WEIL, W. B. (1975). Infantile obesity. In M. Winick (Ed.), *Childhood obesity* (pp. 61–72. New York: Wiley.

WEINRAUB, M., CLEMENS, L. P., SOCKLOFF, A., ETHRIDGE, T., GRACELY, E., & MYERS, B. (1984). The development of sex role stereotypes in the third year: Relationships to gender labeling, gender identity, sex-typed toy preference, and family characteristics. *Child Development, 55,* 1493–1503.

WEINRAUB, M., & LEWIS, M. (1977). The determinants of children's responses to separation. *Monographs of the Society for Research in Child Development, 42* (4, Serial No. 172).

WEISNER, T., & GALLIMORE, R. (1977). My brother's keeper: Child and sibling caretaking. *Current Anthropology, 18,* 169–190.

WEISS, G., & HECHTMAN, L. (1986). *Hyperactive children grown up.* New York: Guilford Press.

WEISZ, J. R. (1978). Choosing problem-solving rewards and Halloween prizes: Delay of gratification and preference for symbolic reward as a function of development, motivation, and personal investment. *Developmental Psychology, 14,* 66–78.

WEISZ, J. R., & MCGUIRE, M. (1980). *Sex differences in the relation between attributions and learned helplessness in children.* Unpublished manuscript, University of North Carolina, Chapel Hill.

WEISZ, J. R., & ZIGLER, E. (1979). Cognitive development in retarded and non-retarded persons. Piagetian tests of the similar sequence hypothesis. *Psychological Bulletin, 86,*831–851.

WEITZMAN, L. (1985). *The divorce revolution: The unexpected social and economic consequences for women and children in America.* New York: Free Press.

WELCH, R. L., HUSTON-STEIN, A., WRIGHT, J. C., & PLEHAL, R. (1979). Subtle sex-role cues in children's commercials. *Journal of Communication, 29,(3),* 202–209.

WELLMAN, H. M. (1977). Preschoolers' understanding of memory relevant variables. *Child Development, 48,* 13–21.

WELLMAN, H. M. (1978). Knowledge of the interaction of memory variables: A development study of metamemory. *Developmental Psychology, 14,* 24–29.

WELLMAN, H. M. (1985). The child's theory of mind: The development of conceptions of cognition. In S. R. Yussen (Ed.), *The growth of reflection in children* (pp. 169–206). San Diego, CA: Academic Press.

WELLMAN, H. M. (1988). First steps in the child's theorizing about mind. In J. W. Astington, P. L. Harris, & D. R. Olson (Eds.), *Developing theories of mind* (pp. 64–92). Cambridge, England: Cambridge University Press.

WELLMAN, H. M., COLLINS, J., & GLIEBERMAN, J. (1981). Understand-ing the combination of memory variables: Developing conceptions of memory limitations. *Child Development, 52,* 1313–1317.

WELLMAN, H. M., CROSS, D., & BARTSCH, K. (1987). Infant search and object permanence: A meta-analysis of the A-not-B error. *Monographs of the Society for Research in Child Development, 51*(No. 3, Serial No. 214).

WELLMAN, H. M., & ESTES, D. (1986). Early understanding of mental entities: A reexamination of childhood realism. *Child Development, 57,* 910–923.

WELLMAN, H. M., & JOHNSON, C. N. (1979). Understanding of mental processes: A developmental study of "remember" and "forget." *Child Development, 50,* 79–88.

WELLMAN, H. M., SOMERVILLE, S. C., & HAAKE, R. J. (1979). Development of search procedures in real-life spatial environments. *Developmental Psychology, 15,* 530–542.

WELLS, G. (1986). Variation in child language. In P. Fletcher & M. Garman (Eds.), *Language acquisition* (pp. 109–139). Cambridge, England: Cambridge University Press.

WELLS, G. L., TURTLE, J. W., & LUUS, C. A. E. (1989). The perceived credibility of child eyewitnesses: What happens when they use their own words? In S. J. Ceci, D. F. Ross, & M. P. Toglia (Eds.), *Perspectives on children's testimony* (pp. 23–36). New York: Springer-Verlag.

WERKER, J. F. (1989). Becoming a native listener. *American Scientist, 77,* 54–59.

WERKER, J. F., & TEES, R. C. (1984). Cross-language speech perception: Evidence for perceptual reorganization during the first year of life. *Infant Behavior and Development, 7,* 49–63.

WERNER, E. E., & SMITH, R. S. (1979). An epidemiologic perspective on some antecedents and consequences of childhood mental health problems and learning disabilities. *Journal of the American Academy of Child Psychiatry, 18,* 292–306.

WERNER, E. E., & SMITH, R. S. (1982). *Vulnerable but invincible: A study of resilient children.* New York: McGraw-Hill.

WERNER, J. S., & SIQUELAND, E. R. (1978). Visual recognition memory in the preterm infant. *Infant Behavior and Development, 1,* 79–94.

WERTSCH, J. (1986). *Mind in context: A Vygotskian approach.* Paper presented at the annual meeting of the American Educational Research Association, San Francisco.

WESTOFF, C. F. (1978). Some speculations on the future of marriage and the family. *Family Planning Perspectives, 10,* 79–83.

WETZEL, J. R. (1987). *American youth: A statistical snapshot.* Washington, DC: William T. Grant Foundation.

WHALEN, C. K. (1983). Hyperactivity, learning problems, and the attention deficit disorders. In T. H. Ollendick & M. Hersen (Eds.), *Handbook of child pyschopathology* (pp. 151–199). New York: Plenum.

WHALEN, C. K., HENKER, B., & HINSHAW, S. P. (1985). Cognitive-behavioral therapies for hyperactive children: Premises, problems, and prospects. *Journal of Abnormal Child Psychology, 13,* 391–410.

WHISNANT, L., & ZEGANS, L. (1975). A study of attitudes toward menarche in white middle-class American adolescent girls. *American Journal of Psychiatry, 132,* 809–814.

WHITE, B. (1985). *The first three years of life.* New York: Prentice-Hall.

WHITE, B., & HELD, R. (1966). Plasticity of sensorimotor development in the human infant. In J. F. Rosenblith & W. Allinsmith (Eds.), *The causes of behavior* (pp. 60–70). Boston: Allyn & Bacon.

WHITE, R. W. (1959). Motivation reconsidered: The concept of competence. *Psychological Review, 66,* 297–333.

WHITEHURST, G. J. (1982). Language development. In B. B. Wolman (Ed.), *Handbook of developmental psychology* (pp. 367–386). New York: Wiley.

WHITEHURST, G. J., FISCHEL, J. E., CAULFIELD, M. B., DEBARYSHE, B. D., & VALDEX-MENCHACA, M. C. (1989). Assessment and treatment of early expressive language delay. In P. R. Zelazo & R. Barr (Eds.), *Challenges to developmental paradigms: Implications for assessment and treatment* (pp. 113–135). Hillsdale, NJ: Erlbaum.

WHITEHURST, G. J., & VALDEZ-MENCHACA, M. C. (1988). What is the role of reinforcement in early language acquisition? *Child Development, 59,* 430–440.

WHITEHURST, G., & VASTA, R. (1975). Is language acquired through imitation? *Journal of Psycholinguistic Research, 4,* 37–59.

WHITING, B., & EDWARDS, C. P. (1988a). *Children in different worlds.* Cambridge, MA: Harvard University Press.

WHITING, B., & EDWARDS, C. P. (1988b). A cross-cultural analysis of sex differences in the behavior of children aged 3 through 11. In G. Handel (Ed.), *Childhood socialization* (pp. 281–297). New York: Aldine de Gruyter.

WHITLEY, B. E., JR. (1983). Sex role orientation and self-esteem: A critical meta-analytic review. *Journal of Personality and Social Psychology, 44,*765–778.

WHITLEY, B. E., JR. (1985). Children's causal attributions for success and failure in achievement settings: A meta-analysis. *Journal of Educational Psychology, 77,* 608–616.

WIESENFELD, A. R., MALATESTA, C. Z., & DeLOACHE, J. S. (1981). Differential parental response to familiar and unfamiliar infant distress signals. *Infant Behavior and Development, 4,* 281–295.

WIKOFF, R. L. (1979). The WISC-R as a predictor of achievement. *Psychology in the Schools. 16,* 364–366.

WILCOX, B. L., & VINCENT, T. (1987, November). School dropout: A federal perspective. *Social Policy Report of the Society for Research in Child Development, 2*(No. 3).

WILENSKY, H. L. (1983). Evaluating research and politics: Political legitimacy and consensus as missing variables in the assessment of social policy. In E. Spiro and E. Yuchtman-Yaar (Eds.), *Evaluating the welfare state: Social and political perspectives* (pp. 51–74). New York: Academic Press.

WILLEMS, E. P. (1967). Sense of obligation to high school activities as related to school size and marginality of student. *Child Development, 38,* 1247–1260.

WILLER, B. A. (1988). *The growing crisis in child care: Quality, compensation, and affordability in early childhood programs.* Washington, DC: National Association for the Education of Young Children.

WILLERMAN, L. (1979). Effects of families on intellectual development. *American Psychologist, 34,* 923–929.

WILLIAM T. GRANT FOUNDATION, COMMISSION ON WORK, FAMILY AND CITIZENSHIP. (1988). *The forgotten half: Pathways to success for America's youth and young families.* Washington, DC: Author.

WILLIAMS, J. (1979). Reading instruction today. *American Psychologist, 34,* 917–922.

WILLIAMS, J. E., BENNETT, S. M., & BEST, D. L. (1975). Awareness and expression of sex stereotypes in young children. *Developmental Psychology, 11,* 635–642.

WILLIAMS, J. E., & BEST, D. L. (1982). *Measuring sex stereotypes: A thirty-nation study.* Beverly Hills, CA: Sage.

WILLIAMS, J. E., BEST, D. L., TILQUIN, C., KELLER, H., VOSS, H. G., BJERKE, T., & BAARDA, B. (1979). *Traits associated with men and women by young children in France, Germany, Norway, the Netherlands, and Italy.* Unpublished manuscript, Wake Forest University.

WILLIAMS, K. G., & GOULET, L. R. (1975). The effects of cuing and constraint instructions on children's free recall performance. *Journal of Experimental Child Psychology, 15,* 169–186.

WILLIAMS, T. M. (1986). *The impact of television: A natural experiment in three communities.* Orlando, FL: Academic Press.

WILSON, E. O. (1975). *Sociobiology: The new synthesis.* Cambridge, MA: Harvard University Press.

WILSON, M. N. (1986). The black extended family: An analytical consideration. *Developmental Psychology, 22,* 246–258.

WILSON, M. N. (1989). Child development in the context of the black extended family. *American Psychologist, 44,* 380–385.

WILSON, M. N., & TOLSON, T. F. J. (1985). *An analysis of adult–child interaction patterns in three-generational black families.* Unpublished manuscript, University of Virginia.

WILSON, R. S. (1976). Concordance in physical growth for monozygotic and dizygotic twins. *Annals of Human Biology, 3,* 1–10.

WILSON, R. S. (1983). The Louisville Twin Study: Developmental synchronies in behavior. *Child Development, 54,* 298–316.

WILSON, W. J. (1987). *The truly disadvantaged.* Chicago: University of Chicago Press.

WINCH, R. F. (1971). *The modern family* (3rd ed.). New York: Holt, Rinehart and Winston.

WINER, G. A., HEMPHILL, J., & CRAIG, R. K. (1988). The effect of misleading questions in promoting nonconservation responses in children and adults. *Developmental Psychology, 24,* 197–202.

WINER, G. A., & KRONBERG, D. D. (1974). Children's responses to verbally and pictorially presented class-inclusion items and to a task of number conservation. *Journal of Genetic Psychology, 125,* 141–152.

WINICK, M., ROSSO, P., & WATERLOW, J. (1970). Cellular growth of cerebrum, cerebellum, and brain stem in normal and marasmic children. *Experimental Nuerology, 26,* 393–400.

WINITZ, H. (1969). *Articulatory acquisition and behavior.* New York: Appleton-Century-Crofts.

WINN, S., TRONICK, E. Z., & MORELLI, G. A. (1989). The infant and the group: A look at Efe caretaking. In J. K. Nugent, B. M. Lester, & T. B. Brazelton (Eds.), *Biology, culture, and development* (Vol. 1, pp. 87–109). Norwood, NJ: Ablex.

WINNER, E. (1986, August). Where pelicans kiss seals. *Psychology Today, 20*(8), 25–35.

WINNER, E. (1988). *The point of words: Children's understanding of metaphor and irony.* Cambridge, MA: Harvard University Press.

WISSLER, C. (1901). The correlation of mental and physical traits. *Psychological Monographs, 3,* 1–62.

WITELSON, S. F., & KIGAR, D. L. (1988). Anatomical development of the corpus callosum in humans: A review with reference to sex and cognition. In D. L. Molfese & S. J. Segalowitz (Eds.), *Brain lateralization in children* (pp. 35–57). New York: Guilford Press.

WOHLWILL, J. F. (1973). *The study of behavioral development.* New York: Academic Press.

WOLCHIK, S. A., BRAVER, S. L., & SANDLER, I. W. (1985). Maternal versus joint custody: Children's postseparation experiences and adjustment. *Journal of Clinical Child Psychology, 14,* 5–10.

WOLFF, J. R. (1981). Some morphogenetic aspects of the development of the central nervous system. In K. Immelmann, G. W. Barlow, L. Petrinovich, & M. Main (Eds.), *Behavioral development* (pp. 164–190). Cambridge, England: Cambridge University Press.

WOLFF, P. H. (1963). Observations on the early development of smiling. In B. M. Foss (Ed.), *Determinants of infant behavior* (Vol. 2, pp. 113–138). London: Methuen.

WOLFF, P. H. (1966). The causes, controls and organization of behavior in the neonate. *Psychological Issues, 5* (1, Serial No. 17).

WONG-FILLMORE, L., AMMON, P., McLAUGHLIN, B., & AMMON, M. S. (1985). *Learning English through bilingual instruction.* Rosslyn, VA: National Clearinghouse for Bilingual Education.

WOOD, D. J., BRUNER, J. S., & ROSS, G. (1976). The role of tutoring in problem solving. *Journal of Child Psychology and Psychiatry, 17,* 89–100.

WOODSON, E. M., WOODSON, R. H., BLURTON-JONES, N. G., POLLOCK, S. B., & EVANS, M. A. (1980). *Maternal smoking and newborn behavior.* Paper presented at the International Conference on Infant Studies, New Haven, CT.

WOODSON, R. H., & da COSTA, E. (1989). The behavior of Chinese, Malay, and Tamil newborns from Malaysia. In J. K. Nugent, B. M. Lester, & T. B. Brazelton (Eds.), *Biology, culture, and development* (Vol. 1, pp. 295–317). Norwood, NJ: Ablex.

WOROBEY, J. (1985). A review of Brazelton-based interventions to enhance parent–infant interaction. *Journal of Reproductive and Infant Psychology, 3,* 64–73.

WOROBEY, J., & BLAJDA, V. M. (1989). Temperament ratings at 2 weeks, 2 months, and 1 year: Differential stability of activity and emotionality. *Developmental Psychology, 25,* 257–263.

WRIGHT, H. F. (1967). *Recording and analyzing child behavior.* New York: Harper & Row.

WRIGHT, J. D., HUSTON, A. C., ROSS, R. P., CLAVERT, S. L., ROLANDELLI, D., WEEKS, L. A., RAEISSI, P., & POTTS, R. (1984). Pace and continuity of television programs: Effects on children's attention and comprehension. *Developmental Psychology, 20,* 653–666.

WRIGHT, P., & CROW, R. (1982). Nutrition and feeding. In P. Stratton (Ed.), *Psychobiology of the human newborn* (pp. 339–364). New York: Wiley.

WYLIE, R. (1979). *The self-concept: Theory and research on selected topics,* Lincoln, NE: University of Nebraska Press.

YANDO, R., SEITZ, V., & ZIGLER, E. (1979). *Intellectual and personality characteristics of children: Social-class and ethnic-group differences.* Hillsdale, NJ: Erlbaum.

YAP, J. N. K., & PETERS, R. DeV. (1985). An evaluation of two hypotheses concerning the dynamics of cognitive impulsivity: Anxiety-over-errors or anxiety-over-competence? *Developmental Psychology, 21,* 1055–1064.

YARROW, L. (1975). *Infant and environment: Early cognitive and motivational development.* New York: Halsted.

YARROW, M. R., CAMPBELL, J. D., & BURTON, R. V. (1970). Recollections of childhood: A study of the retrospective method. *Monographs of the Society for Research in Child Development, 35* (5, Serial No. 138).

YARROW, M. R., SCOTT, P. M., & WAXLER, C. Z. (1973). Learning concern for others. *Developmental Psychology, 8,* 240–260.

YATES, G., MacKENZIE, R., PENNBRIDGE, J., & COHEN, E. (1988). A risk profile comparison of runaway and non-runaway youth. *American Journal of Public Health, 78,* 820–821.

YEATES, K. O., MacPHEE, D., CAMPBELL, F. A., & RAMEY, C. T. (1983). Maternal IQ and home environment as determinants of early childhood intellectual competence: A developmental analysis. *Developmental Psychology, 19,* 731–739.

YOGMAN, M. W. (1981). Development of the father-infant relationship. In H. Fitzgerald, B. Lester, & M. W. Yogman (Eds.), *Theory and research in behavioral pediatrics* (Vol. 1, pp. 221–279). New York: Plenum.

YONAS, A., ARTERBERRY, M. E., & GRANRUD, C. E. (1987). Four-month-old infants' sensitivity to binocular and kinetic information for three-dimensional-object shape. *Child Development, 58,* 910–917.

YONAS, A., GRANRUD, E. C., ARTERBERRY, M. E., & HANSON B. L. (1986). Infants' distance perception from linear perspective and texture gradients. *Infant Behavior and Development, 9,* 247–256.

YOUNG, G., & LEWIS, M. (1979). Effects of familiarity and maternal attention on infant peer relations. *Merrill-Palmer Quarterly, 25,* 105–119.

YOUNGER, B. A. (1985). The segregation of items into categories by ten-month-old infants. *Child Development, 56,* 1574–1583.

YOUNISS, J. (1975). Another perspective on social cognition. In A. Pick (Ed.), *Minnesota Symposia on Child Psychology* (Vol. 9, pp. 173–193). Minneapolis: University of Minnesota Press.

YOUNISS, J., & VOLPE, J. (1978.). A relational analysis of children's friendships. In W. Damon (Ed.), *New directions for child development* (Vol. 1, pp. 1–22). San Francisco: Jossey-Bass.

YUILL, N., & PERNER, J. (1988). Intentionality and knowledge in children's judgements of actor's responsibility and recipient's emotional reaction. *Developmental Psychology, 24,* 358–365.

ZABRUCKY, K., & RATNER, H. H. (1986). Children's comprehension monitoring and recall of inconsistent stories. *Child Development, 57,* 1401–1418.

ZAHAVI, S., & ASHER, S. R. (1978). The effect of verbal instructions on preschool children's aggressive behavior. *Journal of School Psychology, 16,* 146–153.

ZAHN-WAXLER, C., KOCHANSKA, G., KRUPNICK, J., & McKNEW, D. (1990). Patterns of guilt in children of depressed and well mothers. *Developmental Psychology, 26,* 51–59.

ZAHN-WAXLER, C., RADKE-YARROW, M., & KING, R. M. (1979). Child-rearing and children's prosocial initiations toward victims of distress. *Child Development, 50,* 319–330.

ZAJONC, R. B. (1976). Family configuration and intelligence. *Science, 192,* 227–236.

ZAJONC, R. B., & MARKUS, G. B. (1975). Birth order and intellectual development. *Psychological Review, 82,* 74–88.

ZAJONC, R. B., MARKUS, H., & MARKUS, G. B. (1979). The birth order puzzle. *Journal of Personality and Social Psychology, 37,* 1325–1341.

ZARBATANY, L., HARTMANN, D., & GELFAND, D. (1985). Why does children's generosity increase with age: Susceptibility to experimenter influence or altruism? *Child Development, 56,* 746–756.

ZASLOW, M. J. (1989). Sex differences in children's response to parental divorce: II. Samples, variables, ages, and sources. *American Journal of Orthopsychiatry, 59,* 118–141.

ZASLOW, M.J., PEDERSON, F. A., SUWALSKY, J., & RABINOVICH, B. (1983, April). *Maternal employment and parent–infant interaction.* Paper presented at the biennial meeting of the Society for Research in Child Development, Detroit.

ZELAZO, P. R. (1983). The development of walking: New findings on old assumptions. *Journal of Motor Behavior, 2,* 99–137.

ZELAZO, P. R., ZELAZO, N. A., & KOLB, S. (1972). ''Walking'' in the newborn. *Science, 176,* 314–315.

ZELNICKER, T., COCHAVI, D., & YERED, J. (1974). The relationship between speed of performance and conceptual style: The effect of imposed modification of response latency. *Child Development, 45,* 779–784.

ZELNICKER, T., JEFFERY, W. E., AULT, R. L., & PARSONS, J. (1972). Analysis and modification of search strategies of impulsive and reflective children on the Matching Familiar Figures Test. *Child Development, 43,* 321–335.

ZESKIND, P. S., & LESTER, B. M. (1978). Acoustic features and auditory perception of the cries of newborns with prenatal and perinatal complications. *Child Development, 49,* 580–589.

ZESKIND, P. S., & LESTER, B. M. (1981). Analysis of cry features in newborns with differential fetal growth. *Child Development, 52,* 207–212.

ZESKIND, P. S., & MARSHALL, T. R. (1988). The relation between variations in pitch and maternal perceptions of infant crying. *Child Development, 59,* 193–196.

ZESKIND, P. S., & RAMEY, C. T. (1978). Fetal malnutrition: An experimental study of its consequences on infant development in two caregiving environments. *Child Development, 49,* 1155–1162.

ZESKIND, P. S., & RAMEY, C. T. (1981). Preventing intellectual and interactional sequelae of fetal malnutrition: A longitudinal, transactional, and synergistic approach to development. *Child Development, 52,* 213–218.

ZIGLER, E. (1978). Controlling child abuse in America: An effort doomed to failure. In R. Bourne & E. Newberger (Eds.), *Critical perspectives on child abuse* (pp. 171–213). Lexington, MA: Heath.

ZIGLER, E. (1985). Assessing Head Start at 20: An invited commentary. *American Journal of Orthopsychiatry, 55,* 603–609.

ZIGLER, E., ABELSON, W. D., & SEITZ, V. (1973). Motivational factors in the performance of economically disadvantaged children on the Peabody Picture Vocabulary Test. *Child Development, 44,* 294–303.

ZIGLER, E., ABELSON, W. D., TRICKETT, P. K., & SEITZ, V. (1982). Is an intervention program necessary in order to improve economically disadvantaged children's IQ scores? *Child Development, 53,* 340–348.

ZIGLER, E., & BERMAN, W. (1983). Discerning the future of early childhood intervention. *American Psychologist, 38,* 894–906.

ZIGLER, E., & BUTTERFIELD, E. C. (1968). Motivational aspects of changes in IQ test performance of culturally deprived nursery school children. *Child Development, 39,* 1–14.

ZIGLER, E. F., & FINN-STEVENSON, M. E. (1988). Applied developmental psychology. In M. H. Bornstein & M. E. Lamb (Eds.), *Developmental psychology: An advanced textbook* (2nd ed., pp. 595–634). Hillsdale, NJ: Erlbaum.

ZIGLER, E., & SEITZ, V. (1982). Social policy and intelligence. In R. J. Sternberg (Ed.), *Handbook of human intelligence* (pp. 586–641). Cambridge, England: Cambridge University Press.

ZIMMERMAN, I. L., & WOO-SAM, J. M. (1978). Intelligence testing today—Relevance to the school aged child. In L. Oettinger (Ed.), *The psychologist, the school, and the child with MBD/LD* (pp. 51–69). New York: Grune & Stratton.

ZIVIN, G. (1977). On becoming subtle: Age and social rank changes in the case of social gesture. *Child Development, 48,* 1314–1321.

ZUCKERMAN, B., FRANK, D. A., HINGSON, R. AMARO, H., LEVENSON, S. M., KAYNE, H., PARKER, S., KAYE, K., ELKIND, L., GOLDBERG, D., & TYTUN, A. (1989). Birth outcomes for infants of drug-abusing mothers. *New York State Journal of Medicine, 89,* 256–261.

Name Index

Siegal, M., 534
Siegal, A. W., 236
Siegal, I. E., 164
Siegel, L. S., 234, 457
Siegler, R. S., 24, 231, 233, 234,
    242, 256, 258, 259, 261, 280,
    286, 291, 292, 292n, 293, 298,
    298n, 314, 315
Sigafoos, A. D., 138
Sigman, M. D., 136
Signiorelli, N., 529
Signorella, M. E., 537
Signorella, M. L., 537, 538
Sikora, D. M., 62n
Silber, R., 356
Silberman, M. L., 639
Silva, P. A., 414
Silverman, N., 674
Simeonsson, R. J., 78
Simkin, P., 103
Simmons, R. G., 182, 440
Simon, H. A., 256
Simons, C, 467
Simons J., 590
Simourd, L., 451
Sinclair, H., 234
Singer, D. G., 48, 624, 627, 629, 631
Singer, J. E., 17
Singer, J. L., 48, 624, 627, 629, 631
Singer, L. T., 135, 135n
Singleton, L. C., 464
Sinnott, J. M., 146
Siqueland, E. R., 133, 135
Sirignano, S. W., 404
Sirotnik, K. A., 639
Skeels, H. M., 109, 162, 323
Skinner, B. F., 345
Skinner, E. A., 442
Skinner, M. L., 579
Skodak, M., 109, 162, 323
Slaby, R. G., 478, 534, 547, 551,
    552, 553, 627
Slade, A., 249
Slater, A., 157
Slavic, S., 374
Slavin, R., 643
Sleator, E. K., 271
Slobin, D. I., 348, 360, 368, 372
Sloman, J., 606
Slone, D., 98
Slotkin, T. A., 100
Smail, B., 518, 521
Smart, M. S., 186n
Smart, R. C., 186n
Smeeding, T. M., 663n, 666, 667n,
    667
Smetana, J., 482
Smilansky, S., 605, 606n
Smiley, S. S., 268
Smith, A. J., 607
Smith, Carole L., 377
Smith, Caroline, 525, 531
Smith, D. F., 447
Smith, E. E., 232
Smith, E. J., 446
Smith, H. W., 607
Smith, I. D., 440
Smith, J. David, 408, 409
Smith, Jacqui, 520
Smith, Joshua H., 359
Smith, M. Brewster, 499, 500
Smith, M. C., 451
Smith, M. L., 635
Smith, M. S., 335
Smith, Mary B., 97
Smith, P. K., 605, 605n, 608, 609, 634
Smith, Robin, 624, 625, 626
Smith, Romayne A., 508
Smith, Ruth, S., 107, 564
Smith, T. E., 333

Smithells, J., 519, 519n
Smokler C. S., 587
Smolucha, F., 249
Snarey, J. R., 492, 497, 498, 502
Snidman, N., 404
Snow, C. E., 347, 349, 350
Snow, M. E., 577
Snow, R. E., 641
Snyder, J. J., 553
Snyder, L., 351
Sobesky, W. E., 493
Society for Research in Child
    Development, 60, 61, 62n
Sodian, B., 272, 284
Sokoloff, B. Z., 82
Solan, L., 371
Solarz, A. L., 664, 665
Solimano, G., 198, 199
Solnit, A. J., 203
Solomon, D., 638
Solomon, J., 419, 422
Solomon, S. K., 462
Somberg, D. R., 453
Somerville, S. C., 269, 269n
Song, M-J., 482, 647
Sonnenschein, S., 376, 377
Sontag, C. W., 313, 314
Sontag, L. W., 52
Sophian, C., 233, 289
Sorce, J., 399
Sorensen, G., 587
Sosniak, L. A., 339
Spanier, G. B., 562
Spanier, G. V., 579, 583
Spearman, C., 301
Spears, G. F. S., 414
Speece, M. W., 238
Speer, J. R., 285
Speidel, G. E., 327
Spelke, E. S., 158, 160, 213, 218,
    220n, 264, 289
Spellacy, W. N., 98
Spence, J. T., 516, 533
Spence, M. J., 88, 147
Spencer, L., 629
Spencer, M. B., 448
Sperry, L. L., 397
Spiker, D., 78
Spinetta, J., 594
Spitz, R. A., 162, 420
Spivack, G., 465, 466
Spock, B., 9
Sprafkin, J., 624, 625n, 627, 629,
    630, 631
Sprague, R. L., 271
Spreen, O., 189, 190, 191
Sprigle J. E., 336
Spuhler, J. N., 318
Sroufe, L. A., 126, 391, 392, 393,
    395, 422, 423, 425, 426, 427,
    568, 596, 604
St. John, N. H., 645
Staats, A., 345
Stabb, S. D., 615
Stambrook, M., 238
Stanbury, J. B., 73n
Stanhope, L., 42, 410, 458
Stankov, L., 309, 319, 320
Stanley, J. C., 51, 541n, 544
Stanley-Hagan, M., 579, 580, 581,
    583
Stanovich, K. G., 267
Stanowicz, L., 372
Stanton, G. C., 436
Stanton, J. C., 439n
Stapp, J., 516, 533
Starfield, B., 670
Stark, L. J., 16
Starkey, P., 289
Starr, R. H., Jr., 593

Stattin, H., 182
Staub, E., 500
Staudt, J., 242
Stayton, D., 419
Stearns, G., 97
Stechler, G., 102, 103, 104
Steele, P. R. M., 91
Stein, Aletha H., 50, 247, 480, 519,
    519n, 521, 627
Stein, Anne, 98
Stein, M. R., 604
Stein, Z., 97
Steinberg, L. D., 183, 390, 427, 564,
    567, 569, 590, 676
Steinberg, R., 609
Steiner, G. Y., 656, 678
Steiner, J. E., 132, 145, 391
Steinman, S. B., 585
Steinmetz, S., 548
Stenberg, C., 388, 394
Stenchever, M. A., 92
Stene, E., 78
Stene, J., 78
Stengel-Rutkowski, S., 78
Stephan, C. W., 182, 612
Stephens, B. R., 155
Stephenson, M. G., 199
Stern, G. S., 126
Stern, M., 105, 524, 525
Stern, P., 641
Sternberg, R. J., 293, 298, 305, 306,
    307, 311, 326, 339, 340
Sternglanz, S. H., 530
Stevens, F., 312
Stevens, J. H., 571
Stevenson, D. L., 564
Stevenson, H. W., 444, 519, 540,
    545, 646, 647, 648, 649, 649n
Stevenson, J., 317
Stevenson, R., 361
Stevenson-Hinde, J., 410
Stewart, A. J., 57
Stewart, D. A., 80
Stewart, F., 677
Stewart, J., 523, 530, 530n
Stewart, P., 604
Stewart, R. B., 333
Stiefvater, K., 467
Stigler, J. W., 291, 646, 647
Stillman, R. J., 92
Stini, W. A., 200
Stipek, D. J., 439, 442, 443, 545,
    642, 672, 673
Stoch, M. B., 198, 199
Stocker, C., 410
Stoddart, T., 536
Stodolsky, S. S., 319, 320n, 639
Stoel-Gammon, C., 353
Stolberg, A. L., 582
Stolz, H. R., 172
Stolz, L. M., 172
Stone, B. P., 272
Stone, R. K., 406
Stoneman, Z., 410, 531, 610
Stotland, E., 401
Strain, P. S., 621
Strauss, C. C., 202
Strauss, M. A., 548
Strauss, N. L., 443
Strauss, S., 293
Strayer, F. F., 21, 529, 620
Strayer, J. A., 21, 401, 620
Streissguth, A. P., 91, 92, 93
Strickland, R., 592
Stuart, P., 363
Stuckey, M. R., 587
Stucki, M., 154
Stunkard, A. J., 200
Sturm, L., 204
Sturner, W. Q., 134

Styczynski, L. E., 181, 612
Sudhalter, V., 371
Sugawara, A. I., 517
Sullivan, H. S., 464
Sullivan, J. W., 147
Sullivan, L. W., 75
Sullivan, M. W., 312, 387, 388n, 398
Suomi, S. J., 21, 188, 190, 191, 526
Super, C. M., 29n, 123
Suransky, V. P., 5
Susanne, C., 196
Suskind, R. M., 198
Susman, E. J., 550
Sutterfield, S. J., 495, 504
Sutton-Smith, B., 98, 237
Swartz, K. B., 148
Sykers, D. H., 104
Szeminska, A., 212, 228

Taebel, D., 520, 521
Tager-Flusberg, H., 370, 377
Taitz, L. S., 201
Takanishi, R., 656, 657
Tamplin, A., 410
Tangri, S. S., 587
Tanner, J. M., 169, 171, 171n, 172,
    173, 173n, 174, 175, 175n, 176,
    177, 178, 184, 186, 187, 188,
    189, 196, 197, 202, 211
Taplin, P. S., 43
Task Force on Pediatric AIDS, 96
Tauber, M. A., 529, 531
Taylor, A. R., 643
Taylor, D. G., 422
Taylor, Marjorie, 364, 456
Taylor, Marylee C., 533
Taylor, S. P., 481
Teberg, A. J., 104, 105
Tees, R. C., 147, 352
Teixeira, R. A., 645
Telleen, S., 401
Teller, D. Y., 149
Templin, M. C., 358
Tennes, K., 126
Tenney, Y. J., 285
Terman, L. M., 8, 9, 316, 316n
Termine, N. T., 398
Terrace, H. S., 346
Teuber, H. L., 265, 265n
Tharp, R. G., 249, 327
Thatcher, R. W., 195
Thelen, E., 122, 140
Thelen, M. H., 610
Theorell, K., 125
Thevenin, D. M., 353
Thoma, S. J., 496, 499
Thomas, A., 402, 403, 403n, 404,
    410, 411
Thomas, D. L., 440
Thomas, E. A. C., 609
Thomas, J. R., 172
Thomas, M. H., 627
Thomas, N. G., 339, 638
Thomas, R. M., 3
Thompson, J. G., 279
Thompson, R. A., 63, 389, 396, 397,
    400, 401, 420, 423, 427, 428,
    593, 597, 659, 660, 661
Thompson, S. K., 517
Thorndike, R. L., 309, 309n, 310n
Thorsen, E. E., 338
Tikenoff, W. J., 379
Tilden, V. P., 95
Tinsley, B. R., 425
Tisak, J., 465
Tizard, B., 44, 421
Tobias, P. V., 187
Tobin-Richards, M. H., 182
Toda, S., 407
Todd, C. M., 272

Subject Index

kinetic, 150, 157
monocular, 151
pictorial, 150–152, 158
Depth perception, 149–152
Desegregation, school, 645
Developing countries, 655, 677
and breast feeding, 200
disease in, 202
literacy in, 677
malnutrition in, 198, 202
poverty in, 677
war in, 677
Developmental pediatrics, 9–10
Developmental psychology, 1
Developmental quotient (DQ), 312
Developmental research strategies, 36, 51–60
improving, 59–60
see also Research; Research designs
Deviation IQ, 308
Dialectical theory, 27, 31, 208, 245–250
educational implications, 249–250
of private speech, 246–247, 248
and social origins of cognitive development, 247–249
Dialects. *See* Black dialect
Diarrhea, 203
Diet
and anorexia nervosa, 184–185
and hyperactivity, 271
PKU, 73, 76
in pregnancy, 73, 93, 97–98, 104
see also Nutrition
Diethylstilbestrol (DES), 92
Differentiation theory
and learning to read, 264–265
in perceptual development, 160–161
of self-esteem, 438
in sensory processing, 264–265, 266
Difficult child, 402, 406, 411
Disadvantaged children. *See* Economic deprivation; Minority children; Social deprivation; Socioeconomic factors
Discipline methods
coercive, 475, 551
of divorced parents, 579
family size and, 574
of fathers, 479
induction, 474–475, 551
love-withdrawal, 474, 475
power assertion, 475
punishment, 5, 478 (*see also* Punishment)
in Puritan America, 4–5
Discrepancy theory, of emotional development, 385–386
Discretionary programs, 666
Disease
and homelessness, 664
malnutrition and, 202–203
maternal, and prenatal development, 89, 94–95
and physical growth, 202–203
and recessive genes, 72–74
Disequilibrium, and cognitive development, 211
Dishabituation, 134. *See also* Habituation-dishabituation paradigm
Distance, understanding of, 235
Distance curve, of physical growth, 168
Distributive justice, 502–504
Divergent thinking, 303, 337–340
genetic influences on, 337–338
play and, 339
stimulation of, 339
Divorce
changing societal attitudes toward, 581–582
custody arrangements, 581, 583
effects on children's development, 578–581
grandparent visitation rights and, 660–661
intervention programs, 584
long-term outcomes, 580–581, 582
rate of, 560, 578
reaction to
maturity and, 580
sex differences in, 579–580
and remarriage, 577, 582–584
Divorce mediation, 584

Domain-specific knowledge, 280, 339–340
Dominance hierarchies, 21, 620
Dominant-recessive inheritance, 72–74, 543
Donor insemination, 82
Down syndrome, 77–78, 98, 136
Dreams
awareness of inner self and, 435
in infancy, 124
Drive reduction theory, 15, 21
of attachment, 412, 413
Drives
primary, 15
secondary, 15
Dropouts, high school, 674–675
Drugs
adolescents and, 618–619, 665
and prenatal development
illicit, 91
obstetric, 102–103, 138
prescription, 90
Drug therapy
for adrenogenital syndrome, 523
for hyperactivity, 271
for prenatal problems, 82
Dwarfism, deprivation, 203, 204

Ear, development of, 146
Early childhood intervention programs, 334–337, 655
Easy child, 402, 406
Eating patterns
and anorexia nervosa, 184–185
and obesity, 200–201
Ecological experiments, 20
Ecological model, Bronfenbrenner's, 17–20, 426–428, 562
and social policy, 654, 655
Ecological psychology, 16
Ecological theory, 16–20, 31
and day care, 426–428
and families, 560–562
and peer relations, 602
and research strategies, 18–19
Ecology of human development, 16–20
Economic deprivation, 204, 570
early intervention and, 334–337
and IQ, 317–320
long-term consequences of, 56–57
Economy
and social policy, 657, 662, 677
Ectoderm, 86
Education
in American society, 644–648, 675
bilingual, 379
cross-national research on, 646–648
desegrated, 645
early intervention, 334–337
gifted children and, 339, 644
for the handicapped, 642–644
infant, 163
information processing, influence on, 24, 294
in Japan and Taiwan, 648–649
and moral reasoning, 496, 502
Piaget's influence on, 23, 207, 244–245
and poverty, 677
emergence of public, 299
quality of, 634
sex, 176, 180
and social policy, 646–648, 675–676, 677
traditional versus open, 39, 52–53, 339, 636–638
Vgotsky's theory of, 249–250
vocational, 676
see also Academic achievement; Schools; Teachers; Teaching
Educational television, 630–631
Education for All Handicapped Children Act, 642, 671–672
Efe infants, 131
Ego, 10, 413
Egocentric speech, 246–247, 249–250
Egocentrism
adolescent, 240–241
decline in, 215, 217

and distributive justice, 503
formal operational, 240–241
imaginary audience and, 240
and moral understanding, 484
personal fable and, 240
and perspective-taking, 451–452
preoperational, 255, 229–231
sensorimotor, 214, 215, 217, 225
Ego ideal, 474
Ego integrity versus despair, 13
Elaboration, memory strategy of, 258, 260, 274, 278
Electra conflict, 10, 474
Electroencephalograph (EEG), 124, 193
Embarrassment, 395
Embryo, period of the, 85, 86–87, 89, 97
Embryo banks, 82
Embryonic disk, 85
Emile (Rousseau), 6
Emotional deprivation, 161–164, 203, 420–421
Emotional development, 383–428
attachment and, 383, 411–426
behaviorism and, 385
caregivers and, 394–395, 398–399
cognitive development and, 25–26, 387–388
cognitive-developmental discrepancy theory of, 385–386
course of, 384–401
emotional expression, 391–398, 399–401
emotional recognition, 398–401
empathy and, 388, 400–401
longitudinal studies of, 55
organizational approach to, 26, 387–391
psychoanalytic theory of, 25
responding to others' emotions, 398–401
social learning theory of, 385
temperament and, 401–411
see also Emotions
Emotional display rules, 390, 397–398
Emotional neglect, 593. *See also* Child maltreatment; Emotional deprivation
Emotional self-arousal, 385
Emotional sensitivity, sex differences in, 545–546
Emotions
adaptive role of, 26, 387–388, 394–395
basic, 391–395
and cognitive processing, 25–26, 387
complex, 395–396, 474
expression of
discrete emotions, 391–398
display rules and, 390, 397–398
facial, 384, 393
in neonates, 391–394
in physically abused children, 401
physiological, 26, 388–390
postural, 384
self-regulation and, 396–397
vocal, 384
and intelligence test performance, 53, 327
maladaptive, 395n
measuring, 26, 384
mixed, 399, 400
negative, 387, 388, 397
and physical health, 26, 388–389, 390
recognition of, 398–401
in childhood, 399–400
empathy, 388, 400–401
social referencing, 399
and social behavior, 25–26, 387–388
Empathy, 388, 400–401, 473
environmental influences on, 19
and morality, 471, 505
sex differences in, 545
training, 554
Employment
maternal (*see* Maternal employment)
youth, 675–677
Encoding, 253, 255, 260, 291
in social problem solving, 465–466
Endocrine glands, 183–186
Endoderm, 86
Endogenous smiles, 392
Engrossment, 424
Enlightenment, and views of childhood, 5–6

Gastrointestinal infections, and physical growth, 200, 203
Gender, understanding of, 517, 524, 555
Gender consistency, 534
Gender constancy, 533, 572
  emergence of, 534–536
  as a predictor of sex-role behavior, 535–536
Gender differences. See Sex differences
Gender identity. See Sex-role identity
Gender labeling, 515, 534, 535–536
Gender schema theory, 515, 537–539, 556
Gender stability, 534
General factor, "g," 301, 305, 307, 315, 319
General growth curve, 169
Generalized other, 436, 437
Generativity versus stagnation, 13
Genes, 70
  dominant and recessive, 72–74, 543
  modifier, 76
  and mutations, 75
  see also Genetics
Genetic code, 68–70
Genetic counseling, 81–83
Genetic disorders, 72, 74, 75, 76–80, 81, 523–524
  sex differences in, 75–76, 541
Genetic influences, 31, 108
  in brain development, 189
  complex behaviors and, 107–110
  on divergent thinking, 337–339
  and environmental influences, interaction of, 110–113
  on intelligence, 78, 109, 314–315, 318, 320–324, 331
  on obesity, 200
  on personality, 109, 404–405, 407
  on physical growth, 196–197
  on sex differences in cognitive abilities, 540
  on temperament, 405–407
Genetics, 67, 68–77
  co-dominance, 74–75
  dominant-recessive relationships, 72–74
  Mendel's work in, 68
  modifier genes, 76
  mutations, 75
  natural selection, 6, 75
  patterns of inheritance, 71–77
  pleiotropism, 76
  polygenic inheritance, 76–77
  X-linked inheritance, 75–76, 543
Genital abnormalities, 523, 523n, 524
Genitalia. See Sex characteristics
Genital stage, 11
Germinal period, 85
Gesell Developmental Schedules, 312
Gestational age, 105, 189
Gestures
  communicating with, 374
  Down syndrome and, 78
  neonatal imitation of, 137
  preverbal, 355
Gifted children
  assessment of, 9, 316, 339–340, 644
  longitudinal research on, 9, 316, 644
  preschool programs for, 644
  teaching, 644
Glial cells, 189, 190, 195
Goal-directed (intentional) behavior, in Piaget's sensorimotor stage, 213, 216
"Goodness-of-fit" model, 410–411, 423
Government programs. See Social policy
Grammar, 344
Grammatical development, 346–348, 364–372
  complex grammatical forms, 370–371
  expansions and, 372
  formal grammatical understandings, 369–370
  holophrases, 365
  infinitive phrases, 371
  language acquisition device (LAD), 345, 348, 350
  language-making capacity (LMC), 372
  mean length of utterance, (MLU), 364–365, 369
  morphemes, 365, 367–368
  negation, 370

overregularization and, 368–369
passive phrases, 348, 371
phases of, 365–371
question forms, 370
recasts and, 372
telegraphic speech, 365
transformational rules, 346
Grandparents
  support from, 18, 571
  visitation rights of, 660–661
Grasping
  and cognitive development, 141, 142, 210, 214
  neonatal, 118, 120, 141
Gratification. See Delay of gratification
Great Depression, children of, 56–57
Gross motor skills, 140, 141, 143, 171
Group factors, in intelligence testing, 301
Groups. See Peer groups
Growth. See Physical growth
Growth curves, 167–170
  distance curve, 168
  velocity curve, 169
Growth hormone (GH), 184, 203
Growth spurts, 169, 172, 175, 176, 178
  brain, 195–196
Guatemalan children, gastrointestinal infections in, 203
Guilt
  emergence of, 395–396
  in Freud's theory, 474–476

Habituation, 134
  in infants, 134–136
Habituation-dishabituation paradigm, 134–136, 144, 150, 218, 221, 312
Handbook of Child Psychology, 31, 384
Handedness, 192, 193–194
Handicapped children
  intelligence testing of, 309
  mainstreaming, 642–644
  peer relations of, 643
Happiness, 391–392
Hawaiian Pidgin English, 347
Head Start. See Project Head Start
Health
  adolescent, 10
  emotions and, 26, 388–389
Health care
  children and adolescents, 674–677
  infant, 668–673
Health insurance, 670
Hearing
  in infancy, 146
  and infant babbling, 353
Heinz dilemma, 487, 488, 490–491, 493, 498, 504
Hemispheric specialization. See Brain lateralization
Hemophilia, 76, 82
Heredity. See Genetic influences; Genetics
Heritability estimates, 108–110, 320
  criticisms of, 323
  of divergent thinking, 338–339
  generalizability of, 322
  of intelligence, 320–323
  of temperament and personality, 405
  see also Genetic influences
Heroin, and prenatal development, 91
Herpes viruses, and prenatal development, 94–95
Heteronomous morality, 483–484, 485, 486, 489
Heterozygous pattern of genetic inheritance, 72, 74
Hierarchical classification, 226–227, 231, 234
Hindbrain, 188
Hispanic children, 329, 379
Holland, caregiving in, 134
Holophrases, 365
Home-based day care, 589, 591, 609
Home delivery, 100–102
Home environment
  and aggression, 551–553
  and creativity, 338–339
  and memory development, 276
  and IQ, 324, 330–334

adoption studies on, 332
between-family influences, 330–332
confluence model, 332–333
longitudinal studies on, 330
within-family influences, 316, 330, 332–334
and personality development, 406–407
Homelessness, 663–664, 665
Home Observation for Measurement of the Environment (HOME), 330, 331, 332
Homework, and academic achievement, 646, 648
Homologous pairs, 69, 70
Homosexuals, 523n
Homozygous pattern of genetic inheritance, 72
Hong Kong, caregiving in, 134
Hopi Indians, infant motor skills of, 140–141
Horizontal décalage, 234, 234n, 235, 262
Hormonal treatment, 79, 80, 184
Hormone levels
  and adrenogenital syndrome, 523
  and aggression, 550
Hormones, 183
  adrenocorticotropic (ACTH), 185
  and aggression, 550
  follicle stimulating (FSH), 185
  growth (GH), 184, 203
  luteinizing (LH), 185
  prenatal, 91–92, 522–523
  sex (androgens and estrogens), 172, 184, 522–523, 550
  stress, 99–100, 397
  thyroid stimulating (TSH), 184
Hostile aggression, 452–453, 547
Human development, 1
Humor, comprehension of, 237
Hunger
  in developing nations, 677
  infant, 412, 413, 414
Hunger cry, 126
Hunters and gatherers, 560–561
Huntington's chorea, 81
Hyaline membrane disease, 104
Hyperactive children, 58, 93, 270–271, 408
  treatment for, 270
Hypothalamus, 183
Hypothesis, 35, 239
Hypothetico-deductive reasoning, 239

Id, 10
Idealism, adolescent, 240–241
Identical (monozygotic) twins, 85
  IQ correlations of, 109, 321–323
  parental treatment of, 109
  physical growth of, 196–197
  rate of physical maturation in, 197
  reared apart, 112
  see also Twin studies
Identification, 474
Identity
  in adolescence, 444–449, 537, 618
  development of, 445–448, 476n
  group, 618
  sex-role, 532–539 (see also Sex-role identity)
  statuses, 446
Identity achievement, 446, 447, 448
Identity constancy, 228–229, 434
Identity crisis, 445
Identity diffusion, 446, 447
Identity foreclosure, 446, 447
Identity versus identity diffusion, 12
Illness. See Disease
Illocutionary intent, 373
Illogical reasoning, and Piaget's preoperational stage, 225–234
Imaginary audience, 240–241, 448
Imagination, television and, 630–631
Imitation
  deferred, 138, 218, 277
  in infancy, 136–138, 155n, 215
  and language development, 345
  in mother-infant interaction, 138
  of peers, 610
  Piaget's sensorimotor stage, 214, 215, 216
  and social development, 138
  see also Modeling

Memory *(Continued)*
  and scripts, 282–283
  and self-regulation, 285–287
  semantic, 260, 282
  sex differences in, 41
  short-term *(see* Short-term memory)
  span, 257, 261, 280
  strategies *(see* Memory strategies)
  working, 260, 263, 274
Memory strategies, 40–41, 257
  anxious time-monitoring, 40–41
  elaboration, 258, 274
  environmental contexts and, 274–275
  home environment and, 276
  organization, 258, 272–273, 276
  rehearsal, 258, 271–272
  strategic time-monitoring, 40–41
Memory system, Atkinson and Shiffrin's
    flowchart of, 257
Menarche, 175, 177, 523
  age of, 176, 186, 187, 196
  reactions to, 178–179, 180
Menstruation, 84, 185, 186
  cessation of, in anorexia nervosa, 184
  see also Menarche
Mental age (MA), 307–308
Mental health, child and adolescent, 674–677
Mental imagery, 274
Mental retardation
  causes of, 73, 78, 80, 93, 189
  genetic transmission of, 73, 80
  identification of, 8, 329
  mainstreaming and, 643, 643n
  mildly retarded, 643n
  and Piaget's stages, 212
Mental rotation tasks, 542, 544
Mental testing. *See* Intelligence tests
Mesoderm, 86
Mesosystem, 18, 427
Metacognition, 283–287, 432
  knowledge of self as a cognitive processor,
      284–285
  knowledge of strategies and task variables, 285
  naive theory of mind, 285, 304
  and self-control, 509
  self-regulation, 284, 285–287
  television and, 633
Metacognitive training, 286
Metalinguistic awareness, 377–378
Metaphors, use of, 362–363
Metatheoretical issues, in child development, 29
Methadone, and prenatal development, 91
Microcephaly, and prenatal environmental
    influences, 93, 96
Microcomputers. *See* Computers
Microsystem, 17–18, 426
  effect of third parties in, 18, 562
Midbrain, 188
Minamata, Japan, 94
Minority children
  and bilingual education, 379–380
  dropouts, 675
  identity achievement of, 448
  intelligence testing of, 309, 311, 326–328
  overlabeling as retarded, 329
  and poverty, 663
  sex stereotyping by, 520
  teacher reactions to, 642, 645
  teenage pregnancy and, 176
Mirrors, as cues to self, 433
Miscarriage, 92, 176. *See also* Abortion
Mismatch, 363
Mitosis, 70, 85, 189
Modeling, 15, 16
  and aggression, 49, 51, 554
  in emotional development, 385
  in moral development, 477–480
  peer, 610, 621–622
  same-sex, 534, 538
  of sex stereotyped behavior, 52, 529, 531
  in social skills training, 554, 614–615
Models, effectiveness of, 15, 479, 538, 610, 621
Modifier genes, 76
Monkeys. *See* Apes and monkeys

Monocular depth cues, 151
Monologues, 246, 247
  collective, 246
Moral development, 62, 471
  assessing, 487–488, 501
  behaviorist theory of, 471, 476–480
  biological perspective of, 472
  cognitive-developmental theory of, 471,
      472–473, 483–502
  cultural differences in, 495, 496–498
  Freud's theory of, 474
  internalization and, 472, 475–476
  Kohlberg's theory of, 486–495, 501–502, 504
  Piaget's theory of, 483–486
  psychoanalytic theory of, 471, 474–476
  and self-control, 472, 506–510
  see also Morality; Moral reasoning
Moral dilemmas, 486–487, 496, 497, 502
  of distributive justice, 502–504
  Heinz dilemma, 487–491, 493, 498, 504
  prosocial, 502, 504–505
Moral education, 496, 502
Morality
  as adoption of societal norms, 473–482
  autonomous, 484–485
  of care, 499
  components of, 471
  consistency across situations and, 480–481
  heteronomous, 483–484, 485, 489
  internalized, 472
  philosophical views of, 472–473
  as rooted in human nature, 472
  as social conformity, 481–482
  and social conventions, 482, 504n
  as social understanding, 483–502
  See also Moral development; Moral reasoning
Moral Judgment of the Child, The (Piaget), 483
Moral judgments, 482, 484, 485
Moral reasoning, 482
  altruistic, 504–505
  and behavior, 482, 500–501, 504–505
  child-rearing practices and, 496
  cognitive conflict and, 494
  cognitive prerequisites for, 493–495
  cultural differences in, 495, 496–498
  distributive justice, 502–504
  environmental influences on, 495–498
  formal education and, 496
  guilt and, 474, 475, 476
  peer interaction and, 495
  perspective-taking and, 488, 490, 491, 493
  prosocial, 504–505
  sex differences in, 499–500
  of young children, 502–505
  see also Moral development; Morality
Moratorium, 446, 447
Moro reflex, 118, 214
Morphemes, 365, 367–368
Morphology, 344
Mortality rates
  childhood, 174
  infant, 97, 668–671
Motherese, 358, 360, 372
Mother-infant attachment. *See* Attachment
Motivation
  achievement, 441, 444, 519, 641
  and intelligence testing, 327–328
  moral, 482, 500
Motor development, 138–144, 191
  cross-cultural research on, 140–141
  maturation versus experience and, 140–141
  organization and sequence of, 139–140
  secular trends in, 139
  vision and, 141–142
  visually guided reaching, 140, 141–144
  walking, 121
  see also Motor skills
Motor regions, of the cortex, 190
Motor skills
  age averages for, 139, 140
  fine, 140, 141–144, 224
  grasping, 118, 120, 141, 143
  gross, 140, 141, 143, 171
  in infancy, 139–140

  reaching, 141–144
M-space (mental space), 262
Muscle tissue growth of, 172
Muscular distrophy, 81
Mutations, 75
Myelinization, 189, 190, 191, 195, 198

Naive theory of mind, 285, 287
Names, socially desirable, 612
Narcotics. *See* Drugs
National Academy of Early Childhood Programs,
    673
National Association for the Education of Young
    Children, 673
National Commission on Excellence in
    Education, 645
National Day Care Home Study, 590
National Day Care Study, 590
National Runaway Switchboard, 665
Nation At Risk, A, 645
Nation's Report Card, The, 646
Nativist theory of language development,
    345–348, 365
Natural childbirth, 100–102
Natural experiments, 51, 52
Naturalistic observation, 8, 16, 21, 40, 41, 43
Natural kind categories, 232
Natural selection, 6, 75
Nature-nuture controversy, 3, 107, 112–113
  in infant perception, 144
  in IQ, 9, 317–318, 321, 539
  in language development, 344–348
  in temperament and personality, 407
Navaho Indians, childbirth and, 100–101
Negatives, use of, 370
Negativism, 388, 397, 506
Neglect, 568, 593. *See also* Child maltreatment
Neglected children, 611, 614, 615. *See also*
    Maltreated children
Neighborhood play, 606
Neighborhood walk, 18–19
Neo-Freudians, 12
Neonatal Behavioral Assessment Scale (NBAS),
    129, 131
Neonates, 118n
  assessment of, 9–10, 129–130, 144
  cries of, 473
  emotional expression of, 391–392, 396
  fear in, 25, 132, 385, 394–395
  learning in, 130–138
  reflexes of, 118–122, 214
  states of, 122–129
  see also Infancy; Infants
Nepal, delivery in, 138
Nervous system, development of, 86. *See also*
    Brain; Central nervous system; Cerebral
    cortex
Neurolinguistic assessment, 349
Neurological impairment, neonatal diagnosis of,
    10, 129
Neuronal development, 188–190
Neurons, 188–190
  stimulation of, 190
New England Primer, 5
New Guinea, sex role behavior in, 522
New York Longitudinal Study, 402–403
Niche-picking, 112, 113, 321
Noble savages, 6
Noise
  apartment, and auditory development, 16–17
  background, and attention, 267
Nonconformity, 482
Nonreversal shift, 255
Nonverbal cues, of dominance and submission, 21
Normal curve, 308
Normative approach, 8–9, 10, 312
Normative period of child study, 8–9
Normative prescriptions, 478, 480
Norms
  of development, 9, 173
  IQ test, for minorities, 311
  and moral development, 473–482
  peer-group, 616, 617–620
  social *(see* Social norms)